Introduction to
Psychology 11e

James W. Kalat

North Carolina State University

CENGAGE
Learning·

Australia • Brazil • Mexico • Singapore • United Kingdom • United States

Introduction to Psychology, Eleventh Edition
James W. Kalat

Product Manager: Clayton Austin

Content Developer: Liz Fraser

Product Assistant: Kimiya Hojjat

Marketing Manager: Andrew Ginsberg

Content Project Manager: Samen Iqbal

Art Director: Vernon Boes

Manufacturing Planner: Karen Hunt

Intellectual Property Analyst: Deanna Ettinger

Intellectual Property Project Manager: Brittani Morgan

Project Manager, Production Service: Jill Traut,
    MPS Limited

Text and Cover Designer: Jeanne Calabrese

Cover Image Credit: Robert Harding Images/Masterfile

Compositor: MPS Limited

For product information and technology assistance, contact us at
Cengage Learning Customer & Sales Support, 1-800-354-9706.

For permission to use material from this text or product,
submit all requests online at **www.cengage.com/permissions**
Further permissions questions can be e-mailed to
permissionrequest@cengage.com.

Library of Congress Control Number: 2015944015

Student Edition:
ISBN: 978-1-305-27155-5

Loose-leaf Edition:
ISBN: 978-1-305-63054-3

Cengage Learning
20 Channel Center Street
Boston, MA 02210
USA

Cengage Learning is a leading provider of customized learning solutions with employees residing in nearly 40 different countries and sales in more than 125 countries around the world. Find your local representative at **www.cengage.com.**

Cengage Learning products are represented in Canada by Nelson Education, Ltd.

To learn more about Cengage Learning Solutions, visit **www.cengage.com.**

Purchase any of our products at your local college store or at our preferred online store **www.cengagebrain.com.**

Printed in the United States of America
Print Number: 03   Print Year: 2017

To my grandchildren: Max and Ann Stapel-Kalat, Ophelia and Liam Floyd

JAMES W. KALAT (rhymes with ballot) is Professor Emeritus at North Carolina State University, where he taught Introduction to Psychology and Biological Psychology for 35 years. Born in 1946, he received an AB degree summa cum laude from Duke University in 1968 and a PhD in psychology in 1971 from the University of Pennsylvania, under the supervision of Paul Rozin. He is also the author of *Biological Psychology*, 12th edition (Boston, MA: Cengage, 2016), and coauthor with Michelle N. Shiota of *Emotion*, 2nd edition (Belmont, CA: Wadsworth, 2012). In addition to textbooks, he has written journal articles on taste-aversion learning, the teaching of psychology, and other topics. A remarried widower, he has three children, two stepsons, and four grandchildren. When not working on something related to psychology, his hobby is bird-watching.

brief contents

contents

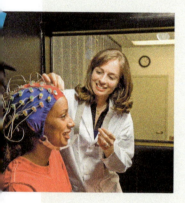

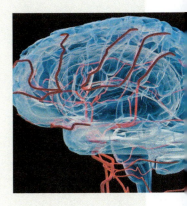

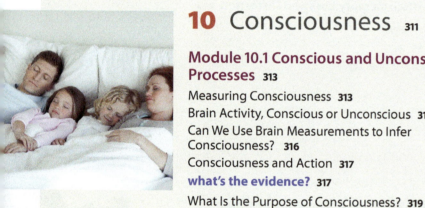

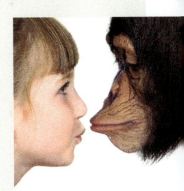

15 Abnormal Psychology: Disorders and Treatment 481

Some years ago, I was on a plane that had to turn around shortly after takeoff because one of its two engines had failed. When we were told to get into crash position, the first thing I thought was, "I don't want to die yet! I was looking forward to writing the next edition of my textbook!" True story.

I remember taking my first course in psychology as a freshman at Duke University in 1965. Frequently, I would describe the fascinating facts I had just learned to my roommate, friends, relatives, or anyone else who would listen. I haven't changed much since then. When I read about new research or think of a new example to illustrate some point, I want to tell my wife, children, and colleagues. Psychology is fun. Although I retired from teaching after 35 years at North Carolina State University, I still volunteer to "pinch hit" when any of my colleagues are ill or out of town. I wake up in the morning and think, "Wow! I get to teach about optical illusions today!" or "Great! Today's topic is emotions!" Do professors in other fields enjoy teaching so much? Does someone in the French department wake up thinking how exciting it will be to teach about adverbs today? I doubt it.

Ideally, a course or textbook in psychology should accomplish two goals. The first is to instill a love of learning so that our graduates will continue to update their education. Even if students permanently remembered everything they learned—and of course they won't—their understanding would gradually go out of date unless they continue to learn about new developments. I hope that some of our students occasionally read *Scientific American Mind* or similar publications. The second goal is to teach students the skills of evaluating evidence and questioning assertions, so that when they do read about some new research, they will ask the right questions before drawing a conclusion. That skill can carry over to fields other than psychology.

Throughout this text, I have tried to model the habit of critical thinking or evaluating the evidence, particularly in the **What's the Evidence?** features that describe research studies in some detail. I have pointed out the limitations of the evidence and the possibilities for alternative interpretations. The goal is to help students ask their own questions, distinguish between good and weak evidence, and ultimately, appreciate the excitement of psychological inquiry.

Approaches, Features, and Student Aids

Many years ago, I read an educational psychology textbook that said children with learning disabilities and attention problems learn best from specific, concrete examples. I remember thinking, "Wait a minute. I do, too! Don't we *all* learn best from specific, concrete examples?" For this reason, science classes use laboratories to let students see for themselves. Few introductory psychology classes offer laboratories, but we can nevertheless encourage students to try procedures that require little or no equipment. At various points, the text describes simple **Try It Yourself** exercises, such as negative afterimages, binocular rivalry, encoding specificity, and the Stroop effect. Additional activities are available as **Online Try It Yourself** activities on MindTap. Students who try these activities will understand and remember the concepts far better than if they merely read about them.

Cognitive psychology researchers find that we learn more if we alternate between reading and testing than if we spend the same amount of time reading. The **Concept Checks** pose questions that attentive readers should be able to answer. Students who answer correctly can feel encouraged. Those who miss a question should use the feedback to reread the relevant passages.

Each chapter of this text is divided into two to five modules, each with its own summary. Modules provide flexibility for instructors who wish to take sections in a different order—for example, operant conditioning before classical conditioning—or who wish to omit a section. Modular format also breaks up the reading assignments so that students read one or two modules for each class. Key terms are listed at the end of each module. At the end of the text, a combined Subject Index and Glossary defines key terms and provides page references.

Education was long a traditional field in which the procedures hardly changed since the invention of chalk. Today, however, educators use the power of new technologies, and this text offers several important technological enhancements. The digital MindTap for *Introduction to Psychology* includes online Try It Yourself exercises as well as an integrated eBook, videos with assessment, mastery training, validated essay assignments, quizzes, and an online glossary.

What's New in the Eleventh Edition?

Anyone familiar with previous editions will notice two changes in the format: A list of learning objectives starts each module, and a few multiple-choice review questions end each module.

This edition has more than 600 new references, including more than 500 from 2012 or later. Nearly every topic in the book has at least a minor revision or update. The three modules of Chapter 2 were combined into two, and the first module of Chapter 10 was substantially reorganized. A few new topics were added, including social neuroscience, individual differences in taste and smell, and how to take notes in class. Many topics were substantially revised, including replicability, epigenetics, and autism. Many of the figures are new or revised. Here are a few of my favorite new studies:

- Hearing loss in old age occurs not only in the ears, but also in the brain. A decrease of inhibitory synapses makes it harder to attend to one voice among many, and the auditory cortex may deteriorate from insufficient input, such as when someone delays getting hearing aids. (Chapter 4)
- The "collectivist attitude" typical of Asian cultures is stronger in some parts of China than others, and correlates strongly with a history of rice farming. Unlike wheat farming, rice farming requires extensive cooperation among neighboring farmers. (Chapter 5)
- In contrast to the previous view that expertise results from 10,000 hours of practice, new research clearly demonstrates important individual differences. Some chess players reach expert levels after only 3,000 hours of practice, whereas others fail to achieve expertise after 25,000 hours. (Chapter 8)
- The brain mechanisms for self-initiated ("spontaneous") movements differ from those for stimulus-elicited movements, and self-initiated movements almost always have a slow, gradual onset. That finding is critical for interpreting Libet's study reporting that brain activity for a muscle movement starts before a conscious decision to move. The problem is that a conscious decision for a spontaneous movement, like the movement itself, is gradual and hard to pinpoint in time. (Chapter 10)
- People at an all-you-can-eat buffet tend to eat until they think they got their money's worth. People given a half-off coupon to a pizza buffet ate less than others did, on average. (Chapter 11)
- People with anorexia nervosa seldom experienced depression or any other psychological troubles prior to becoming anorexic, and treating them for depression is generally ineffective in relieving anorexia. A new study starts with the assumption that the decreased eating is the original problem, and that the increased activity characteristic of anorexia is an unconscious attempt for temperature control. (Chapter 11)
- Sex hormones influence the differentiation of several brain areas, but the chemical mechanisms differ from one brain area to another. Therefore, it is common for a person to be more masculinized or more feminized in one brain area than another, just as someone can be behaviorally more male-typical in some ways and more female-typical in others. (Chapter 11)
- A woman with damage to her amygdala previously seemed unable to experience fear or anxiety. A new study shows that she feels intense anxiety in response to breathing concentrated carbon dioxide. The amygdala damage doesn't prevent fear; it just blocks processing cognitive information relating to fear. (Chapter 12)
- More recent birth cohorts report greater life satisfaction than older birth cohorts, at all ages. (Chapter 12)
- Love doesn't always fade over time. Many older couples continue to experience passionate love. (Chapter 13)

Teaching and Learning Supplements

You're familiar with those television advertisements that offer something, usually for $19.95, and then say, "But wait, there's more!" Same here. In addition to the text, the publisher offers many supplements:

MindTap

MindTap for *Introduction to Psychology,* 11th edition, creates a unique learning path that fosters increased comprehension and efficiency. It engages students and empowers them to produce their best work—consistently. In MindTap, course material is seamlessly integrated with videos, activities, apps, and more.

In MindTap instructors can:

- control the content. Instructors select what students see and when they see it.
- create a unique learning path. In MindTap, the *Introduction to Psychology* text is enhanced with multimedia and activities to encourage and motivate learning and retention, moving students up the learning taxonomy. Materials can be used

as-is or modified to match exactly with an instructor's syllabus.

- integrate their own content. Instructors can modify the MindTap Reader using their own documents or pulling from sources like RSS feeds, YouTube videos, websites, Google Docs, and more.
- follow student progress. Powerful analytics and reports provide a snapshot of class progress, time students spend logging into the course, and completion to help instructors assess level of engagement and identify problem areas.

Test Bank, **powered by Cognero Instant Access.** Written by the author himself, the test bank for *Introduction to Psychology* consists entirely of new or reworded items, with an emphasis on clarity. Nearly all items are worded in the form of a question, and none of them include an "all of the above" or "none of the above" choice. The test bank also includes a special file of items that cut across chapters, intended for inclusion on a comprehensive final exam. That bank is also available in Cognero electronic format.

Online Instructor's Resource Manual is both thorough and creative. It includes suggestions for class demonstrations and lecture material, organized by chapter to allow instructors to easily identify resources to enhance lectures and facilitate learning.

Online PowerPoint® Lecture slide decks are designed to facilitate instructors' use of PowerPoint® in lectures. Slides are provided for each chapter, and contain main concepts, with figures, graphics, and tables to visually illustrate main points from the text. The notes section of the slide provides guidelines and text references to support lecture preparation. Slides have been designed to be easily modifiable for instructors to customize with their own materials.

Acknowledgments

To begin the job of writing a textbook, a potential author needs self-confidence bordering on arrogance and, to complete it, the humility to accept criticism of favorite ideas and carefully written prose. A great many people provided helpful suggestions that made this a far better text than it would have been without them.

My acquisitions editor, Clayton Austin, has been very helpful and supportive throughout the preparation of this edition. I have been delighted to work with Michelle Newhart, my developmental editor, who provided helpful, intelligent advice on everything from the big picture to the details. I thank them for their tireless help.

I greatly appreciate the detailed work of the copy editor, Heather McElwain. Jill Traut and Samen Iqbal did a marvelous job of supervising the production, a complicated task with a book such as this. Vernon Boes, the art director, and Jeanne Calabrese, who designed the cover and interior, had the patience and artistic judgment to counterbalance this very nonartistic author. Andrew Ginsberg planned and executed the marketing strategies. The photo and text researchers at Lumina Datamatics skillfully researched and managed the permissions requests. To each of these, my thanks and congratulations.

My wife, Jo Ellen Kalat, not only provided support and encouragement but also listened to my attempts to explain concepts and offered many helpful suggestions and questions. I thank my department head, Douglas Gillan, my North Carolina State colleagues, and Jack Huber from Meredith College, for their helpful suggestions.

Many reviewers provided helpful and insightful comments. Each edition builds on contributions from reviewers of previous editions. I would like to thank the following reviewers who contributed their insight to one or more editions:

Jennifer Ackil, Gustavus Adolphus College; Jeffrey Adams, Trent University; Judi Addelston, Valencia College; Mark Affeltranger, University of Pittsburgh; Catherine Sanderson, Amherst College; Susan Anderson, University of South Alabama; Bob Arkin, Ohio State University; Melanie M. Arpaio, Sussex County Community College; Susan Baillet, University of Portland; Cynthia Bane, Denison University; Joe Bean, Shorter University; Mark Bodamer, Gonzaga University; Richard W. Bowen, Loyola University Chicago; Rebecca Brand, Villanova University; Michael Brislawn, Bellevue College; Delbert Brodie, St. Thomas University; John Broida, University of Southern Maine; Thomas Brothen, University of Minnesota; Gordon Brown, Pasadena City College; Gregory Bushman, Beloit College; James Calhoun, University of Georgia; Bernardo Carducci, Indiana University Southeast; Thomas Carskadon, Mississippi State University; Mark Casteel, Pennsylvania State University, York Campus; Liz Coccia, Austin Community College; Carolyn Cohen, Northern Essex Community College; Karen Couture, Keene State College; Alex Czopp, Western Washington University; Deana Davalos, Colorado State University; Patricia Deldin, University of Michigan; Katherine Demitrakis, Central New Mexico Community College; Janet Dizinno, St. Mary University; Alicia M. Doerflinger, Marietta College; Karen Douglas, San Antonio College–Alamo Colleges; Kimberly Duff, Cerritos College; Darlene Earley-Hereford, Southern Union State Community College; David J. Echevarria, University of Southern Mississippi; Vanessa Edkins, University of Kansas;

Susan Field, Georgian Court University; Deborah Frisch, University of Oregon; Gabriel Frommer, Indiana University; Rick Fry, Youngstown State University; Robert Gehring, University of Southern Indiana; Judy Gentry, Columbus State Community College; Anna L. Ghee, Xavier University; Bill P. Godsil, Santa Monica College; Kerri Goodwin, Loyola University in Maryland; Joel Grace, Mansfield University; Troianne Grayson, Florida Community College at Jacksonville; Joe Grisham, Indian River State College; Julie A. Gurner, Quinnipiac University; Community College of Philadelphia; Alexandria E. Guzmán, University of New Haven; Richard Hanson, Fresno City College; Richard Harris, Kansas State University; Wendy Hart-Stravers, Arizona State University; W. Bruce Haslam, Weber State University; Christopher Hayashi, Southwestern College; Bert Hayslip, University of North Texas; Manda Helzer, Southern Oregon University; W. Elaine Hogan, University of North Carolina Wilmington; Debra Hollister, Valencia College; Susan Horton, Mesa Community College; Charles Huffman, James Madison University; Linda Jackson, Michigan State University; Alisha Janowsky, University of Central Florida; Robert Jensen, California State University, Sacramento; Andrew Johnson, Park University; James Johnson, Illinois State University; Craig Jones, Arkansas State University; Lisa Jordan, University of Maryland; Dale Jorgenson, California State University, Long Beach; Jon Kahane, Springfield College; Peter Kaplan, University of Colorado, Denver; Arthur Kemp, University of Central Missouri; Mark J. Kirschner, Quinnipiac University; Kristina T. Klassen, North Idaho College; Martha Kuehn, Central Lakes College; Cindy J. Lahar, University of Calgary; Chris Layne, University of Toledo; Cynthia Ann Lease, Virginia Polytechnic Institute and State University; Chantal Levesque, University of Rochester; John Lindsay, Georgia College and State University; Mary Livingston, Louisiana Tech University; Linda Lockwood, Metropolitan State College of Denver; Sanford Lopater, Christopher Newport University; Mark Ludorf, Stephen F. Austin State University; Jonathan Lytle, Temple University; Pamelyn M. MacDonald, Washburn University; Steve Madigan, University of Southern California; Don Marzolf, Louisiana State University; Christopher Mayhorn, North Carolina State University; Michael McCall, Ithaca College; David G. McDonald, University of Missouri; Tracy A. McDonough, Mount St. Joseph University; J. Mark McKellop, Juniata College; Mary Meiners, San Diego Miramar College; Diane Mello-Goldner, Pine Manor College; Nancy J. Melucci, Long Beach City College; Michelle Merwin, University of Tennessee at Martin; Rowland Miller, Sam Houston State University; Gloria Mitchell, De Anza College; Paul Moore, Quinnipiac University; Anne Moyer, Stony Brook University; Jeffrey Nagelbush, Ferris State University; Bethany Neal-Beliveau, Indiana University-Purdue University at Indianapolis; Todd Nelson, California State University, Stanislaus; Jan Ochman, Inver Hills Community College; Wendy Palmquist, Plymouth State University; Elizabeth Parks, Kennesaw State University; Gerald Peterson, Saginaw Valley State University; Brady Phelps, South Dakota State University; Shane Pitts, Birmingham-Southern College; William Price, North Country Community College; Thomas Reig, Winona State University; David Reitman, Louisiana State University; Bridget Rivera, Loyola University in Maryland; Robert A. Rosellini, University at Albany; Jeffrey Rudski, Muhlenberg College; Linda Ruehlman, Arizona State University; Richard Russell, Santa Monica College; Mark Samuels, New Mexico Institute of Mining and Technology; Kim Sawrey, University of North Carolina at Wilmington; Troy Schiedenhelm, Rowan-Cabarrus Community College; Michelle N. Shiota, University of California, Berkeley; Eileen Smith, Fairleigh Dickinson University; Noam Shpancer, Otterbein University; James Spencer, West Virginia State University; Jim Stringham, University of Georgia; Robert Stawski, Syracuse University; Whitney Sweeney, Beloit College; Alan Swinkels, St. Edward's University; Natasha Tokowicz, University of Pittsburgh; Patricia Toney, Sandhills Community College; Terry Trepper, Purdue University Calumet; Warren W. Tryon, Fordham University; Katherine Urquhart, Lake Sumter Community College; Stavros Valenti, Hofstra University; Suzanne Valentine-French, College of Lake County; Douglas Wallen, Minnesota State University, Mankato; Michael Walraven, Jackson College; Donald Walter, University of Wisconsin–Parkside; Jeffrey Weatherly, University of North Dakota; Ellen Weissblum, State University of New York Albany; Fred Whitford, Montana State University; Don Wilson, Lane Community College; David Woehr, Texas A&M University; Jay Wright, Washington State University; John W. Wright, Washington State University.

James W. Kalat

Welcome to introductory psychology! I hope you will enjoy reading this text as much as I enjoyed writing it. I have tried to make this book as interesting and as easy to study as possible.

Features of This Text

Modular Format

Each chapter is divided into two or more modules so that you can study a limited section at a time. Each chapter begins with a table of contents and a list of learning objectives. At the end of each module is a summary of important points, a list of key terms, and a few multiple-choice questions. Although the multiple-choice questions are listed at the end, you may find it a good strategy to try answering them before you read the module. Trying the questions at the start will prime you to pay attention to those topics. Do not assume that the summary points and the review questions include everything you should learn! They are only a sampling.

Key Terms

When an important term first appears in the text, it is highlighted in **boldface** and defined in *italics*. All the boldface terms are listed alphabetically at the end of each module. They appear again with definitions in the combined Subject Index and Glossary at the end of the book. You might want to find the Subject Index and Glossary right now and familiarize yourself with it.

I sometimes meet students who think they have mastered the course because they have memorized the definitions. The title of the course is "psychology," not "vocabulary." You do need to understand the defined words, but don't memorize the definitions word for word. It would be better to try to think of examples of each term. Better yet, when appropriate, think of evidence for or against the concept that the term represents.

Questions to Check Your Understanding

People remember material better if they alternate between reading and testing than if they spend the whole time reading. (We'll consider that point again in the chapter on memory.) At various points in this text are Concept Checks, questions that ask you to use or apply the information you just read. Try to answer each of them before reading the answer. If your answer is correct, you can feel encouraged. If it is incorrect, you should reread the section. In MindTap, Mastery Training is an adaptive tool that allows you to practice concepts over time. As you practice, questions adjust to focus on the items where you need the most review. Reminders help you optimize studying by reviewing at times when it will be most beneficial.

Try It Yourself Activities

The text includes many items marked "Try It Yourself." Most of these can be done quickly with little or no equipment. Online Try It Yourself activities are also available on MindTap. These are like the Try It Yourself activities in the text, except that they include sounds and motion. The description of a psychological principle will be easier to understand and remember after you have experienced it yourself.

"What's the Evidence?" Features

With the exception of the introductory chapter, every chapter includes a section titled "What's the Evidence?" These features highlight research studies in more detail, specifying the hypothesis (idea being tested), research methods, results, and interpretation. In some cases, the discussion also mentions the limitations of the study. These sections provide examples of how to evaluate evidence.

MindTap

MindTap for *Introduction to Psychology* creates a unique learning path that fosters increased comprehension and efficiency. It engages students and empowers them to produce their best work—consistently. In MindTap, course material is seamlessly integrated with videos, activities, apps, and more.

- MindTap delivers real-world relevance with activities and assignments designed to help students build critical thinking and analytical skills that can be applied to other courses and to their professional lives.
- MindTap serves as a single destination for all course materials, so students stay organized and efficient, and have the necessary tools to master the content.

- MindTap shows students where they stand at all times—both individually and compared to the highest performers in class. This information helps to motivate and empower performance.

Indexes and Reference List

A section at the back of the book lists the references cited in the text in case you want to check something for more details. The combined Subject Index and Glossary defines key terms and indicates where in the book to find more information. The name index provides the same information for all names mentioned in the text.

Answers to Some Frequently Asked Questions

Do you have any useful suggestions for improving study habits? Whenever students ask me why they did badly on the last test, I ask, "When did you read the assignments?" The typical answer is that they read everything the night before the test. If you want to learn the subject matter well, read the assigned material before the lecture, review it again after the lecture, and quickly go over it again a few days later. Then reread the textbook assignments and your lecture notes before a test. Memory researchers have established that you will understand and remember something better by studying it several times spread out over days than by studying the same amount of time all at once. Also, of course, the more total time you spend studying, the better.

When you study, don't just read the text but stop and think about it. The more actively you use the material, the better you will remember it. One way to improve your studying is to read by the SPAR method: **S**urvey, **P**rocess meaningfully, **A**sk questions, **R**eview.

Survey: Know what to expect so that you can focus on the main points. When you start a module, first look over the learning objectives. It also helps if you turn to the end and read the summary and try to answer the review questions.
Process meaningfully: Read the chapter carefully, stopping to think from time to time. Tell your roommate something you learned. Think about how you might apply a concept to a real-life situation. Pause when you come to the Concept Checks and try to answer them. Do the Try It Yourself exercises. Try to monitor how well you understand the text and adjust your reading accordingly. Good readers read quickly through easy, familiar content but slowly through difficult material.
Ask questions: When you finish the chapter, try to anticipate what questions your instructor would

ask on a test. What questions would you ask, if you were the professor? Write out the questions, think about them, and hold them for later.
Review: Pause for at least an hour, preferably a day or two. Now return to your questions and try to answer them. Check your answers against the text. Reinforcing your memory a day or two after you first read the chapter will help you retain the material longer and deepen your understanding. If you study the same material several times at lengthy intervals, you increase your chance of remembering it long after the course is over.

What do those parentheses mean, as in "(Ferguson, 2013)"? Am I supposed to remember the names and dates? Psychologists generally cite references in the text in parentheses rather than in footnotes. "(Ferguson, 2013)" refers to an article written by Ferguson, published in 2013. All the references cited in the text are listed in alphabetical order (by the author's last name) in the References section at the back of the book. You will also notice a few citations that include two dates separated by a slash, such as "(Wundt, 1862/1961)." This means that Wundt's document was originally published in 1862 and was republished in 1961. No, you should not memorize the parenthetical source citations. They are provided so interested readers can look up the source of a statement and check for further information. The names that *are* worth remembering, such as B. F. Skinner, Jean Piaget, and Sigmund Freud, are emphasized in the discussion itself.

Can you help me read and understand graphs? You will encounter four kinds of graphs in this text: pie graphs, bar graphs, line graphs, and scatter plots. Let's look at each kind.

A pie graph shows the components of a whole. Figure 1 shows the proportion of psychologists who work in various settings. It shows that many are self-employed, almost as many work in colleges and other educational institutions, and a slightly smaller number work in hospitals and other health care institutions.

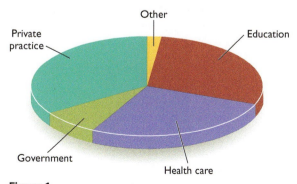

Figure 1

Bar graphs show measurements for two or more groups. Figure 2 shows how much unpleasantness three groups of women reported while they were waiting for a painful shock. The unpleasantness was least if a woman could hold her husband's hand while waiting, intermediate if she held a stranger's hand, and most if she was by herself.

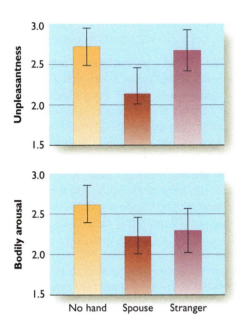

Figure 2

Line graphs show how one variable relates to another variable. Figure 3 shows measurements of conscientiousness in people from age 10 to 80. The upward slope of the line indicates that older people tend to be more conscientious than younger people, on average.

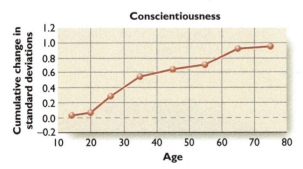

Figure 3

Scatter plots are similar to line graphs, with this difference: A line graph shows averages, whereas a scatter plot shows individual data points. By looking at a scatter plot, we can see how much variation occurs among individuals.

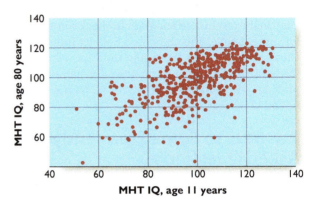

Figure 4

To prepare a scatter plot, we make two observations about each individual. In Figure 4, each person is represented by one point. If you take that point and scan down to the *x*-axis, you find that person's score on an IQ test at age 11. If you then scan across to the *y*-axis, you find that person's score on a similar test at age 80. You can see about how consistent most people's scores are over a lifetime.

We may have to take multiple-choice tests on this material. How can I do better on those tests?

1. Read each choice carefully. Do not choose the first answer that looks correct; first make sure that the other answers are wrong. If two answers fit with what you know, decide which of the two is better.

2. If you don't know the correct answer, make an educated guess. An answer that includes absolute words such as "always" or "never" is probably wrong. Also eliminate any answer that includes unfamiliar terms. If you have never heard of something, it is probably not the right answer. Remember, every test question is about something presented either in lecture or in the text.

3. After you finish, don't be afraid to go back and reconsider your answers. Students have been telling each other for decades that "you should stick with your first answer," but research says that most people who change their answers improve their scores. When you examine a question a second time, you sometimes discover that you misunderstood it the first time.

Last Words Before We Start . . .

Most of all, I hope you enjoy the text. I have tried to include the liveliest examples I can find. The goal is not just to teach you some facts but also to teach you a love of learning so that you will continue to read more and educate yourself about psychology long after your course is over.

James W. Kalat

1 What Is Psychology?

Even when the people we trust seem very confident of their opinions, we should examine their evidence or reasoning.

I f you are like most students, you start off assuming that nearly everything you read in your textbooks and everything your professors tell you must be true. What if it isn't? Suppose impostors have replaced your college's faculty. They pretend to know what they are talking about and they all vouch for one another's competence, but in fact, they are all unqualified. They managed to find textbooks that support their prejudices, but those textbooks are full of false information, too. If so, how would you know?

While we are entertaining such skeptical thoughts, why limit ourselves to colleges? When you read books and magazines or listen to political commentators, how do you know who has the right answers?

No one has the right answers all of the time. One professor starts his first day of class by saying, "At least 10 percent of what I tell you will be wrong. But I don't know which 10 percent it is." Sometimes even the best and most conscientious individuals discover to their embarrassment that a confident opinion was wrong. I don't mean to imply that you should disregard everything you read or hear. But you should expect people to tell you the reasons for their conclusions, so that you can decide which ones to follow with high confidence and which to treat as little better than a guess.

You have just encountered the theme of this book: Evaluate the evidence. You will hear all sorts of claims concerning psychology, as well as medicine, politics, religion, and other fields. Some are valid, some are wrong, some are hard to evaluate for sure, many are valid under certain conditions, and some are too vague to be either right or wrong. When you finish this book, you will be in a better position to examine evidence and decide which claims to take seriously.

module 1.1

Psychologists' Goals

After studying this module, you should be able to:

- Discuss three major philosophical issues important to psychology.

- Distinguish psychology from psychiatry and psychoanalysis.

- Give examples of specializations in psychology, for both research and practice.

Your history text probably doesn't spend much time discussing what the term *history* means, and I doubt that a course on English literature spends the first day defining literature. Psychology is different because so many people have misconceptions about this field. I remember a student who asked when we would get to the kind of psychology he could "use on" people. Another young man bluntly asked me (in my office, not publicly) whether I could teach him tricks to seduce his girlfriend. I told him that (1) psychologists don't try to trick people into doing something against their better judgment, (2) if I did know tricks like that, ethically I couldn't tell him about them, and (3) if I knew powerful tricks to control behavior *and* I had no ethics, I would probably use those powers for my own profit instead of teaching introduction to psychology!

The term *psychology* derives from the Greek roots *psyche,* meaning "soul" or "mind," and *logos,* meaning "word." Psychology is literally the study of the mind or soul, and people defined it that way until the early 1900s. Around 1920, psychologists became disenchanted with the idea of studying the mind. First, research deals with what we observe, and mind is unobservable. Second, talking about "the mind" implies it is a thing or object. Mental activity is a process. It is not like the river but like the flow of the river; not like the automobile but like the movement of the automobile. Beginning in the early 1900s, psychologists defined their field as the study of behavior.

Certainly the study of behavior is important, but is behavior the only thing we care about? When you look at this optical illusion and say that the horizontal part of the top line looks longer than that of the bottom line (although really they are the same length), we wonder why the line *looks* longer, not just why you *said* it looks longer. So as a compromise, let's define psychology as *the systematic study of behavior and experience.* The word *experience* lets us discuss your perceptions without implying that a mind exists independently of your body.

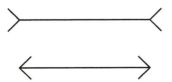

When most people think of psychologists, they think of clinical psychologists—those who try to help worried, depressed, or otherwise troubled people. Clinical psychology is only one part of psychology. Psychology also includes research on sensation and perception, learning and memory, hunger and thirst, sleep, attention, child development, and more. Perhaps you expect that a course in psychology will teach you to "analyze" people and decipher hidden aspects of their personality. It will not. You will learn to understand many aspects of behavior, but you will gain no dazzling powers. Ideally, you will become more skeptical of those who claim to analyze people's personality from small samples of their behavior.

General Points about Psychology

Let's start with three of the most general statements about psychology. Each of these will arise repeatedly throughout this text.

"It Depends"

Hardly anything is true about the behavior of all people all the time. Almost every aspect of behavior depends on age. Infants differ from children, who differ from young adults, who differ from older adults. Behavior also varies with people's genetics, health, past experiences, and whether they are currently awake or asleep. In some ways, behavior differs between males and females or from one culture to another. Some aspects depend on the time of day, the temperature of the room, or how recently someone ate. How someone answers a question depends on the exact wording of the question, the wording of the previous question, and who is asking the questions.

If psychology regards "it depends" as a general truth, you may infer that psychology really doesn't know anything. On the contrary, "it depends" is a serious point. The key is to know *what* it depends on. The further you pursue your studies of psychology, the more you will become attuned to the wealth of subtle influences that people easily overlook. Here is an example: Decades ago, two psychology laboratories were conducting similar studies on human learning but reporting contradictory results. Both researchers were experienced and highly respected, they thought they were following the same procedures, and they did not understand why their results differed. Eventually, one of them traveled to the other's university to watch the other in action. Almost immediately, he noticed a key difference in procedure: the chairs in which the participants sat! His colleague at the other university had obtained chairs from a retired dentist. So the research participants were sitting in *dentist's* chairs, during an era when dental procedures were often painful. The participants were sitting there in a state of heightened anxiety, which altered their behavior (Kimble, 1967).

Progress Depends on Good Measurement

Nobel Prize–winning biologist Sydney Brenner was quoted as saying, "Progress in science depends on new techniques, new discoveries, and new ideas, probably in that order" (McElheny, 2004, p. 71). In any field, from astronomy to zoology, new discoveries and ideas depend on good measurements. Psychologists' understanding has advanced fastest on topics such as sensory processes, learning, and memory, which researchers can measure fairly accurately. Research progress has been slower in such areas as emotion and personality, where we struggle to find clear definitions and accurate measurements. As you proceed through this text, you will note occasional issues such as, "How well do IQ scores really measure intelligence?" or "Are people as happy as they say they are?" Areas of psychology with less certain measurement have less definite conclusions and slower progress.

Confidence in the Conclusions Should Depend on the Strength of the Evidence

Is it all right for young children to spend many hours a day watching television? How much is too much? Is it sometimes all right to spank a child? What should be the limits, if any, on teenagers playing violent video games? To what extent do the behavioral differences between men and women reflect biological influences? You probably have opinions on these questions, and so do many psychologists. However, in many cases, the evidence is not nearly as strong as the confident opinions imply (Ferguson, 2013). It is important to distinguish between opinions based on strong evidence and those based on less. When this text describes research studies in some detail, the reason is to give you an idea of how strong the research evidence is (or isn't) behind some conclusion.

Major Philosophical Issues in Psychology

Psychology began in the late 1800s as an attempt to apply scientific methods to certain questions of the philosophy of mind. Three of the most profound philosophical questions related to psychology are free will versus determinism, the mind–brain problem, and the nature–nurture issue.

Free Will versus Determinism

The scientific approach to anything, including psychology, assumes that we live in a universe of cause and effect. If things "just happen" for no reason at

Behavior is guided by external forces, such as waves, and by forces within the individual. According to the determinist view, even those internal forces follow physical laws.

all, then we have no hope of discovering scientific principles. That is, scientists assume determinism, *the idea that everything that happens has a cause, or determinant, that someone could observe or measure.* This view is an assumption, not a certainty, but the success of scientific research attests to its value.

Does it apply to human behavior? We are, after all, part of the physical world. According to the determinist assumption, everything we do has causes. This view seems to conflict with the impression all of us have that "I make the decisions about my actions. Sometimes, when I am making a decision, like what to eat for lunch or which sweater to buy, I am in doubt right up to the last second. The decision could have gone either way." *The belief that behavior is caused by a person's independent decisions* is known as free will. Do you think your behavior is predictable? How about other people's behavior? Questionnaires show that most people think their own behavior is less predictable than other people's. That is, you think you have free will, but other people, not so much (Pronin & Kugler, 2010).

Some psychologists maintain that free will is an illusion (Wegner, 2002): What you call a conscious intention is more a prediction than a cause of your behavior. When you have the experience of deciding to move a finger, the behavior has already started to happen, controlled unconsciously. We shall explore the evidence for this idea later, in Chapter 10.

Other psychologists and philosophers reply that you do make decisions, in the sense that something within you initiates the action (Baumeister, 2008). When a ball bounces down a hill, its motion depends on the shape of the hill. When you run down a hill, you could change direction if you saw a car coming toward you, or a snake lying in your path. The ball could not.

Nevertheless, the "you" that makes your decisions is itself a product of your heredity and the events of your life. (You did not create yourself.) In a sense, yes, you have a will, an ability to make choices (Dennett, 2003). But your will is the product of your heredity and experiences. It did not emerge from nothing. Whether you do or do not have free will depends on what you mean by "free."

The test of determinism is ultimately empirical: If everything you do has a cause, your behavior should be predictable. Behavior is clearly predictable in some cases, such as reflexes. However, ordinarily psychologists' predictions are more like predicting the weather. The predictions are nearly accurate most of the time, but they cannot be accurate in every detail, simply because so many small influences are operating.

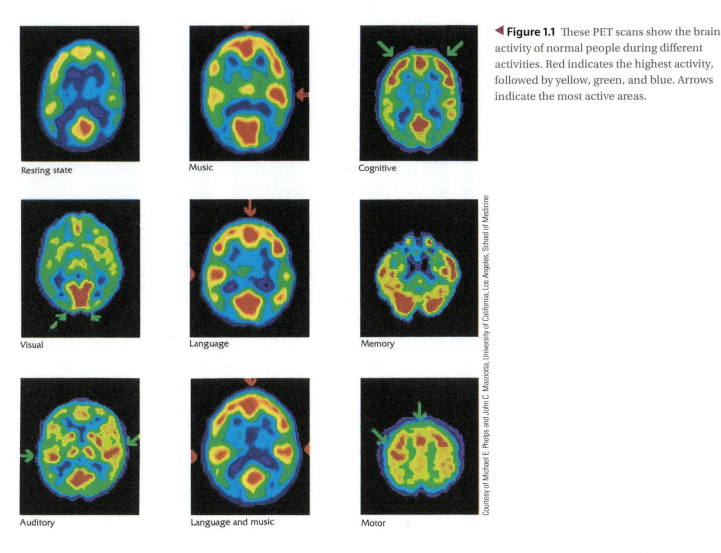

Resting state   Music   Cognitive

Visual   Language   Memory

Auditory   Language and music   Motor

◄ Figure 1.1 These PET scans show the brain activity of normal people during different activities. Red indicates the highest activity, followed by yellow, green, and blue. Arrows indicate the most active areas.

Courtesy of Michael E. Phelps and John C. Mazziotta, University of California, Los Angeles, School of Medicine

Researchers admit one point: Although determinism makes sense theoretically and leads to good research, it doesn't work well as a philosophy of life. One study provides a good illustration of this point: Psychologists asked people to read one of two passages. Some read an argument for determinism, and others read a paper on an irrelevant topic. The participants were then put in a situation in which it would be easy to cheat to gain a personal advantage. A higher percentage of those who had read the determinism essay cheated (Vohs & Schooler, 2008). Apparently, they felt less sense of personal responsibility.

The Mind–Brain Problem

Given that we live in a universe of matter and energy, what, if anything, is the mind? And why does consciousness exist? The *philosophical question of how experience relates to the brain* is the mind–brain problem (or mind–body problem). One view, called dualism, holds that *the mind is separate from the brain but somehow controls the brain and therefore the rest of the body.* However, dualism contradicts the law of conservation of matter and energy, one of the cornerstones of physics. According to that principle, the only way to influence any matter or energy, including the matter and energy that compose your body, is to act on it with other matter or energy. If the mind isn't composed of matter or energy, it cannot *do* anything. For that reason, nearly all brain researchers and philosophers favor monism, *the view that conscious experience is inseparable from the physical brain.* That is, mental activity *is* brain activity. So far as we can tell, consciousness cannot exist without brain activity, and presumably it is also true that certain kinds of brain activity cannot exist without consciousness. The

mind–brain problem inspires much research, some of which we shall consider in Chapter 3 on the brain and Chapter 10 on consciousness.

The photos in **▲ Figure 1.1** show brain activity while a person participated in nine tasks, as measured by a technique called positron-emission tomography (PET). Red indicates the highest degree of brain activity, followed by yellow, green, and blue. As you can see, the various tasks increased activity in different brain areas, although all areas showed some activity at all times (Phelps & Mazziotta, 1985). You might ask: Did the brain activity cause the thoughts, or did the thoughts cause the brain activity? Most brain researchers reply, "Neither," because brain activity and mental activity are the same thing.

Even if we accept this position, we are still far from understanding the mind–brain relationship. What type of brain activity is associated with consciousness? Why does conscious experience exist at all? Could a brain get along without consciousness? Research studies are not about to put philosophers out of business, but results do constrain the philosophical answers that we can seriously consider.

Why do different children develop different interests? They had different hereditary tendencies, but they also had different experiences. Separating the roles of nature and nurture is difficult.

The Nature–Nurture Issue

Why do most little boys spend more time than little girls with toy guns and trucks and less time with dolls? Is it because of biological differences or because parents rear their sons and daughters differently?

Alcohol abuse is common in some cultures and rare in others. Are these differences entirely a matter of social custom, or do genes influence alcohol use also?

Certain psychological disorders are more common in large cities than in small towns and in the countryside. Does life in crowded cities cause psychological disorders? Or do people develop such disorders because of a genetic predisposition and then move to big cities in search of jobs, housing, and welfare services?

Each of these questions relates to the **nature–nurture issue** (or heredity-environment issue): *How do differences in behavior relate to differences in heredity and environment?* The nature–nurture issue shows up in various ways throughout psychology, and it seldom has a simple answer.

concept check

1. **What is meant by determinism?**
2. **What type of evidence supports monism?**

Answers

2. Every type of mental activity is associated with some type of measurable brain activity. Also, as discussed in Chapter 3, any type of brain damage leads to a deficit in some aspect of behavior or experience.

1. Determinism is the assumption that everything that happens has a cause.

What Psychologists Do

We have considered some major philosophical issues related to psychology in general. However, most psychologists deal with smaller, more manageable questions. They work in many occupational settings, as shown in ▼ Figure 1.2. The most common settings are colleges and universities, private practice, hospitals and mental health clinics, and government agencies.

Service Providers to Individuals

It is important to distinguish between several types of mental health professionals. Some of the main kinds of service providers for people with psychological troubles are clinical psychologists, psychiatrists, social workers, and counseling psychologists.

Clinical Psychology

Clinical psychologists *have an advanced degree in psychology (master's degree, doctor of philosophy [PhD], or doctor of psychology [PsyD]), with a specialty in understanding and helping people with psychological problems.* Those problem range from depression, anxiety, and substance abuse to marriage conflicts, difficulties making decisions, or even the feeling that "I should be getting more out of life." Clinical psychologists try, in one way or another, to understand why a person is having problems and then help that person overcome the difficulties. Some clinical psychologists are college professors and researchers, but most are full-time practitioners. A little over half of all new PhDs are for specialists in clinical psychology or other health-related fields.

Psychiatry

Psychiatry is a *branch of medicine that deals with emotional disturbances.* To become psychiatrists, students first earn a medical doctor (MD) degree and then take an additional four years of residency training in psychiatry. Because psychiatrists are medical doctors, they can prescribe drugs, such as antidepressants, whereas most psychologists cannot. In the United States, a few states now permit psychologists with a couple years of additional training to prescribe drugs.

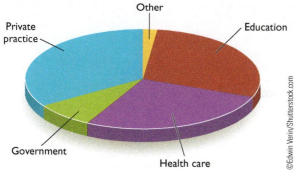

Figure 1.2 Psychologists work in a variety of settings. (Based on data from U.S. Department of Labor, 2008)

More psychiatrists than clinical psychologists work in mental hospitals, and psychiatrists more often treat clients with severe disorders.

Does psychiatrists' ability to prescribe drugs give them an advantage over psychologists in places where psychologists cannot prescribe them? Not always. Drugs can be useful, but relying heavily on them can be a mistake. Whereas a typical visit to a clinical psychologist includes an extensive discussion of the client's troubles, many visits to a psychiatrist focus mainly on checking the effectiveness of a drug and evaluating its side effects. A survey found that over the years, fewer and fewer psychiatrists have been providing talk therapy (Mojtabai & Olfson, 2008).

Other Mental Health Professionals

Several other kinds of professionals also provide help and counsel. **Psychoanalysts** are *therapy providers who rely heavily on the theories and methods pioneered by the early 20th-century Viennese physician Sigmund Freud and later modified by others.* Freud and his followers attempted to infer the hidden, unconscious, symbolic meaning behind people's words and actions, and psychoanalysts today continue that effort.

There is some dispute about who may rightly call themselves psychoanalysts. Some people apply the term to anyone who attempts to uncover unconscious thoughts and feelings. Others apply the term only to graduates of an institute of psychoanalysis, a program that lasts four years or more. These institutes admit mostly people who are already either psychiatrists or clinical psychologists. Thus, people completing psychoanalytic training will be at least in their mid 30s.

A **clinical social worker** *is similar to a clinical psychologist but with different training.* In most cases, a clinical social worker has a master's degree in social work with a specialization in psychological problems. Many health maintenance organizations (HMOs) steer most of their clients with psychological problems toward clinical social workers instead of psychologists or psychiatrists because the social workers, with less formal education, charge less per hour.

Table 1.1 Mental Health Professionals	
Type of Therapist	**Education**
clinical psychologist	PhD with clinical emphasis or PsyD plus internship. Ordinarily, 5+ years after undergraduate degree.
psychiatrist	MD plus psychiatric residency. Total of 8 years after undergraduate degree.
psychoanalyst	Psychiatry or clinical psychology plus 4 or more years in a psychoanalytic institute. Many others who rely on Freudian methods also call themselves psychoanalysts.
psychiatric nurse	From 2-year (AA) degree to master's degree plus supervised experience.
clinical social worker	Master's degree plus 2 years of supervised experience.
counseling psychologist	PhD, PsyD, or EdD plus supervised experience in counseling.
forensic psychologist	Doctorate, ordinarily in clinical psychology or counseling psychology, plus additional training in legal issues.

Some psychiatric nurses (nurses with additional training in psychiatry) provide similar services.

Counseling psychologists *help people with educational, vocational, marriage, health-related, and other decisions.* A counseling psychologist has a doctorate degree (PhD, PsyD, or EdD) with supervised experience in counseling. Whereas a clinical psychologist deals mainly with anxiety, depression, and other emotional distress, a counseling psychologist deals mostly with life decisions and family or career readjustments. Counseling psychologists work in educational institutions, mental health centers, rehabilitation agencies, businesses, and private practice.

You may also have heard of **forensic psychologists,** *who provide advice and consultation to police, lawyers, and courts.* Forensic psychologists are clinical or counseling psychologists who have additional training in legal issues. They advise on such decisions as whether a defendant is mentally competent to stand trial or whether someone eligible for parole is dangerous (Otto & Heilbrun, 2002). Several popular films and television series have depicted forensic psychologists helping police investigators develop a psychological profile of a serial killer. That may sound like an exciting, glamorous profession, but few psychologists engage in such activities (and the accuracy of their profiles is uncertain, as discussed in Chapter 14). Most criminal profilers today have training and experience in law enforcement, not psychology.

■ Table 1.1 compares various types of mental health professionals.

3. How does the education of a clinical psychologist differ from that of a psychiatrist?

Answer

3. A clinical psychologist earns an advanced degree in psychology, generally a PhD or PsyD, that focuses more on research. A psychiatrist earns an MD, like other medical doctors.

Service Providers to Organizations

Psychologists also work in business, industry, and school systems, doing work you might not recognize as psychology. The job prospects in these fields have been good, and you might find these fields interesting.

Industrial/Organizational Psychology

The psychological study of people at work is known as **industrial/organizational (I/O) psychology**. This field deals with such issues as hiring the right person for a job, training people for jobs, developing work teams, determining salaries and bonuses, providing feedback to workers about their performance, planning an organizational structure, and organizing the workplace so that workers will be productive and satisfied. I/O psychologists attend to both the individual workers and the organization, including the impact of economic conditions and government regulations.

Here's an example of a concern for industrial/organizational psychologists (Campion & Thayer, 1989): A company that manufactures complex electronic equipment needed to publish reference and repair manuals for its products. The engineers who designed the devices did not want to spend their time writing the manuals, and none of them were skilled writers anyway. So the company hired a technical writer to prepare the manuals. After a year, she received an unsatisfactory performance rating because the manuals she wrote contained too many technical errors. She countered that, when she asked various engineers in the company to check her manuals or to explain technical details to her, they were always too busy. She found her job complicated and frustrating. Her office was badly lit, noisy, and overheated, and her chair was uncomfortable. Whenever she mentioned these problems, she was told that she "complained too much."

In a situation such as this, an industrial/organizational psychologist helps the company evaluate its options. One solution would be to fire her and hire an expert on electrical engineering who

Human factors specialists help redesign machines to make them easier and safer to use. This field uses principles of both engineering and psychology.

is also an outstanding writer who tolerates a badly lit, noisy, overheated, uncomfortable office. However, if the company cannot find or afford such a person, then it needs to improve the working conditions and provide the current employee with more training and help.

Human Factors

Learning to operate our increasingly complex machinery is one of the struggles of modern life. Sometimes, the consequences are serious. Imagine an airplane pilot who intends to lower the landing gear and instead raises the wing flaps. Or a worker in a nuclear power plant who fails to notice a warning signal. A type of psychologist known as a **human factors specialist** (or **ergonomist**) *attempts to facilitate the operation of machinery so that ordinary people can use it efficiently and safely*. Human factors specialists first worked in military settings, where complex technologies sometimes require soldiers to spot nearly invisible targets, understand speech through deafening noise, track objects in three dimensions, and make life-or-death decisions in a split second. The military turned to psychologists to redesign the tasks to fit the skills that their personnel could master.

Human factors specialists soon applied their expertise to the design of everyday devices, such as cameras, computers, microwave ovens, and cell phones. The field combines features of psychology, engineering, and computer science. It is a growing field with many jobs available.

Military Psychologists

Military psychologists are *specialists who provide services to the military* in many ways. Some are similar to industrial/organizational psychologists, conducting intellectual and personality tests to identify people suitable for certain jobs within the military, and then helping to train people for those jobs. Other military psychologists consult with the leadership about strategies, including the challenges of dealing with allies or enemies from a different culture. Still others provide clinical and counseling services to soldiers dealing with highly stressful experiences. Few experiences in life are more stressful than military combat.

Infants and young children will try to eat almost anything that tastes okay. As they grow older, they begin to avoid foods for reasons other than taste.

let's consider one example: how we select what to eat. Different kinds of psychologists offer different explanations.

Developmental Psychology

Developmental psychologists *study how behavior changes with age,* "from womb to tomb." For example, they might examine language development from age 2 to 4 or memory from age 60 to 80, both describing the changes and trying to explain them.

With regard to food selection, some taste preferences are present from birth. Newborns prefer sweet tastes and avoid bitter and sour substances. However, they appear indifferent to salty tastes, as if they could not yet taste salts (Beauchamp, Cowart, Mennella, & Marsh, 1994). Toddlers will try to eat almost anything they can fit into their mouths, unless it tastes sour or bitter. For that reason, parents need to keep dangerous substances like furniture polish out of toddlers' reach. Older children become increasingly selective about the foods they accept, but up to age 7 or 8, usually the only reason children give for refusing something is that they think it would taste bad (Rozin, Fallon, & Augustoni-Ziskind, 1986). As they grow older, they cite more complex reasons for rejecting foods, such as health concerns.

Also, some psychologists conduct research on such topics as how best to deal with battlefield stress, sleep deprivation, and other difficulties. Matthews (2014) has argued that military psychologists will become increasingly important, as future conflicts pertain more to influencing people than attacking them.

School Psychology

Many if not most children have school problems at one time or another. Some children have trouble sitting still or paying attention. Others get into trouble for misbehavior. Some have problems with reading or other academic skills. Others master their schoolwork quickly and become bored. They too need special attention.

School psychologists are *specialists in the psychological condition of students,* usually in kindergarten through the 12th grade. School psychologists identify children's educational needs, devise a plan to meet those needs, and then either implement the plan themselves or advise teachers how to implement it.

School psychology can be taught in a psychology department, a branch of an education department, or a department of educational psychology. In some countries, it is possible to practice school psychology with only a bachelor's degree. In the United States, the minimum education requirement for a school psychologist is usually a master's degree, but a doctorate may become necessary in the future. Most school psychologists work for a school system, but some work for mental health clinics, guidance centers, and other institutions.

Psychologists in Teaching and Research

Many psychologists, especially those who are not clinical psychologists, teach and conduct research in colleges and universities. To some extent, different kinds of psychologists study different topics. For example, developmental psychologists observe children, and biological psychologists examine the effects of brain damage. However, different kinds of psychologists also sometimes study the same questions, approaching them in different ways. To illustrate,

Learning and Motivation

The research field of **learning and motivation** studies *how behavior depends on the outcomes of past behaviors and current motivations.* How often we engage in any particular behavior depends on the results of that behavior in the past.

We learn our food choices largely by learning what *not* to eat. For example, if you eat something and then feel sick, you form an aversion to the taste of that food, especially if it was unfamiliar. It doesn't matter whether you consciously think the food made you ill. If you eat something at an amusement park and then go on a wild ride and get sick, you may dislike that food, even though you know the ride was at fault.

Cognitive Psychology

Cognition means *thought and knowledge.* A **cognitive psychologist** *studies those processes.* (The root *cogn-* also shows up in the word *recognize,* which literally means "to know again.") Typically, cognitive psychologists focus on how people make decisions, solve problems, and convert their thoughts into language. These psychologists study both the best and the worst of human cognition (expert decision making and why people make costly errors).

Cognitive psychologists seldom study anything related to food selection, but cognitions about food do enter into our food decisions. For example, people often refuse an edible food just because of the very idea of it (Rozin & Fallon, 1987; Rozin, Millman, & Nemeroff, 1986). Most people in the United States refuse to eat meat from dogs, cats, or horses. Vegetarians reject all meat, not because they think it would taste bad, but because they dislike the idea of eating animal parts. On average, the longer people have been vegetarians, the more firmly they regard meat eating as wrong (Rozin, Markwith, & Stoess, 1997).

How would you like to try the tasty morsels in ▶ Figure 1.3? You might be repulsed by the idea of eating insects, even if they are guaranteed to be safe and nutritious (Rozin & Fallon, 1987). Would you be willing to drink a glass of apple juice after you watched someone dip a cockroach into it? What if the cockroach was carefully sterilized? Some people not only refuse to drink that particular glass of apple juice but also say they have lost their taste for apple juice in general (Rozin et al., 1986). Would you drink pure water from a brand-new, never-used toilet bowl? Would you eat a piece of chocolate fudge shaped like dog feces? If not, you are guided by the idea of the food, not its taste or safety.

Biological Psychology

A **biopsychologist** (or **behavioral neuroscientist**) *explains behavior in terms of biological factors, such as activities of the nervous system, the effects of drugs and hormones, genetics, and evolutionary pressures.* How would a biological psychologist approach the question of how people (or animals) select foods?

If you ate corn dogs and cotton candy and then got sick on a wild ride, something in your brain would blame the food, regardless of what you think consciously. This kind of learning helps us avoid harmful substances.

▲ **Figure 1.3** Some cultures consider insects to be good food, whereas others consider them disgusting.

A small part of the difference among people in their taste preferences relates to the fact that some people have up to three times as many taste buds as others do, mostly for genetic reasons. The genes vary within each population, although the relative frequencies of strong tasters and weak tasters are fairly similar for Asia, Europe, and Africa (Wooding, Bamshad, Larsen, Jorde, & Drayna, 2004). People with the most taste buds usually have the least tolerance for strong tastes, including black coffee, black breads, hot peppers, grapefruit, radishes, and Brussels sprouts (Bartoshuk, Duffy, Lucchina, Prutkin, & Fast, 1998; Drewnowski, Henderson, Short, & Barratt-Fornell, 1998). Most of them also dislike foods that are too sweet (Yeomans, Tepper, Rietzschel, & Prescott, 2007).

Hormones also affect taste preferences. Many years ago, one child showed a strong craving for salt. As an infant, he licked the salt off crackers and bacon without eating the food itself. He put a thick layer of salt on everything he ate. Sometimes he swallowed salt directly from the shaker. When deprived of salt, he stopped eating and began to waste away. At the age of $3^{1}/_{2}$, he was taken to the hospital and fed the usual hospital fare. He soon died of salt deficiency (Wilkins & Richter, 1940).

The reason was that he had defective adrenal glands, which secrete the hormones that enable the body to retain salt (Verrey & Beron, 1996). He craved salt because he had to consume it fast enough to replace what he lost in his urine. (Too much salt is bad for your health, but too little salt is also dangerous.) Later research confirmed that salt-deficient animals immediately show an increased preference for salty tastes (Rozin & Kalat, 1971). Becoming salt deficient causes salty foods to taste especially good (Jacobs, Mark, & Scott, 1988). People often report salt cravings after losing salt by bleeding or sweating, and many women crave salt during menstruation or pregnancy.

Evolutionary Psychology

An **evolutionary psychologist** *tries to explain behavior in terms of the evolutionary history of the species, including why evolution might have favored a tendency to act in particular ways.* For example, *why* do people and other animals crave sweets and avoid bitter tastes? Here, the answer is easy: Most sweets are nutritious and almost all bitter substances are poisonous (T. R. Scott & Verhagen, 2000). Ancient animals that ate fruits and other sweets survived to become our ancestors.

However, although some evolutionary explanations of behavior are persuasive, others are debatable (de Waal, 2002). Yes, the brain is the product of evolution, just as any other organ is, but the question is whether evolution has micromanaged our behavior. The research challenge is to separate the evolutionary influences on our behavior from what we have learned during a lifetime.

Social Psychology and Cross-Cultural Psychology

Social psychologists *study how an individual influences other people and how the group influences an individual.* For example, people usually eat together, and on the average we eat about twice as much when we are in a large group as we do when eating alone (de Castro, 2000). If you invite guests to your house, you offer them something to eat or drink as a way to strengthen a social relationship.

Cross-cultural psychology *compares the behavior of people from different cultures.* Comparing people from different cultures is central to determining what is truly characteristic of humans and what varies depending on our background.

Cuisine is one of the most stable and defining features of any culture. In one study, researchers interviewed Japanese high school and college students who had spent a year in another country as part of an exchange program. The students' satisfaction with their year abroad had little relationship to the educational system, religion, family life, recreation, or dating customs of the host country. The main determinant of their satisfaction was the food: Students who could sometimes eat Japanese food had a good time. Those who could not became homesick (Furukawa, 1997).

The similarity between the words *culture* and *agriculture* is no coincidence, as cultivating crops was a major step toward civilization. We learn from our culture what to eat and how to prepare it (Rozin, 1996). Consider, for example, cassava, a root vegetable that is poisonous unless someone washes and pounds it for three days. Can you imagine discovering that fact? Someone had to say, "So far, everyone who ate this plant died, but I bet that if I wash and pound it for three days, then it will be okay." That was a difficult and amazing discovery, but once someone discovered it, culture passed it on to later generations and eventually other countries and continents.

Cassava, a root vegetable native to South America, is now a staple food in much of Africa as well. It grows in climates not suitable for most other crops. However, people must pound and wash it for days to remove the cyanide.

■ **Table 1.2** summarizes some of the major fields of psychology, including several that have not been discussed.

concept check

4. a. Of the kinds of psychological research just described— developmental psychology, learning and motivation, cognitive psychology, biological psychology, evolutionary psychology, social psychology, and cross-cultural psychology— which field concentrates most on children?

b. Which two are most concerned with how people behave in groups?

c. Which concentrates most on thought and knowledge?

d. Which is most interested in the effects of brain damage?

e. Which is most concerned with studying the effect of a reward on future behavior?

5. Why do many menstruating women crave potato chips?

Answers

4. a. Developmental psychology. b. Social psychology and cross-cultural psychology. c. Cognitive psychology. d. Biological psychology. e. Learning and motivation. 5. By losing blood, they also lose salt, and a deficiency of salt triggers a craving for salty tastes.

Should You Major in Psychology?

If your main criterion for choosing a major is to get a high-paying job, your best bet is to major in engineering, computers, business, or one of the natural sciences (Rajecki & Borden, 2011). Nevertheless, psychology majors do get jobs, including many jobs with high interest or high opportunity for a sense of accomplishment. According to one survey, 20 to 25 percent of psychology majors took jobs such as personnel work or social services that relate closely to psychology (Borden & Rajecki, 2000). Others took a variety of jobs in business and government. Whatever the job, psychology courses prepare people to evaluate evidence, organize and write papers, handle statistics, listen carefully to what people say, and respect cultural differences. Those skills are important for almost anything you might do.

Many students major in psychology and then apply to medical school, dental school, law school, divinity school, or other professional schools. Find out what coursework is expected for the professional program of your choice and then

Table 1.2 Some Major Specializations in Psychology

Specialization	General Interest	Example of Interest or Research Topic
Biopsychologist	Relationship between brain and behavior	What body signals indicate hunger and satiety?
Clinical psychologist	Emotional difficulties	How can people be helped to overcome severe anxiety?
Cognitive psychologist	Memory, thinking	Do people have several kinds of memory?
Community psychologist	Organizations and social structures	Would improved job opportunities decrease psychological distress?
Counseling psychologist	Helping people make important decisions	Should this person consider changing careers?
Developmental psychologist	Changes in behavior over age	At what age can a child first distinguish between appearance and reality?
Educational psychologist	Improvement of learning in school	What is the best way to test a student's knowledge?
Environmental psychologist	How factors such as noise, heat, and crowding affect behavior	What building design can maximize the productivity of the people who use it?
Evolutionary psychologist	Evolutionary history of behavior	How did people evolve their facial expressions of emotion?
Human factors specialist	Communication between person and machine	How can an airplane cockpit be redesigned to increase safety?
Industrial/organizational psychologist	People at work	Should jobs be made simple and foolproof or interesting and challenging?
Learning and motivation specialist	Learning in humans and other species	What are the effects of reinforcement and punishment?
Personality psychologist	Personality differences	Why are certain people shy and others gregarious?
Psychometrician	Measuring intelligence, personality, interests	How fair are current IQ tests? Can we devise better tests?
School psychologist	Problems that affect schoolchildren	How should the school handle a child who regularly disrupts the classroom?
Social psychologist	Group behavior, social influences	What methods of persuasion are most effective for changing attitudes?

compare the coursework required for a psychology major. You will probably find that the psychology major is compatible with your professional preparation.

Suppose you want a career as a psychologist. The educational requirements vary among countries, but in the United States and Canada, nearly all jobs in psychology require education beyond a bachelor's degree. People with a master's degree can get jobs in mental health or educational counseling, but in most states, they must work under the supervision of someone with a doctorate. People with a PhD (doctor of philosophy) in clinical psychology or a PsyD (doctor of psychology) degree can provide mental health services. The main difference between the PhD and PsyD degrees is that the PhD includes an extensive research project, leading to a dissertation, whereas the PsyD degree does not. PsyD programs vary strikingly, including some that are academically strong and others with low standards (Norcross, Kohout, & Wicherski, 2005). A college teaching or research position almost always requires a PhD. An increasing percentage of doctorate-level psychologists now work in business, industry, and the military doing research related to practical problems.

For more information about majoring in psychology, prospects for graduate school, and a great variety of jobs for psychology graduates, visit the website of the American Psychological Association.

Types of Psychologists

Experimental psychology researchers, clinical psychologists, human factors specialists, and industrial/organizational psychologists are all psychologists, even though their daily activities have little in common. What unites psychologists is a dedication to progress through research.

This discussion of the various psychological approaches has been simplified in several ways. In particular, biological psychology, cognitive psychology, social psychology, and the other fields overlap significantly. Nearly all psychologists combine insights and information gained from several approaches.

Many like to hyphenate their self-description to emphasize the overlap. For example, "I'm a social-developmental-cognitive neuroscientist."

As we proceed through this book, we shall consider one type of behavior at a time and, generally, one approach at a time. That is simply a necessity; we cannot talk intelligently about many topics at once. But bear in mind that all these processes do ultimately fit together. What you do at any given moment depends on a great many influences.

Summary

The page number after an item indicates where the topic is first discussed.

- *What is psychology?* Psychology is the systematic study of behavior and experience. Psychologists deal with both theoretical and practical questions. (page 3)
- *Three general themes.* Almost any behavior depends on many influences, and few statements apply to everyone all the time. Research progress depends on good measurement. Some conclusions in psychology are based on stronger evidence than others. (page 3)
- *Determinism–free will.* Determinism is the view that everything, including human behavior, has a physical cause. This view is difficult to reconcile with the feeling that humans have free will—that we deliberately, consciously decide what to do. (page 4)
- *Mind–brain.* The mind–brain problem is the question of how conscious experience relates to the activity of the brain. (page 5)
- *Nature–nurture.* Behavior depends on both nature (heredity) and nurture (environment). The relative contributions of nature and nurture vary from one behavior to another. (page 6)

- *Psychology and psychiatry.* Clinical psychologists have a PhD, PsyD, or master's degree. Psychiatrists are medical doctors. Both clinical psychologists and psychiatrists treat people with emotional problems, but psychiatrists can prescribe drugs and other medical treatments, whereas in most states, psychologists cannot. Counseling psychologists help people deal with difficult decisions, and less often deal with serious disorders. (page 6)
- *Service providers to organizations.* Nonclinical fields of application include industrial/organizational psychology, human factors, and school psychology. (page 8)
- *Research fields in psychology.* Psychology as an academic field has many subfields, including biological psychology, learning and motivation, cognitive psychology, developmental psychology, and social psychology. (page 9)
- *Job prospects.* People with a bachelor's degree in psychology enter a wide variety of careers or continue their education in professional schools. Those with an advanced degree in psychology have additional possibilities depending on their area of specialization. (page 11)

Key Terms

You can check the page listed for a complete description of a term. You can also check the glossary/index at the end of the text for a definition of a given term.

biopsychologist (or behavioral neuroscientist) (page 10)

clinical psychologist (page 6)

clinical social worker (page 7)

cognition (page 9)

cognitive psychologist (page 9)

counseling psychologist (page 7)

cross-cultural psychology (page 11)

determinism (page 4)

developmental psychologist (page 9)

dualism (page 5)

evolutionary psychologist (page 10)

forensic psychologist (page 7)

free will (page 4)

human factors specialist (or ergonomist) (page 8)

industrial/organizational (I/O) psychology (page 8)

learning and motivation (page 9)

mind–brain problem (page 5)

military psychologist (page 8)

monism (page 5)

nature–nurture issue (page 6)

psychiatry (page 6)

psychoanalyst (page 7)

psychology (page 3)

school psychologist (page 9)

social psychologist (page 11)

Review Questions

1. Which of the following ideas is essential to determinism?
   (a) People who try harder are more successful.
   (b) People choose their behaviors by free will.
   (c) Most differences in behavior are under genetic control.
   (d) Every behavior has a cause.
2. Which of the following contradicts the idea of dualism?
   (a) Biologists' principle of homeostasis
   (b) Physicists' principle of the conservation of matter and energy
   (c) Chemists' principle of ionic bonding
   (d) Psychologists' principle of reinforcement
3. Of the following, who can prescribe drugs?
   (a) Psychiatrists only
   (b) Clinical psychologists only
   (c) Psychoanalysts only
   (d) Psychiatrists, most psychoanalysts, and a few clinical psychologists
4. Here are four types of psychologists. Which one is correctly matched to a research area?
   (a) Social psychologist—evolution of behavior
   (b) Developmental psychologist—child behavior
   (c) Cognitive psychologist—how people behave in groups
   (d) Biological psychologist—thought and knowledge
5. Why do some people taste certain foods more strongly than others do?
   (a) The taste area of their brain is significantly larger.
   (b) They have up to three times as many taste buds.
   (c) They have higher amounts of a hormone produced by the adrenal gland.
   (d) They come from a culture that puts more value on taste.

Answers: 1d, 2b, 3d, 4b, 5b.

module 1.2

Psychology Then and Now

After studying this module, you should be able to:

- Describe the main research interests of the earliest psychologists.
- List some differences between psychology in its early days and psychology today.
- Explain why early psychologists rejected the study of conscious experience.

Imagine yourself as a young scholar in 1880. Enthusiastic about the new scientific approach in psychology, you decide to become a psychologist. Like other early psychologists, you have a background in either biology or philosophy. You are determined to apply the scientific methods of biology to the problems of philosophy.

So far, so good. But what questions will you address? A good research question is interesting and answerable. (If it cannot be both, it should at least be one or the other!) In 1880, how would you choose a research topic? You cannot get research ideas from a psychological journal because the first issue won't be published until the following year (in German). You cannot follow in the tradition of previous researchers because there haven't *been* any previous researchers. You are on your own.

In the next several pages, we shall explore some of the changes in what psychologists considered good research topics, including projects that dominated psychology for a while and then faded. We shall consider additional historical developments in later chapters. ▼ Figure 1.4 outlines some major historical events inside and outside psychology.

The Early Era

The sciences of astronomy, physics, chemistry, and biology developed gradually over centuries. At first, all practitioners were amateurs. They worked in medicine, law, or other professions and did research in their spare time. Long before any people called themselves scientists, and long before universities began to include these fields as worthy areas of study, the amateur investigators had accumulated a great deal of knowledge.

In contrast, psychology began as a deliberate attempt to start a new science. In the late 1800s, several scholars noted the progress occurring in biology, chemistry, and other fields, and contrasted it to their perception that our understanding of mental processes had not advanced much since the time of Aristotle. They proposed to attack the age-old questions of mind by using the methods of science. Whether a science of mind was even possible, many doubted. But the only way to find out was to try.

Wilhelm Wundt and the First Psychological Laboratory

In 1879, medical doctor and sensory researcher Wilhelm Wundt (pronounced voont) set up in Leipzig, Germany, the first laboratory intended exclusively for psychological research. Wundt's interests were wide-ranging (Zehr, 2000), but one of his goals was to find the elements of experience, comparable to those of chemistry. Psychology's elements were, he maintained, sensations and feelings

(Wundt, 1896/1902).[1] At any moment, you might experience the taste of a fine meal, the sound of good music, and a certain degree of pleasure. These elements would merge into a compound that was your experience. Furthermore, Wundt maintained, your experience is partly under your voluntary control; you can shift your attention from one element to another and get a different experience. To test his idea about the components of experience, Wundt presented various kinds of lights, textures, and sounds, and asked subjects to report the intensity and quality of their sensations. That is, he asked them to introspect—*to look within themselves*. He recorded the changes in people's reports as he changed the stimuli.

Wundt demonstrated the possibility of meaningful psychological research. For example, in one of his earliest studies, he set up a pendulum that struck metal balls and made a sound at two points on its swing. People would watch the pendulum and indicate where it appeared to be when they heard the sound. On average, people reported the pendulum to be about an eighth of a second in front of or behind the ball when they heard the strike (Wundt, 1862/1961). Apparently, the time we think we see or hear something is not the same as when the event occurs. Wundt's interpretation was that a person needs about an eighth of a second to shift attention from one stimulus to another.

Wundt and his students were prolific investigators, and the brief treatment here cannot do him justice. He wrote more than 50,000 pages about his research, but his main impact came from setting the precedent of collecting scientific data to answer psychological questions.

Edward Titchener and Structuralism

At first, most of the world's psychologists received their education from Wundt himself. One of his students, Edward Titchener, came to the United States in 1892 as a psychology professor at Cornell University. Like Wundt, Titchener believed that the main question of psychology was the nature of mental experiences.

[1] A reference citation containing a slash between the years, such as this one, refers to a book originally published in the first year (1896) and reprinted in the second year (1902).

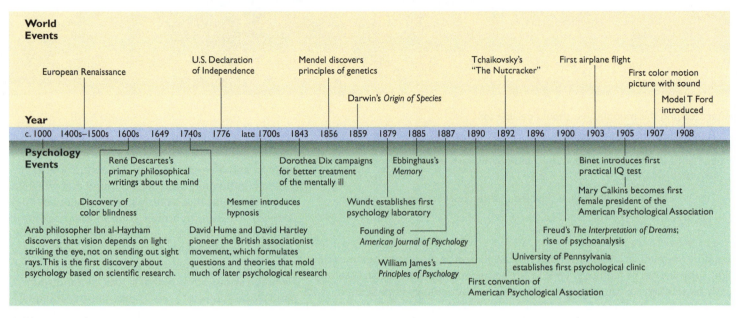

									U.S. Declaration of Independence			Mendel discovers principles of genetics					Tchaikovsky's "The Nutcracker"		First airplane flight				

World Events

European Renaissance — U.S. Declaration of Independence — Mendel discovers principles of genetics — Tchaikovsky's "The Nutcracker" — First airplane flight — First color motion picture with sound

Darwin's *Origin of Species* — Model T Ford introduced

Year

c. 1000 | 1400s–1500s | 1600s | 1649 | 1740s | 1776 | late 1700s | 1843 | 1856 | 1859 | 1879 | 1885 | 1887 | 1890 | 1892 | 1896 | 1900 | 1903 | 1905 | 1907 | 1908

Psychology Events

René Descartes's primary philosophical writings about the mind — Dorothea Dix campaigns for better treatment of the mentally ill — Ebbinghaus's *Memory* — Binet introduces first practical IQ test

Discovery of color blindness — Mesmer introduces hypnosis — Wundt establishes first psychology laboratory — Mary Calkins becomes first female president of the American Psychological Association

Arab philosopher Ibn al-Haytham discovers that vision depends on light striking the eye, not on sending out sight rays. This is the first discovery about psychology based on scientific research. — David Hume and David Hartley pioneer the British associationist movement, which formulates questions and theories that mold much of later psychological research — Founding of *American Journal of Psychology* — Freud's *The Interpretation of Dreams*; rise of psychoanalysis

William James's *Principles of Psychology* — University of Pennsylvania establishes first psychological clinic

First convention of American Psychological Association

▲ **Figure 1.4a-b** Dates of some important events in psychology and elsewhere. (Based partly on Dewsbury, 2000)

Titchener (1910) typically presented a stimulus and asked his subject to analyze it into its separate features—for example, to look at a lemon and describe its yellowness, brightness, shape, and other characteristics. He called his approach structuralism, *an attempt to describe the structures that compose the mind,* particularly sensations, feelings, and images. For example, imagine you are the psychologist: I look at a lemon and try to tell you my experience of its brightness separately from my experience of its yellowness.

Here is the problem. How do you know whether my reports are accurate? After Titchener died in 1927, psychologists soon abandoned both his questions and his methods. Why? Remember that a good scientific question is both interesting and answerable. Regardless of whether Titchener's questions about the elements of the mind were interesting, they seemed unanswerable.

William James and Functionalism

In the same era as Wundt and Titchener, Harvard University's William James articulated some of the major issues of psychology and earned recognition as the founder of American psychology. James's book *The Principles of Psychology* (1890) defined many of the questions that still dominate psychology today.

James had little patience with searching for the elements of the mind. He focused on what the mind *does* rather than what it *is.* That is, instead of seeking the elements of consciousness, he preferred *to learn how people produce useful behaviors.* For this reason, we call his approach functionalism. He suggested the following examples of good psychological questions (James, 1890):

- How can people strengthen good habits?
- Can someone attend to more than one item at a time?
- How do people recognize that they have seen something before?
- How does an intention lead to action?

James proposed possible answers but did little research of his own. His main contribution was to inspire later researchers to address the questions that he posed.

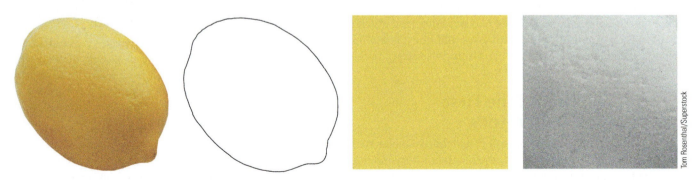

Edward Titchener asked subjects to describe their sensations. For example, they might describe their sensation of shape, their sensation of color, and their sensation of texture while looking at a lemon.

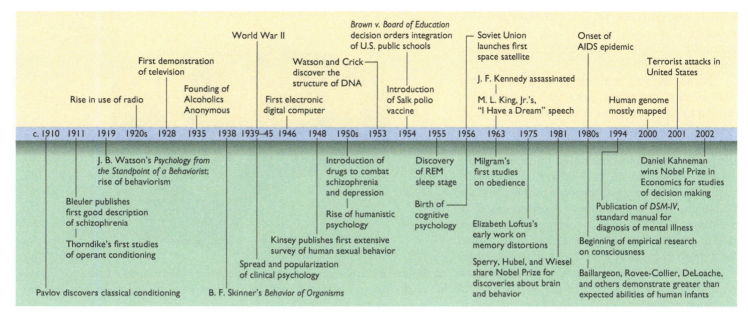

Studying Sensation

In the late 1800s and early 1900s, psychologists paid little attention to abnormal behavior, leaving it to psychiatrists. They devoted much of their research to the study of vision and other sensations. Why? One reason was that they wanted to understand mental experience, and experience consists of sensations. Another reason was that it makes sense to start with relatively easy, answerable questions. Sensation was certainly easier to study than, say, personality.

Early psychologists discovered major differences between physical stimuli and psychological perceptions. For example, a light that is twice as intense as another one does not look twice as bright. ▶ Figure 1.5 shows the relationship between the intensity of light and its perceived brightness. *The mathematical description of the relationship between the physical stimulus and its perceived properties* is called the psychophysical function because it relates psychology to physics. Such research demonstrated the feasibility of scientific research on psychological questions.

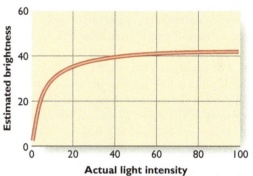

concept check

6. **What topic was the main focus of research for the earliest psychologists and why?**

7. **Why did psychologists abandon Titchener's structuralist approach?**

Answers

7. Structuralists asked people to describe their inner experiences in detail. However, researchers had no way to check the accuracy of the reports.

6. Early psychological research focused mainly on sensation because sensation is central to experience and because the early researchers believed that sensation questions were answerable.

Darwin and the Study of Animal Intelligence

Charles Darwin's theory of evolution by natural selection (Darwin, 1859, 1871) had an enormous impact on psychology as well as biology. Darwin argued that

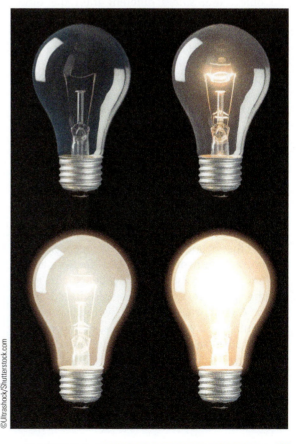

▶ **Figure 1.5** This graph relates the perceived intensity of light to its physical intensity. When a light becomes twice as intense physically, it does not seem twice as bright. (Adapted from Stevens, 1961)

humans and other species share a remote common ancestor. If so, then other animals should share features in common with humans, including some degree of intelligence.

Based on this implication, early comparative psychologists, *specialists who compare different animal species,* did something that seemed more reasonable then than it does now: They set out to measure animal intelligence. They apparently imagined that they could rank-order animals from the smartest to the dullest. They set various species to such tasks as the delayed-response problem and the detour problem. In the *delayed-response problem,* an animal sees or hears a signal indicating where it can find food. After the signal, the animal is restrained for a delay to see how long the animal remembers the signal (see ▶ Figure 1.6). In the *detour problem,* an animal is separated from food by a barrier to see whether it takes a detour away from the food to reach it (▶ Figure 1.7).

However, measuring animal intelligence turned out to be more difficult than it sounded. A species might seem dull-witted on one task but brilliant on another. For example, zebras are generally slow to learn to approach one pattern instead of another for food, unless the patterns happen to be narrow stripes versus wide stripes, in which case they excel (Giebel, 1958) (see ▶ Figure 1.8). Rats don't learn to find food hidden under the object that looks different from the others, but they easily learn to choose the object that *smells* different from the others (Langworthy & Jennings, 1972).

Eventually, psychologists decided that the relative intelligence of nonhuman animals was a pointless question. Different species excel in different ways, and it doesn't make sense to rank-order them.

Psychologists today continue to study animal learning, but the emphasis has changed. The questions are now, "What can we learn from animal studies about the mechanisms of intelligent behavior?" and "How did each species evolve the behavioral tendencies it shows?"

Measuring Human Intelligence

While some psychologists studied animal intelligence, others examined human intelligence. Francis Galton, a cousin of Charles Darwin, was among the first to try to measure intelligence and to ask whether intellectual variations were based on heredity. Galton was fascinated with measurement (Hergenhahn, 1992). For example, he invented the weather map, measured degrees of boredom during lectures, suggested the use of fingerprints to identify individuals, and—in the name of science—attempted to measure the beauty of women in different countries.

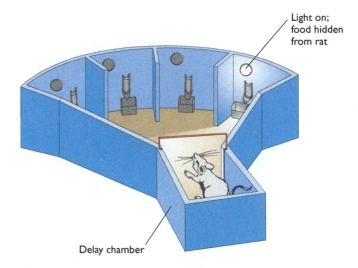

▲ **Figure 1.6** Early comparative psychologists assessed animal intelligence with the delayed-response problem. Variations on this task are still used today with humans as well as laboratory animals.

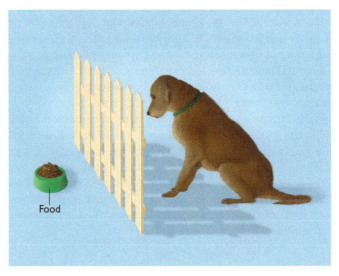

▲ **Figure 1.7** In the detour problem, an animal must go away from the food before it can move toward it.

In an effort to determine the role of heredity in human achievement, Galton (1869/1978) examined whether the sons of famous and accomplished men tended to become eminent themselves. (Women in 19th-century England had little opportunity for fame.) Galton found that the sons of judges, writers, politicians, and other noted men had a high probability of similar accomplishment themselves. He attributed this edge to heredity. (Do you think he had adequate evidence for his conclusion? If the sons of famous men become famous themselves, is heredity the only explanation?)

Galton tried to measure intelligence using simple sensory and motor tasks, but his measurements were unsatisfactory. In 1905, a French researcher named Alfred Binet devised the first useful intelligence test, which we shall discuss further in Chapter 9. At this point, just note that the idea of testing intelligence became popular in the United States and other Western countries. Psychologists,

▲ **Figure 1.8** Zebras learn rapidly when they have to compare stripe patterns (Giebel, 1958).

inspired by the popularity of intelligence tests, developed tests of personality, interests, and other psychological characteristics. Measuring human intelligence faces some of the same problems as animal intelligence: People have many intelligent abilities, and it is possible to be more adept at one than another. Much research goes into trying to make tests of intelligence fair and accurate.

The Rise of Behaviorism

Today it seems reasonable to define psychology as "the systematic study of behavior and experience." For a substantial period of psychology's history, most experimental psychologists would have objected to the words "and experience." Some psychologists still object today, though less strenuously. During the mid-1900s, most researchers described psychology as the study of behavior, period. They had little to say about minds, experiences, or anything of the sort. (According to one quip, psychologists had "lost their minds.")

What was the objection to studying experience? Recall the failure of Titchener's effort to analyze experience into its components. Most psychologists concluded that questions about mind were unanswerable. Instead, they focused on how changes in the environment alter behavior. They explored what learning is and how it occurs.

John B. Watson

Many regard John B. Watson as the founder of **behaviorism,** *a field of psychology that concentrates on observable, measurable behaviors and not on mental processes.* Watson was not the first behaviorist,

but he systematized the approach and popularized it (Watson, 1919, 1925). Here are two quotes from Watson:

> Psychology as the behaviorist views it is a purely objective experimental branch of natural science. Its theoretical goal is the prediction and control of behavior. (1913, p. 158)

> The goal of psychological study is the ascertaining of such data and laws that, given the stimulus, psychology can predict what the response will be; or, on the other hand, given the response, it can specify the nature of the effective stimulus. (1919, p. 10)

Studies of Learning

Inspired by Watson, many researchers set out to study animal behavior, especially animal learning. One advantage of studying nonhuman animals is that the researcher can control the animals' diet, waking/sleeping schedule, and so forth far more completely than with humans. The other supposed advantage was that nonhuman learning might be simpler to understand. Many psychologists optimistically expected to discover simple, stimulus–response laws of behavior. Just as physicists could study gravity by dropping any object in any location, many psychologists in the mid-1900s thought they could learn all about behavior by studying rats in mazes. One highly influential psychologist, Clark Hull, wrote, "One of the most persistently baffling problems which confronts modern psychologists is the finding of an adequate explanation of the phenomena of maze learning" (1932, p. 25). Another wrote, "I believe that everything important in psychology (except perhaps . . . such matters as involve society and words) can be investigated in essence through the

Early behaviorists studied rats in mazes. As they discovered that this behavior was more complicated than they supposed, their interest turned to other topics.

WILL & DENI MCINTYRE/Getty Images

continued experimental and theoretical analysis of the determiners of rat behavior at a choice-point in a maze" (Tolman, 1938, p. 34).

As research progressed, psychologists found that the behavior of a rat in a maze was more complicated than they had expected. Just as psychologists of the 1920s abandoned the structuralist approach to the mind, later psychologists abandoned the hope that studying rats in mazes would quickly uncover universal principles of behavior. Psychologists continue to study animal learning, but the goals and methods have changed.

The behaviorist approach is still alive and well today, but it no longer dominates experimental psychology as it once did. The rise of computer science showed that it was possible to talk about memory, knowledge, and information processing in machines, and if machines can have such processes, presumably humans can, too. Psychologists demonstrated the possibilities of meaningful research on topics that behaviorists had avoided.

concept check

8. Why did behaviorists avoid the topics of thought and knowledge?

Answer

8. Behaviorists concentrate on observable behaviors, whereas thought and knowledge are unobservable processes within an individual. The early behaviorists hoped to find simple stimulus–response laws of behavior.

From Freud to Modern Clinical Psychology

In the early 1900s, clinical psychology was a small field devoted largely to disorders of vision, hearing, movement, and memory (Routh, 2000). The treatment of mental illness remained the province of psychiatry. The Austrian psychiatrist Sigmund Freud revolutionized and popularized psychotherapy with his methods of analyzing patients' dreams and memories. He tried to trace current behavior to early childhood experiences, including children's sexual fantasies. We shall examine Freud's theories in Chapter 14. Freud was a persuasive speaker and writer, and his influence was enormous. By the mid-1900s, most psychiatrists in the United States and Europe were following his methods. However, Freud's influence in psychology has faded substantially since then.

During World War II, many soldiers wanted help in dealing with the traumas caused by their war experiences. Because psychiatrists could not keep up with the need, psychologists began

providing therapy, and clinical psychology as we now know it began to develop. Instead of accepting theories based on the authority of Freud or anyone else, psychologists conducted research to evaluate forms of therapy and developed new, more effective methods.

concept check

9. What event led to the rise of clinical psychology as we know it today?

Answer

9. During and after World War II, the need for services was greater than psychiatrists could provide. Clinical psychologists began providing treatment for psychological distress.

Recent Trends

In its early days, psychology was an ambitious field, expecting to find a grand theory that would revolutionize our understanding and apply widely to all aspects of experience. A review of psychology's early history (Borch-Jacobsen & Shamdasani, 2012) quoted one psychologist who spoke of "a great chance for some future psychologue to make a name greater than Newton's," another one who anticipated that a great psychologist's name will "join those of Copernicus and Darwin," and another who said that "the present psychological situation calls out for a new Darwin of the mind." Sigmund Freud immodestly nominated himself: "Humanity has in the course of time had to endure from the hands of science two great outrages upon its naïve self-love. The first was when it realized that our earth was not the centre of the universe. . . . The second was when biological research robbed man of his peculiar privilege of having been specially created, and relegated him to a descent from the animal world. . . . But man's craving for grandiosity is now suffering the third and most bitter blow from present-day psychological research which is endeavouring to prove to the 'ego' of each one of us that he is not even master in his own house, but that he must remain content with the veriest scraps of information about what is going on unconsciously in his own mind" (Freud, 1915/1935, p. 252). Later, the behaviorists had their own high ambition: to discover simple laws of learning, analogous to the laws of physics. They hoped to state those laws with mathematical precision and apply them generally to explain and predict virtually all of behavior.

Most of today's psychologists are less confident that a grand theory of behavior will ever emerge, or that anyone will qualify as the Copernicus or Darwin of psychology. Most psychologists today attempt to answer more limited questions. **Basic research** seeks theoretical knowledge for its own sake, such as understanding the processes of learning and memory. **Applied research** deals with practical problems, such as how to help children with learning disabilities. The two kinds of research are mutually supportive. Understanding the basic processes helps applied researchers develop effective interventions. Those working toward practical solutions sometimes discover principles that are theoretically important.

Recall that some of the earliest psychological researchers wanted to study the conscious mind but became discouraged with Titchener's introspective methods. Since the 1960s, cognitive psychology (the study of thought and knowledge) has gradually gained in prominence. Although cognitive psychologists sometimes ask people to describe their thoughts, more often they measure the accuracy and speed of responses under various circumstances to draw inferences about the underlying processes.

For many years, the behaviorists who opposed any study of consciousness were right, as researchers had no way to do any meaningful research on the topic. Beginning in the 1980s, several researchers found clever ways to identify the brain processes associated with consciousness.

Another rapidly growing field is neuroscience. New techniques of brain scanning now enable researchers to examine brain activity without opening the skull. Today, neuroscience influences nearly every aspect of psychology. Evolutionary psychology is another new emphasis. Animals that behaved in certain ways survived, reproduced, and became our ancestors. Those whose behaviors did not lead to reproductive success failed to pass on their genes. In some cases, we can cautiously infer the selective pressures that led to our current behaviors.

For many decades, researchers interested in personality concentrated mostly on what can go wrong, such as fear, anger, and sadness. The relatively new field of positive psychology *studies the predispositions and experiences that make people happy, productive, and successful.*

New fields of application have also arisen. Health psychologists study how people's health is influenced by their behaviors, such as smoking, drinking, sexual activities, exercise, diet, and reactions to stress. They also try to help people change their behaviors to promote better health. Sports psychologists apply psychological principles to help athletes set goals, train, and concentrate their efforts.

Psychologists today have also broadened their scope to include more of human diversity. In its early days, around 1900, psychology was more open to women than most other academic disciplines were, but even so, the opportunities for women were limited (Milar, 2000). Mary Calkins, an early memory researcher, was regarded as Harvard's best psychology graduate student, but she was denied a PhD because of Harvard's tradition of granting degrees only to men (Scarborough & Furomoto, 1987). She did, however, serve as president of the American Psychological Association, as did Margaret Washburn, another important woman in the early days of psychology.

Today, women receive nearly three-fourths of the new PhDs in psychology and hold many leadership roles in psychological organizations. Minority students receive bachelor and master's degrees in psychology almost in proportion to their numbers in the total population. However, the number of African American and Hispanic students receiving PhD degrees lags behind the population norms, as shown in ▼ Figure 1.9 (Center for Psychology Workforce Analysis and Research, 2007).

What will psychology be like in the future? A few likely trends are foreseeable. Because advances in medicine have enabled people to live longer, the psychology of aging is increasingly important. Because of depletion of natural resources and climate change, people will need to change their way of life in many ways that we cannot fully anticipate. Persuading people to change their behavior is a task for both politicians and psychologists.

concept check

10. **In what way is psychology today less ambitious than it was in the early 1900s?**

Answer

10. In the early 1900s, leading psychologists expected an insight that would revolutionize psychology in the same way that Darwin revolutionized biology. Fewer psychologists today expect a grand theory.

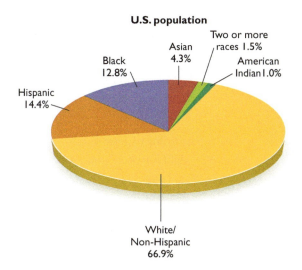

U.S. population

Two or more races 1.5%
Asian 4.3%
American Indian 1.0%
Black 12.8%
Hispanic 14.4%
White/Non-Hispanic 66.9%

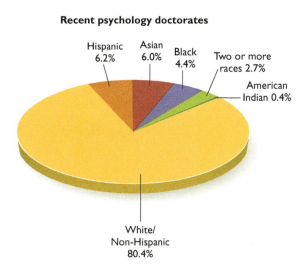

Recent psychology doctorates

Hispanic 6.2%
Asian 6.0%
Black 4.4%
Two or more races 2.7%
American Indian 0.4%
White/Non-Hispanic 80.4%

◀ **Figure 1.9** Ethnic groups as a percentage of the U.S. population and as a percentage of people receiving doctorate degrees in psychology during 2005. (Source: Center for Psychology Workforce Analysis and Research, 2007)

Psychology through the Years

Throughout the early years of psychology, many psychologists devoted enormous efforts to projects that produced disappointing results, such as Titchener's search for the elements of the mind. Not all the efforts of early psychologists were fruitless, and in later chapters, you will encounter many classic studies that we still regard highly. Still, if some past psychologists spent their time on projects we now consider misguided, can we be sure that many of today's psychologists aren't on the wrong track?

We cannot, of course. Of all the theories and research projects that we now respect most dearly, some will stand the test of time and others will not. That is not a reason for despair. Much like a rat in a maze, researchers make progress by trial and error. They advance in a certain direction, and sometimes it leads to progress, and sometimes it leads to a dead end. But even exploring a dead end and eliminating it is progress, of a sort. Eventually, even when research doesn't lead to clear answers, at least it leads to better questions.

Summary

- *Choice of research questions.* During the history of psychology, researchers have several times changed their opinions about what constitutes an interesting, important, answerable question. (page 15)
- *First research.* In 1879, Wilhelm Wundt established the first laboratory devoted to psychological research. (page 15)
- *Limits of self-observation.* One of Wundt's students, Edward Titchener, attempted to analyze the elements of mental experience, relying on people's own observations. Other psychologists became discouraged with this approach. (page 15)
- *The founding of American psychology.* William James, the founder of American psychology, focused attention on how the mind guides useful behavior rather than on the contents of the mind. By doing so, he paved the way for the rise of behaviorism. (page 16)
- *Early sensory research.* In the late 1800s and early 1900s, many researchers concentrated on studies of the senses, partly because sensation is central to mental experience. (page 17)
- *Darwin's influence.* Charles Darwin's theory of evolution by natural selection influenced psychology in many ways. It prompted some prominent early psychologists to compare the intelligence of different species. That question turned out to be more complicated than expected. (page 17)
- *Intelligence testing.* The measurement of human intelligence was one concern of early psychologists that has persisted through the years. (page 18)

- *The era of behaviorist dominance.* As psychologists became discouraged with their attempts to analyze the mind, they turned to behaviorism. For many years, psychological researchers studied behavior, especially animal learning, to the virtual exclusion of mental experience. (page 19)
- *Maze learning.* During the mid-1900s, many experimental psychologists studied rats in mazes. As this approach failed to produce general laws of learning and behavior, researchers became discouraged with it and largely abandoned it. (page 19)
- *Freud.* Sigmund Freud's theories heavily influenced the early development of psychotherapy, although other methods are more widespread today. (page 20)
- *Clinical psychology.* At one time, psychiatrists provided nearly all the care for people with psychological disorders. After World War II, clinical psychology began to assume much of this role. (page 20)
- *Psychological research today.* Today, few psychologists expect a grand theory that will revolutionize our understanding in the same way that Darwin revolutionized biology. Today's psychologists study a wide variety of topics. Cognitive psychology has replaced behaviorist approaches to learning as the dominant field of experimental psychology. Neuroscience now influences researchers in almost all fields. Other new approaches are also becoming widespread. (page 20)

Key Terms

You can check the page listed for a complete description of a term.

applied research (page 20)

basic research (page 20)

behaviorism (page 19)

comparative psychologist (page 18)

functionalism (page 16)

introspect (page 15)

positive psychology (page 21)

psychophysical function (page 17)

structuralism (page 16)

Review Questions

1. Which of these topics was a major research concern for the earliest psychologists?
   (a) Vision and other sensations
   (b) Mental illness
   (c) Social conformity
   (d) Expert problem solving

2. In the early days of psychology, structuralists wanted to discover _____ and functionalists wanted to understand _____.
   (a) what mind can do . . . the elements that compose mind
   (b) the elements that compose mind . . . what mind can do
   (c) treatments for mental illness . . . the best ways to rear children
   (d) the best ways to rear children . . . treatments for mental illness

3. Which of these topics would a behaviorist probably avoid?
   (a) Stimulus–response connections
   (b) Animal behavior
   (c) Learning
   (d) Thought and knowledge

4. What event led to the rise of clinical psychology as we know it today?
   (a) World War II
   (b) Popular films that depicted mental illness
   (c) The writings of Sigmund Freud
   (d) Economic collapse

5. How does basic research differ from applied research?
   (a) Basic research is simpler, and requires less training.
   (b) Basic research is more complex, and requires greater training.
   (c) Basic research seeks solutions to current problems, rather than theoretical understanding.
   (d) Basic research seeks theoretical understanding, rather than a solution to a current problem.

Answers: 1a, 2b, 3d, 4a, 5d.

2 Scientific Methods in Psychology

William Taufic/Curtis

Years ago, I was watching a Discovery Channel nature documentary about elephants. After the narrator discussed the enormous amount of food elephants eat, he started on their digestive system. He commented that the average elephant passes enough gas in a day to propel a car for 20 miles (32 km). I thought, "Wow, isn't that amazing!" and I told a couple of other people about it.

Later I started to think, "Wait a minute. *Who measured that?* Did someone attach a balloon to an elephant's rear end and collect gas for 24 hours? And then put it into a car and drive it? Was that a full-sized car or an economy car? City traffic or highway? How do they know they measured a typical elephant? Did they determine the mean for a broad sample of elephants?" My doubts quickly grew.

"Oh, well," you might say. "Who cares?" You're right; how far someone could propel a car on elephant gas doesn't matter. However, my point is not to ridicule the makers of this documentary but to ridicule *me*. Remember, I said I told two people about this claim before I started to doubt it. For decades, I had taught students to question assertions and evaluate the evidence, and here I was, uncritically accepting a silly statement and telling other people, who for all I know, may have gone on to tell other people. The point is that all of us yield to the temptation to accept unsupported claims, and we all need to discipline ourselves to question the evidence, especially evidence supporting claims that we would like to believe. This chapter concerns evaluating evidence in psychology.

©Graeme Shannon/Shutterstock.com

module 2.1

Evaluating Evidence and Thinking Critically

After studying this module, you should be able to:

- Discuss the importance of replicable results.
- Define burden of proof.
- Explain why scientists seek the most parsimonious explanation of any result.
- Explain why most psychologists are skeptical of claims of extrasensory perception.

What constitutes an explanation? Consider the following quote ("The Medals and the Damage Done," 2004, p. 604):

> In 2002, [Michael] Brennan was a British national rowing champion. . . . As the UK Olympic trials loomed, Brennan was feeling confident. But . . . for much of the past 12 months, Brennan's performance has been eroded by constant colds, aching joints and fatigue. . . . When the trials rolled round this April, Brennan . . . finished at the bottom of the heap. "I couldn't believe it," he says. To an experienced sports doctor, the explanation is obvious: Brennan has "unexplained underperformance syndrome" (UPS).

What do you think? Is "unexplained underperformance syndrome" an *explanation*?

Consider other examples: Birds fly south for the winter "because they have an instinct." Certain people get into fights "because they are aggressive." Certain students have trouble paying attention "because they have attention deficit disorder." Are these statements explanations? Or are they no better than unexplained underperformance syndrome? A good explanation goes beyond giving something a name, and finding good explanations requires good research.

Psychological Science

The word *science* derives from a Latin word meaning "knowledge." Psychologists insist that their field is a science, and they are often defensive about it, when faced with skepticism. To be fair, psychology differs from other scientific fields in many ways.

One way is its history. Other sciences began gradually from the work of amateurs. For centuries, people employed as physicians or other professions devoted some of their leisure time to recording the positions of the stars and planets, observing the result when they mixed chemicals, or watching animals. By the time anyone first thought of science as a job, and by the time universities first offered courses in sciences, the early scientists already had much to teach. Psychology, in contrast, began as a deliberate attempt to start a new science, applying the methods of the natural sciences to some of the questions of philosophy. The early psychology professors frankly didn't have much to teach, other than what biologists had already discovered about the sense organs.

Another issue is ethics. Chemists can do almost anything they want to a jar of chemicals, as long as they don't blow up the building. Psychologists dealing with people have stringent limits.

Gathering Evidence

Science is a search for knowledge based on carefully observed, replicable data. Let's first consider data collection, and then examine that word *replicable*.

Research starts with careful observation. A great deal of scientific research consists of observing and measuring. For example, Robert Provine (2000) studied laughter by visiting shopping malls and recording who laughed and when.

Good observations and measurements often suggest a pattern that leads to a hypothesis, which is *a clear predictive statement*, often an attempt to explain the observations. A test of a hypothesis goes through the series of steps described in the following four sections and illustrated in ▼ Figure 2.1. Articles in most scientific publications follow this sequence, too. In each of the remaining chapters of this book, you will find at least one example of a psychological study described in a section entitled "What's the Evidence?" Each of those will go through the sequence from hypothesis to interpretation.

Hypothesis

A hypothesis can start with observations, such as noticing that some children who watch much televised violence are themselves aggressive. You might then form a hypothesis that watching violence leads to violence. A hypothesis can also be based on a more general statement, such as "children tend to imitate the behavior they see." A good hypothesis leads to predictions. For example, "if we let children watch violent television, they will behave more aggressively," or "if we decrease the amount of violence on television, the crime rate will decrease."

Method

Any hypothesis could be tested in many ways. One way to test the effects of televised violence would be to examine whether children who watch more violent programs are more violent themselves. When we find that on average they are, that result is only the start. It does not tell us about cause and effect: Does watching violence lead to violence? Or is it simply that people who are already violent like to watch violence?

A better method is to take a set of children, such as those attending a summer camp, randomly assign them to two groups and let one group watch violent programs while the other group watches nonviolent programs, and see whether the two groups differ in their violent behaviors (Parke, Berkowitz, Leyens, West, & Sebastian, 1977). The limitation is that researchers control what people watch for only a few days.

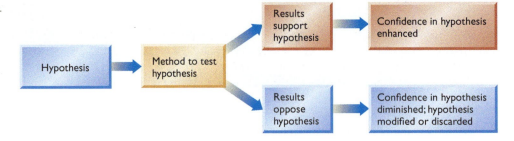

▶ Figure 2.1 An experiment tests the predictions that follow from a hypothesis. Results either support the hypothesis or indicate a need to revise or abandon it.

Because any method has strengths and weaknesses, researchers vary their methods. If studies using different methods all point to the same conclusion, we gradually increase our confidence in the conclusion. A single study is almost never decisive (Greenwald, 2012).

Results

Fundamental to any research is measuring the outcome. A phenomenon such as "violent behavior" is tricky to measure. (Do threats count? Does verbal abuse? When does a push or shove cross the line between playfulness and violence?) It is important for an investigator to set clear rules about measurements. After making the measurements, the investigator determines whether the results are impressive enough to call for an explanation or whether the apparent trends might have been due to chance.

Interpretation

Researchers' final task is to consider what the results mean. If the results contradict the hypothesis, researchers should abandon or modify the original hypothesis. If the results match the prediction, investigators gain confidence in the hypothesis, but they also should consider other hypotheses that fit the results.

Replicability

Most scientific researchers are scrupulously honest in stating their methods and results. A major reason is that anyone who reports a scientific study must include the methods in enough detail for other people to repeat the procedure and, we hope, get similar results. Someone who reports results falsely runs a risk of being caught, and therefore distrusted from then on.

Replicable results are *those that anyone can obtain, at least approximately, by following the same procedures.* Scientists do make certain allowances for small effects. For example, one method of teaching might work better than another, but only slightly, so the advantage might not appear in all studies, especially those with a small number of participants. When researchers try to verify a small

effect, they use a **meta-analysis**, *which combines the results of many studies as if they were all one huge study.* A meta-analysis also determines which variations in procedure increase or decrease the effects. However, if no one can find conditions under which the phenomenon occurs fairly consistently, we do not take it seriously. This rule may seem harsh, but it is our best defense against error.

Consider an example of a nonreplicable result. In the 1960s and early 1970s, several researchers trained rats to do something, chopped up the rats' brains, extracted certain chemicals, and injected those chemicals into untrained animals. The recipients then apparently remembered what the first group of rats had learned to do. From what we know of brain functioning, theoretically this procedure shouldn't work, but if it did, imagine the possibilities. Some people proposed, semiseriously, that someday you could get an injection of European history or introduction to calculus instead of going to class. Alas, the results were not replicable. When other researchers repeated the procedures, most of them found no effect from the brain extracts (L. T. Smith, 1975).

Psychological researchers have become increasingly concerned about the replicability of their findings. We shall consider the issue in more detail in the second module of this chapter.

1. How does a meta-analysis relate to replicability?

Answer

1. If some studies replicate an effect and others do not, a researcher may conduct a meta-analysis that combines all studies as if they were one large study.

Evaluating Scientific Theories

If replicable data support some hypothesis, eventually researchers propose a theory. A scientific **theory** is more than a guess. It is *an explanation or model that fits many observations and makes accurate predictions.* A good theory starts with as few assumptions as possible and leads to many correct predictions. In that way, it reduces the amount of information we must remember. The periodic table in chemistry is an excellent example: From the information about the elements, we can predict the properties of an enormous number of compounds.

One important reason for scientific progress is that scientists generally agree on how to evaluate theories. Whereas most people can hardly imagine evidence that would change their religious or political views, scientists can generally imagine evidence that would make them abandon their favorite theories in favor of other ones. (Oh, not always, of course. Some people can be stubborn.)

Burden of Proof

The philosopher Karl Popper emphasized scientists' willingness to disconfirm their theories by saying that the purpose of research is to find which theories are *incorrect.* That is, the point of research is to *falsify* the incorrect theories, and a good theory is one that withstands all attempts to falsify it. It wins by a process of elimination.

A well-formed theory is falsifiable—that is, *stated in such clear, precise terms that we can see what evidence would count against it*—if, of course, such evidence existed. For example, the theory of gravity makes precise predictions about falling objects. Because people have tested these predictions many times, and none of the observations have disconfirmed the predictions, we have high confidence in the theory.

This point is worth restating because "falsifiable" sounds like a bad thing. Falsifiable does not mean we actually have evidence against a theory. (If we did, it would be falsi*fied.*) Falsifiable means we can *imagine* something that would count as evidence against the theory. A theory that makes no definite prediction is not falsifiable. For example, many physicists believe that ours is just one among a huge number, perhaps an infinite number, of other universes. Can you imagine any evidence *against* that view? If not, it doesn't qualify as a good theory (Steinhardt, 2014). For a psychology example, Sigmund Freud claimed that all dreams are motivated by wish fulfillment. If you have a happy dream, it appears to be a wish fulfillment. However, if you have an unhappy dream, then Freud claimed that a censor in your brain disguised the wish. As Domhoff (2003) noted, Freud stated his theory in such a way that any observation counted for it or at least not against it (see ▶ Figure 2.2). If no possible observation could falsify the theory, it is too vague to be useful.

However, when Popper wrote that research is *always* an attempt to falsify a theory, he went too far. "All objects fall" (the law of gravity) is falsifiable. "Some objects fall" is not falsifiable, although it is certainly true—a pitifully weak statement, but nevertheless true. If "some objects fall" *were* false, you could not *demonstrate* it to be false!

Instead of insisting that all research is an effort to falsify a theory, another approach is to discuss burden of proof, *the obligation to present evidence to support one's claim.* In a criminal trial, the burden of proof is on the prosecution. If the prosecution does not make a convincing case, the defendant goes free. The reason is that the prosecution should be able to find convincing evidence if someone is guilty, but in many cases innocent defendants could not possibly demonstrate their innocence.

Similarly in science, the burden of proof is on anyone who makes a claim that should be demonstrable, if it is true. For the claim "some objects fall," the burden of proof is on anyone who supports the claim. (It's easy to fulfill that burden of proof, of course.) For the claim "every object falls," we cannot expect anyone to demonstrate it to be true for every object, and so the burden of proof is on someone who doubts the claim. (We continue to believe the statement unless someone shows an exception.) For a claim such as "UFOs from outer space have visited Earth" or "some people have psychic powers to perceive things without any sensory information," the burden of proof is on anyone who supports these statements. If they are true, someone should be able to show clear evidence.

Parsimony

What do we do if several theories fit the known facts? Suppose you notice that a picture on your wall is hanging on an angle. You consider four explanations:

- The ground shook when a big truck drove by.
- A gust of wind moved the picture.
- One of your friends bumped it without telling you.
- A ghost moved it.

▲ **Figure 2.2** According to Freud, every dream is based on wish fulfillment. If a dream seems unhappy, it is because a censor in your head disguised the wish. Can you imagine any observation that would contradict this theory?

All four explanations fit the observation, but we don't consider them on an equal basis. When given a choice among explanations that seem to fit the facts, we prefer the one whose assumptions are fewer, simpler, or more consistent with other well-established theories. This is known as the principle of parsimony (literally "stinginess") or *Occam's razor* (after the philosopher William of Occam). The principle of parsimony is a conservative idea: We stick with ideas that work and try as hard as we can to avoid new assumptions (e.g., ghosts).

Parsimony and Degrees of Open-Mindedness

The principle of parsimony tells us to adhere to what we already believe, to resist radically new hypotheses. You might protest: "Shouldn't we remain open-minded to new possibilities?" Yes, if open-mindedness means a willingness to consider proper evidence, but not if it means the assumption that "anything has as much chance of being true as anything else." The stronger the reasons behind a current opinion, the more evidence you should need before replacing it.

For example, many people have attempted to build a "perpetual motion machine," one that generates more energy than it uses. (▼ Figure 2.3 shows an example.) The U.S. Patent Office is officially closed-minded on this issue, refusing even to consider patent applications for such machines. Physicists are convinced, both for logical reasons and because of consistent observations, that any work wastes energy, and that keeping a machine going always requires energy. If someone shows you what appears to be a perpetual motion machine, look for a hidden battery or other power source. If you don't find one, you can assume that you overlooked it. A claim as extraordinary as a perpetual motion machine requires extraordinary evidence.

Let's consider a couple of examples from psychology in which people have claimed very surprising results. Although it is fair to examine the evidence, it is also important to maintain a skeptical attitude and look as closely as possible for a simple, parsimonious explanation.

Applying Parsimony: Clever Hans, the Amazing Horse

Early in the 20th century, Wilhelm von Osten, a German mathematics teacher, set out to demonstrate the intellectual ability of his horse, Hans. To teach Hans arithmetic, he first showed him an object, said "one," and lifted Hans's foot. He raised Hans's foot twice for two objects and so on. With practice, Hans learned to look at a set of objects and tap the correct number of times. Soon it was no longer necessary for Hans to see the objects. Von Osten would just call out a number, and Hans would tap the appropriate number.

Mr. von Osten moved on to addition and then to subtraction, multiplication, and division. Hans caught on quickly, soon responding with 90 to 95 percent accuracy. Then von Osten and Hans began touring Germany, giving public demonstrations. Hans's abilities grew until he could add fractions, convert fractions to decimals or vice versa, do algebra, tell time to the minute, and give the values of German coins. Using a letter-to-number code, he could spell the names of objects and identify musical notes such as B-flat. (Evidently, he had perfect pitch.) He was usually correct even when questions were put to him by people other than von Osten, with von Osten out of sight.

Given this evidence, many people were ready to believe that Hans had great intellectual powers. But others sought a more parsimonious explanation. Oskar Pfungst (1911) observed that Hans could answer a question correctly only if the questioner knew the answer. Apparently, the questioner was giving away the answer. Also, Hans was accurate only when the questioner stood in plain sight.

Eventually, Pfungst observed that anyone who asked Hans a question would lean forward to watch Hans's foot. Hans had learned to start tapping whenever someone stood next to his forefoot and leaned forward. After Hans reached the correct number of taps, the questioner would give a slight upward jerk of the head and a change in facial expression,

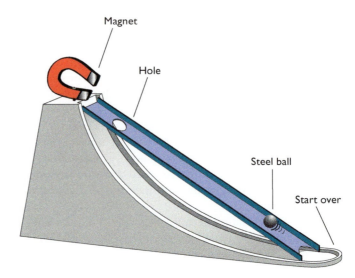

▲ **Figure 2.3** A proposed perpetual motion machine: The magnet pulls the metal ball up the inclined plane. When the ball reaches the top, it falls through the hole and returns to its starting point, from which the magnet will again pull the ball up. Can you see why this device is sure to fail? (See answer A on page 33.)

anticipating that this might be the last tap. (Even skeptical scientists who tested Hans did this involuntarily. After all, they thought, wouldn't it be exciting if Hans got it right?) Hans simply continued tapping until he saw that cue.

In short, Hans was indeed a clever horse, but we do not believe that he understood mathematics. Note that Pfungst did not demonstrate that Hans *didn't* understand mathematics. Pfungst merely demonstrated that he could explain Hans's behavior in the parsimonious terms of responses to facial expressions, and therefore, no one needed to assume anything more complex.

Applying Parsimony: Extrasensory Perception

The possibility of extrasensory perception (ESP) has long been controversial in psychology. Supporters of extrasensory perception claim that *some people*

Clever Hans and his owner, Mr. von Osten, demonstrated that the horse could answer complex mathematical questions with great accuracy. The question was, "How?" (After Pfungst, 1911, in Fernald, 1984.)

1. The great man will be struck down in the day by a thunderbolt. An evil deed, foretold by the bearer of a petition. According to the prediction another falls at night time. Conflict at Reims, London, and pestilence in Tuscany.

2. When the fish that travels over both land and sea is cast up on to the shore by a great wave, its shape foreign, smooth, and frightful. From the sea the enemies soon reach the walls.

3. The bird of prey flying to the left, before battle is joined with the French, he makes preparations. Some will regard him as good, others bad or uncertain. The weaker party will regard him as a good omen.

4. Shortly afterwards, not a very long interval, a great tumult will be raised by land and sea. The naval battles will be greater than ever. Fires, creatures which will make more tumult.

◀ **Figure 2.4** According to the followers of Nostradamus, each of these statements is a specific prophecy of a 20th-century event (Cheetham, 1973). What do you think the prophecies mean? Compare your answers to answer B on page 33.

sometimes acquire information without receiving any energy through any sense organ. Supporters claim that people with ESP can identify someone else's thoughts (telepathy) even from a great distance and despite barriers that would block any known form of energy. Supporters also claim that certain people can perceive objects that are hidden from sight (clairvoyance), predict the future (precognition), and influence such physical events as a roll of dice by mental concentration (psychokinesis).

Accepting any of these claims would require us not only to overhaul major concepts in psychology but also to discard the most fundamental tenets of physics. What evidence is there for ESP?

Anecdotes

Anecdotes are people's reports of isolated events, such as a dream or hunch that comes true. Such experiences often seem impressive, but they are not scientific evidence. Sooner or later, occasional bizarre coincidences are almost sure to occur, and people tend to remember them. At one point a company in North Carolina had two employees named Suresh C. Srivastava. What are the odds against that? Well, this is the wrong question. The odds against that particular coincidence may be high, but the chance of *some* strange coincidence occurring is highly likely, given a long enough wait.

Furthermore, we tend to remember, talk about, and sometimes exaggerate the hunches and dreams that do come true and forget the ones that don't. We could evaluate anecdotal evidence only if people recorded their hunches and dreams *before* the predicted events.

You may have heard of the "prophet Nostradamus," a 16th-century French writer who allegedly predicted many events of later centuries. ▲ **Figure 2.4** presents four samples of his writings. All of his predictions are at this level of vagueness. After something happens, people imaginatively reinterpret his writings to fit the event. (If we don't know what a prediction means until *after* it occurs, is it really a prediction?)

Professional Psychics

Various stage performers claim to read other people's minds and perform other amazing feats. The Amazing Kreskin prefers to talk of his "extremely sensitive" rather than "extrasensory" perception (Kreskin, 1991). Still, part of his success as a performer comes from allowing people to believe he has uncanny mental powers.

After carefully observing Kreskin and others, David Marks and Richard Kammann (1980) concluded that they used the same kinds of deception commonly employed in magic acts. For example, Kreskin sometimes begins his act by asking the audience to read his mind. Let's try to duplicate this trick right now: Try to read my mind. I am thinking of a number between 1 and 50. Both digits

are odd numbers, but they are not the same. For example, it could be 15 but it could not be 11. (These are the instructions Kreskin gives.) Have you chosen a number? Please do.

All right, my number was 37. Did you think of 37? If not, how about 35? You see, I started to think 35 and then changed my mind, so you might have got 35.

If you successfully "read my mind," are you impressed? Don't be. At first, it seemed that you had

Magician Lance Burton can make people and animals seem to suddenly appear, disappear, float in the air, or do other things that we know are impossible. Even if we don't know how he accomplishes these feats, we take it for granted that they are based on methods of misleading the audience.

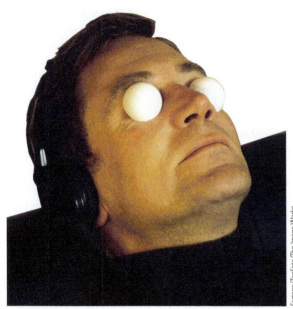

▲ **Figure 2.5** In the ganzfeld procedure, a "receiver," who is deprived of most normal sensory information, tries to describe the photo or film that a "sender" is examining.

many numbers to choose from (1 to 50), but by the end of the instructions, you had only a few. The first digit had to be 1 or 3, and the second had to be 1, 3, 5, 7, or 9. You eliminated 11 and 33 because both digits are the same, and you probably eliminated 15 because I cited it as a possible example. That leaves only seven possibilities. Most people stay far away from the example given and tend to avoid the highest and lowest possible choices. That leaves 37 as the most likely choice and 35 as the second most likely.

Second act: Kreskin asks the audience to write down something they are thinking about while he walks along the aisles talking. Then, back on stage, he "reads people's minds." He might say something like, "Someone is thinking about his mother. . . ." In any large crowd, someone is bound to shout, "Yes, that's me. You read my mind!" On occasion he describes something that someone has written out in great detail. Generally, that person was sitting along the aisle where Kreskin was walking.

After a variety of other tricks (see Marks & Kammann, 1980), Kreskin goes backstage while the mayor or some other dignitary hides Kreskin's paycheck somewhere in the audience. Then Kreskin comes back, walks up and down the aisles, across the rows, and eventually shouts, "The check is here!" The rule is that if he guesses wrong, then he does not get paid. (He hardly ever misses.)

How does he do it? It is a Clever Hans trick. Kreskin studies people's faces. Most people want him to find the check, so they get more excited as he gets close to it and more disappointed or distressed

if he moves away. In effect they are saying, "Now you're getting closer" and "Now you're moving away." Gradually he closes in on the check.

concept check

2. **Suppose a new performer demonstrates what appears to be an amazing ability to read people's minds or predict the future. Before anyone investigates, why do scientists assume it is more likely to be a trick than a supernatural power?**

Answer

2. Scientists prefer the more parsimonious explanation. They resist an extraordinary conclusion if they can find a simpler one.

Experiments

Because anecdotes and stage performances occur under uncontrolled conditions, they are nearly worthless as scientific evidence. Laboratory experiments provide the only evidence about ESP worth serious consideration.

Over the years, researchers have tried many procedures, including guessing the order of a deck of cards, guessing numbers generated by a random-number generator, and describing a remote setting that someone else is viewing. In each case, initial studies generated excitement that subsided after other researchers failed to replicate the findings. For example, in the *ganzfeld* procedure (from German words meaning "entire field"), a "sender" views a photo or film, selected at random from four possibilities, and a "receiver" in another room is asked to describe the sender's thoughts and images. Typically, the receiver wears half Ping-Pong balls over the eyes and listens to static noise through earphones to minimize normal stimuli that might overpower the presumably weak extrasensory stimuli (see ◄ Figure 2.5). Later, a judge examines a transcript of what the receiver said and compares it to the four photos or films, determining which one it matches most closely. On average, it should match the target about one in four times. If a receiver "hits" more often than one in four, we can calculate the probability of accidentally doing that well. One review reported that 6 of the 10 laboratories using this method found positive results (Bem & Honorton, 1994). However, 14 later studies from 7 laboratories failed to find evidence that differed from chance (Milton & Wiseman, 1999).

In 2011, a prestigious journal published a series of studies claiming to show that people can foresee the future (Bem, 2011). In one study, college students clicked on the left or right side of the screen to predict which side would show a picture. After the guess, the computer randomly chose one side or the other. If it matched the student's guess, it displayed an erotic photograph of a couple engaged in a sex act. The experimenter reported that students' guesses matched the computer's choice 53 percent of the time, suggesting an ability to predict the future. In another of the studies, students read a list of words, tried to recall them, and then studied half of the list again. The claim was that the students remembered more of the words that they studied again afterward. That is, you could improve your score on a test by studying the material after the test was over! (If you believe this can work, you are welcome to try it.)

Before you revise your study habits, however, you should know that other psychologists have noted many problems and oddities in both the research procedures and the statistical analysis of results (Alcock, 2011; Rouder & Morey, 2011). Also, researchers at three universities repeated the procedures exactly and failed to find any hint of an effect (Ritchie, Wiseman, & French, 2012). Then another lab tried a modified procedure and also failed to find any benefit from studying again after the test (Traxler, Foss, Polali, & Zirnstein, 2012). Given the long history of promising results that other researchers could not replicate, most psychologists remain skeptical of these and similar claims.

The lack of replicability is one major reason to be skeptical of ESP, but another reason is parsimony. If someone claims that a horse does mathematics or a person foresees random events, we should search thoroughly for a simple explanation.

Scientific Thinking in Psychology

What have we learned about science in general? Science does not deal with proof or certainty. All scientific conclusions are tentative and are subject to revision. Nevertheless, this tentativeness does not imply a willingness to abandon well-established theories without excellent reasons.

Scientists always prefer the most parsimonious theory. Before they accept any claim that requires a major new assumption, they insist that it be supported by replicable experiments that rule out simpler explanations and by a new theory that is clearly superior to the theory it replaces.

Summary

- *Steps in a scientific study.* A scientific study goes through the following sequence of steps: hypothesis, method, results, and interpretation. Because almost any study is subject to more than one possible interpretation, we base our conclusions on a pattern of results from many studies. (page 27)

- *Replicability.* The results of a given study are taken seriously only if other investigators following the same method obtain similar results. (page 28)

- *Burden of proof.* In any dispute, the side that should be capable of presenting clear evidence has the obligation to do so. (page 29)

- *Parsimony.* All else being equal, scientists prefer the theory that relies on simpler assumptions, or assumptions consistent with other theories that are already accepted. (page 29)

- *Skepticism about extrasensory perception.* Psychologists carefully scrutinize claims of extrasensory perception because the evidence reported so far has been unreplicable and because the scientific approach includes a search for parsimonious explanations. (page 30)

Key Terms

burden of proof (page 29)

extrasensory perception (ESP) (page 30)

falsifiable (page 29)

hypothesis (page 27)

meta-analysis (page 28)

parsimony (page 29)

replicable result (page 28)

theory (page 28)

Answers to Other Questions in the Module

A. Any magnet strong enough to pull the metal ball up the inclined plane would not release the ball when it reached the hole at the top. It would pull the ball across the hole. (page 30)

B. The prophecies of Nostradamus (see page 31), as interpreted by Cheetham (1973), refer to the following: (1) the assassinations of John F. Kennedy and Robert F. Kennedy, (2) Polaris ballistic missiles shot from submarines, (3) Hitler's invasion of France, and (4) World War II.

Review Questions

1. What does it mean to say that a theory is "falsifiable"?
   (a) Research has contradicted the theory.
   (b) We can imagine results that would contradict the theory.
   (c) Most people disagree with the theory.
   (d) People are still debating whether the theory is correct.

2. Of the following, which would be the most important step in evaluating the accuracy of Nostradamus's predictions?
   (a) Take several predictions that someone claims to have been correct. Ask a large number of people to evaluate whether they seem to be correct.
   (b) Count what percentage of his predictions seems to have come true and what percentage has not.
   (c) Compare the percentage of his predictions that seems to have come true to the percentage for other people who claim to have psychic powers.
   (d) Ask proponents of his predictions to state predictions of events before they happen. Then see how many come true, as compared to the percentage we could expect to come true by accident.

Answer: 1b, 2d.

Thought Question

For the statement, "Ours is just one of an infinite number of universes," who has the burden of proof—those who support the statement or those who deny it? How should we handle a statement when it may be impossible to get firm evidence either for it or against it?

After studying this module, you should be able to:

- Give examples of operational definitions.

- Distinguish between convenience samples, representative samples, random samples, and cross-cultural samples.

- Explain why experiments can lead to cause-and-effect conclusions, whereas correlational studies do not.

- Cite some pitfalls that might compromise the effectiveness of a survey or an experiment.

- Describe how researchers use descriptive and inferential statistics to evaluate the results of a study.

- Discuss again the importance of replicable results.

- Discuss how psychological researchers deal with ethical issues.

Psychology, like any other field, makes progress only when its practitioners distinguish between strong evidence and weak evidence. The goal of this module is not necessarily to prepare you to conduct psychological research but to help you interpret research results intelligently. When you hear about a new study, you should be able to ask pertinent questions to decide how good the evidence is, what conclusion follows, and how confidently one should accept that conclusion.

General Research Principles

Psychological researchers use scientific methods, but they face problems that chemists and physicists do not. One problem is sampling. A psychologist who studies a group of people has to worry about whether those people might be unusual in some way. A chemist studying, say, a methane molecule doesn't have that worry. If you see one methane molecule, you've seen them all. Still another problem is that people who know they are in a research study often behave differently just because they know someone is watching

them. Chemists don't have that worry about a jar of chemicals. In this module, we explore some of the special ways that psychologists adapt scientific principles.

Operational Definitions

Suppose a physicist asks you to measure the effect of temperature on the length of an iron bar. You reply, "What do we *really mean* by temperature?" The physicist sighs, "Don't worry about it. Here is a thermometer and a ruler. Go measure them."

Psychological researchers use the same strategy. If we want to measure the effect of anger on some behavior, we could debate forever about what anger really is, or we could choose a way to measure it. We might ask people to tell us how angry they are, or we might count frowns per minute or swear words per minute, or we might find some other way to measure anger. In doing so, we are using an operational definition, *a definition that specifies the operations (or procedures) used to produce or measure something, ordinarily a way to give it a numerical value.* You might object that "frowns per minute" is not what anger really is. Of course not, but the reading on a thermometer is also not what temperature really is. An operational definition just says how to measure something. It lets us get on with research.

Suppose we want to investigate friendliness. We would need an operational definition of friendliness—that is, a way to measure it. We might define your friendliness as the number of people you smile at during an hour or the number of people you list as close friends. We might operationally define *love* as "how many hours you spend with someone who asks you to stay nearby."

concept check

3. **Which of the following is an operational definition of intelligence?**
   a. The ability to comprehend relationships
   b. A score on an IQ test
   c. The ability to survive in the real world
   d. The product of the cerebral cortex of the brain

4. **What would you propose as an operational definition of sense of humor?**

Answers

3. (b) A score on an IQ test is an operational definition of intelligence, because it provides a measurement—perhaps not a completely accurate measure, but that is a separate issue. None of the other answer choices tells us how to measure or produce intelligence. 4. We might define sense of humor as the number of times someone laughs during a movie or the number of times someone says something that makes other people laugh. Other definitions are possible if they include a method of measurement.

Population Samples

In a chemistry lab, if you find the properties of some compound, your results apply to that same compound anywhere. Psychology is different. The results of a study on one group of people may or may not apply to other groups of people.

For some purposes, the worry is small. For example, research on certain aspects of vision and hearing can use anyone who is available, and in some cases even laboratory animals. Researchers who expect the results to be about the same for almost everyone can use a **convenience sample**, *a group chosen because of its ease of study*. Unfortunately, many researchers overuse research on college students, a convenience sample that is satisfactory for some purposes but not all.

When comparing two populations, researchers need similar samples of those populations. Consider this example: Every fall, the newspapers report the average SAT scores for each American state, and certain states do consistently better than others. At least part of the explanation relates to sampling. In certain states, nearly all college-bound students take the SAT, whereas in others the in-state colleges require the ACT instead, and the only students taking the SAT are those applying to an out-of-state college (maybe one of the Ivy League colleges, for example). We cannot meaningfully compare the results if we test the average students in one state and the best students in another.

A big improvement over a convenience sample is a **representative sample**, *one that resembles the population* in its percentage of males and females, various ethnic groups, young and old, city dwellers and farmers, or whatever other characteristics seem likely to affect the results. To get a representative sample of the people in a region, an investigator first determines what percentage of the residents belong to each category and then selects people to match those percentages. Of course, a sample that is representative in one way might be unrepresentative in another.

Better yet is a **random sample**, *one in which every individual in the population has an equal chance of being selected*. To produce a random sample of Toronto residents, an investigator might start with a map of Toronto and select a certain number of city blocks at random, randomly select one house from each of those blocks, and then randomly choose one person from each of those households. *Random* here has a special meaning. If you simply say, "Okay, I'll pick this block, this block, and this block," the results are not random, because you may be following a pattern, even if you don't realize it. A better procedure is to draw cards out of a hat or some similar procedure that gives every block an equal chance of being chosen, without human interference. A random sample has this advantage: The larger a random sample, the smaller the probability that its results differ substantially from the whole population. However, although a random sample is theoretically the best, it is difficult to achieve. For example, some of the people you randomly choose might refuse to participate!

If we want results that apply to all of humanity, we need to compare people from several cultures. Most people in the United States have been described as Western, Educated, Industrial, Rich (compared to most of the rest of the world), and Democratic—abbreviated WEIRD (Henrich, Heine, & Norenzayan, 2010). You might not like the abbreviation, but the point is that we need to take cultural differences seriously.

We know to expect cultural differences in matters of diet and leisure activities (Kobayashi, 2011), religion, politics, and sexual behavior. Differences also emerge where we might not have expected them. Here are two examples: First, in the United States, on average people of lower social status show more anger, presumably because they experience more frustration. In Japan, people of higher status show more anger, because anger is associated with authority (Park et al., 2013). Second, if you were asked to arrange a series of pictures in order from the first event to the most recent to tell a logical story, you would probably arrange the pictures from left to right, or possibly from top to bottom. Australian aborigines arrange the pictures from east to west, regardless

College students are often used as convenience samples.

of which direction the people themselves are facing (Boroditsky & Gaby, 2010). Doing so, of course, requires them to know exactly which direction is east. For them, the arrow of time goes east to west, just as Americans think of it as going from left to right.

A psychologist who wants to talk about humans throughout the world, and not just one culture, needs a **cross-cultural sample**, *groups of people from at least two cultures*. Cross-cultural sampling is difficult because of the expense, language barriers, and reluctance of people in some cultures to participate in unfamiliar tasks. ■ **Table 2.1** reviews the major types of samples.

concept check

5. **Suppose you stand on a street and you interview every 10th person who walks by. What kind of sample is this—convenience, representative, or random?**

Answer

5. This is a convenience sample. You made no effort to get a sample that matches the total population in age or anything else, so it is not a representative sample. Everyone in the population did not have an equal chance of participating, because not all kinds of people are equally likely to be walking down that street at that time of day.

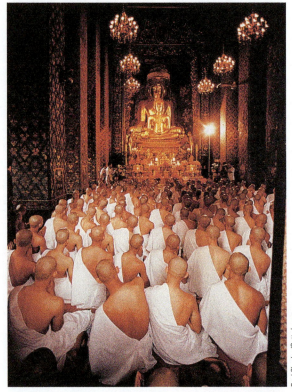

A psychological researcher tests generalizations about human behavior by comparing people from different cultures.

Table 2.1 Types of Samples		
Sample	**Individuals Included**	**Advantages and Disadvantages**
Convenience sample	Anyone who is available	Easiest to get, but results may not generalize to the whole population
Representative sample	Same percentage of male/female, white/black, etc., as the whole population	Results probably similar to whole population, although sample may be representative in some ways but not others
Random sample	Everyone in population has same chance of being chosen	Difficult to get this kind of sample, but it is the best suited for generalizing to the whole population
Cross-cultural	People from different cultures	Difficulties include language barriers, cooperation problems, etc., but essential for studying many issues

Observational Research Designs

Most research starts with description: What happens and under what circumstances? Let's first examine several kinds of observational studies. Later we consider experiments, which are designed to explore cause-and-effect relationships.

Naturalistic Observations

A naturalistic observation is *a careful examination of what happens under more or less natural conditions.* For example, biologist Jane Goodall (1971) spent years observing chimpanzees in the wild, recording their food habits, social interactions, gestures, and way of life (see ▼ Figure 2.6).

Similarly, psychologists sometimes try to observe human behavior "as an outsider." A psychologist might observe whether strangers smile at each other when they pass on a street. How much does the behavior differ between small towns and crowded cities? Who smiles more, women or men? Young people or old people?

Case Histories

Some fascinating conditions are rare. For example, some people are almost completely insensitive to pain. People with Capgras syndrome believe that some of their relatives have been replaced with impostors, who look, sound, and act like the real people. People with Cotard's syndrome insist that they are dead or do not exist. A psychologist who encounters someone with a rare condition like these may report a case history, *a thorough description of someone, including abilities and disabilities, medical condition, life history, unusual experiences, and whatever else seems relevant.* A case history is a kind of naturalistic observation, but we distinguish it because it focuses on a single individual.

A case history can be interesting, but it has major limitations. For example, after the famous scientist Albert Einstein died, researchers examined his brain and reported several unusual features, such as a larger than average ratio of glia cells to neurons in one part of the left hemisphere of his brain. However, given that researchers examined dozens of aspects of his brain, finding a few unusual features is hardly surprising, and possibly irrelevant to Einstein's scientific insights (Hines, 2014). Unless someone reports similar features in the brains of other brilliant scientists, we should draw no conclusions.

▲ **Figure 2.6** In a naturalistic study, observers record the behavior in a natural setting. Here noted biologist Jane Goodall records her observations on chimpanzees. By patiently staying with the chimps, Goodall gradually won their trust and learned to recognize individual animals.

Surveys

A survey is *a study of the prevalence of certain beliefs, attitudes, or behaviors based on people's responses to questions.* No matter what your occupation, at some time you will probably conduct a survey of your employees, your customers, your neighbors, or fellow members of an organization. You will also frequently read and hear about survey results. You should be aware of the ways in which survey results can be useful or misleading.

Sampling

Getting a random or representative sample is important in any research, but especially with surveys. In 1936, the *Literary Digest* mailed 10 million postcards, asking people their choice for president of the United States. Of the 2 million responses, 57 percent preferred the Republican candidate, Alfred Landon.

Later that year, the Democratic candidate, Franklin Roosevelt, defeated Landon by a wide margin. Why was the survey so wrong? The problem was that the *Literary Digest* had selected names from the telephone book and automobile registration lists. In 1936, near the end of the Great Depression, few poor people (who were mostly Democrats) owned telephones or cars.

The Seriousness of Those Being Interviewed

When taking a survey, how carefully do you consider your answers? In one survey, only 45 percent of the respondents said they believed in the existence of intelligent life on other planets. However, a few questions later on the survey, 82 percent said they believed the U.S. government was "hiding evidence of intelligent life in space" (Emery, 1997). Did 37 percent of the people *really* think that the U.S. government is hiding evidence of something that doesn't exist? Or did they answer impulsively without much thought?

Try It Yourself Here's another example: Which of the following programs would you most like to see on television reruns? Rate your choices from highest (1) to lowest (10). (Please fill in your answers, either in the text or on a separate sheet of paper, before continuing to the next paragraph.)

___South Park	___Xena: Warrior Princess
___Lost	___The X-Files
___Cheers	___House
___Seinfeld	___Space Doctor
___I Love Lucy	___Homicide

When I conducted this survey with my own students at North Carolina State University, nearly all did exactly what I asked—they gave every program a rating, including *Space Doctor,* a program that never existed. More than 10 percent rated it in the top five, and a few ranked it as their top choice. (This survey was inspired by an old *Candid Camera* episode in which interviewers asked people their opinions of the nonexistent program *Space Doctor* and received many confident replies.)

Students who rated *Space Doctor* did nothing wrong, of course. I asked them to rank programs, and they did. The fault lies with anyone who interprets such survey results as if they represented informed opinions.

The Wording of the Questions

Try It Yourself Let's start with a little demonstration. Please answer these two questions:

1. I oppose raising taxes. (Circle one.)

1	2	3	4	5	6	7

Strongly agree   Strongly disagree

2. I make it a practice to never lie. (Circle one.)

1	2	3	4	5	6	7

Strongly agree   Strongly disagree

Now cover up those answers and reply to these similar questions:

3. I would be willing to pay a few extra dollars in taxes to provide high-quality education to all children. (Circle one.)

1	2	3	4	5	6	7

Strongly agree   Strongly disagree

4. Like all human beings, I occasionally tell a white lie. (Circle one.)

1	2	3	4	5	6	7

Strongly agree   Strongly disagree

Most students in one study indicated agreement to all four items (Madson, 2005). Note that item 1 contradicts 3, and 2 contradicts 4. You cannot be opposed to raising taxes and in favor of raising taxes. You cannot

Some odd survey results merely reflect the fact that people did not take the questions seriously or did not understand the questions.

be honest all the time and occasionally lie. However, the wording of a question changes its connotation. Question 3 talks about raising taxes "a few extra dollars" for a worthy cause. That differs from raising taxes by an unknown amount for unknown reasons. Similarly, depending on what you mean by a "white lie," you might tell one occasionally while still insisting that you "make it a practice to never lie"—at least not much. The point is that someone can bias your answers one way or the other by rewording a question.

Here is another example. Imagine yourself as the judge in a divorce case, where you have to decide whether to give parent A or parent B primary custody of their child. Never mind whether which parent is the father and which is the mother. Parent A is satisfactory in all ways, but not outstanding. Parent B has some major positives and major negatives. B has a better house, a higher income, and a closer relationship with the child. However, B also has to do much work-related travel and has some minor health problems. To which parent would you award custody? Most people reply B. However, if asked to which parent would you *deny* custody, again most people reply B. The term *award* gets people to focus on the positives, and the

word *deny* gets them to emphasize the negatives, resulting in a different outcome (Shafir, 1983).

In short, the next time you hear the results of some survey, ask how the question was worded and what choices were offered. Even a slightly different wording could yield a different percentage.

Surveyor Biases

Sometimes, an organization words the questions of a survey to encourage the answers they hope to receive. According to a 1993 survey, 92 percent of high school boys and 98 percent of high school girls said they were victims of sexual harassment (Shogren, 1993). Shocking, isn't it? However, perhaps the designers of the survey *wanted* to show that sexual harassment is rampant. The survey defined sexual harassment by a long list of acts ranging from major offenses (e.g., having someone rip your clothes off in public) to minor annoyances. For example, if you didn't like some of the sexual graffiti on the restroom wall, you could consider yourself sexually harassed. If you tried to make yourself look sexually attractive (as most teenagers do, right?) and then attracted a suggestive look from someone you *didn't* want to attract, that stare would count as sexual harassment. (I worry about those who said they *weren't* sexually harassed! They liked *all* the graffiti on the restroom walls? No one ever looked at them in a sexual way? That would be sad.) Sexual harassment is, of course, a serious problem, but a survey that combines major and minor offenses is likely to mislead.

▼ Figure 2.7 shows the results for two surveys conducted on similar populations at about the same time. The issue is whether stem cells derived from aborted

▶ **Figure 2.7** The question on the left led most people to express opposition. The question on the right, worded differently, led most people to express support.

Stem cells are the basic cells from which all of a person's tissues and organs develop. Congress is considering whether to provide federal funding for experiments using stem cells from human embryos. The live embryos would be destroyed in their first week of development to obtain these cells. Do you support or oppose using your federal tax dollars for such experiments?

Sometimes fertility clinics produce extra fertilized eggs, also known as embryos, that are not implanted in a woman's womb. These extra embryos either are discarded, or couples can donate them for use in medical research called stem cell research. Some people support stem cell research, saying it's an important way to find treatments for many diseases. Other people oppose stem cell research, saying it's wrong to use any human embryos for research purposes. What about you—do you support or oppose stem cell research?

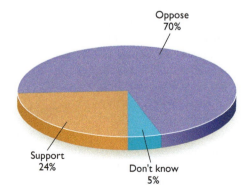
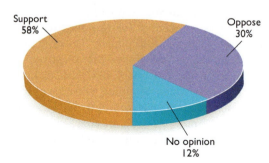

fetuses can be used in medical research. The question on the left was written by an organization opposed to abortion and stem cell research. The question on the right was worded by an organization that is either neutral or favorable to stem cell research (Public Agenda, 2001). As you can see, the wording of the question influenced the answers.

Correlational Studies

Another type of research is a correlational study. A **correlation** is *a measure of the relationship between two variables.* (A variable is anything measurable that differs among individuals, such as age, years of education, or reading speed.) In a correlational study, investigators measure the relation between two variables without controlling either of them. For example, one might measure the correlation between people's height and weight, or the correlation between scores on an extraversion questionnaire and how many friends someone has.

The Correlation Coefficient

Some pairs of variables are related more strongly than others. To measure the strength of a correlation, researchers use a **correlation coefficient**, *a mathematical estimate of the relationship between two variables.* A correlation coefficient of zero indicates no consistent relationship. A coefficient of +1 or −1 indicates a perfect relationship—that is, if you know the value of one variable, you can predict the other with perfect accuracy. (In psychology you probably will never see a perfect +1 or −1 correlation coefficient.) A positive coefficient, such as +1, means that as one variable increases, the other increases also. A negative coefficient, such as −1, means that as one variable increases, the other decreases. A negative correlation is just as useful as a positive correlation. For example, the more often people practice golf, the lower their golf scores, so golf practice is negatively correlated with scores. In nations where people eat more seafood, depression is less common, so seafood consumption is negatively correlated with depression, as shown in ▶ Figure 2.8 (Gómez-Pinilla, 2008).

A 0 correlation indicates that as one variable goes up, the other does not consistently go up or down. A correlation near 0 can mean that two variables really are unrelated or that one or both of them were poorly measured. For example, if you ask students how eager they are to do well in school, their answers correlate almost zero with academic success (Dompnier, Darnon, & Butera, 2009). Does that mean that motivation is unimportant for school success? Hardly. How motivated students *say* they are isn't the same as how motivated they *actually* are. If a measurement is poor—in this case, answers to certain questions—we can hardly expect the measurement to correlate with anything else.

▼ Figure 2.9 shows scatter plots for three correlations (real data). In a scatter plot, *each dot represents a given individual, with one measurement for that individual on the* x-*axis (horizontal) and another measurement on the* y-*axis (vertical).* In Figure 2.9, each dot represents one student in an introductory psychology class. The value for that student along the y-axis represents percentage correct on the final exam. In the first graph, values along the x-axis represent scores on the first test in the course. Here the correlation is +0.72, indicating a fairly strong relationship. Most of the students who did well on the first test also did well on the final, and most who did poorly on the first test also did poorly on the final. In the second graph, the x-axis represents times absent out of 38 class meetings. Here you see a correlation of −0.44. This negative correlation indicates that, in general, those with more absences had lower exam scores. The third graph shows how the final exam scores related to the last three digits of each student's Social Security number. As you would expect, the correlation is close to 0. If we examined the data for a larger population of students, the correlation would no doubt come closer and closer to 0.

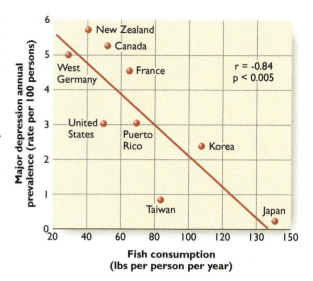

▲ **Figure 2.8** Each dot represents one country. The value along the *x*-axis indicates the amount of seafood that an average person eats in a year. The value along the *y*-axis indicates the probability of developing major depression. As seafood consumption increases, the probability of depression decreases.

concept check

6. **Identify each of these as a positive, zero, or negative correlation:**

   a. The more crowded a neighborhood, the lower the income.

   b. People with high IQ scores are neither more nor less likely than other people to have high telephone numbers.

   c. People who awaken frequently during the night are more likely than other people to feel depressed.

7. **Which indicates a stronger relationship between two variables, a +0.50 correlation or a −0.75 correlation?**

8. **The correlation between students' grades and their scores on a self-esteem questionnaire is very low, not much above 0. Why might that be?**

Answers

8. One possibility is that grades are unrelated to self-esteem. Another possibility is that we used an inaccurate measurement of either self-esteem or grades or both. If anything is measured poorly, it cannot correlate strongly with anything else.

7. The −0.75 correlation indicates a stronger relationship—that is, a greater accuracy of predicting one variable based on measurements of the other. A negative correlation is just as useful as a positive one.

6. a. Negative correlation between crowdedness and income. b. Zero correlation between telephone numbers and IQ scores. c. Positive correlation between awakenings and depression.

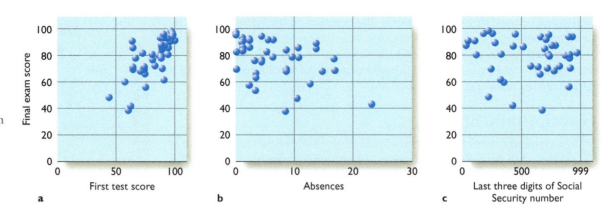

▶ **Figure 2.9** In these scatter plots, each dot represents measurements of two variables for one person. **(a)** Scores on first test and scores on final exam (correlation = +0.72). **(b)** Times absent and scores on final exam (correlation = −0.44). **(c)** Last three digits of Social Security number and scores on final exam (correlation = −0.08).

Illusory Correlations

Sometimes we think we see a correlation that doesn't really exist. For example, many people believe that consuming sugar makes children hyperactive. However, extensive research found little effect of sugar on activity levels, and some studies found that sugar *calms* behavior (Milich, Wolraich, & Lindgren, 1986; Wolraich et al., 1994). Why, then, do many people believe that sugar makes children hyperactive? Researchers watched two sets of mothers with their 5- to 7-year-old sons after telling one group that they had given the sons sugar and the other that they had given the sons a placebo, *a pill*

People's expectations and faulty memories produce illusory correlations, such as that between the full moon and abnormal behavior.

with no known pharmacological effects. In fact, they had given both a placebo. The mothers who *thought* their sons had been given sugar rated their sons hyperactive during the observation period, whereas the other mothers did not (Hoover & Milich, 1994). That is, people see what they expect to see.

When people expect to see a connection between two events (e.g., sugar and activity levels), they remember the cases that support the connection and disregard the exceptions, thus perceiving an **illusory correlation**, *an apparent relationship based on casual observations of unrelated or weakly related events.* Many stereotypes about groups of people are illusory correlations.

As another example, consider the common belief that a full moon affects human behavior. For hundreds of years, many people have believed that crime and various kinds of mental disturbance are more common under a full moon than at other times. The term *lunacy* (from the Latin word *luna,* meaning "moon") originally meant mental illness caused by the full moon. Some police officers claim that they receive more calls on nights with a full moon, and some hospital workers say they have more emergency cases on such nights. However, careful reviews of the data have found no relationship between the moon's phases and either crime or mental illness (Raison, Klein, & Steckler, 1999; Rotton & Kelly, 1985). Why, then, does the belief persist? People remember events that fit the belief and disregard those that do not.

Correlation ≠ Causation

"Correlation does not mean causation." You will hear that statement again and again in psychology and other fields. A correlation indicates how strongly two variables are related to each other. It does not tell us *why* they are related. If two variables—let's call them A and B—are positively correlated, it could be that A causes B, B causes A, or some third variable, C, causes both of them.

For example, how much sunscreen people use is positively correlated with their chance of getting skin cancer. Does that mean that sunscreen causes cancer? It is more likely that people who are at risk of skin cancer, because they spend much time in the sun, are the ones who use more sunscreen.

There is also a positive correlation between how often parents spank their children and how often the children misbehave. Does this correlation indicate that spankings lead to misbehavior? Or does misbehavior lead to spankings? Yet another possibility is that the parents had genes promoting aggressive behavior that led them to spank, and the children inherited those genes, which led to misbehaviors. Because all these explanations are possible, we cannot draw a conclusion about causation.

"Then what good is a correlation?" you might ask. First, correlations help us make predictions. Second, correlational studies pave the way for later experimentation that might lead to a conclusion. For example, if we could persuade half the parents to stop spanking, we might see whether their children's behavior improves.

Here are more examples of why we cannot draw conclusions regarding cause and effect from correlational data (see also ▶ Figure 2.10):

- *Political conservativeness correlates with happiness.* Political conservatives rate themselves as happier than liberals (Napier & Jost, 2008), although these self-reports may not be fully accurate (Wojcik, Hovasapian, Graham, Motyl, & Ditto, 2015). Does a positive correlation mean that being conservative makes you happier? Or that being happy makes you more conservative? Maybe it's neither. Maybe financially secure people are more likely than poor people to be political conservatives, and more likely to be happy.

- *According to one study, people who sleep about seven hours a night are less likely to die within the next few years than those who sleep either more or less* (Kripke, Garfinkel, Wingard, Klauber, & Marler, 2002). Should we conclude (as some people did) that sleeping too much impairs your health? Here is an alternative: People who already have life-threatening illnesses tend to sleep more than healthy people. So perhaps illness causes extra sleep rather than extra sleep causing illness. Or perhaps advancing age increases the probability of both illness and extra sleep. (The study included people ranging from young adulthood through age 101!)

Now, let me tell you a dirty little secret: In rare circumstances, correlational results *do* imply cause and effect. It is a "dirty little secret" because professors want students to avoid cause-and-effect conclusions from correlations, and mentioning the exceptions is risky. Still, consider the fact that people are generally in a better mood when the weather improves (Keller et al., 2005). A likely explanation is that the weather changes your mood. What other possibility is there? Your mood changes the weather? Surely not. Might something else control both the weather and your mood? If so, what? In the absence of any other hypothesis, we conclude that the weather changes your mood. Also, consider that how often a U.S. congressional representative votes a pro-feminist position (as defined by the National Organization for Women) correlates with how many daughters the representative has (Washington, 2006). It is implausible that someone's voting record would influence the sex of his or her children. It is highly likely that having daughters could influence political views. Again, the results suggest cause and effect. Nevertheless, the point remains: We should almost always be skeptical of causal conclusions that anyone draws from a correlational study.

9. **Suppose we find a 0.8 correlation between students' reported interest in psychology and their grades on a psychology test. What conclusion can we draw?**

10. **On average, the more medicines people take, the more likely they are to die young. Propose alternative explanations for this correlation.**

11. **On average, drug addicts who regularly attend counseling sessions are more likely to stay drug-free than those who drop out. Propose alternative explanations for this correlation.**

Answers

11. Perhaps the counseling sessions are helpful to people who want to quit drugs. Or perhaps the people with the most serious addictions are the ones who quit.

10. Perhaps people get sick from complications caused by taking too many pills. Or maybe the people who take many medicines are those who already had serious illnesses.

9. We can conclude only that if we know either someone's interest level or test score, we can predict the other with reasonably high accuracy. We *cannot conclude* that an interest in psychology will help someone learn the material or that doing well on psychology tests increases someone's interest in the material. Either conclusion might be true, of course, but neither conclusion follows from these results. A correlational study cannot demonstrate a cause-and-effect relationship.

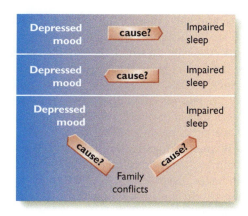

▲ **Figure 2.10** A strong correlation between depression and impaired sleep does not tell us whether depression interferes with sleep, poor sleep leads to depression, or whether another problem leads to both depression and sleep problems.

Experiments

To determine causation, an investigator uses an **experiment**, *a study in which the investigator manipulates at least one variable while measuring at least one other variable.* The **independent variable** is *the item that an experimenter changes or controls*—for example, the type of training that people receive or the wording of the instructions before they start some task. The **dependent variable** is *the item that an experimenter measures to determine the outcome*—for example, how many questions people answer correctly or how rapidly they respond to signals. If the procedure causes different groups to behave differently, you can think of the independent variable as the cause and the dependent variable as the effect.

An **experimental group** *receives the treatment that an experiment is designed to test.* For example, the experimental group might receive some special experience that we think will influence later behavior. The **control group** is *a set of individuals treated in the same way as the experimental group except for the procedure that the experiment is designed to test.* If the people in the experimental group received a special experience, those in the control group do something else during the same time. If those in the experimental group receive a medication, those in the control group receive a placebo. ■ Table 2.2 contrasts experiments with observational studies.

A key procedure for any experiment is **random assignment** of participants to groups: *The experimenter uses a chance procedure, such as drawing names out of a hat, to make sure that all participants have the same probability of being assigned to a given group.* Why is this so important? Consider a couple of examples.

Women at menopause have decreased release of estrogens and related hormones. For years physicians recommended hormone replacement therapy, and the women receiving that therapy tended to be healthier than other women their age. However, women who follow their physicians' advice tend to be more health-conscious in other ways, such as diet and exercise, so they could be healthy for reasons other than the hormones. In an experiment, more than 160,000 women agreed to receive either the hormones or a placebo. The result: Women taking the hormones had decreased risk of hip fractures and colon cancer, but increased risk of heart disease, stroke, and breast cancer (Writing Group for the Women's Health Initiative Investigators, 2002). Overall, the harms were at least as great as the benefits.

Another example: Several studies have found that moderate alcohol drinkers (about one glass of beer or wine per day) tend in the long run to be healthier than heavy drinkers or nondrinkers. It's clear that heavy drinking would be bad, but if you are a nondrinker, should you take up beer or wine? We cannot be sure. First, this is a small effect. In one study, nondrinkers constituted 22 percent of the healthier old people, compared to 25 percent of the less healthy old people (Sun et al., 2011). Second, nondrinkers could differ from moderate drinkers in other ways. Maybe healthy people are more likely to drink than are people who are prone to illness. We cannot be sure, unless someone does a study with random assignment to drinking and not drinking. (That would be a hard study to do.)

12. **An instructor wants to find out whether the frequency of testing in an introductory psychology class influences students' final exam performance. The instructor gives weekly tests in one class, just three tests in a second class, and only a single midterm exam in the third class. All three classes take the same final exam, and the instructor then compares their performances. Identify the independent variable and the dependent variable in this experiment.**

Answer

12. The independent variable is the frequency of tests during the semester. The dependent variable is the students' performance on the final exam.

Reducing the Influence of Expectations

Experiments can go wrong in many ways, if we're not careful. Let's consider several possible problems and how researchers overcome them.

Table 2.2 Comparison of Five Methods of Research	
Observational Studies	
Case Study	Detailed description of single individual; suitable for studying rare conditions
Naturalistic Observation	Description of behavior under natural conditions
Survey	Study of attitudes, beliefs, or behaviors based on answers to questions
Correlation	Description of the relationship between two variables that the investigator measures but does not control; determines whether two variables are closely related but does not address questions of cause and effect
Experiment	
	Determination of the effect of a variable controlled by the investigator on some other variable that is measured; the only method that can inform us about cause and effect

Experimenter Bias and Blind Studies

Experimenter bias is *the tendency of an observer (unintentionally, as a rule) to misperceive the results.* That bias shows up in experiments, but in the outside world, too. Imagine you are a forensic psychologist, asked to testify in court about how dangerous a particular offender is, and therefore what punishment is appropriate. You interview the offender and examine all the relevant evidence. Would you alter your testimony depending on whether the prosecution or the defense had hired you? Studies show that you probably would (Murrie, Boccaccini, Guarnera, & Rufino, 2013). Even when you try to be objective and fair, you cannot easily ignore your desires and expectations. Now imagine you are a baseball umpire, calling balls and strikes. You see a pitch that is a borderline case. If you know the pitcher is one of the best in the league, do you give the benefit of the doubt and call it a strike? A research study showed that you probably would (Kim & King, 2014). The same problem arises whenever a researcher is testing a hypothesis and hoping to get a particular result.

To minimize the influence of expectations, it is best to use a **blind observer**—*someone who records data without knowing the researcher's predictions.* Ideally, the experimenter conceals the procedure from the participants also. Suppose experimenters give children a treatment that is supposed to increase their ability to pay attention. If the children know the prediction, their expectations may influence their behavior. In a **single-blind study**, *either the observer or the participants are unaware of which participants received which treatment* (see ■ Table 2.3). In a **double-blind study**, *both the observer and the participants are unaware of which participants received which treatment.* Of course, the experimenter who organized the study would need to keep records of which participants received which procedure. (If *everyone* loses track of the procedure, it is known jokingly as "triple blind.")

Double-blind studies are difficult in many fields of psychology. In a study to determine the effects of psychotherapy, it is not possible to conceal from participants whether they did or did not receive therapy. In a study of the effects of playing violent video games, researchers might ask some people to play violent games and others to play peaceful games (like *The Sims*), but the peaceful game is not exactly a placebo, because the players might have different expectations of effects (Boot, Simons, Stothart, & Stutts, 2013).

Table 2.3 Single-Blind and Double-Blind Studies

Who is aware of which participants are in which group?

	Experimenter Who Organized the Study	Observer	Participants
Single-blind	aware	unaware	aware
Single-blind	aware	aware	unaware
Double-blind	aware	unaware	unaware

Demand Characteristics

People in a psychological experiment know they are in an experiment. Ethically, the researcher is required to tell them and to obtain their consent. If you know you are in a study and someone is watching you, might that influence your behavior? Furthermore, suppose you know or guess what the experimenter hopes to see. Might that expectation alter your behavior?

Here is an example: Experimenters told one group of men that there was reason to believe that seeing the color pink decreases one's strength. They told another group that seeing the color pink increases one's strength. Then they tested the men's grip strength while looking at a pink panel. Those who expected pink to increase their strength showed a 10 percent stronger grip (Smith, Bell, & Fusco, 1986; see ▼ Figure 2.11).

Here is another example: Many years ago a British television program about the chemical senses concluded by saying (falsely) that smells depend on the rate of vibration of molecules, and the announcer offered to demonstrate. Viewers saw electrodes leading from a cone to an array of electronic equipment. The announcer explained that the electrodes would detect the vibration of molecules in the container, and then relay it to equipment that would produce a sound of the same frequency. Viewers were asked to listen to that frequency and then call or write to the station to say what, if anything, they had smelled. (The next day, the program explained that this had been an experiment and smell doesn't really work that way.) Of 179 people who called

or wrote, 155 claimed to have smelled something, including 6 who complained that the smell had provoked an attack of hay fever, sneezing, or other distress (O'Mahony, 1978).

Even when researchers don't tell people what they expect, people's guesses influence their behavior. Martin Orne (1969) defined demand characteristics as *cues that tell participants what is expected of them and what the experimenter hopes to find.* To minimize demand characteristics, experimenters often try to conceal the purpose of the experiment. A double-blind study also serves the purpose: If two groups share the same expectations but behave differently because of a treatment, then the differences are not due to their expectations.

Problems related to demand characteristics show up in many contexts, not just in experiments. Often an interviewer unintentionally suggests an answer, or poses a question in a way that lets the interviewee guess what answer is expected. Psychotherapists sometimes suggest, intentionally or otherwise, that they are looking for certain kinds of memories or thoughts. Suggestion can be a powerful thing, and often difficult to avoid.

concept check

13. **Which of the following would an experimenter try to minimize or avoid? Falsifiability, independent variables, dependent variables, blind observers, or demand characteristics.**

Answer 13. Of these, only demand characteristics are to be avoided. If you did not remember that falsifiability is a good feature of a theory, check page 29. Every experiment must have at least one independent variable (what the experimenter controls) and at least one dependent variable (what the experimenter measures). Blind observers provide an advantage.

Problems with a Before-and-After Study

Imagine a chemist adding one clear liquid to another. Suddenly the mixture turns green and explodes. We would conclude cause and effect, as we have no reason to expect that the first liquid was about to turn green and explode on its own. Now imagine some procedures in psychology: Researchers give children language training and find that their language skills improve over the next few months. They provide therapy for patients with depression and find that many become gradually less depressed. They provide special training for teenagers who exhibit violence, and find that many of them become less violent. In any of these cases, can we conclude cause and effect? No, because it

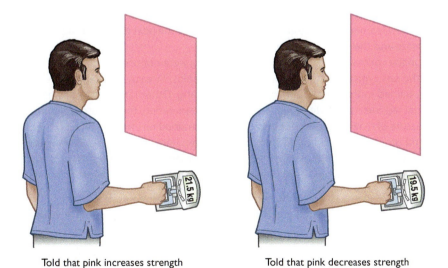

Told that pink increases strength   Told that pink decreases strength

▲ **Figure 2.11** Men who expected to feel stronger while looking at pink were in fact stronger than those who expected to feel weaker while looking at pink.

is possible, even likely, that many of these people would have improved over time without treatment.

Instead of a before-and-after study, a better design is to compare two groups: An investigator provides the treatment for one group (the *experimental group*) and not the other (the *control group*), with participants randomly assigned to the two groups. The difference, if any, that emerges between the groups is an indication of the treatment's effect. Even then, we should beware of generalizing the results too far. Maybe the procedure works only in one culture or under special circumstances. It is important to be cautious about the results of any single study.

what's the evidence?

Inheritance of Acquired Characteristics? Problems in a Before-and-After Study

Let's examine a specific study that illustrates the limitations of a before-and-after study. It pertains to evolution, but the point here is not so much evolution itself as some pitfalls of research.

Charles Darwin's theory of evolution by natural selection makes a simple point: If individuals with one kind of genes reproduce more than those with other genes, then the first set of genes will become more common from one generation to the next. Eventually, the whole population will resemble those who were most successful at reproducing. Prior to Darwin, Jean-Baptiste Lamarck had offered a different theory, evolution by inheritance of acquired characteristics. According to that theory, if you exercise your muscles, your children will be born with larger muscles. If you fail to use your little toe, your children will be born with a smaller little toe than you had. The evidence never supported that theory, and by the early 1900s, nearly all biologists abandoned it in favor of Darwin's theory. However, a few holdouts continued defending Lamarckian evolution.

First Study (McDougall, 1938)

Hypothesis If rats learn to swim through a maze, their offspring will learn the maze more quickly.

Method Rats had to learn to swim a particular route to get out of a tank of water. The experimenter trained them until each rat was consistently swimming quickly the correct route. Then he let them breed. He did not select the best learners for breeding, but simply chose rats at random. When rats of the next generation were old enough, he trained them and then let them reproduce. This procedure continued for one generation after another.

Results The average performance of the rats improved from one generation to the next for the first few generations. That is, the second generation learned faster than the first, the third faster than the second, and so on for a few generations. Later, the results fluctuated.

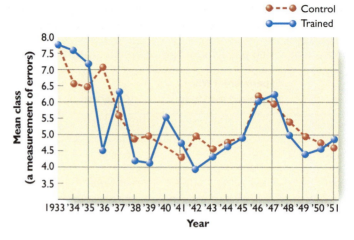

▲ **Figure 2.12** Rats in the experimental group and the control group improved at equal rates from one generation to the next. (From Agar, W. E., Drummond, F. H., Tiegs, O. W., & Gunson, M. M. (1954). Fourth (final) report on a test of McDougall's Lamarckian experiment on the training of rats. *Journal of Experimental Biology, 31*, 307−321.)

Interpretation These results are consistent with the hypothesis, but we should consider other hypotheses, too. If these results really indicate inheritance of acquired characteristics, we would have to imagine that the experience of learning the maze somehow directed the genes to mutate in the right way to help the next generation learn the same maze. It is difficult to imagine how this could happen.

When results conflict so strongly with what we think we know, scientists ask these questions: Are the results replicable? Is there a more parsimonious explanation? And is there any flaw in the design of the study?

Do you, in fact, see anything wrong with the procedure? One group of researchers noticed that this is a before-and-after study with no control group. What would happen, they wondered, if they repeated the study using a control group that was not trained in the maze? Would their offspring improve as much as the offspring of the trained rats?

Second Study (Agar, Drummond, Tiegs, & Gunson, 1954)

Hypothesis If it is possible to replicate McDougall's results, the improvement will also occur in a control group that receives no training in the maze.

Method Rats in the trained group were treated the same as those in McDougall's study: Rats learned the maze and then mated. Rats of the next generation also learned the maze and then mated and so forth.

In the control group, the rats used for training were not used for breeding. Young, healthy rats typically have a litter of about 12 babies. In each generation, a few rats were trained in the maze but not used for breeding. Other rats from the same litter, not trained, were permitted to breed. So in each generation, the researchers obtained a measure of maze learning, but because only untrained rats mated, all the rats in the control group were descended from untrained rats. Any improvement over generations could not be due to the training. The experiment continued for 18 years, with a few generations of rats per year. (Rats reach sexual maturity at about age 60 days.)

Results ▲ Figure 2.12 shows the results. For the first few years, on average, both the trained group and the control group improved from one generation to the next. In later years, the results fluctuated. The two groups performed similarly throughout the study.

Interpretation To most people's surprise, McDougall's results were replicable. However, because the trained group did not differ from the control group, training had nothing to do with the improvement over generations. That is, the results showed no evidence for inheritance of acquired characteristics.

How, then, can we explain the improvement over generations? One possibility is that rats of the first generation were stressed. They had just been shipped in by train, in crowded boxes, from rat-breeding facilities to McDougall's laboratory. (Yes, there are companies that specialize in breeding and selling rats.) The second generation grew up in the laboratory, but they were the offspring of highly stressed parents. Conceivably, those effects could persist for several generations.

Another possibility is that the experimenters gradually got better at taking care of rats and running the experiment. We might be seeing a change in the experimenters, not a change in the rats.

A third possibility is that because the experimenters always mated brother with sister, later generations may have become less vigorous. Ordinarily, we expect inbreeding to be a disadvantage, but perhaps less vigorous rats swam more slowly and therefore had more time to consider which direction to turn in the maze. This idea sounds a little far-fetched but not impossible.

We don't know which explanation is correct. The question isn't important enough for anyone to do the additional research necessary to find out. The main conclusion is that we can account for the results without assuming inheritance of acquired characteristics.

This episode illustrates several points about research: (1) If the results seem unlikely, look for a more parsimonious explanation. (2) Beware of before-and-after studies in psychology, biology, or medicine. Without a control group, we don't know what the results mean. (3) If behavior changes from one generation to the next, the explanation doesn't have to be genetic. It might reflect a change in the environment. For example, your environment differs from the one in which your grandparents grew up.

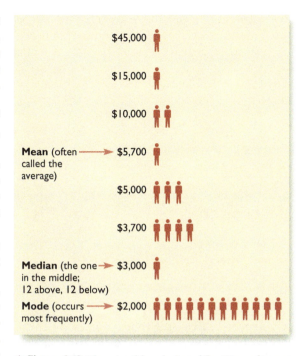

▲ **Figure 2.13** The monthly salaries of the 25 employees of company X, showing the mean, median, and mode. (After Huff, 1954)

Evaluating the Results

Suppose you conduct a well-designed experiment and now you get the results. In psychology, the usual result includes considerable variation among individuals. Perhaps most of the people in the experimental group acted one way and most of those in the control group acted another, but neither group was 100 percent consistent. We need some guidelines on how to decide whether the difference is worth taking seriously.

Descriptive Statistics

First, an investigator summarizes the results, using descriptive statistics, which are *mathematical summaries of results*. We care about the central score—that is, the middle or average. Three ways of representing the central score are the mean, median, and mode. The **mean** is *the sum of all the scores divided by the total number of scores*. When people say "average," they generally refer to the mean. For example, the mean of 2, 10, and 3 is 5 (15 ÷ 3). The mean is especially useful if the scores approximate the normal distribution (or normal curve), *a symmetrical frequency of scores clustered around the mean*.

The mean can be misleading, however. For example, every member of my family has a greater than average number of arms and legs! It's true. Think about it. What is the average (mean) number of arms or legs for a human being? It is not 2, but 1.99 . . . because a few people have had an arm or leg amputated. So if the "average" refers to the mean, it is possible for almost everyone to be above or below average. Here is another example: A survey asked people how many sex partners they hoped to have, ideally, over the next 30 years. The mean for women was 2.8 and the mean for men was 64.3 (L. C. Miller & Fishkin, 1997). However, almost two-thirds of women and about half of men replied "1." They wanted a loving relationship with one partner. Most of the others said they hoped for a few partners, but a small number of men said they hoped for hundreds or thousands. The result was a mean of 64.3, a misleading figure.

When the population distribution is far from symmetrical, we can better represent the typical scores by the median instead of the mean. To determine

the median, *arrange the scores in order from the highest to the lowest. The middle score is the median.* For example, for the set of scores 2, 10, and 3, the median is 3. For the set of scores 1, 1, and 950, the median is 1. Extreme scores greatly affect the mean but not the median.

The third way to represent the central score is the **mode**, *the score that occurs most frequently*. For example, in the distribution of scores 1, 1, 1, 4, 7, 9, and 10, the mode is 1. The mean and median are more useful for most purposes, but the mode calls attention to a common score.

To summarize: The mean is what most people intend when they say "average." It is the sum of the scores divided by the number of scores. The median is the middle score after the scores are ranked from highest to lowest. The mode is the most common score (see ▲ Figure 2.13).

14. a. For the following distribution of scores, determine the mean, the median, and the mode: 5, 2, 2, 2, 8, 3, 1, 6, 7.

b. Determine the mean, median, and mode for this distribution: 5, 2, 2, 2, 35, 3, 1, 6, 7.

Answer 14. a. mean = 4; median = 3; mode = 2. b. mean = 7; median = 3; mode = 2. Note that changing just one number in the distribution from 8 to 35 greatly altered the mean without affecting the median or the mode.

▲ **Figure 2.14** Radivoke Lajic holds the six meteorites that he claims have struck his house.

Inferential Statistics

Suppose researchers randomly assign people to two groups to help them quit smoking cigarettes. One group receives punishments for smoking, and the other group gets rewards for not smoking. Before treatment, both groups average about 10 cigarettes per day. At the end of 6 weeks of therapy, those in the punishment group average 7.5 cigarettes per day, whereas those in the reward group average 6.5 cigarettes per day. How seriously should we take this difference?

To answer this question, we obviously need to know more than just the numbers 7.5 and 6.5. How many smokers were in the study? (Just a few? Hundreds? Thousands?) Also, are most people's behaviors close to the group means, or did a few extreme scores distort the averages?

We evaluate the results with inferential statistics, which are *statements about a large population based on an inference from a small sample.* Certain kinds of statistical tests determine the probability that purely chance variation would achieve a difference as large as the one observed. The result is summarized by a *p* (as in *probability)* value. For example, **$p < 0.05$** indicates that *the probability that randomly generated results would resemble the observed results is less than 5 percent.* The smaller the *p* value, the more impressive the results.

The usual agreement is that, if *p* is less than 0.05, researchers consider the results statistically significant or statistically reliable—that is, *results that chance alone would be unlikely to produce.* Statistical significance depends on three factors: the size of the difference between the groups, the number of research participants in each group, and the amount of variation among individuals within each group.

The implication of statistical significance is that such results are worth considering, worth an attempt to explain them. However, saying that it would be unlikely for chance alone to produce such results does not mean it is unlikely that chance alone *did* produce these results. It sounds as if those statements might mean the same thing, but they do not. For example, suppose you flip a coin 6 times and you get 6 heads in a row. Pure chance produces a string like that less than 5 percent of the time, but in this case we know that chance *did* produce the result (presuming that it's a normal coin). Another example: A man in Bosnia, Radivoke Lajic, has had his house hit by meteorites six times (see ◄ Figure 2.14). One meteor hitting a house is a rare event, and the chance of six such events is, in this case, literally astronomical. So, are we 99.99999 . . . percent sure it was not a coincidence? No. Extremely unlikely coincidences do sometimes occur. If this result was not due to chance, then what? Lajic believes that aliens have singled him out for attack. If so, why? And why are they pelting him with such tiny meteorites? The extreme unlikelihood of this coincidence invites us to look for an explanation, but it does not guarantee that we will find one. Until or unless we do, chance remains a reasonable explanation. (Besides that, asking what is the probability of having six meteorites hit your house is the wrong question. The better question is, "What is the chance that *some* extreme and bizarre coincidence will happen, somewhere and at some time?")

Although a procedure yielding a *p* value has been common through most of psychology's history, objections to it have been growing (Cumming, 2014). One objection is that it falsely implies an all-or-nothing judgment: Either something is significant, or it is not. More realistically, results range along a continuum from convincing to unimpressive. A second objection is that we should care about the size of the effect, not just whether or not it occurred. Given a large enough sample, it would be possible to get a low *p* value even for a tiny effect with no practical importance.

For these and other reasons, a growing trend is for researchers to show the means and 95 percent confidence intervals for each group, as shown in ▼ Figure 2.15 (Cumming, 2008). The 95 percent confidence interval is *the range within which the true mean lies, with 95 percent certainty.*

"Wait a minute," you protest. "We already know the means: 7.5 and 6.5. Aren't *those* the 'true' means?" No, those are the means for particular samples of the population. Someone who studies another group may not get the same

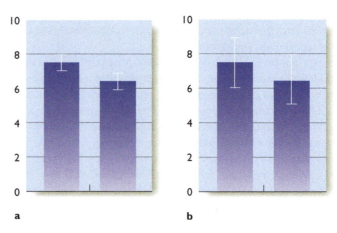

▲ **Figure 2.15** The vertical lines indicate 95 percent confidence intervals. The pair of graphs in part **a** indicate that the true mean has a 95 percent chance of falling within a very narrow range. The graphs in part **b** indicate a wider range.

results. What we care about is the mean for everyone. It is impractical to measure that mean, but if we know the sample mean, the size of the sample, and the amount of variation among individuals (measured by a term called the *standard deviation*), we can estimate how close the sample mean is, probably, to the population mean.

In Figure 2.15a, the 95 percent confidence intervals are small. In other words, the samples were large, the individual variation was small, and the sample means are probably close to the true population means. In Figure 2.15b, the confidence intervals are larger, so the sample means are just approximations of the true population means. Presenting data with confidence intervals enables readers to judge for themselves how large and impressive the difference is between groups (Hunter, 1997; Loftus, 1996).

15. **Should we be more impressed with results when the 95 percent confidence intervals are large or small? Should we be more impressed if the *p* value is large or small?**

Answer

15. In both cases, smaller. A small 95 percent confidence interval indicates high confidence in the results. A small *p* value indicates a low probability of getting such a large difference merely by chance.

Replicability Issues

Here is a hypothetical study. Let's hope no one ever did anything quite this silly, but it illustrates an important point. Dr. Hopeful measures how long 100 college students can balance on one foot with their eyes closed. Then he tests whether the men differed from the women. No, he finds, on average they did not. How about freshmen versus advanced students? Tall people versus short people? Science majors versus humanities majors? One by one, he tries many hypotheses, finding little or no difference. Then he runs another comparison and finds that people with last names near the end of the alphabet could balance longer than those near the start of the alphabet, with *p* < 0.05 and 95 percent confidence intervals that don't overlap. Aha! Maybe people near the end of the alphabet are used to standing in lines for a long time when people line up alphabetically, so they developed this skill. It's a new finding! Calls for a celebration!

Ah, but wait. If you test enough hypotheses, you increase your chance of confirming one or more of them just by accident. The reported difference probably represents a random fluctuation in the data, nothing more (Nuzzo, 2014).

What if Dr. Hopeful had tested *only* this one hypothesis, concerning names at the beginning or end of the alphabet? The results would still run a serious risk of being just a random fluctuation. Researchers throughout the world conduct huge numbers of studies, and some of them produce what appear to be impressive results. They seldom publish the unimpressive results. So, of all the published results, some of them—we don't know how many—are probably accidental findings. We should be skeptical of any result until it has been replicated, especially if we had no good theoretical reason for expecting it.

Unfortunately, in spite of the agreed importance of replication, not many psychologists try to replicate someone else's finding (Pashler & Harris, 2012). The same problem occurs in other fields also. Researchers in neuroscience and medicine are equally concerned about how many published results might be accidents, or at least overstatements of small effects (Tsilidis et al., 2013).

The custom has been changing, however. More and more scientists have been calling for attempts to replicate a result, using exactly the same procedure as the original study (Simons, 2014), and several journals have agreed to publish the results, whatever they may be. As a start, 36 laboratories across several countries attempted replications of 13 well-known psychological experiments, each of them brief enough to conduct quickly. Of the 13, 10 were convincingly

replicated, one was replicated but with weaker results than originally reported, and two consistently failed to be replicated (Klein et al., 2014).

What does it mean when researchers cannot replicate a result? The simplest answer is that the original result was an accident or error, but other answers are possible. A single failure to replicate a finding might mean nothing, especially if the second study had a small number of participants or imprecise measurements (Lakens & Evers, 2014; Stanley & Spence, 2014). Repeated failures might mean that the effect depends on special circumstances (Cesario, 2014; Stroebe & Strack, 2013). For example, asking young women in the United States to read aloud a list of "dirty" words produced intense embarrassment many years ago, but today yields mostly laughter. The original results were correct, but they cannot be replicated because times have changed. Sometimes subtle changes in procedure make a big difference. For certain types of experiments with rats, female researchers get different results from male researchers. The reason is that rats have a stress response to the smell of males, including human males. Just the nearby presence of a T-shirt that a man wore overnight increases rats' stress responses (Sorge et al., 2014). Nevertheless, we need to know whether or not a result is easy to replicate. If it occurs only under certain conditions, we need to know those conditions. If we cannot find conditions in which a result consistently occurs, we should ignore it in theory and in practice (Simons, 2014).

Ethical Considerations in Research

In any experiment, psychologists manipulate a variable to determine how it affects behavior. Perhaps you object to the idea of someone trying to alter your behavior. If so, consider that every time you talk to people, you are trying to alter their behavior at least slightly. Most experiments in psychology are no more manipulative than a conversation. Still, some experiments do raise difficult issues, and researchers are bound by both law and conscience to treat their participants ethically.

Ethical Concerns with Humans

Consider the question of televised violence. If psychologists believed that watching violent programs might really transform viewers into murderers, it would be unethical to conduct experiments to find out for sure. It is also unethical to perform procedures that pose serious risks to the participants.

Before conducting any study on people, researchers ask for their informed consent, *a statement that* they have been told what to expect and that they agree to continue. When researchers ask for volunteers, they describe what will happen. Most procedures are innocuous, such as tests of perception, memory, or attention. Occasionally, however, the procedure includes something that people might not wish to do, such as examining disgusting photographs, drinking concentrated sugar water, or receiving electrical shocks. Participants are told they have the right to quit if they find the procedure too disagreeable.

Special problems arise in research with children, people with mental retardation, or others who might not understand the instructions well enough to provide informed consent (Bonnie, 1997). Individuals with severe depression pose a special problem (Elliott, 1997) because some seem to have lost interest in protecting their own welfare. In such cases, researchers either consult the person's guardian or nearest relative or simply decide not to proceed.

Research at a college must first be approved by an Institutional Review Board (IRB). An IRB judges whether the proposed studies include procedures for informed consent and whether they safeguard each participant's confidentiality. An IRB also tries to prevent risky procedures. It probably would reject a proposal to offer cocaine, even if people were eager to give their informed consent. A committee would also ban procedures that they consider seriously embarrassing or degrading. Many "reality television" shows would be banned if they needed approval from an IRB (Spellman, 2005).

The committee also judges procedures in which investigators want to deceive participants temporarily. If a researcher tells participants the purpose of the study, then they know the researcher's expectations, and demand characteristics will contaminate the results. Therefore, researchers often disguise the purpose of the study. Most people consider that temporary deception to be harmless, but the institutional committee makes the decision.

The American Psychological Association (APA) published a book discussing the proper ethical treatment of volunteers in experiments (Sales & Folkman, 2000). The APA censures or expels any member who disregards these principles.

Ethical Concerns with Nonhumans

Some psychological research deals with nonhuman animals, especially research on basic processes such as sensation, hunger, and learning (see ▲ Figure 2.16). Researchers use nonhumans if they want to control aspects of life that people will not let them control (e.g., who mates with whom), if they want to study behavior continuously over weeks or months (longer than people are willing to participate), or if the research poses health risks. Animal research has

▲ **Figure 2.16** Some animal research consists of observations under natural or nearly natural conditions. Other research raises ethical controversies.

long been essential for preliminary testing of most new drugs, surgical procedures, and methods of relieving pain. People with untreatable illnesses argue that they have the right to hope for cures that might result from animal research (Feeney, 1987). Much of our knowledge in psychology, biology, and medicine made use of animal studies at some point.

Nevertheless, some people oppose much or all animal research. Animals, after all, cannot give informed consent. Some animal rights supporters insist that animals should have the same rights as humans, that keeping animals (even pets) in cages is slavery, and that killing any animal is murder. Others oppose some kinds of research but are willing to compromise about others.

Psychologists vary in their attitudes. Most support some kinds of animal research but draw a line somewhere separating acceptable from unacceptable research (Plous, 1996). Naturally, disagreement arises about where to draw that line.

In this debate, as in many other political controversies, a common tactic is for each side to criticize the most extreme actions of its opponents. For example, animal rights advocates point to studies that exposed monkeys or puppies to painful procedures that seem difficult to justify. Researchers point to protesters who have vandalized laboratories, planted bombs, banged on a researcher's children's windows at night, and inserted a garden hose through a window to flood a house (G. Miller, 2007a). Some protesters have stated that they oppose using any drug, even a medication for AIDS, if its discovery came from research with animals. Unfortunately, when both sides concentrate on criticizing their most extreme opponents, they make points of agreement harder to find.

A careful study by a relatively unbiased outsider concluded that the truth is messy: Some research is painful to the animals *and* nevertheless valuable for scientific and medical progress (Blum, 1994). We must, most people conclude, seek a compromise.

Professional organizations such as the Society for Neuroscience and the American Psychological Association publish guidelines for the proper use of animals in research. Colleges and other research institutions maintain laboratory animal care committees to ensure that laboratory animals are treated humanely, that their pain and discomfort are kept to a minimum, and that experimenters consider alternatives before imposing potentially painful procedures.

How can we determine in advance whether the value of the expected experimental results (which is hard to predict) will outweigh the pain the animals will endure (which is hard to measure)? As is common with ethical decisions, reasonable arguments can be raised on both sides of the question, and no compromise is fully satisfactory.

Psychological Research

Most scientists avoid the word *prove*, because it sounds too final. Psychologists certainly do. (The joke is that psychology courses don't have true–false tests, just maybe–perhaps tests.) The most complex and most interesting aspects of human behavior are products of genetics, a lifetime of experiences, and countless current influences. Given the practical and ethical limitations for untangling all these factors, it might seem that psychological researchers would become discouraged. However, the difficulties have inspired researchers to design clever and complex methods. A single study rarely answers a question decisively, but many studies converge to increase our total understanding.

Summary

- *Operational definitions.* For many purposes, psychologists use operational definitions, which state how to measure a phenomenon or how to produce it. (page 34)

- *Sampling.* Because psychologists hope to draw conclusions that apply to a large population, they try to select a sample that resembles the total population—either a representative sample or a random sample. To apply the results to people worldwide, they need a cross-cultural sample. (page 35)

- *Naturalistic observations.* Naturalistic observations provide descriptions of humans or other species under natural conditions. (page 36)

- *Case histories.* A case history is a detailed research study of a single individual, generally someone with unusual characteristics. (page 36)

- *Surveys.* A survey is a report of people's answers on a questionnaire. It is easy to conduct a survey and, unfortunately, easy to get misleading results. (page 37)

- *Correlations.* A correlational study examines the relationship between variables that are outside the investigator's control. The strength of this relationship is measured by a correlation coefficient that ranges from 0 (no relationship) to plus or minus 1 (a perfect relationship). (page 39)

- *Illusory correlations.* Beware of illusory correlations—relationships that people think they observe between variables after casual observation. (page 40)

- *Inferring causation.* A correlational study cannot uncover cause-and-effect relationships, but an experiment can. (page 40)

- *Experiments.* In an experiment, an investigator manipulates an independent variable to determine its effect on the dependent variable. A before-and-after study often leads to results that are hard to interpret. It is better to compare the results for different groups. (page 41)

- *Random assignment.* An experimenter randomly assigns individuals to the experimental and control groups. All participants should have an equal probability of being chosen for the experimental group. (page 41)

- *Overcoming experimenter bias.* An experimenter's expectations influence the interpretations of behavior and the recording of data. To ensure objectivity, investigators use blind observers who do not know what results are expected. In a double-blind study, neither the observer nor the participants know the researcher's predictions. (page 42)

- *Demand characteristics.* Researchers try to minimize the effects of demand characteristics, which are cues that tell participants what the experimenter expects them to do. (page 43)

- *Mean, median, and mode.* One way of presenting the central score of a distribution is via the mean, determined by adding all the scores and dividing by the number of individuals. Another way is the median, which is the middle score after all the scores have been arranged from highest to lowest. The mode is the score that occurs most frequently. (page 45)

- *Inferential statistics.* Inferential statistics are attempts to deduce the properties of a large population based on the results from a small sample of that population. (page 46)

- *Probability of chance results.* Traditionally, psychologists have used inferential statistics to calculate the probability that a given research result could have arisen by chance. That probability is low if the difference between the two groups is large, if the variability within each group is small, and if the number of individuals in each group is large. Currently, the trend is to present the means and 95 percent confidence intervals for each group and let readers see the size of the effect. (page 46)

- *Replicability.* Because researchers generally publish only the results that look impressive, an unknown number of the reported results may have arisen by accident. Psychologists are becoming more interested in trying to replicate results. (page 47)

- *Ethics of experimentation.* Research on human participants should not proceed until the participants have given their informed consent. Psychologists try to minimize risk to their participants, but they sometimes face difficult ethical decisions. (page 47)

Key Terms

95 percent confidence interval (page 46)

blind observer (page 42)

case history (page 36)

control group (page 41)

convenience sample (page 35)

correlation (page 39)

correlation coefficient (page 39)

cross-cultural sample (page 35)

demand characteristics (page 42)

dependent variable (page 41)

descriptive statistics (page 45)

double-blind study (page 42)

experiment (page 41)

experimental group (page 41)

experimenter bias (page 42)

illusory correlation (page 40)

independent variable (page 41)

inferential statistics (page 46)

informed consent (page 47)

mean (page 45)

median (page 45)

mode (page 45)

naturalistic observation (page 36)

normal distribution (or normal curve) (page 45)

operational definition (page 34)

$p < .05$ (page 46)

placebo (page 40)

random assignment (page 41)

random sample (page 35)

representative sample (page 35)

scatter plot (page 39)

single-blind study (page 42)

statistically significant (or statistically reliable) results (page 46)

survey (page 37)

Review Questions

1. Which of the following is an operational definition of ambition?
   (a) A desire to get ahead in life
   (b) The number of times one has applied for a new or better job
   (c) Setting high goals and trying to achieve them
   (d) The ability to overcome obstacles and persist until succeeding at some task

2. Which of the following could be an operational definition of political activism?
   (a) The number of hours one has devoted to political campaigns
   (b) A tendency to read about political issues and discuss them
   (c) Willingness to stick to one's own political opinion even when friends disagree
   (d) A set of firm and well considered opinions on political issues

3. Which of these procedures produces a random sample of the students in your class?
   (a) Interview all the students whose telephone numbers end with 3.
   (b) Interview the first person in each row.
   (c) Interview the last 10 people who show up for class.
   (d) Interview anyone who is willing to volunteer.

4. Suppose someone reports that blood levels of a certain chemical are negatively correlated with aggressive behavior. What does that mean?
   (a) The higher the level of that chemical, the lower the probability of aggression.
   (b) The lower the level of that chemical, the lower the probability of aggression.
   (c) Levels of that chemical have no consistent relationship to the probability of aggression.
   (d) As people grow older, that chemical declines and so does the probability of aggression.

5. Of the following correlation coefficients, which one indicates the *weakest* relationship between two variables—that is, the lowest accuracy of using one variable to predict the other one?
   (a) 0
   (b) +0.5
   (c) −0.75

6. Suppose some researcher reports a low correlation between stress and depression. One possible explanation is that stress had little to do with depression in that researcher's sample of the population. What is another possible explanation for these results?
   (a) The people varied widely in their level of stress.
   (b) The researcher made inaccurate measurements of either stress or depression.
   (c) People with great stress are likely to become depressed.
   (d) Depression is more common in some countries than in others.

7. Suppose researchers find a +0.4 correlation between the number of vitamin pills people take and their mental health. Which conclusion, if any, can we draw from this result?
   (a) Taking vitamin pills improves mental health.
   (b) Strong mental health improves people's probability of taking action to maintain health.
   (c) Wealthier people are more likely than average to take vitamin pills, and also to be mentally healthy.
   (d) We can draw none of these conclusions.

8. On average, old people who read more books are less likely to develop Alzheimer's disease. What conclusion can we draw from this result?
   (a) Reading books tends to prevent Alzheimer's disease.
   (b) People who are already starting to develop Alzheimer's disease don't read many books.
   (c) We can draw neither of these conclusions.

9. On average, students who attend class every day get better grades than those who frequently miss. Which conclusion, if any, can we draw from this result?
   (a) Attending class helps people improve their grades.
   (b) Brighter students, who are likely to get good grades, are more likely than average to attend class conscientiously.
   (c) We can draw neither of these conclusions.

10. An elementary school tests whether physical exercise influences children's performance. Children in each class are randomly assigned to physical exercise or movie watching for 30 minutes each afternoon. All children take the same tests, and the instructors compare their performances. The independent variable is _____, and the dependent variable is _____.
   (a) exercise versus movie watching . . . scores on tests
   (b) scores on tests . . . the number of students in each class
   (c) the number of students in each class . . . exercise versus movie watching
   (d) scores on tests . . . exercise versus movie-watching

11. A double-blind study helps alleviate the problems caused by which of the following?
   (a) Falsifiability
   (b) Independent variables
   (c) Failure to replicate a study
   (d) Demand characteristics

12. Consider the following distribution of scores: 6, 4, 17, 1, 10, 4, 14, 4, 12. The mean is _____, the median is _____, and the mode is _____.
   (a) 8 . . . 6 . . . 4
   (b) 8 . . . 10 . . . 4
   (c) 6 . . . 8 . . . 4
   (d) 4 . . . 6 . . . 8

13. We should be more impressed with a result if the 95 percent confidence intervals are _____. We should be more impressed with a result if the p value is _____.
   (a) large . . . large
   (b) large . . . small
   (c) small . . . large
   (d) small . . . small

Answers: 1b, 2a, 3a, 4a, 5a, 6b, 7d, 8c, 9c, 10a, 11d, 12a, 13d.

This appendix provides a little more detail about certain statistics and how to calculate them. It is intended primarily to satisfy your curiosity. Ask your instructor whether you should use this appendix for any other purpose.

Measures of Variation

▼ Figure 2.17 shows two distributions of scores, which might be the results for two tests in an introductory psychology class. Both tests have the same mean, 70, but different distributions. If you had a score of 80, you would beat only 75 percent of the other students on the first test, but with the same score, you would beat 95 percent of the other students on the second test.

To describe the difference between the graphs in Figure 2.17a and b, we need a measurement of the variation (or spread) around the mean. The simplest such measurement is the range of a distribution, *a statement of the highest and lowest scores.* The range in Figure 2.17a is 38 to 100, and in Figure 2.17b, it is 56 to 94.

The range is simple but not the most useful calculation because it reflects only the extremes. A better measure is the standard deviation (SD), *a measurement of the amount of variation among scores in a normal distribution.* When the scores are closely clustered near the mean, the standard deviation is small. When

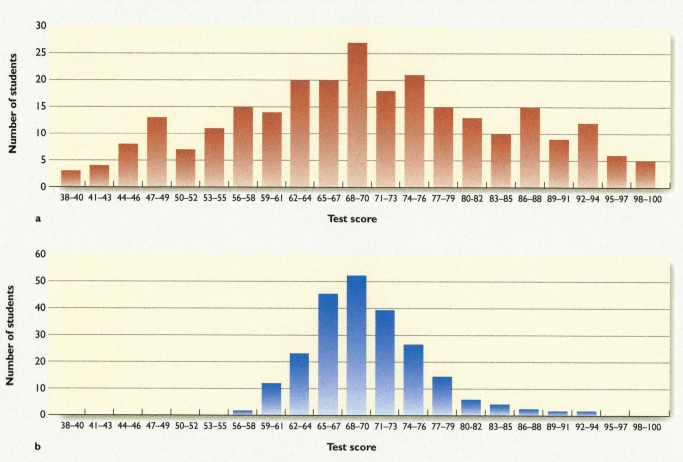

▲ **Figure 2.17** These distributions of test scores have the same mean but different variances and different standard deviations.

the scores are more widely scattered, the standard deviation is large. So, Figure 2.17a has a larger standard deviation, and Figure 2.17b has a smaller one.

As ▶ **Figure 2.18** shows, the Scholastic Assessment Test (SAT) was designed to produce a mean of 500 and a standard deviation of 100. Of all people taking the test, 68 percent should score within 1 standard deviation above or below the mean (400 to 600), and 95 percent score within 2 standard deviations (300 to 700). Only 2.5 percent score above 700. Another 2.5 percent score below 300. That was the original intention, anyway. In fact, the results do not quite match the intended distribution.

Standard deviations enable us to compare scores on different tests. For example, if you scored 1 standard deviation above the mean on the SAT, you tested about as well, relatively speaking, as someone who scored 1 standard deviation above the mean on a different test, such as the American College Test.

To calculate the standard deviation (SD):
1. Determine the mean of the scores.
2. Subtract the mean from each of the individual scores.
3. Square each of those results, add the squares together, and divide by the total number of scores.

The result is called the *variance*. The standard deviation is the square root of the variance. Here is an example:

Individual scores	Each score minus the mean	Difference squared
12.5	−2.5	6.25
17.0	+2.0	4.00
11.0	−4.0	16.00
14.5	−0.5	0.25
16.0	+1.0	1.00
16.5	+1.5	2.25
17.5	+2.5	6.25
105		36.00

The mean is 15.0 (the sum of the first column, divided by 7). The variance is 5.143 (the sum of the third column, divided by 7). The standard deviation is 2.268 (the square root of 5.143).

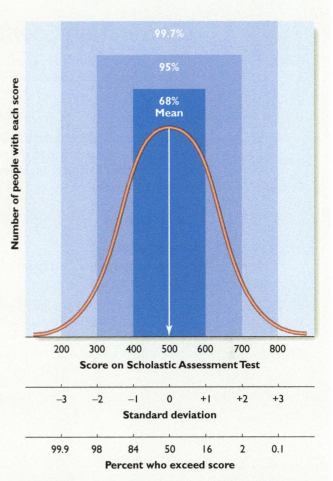

▲ **Figure 2.18** In a normal distribution of scores, the amount of variation from the mean can be measured in standard deviations. In this example, scores between 400 and 600 are said to be within 1 standard deviation from the mean; scores between 300 and 700 are within 2 standard deviations from the mean.

15. **Suppose that you score 80 on your first psychology test. The mean for the class is 70, and the standard deviation is 5. On the second test, you receive a score of 90. This time the mean for the class is also 70, but the standard deviation is 20. Compared to the other students in your class, did your performance improve, deteriorate, or stay the same?**

Answer

15. Even though your score rose from 80 on the first test to 90 on the second, your performance actually deteriorated in comparison to other students' scores. A score of 80 on the first test was 2 standard deviations above the mean, better than 98 percent of all other students. A 90 on the second test was only 1 standard deviation above the mean, a score that beats only 84 percent of the other students.

Correlation Coefficients

To determine a correlation coefficient, we designate one of the variables x and the other one y. We obtain pairs of measures, x_i and y_i. Then we use the following formula:

$$r = \frac{[(\sum x_i y_i)] - n \cdot \bar{x} \cdot \bar{y}}{n \cdot sx \cdot sy}$$

In this formula, $(\sum x_i y_i)$ is the sum of the products of x and y. For each pair of observations (x, y), we multiply x times y and then we add all the products. The term $n \cdot \bar{x} \cdot \bar{y}$ means n (the number of pairs) times the mean of x times the mean of y. The denominator, $n \cdot sx \cdot sy$, means n times the standard deviation of x times the standard deviation of y.

Key Terms

range (page 52)

standard deviation (SD) (page 52)

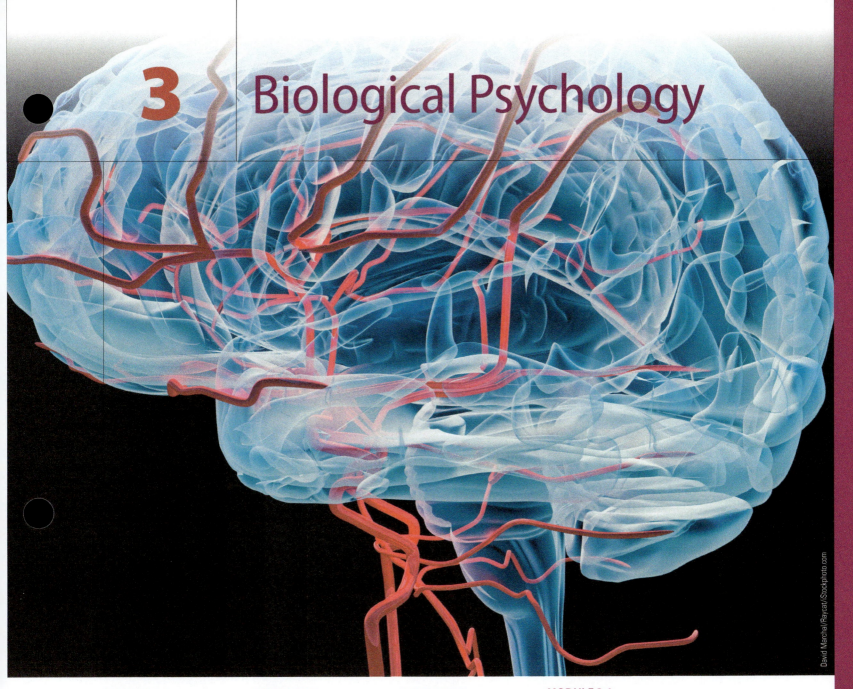

3 | Biological Psychology

David Marchal/Raycat/iStockphoto.com

Townsend Dickinson/The Image Works

A bee has amazingly complex behavior, but we have no way to get inside the bee's experience to know what (if anything) it feels like to be a bee.

A human brain weighs only 1.2 to 1.4 kg (2.5 to 3 lb), and a bee's brain weighs only a milligram. A dollar bill weighs about a gram, so if you imagine a bill chopped into a thousand pieces, one of those pieces weighs about as much as a bee's brain. With that tiny brain, a bee locates food, evades predators, finds its way back to the hive, and then does a dance that directs other bees to the food. It also takes care of the queen bee and protects the hive against intruders.

Everything you perceive or do is a product of your brain activity. How does the brain do all that? We would like to know for both practical and theoretical reasons. Some of the practical issues relate to abnormal behavior. Are psychological disorders biological in origin? Can we treat them effectively with drugs or other biological interventions? Can we prevent deterioration in old age? Theoretical issues relate to what makes us tick. How does brain activity relate to consciousness? Do people differ in personality because of differences in their brains? The fascination of such questions impels researchers to tireless efforts.

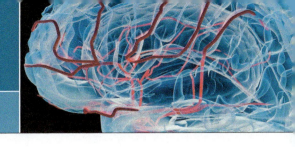

Neurons and Behavior

After studying this module, you should be able to:

- Identify the main structures of a neuron.

- Describe the action potential.

- State the all-or-none law of the action potential.

- Describe communication at synapses.

How do you differ from a machine? We usually think of a machine as something made of metal, but really a machine is anything that converts one type of energy into another, such as converting gasoline into the operation of a car. In that sense, you don't differ from a machine at all, because you are a machine. Your body converts the energy in your food into all the actions of your body. Your brain is part of that machine, and one way to understand your thoughts and actions is to analyze how your brain works. Researchers examine the functions of different parts of the brain, just as someone might study a car by examining what each of the car's parts does.

We start with the individual cells that compose the nervous system. Studying a single cell doesn't take us far toward understanding your behavior, any more than studying a single silicon chip explains a computer. Still, it's a place to start, and it does shed light on a few matters of psychological interest.

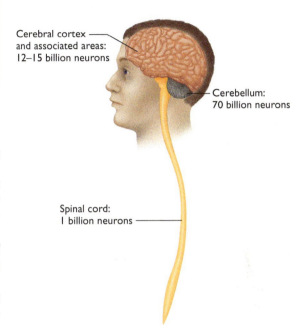

▲ **Figure 3.1** Estimated distribution of the neurons in the adult human central nervous system. An exact count is not feasible, and the number varies from one person to another. (Based on data of R. W. Williams & Herrup, 1988)

Nervous System Cells

You experience your "self" as a single entity that senses, thinks, and remembers. However, your brain consists of an enormous number of separate cells called **neurons** (NOO-rons). ▶ Figure 3.1 shows estimates of the numbers of neurons in various parts of the human nervous system (R. W. Williams & Herrup, 1988). The nervous system also contains other kinds of cells called **glia** (GLEE-uh) *that support the neurons in many ways such as by insulating them, synchronizing activity among neighboring neurons, and removing waste products.* The glia are smaller but more numerous than neurons.

Neurons are similar to other body cells in most ways. The most distinctive feature of neurons is their shape, which varies depending on whether they receive information from a few sources or many and whether they send impulses over a short or a long distance (see ▼ Figure 3.2). A neuron consists of three parts: a cell body, dendrites, and an axon (see ▼ Figure 3.3). The **cell body** *contains the nucleus of the cell.* The **dendrites** (from a Greek word meaning "tree") are *widely branching structures that receive input from other neurons.* The **axon** is a *single, long, thin, straight fiber with branches near its tip.* Some vertebrate axons are covered with **myelin,** *an insulating sheath that speeds up the transmission of impulses along an axon.* As a rule, an axon transmits information to other cells, and the dendrites or cell body receives that information. (Almost any statement about the nervous system has exceptions. In some cases cell bodies pass information to other cell bodies, and even dendrites sometimes send information. Sometimes an axon transmits a message to another axon. The nervous system is complicated.) The information can be either excitatory or inhibitory. That is, it can increase or decrease the probability that the next cell will send a message of its own.

concept check

1. **Which part of a neuron receives input from other neurons (ordinarily)? Which part sends messages to other neurons?**

Answer

1. Dendrites receive input from other neurons. Axons send messages.

▶ **Figure 3.2** Neurons vary enormously in shape. The neurons in **(a)** and **(b)** receive input from many sources, the neuron in **(c)** from only a few sources, and the neuron in **(d)** from an intermediate number of sources. The sensory neurons **(e)** carry messages from sensory receptors to the brain or spinal cord. Inset: Electron micrograph showing cell bodies in brown and axons and dendrites in green. The color was added artificially; electron micrographs are made with electron beams, not light, and therefore, they show no color.

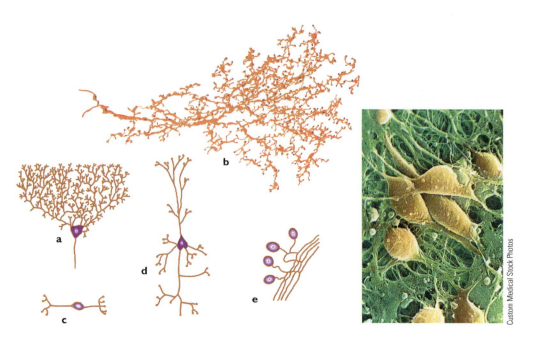

The Action Potential

The function of an axon is to convey information over long distances, such as from the skin to the spinal cord, or from the spinal cord to a muscle.

Electrical conduction would convey information almost instantaneously, but your body is a relatively poor conductor of electricity. If axons conducted electrically, impulses would get weaker and weaker as they traveled. Short people would feel a pinch on their toes more intensely than tall people would—if either felt their toes at all.

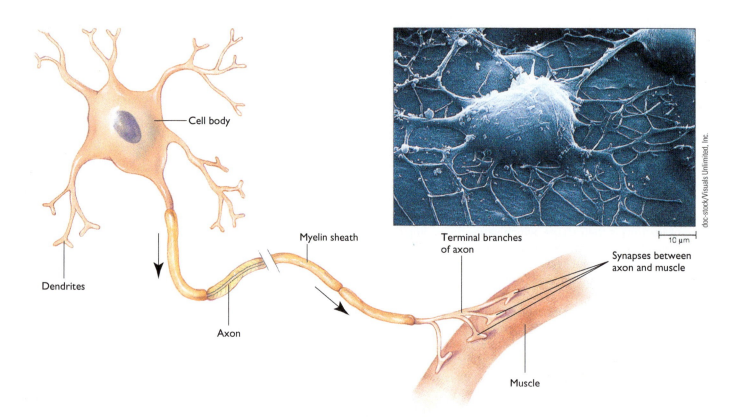

▲ **Figure 3.3** The generalized structure of a motor neuron shows the dendrites, the branching structures that receive transmissions from other neurons, and the axon, a long fiber with branches near its tip. Inset: A photomicrograph of a neuron.

Instead, axons convey information by a process called an action potential, *an excitation that travels along an axon at a constant strength, no matter how far it travels.* An action potential is a yes–no or on–off message, like flicking a light switch (without a dimmer). *The fact that an axon cannot vary the strength or velocity of its action potentials* is known as the all-or-none law of the action potential.

The advantage of an action potential over simple electrical conduction is that action potentials reach your brain at full strength. The disadvantage is that action potentials take time. Your knowledge of what is happening to your toes is at least a 20th of a second out of date. Pain and itch sensations are even slower. A 20th of a second delay will seldom inconvenience you, but that delay is theoretically interesting. When researchers first demonstrated that your touch perceptions are delayed while the message travels to the brain, their result showed that perceptions occur in your head, not in your fingers. When you touch something, it *seems* that the sensation is in your finger, but no, it is in your head. Other evidence for this conclusion is that direct stimulation of certain brain areas produces touch sensation, even if a finger was amputated, and touching the finger produces no sensation if the relevant brain area is damaged.

Here is a quick description of how the action potential works:

1. When the axon is not stimulated, its membrane has a resting potential, *an electrical polarization across the membrane (or covering) of an axon.* Typically, the inside has a charge of about –70 millivolts relative to the outside. It gets this value from the negatively charged proteins inside the axon. In addition, a mechanism called the sodium-potassium pump pushes sodium ions out of the axon while pulling potassium ions in. Consequently, sodium ions are more concentrated outside the axon, and potassium ions are more concentrated inside.
2. An action potential starts in either of two ways: First, many axons produce spontaneous activity. Second, input from other neurons can excite a neuron's membrane. In either case, if the excitation reaches the *threshold* of the axon (typically about –55 millivolts), it briefly opens some *gates* in the axon through which sodium and potassium ions can flow. Sodium ions, which are highly concentrated outside the membrane, rush into the cell, attracted by the negative charge inside. The influx of positively charged sodium ions is the action potential. As the positive charge enters the axon at one point, it stimulates the next point along the axon, which then starts opening sodium channels and repeating the process, as shown in ▲ Figure 3.4.

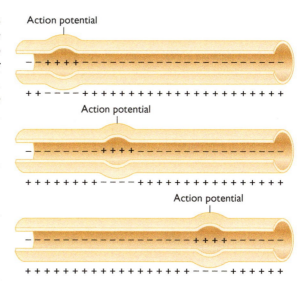

▲ **Figure 3.4** Ion movements conduct an action potential along an axon. At each point along the membrane, sodium ions enter the axon. As each point along the membrane returns to its original state, the action potential flows to the next point.

3. After the sodium gates have been open for a few milliseconds, they snap shut, but the potassium gates remain open a little longer. Because the sodium ions have brought positive charges into the cell, the inside of the cell no longer attracts potassium ions, and because they are more concentrated inside the cell than outside, they tend to flow out of the cell, carrying positive charges with them. Their exit drives the inside of the axon back to its resting potential (see ▼ Figure 3.5b).
4. Eventually, the sodium-potassium pump removes the extra sodium ions and recaptures the escaped potassium ions.

These are the highlights: Sodium enters the cell (excitation). Then potassium leaves (return to the resting potential).

Conduction along an axon is analogous to a fire burning along a string: The fire at each point ignites the next point, which in turn ignites the next point. In an axon, after sodium ions enter the membrane, some of them diffuse to the neighboring portion of the axon, exciting it enough to open its own sodium gates. The action potential spreads to this next area and so on down the axon, as shown in ▼ Figure 3.5. In this manner, the action potential remains equally strong all the way to the end of the axon.

How does this information relate to psychology? First, it explains why sensations from your fingers and toes do not fade away by the time they reach your brain. Second, an understanding of action potentials is one step toward understanding the communication between neurons. Third, anesthetic

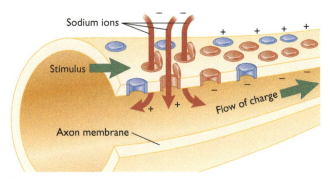

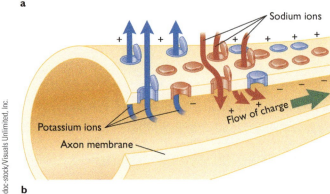

Sodium ions

Stimulus

Flow of charge

Axon membrane

a

doc-stock/Visuals Unlimited, Inc.

Sodium ions

Potassium ions

Flow of charge

Axon membrane

b

▲ **Figure 3.5 (a)** During an action potential, sodium gates open, and sodium ions enter the axon, bearing a positive charge. **(b)** After an action potential occurs, the sodium gates close at that point and open at the next point along the axon. As the sodium gates close, potassium gates open, and potassium ions flow out of the axon. (Modified from Starr & Taggart, 1992)

drugs (e.g., Novocain) operate by clogging sodium gates and therefore silencing neurons. When your dentist drills a tooth, the receptors in your tooth send out the message "Pain! Pain! Pain!" But that message does not reach your brain because the sodium gates are blocked.

concept check

2. **If a mouse and a giraffe both get pinched on the toes at the same time, which will respond faster? Why?**

3. **Fill in these blanks: When the axon membrane is at rest, the inside has a _____ charge relative to the outside. When the membrane reaches its threshold, _____ ions enter from outside to inside, bringing with them a _____ charge. That flow of ions constitutes the _____ _____ of the axon.**

Answers

3. negative . . . sodium . . . positive . . . action potential.

2. The mouse will react faster because the action potentials have a shorter distance to travel in the mouse's nervous system than in the giraffe's.

Synapses

How do so many separate neurons combine forces to produce your stream of experiences? The answer is communication. Communication between one neuron and the next is not like transmission along an axon. At a synapse (SIN-aps), *the specialized junction between one neuron and another* (see ▼ Figure 3.6), *a neuron releases a chemical that either excites or inhibits the next neuron.* That is, the chemical makes the next neuron either more or less likely to produce its own action potential.

A typical axon has branches, each ending with a little bulge called a *presynaptic ending,* or terminal bouton, as shown in ▼ Figure 3.7. (*Bouton* is French for "button.") When an action potential reaches the terminal bouton, it releases a neurotransmitter, *a chemical that activates receptors on other neurons* (see Figure 3.7). Various neurons use dozens of chemicals as neurotransmitters, but a given neuron releases only one or a few of them. The neurotransmitter molecules diffuse across a narrow gap to receptors on the postsynaptic neuron, *the neuron on the receiving end of the synapse.* A neurotransmitter fits into its receptor as a key fits into a lock, and it either excites or inhibits the postsynaptic neuron.

The messages in a computer are simply on/off (represented as 1 or 0), and scientists used to assume that synaptic messages were like that, too. We now know that synaptic messages are highly variable. Depending on the transmitter and its receptor, the effect might have a sudden onset and last only milliseconds, or it might develop more gradually and last for seconds. *Peptide* transmitters diffuse to a wider brain area and produce effects that last minutes. A quick, sudden message is important for vision and hearing. Slower, longer-lasting messages are more appropriate for taste and smell. Very slow, minutes-long messages are useful for hunger, thirst, and sex drive. ▼ Figure 3.8 summarizes synaptic transmission.

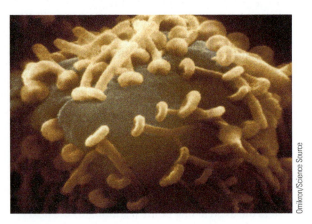

Omikron/Science Source

▲ **Figure 3.6** This synapse is magnified thousands of times in an electron micrograph. The tips of axons swell to form terminal boutons.

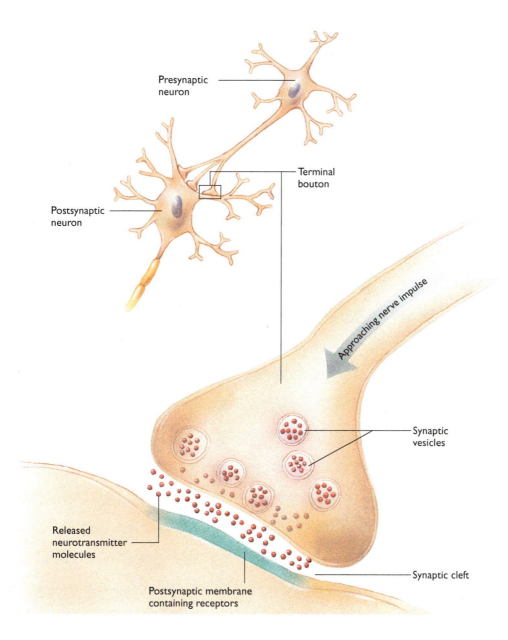

◀ **Figure 3.7** A synapse is a junction of a presynaptic (message-sending) cell and a postsynaptic (message-receiving) cell. The terminal bouton at the tip of the presynaptic axon contains the neurotransmitter.

Presynaptic neuron

Terminal bouton

Postsynaptic neuron

Approaching nerve impulse

Synaptic vesicles

Released neurotransmitter molecules

Synaptic cleft

Postsynaptic membrane containing receptors

Inhibitory messages are essential for many purposes. For example, during a period of painful stimulation, your brain has mechanisms to inhibit further sensation of pain. If you step on a tack and reflexively raise your foot, inhibitory synapses prevent you from trying to raise your other foot at the same time.

After a neurotransmitter excites or inhibits a receptor, it separates from the receptor, ending the message. From that point on, the fate of the receptor molecule varies. It could bounce back to reexcite the postsynaptic receptor, it could diffuse away from the synapse, or it could be reabsorbed by the axon that released it (through a process called *reuptake)*. Most antidepressant drugs act by blocking reuptake, thus prolonging a transmitter's effects.

what's the evidence?

Neurons Communicate Chemically

You have just learned that neurons communicate by releasing chemicals at synapses. What evidence led to this important conclusion?

Today, neuroscientists have a wealth of evidence that neurons release chemicals at synapses. They radioactively trace where chemicals go and what happens when they get there. They inject purified chemicals and use extremely fine electrodes to measure the responses of neurons. In 1920, Otto Loewi conducted a clever experiment with only the simple tools available at the time, to demonstrate that neurons communicate with

concept check

4. **What is the difference between the presynaptic neuron and the postsynaptic neuron?**

Answer

4. The presynaptic neuron releases a neurotransmitter that travels to the postsynaptic neuron, where it activates an excitatory or inhibitory receptor.

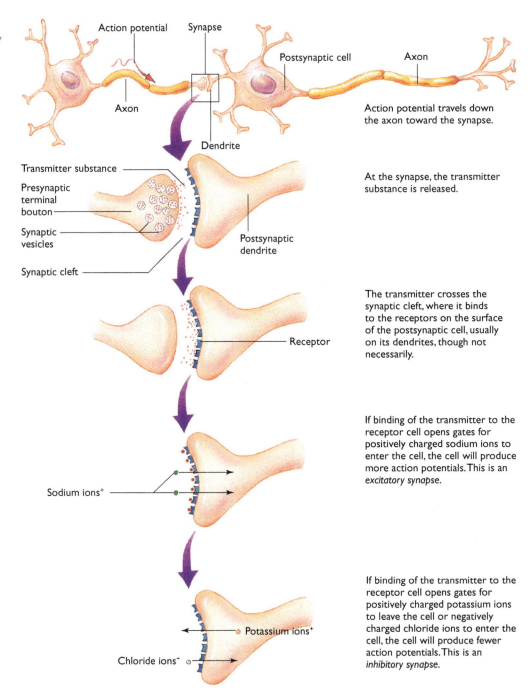

▶ **Figure 3.8** The complex process of neural communication takes only 1 to 2 milliseconds.

Action potential   Synapse

Axon

Postsynaptic cell   Axon

Dendrite

Action potential travels down the axon toward the synapse.

Transmitter substance

Presynaptic terminal bouton

Synaptic vesicles

Synaptic cleft

Postsynaptic dendrite

At the synapse, the transmitter substance is released.

Receptor

The transmitter crosses the synaptic cleft, where it binds to the receptors on the surface of the postsynaptic cell, usually on its dendrites, though not necessarily.

Sodium ions⁺

If binding of the transmitter to the receptor cell opens gates for positively charged sodium ions to enter the cell, the cell will produce more action potentials. This is an *excitatory synapse*.

Potassium ions⁺

Chloride ions⁻

If binding of the transmitter to the receptor cell opens gates for positively charged potassium ions to leave the cell or negatively charged chloride ions to enter the cell, the cell will produce fewer action potentials. This is an *inhibitory synapse*.

chemicals, as he later described in his autobiography (Loewi, 1960).

Hypothesis If a neuron releases chemicals, an investigator should be able to collect some of those chemicals, transfer them to the same site on another animal, and thereby get the second animal to react the way the first animal had been doing. Loewi could not collect chemicals within the brain, so he worked with axons to the heart muscles. (A neuron stimulates a muscle at a junction that is like the synapse between two neurons.)

Method Loewi electrically stimulated certain axons that slowed a frog's heart. As he continued the stimulation, he collected fluid around that heart and transferred it to the heart of a second frog.

Results When Loewi transferred the fluid from the first frog's heart, the second frog's heart rate also slowed (see ▼ **Figure 3.9**).

Interpretation Evidently, the stimulated axons had released a chemical that slows heart rate. At least in this case, neurons send messages by releasing chemicals.

Loewi won a Nobel Prize in physiology for this and related research. Even outstanding experiments have limitations, however. Loewi's results did not indiate

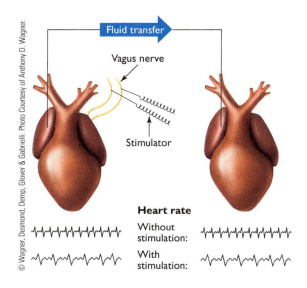
Fluid transfer

Vagus nerve

Stimulator

Heart rate

Without stimulation:

With stimulation:

◀ **Figure 3.9** Otto Loewi stimulated axons known to decrease a frog's heart rate. He collected fluid from around the heart and transferred it to another frog's heart. When that heart slowed its beat, Loewi concluded that the axons in the first heart released a chemical that slows heart rate.

whether axons release chemicals at all synapses, most, or only a few. Answering that question required technologies not available until several decades later. The answer is that the great majority of synapses use chemicals, although a few communicate electrically.

Neurotransmitters and Behavior

The brain has dozens of neurotransmitters, some of them listed in ■ Table 3.1, each of which activates many types of receptors. For example, the brain has at least 26 types of GABA receptors and at least 7 families of serotonin receptors, differing in their structure and their response to drugs (C. Wang et al., 2013). Each receptor type controls somewhat different aspects of behavior. For example, because serotonin type 3 receptors are responsible for nausea, researchers have developed drugs to block nausea (Perez, 1995). However, most complex behaviors rely on a combination of several transmitters and receptor types.

A disorder that increases or decreases a particular transmitter or receptor alters behavior in predictable ways. One example is Parkinson's disease, *a condition that affects 1 to 2 percent of people over the age of 65. The main symptoms are difficulty in initiating voluntary movement, slow movement,*

Table 3.1 Some of the Most Important Neurotransmitters

Neurotransmitter	Functions	Comment
Glutamate	The brain's main excitatory transmitter, present at most synapses; essential for almost all brain activities, including learning.	Strokes kill neurons mostly by releasing extra glutamate that overstimulates them.
GABA (gamma-amino-butyricw acid)	The brain's main inhibitory transmitter.	Anti-anxiety drugs and anti-epileptic drugs increase activity at GABA synapses.
Acetylcholine	Increases brain arousal.	Acetylcholine is also released by motor neurons to stimulate skeletal muscles.
Dopamine	One path is important for movement (damaged in Parkinson's disease). Another path is important for memory and cognition.	Most antipsychotic drugs decrease activity at dopamine synapses. L-dopa, used for Parkinson's disease, increases availability of dopamine.
Serotonin	Modifies many types of motivated and emotional behavior.	Most antidepressant drugs prolong activity at serotonin synapses.
Norepinephrine	Enhances storage of memory of emotional or otherwise meaningful events.	All or nearly all axons releasing norepinephrine originate from one small brain area, called the locus coeruleus.
Histamine	Increases arousal and alertness.	Antihistamines (for allergies) block histamine and therefore lead to drowsiness.
Endorphins	Decrease pain and increase pleasure.	Morphine and heroin stimulate the same receptors as endorphins.
Nitric oxide	Dilates blood vessels in the most active brain areas.	This is the only known transmitter that is a gas.
Anandamide, 2AG, and others	Sent by the postsynaptic neuron back to the presynaptic neuron to decrease further release of transmitters.	THC, the active chemical in marijuana, stimulates these same presynaptic receptors.

tremors, rigidity, and depressed mood. All of these symptoms can be traced to a gradual decay of a pathway of axons that release *the neurotransmitter* dopamine (DOPE-uh-meen). Unlike so many medications discovered by accident, the treatment for Parkinson's disease emerged from knowledge of the underlying mechanism of the disease. Researchers knew they needed to increase dopamine levels in the brain. Dopamine pills or injections would not work because dopamine (like many other chemicals) cannot cross from the blood into the brain. However, a drug called L-dopa does cross into the brain. Neurons absorb L-dopa, convert it to dopamine,

and thereby increase their supply of dopamine. As we shall see in Chapter 15, drugs that alleviate depression and schizophrenia also act on dopamine and serotonin synapses.

concept check

Answer

5. **Some people with schizophrenia take haloperidol, a drug that blocks dopamine synapses. How would haloperidol affect someone with Parkinson's disease?**

5. Haloperidol would increase the severity of Parkinson's disease. In fact, large doses of haloperidol induce symptoms of Parkinson's disease in anyone.

---

in closing | module 3.1

Neurons, Synapses, and Behavior

Even what seems a simple behavior, such as saying a few words, corresponds to a complicated sequence of well-timed movements. Those complex behaviors emerge from synapses, which in their basic outline are simple processes: A cell releases a chemical, which excites or inhibits a second cell for various periods of time. Then the chemical washes away or reenters the first cell to be used again.

Complex behavior is possible because of the connections among huge numbers of neurons. No one neuron or synapse does much by itself. Your experience results from dozens of types of neurotransmitters, billions of neurons, and trillions of synapses, each contributing in a small way.

Summary

- *Neuron structure.* A neuron, or nerve cell, consists of a cell body, dendrites, and an axon. The axon conveys information to other neurons. (page 57)
- *The action potential.* Information is conveyed along an axon by an action potential, which is regenerated without loss of strength at each point along the axon. (page 58)
- *Mechanism of the action potential.* An action potential depends on the entry of sodium into the axon. Anything that blocks this flow stops the action potential. (page 59)

- *How neurons communicate.* A neuron communicates with another neuron by releasing a chemical called a neurotransmitter at a specialized junction called a synapse. A neurotransmitter can either excite or inhibit the next neuron, with varying durations of effect. (page 60)
- *Neurotransmitters and behavioral disorders.* An excess or deficit of a particular neurotransmitter can lead to abnormal behavior, such as that exhibited by people with Parkinson's disease. (page 63)

Key Terms

action potential (page 59)

all-or-none law (page 59)

axon (page 57)

cell body (page 57)

dendrite (page 57)

dopamine (page 64)

glia (page 57)

myelin (page 57)

neuron (page 57)

neurotransmitter (page 60)

Parkinson's disease (page 63)

postsynaptic neuron (page 60)

resting potential (page 59)

synapse (page 60)

terminal bouton (page 60)

Review Questions

1. Compared to other cells of the body, neurons vary more widely in which of these aspects?
   (a) Acid-to-base ratio
   (b) Color
   (c) Chromosomes
   (d) Shape
2. What is meant by the "all-or-none" law of the axon?
   (a) Either the axon produces an action potential, or it doesn't.
   (b) When one axon produces an action potential, all of them do.
   (c) All axons throughout the nervous system produce action potentials of equal strength.
   (d) Incoming input must excite all the dendrites, or the axon won't produce an action potential.
3. What is an action potential?
   (a) An impulse that flows down an axon by electrical conduction
   (b) An impulse that flows down an axon by movement of chemical ions
   (c) A decision someone makes to start doing something
   (d) A machine that measures brain activity
4. When a neurotransmitter excites the postsynaptic neuron, how long do the effects last?
   (a) Just milliseconds
   (b) About a tenth of a second
   (c) Several seconds or longer
   (d) The results vary from one synapse to another.
5. Which of the following is true of receptors for neurotransmitters?
   (a) All neurotransmitters attach to the same type of receptor.
   (b) Excitatory transmitters attach to one type of receptor, and inhibitory transmitters use another.
   (c) Each neurotransmitter has its own receptor.
   (d) Each neurotransmitter can attach to several types of receptors with different properties.

Answers: 1d, 2a, 3b, 4d, 5d.

After studying this module, you should be able to:

- Describe how our knowledge of synapses helps explain how drugs affect behavior.

- Distinguish among classes of drugs such as stimulants, hallucinogens, anxiolytics, and opiates.

- Outline what is known about the mechanisms of some commonly abused drugs.

Ritalin, a drug given to calm hyperactive children, has the same synaptic effects as cocaine. The difference is quantitative. A Ritalin pill slowly and slightly increases dopamine activity in the brain, whereas cocaine produces a sudden rush of effects.

If you were to change a few of a computer's connections at random, you could produce an "altered state," which would almost certainly not be an improvement. Giving drugs to a human brain is a little like changing the connections of a computer, and most drugs temporarily impair brain functioning in some way. By examining the effects of drugs on the brain, we gain greater insight into the brain's normal processes and functions. In Chapter 15, we shall consider drug abuse and addiction, including alcoholism. Here the emphasis is on how drugs operate.

Psychoactive drugs affect synapses in many ways. Some attach to receptors and activate them. Some attach imperfectly, like an almost-fitting key that gets stuck in a lock. Drugs increase or decrease the release of transmitters or decrease reuptake (the return of released transmitters to the neuron that released them). A drug that increases activity at a synapse is called an *agonist,* based on the Greek word for a "contestant" or "fighter." A drug that decreases activity at a synapse is an *antagonist,* from the Greek word for an "enemy."

Stimulants

Stimulants are *drugs that increase energy, alertness, and activity.* Amphetamine, methamphetamine, and cocaine block the protein that the presynaptic neuron uses to reabsorb dopamine or serotonin after releasing them, or reverse it so that it releases dopamine instead of reabsorbing it (Beuming et al., 2008; Calipari & Ferris, 2013). As a result, stimulant drugs increase the effects of those transmitters at their receptors. Dopamine synapses are critical for almost anything that strongly motivates people, ranging from sex and food to music, gambling, and video games (Koepp et al., 1998; Maldonado et al., 1997; Salimpoor et al., 2013).

Cocaine has long been available in the powdery form of cocaine hydrochloride, which can be sniffed. Before 1985, the only way to get a more intense effect from cocaine hydrochloride was to transform it into *freebase cocaine*—cocaine with the hydrochloride removed. Freebase cocaine enters the brain rapidly, and fast entry intensifies the experience. *Crack cocaine*, which first became available in 1985, is cocaine that has already been converted into freebase rocks, ready to be smoked (Brower & Anglin, 1987; Kozel & Adams, 1986). It is called "crack" because it makes popping noises when smoked. Crack produces a rush of potent effects within a few seconds.

The behavioral effects of stimulant drugs depend on the dose. Low levels enhance attention. In fact, amphetamine is often prescribed for attention deficit disorder, under the trade name Adderall. At higher doses, amphetamine and cocaine lead to confusion, impaired attention, and impulsiveness (Simon, Mendez, & Setlow, 2007; Stalnaker et al., 2007). Physical effects include higher heart rate, blood pressure, and body temperature, and a risk of convulsions, lung damage, and heart attack.

As amphetamine or cocaine enters the brain, it increases arousal and produces mostly pleasant effects. However, because these drugs are inhibiting the reuptake of dopamine and other transmitters, the transmitters wash away from synapses faster than the presynaptic neurons can replace them. Over the next few hours, the presynaptic neurons' supply of transmitters dwindles and users begin to experience mild lethargy and depression that last until the neurons rebuild their supply.

Methylphenidate (Ritalin), a drug often prescribed for attention deficit disorder, works the same way as cocaine, at the same synapses (Volkow, Wang, & Fowler, 1997; Volkow et al., 1998). The difference is that methylphenidate, taken as pills, reaches the brain gradually over an hour or more and declines slowly over hours. Therefore, it does not produce the sudden "rush" that makes crack cocaine so addictive.

If people take methylphenidate for attention deficit disorder, do they become more likely to abuse drugs later? A review of longitudinal studies concluded that people who were given stimulant drugs in childhood were neither more likely nor less likely than other people to abuse any drug during adulthood (Humphreys, Eng, & Lee, 2013).

Tobacco delivers nicotine, which increases wakefulness and arousal by stimulating synapses responsive to the neurotransmitter *acetylcholine*. Although nicotine is classed as a stimulant, most smokers say it relaxes them. The research suggests an explanation for this paradox. Although smoking increases tension levels, abstaining from cigarettes increases tension even more. Smoking another cigarette relieves the withdrawal symptoms and restores the usual mood (Parrott, 1999). One reason why it is difficult to quit smoking is that nicotine alters certain cells so that they become more responsive to nicotine and less responsive to other kinds of pleasant events (Changeux, 2010). As this happens, people find it more and more difficult to give up smoking.

▲ **Figure 3.10** Tablas, or yarn paintings, created by members of the Huichol tribe (Mexico) evoke the beautiful lights, vivid colors, and "peculiar creatures" experienced after the people eat the hallucinogenic peyote cactus in ritualized ceremonies.

concept check

6. **The drug AMPT (alpha-methyl-para-tyrosine) prevents the body from making dopamine. How would a large dose of AMPT affect someone's later responsiveness to cocaine, amphetamine, or methylphenidate?**

7. **Some people with attention deficit disorder report that they experience benefits for the first few hours after taking methylphenidate pills but begin to deteriorate in the late afternoon and evening. Why?**

Answers
6. Someone who took AMPT would become less responsive than usual to amphetamine, cocaine, or methylphenidate. These drugs prolong the effects of dopamine, but if the neurons cannot make dopamine, they cannot release it.
7. Remember what happens after taking cocaine: Neurons release dopamine and other transmitters faster than they resynthesize them. Because cocaine blocks reuptake, the supply of transmitters dwindles, and the result is lethargy and mild depression. The same process occurs with methylphenidate but more slowly and to a smaller degree.

Hallucinogens

Drugs that induce sensory distortions are called hallucinogens or *psychedelics*. Many of these drugs are derived from mushrooms or plants, and others are manufactured. Hallucinogenic drugs such as LSD (lysergic acid diethylamide) produce sensory distortions that are not exactly hallucinations in the usual sense, because the person generally recognizes that the strange sensory experience is not real. Hallucinogens also sometimes produce sudden emotional changes, a dreamlike state, or an intense mystical experience. Although LSD is considered a high-risk drug, it has sometimes been used under controlled conditions as an adjunct to psychotherapy and for relief of severe anxiety, such as the anxiety people face when they expect to die soon (Smith, Raswyck, & Davidson, 2014). Peyote, a hallucinogen derived from a cactus plant, has a long history of use in Native American religious ceremonies (see ▲ Figure 3.10).

LSD attaches mainly to one kind of serotonin receptor (Jacobs, 1987). It stimulates those receptors at irregular times and prevents neurotransmitters from stimulating them at the normal times. One result is a decrease in communication among brain areas, such that sensory and emotional experiences occur without the usual guidance and restraint that the frontal cortex would provide.

The drug MDMA (methylenedioxymethamphetamine), popularly known as "ecstasy," produces stimulant effects similar to amphetamine at low doses and hallucinogenic effects similar to LSD at higher doses. Many young adults use MDMA at parties to increase their energy. However, as the

Manu Sassoonian/Art Resource, NY

drug wears off, people feel depressed and lethargic. MDMA increases body temperature, sometimes to dangerous levels. Several studies have reported persisting depression, anxiety, and memory loss in heavy users of MDMA, although it is not certain how much of the damage comes from MDMA and how much from other drugs these people may have taken (Capela et al., 2009; Hanson & Luciana, 2010). Another risk is that MDMA, in combination with its breakdown products, can produce liver damage, especially when they are combined with elevated body temperature (da Silva, Silva, Carvalho, & Carmo, 2014).

Depressants

Depressants are *drugs that decrease arousal,* such as alcohol and *anxiolytics* (anxiety-reducing drugs). People have been using alcohol since prehistoric times. When archeologists unearthed a Neolithic village in Iran's Zagros Mountains, they found a jar that had been constructed about 5500 to 5400 B.C., one of the oldest human-made crafts ever found (see ▼ Figure 3.11). Inside the jar, especially at the bottom, the archeologists found a yellowish residue. They were curious to know what the jar had held, so they sent the residue for chemical analysis. The unambiguous answer came back: It was wine. The jar had been a wine vessel (McGovern, Glusker, Exner, & Voigt, 1996).

Alcohol is a *class of molecules that includes methanol, ethanol, propyl alcohol (rubbing alcohol), and others. Ethanol is the type that people drink.* At moderate doses, alcohol relaxes people by facilitating activity at inhibitory synapses. In greater amounts, it increases risk-taking behaviors, including aggression, by suppressing the fears and inhibitions that ordinarily limit such behaviors. In still greater amounts, as in binge drinking, alcohol suppresses breathing and heart rate to a dangerous degree. Excessive use damages the liver and other organs, aggravates medical conditions, and impairs memory and motor control. A woman who drinks alcohol

▲ **Figure 3.11** This wine jar, dated about 5500 to 5400 B.C., is one of the oldest human crafts ever found.

Courtesy of Penn Museum, image#151075

during pregnancy risks damage to her baby's brain, health, and appearance.

Anxiolytic drugs or **tranquilizers** *help people relax.* The most common examples are *benzodiazepines,* including diazepam (Valium) and alprazolam (Xanax). Benzodiazepines calm people by facilitating transmission at inhibitory synapses. Taking these drugs at the same time as alcohol can produce dangerous suppression of breathing and heart rate.

One benzodiazepine drug, flunitrazepam (Rohypnol), has attracted attention as a "date rape drug." It has also been used to sedate people to facilitate a robbery (Ramadan et al., 2013). The drug dissolves quickly in water and has no color, odor, or taste to warn the person who is consuming it. As with other anxiolytics, it induces drowsiness, clumsiness, and memory impairment (Anglin, Spears, & Hutson, 1997; Woods & Winger, 1997). Someone under the influence of the drug does not have the strength to fight off an attacker and may not remember the event clearly. A hospital that suspects someone has been given this drug can detect its presence with a urine test up to three days later. If the drink is still available, the drug can be detected weeks later (Gautam, Sharratt, & Cole, 2014). This drug is no longer available legally in the United States.

Another date rape drug, GHB (gamma hydroxybutyrate), has become widespread because it can be made easily (though impurely) with household ingredients. Like flunitrazepam, it relaxes the body and impairs muscle coordination. Large doses induce vomiting, tremors, coma, and death.

concept check

8. What is the behavioral effect of anxiolytic drugs?

Answer

8. Anxiolytic drugs reduce anxiety and help people relax.

Narcotics

Narcotics are *drugs that produce drowsiness, insensitivity to pain, and decreased responsiveness.* **Opiates** are *either natural drugs derived from the opium poppy or synthetic drugs with a chemical structure resembling natural opiates.* Opiates make people feel happy, warm, and content, with little anxiety or pain. Morphine (named after Morpheus, the Greek god of dreams) has important medical use as a painkiller. Undesirable consequences include nausea and withdrawal from the world. After the drug leaves the brain, elation gives way to anxiety, pain, and exaggerated responsiveness to sounds and other stimuli. These withdrawal symptoms become especially strong after habitual use.

Opiate drugs such as morphine, heroin, methadone, and codeine bind to specific receptors in the brain (Pert & Snyder, 1973). The discovery of neurotransmitter receptors demonstrated that opiates block pain in the brain, not in the skin. Neuroscientists then found that the brain produces several chemicals, called endorphins, that *bind to the opiate receptors* (Hughes et al., 1975). Endorphins inhibit chronic pain. The brain also releases endorphins during pleasant experiences, such as the "runner's high" or the chill you feel down your back when you hear especially thrilling music (A. Goldstein, 1980).

Although opiates have a strong potential to become addictive, most people who take morphine for pain control under medical care do not develop an addiction. Nevertheless, many people do abuse codeine and other prescription drugs (Bali, Raisch, Moffett, & Khan, 2013).

Marijuana

Marijuana (*cannabis*) is difficult to classify. It softens pain but not as powerfully as opiates. It produces an illusion that time is passing more slowly than usual, but marijuana's effects do not include the more extreme sensory distortions that LSD causes. It has a calming effect but not like that of alcohol or tranquilizers.

Many reports of memory problems in marijuana users are hard to interpret. Does marijuana impair memory or do people with memory problems like

A store owner smiles while selling marijuana legally for the first time in Colorado.

to use marijuana? Remember, correlation does not indicate causation. Both explanations have merit. Students doing poorly in school are more likely than others to start using marijuana early, and to use it often (Hooper, Woolley, & De Bellis, 2014). Also, two studies found that after people quit using marijuana, their memory gradually improved (Bosker et al., 2013; Pope, Gruber, Hudson, Huestis, & Yurgelun-Todd, 2001). Those results imply that memory impairment was partly a result of marijuana use, not just a characteristic of those who chose to use marijuana. The results also indicate that the impairment is not permanent.

Marijuana has several potential medical uses. It reduces nausea, suppresses tremors, reduces pressure in the eyes, and decreases cell loss in the brain after a stroke (Glass, 2001; Panikashvili et al., 2001). However, animal research shows that marijuana is most effective in protecting the brain from stroke damage if it is administered as quickly as possible after the stroke, or better yet *before* the stroke (Schomacher, Müller, Sommer, Schwab, & Schäbitz, 2008). (It's a little impractical to recommend that everyone at risk for stroke should remain more or less permanently stoned.) Because of legal restrictions, research on these medical uses has been limited.

You may have heard that marijuana is dangerous as a "gateway drug." That is, many heroin and cocaine users had used marijuana first. True, but they also tried cigarettes and alcohol first, as well as other risky experiences. It is unclear that the use of marijuana encourages the use of other drugs.

The active ingredient in marijuana is THC, or tetrahydrocannabinol. THC attaches to receptors that are abundant throughout the brain (Herkenham, Lynn, deCosta, & Richfield, 1991). The brain produces large amounts of its own chemicals, anandamide and 2-AG, that attach to those receptors (Devane et al., 1992; Stella, Schweitzer, & Piomelli, 1997). These receptors are abundant in brain areas that control memory and movement, but they are nearly absent from the medulla, which controls heart rate and breathing (Herkenham et al., 1990). In contrast, the medulla has many opiate receptors.

Unlike most other neurotransmitter receptors, those for anandamide and 2-AG (and therefore marijuana) are located on the *pre*synaptic neuron. When the presynaptic neuron releases a transmitter, such as glutamate or GABA, the postsynaptic (receiving) cell releases anandamide or 2-AG, which returns to the presynaptic cell to inhibit further release (Kreitzer & Regehr, 2001; Oliet, Baimoukhametova, Piet, & Bains, 2007; R. I. Wilson & Nicoll, 2002). In effect it says, "I received your signal. You can slow down on sending any more of it." Marijuana, by resembling these natural

Gary C. Caskey/UPI/Newscom

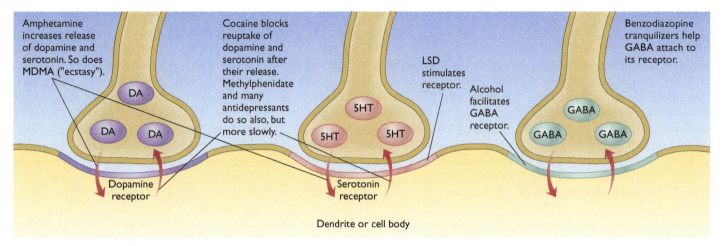

▲ **Figure 3.12** Both legal and illegal drugs operate at the synapses. Drugs can increase the release of neurotransmitters, block their reuptake, or directly stimulate or block their receptors.

reverse transmitters, has the same effect, except that it slows the signal even before it has been sent. It is as if the presynaptic cell "thinks" it has sent a signal when in fact it has not.

Marijuana has many behavioral effects that researchers need to explain. It decreases nausea by blocking the type of serotonin receptor responsible for nausea (Fan, 1995). It increases activity in brain areas responsible for feeding and appetite (DiMarzo et al., 2001). How it produces the illusion that time is passing slowly is hard to explain, but the same phenomenon occurs in laboratory animals. Under the influence of marijuana smoke, rats show impairments when they have to respond at certain time intervals. They respond too quickly, as if 10 seconds felt like 20 seconds (Han & Robinson, 2001).

9. An overdose of opiates produces a life-threatening decrease in breathing and heart rate. Large doses of marijuana do not produce those effects. Why not?

Answer

9. Opiate receptors are abundant in the medulla, which controls heart rate and breathing. The medulla has few receptors sensitive to marijuana.

▲ Figure 3.12 diagrams the effects of several drugs. ■ Table 3.2 summarizes the drugs we have been considering. The list of risks is incomplete because of space. Large or repeated doses of any drug can be dangerous.

Table 3.2 Commonly Abused Drugs and Their Effects

Drug Category	Effects on the Nervous System	Short-Term Effects	Risks (Partial List)
Stimulants			
Amphetamine	Increases release of dopamine and decreases reuptake, prolonging effects	Increases energy and alertness	Psychotic reaction, agitation, heart problems, sleeplessness, stroke
Cocaine	Decreases reuptake of dopamine, prolonging effects	Increases energy and alertness	Psychotic reaction, heart problems
Methylphenidate (Ritalin)	Decreases reuptake of dopamine but with slower onset and offset than cocaine	Increases alertness; much milder withdrawal effects than cocaine	Increased blood pressure
Caffeine	Blocks a chemical that inhibits arousal	Increases energy and alertness	Sleeplessness
Nicotine	Stimulates some acetylcholine synapses; stimulates some neurons that release dopamine	Increases arousal; abstention by a habitual smoker produces tension and depression	Lung cancer from the tars in cigarettes

(continued)

Table 3.2 (*continued*)

Drug Category	Effects on the Nervous System	Short-Term Effects	Risks (Partial List)
Depressants			
Alcohol	Facilitates effects of GABA, an inhibitory neurotransmitter	Relaxation, reduced inhibitions, impaired memory and judgment	Automobile accidents, loss of job
Benzodiazepines	Facilitate effects of GABA, an inhibitory neurotransmitter	Relaxation, decreased anxiety, sleepiness	Dependence. Life-threatening if combined with alcohol or opiates
Narcotics			
Morphine, heroin, other opiates	Stimulate endorphin synapses	Decrease pain; withdrawal from interest in real world; unpleasant withdrawal effects during abstention	Heart stoppage
Marijuana			
Marijuana	Excites negative feedback receptors of both excitatory and inhibitory synapses	Decreases pain and nausea; distorted sense of time	Impaired memory; lung diseases
Hallucinogens			
LSD	Stimulates serotonin type 2 receptors at inappropriate times	Hallucinations, sensory distortions	Psychotic reaction, accidents, panic attacks, flashbacks
MDMA ("ecstasy")	Stimulates neurons that release dopamine; at higher doses also stimulates neurons that release serotonin	At low doses increases arousal; at higher doses, hallucinations	Dehydration, fever
Rohypnol and GHB	Facilitate action at GABA synapses (which are inhibitory)	Relaxation, decreased inhibitions	Impaired muscle coordination and memory
Phencyclidine (PCP or "angel dust")	Inhibits one type of glutamate receptor	Intoxication, slurred speech; hallucinations, thought disorder, impaired memory and emotions	Psychotic reaction at higher doses

Drugs and Synapses

Except for Novocain and related drugs that block action potentials, every drug with psychological effects acts at synapses. That statement includes the abused drugs that this module has emphasized as well as antidepressant drugs, antianxiety drugs, drugs to combat schizophrenia, and so forth. Many drugs have medical uses as well as potential for abuse. Examples include opiates, stimulants, and marijuana. Much of the difference between "good" psychiatric drugs and "bad" abused drugs is a matter of how much someone uses, and when, and why.

Summary

- *Stimulants.* Stimulant drugs such as amphetamines and cocaine increase activity levels and pleasure by increasing the release, and decreasing reuptake, of dopamine and certain other neurotransmitters. Compared to other forms of cocaine, crack enters the brain faster and therefore produces more intense effects. (page 66)
- *Hallucinogens.* Hallucinogens induce sensory distortions. LSD acts at one type of serotonin synapse. MDMA produces stimulant effects at low doses and hallucinogenic effects at higher doses. (page 67)
- *Alcohol.* Alcohol, the most widely abused drug in our society, relaxes people and relieves their inhibitions. It can also impair judgment and reasoning. (page 68)
- *Anxiolytics.* Benzodiazepines, widely used to relieve anxiety, can also relax muscles and promote sleep. Anxiolytics and alcohol act by facilitating inhibitory synapses. (page 68)
- *Opiates.* Opiate drugs bind to endorphin receptors in the nervous system. The immediate effect of opiates is pleasure and relief from pain. (page 68)
- *Marijuana.* Marijuana's active compound, THC, acts on abundant receptors. Marijuana acts on receptors on the presynaptic neuron, putting the brakes on release of both excitatory and inhibitory transmitters. (page 69)

Key Terms

alcohol (page 68)

anxiolytic drugs (tranquilizers) (page 68)

depressant (page 68)

endorphins (page 69)

hallucinogens (page 67)

narcotics (page 68)

opiates (page 68)

stimulants (page 66)

Review Questions

1. How do stimulant drugs such as cocaine affect neurons?
   (a) They attach to the same synapses as dopamine and serotonin.
   (b) They increase reuptake of dopamine and serotonin by the presynaptic neuron.
   (c) They block reuptake of dopamine and serotonin by the presynaptic neuron.
   (d) They inhibit release of dopamine and serotonin.

2. In what way do the effects of methylphenidate (Ritalin) differ from those of cocaine?
   (a) Cocaine increases activity at dopamine synapses, whereas methylphenidate decreases the activity.
   (b) Cocaine decreases activity at dopamine synapses, whereas methylphenidate increases the activity.
   (c) Cocaine and methylphenidate attach to different types of receptors.
   (d) Methylphenidate, taken as a pill, reaches the brain more slowly and its effects decline more slowly.

3. Alcohol and anxiolytic drugs (tranquilizers) facilitate synapses that release which transmitter?
   (a) Dopamine
   (b) Serotonin
   (c) GABA
   (d) Glutamate

4. THC, the active component of marijuana smoke, produces its behavioral effects by what action on neurons?
   (a) It blocks the reuptake of dopamine and serotonin.
   (b) It decreases release of glutamate or GABA.
   (c) It attaches to serotonin receptors.
   (d) It facilitates transmission at inhibitory synapses.

Answers: 1c, 2d, 3c, 4b.

Brain and Behavior

After studying this module, you should be able to:

- Explain why most scientists favor the position called monism.
- Cite examples of how brain damage affects behavior.
- Describe methods of studying and measuring brain activity.
- Cite examples of brain plasticity.
- Define the binding problem.

When studying the brain, you can easily get bogged down in memorizing the names and functions of brain areas. Before we get into all those facts, let's start with two points that are important to remember.

The first is that you use all of your brain. You may have heard that "they say" we use only 10 percent of our brains. No one is sure where this idea originated, but people have been telling it to one another for at least a century. What does it mean? Does anyone believe you could lose 90 percent of your brain and still do as well as you are doing now? Presumably not. Some people say, "Surely we could do so much more with our brains!" Well, yes, but that has nothing to do with using 10 percent. A poor athlete uses all of his or her muscles, just not very skillfully. Similarly, someone who uses the brain poorly nevertheless uses all of it. A slightly less ridiculous idea is that at any moment some brain areas are more active than usual and others are less active. That's true, but it is wrong to assume that you would be smarter if you increased activity in all of your brain. Simultaneous contraction of every muscle in your body wouldn't give you great athletic performance; it would give you spasms. Similarly, simultaneous activation of every neuron wouldn't give you great thoughts; it would give you convulsions. Useful brain activity requires a pattern of activating some neurons while inhibiting others, and the inhibition is just as important as the excitation.

The second point to remember is the concept of monism, the idea that mental activity and brain activity are inseparable. I (your author) remember as a young college student taking it for granted that my mind and brain were separate. And then I learned that nearly all scientists and philosophers reject that idea. You should at least know not to take dualism for granted, and this module will discuss some of the evidence against dualism: If you lose part of your brain, you lose part of your mind. So far as we can tell, you

cannot have mental activity without brain activity, and you cannot have certain kinds of brain activity without mental activity. According to monism, mental activity *is* brain activity.

The central nervous system, consisting of *the brain and the spinal cord,* communicates with the rest of the body by the peripheral nervous system, consisting of *nerves connecting the spinal cord with the rest of the body.* Within the peripheral nervous system, we distinguish the *somatic nervous system,* which connects to the skin and muscles, and the *autonomic nervous system,* which connects to the heart, stomach, and other organs. Sensory nerves bring information from other body areas to the spinal cord, and motor nerves take information from the spinal cord to the muscles, where they cause contractions. ▼ Figure 3.13 summarizes these major divisions of the nervous system.

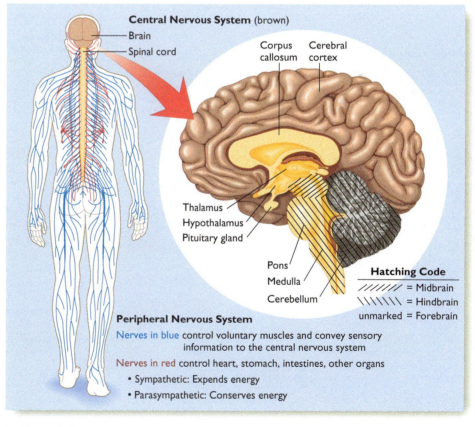

Central Nervous System (brown)
- Brain
- Spinal cord

Corpus callosum Cerebral cortex

Thalamus
Hypothalamus
Pituitary gland

Pons
Medulla
Cerebellum

Hatching Code
////// = Midbrain
\\\\\\ = Hindbrain
unmarked = Forebrain

Peripheral Nervous System

Nerves in blue control voluntary muscles and convey sensory information to the central nervous system

Nerves in red control heart, stomach, intestines, other organs
- Sympathetic: Expends energy
- Parasympathetic: Conserves energy

▲ **Figure 3.13** The major components of the nervous system are the central nervous system and the peripheral nervous system, which includes the somatic nervous system and the autonomic nervous system.

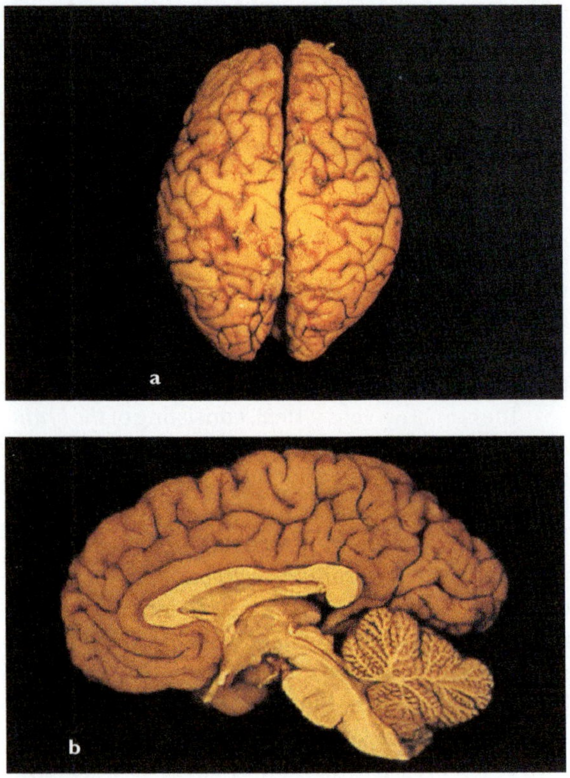

The Cerebral Cortex

The vertebrate brain has three major divisions—hindbrain, midbrain, and forebrain—as shown in Figure 3.13. In fish, amphibians, reptile, and birds, the midbrain constitutes a large portion of the brain. In mammals including humans, the forebrain is by far the largest area. It consists of hemispheres, *the left and right halves of the forebrain* (see ◄ Figure 3.14). Each hemisphere controls sensation and movement on the opposite side of the body. (Why does it control the opposite side instead of its own side? No one knows, but the same is true for all vertebrates and some invertebrates.) We consider the differences between the left and right hemispheres later in this module. The *outer covering of the forebrain,* known as the cerebral cortex, is especially prominent in humans.

The Occipital Lobe of the Cortex

Researchers describe the cerebral cortex in terms of four *lobes:* occipital, parietal, temporal, and frontal, as shown in ▼ Figure 3.15. The occipital lobe, *at the rear of the head, is specialized for vision.* People with damage in this area have *cortical blindness.* Cortical blindness differs from the usual kind of blindness resulting from eye damage. Someone who used to have normal vision and then suffered eye damage can imagine visual scenes and continues (for years, if not necessarily forever) to have visual dreams. People with cortical blindness have no visual imagery, even in dreams. However, the intact eyes continue sending messages to other brain areas, including one that controls wakefulness and sleep. Therefore, someone with cortical blindness continues feeling wakeful during the day and sleepy at night.

Some (not all) people with cortical blindness experience blindsight, *the ability to point to or otherwise indicate the direction to a visual stimulus, without*

▲ **Figure 3.14** The human cerebral cortex: **(a)** left and right hemispheres; **(b)** a view from inside. The folds greatly extend the brain's surface area.

Dr. Colin Chumbley/Science Source

Dr. Colin Chumbley/Science Photo Library/Science Source

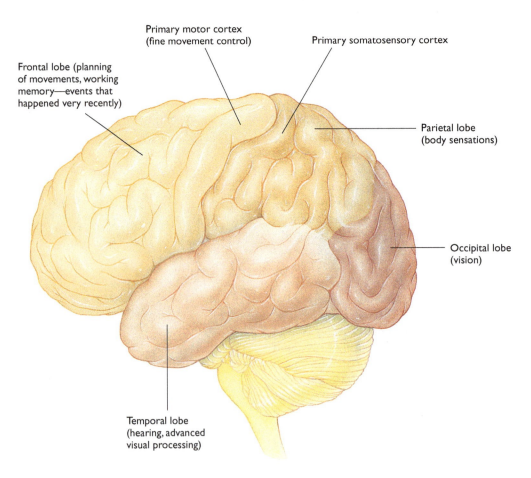

▶ **Figure 3.15** The four lobes of the human forebrain, with some of their functions.

Frontal lobe (planning of movements, working memory—events that happened very recently)

Primary motor cortex (fine movement control)

Primary somatosensory cortex

Parietal lobe (body sensations)

Occipital lobe (vision)

Temporal lobe (hearing, advanced visual processing)

any conscious perception of seeing anything at all (Weiskrantz, Warrington, Sanders, & Marshall, 1974; Striemer, Chapman, & Goodale, 2009). Some can correctly state an object's color, direction of movement, or approximate shape, again insisting that they are just guessing (Radoeva, Prasad, Brainard, & Aguirre, 2008). Some respond to the emotional expression of a face that they do not see consciously (Gonzalez Andino, de Peralta Menendez, Khateb, Landis, & Pegna, 2009; Tamietto et al., 2009).

What is the explanation? In some cases, small islands of healthy tissue remaining in the damaged visual cortex are large enough for certain functions, though not for conscious perception (Fendrich, Wessinger, & Gazzaniga, 1992; Radoeva et al., 2008). Also, several areas outside the primary visual cortex continue to receive visual information—again, enough to control certain functions but not enough for conscious perception (Schmid et al., 2010). Blindsight demonstrates that many functions occur without consciousness. It also provides an example of one of the many possible ways that brain damage can alter experience.

concept check

10. **How does cortical blindness differ from blindness caused by eye damage?**

Answer

10. Someone with cortical blindness loses visual imagery, even in dreams. However, sunlight continues to regulate the person's wake-sleep cycle. Also, some people with cortical blindness have blindsight, in which they can indicate the location of a stimulus or other properties of the stimulus without conscious perception of it. Someone with total eye damage can continue to have visual imagery, but light does not drive the wake-sleep cycle, and blindsight cannot occur.

The Temporal Lobe of the Cortex

The temporal lobe of each hemisphere, *located toward the left and right sides of the head, is the main area for hearing and certain aspects of vision.* People with damage in the auditory parts of the temporal lobe do not become deaf, but they are impaired at recognizing sequences of sounds, as in music or speech. The temporal cortex is also important for feeling something with your fingers and detecting the rate of vibration (Yau, Celnik, Hsiao, & Desmond, 2014). Hearing is, of course, also a perception of rate of vibration (of sound waves in the air).

Language comprehension depends on part of the temporal lobe, in most cases the left temporal lobe. People with damage in that area have trouble understanding speech and remembering the names of objects. Their own speech, grammatical but lacking most nouns, is hard to understand.

In other parts of the temporal lobe, damage produces visual deficits. One area in the temporal lobe, called the *fusiform gyrus,* responds mainly to the sight of faces (Kanwisher & Yovel, 2006). People with damage in that area no longer recognize faces, although they see well in other regards and recognize people by their voices (Tarr & Gauthier, 2000). They can describe facial features, such as this is a person with a rounded face, short brown hair, and so forth, but they don't easily recognize the individual. You can experience the same difficulty if you look at faces just briefly and upside-down.

Among healthy people, the development of the fusiform gyrus and its connections varies from one person to another. People with extensive connections to and from the fusiform gyrus learn to recognize faces easily, and may even recognize someone they met just once, years ago. People with fewer than average connections have difficulty recognizing even familiar people (Grueter et al., 2007; C. Thomas et al., 2009). Oliver Sacks, a famous neurologist, has this problem himself. He has trouble recognizing even his relatives and closest friends,

and sometimes looks at himself in the mirror and thinks he is looking at some other bearded man (Sacks, 2010). So, if you have much difficulty recognizing faces, it's probably not that you just aren't trying hard enough. The explanation may relate to your brain anatomy.

People with damage to another part of the temporal lobe become motion blind: Although they see the size, shape, and color of objects, they do not track speed or direction of movement (Zihl, von Cramon, & Mai, 1983). They eventually notice that someone who used to be one place is now in another, and therefore must have moved, but they don't see the movement moment by moment. Crossing a street is hazardous, because the cars seem stationary. Pouring coffee is difficult, as the person cannot monitor the rising level.

It is hard to imagine vision without motion perception, but here is how to demonstrate a small sample of the experience. Look at yourself in the mirror and focus on your left eye. Then move your focus to the right eye. Do you see your eyes moving in the mirror? (Go ahead; try it.) People agree that they do not see their eyes move.

try it yourself

"Oh, but wait," you say. "That movement in the mirror was simply too quick and too small to see." Wrong. Get someone else to look at your left eye and then shift gaze to your right eye. You *do* see the other person's eye movement. You see someone else's eyes move, but you do not see your own eyes move in the mirror.

Why not? During voluntary eye movements, called *saccades,* and in fact beginning 75 milliseconds before such movements, your brain suppresses activity in the part of the temporal cortex responsible for motion perception (Bremmer, Kubischik, Hoffmann, & Krekelberg, 2009; Burr, Morrone, & Ross, 1994; Paus, Marrett, Worsley, & Evans, 1995; Vallines & Greenlee, 2006). That is, you become temporarily motion blind. Now, try to imagine what it would be like to have this condition all the time.

Other parts of the temporal lobe are critical for certain aspects of emotion. The amygdala (see ▼ **Figure 3.16**), *a structure in the temporal lobe, responds strongly to emotional situations.* People with damage to the amygdala are slow to process emotional information, such as facial expressions and descriptions of emotional situations (Baxter & Murray, 2002). In contrast, people with an easily aroused amygdala tend to be shy and fearful (Hariri et al., 2002; Rhodes et al., 2007).

A simple way to gauge amygdala arousal is to make a sudden, loud sound and measure the startle response. All people except the deaf show some startle response, but some respond more than others, and some *habituate* (decline in response) faster than others. People with a highly reactive amygdala respond strongly and habituate slowly to a loud noise, indicating anxiety. That response correlates with political attitudes: People who favor vigorous military and police action to protect against potentially dangerous people tend to show strong amygdala responses, whereas those who are more relaxed about such dangers show weaker amygdala responses (Oxley et al., 2008). ▼ Figure 3.17 shows the results of one study. This research says nothing about which group is correct on the political issues, but it indicates that even our political leanings relate to our brain activities.

11. Under what condition does a person with full vision experience temporary motion blindness?

Answer

11. During and slightly before a voluntary eye movement.

The Parietal Lobe of the Cortex

The parietal lobe, just anterior (forward) from the occipital lobe, is specialized for the body senses, including touch, pain, temperature, and awareness of the location of body parts in space. The primary somatosensory (so-ma-toh-SEN-so-ree, meaning body-sensory) cortex, a strip in the anterior portion of the parietal lobe, has cells sensitive to touch in various body areas, as shown in ▼ Figure 3.18. In that figure, note that the largest areas are devoted to touch in the most sensitive areas, such as the lips and hands. Damage to any part of the somatosensory cortex impairs sensation from the corresponding body part.

Although the somatosensory cortex is the primary site for touch sensations, touch also activates other areas that are important for emotional responses. Consider someone who has lost input to the somatosensory cortex. You gently stroke her arm, and she smiles without knowing why. She has the pleasant emotional experience despite no touch sensation (Olausson et al., 2002). You see again that brain damage produces surprisingly specialized changes in behavior and experience.

Parietal lobe damage also interferes with spatial attention. People with such damage see what an object is but not where it is. They have trouble reaching toward it, walking around it, or shifting attention from one object to another. When walking, they can describe what they see, but they bump into objects instead of walking around them. They can describe their furniture from memory but not how it is arranged in the house. Sometimes they have trouble finding various parts of their body (Schenk, 2006).

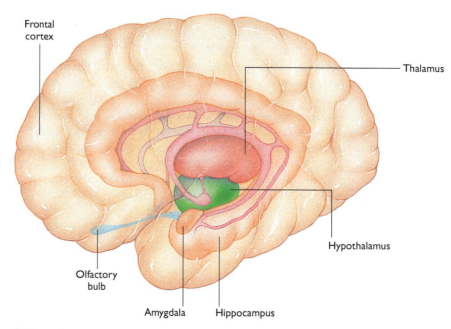

▲ **Figure 3.16** A view of the forebrain, showing internal structures as though the outer structures were transparent.

12. Parietal lobe damage interferes with which aspect of vision?

Answer

12. It interferes with identifying the object's location.

The Frontal Lobe of the Cortex

The frontal lobe, *at the anterior (forward) pole of the brain,* includes the primary motor cortex, *important for controlling fine movements,* such as moving a finger or wiggling a toe. Each area of the primary motor cortex controls a different part of the body, and larger areas are devoted to the areas we control with precision, such as the tongue and fingers, than others such as the shoulder and elbow

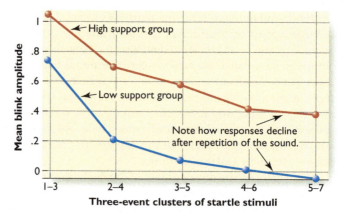

▲ **Figure 3.17** People with high support for military action, capital punishment, and immigration control show enhanced eye-blink responses to a sudden loud noise relative to those with low support for these positions. Those with low support show a more rapid decline in response as the noise is repeated.

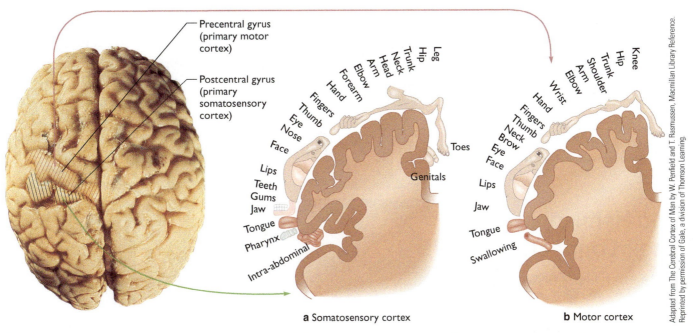

Figure 3.18 (a) The primary somatosensory cortex and (b) the primary motor cortex, illustrating which part of the body each brain area controls. Larger areas of the cortex are devoted to body parts that need to be controlled with great precision, such as the face and hands. (parts a and b after Penfield & Rasmussen, 1950)

muscles. The *anterior sections of the frontal lobe,* called the prefrontal cortex, are important for memory of what has just happened and what you are planning to do next. The prefrontal cortex is also critical for directing attention. Suppose you look at pictures of a house superimposed on pictures of a face. Sometimes you are told to pay attention to the house and sometimes you are to attend to the face. The prefrontal cortex then facilitates activity in either the part of the temporal cortex that attends to faces or the part that attends to houses (Baldauf & Desimone, 2014).

The prefrontal cortex also participates heavily in decision making, especially for bypassing a current pleasure in favor of a greater pleasure later. Suppose you have a choice between going to a movie tonight and finishing a paper that is due tomorrow, which will have a big effect on your grade at the end of the semester. That decision depends on your prefrontal cortex (Frank & Claus, 2006). People with impairments of the prefrontal cortex often make impulsive decisions because they have trouble imagining how good they might feel after one outcome and how sad or guilty they might feel after another (S. W. Anderson, Bechara, Damasio, Tranel, & Damasio, 1999; Damasio, 1999). Generally, people who are easily distracted and people who tend to make impulsive decisions have weak responses in the prefrontal cortex.

Since the late 1990s, psychologists have become excited about mirror neurons, found in several brain areas but especially in the frontal cortex. Mirror neurons *are active when you make a movement and also when you watch someone else make a similar movement* (Dinstein, Hasson, Rubin, & Heeger, 2007). For example, certain neurons in the frontal cortex become active when you smile or when you see someone else smile (Montgomery, Seeherman, & Haxby, 2009). Do mirror neurons enable you to copy other people's actions? Do they enable you to identify with other people and understand them better? You can see how psychologists would speculate that mirror neurons are the basis for human civilization.

However, before we speculate too far, researchers need to address some important questions. In particular, were you born with mirror neurons that

helped you learn to copy other people? Or did you learn to copy other people, and in the process develop mirror neurons? That is, perhaps after you have learned the parallels between what you see and what you can do, seeing someone do something reminds you of your own ability to do the same thing and therefore activates neurons responsible for those actions.

We probably have several kinds of mirror neurons. Sometimes infants imitate a few facial movements, as shown in ▼ **Figure 3.19**. That result implies built-in mirror neurons that connect the sight of a movement to the movement itself (Meltzoff & Moore, 1977). However, other mirror neurons develop their properties by learning. For example, expert dancers show activity in certain brain areas when they perform certain well-practiced movements or watch others perform the same movements. They don't show such activity when they watch movements that they themselves don't perform (Calvo-Merino, Grèzes, Glaser, Passingham, & Haggard, 2006).

If you consistently watch someone else move the little finger every time you move your index finger, certain cells in your frontal cortex come to respond whenever you move your *index* finger or see someone else move the *little* finger (Catmur, Walsh, & Heyes, 2007). In other words, at least some—probably many—neurons develop their mirror quality (or in this case an anti-mirror quality) by learning.

concept check

13. What evidence suggests that imitation produces mirror neurons as opposed to the idea that mirror neurons produce imitation?

Answer

13. It is possible to train neurons to respond to one kind of movement while the person produces and a different movement the person watches. If people can learn to develop these "anti-mirror" neurons, then presumably, they could also learn to develop mirror neurons.

The Two Hemispheres and Their Connections

Let's focus on a type of brain damage that produces highly interesting results. Each hemisphere of the brain gets sensory input mostly from the opposite side of the body and controls muscles on the opposite side. The hemispheres differ in other ways, too. For almost all right-handed people and more than 60 percent of left-handed people, parts of the left hemisphere control speech. For most other left-handers, both hemispheres control speech. Few people have complete right-hemisphere control of speech. The right hemisphere is more important for certain other functions, including the ability to imagine what an object would look like after it rotates and the ability to understand the emotional connotations of facial expressions, gestures, and tone of voice (Adolphs, Damasio, & Tranel, 2002; Stone, Nisenson, Eliassen, & Gazzaniga, 1996).

In one study, people watched videotapes of 10 people speaking the truth half the time and lying half the time. Do you think you could tell the difference between truth and lies? The average for MIT undergraduates was 47 percent correct, slightly less than they should have done by random guessing. One group that did better than chance was a set of people with left-hemisphere brain damage! They understood little of what people were saying, so they relied on gestures and facial expressions, which the right hemisphere interprets quite well (Etcoff, Ekman, Magee, & Frank, 2000).

The two hemispheres constantly exchange information. If you feel something with the left hand and something else with the right hand, you can tell whether they are made of the same material because the hemispheres pass information back and forth through the **corpus callosum**, *a set of axons that connect the left and right hemispheres of the cerebral cortex* (see ▼ Figure 3.20). What would happen if the corpus callosum were cut?

In certain cases, brain surgeons cut the corpus callosum to relieve **epilepsy**, *a condition in which cells somewhere in the brain emit abnormal rhythmic,*

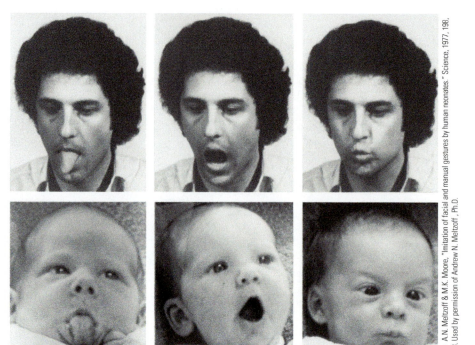

▲ **Figure 3.19** Newborn infants sometimes imitate facial expressions. Because they have not had an opportunity to learn to imitate, their behavior implies built-in mirror neurons. (From Meltzoff & Moore, 1977)

From: A.N. Meltzoff & M.K. Moore, "Imitation of facial and manual gestures by human neonates." Science, 1977, 198, 75-78. Used by permission of Andrew N. Meltzoff , Ph.D.

spontaneous impulses. Most people with epilepsy respond well to antiepileptic drugs and live normal lives, but a few continue having frequent major seizures. When all else failed, surgeons sometimes severed the corpus callosum. The original idea was that this surgery would limit epileptic seizures to one hemisphere and therefore make the epilepsy less incapacitating. (Because other methods have arisen, this surgery is seldom if ever performed today.)

The operation was more successful than expected. Not only did it limit seizures to one side of the body, but also it decreased their frequency. The operation interrupts a feedback loop that lets an epileptic seizure echo back and forth between the hemispheres. However, although these split-brain patients (whose corpus callosum has been cut) resume a normal life, they show some fascinating behavioral effects.

If you have left-hemisphere control of speech, like most people, the information that enters your right hemisphere passes quickly across the corpus callosum to your left (speaking) hemisphere, enabling you to describe what you see or feel in words. However, when a split-brain patient feels something with the left hand, the information goes only to the right (nonspeaking) hemisphere (Nebes, 1974; Sperry, 1967). If asked to point to the object, the person points correctly with the left hand (controlled by the right hemisphere) while saying (with the left hemisphere), "I have no idea what it was. I didn't feel anything."

Now consider what happens when a split-brain patient sees something (see ▼ Figure 3.21). The person in Figure 3.21 focuses on a point in the middle of the screen. The investigator flashes a word such as *hatband* on the screen for a split second, too briefly for an eye movement, and asks for the word. The person replies, "band," which is what the left hemisphere saw. (The left hemisphere sees the right side of the world.) To the question of what *kind* of band, the reply might be, "I don't know. Jazz band? Rubber band?" However, the left hand (controlled by the right hemisphere) points to a hat (which the right hemisphere saw).

A split-brain person reports feeling the same as before the operation and still reports just one consciousness. Of course, it is the left hemisphere that is

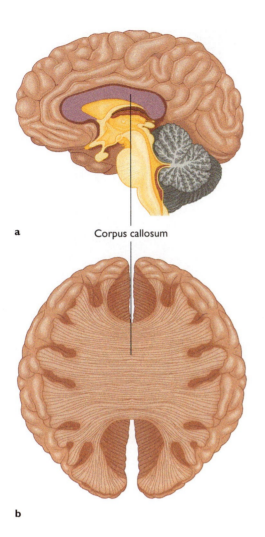

a   Corpus callosum

b

▲ **Figure 3.20** The corpus callosum is a large set of fibers that convey information between the two hemispheres of the cerebral cortex. **(a)** A midline view showing the location of the corpus callosum. **(b)** A horizontal section showing how each axon of the corpus callosum links one spot in the left hemisphere to a corresponding spot in the right hemisphere.

talking, and it doesn't know about the experiences of the right hemisphere! The left hemisphere continues trying to make sense of everything the body does, as if it were completely in control. Consider this study: While the person stares straight ahead, two pictures flash briefly on a screen so that the left hemisphere sees one and the right hemisphere sees the other. Then, from a set of pictures on cards, each hemisphere uses the hand it controls to select an item related to what it saw. In one case, the left hemisphere saw a chicken claw and pointed with the right hand to a chicken. The right hemisphere saw a snow scene and pointed to a snow shovel (see ▼ Figure 3.22). When asked to explain the choices, the left (talking) hemisphere said the chicken claw goes with the chicken, and you need a shovel to clean out the chicken shed. Gazzaniga (2000) infers that the left hemisphere has a function that he calls the interpreter. It makes up a story to explain what it sees happening, even if the behaviors actually happened for a different reason. We shall encounter this point again in later chapters: We often don't know all the reasons for our own behavior, and we make up reasons that may or may not be correct.

Split-brain surgery is rare. We study such patients not because you are likely to meet one but because they teach us something about brain organization, and raise important questions about what it means to be conscious.

✓ concept check

14. After damage to the corpus callosum, a person can describe some, but not all, of what he or she feels. With which hand must the person feel an object before speaking about it?

Answer

14. The person must feel something with the right hand, the hand that the left hemisphere feels.

a

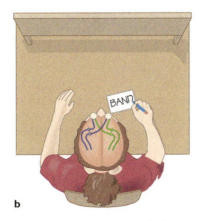

b

c

▲ **Figure 3.21** **(a)** When the word *hatband* flashes on a screen, a split-brain patient reports only what the left hemisphere saw, *band*, and **(b)** writes *band* with the right hand. However, **(c)** the left hand (controlled by the right hemisphere) points to a hat, which is what the right hemisphere saw.

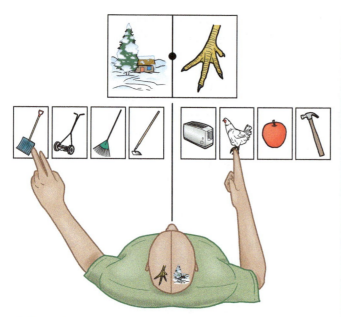

▲ **Figure 3.22** After the two hemispheres see a snow scene and a chicken claw, the two hands point to a chicken and a shovel as the related items. However, the left (talking) hemisphere tries to explain both choices in terms of what it saw, the chicken claw. (From Gazzaniga, M. S., "Cerebral specialization and interhemispheric communication: Does the corpus callosum enable the human condition?" *Brain, 123,* pp. 1293–1326 (Fig. 19a, p. 1318). Copyright © 2000 Oxford University Press. Reprinted by permission.)

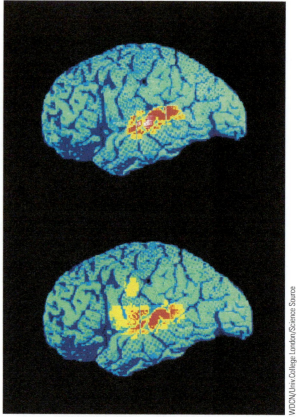

▲ **Figure 3.23** A PET scan of the human brain. Red shows areas of most increased activity during some task; yellow shows areas of next most increased activity.

Measuring Brain Activity

How did researchers discover the functions of various brain areas? In earlier times, nearly all research concerned patients with brain damage, and much of it still does. However, researchers now also have techniques to examine brain activity in healthy people.

An electroencephalograph (EEG) *uses electrodes on the scalp to record rapid changes in brain electrical activity.* A similar method is a magnetoencephalograph (MEG), *which records magnetic changes.* Both methods provide data on a millisecond-by-millisecond basis, measuring the brain's reactions to lights, sounds, and other events. However, because they record from the surface of the scalp, they provide little precision about the location of the activity.

Another method offers better anatomical localization but less information about timing: Positron-emission tomography (PET) *records radioactivity of various brain areas emitted from injected chemicals* (Phelps & Mazziotta, 1985). First, someone receives an injection of a radioactively labeled compound such as glucose. The most active brain areas rapidly absorb glucose, a sugar that is the brain's main fuel. Therefore, the labeled glucose emits radioactivity primarily from the most active areas. Detectors around the head record the radioactivity

and send results to a computer that generates an image such as the one in ▲ Figure 3.23. Red indicates areas of greatest activity, followed by yellow, green, and blue. Unfortunately, PET scans require exposing the brain to radioactivity.

Another technique, functional magnetic resonance imaging (fMRI), *uses magnetic detectors outside the head to compare the amounts of hemoglobin with and without oxygen in different brain areas* (J. D. Cohen, Noll, & Schneider, 1993). (Adding or removing oxygen changes the response of hemoglobin to a magnetic field.) The most active brain areas use the most oxygen and therefore decrease the oxygen bound to the blood's hemoglobin. The fMRI technique indicates relative amounts of brain activity on a second-by-second basis, as shown in ▼ Figure 3.24.

If we want to use a PET or fMRI scan to measure the brain activity during some task, the data tell us nothing except by comparison to the activity that occurs otherwise. Suppose we want to find the brain areas important for memory. We record activity while someone is engaged in a memory task and compare that activity to times when the person is doing . . . what? Doing nothing? That comparison wouldn't work; the memory task presumably includes

WDCN/Univ College London/Science Source

sensory stimuli, motor responses, attention, and other processes. Besides that, "doing nothing" (mind wandering) activates certain brain areas, too (Mason et al., 2007). Researchers must design a comparison task that requires attention to the same sensory stimuli, the same hand movements, and so forth as the memory task. Then they set a computer to subtract the activity in the comparison task from the activity in the memory task. The areas with the largest difference between the tasks are presumably important for some aspect of memory.

Brain scans sometimes lead to important insights about behavior. For example, an fMRI study showed that when people taking a placebo say that they feel less pain, the brain areas responsible for pain actually show decreased responses (Wager & Atlas, 2013). However, the impressive pictures sometimes lure people to careless interpretations. After one study reported that the sight of chocolate excites certain brain areas in "chocolate cravers" (Rolls & McCabe, 2007), some people in the media exclaimed, "Wow, now we understand *why* they craved chocolate!" Do we? Knowing which brain areas become excited tells us nothing about why they became more excited in some people than in others.

Another issue: Suppose researchers find that a particular brain area becomes more active when you are angry. Later, when that area becomes active again, can they conclude that you are angry again? No, not unless research shows that the area is active *only* when you are angry. Perhaps that area also becomes active when you are frightened, excited, paying attention to nearby people, or something else. A good test of understanding is this: Can we take fMRI measures at one time, while we know what you are doing, and then use measures at a later time to infer what you are seeing, hearing, or planning to do? A few such studies have reported success (Haynes et al., 2007; Kay, Naselaris, Prenger, & Gallant, 2008). However, in most cases we should interpret fMRI data cautiously.

15. What is an advantage of fMRI in comparison to PET scans?

Answer
15. An fMRI scan does not expose the body to radiation.

Subcortical Areas

Figure 3.16 shows some of the structures in the interior of the forebrain. At the center is the *thalamus,* the last stop for almost all sensory information on the way to the cerebral cortex. Surrounding the thalamus are areas called the *limbic system.* (A limbus is a margin or border.) The hippocampus, important

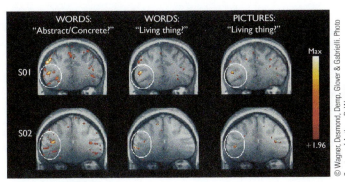

▲ **Figure 3.24** This brain scan was made with functional magnetic resonance imaging (fMRI). Participants looked at words or pictures and judged whether each item was abstract or concrete, living or nonliving. Yellow shows the areas most activated by this decision; red shows areas less strongly activated. (From Wagner, Desmond, Demb, Glover, & Gabrieli, 1997. Photo courtesy of Anthony D. Wagner)

for memory, will appear again in Chapter 7. The hypothalamus, *located just below the thalamus, is important for hunger, thirst, temperature regulation, sex, and other motivated behaviors.*

The cerebral cortex does not directly control the muscles. It sends output to the pons and medulla, *which control the muscles of the head* (e.g., for chewing, swallowing, breathing, and talking), and to the spinal cord, *which controls the muscles from the neck down* (see ▲ Figures 3.13 and ▼ 3.25). The spinal cord also controls many reflexes, such as the knee-jerk reflex. A reflex is a *rapid, automatic response to a stimulus,* such as unconscious adjustments of your legs while you are walking or quickly jerking your hand away from something hot.

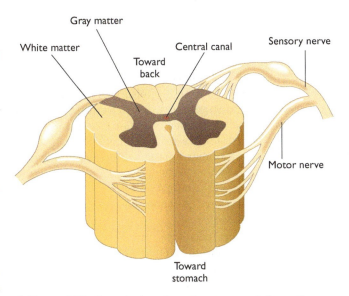

▲ **Figure 3.25** The spinal cord receives sensory information from all body parts except the head. Motor nerves in the spinal cord control the muscles and glands.

The cerebellum (Latin for "little brain"), *part of the hindbrain,* is important for any behavior that requires aim or timing, such as tapping out a rhythm, judging which of two visual stimuli is moving faster, and judging whether one musical tempo is faster or slower than another (Ivry & Diener, 1991; Keele & Ivry, 1990). It is also essential to learned responses that require precise timing, such as quickly responding to a warning signal (Krupa, Thompson, & Thompson, 1993). People with damage to the cerebellum show motor problems like those of alcoholic intoxication, including slurred speech, staggering, and inaccurate eye movements. The reason for the similarity is that alcohol suppresses activity in the cerebellum.

16. Someone with a cut through the upper spinal cord still shows many reflexive movements but no voluntary movements of the arms or legs. Why not?

Answer

16. The spinal cord controls many reflexes by itself. However, voluntary control of muscles depends on messages from the brain to the spinal cord, and a cut through the upper spinal cord interrupts those messages.

The Autonomic Nervous System and Endocrine System

The autonomic nervous system, closely associated with the spinal cord, *controls the heart, digestive system, and other organs.* The term *autonomic* means involuntary, or automatic. You cannot decide to increase your heart rate in the same way that you could decide to wave your hand. Brain activity does, however, influence the autonomic nervous system. For example, your autonomic nervous system reacts more strongly when you are nervous than when you are relaxed. Thinking a frightening thought could increase your heart rate.

The autonomic nervous system has two parts: (a) The *sympathetic nervous system,* controlled by a chain of cells lying just outside the spinal cord, increases heart rate, breathing rate, sweating, and other processes that are important for vigorous fight-or-flight activities. It inhibits digestion and sexual arousal, which can wait until the emergency is over. (b) The *parasympathetic nervous system,* controlled by cells at the top and bottom levels of the spinal cord, decreases heart rate, increases digestive activities, and in general, promotes "vegetative" activities that take place during rest and relaxation (see ▶ Figure 3.26). If you are driving and you see a police car wailing its siren behind you, your sympathetic nervous system arouses. Your heart starts racing, you breathe heavily, and you

Sympathetic system	Parasympathetic system
Preparation for vigorous activity	**Body at rest**
• Pupils open	• Pupils constrict
• Saliva decreases	• Saliva flows
• Pulse quickens	• Pulse slows
• Sweat increases	• Stomach churns
• Stomach less active	
• Epinephrine (adrenaline) secreted	

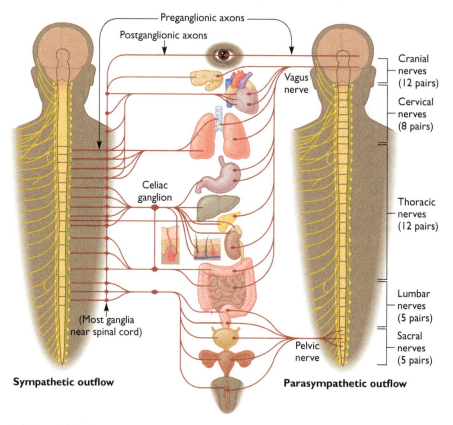

▲ **Figure 3.26** The sympathetic nervous system prepares the organs for a brief bout of vigorous activity. The parasympathetic nervous system puts the brakes on vigorous activity and prepares the body for rest and digestion.

start sweating. When the police car passes and you see that it is chasing someone else, your parasympathetic nervous system kicks in, and you suddenly relax.

Over-the-counter cold remedies act by decreasing parasympathetic actions, such as sinus flow. The side effects come from increased sympathetic actions, such as heart rate, blood pressure, and arousal.

The autonomic nervous system influences the endocrine system, *glands that produce hormones and release them into the blood.* Hormones controlled by the hypothalamus and *pituitary gland* regulate the other endocrine organs. ▼ Figure 3.27 shows some of the endocrine glands. Hormones are *chemicals released by glands and conveyed by the blood to alter activity in various organs.* Some hormonal effects are brief, such as changes in heart rate or blood pressure. Other hormonal effects prepare an animal for pregnancy, migration, hibernation, or other long-lasting activities. Within the brain, hormones produce temporary changes in the excitability of cells, and they also influence the survival, growth, and connections of cells. The sex hormones (*androgens* and *estrogens*) have strong effects during early development, when they produce differences between male and female anatomies, including certain brain areas as well as the rest of the body (Cahill, 2006).

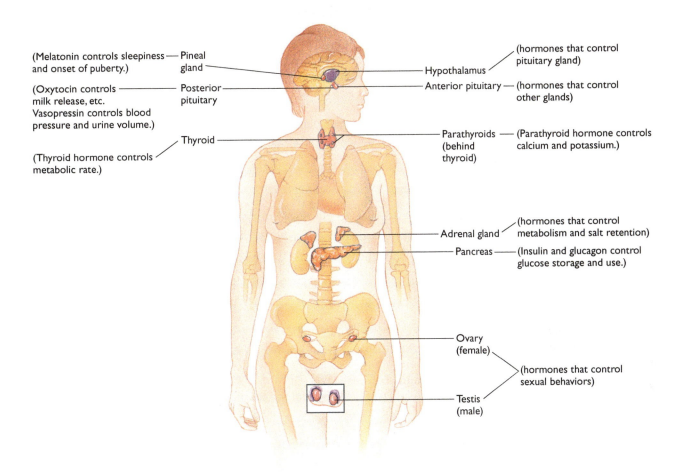

▲ **Figure 3.27** Glands in the endocrine system produce hormones and release them into the bloodstream.

concept check ✔

17. While someone is trying to escape danger, the heart rate and breathing rate increase. After the danger passes, heart rate and breathing rate fall below normal. Which part of the autonomic nervous system is more active during the danger, and which is more active after it?

Answer

17. The sympathetic nervous system predominates during the danger, and the parasympathetic system predominates afterward.

Experience and Brain Plasticity

When we talk about brain anatomy, it is easy to get the impression that the structures are fixed. In fact, brain structure shows considerable plasticity—that is, *change as a result of experience*.

Early researchers believed that the nervous system produced no new neurons after early infancy. Later researchers found that *undifferentiated cells* called stem cells develop into new neurons in certain brain areas and not others (Gage, 2000; Graziadei & deHan, 1973; Song, Stevens, & Gage, 2002). In the adult human brain, new neurons develop in the hippocampus, which is important for establishing memory of specific events, and a subcortical area called the *basal ganglia*, important for gradually learning skills and pattern recognition (Ernst et al., 2014; Kee, Teixeira, Wang, & Frankland, 2007). After a stroke or other damage in the cerebral cortex, behavioral recovery can occur in other ways, but no new neurons form to replace the lost ones (Huttner et al., 2014).

Although formation of new neurons is limited, new experiences stimulate axons and dendrites to expand and withdraw their branches. These changes, which occur more rapidly in young people but continue throughout life, enable the brain to adapt to changing circumstances (Boyke, Driemeyer,

Gaser, Büchel, & May, 2008). For example, one man lost his hand in an accident at age 19. Thirty-five years later, surgeons grafted a new hand onto his arm. Within a few months, axons connected the new hand to his brain, and he regained partial sensation from the hand (Frey, Bogdanov, Smith, Watrous, & Breidenbach, 2008).

Substantial brain changes also occur after people learn to read, even if they learn in adulthood (Carreiras et al., 2009; Dehaene et al., 2010). Many studies have examined what happens after people learn to play music. One brain area devoted to hearing is 30 percent larger than average in professional musicians (Schneider et al., 2002), and an area responsive to finger sensations is larger than average in people who play stringed instruments (Elbert, Pantev, Wienbruch, Rockstroh, & Taub, 1995). We might wonder whether musical training caused those changes, or whether people with certain kinds of brains are more likely than others to become musicians. One study found measurable changes in children's brains as a result of 15 months of music training, as compared to similar children who did not undergo such training (Hyde et al., 2009). The implication is that music training alters the brain.

18. In the study showing changes in children's brains as they learn to play music, why was it necessary to have a control group of untrained children?

Answer

18. It was important to separate the effects of music from the effects of growing 15 months older.

Social Neuroscience

Social neuroscience, the study of the biological bases of social behavior, is developing into an exciting area of research. In certain ways, the brain reacts to social stimuli in special ways. One study found that when a mouse makes a nonaggressive social approach to another mouse, it activates a particular dopamine pathway between two brain areas—the *ventral tegmentum* and the *nucleus accumbens*—that both pertain to reward and positive feelings. Approaches to nonsocial objects did not activate this path. Furthermore, artificially stimulating this path enhanced social approaches (Gunaydin et al., 2014).

The hormone oxytocin, released by women when nursing a baby and by both men and women during sexual activity, has received much publicity as the "love hormone." "Love-magnifying" hormone would be a more accurate term. One study examined men who reported being deeply in love. They rated the attractiveness of their female partner and other women, while viewing photos of each. When under the influence of extra oxytocin, each man increased his ratings of the woman he loved, compared to ratings under a placebo, but he did not significantly change ratings of the other women (Scheele et al., 2013). So oxytocin increased love that was already present, but it didn't create new love.

In another study, researchers measured how far away from an attractive woman each man stood, after receiving either oxytocin or a placebo. Unattached men approached the woman equally closely under either condition, but men in a monogamous relationship stood *farther* away after the oxytocin (Scheele et al., 2012). That is, oxytocin apparently enhanced a man's relationship to his partner, increasing his resistance to the temptation of another attractive woman.

What would you guess: Would oxytocin increase conformity to other people's opinions? It depends. Oxytocin increases conformity only to the opinions of people whom you perceive to be like yourself (Stallen, De Dreu, Shalvi, Smidt, & Sanfey, 2012). Would you guess that oxytocin increases trust? In certain economic games, you have the opportunity to invest money in a cooperative venture with someone else, trusting that the other person won't cheat you. In such situations, oxytocin can increase, decrease, or have no effect on your trust, depending on how much you initially liked or disliked the other person (van Ijzendoorn & Bakermans-Kranenburg, 2012).

The effects of oxytocin are not always prosocial. In a threatening situation, oxytocin increases people's attention to possible dangers and heightens their avoidance of strangers (Olff et al., 2013; Poulin, Holman, & Buffone, 2012). People tending to be distrustful in general become even more distrustful under the influence of oxytocin (Bartz et al., 2011).

The apparent pattern is that oxytocin increases attention to social information (Olff et al., 2013). The result is stronger positive responses to people whom you love or trust, but only to those people.

The Binding Problem

We end this module with a theoretical problem that researchers first began to notice around 1990: Vision takes place in one part of your brain, hearing in another, and touch in still another. Those areas do not share much information with one another, nor do they send information to a central location. That is, no "little person in the head" puts it all together. So, when you play a piano, how do you know that the piano you see is also what you hear and feel? When you eat something, how do the taste, smell, and texture combine into a single experience (Stevenson, 2014)? *The question of how separate brain areas combine forces to produce a unified perception of a single object* is the binding problem (Treisman, 1999). The binding problem relates to the mind–brain problem mentioned in Chapter 1.

Part of the answer lies with spatial perception. Consider the piano: If you identify the location of the hand that you feel, the location of the piano you see, and the location of the sound you hear, and all those locations are the same, you link the sensations together. If you cannot locate something in space, you probably won't bind sensations correctly into a single experience. You might look at a yellow lemon and a red tomato and report seeing a yellow tomato and no lemon at all (L. C. Robertson, 2003). People with parietal lobe damage have trouble binding aspects of an experience, because they do not perceive locations accurately (Treisman, 1999; Wheeler & Treisman, 2002). People with intact brains experience the same problem if they see something very briefly while distracted (Holcombe & Cavanagh, 2001).

We also know that binding occurs only for simultaneous events. Have you ever watched a film or television show in which the soundtrack is noticeably

When you watch a movie, the sound seems to come from the actors' mouths. You bind the sound and the action because they are simultaneous.

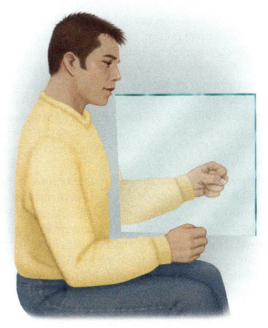

Warner Bros. Pictures/Courtesy Everett Collection

ahead of or behind the picture? If so, you knew that the sound wasn't coming from the performers on screen. You get the same experience watching a poorly dubbed foreign-language film. However, when you watch a ventriloquist, the motion of the dummy's mouth simultaneous with the sound lets you perceive the sound as coming from the dummy.

You can experience a demonstration of binding by trying the following (I. H. Robertson, 2005): Stand or sit by a large mirror as in ▶ Figure 3.28, watching both your right hand and its reflection in the mirror. Hold your left hand out of sight. Then repeatedly clench and unclench both hands, and touch each thumb to your fingers and palm, in unison. You will feel your left hand doing the same thing that you see the hand in the mirror doing. After a couple of minutes, you may start to experience the hand in the mirror as your own left hand. You are binding your touch and visual experiences because they occur at the same time, apparently in the same location. For most people, this procedure is just an amusing demonstration, but for someone who has had an arm amputated, a procedure similar to this helps the person feel an artificial arm as being part of the body.

▲ **Figure 3.28** Move your left and right hands in synchrony while watching the image of one hand in a mirror. Within minutes, you may experience the one in the mirror as being your own hand. This demonstration illustrates how binding occurs.

concept check

19. **What two elements must take place for binding to occur?**

Answer

19. For binding to occur, the brain must be able to identify that different aspects of the stimulus come from the same location. Also, the different aspects must occur simultaneously.

try it yourself

---

in closing | module 3.3

Brain and Experience

The main point of this module is that mind and brain activity are tightly linked—indeed, apparently synonymous. If you lose part of your brain, you lose part of your mind. If you have some mental experience, you simultaneously alter activity in some brain area. If two people's behaviors differ, their brains differ too, in some way.

Another major point is that although different brain areas handle different functions without feeding into a central processor, they still manage to function as an organized whole. We could compare the brain to a flock of birds or a school of fish: It has no leader, but the individuals coordinate their actions to work as a unit anyway. Similarly, brain areas act individually and nevertheless produce a single experience.

Research on brain functioning is challenging because the brain itself is so complex. Just think about all that goes on within this 1.3 kg mass of tissue composed mostly of water. It is an amazing structure.

Summary

- *Two key points.* You use all of your brain, not some percentage of it. Although most people take for granted that their mind is separate from the brain, the evidence points to the contrary: Mind activity and brain activity are the same thing. To lose part of one is to lose part of the other. (page 73)
- *Central and peripheral nervous systems.* The central nervous system consists of the brain and the spinal cord. The peripheral nervous system consists of nerves that communicate between the central nervous system and the rest of the body. (page 73)
- *The cerebral cortex.* The cerebral cortex has four lobes: occipital lobe (vision), temporal lobe (hearing and some aspects of vision), parietal lobe (body sensations), and the frontal lobe (preparation for movement). Damage in the cerebral cortex produces specialized behavioral deficits. (page 74)
- *Hemispheres of the brain.* Each brain hemisphere controls the opposite side of the body. The left hemisphere of the human brain is specialized for language in most people. The right hemisphere is important for understanding spatial relationships and for interpreting emotional expressions. (page 78)
- *Corpus callosum.* The corpus callosum enables the left and right hemispheres of the cortex to communicate with each other. If the corpus callosum is damaged, the two hemispheres cannot share information (page 78)
- *Split-brain patients.* After damage to the corpus callosum, people can describe information only if it enters the left hemisphere. Such people in some ways act as if they have separate fields of consciousness, and in some ways they act as if they are unified. (page 78)
- *Learning about brain functions.* Modern technology enables researchers to develop images showing the structure and activity of various brain areas in living, waking people. Such methods are powerful, but the results should be interpreted with caution. (page 80)
- *Communication between the cerebral cortex and the rest of the body.* Information from the cerebral cortex passes to the medulla and then into the spinal cord. The medulla and spinal cord receive sensory input from the periphery and send output to the muscles and glands. (page 81)
- *Autonomic nervous system and endocrine system.* The autonomic nervous system controls the body's organs, preparing them for emergency activities or for relaxed activities. The endocrine system consists of organs that release hormones into the blood. (page 82)
- *Brain plasticity.* Experiences alter brain connections. Prolonged unusual experiences—such as in musicians who practice many hours a day—change the brain in profound ways. (page 83)
- *Social neuroscience.* Biological mechanisms of social behavior have received increasing attention. The hormone oxytocin enhances love and trust toward people that you already regarded highly. (page 84)
- *The binding problem.* Theoretically, it is problematic to understand how one brain area responsible for vision, another area responsible for hearing, and another area responsible for touch combine forces to yield a unified perception of an object. Binding different senses into one experience requires perceiving the various aspects as occurring in the same place at the same time. (page 84)

Key Terms

amygdala (page 75)

autonomic nervous system (page 82)

binding problem (page 84)

blindsight (page 74)

central nervous system (page 73)

cerebellum (page 82)

cerebral cortex (page 74)

corpus callosum (page 78)

electroencephalograph (EEG) (page 80)

endocrine system (page 82)

epilepsy (page 78)

frontal lobe (page 76)

functional magnetic resonance imaging (fMRI) (page 80)

hemisphere (page 74)

hormone (page 82)

hypothalamus (page 81)

interpreter (page 79)

magnetoencephalograph (MEG) (page 80)

medulla (page 81)

mirror neurons (page 77)

monism (page 73)

occipital lobe (page 74)

oxytocin (page 84)

parietal lobe (page 76)

peripheral nervous system (page 73)

plasticity (page 83)

pons (page 81)

positron-emission tomography (PET) (page 80)

prefrontal cortex (page 77)

primary motor cortex (page 76)

primary somatosensory cortex (page 76)

reflex (page 81)

social neuroscience (page 84)

spinal cord (page 81)

stem cells (page 83)

temporal lobe (page 75)

Review Questions

1. What is meant by "blindsight"?
   (a) The ability of blind people to find their way around by using other senses
   (b) The ability to perceive objects without using any sensory information
   (c) The tendency to see optical illusions, such as thinking one line is longer than another when both are really the same
   (d) The ability to respond to visual stimuli without conscious awareness of those stimuli

2. If someone has trouble recognizing faces despite normal vision in other regards, what is a possible explanation?
   (a) Fewer than average connections from the fusiform gyrus in the left temporal cortex
   (b) Abnormal shape of the eyeball, with one axis longer than the other
   (c) Damage to the primary visual cortex in the occipital cortex of both hemispheres
   (d) Damage to the language areas in the temporal lobe of the left hemisphere

3. In the primary somatosensory cortex in the parietal lobe, the greatest amount of space is devoted to which parts of the body?
   (a) The most sensitive areas, such as the lips and hands
   (b) The areas with the most muscle, especially the arms and legs
   (c) The areas closest to the brain, such as the face and neck
   (d) The areas with the greatest amount of skin, such as the abdomen and back

4. When people moved one finger while they saw someone else move a different finger, certain neurons began responding to both of these events. What does this finding imply about mirror neurons?
   (a) Some mirror neurons develop their properties by learning.
   (b) Mirror neurons make it possible for us to imitate.
   (c) Each mirror neuron corresponds to a different movement.
   (d) Each mirror neuron has a corresponding mirror neuron with similar properties on the opposite side of the brain.

5. After damage to the corpus callosum, a person can describe what he or she feels only after feeling it with the ____ hand, which sends information to the ____ hemisphere.
   (a) left . . . left
   (b) left . . . right
   (c) right . . . left
   (d) right . . . right

6. PET measures ____ and fMRI measures ____.
   (a) electrical activity on the scalp . . . magnetic activity on the scalp
   (b) magnetic activity on the scalp . . . electrical activity on the scalp
   (c) oxygen use in brain areas . . . glucose supply to brain areas
   (d) glucose supply to brain areas . . . oxygen use in brain areas

7. The cerebellum is important for behaviors that require which of the following?
   (a) Prolonged exertion
   (b) Accurate timing
   (c) Reflexive action
   (d) Coordinating vision with hearing

8. Why do many cold remedies interfere with sleep?
   (a) They decrease sympathetic nervous system activity and increase parasympathetic activity.
   (b) They decrease parasympathetic nervous system activity and increase sympathetic activity.
   (c) They increase production of hormones, especially the sex hormones.
   (d) They decrease production of hormones, especially the sex hormones.

9. In what parts of the adult human brain, if any, can new neurons form?
   (a) In all parts of the brain
   (b) Only in the cerebral cortex
   (c) Only in the hippocampus and basal ganglia
   (d) In none of the brain

10. Which of the following defines the binding problem?
    (a) The question of how the brain creates a unified experience from sensations analyzed by separate brain areas
    (b) The question of how a person converts sensory information into motor output
    (c) The question of how the brain compares information in the left hemisphere to information in the right hemisphere
    (d) The question of how people coordinate movement of the left hand with movement of the right hand

Answers: 1d, 2a, 3a, 4a, 5c, 6d, 7b, 8b, 9c, 10a.

After studying this module, you should be able to:

- Outline some of the basic principles of genetics.

- Discuss epigenetics as a mechanism influencing development.

- Explain how researchers estimate heritability.

- Describe the assumptions and goals of evolutionary psychology.

Everyone has tens of thousands of genes that control development. If we could go back in time and change just one of the genes you were born with, how would your experience and personality be different?

Obviously, it depends! *Which* gene? Hundreds of your genes control olfactory receptors. A mutation in one of them would decrease your sensitivity to a few smells, and you might not even notice your deficiency. Mutations in certain other genes would change your life drastically or end it quickly.

The effect of changing a gene also depends on your environment. Suppose you had a gene that magnifies your reactions to stressful experiences. That gene would make a big difference if you live under highly stressful conditions, but much less if you live in calmer circumstances.

It makes no sense to ask whether your behavior depends mainly on heredity or environment. Without either heredity or environment, you could not exist. However, if your behavior differs from someone else's, we can ask whether that difference depends more on differences in heredity or environment. Most behavioral differences depend on differences in both heredity and environment.

The study of genetics has become increasingly important for citizens of the 21st century. Let's first review some basic points about genetics and then explore their application to human behavior.

Genetic Principles

Except for your red blood cells, all of your cells contain a nucleus that includes *strands of hereditary material* called chromosomes (see ▲ Figure 3.29). Each human nucleus has 23 pairs of chromosomes, except that egg and sperm cells have 23 single, unpaired chromosomes. At fertilization, the 23 chromosomes

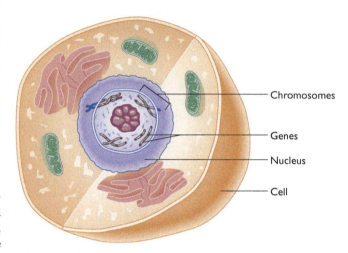

▲ **Figure 3.29** Genes are sections of chromosomes in the nuclei of cells. (Scale is exaggerated for illustration purposes.)

from an egg cell combine with the 23 of a sperm cell to form 23 pairs for the new person (see ▼ Figure 3.30).

Sections along each chromosome, known as genes, *control the chemical reactions that direct development*—for example, those that influence

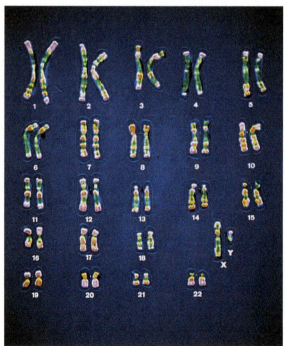

Science Photo Library/Science Source

▲ **Figure 3.30** The nucleus of each human cell contains 46 chromosomes, 23 from the sperm and 23 from the ovum, united in pairs.

Albinos occur in many species, always because of a recessive gene. (**a**) Striped skunk. (**b**) American alligator. (**c**) Mockingbird.

height or hair color. Genes are composed of the chemical DNA, which controls the production of another chemical called RNA, which among other functions controls the production of proteins. The proteins either become part of the body's structure or control the rates of chemical reactions in the body. To explain the concept of genes, educators often use an example such as eye color. If you have either one or two genes for brown eyes, you will have brown eyes because the brown-eye gene is dominant—*that is, a single copy of the gene is sufficient to produce its effect.* The gene for blue eyes is recessive—*its effects appear only if the dominant gene is absent.* You have blue eyes only if you have two genes for blue eyes.

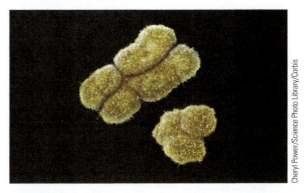

▲ **Figure 3.31** An electron micrograph shows that the X chromosome is longer than the Y chromosome. (From Ruch, 1984)

Sex-Linked and Sex-Limited Genes

Because chromosomes come in pairs (one from the mother and one from the father), you have two of almost all genes. The exceptions are those on the chromosomes that determine whether you developed as a male or as a female. Mammals' sex chromosomes are known as X and Y (see ▶ Figure 3.31). *A female has two X chromosomes* in each cell. *A male has one X chromosome and one Y chromosome.* The mother contributes an X chromosome to each child, and the father contributes either an X or a Y. Because men have one X chromosome and one Y chromosome, they have unpaired genes on these chromosomes. Women have two X chromosomes, but in each cell, one of the X chromosomes is activated and the other is silenced, apparently at random.

Genes located on the X or Y chromosome are known as sex-linked genes. A recessive gene on the X chromosome shows its effects more in men than in women. For example, red-green color deficiency depends on an X-linked recessive gene. A man with that gene on his X chromosome will be red-green deficient because he has no other X chromosome. A woman with that gene probably has a gene for normal color vision on her other X chromosome. Consequently, far more men than women have red-green deficiency (see ▶ Figure 3.32).

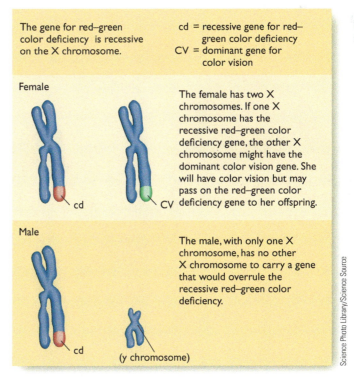

The gene for red–green color deficiency is recessive on the X chromosome.

cd = recessive gene for red–green color deficiency
CV = dominant gene for color vision

Female

The female has two X chromosomes. If one X chromosome has the recessive red–green color deficiency gene, the other X chromosome might have the dominant color vision gene. She will have color vision but may pass on the red–green color deficiency gene to her offspring.

cd   CV

Male

The male, with only one X chromosome, has no other X chromosome to carry a gene that would overrule the recessive red–green color deficiency.

cd   (y chromosome)

▲ **Figure 3.32** Why males are more likely than females to be red-green color deficient.

A *sex-limited gene* occurs equally in both sexes but exerts its effects mainly or entirely in one or the other. For example, both men and women have the genes for facial hair, but men's hormones activate those genes. Both men and women have the genes for breast development, but women's hormones activate those genes.

20. **Suppose a father is red-green deficient and a mother has two genes for normal color vision. What sort of color vision will their children have?**

Answer

20. The sons receive a gene for normal color vision from the mother, and a Y chromosome (irrelevant to color vision) from the father. They will have normal color vision. The daughters receive a gene for normal color vision from the mother and a gene for red-green color deficiency from the father. They will also have normal color vision, but they will be carriers who can pass the red-green deficiency gene to some of their children.

A More Complex View of Genes

To talk about "the gene for" something is convenient at times, but also misleading. Even for the supposedly simple case of eye color, researchers have found at least 10 genes with a significant influence (Liu et al., 2010). Variations in height depend on at least 180 genes as well as the effects of diet, health, and other environmental influences (Allen et al., 2010). We can

barely imagine all the influences on behavior. Furthermore, each gene affects many outcomes, not just eye color, height, or whatever else we happen to have measured.

Furthermore, the nature of a gene is more complicated than we once thought. In some cases, part of one gene overlaps part of another one, or parts of a gene are located in different places. The newly emerging field of epigenetics *deals with changes in gene expression without modification of the DNA sequence* (Tsankova, Renthal, Kumar, & Nestler, 2007). Every cell in your body has the same genes, but the genes active in one cell differ from those active in another, and even within a given cell, a gene can be more active at one time and less at another. For an obvious example, puberty turns on certain genes that had been less active before (Lomniczi et al., 2013). Learning is a less obvious but very important example; when you learn something, you increase activity of certain genes in certain neurons, while decreasing their activity in others (Feng, Fouse, & Fan, 2007). Drug addiction produces epigenetic changes in gene expression in the brain, and so does the feeling of being socially isolated (Sadri-Vakili et al, 2010; Slavich & Cole, 2013).

How does an experience modify genetic activity? Proteins called *histones* wrap the DNA of a chromosome into little balls, as shown in ▼ Figure 3.33. When certain chemicals (called *acetyl* groups) attach to a histone, they loosen the ball and increase the expression of genes in that ball. Other chemicals (called *methyl* groups) can attach to a gene and inactivate it. In short, an experience affects you at once and also alters the way you react to a future event.

In some cases epigenetic changes can extend to later generations. We have long known that changes in the mother's experience can affect her offspring, but the explanation was unclear, because it might relate to either epigenetics or prenatal environment. Studies with laboratory animals have now shown that the father's experience can also affect the offspring, confirming the role of epigenetic changes. For example, exposing male mice to extreme stress alters their own behavior, alters the pattern of RNA in their sperm, and alters the behavior of their offspring (Gapp et al., 2014). Also, after male mice have been fed a high-fat diet, they gain weight, they increase the number of methyl groups on certain genes in their sperm, and their offspring show low sensitivity to

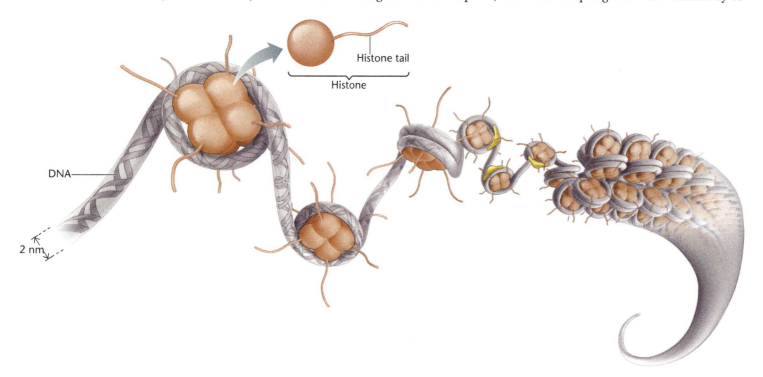

▲ **Figure 3.33** DNA is wrapped into little balls. Attaching or removing certain chemicals from a histone tail can loosen or tighten the ball, thereby increasing or decreasing the expression of genes in that ball.

insulin and a predisposition to diabetes (Ng et al., 2010; Wei et al., 2014). Human studies have also suggested that a man's nutrition can affect the health and life expectancy of his children and grandchildren (Pembrey et al., 2006).

How does an experience lead to epigenetic changes in specific genes, as opposed to some other genes? For that question, we need to await further research. In any case, epigenetics will play an increasingly important role in psychology.

21. Why is it misleading to talk about "the gene" for some behavior or ability?

22. What are the effects of acetyl and methyl groups on a gene?

Answers

21. Almost every aspect of behavior depends on the combined influence of many genes and environmental influences. Also, any gene affects more than one outcome.
22. Acetyl groups loosen a ball of DNA and expose the genes within it to greater expression. Methyl groups attach to a gene and inactivate it.

Estimating Heritability in Humans

All behavior depends on both heredity and environment, but variations might depend more on the variation in genes or variations in the environment. Suppose we want to estimate how much of the variation in some behavior depends on differences in genes. The answer is summarized by the term **heritability**, *an estimate of the variance within a population that is due to heredity*. Heritability ranges from 1, indicating that heredity controls all the variance, to 0, indicating that it controls none of it. For example, red-green color vision deficiency has a heritability of almost 1, whereas which language you speak (such as English or Chinese) has a heritability of 0. Note that the definition of heritability includes the phrase "within a population." For certain characteristics the results for one population might differ from those of another, depending on how much genetic variation each population has, and how much environmental variation. To estimate the heritability of a behavior, researchers have traditionally relied on evidence from twins and adopted children.

23. If our society changed so that it provided an equally good environment for all children, would the heritability of behaviors increase or decrease?

Answer

23. If all children had equally supportive environments, the total amount of variation in behavior would decrease, but whatever variation remained would have to depend largely on heredity (because differences in the environment have been minimized). Therefore heritability would *increase*.

Twin Studies

Monozygotic (mon-oh-zie-GOT-ik) **twins** *develop from a single fertilized egg (zygote) and therefore have identical genes.* Most people call them "identical" twins, but that term is misleading. Some monozygotic twins are mirror images—one right-handed and the other left-handed. It is also possible for various genes to be activated in one twin and suppressed in the other. **Dizygotic** (DIE-zie-GOT-ik) **twins** *develop from two eggs and share only half their genes* (see ▼ Figure 3.34). They are often called "fraternal" twins because they are only as closely related as brother and sister. If dizygotic twins resemble each other almost as much as monozygotic twins do in some trait, then the heritability of that trait is low, indicating that genetic similarity had little influence. If monozygotic twins resemble each other more strongly than dizygotic twins do, then the heritability is probably high. An alternative explanation, valid in some cases, is that monozygotic twins resemble each other so strongly because people treat them the same way.

Researchers also examine pairs of monozygotic twins who grew up in separate environments. Today's adoption agencies place twins in the same family, but in previous times, many twins were adopted separately (see ▼ Figure 3.35). One pair of monozygotic twins, reunited in adulthood after being reared separately, quickly discovered that they had much in common. Both had been named Jim by their adoptive parents. Each liked carpentry and drafting, had built a bench around a tree in his yard, and worked as a deputy sheriff. Both chewed their fingernails, gained weight at the same age, smoked the same brand of cigarettes, drove Chevrolets, and took their vacations in western Florida. Each married a woman named Linda, divorced her, and married a woman named Betty. One had a son named James Alan and the other had a son named James Allen, and each had a pet dog named Toy. It is, of course, difficult to know how many of these similarities are mere coincidences. However, many other sets of twins reunited in adulthood also reported detailed similarities (Lykken, McGue, Tellegen, & Bouchard, 1992).

Researchers examined about 100 pairs of twins, some monozygotic and others dizygotic, who were reared separately and reunited as adults. On the average, the monozygotic twins resembled each other more strongly with regard to hobbies, vocational interests, answers on personality tests, tendency to trust other people, political beliefs, probability

Figure 3.34 Monozygotic twins develop from the same fertilized egg. Dizygotic twins grow from two eggs fertilized by different sperm.

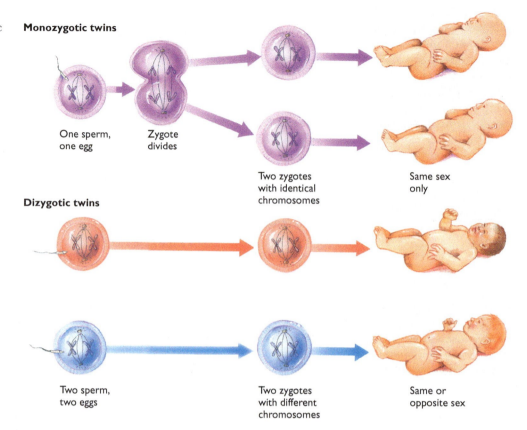

Monozygotic twins

One sperm, one egg

Zygote divides

Two zygotes with identical chromosomes

Same sex only

Dizygotic twins

Two sperm, two eggs

Two zygotes with different chromosomes

Same or opposite sex

▲ **Figure 3.35** Anaïs Bordier and Samantha Futerman were born in Korea and adopted in infancy, one in France and the other in the United States. When one spotted the other on a YouTube video, they connected and discovered many detailed similarities.

of voting, job satisfaction, life satisfaction, probability of mental illness, consumption of coffee and fruit juices, and preference for awakening early in the morning or staying up late at night (Bouchard & McGue, 2003; Cesarini et al., 2008; DiLalla, Carey, Gottesman, & Bouchard, 1996; Fowler, Baker, & Dawes, 2008; Hur, Bouchard, & Eckert, 1998; Hur, Bouchard, & Lykken, 1998; Lykken, Bouchard, McGue, & Tellegen, 1993; McCourt, Bouchard, Lykken, Tellegen, & Keyes, 1999). The implication is that genes influence a wide variety of behaviors.

Studies of Adopted Children

Another kind of evidence for heritability comes from studies of adopted children. Resemblance to their adopting parents implies an environmental influence. Resemblance to their biological parents implies a genetic influence.

However, the results are sometimes hard to interpret. For example, consider the evidence that many adopted children with an arrest record had biological mothers with a criminal history (Mason & Frick, 1994). The resemblance could indicate a genetic influence, but the mothers also provided the prenatal environment. Chances are, many of the mothers with a criminal record smoked, drank alcohol, perhaps used other drugs, and in other ways endangered the fetus's brain development. Prenatal environment is an important influence on development.

concept check

24. **Suppose someone studies adopted children who developed severe depression and finds that many of their biological parents had depression, whereas few of their adopting parents did. One possible interpretation is that genetic factors influence depression more than family environment does. What is another interpretation?**

Answer

24. Perhaps biological mothers who are becoming depressed eat less healthy foods, drink more alcohol, or in some other way impair the prenatal environment of their babies.

Dustin Finkelstein/Getty Images

Examination of Chromosomes

A third type of evidence: Now that biologists have mapped the human genome (the set of all genes on our chromosomes), it is possible to examine the chromosomes and identify genes that are linked to a particular condition. One gene is strongly linked to Huntington's disease. Several genes are linked to increased risk of certain types of cancer.

Researchers have spent enormous efforts seeking a gene that might explain schizophrenia, depression, alcoholism, or other behavioral conditions. They have found many genes that slightly increase the probability of one condition or another, but so far it appears that no important aspect of behavior is strongly related to variations in any single gene. That is, nearly every behavioral variation depends on many genes with small contributions, as well as variations in the environment.

How Genes Influence Behavior

Based on studies of twins and adopted children, researchers have found at least moderate heritability for almost every behavior they have examined, including loneliness (McGuire & Clifford, 2000), neuroticism (Lake, Eaves, Maes, Heath, & Martin, 2000), time spent watching television (Plomin, Corley, DeFries, & Fulker, 1990), and religious devoutness (Waller, Kojetin, Bouchard, Lykken, & Tellegen, 1990). About the only behavior for which researchers have reported zero heritability is choice of religious denomination (Eaves, Martin, & Heath, 1990). That is, genes apparently influence how often you attend religious services but not which services you attend (or don't). How could genes influence this range of behaviors?

Direct and Indirect Influences

In some cases, genes influence behavior by altering development of the brain or sensory receptors. For example, one influence on people's food preferences is the number of taste buds they have on the tongue, largely influenced by genetics. In other cases, genes influence behavior in an indirect manner by altering something outside the nervous system. Consider dietary choices: Almost all infants can digest *lactose,* the sugar in milk. Within a few years, nearly all Asian children and many others lose the ability to digest it. (The loss depends on genes, not on how often people drink milk.) People who cannot digest lactose can enjoy a little milk and more readily enjoy cheese and yogurt, which are easier to digest, but they get gas and cramps if they consume much milk or ice cream (Flatz, 1987; Rozin & Pelchat, 1988). ▼ Figure 3.36 shows how the ability to digest dairy products varies among ethnic groups. The point is that a gene can affect behavior—in this case, preference for dairy products—by altering chemical reactions outside the brain.

Genes also influence behaviors by altering body anatomy. Consider genes that make you unusually good-looking. Because many people smile at you, invite you to parties, and try to become your friend, you develop increased self-confidence and social skills. The genes changed your behavior by changing how other people treated you.

The Multiplier Effect

Imagine you have genes that make you tall, and other genes that help you develop fast running skills. At first you have a slight natural advantage in basketball playing, compared to others your age. Therefore, you get to be on basketball teams, you receive coaching, and your skills improve. As your skills improve, you experience more success and receive further encouragement. What started as a small natural advantage becomes greater and greater as a result of environmental influences as well as genetics. Researchers call this tendency a multiplier effect—*A small initial advantage in some behavior, possibly genetic in origin, alters the environment and magnifies that advantage* (Dickens & Flynn, 2001). The same could occur for almost any aspect of behavior. For example, someone who is inclined to be active and vigorous tends to choose outgoing friends and stimulating social situations. Someone with a more reserved temperament gravitates toward

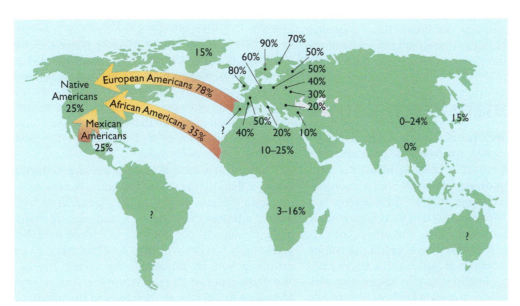

◄ **Figure 3.36** Adult humans vary in their ability to digest lactose, the main sugar in milk. The numbers refer to the percentage of each population's adults that can easily digest lactose. (Based on Flatz, 1987; Rozin & Pelchat, 1988)

quiet activities and smaller social groups. The initial behavioral tendency increases by altering the environment. Thus, it is often difficult to separate the contributions of heredity and environment.

Genes ⟶ Initial tendencies ⟶ Learning and encouragement

Improvements in the behavior

25. **Because of the multiplier effect, should we expect estimates of heritability to be higher for children or for adults?**

Answer

25. In most cases, heritability estimates should be higher for adults. As people grow older, their behavior tendencies alter their environment in ways that increase or exaggerate the initial differences that genes produced.

Environmental Modification of Genetic Effects

Some people assume that if a gene has a strong influence on some behavior, then we can do nothing about it, short of genetic modification. An example that refutes this assumption is phenylketonuria (PKU), *an inherited condition that, if untreated, leads to mental retardation.* About 2 percent of people with European or Asian ancestry, and almost no Africans, have the recessive gene that leads to PKU, but because the gene is recessive, one copy is nearly harmless. People with copies from both parents cannot metabolize *phenylalanine,* a common constituent of proteins. On an ordinary diet, an affected child accumulates phenylalanine in the brain and becomes mentally retarded. However, a diet low in phenylalanine protects the brain. Thus, a special diet prevents a disorder that would otherwise show high heritability.

Evolutionary Psychology

Since ancient times, people have practiced selective breeding. Farmers use the best egg-laying chickens and best milk-producing cows to breed the next generation. People have selectively bred friendly lap dogs, reliable guard dogs, and dutiful sheepherding dogs. We have improved crops by selecting seeds of the best-yielding plants. Maize (American corn) is the product of prolonged selective breeding by Native Americans (Gallavotti et al., 2005; see ▲ Figure 3.37). Charles Darwin's insight was that nature also acts as a selective breeder. If certain kinds of individuals

▲ **Figure 3.37** Many centuries ago, Native Americans selectively bred *teosinte,* a plant with barely edible hard kernels, until they developed what we now know as maize (American corn).

are more successful than others at surviving and reproducing—especially reproducing—then they pass on their genes, and the next generation resembles them more than it does the less successful individuals. Over time, the species as a whole can change. Darwin's preferred term was *descent with modification,* but the concept quickly became known as evolution, defined as *a gradual change in the frequency of various genes from one generation to the next.* Why do you have the genes that you do? Simply, your parents had those genes and survived long enough to reproduce. So did your parents' parents and so on. Any gene that is common in a large population presumably had benefits in the past, though not necessarily today.

Natural selection acts on brain and behavior, just as it does on the rest of the body. For example, the dodo was a large bird in the pigeon/dove family that adapted to life on an island with no mammals. Living without needing to escape enemies, it gradually lost the ability to fly. (Flightless dodos evidently had an advantage by saving energy.) The dodo also lost all fear. When humans eventually came to the island, they hunted the flightless,

▲ **Figure 3.38** Human infants tightly grasp anything in the palm of their hands. In our remote monkey-like ancestors, this reflex helped infants hold onto their mothers.

fearless dodos for meat or for sport, and quickly exterminated them.

Kittiwakes, unlike other members of the gull family, usually breed on the narrow ledges of steep cliffs. Many of their behaviors are adapted to this setting, including the fact that their chicks stay in place until they are old enough to fly (Tinbergen, 1958). Even if they are placed on a safe, flat surface, they remain motionless. On the other hand, the chicks of other gull species start walking around at an early age—even if they are placed on a narrow ledge, like the ones where kittiwakes nest. (They, of course, fall off.) The stationary behavior that is so clearly adaptive for kittiwake chicks is a product of evolution, not learning or reasoning.

It would be easy to cite other examples of animal behavior that have evolved to special circumstances, but what about humans? Have we evolved specializations in our behavior? Some aspects of human behavior make no sense except in the context of evolution. For example, consider the "goose bumps" you get when you are cold. What good do they do for you? None. However, other mammals, with hairier skin, gain an advantage by erecting their hairs when they are cold. Their raised hairs provide extra insulation. Hair erection in a cold environment was useful to your ancient ancestors, and you continue to show that reaction, even though your body hairs are short, usually covered with clothing, and generally useless.

Also consider a human infant's grasp reflex: An infant's hand tightly grasps anything placed into the palm, such as a finger or pencil. This behavior serves no function today, but for our ancient ancestors, it helped an infant hold onto the mother as she traveled (see ▲ Figure 3.38). Again, in humans this behavior makes sense only as an evolutionary carryover.

Evolutionary psychologists try to infer the benefits that favored certain genes and behaviors. Some of the most controversial interpretations pertain to human sexual behavior. For example, in many species throughout the animal kingdom, males seek mating opportunities with multiple partners more vigorously than females seek multiple partners. When we see this tendency in frogs, birds, or lions, an evolutionary explanation seems clear: A male can spread his genes by mating with many females, whereas a female cannot produce more babies by mating with more males. (She might gain some advantage by additional partners, especially if the first male is infertile, but her potential gain is less than a male's.) In humans, too, as shown in ▼ Figure 3.39, more men than women are eager for more than one sexual partner (Schmitt et al., 2003). Many men will accept almost any partner for a short-term sexual relationship, whereas most women either refuse a short-term sexual relationship or accept only a very appealing partner. The proposed evolutionary explanation parallels that for other species (Bjorklund & Shackelford, 1999; Buss, 2000; Gangestad, 2000; Geary, 2000): A man can spread his genes by either of two strategies: He can devote full efforts to helping one woman rear his children, or have sex with many women and hope they can rear the children without his help (Gangestad & Simpson, 2000). Women can gain possible advantages from multiple partners (Hrdy, 2000), but they cannot multiply their number of children by multiplying their number of sex partners.

This interpretation has been controversial. One objection is that it seems to give men an excuse for sexual infidelity. Evolutionary psychologists respond that explaining what *is* does not equal saying what *ought to be*. Pain is also a product of evolution, for example, but we are quite happy to restrain it.

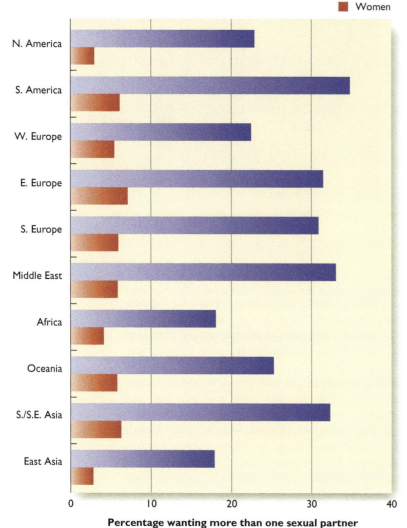

Figure 3.39 legend:
- Men
- Women

Percentage wanting more than one sexual partner

Labels (top to bottom): N. America, S. America, W. Europe, E. Europe, S. Europe, Middle East, Africa, Oceania, S./S.E. Asia, East Asia

x-axis: 0, 10, 20, 30, 40

▲ **Figure 3.39** In all 52 countries that were surveyed, more men than women hoped for more than one sexual partner within the next month. (Source: Based on data of Schmitt et al., 2003)

Another objection is that even if the evolutionary explanation applies to other animal species, it does not necessarily have the same force in humans. With humans, it is harder to separate our presumably innate tendencies from what we have learned (Eagly & Wood, 1999).

Here is another example of a possible evolutionary explanation of a male-female difference: Whom would you prefer for a long-term mating relationship, someone who is more physically attractive, or someone who is more financially successful? Women are more likely than men to prefer the financially successful partner (Buss, 2000). An evolutionary interpretation is that a woman needs a good provider during her time of pregnancy and infant care, when she is limited in her ability to find food and supplies. Therefore, perhaps women evolved to prefer a mate who has this ability. Although this explanation is plausible, it is not convincing. First, the amount of women's preference for a good provider varies considerably among cultures. In countries where women have no economic resources of their own, they prefer a wealthy husband, but where women can get good jobs, they choose a husband for other reasons (Zentner & Mitura, 2012). Second, this tendency is far from universal even among other mammals. In many mammalian species, the male separates from the female after mating and contributes nothing to caring for her or her babies. So if this is an evolved tendency, it had to evolve specifically in humans.

In short, it is important to distinguish between the most convincing evolutionary explanations (such as for goose bumps and infant grasp reflex) and the more speculative interpretations (de Waal, 2002). In many cases, it is easy to propose an evolutionary explanation and more difficult to test it.

concept check

26. **What explanation do evolutionary psychologists offer for the human infant's grasp reflex?**

Answer

26. Although the reflex is useless for humans, it was important to ancestral species in which infants had to cling to their mothers while the mothers were walking.

Genes and Experience

Physicists say that the development of the universe depended on its "initial conditions"—the array of matter and energy a fraction of a second after the "big bang." The outcome of any experiment in physics or chemistry depends on the initial conditions—the type of matter, its temperature and pressure, and so forth. You had initial conditions, too—your genes. Understanding your genes is important for understanding why you developed differently from someone else, but it would not be enough. Your genes influence how you react to your environment, and your environment activates certain genes and inactivates others. In this module we have explored just a little of the complex ways in which genes interact with experiences.

Summary

- *Genes.* Genes control heredity. A recessive gene exerts its effects only in someone with two copies of the gene per cell. A dominant gene exerts its effects even if one has only a single copy per cell. (page 88)
- *Sex-linked and sex-limited genes.* Genes on the X or Y chromosome are sex linked. An X-linked recessive gene will show its effects more frequently in males than in females. A sex-limited gene is present in both sexes, but it affects one more than the other. (page 89)
- *Epigenetics.* Experiences can modify the expression of genes. (page 90)
- *Heritability.* Researchers estimate heritability by comparing monozygotic and dizygotic twins, by comparing twins reared in separate environments, by examining how adopted children resemble their biological parents, and by finding associations between particular genes and observed outcomes. (page 91)
- *How genes affect behavior.* Genes affect behaviors by altering the chemistry of the brain. They also exert indirect effects by influencing other organs that in turn influence behavior. (page 93)
- *Multiplier effect.* If a gene promotes an advantage in some aspect of behavior, the individual may practice that behavior in ways that multiply the initial slight advantage. (page 93)
- *Environmental modification of genetic effects.* A change in the environment can alter or cancel what would otherwise be a major genetic effect. The phenylketonuria gene would lead to mental retardation, but a special diet minimizes its effects. (page 94)
- *Evolution.* Genes that increase the probability of survival and reproduction become more common in the next generation. (page 94)
- *Evolution of behavior.* Many examples of animal behavior can be explained as evolutionary adaptations to a particular environment or way of life. (page 94)
- *Evolution of human behavior.* Certain aspects of human behavior, such as the infant grasp reflex, make no sense except as an evolutionary carryover from ancestors for whom the behavior was useful. However, it is important to distinguish between convincing evolutionary explanations and speculative explanations that await further research. (page 95)

Key Terms

chromosome (page 88)	gene (page 88)	recessive (page 89)
dizygotic twins (page 91)	heritability (page 91)	sex-limited gene (page 90)
dominant (page 89)	monozygotic twins (page 91)	sex-linked gene (page 89)
epigenetics (page 90)	multiplier effect (page 93)	X chromosome (page 89)
evolution (page 94)	phenylketonuria (PKU) (page 94)	Y chromosome (page 89)

Review Questions

1. What is meant by a "sex-limited" gene?
   (a) A gene that exerts its effects only or mainly on one sex or the other
   (b) A gene that occurs on the X chromosome
   (c) A gene that occurs on the Y chromosome
   (d) A gene that occurs on either the X or Y chromosome

2. In what way does the field of epigenetics blur the distinction between hereditary effects and environmental effects?
   (a) In epigenetics, some gene causes a change in the environment.
   (b) In epigenetics, a particular environment alters behavior only for someone with a particular gene.

(c) In epigenetics, the effects of a gene multiply by the effects of the environment.

(d) Epigenetic changes are alterations in gene expression caused by environmental influences.

3. How do monozygotic twins differ from dizygotic twins?
   (a) Monozygotic twins develop from a single fertilized egg, whereas dizygotic twins develop from two eggs.
   (b) Dizygotic twins develop from a single fertilized egg, whereas monozygotic twins develop from two eggs.
   (c) Monozygotic twins are the same sex, whereas dizygotic twins are of different sexes.
   (d) Dizygotic twins are the same sex, whereas monozygotic twins are of different sexes.

4. Researchers estimate heritability of a behavior by examining three types of evidence. Which of the following is NOT one of those types?
   (a) Differences among cultures
   (b) Examination of chromosomes
   (c) Comparisons between monozygotic and dizygotic twins
   (d) Comparisons of adopted children to their biological and adopting parents

5. Genes influence people's likelihood of drinking milk by controlling which of these?
   (a) Taste buds on the tongue
   (b) Ability to metabolize lactose

(c) Pleasure areas in the brain
(d) Stomach contractions

6. Observations about phenylketonuria provide evidence *against* which of the following statements?
   (a) A single gene can have a major effect on behavior.
   (b) Behaviors depend on both genetic and environmental influences.
   (c) Most children's temperament is consistent over long periods of time.
   (d) If something is under genetic control, it is fixed and unchangeable.

7. What explanation do evolutionary psychologists offer for the "goose bumps" we get when we are cold?
   (a) Activity of the sympathetic nervous system erects the skin's hairs.
   (b) For our ancient ancestors, hair erection increased insulation.
   (c) Goose bumps increase our probability of attracting a mate.
   (d) Goose bumps may be useful at some time in the future.

Answers: 1a, 2d, 3a, 4a, 5b, 6d, 7b.

4 Sensation and Perception

Olivy/Shutterstock.com

When my son Sam was 8 years old, he asked me, "If we went to some other planet, would we see different colors?" He meant colors that were as different from familiar colors as yellow is from red or blue. I told him that would be impossible, and I tried to explain why. No matter where we go in outer space, we could never experience a color, sound, or other sensation that would be fundamentally different from what we experience on Earth. Different combinations, perhaps, but not fundamentally different sensory experiences.

Three years later, Sam told me he wondered whether people who look at the same thing are all having the same experience: When different people look at something and call it "green," how can we know whether they are having the same experience? I agreed that there is no way to be sure.

Why am I certain that colors on a different planet would look the same as on Earth but uncertain whether colors look the same to different people here? If the answer isn't clear to you, perhaps it will be after you read this chapter.

Sensation is the *conversion of energy from the environment into a pattern of response by the nervous system*. It is the registration of information. **Perception** is *the interpretation of that information.* For example, light rays striking your eyes produce sensation. Your experience of recognizing your roommate is a perception. In practice, the distinction between sensation and perception is often difficult to make.

A. Gragera/Latin Stock/Science Source

No matter how exotic some other planet might be, it could not have colors we do not have here. The reason is that our eyes can see only certain wavelengths of light, and color is the experience our brains create from those wavelengths.

module 4.1

Vision

After studying this module, you should be able to:

- Remember that vision occurs because light strikes the retina.
- Identify the structures of the eye.
- Explain how the route from the receptors to the brain produces a blind spot.
- Explain why vision in the fovea differs from that in the periphery.
- Outline the processes necessary for dark adaptation.
- Compare and contrast three theories of color vision.

Around 1990, someone at the University of Michigan asked every academic department to offer one question that they thought every student should be able to answer before graduation. That is, it was so important that if you cannot answer it, you shouldn't get your diploma, regardless of your major.

One of the most impressive questions came from the chemistry department: Suppose in the middle of a well-insulated, airtight room, you plug in a refrigerator with its door wide open. Will the result be to cool the room, heat the room, or have no effect on room temperature? (Think about it and answer before you read further.)

To answer, you have to know that a refrigerator doesn't create coldness; it moves heat from its inside to the outside. Then compare the heat added on the outside to the heat removed from the inside. For the two to break even, the refrigerator would have to operate at 100 percent efficiency, and to cool the room, it would have to operate at more than 100 percent efficiency. One of the most important physical principles is that every machine wastes some energy. Therefore, the refrigerator will heat the room. Another way to think about it: The refrigerator uses electricity. Using electricity always generates some heat. That question requires an application of the principles of entropy, or the second law of thermodynamics, an important concept even if you don't know the term itself.

By contrast to chemistry's clever question, the psychology department asked, "What is the current definition of psychology?" How embarrassing. After all the research we have done, we have nothing better to offer the world than a definition of ourselves?

Here is a better question. It doesn't represent all of psychology, and it may seem simple-minded, but it's a question that certainly every educated person should be able to answer: What enables you to see something? Do you see because light enters your eyes, or do you send out sight rays?

The correct answer is that light enters your eyes. When you see a tree, your perception of the tree is in your head, not in the tree. If you *did* send sight rays that struck an object, you wouldn't know about it, unless those rays bounced back into your eyes. However, a survey found that one-third of college students believed they sent out sight rays (Winer & Cottrell, 1996; Winer, Cottrell, Gregg, Fournier, & Bica, 2002).

The discovery of how vision works was the first research discovery in psychology (Steffens, 2007). About a thousand years ago, the Islamic scholar Ibn al-Haytham reasoned that people see the stars as soon as they open their eyes, and it is implausible that sight rays would travel that fast to something so distant. Further, he demonstrated that when light strikes an object, a viewer sees only the light rays that reflect directly to the viewer's eyes.

In addition to the idea of sight rays, people have other misconceptions about vision. We are often led astray because we imagine that what we see is a copy of the outside world. It is not. Just as a computer translates a sight or sound into a series of 1s and 0s, your brain *translates* stimuli into very different representations.

1. How far can an ant see?

Answer

1. Ants, like any other animal, see as far as the light travels. (Presumably they can see the sun at a distance of 93 million miles or 150 million kilometers.) How far anyone can see has nothing to do with the eyes, if the eyes work at all.

Detecting Light

Sensation is the detection of stimuli—*energies from the world around us that affect us in some way.* Our eyes, ears, and other sensory organs are packed with receptors—*specialized cells that convert environmental energies into signals for the nervous system.*

What we call *light* is part of the electromagnetic spectrum, *the continuum of all frequencies of radiated energy,* from gamma rays and X-rays with very short wavelengths, through ultraviolet, visible light, and infrared, to radio and TV transmissions with very long wavelengths (see ▼ Figure 4.1). Light is visible only because our receptors respond to wavelengths from 400 to 700 nanometers (nm). With different receptors, we would see a different range of wavelengths. Many insects and birds, in fact, see ultraviolet wavelengths that we do not.

The Structures of the Eye

When we see something, light reflected from the object passes through the pupil, an *adjustable opening that widens and narrows to control the amount of light entering the eye.* The iris, the *colored structure on the surface of the eye surrounding the pupil,* is what we describe when we say someone has brown, green, or blue eyes.

Light passing through the pupil travels through the *vitreous humor* (a clear jellylike substance) to strike the retina, *a layer of visual receptors covering the back surface of the eyeball.* The cornea and the lens focus the light on the retina, as shown in ▼ Figure 4.2. The cornea, *a rigid transparent structure* on the surface of the eyeball, always focuses light in the same way. The **lens**, *a flexible structure that varies its thickness,* enables **accommodation of the lens**—that is, *you adjust its focus for objects at different distances.* When you focus on a distant object, your eye muscles relax and let the lens become thinner and flatter, as shown in ▼ **Figure 4.3a**. When you focus on a close object, your eye muscles tighten and make the lens thicker and rounder (see ▼ **Figure 4.3b**).

The **fovea** (FOE-vee-uh), *the central area of the human retina,* is adapted for detailed vision (see Figure 4.2). Of all retinal areas, the fovea has the greatest density of receptors. Also, more of the cerebral cortex is devoted to analyzing input from the fovea than input from other areas.

Hawks, owls, and other predatory birds have a greater density of receptors on the top of the retina (for looking down) than on the bottom of the retina (for looking up). When they fly, this arrangement lets them see the ground beneath them in detail. When on the ground, however, they have trouble seeing above themselves (see ▼ **Figure 4.4**).

Some common disorders of vision are described in ■ **Table 4.1**.

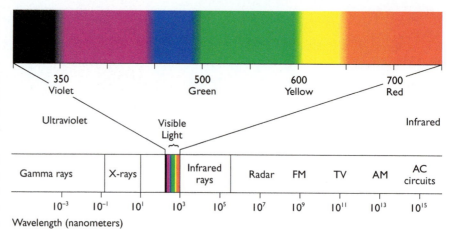

▲ **Figure 4.1** Visible light is a small part of the electromagnetic spectrum. We see these wavelengths because our receptors respond to them.

concept check

2. **As people grow older, the lens becomes more rigid. How would that rigidity affect vision?**

Answer

2. Because the lens is more rigid, older people are less able to change their focus for objects at different distances. In particular, they find it difficult to focus on nearby objects.

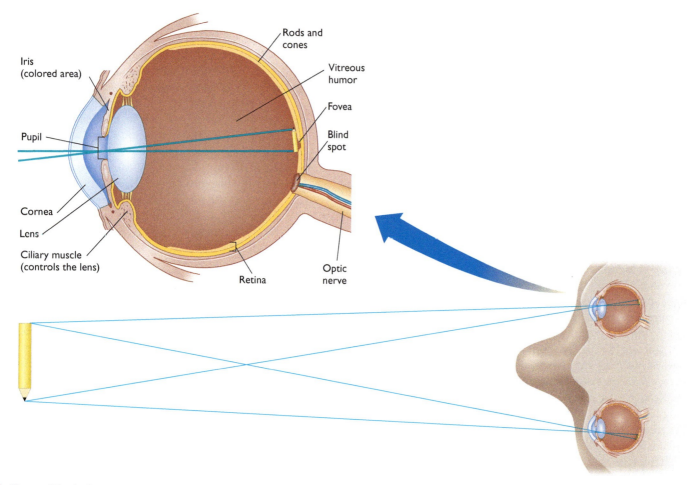

▲ **Figure 4.2** The lens gets its name from the Latin word *lens,* meaning "lentil." This reference to its shape is an appropriate choice, as this cross-section of the eye shows. The names of other parts of the eye also refer to their appearance.

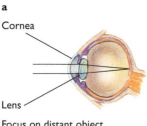

Cornea

Lens

Focus on distant object
(lens thin)

b

Cornea

Lens

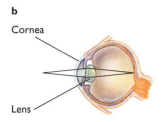

Focus on close object
(lens thick)

▲ **Figure 4.3** The flexible, transparent lens changes shape so that objects (**a**) far and (**b**) near can come into focus. The lens bends entering light rays so that they fall on the retina.

© Chase Swift Photography

▲ **Figure 4.4** Birds of prey, such as these owlets, can see down much more clearly than up. In flight that arrangement is helpful. On the ground, they have to turn their heads almost upside down to look up.

The Visual Receptors

The retina's two types of visual receptors, cones and rods, differ in function and appearance, as ▼ **Figure 4.5** shows. The **cones** are *adapted for perceiving color and detail in bright light*. The **rods** are *adapted for vision in dim light*.

Of the visual receptors in the human retina, about 5 percent are cones. Although 5 percent may not sound like much, the cone-rich parts of the retina send more axons to the brain than do the rod-rich areas, and cone responses dominate the human visual cortex. Most birds also have many cones and good color vision. Species that are active at night—rats and mice, for example—have mostly rods.

The proportion of cones rises toward the center of the retina. The fovea consists solely of cones (see Figure 4.2). Toward the periphery, the proportion of rods increases sharply, and color vision becomes weaker.

Try this experiment: Hold several pens or pencils of different colors behind your back. (Any objects will work if they are similar in size, shape, and brightness.) Pick one without looking at it. Hold it behind your head and bring it slowly into your field of vision, while focusing your eyes straight ahead. When you begin to see the object, you will probably not see its color.

try it yourself

Table 4.1 Common Disorders of Vision	
Disorder	
Presbyopia	Impaired ability to focus on nearby objects because of decreased flexibility of the lens
Myopia	Nearsightedness—impaired ability to focus on distant objects because of the shape of the eyeball
Hyperopia	Farsightedness—impaired ability to focus on close objects because of the shape of the eyeball
Glaucoma	Damage to the optic nerve, usually caused by increased pressure in the eyeball
Cataract	A disorder in which the lens becomes cloudy

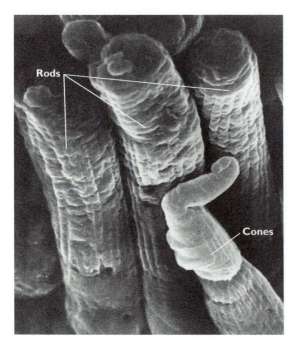

▲ **Figure 4.5** Rods and cones seen through a scanning electron micrograph. The rods, numbering more than 120 million in humans, enable vision in dim light. The 6 million cones in the retina distinguish gradations of color in bright light. (Reprinted from "Scanning electron microscopy of vertebrate visual receptors," by E. R. Lewis, F. S. Werb, & Y. Y. Zeevi, 1969. *Brain Research, 15,* pp. 559–562. Copyright 1969, with permission from Elsevier.)

Rods are more effective than cones for detecting dim light for two reasons: First, a rod responds to faint stimulation more than a cone does. Second and more importantly, the rods pool their resources. Only one or a few cones converge messages onto the next cell, called a *bipolar cell,* whereas many rods converge their messages. In the far periphery of the retina, more than 100 rods send messages to a bipolar cell (see ▶ Figure 4.6). ■ Table 4.2 summarizes differences between rods and cones.

3. **Why is it easier to see a faint star in the sky if you look slightly to the side of the star instead of straight at it?**

Answer

3. The center of the retina has only cones. If you look slightly to the side, light falls on a retinal area with more rods, which respond better to faint light. Also, in the periphery, more receptors converge their output onto the next cell.

Dark Adaptation

Suppose you go into a basement at night looking for a flashlight. The only light bulb is burned out. Just a little moonlight comes through the basement

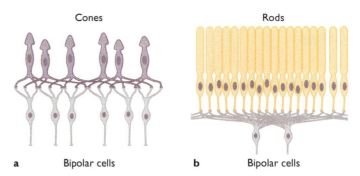

Cones   Rods

a   Bipolar cells   b   Bipolar cells

▲ **Figure 4.6** Because so many rods converge their output to the next layer of the visual system, known as bipolar cells, even a little light falling on the rods stimulates a bipolar cell. Thus, the periphery of the retina, with many rods, readily detects faint light. However, because bipolar cells in the periphery get input from so many receptors, they have only imprecise information about the location and shape of objects.

windows. At first, you see hardly anything, but as time passes, your vision gradually improves. *Gradual improvement in the ability to see in dim light* is called dark adaptation.

Here is the mechanism: Exposure to light chemically alters molecules called *retinaldehydes,* thereby stimulating the visual receptors. (Retinaldehydes are derived from vitamin A.) Under moderate light the receptors *regenerate* (rebuild) the molecules about as fast as the light keeps breaking them down. In dim light, receptors regenerate their molecules without competition, improving your detection of faint light.

Cones and rods adapt at different rates. When you enter a dark place, your cones regenerate their retinaldehydes first, but by the time the rods finish, the rods are more sensitive to faint light than the cones are. At that point, you see mostly with rods.

Here is how a psychologist demonstrates dark adaptation (E. B. Goldstein, 2007): You enter a room that is completely dark except for a tiny flashing light. You use a knob to adjust the light so that you barely see it. Over 3 or 4 minutes, you gradually decrease the intensity of the light, as shown in ▼ Figure 4.7a. Note that a decrease in the intensity of the light indicates increased sensitivity of your eyes. If you stare straight at the point of light, your results demonstrate the adaptation of your cones to the dim light. (You are focusing the light on your fovea, which has no rods.)

Now the psychologist repeats the study with a change in procedure: You stare at a faint light while another light flashes to the side, where it stimulates rods as well as cones. You adjust a knob until the flashing light in the periphery is

Table 4.2 Differences between Rods and Cones

	Rods	Cones
Shape	Nearly cylindrical	Tapered at one end
Prevalence in human retina	95 percent	5 percent
Abundant in	All vertebrate species	Species active during the day
Area of the retina	Toward the periphery	Toward the fovea
Important for color vision?	No	Yes
Important for detail?	No	Yes
Important in dim light?	Yes	No
Number of types	Just one	Three

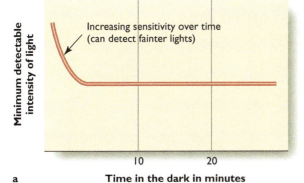

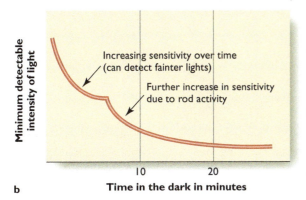

▲ Figure 4.7 These graphs show dark adaptation to **(a)** a light you stare at directly, using only cones, and **(b)** a light in your peripheral vision, which you see with both cones and rods. (Based on E. B. Goldstein, 1989)

barely visible. (**▲ Figure 4.7b**.) During the first 7 to 10 minutes, the results are the same as before. But then your rods become more sensitive than your cones, and you begin to see even fainter lights. Your rods continue to adapt over the next 20 minutes or so.

To demonstrate dark adaptation without any apparatus, try this: At night, turn on one light in your room. Close one eye and cover it tightly with your hand for a minute or more. Your covered eye will adapt to the dark while your open eye remains adapted to the light. Then turn off the light and open both eyes. You will see better with your dark-adapted eye than with the light-adapted eye. (This instruction assumes you still have some faint light coming through a window. In a *completely* dark room, of course, you see nothing.)

concept check

4. After you have thoroughly adapted to extremely dim light, will you see more objects in your fovea or in the periphery of your eye?

Answer

4. You will see more objects in the periphery. The fovea contains only cones, which do not become as sensitive as the rods in the periphery.

The Visual Pathway

If you or I were designing an eye, we would probably run connections from the receptors directly back to the brain. Although that route sounds logical, it is not how your eyes actually work. The visual receptors send their impulses *away from* the brain, toward the center of the eye, where they contact neurons called bipolar cells. *The bipolar cells contact still other neurons,* the **ganglion cells**. *The axons from the ganglion cells join to form* the **optic nerve**, *which turns around and exits the eye,* as **▼ Figures** 4.2 and 4.8 show. Half of each optic nerve crosses to the opposite side of the brain at the optic chiasm (KI-az-m). Most of the optic nerve goes to the thalamus, which sends information to the primary visual cortex in the occipital lobe. Some people have up to three times as many axons in their optic nerve as others have. Those with thicker optic nerves are better at detecting faint lights and tiny movements (Andrews, Halpern, & Purves, 1997; Halpern, Andrews, & Purves, 1999).

The *retinal area where the optic nerve exits* is called the **blind spot**. That part of the retina has no room for receptors because the exiting axons take up all the space. Also, blood vessels enter the eye at this point. Ordinarily, you are unaware of your blind spot.

To illustrate, close your left eye and stare at the center of **▼ Figure 4.9**; then slowly move the page forward and backward. When your eye is about 25 to 30 cm (10 to 12 inches) away from the page, the lion disappears because it falls into your blind spot. In its place you perceive a continuation of the circle.

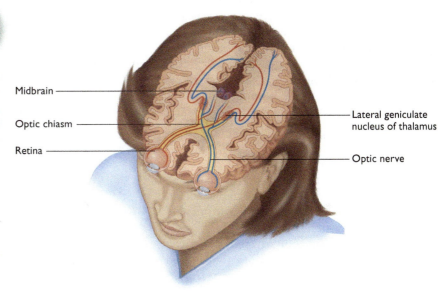

Midbrain

Optic chiasm

Retina

Lateral geniculate nucleus of thalamus

Optic nerve

▲ Figure 4.8 Axons from ganglion cells in the retina depart the eye at the blind spot and form the optic nerve. In humans, about half the axons in the optic nerve cross to the opposite side of the brain at the optic chiasm.

▶ **Figure 4.9** Close your left eye and focus your right eye on the animal trainer. Move the page toward your eyes and away from them until the lion on the right disappears. At that point, the lion is focused on the blind spot of your retina, where you have no receptors.

Color Vision

How does the visual system convert wavelengths of light into a perception of color? The process begins with three kinds of cones. Later, cells in the visual path code this wavelength information in terms of pairs of opposites—red versus green, yellow versus blue, and white versus black. Finally, cells in the cerebral cortex compare the input from various parts of the visual field to synthesize a color experience. Let's examine these stages in turn.

The Trichromatic Theory

Thomas Young was an English physician of the 1700s who, among other accomplishments, helped to decode the Rosetta stone (making it possible to understand Egyptian hieroglyphics), introduced the modern concept of energy, revived and popularized the wave theory of light, showed how to calculate annuities for insurance, and offered the first theory about how people perceive color (Martindale, 2001). His theory, elaborated and modified by Hermann von Helmholtz in the 1800s, came to be known as the **Young-Helmholtz**

theory, or the **trichromatic theory**. (*Trichromatic* means "three colors.") Phrased in modern terms, it says that *color vision depends on the relative responses of three types of cones* (see ▼ Figure 4.10). One type is most sensitive

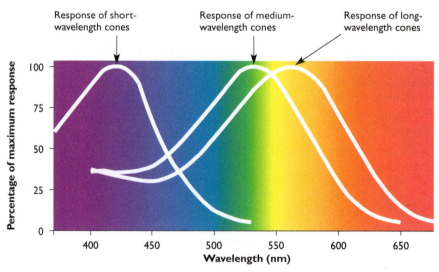

▲ **Figure 4.10** Sensitivity of three types of cones to different wavelengths of light. (Based on data of Bowmaker & Dartnall, 1980)

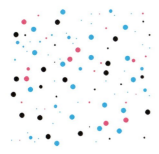

▲ **Figure 4.11** Blue dots look black unless they cover enough area. Count the red dots; then count the blue dots. Try again while standing farther from the page. You will probably count as many red dots as before but fewer blue dots.

to short wavelengths (which we generally see as blue), another to medium wavelengths (green), and another to long wavelengths (red). Every wavelength of light produces its own distinct ratio of responses by the three kinds of cones. White light excites all three kinds equally. From the ratio among the three types of cones, the brain determines color.

Young and Helmholtz proposed their theory long before anatomists confirmed the existence of three types of cones (Wald, 1968). Helmholtz found that observers could mix various amounts of three wavelengths of light to match all other colors. (Mixing lights is different from mixing paints. Mixing yellow and blue *paints* produces green; mixing yellow and blue *lights* produces white.)

The short-wavelength cones, which respond most strongly to blue, are the least numerous. For the retina to detect blueness, the blue must extend over a somewhat larger area than other colors. ▲ **Figure 4.11** illustrates this effect.

concept check

5. If the medium- and long-wavelength cones are about equally active, while the short-wavelength cones are much less active, what do you see?

Answer

5. You see yellow. Check Figure 4.10.

The Opponent-Process Theory

Young and Helmholtz were right about how many cones we have, but our perception of color has features that the trichromatic theory does not handle easily. For example, if you stare for a minute or so at something red and look away, you

see a green afterimage. If you stare at something green, yellow, or blue, you see a red, blue, or yellow afterimage. To account for these afterimages, a 19th-century scientist, Ewald Hering, proposed the **opponent-process theory** of color vision: *We perceive color in terms of paired opposites—red versus green, yellow versus blue, and white versus black.* To illustrate, please follow the instructions in ▼ **Figure 4.12**.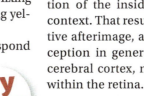

When you looked away, you saw the logo in its normal coloration. After staring at an image, you replace blue with yellow, yellow with blue, red with green, green with red, white with black, and black with white. *Experiences of one color after the removal of another* are called **negative afterimages**.

Presumably, the explanation depends on cells somewhere in the nervous system that increase their activity in the presence of, say, blue, and decrease it in the presence of yellow. Then after you have stared at something blue, these cells become fatigued and decrease their response. Your brain then interprets the decrease as the color yellow. We could imagine such cells in the retina itself, but here is an observation that argues against that interpretation: Stare at the center of ▼ **Figure 4.13** for a minute or more, and then look at a white surface. The afterimage you see is red on the outside, as expected. But you see *green,* not gray or black, for the inside circle. Your perception of the inside depends on the surrounding context. That result strongly implies that the negative afterimage, and indeed color perception in general, depends on the cerebral cortex, not just interactions within the retina.

▲ **Figure 4.12** Stare at any one point that you choose under a bright light for a minute. Don't move your eyes. Then look at a white page and you will see the golden arches.

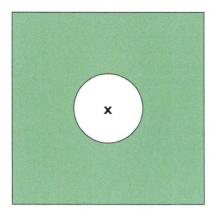

▲ **Figure 4.13** Stare at the center for a minute or more and then look at a white surface. What color do you see in the center?

6. **The negative afterimage that you created by staring at Figure 4.12 may seem to move against the background. Why doesn't it stay in one place?**

Answer

6. The afterimage is on your eye, not on the background. When you try to focus on a different part of the afterimage, you move your eyes and the afterimage moves with them.

The Retinex Theory

What you see at any point in space depends on more than the object itself. It depends on contrast with the objects around it. Brightness contrast *is the increase or decrease in an object's apparent brightness by comparison to objects around it.* In ▼ Figure 4.14, the pink bars on the right probably look darker than those on the left, but in fact, they are the same. The brain uses its past experience to calculate how that pattern of light probably was generated, taking into account all the contextual information (Purves, Williams, Nundy, & Lotto, 2004). In Figure 4.14, you see what appears to

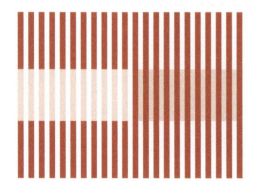

▲ **Figure 4.14** The pink bars in the left center area are in fact the same as the pink bars in the right center area, but those on the left seem lighter.

▲ **Figure 4.15** (a) When the block is under yellow light (left) or blue light (right), you still recognize the colors of individual squares. Parts **b** and **c** show what happens if we remove the context: The "blue" squares in the left half of part **a** and the "yellow" squares in the right half are actually the same as each other, and gray. (From *Why we see what we do,* by D. Purves and R. B. Lotto, Figure 6.10, p. 134. Copyright 2003 Sinauer Associates, Inc. Reprinted by permission.)

be a partly clear white bar covering the center of the left half of the grid, and the pink bars look light. In the corresponding section to the right, the pink bars appear to be under the red bars and on top of a white background. Here the pink looks darker because you contrast the pink against the white background above and below it.

Color perception also depends on contrast. Suppose you look at a large white screen illuminated with green light in an otherwise dark room. How would you know whether this is a white screen illuminated with green light or a green screen illuminated with white light? Or a blue screen illuminated with yellow light? You wouldn't know. Now someone wearing a brown shirt and blue jeans stands in front of the screen. Suddenly, you see the shirt as brown, the jeans as blue, and the screen as white, even though all the objects are reflecting mostly green light. You perceive color by comparing the light one object reflects to the light that other objects reflect. That is, the apparent color of an object depends on the objects surrounding it.

In contrast, suppose you take a complex array of objects and shine yellow light on them, or shine blue light on them. Even though everything is now yellowish or bluish, you have no difficulty perceiving which objects are red, green, yellow, blue, black, or white. This *tendency of an object to appear nearly the same color under a variety of lighting conditions* is called color constancy (see ▲ Figure 4.15).

In response to such observations, Edwin Land (the inventor of the Polaroid Land camera) proposed the retinex theory. According to this theory, *the cerebral cortex compares the patterns of light coming from different parts of the retina and synthesizes a color perception for each area* (Land, Hubel, Livingstone, Perry, & Burns, 1983; Land & McCann, 1971). (*Retinex* is a combination of the words *retina* and *cortex.*)

As Figure 4.15 emphasizes, we should not call short-wavelength light "blue" or long-wavelength light "red." A gray square can look blue in one context and yellow in another (Lotto & Purves, 2002; Purves & Lotto, 2003). Color is something our brain constructs, not a property of the light itself.

Each of the trichromatic, opponent-process, and retinex theories is correct with regard to certain aspects of vision. The trichromatic states that human color vision starts with three kinds of cones. The opponent-process theory explains how later cells organize color information. The retinex theory notes that the cerebral cortex compares color information from various parts of the visual field.

Color Vision Deficiency

Centuries ago, people assumed that anyone who was not blind could see and recognize colors (Fletcher & Voke, 1985). Then during the 1600s, the phenomenon of color vision deficiency (or color-blindness) was unambiguously recognized. Here was the first indication that color vision is a function of our eyes and brains and not just of the light itself.

The older term color-*blindness* is misleading because very few people are totally unable to distinguish colors. About 8 percent of men and less than 1 percent of women have difficulty distinguishing red from green (Bowmaker, 1998). The cause is a recessive gene on the X chromosome. Because men have only one X chromosome, they need just one gene to become red-green color deficient. Women, with two X chromosomes, need two such genes to develop the condition. Red-green color-deficient people have only the short-wavelength cone and either the long-wavelength or the medium-wavelength cone (Fletcher & Voke, 1985).

▶ Figure 4.16 gives a crude but usually satisfactory test for red-green color vision deficiency. What do you see in each part of the figure?

How does the world look to people with color vision deficiency? They describe the world with the usual color words: Roses are red, bananas are yellow, and grass is green. But their answers do not mean that they perceive colors the same as other people do. Certain rare individuals are red-green color deficient in one eye but have normal vision in the other eye. Because they know

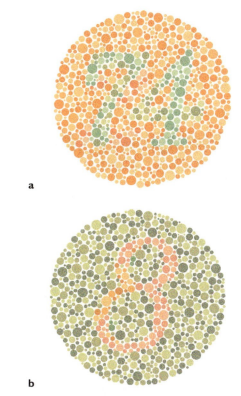

a

b

▲ **Figure 4.16** These items provide an informal test for red-green color vision deficiency. What do you see? Compare your answers to answer A on page 110.

what the color words really mean (from experience with their normal eye), they can describe what their deficient eye sees. They say that objects that look red or green to the normal eye look yellow or yellow-gray to the other eye (Marriott, 1976).

If you have normal color vision, ▼ Figure 4.17 will show you what it is like to be color deficient. First, cover part b, a typical item from a color deficiency test, and stare at part a, a red field, under a bright light for about a minute. (The brighter the light and the longer you stare, the greater the effect will be.) Then look at part b. Staring at the red field fatigued your long-wavelength cones, weakening your red sensation.

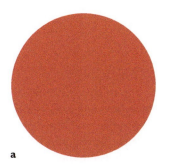

a

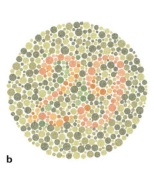

b

c

◀ **Figure 4.17** First, stare at pattern (**a**) under bright light for about a minute and then look at (**b**). What do you see? Next stare at (**c**) for a minute and look at (**b**) again. Now what do you see? See answer B on page 110.

Now stare at part c, a green field, for about a minute and look at part b again. Because you have fatigued your green cones, the figure in b will stand out even more strongly than usual. In fact, certain people with red-green color deficiency may be able to see the number in b after staring at c.

Color vision deficiency illustrates a more general point. Before people knew about color vision deficiency, they easily assumed that the world looked the same to everyone. Still today it is easy to assume that everything tastes the same and smells the same to other people as it does to you. As you will learn in the next module, that assumption is untrue.

in closing | module 4.1

Vision as an Active Process

Before the existence of people or other color-sighted animals on Earth, was there any color? *No.* Light was present, to be sure, and different objects reflected different wavelengths of light, but color exists only in brains.

Your brain does an enormous amount of processing to determine what you are seeing. Imagine building a robot with

vision. Light strikes the robot's visual sensors, and then . . . what? How will the robot know what objects it sees or what to do about them? All those processes—which are so difficult to mimic in a robot—happen in your brain in a fraction of a second.

Summary

- *How vision works.* Vision occurs when light rays strike the retina at the back of the eye, causing cells to send messages to the brain. We do not send sight rays out of the eyes. (page 101)
- *Light.* Light is the part of the electromagnetic spectrum that excites receptors in the eyes. If we had different types of receptors, we would define other wavelengths as light. (page 101)
- *Focus.* The cornea and lens focus light onto the retina. (page 101)
- *Cones and rods.* Cones, found mainly in and near the fovea, are essential for color vision. Rods, more numerous toward the periphery, detect dim light. (page 103)
- *Blind spot.* The blind spot is the area of the retina through which the optic nerve exits. (page 105)

- *Color vision.* Color vision depends on three types of cones, each sensitive to a particular range of light wavelengths. Cones transmit messages so that later cells in the visual system indicate one color (e.g., blue) by an increase in activity and another color (e.g., yellow) by a decrease. The cerebral cortex compares responses from different parts of the retina to determine color experiences. (page 106)
- *Color vision deficiency.* Complete color-blindness is rare. Certain people have difficulty distinguishing reds from greens for genetic reasons. (page 109)

Key Terms

accommodation of the lens (page 102)

blind spot (page 105)

brightness contrast (page 108)

color constancy (page 108)

cone (page 103)

cornea (page 101)

dark adaptation (page 104)

electromagnetic spectrum (page 101)

fovea (page 102)

ganglion cells (page 105)

iris (page 101)

lens (page 102)

negative afterimage (page 107)

opponent-process theory (page 107)

optic nerve (page 105)

perception (page 100)

pupil (page 101)

receptor (page 101)

retina (page 101)

retinex theory (page 108)

rod (page 103)

sensation (page 100)

stimulus (page 101)

trichromatic theory (or Young-
    Helmholtz theory) (page 106)

Answers to Other Questions in the Module

A. In Figure 4.16a, a person with normal color vision sees the numeral 74; in Figure 4.16b, the numeral 8.

B. In Figure 4.17b, you should see the numeral 29. After you have stared at the red circle in part a, the 29 in part b may look less

distinct than usual, as though you were red-green color deficient. After staring at the green circle, the 29 may be even more distinct than usual. If you do not see either of these effects at once, try again, but this time stare at part a or c longer *and* continue staring at part b a little longer. The effect does not appear immediately.

Review Questions

1. You may have heard people say that cats can see in total darkness. Is that possible?
   - (a) Yes, they send rays out of their eyes that enable them to see in the dark.
   - (b) Yes, they see in the dark, although no one knows how they do it.
   - (c) Don't be ridiculous. Vision is the detection of light, so vision in darkness is impossible.

2. Why do we have our most detailed vision from the part of the retina called the fovea?
   - (a) The fovea has the greatest density of receptors.
   - (b) The lens and cornea focus light most clearly on the fovea.
   - (c) The fovea is the point most distant from the blind spot.
   - (d) The fovea has an equal ratio of cones and rods.

3. Why do we detect faint light more effectively in the periphery of the retina than in the fovea?
   - (a) The periphery has more tightly packed receptors.
   - (b) The center of the retina is in the shadow of the pupil.
   - (c) The periphery of the retina has more cones, which are more sensitive to faint light.
   - (d) In the periphery, more receptors converge their output onto the next cell.

4. After light stimulates receptors at the back of your retina, where do the receptors send their output?
   - (a) Directly to the thalamus
   - (b) Directly to the cerebral cortex
   - (c) To other neurons that are closer to the center of the eye

5. What fills the blind spot of the retina?
   - (a) The lens
   - (b) The fovea
   - (c) A bone
   - (d) Axons and blood vessels

6. According to the trichromatic theory, how does our nervous system tell the difference between bright yellow-green and dim yellow-green light?
   - (a) By the relative rates of response by medium-wavelength and long-wavelength cones
   - (b) By the relative rates of response by medium-wavelength and short-wavelength cones
   - (c) By the relative rates of response by all three types of cones
   - (d) By the total amount of activity by all three types of cones

7. Which of these phenomena does the opponent-process theory explain better than the trichromatic theory does?
   - (a) The tendency of an object's apparent color to change depending on variations in the objects surrounding it
   - (b) The fact that color vision is better in the fovea than in the periphery
   - (c) Negative color afterimages
   - (d) The fact that people can mix three colors of light to match any other color

8. Which of these phenomena does the retinex theory explain better than the trichromatic theory or the opponent-process theory does?
   - (a) The tendency of an object's apparent color to change depending on variations in the objects surrounding it
   - (b) The fact that color vision is better in the fovea than in the periphery
   - (c) Negative color afterimages
   - (d) The fact that people can mix three colors of light to match any other color

Answers: 1c, 2a, 3d, 4c, 5d, 6d, 7c, 8a.

After studying this module, you should be able to:

- Outline the mechanisms of hearing, touch, pain, taste, and smell.

- Distinguish between two types of deafness.

- Describe the mechanisms of pitch perception.

- Explain how we localize sounds.

- List factors that increase or decrease perception of pain.

- Describe the basis for phantom limbs.

Consider these common expressions:

- I *see* what you mean.
- I *feel* your pain.
- I am deeply *touched* by everyone's support and concern.
- She is a person of fine *taste*.
- He was *dizzy* with success.
- The policies of this company *stink*.
- That *sounds* like a good job offer.

The metaphorical use of sensation terms is no accident. Our thinking and brain activity deal only with sensory stimuli and concepts derived from them. Perhaps you doubt that assertion and object, "Sometimes, I think about numbers, time, love, justice, and all sorts of other nonsensory concepts." Yes, but how did you learn those concepts? Didn't you learn numbers by counting objects you could see or touch? Didn't you learn about time by observing changes in sensations? Didn't you learn about love and justice from events that you saw, heard, and felt? Could you explain any abstract concept without referring to something you detected with your senses? In this module we consider sensations from sounds, head tilt, skin stimulation, and chemicals.

Hearing

What we familiarly call the "ear" is a fleshy structure technically known as the *pinna*. It funnels sounds to the inner ear, where the receptors lie. The mammalian ear converts sound waves into mechanical displacements along a row of receptor cells. Sound waves are *vibrations of the air, water, or other medium.* They vary in frequency and amplitude

(see ▼ Figure 4.18). The frequency of a sound wave is the number of *cycles (vibrations) per second,* designated hertz (Hz). Pitch is a *perception closely related to frequency.* We perceive a high-frequency sound wave as high pitched and a low-frequency sound as low pitched.

Loudness is a *perception of the intensity of sound waves.* Other things being equal, the greater the amplitude of a sound, the louder it sounds. Because loudness is a psychological experience, however, other factors influence it also. For example, someone who speaks rapidly seems louder than someone speaking slowly at the same amplitude.

In addition to amplitude and pitch, sounds vary in timbre (TAM-ber), which refers to tone complexity. Any instrument playing a note at 256 Hz will simultaneously produce some sound at 128 Hz, 512 Hz, and so forth, known as harmonics of the principal note. Because each instrument or voice has a different ratio of harmonics, each sounds different from the others, even when they are playing the same note. That difference is due to timbre.

Variations in pitch, loudness, and timbre can convey emotion in many ways. An emphatic "I'm ready" indicates eagerness. A slower "I'm ready" with a different accent means you are sadly resigned to doing something unpleasant but necessary. Strong emphasis on the first word says you are ready but why isn't everyone else? Conveying emotional information by tone of voice is known as *prosody.*

The ear converts relatively weak sound waves into more intense waves of pressure in the *fluid-filled canals of the snail-shaped organ* called the cochlea (KOCK-lee-uh), *which contains the receptors for hearing* (see ▼ Figure 4.19). When

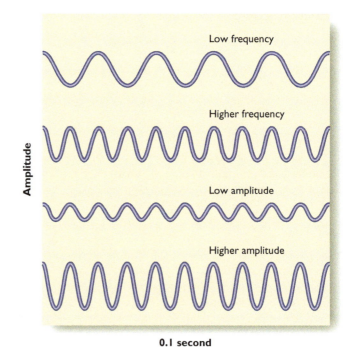

Low frequency

Higher frequency

Low amplitude

Higher amplitude

Amplitude

0.1 second

▲ **Figure 4.18** The time between the peaks of a sound wave determines the frequency of a sound. We experience frequencies as different pitches. The vertical range, or amplitude, of a wave determines the sound's intensity.

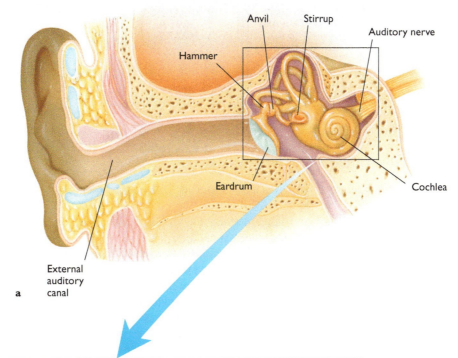

◀ **Figure 4.19** Sound waves vibrate the eardrum (**a**). Three tiny bones convert the eardrum's vibrations into vibrations in the fluid-filled cochlea (**b**). These vibrations displace hair cells along the basilar membrane in the cochlea, aptly named after the Greek word for "snail." Here, the dimensions of the cochlea have been changed to make the principles clear.

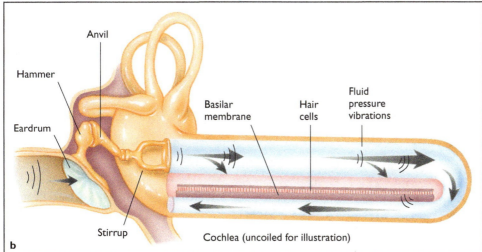

sound waves strike the eardrum, they cause it to vibrate. The eardrum connects to three tiny bones—the hammer, anvil, and stirrup (also known by their Latin names *malleus, incus,* and *stapes*). As the weak vibrations of the large eardrum travel through these bones, they transform into stronger vibrations of the much smaller stirrup. The stirrup in turn transmits the vibrations to the fluid-filled cochlea, where the vibrations displace hair cells along the basilar (BASS-uh-ler) membrane in the cochlea. These hair cells, which act like touch receptors on the skin, connect to neurons whose axons form the auditory nerve. The auditory nerve transmits impulses to the brain areas responsible for hearing.

Understanding the mechanisms of hearing helps us explain hearing loss. One kind of hearing loss is conduction deafness, which *results when the bones connected to the eardrum fail to transmit sound waves properly to the cochlea.* Surgery can correct conduction deafness by removing whatever is obstructing the bones' movement. People with conduction deafness still hear their own voice because it is conducted through the skull bones to the cochlea, bypassing the eardrum altogether. The other type of hearing loss is nerve deafness, *resulting from damage to the cochlea, hair cells, or auditory nerve.* Disease, heredity, and exposure to loud noises are common causes of nerve deafness.

Hearing aids compensate for hearing loss, except in cases of severe nerve deafness. People with damage to certain parts of the cochlea have trouble hearing only the high or medium-range frequencies. Modern hearing aids can be adjusted to amplify one set of frequencies and not another. However, despite hearing aids, many older people continue to have hearing difficulties, especially in noisy surroundings. One reason is that before they got their hearing aids, their brain areas for language comprehension started deteriorating due to inadequate input (Peelle, Troiani, Grossman, & Wingfield, 2011). A second reason is impaired attention

Figure 4.20 People with impaired hearing supplement it by watching the speaker's lips.

Pickles

OPAL, WHAT WAS THAT RESTAURANT WE USED TO GO TO ALL THE TIME?

HOLD ON JUST A MINUTE...

THERE, NOW. SAY IT AGAIN. I COULDN'T HEAR YOU WITHOUT MY GLASSES.

due to difficulty filtering out the irrelevant sounds (Anderson, Parbery-Clark, White-Schwoch, & Kraus, 2012). Understanding improves when the listener watches the speaker's face, combining the sound with a bit of lip-reading (Golumbic, Cogan, Schroeder, & Poeppel, 2013; see ▲ Figure 4.20). Familiarity also helps. Older people are better at understanding their spouse's voice than someone else's voice in a crowded setting. They are also better at *ignoring* the spouse's voice when they are trying to listen to someone else (Johnsrude et al., 2013).

Pitch Perception

Adult humans hear sound waves from about 15–20 hertz to about 15,000–20,000 Hz (cycles per second). The upper limit of hearing declines with age and also after exposure to loud noises. Thus, children hear higher frequencies than adults do. Low frequencies are perceived as low pitch, and high frequencies are perceived as high pitch, but frequency is not the same as pitch. For example, doubling the frequency doesn't make the pitch seem twice as high; it makes it one octave higher.

We hear pitch by different mechanisms at different frequencies. At low frequencies (up to about 100 Hz), *a sound wave through the fluid of the cochlea vibrates all the hair cells, which produce action potentials in synchrony with the sound waves.* This is the frequency principle. For example, a sound at a frequency of 50 Hz makes each hair cell send the brain 50 impulses per second.

Beyond about 100 Hz, hair cells cannot keep pace. Still, each sound wave excites at least a few hair cells, and *"volleys" (groups) of them respond to each vibration with an action potential* (Rose, Brugge, Anderson, & Hind, 1967). This is known as the volley principle. Thus, a tone at 1000 Hz might produce 1,000 impulses per second, even though no neuron fires that rapidly. Volleys keep pace with sounds up to about 4000 Hz, good enough for almost all speech and music. (The highest note on a piano is 4224 Hz.)

At still higher frequencies, we rely on a different mechanism. At each point along the cochlea, the hair cells are tuned resonators that vibrate only for sound waves of a particular frequency. *The highest frequency sounds vibrate hair cells near the stirrup end, and lower frequency sounds (down to about 100 to 200 Hz) vibrate hair cells at points farther along the membrane* (Warren, 1999). This is the place principle. Tones less than 100 Hz excite all hair cells equally, and we hear them by the frequency principle. We identify tones from 100 to 4000 Hz by a combination of the volley principle and the place principle. Beyond 4000 Hz, we identify tones only by the place principle. ▼ Figure 4.21 summarizes the three principles of pitch perception.

concept check

7. **Suppose a mouse emits a soft high-frequency squeak in a room full of people. Which kinds of people are least likely to hear the squeak?**

Answer

7. Obviously, the people farthest from the mouse are least likely to hear it. In addition, older people would be less likely to hear the squeak because of declining ability to hear high frequencies. Another group unlikely to hear the squeak are those who had damaged their hearing, such as by repeated exposure to loud noises.

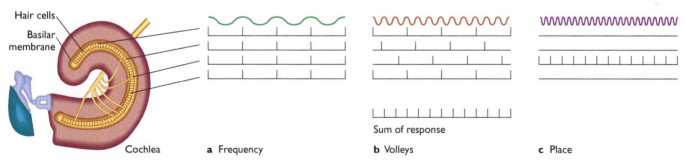

Hair cells

Basilar membrane

Cochlea

a Frequency

Sum of response

b Volleys

c Place

▲ **Figure 4.21** (a) At low frequencies, hair cells along the basilar membrane produce impulses in synchrony with the sound waves. (b) At medium frequencies, different cells produce impulses in synchrony with different sound waves, but a volley (group) produces one or more impulses for each wave. (c) At high frequencies, only one point along the basilar membrane vibrates.

Probably you have heard of people who can listen to a note and identify its pitch by name: "Oh, that's a C-sharp." People either name pitches well or not at all. Hardly anyone is intermediate. The main influence on this ability is early music training. Not everyone with musical training develops absolute pitch, but almost everyone with absolute pitch had musical training (Athos et al., 2007). The ability is more widespread among people who speak tonal languages, such as Vietnamese and Mandarin Chinese, in which children learn from the start to pay close attention to the pitch of a word (Deutsch, Henthorn, Marvin, & Xu, 2006). For example, in Mandarin Chinese, dá (with a rising tone) means dozen, and dà (with a falling tone) means big.

If you are amazed by people with absolute pitch, your own ability to recognize (though not name) a specific pitch might surprise you. In one study, 48 college students with no special talent or training listened to 5-second segments from television theme songs, played in their normal key or a slightly higher or lower key. The students usually chose the correct version, but only of programs they had watched (Schellenberg & Trehub, 2003). That is, they remembered the familiar pitches.

People who are said to be "tone-deaf" are not completely tone-deaf, and if they were, they could not understand speech. However, they are impaired at detecting changes in sound frequency smaller than 10 percent, whereas most people detect changes smaller than 1 percent (Hyde & Peretz, 2004; Loui, Alsop, & Schlaug, 2009). Tone-deaf people don't detect when someone is singing off-key, and they don't detect a wrong note in a melody. Many of them have relatives with the same condition, so it probably has a genetic basis (Peretz, Cummings, & Dube, 2007). If you do an Internet search for "amusia test," you can find a quick way to test yourself or your friends.

Localizing Sounds

When you hear, the activity is in your ear, but you experience the sound as "out there," and you can generally estimate its place of origin. What cues do you use?

The auditory system determines the direction of a sound source by comparing the messages from the two ears. When a sound comes from the front, the messages reach the two ears simultaneously at equal intensity. When it comes from the left, it reaches the left ear first and is more intense there (see ▶ Figure 4.22). The timing is important for localizing low-frequency sounds. Intensity helps us localize high-frequency sounds.

You also detect the approximate distance of sound sources. If a sound grows louder, you interpret it as coming closer. If two sounds differ in pitch, you assume the higher frequency tone is closer. (Low-frequency tones carry better over distance, so if you hear a high-frequency tone, its source is probably close.) However, loudness and frequency tell you only the *relative* distances, not *absolute* distances. The only cue for absolute distance is the amount of reverberation (Mershon & King, 1975). In a closed room, you first hear the sound waves coming directly from the source and then the waves that reflected off the walls, floor, ceiling, or other objects. If you hear many echoes, you judge the source of the sound to be far away. It is hard to localize sound sources in a noisy room where echoes are hard to hear (McMurtry & Mershon, 1985).

concept check

8. Why is it sometimes difficult to tell whether a sound is coming from directly in front of or directly behind you?

9. If someone who ordinarily uses hearing aids in both ears currently wears one in only the left ear, what will be the effect on sound localization?

▲ **Figure 4.22** The ear located closest to the sound receives the sound waves first. That cue is important for localizing low-frequency sounds.

Answers
8. We localize sounds by comparing the input into the two ears. If a sound comes from straight ahead or from directly behind (or from straight above or below), the input into the left and right ears is identical.
9. Sounds will be louder in the left ear than in the right, and therefore, they may seem to be coming from the left side even when they aren't. However, a sound from the right will still strike the right ear before the left, so time of arrival at the two ears will compete against the relative loudness.

The Vestibular Sense

Imagine yourself riding a roller coaster with your eyes closed. The up and down, back and forth sensations you feel come from structures called *vestibules* in the inner ear on each side of your head. The **vestibular sense** detects *the tilt and acceleration of the head, and the orientation of the head with respect to gravity.* It plays a key role in posture and balance. Intense vestibular sensations are responsible for motion sickness.

The vestibular sense also enables you to keep your eyes fixated on a target as your head moves. When you walk down the street, you can keep your eyes fixated on a street sign, even though your head is bobbing up and down. The vestibular sense

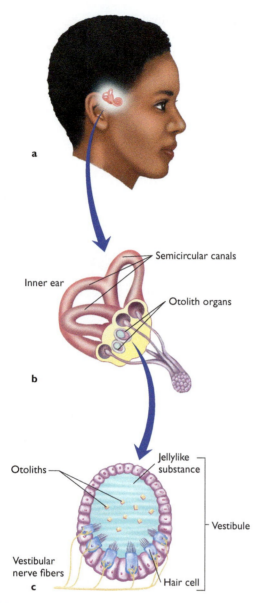

▲ **Figure 4.23** (**a**) Location of and (**b**) structures of the vestibule. (**c**) Moving your head or body displaces hair cells that report the tilt of your head and the direction and acceleration of movement.

detects head movements and compensates with eye movements.

To illustrate, try to read this page while you jiggle the book up and down or side to side, keeping your head steady. Then hold the book steady and move your head up and down and from side to side. You probably find it much easier to read when you are moving your head than when you are jiggling the book. The reason is that your vestibular sense keeps your eyes fixated on the print during head movements, but it cannot compensate for movements of the book. After damage to the vestibular sense, people report blurry vision while they

are walking. To read street signs, they must come to a stop.

The vestibular system consists of three semi-circular canals oriented in different directions, and two otolith organs (see ◀ Figure 4.23b). The *semicircular canals* are lined with hair cells and filled with a jellylike substance. When the body accelerates in any direction, the jellylike substance in the corresponding semicircular canal pushes against the hair cells, which send messages to the brain. The *otolith organs* shown in ◀ Figure 4.23b also contain hair cells (see ◀ Figure 4.23c), which lie next to the *otoliths* (calcium carbonate particles). Depending on which way the head tilts, the particles excite different sets of hair cells. The otolith organs report the direction of gravity and therefore which way is up.

For astronauts in the zero-gravity environment of outer space, the vestibular sense cannot identify up or down. Instead, astronauts learn to rely on visual signals, such as the walls of the ship (Lackner, 1993).

The Cutaneous Senses

What we commonly think of as touch consists of several partly independent senses: pressure on the skin, warmth, cold, pain, itch, vibration, movement across the skin, and stretch of the skin. These sensations depend on several kinds of receptors, as ▼ Figure 4.24 shows (Iggo & Andres, 1982). A pinprick on the skin feels different from a light touch, and both feel different from a burn because each excites different receptors. Collectively, these sensations are known as the cutaneous senses, meaning the *skin senses*. They are also known as the *somatosensory system*, meaning *body-sensory system*.

Have you ever wondered about the sensation of itch? Is it a kind of touch, pain, or what? Itch depends on a special type of receptor that sends messages through a special path in the spinal cord (Y.-G. Sun et al., 2009). Itch is unlike pain. In fact, pain inhibits itch (Andrew & Craig, 2001). If a dentist anesthetizes your mouth for dental surgery, as the anesthesia wears off, the itch receptors recover before the pain and touch receptors do. If you scratch the itchy spot, you don't feel the scratch and you don't relieve the itch.

Tickle is another kind of cutaneous sensation. Have you ever wondered why you cannot tickle yourself? Some people can, a little, especially when they are just starting to wake up, but it's not the same as when someone else tickles them. The reason is that tickle requires surprise. When you are about to touch yourself, certain parts of your brain build up an anticipation response that is similar to the actual

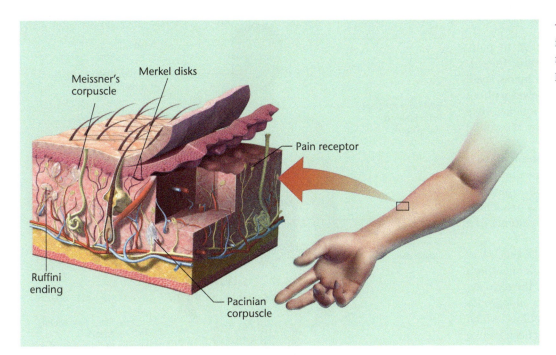

◀ **Figure 4.24** Cutaneous sensation is the product of many kinds of receptors, each sensitive to a particular kind of information.

Meissner's corpuscle

Merkel disks

Pain receptor

Ruffini ending

Pacinian corpuscle

stimulation (Carlsson, Petrovic, Skare, Petersson, & Ingvar, 2000). When you try to tickle yourself, the sensation is no surprise.

Pain

Pain is important for its own sake and because of its relation to depression and anxiety. The experience of pain is a mixture of body sensation and emotional reaction, which depend on different brain areas (Craig, Bushnell, Zhang, & Blomqvist, 1994; Fernandez & Turk, 1992). An area in the parietal cortex responds to the sensation itself. The brain area responsive to the emotional aspect—the *anterior cingulate cortex*—also responds to the emotional pain of watching someone else get hurt (Singer et al., 2004). Physical pain can be intense at the moment, but emotional pain is more enduring. Try to remember how you felt during a painful injury. Then try to remember how you felt at the death of a loved one. Most people relive the emotional pain more intensely (Chen, Williams, Fitness, & Newton, 2008).

People often talk of "hurt feelings." Is that just a saying, or is social distress really like pain? It is like pain in a couple of ways. First, when someone feels rejected by others, activity increases in the anterior cingulate gyrus, the area responsive to the emotional aspect of pain (Eisenberger, Lieberman, & Williams, 2003). More intense emotional distress, such as that from a difficult romantic breakup, activates that emotional area and also the area associated with the sensation of pain itself (Kross, Berman, Mischel, Smith, & Wager, 2011). Second, you can relieve hurt feelings by taking acetaminophen (Tylenol®)! College students kept a daily log of hurt feelings while taking either acetaminophen or a placebo. Those taking acetaminophen reported fewer hurt feelings, and the frequency declined as they continued taking the drug (De Wall et al., 2010). (So, the next time you hurt people's feelings, don't apologize. Just hand them a pill.)

The Gate Theory of Pain

You visit a physician because of severe pain, but as soon as the physician tells you the problem is nothing to worry about, the pain starts to subside. Have you ever had such an experience?

Recall the term *placebo* from Chapter 2: A placebo is a drug or other procedure with no important effects beyond those that result from people's expectations. Placebos have little effect on most medical conditions, with two exceptions—pain and depression (Hróbjartsson & Gøtzsche, 2001; Wager et al., 2007). In one experiment, college students had a smelly brownish liquid rubbed onto one finger. It was in fact a placebo, but they were told it was a painkiller. Then they were painfully pinched on that finger and a finger of the other hand. They consistently reported less pain on the finger with the placebo (Montgomery & Kirsch, 1996). How placebos work is unclear, but these results eliminate mere relaxation as an explanation, because relaxation would affect both hands equally.

Because of observations such as these, Ronald Melzack and P. D. Wall (1965) proposed the gate theory of pain, the idea that *pain messages must pass through a gate, presumably in the spinal cord, that can block the messages.* That is, other kinds of input close the gate, preventing pain messages from reaching the brain. If you injure yourself, rubbing the surrounding skin sends inhibitory messages to the spinal cord, closing the pain gates. Pleasant or distracting events also send inhibitory messages. In contrast, a barrage of painful stimuli cause pain at the time and increase response to similar stimuli in the future (Walters, 2009). You could say the brain learns how to feel pain and gets better at it (see ▼ Figure 4.25).

Ways to Decrease Pain

Some people are completely insensitive to pain. Before you start to envy them, consider this: They often burn themselves by picking up hot objects, scald their tongues on hot coffee, cut themselves without realizing it, or bite off the tip of the tongue. They don't learn to avoid danger, and many die young (Cox et al., 2006).

Although we shouldn't rid ourselves of pain altogether, we would like to limit it. Distraction is one way. Postsurgery patients in a room with a pleasant view complain less about pain, take less painkilling medicine, and recover faster than do patients in a windowless room (Ulrich, 1984).

Several medications also reduce pain. Endorphins are *neurotransmitters that weaken pain sensations* (Pert & Snyder, 1973; see ▼ Figure 4.26). The term *endorphin* is a combination of the terms *endogenous* (self-produced) and *morphine*. Morphine, which stimulates endorphin synapses, has long been known for its ability to inhibit dull, lingering pains. Pleasant experiences, such as sexual activity or thrilling music, also release endorphins (A. Goldstein, 1980).

Paradoxically, another method of decreasing pain begins by inducing it. The *chemical* capsaicin *stimulates receptors that respond to painful heat.* Capsaicin is what makes jalapeños and similar peppers taste hot. Rubbing capsaicin on the skin produces a temporary burning sensation. As it subsides, the skin loses some of its pain sensitivity. Several skin creams with capsaicin are used to relieve aching muscles. High doses of capsaicin cause a buildup of calcium in heat receptors, damaging the receptors and making them temporarily unresponsive (Anand & Bley, 2011).

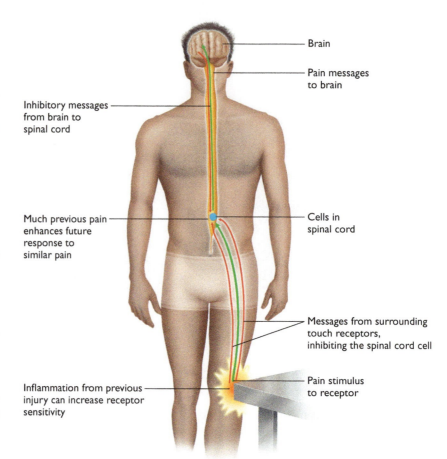

▲ **Figure 4.25** Pain messages from the skin are relayed from the spinal cord to the brain. According to the gate theory of pain, spinal cord cells can block or enhance the signal. Green lines indicate axons with excitatory inputs; red lines indicate axons with inhibitory inputs.

10. Pain activates two brain areas. How do the functions of those areas differ?

Answer

10. One area responds to the sensation itself. The other responds to the emotional consequence.

Phantom Limbs

Some people report *continuing sensations, including pain, in a limb long after it has been amputated.* This phenomenon, known as a phantom limb, might last days, weeks, or years after the amputation (Ramachandran & Hirstein, 1998). Physicians and psychologists have long wondered about the cause. Research in the 1990s found the problem within the brain.

Figure 3.18 showed the input from various body areas to the somatosensory cortex. ▼ Figure 4.27a repeats part of that illustration. Part b shows what happens immediately after a hand amputation: The hand area of the cortex becomes inactive because the axons from the hand are inactive. As time passes, axons from the face, which ordinarily excite only the face area of the cortex, strengthen connections to the nearby hand area of the cortex (see ▼ Figure 4.27c). From then on, stimulation of the face continues to excite the face area but now also excites the hand area. When the axons from the face area stimulate the hand area, they produce a hand experience—that is, a phantom limb (Flor et al., 1995; Ramachandran & Blakeslee, 1998).

It is possible to relieve phantom sensations: People who learn to use an artificial hand or limb lose their phantoms (Lotze et al., 1999). The relevant areas of the cortex start reacting to the artificial limb, and this sensation displaces the abnormal sensations (Di Pino, Guglielmelli, & Rossini, 2009).

11. A phantom hand sensation would be strongest after touch to what body part?

Answer

11. The phantom hand sensation would be strongest when something touches the face.

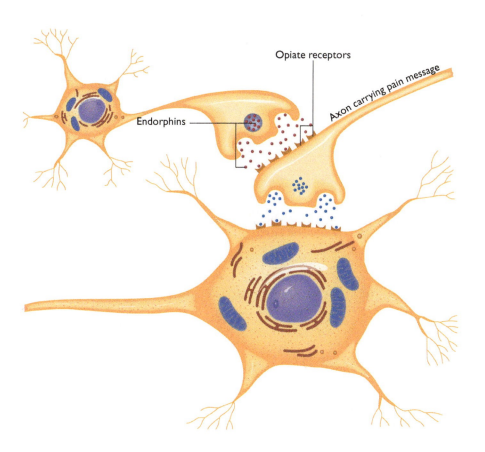

Opiate receptors

Endorphins

Axon carrying pain message

◀ **Figure 4.26** Endorphins block the release of a transmitter conveying pain sensations. Opiates imitate the effects of endorphins.

The Chemical Senses

Humans' heavy reliance on vision and hearing is unusual in the animal kingdom. Most animals depend mainly on taste and smell to find food and mates. We humans often overlook the importance of these sensations.

Taste

The sense of **taste**, which *detects chemicals on the tongue,* serves just one function: It governs eating and drinking. The *taste receptors are* in the **taste buds**,

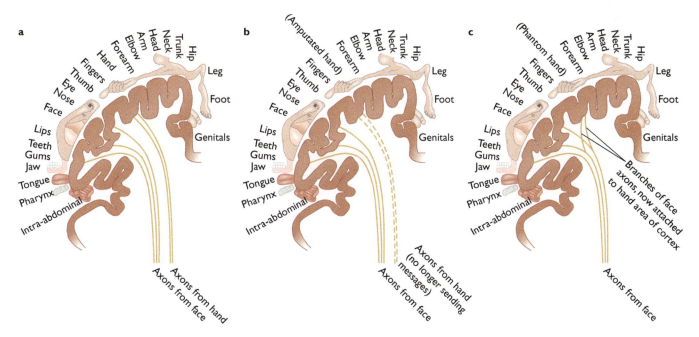

▲ **Figure 4.27** (a) Each area of the somatosensory cortex gets input from a different body area. (b) If one body part, such as the hand, is amputated, its area of the cortex no longer gets its normal input. (c) Axons from a neighboring area branch out to excite the vacated area. Now, stimulation of the face excites both the face area and the hand area, producing both a facial sensation and a phantom hand sensation.

located in the folds on the surface of the tongue, mainly along the edge of the tongue in adults (see ▼ Figure 4.28). Children's taste buds are more widely distributed.

Try this demonstration (based on Bartoshuk, 1991): Soak something small (the tip of a cotton swab will do) in sugar water, salt water, or vinegar. Touch it to the center of your tongue, not too far back. You will feel it but taste nothing. Slowly move the soaked substance toward the side or front of your tongue. Suddenly, you taste it. If you go in the other direction (first touching the side of the tongue and then moving toward the center), you will continue to taste the substance even at the center of your tongue. The explanation is that your taste buds do not tell you *where* you taste something. When you stimulate touch receptors on your tongue, your brain interprets the taste perception as coming from wherever it feels touch.

Types of Taste Receptors

Traditionally, Western cultures have talked about four primary tastes: sweet, sour, salty, and bitter. However, the taste of monosodium glutamate (MSG), common in Asian cuisines and similar to the taste of unsalted chicken soup, cannot be described in these terms (Kurihara & Kashiwayanagi, 1998; Schiffman & Erickson, 1971), and researchers found a taste receptor specific to MSG (Chaudhari, Landin, & Roper, 2000). Because English had no word for the taste of MSG, researchers adopted the Japanese word *umami.*

Bitter taste is puzzling because such diverse chemicals taste bitter. The only thing they have in common is being poisonous or at least harmful in large amounts. How could such diverse chemicals all excite the same receptor? The answer is, they don't. We have 25 or more types of bitter receptors, each sensitive to different chemicals (Adler et al., 2000; Behrens, Foerster, Staehler, Raguse, & Meyerhof,

▶ **Figure 4.28** (**a**) Taste buds, which react to chemicals dissolved in saliva, are located along the edge of the tongue in adult humans. (**b**) A cross section through part of the surface of the tongue showing taste buds.

After someone with an amputation gains experience using an artificial limb, phantom limb sensations fade or disappear.

2007; Matsunami, Montmayeur, & Buck, 2000). Any chemical that excites any of these receptors produces the same bitter sensation. One consequence is that a wide variety of harmful chemicals taste bitter. Another consequence is that we do not detect low concentrations of bitter chemicals, because we do not have many of any one type of bitter receptor.

concept check

12. **Why are people more sensitive to a very dilute sugar or salt taste than they are to an equally dilute bitter taste?**

Answer

12. People have many types of bitter receptors, but not a huge number of any one type.

Smell

The *sense of smell* is known as olfaction. The olfactory receptors, located on the mucous membrane in the rear air passages of the nose (see ▼ Figure 4.29),

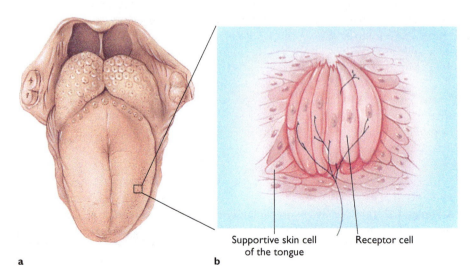

Supportive skin cell of the tongue   Receptor cell

a   b

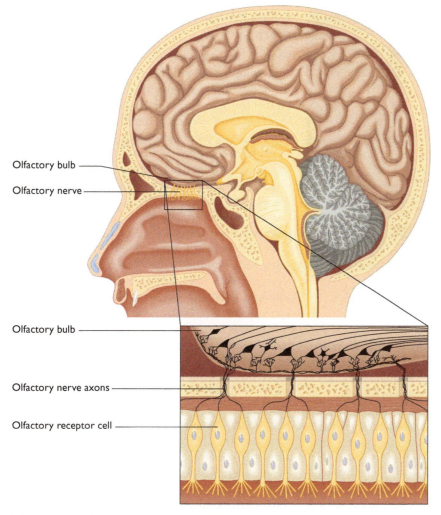

Olfactory bulb

Olfactory nerve

Olfactory bulb

Olfactory nerve axons

Olfactory receptor cell

▲ **Figure 4.29** The olfactory receptor cells lining the nasal cavity send information to the olfactory bulb in the brain.

see ▼ Figure 4.30). Through combinations of the responses of our hundreds of types of receptors, we can distinguish among a huge number of odors and their mixtures—more than a trillion, according to one estimate (Bushdid, Magnasco, Vosshall, & Keller, 2014).

Many odors produce strong emotional responses. People who lose the sense of smell lose much of their joy in life and in many cases become depressed (Herz, 2007). Our emotional reactions to odors are not built-in, however. Americans experience wintergreen odor only in association with candy. In Britain, wintergreen is often included in rub-on pain medications. Guess what: Most Americans like the odor, and British people do not. One woman reported hating the smell of roses because she first smelled them at her mother's funeral. Another woman reported liking the smell of skunk (from a distance) because it reminded her of a joyful trip through the country when she was a child (Herz, 2007).

Suppose I ask you to smell something labeled "odor of Parmesan cheese." You say you like it. Then I say, "Oops, I'm sorry, that was mislabeled. It's actually the smell of vomit." Oh, no! Now you hate the smell—the same smell! "Wait, my mistake. I was right the first time. It really is Parmesan." Now do you like it or not? Your emotional reaction to an odor depends on what you think it is (Herz & von Clef, 2001).

Olfaction serves important social functions in most nonhuman mammals. In many species, individuals use olfaction to recognize one another and to identify when a female is sexually receptive. Most humans prefer *not* to recognize one another by smell. The deodorant and perfume industries exist for the

detect airborne molecules. The axons of the olfactory receptors form the olfactory tract, which extends to the olfactory bulbs at the base of the brain.

The human sense of smell is not as good as that of dogs or many other species, but it is better than we might guess. We watch a dog track someone through the woods and think, "Wow, I could never do that." Well, of course not, if you stand with your nose far above the ground! Experimenters asked young adults to get down on all fours, touch their nose to the ground, and try to follow a scent trail, blindfolded. Most succeeded (J. Porter et al., 2007).

How many kinds of olfactory receptors do we have? Until 1991, researchers did not know. In contrast, researchers in the 1800s established that people have three kinds of color receptors. They used behavioral methods, showing that people can mix three colors of light in various amounts to match any other color. Regarding olfaction, however, no one reported comparable studies. Can people match all possible odors by mixing appropriate amounts of three, four, seven, ten, or some other number of odors?

It is good that no one spent a lifetime trying to find out. Linda Buck and Richard Axel (1991), using modern biochemical technology, demonstrated that humans have hundreds of types of olfactory receptors. Rats and mice have about a thousand (Zhang & Firestein, 2002;

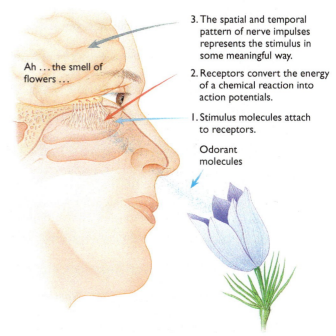

Ah ...the smell of flowers ...

3. The spatial and temporal pattern of nerve impulses represents the stimulus in some meaningful way.

2. Receptors convert the energy of a chemical reaction into action potentials.

1. Stimulus molecules attach to receptors.

Odorant molecules

▲ **Figure 4.30** Olfaction, like any other sensory system, converts physical energy into a complex pattern of brain activity.

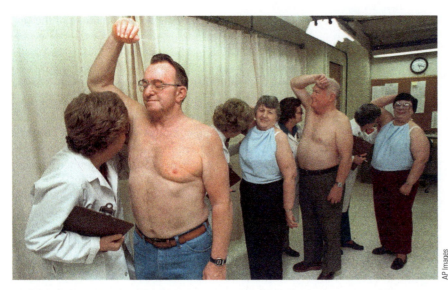

Professional deodorant tester: That's a career option you probably never considered. U.S. industries spend millions of dollars to eliminate the kinds of personal odors that are essential to other mammalian species.

Individual Differences in Taste and Smell

Suppose we ask many people to rate "how strong" something tastes or smells. They all give it about the same rating, and we might conclude that they all had the same experience. However, this conclusion would be wrong. When you rate the strength of something, you rate it based on your own range of experiences. So, if you rate something as "very strong," you mean it is strong compared to your other experiences, but you cannot compare it to someone else's experiences.

Some people have three times as many taste buds on the tongue as other people do (Hayes, Bartoshuk, Kidd, & Duffy, 2008). Those with more taste buds experience stronger tastes, tend to have stronger food likes and dislikes than other people, and generally dislike strong-tasting or highly spiced foods.

People also vary in olfaction. Remember, we have hundreds of types of olfactory receptors, each controlled by its own gene. Many of these genes differ slightly from one person to another, and as a result, a particular odor might seem stronger or weaker to you than to someone else (Mainland et al., 2014). People vary in olfaction for other reasons also. On average, women are more sensitive to smells than men are (Yousem et al., 1999) and young people are more sensitive than older people. Sharply deteriorating olfaction is often one of the first symptoms of Alzheimer's disease or Parkinson's disease (Doty & Kamath, 2014).

sole purpose of removing and covering up human odors. But olfaction is more important to our social behavior than we generally acknowledge. The smell of a sweaty woman—especially a woman near her time of ovulation—causes a heterosexual man to increase his testosterone secretion (Miller & Maner, 2010; Savic, Berglund, & Lindström, 2005). Something in his brain says, "Ooh. I smell a sweaty woman. I bet she is *hot*!" It's different for women (Wyart et al., 2007). We have no evidence that the smell of a sweaty man increases a woman's sexual arousal. In fact, it causes a woman to increase her secretion of stress hormones! Something in her brain says, "I smell a sweaty man. Uh, oh."

Imagine you are exposed to just the smells of several people, and you are to rate each one's desirability as a potential romantic partner. You can make certain surmises from body odor, including a person's health, because people smell better when they are healthy than when ill (Olsson et al., 2014). Also, most people give a low rating to anyone who smells too much like their own relatives (Havlicek & Roberts, 2009). Women show this tendency more strongly if they are capable of becoming pregnant, and less if they are taking contraceptive pills (Roberts, Gosling, Carter, & Petrie, 2008). Avoiding a potential mate who smells like your relatives is a good way to avoid inbreeding, and to provide your child with a variety of genes for immunities.

Synesthesia

We end our tour of the senses with synesthesia, a *condition in which a stimulus of one type, such as sound, also elicits another experience, such as color*. The most common type is perceiving each letter or number as a color, such as seeing E as green or red. One man reported seeing synesthetic colors that he never saw in real life because he was red-green color deficient. He called them "Martian colors" (Ramachandran, 2003). Evidently, although his retina could not send messages for those colors, the brain was organized to perceive them. Other types of synesthesia are uncommon but fascinating. One woman experiences most words and sounds as mouth sensations. As she listens, reads, or speaks, she experiences one taste or smell after another, and occasionally other mouth sensations such as feeling her mouth as full of marbles or feeling as if she just swallowed a button (Colizoli, Murre, & Rouw, 2013). A man with a similar word-taste synesthesia reported sometimes tasting a word before he could think of it. He said he couldn't quite remember what the

13. What accounts for people's emotional responses to smells?

Answer

13. Emotional responses to smells are mostly learned by association with other events.

word was, but it tasted like tuna (Simner & Ward, 2006). (It gives a new meaning to the term "tip of the tongue" experience.)

A synesthetic perception is quick and automatic. In one study, people listened to sentences such as, "The clear lake was the most beautiful hue of 7." For people with synesthesia who experienced 7 as blue, this sentence evoked a strong brain response within a tenth of a second after hearing the 7. For those who experienced 7 as some other color, the response was weaker, as it is for people without synesthesia (Brang, Edwards, Ramachandran, & Coulson, 2008).

try it yourself

For another example, find the 2s and As in the following displays as quickly as possible.

```
555555555555  555555555555  555555555555  5555555525555
555555555555  555555555525  555555555555  555555555555
555555555555  555555555555  555255555555  555555555555
552555555555  555555555555  555555555555  555555555555
555555555555  555555555555  555555555555  555555555555


444444444444  444444444444  444444444444  444444444444
444444444444  44A444444444  444444444444  444444444444
44444A444444  444444444444  444444444444  4444444A44444
444444444444  444444444444  444444444444  444444444444
444444444444  444444444444  44444444A44   444444444444
```

One person with synesthesia found it just as hard as anyone else to find the As among 4s because both of them looked red to her. However, because 2s look violet and 5s look yellow to her, she was quicker than average to find the 2s, almost as if—but not quite as if—the displays had been printed like this (Laeng, Svartdal, & Oelmann, 2004):

```
555555555555  555555555555  555555555555  5555555525555
555555555555  555555555525  555555555555  555555555555
555555555555  555555555555  555255555555  555555555555
552555555555  555555555555  555555555555  555555555555
555555555555  555555555555  555555555555  555555555555
```

These results are surprising. The colors helped her find the 2s, but somehow her brain had to know the 2s from the 5s *before* it could produce the color experiences. At this point, synesthesia remains a fascinating mystery. In most cases it develops gradually during childhood. Many 6- and 7-year-old children show some degree of synesthesia. By the time they are a few years older, some have lost it, whereas others have developed a stronger, more consistent experience (Simner & Bain, 2013).

Synesthesia tends to run in families (Barnett et al., 2008), and curiously it often occurs in the same families as people with absolute pitch (Gregerson et al., 2013). In some cases we have a clue as to how it develops. Ten people are known to have developed letter-color synesthesia in which the colors matched the Fisher-Price refrigerator magnets they had played with as children, such as red A, yellow C, and green D (Witthoft & Winawer, 2013). Why these particular children developed synesthesia and others did not, we do not know.

concept check

14. What is evidence that synesthesia is a real phenomenon, not just pretended or imagined?

Answer

14. People who see 2 as one color and 5 as a different color can find the 2s among a group of 5s more easily than other people do.

---

in closing | module 4.2

Sensory Systems

The world as experienced by a bat (which hears frequencies up to 100,000 Hz) or a mouse (which depends on its whiskers to explore the world) is in many ways a different world from the one that you experience. The function of the senses is not to tell you about everything in the world but to alert you to the information you are most likely to use, given the human way of life.

Summary

- *Pitch.* At low frequencies of sound, we identify pitch by the frequency of vibrations of hair cells in our ears. At intermediate frequencies, we identify pitch by volleys of responses from many neurons. At high frequencies, we identify pitch by the location where the hair cells vibrate. (page 114)
- *Localizing sounds.* We localize a sound source by detecting differences in the time and loudness of the sounds in the two ears. We localize the distance of a sound source primarily by the amount of reverberation following the main sound. (page 115)
- *Vestibular system.* The vestibular system tells us about the movement of the head and its position with respect to gravity.

It enables us to keep our eyes fixated on an object while the rest of the body is in motion. (page 115)
- *Cutaneous receptors.* We experience many types of sensation on the skin, each dependent on different receptors. Itch is a sensation based on tissue irritation, inhibited by pain. Tickle depends on the unpredictability of the stimulus. (page 116)
- *Pain.* The experience of pain can be greatly inhibited or enhanced by other simultaneous experiences, including touch to surrounding skin. Expectations also influence pain. Hurt feelings resemble physical pain, especially in their emotional aspect. (page 117)

- *Phantom limbs.* After an amputation, the corresponding portion of the somatosensory cortex stops receiving its normal input. Axons from neighboring cortical areas form branches that excite the silenced areas of cortex. When these cortical areas receive the new input, they react in the old way, producing a phantom sensation. (page 118)
- *Taste receptors.* People have receptors sensitive to sweet, sour, salty, bitter, and umami (MSG) tastes. We have many kinds of bitter receptors, but not many of any one kind. (page 119)
- *Olfactory receptors.* The olfactory system—the sense of smell—depends on hundreds of types of receptors. We have strong emotional reactions to many odors based on previous experiences. Olfaction influences our social responses more than most people realize. (page 120)
- *Individual differences.* Some people have three times as many taste buds as others do, giving them greater sensitivity to taste. People vary in their genes for olfactory receptors, causing certain odors to seem stronger. (page 122)
- *Synesthesia.* Some people have consistent experiences of one sensation evoked by another. For example, they might experience particular letters or numbers as having a color. (page 122)

Key Terms

capsaicin (p. 118)

cochlea (page 112)

conduction deafness (page 113)

cutaneous senses (page 116)

endorphin (page 118)

frequency principle (page 114)

gate theory (page 117)

hertz (Hz) (page 112)

loudness (page 112)

nerve deafness (page 113)

olfaction (page 120)

phantom limb (page 118)

pitch (page 112)

place principle (page 114)

sound waves (page 112)

synesthesia, (page 122)

taste (page 119)

taste bud (page 119)

timbre (page 112)

vestibular sense (page 115)

volley principle (page 114)

Review Questions

1. When hair cells at one point along the basilar membrane become active, we hear a tone at 5000 Hz. What do we hear when the same hair cells double their rate of activity?
   (a) A pitch one octave higher.
   (b) The same pitch as before, but louder.

2. Suppose you are listening to a monaural (nonstereo) radio. Can it play sounds that you localize as coming from different directions or distances?
   (a) Yes. It can play sounds that you localize as coming from different directions (left/right) and different distances.
   (b) It can play sounds that you localize as coming from different directions (left/right), but not from different distances.
   (c) It can play sounds that you localize as coming from different distances, but not from different directions (left/right).
   (d) No. It cannot play sounds that you localize as coming from either different directions or different distances.

3. What is the relationship between itch and pain?
   (a) Itch is just a lesser stimulation of pain receptors.
   (b) The same axons that convey pain messages convey itch, but in different ways.
   (c) Pain sensation inhibits itch sensation.

4. Psychologist Linda Bartoshuk recommends candies containing moderate amounts of jalapeño peppers as a treatment for pain in the mouth. Why?
   (a) Jalapeños excite pleasure centers in the brain.
   (b) Jalapeños decrease overall brain activity.
   (c) After the immediate heat experience, pain receptors become less responsive.
   (d) Jalapeños distract attention from other pain.

5. Which of the following is responsible for the phantom limb experience?
   (a) Crossed connections from the normal limb on the other side of the body
   (b) Anxiety and other psychological reactions to the amputation
   (c) Irritation at the stump where the amputation took place
   (d) Reorganization of connections in the brain

6. In addition to sweet, sour, salty, and bitter, people have taste receptors for what additional taste?
   (a) Hot (the taste of jalapeños)
   (b) Umami (the taste of MSG)
   (c) Cool (the taste of menthol)
   (d) Garlic

7. How many types of olfactory receptors do people have?
   (a) Three
   (b) Seven
   (c) Hundreds
   (d) Unknown

8. Of people with letter-color synesthesia, why do many see red as A, yellow as C, and green as D?
   (a) Red uses the same neurotransmitter as A, yellow as C, and so forth.
   (b) They learned to copy one child who started with those associations.
   (c) The brain areas for those colors are near the brain areas for those letters.
   (d) As children, they played with refrigerator magnets of those colors.

Answers: 1b, 2c, 3c, 4c, 5d, 6b, 7c, 8d.

module 4.3

Interpreting Sensory Information

After studying this module, you should be able to:

- Explain why it is difficult to specify the minimum detectable stimulus.
- List some things that subliminal perception can and cannot do.
- Discuss the evidence for feature detectors
- Discuss the evidence Gestalt psychologists present to show limitations of the feature detector approach.
- List some factors that enable us to perceive depth.
- Give an example of an optical illusion and explain it.

According to a popular expression, "a picture is worth a thousand words." If so, what is a thousandth of a picture worth? One word? Perhaps not even that.

Printed photographs, such as the one on page 122, are composed of a great many dots, which you can see if you magnify the photo, as in ▼ Figure 4.31. Although one dot by itself tells us nothing, the pattern of many dots becomes a meaningful picture.

Our vision is like this all the time. Your retina includes more than a hundred million rods and cones, each of which sees one dot of the visual field. What you perceive is not dots but lines, curves, and objects. Your nervous system starts with a vast amount of information and extracts the important patterns.

Perceiving Minimal Stimuli

Some of the earliest psychological researchers tried to determine the weakest sounds, lights, and touches that people could detect. They also measured the smallest difference that people could detect between one stimulus and another—the *just noticeable difference* (JND). Although these questions seemed easy, the answers were more complicated. First, the answer depends on what someone had been doing just before the test. If you had spent the last hour on the beach on a sunny day, you will be poor at detecting faint lights. If you spent the last hour listening to loud music, you will be poor at hearing soft sounds. But even if you spent the last hour in a quiet, dark room, your responses can be hard to interpret.

Sensory Thresholds and Signal Detection

Imagine a typical experiment to determine your threshold of hearing—that is, the minimum intensity that you can hear: On each trial, the experimenter presents either no tone or a faint tone, and you report hearing or not hearing something. ▼ Figure 4.32 presents typical results. Notice that no sharp line separates sounds that people hear from sounds they do not. Researchers therefore define an absolute sensory threshold as the *intensity at which a given individual detects a stimulus 50 percent of the time.* However, people sometimes report hearing a tone when none was present. We should not be surprised. Throughout the study, they have been listening to faint tones and saying "yes" when they heard almost nothing. The difference between nothing and almost nothing is slim. Still, if someone reports a tone when

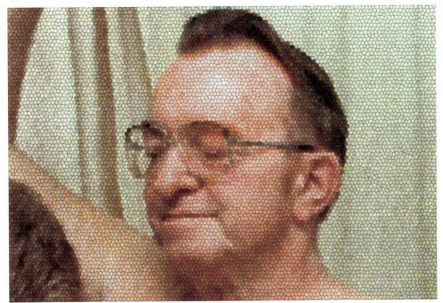

▲ **Figure 4.31** From a photograph composed of dots, we see objects and patterns.

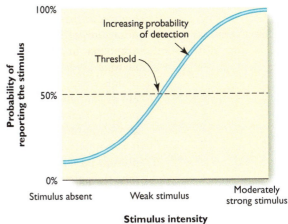

▲ **Figure 4.32** Typical results of an experiment to measure an absolute sensory threshold. No sharp boundary separates stimuli that you perceive from those you do not.

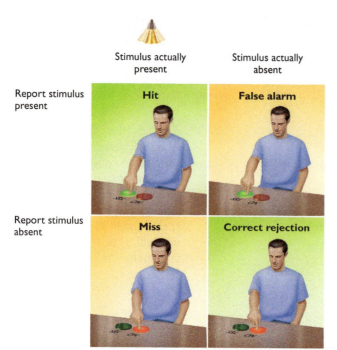

Stimulus actually present   Stimulus actually absent

Report stimulus present

Hit   **False alarm**

Report stimulus absent

Miss   **Correct rejection**

▲ **Figure 4.33** People make two kinds of correct judgments (green backgrounds) and two kinds of errors (yellow backgrounds). If you tend to say the stimulus is present when you are in doubt, you will get many hits but also many false alarms.

none was present, we have to be cautious in interpreting the other responses. How often were they really hearing something, and how often were they just guessing?

When people try to detect weak stimuli, they can be correct in two ways: reporting the presence of a stimulus (a "hit") and reporting its absence (a "correct rejection"). They can also be wrong in two ways: failing to detect a stimulus (a "miss") and reporting it present when it was absent (a "false alarm"). ▲ Figure 4.33 outlines these possibilities.

Signal-detection theory is the *study of people's tendencies to make hits, correct rejections, misses, and false alarms* (D. M. Green & Swets, 1966). The theory originated in engineering, where it applies to such matters as detecting radio signals in the presence of noise. Suppose someone reports a stimulus present on 80 percent of the trials when the stimulus is present. That statistic is meaningless unless we also know how often the person said it was present when it was not. If the person also reported the stimulus present on 80 percent of trials when it was absent, then the person is just guessing.

In a signal-detection experiment, people's responses depend on their willingness to risk misses or false alarms. (When in doubt, you have to risk one or the other.) Suppose you are the participant and you are told that you will receive a 10-cent reward whenever you correctly report that a light is

present, but you will be fined 1 cent if you say "yes" when it is absent. When you are in doubt, you guess "yes," with results like those in ▼ Figure 4.34a. Then the rules change: You receive a 1-cent reward for correctly reporting the presence of a light, but you suffer a 10-cent penalty and an electrical shock if you report a light when it was absent. Now you say "yes" only when certain, with results like those in ▼ Figure 4.34b.

People become cautious about false alarms for other reasons, too. In one experiment, participants were asked to read words that flashed briefly on a screen. They performed well with ordinary words such as *river* or *peach*. For emotionally loaded words such as *penis* or *bitch,* however, they generally said they were not sure what they saw. Several explanations are possible (e.g., G. S. Blum & Barbour, 1979). One is that participants hesitate to blurt out an emotionally charged word unless they are certain they are right.

The signal-detection approach is important in many settings remote from the laboratory. For

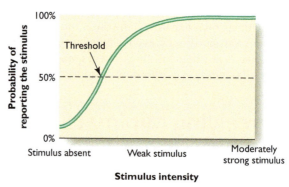

Instructions: You will receive a 10-cent reward for correctly reporting that a light is present. You will be penalized 1 cent for reporting that a light is present when it is not.

a

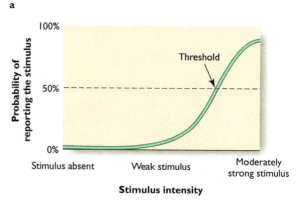

Instructions: You will receive a 1-cent reward for correctly reporting that a light is present. You will be penalized 10 cents *and* subjected to an electric shock for reporting that a light is present when it is not.

b

▲ **Figure 4.34** Results of measuring a sensory threshold with different instructions.

example, the legal system is also a signal-detection situation. A jury can be right in two ways and wrong in two ways:

	Defendant is guilty	**Defendant is innocent**
Jury votes "guilty"	Hit	False alarm
Jury votes "not guilty"	Miss	Correct rejection

Judges instruct juries to vote "not guilty" when in doubt. A miss, setting a guilty person free, is more acceptable than a false alarm that convicts an innocent person.

Another example is screening baggage at an airport. Screeners can err by thinking they see a weapon that is not present, or missing one that is there. A special problem in this case is that extremely few air travelers actually pack weapons. If you haven't seen a weapon in weeks, you expect not to see one, and you probably overlook a weapon even if you do see it (Mitroff & Biggs, 2014; Wolfe, Horowitz, & Kenner, 2005). Forcing people to slow down doesn't help much (Kunar, Rich, & Wolfe, 2010). (It just slows down the line at airport security.)

Radiologists encounter a related problem. A radiologist might scan through hundreds of X-ray scans, looking for small nodules that might indicate illness. With increasing expertise, they do find most of them, but they sometimes overlook something they hadn't expected to see. In one study, 24 expert radiologists examined chest scans of five people, looking for nodules. In the fifth one, researchers had added a drawing of a gorilla (see ▶ Figure 4.35). Although they found most of the nodules, only 4 of the 24 noticed the gorilla (Drew, Vō, & Wolfe, 2013).

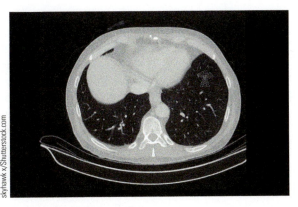

skyhawk x/Shutterstock.com

▲ **Figure 4.35** Most radiologists who were looking for lung nodules overlooked the much larger gorilla in this chest X-ray. From "The invisible gorilla strikes again: Sustained inattentional blindness in expert observers," by Drew, T., Vō, M. L.-H., & Wolfe, J. M., 2013. *Psychological Science, 24,* pp. 1848–1853.

concept check ✓

15. **Suppose a particular chemical is present in 90 percent of people with a particular kind of cancer. What, if anything, can we conclude? Think about this problem in terms of signal detection.**

Answer

15. We cannot conclude anything. After all, 100 percent of people with cancer have water in their bodies. The 90 percent figure means nothing unless we know how many people without cancer also have this chemical.

Subliminal Perception

Subliminal perception is the phenomenon that *a stimulus can influence behavior even when it is presented so faintly or briefly that the observer has no conscious perception of it.* (*Limen* is Latin for "threshold." Thus, subliminal means "below the threshold.") Is subliminal perception powerful, impossible, or something in between?

What Subliminal Perception Doesn't Do

Many years ago, claims were made that subliminal messages could control people's buying habits. For example, a theater owner might insert a single frame, "EAT POPCORN," in the middle of a film. Viewers, unaware of the message, supposedly would flock to the concession stand to buy popcorn. Many tests of this hypothesis found little or no effect (Cooper & Cooper, 2002), and the advertiser eventually admitted he had no evidence (Pratkanis, 1992).

Another claim is that certain rock-'n'-roll recordings contain "satanic" messages that were recorded backward and superimposed on the songs. Some people allege that listeners unconsciously perceive these messages and then follow the evil advice. If you spend hours listening to rock music played backward—and I hope you have something better to do with your time—with some imagination you can think you hear a variety of messages, regardless of whether the artists intended any such thing. However, for practical purposes it doesn't matter, because repeated studies have found that when you listen to music played

forward, you cannot decipher any backward message, and any backward message has no effect on your behavior (Kreiner, Altis, & Voss, 2003; Vokey & Read, 1985).

A third unsupported claim: "Subliminal audiotapes" with faint, inaudible messages can help you improve your memory, quit smoking, lose weight, or raise your self-esteem. In one study, psychologists asked more than 200 volunteers to listen to a popular brand of audiotape. However, they intentionally mislabeled some of the self-esteem tapes as "memory tapes" and some of the memory tapes as "self-esteem tapes." After a month of listening, most people who *thought* they were listening to self-esteem tapes said they had improved their self-esteem, and those who *thought* they were listening to memory tapes said they had improved their memory. The actual content made no difference. The improvement depended on people's expectations, not the tapes (Greenwald, Spangenberg, Pratkanis, & Eskanazi, 1991).

What Subliminal Perception Can Do

Subliminal messages do produce effects, although most are brief or subtle. For example, in several studies, people viewed pictures of faces with neutral, pleasant, or unpleasant expressions for a tiny fraction of a second, followed by an interfering pattern. Under these conditions, people have no conscious perception of the face. However, after seeing a happy face, they usually move their facial muscles briefly and slightly in the direction of a smile, and after seeing an angry face, they tense their muscles slightly in the direction of a frown (Dimberg, Thunberg, & Elmehed, 2000). If they view a face with an expression subliminally and shortly thereafter see the same face longer, with a neutral expression, they are more likely to evaluate the face favorably if the subliminal face had a pleasant expression, and to evaluate it unfavorably if the subliminal face had an unpleasant expression (Prochnow et al., 2013). In another study, young men viewed a variety of pictures for a tiny fraction of a second, followed by interfering pictures, and had no conscious response to any of them. However, some of the pictures showed naked loving couples. After those pictures, the men's brains showed increased activity in reward-related areas (Oei, Both, van Heemst, & van der Grond, 2014).

Subliminal perception effects emerge only as small changes in average performance, ordinarily in measurements taken shortly after the subliminal stimulus. However, the fact that such effects occur at all demonstrates the possibility of unconscious influences (Greenwald & Draine, 1997).

concept check

16. **Suppose someone claims that broadcasting the subliminal words "Don't shoplift," intermixed with music at a store, decreases shoplifting. What would be the best way to test that claim?**

Answer

16. Play that message on half of all days, randomly chosen, for a period of weeks. On other days, play no subliminal message or an irrelevant one. See whether the frequency of shoplifting decreases on days with the message.

Perceiving and Recognizing Patterns

People become amazingly good at recognizing objects and patterns. For example, you may someday go to a high school reunion and see people you haven't seen in many years. Some have grown fat or bald, or changed in other ways, but you will still recognize many of them (Bruck, Cavanagh, & Ceci, 1991). Although we recognize people mostly by facial features, we attend to the hair also. Can you identify the person in ▶ Figure 4.36?

The Feature-Detector Approach

How do we recognize people, objects, or any patterns at all? According to one explanation, we begin by breaking a stimulus into its parts. For example, when we look at a letter of the alphabet, *specialized neurons in the visual cortex,* called feature detectors, *respond to the presence of simple features, such as lines and angles.* One neuron might detect the feature "horizontal line," while another detects a vertical line, and so forth.

▲ **Figure 4.36** Who is this? We recognize people by hair as well as facial features. If you're not sure who it is, check answer C on page 140.

what's the evidence?

Feature Detectors

What evidence do we have for feature detectors in the brain? The evidence includes studies of laboratory animals and humans.

First Study

Hypothesis Neurons in the visual cortex of cats and monkeys respond only when light strikes the retina in a particular pattern.

Method Two pioneers in the study of the visual cortex, David Hubel and Torsten Wiesel (1981 Nobel Prize winners in physiology and medicine), inserted thin electrodes into cells of the occipital cortex of cats and monkeys and recorded the cells' activity as various light patterns struck the animals' retinas. At first, they used mere points of light that produced little response. Later they tried lines (see ▼ **Figure 4.37**).

Results They found that each cell responds best in the presence of a particular stimulus (Hubel & Wiesel, 1968). Some cells become active only at the sight of a vertical bar of light. Others become active only for a horizontal bar. In other words, the cells appear to be feature detectors. Later investigators found cells that respond to other features, such as movement in a particular direction.

Interpretation Hubel and Wiesel reported feature-detector neurons in cats and monkeys. If the organization of the visual cortex is similar in species as distantly related as cats and monkeys, it is likely (though not certain) to be similar in humans as well.

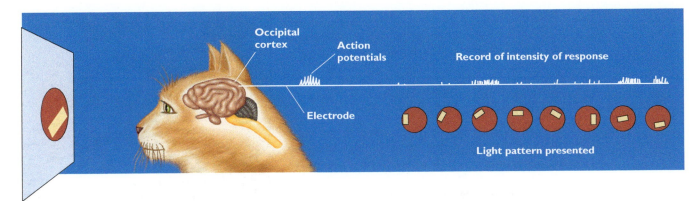

▲ **Figure 4.37** Hubel and Wiesel recorded the activity of neurons in the visual cortex. Most neurons responded vigorously only when a portion of the retina saw a bar of light oriented at a particular angle.

A second line of evidence follows this reasoning: If the human cortex has feature-detector cells, overstimulation of certain cells should fatigue them. Afterward, someone should see an aftereffect based on the inactivity of that those cells. (Recall negative color afterimages, as in Figure 4.12.) An example is the waterfall illusion: *If you stare at a waterfall for a minute or more and then turn your eyes to nearby cliffs, the cliffs appear to flow upward.* Staring at the waterfall fatigues neurons that respond to downward motion. When they fatigue, they become inactive, while neurons responding to upward motion remain active. The result is an illusion of upward motion.

Here is another demonstration:

Second Study

Hypothesis After you stare at vertical lines, you fatigue feature detectors responding to lines of that width. If you then look at wider or narrower lines, they will appear to be even wider or narrower than they really are.

Method Cover the right half of ▶ **Figure 4.38** and stare at the little rectangle in the middle of the left half for a minute or more. Do not stare at one point, but move your focus around within the rectangle. Then look at the square in the center of the right part of the figure and compare the spacing between the lines of the top and bottom gratings (Blakemore & Sutton, 1969).

Results What did you perceive in the right half? People generally report that the top lines look narrower and the bottom lines look wider.

Interpretation Staring at the left part of the figure fatigues neurons sensitive to wide lines in the top part of the figure and neurons sensitive to narrow lines in the bottom part. Then, when you look at lines of medium width, the fatigued cells are inactive. Cells sensitive to narrower lines dominate your perception in the top part, and those sensitive to wider lines dominate in the bottom part.

To summarize, two types of evidence support the existence of visual feature detectors: (a) The brains of other species contain cells with the properties of feature detectors, and (b) after staring at certain patterns, we see aftereffects that imply fatigue of feature-detector cells in the brain.

The research on feature detectors started an enormous amount of activity by laboratories throughout the world. Later results revised our views of what the earlier results mean. For example, even though certain neurons respond well to a single vertical line,

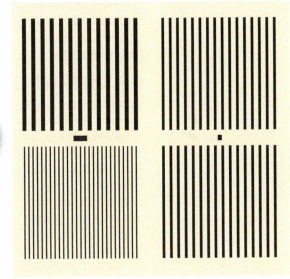

▲ **Figure 4.38** To fatigue your feature detectors and create an afterimage, follow the directions for the second study. (From Blakemore & Sutton, 1969)

most respond even more strongly to a sine-wave grating of lines:

Thus, the feature that cells detect is probably more complex than just a line. Furthermore, because each cell responds to a range of stimuli, no cell provides an unambiguous message about what you see at any moment.

An important point about scientific advances: A single line of evidence—even Nobel Prize–winning evidence—seldom provides the final answer to a question. We look for multiple ways to test a hypothesis.

17. **What is a feature detector?**

a

Do Feature Detectors Explain Perception?

The neurons just described are active in the early stages of visual processing. Do we simply add up the responses from various feature detectors to perceive a face?

No, feature detectors cannot completely explain how we perceive letters, much less faces. For example, we perceive the words in ▼ Figure 4.39a as CAT and HAT, even though the H and A symbols are identical. Likewise, the character in the center of ▼ Figure 4.39b can be read as either B or 13. Perceiving a pattern depends on context, not just adding up feature detectors.

Gestalt Psychology

Your ability to perceive something in more than one way, as in ▼ Figure 4.39, is the basis of Gestalt psychology, *a field that emphasizes perception of overall patterns. Gestalt* (geh-SHTALT) is a German word that means pattern or configuration. The founders of Gestalt psychology rejected the idea of breaking down a perception into its component parts. A melody broken into individual notes is no longer a melody. Their slogan was, "The whole is different from the sum of its parts."

Gestalt psychology does not deny the importance of feature detectors. It merely insists that feature detectors are not enough. Feature detectors represent a bottom-up process, *in which tiny elements combine to produce larger items.* However, perception also includes a top-down process, *in which you apply your experience and expectations to interpret each item in context.* Here are some examples.

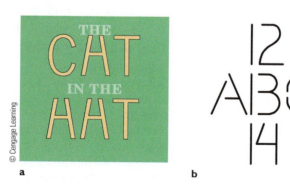

a   b

© Cengage Learning

▲ **Figure 4.39** Context determines our perception. In **(a)** you see the same item as A or H depending on context. In **(b)** the central character can appear as B or the number 13 depending on whether you read horizontally or vertically. (Part b from Kim, 1989)

b

▲ **Figure 4.40** Do you see an animal in each picture? If not, check answer D on page 140. (From "A puzzle picture with a new principle of concealment," by K. M. Dallenbach, 1951. *American Journal of Psychology, 54,* pp. 431–433. Copyright by the Board of Trustees of the University of Illinois.)

In either the top or bottom part of ▲ Figure 4.40, you might see only meaningless black and white patches for a while and then suddenly you might see an animal. To perceive the animals, you separate figure and ground—that is, you distinguish the *object from the background.* Ordinarily, you make that distinction almost instantly. You become aware of the process only when it is difficult (as it is here).

▼ Figure 4.41 shows four reversible figures *that can be perceived in more than one way.* In effect, we test hypotheses: "Is this the front of the object or is that the front? Is this section the foreground or the background?" The longer you look at a reversible figure, the more frequently you alternate between one perception and another (Long & Toppine, 2004). Part a is called the *Necker cube,* after the psychologist who first called attention to it. Which is the front face of the cube? You can see it either way. Part b is either a vase or two profiles. Does part c show an old woman or a young woman? Almost everyone sees one or the other immediately, but many people lock

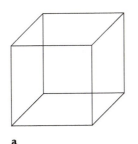

a b c d

▲ **Figure 4.41** Reversible figures: **(a)** The Necker cube. Which is the front face? **(b)** Faces or a vase? **(c)** An old woman or a young woman? **(d)** A face or what? (part c: From "A new ambiguous figure," by E. G. Boring. *American Journal of Psychology, 42*, pp. 444–445. Copyright 1930 by the Board of Trustees of the University of Illinois. Used by permission of the University of Illinois Press.)

into one perception so tightly that they do not see the other one. The 8-year-old girl who drew part d intended it as a face. Can you find another possibility? If you have trouble with parts c or d, check answers E, F, and G on page 140. The point of the reversible figures is that we perceive by imposing order (top-down), not just by adding up lines and points (bottom-up).

concept check

18. **In what way does the phenomenon of reversible figures conflict with the idea that feature detectors fully explain vision?**

Answer

18. If vision were simply a matter of stimulating feature detectors and adding up their responses, then a given display would always produce the same perception.

The Gestalt psychologists described principles of how we organize perceptions into meaningful wholes, as illustrated in ▼ **Figure 4.42**. **Proximity** is the *tendency to perceive objects that are close together as belonging to a group.* The objects in part a form two groups because of their proximity. The *tendency to perceive similar as being a group* is, quite reasonably, called **similarity**. In part b, we group the Xs together and the ●'s together because of similarity.

When lines are interrupted, as in part c, we perceive **continuation**, *a filling in of the gaps.* You probably perceive this illustration as a rectangle covering the center of a very long hot dog.

When a familiar figure is interrupted, as in part d, we perceive a **closure** of the figure; that is, *we imagine the rest of the figure* to see something that is simple, symmetrical, or consistent with our past experience (Shimaya, 1997). For example, you probably see the following as an orange rectangle overlapping a blue diamond, although you don't really know what, if anything, is behind the rectangle:

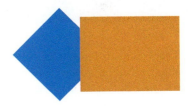

The principle of closure resembles continuation. With a complicated pattern, however, closure deals with more information. For example, in Figure 4.42c, you fill in the gaps to perceive one long hot dog. With additional context, you might perceive the same pattern as two shorter hot dogs:

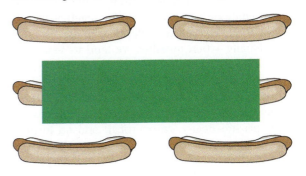

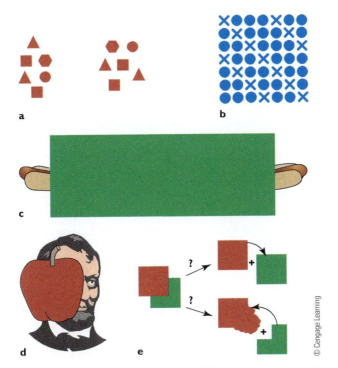

a b c d e

© Cengage Learning

▲ **Figure 4.42** Gestalt principles of **(a)** proximity, **(b)** similarity, **(c)** continuation, **(d)** closure, and **(e)** good figure.

a

b

c

▲ **Figure 4.43** From part a to part b, the head and tail move the same way, and it appears to be one lizard. From part a to part c, the head moves and the tail doesn't, so it must be two lizards.

Another Gestalt principle is **common fate**: *We perceive objects as part of the same group if they change or move in similar ways at the same time.* If you see two objects move in the same direction and speed, you see them as parts of the same thing, as in ▲ Figure 4.43. Also, if they grow brighter or darker together, you see them as related (Sekuler & Bennett, 2001).

Finally, when possible, we tend to perceive a **good figure**—*a simple, familiar, symmetrical figure.* Many familiar objects are geometrically simple or close to it: The sun and moon are round, tree trunks meet the ground at almost a right angle, faces and animals are nearly symmetrical, and so forth. If we can interpret something as a circle, square, or straight line, we do. In Figure 4.42e, the part on the

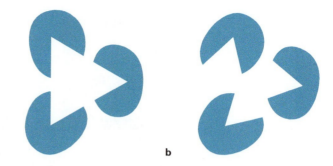

a   b

▲ **Figure 4.44** In **(a)** we see a triangle overlapping three irregular ovals. We see it because triangles are "good figures" and symmetrical. If we tilt the ovals, as in **(b)**, the illusory triangle disappears. (From Singh, Hoffman, & Albert, 1999)

left could represent a red square overlapping a green one or a green backward L overlapping a red object of almost any shape. We are powerfully drawn to the first interpretation because it includes "good," regular, symmetrical objects.

In ▲ Figure 4.44a, we perceive a white triangle overlapping three ovals (Singh, Hoffman, & Albert, 1999). However, if we tilt the blue objects, as in ▲ Figure 4.44b, the illusion of something on top of them disappears. We "see" the overlapping object only if it is a symmetrical, good figure.

Does the principle of good figure apply only in Westernized societies, where people become familiar with squares, triangles, and so forth from an early age? Apparently not. Researchers studied the Himba, a southwest African culture with no manufactured products and few words for shapes. Even they noticed the difference between squares and almost-square shapes, about as well as U.S. college students did (Biederman, Yue, & Davidoff, 2009).

Similarities between Vision and Hearing

The perceptual organization principles of Gestalt psychology apply to hearing also. Like reversible figures, some sounds can be heard in more than one way. You can hear a clock going "tick, tock, tick, tock" or "tock, tick, tock, tick." You can hear your windshield wipers going "dunga, dunga" or "gadung, gadung."

The Gestalt principles of continuation and closure work best when one item interrupts something else. In ▼ Figure 4.45, the context in parts c and d suggests objects partly blocking our view of a three-dimensional cube. In parts a and b, we are much less likely to see a cube, as nothing suggests something occluding

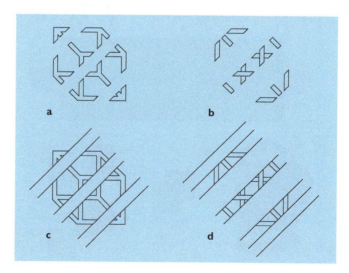

a   b

c   d

▲ **Figure 4.45** **(a)** and **(b)** appear to be arrays of flat objects. Introducing a context of overlapping lines causes a cube to emerge in **(c)** and **(d)**. (From Kanizsa, 1979)

© Cengage Learning

a

b

◀**Figure 4.46** Why is the word *psychology* easier to read in (**b**) than in (**a**)? (After Bregman, 1981)

the view. Similarly, in ▲ Figure 4.46a, we see a series of meaningless patches. In ▲ Figure 4.46b, the addition of some black glop helps us see these patches as the word *psychology* (Bregman, 1981).

The same is true in hearing. If a speech or song is broken up by periods of silence, we do not fill in the gaps and we find the utterance hard to understand. However, if the same gaps are filled with noise, we "hear" what probably occurred during the gaps. That is, we apply continuation and closure (C. T. Miller, Dibble, & Hauser, 2001; Warren, 1970).

Perceiving Movement and Depth

As an automobile moves away from us, its image on the retina grows smaller, but we perceive it as moving, not shrinking. That perception illustrates visual constancy—our *tendency to perceive objects as keeping their shape, size, and color, despite distortions in the actual pattern reaching the retina.* ▼ Figure 4.47 shows

a

b

▲ **Figure 4.47** (**a**) Shape constancy: We perceive all three doors as rectangles. (**b**) Size constancy: We perceive all three hands as equal in size.

examples of shape constancy and size constancy. Constancies depend on our familiarity with objects and on our ability to estimate distances and angles of view. For example, we know that a door is still rectangular even when we view it from an odd angle. But to recognize that an object keeps its shape and size, we have to perceive movement or changes in distance. How do we do so?

Perception of Movement

Moving objects capture attention for a good reason. Throughout our evolutionary history, moving objects have been more likely than stationary objects to require action. A moving object might be another person, or something you could catch and eat, or something that wants to catch and eat you. People are particularly adept at perceiving a body in motion. Suppose we attach small lights to someone's shoulders, elbows, hands, hips, knees, and ankles. Then we turn out all other lights so that you see just the lights on this person. As soon as the person starts to walk, you see the lights as a person in motion. In fact, you have a brain area specialized for just this task (Grossman & Blake, 2001). If you do an Internet search for Biomotion, you can find a marvelous illustration of this process.

Try this simple demonstration: Hold an object in front of your eyes and then move it to the right. Now hold the object in front of your eyes and move your eyes to the left. The image of the object moves across your retina in the same way when you move the object as when you move your eyes. Yet you perceive the object as moving in one case but not in the other. Why?

The object looks stationary when you move your eyes for two reasons. One is that the vestibular system informs the visual areas of the brain about your head and eye movements. When your brain knows that your eyes have moved to the left, it interprets what you see as the result of eye movement. One man with a rare kind of brain damage could not connect his eye movements with his perceptions. Whenever he moved his head or eyes, the world appeared to be moving. Frequently, he became dizzy and nauseated (Haarmeier, Thier, Repnow, & Petersen, 1997).

The other reason is that you perceive motion when an object moves *relative to the background* (Gibson, 1968). When you walk, stationary objects move across your retina but do not move relative to the background.

What do you perceive when an object is stationary and the background moves? In that unusual case, you *incorrectly perceive the object as moving,* a phenomenon called induced movement. When you watch clouds moving across the moon, you might perceive the clouds as stationary and the moon as moving. Induced movement is *apparent movement,* as opposed to *real movement.*

You have already read about the waterfall illusion (page 129), another example of apparent movement. Yet another is stroboscopic movement, an *illusion of movement created by a rapid succession of stationary images.* When a scene flashes on a screen, followed a split second later by a slightly different scene, you perceive objects as moving smoothly (see ▼ Figure 4.48). Motion pictures are actually a series of still photos flashed on the screen.

The ability to detect visual movement played an interesting role in the history of astronomy. In 1930, Clyde Tombaugh was searching the skies for a possible undiscovered planet beyond Neptune. He photographed each region of the sky twice, several days apart. A planet, unlike a star, moves from one photo to the next. However, how would he find a small dot that moved among all the countless unmoving dots in the sky? He put each pair of photos on a machine that would flip back and forth between one photo and the other. When he came to one pair of photos, he immediately noticed one dot moving as the machine flipped back and forth (Tombaugh, 1980). He identified that dot as Pluto, which astronomers now list as a dwarf planet (see ▶ Figure 4.49).

▲ **Figure 4.49** Clyde Tombaugh photographed each area of the sky twice, several days apart. Then he used a machine to flip back and forth between the two photos of each pair. When he came to one part of the sky, he noticed a dot moving between the two photos. That dot was Pluto.

Perception of Depth

Although we live in a world of three dimensions, our retinas are in effect two-dimensional surfaces. Depth perception, the *perception of distance,* enables us to experience the world in three dimensions. This perception depends on several factors.

One factor is retinal disparity—*the difference in the apparent position of an object as seen by the left and right retinas.* Try this: Hold a finger at arm's length. Focus on it with one eye and then the other. Note that the apparent position of your finger shifts with respect to the background. Now hold your finger closer to your face and repeat. The apparent position of your finger shifts even more. The amount of discrepancy between the two eyes is one way to gauge distance.

A second cue for depth perception is the convergence of the eyes—that is, the *degree to which they turn in to focus on a close object.* When you focus on something close, your eyes turn in, and you sense the tension of your eye muscles. The more the muscles pull, the closer the object must be.

Retinal disparity and convergence are called binocular cues because they *depend on both eyes.* Monocular cues enable you to *judge depth and distance with just one eye* or when both eyes see the same image, as when you look at a picture, such as ▼ Figure 4.50. The ability to interpret depth in a picture depends

▲ **Figure 4.50** We judge depth and distance in a photograph using monocular cues (those that would work even with just one eye). Closer objects occupy more space on the retina (or in the photograph) than do distant objects of the same type. Nearer objects show more detail. Closer objects overlap distant objects. Objects in the foreground look sharper than objects do on the horizon.

▲ **Figure 4.48** A movie consists of a series of still photographs flickering at 86,400 per hour. Here you see a series of stills spread out in space instead of time.

on experience. For example, in ▶ Figure 4.51, does it appear to you that the hunter is aiming his spear at the antelope? When this drawing was shown to African people who had seldom or never seen drawings, many said the hunter was aiming at a baby elephant (Hudson, 1960).

Let's consider some of the monocular cues we use to perceive depth:

Object size: Other things being equal, a nearby object produces a larger image than a distant one. This cue helps only for objects of known size. For example, the backpacker in Figure 4.50 produces a larger image than do the mountains, which we know are larger. So we see the person as closer. However, the mountains in the background differ in actual as well as apparent size, so we cannot assume the ones that look bigger are closer.

Linear perspective: As parallel lines stretch out toward the horizon, they come closer together. Examine the road in Figure 4.50. At the bottom of the photo (close to the viewer), the edges of the road are far apart. At greater distances they come together.

Detail: We see nearby objects, such as the backpacker, in more detail than distant objects.

Interposition: A nearby object interrupts our view of a more distant object. For example, the tree on the right interrupts our view of the mountains, so we see that the tree is closer than the mountains.

Texture gradient: The bushes and leaves on the left of the photo are more clearly separated, whereas those toward the center look less distinct from one another. The "packed together" appearance of objects gives us another cue to their approximate distance.

Shadows: Shadows help us gauge sizes as well as locations of objects.

Accommodation: The lens of the eye *accommodates*—that is, it changes shape—to focus on nearby objects, and your brain detects that change and thereby infers the distance to an object. Accommodation could help tell you how far away the photograph itself is, although it provides no information about the relative distances of objects in the photograph.

Motion parallax: Another monocular cue helps us perceive depth while we are moving, although it does not help with a photograph. If you are walking or riding in a car and fixating at the horizon, nearby objects move rapidly across the retina, while those farther away move less. The *difference in speed of movement of images across the retina as you travel* is the principle of motion parallax. Television and film crews use this principle. If the camera moves slowly, you see closer objects move more than distant ones and get a sense of depth.

▲ **Figure 4.51** Which animal is the hunter attacking? Many people unfamiliar with drawings and photographs said he was attacking a baby elephant. (From Hudson, 1960)

concept check

19. **Which monocular cues to depth are available in Figure 4.51?**

Answer

19. Object size and linear perspective are cues that the elephant must be far away.

Steve McGurry/Magnum Photos

If you were a passenger on this train looking toward the horizon, the ground beside the tracks would appear to pass by more quickly than more distant parts of the landscape. In this photo's version of motion parallax, the ground is blurred and more distant objects are crisp.

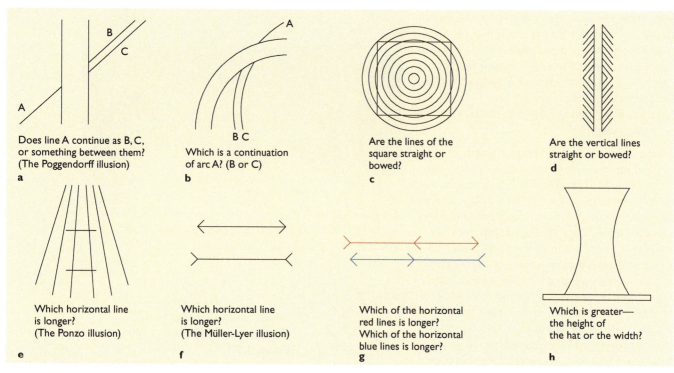

▲ **Figure 4.52** These geometric figures illustrate optical illusions. Answers (which you are invited to check with ruler and compass): **(a)** B, **(b)** B, **(c)** straight, **(d)** straight, **(e)** equal, **(f)** equal, **(g)** equal, **(h)** equal.

Optical Illusions

Vision is well adapted to understanding what we see, but special situations can fool it. An **optical illusion** is a *misinterpretation of a visual stimulus.* ▲ Figure 4.52 shows a few examples. If you do an Internet search for optical illusions, you will find a treasure trove of amusing and instructive examples.

Psychologists would like to explain the optical illusions as simply and parsimoniously as possible. One approach that applies to many but not all illusions pertains to mistakes of depth perception.

Depth Perception and Size Perception

As you see in ▶ Figure 4.53, an image on the retina may represent either a small, close object or a large, distant object. If you know the size or the distance, you can estimate the other one. However, if you misjudge size or distance, you will be wrong about the other also.

Watch what happens when you take a single image and change its apparent distance: Stare at Figure 4.12 again to form a negative afterimage. Examine the afterimage while looking at a sheet of paper. As you move the paper backward and forward, you can change the apparent size.

The world provides many cues about the size and distance of objects, but not always for objects in the sky. If you see an unfamiliar object in the sky, you might misjudge its distance, and if so, you will also misjudge its size and speed. For example, if you see an odd-looking small object floating by in the sky but you interpret it as far away, you could easily think you are seeing a large UFO traveling at an incredible speed.

Many optical illusions occur based on misjudging distance. ▼ Figure 4.54a shows people in the Ames room (named for its designer, Adelbert Ames). The room looks like a normal rectangular room, but one corner is actually much closer than the other. If we eliminated all the background cues, we would correctly perceive the woman as being about the same size as the man, and farther

▲ **Figure 4.53** No, it's not a bird on steroids. This night heron was close to the camera. If you misjudge the distance to something, you misjudge its size.

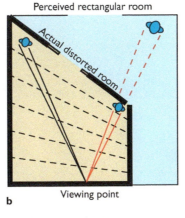

Perceived rectangular room

Actual distorted room

Viewing point

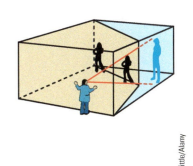

Michael Doolittle/Alamy

Michael Doolittle/Alamy

a

b

▲ **Figure 4.54** The Ames room is designed to view through a peephole with one eye. (**a**) The man on the right appears much larger than the woman to the left. (**b**) This diagram shows how the shape of the room distorts the viewer's perception of distance. (Part b from J. R. Wilson et al., 1964)

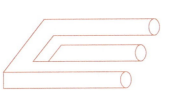

▲ **Figure 4.55** These two-dimensional drawings puzzle us because we try to interpret them as three-dimensional objects.

away. However, the apparently rectangular room provides such misleading cues to distance that the man appears to be unrealistically tall.

Many two-dimensional drawings offer misleading depth cues. Because of your long experience with photos and drawings, you interpret most drawings as representations of three-dimensional scenes. ▲ Figure 4.55 shows a bewildering two-prong/three-prong device and a round staircase that seems to run uphill all the way clockwise or downhill all the way counterclockwise. Both drawings puzzle us when we try to see them as three-dimensional objects.

In ▶ Figure 4.56, linear perspective suggests that the right of the picture is farther away than the left. We therefore see the cylinder on the right as being the farthest away. If it is the farthest and still produces the same size image on the retina as the other two, then it would have to be the largest. When we are misled by the cues that ordinarily ensure constancy in size and shape, we experience an optical illusion (Day, 1972).

▼ Figure 4.57 shows the tabletop illusion (Shepard, 1990). Here, almost unbelievably, the vertical dimension of the blue table equals the horizontal dimension of the yellow table, and the horizontal dimension of the blue table equals the vertical dimension of the yellow table. The blue table appears long and thin compared to the yellow one because we interpret it in depth. In effect, your brain constructs what each table would have to really *be* to look this way (Purves & Lotto, 2003).

Here is a possible application of optical illusions: In the display on the right, the central circles are equal, but most people see the one on the right as larger. Researchers set up putting greens and let golfers try to sink putts, sometimes with large circles surrounding the hole (as on the left) and sometimes with small circles surrounding it (as on

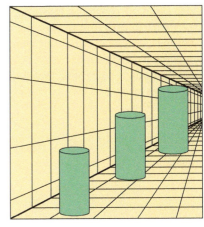

▲ **Figure 4.56** The cylinder on the right seems larger because the context makes it appear farther away.

the right). People sank almost twice as many putts for the version on the right, where the hole *looked* bigger (Witt, Linkenauger, & Proffitt, 2012). I don't know whether they will let you put little circles on the ground during your next golf tournament.

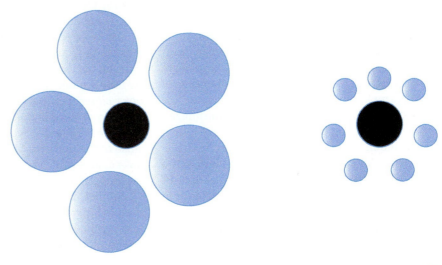

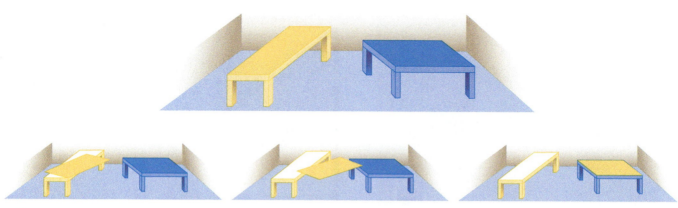

▲ **Figure 4.57** The tabletop illusion. The blue table is as wide as the yellow table is long, and as long as the yellow table is wide. The parts below show rotation of the yellow table to overlap the blue one.

▶ **Figure 4.58** Ordinarily, the moon looks much larger at the horizon than it does overhead. In photographs, this illusion disappears almost completely, but the photographs demonstrate that the physical image of the moon is the same in both cases. The moon illusion requires a psychological explanation, not a physical one.

Mark Artman/The Image Works

The Moon Illusion

To most people, the *moon at the horizon appears about 30 percent larger than it appears when it is higher in the sky.* This moon illusion is so convincing that many people have tried to explain it by referring to the bending of light rays by the atmosphere or other physical phenomena. However, if you photograph the moon and measure its image, you will find that it is the same size at the horizon as it is higher in the sky. ▲ Figure 4.58 shows the moon at two positions in the sky. You can measure the two images to demonstrate that they are really the same size. (The atmosphere's bending of light rays makes the moon look orange near the horizon, but it does not increase the size of the image.) However, photographs do not capture the strength of the moon illusion as we see it in real life. In Figure 4.58 or any similar pair of photos, the moon looks almost the same at each position. In the actual night sky, the moon looks enormous at the horizon.

One explanation is size comparison. When you see the moon low in the sky, it seems large compared

to the tiny buildings or trees you see at the horizon. When you see the moon high in the sky, it appears small compared to the vast, featureless sky (Baird, 1982; Restle, 1970).

A second explanation is that the terrain between the viewer and the horizon gives an impression of great distance. When the moon is high in the sky, we have no basis to judge distance, and we unconsciously see the overhead moon as closer. Because we see the horizon moon as more distant, we perceive it as larger (Kaufman & Rock, 1989; Rock & Kaufman, 1962). This explanation is appealing because it relates the moon illusion to perception of distance, a factor already accepted as important for other illusions.

Many psychologists are not satisfied with this explanation, however, because they are not convinced that the horizon moon looks farther away than the overhead moon. If we ask which looks farther away, many people say they are not sure. If we insist on an answer, most say the horizon moon looks *closer,* contradicting the theory. Some psychologists reply that the situation is complicated: We unconsciously perceive the horizon as farther away. Consequently, we perceive the horizon moon as very large. Then, because of the perceived large size of the horizon moon, we consciously say it looks closer, while continuing unconsciously to perceive it as farther (Rock & Kaufman, 1962).

Studies of optical illusions confirm what other phenomena already indicated: What we perceive is not the same as what is "out there." Our visual system does an amazing job of providing us with useful information about the world around us, but under unusual circumstances, we have distorted perceptions.

Making Sense of Sensory Information

You have probably heard the expression, "Seeing is believing." The saying is true in many ways, including that what you believe influences what you see. Perception is not just a matter of adding up the events striking the retina. We look for what we expect to see, we impose order on haphazard patterns, we see three dimensions in two-dimensional drawings, and we see optical illusions. The brain does not compute what light is striking the retina but tries to learn what the objects really are and what they are doing.

Summary

- *Perception of minimal stimuli.* No sharp dividing line distinguishes sensory stimuli that can be perceived and sensory stimuli that cannot be perceived. (page 125)
- *Signal detection.* To determine how accurately someone detects a signal, we need to consider not only the ratio of hits to misses when the stimulus is present but also the ratio of false alarms to correct rejections when the stimulus is absent. (page 126)
- *Detecting rare stimuli.* When people are trying to detect some item, they are more likely to overlook it if it occurs rarely. (page 127)
- *Subliminal perception.* Under some circumstances, a weak stimulus that we do not consciously identify influences our behavior, at least briefly. (page 127)
- *Feature detectors.* In the first stages of the process of perception, feature-detector neurons identify lines, points, and simple movement. Visual aftereffects can be interpreted in terms of fatiguing certain feature detectors. (page 128)
- *Perception of organized wholes.* According to Gestalt psychologists, we perceive an organized whole by identifying patterns in a top-down manner. (page 130)
- *Visual constancies.* We ordinarily perceive the shape, size, and color of objects as constant, even when the pattern of light striking the retina varies. (page 133)
- *Motion perception.* We perceive an object as moving if it moves relative to its background. We can distinguish between an object that is actually moving and a similar pattern of retinal stimulation that results from our own movement. (page 133)
- *Depth perception.* To perceive depth, we use the accommodation of the eye muscles and retinal disparity between the views that our two eyes see. We also learn to use several other cues that are just as effective with one eye as with two. (page 134)
- *Optical illusions.* Some optical illusions occur because we misperceive the relative distances of objects. We perceive displays by comparing them to our previous experiences with similar objects. (page 136)

Key Terms

absolute sensory threshold (page 125)

binocular cues (page 134)

bottom-up process (page 130)

closure (page 131)

common fate (page 132)

continuation (page 131)

convergence (page 134)

depth perception (page 134)

feature detector (page 128)

figure and ground (page 130)

Gestalt psychology (page 130)

good figure (page 132)

induced movement (page 134)

monocular cues (page 134)

moon illusion (page 138)

motion parallax (page 135)

optical illusion (page 136)

proximity (page 131)

retinal disparity (page 134)

reversible figure (page 130)

signal-detection theory (page 126)

similarity (page 131)

stroboscopic movement (page 134)

subliminal perception (page 127)

top-down process (page 130)

visual constancy (page 133)

waterfall illusion (page 129)

Answers to Other Questions in the Module

C. Marilyn Monroe

E.

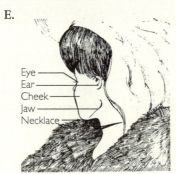

Eye —
Ear —
Cheek —
Jaw —
Necklace —

Young woman

G.

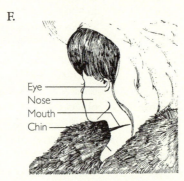

D.

F.

Eye —
Nose —
Mouth —
Chin —

Old woman

Review Questions

1. Suppose 70 percent of people with depression show recovery over 6 months on a particular type of therapy. Before we draw any conclusion about the effectiveness of the therapy, what is the most important thing we need to know?
   (a) Were these people a random sample of all people with depression?
   (b) What was the nature of the therapy and did it have any bad side effects?
   (c) How long did they remain in a state of recovery?
   (d) How many people without the therapy also recovered over 6 months?

2. Subliminal perception has been demonstrated to produce which of these effects?
   (a) A subliminal message during a movie to "buy popcorn" greatly increases popcorn sales.
   (b) Messages recorded backward on rock music turn teenagers to evil deeds.
   (c) Listening to subliminal messages on a recording can improve memory or self-esteem.
   (d) Seeing a facial expression subliminally has temporary emotional effects.

3. What evidence supports the idea of feature detectors?
   (a) People who have lost a particular brain neuron become unable to recognize a particular object.
   (b) Recordings from laboratory animals show that each neuron in the visual system responds mainly to a particular kind of stimulus.
   (c) People who have stared at a particular stimulus for a minute or more become better able to detect the same stimulus.
   (d) People can easily recognize an object even after it has changed in color, shape, or direction.

4. What is the emphasis of Gestalt psychology with regard to vision?
   (a) Top-down processes are important for perception.
   (b) Bottom-up processes are important for perception.
   (c) Mechanisms of vision differ from one animal species to another.

5. With three-dimensional photography, cameras take two views of the same scene from different locations through lenses with different color filters or with different polarized-light filters. The two views are then superimposed. The viewer looks at the

composite view through special glasses so that one eye sees the view taken with one camera and the other eye sees the view taken with the other camera. Which depth cue is at work here?

(a) Motion parallax
(b) Interposition
(c) Retinal disparity
(d) Convergence

6. Of the various cues to distance, which ones are binocular cues?
(a) Object size and linear perspective
(b) Retinal disparity and convergence
(c) Interposition and texture gradient
(d) Accommodation and motion parallax

7. Which of the following explains many optical illusions?
(a) Horizontal eye movements are more difficult than vertical eye movements.
(b) If you misjudge distance, you also misjudge size.
(c) Light bends as it travels through the atmosphere.
(d) What other people say about something influences your judgment.

Answers: 1d, 2d, 3b, 4a, 5c, 6b, 7b.

5 Development

Suppose you buy a robot. When you get home, you discover that it does nothing useful. It cannot even maintain its balance. It makes irritating, high-pitched noises, moves its limbs haphazardly, and leaks. The store you bought it from refuses to take it back. And you're not allowed to turn it off. So you are stuck with this useless machine.

A few years later, your robot walks and talks, reads and writes, draws pictures, and does arithmetic. It follows your directions (usually) and sometimes does useful things without being told. It beats you at memory games.

How did all this happen? After all, you knew nothing about how to program a robot. Did your robot have some sort of built-in programming that simply took a long time to phase in? Or was it programmed to learn all these skills?

Children are like that robot. Parents wonder, "How did my children get to be the way they are? And why did my two children turn out so different?" Developmental psychology seeks to understand how nature and nurture combine to produce human behavior "from womb to tomb."

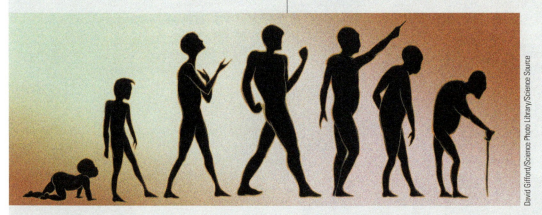

David Gifford/Science Photo Library/Science Source

As we grow older, our behavior changes in many ways. Developmental psychologists seek to describe and understand these changes.

module 5.1

Cognitive Development in Infancy and Childhood

After studying this module, you should be able to:

- Contrast cross-sectional designs and longitudinal designs.
- Give examples of cohort effects.
- Explain how psychologists infer the cognitive abilities of infants.
- List and describe Piaget's stages of cognitive development.
- Discuss two methods of inferring the concept of object permanence.
- Give examples to show that infants develop cognitive abilities gradually.

Young children's artwork is amazingly inventive and revealing. One toddler, 1½ years old, proudly showed off a drawing that consisted only of dots. Adults were puzzled. It is a rabbit, the child explained, while making more dots: "Look: hop, hop, hop . . . " (Winner, 1986). When my daughter, Robin, was 6 years old, she drew a picture of a boy and a girl wearing Halloween costumes and drawing pictures (see ▶ Figure 5.1). For the little girl's drawing, Robin pasted on some wildlife photos that, she insisted, were the little girl's drawings. The little boy's drawing was just a scribble. When I asked why the little girl's drawing was so much better than the little boy's, Robin replied, "Don't make fun of him, Daddy. He's doing the best he can."

Often, as in this case, a drawing expresses the child's worldview. As children grow older, their art becomes more skillful, but often less expressive. As we grow older, we gain many new abilities and skills, but we lose something, too.

Studying the abilities of young children is challenging. They misunderstand our questions and we misunderstand their answers. Our estimate of children has progressed enormously as developmental psychologists have developed clever new ways to test children. One theme you will encounter repeatedly in this module is that we reach different conclusions about children depending on how we measure some ability.

© Robin Kalat

▲ **Figure 5.1** A drawing of two children drawing pictures, courtesy of 6-year-old Robin Kalat.

Research Designs for Studying Development

Studying psychological development poses a special problem. Should a researcher study younger and older people at the same time, or study one group of people repeatedly as they advance from one age to another? Each method has strengths and limitations.

Myrleen Ferguson Cate/PhotoEdit

As we grow older, we mature, but we revert to childlike behaviors when such behavior is acceptable.

Table 5.1 Cross-Sectional and Longitudinal Studies

	Description	Advantages	Disadvantages	Example
Cross-sectional	Several groups of subjects of various ages studied at one time	1. Quick 2. No risk of confusing age effects with effects of changes in society	1. Risk of sampling error by getting different kinds of people at different ages 2. Risk of cohort effects	Compare memory abilities of 3-, 5-, and 7-year-olds
Longitudinal	One group of subjects studied repeatedly as the members grow older	1. No risk of sampling differences 2. Can study effects of one experience on later development 3. Can study consistency within individuals over time	1. Takes a long time 2. Some participants quit 3. Sometimes hard to separate effects of age from changes in society	Study memory abilities of 3-year-olds, and of the same children again 2 and 4 years later

Cross-Sectional and Longitudinal Designs

A cross-sectional study *compares groups of individuals of different ages at the same time.* For example, we could compare drawings by 6-year-olds, 8-year-olds, and 10-year-olds. Cross-sectional studies are acceptable for many purposes, but not always. For example, if you compared a random sample of 55-year-olds with a random sample of 85-year-olds, you would find that the 85-year-olds have less interest in sports. You would also find that, on average, 85-year-olds are shorter and have smaller heads. Why? One explanation is that, on average, women live longer than men. Women tend to be smaller, have smaller heads, and show less interest in sports. The sample of 55-year-olds you studied was not comparable to the 85-year-olds.

A longitudinal study *follows a single group of individuals as they develop.* For example, we could study a group of children from, say, age 6 to age 12. ■ Table 5.1 contrasts the two kinds of studies. A longitudinal study necessarily takes years to complete. Also, not everyone who participates the first time is willing and available later. Selective attrition is *the tendency for certain kinds of people to drop out of a study* for many reasons, including health, moving far away, or loss of interest. The kind of people who stay in the study may differ in many ways from those who quit. Psychologists can compensate for selective attrition by discarding the earlier data for people who left the study.

Certain questions logically require a longitudinal study. For example, to study the effects of divorce on children, researchers compare how each child reacts at first with how that same child reacts later. To study whether happy children become happy adults, researchers follow a single group over time.

A sequential (or cross-sequential) design combines cross-sectional and longitudinal designs. In a sequential design, a researcher starts with people of different ages and studies them again at later times. For example, one might study 6-year-olds and 8-year-olds and then examine the same children 2 years later:

First study	2 years later
Group A, age 6 years	Group A, now 8 years old
Group B, age 8 years	Group B, now 10 years old

1. **At Santa Enigma College, the average first-year student has a C-minus average, and the average senior has a B-plus average. An observer concludes that, as students progress through** college, they improve their study habits. Based on the idea of selective attrition, **propose another possible explanation.**

Cohort Effects

If you had been born in 1940, your childhood and adolescence would have been very different from today: no Internet, computers, iPods, cell phones, air conditioners, automatic dishwashers, or appliances for washing and drying clothes. You would have listened to radio instead of watching television. Telephone calls to someone outside your hometown were an expensive luxury. Few women or minorities went to college, and they had limited job opportunities afterward. If you had lived then, how would you have been different?

People of different generations differ in many ways, called *cohort effects* (see ▼ **Figure 5.2**). A **cohort** is *a group of people born at a particular time or a group of people who enter an organization at a particular time.* (We could talk about the cohort of students entering a college in a given year, or the cohort of workers a corporation hires in a given year.)

The era in which you grew up is a powerful influence on your psychological development. For example, Americans whose youth spanned the Great Depression and World War II learned to save money and to sacrifice for the needs of the country. Even after the war was over and prosperity reigned, most remained thrifty and cautious (Rogler, 2002). In contrast, young people of today have had much more leisure time and more opportunity for recreation (Larson, 2001). Today's youth tend to be more self-satisfied than young people of the past (Twenge & Campbell, 2008).

In the United States long ago, as in many countries today, it was customary for most people to spend their lives in or near the neighborhood where they were born. Today many people move great distances, perhaps repeatedly, in search of a better job. The results include less identification with their community, few lasting friendships, and less feeling of obligation to help their neighbors (Oishi, 2010). According to Jean Twenge (2006), cohort effects are similar to cultural differences. Much of today's technology is so unfamiliar to many older people that they feel like immigrants to this culture.

2. **Suppose you want to study the effect of age on choice of clothing. Would cohort effects have greater influence on a longitudinal study or a cross-sectional study?**

▲ **Figure 5.2** People born at different times grow up with different experiences. In an earlier era, bathing suit inspectors prohibited "overly revealing" outfits that would seem modest today.

The Fetus and the Newborn

Let's begin at the beginning. During prenatal development, everyone starts as a *fertilized egg cell,* or **zygote**, that develops through its first few stages until it becomes a **fetus** *about 8 weeks after conception.* As soon as 6 weeks after conception, the nervous system is mature enough to produce a few movements. The first movements are spontaneous—that is, not elicited by any stimulus. Contrary to what we might have guessed, the muscles and the nerves controlling these movements mature before the sense organs. Those spontaneous movements are essential, and without them the spinal cord does not develop properly. Later, but still before birth, the sense organs appear, the head and eyes begin to turn toward sounds, and the brain alternates between waking and sleeping (Joseph, 2000). The fetus does a good bit of yawning and hiccupping. Presumably these behaviors serve some function, although that function remains unclear (Provine, 2012).

A serious risk arises if a fetus is exposed to alcohol. Any drugs that a mother takes reach the fetus's vulnerable developing brain (Hubbs-Tait, Nation, Krebs, & Bellinger, 2005). *If the mother drinks alcohol during pregnancy,* the infant may develop **fetal alcohol syndrome**, *a condition marked by malformations of the face, heart, and ears; and nervous system damage, including seizures, hyperactivity, and impairments of learning, memory, problem solving, attention, and motor coordination* (Mattson, Crocker, & Nguyen, 2011). The severity varies from severe to barely noticeable, depending on the amount and timing of the mother's drinking (see ▼ Figure 5.3).

Binge drinking is particularly dangerous, and prolonged drinking is worse than brief drinking, but researchers cannot identify any level as "safe" (May et al., 2013).

The reason for the nervous system damage is now understood: Developing neurons require persistent excitation to survive. Without it, they activate a self-destruct program, which is a way of weeding out the less useful neurons. Alcohol interferes with the brain's main excitatory neurotransmitter (glutamate) and facilitates the main inhibitory neurotransmitter (GABA). It therefore decreases neurons' arousal and makes many of them self-destruct (Ikonomidou et al., 2000). Other drugs that interfere with excitatory transmission may be dangerous also, possibly including repeated exposure to anesthetic drugs (Gleich, Nemergut, & Flick, 2013).

Still, it is remarkable that an occasional "high-risk" child—small at birth, exposed to alcohol or other drugs before birth, from a disadvantaged family, a victim of prejudice, and so forth—overcomes all obstacles to become healthy and successful. Resilience (the ability to overcome obstacles) is poorly understood, but it relates partly to genetic influences, education, and supportive relatives and friends (Bonanno & Mancini, 2008).

concept check

_____

3. By what mechanism does alcohol harm the brain of a fetus?

_____

Answer

3. Alcohol impairs excitatory transmission in neurons. Neurons that do not get enough excitation during early development execute a self-destruct program.

Infancy

Research progress depends on good measurement. How can we measure psychological processes in infants who cannot talk and can barely control a few muscles? A researcher monitors the few actions available to infants, drawing inferences about their growing understanding of the world.

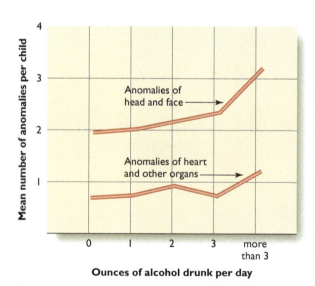

▲ **Figure 5.3** **(a)** The more alcohol a woman drinks during pregnancy, the more likely her baby is to have anomalies of the head, face, and organs. (Based on data of Ernhart et al., 1987) **(b)** A child with fetal alcohol syndrome: Note the wide separation between the eyes, a common feature of this syndrome.

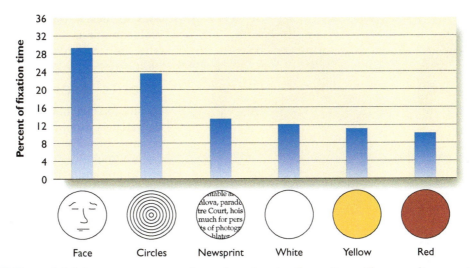

▲ **Figure 5.4** Infants pay more attention to faces than to other patterns. These results suggest that infants are born with certain visual preferences. (Based on Fantz, 1963)

Infants' Vision

William James, the founder of American psychology, said that as far as an infant can tell, the world is a "buzzing confusion," full of meaningless sights and sounds. Since James's time, psychologists have substantially increased their estimates of infants' vision.

We can start by recording an infant's eye movements. Even 2-day-old infants spend more time looking at drawings of human faces than at other patterns with similar areas of light and dark (Fantz, 1963; see ▲ Figure 5.4). However, infants do not have the same concept of "face" that adults do. As shown in ▼ Figure 5.5, newborns gaze equally at distorted and normal faces. However, they gaze longer at right-side-up faces than upside-down faces regardless of distortion. Evidently, the newborn's concept of face is just an oval with most of its content toward the top (Cassia, Turati, & Simion, 2004).

The ability to recognize faces continues developing for years. Parents in one study repeatedly read a storybook with photographs of two children's faces from many angles and with many expressions. After 2 weeks, 4-year-old children easily recognized pictures of the two children. However, when they had to choose between a normal picture and one with altered spacing among the features, they guessed randomly (Mondloch, Leis, & Maurer, 2006). By age 6, a child easily sees the difference between the photos in ▼ Figure 5.6, but 4-year-olds evidently do not.

The gradual improvement of face recognition depends on experience, and infants, like all

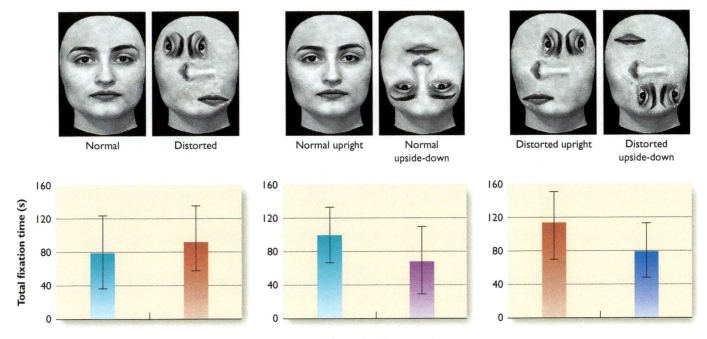

▲ **Figure 5.5** Infants gaze about equally at normal and distorted faces, but they stare longer at upright than upside-down faces. (Source: Cassia, Turati, & Simion, 2004)

▲ **Figure 5.6** These faces differ only in the positions of the eyes, nose, and mouth. Four-year-olds do not recognize which face is familiar. (Source: Mondloch, Leis, & Maurer, 2006)

of us, become best at recognizing the kinds of faces they frequently see. At age 6 months, infants are about as good at recognizing monkey faces as human faces. (The test is to show one monkey or human face for 30 seconds, and then that face and another one. If the infant looks more at the new face, we infer that it recognized the old face.) Over the next 3 months, infants' ability to recognize monkey faces declines, unless they have had special training to pay attention to monkey faces (Scott & Monesson, 2009).

By age 5 months, infants have had much visual experience but almost no experience at crawling or reaching. Over the next several months, as they increase their control of arm and leg movements, they learn to pick up toys, crawl around objects, and in other ways coordinate what they see with what they do. At first, they crawl indiscriminately, and parents need to supervise constantly to prevent the infants from crawling off a bed or tumbling down the stairs. After a couple weeks of practice, they learn to avoid crawling off unsafe edges (Adolph, 2000). They learn that avoidance regardless of whether or not they have had any experience of falling; the act of crawling gives them a sense of distance and depth (Anderson et al., 2013). They more quickly learn to avoid crawling off ledges if they had the experience of moving around in a powered "baby go-cart" before they were old enough to crawl (Dahl et al., 2013). Have they learned fear of heights? Well, yes and no. It depends on how we test them. Infants who have learned not to crawl over an unsafe ledge show increased heart rate when held over what would be an unsafe drop (Dahl et al., 2013). However, when the same infants start to walk a few months later, they again step indiscriminately, and parents need to supervise them until they learn what is and is not a safe step-off distance (Kretsch & Adolph,

2013; see also ▼ Figure 5.7). Evidently, for any kind of locomotion, young children gradually learn what they can and cannot do.

Infants' Hearing

Infants don't do much, but one thing they do is suck. Researchers use that response to measure hearing, because infants suck more vigorously when certain kinds of sounds arouse them.

In one study, the experimenters played a brief sound and noted how it affected infants' sucking rate (see ▼ Figure 5.8). On the first few occasions, the sound increased the sucking rate. A repeated sound produced less and less effect. We say that the infant became *habituated* to the sound. **Habituation** is *decreased response to a repeated stimulus*. When the experimenters substituted a new sound, the sucking rate increased. Evidently, the infant was aroused by the unfamiliar sound. *When a change in a stimulus increases a previously habituated response*, we say that the stimulus produced **dishabituation**.

Monitoring dishabituation tells us whether infants detect a difference between two sounds. For example, infants who have become habituated to the sound *ba* will increase their sucking rate when they hear the sound *pa* (Eimas, Siqueland, Jusczyk, & Vigorito, 1971). Apparently, even month-old infants notice the difference between *ba* and *pa*, an important distinction for later language comprehension.

Infants, in fact, appear to distinguish among all sounds that occur in any language. Within a few months, however, they begin to distinguish more

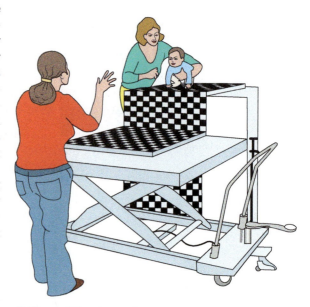

▲ **Figure 5.7** Infants who are starting to crawl learn not to go over deep edges. A few months later when they are starting to walk, they have to learn again what is safe and what is unsafe.

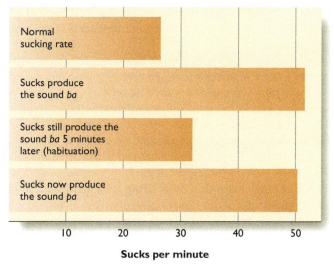

Normal sucking rate			
Sucks produce the sound *ba*			
Sucks still produce the sound *ba* 5 minutes later (habituation)			
Sucks now produce the sound *pa*			

10   20   30   40   50

Sucks per minute

▲ **Figure 5.8** After repeatedly hearing a *ba* sound, the infant's sucking habituates. When a new sound, *pa*, follows, the sucking rate increases. (Based on results of Eimas, Siqueland, Jusczyk, & Vigorito, 1971)

accurately among the sounds that are important in the language they are about to learn. For example, the Japanese language does not distinguish between the sounds *l* and *r*. At first, Japanese infants respond differentially to the two sounds, but within a few months they stop. Similarly, in German the difference between *u* and *ü* alters the meaning of a word, but in English it doesn't. In some of the languages of India, the difference between *k* and a harder version of *k* makes a difference, but in English, it doesn't. In English, the accent on one syllable or the other changes the meaning (consider *decade* vs. *decayed* and *weakened* vs. *weekend*), but in French, accent doesn't matter. At first, infants distinguish among all these sound differences, but within a few months, they get better at distinguishing among sounds important in their language, and worse at distinguishing sound differences meaningless in their language (Byers-Heinlein & Fennell, 2014; Kuhl, Williams, Lacerda, Stevens, & Lindblom, 1992; Tsuji & Cristia, 2014). All this takes place long before they understand what any of those words mean.

concept check

4. **Suppose an infant habituates to the sound *ba*, but when we substitute the sound *bla*, the infant fails to increase the sucking rate. What interpretation would be likely?**

Answer

4. Evidently, the infant does not hear a difference between *ba* and *bla*. (This is a hypothetical result; the study has not been done.)

Infants' Learning and Memory

How could we measure learning and memory in infants who cannot speak? Many studies have used the fact that infants learn to suck harder on a nipple if their sucking turns on a sound. Investigators then determined whether infants suck harder for some sounds than for others. In one study, babies younger than 3 days old could turn on a tape recording of a woman's voice by sucking on a nipple. The results: They sucked more frequently to turn on recordings of their own mother's voice than another woman's voice (DeCasper & Fifer, 1980). Apparently, they preferred their own mother's voice. Because they showed this preference as early as the day of birth, psychologists believe that the infants learned the sound of the mother's voice before birth.

In a follow-up study, pregnant women read a nursery rhyme three times in a row, twice a day. By age 38 weeks postconception (shortly before birth), fetuses showed a heart rate response to the familiar rhyme, and not to a different rhyme (Krueger & Garvan, 2014). In another study, researchers played a simple piano melody for fetuses to hear twice daily for the last three weeks before birth. Six weeks later, those infants (and not other infants) showed a larger heart rate response to the familiar melody than to a different melody (Granier-Deferre, Bassereau, Ribeiro, Jacquet, & deCasper, 2011). This study shows memory of prenatal experiences lasting at least six weeks.

concept check

5. **Suppose a newborn sucks to turn on a tape recording of its father's voice. Eventually, the baby habituates and the sucking frequency decreases. Now the experimenters substitute the recording of a different man's voice. What would you conclude if the sucking frequency increased? What if it remained the same? What if it decreased?**

Answer

5. If the frequency increased, we would conclude that the infant recognizes the difference between the father's voice and the other voice. If the frequency remained the same, we would conclude that the infant did not notice a difference. If the sucking frequency decreased, we would conclude that the infant recognizes a difference, and we would assume that the infant preferred the sound of the father's voice.

Carolyn Rovee-Collier (1997, 1999) demonstrated that infants can learn a response and remember it. She attached a ribbon to an ankle so that an infant could activate a mobile by kicking with one leg (see ▼ Figure 5.9). Two-month-old infants quickly

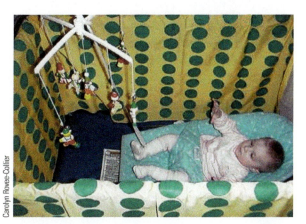

▲ **Figure 5.9** Two-month-old infants rapidly learn to kick to activate a mobile attached to their ankles with a ribbon. They remember how to activate the mobile when tested days later. (From Hildreth, Sweeney, & Rovee-Collier, 2003)

learned this response and generally kept the mobile going nonstop for a full 45-minute session. (Infants have little control over their leg muscles, but they don't need much control to keep the mobile going.) They remembered what to do when the ribbon was reattached several days later, to the infants' evident delight. Six-month-old infants remembered the response for 2 weeks. Even after they forgot it, they quickly relearned it (Hildreth, Sweeney, & Rovee-Collier, 2003).

Jean Piaget's View of Cognitive Development

Somewhat older children are much easier to test, and one quickly discovers that their thinking differs from that of adults. The theorist who made this point most influentially was Jean Piaget (pee-ah-ZHAY; 1896–1980).

Early in his career, while administering IQ tests to French-speaking children in Switzerland, Piaget was fascinated that so many children of a given age gave the same incorrect answer to certain questions. He concluded that children have qualitatively

Jean Piaget (on the left) demonstrated that children with different levels of maturity react differently to the same experience.

different thought processes from adults. According to Piaget, as children develop intellectually, they do more than accumulate facts. They construct new mental processes.

In Piaget's terminology, behavior is based on schemata (the plural of *schema*). A schema is *an organized way of interacting with objects*. For instance, infants have a grasping schema and a sucking schema. Older infants gradually add new schemata and adapt their old ones through the processes of assimilation and accommodation. Assimilation means *applying an old schema to new objects or problems*. For example, when a child sees animals move and then sees the sun and moon move, the child may assume that the sun and moon are alive, like animals. Accommodation means *modifying an old schema to fit a new object or problem*. A child may learn that "only living things move on their own" is a rule with exceptions and that the sun and moon are not alive.

Infants shift back and forth between assimilation and accommodation. Equilibration is *the establishment of harmony or balance between the two*. A discrepancy occurs between the child's current understanding and some evidence to the contrary. The child accommodates to that discrepancy and achieves an equilibration at a higher level. Similar processes occur in adults. When you see a new mathematical problem, you try several familiar methods until you find one that works. That is, you assimilate the new problem to an old schema. However, if the new problem is sufficiently different, you modify (accommodate) your schema to find a solution. In this way, said Piaget, intellectual growth occurs.

Piaget contended that children progress through four major stages of intellectual development:

1. *The sensorimotor stage* (from birth to almost 2 years)
2. *The preoperational stage* (from just before 2 to 7 years)
3. *The concrete operations stage* (from about 7 to 11 years)
4. *The formal operations stage* (from about 11 years onward)

The ages are variable, and not everyone reaches the formal operations stage. However, all people progress through the stages in the same order. Let's consider each of Piaget's stages.

Piaget's Sensorimotor Stage

Piaget called the first stage of intellectual development the sensorimotor stage because *at this early age (the first 1½ to 2 years) behavior is mostly simple motor responses to sensory stimuli*—for example, the grasp reflex and the sucking reflex. According to Piaget, infants respond only to what they see and hear at the moment. In particular, he believed that children during this period fail to respond to objects they remember seeing even a few seconds ago. What evidence could he have for this view?

what's the evidence?

The Infant's Concept of Object Permanence

Piaget argued that infants in the first few months of life lack the concept of object permanence, *the idea that objects continue to exist even when we do not see or hear them.* That is, for an infant, "Out of sight, out of existence."

How would he know that? Piaget drew his inferences from observations like this: Place a toy in front of a 6-month-old infant, who reaches out for it. Later, place a toy in the same place, but before the infant has a chance to grab it, cover it with a clear glass. The infant removes the glass and takes the toy. Now repeat that procedure but use an opaque (nonclear) glass. The infant, who watched you place the glass over the toy, makes no effort to remove the glass and obtain the toy. Next, place a thin barrier between the infant and the toy. An infant who cannot see the toy does not reach for it (Piaget, 1937/1954) (see ▶ Figure 5.10).

According to Piaget, the infant does not know that the hidden toy continues to exist. However, the results vary depending on circumstances. For example, if you show a toy and then turn out the lights, a 7-month-old infant reaches out toward the unseen toy if it was a familiar toy but not if it was unfamiliar (Shinskey & Munakata, 2005). A study by Renee Baillargeon (1986) also suggests that infants show signs of understanding object permanence when they are tested differently.

Hypothesis An infant who sees an event that would be impossible (if objects are permanent) will be surprised and therefore will stare longer than will an infant who sees a similar but possible event.

Method Infants aged 6 or 8 months watched a series of events. The infant watched the experimenter raise a screen to show the track and then watched a toy car go down a slope and emerge on the other side of the screen, as shown here. This was called a "possible" event.

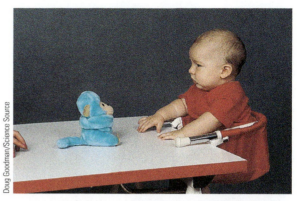

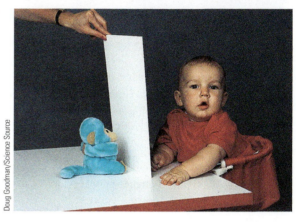

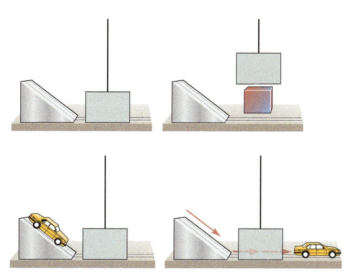

Possible event. The box is behind the track, and the car passes by the box.

The researchers measured how long the child stared after the car passed by. They repeated the procedure until the child's staring time decreased for three trials in a row (showing habituation). Then the experimenters presented a series of "possible" events, as just described, and "impossible" events like this:

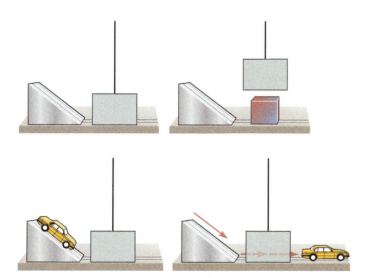

Impossible event. The raised screen shows a box on the track where the car would pass. After the screen lowers, the car goes down the slope and emerges on the other side.

▲ **Figure 5.10** (**a**) A 6- to 9-month-old child reaches for a visible toy but not one that is hidden behind a barrier (**b**) even if the child sees someone hide the toy. According to Piaget, this observation indicates that the child hasn't yet grasped the concept of object permanence.

In an impossible event, the raised screen showed a box on the track where the car would pass. After the screen lowered, the car went down the slope and emerged on the other side. (The experimenters pulled the box off the track after lowering the screen.) The experimenters measured each child's staring times after both kinds of events. They repeated both events two more times, randomizing the order of events.

Results As shown in ▼ Figure 5.11, infants stared longer after seeing an impossible event. They also stared longer after the first pair of events than after the second and third pairs (Baillargeon, 1986).

Interpretation Why did the infants stare longer at the impossible event? The inference—admittedly only an inference—is that the infants found the impossible event surprising. To be surprised, infants had to expect that the box would continue to exist. If so, even 6-month-old infants have some understanding of object permanence, as well as elementary physics. A later study with a slightly different method demonstrated object permanence in infants as young as 3½ months (Baillargeon, 1987).

Still, remember that 9-month-olds failed Piaget's object permanence task of reaching out to pick up a

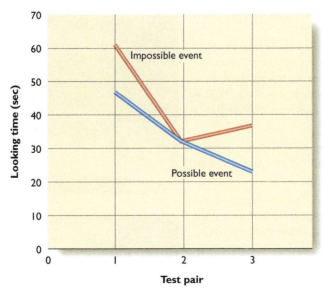

▲ Figure 5.11 Infants stared longer after watching impossible events than after watching possible events. (From Baillargeon, 1986)

hidden object. Do infants understand object permanence or not? Evidently, it is not a good question. Infants use a concept in some situations and not others. The same is true for all of us. Did you ever learn a grammatical rule in English class and then violate it in your own speech? Did you ever learn a math formula and then fail to apply it to a new situation?

Other psychologists modified this procedure to test many other infant concepts. Researchers put five objects behind a screen, added five more, and removed the screen. Nine-month-olds stared longer when they saw just five objects than when they saw ten, suggesting some understanding of addition (McCrink & Wynn, 2004). Researchers buried a ball in the sand and then retrieved apparently the same ball from the same or a different location. Infants stared longer when the ball emerged from the new location (Newcombe, Sluzenski, & Huttenlocher, 2005). When infants watched an animated display in which a larger figure and a smaller figure crossed paths, 10-month-olds stared longer if the larger one bowed and stepped aside to let the smaller one pass (Thomsen, Frankenhuis, Ingold-Smith, & Carey, 2011). If we assume that staring means surprise, then infants apparently understand something about social dominance. Related studies suggest that 5-month-olds understand that liquids can pass through a barrier, but solids cannot (Hespos, Ferry, & Rips, 2009). However, infants as old as 12 months show no surprise if you place a toy into a container and then pull out a toy of different shape or color (Baillargeon, Li, Ng, & Yuan, 2009). Evidently, infants imagine that objects can magically change shape or color.

Here are two conclusions: First, we should be cautious about inferring what infants or anyone else can or cannot do, because the results vary with the procedures.

Second, concepts develop gradually. An infant may show a concept in one situation and not another.

Sense of Self

Do young children have a concept of "self"? How would we know? Here is the evidence: Someone puts a spot of unscented rouge on an infant's nose and then puts the infant in front of a mirror. Infants younger than 1½ years old either ignore the red spot on the baby in the mirror or reach out to touch the mirror. At some point after age 1½ years, infants instead touch themselves on the nose, indicating that they recognize themselves in the mirror (see ▼ Figure 5.12). Infants show this sign of self-recognition at varying ages; the age when they first show self-recognition is about the same as when they begin to act embarrassed (M. Lewis, Sullivan, Stanger, & Weiss, 1991). They show a sense of self in both situations or in neither.

Before this time, do infants fail to distinguish between self and other? Perhaps, but we cannot be sure. Before age 1½, we see no evidence for a sense of self, but absence of evidence is not evidence of absence. Perhaps younger infants would show a sense of self in some other test that we have not yet devised.

▲ Figure 5.12 If someone places a bit of unscented rouge on a child's nose, a 2-year-old looking at a mirror shows self-recognition by touching his or her own nose.

Piaget's Preoperational Stage

By age 1½ to 2, children begin speaking. A child who asks for a toy obviously understands object permanence. Nevertheless, young children still misunderstand much. They do not understand how a mother can be someone else's daughter. A boy with one brother will assert that his brother has no brother. Piaget refers to this period as the preoperational stage because *the child lacks operations, which are reversible mental processes.* For a boy to understand that his brother has a brother, he must be able to reverse the concept of "having a brother." According to Piaget, three typical aspects of preoperational thought are egocentrism, difficulty distinguishing appearance from reality, and lack of the concept of conservation.

Egocentrism: Failing to Understand Other People's Perspective

According to Piaget, young children's thought is egocentric. Piaget did *not* mean selfish. Instead, he meant that *a child sees the world as centered around himself or herself and cannot easily take another person's perspective.* If you sit opposite a preschooler, the child can describe how the blocks on the table look from the child's side but not how they would look from your side.

Another example: Young children hear a story about Lucy, who wants her old pair of red shoes. Lucy's brother Linus enters the room, and she asks him to bring her red shoes. He goes and brings back her new red shoes, and she is angry because she wanted the old red shoes. Young children hearing the story are surprised that he brought the wrong shoes because *they* knew which shoes she wanted (Keysar, Barr, & Horton, 1998).

However, young children do sometimes understand another person's perspective. In one study, 5- and 6-year-old children had to tell an adult to pick up a particular glass. If a child saw that the adult could see two glasses, the child usually said to pick up the "big" or "little" glass to identify the right one. If the child saw that the adult could see only one glass, the child often said just "the glass" (Nadig & Sedivy, 2002; ▶ Figure 5.13).

▲ **Figure 5.13** Sometimes, a child saw that the adult could see two glasses. At other times, it was clear that the adult could see only one. If two glasses were visible, the child usually told the adult which glass to pick up, instead of saying, "pick up the glass." (From Nadig & Sedivy, 2002)

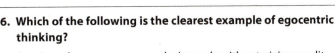

6. Which of the following is the clearest example of egocentric thinking?

a. A writer who uses someone else's words without giving credit
b. A politician who blames others for everything that goes wrong
c. A professor who gives the same complicated lecture to a freshman class as to a convention of professionals

Answers

6. c is a case of egocentric thought, a failure to recognize another person's point of view.

Theory of Mind: Understanding that Different People Know Different Things

To say that a child is egocentric implies that he or she does not understand what other people know or don't know. Psychologists say that a young child lacks, but gradually develops theory of mind, which is *an understanding that other people have a mind, too, and that each person knows some things that other people don't know.* How can we know whether a child has this understanding? Here is an example of a research effort.

Children's Understanding of Other People's Knowledge and Beliefs

How and when do children first understand that other people have minds and knowledge? Researchers have devised clever experiments to explore this question.

Hypothesis A child who understands that other people have minds knows that someone could have a false belief.

Method A child watches and listens as an adult acts out this story: Maxi sees his mother put chocolate into the blue cupboard. He plans to return later and get some. However, while he is absent, his mother moves the chocolate to the green cupboard. The questions are: Where will Maxi look for the chocolate? If his grandfather is available to help, where will Maxi tell him to look? If an older brother wants to take the chocolate, and Maxi wants to prevent the brother from finding the chocolate, where will he point? (See ▼ Figure 5.14.)

Results Older children answer correctly: Maxi looks in the blue cupboard and tells his grandfather to get chocolate from the blue cupboard, but tells his brother to look in the green cupboard. Younger children answer incorrectly, as if they thought Maxi had all the correct

Answer

7. It means that the child has "theory of mind." The child understands that Maxi, who was absent while the mother moved the chocolate, will have a false belief.

We might be tempted to the simple interpretation that young children lack theory of mind, but at some point they suddenly gain it. However, development is seldom a sudden, all-or-nothing process. In the "Maxi" situation, it is likely that many 3-year-olds don't fully understand the questions. In a later study, 3-year-olds watched as a Lego figure representing a girl put bananas (which she liked to eat) in one of two refrigerators. Then the girl moved forward, with her back to the refrigerators, while the experimenter moved the bananas from one refrigerator to the other. When the experimenter invited the child to play with the girl figure and asked, "What is she going to do now?" in most cases the child moved the figure to the refrigerator that *previously* had the bananas, indicating theory of mind. However, if the experimenter asked where the girl would look for the bananas, the child answered with the wrong refrigerator (Rubio-Fernández & Geurts, 2013). That is, a nonverbal response showed that the child understood what the girl would know, but answering in words caused confusion. In an even more simplified task, even 18-month-olds showed an understanding of theory of mind (Senju, Southgate, Snape, Leonard, & Casibra, 2011). In short, gaining theory of mind—or any other concept—is not a sudden transition. A child can show indications of understanding in some ways or situations and not in others.

Distinguishing Appearance from Reality

During Piaget's preoperational stage, children apparently do not distinguish clearly between appearance and reality. For example, a child who sees you put a white ball behind a blue filter will say that the ball is blue. When you ask, "Yes, I know the ball *looks* blue, but what color is it *really*?" the child replies that it really *is* blue (Flavell, 1986). Similarly, a 3-year-old who encounters a sponge that looks like a rock will say that it really is a rock, but a child who says it is a sponge will also insist that it *looks like* a sponge.

However, the results depend on exactly how we ask the question. Psychologists showed 3-year-olds a sponge that looked like a rock and let them touch it. When the investigators asked what it looked like and what it was *really*, most of the children said "rock" both times or "sponge" both times. However, if the investigators asked, "Bring me something so I can wipe up some spilled water," the children brought the sponge. And when the investigators asked, "Bring me something so I can take a picture of a teddy bear with something that looks like a rock," they brought the same object. So evidently, the children did understand that something could be a sponge and

▲ **Figure 5.14** Maxi watches his mother place chocolate in one place. While he is absent, she moves it. Where will Maxi look for it? Younger children point to the new location, suggesting they do not understand that Maxi will have an incorrect belief.

information that the observers themselves had. The percentage of children answering correctly increases from age 3 to age 6, and most children beyond about 4½ answer correctly (Wellman, Cross, & Watson, 2001; Wimmer & Penner, 1983).

Interpretation Evidently, children gradually develop in their ability to understand other people's thoughts, beliefs, and knowledge.

concept check

7. If the chocolate is now in the green cupboard, what does it mean if a child says Maxi will look in the blue cupboard?

a   A 2½-year-old is shown a small room where a stuffed animal is hidden.

Child is unable to find the stuffed animal in the larger room.

Child is told that the machine expands the room. Child stands out of the way during some noises and then returns.

b   Child is shown a small room where a stuffed animal is hidden.

Child is able to find the stuffed animal in the "blown-up" room.

▲ **Figure 5.15** If an experimenter hides a small toy in a small room and asks a child to find a larger toy "in the same place" in the larger room, most 2½-year-olds search haphazardly. (**a**) However, the same children know where to look if the experimenter says this is the same room as before, but a machine has expanded it (**b**).

look like a rock, even if they didn't say so (Sapp, Lee, & Muir, 2000). Repeatedly, we are seeing this pattern: A child can show a concept in one way and not another.

Also consider this experiment: A psychologist shows a child a playhouse room that is a scale model of a full-size room. The psychologist hides a tiny toy in the small room and explains that a bigger toy just like it is "in the same place" in the bigger room. (For example, if the little toy is behind the sofa in the little room, the big toy is behind the sofa in the big room.) Then the psychologist asks the child to find the big toy in the big room. Most 3-year-olds go to the correct place at once (DeLoache, 1989). Most 2½-year-old children, however, search haphazardly (see ▲ Figure 5.15a).

Again, the results depend on how we ask the question. As before, a psychologist hides a toy in the small room while the child watches. Then the psychologist shows the child a "machine that can make things bigger." The psychologist aims a beam from the machine at the room and takes the child out of the way. They hear some chunkata-chunkata sounds, and then the psychologist shows the full-size "blown-up" room and asks the child to find the hidden toy. Even 2½-year-olds go immediately to the correct location (DeLoache, Miller, & Rosengren, 1997; see ▲ Figure 5.15b). (Incidentally, the children had no doubt that the machine had expanded the room. Many continued to believe it even after the psychologist explained what happened!)

Developing the Concept of Conservation

According to Piaget, preoperational children lack the concept of conservation. They fail to *understand that objects conserve such properties as number, length, volume, area, and mass after changes in the shape or arrangement of the objects.* They cannot perform the mental operations necessary to understand the trans-

formations. ■ Table 5.2 shows typical conservation tasks. For example, if we show two equal glasses with the same amount of water and then pour the contents of one glass into a third glass that is taller and thinner, preoperational children say that the third glass contains more water (see ▼ Figure 5.16).

I once thought perhaps the phrasing of the questions tricks children into saying something they do not believe. If you have the same doubts, find a 6-year-old child and try it yourself with your own wording. Here's my experience: Once when I was discussing Piaget in my introductory psychology class, I invited my son Sam, then 5½ years old, to take part in a class demonstration. I started with two glasses of water, which he agreed contained equal amounts of water. Then I poured the water from one glass into a wider glass, lowering the water level. When I asked which glass contained more water, Sam confidently pointed to the tall, thin one. After class he complained, "Daddy, why did you ask me such an easy question? Everyone could see that there was more water in that glass! You should have asked me something harder to show how smart I am!" The following year, I brought Sam, now 6½ years old, to class for the same demonstration. I poured the water from one of the tall glasses into

Table 5.2 Typical Tasks Used to Measure Conservation

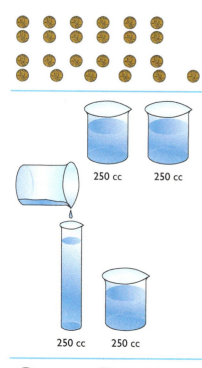

Conservation of number
Preoperational children say that these two rows contain the same number of pennies.

Preoperational children say that the second row has more pennies.

Conservation of volume
Preoperational children say that the two same-size containers have the same amount of water.

250 cc   250 cc

Preoperational children say that the taller, thinner container has more water.

250 cc   250 cc

Conservation of mass
Preoperational children say that the two same-size balls of clay have the same amount of clay.
Preoperational children say that a squashed ball of clay contains a different amount of clay than the same-size round ball of clay.

a wider one and asked him which glass contained more water. He looked and paused. His face turned red. Finally, he whispered, "Daddy, I don't know!" After class he complained, "Why did you ask me such a hard question? I'm never coming back to any of your classes again!" The question that used to be embarrassingly easy had become embarrassingly difficult.

The next year, when he was 7½, I tried again (at home). This time he answered confidently, "Both glasses have the same amount of water, of course. Why? Is this some sort of trick question?"

▲ **Figure 5.16** Preoperational children don't understand that the volume of water remains constant despite changes in its appearance. During the transition to concrete operations, a child finds conservation tasks difficult and confusing.

Piaget's Stages of Concrete Operations and Formal Operations

At about age 7, children enter the stage of concrete operations and begin to understand the conservation of physical properties. The transition is gradual, however. A 6-year-old may understand that squashing a ball of clay does not change its weight but still think that squashing it changes how much water it displaces when dropped into a glass.

According to Piaget, during the stage of concrete operations, *children perform mental operations on concrete objects but still have trouble with abstract or hypothetical ideas.* For example, ask this question: "How could you move a mountain of whipped cream from one side of the city to the other?" Older children enjoy devising imaginative answers, but children in the concrete operations stage complain that the question is silly.

Or ask, "If you could have a third eye anywhere on your body, where would you put it?" Children in this stage generally respond immediately that they would put it right between the other two, on their foreheads. Older children suggest more imaginative ideas such as on the back of their head, in the stomach (so they could watch food digesting), or on the tip of a finger (so they could peek around corners).

Finally, in Piaget's stage of formal operations, adolescents develop *logical, deductive reasoning and systematic planning.* According to Piaget, children reach the stage of formal operations at about age 11. Later researchers found that many people reach this stage later or not at all. Thinking with formal operations demonstrates planning. For example, we set up five bottles of clear liquid and explain that it is possible to mix some combination to produce a yellow liquid. The task is to find that combination. Children in the concrete operations stage plunge right in with no plan. They try combining bottles A and B, then C and D, then perhaps A, C, and E. Soon they have forgotten which combinations they've already tried. Adolescents in the formal operations stage approach the problem more systematically. They may first try all the two-bottle combinations: AB, AC, AD, AE, BC, and so forth. If those fail, they try three-bottle combinations: ABC, ABD, ABE, ACD, and so on. By trying every possible combination only once, they are sure to succeed. ■ Table 5.3 summarizes Piaget's four stages.

Are Piaget's Stages Distinct?

Piaget regarded the four stages of intellectual development as distinct. He believed a transition from one stage to the next required a major reorganization of thinking, like a caterpillar metamorphosing into a chrysalis or a chrysalis metamorphosing into a butterfly. That is, intellectual growth has periods of revolutionary reorganization.

Later research casts doubt on this conclusion. If it were true, then a child in a given stage of development—say, the preoperational stage—should perform consistently at that level. In fact, children's performance fluctuates as a task is made more or less difficult. For example, consider the conservation-of-number task, in which an investigator presents two rows of seven or more objects, spreads out one row, and asks which row has more.

Table 5.3 Summary of Piaget's Stages of Cognitive Development

Stage and Approximate Age	Achievements and Activities	Limitations
Sensorimotor (birth to 1½ years)	Reacts to sensory stimuli through reflexes and other responses	Little use of language; seems not to understand object permanence in the early part of this stage
Preoperational (1½ to 7 years)	Develops language; can represent objects mentally by words and other symbols; can respond to objects that are remembered but not present	Lacks operations (reversible mental processes); lacks concept of conservation; focuses on one property at a time (such as length or width), not on both at once; still has trouble distinguishing appearance from reality
Concrete operations (7 to 11 years)	Understands conservation of mass, number, and volume; can reason logically with regard to concrete objects that can be seen or touched	Has trouble reasoning about abstract concepts and hypothetical situations
Formal operations (11 years onward)	Can reason logically about abstract and hypothetical concepts; develops strategies; plans actions in advance	None beyond the occasional irrationalities of all human thought

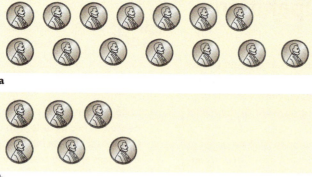

a

b

▲ **Figure 5.17** **(a)** With the standard conservation-of-number task, preoperational children answer that the spread-out row has more items. **(b)** With a simplified task, the same children say that both rows have the same number of items.

Preoperational children reply that the spread-out row has more. However, when Rochel Gelman (1982) presented two rows of only three objects each (see ▲ Figure 5.17) and then spread out one of the rows, even 3- and 4-year-old children usually answered that the rows had the same number of items.

Whereas Piaget believed children made distinct jumps from one stage to another, most psychologists today see development as gradual and continuous (Courage & Howe, 2002). That is, the difference between older children and younger children is not so much a matter of gaining a new ability. It is a matter of using their abilities in more and more situations.

Differing Views: Piaget and Vygotsky

One implication of Piaget's view is that children must discover certain concepts, such as the concept

of conservation, mainly on their own. Teaching a concept means directing children's attention to the key aspects and letting them discover the concept. In contrast, Russian psychologist Lev Vygotsky (1978) argued that educators should not wait for children to rediscover the principles of physics and mathematics. Indeed, the value of language is that it lets us profit from the experience of previous generations.

Vygotsky certainly did not mean that adults should ignore a child's developmental level. Rather, every child has a zone of proximal development, *the distance between what a child can do alone and what is possible with help.* Instruction should remain within that zone. For example, one should not try to teach a typical 4-year-old the concept of conservation of volume. However, a 6-year-old who does not yet understand the concept might learn it with help and guidance. Similarly, children improve their recall of lists or stories if adults help them understand and organize the information (Larkina, Güler, Kleinknecht, & Bauer, 2008). Vygotsky compared this help to *scaffolding,* the temporary supports that builders use during construction: After a building is complete, the scaffolding is removed. Good advice for educators is to be sensitive to a child's zone of proximal development and pursue how much further they can push a child.

concept check

9. **What would Piaget and Vygotsky think about the feasibility of teaching the concept of conservation?**

Answer

9. Piaget recommended waiting for a child to discover the concept by himself or herself. For Vygotsky, the answer depends on the child's zone of proximal development. An adult can help a child at the right age.

The zone of proximal development is the gap between what a child does alone and what the child can do with help.

How Grown Up Are We?

Both Piaget and Vygotsky implied that we start with infant cognition and eventually attain adult thinking, which we practice from then on. Are they right, or do we sometimes slip into childish ways of thought?

Consider egocentric thinking. Young children seem to assume that whatever they know or understand, other people will know or understand also. Sometimes, adults make the same mistake. Suppose you say, "The daughter of the man and the woman arrived." Did one person arrive (who is the daughter of the man and the woman) or two people (the man's daughter and some other woman)? You know what you meant, but you might overestimate how well other people understand you (Keysar & Henly, 2002).

Another example: According to Piaget, after about age 7, we all understand conservation of number, volume, and so forth. If we show two equally tall, thin containers of water and pour the water from one of them into a wider container, older children and adults confidently say that the two containers have equal amounts of water. However, let's test in a different way: We give people a tall, thin glass or a short, wide glass and invite them to add as much juice as they want. Adults as well as children usually put more juice into the short, wide glass, while thinking that they are getting less juice than usual. Even professional bartenders generally pour more liquor into a short, wide glass than into a tall, thin one (Wansink & van Ittersum, 2003). Evidently, even adults don't fully understand conservation of volume if they are tested in this way. In short, as we grow older, we suppress our childlike ways of thinking, but we don't lose them completely. You still have a child's mind hidden inside you.

concept check

10. **How could you get someone to pour you a larger than average drink?**

Answer

10. Ask to have the drink in a short, wide glass.

Understanding Children

Jean Piaget called attention to the ways in which children differ from adults. They are not just slower or less well informed; they process information differently. Everything that we do develops over age. But as you can see, it takes much work to pin down exactly what infants and small children understand, and what they misunderstand.

Furthermore, the changes are gradual and incomplete. Even adults revert to childlike thinking at times. Development is not a matter of suddenly gaining cognitive skills. It is a matter of applying skills more consistently and under a wider variety of conditions.

Summary

- *Cross-sectional and longitudinal studies.* Cross-sectional studies examine people of different ages at the same time. Longitudinal studies monitor people as they grow older. A sequential design combines both methods. (page 146)
- *Cohort effects.* Many differences between young people and old people are not due to age but to the era in which they grew up. (page 147)
- *Prenatal development.* The brain begins to mature long before birth. Exposure to drugs such as alcohol decreases brain activity and releases neurons' self-destruct programs. Some people manage to do well in life despite unpromising circumstances. (page 148)
- *Inferring infant capacities.* We easily underestimate newborns' capacities because they have so little control over their muscles. Careful testing demonstrates greater abilities than we might have supposed. (page 148)
- *Infant vision and hearing.* Newborns stare at some visual patterns longer than others. They habituate to a repeated sound but dishabituate to a slightly different sound, indicating that they hear a difference. (page 149)
- *Infant memory.* Newborns suck more vigorously to turn on a recording of their own mother's voice than some other woman's voice, indicating that they recognize the sound of the mother's voice. Infants just 2 months old learn to kick and move a mobile, and they remember how to do it several days later. (page 151)

- *Piaget's view of children's thinking.* According to Jean Piaget, children's thought differs qualitatively from adults' thought. He believed children grow intellectually through accommodation and assimilation. (page 152)
- *Piaget's stages of development.* Children in the sensorimotor stage respond to what they see, hear, or feel at the moment. In the preoperational stage, they lack reversible operations. In the concrete operations stage, children reason about concrete problems but not abstractions. Adults and older children are in the formal operations stage, in which they plan strategies and deal with hypothetical or abstract questions. (page 152)
- *Egocentric thinking.* Young children often fail to understand other people's point of view. (page 155)
- *Theory of mind.* Children gradually develop their ability to assess other people's knowledge and beliefs, including false beliefs. (page 155)
- *Appearance and reality.* Young children sometimes seem not to distinguish between appearance and reality. However, with a simpler task, they do distinguish. Children may show a concept under some conditions and not others. (page 156)
- *Vygotsky.* According to Lev Vygotsky, children must learn new abilities from adults or older children, but only within their zone of proximal development. (page 160)
- *Adults.* Adults revert to childlike reasoning in certain situations. (page 160)

Key Terms

accommodation (page 152)

assimilation (page 152)

cohort (page 147)

conservation (page 157)

cross-sectional study (page 146)

dishabituation (page 150)

fetal alcohol syndrome (page 148)

fetus (page 148)

egocentric (page 155)

equilibration (page 152)

habituation (page 150)

longitudinal study (page 146)

object permanence (page 152)

operation (page 155)

preoperational stage (page 155)

schema (pl. schemata) (page 152)

selective attrition (page 146)

sensorimotor stage (page 152)

sequential design (page 146)

stage of concrete operations (page 159)

stage of formal operations (page 159)

theory of mind (page 155)

zone of proximal development (page 160)

zygote (page 148)

Review Questions

1. Which of these characterizes a cross-sectional study of development?
   (a) Researchers compare people from several cultures.
   (b) Researchers compare one group of people at several times as they grow older.
   (c) Researchers compare people of different ages, at the same time.
   (d) Researchers examine many aspects of behavior, for one group of people at one point in time.

2. Suppose a survey reports different political leanings by older adults than younger adults. A possible explanation is that people change their views as they age. Another is that older people have different priorities from younger people. What is still another possibility?
   (a) Demand characteristics
   (b) A cohort effect
   (c) Zone of proximal development
   (d) Equilibration

3. Theoretically, which of the following drugs should produce effects similar to those of fetal alcohol syndrome, if a mother takes them during pregnancy?
   (a) Cocaine (which increases activity at dopamine synapses)
   (b) Anti-anxiety drugs (which increase activity at inhibitory synapses)
   (c) Nicotine (which stimulates acetylcholine synapses)
   (d) Caffeine (which increases heart rate)

4. Suppose an infant habituates to the sound *ba*, but when we substitute the sound *boo*, the infant fails to increase the sucking rate. What interpretation would be likely?
   (a) The infant hears a difference between the two sounds.
   (b) The infant does not hear a difference between the two sounds.
   (c) The infant prefers the sound *ba*.
   (d) The infant prefers the sound *boo*.

5. Suppose a newborn sucks to turn on a tape recording of its father's voice. Eventually the infant habituates and the sucking frequency decreases. Now the experimenters substitute the recording of a different man's voice. Which of the following results would indicate that the infant detects a difference between the two voices?
   (a) The sucking rate increases.
   (b) The sucking rate decreases.
   (c) The sucking rate remains the same.

6. What evidence suggests that even 6- to 8-month-old infants understand object permanence?
   (a) They reach around an opaque barrier to grasp an unseen toy.
   (b) They ask for toys that they do not currently see.
   (c) They stare longer at events that would be impossible if unseen objects continue to exist.
   (d) After they have repeatedly seen one toy and habituated to it, they dishabituate when they see a new toy.

7. To demonstrate "theory of mind," what must a child understand?
   (a) That someone else can have a false belief
   (b) That human mental abilities are more advanced than those of other species
   (c) That mental activity is inseparable from brain activity
   (d) That all mental activity requires sensory input

8. A child watches an experimenter hide a small toy in a small room, and then tries to find a larger version of the same toy hidden "in the same place" in a larger room. At what age can most children first succeed on this task?
   (a) 4 years old
   (b) 3 years old
   (c) It depends on how you ask the question.
   (d) It depends on the child's interest in the toy.

9. One year ago, Sarah did not seem to understand conservation of number, volume, or mass. Today she does. According to Piaget, Sarah has progressed from which stage to which other stage?
   (a) Preoperational stage to concrete operations stage
   (b) Sensorimotor stage to preoperational stage
   (c) Concrete operations stage to formal operations stage
   (d) Formal operations stage to concrete operations stage

10. Which of the following would be evidence in favor of Vygotsky's "zone of proximal development"?
    (a) Most 3-year-olds can observe a toy hidden in a small room and use it to locate a larger toy in a larger room, but 2½-year-olds cannot.
    (b) It is possible to teach conservation of volume to many 6-year-olds but not many 4-year-olds.
    (c) Children in the stage of concrete operations have trouble with abstract or hypothetical ideas.
    (d) Intellectual development varies from one culture to another.

Answers: 1c, 2b, 3b, 4b, 5a, 6c, 7a, 8c, 9a, 10b.

module 5.2

Social and Emotional Development

After studying this module, you should be able to:

- Characterize Erikson's stages of social and emotional development.

- Explain how psychologists measure attachment in young children.

- Discuss the major social and emotional issues people face during adolescence, adulthood, and old age.

You are a contestant on a new TV game show, *What's My Worry?* Behind the curtain is someone you cannot see, who has an overriding concern. You are to identify that concern by questioning a psychologist who knows this person well, asking only questions that can be answered with a single word or phrase. Here's the catch: The more questions you ask, the smaller the prize. If you guess correctly after the first question, you win $64,000. After two questions, you win $32,000 and so on. Your best strategy is to ask as few questions as possible and then make an educated guess.

What would your first question be? A good one would be: "How old is this person?" The worries of teenagers differ from those of 20-year-olds, which differ from those of older adults. Each age has its own concerns, opportunities, and pleasures.

Erikson's Description of Human Development

Erik Erikson divided the human life span into eight periods that he called ages or stages. At each stage, he said, people have specific tasks to master, and each stage generates its own social and emotional conflicts. ■ Table 5.4 summarizes Erikson's stages.

According to Erikson, failure to master the task of any stage leaves unfortunate consequences that carry over to later stages. For example, an infant deals with basic trust versus mistrust. An infant with a supportive environment forms strong attachments that positively influence future relationships with other people (Erikson, 1963). An infant who is mistreated fails to form a trusting relationship and has trouble developing close ties with people later.

In adolescence, the key issue is identity. Most adolescents in Western societies consider many options of how they will spend the rest of their lives.

Erik Erikson emphasized that each age has special conflicts.

Table 5.4 Erikson's Stages of Human Development		
Stages	**Main Conflict**	**Typical Question**
Infant	Basic trust versus mistrust	Is my social world predictable and supportive?
Toddler (ages 1–3)	Autonomy versus shame and doubt	Can I do things by myself or must I always rely on others?
Preschool child (ages 3–6)	Initiative versus guilt	Am I good or bad?
Preadolescent (ages 6–12)	Industry versus inferiority	Am I successful or worthless?
Adolescent (early teens)	Identity versus role confusion	Who am I?
Young adult (late teens and early 20s)	Intimacy versus isolation	Shall I share my life with another person or live alone?
Middle adult (late 20s to retirement)	Generativity versus stagnation	Will I succeed in my life, both as a parent and as a worker?
Older adult (after retirement)	Ego integrity versus despair	Have I lived a full life or have I failed?

They entertain alternative identities and consider many possible futures.

According to Erikson, the key decision of young adulthood is intimacy or isolation—that is, sharing your life with someone else or living alone. The quality of an intimate relationship has enormous impact throughout adult life.

If you live a full life span, you will spend about half your life in middle adulthood, where the issue is generativity (producing something important, e.g., children or work) versus stagnation (not producing). If all goes well, you take pride in your success. If not, then your difficulties and disappointments continue into old age, where the issue is integrity versus despair.

You might describe the main concerns of certain ages differently from what Erikson said. Nevertheless, two of his general points seem valid: Each stage has its own special difficulties, and an unsatisfactory resolution to the problems of one age produces extra difficulty in later life. Let's examine in more detail some of the major social and emotional issues of particular ages.

Infancy and Childhood

An important aspect of human life is attachment—*a feeling of closeness toward another person.* Attachments begin in infancy. John Bowlby (1973) proposed that infants who develop good attachments have a sense of security and safety, and those without strong attachments have trouble developing close relations later as well. Later research confirms this idea. A longitudinal study found that toddlers who received lower-quality care developed into young adults who had trouble forming strong romantic attachments. They erupted into verbal hostility with their partners significantly more often than most other people do (Oriña et al., 2011).

Most research on attachment has measured it in the Strange Situation (usually capitalized), pioneered by Mary Ainsworth (1979). In this procedure, *a mother and her infant* (typically 12 to 18 months old) *come into a room with many toys. Then a stranger enters the room. The mother leaves and then returns. A few minutes later, both the stranger and the mother leave. Then the stranger returns, and finally, the mother returns.* Through a one-way mirror, a psychologist observes the infant's reactions to each coming and going. Observers classify infants' responses in the following categories:

- *Securely attached.* The infant uses the mother as a base of exploration, cooing at her, showing her toys, and making eye contact with her. The infant shows some distress when the mother leaves but cries only briefly if at all. When she returns,

the infant goes to her with apparent delight, cuddles for a while, and then returns to the toys.
- *Anxious (or resistant).* Responses toward the mother fluctuate between happy and angry. The infant clings to the mother and cries profusely when she leaves, as if worried that she might not return. When she does return, the infant clings to her again but does not use her as a base to explore the toys. A child with an anxious attachment typically shows many fears, including a strong fear of strangers.
- *Avoidant.* While the mother is present, the infant does not stay near her and seldom interacts with her. The infant may or may not cry when she leaves and does not go to her when she returns.
- *Disorganized.* The infant seems not even to notice the mother or looks away while approaching her or covers his or her face or lies on the floor. The infant alternates between approach and avoidance and shows more fear than affection.

The prevalence of the various attachment styles differs from one country to another, but the secure pattern is usually the most common (Ainsworth, Blehar, Waters, & Wall, 1978). Of course, many children do not fit neatly into one category or another, and some who are classified as "secure" or "avoidant" are more secure or avoidant than others. Most children remain stable in their classification from one time to another (Moss, Cyr, Bureau, Tarabulsy, & Dubois-Comtois, 2005). In fact, psychologists can predict later attachment behavior from observations on infants as young as 3 months. In the Still-Face Paradigm, a parent plays with a child and then suddenly shifts to an unresponsive, expressionless face. Infants who continue looking at the parent with little sign of distress are likely to show a strong, secure attachment at a year old and beyond (Braungart-Rieker et al., 2014).

The Strange Situation also can be used to evaluate the relationship between child and father (Belsky, 1996), child and grandparent, or other relationships. As a rule, the quality of one relationship correlates with the quality of others. For example, most children who have a secure relationship with the mother also have a secure relationship with the father, and chances are the parents are happy with each other as well (Elicker, Englund, & Sroufe, 1992; Erel & Burman, 1995). Most infants who have a secure relationship with their parents at age 12 months continue to have a close relationship with them decades later (Waters, Merrick, Treboux, Crowell, & Albersheim, 2000). Those who show a secure attachment in infancy are more likely than others to form high-quality romantic attachments in adulthood (Roisman, Collins, Sroufe, & Egeland, 2005). They are quick to resolve conflicts with romantic partners and other people (Salvatore, Kuo, Steele, Simpson, & Collins, 2011).

Why do some children develop more secure attachments than others? One reason is that children differ genetically in their temperament—their *tendency to be active or inactive, and to respond vigorously or quietly to new stimuli* (Bouchard, Lykken, McGue, Segal, & Tellegen, 1990; Matheny, 1989). Temperament is fairly consistent throughout life for most people (Durbin, Hayden, Klein, & Olino, 2007). Those with a "difficult" temperament are frightened more easily than others from infancy through adulthood (Kagan, Reznick, & Snidman, 1988; Kagan & Snidman, 1991; Schwartz, Wright, Shin, Kagan, & Rauch, 2003). How long an infant fixates on one object at a time at age 8 months correlates with self-control at age 3 years, and impulse control at age 3 years correlates with impulse control in adulthood (Papageorgiou et al., 2014; Slutske, Moffitt, Poulton, & Caspi, 2012).

Attachment style also relates strongly to how responsive the parents are to the infants' needs, including holding, touching, facial expressions, and so forth. Gentle touch can be very reassuring (Hertenstein, 2002). Developing a secure attachment takes time and effort. One study examined children who were reared in an orphanage in Africa, Asia, eastern Europe, or Latin America for one to three years before adoption by a U.S. family. By three months after adoption, about half of the children showed an attachment to their adopting parents, and by nine months, about two-thirds showed a secure attachment (Carlson, Hostinar, Mliner, & Gunnar, 2014).

Patterns of attachment are similar across cultures, with a few apparent exceptions. However, what appears to be a difference in attachment sometimes reflects difficulties in measurement. In one study, Western psychologists observing Black children in South Africa found low consistency between measurements of attachment in one situation and another. When they enlisted local people as co-investigators, the local observers, who understood the local customs, reported data with much greater consistency (Minde, Minde, & Vogel, 2006). Another study reported an unusually high prevalence of "anxious attachment" among Japanese infants. However, Japanese mothers customarily stay with their babies almost constantly, including bathing with them and sleeping in the same bed. When the Japanese mothers were persuaded to leave their infants alone with a stranger, it was in many cases a new experience for the infant, who reacted with horror. The same reaction by a U.S. child would have a different meaning (Rothbaum, Weisz, Pott, Miyake, & Morelli, 2000).

©Syda Productions/Shutterstock.com

concept check

11. If a child in the Strange Situation clings tightly to the mother and cries furiously when she leaves, which kind of attachment does the child have?

Answer

11. In the United States, this pattern would indicate an anxious or insecure attachment. In Japan, however, it is an understandable reaction to a surprising experience.

Social Development in Childhood and Adolescence

Whereas attachment to parents or other caregivers is critical for infants, relationships with age-mates become increasingly important during childhood and adolescence. Around *puberty*, the onset of sexual maturity, sexual interest begins to enter into peer relationships.

The status of adolescents varies among cultures and eras. If you had been born in the 1800s or early 1900s, or in many parts of the world today, your education probably would have ended in your early teens, if not before, and you would have begun working full-time or taking care of your children. In Western societies today, improved health and nutrition have lowered the average age of puberty (Okasha, McCarron, McEwen, & Smith, 2001), but the economic situation encourages young people to stay in school and postpone marriage, family, and career. The result is a long period of physical maturity without adult status.

Adolescence is often described as a time of "storm and stress." Most adolescents report occasional

Doug Menuez/PhotoDisc./Getty Images
Children learn social skills by interacting with brothers, sisters, and friends close to their own age.

Jeremy Horner/Encyclopedia/Corbis
(a) American teenagers are financially dependent on their parents but have the opportunity to spend much time in whatever way they choose. **(b)** In many nontechnological societies, teenagers are expected to do adult work and accept adult responsibilities.

periods of moodiness and conflict with their parents in early adolescence, though the conflicts decrease in later adolescence (Laursen, Coy, & Collins, 1998). As a rule, adolescents who receive sympathetic support and understanding experience less conflict with their parents (R. A. Lee, Su, & Yoshida, 2005). Of course, we need to ask what caused what. Did the sympathetic parents cause the adolescents to feel less conflict, or did calm, well-behaved adolescents bring out the best in their parents?

Adolescence is also a time of risk-taking behaviors, not only in humans but in other species, too (Spear, 2000). Adolescents are certainly aware of the dangers. If asked about the advisability of drunk driving, unprotected sex, and so forth, they describe the dangers as well as adults do. Why, then, don't they behave like adults? Well, most of the time they do, at least when they take time to consider their decisions. They make impulsive, risky decisions mainly when they decide quickly, especially under peer pressure (Luna, Padmanabhan, & O'Hearn, 2010).

One hypothesis to explain impulsive behavior in adolescents is that the prefrontal cortex, important for inhibiting inappropriate behaviors, is slow to mature, not reaching full maturity until the late teens or early 20s (Luna, Padmanabhan, & O'Hearn, 2010). However, this cannot be the full explanation. Take a look at the following items and quickly rate each on a scale from 1 (very bad idea) to 7 (very good idea):

> Ride a bicycle down a staircase.
> Eat a salad.
> Swim with alligators.
> Watch the stars on a clear night.
> Take unknown pills at a party.

People between ages 10 and 30 responded to items like these. If making cautious decisions depended on brain maturation, we should expect ratings on the risky items to be highest in the youngest participants, and gradually decreasing for older ones. In fact, as ▼ **Figure 5.18** shows, acceptance of risky

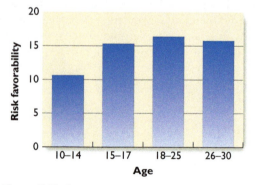

▲ **Figure 5.18** On average, people around age 20 gave higher acceptability ratings to risky activities than did those who were either younger or older. (Based on data from Shulman 2014)

activities increased up to about age 20 before declining (Shulman, 2014). In fact, in many situations 20-year-olds do take greater risks than young teenagers. The reason for the risk taking may not be a lack of inhibition, so much as it is a greater urge for excitement.

Identity Development

As Erikson pointed out, adolescence is a time of "finding yourself," determining "who am I?" or "who will I be?" It is when most people first construct a coherent "life story" of how they got to be the way they are (Habermas & Bluck, 2000).

An adolescent's *concern with decisions about the future and the quest for self-understanding* has been called an identity crisis. The term *crisis* implies more emotional turbulence than is typical. Identity development has two major elements: whether one is actively exploring the issue and whether one has made any decisions (Marcia, 1980). We can diagram the possibilities using the following grid:

	Has explored or is exploring the issues	**Has not explored the issues**
Decisions already made	Identity achievement	Identity foreclosure
Decisions not yet made	Identity moratorium	Identity diffusion

Those who have not yet given any serious thought to making decisions and who have no clear sense of identity are said to have identity diffusion. They are not actively concerned with their identity at the moment. Identity diffusion is more common among people with low self-esteem and a hopeless, pessimistic attitude toward life (Phillips & Pittman, 2007). If you think you have little chance of achieving anything, there is no reason to decide on any goals or ambitions. People in identity moratorium are *considering the issues but not yet making decisions.* They experiment with various possibilities and imagine themselves in different roles, but postpone any choices.

Identity foreclosure is a state of *reaching firm decisions without much thought.* For example, a young man might be told that he is expected to go into the family business with his father, or a young woman might be told that she is expected to marry and raise children. Decrees of that sort were once common in North America and Europe, and they are still common in many societies today. Someone living in such circumstances has little reason to consider alternative possibilities.

Finally, identity achievement is *the outcome of having explored various possible identities and then making one's own decisions.* Identity achievement does not come all at once. For example, you might decide about your career but not about marriage. You might also decide about a career and then reconsider the decision later.

The "Personal Fable" of Teenagers

Answer the following items true or false:

- Other people may fail to realize their life ambitions, but I will realize mine.
- I understand love and sex in a way that my parents never did.
- Tragedy may strike other people but probably not me.
- Almost everyone notices how I look and how I dress.

According to David Elkind, one reason for risky behavior is the "personal fable," which includes the secret belief that "nothing bad can happen to me."

According to David Elkind (1984), teenagers are particularly likely to harbor such beliefs. Taken together, he calls them the "personal fable," the conviction that "I am special—what is true for everyone else is not true for me." Up to a point, this fable supports an optimistic outlook on life, but it becomes dangerous if it leads people to take foolish risks.

This attitude is hardly unique to teenagers, however. Most middle-aged adults regard themselves as more likely than other people to succeed on the job and as less likely than average to have a serious illness (Quadrel, Fischhoff, & Davis, 1993). They also overestimate their own chances of winning a lottery, especially if they get to choose their own lottery ticket (Langer, 1975). That is, few people fully outgrow the personal fable.

Adulthood

From early adulthood until retirement, the main concern of most adults is, as Erikson noted, "What will I achieve and contribute to society and my family? Will I be successful?"

Adulthood extends from one's first full-time job until retirement. We lump so many years together because it seems that little is changing. During your childhood and adolescence, you grew taller each year, and each new age brought new privileges, such as permission to stay out late, your first driver's license, the right to vote, and the opportunity to go to college. After early adulthood, one year blends into the next. Children and teenagers know exactly how old they are, but adults sometimes have to think about it. Important changes do occur during adulthood, but most of them are self-initiated, such as getting married, having children, changing jobs, or moving to a new location (Rönkä, Oravala, & Pulkkinen, 2003).

Daniel Levinson (1986) describes adult development in terms of a series of overlapping eras. After the transition into adulthood at about age 20, give or take a couple of years, comes early adulthood, which lasts until about age 40. During early adulthood, people make big decisions about career, marriage, and having children. Most people stay with their chosen career or something closely related throughout adult life (Low, Yoon, Roberts, & Rounds, 2005). During early adulthood, people devote great energy to pursuing their goals. However, buying a house and raising a family on a young person's salary are difficult and stressful.

During middle adulthood, extending from about age 40 to 65, physical strength begins to decline, on average, but not enough to be a problem (except for pro athletes). At this point, people have already achieved success at work or have come to accept whatever status they have. Many people become more accepting of themselves and others at this time and feel less tyrannized by the stress of the job. In most cases, they also face less day-to-day stress of caring for small children.

In middle adulthood, according to Levinson (1986), people go through a **midlife transition**, *a period of reassessing goals, setting new ones, and preparing for the rest of life*. This transition may occur in response to a divorce, illness, death in the family, a career change, or some other event that causes the person to question past decisions and current goals (Wethington, Kessler, & Pixley, 2004). Just as the adolescent identity crisis is a bigger issue in cultures that offer many choices, the same is true for the midlife transition. If you lived in a society that offered no choices, you would not worry about the paths not taken! In Western society, however, you enter adulthood with high hopes. When my son Sam was getting ready for college, I asked him what his goal was. He replied, "world domination." I thought about that for a while and then asked what he was going to *be*. He replied that he was going to be "awesome." I hope you have similarly high ambitions. However, by middle age you begin to see which of your early goals are achievable, which ones are not, and which ones might be achievable but only if you get started soon. At that point you have your midlife transition and reconsider your goals.

People deal with their midlife transitions in many ways. Most people abandon unrealistic goals and set new goals consistent with the direction their lives have taken. Others decide that they have been ignoring dreams that they are not willing to abandon. They go back to school, set up a new business, or try something else they have always wanted to do. The least satisfactory outcome is to decide, "I can't abandon my dreams, but I can't do anything about them either. I can't take the risk of changing my life, even though I am dissatisfied with it." People with that attitude become discouraged and depressed.

The advice is clear: To increase your chances of feeling good in middle age and beyond, make good decisions when you are young. If you care about some goal, don't wait for a midlife transition. Get started on it now.

concept check

12. How does a midlife transition resemble an adolescent identity crisis?

Answer

12. In both cases, people examine their lives, goals, and possible directions for the future.

Old Age

Finally, people reach late adulthood, beginning around age 65. According to Erikson, people who feel satisfied with their lives experience "ego integrity," and those who are not satisfied feel "despair." How you feel in old age depends on what happened long before.

People age in different ways. Some deteriorate in intellect, coordination, and ability to care for themselves, while others remain alert and active. One way to improve older people's memory and cognition is daily physical exercise (Colcombe & Kramer, 2003; Mattson & Magnus, 2006). Certain video games that require sustained attention to several items at the same time also improve old people's performance (Anguera et al., 2013). Several other types of training programs have shown benefits also (Park et al., 2014; Rebok et al., 2014).

Psychologists have long noticed a conflict between test results that show older people declining intellectually and observations showing older people doing well in everyday life. Part of the explanation, of course, is that some people decline considerably and others do not. Another part of the explanation is that because older people find many tasks more difficult than before, they concentrate their efforts on tasks that seem more relevant or more important. As a result they do well in everyday life and on their jobs, but not so well when their motivation sags, as it often does when taking psychological tests (Hess, 2014). Furthermore, older people can call upon their extensive store of knowledge instead of solving each problem anew (Umanath & Marsh, 2014).

As we shall see in Chapter 12 on emotions, several kinds of evidence indicate that healthy older people are, on average, happier and more satisfied with life than younger people are. That result may seem surprising. However, young people face many pressures from work and raising children, whereas

In Tibet and many other cultures, children are taught to treat old people with respect and honor.

older people have more leisure. Furthermore, older people deliberately focus their attention on family, friends, and other events that bring them pleasure (Carstensen, Mikels, & Mather, 2006).

Your satisfaction in old age will depend largely on how you live while younger. Some older people say, "I hope to live many more years, but even if I don't, I have lived my life well. I did everything that I really cared about." Others say, "I wanted to do so much that I never did." Feeling dignity in old age also depends on how people's families, communities, and societies treat them. African American and Native American families traditionally honor their elders, giving them a position of status in the family and calling on them for advice. Japanese families follow a similar tradition, at least publicly (Koyano, 1991).

Loss of control is a serious issue when health begins to fail. Consider someone who spent half a century running a business who now lives in a nursing home where staff members make all the decisions. Leaving even a few of the choices and responsibilities to the residents improves their self-respect, health, alertness, and memory (Rodin, 1986; Rowe & Kahn, 1987).

The Psychology of Facing Death

This is perhaps the greatest lesson we learned from our patients: LIVE, so you do not have to look back and say, "God, how I have wasted my life!"
—Elisabeth Kübler-Ross (1975, p. xix)

The worst thing about death is the fact that when a man is dead it's impossible any longer to undo the harm you have done him, or to do the good you haven't done him. They say: live in such a way as to be always ready to die. I would say: live in such a way that anyone can die without you having anything to regret.

—Leo Tolstoy (1865/1978, p. 192)

Have you ever heard the advice, "Live each day as if it were going to be your last"? The point is to appreciate every moment, but if you really believed you would die today, you wouldn't plan for the future. You wouldn't save money or worry about the long-term health consequences of your actions. You probably wouldn't study this textbook. If you lived each day as if you expected to live forever, maybe we would be more careful about protecting the environment.

Just thinking about the fact of eventual death evokes distress. To go on with life effectively, we try to shield ourselves from thinking too much about dying. According to **terror-management theory**, *we cope with our fear of death by avoiding thoughts about death and by affirming a worldview that provides self-esteem, hope, and value in life* (Pyszczynski, Greenberg, & Solomon, 2000). When something reminds you of your mortality, you do whatever you can to reduce your anxiety. You reassure yourself that you still have many years to live. "My health is good, I don't smoke, I don't drink too much, and I'm not overweight." If that isn't true, you tell yourself that you plan to quit smoking, you are going to cut down on your drinking, and any day now you are going to start losing weight. You also think about the good job you have (or hope to have), the high salary you earn (or expect to earn), and the exciting things you will do during the rest of your life (Kasser & Sheldon, 2000).

Still, even excellent health merely postpones death, so a reminder of death redoubles your efforts to defend a belief that life is important. You reaffirm your religious beliefs, your patriotism, or other views that help you find meaning in life (Greenberg et al., 2003). You vow to repair damaged relationships with relatives or friends (Anglin, 2014). If you are a parent, you think more about your children, who will survive after you are gone (Yaakobi, Mikulincer, & Shaver, 2014). You do whatever you can to increase your feeling of control over your future (Zaleskiewicz, Gasiorowska, & Kesebir, 2013). You take pride in how you have contributed to your profession or something else that will continue after you are gone (Pyszczynski et al., 2000).

How people react to awareness of death varies somewhat as a function of culture. In Western cultures, people primed to think about death distance themselves from victims of violence or other misfortune, saying, "I'm not like that, so it won't happen to me." In Eastern cultures, people become more likely to identify with others, even the unfortunate, saying, "the welfare of the collective society is what matters" (Ma-Kellams & Blascovich, 2011).

Advances in modern medicine raise new ethical issues with regard to dying. We can now keep people alive after their physical and mental capacities have badly deteriorated. Should we? If someone is bedridden, in pain, and mentally deteriorated, with little hope of recovery, is it acceptable to help the person hasten death? A growing number of people have to face these difficult decisions for themselves and family members.

---

in closing | module 5.2

Social and Emotional Issues through the Life Span

Let's close by reemphasizing a key point of Erik Erikson's theory: Each age or stage builds on the previous ones. The quality of your early attachments to parents and others correlates with your ability to form close, trusting relationships later. How well you handle the identity issues of adolescence affects your adult life. Your productivity as an adult determines how satisfied you will feel in old age. Life is a continuum, and the choices you make at any age link with those you make before and after.

Summary

- *Erikson's view of development.* Erik Erikson described the human life span as a series of eight ages or stages, each with its own social and emotional conflicts. (page 163)
- *Infant attachment.* Infants develop attachments to significant people in their lives, as measured in the Strange Situation. Those with strong early attachments are likely to develop good social and romantic attachments as adults. (page 164)
- *Adolescent identity crisis.* Adolescents deal with the question "Who am I?" (page 166)
- *Adults' concerns.* A major concern of adults is productivity in family and career. Many adults undergo a midlife transition when they reevaluate their goals. (page 167)
- *Old age.* Dignity and independence are key concerns of old age. (page 168)
- *Facing death.* People at all ages face the anxieties associated with the inevitability of death. A reminder of death influences people to defend their worldviews. (page 168)

Key Terms

attachment (page 164)

identity achievement (page 166)

identity crisis (page 166)

identity diffusion (page 166)

identity foreclosure (page 166)

identity moratorium (page 166)

midlife transition (page 167)

Still-Face Paradigm (page 164)

Strange Situation (page 164)

temperament (page 164)

terror-management theory (page 169)

Review Questions

1. The Strange Situation is an effort to measure which aspect of behavior?
   (a) How well an adolescent can resist peer pressure
   (b) A child's attachment to the parents
   (c) How rapidly a child is progressing through Piaget's stages
   (d) A child's ability to coordinate vision with action

2. One explanation for adolescent impulsivity is that the prefrontal cortex, important for inhibiting inappropriate behaviors, is still gradually becoming mature during this period. What evidence indicates that this explanation cannot be the full answer?
   (a) People with damage to the prefrontal cortex tend to make many poor and impulsive decisions.
   (b) Twenty-year-olds rate many risky activities more acceptable than young teenagers do.
   (c) Most teenagers believe the "personal fable" that they are different from everyone else.
   (d) Adolescents make the same decisions regardless of peer pressure.

3. In a society where almost everyone becomes a farmer, which of the following would be most common?
   (a) Identity diffusion
   (b) Identity moratorium
   (c) Identity foreclosure
   (d) Identity achievement

4. Terror-management theory deals with which psychological process?
   (a) How psychologists can control violent people
   (b) How psychologists can treat post-traumatic stress disorder
   (c) How people cope with their fear of dying
   (d) How people learn to deal with abusive relationships

Answers: 1b, 2b, 3c, 4c.

module 5.3

Diversity: Gender, Culture, and Family

After studying this module, you should be able to:

- Describe how men and women differ, on average, and discuss possible explanations.
- Discuss the influences of culture on behavior.
- Evaluate the evidence regarding the influence of birth order and family size.
- Evaluate the evidence about the contributions of parenting styles, nontraditional families, and divorce on children's development.

Suppose we changed you from male to female or female to male. Or suppose we changed your ethnicity or culture. Perhaps we traded you at birth to a different family. How would you be different? With such drastic changes, it is not clear that it would still be *you!* Gender, culture, and family are integral parts of anyone's development and identity.

Gender Influences

Males and females differ biologically in many ways that influence behavior. Some brain areas are proportionately larger in men and other areas proportionately larger in women (Cahill, 2006). Certain genes are more active in male brains, and other genes are more active in female brains, on average (Reinius et al., 2008).

Despite the brain differences, behavioral differences are small to negligible in most regards. However, a few differences are reasonably consistent. Men, being generally larger and stronger, throw harder and get into fights more often (Hyde, 2005). On average, boys are more active, whereas girls have better self-control (Else-Quest, Hyde, Goldsmith, & Van Hulle, 2006). Men are more likely to help a stranger change a flat tire, but women are more likely to provide long-term nurturing support (Eagly & Crowley, 1986). The more pairs of shoes you own, the higher is the probability that you are female. Men and women tend to carry books in different ways, as shown in ▶ Figure 5.19.

On average, females are better than males at recognizing faces and detecting emotional signals (Chen & Haviland-Jones, 2000; Hall & Matsumoto, 2004; Heisz, Pottruff, & Shore, 2013). People have long noted how often men misinterpret a woman's smile, mistaking friendliness for sexual interest. Psychologists used to interpret this trend as wishful thinking until they discovered that the opposite is also true: When a woman is trying to signal sexual interest, many men misinterpret her expression as mere friendliness (Farris, Treat, Viken, & McFall, 2008). Evidently, men are just less accurate at recognizing emotional expressions, one way or the other.

When giving directions, men are more likely to use directions and distances—such as "go four blocks east . . ."—whereas women are more likely to use landmarks—such as "go until you see the library . . ." (Saucier et al., 2002). ▼ Figure 5.20 compares men's and women's ways of giving directions (Rahman, Andersson, & Govier, 2005). Similarly, in monkeys, mice, and several other species, males perform better than females in mazes without landmarks, whereas females remember the landmarks better (Jones, Braithwaite, & Healy, 2003; Williams, Barnett, & Meck, 1990). However, if forced to rely on either landmarks

or distances, both men and women get along fine (Spelke, 2005).

Another difference: Women apologize more than men do. Why? In one study, men and women kept a diary of how often they did something for which they should have apologized, how often they did apologize, how often they thought someone else should have apologized, and how often that person did. Men reported fewer occasions when they should apologize, and fewer occasions when someone else should apologize (Schumann & Ross, 2010). That is, men often shrug something off as unimportant, when women expect to say or hear, "I'm sorry." You see how this difference can be a source of friction between men and women. However, this is the kind of behavior that is likely to vary among cultures, and we should await cross-cultural studies before drawing a broad conclusion. (P.S. A great quote from a man: "If I have done anything for which I should apologize, I am ready to be forgiven.")

Blend Images/Getty Images

▲ **Figure 5.19** Men usually carry books and similar objects at their sides. Women beyond the age of puberty usually carry them at their chest. Of course, this generalization does not apply to people wearing backpacks.

Men often fail to read other people's emotions.
(© *ZITS PARTNERSHIP, King Features Syndicate. Reprinted by permission.*)

Okay, so men and women differ in miscellaneous behavioral ways. To what extent do they differ in intellectual abilities? So far as we can tell, not at all (Halpern et al., 2007; Hyde, 2005; Levine, Vasilyeva, Lourenco, Newcombe, & Huttenlocher, 2005; Spelke, 2005). Most people believe that men are better in mathematics. Males outperform females in math in countries where men have greater economic and political status than women. In countries where men and women have nearly equal status, the difference in average math performance disappears (Guiso, Monte, Sapienza, & Zingales, 2008). In the United States, on average, females do as well as or better than males on standardized math test scores and grades in nearly all math courses from elementary school through college (Hyde, Lindberg, Linn, Ellis, & Williams, 2008; Spelke, 2005).

An exception to this rule is that males do better on geometrical tasks, such as those in ▼ Figure 5.21. With much simpler tasks, we see a hint of a male advantage even among infants (Moore & Johnson, 2008; Quinn & Liben, 2008). However, these results do not necessarily indicate a difference in inborn ability. Boys usually spend more time on activities that require attention to angles and directions, providing the opportunity to learn relevant skills. Young women who spent 10 hours playing action video games significantly narrowed the male–female gap on visuospatial tasks (Feng, Spence, & Pratt, 2007). Thus, it appears that men and women differ more in interests than abilities.

Vastly more men than women become grand masters in chess. However, a study found that boys and girls start at an equal level in chess and progress at equal rates. The main reason more men than women reached the highest level was that vastly more boys than girls *started* playing chess (Chabris & Glickman, 2006).

Males and females do show differences in interests, from childhood through adulthood. Also, males are more likely than females to devote almost all their energies to a single interest, whereas females are more likely to develop a variety of interests (Valla & Ceci, 2014; Wang, Eccles, & Kenny, 2013).

The way people rear children certainly contributes to the development of different interests. For example, children who watch a television commercial showing just boys playing with a particular toy say that this is a toy "just for boys" (Pike & Jennings, 2005). However, biological tendencies may contribute also. Male monkeys prefer to play with what people consider "boys' toys," such as a ball

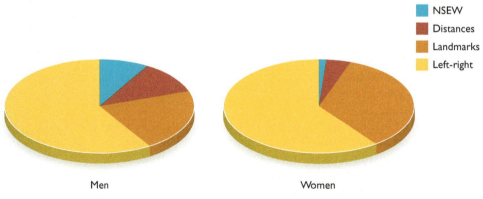

▲ **Figure 5.20** When giving directions, men refer to distances and north, south, east, and west more often than women do. Women describe more landmarks. (Based on data of Rahman, Andersson, & Govier, 2005)

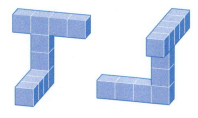

Can the set of blocks on the left be rotated to match the set at the right?

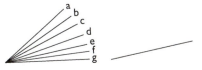

Which of the lines at the left has the same angle as the one at the right?

a
b
c
d
e
f
g

▲ **Figure 5.21** On average, men perform slightly better than women on tasks like these. (The answers are given below.)

Answer

No, the set on the left cannot be rotated to match the one on the right. For the second question, line e matches the model to its right.

and a toy car, and female monkeys prefer to play with "girls' toys," such as a soft doll (Alexander & Hines, 2002; Hassett, Siebert, & Wallen, 2008). Among human infants 3 to 8 months old (too young to have much experience with toys), girls look more at dolls than at toy trucks, whereas boys look at both about equally (Alexander, Wilcox, & Woods, 2009).

More convincingly, researchers have found that girls who were exposed to higher than average levels of the male hormone testosterone during prenatal development tend to play with boys' toys more than the average for other girls (Berenbaum, Duck, & Bryk, 2000; Nordenström, Servin, Bohlin, Larsson, & Wedell, 2002; Pasterski et al., 2005). (Some mothers produce more testosterone, and some of it enters the developing fetus.) Conversely, when pregnant women are exposed to chemicals that interfere with testosterone, their sons show less than average interest in boys' toys at ages 3 to 6 (Swan et al., 2010). These results suggest that males' and females' interests differ for biological as well as socially acquired reasons.

concept check

13. **Describe a study showing a social or cultural influence on interest in boys' or girls' toys. Describe a study suggesting a biological influence.**

Answer

13. Children who watch a commercial showing just boys playing with a toy assume the toy is just for boys. Levels of testosterone during a woman's pregnancy influence her children's later interest in boys' or girls' toys.

Gender Roles

People's behaviors depend partly on **gender roles** (also known as sex roles), *the different activities that society expects of males and females.* Gender roles sometimes constrain people's choices. For example, traditional gender roles discourage some women from pursuing interests or career opportunities that are considered too masculine. Gender roles can be a problem for men, too. In many cultures, young men are required to kill a large animal or withstand great pain to prove their manhood. In the United States, some men feel a need to get into fights or engage in other risky behaviors to prove their manhood (Vandello, Bosson, Cohen, Burnaford, & Weaver, 2008).

Biology influences a few aspects of gender roles: For example, only women can nurse babies, and men generally have an edge in physical strength. However, many gender roles are customs set by our society. Do you regard building a fire as mostly men's work or women's? What about basket weaving? Planting crops? Milking cows? The answers vary from one society to another (Wood & Eagly, 2002). Cultures also determine the relative status of men and women. Generally, if a culture lives in conditions that require hunting, fighting, or other use of physical strength, men have greater status than women. When food is abundant and enemies are few, men and women have more equal status.

Over the last few decades, gender roles have changed in many ways in many countries. In the United States, Canada, and Europe, women have become far more likely than before to get a college education, to pursue a career, and to become financially independent. Women in politics or other positions of leadership, once a rarity, are now common. Dating customs have been more resistant to change, however. Although exceptions occur, most people still expect that a man asks a woman for a date, picks her up, pays for most expenses, drives her home, and takes the initiative for kissing or other sexual contact (Eaton & Rose, 2011).

Reasons behind Gender Differences

Gender differences reflect both biological and social influences. Biological influences include the greater size and strength of males, on average, as well as the apparent influence of prenatal hormones on a child's later interests. Social influences include the expectations that parents convey to their children. Even with 6- and 9-month-old infants, mothers talk to their daughters in a more conversational way and give more instructions to their sons, such as "come here" (Clearfield & Nelson, 2006). At this age, the infants themselves are neither walking nor talking, so the difference demonstrates the mother's behavior, not her reaction to the infants' behavior. Gender roles vary significantly across cultures (see ▼ Figure 5.22).

In one study, researchers set up cameras and microphones to eavesdrop on families in a science museum. Boys and girls spent about equal time looking at each exhibit, and the parents spent about equal time telling boys and girls how to use each exhibit, but on the average, the parents provided about three times as much scientific explanation to the boys as to the girls, regardless of how many questions the children themselves asked (Crowley, Callanen, Tenenbaum, & Allen, 2001).

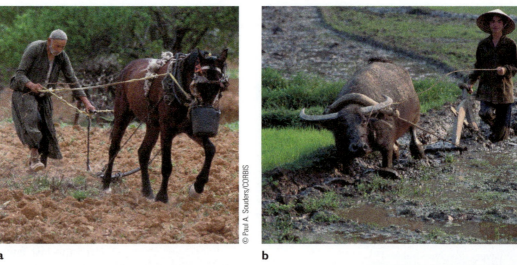

▲ **Figure 5.22** Gender roles vary greatly among cultures and even from one time period to another for a single culture. Here, a Palestinian man (**a**) and a Vietnamese woman (**b**) plow the fields. Men in Bangladesh (**c**) and women in Thailand (**d**) do the wash.

Cultural and Ethnic Influences

Some behaviors are remarkably similar across cultures. Did you know that the average nonromantic hug lasts 3 seconds? The duration is the same for people from all parts of the world (Nagy, 2011). In contrast, many other customs vary enormously across cultures. In Europe and North America, parents put their newborn in a crib, encouraging independence from the start. In Asia, infants sleep in the parents' bed. Europeans and Americans consider the Asian custom strange, and Asians consider the European/American custom cruel.

If you grew up in the United States or a similar country, you spent most of your playtime with other children close to your own age, including few if any of your relatives. If you grew up in parts of Africa or South America, you played in mixed-age groups that almost certainly included your brothers, sisters, and cousins (Rogoff, Morelli, & Chavajay, 2010).

When complaining about some product or service, would you express anger to try to get your way? In Europe or the United States, moderate expressions of anger are generally effective. In Asia, they usually backfire, unless the circumstances clearly and obviously justify the anger (Adam, Shirako, & Maddux, 2010). In the United States, frequent expressions of anger correlate with an increased risk of illness. In Japan, expressions of anger correlate with better health, because only people with high social status are likely to express any anger (Kitayama et al., 2015).

Describing the effects of culture is difficult and often prone to overgeneralizations. One popular generalization is that Western culture, such as the United States, Canada, and most of Europe, is "individualistic." People value independence, strive for individual achievements, and take pride in personal accomplishments. In "collectivist" cultures such as China, people emphasize dependence on one another, strive for group advancement, and take pride in their family's or group's accomplishments more than their own. This generalization is useful in some ways, but overstated (Brewer & Chen, 2007).

To the extent that this generalization holds, *why* is Chinese culture generally more collectivist than Western culture? Historically, it may relate to rice farming. Rice farms, which are common in much of China, require elaborate irrigation systems that need constant maintenance by group efforts. Neighbors have to cooperate so that everyone gets enough water. Farmers need to stagger their planting times so that each one can help the others harvest their crops. Everyone needs to work for the common good, or no one profits. In contrast, wheat farming, common in northern China, requires little or no cooperation from neighbors. Psychologists have found that people who live in southern China, with a long history of rice farming, show a strong collectivist and cooperative attitude, including people in that area who are not farmers. People in northern China show a more independent attitude, even though they share the same religion, government, and ethnic background as the southern Chinese (Talhelm et al., 2014).

Ethnic Minorities

Growing up as a member of an ethnic minority poses special issues. Achieving ethnic identity is comparable to the process adolescents go through in finding an individual identity. In most cases, minority-group members who achieve a strong, favorable ethnic identity have high self-esteem (Phinney, 1990). However, the outcome depends on the status of one's group. In Miami, Florida, researchers found that Cuban Americans with a strong ethnic identification had high self-esteem, but Nicaraguan Americans with a strong ethnic identification had low self-esteem (Cislo, 2008). Cuban Americans dominate Miami politics and culture, so it is easy to see how ethnic identification would work differently for the Cuban and Nicaraguan Americans.

Acculturation

Ethnic identity is especially salient for immigrants to a country. Immigrants need to learn the customs of a different country, and in many cases they need to learn a new language. Immigrants, their children, and sometimes further generations experience biculturalism, *partial identification with two cultures.* For example, Mexican immigrants to the United States speak Spanish and follow Mexican customs at home but switch to the English language and U.S. customs in other places. In most cases, immigrants with this type of bicultural attachment are better adjusted than those who either reject the old ways completely or decline to participate in the surrounding society (Sam & Berry, 2010). Bicultural youth tend to have low rates of substance use, delinquency, and depression (Coatsworth, Maldonado-Molina, Pantin, & Szapocznik, 2005). One reason is that their parents maintain close supervision (Fuligni, 1998). Another reason is that by not feeling fully part of U.S. youth culture, bicultural adolescents are less subject to its peer pressures.

However, bicultural identification is difficult if the minority group is widely distrusted. Many Turkish and Russian immigrants to Germany feel ostracized and unable to identify with German culture (Simon, Reichert, & Grabow, 2013). Similarly, Muslim Americans became targets of distrust after the terrorist attacks in September 2001, and consequently found it more difficult to identify as both American and Muslim (Sirin & Fine, 2007).

Frank Lukasseck/Terra/Corbis

Rice farming requires much cooperation among neighbors, leading to a collectivist culture.

Just as people master a foreign language better if they start young, people who immigrate at a younger age tend to accept the new culture more readily (Cheung, Chudek, & Heine, 2011). People maintain some parts of their original culture longer than others. For example, most immigrants to the United States

Gideon Mendel/Corbis News/Corbis

Many immigrants are bicultural, being familiar with two sets of customs. These immigrant children attend middle school in Michigan.

maintain their ethnic food preferences long after they have switched to American customs of dress and entertainment (Ying, Han, & Wong, 2008).

At least to a small extent, nearly all of us learn to function in multiple subcultures. Unless you live in a small town where everyone has the same background, religion, and customs, you learn to adjust what you say and do in different settings and with different groups of people. The transitions are more noticeable and more intense for ethnic minorities.

Analogous to biculturalism is biracialism. A growing percentage of people in the United States have parents from different origins, such as African and European, European and Hispanic, or Asian and Native American. People of mixed ancestry are especially common in Hawaii, California, and Puerto Rico. Decades ago, psychologists believed that biracial children and adolescents were at a disadvantage, rejected by both groups. Today, however, racially mixed couples are more common, and most biracial youth say they feel reasonably well accepted by both groups. Biracial people generally say their mixed background enables them to see the best in both cultures. The one problem they often mention is how to label themselves. If a form asks for a racial/ethnic identity, they don't want to check just one identity because that would deny the other part of themselves (Shih & Sanchez, 2005). The U.S. Census form now permits people to indicate mixed ancestry.

Many biracial people have achieved great success. Barack Obama is a prominent example.

AP Images/Jack Dempsey

concept check

14. In what way is biracialism similar to biculturalism?

Answer

14. A bicultural person identifies to some extent with two cultures. A biracial person identifies to some extent with two ethnic origins.

The Family

In early childhood, parents and other relatives are the most important people in a child's life. How do those early family experiences mold personality and social behavior?

Birth Order and Family Size

You have probably heard people say that firstborn children are more successful and ambitious than later-born children. Later-born children are said to be more popular, more independent, less conforming, less neurotic, and possibly more creative.

Most of the studies supporting these generalizations used flawed research methods (Ernst & Angst, 1983; Schooler, 1972). A common way to do the research is this: Ask people to tell you their birth order and something else about themselves, such as their grade point average in school. Then measure the correlation between the measurements. Do you see a possible problem here?

The problem is that many firstborns come from families with only one child, whereas later-born children necessarily come from larger families. Many highly educated and ambitious parents have only one child, who then has many advantages. What appears to be a difference between first- and later-born children could be a difference between small and large families (Rodgers, 2001).

A better method is to compare first- and second-born children in families with at least two children, first- and third-born children in families with at least three children, and so forth. ▼ Figure 5.23 shows the results of one study. The average IQ was higher in small families than in large families. However, within a family of a given size, birth order made little difference (Rodgers, Cleveland, van den Oord, & Rowe, 2000).

Many other studies also found that apparent differences between firstborn and later-born children are really differences between small and large families

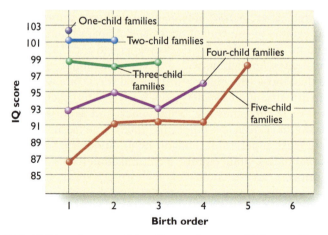

▲ **Figure 5.23** Children from small families tend to score higher on IQ tests than children from large families. However, within a family of a given size, birth order is not related to IQ. (Adapted from Rodgers, Cleveland, van den Oord, & Rowe, 2000)

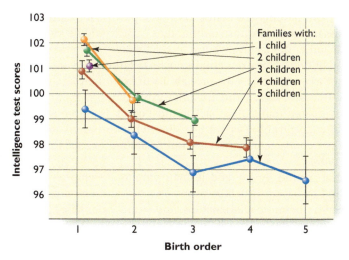

▲ **Figure 5.24** In a Norwegian study, children from small families scored higher than those from larger families. In addition, earlier-born children scored higher than later-born children, even when considering family size. (Adapted from Bjerkedal, Kristensen, Skjeret, & Brevik, 2007)

(Kanazawa, 2012; Wichman, Rodgers, & MacCallum, 2006). However, a large Norwegian study found that firstborn children scored slightly higher on IQ tests than later-born children, even within the same family (Bjerkedal, Kristensen, Skjeret, & Brevik, 2007). Contrast the results in ▲ Figure 5.24 to those in Figure 5.23. The true relationship between birth order and IQ remains uncertain, as is the relationship between birth order and personality. However, these points are clear: First, the effect of birth order, if any, is small. Second, research must carefully separate the effects of birth order from those of family size.

15. **Why is it improper to compare all the firstborns in your class to all the later-borns?**

Answer

15. Many firstborns come from one-child families. Small families differ from large families in various ways.

Effects of Parenting Styles

If you have children of your own, will you be loving and kind or strict and distant? Will you give your children everything they want or make them work for rewards? Will you encourage their independence or enforce restrictions? Moreover, how much does your behavior matter?

Psychologists have done a great deal of research comparing parenting styles to the behavior and personality of the children. Much of this research is based on four parenting styles described by Diana Baumrind (1971):

Authoritative parents: These parents *set high standards and impose controls, but they are also warm and responsive to the child's communications.* They set limits but adjust them when appropriate. They encourage their children to strive toward their own goals.

Authoritarian parents: Like the authoritative parents, authoritarian parents set firm controls, but they tend to be *emotionally more distant from the child. They set rules without explaining the reasons behind them.*

Permissive parents: Permissive parents are *warm and loving but undemanding.*

Indifferent or uninvolved parents: These parents *spend little time with their children and do little more than provide them with food and shelter.*

Of course, not everyone fits neatly into one pattern or another, but most parents are reasonably consistent over time and from one child to another. For example, most parents who are permissive with one child are permissive with the others, too (Holden & Miller, 1999). The research has found small but reasonably consistent links between parenting style and children's behavior. For example, most children of authoritative parents are self-reliant, cooperative, and successful in school. Children of authoritarian parents tend to be law-abiding but distrustful and not very independent. Children of permissive parents are often socially irresponsible. Children of indifferent parents tend to be impulsive and undisciplined.

However, the "best" style of parenting depends on the child. Children with a somewhat fearful temperament respond well to mild discipline, developing a strong conscience. Children with a fearless temperament respond poorly to any kind of discipline and respond better to rewards (Kochanska, Aksan, & Joy, 2007). If you become a parent, use some trial and error to find what works best with your children rather than relying on what some authority says is the "right" way to rear children.

Furthermore, interpreting the results about parenting is not as easy as it may appear. For years, psychologists assumed that parental indifference *leads to* impulsive, out-of-control children. However, as Judith Rich Harris (1998) pointed out, other explanations are possible. Maybe impulsive, hard-to-control children cause their parents to withdraw into indifference. Or maybe the parents and children share genes that lead to uncooperative behaviors (Klahr & Burt, 2014). Similarly, the kindly behaviors of authoritative parents could encourage well-mannered behaviors in their children, but it is also likely that children who are well behaved from the start elicit kindly, understanding behaviors in their parents.

A better approach to evaluating parenting styles is to study adopted children, who are genetically unrelated to the parents rearing them. One study of adult twins who had been adopted by separate families found that the parenting style described by one twin correlated significantly with the parenting style described by the other twin, especially for monozygotic twins (Krueger, Markon, & Bouchard, 2003). That is, if one twin reported being reared by kindly, understanding adoptive parents, the other usually did also, even though they were reared in separate families. The twins' temperaments had either affected their adopting parents, or affected how the twins perceived their environments (or both).

If we examine long-term personality traits of adopted children and their adopting parents, the results surprise most people: Children's personalities correlate almost zero with the parents' personalities (Heath, Neale, Kessler, Eaves, & Kendler, 1992; Loehlin, 1992; Viken, Rose, Kaprio, & Koskenvuo, 1994). For this reason, Harris (1995, 1998) argued that parenting style has little influence on most aspects of personality. Much personality variation depends on genetic differences, and the rest of the variation, she argued, depends mostly on the influence of other children.

As you can imagine, not everyone happily accepted Harris's conclusion. Psychologists who had spent a career studying parenting styles were not pleased to be told that their results were inconclusive. Parents were not pleased to be told that they had little influence on their children's personalities. Harris (2000), however, chose her words carefully. She did not say that it makes no difference how you treat your children. For one thing, obviously, if you treat your children badly, they won't like you! Furthermore, children who grow up in a generally happy, supportive family develop better social relationships later in life than children reared in much less supportive families (Ackerman et al., 2013; Jaffee, Hanscombe, Haworth, Davis, & Plomin, 2012).

Psychologists using improved research methods have shown real, though not huge, effects of parenting style (Collins, Maccoby, Steinberg, Hetherington, & Bornstein, 2000). The controversy has led to greater appreciation of the mutual influences of parents on their children and children on their parents (Kiff, Lengua, & Zalewski, 2011).

In general, two parents are better than one, partly for financial reasons. We might guess that a child whose mother dies early would be more harmed than one whose father died, simply because on average mothers spend more time with their children. However, children whose father died seem to be at more risk, at least as measured by the probability of eventually becoming depressed (Jacobs & Bovasso, 2009). The apparent explanation is that death of a father has been a greater financial setback in most cases. Children reared by a single mother generally do about as well as children in two-parent homes if the single mother has a good income (MacCallum & Golombok, 2004; Weissman, Leaf, & Bruce, 1987).

Children reared by gay and lesbian parents develop about the same as those reared by heterosexuals in terms of social and emotional development, mental health, romantic relationships, and sexual orientation (Bos, van Balen, & van den Boom, 2007; Gartrell, Bos, & Goldberg, 2011; Golombok et al., 2003; Wainright, Russell, & Patterson, 2004). The children's main difficulties relate to the prejudices that their classmates may have against single-sex couples (Bos & Gartrell, 2010).

However, we should be cautious about our conclusions. It is difficult to demonstrate conclusively the *absence* of any difference, and many studies comparing traditional and nontraditional families examined only small samples or a limited range of behaviors (Redding, 2001; Schumm, 2008). We can say that being reared by a single parent or by gays or lesbians does not produce a big effect, but the data don't eliminate the possibility of any effect at all.

Parental Conflict and Divorce

In an earlier era, people in the United States considered divorce shameful. Political commentators attributed Adlai Stevenson's defeat in the presidential campaign of 1952 to the fact that he was divorced. Americans would never vote for a divorced candidate, the commentators said. "Never" didn't last very long. By 1980, when Ronald Reagan was elected president, voters hardly noticed his divorce and remarriage.

The effects of divorce on children are highly variable. On average, the children show at least temporary setbacks in academic performance and social

16. Why is a correlation between parents' behavior and children's behavior inconclusive concerning how parents influence their children? Why does a correlation between adoptive parents' behavior and that of their adopted children provide more useful information?

Answer

16. Children can resemble their parents' behavior because of either genetics or social influences. Adoptive children do not necessarily resemble their adopted parents genetically, so any similarity in behavior would reflect environmental influences. Of course, the question would remain as to whether the parents influenced the children or the children influenced the parents.

Nontraditional Families

Western society has considered a traditional family to be a mother, a father, and their children. A nontraditional family is, therefore, anything else.

Many children today are reared by a single parent or by gay parents. The research indicates that who rears the child has less influence than whether the caregivers are loving and dependable.

relationships. Many pout and seek extra attention, especially in the first year after a divorce (Hetherington, 1989). In the long term, many children reared by a divorced mother have difficulties, partly because of the emotional trauma of the divorce and partly because of financial difficulties. A study across 14 countries found that divorce decreased a child's probability of graduating from college by 7 percent (Bernardi & Radl, 2014). Some children remain distressed for years, whereas others recover quickly. A few seem to do well at first but become more distressed later. Others are resilient throughout their parents' divorce and afterward. They keep their friends, do all right in school, and maintain good relationships with both parents (Hetherington, Stanley-Hagan, & Anderson, 1989).

Research results show that divorce's effects vary somewhat among cultures and ethnic groups. Divorce is more common in Black families, but in most regards, divorced Black women adjust better than White women do (McKelvey & McKenry, 2000). Many Black families ease the burden of single parenthood by having a grandmother or other relative help with child care.

None of the research implies that parents must stay together for their children's benefit. Children do not fare well if their parents are constantly fighting. Children who observe much conflict between their parents tend to be nervous, unable to sleep through the night (El-Sheikh, Buckhalt, Mize, & Acebo, 2006), and prone to violent and disruptive behaviors (Sternberg, Baradaran, Abbott, Lamb, & Guterman, 2006).

17. You may hear someone say that the right way to rear children is with both a mother and a father. Based on the research evidence, what would be a good reply?

Answer

17. According to the evidence so far, children reared by a single parent, gay couple, or divorced parents develop normally.

Many Ways of Life

Children grow up in a great variety of environments. Some of the differences are huge if we compare across cultures, but important differences occur also within a culture. Some of the factors exert less influence than we might expect. For example, adopted children's personalities correlate almost not at all with that of their adopting parents, and being reared by a gay or lesbian couple produces little effect on children's personality development. Indeed, it is difficult to demonstrate a major personality effect from any single influence. Perhaps that is because so many factors come into play.

Summary

- *Gender influences.* Men and women differ on average in various aspects of behavior, including interests. However, researchers have found no clear evidence of differences in intellectual abilities. (page 171)
- *Gender roles.* Parents and others convey certain expectations of how boys and girls will act. These expectations substantially influence behavioral development. (page 173)
- *Cultural and ethnic differences.* Being a member of an ethnic minority raises special issues for identity development. Immigrant children have special difficulties as they try to participate in two cultures. Most bicultural and biracial children develop well. (page 174)
- *Birth order.* Many studies comparing firstborn versus later-born children have failed to separate the effects of birth order from the effects of family size. Much of the apparent difference between firstborns and later-borns is really a difference between children of small versus large families. (page 176)
- *Parenting styles.* Parenting style correlates with the behavior of the children. For example, caring, understanding parents tend to have well-behaved children. However, children affect the parents as much as parents affect the children. (page 177)
- *Nontraditional child care.* Researchers have found no important differences in personality development between children reared by gay or lesbian couples and those reared by heterosexual couples. (page 178)
- *Effects of divorce.* Children of divorced parents often show signs of distress, but the results vary across individuals. (page 178)

Key Terms

authoritarian parents (page 177)

authoritative parents (page 177)

biculturalism (page 175)

gender roles (page 173)

indifferent or uninvolved parents (page 177)

permissive parent (page 177)

Review Questions

1. One reason why nearly all the best chess players are men is that more boys than girls start playing chess. Of the following, what is another plausible explanation?
   (a) Males have greater abilities than females do at mathematics and anything related to mathematics.
   (b) Males are more likely than females are to devote themselves to a single interest.
   (c) The male brain has many structural differences from the female brain, on average.
   (d) Chess is played only in cultures that give females few educational opportunities.

2. Which of the following studies suggests a cultural influence on a child's interest in boys' or girls' toys?
   (a) Girls exposed before birth to higher testosterone levels show greater interest in boys' toys later.
   (b) Boys exposed before birth to chemicals that interfere with testosterone show decreased interest in boys' toys later.
   (c) Children who watch a commercial showing just boys playing with a toy assume it is only for boys.
   (d) Male monkeys show more interest in boys' toys than female monkeys do.

3. A "collectivist" attitude is more common in southern China than in northern China. What is apparently responsible for this difference?
   (a) Greater prevalence of Confucianism in southern China
   (b) A history of rice farming in southern China
   (c) A longer history of communist government in southern China
   (d) A higher level of education in southern China

4. Suppose you want to test the effect of birth order on intelligence by comparing firstborn children to third-born children. To do the study properly, which of the following is most important?
   (a) Use only firstborn children who are unrelated to the third-born children.
   (b) Include only those firstborns who come from a family of at least three children.
   (c) Include an equal percentage of males and females in each group.
   (d) Get results from any first- or third-born child who volunteers to participate.

5. If we want to determine whether children resemble their parents because of genetic influences or because of social influences, which of the following would be the most helpful kind of information?
   (a) Compare monozygotic and dizygotic twins.
   (b) Examine the amount of similarity between adopting parents and their adopted children.
   (c) Compare children's similarity to their mother and their father.

6. According to the evidence so far, what can be expected of children who are reared by a gay or lesbian couple?
   (a) Most have psychological adjustment problems in childhood, although they are normal in adulthood.
   (b) Most seem normal during childhood, but they develop problems during adulthood.
   (c) Most have psychological adjustment problems during both childhood and adulthood.
   (d) Most develop about normally, about the same as those reared by a heterosexual couple.

Answers: 1b, 2c, 3b, 4b, 5b, 6d.

6 Learning

Koji Aoki/Getty Images

Andrea Chu/Getty Images

Newborn humans have almost no control of their muscles, except for their eyes and mouth. Imagine a baby born with complete control of all muscles, including arms, hands, legs, and feet. Would that be a good thing?

After the parents stopped bragging about their precocious youngster, they would discover what a nightmare they had. An infant with extreme mobility but no experience would get into every imaginable danger. From the start, people need to learn what is safe to touch and what isn't, where we can go and where we shouldn't. Just about everything we do requires constant learning and relearning.

Psychologists have devoted an enormous amount of research to learning, and in the process, they developed and refined research methods that they now routinely apply in other areas of psychological investigation. This chapter is about the procedures that change behavior—why you lick your lips at the sight of tasty food, why you turn away from a food that once made you sick, why you handle sharp knives cautiously, and why you shudder if you see someone charging toward you with a knife. In Chapter 7, we proceed to the topic of memory, including the ability to recall specific events.

module 6.1

Classical Conditioning

After studying this module, you should be able to:

- Discuss the assumptions and goals of behaviorism.

- Define classical conditioning and describe the procedures for producing and measuring it.

- State the procedures for extinction in classical conditioning.

- Explain how classical conditioning pertains to drug tolerance.

- Describe how Pavlov tried to explain classical conditioning, and cite later evidence that calls for a different explanation.

During a period in the middle of the 20th century, most of the leading researchers in experimental psychology focused on animal learning, including a huge number of studies of rats in simple mazes and pigeons pecking a disk on the side of the cage. To understand researchers' fixation on these topics, we have to understand something of the history. The interest in animal learning arose from both scientific and philosophical roots.

The Behaviorist View in Relation to Learning

As discussed in Chapter 1, some of the early psychologists, the structuralists, explored mental events by asking people to describe their sensations, experiences, and so forth. Other psychologists wanted to get as far away from that approach as possible, because statements about mental states explained nothing:

> **Q:** Why did she yell at him?
> **A:** She yelled because she was angry.
> **Q:** How do you know she was angry?
> **A:** We know she was angry because she was yelling.

Those who objected to discussions of mental states advocated behaviorism, *the position that psychology should concern itself only with what people and other animals do, and the circumstances in which they do it*, without reference to thoughts, ideas, emotions, or any other internal state. To the question, "Why did she yell at him?" their reply would identify the experiences and stimuli that provoked the outburst. Behaviorists view discussions of mental events as just sloppy language. As B. F. *Skinner* (1990) argued, when you say, "I *intend* to . . . ," what you really mean is "I am about to . . . " or "In situations like this, I usually . . . " or "This behavior is in the preliminary stages of happening." Any statement about mental experiences can be converted into a description of behavior.

The same insistence on description is central to the British and American legal systems: A witness is asked, "What did you see and hear?" An acceptable answer might be, "The defendant was sweating and trembling, and his voice was wavering." A witness should not say, "The defendant was nervous and worried," because that statement requires an inference that the witness is not entitled to make. (Of course, the jury might draw an inference.)

You might be tempted to dismiss behaviorism because, at least at first glance, it seems so ridiculous: "What do you *mean,* my thoughts and beliefs and emotions don't cause my behavior?!" The behaviorists' reply is, "Exactly right. Your thoughts and other internal states do not cause your behav-

ior because events in your environment caused your thoughts. Those events are the real causes of your behavior." Contemplate this: If you believe that your thoughts or other internal states cause behaviors *independently* of your previous experiences, what evidence could you provide to support your claim?

Jacques Loeb was one of the earliest, most extreme advocates of behaviorism. In Loeb's words, "Motions caused by light or other agencies appear to the layman as expressions of will and purpose on the part of the animal, whereas in reality the animal is forced to go where carried by its legs" (Loeb, 1918/1973, p. 14). Why do certain caterpillars approach light? It is not, according to Loeb, because they are "fond" of light. It is because light in front of them increases their rate of locomotion. If light strikes mainly from the left or right side, the caterpillar turns toward the light, not because it "wants to," but because light from the side causes greater muscle tension on one side of the body and therefore causes the animal to move one set of legs more than the other. Loeb applied similar explanations to why certain animals tend to move toward heat or cold, toward or away from water, up (away from gravity) or down, and so forth (see ▼ **Figure 6.1**). Built-in mechanisms caused animals to move in adaptive ways, without the animals necessarily having any desires or intentions. Loeb's view was an example of stimulus–response psychology, *the attempt to explain behavior in terms of how each stimulus triggers a response.*

Although the term *stimulus–response psychology* was appropriate for Loeb, it is a misleading description of today's behaviorists. Behaviorists believe that behavior is a product of not only the current stimuli but also the individual's history of experiences, plus such factors as wakefulness or sleepiness (Staddon, 1999).

Was Loeb's account sufficient to explain all behaviors of caterpillars or other invertebrates? Well, no one had any evidence that it *wasn't* sufficient. The question then was, how far could that approach apply? Could we explain some, much, or all of vertebrate behavior in equally simple terms?

The greatest challenge was to explain learning. Behaviorists' goal was ambitious and optimistic. Their goal was to find basic laws of behavior, especially learning, that would be analogous to the laws of physics. Their goal was the simplest explanation possible, based on the principle of parsimony discussed in Chapter 2. But could they explain learning in simple terms, without reference to understanding, ideas, or other internal processes?

▲ **Figure 6.1** Jacques Loeb, an early student of animal behavior, argued that much or all of invertebrate behavior could be described as responses to simple stimuli, such as approaching light or moving opposite to the direction of gravity.

concept check

1. **Why do behaviorists reject explanations in terms of thoughts?**

2. **How did Loeb explain why certain animals turn toward the light?**

Answers

1. Previous events and current stimuli are responsible for thoughts, and therefore the events and stimuli are the real causes of behavior.
2. According to Loeb, light from the side caused greater muscle tension on one side of the body. Therefore, muscles on one side or the other moved more vigorously than those on the other side. This imbalance of movement continued until the light stimulation on both sides was equal.

Ivan P. Pavlov devised simple principles to describe learned changes in a dog's behavior.

Pavlov and Classical Conditioning

In the early 1900s, Ivan P. Pavlov, a Russian physiologist who had won a Nobel Prize in physiology for his research on digestion, stumbled upon an observation that offered a simple explanation for learning. Given the rise of behaviorism, the mood of the time was ripe for Pavlov's ideas.

One day as Pavlov was pursuing his digestion research, he noticed that a dog secreted digestive juices as soon as it saw the lab worker who customarily fed the dogs. Because this secretion clearly depended on the dog's previous experiences, Pavlov called it a "psychological" secretion. He enlisted the help of other specialists, who discovered that "teasing" a dog with the sight of food produced salivation that was as predictable and automatic as any reflex. Pavlov called it a *conditioned reflex* because it depended on conditions.

Pavlov's Procedures

Pavlov assumed that animals are born with *automatic connections*—called unconditioned reflexes—*between a stimulus such as food and a response such as secreting digestive juices.* He conjectured that animals acquire new reflexes by transferring a response from one stimulus to another. For example, if a particular sound always precedes food, an animal would salivate to the sound as if it were food.

The *process by which an organism learns a new association between two stimuli—a neutral stimulus and one that already evokes a reflexive response—* is known as classical conditioning, or Pavlovian conditioning. It is called classical because it has been known and studied for a long time.

Pavlov selected dogs with a moderate degree of arousal. Highly excitable dogs would not hold still long enough because of what he called their "freedom reflex." Highly inhibited dogs would fall asleep. He attached a tube to one of the salivary ducts in a dog's mouth to measure salivation, as shown in ▼ Figure 6.2. He could have measured stomach secretions, but salivation was easier to measure.

Whenever Pavlov gave a dog food, the dog salivated. The food → salivation connection was automatic, requiring no training. Pavlov called food the unconditioned stimulus, and he called salivation the unconditioned response.

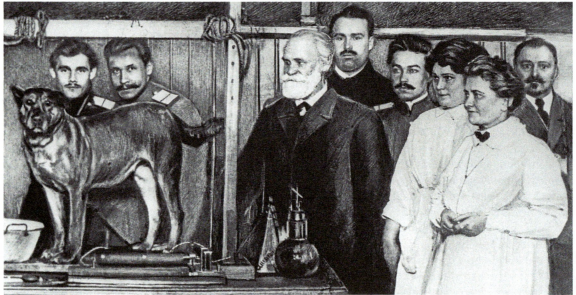

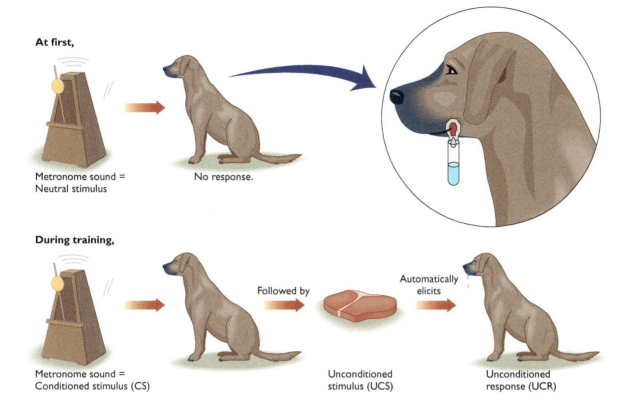

At first,

Metronome sound =
Neutral stimulus

No response.

During training,

Metronome sound =
Conditioned stimulus (CS)

Followed by

Unconditioned
stimulus (UCS)

Automatically
elicits

Unconditioned
response (UCR)

After some number of repetitions,

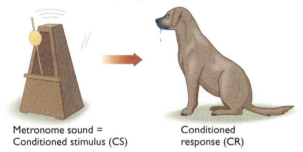

Metronome sound =
Conditioned stimulus (CS)

Conditioned
response (CR)

◄ **Figure 6.2** A conditioned stimulus precedes an unconditioned stimulus. At first, the conditioned stimulus elicits no response, and the unconditioned stimulus elicits the unconditioned response. After sufficient pairings, the conditioned stimulus elicits the conditioned response, which can resemble the unconditioned response.

The **unconditioned stimulus (UCS)** is *an event that automatically elicits an unconditioned response.* The **unconditioned response (UCR)** is *the action that the unconditioned stimulus elicits.*

Next Pavlov introduced a new stimulus, such as a metronome or other sound. Upon hearing the metronome, the dog lifted its ears and looked around but did not salivate, so the metronome was a neutral stimulus with regard to salivation. Pavlov sounded the metronome shortly before giving food to the dog. After a few pairings of the metronome with food, the dog began to salivate as soon as it heard the metronome (Pavlov, 1927/1960).

We call the metronome the **conditioned stimulus (CS)** because a dog's *response to it depends on the preceding conditions*—that is, pairing the CS with the UCS. The salivation that follows the metronome is the **conditioned response (CR)**. The conditioned response is *whatever response the conditioned stimulus elicits as a result of the conditioning (training) procedure.* At the start, the conditioned stimulus elicits no significant response. After conditioning, it elicits a conditioned response.

In Pavlov's experiment, the conditioned response was salivation and so was the unconditioned response. However, in some cases, the conditioned response differs from the unconditioned response. For example, the unconditioned response to an electric shock includes shrieking and jumping. The conditioned response to a stimulus paired with shock (i.e., a warning signal for shock) is a tensing of the muscles and cessation of activity (e.g., Pezze, Bast, & Feldon, 2003).

To review, the *unconditioned stimulus* (UCS), such as food, automatically elicits the *unconditioned response* (UCR), such as salivating. A neutral stimulus, such as a sound, that is paired with the UCS becomes a *conditioned stimulus* (CS). At first, it elicits no response or an irrelevant response, such as looking around. After some number of pairings of the CS with the UCS, the conditioned stimulus elicits the *conditioned response* (CR), which usually resembles the UCR. Figure 6.2 diagrams these relationships.

As a rule, conditioning occurs more rapidly if the conditioned stimulus is unfamiliar. If you have heard a tone many times (followed by nothing) and now start hearing the tone followed by a strong stimulus, you will be slow to show signs of conditioning. Similarly, imagine two people who are bitten by a snake. One has never been near a snake before, and the other has spent years tending snakes at the zoo. You can guess which one will learn a greater fear.

More Examples of Classical Conditioning

Here are more examples of classical conditioning:

- Your alarm clock makes a faint clicking sound a couple of seconds before the alarm goes off. At first, the click by itself does not awaken you, but the alarm does. After a week or so, you awaken when you hear the click.

| Unconditioned stimulus | = | alarm | → | Unconditioned response | = | awakening |
| Conditioned stimulus | = | click | → | Conditioned response | = | awakening |

- You hear the sound of a dentist's drill shortly before the unpleasant experience of the drill on your teeth. From then on, the sound of a dentist's drill arouses anxiety.

| Unconditioned stimulus | = | drilling | → | Unconditioned response | = | tension |
| Conditioned stimulus | = | sound of the drill | → | Conditioned response | = | tension |

- A nursing mother responds to her baby's cries by putting the baby to her breast, stimulating the flow of milk. After a few days of repetitions, the sound of the baby's cry is enough to start the milk flowing.

| Unconditioned stimulus | = | baby sucking | → | Unconditioned response | = | milk flow |
| Conditioned stimulus | = | baby's cry | → | Conditioned response | = | milk flow |

- Whenever your roommate flicks a switch on the stereo, it starts blasting sounds at a deafening level. You flinch as soon as you hear the flick of the switch.

| Unconditioned stimulus | = | very loud music | → | Unconditioned response | = | flinching |
| Conditioned stimulus | = | flick of the switch | → | Conditioned response | = | flinching |

Note the usefulness of classical conditioning. It prepares an individual for likely events.

One more example: Form an image of a lemon, a nice fresh juicy one. You cut it into slices and then suck on a slice. Imagine that sour taste. As you imagine the lemon, do you notice yourself salivating? If so, your imagination produced enough resemblance to the actual sight and taste of a lemon to serve as a conditioned stimulus.

3. **Every time an army drill sergeant calls out "Ready, aim, fire," the artillery shoots, making a painfully loud sound that causes you to flinch. After a few repetitions, you tense your muscles after the word "fire," before the shot itself. In this example, identify the CS, UCS, CR, and UCR.**

Answer

3. The conditioned stimulus is the sound "Ready, aim, fire." The unconditioned stimulus is the artillery shot. The unconditioned response is flinching; the conditioned response is tensing.

Additional Phenomena of Classical Conditioning

The *process that establishes or strengthens a conditioned response* is known as acquisition. After discovering classical conditioning, Pavlov and others varied the procedures to produce other outcomes. Here are some of the main phenomena.

Extinction

Suppose someone sounds a buzzer and then blows a puff of air into your eyes. After a few repetitions, you start to close your eyes as soon as you hear the buzzer (see ▼ Figure 6.3). Now the buzzer sounds repeatedly without the puff of air. What do you do?

You blink your eyes the first time and perhaps the second and third times, but before long, you stop. This decrease of the conditioned response is called extinction. *To extinguish a classically conditioned response, repeatedly present the conditioned stimulus (CS) without the unconditioned stimulus (UCS).* That is, acquisition of a response (CR) occurs when the CS predicts the UCS, and extinction occurs when the CS no longer predicts the UCS.

Extinction is not the same as forgetting. Both weaken a learned response, but they arise in different ways. You forget during a long period without reminders or practice. Extinction occurs because of a specific experience—perceiving the conditioned stimulus without the unconditioned stimulus. If acquisition is learning to make a response, extinction is learning to inhibit it.

Don't be misled by connotations of the term *extinction*. After extinction of an animal or plant species, it is gone forever. In classical conditioning, extinction does *not* mean obliteration. Extinction suppresses a response. Think of it like extinguishing a fire: Pouring water on a huge fire puts out the blazes, but a few smoldering embers may linger long afterward, and they might easily reignite the fire.

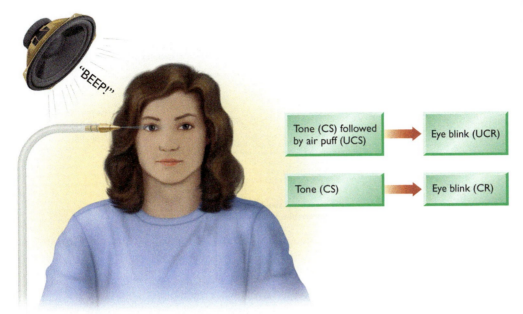

Tone (CS) followed by air puff (UCS) → Eye blink (UCR)

Tone (CS) → Eye blink (CR)

Spontaneous Recovery

Suppose you are in a classical-conditioning experiment. At first, you repeatedly hear a buzzer (CS) that precedes a puff of air to your eyes (UCS). Then the buzzer stops predicting an air puff. After a few trials, your response to the buzzer extinguishes. Next you wait a while with nothing happening until suddenly you hear the buzzer again. What will you do? Chances are, you blink your eyes at least slightly. Spontaneous recovery is *a temporary return of an extinguished response after a delay* (see ▼ Figure 6.4).

Why does spontaneous recovery occur? Think of it this way: At first, the buzzer predicted a puff of air to your eyes, and then it didn't. You behaved in accordance with the more recent experiences.

Hours later, neither experience is much more recent than the other, and the effects of acquisition and extinction are about equally strong.

 concept check

4. **In Pavlov's experiment on conditioned salivation in response to a buzzer, what procedure produces extinction? What procedure produces spontaneous recovery?**

Answer

4. To bring about extinction, present the buzzer repeatedly without presenting food. To bring about spontaneous recovery, first bring about extinction. Then wait and present the buzzer again.

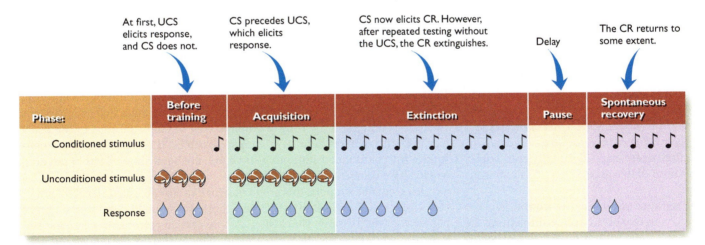

At first, UCS elicits response, and CS does not.

CS precedes UCS, which elicits response.

CS now elicits CR. However, after repeated testing without the UCS, the CR extinguishes.

Delay

The CR returns to some extent.

Phase:	Before training	Acquisition	Extinction	Pause	Spontaneous recovery
Conditioned stimulus					
Unconditioned stimulus					
Response					

▲ **Figure 6.4** If the conditioned stimulus regularly precedes the unconditioned stimulus, acquisition occurs. If the conditioned stimulus is presented by itself, extinction occurs. A pause after extinction yields a brief spontaneous recovery.

Stimulus Generalization

Suppose a bee stings you, and you learn to fear bees. Now you see a wasp or hornet. Will you fear that, too?

You probably will, but you probably will not fear butterflies or other insects that don't resemble bees. The more similar a new stimulus is to the conditioned stimulus, the more likely you are to show a similar response (see ▶ Figure 6.5). **Stimulus generalization** is the *extension of a conditioned response from the training stimulus to similar stimuli.*

However, it is often difficult to specify what we mean by "similar" (Pearce, 1994). After a bee stings you, you might fear the sound of buzzing bees when you are walking through a forest but not when you hear the same sounds in a nature documentary on television. Furthermore, two items that seem similar to you might not seem similar to someone else.

Discrimination

You are walking through a wilderness area carrying a baby. At some point the baby shakes a rattle. You hear the sound and smile. A minute later you hear a slightly different rattle—the sound of a rattlesnake. You react very differently because you have learned to **discriminate**—*to respond differently to stimuli that predict different outcomes.* Similarly, you discriminate between a bell that signals time for class to start and a different bell that signals a fire alarm.

Discrimination training enhances sensitivity to sensory cues. In one study, people sniffed two chemicals that seemed virtually the same. However, one chemical always preceded an electrical shock, and the other always preceded a safe interval without shock. As training proceeded, people got better at detecting the difference, and they reacted to the smell that predicted shock (Li, Howard, Parrish, & Gottfried, 2008).

Drug Tolerance as an Example of Classical Conditioning

Classical conditioning shows up in ways you might not expect. One example is **drug tolerance**: *Users of certain drugs experience progressively weaker effects after taking the drugs repeatedly.* Some longtime users experience only mild effects from an amount of heroin that would kill an average person.

Drug tolerance results partly from automatic chemical changes that occur in cells throughout the body, but it also depends partly on classical conditioning. Consider: When drug users inject themselves with morphine or heroin, the drug injection procedure is a complex stimulus that includes the

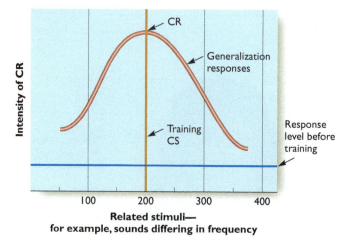

▲ **Figure 6.5** Stimulus generalization is the process of extending a learned response to new stimuli that resemble the one used in training. A less similar stimulus elicits a weaker response.

time and place as well as the needle injection. This total stimulus predicts a second stimulus, the drug's entry into the brain. When the drug reaches the brain, it triggers a variety of body defenses—including changes in hormone secretions, heart rate, and breathing rate—that counteract the effects of the drug itself.

First stimulus	→	**Second stimulus**	→	**Automatic response**
(Injection procedure)		(Drug enters brain)		(Body's defenses)

Whenever one stimulus predicts a second stimulus that produces an automatic response, classical conditioning can occur. The first stimulus is the CS, the second is the UCS, and the response is the UCR. Let's relabel as follows:

Conditioned stimulus	→	**Unconditioned stimulus**	→	**Unconditioned response**
(Injection procedure)		(Drug enters brain)		(Body's defenses)

If conditioning occurs here, what would happen? Suppose the CS (drug injection) produces a CR that resembles the UCR (the body's defenses against the drug). In that case, as soon as the injection starts, before the drug enters the body, the body starts mobilizing its defenses against the drug. Therefore, the drug has less effect, and we say that the body developed tolerance. Shepard Siegel (1977, 1983) conducted several experiments that confirm classical conditioning during drug injections.

Conditioned stimulus	→	**Conditioned response**
(Injection procedure)		(Body's defenses)

The research tested several predictions. One prediction was this: If the injection procedure serves as a conditioned stimulus, then the body's defense reactions should be strongest if the drug is administered in the usual way, in the usual location, with as many familiar stimuli as possible. (The entire experience constitutes the conditioned stimulus.) Therefore, the behavioral effects of the drug would be weakened in the familiar setting.

The evidence supports this prediction for a variety of drugs (Siegel & Ramos, 2002). Much of the research deals with laboratory animals, but observations of people confirm the same conclusion. People drinking alcohol in a familiar setting experience less cognitive impairment than those drinking it in an unfamiliar setting (Birak, Higgs, & Terry, 2011).

A second prediction: If tolerance is classically conditioned, researchers should be able to extinguish it. The procedure for extinction is to present the

CS without the UCS. Given the difficulties of working with human drug users, researchers studied rats. Many drug effects are difficult to measure in nonhumans, but one is easy—the ability of morphine to decrease pain. Researchers first measured the smallest pain necessary to make rats flinch. Then they gave the rats morphine and ran the test again, finding that the drug greatly decreased the pain response. The next step was to produce tolerance by daily drug injections, testing the pain response each time. When the rats showed increased pain response, indicating tolerance to the morphine, researchers went to the final step. They gave the rats daily injections of salt water. If we think of the injection procedure as the CS and morphine as the UCS, then injecting salt water is presenting the CS without the UCS. After a few repetitions, tolerance partly extinguished. Now an injection of morphine substantially decreased the pain response (Siegel, 1977). In short, drug tolerance shows the properties we would expect it to have if tolerance depends on classical conditioning. ▼ Figure 6.6 summarizes this experiment.

Research on the classical conditioning of drug tolerance eventually led to applications to help people quit their addictions. People with a history of addiction experience cravings in the presence of sights, sounds, and smells that remind them of their drug experiences. When psychologists present those stimuli under conditions where the person is able to resist the temptation, the result is partial extinction of the cravings (Loeber, Croissant, Heinz, Mann, & Flor, 2006).

concept check

5. When someone develops tolerance to the effects of a drug injection, what are the conditioned stimulus, the unconditioned stimulus, the conditioned response, and the unconditioned response?

6. How did researchers measure drug tolerance in rats?

Answers

5. The conditioned stimulus is the injection procedure. The unconditioned stimulus is the entry of the drug into the brain. Both the conditioned response and the unconditioned response are the body's defenses against the drug.
6. They first measured the ability of morphine to decrease rats' pain responses. Then they administered morphine daily for a few days and tested the rats' pain responses each day. After repeated injections, the rats showed increased pain responses, and therefore tolerance to the effects of the drug.

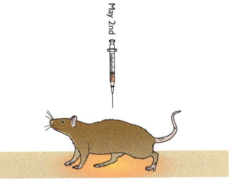

1. Initial response to painful heat: Rat licks its paw.

2. First test under morphine: No response unless heat is turned up much higher.

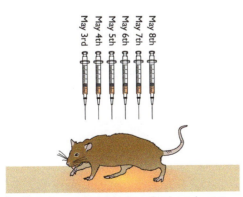

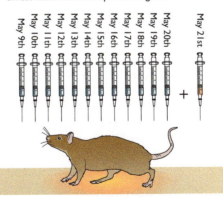

3. After six morphine injections: Rat has tolerance and shows response to pain despite morphine.

4. After 12 saltwater injections, another morphine injection reduces pain. Tolerance is partly extinguished.

▲ **Figure 6.6** Morphine decreases pain, but after a few repetitions, a rat develops tolerance to this effect. Repeated injections of salt water produce extinction of the learned tolerance.

Explanations of Classical Conditioning

What is classical conditioning, really? As is often the case, the process appeared simple at first, but later investigation found it to be more complex and more interesting. Pavlov noted that conditioning depended on the timing between CS and UCS, as shown here:

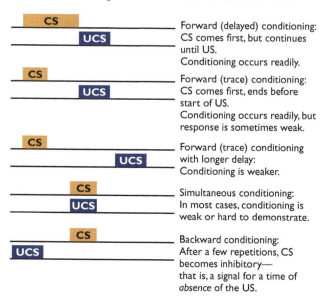

Forward (delayed) conditioning: CS comes first, but continues until US.
Conditioning occurs readily.

Forward (trace) conditioning: CS comes first, ends before start of US.
Conditioning occurs readily, but response is sometimes weak.

Forward (trace) conditioning with longer delay:
Conditioning is weaker.

Simultaneous conditioning: In most cases, conditioning is weak or hard to demonstrate.

Backward conditioning: After a few repetitions, CS becomes inhibitory—that is, a signal for a time of *absence* of the US.

In these displays, read time left to right. Pavlov surmised that presenting the CS and UCS at nearly the same time caused a connection to grow in the brain so that the animal treated the CS as if it were the UCS. ▼ Figure 6.7a illustrates possible connections before the start of training: The UCS excites a UCS center somewhere in the brain, which immediately stimulates the UCR center. ▼ Figure 6.7b illustrates connections that might develop during conditioning: Pairing the CS and UCS develops a connection between their brain representations. After this connection develops, the CS excites the CS center, which excites the UCS center, which excites the UCR center and produces a response.

Later studies contradicted that idea. First, a shock (UCS) causes rats to jump and shriek, but a conditioned stimulus paired with shock makes them freeze in position. They react to the conditioned stimulus as a danger signal, not as if they felt a shock. That is, conditioning did not simply transfer the response from one stimulus to another. Also, in trace conditioning, where a delay separates the end of the CS from the start of the UCS, the animal does not make a conditioned response immediately after the conditioned stimulus but instead waits until almost the end of the usual delay between CS and UCS. Again, it is not treating the CS as if it were the UCS; it is using it as a predictor, a way to prepare for the UCS (Gallistel & Gibbon, 2000).

It is true, as Pavlov suggested, that the longer the delay between the CS and the UCS, the weaker the conditioning, other things being equal. However, just having the CS and UCS close together in time is not enough. It is essential that they occur more often together than they occur apart. That is, the CS must be a good predictor of the UCS. Consider this experiment: For rats in both Group 1 and Group 2, every presentation of a CS is followed by a UCS, as shown in ▼ Figure 6.8. For Group 2, the UCS also appears at many other times without the CS. For this group, the UCS happens frequently anyway, and no more often with the CS than without it. Group 1 learns a strong response to the CS, and Group 2 does not (Rescorla, 1968, 1988).

concept check

7. If classical conditioning depended *entirely* on presenting the CS and UCS at nearly the same time, what result should the experimenters have obtained in Rescorla's experiment?

Answer

7. If classical conditioning depended entirely on presenting the CS and UCS at nearly the same time, the rats in both groups would have responded equally to the conditioned stimulus, regardless of how often they received the unconditioned stimulus at other times.

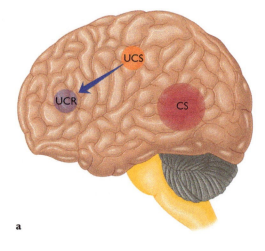
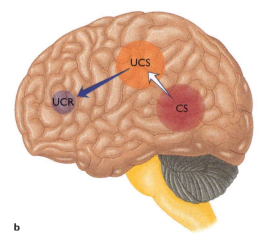

▶ **Figure 6.7** According to Pavlov, **(a)** at the start of conditioning, activity in a UCS center automatically activates the UCR center. **(b)** After sufficient pairings of the CS and UCS, a connection develops between the CS and UCS centers. Afterward, activity in the CS center flows to the UCS center and therefore excites the UCR center.

a   b

Group 1

Group 2

◀ **Figure 6.8** In Rescorla's experiment, the CS always preceded the UCS in both groups, but Group 2 received the UCS frequently at other times also. Group 1 developed a strong conditioned response to the CS, and Group 2 did not.

Now consider this experiment: Rats are shown a light (CS) followed by shock (UCS) until they respond consistently to the light. The conditioned response is that they freeze in place. Then they get a series of trials with both a light and a tone, again followed by shock. Let's test the rats' response to the tone alone. Do they show a conditioned response? No. The same pattern occurs with the reverse order: First, rats learn a response to the tone, and then they get light–tone combinations before the shock. They show a conditioned response to the tone but not to the light (Kamin, 1969; see ▼ Figure 6.9). These results demonstrate the **blocking effect:** *The previously established association to one stimulus blocks the formation of an association to the added stimulus.* Research supports two explanations: First, if the first stimulus predicts the outcome, the second stimulus adds no new information. Second, the rat attends strongly to the stimulus that already predicts the outcome and therefore pays less attention to the new stimulus.

The same principle holds in human reasoning. Suppose you have several experiences when you eat something with peppers and have an allergic reaction. Then you have several experiences when you eat peppers and nuts and have the same reaction. You have already decided to try to avoid peppers. Do you now

strongly avoid nuts also? Probably not (Melchers, Ungor, & Lachnit, 2005).

concept check

8. **Suppose you have already learned to flinch when you hear the sound of a dentist's drill.** Now your dentist turns on some soothing background music during the drilling. The background music is paired with the pain just as much as the drill sound is. Will you learn to flinch at the sound of that background music?

Answer

8. You will not learn to flinch at the sound of the background music. Because the drill sound already predicted the pain, the new stimulus is uninformative and will not be strongly associated with the pain.

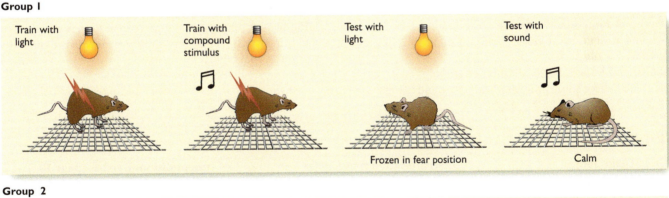

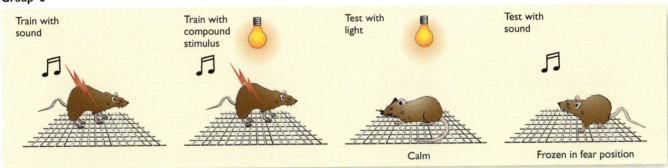

▲ **Figure 6.9** Each rat first learned to associate either light or sound with shock. Then it received a compound of both light and sound followed by shock. Each rat continued to show a strong response to the old stimulus (which already predicted shock) but little to the new stimulus.

Classical Conditioning Is More than Drooling Dogs

If someone had asked you to describe what you hoped to learn from a psychology course, you probably would not have replied, "I want to learn how to make dogs salivate!" I hope you see that the research on conditioned salivation is just a way to explore fundamental mechanisms, much as genetics researchers have studied the fruit fly *Drosophila* or neurophysiologists have studied the nerves of squid. Classical conditioning is important for many important behaviors, ranging from emotional responses to drug tolerance. We shall encounter it again in later chapters.

People sometimes use the term *Pavlovian* to mean simple, mechanical, robotlike behavior. Pavlovian or classical conditioning is not a mark of stupidity. It is a way of responding to relationships among events, a way of preparing us for what is likely to happen.

Summary

- *Behaviorism.* Behaviorists insist that psychologists should study behaviors and not internal states such as intentions or expectations. Previous events led to the internal states, and therefore those events are the real causes of behavior. (page 183)

- *Behaviorists' interest in learning.* Behaviorists' goal is to explain behavior without relying on terms such as *idea* or *understanding.* Much of invertebrate behavior can be described in simple terms, but the greater challenge was to explain learning. (page 183)

- *Classical conditioning.* Ivan Pavlov discovered classical conditioning, the process by which an association forms between a neutral stimulus (the conditioned stimulus) and one that initially evokes a reflexive response (the unconditioned stimulus). The result is a new response (the conditioned response) to the conditioned stimulus. (page 184)

- *Extinction.* A conditioned response can be extinguished by repeatedly presenting the conditioned stimulus by itself. (page 186)

- *Spontaneous recovery.* If the conditioned stimulus is not presented at all for some time after extinction and is then presented again, the conditioned response may return. The return is called spontaneous recovery. (page 187)

- *Stimulus generalization.* A conditioned response to a stimulus will extend to other stimuli to the extent that they resemble the trained stimulus. (page 188)

- *Discrimination.* Animals (including people) learn to respond differently to stimuli that predict different outcomes. (page 188)

- *Drug tolerance.* Drug tolerance results in part from classical conditioning. The drug administration procedure comes to evoke defensive responses. (page 188)

- *Basis for classical conditioning.* Pavlov believed that conditioning occurred because presenting two stimuli close to each other in time developed a connection between their brain representations. Later research showed that animals do not treat the conditioned stimulus as if it were the unconditioned stimulus. Also, being close in time is not enough. Learning occurs if the first stimulus predicts the second stimulus. (page 190)

Key Terms

acquisition (page 186)

behaviorism (page 183)

blocking effect (page 191)

classical conditioning (or Pavlovian conditioning) (page 184)

conditioned response (CR) (page 185)

conditioned stimulus (CS) (page 185)

discrimination (page 188)

drug tolerance (page 188)

extinction (page 186)

spontaneous recovery (page 187)

stimulus generalization (page 188)

stimulus–response psychology (page 183)

unconditioned reflex (page 184)

unconditioned response (UCR) (page 185)

unconditioned stimulus (UCS) (page 185)

Review Questions

1. Which of the following did behaviorists reject?
   (a) The study of conscious thought
   (b) The principle of parsimony
   (c) Darwin's theory of evolution
   (d) The use of scientific methods in psychology

2. In what way is the term *stimulus-response psychology* more appropriate for Jacques Loeb than for the behaviorists of today?
   (a) Today's behaviorists agree that thoughts and emotions are the true causes of behavior.

(b) Today's behaviorists study only humans, not other species.

(c) Today's behaviorists recognize that sleepiness and other internal processes modify responses to a stimulus.

(d) Today's behaviorists study only the stimuli and not the responses.

3. At the start of training, the CS elicits ___ and the UCS elicits ___. After repetitions of the CS followed by the UCS, the CS elicits ___ and the UCS elicits ___.
   (a) CR . . . CR . . . UCR . . . UCR
   (b) CR . . . UCR . . . CR . . . UCR
   (c) no response . . . UCR . . . CR . . . UCR
   (d) UCS . . . UCR . . . UCR . . . CR

4. How does extinction differ from forgetting?
   (a) Extinction is more complete and more permanent.
   (b) Forgetting depends on changes in brain activity. Extinction does not.
   (c) Extinction depends on changes in brain activity. Forgetting does not.
   (d) Forgetting depends on passage of time. Extinction depends on a specific experience.

5. Suppose an individual undergoes extinction, and then a delay ensues with no exposure to either the CS or the UCS. What will probably happen?
   (a) Forgetting
   (b) Consolidation
   (c) Spontaneous recovery
   (d) Stimulus discrimination

6. What evidence indicates that rats' tolerance to morphine injections is at least partly due to classical conditioning?
   (a) Rats that have been exposed repeatedly to morphine salivate when they receive morphine.

(b) Rats that have developed a tolerance to morphine salivate when they receive morphine.

(c) Repeated injections of salt water increase the later effects of morphine.

(d) Repeated injections of salt water decrease the later effects of morphine.

7. Which of the following is evidence against Pavlov's explanation for classical conditioning?
   (a) Conditioning always occurs if a CS repeatedly precedes the UCS.
   (b) Other things being equal, longer CS–UCS delays lead to weaker evidence of conditioning.
   (c) In some cases the CR is different from the UCR.

8. Rats repeatedly received one stimulus followed by a UCS. Then they repeatedly received that stimulus and a second stimulus, followed by the same UCS. What happened, and what is this phenomenon called?
   (a) Rats stopped responding to either of the two stimuli. This is the spontaneous recovery effect.
   (b) Rats learned to respond equally to the first and second stimuli. This is the stimulus generalization effect.
   (c) Rats started responding to the second stimulus instead of the first stimulus. This is the blocking effect.
   (d) Rats showed little response to the second stimulus. This is the blocking effect.

Answers: 1a, 2c, 3c, 4d, 5c, 6c, 7c, 8d.

After studying this module, you should be able to:

- Describe the procedures for operant conditioning and explain how it differs from classical conditioning.

- Define reinforcement and state how punishment differs from it.

- State the procedures for extinction in operant conditioning, and explain how they differ from the procedures in classical conditioning.

- Explain how shaping, chaining, and schedules of reinforcement alter the types and rates of behaviors.

- Give an example of a practical application of operant conditioning.

Growing up in a different environment would change your behavior, but would it completely determine your behavioral development? How much can the environment control, and how much can it not control?

Suppose a family in another country adopted you at birth. You then lived in a land with different language, customs, food, religion, and so forth. Undoubtedly you would be different in many ways. But would that alternative "you" have anything in common with the current "you"? Or does your culture and environment mold your behavior completely? The most extreme statement of environmental determinism came from John B. Watson, one of the founders of behaviorism, who said,

> Give me a dozen healthy infants, well-formed, and my own specified world to bring them up in and I'll guarantee to take any one at random and train him to become any type of specialist I might select— doctor, lawyer, artist, merchant-chief, and yes, even beggar-man thief—regardless of his talents, penchants, tendencies, abilities, vocations, and race of his ancestors. I am going beyond my facts and I admit it, but so have the advocates of the contrary. (1925, p. 82)

Needless to say, Watson never had a chance to demonstrate his point. No one gave him a child and his own specified world. If he or anyone else really did have complete control of the environment, would it be possible to control a child's eventual fate? We may never know, ethics being what they are, after all. Still, one of the goals of researchers studying learning is to see what kinds of behavior change result from changes in the environment.

Thorndike and Operant Conditioning

Shortly before Pavlov's research, Edward L. Thorndike (1911/1970), a Harvard graduate student, began training cats in a basement. Saying that earlier experiments had dealt only with animal intelligence, not animal stupidity, he sought a simple behaviorist explanation of learning. He put cats into puzzle boxes (see ▼ Figure 6.10) from which they could escape by pressing a lever, pulling a string,

▲ **Figure 6.10** Each of Thorndike's puzzle boxes had a device that could open it. Here, tilting the pole will open the door. (Based on Thorndike, 1911/1970)

tilting a pole, or other means. Sometimes, he placed food outside the box, but usually, cats worked just to escape from the box. The cats learned to make whatever response opened the box, especially if the box opened quickly.

They learned by trial and error. When a cat had to tilt a pole to escape from the box, it might at first paw or gnaw at the door, scratch the walls, or pace back and forth. Eventually, it bumped against the pole and the door opened. The next time, the cat went through a similar repertoire of behaviors but might bump against the pole a little sooner. Over many trials, the cat gradually but inconsistently improved its speed of escape. ▶ Figure 6.11 shows a learning curve to represent this behavior. A learning curve is *a graph of the changes in behavior that occur over the course of learning.*

Did the cat understand the connection between bumping against the pole and opening the door? No, said Thorndike. If the cat gained a new insight at some point, its escape should have been quick from that point on. The graph of the cat's escape times shows no sharp break that we could identify as the time of an insight.

Thorndike concluded that learning occurs because certain behaviors are strengthened at the expense of others. An animal enters a situation with a repertoire of responses such as pawing the door, scratching the walls, pacing, and so forth (labeled R_1, R_2, R_3, etc., in ▼ Figure 6.12). It starts with its most probable response (R_1). If nothing special happens, it proceeds to other responses, eventually reaching one that opens the door—for example, bumping against the pole (R_7 in this example). Opening the door reinforces the preceding behavior.

A reinforcement is *the process of increasing the future probability of the most recent response.* Thorndike said that reinforcement "stamps in," or

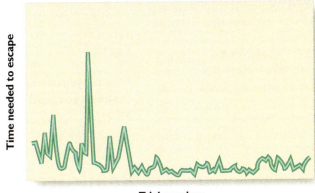

▲ **Figure 6.11** As the data from one of Thorndike's experiments show, a cat's time to escape from a box decreases gradually but sporadically. Thorndike concluded that the cat did not at any point "get an idea." Instead, reinforcement gradually increased the probability of the successful behavior.

strengthens, the response. The next time the cat is in the puzzle box, it has a slightly higher probability of the effective response. If it receives reinforcement again, the probability goes up another notch (see Figure 6.12). You see how this view fit with behaviorists' hope for an explanation that did not rely on thoughts, understanding, or other mental processes.

Thorndike summarized his views in the law of effect (Thorndike, 1911/1970, p. 244):

> Of several responses made to the same situation, those which are accompanied or closely followed by satisfaction to the animal will, other things being equal, be more firmly connected with the situation, so that, when it recurs, they will be more likely to recur.

Hence, the animal becomes more likely to repeat the responses that led to favorable consequences even if it does not understand why. Similarly, a

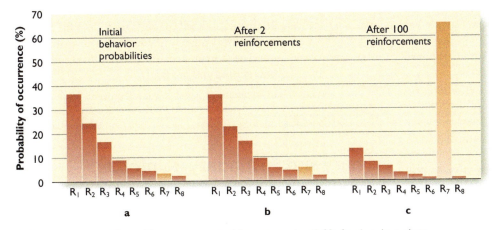

▲ **Figure 6.12** According to Thorndike, a cat starts with many potential behaviors in a given situation. When one of the behaviors leads to reinforcement, the future probability of that behavior increases. We need not assume that the cat understands what it is doing or why.

machine could be programmed to produce random responses and repeat the ones that led to reinforcement.

Was Thorndike's interpretation correct? Another way of putting this question: When an animal learns to make a response that produces some outcome, does it "expect" that outcome, or does it simply register, "Make this response in this situation"? In general, it is difficult to answer this question (Burke, Franz, Miller, & Schoenbaum, 2008). However, it is clear that animals learn more than just muscle movements. An animal that learned to turn left, but now has a muscle impairment that prevents turning left, will instead rotate 270° to the right, accomplishing the same outcome (Seligman, Railton, Baumeister, & Sripada, 2013).

Thorndike revolutionized the study of animal learning, substituting experimentation for collections of anecdotes. He also demonstrated the possibility of simple explanations for apparently complex behaviors (Dewsbury, 1998). On the negative side, his example of studying animals in contrived laboratory situations led researchers to ignore much about how animals learn in nature (Galef, 1998).

The kind of learning that Thorndike studied is called operant conditioning (because the subject *operates* on the environment to produce an outcome) or instrumental conditioning (because the subject's behavior is *instrumental* in producing the outcome). Operant or instrumental conditioning is *the process of changing behavior by providing a reinforcer after a response.* The defining difference between operant conditioning and classical conditioning is the procedure: *In operant conditioning, the subject's behavior produces an outcome that affects future behavior. In classical conditioning, the subject's behavior has no effect on the outcome (the presentation of either the CS or the UCS).* For example, in classical conditioning, the experimenter (or the world) presents two stimuli at particular times, regardless of what the subject does or doesn't do. Those stimuli change future behaviors, but the behaviors do not control the stimuli. In operant conditioning, the subject has to make some response before any outcome occurs.

In general, the two kinds of conditioning also affect different behaviors. Classical conditioning applies mainly to visceral responses (i.e., *responses of the internal organs*), such as salivation and digestion, whereas operant conditioning applies mainly to skeletal responses (i.e., *movements of leg muscles, arm muscles, etc.*). However, this distinction sometimes breaks down. For example, if a tone predicts an electric shock (a classical-conditioning procedure), the tone makes the animal freeze in position (a skeletal response) as well as increase its heart rate (a visceral response).

9. **When a bell rings, an animal sits up on its hind legs and drools; then it receives food. Is the animal's behavior an example of classical conditioning or operant conditioning?** So far, you do not have enough information to answer the question. What else do you need to know before you can answer?

Answer

9. You need to know whether the bell always predicts food (classical conditioning) or whether the animal receives food only when it sits up (operant conditioning).

Reinforcement and Punishment

Some events work extremely well as reinforcers for some individuals and not others. Consider how many hours some people will play a video game just for a high score. In one quirky experiment, mother rats could press a lever to deliver extra baby rats into their cage. They kept on pressing and pressing, adding more and more babies (Lee, Clancy, & Fleming, 1999). Is there any pattern as to what is a good reinforcer and what isn't?

We might guess that reinforcers are biologically useful to the individual, but many are not. For example, saccharin, a sweet but biologically useless chemical, can be a reinforcer. For many people, alcohol and tobacco are stronger reinforcers than vitamin-rich vegetables. So biological usefulness doesn't define reinforcement.

A useful way of defining reinforcement relies on the concept of equilibrium. If you could spend your day any way you wanted, how would you divide your time, on average? Let's suppose you might spend 30 percent of your day sleeping, 10 percent eating, 8 percent exercising, 11 percent reading, 9 percent talking with friends, 2 percent grooming, 2 percent playing the piano, and so forth. Now suppose something kept you away from one of these activities for a day or two. An opportunity to do that activity would get you back toward equilibrium. According to the disequilibrium principle of reinforcement, *anything that prevents an activity produces disequilibrium, and an opportunity to return to equilibrium is reinforcing* (Farmer-Dougan, 1998; Timberlake & Farmer-Dougan, 1991).

Of course, some activities are more insistent than others. If you have been deprived of oxygen, the opportunity to breathe is extremely reinforcing. If you have been deprived of reading time or telephone time, the reinforcement value is less.

10. **Suppose you want to reinforce a child for doing chores around the house, and you don't know what would be a good reinforcer. According to the disequilibrium principle, how should you proceed?**

Answer

10. Begin by determining how the child ordinarily spends his or her time when given unlimited opportunities. Then find which of these activities the child has been deprived of recently. The opportunity to do one of those activities should be reinforcing.

Primary and Secondary Reinforcers

Psychologists distinguish between primary reinforcers (or *unconditioned reinforcers) that are reinforcing because of their own properties,* and secondary reinforcers (or *conditioned reinforcers) that became reinforcing by association with something else.* Food and water are primary reinforcers. Money (a secondary reinforcer) becomes reinforcing because we can exchange it for food or other primary reinforcers. A student learns that a good grade wins approval, and an

What serves as a reinforcer for one person might not for another. Lucy Pearson (left) has collected more than 110,000 hubcaps. Jim Hambrick (right) collects Superman items.

employee learns that increased productivity wins the employer's praise. In these cases, *secondary* means "learned." It does not mean unimportant. We spend most of our time working for secondary reinforcers.

Punishment

In contrast to a *reinforcer,* a punishment *decreases the probability of a response.* A reinforcer can be either a presentation of something (e.g., receiving food) or a removal (e.g., stopping pain). Similarly, punishment can be either a presentation of something (e.g., receiving pain) or a removal (e.g., withholding food). Punishment is most effective when it is quick and predictable. An uncertain or delayed punishment is less effective. For example, the burn you feel from touching a hot stove is highly effective in teaching you something to avoid. The threat that smoking cigarettes might give you cancer many years from now may also be effective, but less so. Punishments are not always effective. If the threat of punishment were always effective, the crime rate would be zero.

B. F. Skinner (1938) tested punishment in a famous laboratory study. He first trained food-deprived rats to press a bar to get food and then he stopped reinforcing their presses. For the first 10 minutes, some rats not only failed to get food, but also received a slap on their paws every time they pressed the bar. (The bar slapped their paws.) The punished rats temporarily suppressed their pressing, but in the long run, they pressed as many times as did the unpunished rats. Skinner concluded that punishment produces no long-term effects.

That conclusion, however, is an overstatement (Staddon, 1993). A better conclusion would be that punishment does not greatly weaken a response when no other response is available. Skinner's food-deprived rats had no other way to seek food. (If someone punished you for breathing, you would continue breathing nevertheless.)

Still, alternatives to punishment are often more effective. How could we get drivers to obey school-zone speed limits? Warning them of fines is not very effective. Even stationing police officers in the area has limited success. A surprisingly effective procedure is to post a driver-feedback sign that posts the speed limit and an announcement of "your speed" based on a radar sensor (Goetz, 2011). Just getting individual feedback heightens a driver's awareness of the law and likelihood of obeying it.

Is physical punishment of children, such as spanking, a good or bad idea? Spanking is illegal in many countries, mostly in Europe (Zolotor & Puzia, 2010). Many psychologists strongly discourage spanking, recommending that parents simply reason with the child or use nonphysical methods of discipline, such as time out or loss of television or other privileges. What evidence backs this recommendation?

All the research presents correlations between physical punishment and behavioral problems. Children who are frequently spanked tend to be ill behaved. You should see the problem in

Many secondary reinforcers are surprisingly powerful. Consider how hard children work for a little gold star that the teacher pastes on an assignment.

interpreting this result: It might mean that spanking causes misbehavior, or it might mean that ill-behaved children provoke their parents to spank them. It could also mean that spanking is more common for families in stressful conditions, families with much parental conflict, or families with other factors that might lead to misbehaviors (Morris & Gibson, 2011). A better type of research compares children who were frequently spanked to children from similar backgrounds who were frequently subjected to nonphysical punishment, such as time out. That type of research shows no difference between those spanked and those given other types of punishment (Larzelere, Cox, & Smith, 2010). So it appears that misbehavior leads to punishment (of whatever type) more than punishment leads to misbehavior.

The conclusions are different with regard to severe punishment bordering on child abuse. Likely outcomes then include antisocial behavior, low self-esteem, and hostility toward the parents (Larzelere & Kuhn, 2005), as well as increased risk for a lifetime of health problems (Hyland, Alkhalaf, & Whalley, 2013).

Categories of Reinforcement and Punishment

As mentioned, a reinforcer can be either presenting something like food or avoiding something like pain. Possible punishments include either presenting pain or avoiding food. Psychologists use different terms to distinguish these possibilities, as shown in ■ Table 6.1.

The upper left and lower right of the table both show reinforcement. Reinforcement *always* *increases* the probability of a behavior. Reinforcement can be either **positive reinforcement**—*presenting something such as food*, or **negative reinforcement**—*avoiding something such as pain*. Many people find the term *negative reinforcement* confusing or misleading (Baron & Galizio, 2005; Kimble, 1993), and most researchers prefer the terms *escape learning* or *avoidance learning*. The individual is reinforced by an opportunity to escape or avoid a danger. Regardless of whether reinforcement comes from gaining something desirable or avoiding something undesirable, the effects on behavior are about the same (Mallpress, Fawcett, McNamara, & Houston, 2012).

Punishment *always decreases* the probability of a behavior. In Table 6.1, the upper right and lower left items show two types of punishment. Punishment can be either presenting something such as pain, or omitting something such as food or privileges. Punishment by omitting something is occasionally known as negative punishment.

To classify some procedure, attend to the wording. If the procedure increases a behavior, it is reinforcement. If it decreases a behavior, it is punishment. If the reinforcer is the presence of something, it is positive reinforcement. If the reinforcer is the absence of something it is negative reinforcement, also known as escape or avoidance learning.

11. **Identify each of the following examples using the terms in Table 6.1:**
   a. Your employer gives you bonus pay for working overtime.
   b. You learn to stop drinking caffeinated beverages at night because they keep you awake.
   c. You put on sunscreen to decrease the risk of skin cancer.
   d. If you get a speeding ticket, you will temporarily lose the privilege of driving the family car.

Answers

11. a. positive reinforcement; b. punishment; c. avoidance learning or negative reinforcement; d. punishment.

Table 6.1 Four Categories of Operant Conditioning		
	Event Such as Food	**Event Such as Pain**
Behavior leads to the event	**Positive Reinforcement** *Result:* Increase in the behavior, reinforced by presentation of food. *Example:* "If you clean your room, I'll get you a pizza tonight."	**Punishment** *Result:* Decrease in the behavior, and therefore a decrease in pain. *Example:* "If you insult me, I'll slap you." 
Behavior avoids the event	**Punishment** *Result:* Decrease in the behavior, and therefore food continues to be available. *Example:* "If you hit your little brother again, you'll get no dessert." 	**Negative Reinforcement = Escape or Avoidance Learning** *Result:* Increase in the behavior, and therefore a decrease in pain. *Example:* "If you go into the office over there, the doctor will remove the thorn from your leg." 

Additional Phenomena of Operant Conditioning

Recall the concepts of extinction, generalization, and discrimination in classical conditioning. The same concepts apply to operant conditioning, with different procedures.

Extinction

No doubt you have heard the saying, "If at first you don't succeed, try, try again." The comedian W. C. Fields said, "If at first you don't succeed, try, try again. Then quit. There's no point in being a damn fool about it."

In operant conditioning, extinction *occurs if responses stop producing reinforcements.* For example, you were once in the habit of asking your roommate to join you for supper. The last few times you asked, your roommate said no, so you stop asking. You used to enjoy a particular video game, but the last few times it seemed boring, so you stop playing. In classical conditioning, extinction is achieved by presenting the CS without the UCS. In operant conditioning, the procedure is response without reinforcement. ■ Table 6.2 compares classical and operant conditioning.

Generalization

Someone who receives reinforcement for a response in the presence of one stimulus will probably make the same response in the presence of a similar stimulus. *The more similar a new stimulus is to the original reinforced stimulus, the more likely is the same response.* This phenomenon is known as stimulus generalization. For example, you might reach for the turn signal of a rented car in the same place you would find it in your own car.

Many animals have evolved an appearance that takes advantage of their predators' stimulus generalization (Darst & Cummings, 2006). A predatory bird that learns to avoid a poisonous snake probably also avoids a harmless look-alike snake. A bird that learns to avoid a bad-tasting butterfly will also avoid other butterflies of similar appearance. ▲ Figure 6.13 shows one example.

Discrimination and Discriminative Stimuli

If reinforcement occurs for responding to one stimulus and not another, the result is discrimination *between them, yielding a response to one stimulus and not the other.* For example, you smile and greet someone you think you know, but then you realize it is someone else. After several such experiences, you learn

Poisonous Harmless

▲ **Figure 6.13** The harmless frog evolved an appearance that resembles a poisonous species, taking advantage of the way birds generalize their learned avoidance responses. (Source: C. R. Darst & M. E. Cummings, 2006).

to recognize the difference between the two people. Mushroom hunters learn to pick the edible types and leave the poisonous ones.

A *stimulus that indicates which response is appropriate or inappropriate* is called a discriminative stimulus. Much of our behavior depends on discriminative stimuli. For example, you learn ordinarily to be quiet during a lecture but you talk when the professor encourages discussion. You learn to drive fast on some streets and slowly on others. Throughout your day, one stimulus after another signals which behaviors will yield reinforcement, punishment, or neither. *The ability of a stimulus to encourage some responses and discourage others* is known as stimulus control.

B. F. Skinner and the Shaping of Responses

One of the most famous psychological researchers, B. F. Skinner (1904–1990), demonstrated many uses of operant conditioning. Skinner was a devoted behaviorist who always sought simple explanations in terms of reinforcement histories rather than mental processes.

One problem confronting any behavior researcher is how to define a response. Imagine watching children and trying to count "aggressive behaviors." What is an aggressive act and what isn't? Skinner simplified the measurement by simplifying the situation (Zuriff, 1995): He set up a box, called an *operant-conditioning chamber* (or *Skinner box,* a term that Skinner himself never used), in which a rat presses a lever or a pigeon pecks an illuminated "key" to receive food (see ▼ Figure 6.14). He operationally defined the response as anything that the animal did to depress the lever or key. So if the rat pressed the lever with its snout instead of its paw, the response still counted. If the pigeon batted the key with its wing instead of pecking it with its beak, it still counted. The behavior was defined by its outcome, not by muscle movements.

Does that definition make sense? Skinner's reply was that it did because it led to consistent results. When deciding how to define a behavior—any

Table 6.2 Classical Conditioning and Operant Conditioning

	Classical Conditioning	Operant Conditioning
Terminology	CS, UCS, CR, UCR	Response, reinforcement
Behavior	Does not control UCS	Controls reinforcement
Paired during acquisition	Two stimuli (CS and UCS)	Response and reinforcement (in the presence of certain stimuli)
Responses	Mostly visceral (internal organs)	Mostly skeletal muscles
Extinction procedure	CS without UCS	Response without reinforcement

▲ **Figure 6.14** B. F. Skinner examines a rat in an operant-conditioning chamber. When the light above the bar is on, pressing the bar is reinforced. A food pellet rolls out of the storage device (left) and down the tube into the cage.

behavior—the best definition is the one that produces the clearest results.

Shaping Behavior

When Thorndike wanted to train a cat to push a pole or pull a string, he simply put the cat in a puzzle box and waited. Skinner wanted to train rats to push levers and pigeons to peck at keys. These behaviors are not part of the animals' normal routine. If he simply put an animal into a box and waited, he might be in for a very long wait. To speed the process, Skinner developed a powerful technique, called **shaping**, for *establishing a new response by reinforcing successive approximations to it.*

To *shape* a rat to press a lever, you might begin by reinforcing the rat for standing up, a common behavior in rats. After a few reinforcements, the rat stands up more frequently. Now you change the rules, giving food only when the rat stands up while facing the lever. Soon it spends more time standing up and facing the lever. It extinguishes its behavior of standing and facing in other directions because those responses are not reinforced.

Next you provide reinforcement only when the rat stands facing the correct direction while in the half

of the cage nearer the lever. You gradually move the boundary, and the rat moves closer to the lever. Then the rat must touch the lever and, finally, apply weight to it. Through a series of short, easy steps, you shape the rat to press a lever.

Shaping works with humans, too, of course. Consider education: First, your parents or teachers praise you for counting your fingers. Later, you must add and subtract to earn their congratulations. Step by step, your tasks become more complex until you are doing advanced mathematics.

Chaining Behavior

Ordinarily, you don't do just one action and then stop. You do a long sequence of actions. To produce a sequence, psychologists use a procedure called **chaining**. Assume you want to train a show horse to go through a sequence of actions. You could *chain* the behaviors, *reinforcing each one with the opportunity to engage in the next one.* The animal starts by learning the final behavior. Then it learns the next to last behavior, which is reinforced by the opportunity to perform the final behavior. And so on.

A rat might be placed on the top platform, as in ▼ Figure 6.15f, where it eats. Then it is put on the intermediate platform with a ladder leading to the top platform. The rat learns to climb the ladder. Then it is placed again on the intermediate platform but without the ladder. It must learn to pull a string to raise the ladder so that it can climb to the top platform. Then the rat is placed on the bottom platform (▼ Figure 6.15a). It now learns to climb the ladder to the intermediate

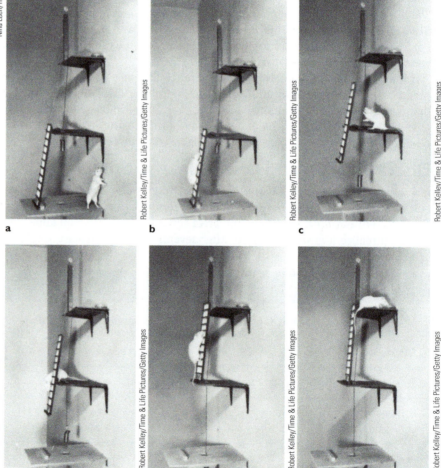

a   b   c

d   e   f

▲ **Figure 6.15** In chaining, each behavior is reinforced by the opportunity to engage in the next behavior. To reach food on the top platform, this rat must climb a ladder and pull a string to raise the ladder so that it can climb again.

platform, pull a string to raise the ladder, and then climb the ladder again. A chain like this can go on and on. Each behavior is reinforced with the opportunity for the next behavior, until the final behavior is reinforced with food.

People learn chains of responses, too. You learn to eat with a fork and spoon. Then you learn to put your own food on the plate before eating. Eventually, you learn to plan a menu, go to the store, buy the ingredients, cook the meal, put it on the plate, and then eat it. Each behavior is reinforced by the opportunity to engage in the next behavior.

To show the effectiveness of shaping and chaining, Skinner performed a demonstration: First, he trained a rat to go to the center of a cage. Then he trained it to do so only when he played a certain piece of music. Next he trained it to wait for the music, go to the center of the cage, and sit up on its hind legs. Step by step, he eventually trained the rat to wait for the music (the "Star-Spangled Banner"), move to the center of the cage, sit up on its hind legs, put its claws on a string next to a pole, pull the string to hoist the U.S. flag, and then stand back and salute. Only then did the rat get its reinforcement. Needless to say, patriotism is not part of a rat's usual repertoire. The point is, chaining can produce complex behaviors.

Schedules of Reinforcement

The simplest procedure in operant conditioning is to *provide reinforcement for every correct response*, a procedure known as continuous reinforcement. However, in the real world, continuous reinforcement is not common.

Reinforcement for some responses and not for others is known as intermittent reinforcement or partial reinforcement. We behave differently when we learn that only some of our responses will be reinforced. Psychologists have investigated the effects of many schedules of reinforcement, which are *rules for the delivery of reinforcement*. In addition to continuous reinforcement, four other schedules for the delivery of intermittent reinforcement are fixed ratio, fixed interval, variable ratio, and variable interval (see ■ Table 6.3). A ratio schedule provides reinforcements depending on the number of responses. An interval schedule provides reinforcements depending on the timing of responses.

Fixed-Ratio Schedule

A fixed-ratio schedule *provides reinforcement only after a certain (fixed) number of correct responses*—after every sixth response, for example. Examples include factory workers who are paid for every ten pieces they turn out or fruit pickers who get paid by the bushel.

A fixed-ratio schedule requiring a small number of responses, such as two or three, produces a steady rate of response. However, if the schedule requires

Table 6.3 Some Schedules of Reinforcement

Type	Description
Continuous	Reinforcement for every response of the correct type
Fixed ratio	Reinforcement following completion of a specific number of responses
Variable ratio	Reinforcement for an unpredictable number of responses that varies around a mean value
Fixed interval	Reinforcement for the first response that follows a given delay since the previous reinforcement
Variable interval	Reinforcement for the first response that follows an unpredictable delay (varying around a mean value) since the previous reinforcement

many responses before reinforcement, the typical result is a pause after each reinforcement, and then resumption of steady responding. Researchers sometimes graph the results with a *cumulative record:* The line is flat when the individual does not respond, and it moves up with each response. For a fixed-ratio schedule requiring ten responses, a typical result would look as shown below. Note that the number of responses per reinforcement is constant, but the time between one reinforcement and another can vary. On average, pauses are longer in schedules requiring greater numbers of responses. For example, if you have just completed 10 math problems, you pause briefly before starting your next assignment. If you had to complete 100 problems, you pause longer.

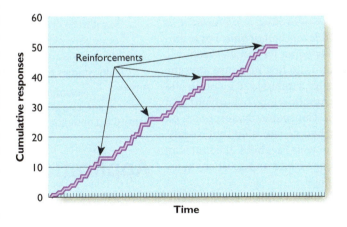

Variable-Ratio Schedule

A variable-ratio schedule is similar to a fixed-ratio schedule, except that *reinforcement occurs after a variable number of correct responses*. For example, reinforcement might sometimes occur after one or two responses, sometimes after five, sometimes after ten, and so on. Variable-ratio schedules generate steady response rates.

Variable-ratio schedules, or approximations of them, occur whenever each response has a nearly equal probability of success. When you apply for a job, you might or might not be hired. The more applications you submit, the better your chances, but you cannot predict how many applications you need to submit before receiving a job offer. Gambling pays off on a variable ratio. If you enter a lottery, each time you enter you have some chance of winning, but you cannot predict how many times you must enter before winning (if ever).

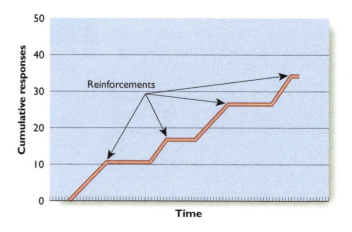

Fixed-Interval Schedule

A **fixed-interval schedule** *provides reinforcement for the first response after a specific time interval.* For instance, an animal might get food for its first response after a 15-second interval. Then it would have to wait another 15 seconds before another response is effective. Animals (including humans) on such a schedule learn to pause after reinforcement and begin to respond again toward the end of the time interval. As the time of the next reinforcement approaches, the rate of responding accelerates. The cumulative record is as shown above and to the right. Note that the delay between one reinforcement and the next is constant, but the number of responses is variable.

Checking your mailbox is an example of behavior on a fixed-interval schedule. If your mail is delivered at about 3 p.m. and you are eagerly awaiting an important package, you might begin to check around 2:30 and continue checking every few minutes until it arrives. Showing up on time for class is another example of a fixed-interval schedule.

Variable-Interval Schedule

With a **variable-interval schedule**, *reinforcement is available after a variable amount of time.* For example, reinforcement may come for the first response after 2 minutes, then for the first response after the next 7 seconds, then after 3 minutes 20 seconds, and so forth. You cannot know how long before your next response is reinforced. Consequently, responses on a variable-interval schedule are slow but steady. Checking your email or your Facebook account is an example: A new message could appear at any time, so you check occasionally.

Stargazing and bird-watching are also reinforced on a variable-interval schedule. The opportunity to see something unusual appears at unpredictable intervals.

Extinction of Responses Reinforced on Different Schedules

Suppose you have two friends, Beth and Becky. Beth has been highly reliable. When she says she will do

something, she does it. Becky, however, sometimes keeps her word and sometimes doesn't. Now both of them go through a period of untrustworthy behavior. With whom will you lose patience sooner? It's Beth. One explanation is that you notice the change more quickly. Because Becky has been unreliable in the past, a new stretch of similar behavior is hardly noteworthy.

Another example: You and a friend go to a gambling casino and bet on the roulette wheel. Amazingly, at the start you win every time. Your friend wins some and loses some. Then both of you go into a prolonged losing streak. Presuming both of you have the same amount of money, which of you will probably continue betting longer?

Your friend will, even though you had the favorable early experience. Responses extinguish more slowly after intermittent reinforcement (either a ratio schedule or an interval schedule) than after continuous reinforcement. Someone who has received intermittent reinforcement is accustomed to playing without winning.

concept check

12. **Identify which schedule of reinforcement applies to each of the following examples:**

   a. You attend every new movie that appears at your local theater, although you enjoy about a quarter of them.
   b. You are told that a company will soon announce a job opportunity, and you want to be one of the first to apply. You don't know when they will post the announcement, so you keep checking every hour or two.
   c. You tune your television set to an all-news cable channel, and you look up from your studies to check the sports scores every 30 minutes.

Answers

12. a. variable ratio. (You will be reinforced for about a quarter of your entries to the theater but on an irregular basis.) b. variable interval. (Checking will be effective after some interval of time, but the length of that time is unpredictable.) c. fixed interval.

Applications of Operant Conditioning

Although operant conditioning arose from theoretical interests, it has a long history of applications. Here are two examples.

Persuasion

How could you persuade someone to do something objectionable? For an extreme example, could a captor convince a prisoner of war to cooperate?

An application of shaping is to start by reinforcing a slight degree of cooperation and then working up to the goal little by little. This principle was applied by people who probably never heard of B. F. Skinner or positive reinforcement. During the Korean War, the Chinese Communists forwarded some of the letters written home by American prisoners of war but intercepted others. (The prisoners could tell from the replies which letters had been forwarded.) The prisoners suspected that they could get their letters through if they wrote something mildly favorable about their captors. So they began including occasional remarks that the Communists were not really so bad, that certain aspects of the Chinese system seemed to work pretty well, or that they hoped the war would end soon.

After a while, the Chinese started essay contests, offering extra food or other privileges to the soldier who wrote the best essay in the captors' opinion. Most of the winning essays contained a statement or two that offered a minor compliment to the Communists or a minor criticism of the United States. Gradually, more and more soldiers started including such statements. Then the Chinese might ask, "You said the United States is not perfect. Could you tell us some of the ways in which it is not perfect, so that we can better understand your system?" As time passed, without torture and with only modest reinforcements, the Chinese induced prisoners to denounce the United States, make false confessions, inform on fellow prisoners, and reveal military secrets (Cialdini, 1993).

The point is clear: Whether we want to get rats to salute the flag or soldiers to denounce it, the most effective training technique is to start with easy behaviors, reinforce those behaviors, and then gradually shape more complex behaviors.

Applied Behavior Analysis/Behavior Modification

In one way or another, people almost constantly try to influence other people's behavior. Psychologists have applied operant conditioning to enhance that influence.

In **applied behavior analysis**, also known as **behavior modification**, a *psychologist removes reinforcement for unwanted behaviors and provides reinforcement for more acceptable behaviors.* For example, school psychologists instituted a program to encourage children with attention-deficit disorder to complete more school assignments. In addition to verbal praise, children received points for each assignment completed and additional points for completing it

accurately. They lost points for any rule violation, such as being out of the seat. At the end of each week, those who had accumulated enough points could go to a party or take a field trip. The result of this program was a significant increase in completion of assignments and better in-class behavior (Fabiano et al., 2007).

Another example: People with a painful injury avoid using the injured arm or leg and receive much sympathy. In some cases the sympathy and the excuse for not working very hard become powerful reinforcers, and people continue acting injured and complaining about the pain after the injury has healed. To overcome this maladaptive behavior, families and friends can praise or otherwise reinforce attempts at increased mobility, and stop providing sympathy for the complaints (Jensen & Turk, 2014). This policy, of course, requires distinguishing between real pain and exaggerated pain.

concept check

13. Of the procedures characterized in Table 6.1, which one applies to supporting attempts at increased mobility? Which one applies to decreasing attention to inappropriate complaints?

Answer

13. Support for increased mobility is positive reinforcement. Decreasing attention for inappropriate complaints is punishment. Reinforcement increases a behavior and punishment decreases it.

---

in closing | module 6.2

Operant Conditioning and Human Behavior

Suppose one of your instructors announces that everyone in the class will receive the same grade at the end of the course, regardless of performance on tests and papers. Will you study hard in that course? Probably not. Or suppose your employer said that all raises and promotions would be made at random, with no regard to how well you do your job. Would you work as hard as possible? Not likely. Our behavior depends on its consequences, just like that of a rat or pigeon. That is the main point of operant conditioning.

Summary

- *Reinforcement.* Edward Thorndike defined reinforcement as the process of increasing the future probability of the preceding response. (page 195)
- *Operant conditioning.* Operant conditioning is the process of controlling the rate of a behavior through its consequences. (page 196)
- *The nature of reinforcement.* If someone has been deprived of the opportunity to engage in a behavior, then the opportunity to return to that behavior is reinforcing. (page 196)
- *Reinforcement and punishment.* Reinforcement occurs by presenting favorable events or omitting unfavorable events. Punishment occurs by presenting unfavorable events or omitting favorable events. (page 196)
- *Extinction.* In operant conditioning, a response is extinguished if it is no longer followed by reinforcement. (page 199)
- *Shaping.* Shaping is a technique for training subjects to perform acts by reinforcing them for successive approximations to the desired behavior. (page 200)

- *Schedules of reinforcement.* The frequency and timing of a response depend on the schedule of reinforcement. In a ratio schedule of reinforcement, an individual is given reinforcement after a fixed or variable number of responses. In an interval schedule of reinforcement, an individual is given reinforcement after a fixed or variable period of time. (page 201)
- *Applications.* People have applied operant conditioning to persuasion and applied behavior analysis. (page 202)

Key Terms

applied behavior analysis (or behavior modification) (page 203)

chaining (page 200)

continuous reinforcement (page 201)

discrimination (page 199)

discriminative stimulus (page 199)

disequilibrium principle (page 196)

extinction (page 199)

fixed-interval schedule (page 202)

fixed-ratio schedule (page 201)

intermittent reinforcement (page 201)

law of effect (page 195)

learning curve (page 195)

negative reinforcement (page 198)

operant conditioning (or instrumental conditioning) (page 196)

positive reinforcement (page 198)

primary reinforcer (page 196)

punishment (page 197)

reinforcement (page 195)

schedule of reinforcement (page 201)

secondary reinforcer (page 196)

shaping (page 200)

skeletal responses (page 196)

stimulus control (page 199)

stimulus generalization (page 199)

variable-interval schedule (page 202)

variable-ratio schedule (page 201)

visceral responses (page 196)

Review Questions

1. What is the defining difference between operant conditioning and classical conditioning?
   (a) Operant conditioning occurs in humans, and classical conditioning occurs in other species.
   (b) Operant conditioning produces an increase in behavior, and classical conditioning produces a decrease in behavior.
   (c) In operant conditioning, the response controls the outcome.
   (d) Operant conditioning occurs rapidly, and classical conditioning is slow.

2. According to the disequilibrium principle, what constitutes a reinforcer?
   (a) An opportunity to do something that you haven't been able to do as much as usual
   (b) Any event or activity that is biologically useful
   (c) Any stimulus that increases brain activity
   (d) A set of stimuli that are more familiar to you than they are to most other people

3. Frequently spanked children are likely to misbehave. What conclusion can we draw from this observation, if any?
   (a) We can conclude that spankings cause misbehavior.
   (b) We can conclude that misbehavior leads to spankings.
   (c) We can draw no cause-and-effect conclusion from this observation.

4. Which of the following is an example of negative reinforcement, also known as escape learning or avoidance learning?
   (a) You learn to stop practicing your accordion at 5 a.m. because your roommate threatens to kill you if you do it again.
   (b) Your swimming coach says you cannot go to the next swim meet (which you are looking forward to) if you break a training rule.
   (c) You turn off a dripping faucet, ending the "drip drip drip" sound.
   (d) You learn to avoid undercooked seafood because you have felt sick after eating it.

5. Shaping a behavior for an experiment in operant conditioning begins with which of the following?
   (a) Placing an animal into the proper position to make the response
   (b) Reinforcing a simple approximation to the desired behavior
   (c) Demonstrating a response for the individual to try to imitate
   (d) Punishing all responses other than the one the experimenter is trying to teach

6. Which schedule of reinforcement describes the following: You phone a company and hear a busy signal. You don't know how soon someone will hang up, so you try again every few minutes.
   (a) Fixed interval
   (b) Fixed ratio
   (c) Variable interval
   (d) Variable ratio

7. Which of the following is an example of a variable-ratio schedule?
   (a) Stargazing in hopes of finding a comet
   (b) Opening oysters in hopes of finding a pearl
   (c) Buying ice cream cones at a place that offers a free one after every 10 purchases
   (d) Taking a test that is given in class once a week

Answers: 1c, 2a, 3c, 4c, 5b, 6c, 7b.

module 6.3

Variations of Learning

After studying this module, you should be able to:

- Explain how conditioned taste aversions and birdsong learning differ from the types of learning that Pavlov and Skinner studied.

- Describe research that supports the idea of predispositions to learn some connections more easily than others.

- Discuss the importance of social learning.

Thorndike, Pavlov, and the other pioneers of research on learning assumed that learning was the same wherever and whenever it occurred. If so, researchers could study any convenient example, such as salivary conditioning or the responses of pigeons in a Skinner box, and discover all the principles of learning.

However, from the start, researchers encountered results that challenge this assumption. At a minimum, some things are easier to learn than others. For example, Thorndike's cats learned to push and pull various devices in their efforts to escape from his puzzle boxes. But when Thorndike tried to teach them to scratch or lick themselves for the same reinforcement, they learned slowly and performed inconsistently (Thorndike, 1911/1970). Why?

One explanation is preparedness, the *concept that evolution has prepared us to learn some associations more easily than others* (Seligman, 1970). Presumably, cats and their ancestors since ancient times have encountered many situations in which pushing or pulling something produced a useful outcome. It makes sense for them to have evolved predispositions to facilitate this type of learning. However, when in nature would licking or scratching yourself move an obstacle and get you out of confinement? We should not expect cats to be prepared for this kind of learning.

Similarly, dogs readily learn that a sound from one direction means "raise your left leg" and a sound from another direction means "raise your right leg." They are slow to learn that a ticking metronome means raise the left leg and a buzzer means raise the right leg (Dobrzecka, Szwejkowska, & Konorski, 1966). These results make sense if we assume that animals are evolutionarily prepared to learn the associations that are useful in their natural habitat. When in nature would one sound mean "turn to the left" (regardless of where the sound came from) and a different sound mean "turn to the right"?

The idea of preparedness has many practical applications. People learn easily to turn a wheel clockwise to move something to the right and counterclockwise to move it to the left (as when turning the steering wheel of a car). If the controls work the opposite way, people often get confused. Many engineers who design machines consult with human-factors psychologists about how to set up the controls so that people can easily learn to use them.

Conditioned Taste Aversions

If a sound (CS) predicts food (UCS), learning proceeds most quickly if the CS precedes the UCS by about half a second. If a rat receives food after pressing a bar, learning is fastest if the reinforcement occurs within a second or two after the response. Based on research of this type, psychologists were at one time convinced that learning occurs only between events happening within seconds of each other (Kimble, 1961).

However, that generalization fails in certain situations. Consider what happens if you eat something and get sick to your stomach an hour or so later. Despite a substantial delay between eating and feeling sick, you learn an aversion to that food. If you try eating it again, you find it repulsive. *Associating a food with illness* is conditioned taste aversion, first documented by John Garcia and his colleagues (Garcia, Ervin, & Koelling, 1966). One of its special features is that it occurs reliably after a single pairing of food with illness, even with a long delay between them. An animal drinks something it would ordinarily prefer, such as sweetened water, and receives a treatment to produce nausea minutes or hours later. The experimenter waits days for the animal to recover and then offers it a choice between sweetened and unflavored water. The animal strongly prefers the unflavored water (Garcia et al., 1966).

If you get sick after eating something, you will learn an aversion regardless of whether the food itself made you sick or you got sick from something else, such as riding a roller coaster. Some part of your brain reacts, "I don't care about that roller coaster. I feel sick, and I'm not taking any chances. From now on, that food is taboo."

You can learn taste aversions to a familiar food, but you acquire much stronger aversions if you had no previous safe experience with the food. If you eat several foods before becoming ill, you learn aversions mainly to the unfamiliar ones, even if you ate familiar foods closer in time to the illness. A further specialization is that you associate illness with something you ate, and not with other types of events. Let's consider the evidence.

what's the evidence?

Predisposition in Learning

In nature, the food you eat predicts whether you will feel full or hungry, healthy or sick. It doesn't predict pain on your skin. In contrast, what you see or hear might predict pain, but it seldom has anything to do with nausea.

Hypothesis Rats that experience foot shock will learn to avoid visual or auditory signals associated with the shock. Rats that experience nausea will learn to avoid foods that they recently ate.

Method Water-deprived rats were offered a tube of saccharin-flavored water. The tube was set up such

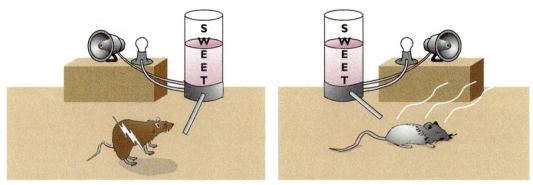

When rats drink, they taste the saccharin-flavored water and turn on a bright light and a clicking sound. Some rats receive electric shock to their feet 2 seconds after they start drinking. Other rats receive X-rays that produce nausea.

Days later: Rats are given a choice between a tube of saccharin-flavored water and a tube of unflavored water hooked up to the light and the buzzer.

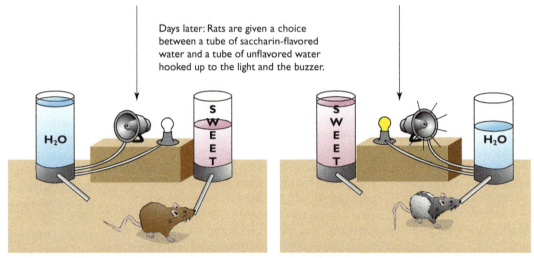

Rats that had been shocked avoid the tube with the lights and noises.

Rats that had been nauseated by X-rays avoid the saccharin-flavored water.

▲ **Figure 6.16** An experiment by Garcia and Koelling (1966): Rats associate illness with what they ate. They associate pain with what they saw or heard.

that when a rat licked the spout of the tube, it turned on a bright light and a clicking sound, as shown in ▲ Figure 6.16. Thus, each rat experienced the taste, light, and noise simultaneously. Half the rats received a mild foot shock 2 seconds after they started licking the tube. The other half received X-rays, which produce mild nausea. After two days to allow rats to recover from the X-rays, the procedure was repeated, and after another two days it was repeated again. In the final test, rats could drink from a tube containing saccharin-flavored water, or from a separate tube containing unflavored water but connected to the light and the clicking sound.

Results Rats that had received shock avoided the tube connected to lights and sounds, but drank normally from the tube with saccharin-flavored water. Rats that had received X-rays avoided the saccharin water but drank normally from the tube connected to lights and sounds.

Interpretation When a rat (or almost any other animal) receives shock to its feet, it learns to avoid the lights or sounds that it detects at the time. When it becomes nauseated, it learns to avoid something that it ate. Animals evidently come with predispositions to learn some connections more than others. This tendency is an excellent example of preparedness.

Conditioned taste aversions have several practical applications. Ranchers have taught coyotes to avoid sheep by giving the coyotes sheep meat laced with chemicals that cause nausea (see ▼ Figure 6.17). This procedure saves the ranchers' sheep without killing the coyotes (Gustavson, Kelly, Sweeney, & Garcia, 1976). One way of treating alcoholism is to ask people to drink alcohol and then administer a drug that causes nausea. This treatment is not widely used, but when it has been used, it has been quicker and more effective than other treatments for alcoholism (Revusky, 2009). Most pregnant women experience food aversions, mainly to meats and eggs. Most of them also experience nausea ("morning sickness") during the first few weeks of pregnancy. Apparently they eat something, feel nausea for reasons unrelated to the food, and develop an aversion to the food. Women with the most nausea during pregnancy tend to be those with the strongest

▲ **Figure 6.17** This coyote previously fell ill after eating sheep meat containing lithium salts. Now it reacts with revulsion toward both live and dead sheep.

food aversions (Bayley, Dye, & Hill, 2009). Similarly, many cancer patients learn aversions to foods they ate just prior to chemotherapy or radiation therapy (Bernstein, 1991; Scalera & Bavieri, 2009). With one treatment after another, they come to dislike more and more foods. A good strategy is to pick one "scapegoat" food and eat it prior to each treatment. In that way, patients learn a strong aversion to just that food while retaining their enjoyment of others.

14. **What evidence indicates that conditioned taste aversion is different from other kinds of learning?**

Answer

14. In addition to the fact that conditioned taste aversion occurs over long delays, animals are predisposed to associate foods and not other events with illnesses.

Birdsong Learning

Birdsongs brighten the day for people who hear them, but they are earnest business for the birds themselves. For most species, song is limited to males during the mating season. A song indicates, "Here I am. I am a male of species ___. If you're a female of my species, please come closer. If you're a male of my species, go away." Some species have a built-in song, but others have to learn it. The male *learns most readily during a* sensitive period *early in his first year of life* (Marler, 1997). Similarly, human children learn language most easily when they are young.

Song learning is unlike standard examples of classical and operant conditioning. During the sensitive period, the infant bird only listens. At that point, it makes no response and receives no reinforcement, and nevertheless learning occurs. The following spring, when the bird starts to sing, we

see a trial-and-error process. At first, his song is a mixture of sounds, like a babbling human infant. As time passes, he eliminates some sounds and rearranges others until he matches the songs he heard the previous summer (Marler & Peters, 1981, 1982). But his only reinforcer is recognizing that he has sung correctly.

Later in life, he may modify his song depending on competing noises. Many birds now live in suburban neighborhoods with cars, trucks, other machinery, children at play, and so forth. Humans are a noisy species. How is a little bird to make itself heard? Compared to birds away from people, those near people spend more time singing (Diaz, Parra, & Gallardo, 2011). They shift some of their singing to night, when the neighborhood tends to be quieter (Fuller, Warren, & Gaston, 2007). Also, they sing higher-pitched songs, omitting the low-pitched sounds that car and truck sounds would mask (Slabbekoorn & den Boer-Visser, 2006). Individual birds adjust their calls depending on the noise levels, so the results indicate learning, not changes in their genetics. The point is that the principles of learning vary among situations in a way that makes sense based on the animal's way of life (Rozin & Kalat, 1971).

A male white-crowned sparrow learns his song in the first months of life but does not begin to sing it until the next year.

15. What aspects of birdsong learning set it apart from classical and operant conditioning?

Answer

15. The most distinctive feature is that birdsong learning occurs when the learner makes no apparent response and receives no apparent reinforcement.

According to the social-learning approach, we learn by imitating behaviors that are reinforced and avoiding behaviors that are punished. This girl is being blessed by the temple elephant. Others who are watching may later imitate her example.

Social Learning

Just as many birds learn their song from other birds, humans obviously learn much from each other. Just think of all the things you did *not* learn by trial and error. You don't throw on clothes at random and wait to see which clothes bring the best reinforcements. Instead, you copy the styles that other people are wearing. If you are cooking, you don't make up recipes at random. You start with what other people have recommended. If you are dancing, you don't randomly try every possible muscle movement. You copy what other people do.

According to the social-learning approach (Bandura, 1977, 1986), *we learn about many behaviors by observing the behaviors of others.* For example, if you want to learn to drive a car, you start by watching people who are already skilled. When you try to drive, you receive reinforcement for driving well and punishments (possibly injuries!) if you drive badly, but your observations of others facilitate your progress.

Social learning is a type of operant conditioning, and the underlying mechanisms are similar. However, social information is usually quicker and more efficient than trying to learn something from scratch on your own.

Modeling and Imitation

If you visit another country with customs unlike your own, you find much that seems bewildering. Even the way to order food in a restaurant may be unfamiliar.

A hand gesture such as [gesture] is considered friendly in some countries but rude and vulgar in others. Many visitors to Japan find the toilets confusing. With effort, you learn foreign customs either because someone explains them to you or because you watch and copy. You *model* your behavior after others or *imitate* others.

In high school, what made certain students popular? No doubt you could cite many reasons, but once they became popular, simply being the center of attention increased their popularity. If a friend showed interest in some boy or girl, you started to notice that person, too. You modeled or imitated your friend's interest. The same is true in nonhumans. If one female shows an interest in mating with a particular male, other females increase their interest in him also (Dubois, 2007).

Why do we imitate? Other people's behavior often provides information. Did you ever have this experience? You tell your parents you want to do something because "everyone else" is doing it. They scream, "If everyone else were jumping off a cliff, would you do it, too?" Well, let's think about it. If literally *everyone* were jumping off a cliff, maybe they have a reason! Maybe you're in great danger where you are. Maybe if you jump, you'll land on something soft. If everyone is jumping off a cliff, you should consider the possibility that they know something you don't.

Another reason for imitation is that other people's behavior establishes a norm or rule. For example, you wear casual clothing where others dress casually and formal wear where others dress formally. You drive on the right side of the road in the United States or on the left side in Britain. Doing the same as other people is often helpful.

A Japanese toilet is a hole in the ground with no seat. Western visitors usually have to ask how to use it. (You squat.)

▲ **Figure 6.18** Does looking at this photo make you want to yawn?

You also imitate automatically in some cases. If someone yawns, you become more likely to yawn yourself. Even seeing a photo of an animal yawning may have the same result (see ▲ Figure 6.18). You are not intentionally copying, and you haven't received any new information. You imitate because seeing a yawn suggested the idea of yawning.

You automatically imitate many other actions that you see, often with no apparent motivation (Dijksterhuis & Bargh, 2001). If you see someone smile or frown, you briefly start to smile or frown. Your expression may be a quick, involuntary twitch that is hard to notice, but it does occur. Spectators at an athletic event sometimes slightly move their arms or legs in synchrony with what some athlete is doing. When expert pianists listen to a composition they have practiced, they start involuntarily tapping their fingers as if they were playing the music (Haueisen & Knösche, 2001). People also copy the hand gestures they see (Bertenthal, Longo, & Kosobud, 2006). You can demonstrate by telling someone, "Please wave your hands" while you clap your hands. Many people copy your actions instead of following your instructions.

try it your self

Albert Bandura, Dorothea Ross, and Sheila Ross (1963) studied the role of imitation for learning aggressive behavior. They asked two groups of children to watch films in which an adult or a cartoon character violently attacked an inflated "Bobo" doll. Another group watched a different film. They then left the children in a room with a Bobo doll. Only the children who had watched films with attacks on the doll attacked the doll themselves, using many of the same movements they had just seen (see ▼ Figure 6.19). The clear implication is that children copy the aggressive behavior they have seen in others.

▲ **Figure 6.19** This girl attacks a doll after seeing a film of a woman hitting it. Witnessing violence increases the probability of violent behavior.

concept check ✓

16. Many American politicians campaign with similar styles and take similar stands on the issues. Explain this observation in terms of social learning.

Answer

16. One reason that most American politicians run similar campaigns and take similar stands is that they all tend to copy the same models—candidates who have won recent elections. Another reason is that they all pay attention to the same public opinion polls.

Vicarious Reinforcement and Punishment

A few months ago, your best friend opened a new restaurant. Now you are considering quitting your job and opening your own restaurant. How do you decide what to do?

You probably start by asking how successful your friend has been. You imitate behavior that has been reinforcing to someone else, especially someone that you like (Mobbs et al., 2009). If you imitate someone you don't like, people will think something is wrong with you (Kavanagh, Suhler, Churchland, & Winkielman, 2011). That is, you learn by **vicarious reinforcement** or **vicarious punishment**—by *substituting someone else's experience for your own*. In one study, people learned a classically conditioned fear response to the sight of one face, paired with shock. Then they watched a video of someone else looking at the same face, showing no fear and receiving no shock. Watching that video decreased their own fear responses (Golkar, Selbing, Flygare, Öhman, & Olsson, 2013).

Whenever a new business venture succeeds, other companies copy it. When a sports team wins consistently, other teams copy its style of play. When a television program wins high ratings, other producers present similar shows the following year. Politicians imitate the campaign tactics of candidates who were previously elected.

Advertisers depend heavily on vicarious reinforcement. They show happy, successful people using their product, with the implication that if you use their product, you too will be happy and successful. The people promoting state lotteries show the ecstatic winners—never the losers!—suggesting that if you play the lottery, you too can win.

Vicarious punishment is generally less effective (Kuroshima, Kuwahata, & Fujita, 2008). Children ages 3 to 7 had an opportunity to cheat on a task while the experimenter was supposedly not looking. Then the experimenter read the stories *Pinocchio* or "The Boy Who Cried Wolf" (in which a child was

Politicians consistently run negative ads against their opponents because these kinds of ads have proven to be effective in previous campaigns. Hence the use of negative campaigning is an example of vicarious reinforcement.

punished for lying) or "George Washington and the Cherry Tree" (in which a child was praised and rewarded for telling the truth. Finally the experimenter asked the children whether they had cheated while the experimenter wasn't looking. Compared to children who had heard an irrelevant story ("The Tortoise and the Hare"), those who heard the "George Washington" story were more likely to tell the truth, but those who heard the other two stories were not (Lee et al., 2014). Similarly with adults, vicarious reinforcement works better than vicarious punishment, largely because most people do not identify with someone who failed or received punishment.

Self-Efficacy in Social Learning

When you watch an Olympic diver win a gold medal, why do you (presumably) *not* try to imitate those dives? You imitate someone else's behavior only if you have a sense of self-efficacy—*the belief of being able to perform the task successfully*. You consider your strengths and weaknesses, compare yourself to the successful person, and estimate your chance of success.

This effect is clear in children's life aspirations. Nearly anyone would like a high-paying, high-prestige profession, but many think they could never rise to that level, so they don't try (Bandura, Barbaranelli, Caprara, & Pastorelli, 2001). One value of getting women and minorities into high-visibility leadership jobs is that they provide role models for others. In 1993, India passed a law that guaranteed leadership roles for women in certain randomly selected villages. Before long, young girls in those villages, and not the others, expressed higher aspirations for their own accomplishments (Beaman, Duflo, Pande, & Topalova, 2012).

Self-Reinforcement and Self-Punishment

If your sense of self-efficacy is strong enough, you try to imitate the behavior of a successful person. But actually succeeding may require prolonged efforts. People typically set a goal for themselves and monitor their progress toward that goal. Sometimes people reinforce or punish themselves, just as if they were training someone else. They say, "If I finish this math assignment on time, I'll treat myself to a movie and a new magazine. If I don't finish on time, I'll make myself clean the sink and the toilets." (Nice threat, but people usually forgive themselves without imposing the punishment.)

Some therapists teach clients to use self-reinforcement. One 10-year-old boy had a habit of biting his fingernails, sometimes down to the skin and even drawing blood. He learned to keep records of how much nail biting he did at various times of day, and then he set goals for himself. If he met the goals

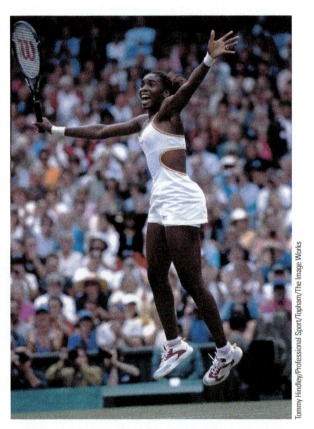

We tend to imitate the actions of successful people but only if we feel self-efficacy, a belief that we could perform the task well.

of reducing his nail biting, he wrote compliments such as "I'm great! I did wonderful!" The penalty for doing worse was that he would return his weekly allowance to his parents. An additional reinforcement was that his father promised that if the son made enough progress, he would let the son be the "therapist" to help the father quit smoking. Over several weeks, the boy quit nail biting altogether (Ronen & Rosenbaum, 2001).

One amusing anecdote shows the limits of self-reinforcement and self-punishment: To try to quit smoking cigarettes, psychologist Ron Ash (1986) vowed to smoke only while he was reading *Psychological Bulletin* and other highly respected but tedious journals. He hoped to associate smoking with boredom. Two months later, he was smoking as much as ever, but he was starting to *enjoy* reading *Psychological Bulletin!*

in closing | module 6.3

All Learning Is Not the Same

When investigators examine how synapses change during learning, they find similar mechanisms in all species and many situations. Nevertheless, we find multiple variations. The ways we learn are adapted to different situations, such as food choice and birdsong. We use social mechanisms to facilitate and hasten learning. The outcome of these specializations increases the efficiency of learning.

Summary

- *Preparedness.* Evolution has prepared us and other animals to learn some associations more readily than others. (page 205)
- *Conditioned taste aversions.* Animals, including people, learn to avoid foods, especially unfamiliar ones, if they become ill afterward. This type of learning occurs reliably after a single pairing, even with a long delay between the food and the illness. Illness is associated much more strongly with foods than with other stimuli. (page 205)
- *Birdsong learning.* Infant birds of some species must hear their songs during a sensitive period early in life if they are to develop a fully normal song the following spring. During the early learning, the bird makes no response and receives no reinforcement. (page 207)

- *Imitation.* We learn much by observing other people's actions and their consequences. (page 208)
- *Vicarious reinforcement and punishment.* We tend to imitate behaviors that lead to reinforcement for other people. We are less consistent in avoiding behaviors that are unsuccessful for others. (page 209)
- *Self-efficacy.* Whether we imitate a behavior depends on whether we believe we are capable of duplicating it. (page 210)
- *Self-reinforcement and self-punishment.* Once people have decided to try to imitate a certain behavior, they set goals for themselves and sometimes provide their own reinforcements. (page 210)

Key Terms

conditioned taste aversion (page 205)

preparedness (page 205)

self-efficacy (page 210)

sensitive period (page 207)

social-learning approach (page 208)

vicarious reinforcement (or vicarious punishment) (page 209)

Review Questions

1. Which kind of learning takes place despite a long delay between the events to be associated?
   (a) Associating food with illness (conditioned taste aversions)
   (b) Associating a muscle response with receiving food (operant conditioning)
   (c) Associating a sound with food (classical conditioning)

2. In which of these ways is a conditioned taste aversion different from other types of learning?
   (a) Conditioned taste aversions undergo extinction faster than other types of learning.
   (b) Illness is more strongly associated with tastes than with other stimuli.

(c) Conditioned taste aversions do not generalize to other tastes.

(d) Conditioned taste aversions are stronger with familiar tastes than with unfamiliar tastes.

3. In what way is birdsong learning similar to language learning?

(a) Each of them evolved from sign language.

(b) Birds can learn any song, just as children can learn any language.

(c) Both are most easily learned early in life.

(d) Both are learned mainly by listening to the mother.

4. What does the social-learning approach emphasize?

(a) Fixed-ratio schedules of reinforcement

(b) Learning by imitation

(c) Classical conditioning of emotional responses

(d) Primary reinforcement

Answers: 1a, 2b, 3c, 4b.

7 Memory

iStockphoto.com/Rich Legg

With a suitable reminder, you remember some events distinctly, even after a long delay. Other memories are lost or distorted.

Suppose I offer you, for a price, an opportunity to do absolutely anything you want for a day. You will not be limited by the usual physical constraints. You can travel in a flash and visit as many places as you wish, even outer space. You can travel forward and backward through time, finding out what the future holds and witnessing the great events of the past. (You will not be able to alter history.) Anything you want to do—just name it and it is yours. Furthermore, I guarantee your safety: No matter where you choose to go or what you choose to do, you will not get hurt.

How much would you pay for this amazing opportunity? Oh, yes, I should mention, there is one catch. When the day is over, you will completely forget everything that happened. Any notes or photos will vanish. And anyone else who takes part in your special day will forget it, too.

Now how much would you be willing to pay? Much less, no doubt, and perhaps nothing. Living without remembering is hardly living at all: Our memories are almost the same as our selves.

Ariel Skelley/Getty Images

After studying this module, you should be able to:

- Differentiate among ways of testing memory.

- Describe ways to minimize errors in eyewitness testimony and suspect lineups.

- Distinguish types of memory and describe their main features: short-term, long-term, working, semantic, episodic, declarative, procedural, and probabilistic.

▲ **Figure 7.1** Hermann Ebbinghaus pioneered the scientific study of memory by observing his own capacity for memorizing lists of nonsense syllables.

Every year, people compete in the World Memory Championship (You can read about it at this website: **www.worldmemorychampionships.com.**) One event is speed of memorizing a shuffled deck of 52 cards. The all-time record is 21.19 seconds. Another is memorizing a list of numbers after hearing them once. The record is 364 numbers. People also compete at memorizing dates of fictional events, names of unfamiliar faces in photos, and so forth. Dominic O'Brien, eight-time world champion, gives speeches and writes books about how to train your memory. However, he admits that one time while he was practicing card memorization, an irate friend called from an airport to complain that O'Brien had forgotten to pick him up. O'Brien apologized and drove to London's Gatwick Airport, practicing card memorization along the way. When he arrived, he remembered that his friend was at Heathrow, London's other major airport (Johnstone, 1994).

Anyone—you, me, or Dominic O'Brien—remembers some information and forgets the rest. **Memory** is *the retention of information*. It includes skills such as riding a bicycle or tying your shoelaces. It also includes facts that never change (your birthday), facts that seldom change (your mailing address), and facts that frequently change (where you left your keys). You remember your most important experiences and some of your unimportant ones, many useful facts and much trivia that you cannot imagine ever using.

Advice: This chapter includes many Try It Yourself activities. You will gain much more from this chapter if you take the time to try them.

Ebbinghaus's Pioneering Studies of Memory

Suppose you wanted to study memory, but no one had ever done memory research before. Where would you start?

Dominic O'Brien, eight-time winner of the World Memory Championships and author of several books on training your memory, admits he sometimes forgets practical information, such as promising to meet a friend at Heathrow Airport.

If you asked people to describe their memories, you would not know when the memories formed, how often people had rehearsed them, or even whether the memories were correct. German psychologist Hermann Ebbinghaus (1850–1909) avoided these problems by an approach that we now take for granted: He taught new material so that he knew exactly what someone had learned and when. Then he measured memory after various delays. To be sure the material was new, he used lists of nonsense syllables, such as *GAK* or *JEK*. He wrote out 2,300 syllables, assembled them randomly into lists (see ▲ Figure 7.1), and then set out to study memory. He had no cooperative introductory psychology students to enlist in his study, and no friends eager to memorize nonsense syllables, so he ran all the tests on himself. For six years, he memorized thousands of lists of nonsense syllables. (He was either very dedicated to his science or uncommonly tolerant of boredom.)

Many of his findings were hardly surprising. For example, as shown in ▼ Figure 7.2, he took longer to memorize longer lists than shorter lists. "Of course!" you might scoff. But Ebbinghaus was not just demonstrating the obvious. He measured *how much* longer it took to memorize a longer list. You might similarly object to the law of gravity: "Of course the farther something falls, the longer it takes to hit the ground!" However, measuring the acceleration of gravity was essential to progress in physics, and measuring how long it takes to learn a list enables psychologists to compare conditions: Do adults learn faster than children? Do we learn some kinds of lists faster than other lists? Ebbinghaus's approach led to all the later research on memory.

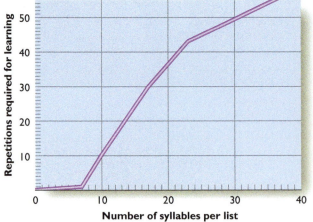

▲ **Figure 7.2** Ebbinghaus counted how many times he had to read a list of nonsense syllables before he could recite it once correctly. For a list of seven or fewer, one reading was usually enough. Beyond seven, the longer the list, the more repetitions he needed. (From Ebbinghaus, 1885/1913)

Methods of Testing Memory

Nearly everyone occasionally has a tip-of-the-tongue experience (Brown & McNeill, 1966). You want to remember a word or a name, and all you can think of is something similar that you know isn't right. Once I was trying to remember the name of a particular researcher, and all I could think of was *Bhagavad Gita* (the Hindu holy writings). Eventually I remembered the name: Paul Bach-y-Rita. In a tip-of-the-tongue experience, you might know the first letter, the number of syllables, and much else, even if you cannot generate the word itself.

In other words, memory is not an all-or-none thing. You might or might not remember something depending on how someone tests you. Let's survey the main methods of testing memory. Along the way, we begin to distinguish different types of memory.

Free Recall

A simple method for the researcher (though not for the person tested) is to ask for free recall. To recall something is *to produce a response, as you do on essay tests or short-answer tests.* For instance, "Tell me what you did today." Most people will respond with a very brief synopsis, although they could elaborate in detail to follow-up questions. Free recall almost always understates the actual amount you know. If you try to name all the children who were in your second-grade class, you might not do well, but your low recall does not mean that you have completely forgotten them.

Cued Recall

Your accuracy improves with cued recall, in which you *receive significant hints about the material.* For example, a photograph of the children in your second-grade class (see ▼ Figure 7.3) or a list of their initials will help you remember. Try this: Cover the right side of ■ Table 7.1 and try to identify the authors of each book on the left. Then uncover the right side, revealing each author's initials, and try again. (This method is cued recall.) Note how much better you do with these hints.

Recognition

With recognition, a third method of testing memory, someone *chooses the correct item among several options.* People usually recognize more items than they recall. For example, someone might give you a list of 60 names and ask you to check off the correct names of children in your second-grade class. Multiple-choice tests use the recognition method.

Savings

A fourth method, the savings method (also known as the relearning method), detects weak memories *by comparing the speed of original learning to the speed of relearning.* Suppose you cannot name the children in your second-grade class and cannot even pick out their names from a list of choices. You would nevertheless learn a correct list of names faster than a list of people you had never met. That is, you save time when you relearn something. The amount of time saved (time needed for original learning minus the time for relearning) is a measure of memory.

Implicit Memory

Free recall, cued recall, recognition, and savings are tests of explicit (or direct) memory. That is, *someone who states an answer regards it as a product of memory.* In implicit memory (or indirect memory), *an experience influences what you say or do even though you might not be aware of the influence.* If you find that definition unsatisfactory, you are not alone (Frensch & Rünger, 2003). Defining something in terms of a vague concept like "awareness" is not a good practice. This definition is tentative until we develop a better one.

▲ **Figure 7.3** Can you recall the names of the students in your second-grade class? Trying to remember without any hints is *free recall*. Using a photo or a list of initials is *cued recall*.

Table 7.1 Cued Recall

Book	Author
Instructions: First try to identify the author of each book listed in the left column while covering the right column. Then expose the right column, which gives each author's initials, and try again (cued recall).	
Moby Dick	H. M.
Emma and *Pride and Prejudice*	J. A.
Hercule Poirot stories	A. C.
Sherlock Holmes stories	A. C. D.
I Know Why the Caged Bird Sings	M. A.
War and Peace	L. T.
This textbook	J. K.
The Canterbury Tales	G. C.
The Origin of Species	C. D.
Gone with the Wind	M. M.
Les Miserables	V. H.

(For answers, see page 224, answer A.)

The best way to explain implicit memory is by examples: Suppose you are in a conversation while other people nearby are discussing something else. You ignore the other discussion, but a few words from that background conversation probably creep into your own. You do not even notice the influence, although an observer might.

Here is a demonstration of implicit memories. For each of the following three-letter combinations, fill in additional letters to make any English word:

> CON___
> SUP___
> DIS___
> PRO___

You could have thought of any number of words—the dictionary lists well over 100 familiar CON___ words alone. Did you happen to write any of the following: *conversation, suppose, discussion,* or *probably?* Each of these words appeared in the preceding paragraph. *Reading or hearing a word temporarily* results in priming *that word and increasing the chance that you will use it yourself,* even if you are not aware of the influence (Graf & Mandler, 1984; Schacter, 1987). This demonstration works better if you listen to spoken words than if you read them.

■ Table 7.2 contrasts some memory tests.

Table 7.2 Ways to Test Memory

Title	Description	Example
Recall	You are asked to say what you remember.	Name the Seven Dwarfs.
Cued recall	You are given significant hints to help you remember.	Name the Seven Dwarfs. Hint: One was always smiling, one was smart, one never talked, one always seemed to have a cold . . .
Recognition	You are asked to choose the correct item from among several items.	Which of the following were among the Seven Dwarfs: Sneezy, Sleazy, Dopey, Dippy, Hippy, Happy?
Savings (relearning)	You are asked to relearn something: If it takes you less time than when you first learned that material, some memory has persisted.	Try memorizing this list: Sleepy, Sneezy, Doc, Dopey, Grumpy, Happy, Bashful. Can you memorize it faster than this list: Sleazy, Snoopy, Duke, Dippy, Gripey, Hippy, Blushy?
Implicit memory	You are asked to generate words, without necessarily regarding them as memories.	You hear the story "Snow White and the Seven Dwarfs." Later you are asked to fill in these blanks to make any words that come to mind: _ L _ _ P _ _ N _ _ Z _ _ _ C _ O _ EY _ R _ _ P _ _ _ P P _ _ A _ H _ U _

Procedural Memories and Probabilistic Learning

Procedural memories, *memories of how to do something,* such as walking or eating with chopsticks, are a special kind of implicit memories. Psychologists distinguish procedural memories from declarative memories, *memories we can readily state in words.* For example, if you type, you know the locations of the letters well enough to press the right key at the right time (a procedural memory), but can you state that knowledge explicitly? For example, which letter is directly to the right of C? Which is directly to the left of P?

Procedural memory, or habit learning, differs from declarative memory in several ways. First, the two types of memory depend on different brain areas, and brain damage can impair one without impairing the other. Second, procedural memory or habit learning develops gradually, whereas you often form a declarative memory all at once. For example, you need much practice to develop the procedural memories of how to play a piano or how to shoot a basketball. You might very quickly form the declarative memory, "the men's room is on the left and the women's room is on the right." Habit learning is also well suited for learning something that is usually true or true only under certain circumstances (Shohamy, Myers, Kalanithi, & Gluck, 2008). For example, you might notice that a particular pattern of wind, clouds, and barometric pressure predicts rain, although no one of these cues is reliable by itself. Or you might notice that certain dogs are unfriendly when they hold their head, ears, and tail in certain postures. People sometimes learn to pick up on a variety of cues without realizing that they are doing so.

concept check

1. For each of these examples, identify the type of memory test—free recall, cued recall, recognition, savings, or implicit.

   a. Although you thought you had forgotten your high school French, you do better in your college French course than your roommate, who never studied French before.

   b. You are trying to remember the phone number of the local pizza parlor without looking it up in the phone directory.

   c. You hear a song on the radio without paying much attention to it. Later, you find yourself humming a melody, but you don't know what it is or where you heard it.

   d. You forget where you parked your car, so you scan the parking lot hoping to find your car among all the others.

   e. Your friend asks, "What's the name of our chemistry lab instructor? I think her name starts with an S."

Answers

1. a. savings; b. free recall; c. implicit; d. recognition; e. cued recall.

Application: Suspect Lineups as Recognition Memory

Suppose you witness a crime, and now the police want you to identify the guilty person. You look at suspects in a lineup or examine a book of photos. Your task is an example of recognition memory, as you try to identify the correct item among distracters.

The task raises a problem, familiar from your own experience. When you take a multiple-choice test, which is also recognition memory, sometimes none of the choices seems exactly right, but you select the best one available. What happens if you do the same with a book of photos? You look through the choices and pick the one who looks most like the perpetrator of the crime. You tell the police you think suspect #4 is the guilty person. "Think?" the police ask. "Your testimony won't be worth much in court unless you're sure." You look again, eager to cooperate. Finally, you say you're sure. The police say, "Good, that's the person we thought did it." Getting that feedback strengthens your confidence in that choice. You testify in court, and the suspect is convicted. But is justice done? Many people have been convicted of crimes because of eyewitness testimony and later exonerated by DNA evidence.

Psychologists have proposed ways to improve suspect lineups:

1. Instruct the witness that the guilty person may or may not be in the lineup. The witness doesn't have to identify someone.

2. The officer supervising the lineup should be a "blind" observer—that is, someone who doesn't know which person the investigators suspect. Otherwise the officer might unintentionally bias the witness.

Cotton

Poole

In 1985, Ronald Cotton (left) was convicted of rape, based on a victim's identification from a set of photos. Ten years later, DNA evidence demonstrated that Cotton was innocent and that the real culprit was Bobby Poole (right). Eyewitness testimony has in many cases led to the conviction of innocent people.

3. If the witness said that the culprit had some distinctive feature, such as a scar above the left eye, all the suspects in the lineup should have that feature (Zarkadi, Wade, & Stewart, 2009). Otherwise the witness would just pick the one with a scar, who may or may not be guilty.

4. Postpone as long as possible any feedback about whether the witness chose someone whom the police suspected (Wells, Olson, & Charman, 2003; Zaragoza, Payment, Ackil, Drivdahl, & Beck, 2001). Any sign of agreement adds to a witness's confidence, even if the witness was wrong (Hasel & Kassin, 2009; Semmler, Brewer, & Wells, 2004; Wright & Skagerberg, 2007).

5. Instead of asking for a definite yes/no decision, ask the witness to specify for each person in the lineup, "How confident are you that this person committed the crime?" A witness could say "90 percent," "75 percent," or any other number, and might give non-zero replies to more than one suspect (Brewer, Weber, Wootton, & Lindsay, 2012).

6. The most controversial recommendation is to present the lineup sequentially (Wells et al., 2000; Wells, Memon, & Penrod, 2006). In a sequential lineup, the witness says "yes" or "no" to each suspect, one at a time. If the witness says yes, the procedure is finished. After all, there is no point in looking at additional suspects if the witness has already decided. The witness has no opportunity to go back and reexamine photos after rejecting them. In this procedure, the witness makes a definite identification or none at all, rather than choosing the best suspect available.

Each of these procedures leads to a smaller number of total identifications, but an increased probability that someone the witness identifies really is guilty (Clark, 2012). The last suggestion, a sequential lineup, is particularly likely to lead to no identification at all. The advantages and disadvantages depend on how we weigh the risk of setting a guilty person free versus the risk of imprisoning an innocent person.

concept check

2. **How does a sequential lineup avoid one of the problems inherent in a multiple-choice test?**

Answer

2. With a multiple-choice test, a person chooses the best available answer, even if it is not exactly correct. The same is often true in a simultaneous lineup. With a sequential lineup, a person chooses only when confident.

Children as Eyewitnesses

While on the topic of eyewitness memory, let's consider young children. How much should we trust their reports when they are witnesses or victims of a crime? How could we measure their accuracy?

One research approach is to ask a child to recall an event in which the facts are known, such as a medical or dental examination. How well can the child report those events? Researchers find that children as young as 3 years old report with reasonable accuracy even 6 weeks later (Baker-Ward, Gordon, Ornstein, Larus, & Clubb, 1993).

Several factors influence the accuracy of young children's reports:

- **Delay of questioning.** After a traumatic experience such as an injury, a child's memory is best at first and becomes less accurate over a long delay. The same is true for people at any age, of course. However, with very young children, a delayed report is sometimes more detailed, simply because the child has become more articulate in use of the language (Peterson, 2011).
- **Repeating the question.** If you ask a child a question, and then shortly thereafter ask the same question again, the child often changes the answer

(Krähenbühl & Blades, 2006; Poole & White, 1993). Apparently the child thinks, "Why is she asking me again? My first answer must have been wrong!" However, if someone else repeats the question, the child will probably give the original answer. Also, it is appropriate for you to ask the question again after a delay, and you might get more information the second time. A researcher observed 37 cases in which 3- to 12-year-old children were removed from an abusive family and interviewed about this event one week later and three months later. The accuracy of reports was about equally good both times, and children often reported information the second time that they had neglected to mention the first time (Baugerud, Magnussen, & Melinder, 2014).

- **Type of question.** To an open-ended question such as, "Tell me what happened," a young child's answer is usually short but accurate. After a suggestive question such as, "Did he touch you under your clothing?" children's accuracy is less dependable (Lamb, Orbach, Hershkowitz, Horowitz, & Abbott, 2007). A suggestive question is especially dangerous after a delay, when the memory has weakened (Quas et al., 2007).
- **Hearing other children.** A child who hears other children reporting something is likely to say the same thing, even if it is wrong (Principe, Kanaya, Ceci, & Singh, 2006).
- **Using physical representations.** To investigate suspicions of sexual abuse, some psychologists try to prod a child's memory by providing anatomically detailed dolls and asking the child to act out some event. However, children sometimes act out fantasies instead of memories. When researchers ask children to act out a doctor's exam (where they know what happened), children act out many events that did not happen (Greenhoot, Ornstein, Gordon, & Baker-Ward, 1999). Although dolls apparently don't help, drawings do. If a child is asked to draw an event as well as describe it, the result is usually a more detailed description, with no loss of accuracy (Patterson & Hayne, 2011). Of course, some children draw much better than others.
- **Understanding a question.** Have you ever seen someone imbosk a lecythus? You probably answer either "I don't know," or "What do you mean?" A 3-year-old child who doesn't understand a question usually answers "yes" (Imhoff & Baker-Ward, 1999).

Adults easily overestimate how well a child understands something. A couple took their 3-year-old daughter on a trip and said they would stop at a barbecue restaurant for dinner. She was so excited that she could hardly wait. She spent most of the trip asking, "Now how long till barbecue?" As they finally approached the restaurant, she asked, "Will other children be there too, with their Barbies?" Suddenly it dawned on the parents, "Ah, that's what she thought 'barbie-cue' meant!"

Can we trust a child's testimony? In short, it depends. With proper questioning, even a 3-year-old provides accurate information. With delayed or biased questioning, the accuracy declines. To a yes/no question, make sure the child understands the question.

The Information-Processing View of Memory

Over the years, psychologists have repeatedly tried to explain the mechanisms of behavior by analogy to the technologies of their time. In the 1600s, René Descartes compared animal behavior to the actions of a hydraulic pump. Psychologists of the early 1900s suggested that learning worked like a telephone switchboard. In the early days of radio, some researchers compared the nervous system to a radio. Today's most modern technology is a computer, and the information-processing model compares human memory to that of a computer: *Information that enters the system is processed, coded, and stored*, as in ▼ Figure 7.4. When you type something on the keyboard, the computer stores it in a temporary memory. When you store something on the hard drive,

you set up a stable, long-lasting representation. According to the information-processing model, information first enters short-term memory (a temporary store), and some of the short-term memory transfers into long-term memory (like a hard disk). Eventually, a cue from the environment prompts the system to retrieve stored information (Atkinson & Shiffrin, 1968). Let's examine this model.

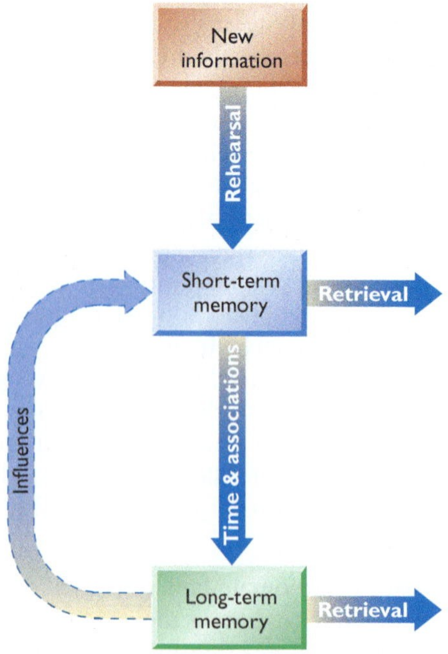

Short-Term and Long-Term Memory

Information-processing theory distinguishes between short-term memory, *temporary storage of recent events*, and long-term memory, *a relatively permanent store*. For example, while you are playing a game, the current score is in your short-term memory, and the rules of the game are in your long-term memory.

Psychologists distinguish two types of long-term memory, semantic and episodic. Semantic memory is *memory of principles and facts*, like what you are taught in school. Episodic memory is *memory for specific events in your life* (Tulving, 1989). For example, your memory of the law of gravity is a semantic memory, whereas remembering the time you dropped your grandmother's vase is an episodic memory. Remembering who is the mayor of your city is a semantic memory, and remembering the time you met the mayor is an episodic memory.

Episodic memories are more fragile than semantic memories. If you don't play tennis for a few years, you will still remember the rules, but your memory of a particular tennis game will fade. When you try to recall an event from long ago, you might be wrong or uncertain about many of the details. People with certain kinds of brain damage lose most of their episodic memories but keep their semantic memories.

concept check

3. **Classify each of these as semantic memory or episodic memory: (a) Naming the first president of the United States. (b) Defining "classical conditioning." (c) Describing your trip to Disney World. (d) Remembering where you had dinner last night, who ate with you, and what you ate.**

Answer

3. (a) semantic. (b) semantic. (c) episodic. (d) episodic.

People often remember a semantic memory, but forget the episodic memory of when or where they learned it (Friedman, Reese, & Dai, 2011). *Forgetting when, where, or how you learned something* is source amnesia.

Here is the danger: You might read a novel containing some factual material and other items that might or might not be true. Or you hear a rumor from an unreliable source, but later forget the source. You remember information from the novel or the rumor, but you don't remember that it came from an unreliable source, so you start to take the statement seriously (Johnson, Hashtroudi, & Lindsay, 1993; Riccio, 1994). Of course, the risk is even greater if you don't know that the source was unreliable.

In one study, students read fictional stories that included statements such as "a sextant is a tool used at sea to navigate by the stars." Later, they were asked such questions as, "what tool is used at sea to navigate by the stars?" People who had just read that fact were more likely than other people to answer correctly. Most remembered seeing it in the story, but many said they had already known the fact before reading the story. Another group of students read stories with misinformation such as "a compass is a tool used at sea to navigate by the stars." Many of these students later answered the question incorrectly, saying that a compass is a tool to navigate by the stars. Many insisted that they too had "already" known this fact before reading the story! This example illustrates source amnesia (Marsh, Meade, & Roediger, 2003).

How far could we push this tendency? Researchers took students who had correctly answered certain questions (such as "Who invented the lightbulb?"

New information

Rehearsal

Short-term memory → Retrieval

Influences

Time & associations

Long-term memory → Retrieval

▲ **Figure 7.4** The information-processing model of memory resembles a computer's memory system, including temporary and permanent memory.

Answer: "Edison"), and had them read stories with misinformation, such as that Franklin invented the lightbulb. Afterward, 20 percent of them incorporated the misinformation, replying that Franklin invented the lightbulb (Fazio, Barber, Rajaram, Ornstein, & Marsh, 2013). Another study had college students read stories with plausible misinformation (listing St. Petersburg as the capital of Russia instead of Moscow, or listing the Gobi as the world's largest desert instead of the Sahara), or stories with implausible information (such as the Pilgrims sailed to the new world on the *Titanic*, or Detroit is the capital of Finland). More students accepted the plausible misinformation and incorporated it into their answers, but a few accepted the implausible, even ridiculous misinformation (Hinze, Slaten, Horton, Jenkins, & Rapp, 2014).

Capacity of Short-Term and Long-Term Memory

Psychologists have traditionally drawn several distinctions between short-term and long-term memory. One difference is capacity. Long-term memory has a vast, hard-to-measure capacity. Asking how much information long-term memory can store is like asking how many books a library can hold. The answer depends on the size of the books and how you arrange them. Short-term memory, in contrast, has a limited capacity. Read each of the following letter sequences and then try to repeat them from memory. Or read each aloud and ask a friend to repeat it.

try it your self

    EHGPH
    JROZNQ
    SRBWRCN
    MPDIWFBS
    ZYBPIAFMO

Most healthy, educated adults can repeat a list of about seven letters, numbers, or words. Some remember eight or nine; others, only five or six. George Miller (1956) referred to short-term memory capacity as "the magical number seven, plus or minus two." When people try to repeat a longer list, they may fail to remember even the first seven items. It is like trying to hold objects in one hand: If you try to hold too many, you drop them all. However, don't take this analogy too seriously. Memory depends on changes in synapses spread out over a huge population of cells. It is not like objects you put in one place.

Sometimes we forget where we heard or read something, and believe it more than we should.

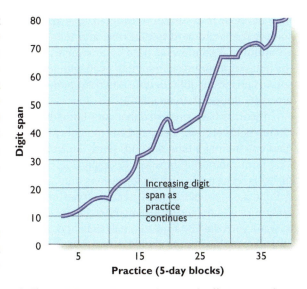

▲ **Figure 7.5** A college student gradually increased his ability to repeat a list of numbers. However, his short-term memory for letters or words did not increase. (From Ericsson, Chase, & Faloon, 1980)

You can store more information in short-term memory by chunking—*grouping items into meaningful sequences or clusters*. For example, the sequence "ventysi" has seven letters, at the limit of most people's capacity. However, "seventysix" with three additional letters can be easily remembered as "76," a two-digit number. "Seventeenseventysix" is even longer, but if you think of it as 1776, an important date in U.S. history, it is a single item to store.

One college student in a lengthy experiment initially could repeat about seven digits at a time. Over a year and a half, working 3 to 5 hours per week, he gradually improved until he could repeat 80 digits, as shown in ▲ **Figure 7.5**, by chunking. He was a competitive runner, so he might store the sequence "3492 . . ." as "3 minutes, 49.2 seconds, a near world-record time for running a mile." He might store the next set of numbers as a good time for running a kilometer, a mediocre marathon time, or a date in history. With practice, he started recognizing larger and larger chunks of numbers. However, when he was tested on his ability to remember a list of letters, his performance was only average, because he had not developed any chunking strategies for letters (Ericsson, Chase, & Faloon, 1980).

Because people are so good at chunking, not always realizing that they are doing it, psychologists have come to doubt that short-term memory really does hold seven items. When you remembered S R B W R C N, did you really remember it as seven items? Or did you group them, such as SR . . . B . . . WR . . . CN? More recent research indicates that the true limit of adult short-term memory is about four chunks rather than seven items (Cowan, 2010; Mandler, 2013). With unfamiliar stimuli, the limit may be even less. Students listened to a series of sounds that were hard to describe, and then heard an additional sound and tried to answer which of the first set of sounds it matched. Even with just two sounds this was a difficult task, and they made many errors (Golubock & Janata, 2013).

Theorists have suggested that your immediate attention holds only one item, and any memory for more than one item at a time depends partly on storage in long-term memory (Shipstead & Engle, 2013). Other theorists argue that we are wrong even to think about a definite capacity of short-term memory. If you look at an array of a few items and try to remember them shortly afterward, you could be approximately right about several of them or exactly right about just one (Ma, Husain, & Bays, 2014; Spachtholz, Kuhbandner, & Pekrun, 2014). That is, you can trade capacity for accuracy.

Decay of Memories over Time

A short-term memory, by definition, lasts only a short time unless you continue rehearsing it. Here is the classic demonstration: Lloyd Peterson and Margaret Peterson (1959) presented meaningless sequences of letters, like HOXDF, and then tested people's memory after various delays. If you were in this study, knowing that the experimenter was going to ask you to repeat the letters, you would spend the delay rehearsing, "HOXDF, HOXDF, . . ." To prevent rehearsal, the experimenters used a second task. When they presented the letters, they also presented a number, such as 231. You were supposed to start with that number and count backward by 3s, such as "231, 228, 225, 222, 219, . . ." until the experimenter signaled the end of the delay. At that point, you should say the letters.

▶ Figure 7.6 shows the results. On average, only about 10 percent of the participants could recall the letters after 18 seconds. In other words, short-term memory fades rapidly.

Peterson and Peterson were dealing with nonsense information, such as HOXDF. With more meaningful material, people store information quickly. If someone told you to leave the building by the west exit instead of the east exit because a venomous snake is lurking at the east exit, you don't need to worry that you will forget this advice in the next 18 seconds.

Why do short-term memories fade? The simplest hypothesis is that the brain representation decays over time. Neuroscientists identified a brain protein that weakens a memory trace, presumably to avoid permanently storing unimportant information (Genoux et al., 2002). Another hypothesis is that short-term memories fade because we confuse one with another. Suppose you try a Peterson-type experiment: You see or hear a set of five letters and then you count backward by 3s for some

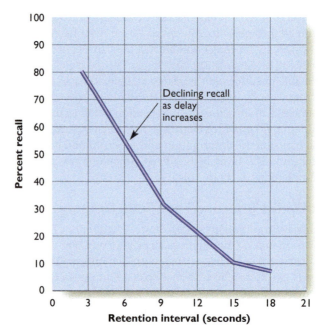

▲ **Figure 7.6** People's memory of a set of letters faded quickly if they were prevented from rehearsing.

period of time. On the first trial you will probably remember those letters, even with a fairly long delay. On later trials, the task gets more and more difficult, largely because memory of the old items is interfering with the new items. Similar results occur for visual memories: You view 100 pictures, 4 per second, and then see another set of pictures and try to remember which ones you had seen. On average, you would identify about 30 of them correctly. But then you have to do it again and again, and some of the pictures from the first set reappear, but you have to remember which pictures were in the new set. Under these conditions the interference mounts, and it is a struggle to get 3 or 4 correct (Endress & Potter, 2014).

How long does a long-term memory last? It depends (Altmann & Gray, 2002). If you are playing basketball, you remember the score, approximately how much time is left in the game, what defense your team is using, what offense, how many fouls you have committed, and so forth. You won't (and wouldn't want to) remember that information for the rest of your life, but you also don't need to rehearse it constantly to prevent it from fading. Similarly, right now you probably remember approximately how much money is in your wallet, where and when you plan to meet someone for dinner, what you plan to do next weekend, how long until your next psychology test, and much other information you need to store until you update it with new information.

Many long-term memories last a lifetime. Old people can describe events that happened in their childhood. Harry Bahrick (1984) found that people who had studied Spanish 1 or 2 years ago remembered more than those who had studied it 3 to 6 years ago, but beyond 6 years, the retention appeared to be stable (see ▼ **Figure 7.7**).

concept check

4. What are two differences between short-term memory and long-term memory?
5. Studies in the 1950s indicated that short-term memories, unless rehearsed, decay within seconds. What is an alternative explanation for the unavailability of those memories, other than decay?

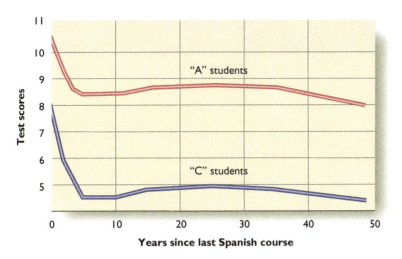

▲ Figure 7.7 Spanish vocabulary as measured by a recognition test declines in the first few years but then becomes stable. The students who received an "A" performed better, but each group showed similar rates of forgetting. (From Bahrick, 1984)

Answers

4. Short-term memory has a small capacity, whereas long-term memory has a huge capacity. Also, short-term memory fades within seconds unless you rehearse it. 5. We forget short-term memories because of interference from similar memories.

Working Memory

"Clarence Birdseye patented a method for selling frozen fish." You probably didn't know that. It is now in your short-term memory, and it may or may not become a long-term memory. "Read the first three paragraphs on page 42 and summarize the main points." That instruction is also in short-term memory, but it is of a different kind. Whereas you might want to remember the fact about Clarence Birdseye, you have no reason to remember the instruction about page 42 after you complete it.

Originally, psychologists thought of short-term memory as the way to store something while your brain moves it into long-term storage. That is, you gradually consolidate your memory. Consolidation—*converting a short-term memory into a long-term memory*—does occur, but not all short-term memories become long-term memories, even after long rehearsal. You might watch a hockey game in which the score remains 1-0 for two hours, but you don't store that score permanently. In contrast, if someone tells you, "Your sister just had a baby," you form a lasting memory quickly.

Today, most researchers emphasize temporary memory storage as the information you are using at the moment. To emphasize this different perspective, they speak of working memory, which is *a system for working with current information*. Working memory is almost synonymous with your current sphere of attention (Baddeley, 2001; Baddeley & Hitch, 1994; Repovš & Baddeley, 2006). It includes information you use and then forget, like "summarize the material on page 42" or "go to the first intersection and turn right." It also includes the executive functioning that *governs shifts of attention*. The hallmark of good working memory is the ability to shift attention as needed among different tasks. A hospital nurse has to keep track of the needs of several patients, sometimes interrupting the treatment of one patient to take care of an emergency and then returning to complete work with the first patient.

Here is a simple way to measure how long it takes the central executive to shift attention: Recite aloud a poem, song, or other passage that you know well. (If you cannot think of a more interesting example, recite the alphabet.) Time how long it takes. Then measure how long it takes you to say the same thing silently. Finally, time how long it takes you to alternate—the first word aloud, the second silent, the third aloud, and so forth. Alternating takes longer because you keep shifting attention.

Here is another way to measure executive processes: You hear a list of words such as *maple, elm, oak, hemlock, chestnut, birch, sycamore, pine, redwood, walnut, dogwood, hickory*. After each word, you are supposed to say the *previous* word. So after "maple, elm," you should say "maple." After "oak" you reply "elm." If you do well on that task, proceed to a more difficult version: You should repeat what you heard *two* words ago. So you wait for "maple, elm, oak" and reply "maple." Then you hear "hemlock" and reply "elm." You shift back and forth between listening to a new word and repeating something from memory. For a still harder task, you can try for three back or four back.

People who do well on tasks like these have a high capacity of working memory. They generally do well on many other tasks, including school performance (Rose, Feldman, & Jankowitz, 2011), understanding other people's point of view (Barrett, Tugade, & Engle, 2004), learning a second language (Linck, Osthus, Koeth, & Bunting, 2013), and resisting impulses to heavy drinking (Houben, Wiers, & Jansen, 2011). They have less than average "mind wandering" while they need to concentrate on a difficult task but more than average mind wandering when performing easy tasks (Kane et al., 2007).

6. **What do the differences about "mind wandering" tell us about attention?**

Answer

6. People with good working memory can control their attention when necessary, to complete a difficult task.

Varieties of Memory

Although researchers cannot clearly say what memory is, they agree about what it is *not:* Memory is not a single store into which we simply dump things and later take them out. When Ebbinghaus conducted his studies of memory in the late 1800s, he thought he was measuring the properties of memory, period.

We now know that the properties of memory depend on the type of material memorized, its relationship to previous memories, the method of testing, and the recency of the event. Memory is not one process, but many.

Summary

- *Ebbinghaus's approach.* Hermann Ebbinghaus pioneered the experimental study of memory by testing his own ability to memorize and retain lists of nonsense syllables. (page 215)
- *Methods of testing memory.* The free recall method reveals only relatively strong memories. Progressively weaker memories can be demonstrated by the cued recall, recognition, and savings methods. Implicit memories are changes in behavior under conditions in which the person cannot verbalize the memory or is unaware of the influence. (page 216)
- *Procedural memory.* Procedural memory, or habit learning, develops gradually, unlike declarative memory. Procedural memory is also well suited to remembering information that is usually true under certain circumstances, as opposed to re-membering a single event. (page 218)
- *Suspect lineups.* Suspect lineups are an example of the recog-nition method of testing memory. Unfortunately, witnesses sometimes choose the best available choice, which may not be

correct. Psychologists have recommended ways to decrease inaccurate identifications. (page 218)
- *Children as eyewitnesses.* Even young children can provide ac-curate eyewitness reports if they are asked unbiased questions soon after the event. (page 219)
- *Short-term and long-term memory.* Short-term memory has a capacity of only a few items in normal adults, although chunk-ing can enable us to store much information in each item. Short-term memory shows a trade-off between number of items stored and the precision of storage. Long-term memory has a huge capacity. Short-term memories fade over time if not rehearsed, partly because of interference from similar memories. Long-term memories last varying periods, up to a lifetime. (page 220)
- *Working memory.* Working memory is a system for dealing with current information, including the ability to shift atten-tion back and forth among tasks as necessary. (page 223)

Key Terms

chunking (page 221)

consolidation (page 223)

cued recall (page 216)

declarative memory (page 218)

episodic memory (page 220)

executive functioning (page 223)

explicit memory (or **direct memory**) (page 216)

free recall (page 216)

implicit memory (or **indirect memory**) (page 216)

information-processing model (page 220)

long-term memory (page 220)

memory (page 215)

priming (page 217)

procedural memory (page 218)

recognition (page 216)

savings method (or **relearning method**) (page 216)

semantic memory (page 220)

short-term memory (page 220)

source amnesia (page 220)

working memor (page 223)

Answer to Other Question in the Module

A. Herman Melville, Jane Austen, Agatha Christie, Arthur Conan Doyle, Maya Angelou, Leo Tolstoy, James Kalat, Geoffrey Chaucer, Charles Darwin, Margaret Mitchell, Victor Hugo. (page 217)

Review Questions

1. What is one major difference between procedural (habit) and declarative memory?
   - (a) Procedural memory develops gradually and is sensitive to information that is usually but not always correct.
   - (b) Procedural memory depends on a single experience.
   - (c) Procedural memory occurs only in adulthood.
   - (d) Procedural memory is forgotten quickly.

2. When police ask a witness to identify a suspect from a lineup, which of the following procedures do psychologists recommend?
   - (a) Ask for a percent confidence answer instead of a yes/no answer.
   - (b) Inform the witness that the police strongly suspect one of the people in this lineup.
   - (c) Use an array of suspects who vary greatly in their appearance.
   - (d) Encourage a witness who has identified the same person that the police suspect.

3. To investigate a possible case of sexual abuse of a young child, what is the best way to ask the child?
   - (a) Provide the child with an anatomically detailed doll and ask the child to demonstrate what happened.
   - (b) Ask, "tell me what happened," as soon as possible.
   - (c) Ask, "Did the man manipulate your genitals?"
   - (d) First tell the child what other children have reported after being sexually abused.

4. Which of the following is an example of an episodic memory?
   - (a) "I remember that Tokyo is the largest city in Japan."
   - (b) "People in Japan eat large amounts of seafood and rice."
   - (c) "Let me tell you about my trip to Japan . . ."
   - (d) "Kabuki theater and sumo wrestling originated in Japan."

5. Which of the following is an example of source amnesia?
   - (a) "I forget what is the capital of Poland, but I think it starts with a W."
   - (b) "I don't remember where I heard this, but I heard that apricot pits can cure cancer."
   - (c) "For a while this morning I couldn't remember where I was, but then I remembered."
   - (d) "I studied the periodic table in high school, but now I forget it."

6. Theorists today believe that short-term memory can hold only four items at most. Why can you nevertheless repeat a list of seven or more items?
   - (a) Episodic memory
   - (b) Chunking
   - (c) Procedural memory
   - (d) Repression

7. The "central executive" aspect of working memory is responsible for what?
   - (a) Storing a short-term memory long enough for the brain to form a long-term memory
   - (b) Rehearsing a short-term memory to prevent it from fading
   - (c) Converting thought into language
   - (d) Shifting attention between one task and another

Answers: 1a, 2a, 3b, 4c, 5b, 6b, 7d.

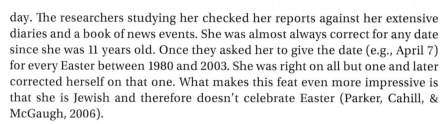

After studying this module, you should be able to:

- List influences that improve or interfere with encoding.
- Discuss ways to organize and improve studying.
- Give examples of mnemonic devices.
- Discuss memory as a process of reconstruction.

Have you ever felt distressed because you cannot remember some experience? One woman reports feeling distressed because she cannot stop remembering! When she sees or hears a date—such as April 27, 1994—a flood of episodic memories descends on her. "That was Wednesday. . . . I was down in Florida. I was summoned to come down and to say goodbye to my grandmother who they all thought was dying but she ended up living. My Dad and my Mom went to New York for a wedding. Then my Mom went to Baltimore to see her family. I went to Florida on the 25th, which was a Monday. This was also the weekend that Nixon died. And then I flew to Florida and my Dad flew to Florida the next day. Then I flew home and my Dad flew to Baltimore to be with my Mom" (Parker, Cahill, & McGaugh, 2006, p. 40). Tell her another date, and she might describe where she went to dinner and with whom, as well as the major news event of that

day. The researchers studying her checked her reports against her extensive diaries and a book of news events. She was almost always correct for any date since she was 11 years old. Once they asked her to give the date (e.g., April 7) for every Easter between 1980 and 2003. She was right on all but one and later corrected herself on that one. What makes this feat even more impressive is that she is Jewish and therefore doesn't celebrate Easter (Parker, Cahill, & McGaugh, 2006).

You might not want to have the detailed episodic memory of this woman, who says her memories so occupy her that she can hardly focus on the present. Still, you might like to improve your memory of items you do want to remember. Memory consists of three aspects—encoding, storage, and retrieval. The main point of this module is simple: When you want to retrieve a memory, it's too late if you didn't encode it well in the first place. To improve your memory, improve the way you study.

Encoding

If you want to memorize a definition, would you repeat it over and over? Repetition by itself is a poor study method, especially if you do it all at one time.

To illustrate, examine ▼ Figure 7.8, which shows a real U.S. penny and 14 fakes. If you live in the United States, you have seen pennies countless times, but can you now identify the real one? Most U.S. citizens guess wrong (Nickerson & Adams, 1979). (If you do not have a penny in your pocket, check answer B on page 236. If you are not from the United States, try drawing the front or back of a common coin in your own country.) In short, mere repetition, such as looking at a coin many times, does not guarantee a strong memory.

try it yourself

Factors that Influence Encoding

One influence on how well you remember something is whether you try to remember it! If you don't expect to need certain information very often, and you

Most actors preparing for a play spend much time thinking about the meaning of what they will say (a deep level of processing) instead of just repeating the words.

Paul Doyle/Alamy

▲ **Figure 7.8** Can you spot the genuine penny among 14 fakes? (Based on Nickerson & Adams, 1979)

know you can easily find it on the Internet when you do need it, you put little effort into remembering it (Sparrow, Liu, & Wegner, 2011). In one study, students were told they would play a *Concentration* game in which they needed to remember the locations of various items in an array. Half the students saw all the items and tried to memorize their locations. The other half saw the items and took notes, but then to their surprise the experimenters took the notes away. The first group remembered much better than the second group. Evidently, those taking notes expected to rely on the notes, and they didn't bother trying to remember (Eskritt & Ma, 2014).

Emotional arousal also enhances memory encoding. Chances are, you vividly remember your first day of college, your first kiss, the time your team won the big game, and times you were frightened. Extreme panic interferes with memory, but moderate emotion provides benefits, largely by increasing the release of the hormones cortisol and epinephrine (adrenaline) from the adrenal gland. Those hormones stimulate brain areas that enhance memory storage (Andreano & Cahill, 2006).

The effects of arousal on memory have been known for centuries. In England in the early 1600s, when people sold land, they did not yet have the custom of recording the sale on paper. Paper was expensive and few people could read anyway. Instead, local residents would gather while someone announced the sale and instructed everyone to remember it. Of all those present, whose memory of the sale was most important? It was the children, because they would live the longest. And of all those present, who were least interested? Right, again, it's the children. To increase the chances that the children would remember, the adults would kick them while telling them about the business deal. The same idea persisted in the custom, still common in the early 1900s, of slapping schoolchildren's hands with a stick to make them pay attention. (However, no one did controlled experiments to test the effectiveness of this intervention!)

Many people report intense, detailed "flashbulb" memories from when they heard highly emotional news. They remember who told them, where they were, what they were doing, often even the weather and other irrelevant details. When researchers interviewed people both at the time and years later, they found that occasionally people's reports change, while remaining confident and vivid. One person originally reported hearing about the terrorist attacks of September 11, 2001 on a car radio, and 2 years later reported having heard about it while standing in line at an airport (Kvavilashvili, Mirani, Schlagman, Foley, &

Kornbrot, 2009). Confident, vivid memories aren't always correct.

concept check ✓

7. Most people with post-traumatic stress disorder have lower than normal levels of cortisol. What would you predict about their memory?

Answer

7. Because of the lower cortisol levels, they should have trouble storing memories and they should experience frequent memory lapses.

In addition to attention and emotion, many other factors influence how well you store your memories. To illustrate, read the following list, look away from the book, and write as many of the words as you can. The demonstration would work better if you saw the words one at a time on a screen. You can approximate that procedure by covering the list with a sheet of paper and pulling it down to reveal one word at a time.

try it yourself

LEMON
GRAPE
POTATO
COCONUT
CUCUMBER
TOMATO
BROCCOLI
APPLE
SPINACH
TOMATO
ORANGE
LETTUCE
CARROT
STRAWBERRY
BANANA
TOMATO
PEACH
NAKED
LIME
PINEAPPLE
TURNIP
MANGO
TOMATO
BLUEBERRY
TOMATO
APRICOT
WATERMELON

I hope you tried the demonstration. If so, *TOMATO* was probably one of the words you remembered because it occurred five times instead of just once. Other things being equal, repetition helps, especially if the repetitions are spread out. You probably also remembered *LEMON* and *WATERMELON* because they were the first and last items on the list. The primacy effect is *the tendency to remember well the first items.* The recency effect is *the tendency to*

People recall emotionally arousing events in great detail, although not always accurately.

Anadolu Agency/Getty Images

remember the final items. The primacy and recency effects are robust for almost any type of memory. If you try to list all the vacations you have ever taken or all the sporting events you have ever watched, you will probably include the earliest ones and the most recent.

You probably also remembered *CARROT* and *NAKED.* The word *CARROT* was distinctive because of its size, color, and font. *NAKED* stood out as the only item on the list that was neither a fruit nor a vegetable. In a list of mostly similar items, the unusual ones are easier to remember. We also tend to remember unusual people. If you meet several women of average appearance with similar names, like Jennifer Stevens, Stephanie Jensen, and Jenny Stevenson, you will have trouble remembering their names. You will more quickly remember a tall, red-headed woman named Bimbo Sue Budweiser.

You might not have remembered *MANGO* if you didn't grow up eating mangoes in childhood. People find it easier to remember words they learned in early childhood (e.g., *APPLE, ORANGE,* and *BANANA*) than words they learned later (Juhasz, 2005). Similarly, if you grew up watching *Sesame Street,* you can probably name Bert, Ernie, and Oscar the Grouch more quickly than many of the characters you have watched on television more recently.

Did you remember the word *LIME?* Probably not, because it came right after the word *NAKED.* When people see an unexpected sex-related word, it grabs attention so strongly that they pay less attention to the next word and sometimes up to the next four or five words (Arnell, Killman, & Fijavz, 2007). The effect would be even stronger if you were watching a series of slides, and one of them had a photo of naked people. Some people also forget the word that came *before* a highly emotional word or image (Strange, Kroes, Roiser, Yan, & Dolan, 2008).

One more determinant: Other things being equal, you would probably remember a list of people or animals better than a list of inanimate objects, even if they are familiar objects like *stove* and *hat* (Nairne, VanArsdall, Pandeirada, Cogdill, & Le Breton, 2013). People and animals grab our attention and interest more than almost anything else does.

8. What are some factors that increase or decrease your probability of remembering a word on a list?

Answer

8. Moderate emotion enhances memory. Memory is enhanced by repetition, distinctiveness, and being either first or last on a list. We also tend to remember words we learned early in life more easily than those we learned later. We tend to forget an item that came right after something unusually arousing.

Let's try another demonstration. Below are two lists. As you read through one of the lists—it doesn't matter which one—repeat each word for a couple of seconds. So, if the word were *insect,* you would say, "Insect, insect, insect . . ." and then proceed to the next word. For the other list, imagine yourself stranded in the middle of a vast grassland in some foreign country, where you need to find food and water and protect yourself from snakes, lions, and other dangers. As you go through the list, again spend a couple of seconds on each word, thinking about how useful this item would be for survival under these conditions. Give it a rating from 1 (useless) to 5 (extremely valuable). You choose whether to do the repetition list first or the rating-for-survival list first. At the end, pause awhile and then try to recall the items you read.

List A	List B
toothbrush	firecracker
thermometer	rollerblades
marionette	umbrella
jewelry	hammock
tuxedo	binoculars
washcloth	encyclopedia
bandage	saxophone
trampoline	camera
metronome	mirror
flashlight	scissors
chain	string
knife	bottle
balloon	radio
carpet	envelope
overcoat	candy
matches	pencil

Most people remember far more words from the survival list than from the repetition list (Nairne, Pandeirada, & Thompson, 2008; Nairne, Thompson, & Pandeirada, 2007). If, instead of rating the words for survival relevance, you rated them for pleasantness, that procedure would help, too, but not as much as rating words for survival. Evidently, thinking about survival engages attention and memory better than anything else does. It makes sense for our brains to have evolved this way. In a follow-up study, people read words while rating their value for a hunting contest, or for hunting food for your tribe. Even though it was the same act in both cases—hunting—people remembered more words if they thought of hunting in terms of survival instead of a contest (Nairne, Pandeirada, Gregory, & Van Arsdall, 2009).

Moreover, simply repeating the words is one of the least effective ways to study, if you want long-term

Table 7.3	Depth-of-Processing Model of Memory
Superficial processing	Simply repeat the material to be remembered: "Hawk, Oriole, Tiger, Timberwolf, Blue Jay, Bull."
Deeper processing	Think about each item. Note that two start with T and two with B.
Still deeper processing	Note that three are birds and three are mammals. Also, three are major league baseball teams and three are NBA basketball teams. Use whichever associations mean the most to you.

▲ **Figure 7.9** If you think of the word *queen* as *queen bee*, then the cue *playing card* will not remind you of the word later. If you think of the *queen of England*, then *chess piece* will not be a good reminder.

retention. Actors spend little time simply repeating their lines when rehearsing for a play. Rather, they think about the goal and meaning of each statement and how it develops the character and the story (Noice & Noice, 2006). According to the **depth-of-processing principle** (Craik & Lockhart, 1972), *how easily you retrieve a memory depends on the number and types of associations you form.* When you read a list or read a chapter, simply reading the words without much thought is "shallow processing," which produces only fleeting memories. Alternatively, you might stop and consider various points as you read them, relate them to your own experiences, and think of your own examples to illustrate each principle. The more ways you think about the material, the deeper your processing and the more easily you will remember later. The difference isn't apparent at once. Immediately after you read something, you may remember it just as well after shallow processing as after deep processing. But after a longer delay, you will remember significantly more after deep processing (Rose, Myerson, Roediger, & Hale, 2010). ■ Table 7.3 summarizes the depth-of-processing model.

prompt your memory later. According to the **encoding specificity principle** (Tulving & Thomson, 1973), *the associations you form at the time of learning will be the most effective retrieval cues later* (see ▲ Figure 7.9). Here is an example (modified from Thieman, 1984). First, read the pairs of words (which psychologists call *paired associates*) in ■ Table 7.4a. Then turn to ■ Table 7.4b on page 231. For each of the words on that list, try to recall a related word on the list you just read. *Please do this now.* (The answers are on page 236, answer B.)

Most people find this task difficult. If they initially coded the word *cardinal* as a type of clergyman, the retrieval cue *bird* doesn't remind them of it. If they thought of it as a bird, then *clergyman* is not a good reminder.

The principle of encoding specificity extends to other aspects of experience at the time of storage. In one study, college students who were fluent in both English and Russian were given a list of words such as *summer, birthday,* and *doctor,* some in English and some in Russian. For each word, they were asked to describe any related event they

concept check

9. **Many students who get the best grades in a course read the assigned text chapters more slowly than average. Why?**

Answer

9. Students who pause to think about the meaning are engaging in deep processing. They will remember the material better than those who read a chapter quickly.

Encoding Specificity

When you encode (store) a memory, you form associations. If you form many associations, many possible *reminders*—called **retrieval cues**—can

Table 7.4a	
Clergyman—Cardinal	Geometry—Plane
Trinket—Charm	Tennis—Racket
Type of wine—Port	Music—Rock
U.S. politician—Bush	Magic—Spell
Inch—Foot	Envelope—Seal
Computer—Apple	Graduation—Degree

remembered. In response to Russian words, they recalled mostly events that happened when they were speaking Russian. In response to English words, they recalled mostly events that happened when they were speaking English (Marian & Neisser, 2000). In another study, people viewed objects in various locations on a computer screen, and later remembered the items better if they looked toward the same location on a now-blank screen (Johansson & Johansson, 2014). Even distraction pertains to encoding specificity: One study found that people who learned a skill while distracted by something else remembered the skill better if they were tested with the same distraction present (Song & Bédard, 2015). So don't listen to music while you are studying unless you expect to listen to music again when you are taking the test!

Some police interviewers use encoding specificity when questioning crime witnesses. They start by asking the witnesses to imagine the original conditions as closely as possible—the location, the weather, the time of day, how they were feeling at the time. Getting back to the original event, at least in imagination, helps people remember more details of what they saw (Fisher, Geiselman, & Amador, 1989).

The encoding specificity principle has this implication: If you want to remember something at a particular time and place, study under the same conditions where you will try to remember. However, if you want to remember something always, you should vary your study habits so that your memory does *not* become too specific to one setting.

10. Suppose someone cannot remember what happened at a party last night. What steps might help improve the memory?

Answer

10. Presuming the person really wants to remember, it might help to return to the place of the party with the same people present, perhaps even at the same time of day. The more similar the conditions of original learning and later recall, the better the probability of remembering.

How to Organize Your Studying

Did you ever have this experience? You read something over and over. You are sure you have studied it hard and know it well. Then you take a test and you don't remember it nearly as well as you had expected. What went wrong?

Studying All at Once or Spread Out

Should you study a little at a time or wait and do it all shortly before the test? You know that waiting until just before the test is risky. An unexpected interruption might prevent you from studying at all. Let's change the question to make the answer less obvious: You don't wait until just before the test, but you nevertheless study all at once. Will your result be better, worse, or the same as if you studied a little at a time over several days?

Studying all at once is okay if you need to remember it immediately and never again. However, if you care about long-term memory, studying all at once is worse for every kind of learning that researchers have tested, including language, math, music, and sports (Cepeda, Pashler, Vul, Wixted, & Rohrer, 2006; Kornell & Bjork, 2008; Küpper-Tetzel, 2014; McDaniel, Fadler, & Pashler, 2013). Suppose you are trying to learn a foreign language. You study a list of words until you know their meanings. Now, you spend another 10 minutes going over the same list again and again. How much do you gain? The research says that the extra 10 minutes is almost completely wasted (Rohrer & Pashler, 2007). You would do much better to do something else now and review the vocabulary list later.

When you wait to study again, how long should you wait? It depends. To remember something next week, you get the best results if you review tomorrow. To remember something next month, you should wait a week and a half before you review. To remember next year, wait about 3 weeks. In each case, it is better to wait a little longer than a little less (Cepeda, Vul, Rohrer, Wixted, & Pashler, 2008). Better yet, of course, review several times.

When you study something all at once, it *seems* that you are learning well because the material is so fresh in your memory at the time. However, people almost always underestimate how much they are going to forget (Koriat, Bjork, Sheffer, & Bar, 2004). To remember something well, you need to practice retrieving the memory—that is, finding it. While you are reading something over and over, it is so fresh in your memory that you gain no practice at retrieving it. If you go away and come back later, you need effort to refresh the ideas, and that effort strengthens the memory.

Advantages of Varied Study

Within a study session, you gain by adding variety, although it won't seem that way. Suppose you are trying to learn the artistic styles of several painters so that you can identify new paintings by the same artists. Would you learn better by seeing many paintings by artist A, then many by artist B, many by C, and so forth? Or would it be better to see one by each, and then another by each, and so forth? Most people assume the first way is better, seeing many examples by a given artist all at one time. However, the results show that spacing them out works substantially better (Kornell, Castel, Eich, & Bjork, 2010). Suppose you are trying to learn to solve four types of math problems. It seems easier to solve several examples of one type, then several examples of the next type, and so forth. (Nearly all math textbooks are organized that way.) But if you want to remember the skills for long, your best strategy is to mix up one type with another until you can solve each of them, then wait a week or so and try again, also mixing up one type with another (Rohrer & Taylor, 2007). When you are reading a textbook like this one, you should occasionally go back to previous chapters and try to answer the review questions and concept checks (Dunlosky, Rawson, Marsh, Nathan, & Willingham, 2013).

Varying the conditions of learning makes a task seem more difficult, but in the long run, it helps. In one experiment, a group of 8-year-old children practiced throwing a beanbag at a target 3 feet away. Another group practiced with a target sometimes 2 feet away and sometimes 4 feet away but never 3 feet away. Then both groups were tested with the target 3 feet away. The children who had practiced with the 3-foot target missed it by a mean of 8.3 inches. The children who had been practicing with 2-foot and 4-foot targets missed by only 5.4 inches, even though they were aiming at the 3-foot target for the first time (Kerr & Booth, 1978). In another experiment, young adults practiced a technique for mentally squaring two-digit numbers—for example, $23 \times 23 = 529$. Those who practiced with a small range of numbers learned the technique quickly but forgot it quickly. Those who practiced with a wider range of numbers learned more slowly but remembered better later (Sanders, Gonzalez, Murphy, Pesta, & Bucur, 2002).

Taking Notes During Class

Taking notes in class focuses attention at the time, and provides material for review later. However, students seldom get much training on how to take notes. Extremely brief notes do little good, but trying to record every word is problematical also. Trying to record everything is tiring, and if you succeed, your notes will be so long that you may be intimidated about reviewing them later. Generally, the best strategy is to try to record the main ideas in an organized fashion.

Is it a good idea to bring a laptop computer to class and type notes on the computer? Opinions are divided on this issue. On the plus side, most people type faster than they write, and they take more detailed notes with the laptop (Bui, Myerson, & Hale, 2013). On the minus side, highly detailed notes are not always an advantage. Often it is better to think about the content and try to summarize the main ideas (Mueller & Oppenheimer, 2014). Furthermore, laptops provide a distraction, and many students who bring laptops to class use them for email and other tasks unrelated to class (Kraushaar & Novak, 2010). On average students who bring laptops to class get lower grades than other students (Fried, 2008).

What You Learn During Testing

Most people assume that they learn while reading something but not while recalling it. In fact, to strengthen a memory, it is essential to practice recalling it. In several studies, one group of students spent a certain amount of time reading and rereading. Another group spent the same time alternating between reading and answering questions about what they had read. Both groups did equally well at the end of the study session, but when tested later, a difference was clear and consistent: The students who alternated between reading and testing did better (Karpicke & Blunt, 2011; McDaniel, Howard, & Einstein, 2009; Roediger & Karpicke, 2006). The advantage is greatest with difficult material or difficult tests (Halamish & Bjork, 2011).

A test forces you to generate the material instead of passively reading it. Also, it shows what you don't know, encouraging you to pay more attention to that material or to study it in a different way (Karpicke & Roediger, 2008; Pyc & Rawson, 2010). Here is a related finding: Suppose your instructor starts a lecture by asking a question, such as, "What is meant by depth of processing?" You don't know, so either you say you don't know or you offer a guess that's probably wrong. Then the instructor gives the correct information. Research shows that you will remember the information better than if the instructor had merely stated it without asking the question (Kornell, Hays, & Bjork, 2009). Asking the question builds your curiosity and increases your attention to the answer.

Table 7.4b

Instructions: For each of these words, write one of the second of the paired terms from the list in Table 7.4a.

Animal—	Stone—
Part of body—	Personality—
Transportation—	Write—
Temperature—	Bird—
Crime—	Harbor—
Shrubbery—	Fruit—

Here is how you can apply this idea: Each module in this book ends with review questions. From now on, turn to those review questions *before* you read the chapter and try to answer them. Then read the module.

Conclusions: (1) You generally overestimate how well you have learned something if you haven't waited long enough to see how much you will forget. (2) Studying once is seldom effective, no matter how hard you study that one time. (3) Varying the conditions of studying improves long-term memory. (4) You remember better if you test yourself.

concept check

11. So, why is it a good idea to answer Concept Checks like this one?

12. Is the advice to spread out your study over a long time instead of doing it all at one sitting consistent with the encoding specificity principle?

Answers

11. Practicing the retrieval of a memory strengthens it. Students who spent part of their study time answering test questions did better than those who spent the whole time reading.
12. The ideas are compatible. If you study all at one sitting, you encode the memory to what you are thinking about at that time. If you study at several times, the memory attaches to a greater variety of retrieval cues.

Mnemonic Devices

If you need to memorize a long, not very exciting list—for example, a list of the 50 largest cities in South America—how would you do it? One effective strategy is to attach systematic retrieval cues to each term so that you can remind yourself of the terms when you need them. A **mnemonic device** is *any memory aid based on encoding items in a special way.* The word *mnemonic* (nee-MAHN-ik) comes from a Greek root meaning "memory." The same root appears in the word *amnesia,* "lack of memory." Some mnemonic devices are simple, such as "Every Good Boy Does Fine" to remember the notes EGBDF on the treble clef in music. To remember the functions of the sympathetic and parasympathetic nervous systems, you might try making connections like those shown in ▶ Figure 7.10 (Carney & Levin, 1998).

Suppose you have to memorize a list of Nobel Peace Prize winners (see ▶ Figure 7.11). You might make up a little story: "Dun (Dunant) passed (Passy) the Duke (Ducommun) of Gob (Gobat) some cream (Cremer). That made him internally ILL (Institute of International Law). He suited (von Suttner) up with some roses (Roosevelt) and spent some money (Moneta) on a Renault (Renault)..." You still have to study the names, but your story helps.

Another mnemonic device is the **method of loci** (method of places). *First, you memorize a series of places, and then you use a vivid image to associate each location with something you want to remember.* For example, you might start by memorizing every location along the route from your dormitory room to your psychology classroom. Then you link the locations, in order, to the names.

Suppose the first three locations you pass are the desk in your room, the door to your room, and the corridor. To link the first Nobel Peace Prize winners, Dunant and Passy, to your desk, you might imagine a Monopoly game board on your desk with a big sign "DO NOT (Dunant) PASS (Passy) GO." Then you link the second pair of names to the second location, your door: A DUKE student (as in Ducommun) is standing at the door, giving confusing signals. He says "DO COME IN (Ducommun)" and "GO BACK (Gobat)." Then you link the corridor to Cremer, perhaps by imagining someone has spilled CREAM (Cremer) all over the floor (see ▼ Figure 7.12). You continue in this manner until you have linked every name to a location. Now, if you can remember all those locations in order and if you have good visual images for each one, you can recite the list of Nobel Peace Prize winners.

Simpler mnemonic devices often help, such as when remembering people's names. You might remember someone named Harry Moore by picturing him as "more hairy." To memorize a traditional wedding vow, you might remember "BRISTLE" to remind you of "**B**etter or worse, **R**icher or poorer, **I**n **S**ickness and health, **T**o **L**ove and to cherish."

A parachute lets you coast down slowly, like the parasympathetic nervous system.

If the symphony excites you, it arouses your sympathetic nervous system.

▲ **Figure 7.10** One mnemonic device is to think of an image that will remind you of what you need to remember.

Storage

Most of the work of forming a memory pertains to encoding. Storing or maintaining a memory sounds like a passive process, but important things happen here, too. As time passes after initial learning, some memories change in ways that make them available much later, perhaps forever. This process is called consolidation.

Nobel Peace Prize Winners

1901	H. Dunant and F. Passy
1902	E. Ducommun and A. Gobat
1903	Sir W. R. Cremer
1904	Institute of International Law
1905	Baroness von Suttner
1906	T. Roosevelt
1907	E. T. Moneta and L. Renault
1908	K. P. Arnoldson and F. Bajer
1909	A. M. F. Beernaert and Baron d'Estournelles de Constant

2007	Al Gore and the Intergovernmental Panel on Climate Change
2008	Martti Ahtisaari
2009	Barack Obama
2010	Liu Xiaobo
2011	Ellen Johnson Sirleaf, Leymah Gbowee, and Tawakkol Karman
2012	European Union
2013	Organisation for the Prohibition of Chemical Weapons

▲ **Figure 7.11** A list of Nobel Peace Prize winners: Mnemonic devices can be useful when people try to memorize long lists like this one.

events from that age range may be largely a matter of heightened interest, rather than consolidation of memory.

▲ **Figure 7.12** With the method of loci, you first learn a list of places, such as "my desk, the door of my room, the corridor, . . ." Then you link each place to an item on a list.

Decades ago, psychologists imagined consolidation as a chemical process that took a fixed amount of time. However, some memories consolidate much more easily than others. When you hear, "Jakarta is the capital of Indonesia," you might have to work at it to form a lasting memory. If someone says, "Yes, I will go with you to the dance on Friday," you store the memory almost immediately.

You can try a couple of ways to enhance consolidation after learning something. One is to take some caffeine shortly after learning something. A study found that 200 to 300 mg of caffeine, a little more than you would get from an average cup of coffee, enhanced the detail of people's memories when tested a day later (Borota et al., 2014). Another strategy is to sleep or rest quietly shortly after learning (Dewar, Alber, Butler, Cowan, & Della Salla, 2012). Yes, it seems paradoxical that either increased arousal or decreased arousal enhances consolidation, but those are the results.

How long does consolidation continue? Certain kinds of evidence suggest that it continues for decades, but the interpretation of that evidence is ambiguous. Studies found that people in their 60s and 70s remember events from their adolescence and early adulthood better than more recent events (Haist, Gore, & Mao, 2001; Maguire & Frith, 2003; Niki & Luo, 2002). For example, older adults generally remember the music, movies, and politicians from their youth better than they remember comparable items from recent years. One interpretation is that the memories continued to consolidate, year after year. Another is that memories in young adulthood formed more strongly in the first place (Berntsen & Rubin, 2002). To most people, the teenage and young adult years are especially interesting and important. Most movies, television shows, and novels focus on that era of life. When children describe their future lives, they describe more events from their teenage and young adult lives than from any other period (Bohn & Berntsen, 2011). Thus, the enhanced recall of

concept check

13. **If you have just learned something, what are two things you could do that might improve consolidation of the memory?**

Answer

13. You could consume some caffeine or take a nap. (Of course, if you need to study five topics tonight, you cannot do either of these strategies after every one of them!)

Retrieval

People sometimes imagine that memory is like playing back a recording of an event. Memory differs from a recording in many ways. Here is one: Suppose you try to list all the cities you have ever visited. You describe all you can, and then you come back a day or two later and try again. On your second try, you will probably recall *more* than you did the first time (Erdelyi, 2010). Whereas loss of memory is called amnesia, this *gain of memory over time* is called hypermnesia. On the second try, you recall most or all of what you said the first time, plus in the meantime something may have reminded you of something you left out the first time. For this reason, police sometimes interview a witness several times. It is possible to omit something at first and remember it later.

Here is another difference between memory and a recording: Suppose someone asks you to describe a particular part of an experience—perhaps, "Tell me about the meals you had on your beach trip." Then someone else asks you to describe the beach trip in general. Answering the first question strengthens your memory of the meals but weakens your memory of everything else about the trip (Bäuml & Samenieh, 2010). Furthermore, someone who accompanied you on the beach trip and heard you describing the meals will also tend to forget the events other than meals (Coman, Manier, & Hirst, 2009). Focusing on one part of a memory weakens the rest of it, at least temporarily.

Here is a third, and most important difference between memory and a recording: When you try to remember an experience, you start with the details you remember clearly and fill in the gaps with reconstruction: *During an experience, you construct a memory. When you try to retrieve that memory, you reconstruct an account based partly on distinct memories and partly on your expectations of what must have happened.* Suppose you try to recall studying in the library three nights ago. With a little effort, you might remember where you sat, what you were reading, who sat next to you, and where you went for a snack afterward. If you aren't quite sure, you fill in the gaps with what usually happens during an evening at the library. Within weeks, you gradually forget that evening, and if you try to remember it, you will rely more and more on "what must have happened," omitting more and more details (Schmolck, Buffalo, & Squire, 2000). However, if you happen to fall in love with the person who sat next to you that evening, the evening is important enough to become a lifetime memory. Still, when you try to recall it, you reconstruct the details. You remember where you went for a snack and some of what the two of you said, but if you want to recall the book you were reading in the library, you have to reason it out: "Let's see, that semester I was taking a chemistry course that took a lot of study, so maybe I was reading a chemistry book. No, wait, I remember. When we went out to eat, we talked about politics. So maybe I was reading my political science text."

Reconstruction and Inference in List Memory

Please try this demonstration: Read the words in list A once; then turn away from the list, pause for a few seconds, and write as many of the words as you can remember. Repeat the same procedure for list B. *Please do this now, before reading the following paragraph.*

List A	List B
bed	candy
rest	sour
weep	sugar
tired	dessert
dream	salty
wake	taste
snooze	flavor
keep	bitter
doze	cookies
steep	fruits
snore	chocolate
nap	yummy

After you have written your lists, check how many of the words you got right. If you omitted many, you are normal. The point of this demonstration is not how many you got right but whether you included *sleep* on the first list or *sweet* on the second. Many people include one of these words (which are not on the lists), and some do so with confidence

(Deese, 1959; Roediger & McDermott, 1995; Watson, Balota, & Roediger, 2003). In list B, *sweet* is related to the other words in meaning. In list A, *sleep* is related to most of the words in meaning, and the list also includes three words that rhyme with sleep (*weep*, *keep*, and *steep*). This combined influence produces false recall in a higher percentage of people. Apparently, while learning the individual words, people also learn the gist of what they are all about. When they try to retrieve the list later, they reconstruct a memory of what "must have" been on the list (Seamon et al., 2002).

This effect occurs mainly if you have a memory of intermediate strength. If a list is short or if you learn it well, you probably won't add an extra word that is not on the list. If you remember few or none of the words on the list, you cannot use them to infer another word (Schacter, Verfaellie, Anes, & Racine, 1998).

concept check

14. What are some ways in which memory differs from a recording?

Answer

14. You reconstruct a memory, using inferences to fill in the gaps. Also, if you recall something repeatedly, you sometimes remember more on later tries than you did the first time. Recalling one aspect of an experience may weaken memory of other aspects of the experience.

Reconstructing Stories

Suppose you listen to a story about a teenager's day, including both normal events (watching television) and oddities (parking a bicycle in the kitchen). Which would you remember better—the normal events or the oddities? It depends. If you are tested immediately, while your memory is still strong, you remember the unusual and distinctive events best. However, as you start forgetting the story, you begin to omit the unlikely events, reconstructing a more typical day for the teenager, including some that the story omitted, such as "the teenager went to school in the morning." In short, the less certain your memory is, the more you rely on your expectations (Heit, 1993; Maki, 1990). If you retell something repeatedly—either a story you heard or an event from your own experience—the retellings gradually become more coherent (Ackil, Van Abbema, & Bauer, 2003; Bartlett, 1932). They make more sense because you rely more on the gist, keeping the details that fit the overall theme and omitting or modifying the others.

In a study that highlights the role of expectations, U.S. and Mexican adults tried to recall three stories. Some heard U.S. versions of the stories, and others heard Mexican versions. (For example, in the "going on a date" story, the Mexican version had the man's sister go along as a chaperone.) On the average, U.S. participants remembered the U.S. versions better, whereas Mexicans remembered the Mexican versions better (Harris, Schoen, & Hensley, 1992).

concept check

15. In books about history, it seems that one event led to another in a logical order, but in everyday life, events seem illogical, unconnected, and unpredictable. Why?

Answer

15. Long after the fact, a historian puts together a coherent story based on the gist of events, emphasizing details that fit the pattern and omitting others. In your everyday life, you are aware of all the facts, including those that do not fit any pattern.

Hindsight Bias

Three weeks before the impeachment trial of U.S. President Clinton in 1999, college students were asked to predict the outcome. On the average, they estimated the probability of a conviction at 50.5 percent. A week and a half after Clinton was not convicted, they were asked, "What would you have said 4½ weeks ago was the chance [of a conviction]?" On the average, they reported a 42.8 percent estimate (Bryant & Guilbault, 2002). Their behavior illustrates **hindsight bias**, *the tendency to mold our recollection of the past to fit how events later turned out.* Something happens and we then say, "I *knew* that was going to happen!" Hindsight bias occurs for several reasons. We would like to think the world is an orderly, predictable place and that we are smart enough to predict what will happen. We confuse the facts we know now with those we knew earlier. We focus on the facts we knew earlier that fit with the later outcome, and disregard those that didn't fit. Then we put together a meaningful story in which the earlier events seem to lead inevitably to the outcome (Roese & Vohs, 2012).

Another example: As you can see in ▶ **Figure 7.13**, an image gradually morphs from a blur to an elephant. At what point do you think the average person would identify it as an elephant? It is hard to imagine not knowing it will be an elephant. On this and similar sequences, most people overestimate how soon people will recognize the image (Bernstein, Atance, Loftus, & Meltzoff, 2004). That is, they show hindsight bias.

Hindsight bias affects judgments in legal cases. Suppose a physician makes a diagnosis that turns out to be wrong. After we learn the correct diagnosis, it seems "obvious" that the physician should have known it also, and a malpractice suit is the result (Arkes, 2013). When people were told about the possible hazards of a train going around a mountain track, only one-third said they thought the company should cease operations for safety reasons. However, other participants knew a train had derailed, spilling toxic chemicals into a river, and two-thirds of them said the company should pay punitive damages for continuing operations in spite of the foreseeable dangers (Hastie, Schkade, & Payne, 1999). That is, after people know the result, they believe it was foreseeable. One way to minimize hindsight bias is to ask someone how else things might have happened, and how those alternative outcomes might be explained (Roese & Vohs, 2012).

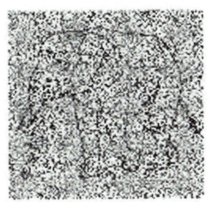

▲ **Figure 7.13** At what point in this sequence do you think the average person would recognize it as an elephant? (Source: From Bernstein, Atance, Loftus, & Meltzoff, 2004)

Improving Your Memory

If you want to improve your memory for something that happened years ago, what can you do? Not much. You might try returning to where the event happened or finding some other reminder. If you remember little at first, you might try again a few days later. Still, your prospects for finding a lost memory are limited. To improve your memory, by far the best strategy is to improve your storage. Think carefully about anything you want to remember, study it under a variety of conditions, and review it frequently.

Summary

- *Repetition.* Although repetition aids memory, other things being equal, repetition by itself is a poor way to study. (page 226)
- *Influences on memory encoding.* Arousal enhances memory coding. Memory is best for the first and last items of a list, anything that is unusual, and items familiar since childhood. (page 226)
- *Depth of processing.* A memory becomes stronger if you think about the meaning of the material and relate it to other material. A memory is particularly enhanced if you think about how it could pertain to your survival. (page 229)
- *Encoding specificity.* When you form a memory, you link it to the way you thought about it at the time. When you try to recall the memory, a cue is most effective if it resembles the links you formed at the time of storage. (page 229)
- *Timing of study.* Spreading out your study is more effective than studying in a single session. During a single session, you underestimate how much you will forget later, and you do not practice retrieving a memory, because it is still fresh. (page 230)
- *Variation in learning.* Long-term memory is best if you study under varying conditions. Spreading out examples is better than studying many examples of the same thing at one time. (page 230)
- *Advantages of testing.* Alternating between reading and testing enhances long-term memory better than spending the same amount of time just reading. (page 231)
- *Mnemonics.* Specialized techniques for using systematic retrieval cues help people remember lists of items. (page 231)
- *Storage and consolidation.* Whereas some memories are lost, others gradually strengthen over time. (page 232)
- *Retrieval.* Memory is unlike a recording. Something that you forget at first, you may recall later. Focusing on one aspect of a memory weakens other aspects. (page 233)
- *Reconstructing memories.* Few memories are recalled intact. Ordinarily, we recall parts of an event and fill in the rest with logical reconstructions. (page 234)
- *Reconstructions from a word list.* If people read or hear a list of related words and try to recall them, they often include related words that were not on the list. They remember the gist and reconstruct what must have been on the list. (page 234)
- *Story memory.* Someone whose memory of a story has faded relies on the gist, omits details that seemed irrelevant, and adds or changes other facts to fit the logic of the story. (page 234)
- *Hindsight bias.* People often revise their memories, saying that how an event turned out was what they expected all along. (page 235)

Key Terms

depth-of-processing principle (page 229)

encoding specificity principle (page 229)

hindsight bias (page 235)

hypermnesia (page 233)

method of loci (page 232)

mnemonic device (page 232)

primacy effect (page 227)

recency effect (page 227)

reconstruction (page 233)

retrieval cue (page 229)

Answers to Other Questions in the Module

A. The correct coin is A. (page 236)

B. Animal—Seal; Part of body—Foot; Transportation—Plane; Temperature—Degree; Crime—Racket; Shrubbery—Bush; Stone—Rock; Personality—Charm; Write—Spell; Bird—Cardinal; Harbor—Port; Fruit—Apple. (page 229)

Review Questions

1. Emotional arousal enhances memory storage by increasing the release of which hormones?
   (a) Insulin and glucagon
   (b) Testosterone and estradiol
   (c) Cortisol and epinephrine
   (d) Thyroid hormone and parathyroid hormone

2. Other things being equal, you remember a list of words best if you think about them in what way?
   (a) How the items might relate to important events in history
   (b) How hard it would be to manufacture each item
   (c) Which store you would have to visit to purchase each item
   (d) How well the items could aid you in a survival situation

3. According to the depth-of-processing principle, what should you do to improve your chances of remembering something later?
   (a) Repeat the information to be remembered as many times as possible.
   (b) Strengthen synapses near the center of your brain.
   (c) Associate the information with your own interests and experiences.
   (d) First memorize a list of places and then associate each item on a list with one of those places.

4. According to the encoding specificity principle, how should you study if you want to remember something for a lifetime?
   (a) Do all your studying in the same location, such as one place in the library.
   (b) Study something over and over, all at one time, until you master it.
   (c) Study something in a variety of times and place.

5. If you want to do well on the final exam in this course, what should you do now?
   (a) Continue reviewing this chapter over and over again.
   (b) After you finish this chapter, review some of the earlier chapters in the book.

6. Old people remember events from young adulthood better than those from middle adulthood. One explanation is that memories continue to consolidate, year after year. What is another explanation?
   (a) Old people don't want to remember their middle adult years.
   (b) Memories from middle adulthood are stored in a different part of the brain.
   (c) Memories of young adulthood formed more strongly at the time.

7. If you studied a list such as "candy, sour, sugar, dessert, salty, taste, . . . " thoroughly instead of hearing it just once, would you be more likely or less likely to include "sweet," which isn't on the list?
   (a) More likely
   (b) Less likely
   (c) About equally likely

8. As discussed in Chapter 5, children who fail to display "theory of mind" seem to assume that if they know something, everyone else would know it too. Which of the following phenomena is similar to that assumption?
   (a) Encoding specificity principle
   (b) Hypermnesia
   (c) Hindsight bias
   (d) Depth-of-processing principle

Answers: 1c, 2d, 3c, 4c, 5b, 6c, 7b, 8c.

After studying this module, you should be able to:

- Explain how interference leads to forgetting.

- Describe evidence regarding how suggestions can lead to false memory reports.

- Discuss amnesia and the light it sheds on memory.

- State what currently appears to be the best explanation for infantile amnesia.

He: We met at nine.

She: We met at eight.

He: I was on time.

She: No, you were late.

He: Ah, yes! I remember it well. We dined with friends.

She: We dined alone.

He: A tenor sang.

She: A baritone.

He: Ah, yes! I remember it well. That dazzling April moon!

She: There was none that night. And the month was June.

He: That's right! That's right!

She: It warms my heart to know that you remember still the way you do.

He: Ah, yes! I remember it well.

—"I Remember It Well" from the musical *Gigi* by Alan Jay Lerner and Frederick Loewe

We all forget, and forgetting doesn't surprise us. A little more surprising is the fact that sometimes we think we remember something clearly, though we are wrong. Here we explore why memory sometimes fails.

Retrieval and Interference

When you try to remember something, you might confuse it with something else you have learned. Remember Hermann Ebbinghaus, who pioneered memory research. Ebbinghaus measured how long he could remember various lists of 13 nonsense syllables. The results appear as the green line on ▲ Figure 7.14. On average, he forgot more than half of each list within the first hour (Ebbinghaus, 1885/1913). What a discouraging graph! If people typically forget that fast, then education would be pointless. However,

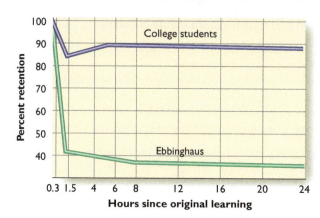

▲ **Figure 7.14** Recall of lists of syllables by Ebbinghaus (1885/1913) and by college students after delays of various lengths (based on Koppenaal, 1963). Ebbinghaus learned as fast as other people but forgot faster.

most college students remember nearly 90 percent of a list of nonsense syllables 24 hours later, as shown in the purple line of Figure 7.16 (Koppenaal, 1963).

Why do you suppose college students remember a list so much better than Ebbinghaus did? You may be tempted to say that college students are very intelligent. Well, yes, but Ebbinghaus was too. Or you might suggest that college students "have had so much practice at memorizing nonsense." (Sorry if you think so.) The explanation is the opposite: Ebbinghaus had memorized *too much* nonsense—thousands of lists of syllables. After you memorize many similar lists, your memory is like a cluttered room: The clutter doesn't prevent you

Ebbinghaus quickly forgot new lists of nonsense syllables because of interference from the previous lists he had learned.

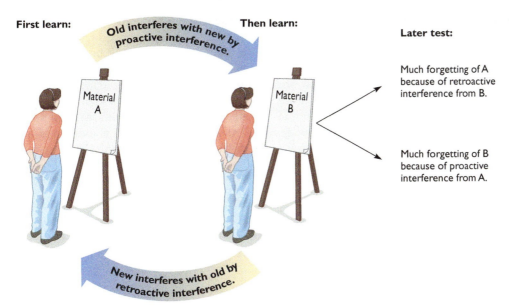

First learn:

Old interferes with new by proactive interference.

Material A

Then learn:

Material B

New interferes with old by retroactive interference.

Later test:

Much forgetting of A because of retroactive interference from B.

Much forgetting of B because of proactive interference from A.

◀ **Figure 7.15** If you learn similar materials, each interferes with retrieval of the other.

from bringing in still more clutter, but it interferes with finding what you want. Ebbinghaus quickly forgot new lists because of interference from older lists.

If you learn several sets of related materials, they interfere with each other. The *old materials increase forgetting of new materials* by proactive interference (acting forward in time). The *new materials increase forgetting of old materials* by retroactive interference (acting backward). ▲ Figure 7.15 contrasts the two kinds of interference.

Interference is a major cause of forgetting. You forget where you parked your car today because of proactive interference from the previous times you parked your car. You forget last week's French vocabulary list because of retroactive interference from this week's list.

concept check

16. **Professor Tryhard learns the names of his students every semester. After several years, he learns them as quickly as ever but forgets them faster. Does he forget because of retroactive or proactive interference?**

17. **Remember the concept of spontaneous recovery from Chapter 6? Can you explain it in terms of proactive interference? (Hint: Original learning comes first and extinction comes second. What would happen if the first interfered with the second?)**

Answers

16. It is due to proactive interference—interference from memories learned earlier.

17. First, someone learns the response; the second learning is the extinction of the response. If the first learning actively interferes with the later extinction, spontaneous recovery will result.

A Controversy: "Recovered Memories" or "False Memories"?

Is it possible to recover forgotten memories? Suppose you tell a therapist about vague distress, and the therapist replies, "Symptoms like yours are common among people who were sexually abused in childhood. Do you think you were?" You reply, "no," but the therapist persists: "The fact that you don't remember doesn't mean that it didn't happen. Perhaps it was so painful that you repressed the memory." The therapist recommends hypnosis, repeated attempts to remember, or trying to imagine how it would have happened if it did. (This procedure reflects the assumption that reliving painful old memories is beneficial—an assumption for which there is little evidence and much reason to doubt.) A few sessions later, you say, "It's starting to come back. . . . I think I do remember. . . . " Most therapists would not use such aggressive techniques to recover old memories, but some do. *Reports of long-lost memories, prompted by clinical techniques,* are known as recovered memories.

When people claim to recover long-forgotten memories, has the therapist uncovered the truth, distorted the truth, or convinced someone to believe an imagined event? This issue was for many years one of the most heated debates in psychology.

Some reports are bizarre. In one case, two sisters accused their father of repeatedly raping them both vaginally and anally, bringing his friends over on Friday nights to rape them, and forcing them to participate in satanic rituals that included cannibalism and the slaughter of babies (Wright, 1994). The sisters had not remembered any of these events before repeated sessions with a therapist. In another case, 3- and 4-year-old children, after repeated urgings from a therapist, accused their Sunday school teacher of sexually abusing them with a curling iron, forcing them to drink blood and urine, hanging them upside down from a chandelier, dunking them in toilets, and killing an elephant and a giraffe during Sunday school class (Gardner, 1994). No one found any physical evidence to support the claims, such as scarred tissues or giraffe bones.

Even when claims of recovered memories are much less bizarre, their accuracy is doubtful. Researchers compared people who recovered a memory as a result of therapy with others who spontaneously remembered an episode of childhood sexual abuse that they hadn't thought about in years. For those who spontaneously reported a long-lost memory, investigators were usually able to find supporting evidence, such as other people who reported being abused by the same perpetrator. For the people who reported recovering a memory only as a result of therapy, investigators did not find supporting evidence in a single case (Geraerts et al., 2007).

When people have abusive experiences, are they likely to forget them for years? And can repeated suggestions get someone to recall an event that never happened?

Memory for Traumatic Events

Sigmund Freud, whom we consider more fully in Chapter 14, introduced the term **repression** as *the process of moving an unacceptable memory or impulse from the conscious mind to the unconscious mind*. Many clinicians now prefer the term **dissociation**, referring to *memory that one has stored but cannot retrieve* (Alpert, Brown, & Courtois, 1998). However, the idea is the similar, and researchers have found no clear evidence that either process occurs (Holmes, 1990).

Do people ever forget highly emotional events? One study examined 16 children who had witnessed the murder of one of their parents, about as traumatic an event as one could imagine. All had recurring nightmares and haunting thoughts of the experience, and none had forgotten (Malmquist, 1986). Other studies examined prisoners of war who had been severely mistreated (Merckelbach, Dekkers, Wessel, & Roefs, 2003), children who had been kidnapped or forced to participate in pornographic movies (Terr, 1988), and people with other horrible experiences. People either remembered the events, or forgot only about as much as one might expect for early childhood events. If repression doesn't occur under these circumstances, when does it?

Whether someone remembers a traumatic experience depends on the age at the time of the event, its severity, and the reaction of other family members. Several studies examined young adult women who had been victims of childhood sexual abuse, documented by either hospital records or criminal proceedings. In each study, those who were older at the time of the offense remembered it better than those who were younger. Memory was better among those who had more severe or repeated abuse and those who received more family support and encouragement (Alexander et al., 2005; Goodman et al., 2003; Williams, 1994). In these regards traumatic memories are similar to any other memories.

18. Based on material earlier in this chapter, why should we expect traumatic events to be remembered better than most other events?

Answer

18. Emotionally arousing memories are usually more memorable than other events. Any emotionally arousing event stimulates release of cortisol and epinephrine, which stimulate brain areas important for storing memories. Also, highly unusual events tend to be memorable.

Influence of Suggestion

For psychologists skeptical of claims that therapy recovers repressed memories, what is the alternative? Memory recall is a process of reconstruction. Perhaps repeated suggestions to recall a memory of childhood abuse (or anything else) can implant a **false memory** (or false report), *an inaccurate report that someone believes to be a memory* (Lindsay & Read, 1994; Loftus, 1993). Early research found that asking misleading questions about a videotape, such as "Did you see the children getting on the school bus?" caused many people falsely to report having seen a school bus (Loftus, 1975). Could an experimenter mislead people into reporting false memories about their own lives? Let's examine two experiments.

what's the evidence?

Suggestions and False Memories

First Study

Hypothesis In some cases, people who are told about a childhood event will come to believe it happened, even if in fact it did not.

Method Participants were told that the study concerned their childhood memories. Each participant was given paragraphs describing four events. Three of the events had actually happened. (The experimenters had contacted parents to get descriptions of childhood events.) A fourth event was a plausible but false story about getting lost. An example for one Vietnamese woman: "You, your Mom, Tien, and Tuan, all went to the Bremerton Kmart. You must have been 5 years old at the time. Your Mom gave each of you some money to get a blueberry ICEE. You ran ahead to get into the line first, and somehow lost your way in the store. Tien found you crying to an elderly Chinese woman. You three then went together to get an ICEE." After reading the four paragraphs, each participant was asked to write whatever additional details he or she could remember of the event. Participants were asked to try again a week later and then again after another week (Loftus, Feldman, & Dashiell, 1995).

Results Of 24 participants, 6 reported remembering the suggested false event, and some of them elaborated with additional details. The woman in the foregoing example said, "I vaguely remember walking around Kmart crying and looking for Tien and Tuan.

I thought I was lost forever. I went to the shoe department, because we always spent a lot of time there. I went to the handkerchief place because we were there last. I circled all over the store it seemed 10 times. I just remember walking around crying. I do not remember the Chinese woman, or the ICEE (but it would be raspberry ICEE if I was getting an ICEE) part. I don't even remember being found."

Interpretation A suggestion can sometimes provoke a memory report of an event that never happened. Granted, this suggestion influenced only a quarter of the people tested, and most of them reported only vague memories. Still, the researchers achieved the effect after just a single brief suggestion. In a similar study, 13 of 47 participants reported detailed false memories of getting lost or getting attacked by an animal or another child, and 18 more participants reported partial recollection (Porter, Birt, Yuille, & Lehman, 2000). After being told of getting sick after eating an egg in childhood, many people avoided eggs, and after being told of liking asparagus the first time they tried it, many increased their preference for asparagus (Bernstein & Loftus, 2009).

One objection is that perhaps these false memories were not entirely false. Maybe the young woman *was* lost at some point—if not in a Kmart at age 5, then somewhere else at some other age. In other studies, researchers suggested virtually impossible events. For example, college students read fake advertisements for Disneyland that depicted people meeting and shaking hands with Bugs Bunny, a Warner Brothers character who would never appear at Disneyland. About 30 percent of those who read this ad later reported that they too had met Bugs Bunny at Disneyland. Some reported touching his ears or tail (Loftus, 2003). In another study, British students who were asked to imagine certain experiences later reported that they remembered them, including "having a nurse remove a skin sample from my little finger"—a procedure that British physicians never use (Mazzoni & Memon, 2003). In short, suggestions can lead people to report memories of events that never happened.

Second Study

Some therapists ask their clients to examine childhood photographs to help evoke old memories. They are certainly right that photographs bring back memories. However, might old photographs also facilitate false memories?

Hypothesis A false suggestion about a childhood event will evoke more memory reports if people have examined photographs from that time period.

Method Researchers asked the parents of 45 college students to describe an event that happened while these students were in third or fourth grade and another that happened in fifth or sixth grade. Both were supposed to be events that the student might or might not remember rather than events the family had repeatedly discussed. The researchers also asked the parents to confirm that the following event—the one they planned to suggest—had *not* happened: In the first grade, the child took a "Slime" toy to school, and then she and another child slid it into the teacher's desk and received a mild punishment later. The researchers also asked the parents for copies of class photographs from first grade, third or fourth grade, and fifth or sixth grade.

After these preparations, they brought in the students and briefly described for each student the three events (two provided by the parents and the one false event). They asked the students to provide whatever additional information they remembered about each event. Half of them (randomly selected) were shown their class photographs and half were not. At the end of the session, they were asked to think about the first-grade event for the next week and try to remember more about it. Those in the photograph group took the photo with them. A week later, the students returned and again reported whatever they thought they remembered (Lindsay, Hagen, Read, Wade, & Garry, 2004).

Results Most students reported clear memories of the two real events. For the false event of first grade, ▲ Figure 7.16 shows the percentage of students who reported the event in the first and second sessions. Memories increased from the first to the second session, and students who saw the photographs reported more memories

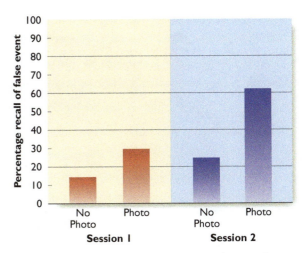

▲ **Figure 7.16** More students who saw a first-grade class photograph reported remembering the suggested (false) event. (From "True photographs and false memories, by D. S. Lindsay, L. Hagen, J. D. Read, K. A. Wada, and M. Garry, 2004. *Psychological Science* 15, pp. 149–154. Copyright 2004 Blackwell Publishing. Reprinted with permission.)

than those who did not see photographs. By the second session, almost two-thirds of the students who saw a class photograph reported some memory of the false event.

At the end of the study, the researchers explained that the first-grade event did not really happen. Many of the students expressed surprise, such as, "No way! I remember it! That is so weird!" (Lindsay et al., 2004, p. 153).

Interpretation Examining an old photograph increases suggestibility for false memories. Why? When you are trying to decide whether you remember something, you try to call up related thoughts and images. If you can recall extra details, it is probably a real memory. A photo makes it easier for you to recall details and think the event is real (Henkel, 2011; Strange, Garry, Bernstein, & Lindsay, 2011). If you are trying to remember when you and a friend pulled a prank on the teacher, the visual image makes the memory more vivid and more convincing.

In related studies, researchers manipulated photos by computers, showing childhood pictures of people having tea with Prince Charles of England or riding with their families in a hot-air balloon—false events in each case. Many of the participants claimed to remember the events and provided additional details (Strange, Sutherland, & Garry, 2004; Wade, Garry, Read, & Lindsay, 2002). People who viewed doctored photos of historical events misremembered the events to match the photos (Sacchi, Agnoli, & Loftus, 2007; ▼ Figure 7.17.) The effect of photos relates to source amnesia, as described earlier. Source amnesia occurs if you remember something but don't remember where you learned it. In the case of photos, you see something in the photo and think you remember it from an experience long ago.

▲ **Figure 7.17** If you saw a photo of this train wreck and later saw an altered photo with people added to it, you might report remembering that you had seen the people at first also.

Areas of Agreement and Disagreement

What was once an extremely bitter dispute between clinical psychologists and psychological researchers has calmed somewhat, but disagreements remain. Everyone agrees it is possible to have a childhood experience, not think about it for years, and remember it later (McNally & Geraerts, 2009). The question is how often (if ever) therapeutic techniques such as suggestion and hypnosis increase the accurate recall of old memories, and how often they implant false memories. Over the years, most psychotherapists have become less confident that therapy can recover old memories, and more accepting of the idea that suggestions can implant false memories, but on average the therapists are more likely to believe in repression than researchers are, and more likely to believe they can restore repressed memories (Patihis, Ho, Tingen, Lilienfeld, & Loftus, 2014). Curiously, members of the general public—including judges, jurors, and police officers—are if anything even more likely than psychotherapists to believe in repression and the possibility of recovered memories (Benton, Ross, Bradshaw, Thomas, & Bradshaw, 2006; Patihis et al., 2014). Researchers do not insist on rejecting every report of a recovered memory, but they strongly recommend treating those reports as uncertain until and unless independent evidence supports the report.

concept check

19. In what way is hindsight bias similar to an implanted "false memory"?

Answer

19. In a case of hindsight bias, something that you learn later operates like a suggestion, so that when you try to remember what you previously thought, you are influenced by that suggestion and change your reported memory to fit it.

Amnesia

Imagine you defied the advice given to computer owners and passed your computer through a powerful magnetic field. Suppose that instead of erasing all the memories you erased only the text files and not the graphics files. Or suppose the old memories were intact but you could no longer store new ones. From the damage, you would gain hints about how your computer's memory works.

The same is true of human memory. Various kinds of brain damage impair one kind of memory but not another, helping us infer how memory is organized.

Amnesia after Damage to the Hippocampus

Amnesia is a *loss of memory*. Even in the most severe cases of amnesia, people don't forget everything they ever learned. They don't forget how to walk, talk, or eat. (If they did, we would call it *dementia*, not amnesia.) In many cases they remember most of their factual knowledge. What they most often forget is their personal experiences. Amnesia results from many kinds of brain damage, including damage to the hippocampus.

In 1953 Henry Molaison, known in the research literature by his initials H. M., was suffering from many small daily epileptic seizures and about one major seizure per week. He did not respond to any antiepileptic drugs, and in desperation, surgeons removed most of his **hippocampus**, *a large forebrain structure in the interior of the temporal lobe* (see ▼ Figure 7.18), based on two previous cases in which hippocampal damage reduced the frequency of epileptic seizures. At the time, researchers knew little about what to expect after damage to the hippocampus. Since then, animal research has established that the hippocampus is important for encoding and retrieving memories.

The surgery greatly decreased the frequency and severity of H. M.'s seizures. His personality remained the same, except that he became more passive (Eichenbaum, 2002). His IQ score increased slightly, presumably because he had fewer epileptic seizures. However, he suffered severe memory problems (Corkin, 1984; Milner, 1959). H. M. suffered massive **anterograde** (ANT-eh-ro-grade) **amnesia**, *inability to store new long-term memories.* For years after the operation, he cited the year as 1953 and his own age as 27. Later, he took wild guesses (Corkin, 1984). He would read the same issue of a magazine repeatedly without recognizing it. He could not remember where he lived. He also suffered partial **retrograde amnesia**, *loss of memory for events that occurred shortly before the brain damage* (see ▼ Figure 7.19). Initial reports said that H. M.'s retrograde amnesia was limited to the last couple of years before the surgery. Later reports said it extended much further, especially for episodic (autobiographical) memories. Another person with amnesia following diffuse brain damage suffered a complete loss of his episodic memory. When he looks at old family photos, he names the people, but he cannot describe the event in the photo or any other event including those people (Rosenbaum et al., 2005).

H. M. had normal short-term memory and working memory, as do most other patients with amnesia (Shrager, Levy, Hopkins, & Squire, 2008). If someone told him to remember a number, he could recall it minutes later, if nothing distracted him. However, after any distraction he forgot the number, and forgot that he had tried to remember a number. He often told the same person the same story several times within a few minutes, forgetting that he had told it before (Eichenbaum, 2002).

Like Rip van Winkle, the story character who slept for 20 years and awakened to a vastly changed world, H. M. became more and more out of date with each passing year (Gabrieli, Cohen, & Corkin, 1988; Smith, 1988). He did not recognize people who became famous after the mid-1950s, although when

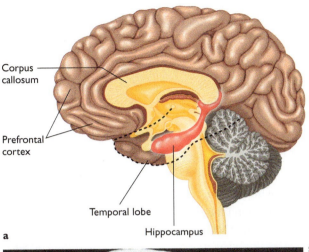

Corpus
callosum

Prefrontal
cortex

Temporal lobe

Hippocampus

a

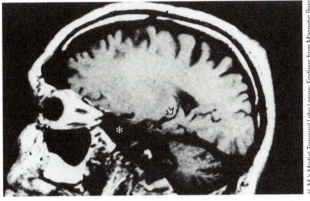

H. M.'s Medial Temporal Lobe Lesion: Findings from Magnetic Resonance Imaging, The Journal of Neuroscience, Volume 17, Number 10, 1997 pp. 3964-3979 Copyright ©1997 Society for Neuroscience

b

▲ **Figure 7.18** (a) The hippocampus is a large subcortical brain structure. (b) The photo shows an MRI scan of H. M.'s brain. The asterisk indicates the area from which the hippocampus is missing. The arrow indicates a portion of the hippocampus that is preserved. (Photo courtesy of Suzanne Corkin and David Amaral)

given a famous person's name, he sometimes provided a bit of correct information (O'Kane, Kensinger, & Corkin, 2004). He did not understand the words and phrases that entered the English language after his surgery, such as *Jacuzzi* and *granola* (Corkin, 2002). He guessed that *soul food* meant "forgiveness" and that a *closet queen* might be "a moth" (Gabrieli, Cohen, & Corkin, 1988).

In spite of H. M.'s massive memory difficulties, he could still acquire and retain new skills. Recall the distinction between declarative (factual) memory and procedural memory (skills and habits). H. M. learned to read material written in mirror fashion (Cohen & Squire, 1980), such as shown below. However, he did not remember having learned this or any other new skill and always expressed surprise at his success.

He could read sentences written backwards, like this. (shown mirror-reversed)

Difficulty retrieving
old memories =
Retrograde amnesia

**Time of
damage**

Difficulty learning new
information =
Anterograde amnesia

▲ **Figure 7.19** Brain damage induces retrograde amnesia (loss of old memories) and anterograde amnesia (difficulty storing new memories).

The results for H. M. led researchers to study both people and laboratory animals with similar damage. The following points have emerged:

- Storing declarative memory requires the hippocampus. Procedural memories depend on a different brain area, the basal ganglia.
- The hippocampus is especially important for episodic memories—memories of specific events in one's life. Episodic memories form all at once, unlike procedural memories that develop gradually.
- The hippocampus is more important for explicit memory than for implicit memory and more important for difficult tasks than for easy tasks (Reed & Squire, 1999; Ryan, Althoff, Whitlow, & Cohen, 2000).
- The hippocampus is especially important for spatial memories—remembering where something is or how to get from one place to another (Jacobs et al., 2013; Miller et al., 2013).
- Patients with hippocampal damage have trouble imagining the future, just as they have trouble recalling the past. When you imagine a future event, such as a trip to the beach or a visit to a museum, you rearrange and modify your recollections of similar events in the past. If you cannot remember your past, you cannot put much detail into your imagined future (Hassabis, Kumaran, Vann, & Maguire, 2007). A patient with amnesia truly lives in the present moment, without a past or a future.

Exactly what is the role of the hippocampus in memory? According to one influential theory, the hippocampus is critical for remembering the details and context of a memory. It connects to many areas of the cerebral cortex and synchronizes their activity, enabling them to combine their information in recalling an event (Watrous, Tandon, Conner, Pieters, & Ekstrom, 2013). When you recall something you did yesterday, your memory is rich in details, including who, what, where, and when. Those details depend on the hippocampus. As time passes, your memory consolidates, but as it consolidates, it changes. You remember the "gist" of what happened but fewer details (Winocur, Moscovitch, & Sekeres, 2007).

concept
check

20. Which kinds of memory were most impaired in H. M.? Which kinds were least impaired?

Answer

20. H. M. was greatly impaired at forming new declarative memories. His short-term memory was intact, as was his ability to form new procedural memories. His recall of old semantic memories was largely intact. His recall of old episodic memories from before the damage was greatly impaired but not entirely lost.

Amnesia after Damage to the Prefrontal Cortex

Damage to the prefrontal cortex also produces amnesia (see Figure 7.18). Because the prefrontal cortex receives extensive input from the hippocampus, the symptoms of prefrontal cortex damage overlap those of hippocampal damage. However, some special deficits also arise.

Prefrontal cortex damage can be the result of a stroke, head trauma, or **Korsakoff's syndrome**, *a condition caused by a prolonged deficiency of vitamin B₁ (thiamine), usually as a result of chronic alcoholism.* This deficiency leads to widespread loss or shrinkage of neurons, especially in the prefrontal cortex. Patients suffer apathy, confusion, and amnesia (Squire, Haist, & Shimamura, 1989). If given a list of words to remember, they forget those at the beginning of the list before they reach the end and they soon forget those at the end also (Stuss et al., 1994).

Patients with prefrontal cortex damage answer many questions with **confabulations**, *which are attempts to fill in the gaps in their memory.* Most often they answer a question about what's happening today by describing something from their past (Borsutzky, Fujiwara, Brand, & Markowitsch, 2008; Schnider, 2003). For example, an aged hospitalized woman might insist that she had to go home to feed her baby. Sometimes patients act out their confabulations, trying to leave the hospital to go home or go to work (Nahum, Bouzerda-Wahlen, Guggisberg, Ptak, & Schnider, 2012). Confabulations are not exactly attempts to hide an inability to answer a question, as Korsakoff's patients almost never confabulate on a question such as "Where is Premola?" or "Who is Princess Lolita?" (Schnider, 2003). That is, people who never knew the answer freely admit not knowing. The following interview is a typical example (Moscovitch, 1989, pp. 135–136). Note the mixture of correct information, confabulations that were correct at some time in the past, and imaginative attempts to explain the discrepancies between one answer and another:

Psychologist: How old are you?

Patient: I'm 40, 42, pardon me, 62.

Psychologist: Are you married or single?

Patient: Married.

Psychologist: How long have you been married?

Patient: About 4 months.

Psychologist: What's your wife's name?

Patient: Martha.

Psychologist: How many children do you have?

Patient: Four. (He laughs.) Not bad for 4 months.

Psychologist: How old are your children?

Patient: The eldest is 32; his name is Bob. And the youngest is 22; his name is Joe.

Psychologist: How did you get these children in 4 months?

Patient: They're adopted.

Psychologist: Who adopted them?

Patient: Martha and I.

Psychologist: Immediately after you got married you wanted to adopt these older children?

Patient: Before we were married we adopted one of them, two of them. The eldest girl Brenda and Bob, and Joe and Dina since we were married.

Psychologist: Does it all sound a little strange to you, what you are saying?

Patient: I think it is a little strange.

Psychologist: I think when I looked at your record it said that you've been married for over 30 years. Does that sound more reasonable to you if I told you that?

Patient: No.

Psychologist: Do you really believe that you have been married for 4 months?

Patient: Yes.

Patients with prefrontal cortex damage confidently defend their confabulations and often maintain the same confabulation from one time to the next. Actually, normal people sometimes show the same tendency. College students listened to complicated 2-minute descriptions of topics they knew little about and then answered detailed questions. Once a week for the next 4 weeks, they heard the same description and answered the same questions. Most people repeated the same incorrect guesses from one week to the next (Fritz, Morris, Bjork, Gelman, & Wickens, 2000).

Why do people with prefrontal damage confabulate so much more than the rest of us? According to Morris Moscovitch (1992), the prefrontal cortex is necessary for *working with memory,* the strategies we use to reconstruct memories that we cannot immediately recall. If you are asked what is the farthest north that you have ever traveled or how many salads you ate last week, you reason out your answer. People with prefrontal cortex damage have difficulty making reasonable inferences.

Despite their impoverished memory in other regards, people with brain damage perform well on most tests of implicit memory. For example, after hearing a list of words, a patient may not be able to say any of the words on the list and may not even remember that there was a list. However, when given a set of three-letter stems such as CON—, the patient completes them to make words that were on the list (Hamann & Squire, 1997).

Another example: After patients repeatedly practiced playing the video game *Tetris,* they said they did not remember playing the game before, although they did improve from one session to the next. When they closed their eyes to go to sleep at night, they said they saw little images of blocks and wondered what they were (Stickgold, Malia, Maguire, Roddenberry, & O'Connor, 2000).

One important conclusion emerges from all the studies of brain damage and amnesia: We have several different types of memory. It is possible to impair one type without equally damaging another.

concept check

21. **Although confabulation is a kind of false memory, how does it differ from the suggested false memories discussed earlier in this module?**

Answer

21. Most confabulated statements were true at one time, though not now. They seldom make up new information.

Memory Impairments in Alzheimer's Disease

A more common disorder is Alzheimer's (AHLTZ-hime-ers) disease, *a condition occurring mostly in old age, characterized by increasingly severe memory loss, confusion, depression, disordered thinking, and impaired attention.* Although several genes have been linked to an onset of Alzheimer's disease before age 60, most cases of the late-onset form (which is far more common) are not linked with any genetic mutation. A more likely explanation lies with epigenetics—that is, changes in the expression of the genes (De Jager et al., 2014; Lunnon et al., 2014). Environmental factors are undoubtedly important, though not well understood. The Yoruba people of Nigeria almost never get Alzheimer's disease, even if they have the genes that increase the risk for Americans to get the disease (Hendrie, 2001). Which aspect of their culture shields them from Alzheimer's is uncertain, although diet is a possibility.

Alzheimer's disease is marked by accumulation of harmful proteins in the brain and deterioration of brain cells, impairing arousal and attention. The memory problems include both anterograde and retrograde amnesia. Performance varies from one time to another, depending on alertness (Palop, Chin, & Mucke, 2006). Sometimes a cup of coffee or a brisk walk helps by increasing blood flow.

Because the areas of damage include the hippocampus and the prefrontal cortex, memory deficits of people with Alzheimer's disease overlap those of H. M. and patients with Korsakoff's syndrome. Their mixture of memory problems is hardly surprising, given the overall decrease of arousal and attention. Weak arousal and impaired attention impair almost any aspect of memory. However, like H. M., as a rule they can learn new skills, such as how to use a cell phone (Lekeu, Wojtasik, Van der Linden, & Salmon, 2002).

concept check

22. **What kinds of memory are impaired in patients with Alzheimer's disease?**

Answer

22. Patients with Alzheimer's disease have weaknesses in almost all types of memory, although they can learn new skills (procedural memory).

Early Childhood Amnesia

Let's end with a type of amnesia we all experience. How much do you remember from when you were 6 years old? How about age 4? Age 2? Most adults report at most a few fragmentary memories of early childhood (Bauer, Wenner, & Kroupina, 2002; Nelson & Fivush, 2004). The *scarcity of early episodic memories* is known as early childhood amnesia or infantile amnesia.

Sigmund Freud called attention to this phenomenon by his provocative suggestion that we *repress* (that is, ban from consciousness) all memories from early childhood because so many of them were sexual in nature and highly disturbing. Not many psychologists today take that theory seriously. Observers of young children note occasional signs of sexual interest, but hardly enough to make that whole era of life seem traumatic.

Later psychologists proposed several theories for why young children fail to form long-term memories. One proposal is that long-term episodic memories require a "sense of self" that develops between ages 3 and 4 (Howe & Courage, 1993). Another idea is that the hippocampus, known to be important for episodic memory, is slow to mature, so memories from the first few years are not stored well (Moscovitch, 1985). However, these proposals are answering the wrong question, trying to explain why young children don't form long-term memories. Young children *do* form long-term memories. Freud's explanation may seem preposterous, but he was asking the right question: Why do we *forget* the memories we formed in early childhood?

Three- and four-year-olds clearly remember their last birthday party, Christmas or other celebrations, and other events from months ago. One extremely articulate 2-year-old reported details about a 3-day hospitalization at age 5 months, although his parents and grandparents had not talked about the experience since then (Solter, 2008). However, a year later he had forgotten about it. Researchers asked 4- to 13-year-old children to report their earliest memories. Some of the youngest children recalled events from ages 2 and 3. However, as children grew older, they forgot their earliest memories. ▼ Figure 7.20 shows how as children grow older, they become less likely to recall events from their earliest years (Peterson, Warren, & Short, 2011). In another study, 4- and 6-year-old children described events from months ago. A year later, they had forgotten most of those events (Morris, Baker-Ward, & Bauer, 2010).

Infantile amnesia occurs not only in humans, but in rats, mice, and many other species also. That is, infant animals learn much, but unless they continue to practice what they learn, they forget within a couple of days. Studies in several rodent species offer an explanation for infantile amnesia: Early in life, the hippocampus rapidly forms new neurons that facilitate new learning. However, as an infant rodent (or human) continues forming new neurons and replacing many of the old ones with new ones, the result is a loss of many older memories. It is possible to increase the formation of new neurons in older animals by physical exercise. The result is improved learning, but also more rapid forgetting.

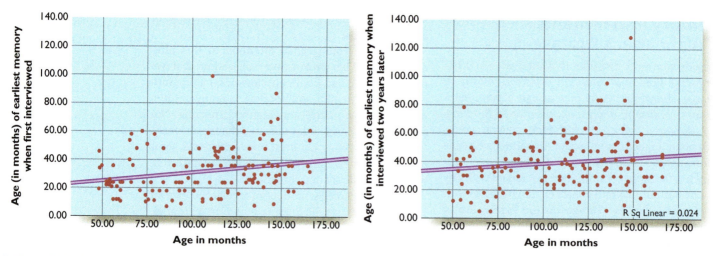

▲ **Figure 7.20** Children from ages 4 to 14 reported their oldest episodic memory. In general, the older children's memories went less far back into early childhood. From Peterson, Warren, & Short, 2011. Used by permission.

Chemical procedures that decrease formation of new neurons can impair learning in young animals, but it also decreases their forgetting. Guinea pigs are born more mature than most other animals, capable of walking around and eating solid food on the day of birth. They have relatively low rates of neuron formation in the hippocampus, and they do not show the tendency to forget their early memories. Overall, it appears that we have an explanation for childhood/infantile amnesia: Rapid formation of new hippocampal neurons early in life not only promotes rapid learning but also promotes rapid forgetting (Akers et al., 2014).

concept check

23. **What evidence indicates that infant amnesia is not due to a failure to establish long-term memories?**
24. **Rats and other species also show forgetting of their earliest memories. How does that observation support or contradict several possible theories of infantile amnesia?**

Answers

23. Young children remember events that happened months or even years ago. However, over time they lose those memories.
24. It seems doubtful to suppose that rats a few months old gain a "sense of self" that they lacked earlier. It also seems doubtful to suppose that they have traumatic sexual fantasies that cause them to repress memories of their early experiences. However, an explanation in terms of maturation of the nervous system makes sense.

---

in closing | module 7.3

Memory Loss and Distortion

When we try to recall something from long ago, we often find that the details have faded and we need to infer or reconstruct much of the information. The fact that we are built this way is not really a failing. Computers store every detail that we give them indefinitely, but our brains don't need to. The older some experience is, the less likely we are to need all the details. If we do need the details, we can usually reason them out well enough for most purposes.

Summary

- *Interference.* When someone learns several similar sets of material, the earlier ones interfere with retrieval of later ones by proactive interference. The later ones interfere with earlier ones by retroactive interference. Interference is a major cause of forgetting. (page 238)
- *The "recovered memory" versus "false memory" debate.* Some therapists have used hypnosis or suggestions to try to help people remember painful experiences. Many researchers doubt the accuracy of those recovered memories. Suggestions can induce people to distort memories or report events that did not happen. (page 239)
- *Amnesia after damage to the hippocampus.* H. M. and other patients with damage to the hippocampus have great difficulty storing new long-term declarative memories, especially episodic memories, although they form normal short-term, procedural, and implicit memories. (page 242)

- *Role of the hippocampus.* The hippocampus serves many functions in memory. One is to bind together all the details and context of an event. In the absence of a healthy hippocampus or after the information in the hippocampus weakens, one is left with only the "gist" of the event. (page 243)
- *Damage to the prefrontal cortex.* Patients with damage to the prefrontal cortex give confident wrong answers, known as confabulations. Most confabulations were correct information earlier in the person's life. (page 244)
- *Alzheimer's disease.* People with Alzheimer's disease, a condition that occurs mostly after age 60 to 65, have a variety of memory problems, although procedural memory is more intact than explicit, declarative memory. Their problems stem largely from impairments of arousal and attention. (page 245)
- *Infant amnesia.* Most people remember little from early childhood, even though preschoolers have clear recollections of experiences that happened months or even years ago. The apparent explanation is that infants rapidly form new neurons in the hippocampus, facilitating rapid learning. However, the turnover of neurons means that many old ones are replaced, leading to forgetting. (page 245)

Key Terms

Alzheimer's disease (page 245)

amnesia (page 242)

anterograde amnesia (page 242)

confabulations (page 244)

dissociation (page 240)

early childhood amnesia or infantile amnesia (page 245)

false memory (page 240)

hippocampus (page 242)

Korsakoff's syndrome (page 244)

proactive interference (page 239)

recovered memory (page 239)

repression (page 240)

retroactive interference (page 239)

retrograde amnesia (page 242)

Review Questions

1. Last week you read a magazine article and discussed it. Since then you have read several additional articles. When you try to discuss the article you read last week, you find that you cannot remember it clearly. Why?
   (a) Proactive interference
   (b) Retroactive interference

2. One explanation of the primacy effect is that the first item on a list is not blocked by _____ interference. One explanation of the recency effect is that the last item on the list is not blocked by _____ interference.
   (a) proactive . . . proactive
   (b) proactive . . . retroactive
   (c) retroactive . . . proactive
   (d) retroactive . . . retroactive

3. In which of these ways does a memory recovered by therapy differ, on average, from traumatic memories that people recover spontaneously?
   (a) Recovered memories include much more detail.
   (b) Recovered memories are more likely to emerge suddenly.
   (c) Recovered memories are seldom supported by evidence.
   (d) Recovered memories generally pertain to abuse by strangers.

4. Based on studies of children known to have experienced highly traumatic experiences, what are the implications for the concept of repression?
   (a) Repression is a common event.
   (b) Only highly traumatic experiences trigger repression.
   (c) If repression occurs at all, it occurs under rare and unknown circumstances.

5. If someone is trying to remember an event that may have happened long ago, what is the probable consequence of showing a photograph from that period of time?
   (a) The person becomes more likely to recall the possible event accurately and in detail.
   (b) The person becomes more susceptible to suggestion of something that didn't happen.
   (c) The person becomes more likely to deny that any such event occurred.

6. Which kind of memory was most impaired in patient H. M.?
   (a) Short-term memory
   (b) Declarative memory, especially episodic memory
   (c) Procedural memory
   (d) Memory for semantic facts learned long before his operation

7. Which of the following is most characteristic of people with Korsakoff's syndrome?
   (a) Retrograde amnesia without anterograde amnesia
   (b) Loss of implicit memory
   (c) Confabulations
   (d) Inability to recognize faces

8. Most adults remember very few events from early childhood. Studies on mice support which explanation for this infantile amnesia?
   (a) In infants, the hippocampus is not yet mature enough to form long-term memories.
   (b) Infants do not yet have mature sense organs.
   (c) Infants have not yet formed a sense of self.
   (d) Infants form many new neurons that not only facilitate new learning but also forgetting.

Answers: 1b, 2b, 3c, 4c, 5b, 6b, 7c, 8d.

8 Cognition and Language

©Nolte Lourens/Shutterstock.com

Owen Franken/Corbis

Cognitive psychology studies how people think and what they know.

onsider the statement, "This sentence is false." Is the statement itself true or false? Declaring the statement true agrees with its own assessment that it is false. But declaring it false would make its assessment correct. A sentence about itself, called a *self-referential* sentence, can be confusing. It can be true (like this one!). It can be false ("Anyone who reads this sentence will be transported suddenly to the planet Neptune"), untestable ("Whenever no one is reading this sentence, it changes its font"), or amusing ("This sentence no verb").

In this chapter, you will be asked to think about thinking. Doing so is self-referential, and if you try to "think about what you are thinking now," you can go into a confusing loop like the one in "This sentence is false." Thus, psychological researchers focus as much as possible on results obtained from carefully controlled experiments, not just on what people say that they think about their thought processes.

module 8.1

Attention and Categorization

After studying this module, you should be able to:

- Distinguish between attentive and preattentive processes.
- Give examples of phenomena related to attention, such as change blindness.
- Discuss what is known about attention deficit disorder.
- Discuss the importance of categorization and how categorization affects thinking.

Cognition means *thinking and using knowledge.* Cognitive psychologists also deal with how people organize their thoughts into language. Cognition begins with attending to something and categorizing what it is. How can researchers learn about cognitive processes? Since about 1970, psychologists have developed many ways to infer processes they cannot observe, generally by measuring the speed and accuracy of responses.

Research in Cognitive Psychology

You might think cognitive psychology should be simple. "If you want to find out what people think or know, why not ask them?" Sometimes, psychologists do ask, but people don't always know their own thought processes. Consider

Fig 1. From Johansson, Hall, Sikstroöm, & Olsson, 2005. Science, 310, 116-119. Used by permission of the author

▲ **Figure 8.1** The participant identified the face considered more attractive. Then the experimenter switched cards and asked why this face seemed more attractive. (From Johansson, Hall, Sikström, & Olsson, 2005)

this experiment: The experimenter presents two cards at a time, each showing a female face, and asks which one looks more attractive. Sometimes the experimenter also asks for an explanation. Occasionally, the experimenter surreptitiously switches cards, so he asks why someone chose a particular face, when in fact it was the face *not* chosen, as shown in ▼ Figure 8.1. People usually don't notice the switch, and on average, their explanations are as long, as specific, and as confident for the switched cards as for the originally chosen cards (Johansson, Hall, Sikström, & Olsson, 2005). Psychologists call this phenomenon choice blindness because people act as if they don't know what they had chosen. Clearly, when people "explain" a choice they hadn't actually made, they must be stating reasons that they made up afterward. Therefore, we suspect that even on the trials without a switch, people often chose without knowing a reason and then made up a reasonable-sounding explanation afterward.

If we cannot always find out people's thought processes just by asking, how can we discover them? Let's consider one of the first experiments that showed how to measure a mental process.

what's the evidence?

Mental Imagery

If you look at something and try to describe how it would look from a different angle, you would probably say you imagined rotating the object. Roger Shepard and Jacqueline Metzler (1971) reasoned that if people use mental images, then the time it takes to rotate a mental image should be similar to the time needed to rotate a real object.

Hypothesis When people have to rotate a mental image to answer a question, the farther they have to rotate it, the longer it will take to answer the question.

Method Participants examined pairs of drawings of three-dimensional objects, like those in ▼ Figure 8.2, and indicated whether it would be possible to rotate one object to match the other. (Try to answer this question yourself before reading further.)

People pulled one lever to indicate *same* and another lever to indicate *different.* When

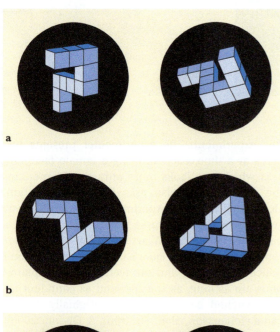

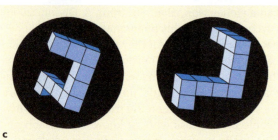

▲ **Figure 8.2** Examples of pairs of drawings used in an experiment by Shepard and Metzler (1971). Do the drawings for each pair represent the same object being rotated, or are they different objects? (See answer A on page 261.) (From "Mental rotation of three-dimensional objects" by R. N. Shepard and J. N. Metzler, 1971. *Science,* 171, pp. 701–703. Copyright 1971. Reprinted with permission from AAAS.)

the correct answer was *same*, someone might determine that answer by rotating a mental image of the first picture until it matched the second. If so, the delay should depend on how far the image had to be rotated.

Results Participants answered nearly all items correctly. As predicted, their reaction time when they responded *same* depended on the angular difference in orientation between the two views, as ▲ **Figure 8.3** shows. For every additional 20 degrees of rotation, the time to respond increased by a constant amount. That is, people reacted as if they were watching an object rotate at a constant speed.

Interpretation Viewing a mental image is partly like vision. In this case, common sense appears to be correct. However, the main point is that researchers can infer thought processes from people's delay in answering a question. Much research in cognitive psychology leads to inferences from the timing of responses.

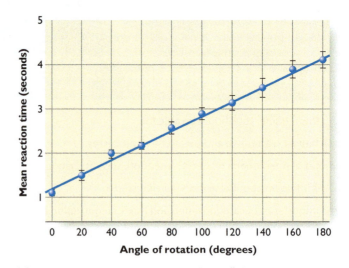

▲ **Figure 8.3** Mean times for correctly saying "same" depending on the required degree of rotation. (From "Mental rotation of three-dimensional objects" by R. N. Shepard and J. N. Metzler, 1971. *Science,* 171, pp. 701–703. Copyright 1971. Reprinted with permission from AAAS.)

Attention

You are constantly bombarded with more sights, sounds, smells, and other stimuli than you can process. **Attention** is *the tendency to respond to and remember some stimuli more than others.*

Sometimes, something such as a loud noise or flashing light suddenly grabs your attention. Psychologists call this a **bottom-up process** because the *peripheral stimuli control it*. Magicians use this tendency. A magician pulls a rabbit or a dove out of a hat, and the surprised viewers automatically watch the rabbit hop away or the dove fly away. During the brief time that their attention is occupied, the magician sets up the next trick, unnoticed (Macknik et al., 2008).

In contrast to a bottom-up process, you can *deliberately decide to shift your attention* in a **top-down process**. To illustrate, fixate your eyes on the x in the center and then, without moving your eyes, read the letters in the circle around it clockwise:

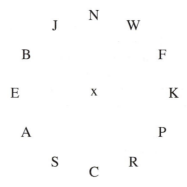

As you see, it is possible to control your attention without moving your eyes. When you increase your attention to something in your visual field, the part of your visual cortex sensitive to that area becomes more active and receives more blood flow (Müller, Malinowski, Gruber, & Hillyard, 2003). If you focus on a word, such as THIS, and attend to the letters, you increase activity in the language areas of the brain, but if you attend to the color, you shift activity to the color-detecting areas (Polk, Drake, Jonides, Smith, & Smith, 2008).

Let's go back to bottom-up processes, in which a stimulus automatically grabs your attention. Hearing your name or seeing your photograph is almost sure to attract your attention (Brédart, Delchambre, & Laureys, 2006; Shapiro, Caldwell, & Sorensen, 1997). An angry face in a crowd is easy to spot, unless everyone in the crowd is angry (Schmidt-Duffy, 2011). If you glance at a written page, emotionally charged words get your attention, such as those referring to moral or immoral behavior (Gantman & Van Bavel, 2014). A moving object in an otherwise stationary scene grabs attention, especially if it is moving irregularly, like a meandering animal, or moving directly toward you, posing possible threat (Lin, Franconeri, & Enns, 2008; Pratt, Radulescu, Guo, & Abrams, 2010).

Your attention flows to anything unusual. I once watched a costume contest in which people were told to dress so distinctively that their friends could find them quickly in a crowd. The winner was a young man who came onto the stage naked. Although he certainly earned the prize, the contest had a problem: The most distinctive clothing (or lack of it) depends on what everyone else is wearing. A naked man is easy to spot in most places, but at a nudist beach, you would more quickly notice a man in a coat and tie. What is unusual depends on the context.

To illustrate how an unusual object draws attention, find the one whooping crane in ▲ Figure 8.4 within the flock of sandhill cranes. That was easy, wasn't it? When anything differs drastically from items around it in size, shape, color, or movement, we find it by a preattentive process, meaning that it *stands out immediately*. You would find that whooping crane just as fast in a larger flock or smaller flock.

Contrast that task with ▼ Figure 8.5. Here, all the birds are marbled godwits. Your task is to find the one that faces to the right. Here, you have to check each bird separately. The more birds present, the longer you will probably need to find the unusual one. (You might find it quickly if you luckily start your search in the correct corner of the photograph.) You had to rely on an attentive process—*one that requires searching through the items in series* (Enns & Rensink, 1990; Treisman & Souther, 1985). The *Where's Waldo* books are an excellent example of a task requiring an attentive process.

The distinction between attentive and preattentive processes has practical applications. Imagine yourself as a human factors psychologist designing a machine with many gauges. Suppose that when the machine is running well, the first gauge should read about 70, the second 40, the third 30, and the fourth 10. If you arrange the gauges as in the top row of ▼ Figure 8.6, then people must check each gauge separately to find anything dangerous. In the bottom row, the gauges are arranged so that all the safe ranges are on the right. Now someone glances at the display and quickly (preattentively) notices anything out of position.

▲ **Figure 8.4** Demonstration of preattentive processes: You find the one whooping crane immediately, regardless of how many sandhill cranes are present.

The Attention Bottleneck

Much evidence indicates that attention is limited, as if various items were trying to get through a bottleneck that permits only a little to pass through at a time. If two or three objects flash briefly on a screen, you can identify their colors. If six objects flash on a screen, you still know the colors of only two or three (Zhang & Luck, 2008). You can more effectively attend to a couple of items at the same time if they are not similar to each other, such as a face and a picture of a lake. The apparent reason is that two similar items, such as two faces or two natural scenes, activate overlapping populations of neurons in the brain, and therefore interfere with

▲ **Figure 8.5** Demonstration of attentive processes: Find the marbled godwit that is facing to the right. In this case, you need to check the birds one at a time.

concept check

1. What is the relationship between top-down versus bottom-up processes, and attentive versus preattentive processes?

Answer

1. Bottom-up processes are preattentive. Top-down processes are attentive.

▲ **Figure 8.6** Each gauge measures something a machine does. The green area of the dial is the safe zone. In the top row, an operator must check gauges one at a time. In the bottom row, all the safe ranges are in the same place, and an unsafe reading stands out.

Kunar, Carter, Cohen, & Horowitz, 2008). An exception to this rule arises if the conversation is a heated argument with a romantic partner. A heated argument while driving is a serious distraction under any conditions, but even worse if the driver and partner are side by side. The driver tends to look at the partner, gesture, and therefore decrease attention to the driving (Lansdown & Stephens, 2013).

What if a passenger in the car is talking on a cell phone to someone else? In that case, the driver hears a "half-alogue," half of a conversation, which is more distracting than a full conversation (Emberson, Lupyan, Goldstein, & Spivey, 2010). A half-conversation has unpredictable starts and stops. Also, a nonparticipant who overhears it tends to fill in the blanks with imagined content, and doing so takes mental effort.

each other (Cohen, Konkle, Rhee, Nakayama, & Alvarez, 2014). To test your own attention bottleneck and explore related topics, visit this website: dualtask.org.

Imagine yourself in the control room of the Three Mile Island nuclear power plant, the site of a nearly disastrous accident in 1979. ▶ Figure 8.7 shows a small portion of the room as it appeared then, with an enormous number of knobs and gauges. (Since then, the controls have been redesigned to simplify the task.) A poorly designed control system overwhelms someone's ability to pay attention. Let's consider examples of the limits of human attention.

Conflict in Attention

Can you do two things at once? You can easily when two activities are highly compatible, such as walking and chewing gum (Hemond, Brown, & Robertson, 2010). However, people who try to "multitask," doing two or more unrelated tasks at once, are often more impaired than they realize.

Even when you are doing only one task, your attention level varies. While "your mind wanders," you are thinking about something unrelated to the task, and your ability to process the relevant information decreases (Barron, Riley, Greer, & Smallwood, 2011). Mind wandering interferes especially with performance on difficult tasks (Cohen & Maunsell, 2011).

Many years ago when automobile radios were introduced, people worried that listening to the radio would distract drivers and cause accidents. We no longer worry about radio, but we do worry about drivers using cell phones. A cell phone conversation is generally more distracting than a conversation with a passenger in the car, because most passengers pause a conversation when driving conditions are difficult (Drews, Pasupathi, & Strayer, 2008;

GPU Nuclear Corp

▲ **Figure 8.7** The Three Mile Island TMI-2 nuclear power plant had a confusing control system, a small portion of which is shown here. Some of the important gauges were not easily visible, some were poorly labeled, and many alarm signals had ambiguous meanings. After the accident in 1979, the system was redesigned.

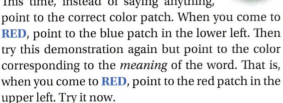

▲ **Figure 8.8** Read (left to right) the color of the ink in each part. Try to ignore the words themselves.

The Stroop Effect

In ▲ Figure 8.8, examine the blocks of color at the top of the figure. Scanning from left to right, name each color as fast as you can. Then examine the nonsense syllables in the center of the figure. Again, say the color of each one as fast as possible. Then turn to the real words at the bottom. Instead of reading them, quickly state each one's color.

Most people read the colors quickly for the first two parts, but they slow down greatly for the colored words (which happen to be the names of colors). After all of your years of reading, you can hardly bring yourself to look at **RED** and say "green." Reading the words distracts from your attention to the colors. *The tendency to read the words instead of saying the color of ink* is known as the **Stroop effect**, after the psychologist who discovered it. People do better on this task if they blur their vision, say the colors in a different language, or manage to regard the color words as meaningless (Raz, Kirsch, Pollard, & Nitkin-Kaner, 2006).

Do words always take priority over colors? Not necessarily. Try the following: Go back to Figure 8.8 and notice the colored patches at the four corners. This time, instead of saying anything, point to the correct color patch. When you come to **RED**, point to the blue patch in the lower left. Then try this demonstration again but point to the color corresponding to the *meaning* of the word. That is, when you come to **RED**, point to the red patch in the upper left. Try it now.

You probably found it easy to point to the patch that matches the color of the ink and harder to point to the color matching the word meaning (Durgin, 2000). When you are speaking, you are primed to read the words you see, but when you are pointing, you are more primed to attend to nonverbal cues, such as ink color.

Change Blindness

Movie directors discovered long ago that if they shot different parts of a scene on different days, few viewers noticed the changes in the cloud pattern, the background props, or the actors' clothes (Simons & Levin, 2003). Why is that? Most people believe they see a whole scene at once. In one sense you do: In one study, people viewed nearly 3,000 complex scenes for 3 seconds each. Occasionally, one of the scenes was repeated, and when that happened, the viewer was to press a key to report recognition. On average, people correctly noted more than 75 percent of the repeated scenes (Konkle, Brady, Alvarez, & Oliva, 2010).

However, seeing the gist of the scene is different from noticing every detail. When you look at a complex scene, your eyes dart around from one fixation point to another, fixating about three times per second (Henderson, 2007). During each fixation you attend to only a few details (Franconeri, Alvarez, & Enns, 2007). If one of those details changed while you were fixating on it, you would notice. A big, sudden change somewhere else would also grab your attention. But you cannot attend to every detail at

a Change in marginal interest (MI)

b Change in central interest (CI)

▲ **Figure 8.9** How quickly can you find the difference in each pair of pictures? If you need help, check answer B, page 261.

once, and you can easily overlook changes that occur gradually or during an eyeblink (Cohen, Alvarez, & Nakayama, 2011; Henderson & Hollingworth, 2003).

Psychologists call this phenomenon **change blindness**—*the failure to detect changes in parts of a scene.* ▲ Figure 8.9 shows two pairs of photos. In each pair, one differs from the other in a single regard. How quickly can you find those differences? Most people need 10 seconds or longer (Rensink, O'Regan, & Clark, 1997).

2. Did you find the changes in Figure 8.9 by a preattentive or an attentive mechanism?

Answer

2. The changes did not jump out by a preattentive mechanism. You had to use an attentive process to check each part of the scene one at a time.

The conclusion is that you do not maintain a detailed representation of what you see or hear. You hold a few details, but you cannot notice everything. One implication is that eyewitness reports are invariably incomplete. Much may have

happened that a witness overlooked. Magicians exploit change blindness (Macknik et al., 2008). A magician throws a ball into the air and catches it a few times and then pretends to throw it again, "watching" it go up. Many viewers do not immediately notice the change. They "see" the ball going up . . . and then disappearing!

Attention Deficit Disorder

People vary in their ability to maintain attention, as in anything else. **Attention deficit disorder (ADD)** is characterized by *easy distraction, impulsiveness, moodiness, and failure to follow through on plans.* **Attention-deficit hyperactivity disorder (ADHD)** is *the same except with excessive activity and "fidgetiness."* The symptoms vary considerably in type and intensity. Some people have problems mostly with attention, some mainly with impulsivity, and some with both.

The underlying causes almost certainly vary. In some cases, ADHD results from fetal alcohol exposure, lead poisoning, epilepsy, or emotional stress (Pearl, Weiss, & Stein, 2001). Researchers have found much evidence for a genetic predisposition, but no common gene produces a large effect. Evidently many genes can produce a small to moderate effect (Franke et al., 2012; Li, Chang, Zhang, Gao, & Wang, 2014). Another possibility is epigenetics—that is, changes in the expression of genes, rather than changes in the genes themselves.

Both children and adults with ADHD show mild abnormalities in certain brain areas, on average, especially in the frontal cortex (Cubillo, Halari, Smith, Taylor, & Rubia, 2012). It is also reported that people with ADHD have greater overall brain activity, implying a lack of inhibitory transmission (Wang, Jiao, Tang, Wang, & Lu, 2013). All of the reported brain abnormalities, like the reported genetic abnormalities, vary from one person to another. Many psychologists doubt that ADHD is a single disorder (Furman, 2008).

What exactly do we mean by "attention deficit"? The problem is not an inability to pay attention. People with ADHD easily pay attention to anything they care about. The problem relates to shifting attention quickly and appropriately. Here are two tasks sensitive to attention deficit disorder:

- **Choice-Delay Task** Would you prefer a small reward now or a bigger reward later? Obviously, it depends on *how much* bigger and *how much* later. On average, people with ADHD are more likely than other people their age to opt for the immediate reward (Solanto et al., 2001).
- **Stop-Signal Task** Suppose your task is to press the X key whenever you see an X on the screen and

the O key whenever you see an O. However, if you hear a "beep" shortly after either letter, then you should not press. If the letter and beep occur simultaneously, you easily inhibit your urge to press the button. If the beep occurs after you have already started to press, it's too late. The interesting results are with short delays: After how long a delay could you still manage to stop your finger from pressing the button? Most people with ADD or ADHD have trouble inhibiting their response after short delays (Lipszyc & Schachar, 2010).

The choice-delay task and stop-signal task measure different attentional problems. Some children show impairments on one task but not the other (Solanto et al., 2001; Sonuga-Barke, 2004).

3. Describe one of the behavioral tests used to measure deficits of attention or impulse control.

Answer

3. In the choice-delay task, the question is under what conditions someone will sacrifice a reward now for a larger one later. In the stop-signal task, one signal calls for a response and a second signal cancels the first signal; the question is under what circumstances a person can inhibit the response.

The most common treatment for ADD or ADHD is stimulant drugs such as methylphenidate (Ritalin) or amphetamines (Adderall). Stimulant drugs reduce the impulsivity and attention deficit problems in most cases, especially at first. For studies lasting much more than one year, the evidence is not clear on whether the drugs continue to have significant benefits, especially for academic performance (Langberg & Becker, 2012; Molina et al., 2009; Parker, Wales, Chalhoub, & Harpin, 2013).

A fair number of healthy, normal people have been taking stimulant drugs in an attempt to enhance their already normal abilities. That practice raises the ethical question of whether it is fair for students to use drugs to get better grades, or for professionals in a competitive field to gain an advantage by using drugs. However, the concern may be misplaced. Research suggests that stimulant drugs are no better than placebos, and possibly worse, for people who are already performing well (Ilieva, Boland, & Farah, 2013).

Sometimes our society relies too heavily on medication, and that statement is particularly true for the issue of ADHD. Studies in the United States and in Iceland found that stimulant drugs are prescribed more often for children who are young for their grade than those older for their grade. That is, if the cutoff for entering first grade is 6 years old, those who are just barely 6 are more likely to get an ADHD diagnosis, and to be treated with stimulant drugs, than those who are almost 7 (Elder, 2010; Zoëga, Valdimarsdóttir, & Hernández-Díaz, 2012). We can infer that some teachers and psychiatrists are confusing immaturity with a medical problem.

To minimize use of medications, what other procedures work? Exercise and adequate sleep help (Gapin, Labban, & Etnier, 2011; Gruber et al., 2011). Behavioral therapy is also effective, either in addition to the drugs or instead of them (Evans, Owens, & Bunford, 2014). Those methods include classroom use of rewards for good behavior and time-outs for inappropriate behavior, as well as techniques that parents learn to use. The research finds that behavior therapies are more effective than stimulant drugs for improving social skills, improving academic performance, and decreasing conduct problems (Daley et al., 2014; Sibley, Kuriyan, Evans, Waxmonsky, & Smith, 2014).

Categorizing

Putting things into categories makes our thinking more efficient. What you learn about amphibians tells you what to expect of all amphibians, including a species you meet for the first time. What you learn about cars tells you what to expect of cars in general. And so forth. However, categorizing sometimes proves a disadvantage (Peterson, Schroijen, Mölders, Zenker, & Van den Bergh, 2014). If you categorize some politician as "member of the party I oppose," then you are inclined to oppose every idea that politician advocates. If you think of someone as a "person with schizophrenia," then almost anything that person says or does may seem like a symptom of the disorder. In short, categories are necessary, but heavy reliance on them is sometimes misleading. How do we form categories?

Ways to Describe a Category

Do we look up our concepts in a mental dictionary to determine their meaning? A few words have simple, unambiguous definitions. For example, a *line* is the shortest distance between two points.

Many concepts are hard to define, however. You can probably recognize country music, but can you define it? What's the border between being bald and not bald? Is a man who loses one hair bald? Of course not. Then he loses one more hair, then another, and another. Eventually, he *is* bald. At what point did losing one more hair make him bald?

Eleanor Rosch (1978; Rosch & Mervis, 1975) argued that many categories are best described by *familiar or typical examples* called **prototypes**. After we identify good prototypes of country music or a bald person, we compare other items to them. Depending on how closely something matches, we call it a member of the category, a nonmember, or a borderline case. For example, cars and trucks are members of the category "vehicle." Flowers are nonmembers. Escalators and water skis are borderline cases.

However, some categories are harder to describe by prototypes (Fodor, 1998). We can think about "bug-eyed monsters from outer space" without ever encountering a prototype of that category.

Conceptual Networks and Priming

Try to think about one word and nothing else. You will soon discover the difficulty. If you don't relate that word to something else, you're just repeating it, not thinking about it. For example, when you think about *bird,* you link it to more specific examples, such as *sparrow,* more general categories, such as *animals,* and related terms, such as *flight* and *eggs.*

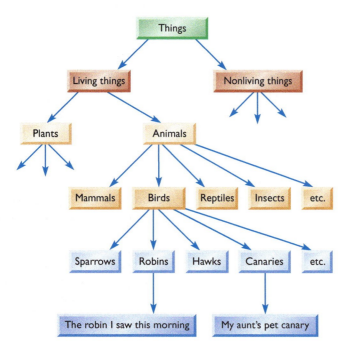

We organize items into hierarchies, such as animal as a high-level category, bird as intermediate, and sparrow as a lower-level category. Researchers demonstrate the reality of this kind of hierarchy by measuring the delay for people to answer various questions (Collins & Quillian, 1969, 1970). Answer the following true–false questions as quickly as possible:

- Canaries are yellow.
- Canaries sing.
- Canaries lay eggs.
- Canaries have feathers.
- Canaries have skin.

All five items are true, but people answer some faster than others. Most people answer fastest on the *yellow* and *sing* items, slightly slower on the *eggs* and *feathers* items, and still slower on the *skin* item. Why? Yellowness and singing are distinctive of canaries. Because you do not think of eggs or feathers specifically as canary features, you reason, "Canaries are birds, and birds lay eggs. So canaries must lay eggs." For skin, you have to reason, "Canaries are birds and birds are animals. Animals have skin, so canaries must have skin." This way of categorizing things saves you enormous effort overall. When you learn some new fact about birds or animals in general, you don't have to learn it again separately for every species.

4. **Which would people answer faster: whether politicians give speeches or whether they sometimes eat spaghetti? Why?**

Answer

4. It would take longer to answer whether politicians eat spaghetti. Giving speeches is a distinctive feature of politicians. Eating spaghetti is not. To answer the second question, you have to reason that politicians are people, and most people eat spaghetti.

We also link a word or concept to related concepts. ▼ **Figure 8.10** shows a possible network of conceptual links that someone might have at a particular moment (Collins & Loftus, 1975). Suppose this network describes your own concepts. *Thinking about one of the concepts shown in this figure will activate, or prime, the concepts linked to it* through a process called **spreading activation** (Collins & Loftus, 1975). For example, if you hear *flower,* you are primed to think of *rose, violet,* and other flowers. If you also hear *red,* the combination of *flower* and *red* primes you to think of *rose.* Priming that word helps you recognize it more easily than usual if it were flashed briefly on a screen or spoken very softly.

The idea of priming a concept is analogous to priming a pump: If you put some water in the pump to get it started, you can continue using the pump to draw water from a well. Similarly, **priming** *a concept gets it started. Reading or hearing one word makes it easier to think or recognize a related word. Seeing something makes it easier to recognize a related object.* Priming is important in language. When you read a word that you barely know or have trouble hearing a word someone has said, the context helps you understand it if the preceding sentences were about closely related concepts (Plaut & Booth, 2000).

Priming occurs in many situations. For example, if you look at pictures and try to identify the people or objects in the foreground, you will find the task easier if the background primes the same answer as the object in the foreground (Davenport & Potter, 2004) (see ▼ **Figure 8.11**).

Here is an illustration that can be explained in terms of spreading activation. Quickly answer each of the following questions (or ask someone else):

1. How many animals of each kind did Moses take on the ark?
2. What was the famous saying uttered by Louis Armstrong when he first set foot on the moon?
3. Some people pronounce St. Louis "saint loo-iss" and some pronounce it "saint loo-ee." How would you pronounce the capital city of Kentucky?

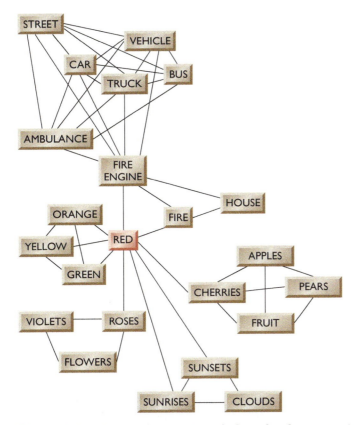

▲ **Figure 8.10** We link each concept to a variety of other related concepts. Any stimulus that activates one of these concepts will also partly activate (or prime) the ones that are linked to it. (From Collins & Loftus, 1975)

You can check answer C at the end of this module, page 261. Why do so many people miss these questions? ▼ Figure 8.12 offers an explanation in terms of spreading activation (Shafto & MacKay, 2000): The question about Louis Armstrong activates a series of sounds and concepts that are linked to one another and to other items. The sound *Armstrong* and the ideas *first astronaut on the moon* and *famous sayings* are all linked to "One small step for a man . . ." Even the name *Louis Armstrong* is loosely linked to *Neil Armstrong* because both are famous people. The combined effect of all these influences automatically triggers the answer, "One small step for a man . . ."

concept check

5. **Suppose someone says "cardinal" and then briefly flashes the word *bird* on a screen. Some viewers identify the word correctly, suggesting priming, and some do not. Considering both priming and the encoding specificity idea from Chapter 7, how might you explain why some people and not others identified the word *bird*?**

Answer bird. and words of set different very a prime to activation spreading have would church Catholic the in cer off- an as "cardinal" of thought who people other However, bird. word the prime to activation spreading had have would bird a as it of thought and "cardinal" heard who People 5.

◀ **Figure 8.11** A bullfight setting primes recognition of a matador, and a library setting primes recognition of a librarian. When people are placed in the opposite settings, we take longer to identify them.

Pisaphotography/Shutterstock.com, Filipe B. Varela/Shutterstock.com

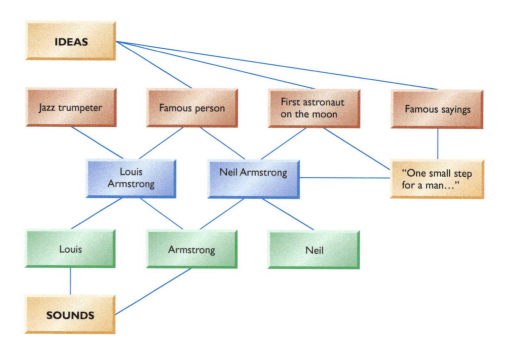

▶ **Figure 8.12** According to one explanation, the word *Armstrong* and the ideas *astronaut, first person on the moon,* and *famous sayings* all activate the linked saying "One small step for a man. . . ."

Thinking about Attention and Concepts

Behaviorists traditionally avoided the topic of cognition because thinking and knowledge are unobservable. Although this module has demonstrated the possibilities for research on cognition, you should also see that the behaviorists' objections were not frivolous. Research on cognition is difficult, and requires inferences from masses of data. Nevertheless, the research is important, for practical as well as theoretical reasons. For example, the better we can specify what we mean by "attention," the better we can help people with attention deficits.

Summary

- *Research methods in cognitive psychology.* Researchers infer mental processes from measurements of speed and accuracy. (page 251)
- *Mental imagery.* Mental images resemble vision in certain respects. The time required to answer questions about a rotating object depends on how far the object would actually rotate between one position and another. (page 251)
- *Top-down and bottom-up processes.* Some stimuli grab our attention automatically. We also control our attention, deliberately shifting it from one item to another. (page 252)
- *Attentive and preattentive processes.* We quickly notice items that are unusual in certain salient ways, regardless of potential distracters. Noticing less distinct items requires attention to one target after another. (page 253)
- *Attention bottleneck.* Attention is limited, and items compete for it. (page 253)
- *Distraction.* Directing attention to one item means subtracting it from another. For example, talking on a cell phone distracts from attention to driving. (page 254)

- *The Stroop effect.* When we are speaking, written words grab attention, making it difficult to attend to the color of the letters. (page 255)
- *Change blindness.* We often fail to detect changes in a scene if they occur slowly or during an eye movement. (page 255)
- *Attention deficit disorder.* People with attention deficit disorder have trouble shifting attention. Two tests of attention problems are the choice-delay task and the stop-signal task. Treatment with stimulant drugs has advantages and disadvantages. (page 256)
- *Categorization.* People use many categories that are hard to define. Many items are marginal examples of a category, so we cannot insist on a yes–no decision. (page 257)
- *Conceptual networks and priming.* We represent words or concepts with links to related concepts. Thinking about a concept primes one to think of related concepts. (page 257)

Key Terms

attention (page 252)

attention deficit disorder (ADD) (page 256)

attention-deficit hyperactivity disorder (ADHD) (page 256)

attentive process (page 253)

bottom-up process (page 252)

change blindness (page 256)

choice blindness (page 251)

choice-delay task (page 256)

cognition (page 251)

preattentive process (page 253)

priming (page 258)

prototype (page 257)

spreading activation (page 258)

stop-signal task (page 256)

Stroop effect (page 255)

top-down process (page 252)

Answers to Other Questions in the Module

A. The objects in pair a are the same; in b they are the same; and in c they are different. (page 252)

B. In the top scene, a horizontal bar along the wall has changed position. In the lower scene, the location of the helicopter has changed. (page 256)

C. 1. None. Noah had an ark, not Moses. 2. Neil Armstrong, not Louis Armstrong, set foot on the moon. 3. The correct pronunciation of Kentucky's capital is "frank-furt." (Not "loo-ee-ville"!) (page 258)

Review Questions

1. In a pioneering study, Shepard and Metzler concluded that imagining how something would look from a different angle is something like actually watching something rotate. They drew this conclusion by measuring what?
   (a) The delay of people's responses
   (b) The accuracy of people's responses
   (c) Brain activity
   (d) People's self-reports of how they answered the question

2. Suppose you are in a field of brownish bushes and one motionless brown rabbit. You will find it by _____.
   If the rabbit starts hopping, you will find it by _____.
   (a) an attentive process . . . an attentive process
   (b) an attentive process . . . a preattentive process
   (c) a preattentive process . . . an attentive process
   (d) a preattentive process . . . a preattentive process

3. What does the Stroop effect demonstrate?
   (a) Familiarity with a word can interfere with saying the color of its ink.
   (b) An item that looks different from all the others captures attention automatically.
   (c) We often fail to detect visual changes that occur slowly or during an eyeblink.
   (d) People find it possible to deal with categories even when they are hard to define.

4. Other things being equal, which children in a class are most likely to be treated for ADHD?
   (a) Children who are taller than average for the grade in school
   (b) Children who are younger than average for the grade in school
   (c) Children whose parents have low expectations for their school performance
   (d) Children with greater than average athletic ability

5. Priming a concept is responsible for which of the following?
   (a) Change blindness
   (b) The Stroop effect
   (c) The stop-signal task
   (d) Spreading activation

Answers: 1a, 2b, 3a, 4b, 5d.

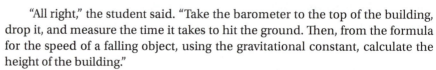

After studying this module, you should be able to:

- Distinguish between System 1 and System 2 thinking.

- Explain the advantages and disadvantages of maximizing, as opposed to satisficing.

- List some of the common errors of thinking.

- Discuss the bases for developing expertise, and what experts do that makes them experts.

▼ **Figure 8.13** shows an object that was made by cutting and bending an ordinary piece of cardboard (Gardner, 1978). How was it made? Take a piece of paper and try to make it yourself. (The solution is on page 272, answer D.)

This is an "insight" or "aha!" problem. If you solve it, you probably cannot explain how you found the answer. You say, "It just came to me."

Here is another example of creative problem solving: A college physics exam asked how to use a barometer to determine the height of a building. One student answered that he would tie a long string to the barometer, go to the top of the building, and lower the barometer to the ground. Then he would cut the string and measure its length.

When the professor marked this answer incorrect, the student asked why. "Well," said the professor, "your method would work, but it's not the method I wanted you to use." When the student objected, the professor offered to let him try again.

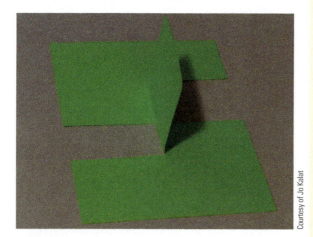

▲ **Figure 8.13** This object was made by cutting and folding an ordinary piece of cardboard with nothing left over. How was it done?

"All right," the student said. "Take the barometer to the top of the building, drop it, and measure the time it takes to hit the ground. Then, from the formula for the speed of a falling object, using the gravitational constant, calculate the height of the building."

"Hmmm," replied the professor. "That too would work. And it does make use of physical principles. But it still isn't what I had in mind. Can you think of another way?"

"Another way? Sure," he replied. "Place the barometer next to the building on a sunny day. Measure the height of the barometer and the length of its shadow. Also measure the length of the building's shadow. Then use this formula:"

$$\frac{\text{height of barometer}}{\text{height of building}} = \frac{\text{length of barometer's shadow}}{\text{length of building's shadow}}$$

The professor was impressed but still reluctant to give credit, so the student persisted with another method: "Measure the barometer's height. Then walk up the stairs of the building, marking it off in units of the barometer's height. At the top, take the number of barometer units and multiply by the height of the barometer to get the height of the building."

The professor sighed: "Give me one more way—any other way—and I'll give you credit, even if it's not the answer I wanted."

"Really?" asked the student with a smile. "*Any* other way?"

"Yes, any other way."

"All right," said the student. "Go to the man who owns the building and say, 'Hey, buddy, if you tell me how tall the building is, I'll give you this great barometer!'"

Sometimes, people develop creative, imaginative solutions like the ones that the physics student proposed. At other times, they suggest a creative idea that couldn't possibly work. ▼ **Figure 8.14** shows an example. Psychologists

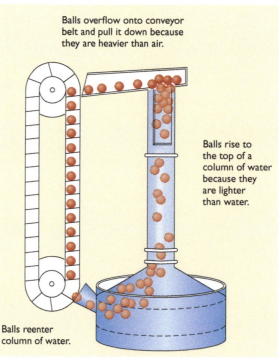

Balls overflow onto conveyor belt and pull it down because they are heavier than air.

Balls rise to the top of a column of water because they are lighter than water.

Balls reenter column of water.

◀**Figure 8.14** An inventor applied for a patent on this "perpetual motion machine." Rubber balls, lighter than water, rise in a column of water and flow over the top. They are heavier than air, so they fall, moving a belt and generating energy. At the bottom, they reenter the water column. Why couldn't this system work? (Check answer E on page 272.)

study problem-solving behavior and decision making partly to understand the thought processes and partly to look for ways to help people reason more effectively.

Two Types of Thinking and Problem Solving

Daniel Kahneman (2011) described human thinking in terms of two systems. We use System 1 (or Type 1 thinking) *for quick, automatic processes* (such as recognizing familiar faces and routine actions) *and for questions we think are easy.* System 1 generally proceeds without much effort. We use System 2 (or Type 2 thinking) *for mathematical calculations, evaluating evidence, and anything else that requires attention.* System 2 relies heavily on working memory, and if your working memory is already loaded, because you are trying to remember something else, you tend to fall back onto System 1 (Evans & Stanovich, 2013). In fact, because System 1 saves time and energy, we rely on it whenever we can. Answer the following:

A bat and a ball together cost $1.10. The bat costs $1 more than the ball. What does the ball cost?

System 1 provides the intuitive answer that the ball costs $0.10. But that is wrong. If the ball costs $0.10 and the bat costs $1 more than the ball, the bat costs $1.10, and the total is $1.20. With a little effort, you can calculate that the ball must cost $0.05. But you might jump to a conclusion before realizing that you need your System 2 to do the calculation. If the question had been printed in small, blurry print, so that you had to exert some effort just to read it, you would be more likely to think about it and answer correctly (Alter, Oppenheimer, Epley, & Eyre, 2007). Yes, you actually do better if you have trouble reading the question! Anything that gets you to slow down and think about it improves your performance.

In many cases, System 2 solves problems by an algorithm, *an explicit procedure for calculating an answer or testing every hypothesis.* Suppose you are a traveling salesperson in Ames, Iowa (see ▶ Figure 8.15). You want to visit 10 cities and return home by the shortest route. You might list all possible routes, measure them, and determine which one is shortest.

However, it would take a long time to calculate all those routes, and if you had to visit hundreds of cities instead of 10, you couldn't possibly consider every possibility. You would turn to heuristics, *strategies for simplifying a problem and generating a satisfactory guess.* Heuristics provide quick guidance when you are willing or forced to accept some possibility of error, and they work well most of the time (Gigerenzer, 2008).

System 1 relies heavily on heuristics. Examples: If you want to guess which child is oldest, choose the tallest. If one product is more expensive than another, it is probably of higher quality. If the instructions for a task are difficult to understand, the task itself is probably difficult to do, but probably also important (Labroo, Lambotte, & Zhang, 2009). Each of these heuristics works most of the time but not always. We also tend to follow several heuristics that are not defensible at all. For example, *if the instructions are written in an unfamiliar or unclear font,* people overestimate the difficulty of the task itself (Song & Schwarz, 2008). We tend to distrust people whose names are difficult to pronounce (Newman et al., 2014). If a medicine or food additive has a name that is difficult to pronounce, people assume it is unsafe (Song & Schwarz, 2009).

Maximizing and Satisficing

You also use heuristics for questions such as, "Which job shall I take?" or "How shall I spend my money?" You don't have all the information you need, and there is no single correct answer. Instead, you generate a few possibilities,

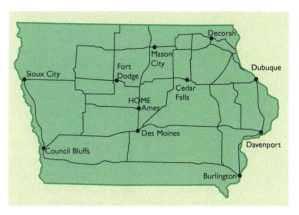

▲ **Figure 8.15** In the traveling salesperson task, you want to find the shortest route connecting all the points you need to visit.

consider them, and try to make the best choice you can. (Note that not every decision falls neatly into System 1 or System 2. When you use heuristics to simplify a decision and then ponder your decision carefully, you are using both types of thinking.)

Before making a decision, how many possibilities do you consider and how thoroughly do you investigate them? One strategy, maximizing, is *thoroughly considering all available choices to find the best one.* Satisficing is *searching only until you find something satisfactory.* If you have a choice with much at stake—for example, what is the safest design for a new bridge over some river—you should carefully consider every reasonable possibility. However, most of our daily decisions have much less at stake. Some people habitually follow the maximizing strategy and others prefer satisficing for most of their decisions, big and small. Researchers classify people as mainly maximizers or satisficers based on questions like the following (Schwartz et al., 2002). Rate yourself from 1 (not at all true) to 7 (definitely true):

- When I listen to the car radio, I frequently check other stations.
- I frequently channel-surf to find the best show.
- I shop at many stores before deciding which clothes to buy.
- I expect to interview for many jobs before I accept one.

The higher your score, the more you are a maximizer. Researchers find that high maximizers usually make better choices, according to objective criteria. They get jobs with higher starting pay than do satisficers, in spite of being about equal in their college grade point average. However, they have more difficulty making a choice (Paivandy, Bullock, Reardon, & Kelly, 2008), and they are usually *less* satisfied with their choices. Satisficers look for something "good enough" and find it. Maximizers look for "the best" and continue to wonder whether they were right

(Iyengar, Wells, & Schwartz, 2006). If two or more choices appear to be almost equally good, they worry about their choice and second-guess themselves afterward (Shenhav & Buckner, 2014). College students who are maximizers often brood about whether they chose the right major (Leach & Patall, 2013). Maximizers in romantic relationships tend to feel less satisfied with their partner and less committed to the relationship (Mikkelson & Pauley, 2013).

When you want to make a choice, how many options do you want to consider? If you know exactly what you want—suppose you are passing through a town and you want the cheapest motel room available—then you want to see as many options as possible. However, if you are planning a beach vacation, you care about quality and location as well as price. If you consider too many options that differ in too many ways, you might become overwhelmed and make no choice at all (Hadar & Sood, 2014; Park & Jang, 2013; Schwartz, 2004).

In many countries today, decisions are difficult just because of the huge number of options available. Your local supermarket may offer 50 or so types of breakfast cereals and almost as many types of potato chips. In one study, researchers at a supermarket offered free samples of jams. If they offered 6 types of jam, 12 percent of people bought one. If they offered 24 types, a larger number of people stopped to sample a few, but almost no one bought anything (Iyengar & Lepper, 2000). Similarly, retired people in the United States can choose from about 50 prescription drug plans under Medicare Part D. Research shows that it is hard to make a good choice among so many (Wood et al., 2011). As a rule, people are most likely to make a good choice if they consider no more than 20 possibilities (Lenton, Fasolo, & Todd, 2008; Reed, Mikels, & Simon, 2008; Shah & Wolford, 2007).

6. Who would have more trouble choosing a meal from a six-page menu, maximizers or satisficers?

Answer

6. Maximizers would have more trouble, because they want to consider every choice. A satisficer might find an acceptable choice quickly.

The Representativeness Heuristic and Base-Rate Information

Although heuristic thinking is often helpful, it leads us astray when we rely on it inappropriately. In 2002, Daniel Kahneman won the Nobel Prize in economics for research showing examples of inappropriate use of heuristics. For example, consider the saying:

"If something looks like a duck, waddles like a duck, and quacks like a duck, chances are it's a duck." This saying is an example of the **representativeness heuristic**, *the assumption that an item that resembles members of a category is probably also in that category*. This heuristic is usually correct, except when we deal with uncommon categories. If you see something that looks like a rare bird, you should check carefully to make sure it isn't a similar, more common species. In general, to decide whether something belongs in one category or another, you should consider the **base-rate information**—that is, *how common the two categories are*.

When people apply the representativeness heuristic, they frequently overlook base-rate information. For example, consider the following question (modified from Kahneman & Tversky, 1973):

Psychologists interviewed 30 engineers and 70 lawyers. One of them, Jack, is a 45-year-old married man with four children. He is generally conservative, cautious, and ambitious. He shows no interest in political and social issues and spends most

In 2002, Princeton psychologist Daniel Kahneman (left) won the Nobel Prize in economics. Although others have won Nobel Prizes for research related to psychology, Kahneman was the first winner who had a PhD in psychology.

Table 8.1 The Representativeness Heuristic and the Availability Heuristic

	A Tendency to Assume That	Leads Us Astray When	Example of Error
Representativeness Heuristic	An item that resembles members of a category probably belongs to that category.	Something resembles members of a rare category.	Something looks like it might be a UFO, so you decide it is.
Availability Heuristic	The more easily we can think of members of a category, the more common the category is.	One category gets more publicity than another or is more memorable.	You remember more reports of airplane crashes than car crashes, so you think air travel is more dangerous.

of his free time on home carpentry, sailing, and solving mathematical puzzles. What is the probability that Jack is one of the 30 engineers in the sample of 100?

Most people estimate a rather high probability—perhaps 80 or 90 percent—because the description sounds more like engineers than lawyers. That estimate isn't wrong, as we cannot know the true probability. The key point is that if some people hear that the sample included 30 engineers and 70 lawyers, and others hear it included 70 engineers and 30 lawyers, both groups make about the same estimate for Jack (Kahneman & Tversky, 1973). Certainly, the base-rate information (the number of engineers in the sample) should have some influence.

Here is another example of misusing the representativeness heuristic:

Linda was a philosophy major. She is 31, bright, outspoken, and concerned about issues of discrimination and social justice.

What would you estimate is the probability that Linda is a bank teller? What is the probability that she is a feminist bank teller? (Answer before you read on.)

The true probabilities are not the point. The interesting result is that many people estimate a higher probability that Linda is a *feminist* bank teller than that she is a bank teller (Tversky & Kahneman, 1983). She couldn't be a feminist bank teller without being a bank teller. Apparently, the word "feminist" triggers people's representativeness heuristic to say, "Yes, that would fit" (Shafir, Smith, & Osherson, 1990).

The Availability Heuristic

When you estimate how common something is, you usually start by thinking of examples. If you remember enjoying your astronomy class more times than you remember enjoying any other class, probably that astronomy class really was interesting. If you remember many summer days when mosquitoes bit you and no winter days when they bit you, you conclude that mosquitoes are more common in summer. The availability heuristic is *the tendency to assume that if we easily think of examples of a category, then that category must be common.* However, this heuristic leads us astray when uncommon events are highly memorable. For example, you remember a few highly publicized cases of shootings in schools or colleges, and greatly overestimate the risk of danger. Also, you might remember the occasional times when a hunch or dream seemed to predict a future event, but forget the vast number of times it did not, thereby incorrectly attributing predictive value to your hunches or dreams.

Another example: How would you feel if your favorite team wins its next game? How would you feel if you missed your bus? Most people overestimate how good they would feel after good events and how bad they would feel after bad events. One reason is that you try to remember how you felt after similar experiences in the past, and memories of your most extreme experiences are easily available (Gilbert & Wilson, 2009). Because they are easily available, you assume they are typical.

Also, consider the widespread belief that "you should stick with your first impulse on a multiple-choice test." Researchers have consistently found this claim

to be wrong (Johnston, 1975; Kruger, Wirtz, & Miller, 2005). Changing an answer can help for several reasons. When you reread a question, you might discover that you misunderstood it the first time. Sometimes, a question later in the test reminds you of the correct answer to an earlier item. Why, then, do most students believe that their first impulse is correct? When you get your test back, which questions do you check? You check the questions you got wrong, therefore noticing the ones you changed from right to wrong. However, you overlook the larger number you changed from wrong to right. Your availability heuristic leads you to believe that changing an answer hurts you. Table 8.1 summarizes the representativeness and availability heuristics.

concept check

7. **Although fatal automobile crashes are far more common than airplane crashes, many people fear airplane travel, partly because they vividly remember hearing about airplane crashes. Is this an example of the representativeness heuristic or the availability heuristic?**

8. **You meet a tall man and guess that he is more likely to be a professional basketball player than a salesperson. Is this an example of the representativeness heuristic or the availability heuristic?**

Answers

7. It is an example of the availability heuristic. 8. It is an example of the representativeness heuristic.

Other Common Errors in Human Cognition

In addition to sometimes relying inappropriately on the representativeness heuristic and availability heuristic, people make other errors. For decades, college professors have emphasized critical thinking, *the careful evaluation of evidence for and against any conclusion.* However, even professors (and textbook writers) who teach critical thinking sometimes find themselves accepting nonsense that they should have questioned. Why do intelligent people sometimes make major mistakes? Here are a few of the reasons.

Overconfidence

How long is the Nile River? You probably don't know, but please guess an approximate range, such as "between X and Y" in miles or kilometers. Then state your confidence in your answer. If you say "0 percent," you mean that you *know* your range is wrong. If so, widen the range until you are fairly confident you must be right.

On difficult questions like this, most people are overconfident of their answers. On questions where they say they are 90 percent confident, they are actually correct far less than 90 percent (Plous, 1993). On easy questions, the trend is reversed and people tend to be underconfident (Erev, Wallsten, & Budescu, 1994; Juslin, Winman, & Olsson, 2000). (Incidentally, the Nile River is 4,187 miles long, or 6,738 kilometers.)

Overconfidence is sometimes helpful (Johnson & Fowler, 2011). Highly confident people tend to get good job offers and promotions. Highly confident politicians win elections. If you act certain of winning a fight, a stronger opponent may back down. However, overconfidence can be harmful, too. If the stronger opponent doesn't back down, you could get badly hurt. Overconfident leaders often blunder into costly mistakes. Investors may lose money, especially by expecting that stocks that have been growing in value will continue to do so (Critcher & Rosenzweig, 2014).

Philip Tetlock (1992) studied government officials and consultants, foreign policy professors, newspaper columnists, and others who make their living by analyzing and predicting world events. He asked them to predict world events over the next 1 to 10 years—what would happen in Korea, the Middle East, and so forth. Later, he compared predictions to actual results and found very low accuracy, especially among those who were the most confident. Later research did, however, show ways to improve accuracy. People who pay attention to their errors learn to reduce their biases, and people who work together in groups profit by sharing information and ideas (Mellers et al., 2014).

Confirmation Bias

We often err by *accepting a hypothesis and then looking for evidence to support it instead of considering other possibilities.* This tendency, the confirmation bias, occurs in all walks of life. People listen mostly to others who agree with them on matters of science, politics, or religion—and then they accuse their opponents of being biased.

Once we have made a decision, we look for reasons to stick with it. Peter Wason (1960) asked students to discover a certain rule he had in mind for generating sequences of numbers. One example of the numbers the rule might generate, he explained, was "2, 4, 6." He told the students that they could ask about other sequences, and he would tell them whether or not those sequences fit his rule. They should tell him as soon as they thought they knew the rule.

Most students started by asking, "8, 10, 12?" When told "yes," they proceeded with "14, 16, 18?" Each time, they were told, "Yes, that sequence fits the rule." Soon most of them guessed, "The rule is three consecutive even numbers." "No," came the reply. "That is not the rule." Many students persisted, trying "20, 22, 24?" "26, 28, 30?" "250, 252, 254?" They continued testing sequences that fit their rule, ignoring other possibilities. The rule Wason had in mind was, "Any three positive numbers of increasing magnitude." For instance, 1, 2, 3 would be acceptable, and so would 21, 25, 601.

A special case of confirmation bias is functional fixedness, *the tendency to adhere to a single approach or a single way of using an item.* Here are three examples:

1. You are provided with a candle, a box of matches, some thumbtacks, and a tiny piece of string, as shown in ▼ Figure 8.16. Using no other equipment, find a way to mount the candle to the wall so that it can be lit.

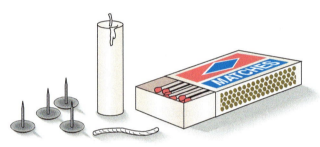

▲ **Figure 8.16** Given only these materials, what is the best way to attach the candle to a wall so that it can be lit?

2. Consider an array of nine dots:

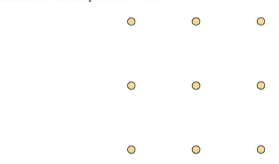

Connect all nine dots with a series of connected straight lines, such that the end of one line is the start of the next. For example, one way would be:

But use the fewest lines possible.

3. There are some students in a room. All but two of them are psychology majors, all but two are chemistry majors, and all but two are history majors. How many students are present? (If your System 1 blurts out, "two of each," try out your answer: It doesn't work.) Now here's the interesting part: There are two possible solutions. After you have found one solution, discard it and find another. After you have either found solutions or given up, check answer F on page 272. (Solve these problems before reading further.)

Question 1 was difficult because most people think of the matchbox as a container for matches, not as a tool on its own. The box is "functionally fixed" for one way of using it. A similar question was put to people in a subsistence society with few tools. They were given a set of objects and asked how they could use them to build a tower to reach a person in distress. If the objects included an empty box, they used it, but if the box contained other objects, they didn't quickly think of emptying the box and using it (German & Barrett, 2005).

Question 2 was difficult because most people assume that the lines must remain within the area defined by the nine dots. On question 3, it is difficult to think of even one solution, and after thinking of it, it is hard to abandon it to think of a different approach.

Framing Questions

A logical person should give the same answer no matter how a question is worded, right? However, most people change their answers depending on the wording of the questions, as you may recall from the discussion of surveys in Chapter 2. *The tendency to answer a question differently when it is framed differently* is called the framing effect.

An example: A company that provides health insurance will charge higher rates to overweight people. If they describe it as "a discount for lower weight," people like it better than if they call it "a penalty for higher weight," even though the effect is the same (Tannenbaum, Valasek, Knowles, & Ditto, 2013).

Another example: You are debating between two cars—let's call them B and C. Car B is a better car, but more expensive. While you are pondering, the salesperson also suggests car A, which is even more luxurious than B, but also a great deal more expensive. You won't pick A, but now you are more likely to choose B, which seems like a good compromise.

Plan	How question was framed	Plan preferred by	Outcome
A	Save 200 people	72%	
C	400 people will die	22%	200 live, 400 die
B	33% chance of saving all 600; 67% chance of saving no one	28%	
D	33% chance no one will die; 67% chance all 600 will die	78%	33% chance 600 live or 67% chance 600 die

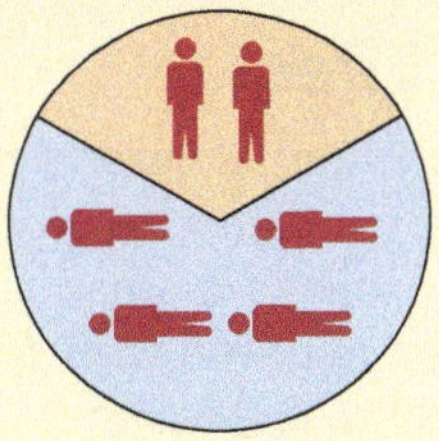

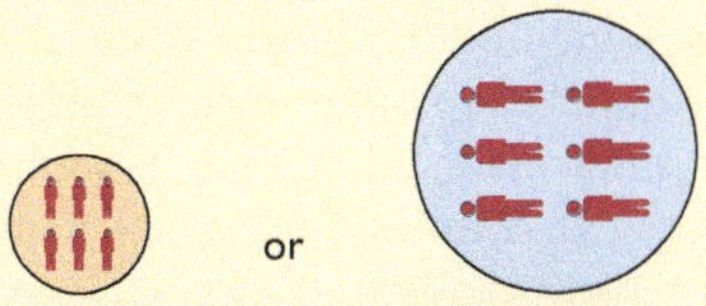

▲ **Figure 8.17** Most people chose plan A over B and D over C, although A produces the same result as C and B produces the same result as D. Amos Tversky and Daniel Kahneman (1981) proposed that most people play it safe to gain something but accept a risk to avoid a loss.

If, instead of car A, someone had suggested car D, which is extremely cheap but also of extremely low quality, now you would probably choose car C, because it now seems like the compromise choice (Trueblood, Brown, Heathcote, & Busemeyer, 2013).

Another example of the framing effect: You have been appointed head of the Public Health Service, and you need to choose a plan to deal with a disease that endangers the lives of 600 people. Plan A will save the lives of 200 people. Plan B has a 33 percent chance to save all 600 and a 67 percent chance to save no one. *Choose plan A or B before reading further.*

Now another disease breaks out, and again, you must choose between two plans. If you adopt plan C, 400 people will die. If you adopt plan D, there is a 33 percent chance that no one will die and a 67 percent chance that 600 will die. *Choose plan C or D now.*

▲ **Figure 8.17** shows the results for how a large group of people responded when given these choices. Most chose A over B and D over C. However, plan A is exactly the same as C (200 live, 400 die), and plan B is exactly the same as D. Why then did so many people choose both A and D? As Tversky and Kahneman (1981) demonstrated, most people avoid taking a risk to gain something (e.g., saving lives), because we know that even a small gain will feel good. However, we willingly take a risk to avoid loss (e.g., not letting people die), because any loss will feel bad. Similar results have been found in other studies, with people of all ages (Reyna, Chick, Corbin, & Hsia, 2014).

The Sunk Cost Effect

The sunk cost effect is a special case of the framing effect. Suppose that months ago you bought an expensive ticket for today's football game, but the weather is miserably cold. You wish you hadn't bought the ticket. Do you go to the game?

Many people attend the game anyway because they don't want to waste the money. This example illustrates the **sunk cost effect**, *the willingness to do something undesirable because of money or effort already spent* (Arkes & Ayton, 1999). This tendency arises in many situations. A company or government continues investing money in an unsuccessful project because it doesn't want to admit that the money already spent was wasted. A professional sports team is disappointed with a high-salaried player's performance, but keeps using that player to avoid wasting the money.

9. Someone says, "More than 90 percent of all college students like to watch late-night television, but only 20 percent of adults over 50 do. Therefore, most watchers of late-night television are college students." What error in thinking has this person made?

10. Which of the following offers by your professor would probably be more persuasive? (a) "If you do this extra project, there's a chance I will add some points to your grade." (b) "I'm going to penalize this whole class for being inattentive today, but if you do this extra project, there's a chance I won't subtract anything from your grade."

Answers

9. Failure to consider the base rate: 20 percent of all older adults is a larger number than 90 percent of all college students. This is an example of inappropriately using the representativeness heuristic.
10. Probably (b). People are generally more willing to take a risk to avoid losing something than to gain something.

Expertise

Although all of us make mistakes in our reasoning, some people develop expertise within a given field that enables them to solve problems quickly with a minimum of error. They apply the appropriate algorithms quickly, and they recognize which heuristics do or do not work in a particular situation. Reaching that point requires much effort.

Practice, Practice, Practice, but Have Some Talent, Too

Expert performance is impressive. Some people complete the most difficult crossword puzzles rapidly. Some physicians look at an X-ray and immediately notice a dot that indicates a major illness. Someone else might see a bird for a split second and identify its species, sex, and age. Are experts born, made, or some of each?

In fields ranging as diverse as chess, sports, and violin playing, expertise requires about 10 years of intense practice (Ericsson & Charness, 1994; Ericsson, Krampe, & Tesch-Römer, 1993). The top violin players practice three to four hours every day beginning in early childhood. A world-class athlete spends hours at a time perfecting skills. Whereas most average players like to practice the skills they do best, the best players spend most of their practice time on what they do the worst. They also tend to alternate between practicing one skill and another (Coughlan, Williams, McRobert, & Ford, 2014). As discussed in Chapter 7, varying your study within a session makes it more effective.

Hungarian author Laszlo Polgar set out to demonstrate that almost anyone can achieve expertise with sufficient effort. He devoted enormous efforts to nurturing his three daughters' chess skills. All three became outstanding, and one, Judit, became the first woman and the youngest person ever to reach grand master status.

Based on these results, it became popular to say that expertise depends on 10,000 hours of practice. According to later research, that rule is only an approximation, because it overlooks individual differences (Macnamara, Hambrick, & Oswald, 2014). Two people who practice a skill such as piano or chess for the same number of hours are not necessarily equal at the end. On average, chess players reach master level after 11,000 hours of practice, but some reach that level after just over 3,000 hours, whereas others accumulate more than 25,000 hours without ever reaching master level (Gobet & Campitelli, 2007). In general, those who learn faster in school also develop expertise faster (Campitelli & Gobet, 2011; Meinz & Hambrick, 2010). Also, a few thousand hours starting in childhood count for more than the same number of hours in adulthood (Gobet & Campitelli, 2007).

An additional factor is that people who start off doing well at something are more likely than others to develop an interest and therefore devote the needed hours to improving their skill. Consider music: Many studies have found that highly practiced musicians are better than average at discriminating

Judit Polgar confirmed her father's confidence that prolonged effort could make her a grand master chess player.

pitches, melodies, and rhythms (that is, detecting the difference between one and another). It seems natural to assume that their practice improved their recognition of sounds. However, the alternative is that people who originally had more precise hearing were more likely than others to develop an interest in music. Miriam Mosing and colleagues compared thousands of pairs of adult twins. They found that even in cases where one twin had practiced a musical instrument extensively and the other one hardly at all, both twins were about equally good at discriminating pitches, melodies, and rhythms (Mosing, Madison, Pederson, Kuja-Halkola, & Ullén, 2014). That is, although practice undeniably improves someone's skill at playing an instrument, it doesn't measurably affect hearing. The reason that most of the top musicians hear so well is that people who hear well are more likely than others to become musicians.

For practice to be effective, people need feedback based on the practice (Kahneman & Klein, 2009). Athletes see at once whether their performance was better or worse than a previous attempt, and how they compared to their competitors. Computer programmers get excellent feedback: If they program something correctly, it works. If they make a mistake, the computer crashes or does something it wasn't supposed to do. Weather forecasters also get good, quick feedback. People who get good feedback have a chance to improve with practice.

In contrast, psychotherapists get relatively weak feedback. With depression and many other conditions, some patients would improve over time even without treatment, whereas others would remain troubled for long times regardless of treatment. Consequently, therapists get only slow and unreliable feedback on the effectiveness of their techniques. On average, psychotherapists show little or no improvement over years of experience (Tracey, Wampold, Lichtenberg, & Goodyear, 2014).

What about politicians? Do they improve with practice? Certainly they improve at their ability to win elections, a task on which they get good feedback. However, experience in office doesn't greatly improve their ability to make the right decisions on public policy. (If it did, then we should expect experienced legislators to agree with one another.) The problem is a lack of feedback: When the government enacts a policy, we seldom know how much better or worse things might have been under some other policy.

▲ **Figure 8.18** Master chess players quickly recognize and memorize chess pieces arranged as they might occur in a normal game (**a**). However, they are no better than average at memorizing a random pattern (**b**).

11. **If you and your 6-year-old cousin spent 10,000 hours practicing chess, starting today, who would probably reach master level first?**

Answer

11. Probably your cousin would. Other things being equal, practice is more effective if it begins at an early age.

Expert Pattern Recognition

What exactly do experts do that sets them apart from others? Primarily, they can look at a pattern and recognize its important features quickly.

In a typical experiment (de Groot, 1966), chess experts and novices briefly examined pieces on a chessboard, as in ▶ Figure 8.18, and tried to recall the positions. When the pieces were arranged as might occur in a normal game, expert players recalled 91 percent of the positions correctly, whereas novices recalled only 41 percent. When the pieces were arranged randomly, however, experts and novices were about equal at recalling the positions. That is, experts do not have a superior memory overall, but they have learned to recognize common chessboard patterns. (Recall from Chapter 7 the concept of chunking, the process of remembering a cluster of items as a unit.)

Another example comes from basketball. Imagine you watch a video clip of someone shooting a free throw, but the clip is interrupted before the ball reaches the net. How much would you have to see before you could guess

whether the ball will go through the hoop? Most people aren't sure until the ball is well on the way to the basket. Professional basketball players usually know the answer before the ball leaves the shooter's hands (Aglioti, Cesari, Romani, & Urgesi, 2008; ▼ Figure 8.19). In areas from bird identification to reading X-rays to judging gymnastic competitions, experts recognize important patterns almost immediately (Murphy & Medin, 1985; Ste-Marie, 1999; Tanaka, Curran, & Sheinberg, 2005).

12. **The introduction to Module 7.1 mentioned the World Memory Championships, in which contestants compete at memorizing long lists of words, numbers, or cards. How would practice enable them to develop this kind of expertise? That is, what must they do differently from other people?**

Answer

12. As with other kinds of expertise, experts at memorizing learn to recognize patterns. Whereas most people would see "king of hearts, two of spades, three of clubs, seven of clubs, ace of diamonds" as five items, someone who has practiced memorizing cards might see this as a single familiar pattern or as a part of an even larger pattern.

Most viewers can tell whether the ball will go in (above) or not (below) at about this point.

Professional players can tell whether the ball will go in or not at about this point.

▲ **Figure 8.19** Professional basketball players recognize whether or not the ball will go into the basket before the ball leaves the shooter's hands. The rest of us need longer.

Near Transfer and Far Transfer

If you develop expertise in one area, will it help you with anything else? The assumption that it will is an old one. Long ago, college education in Britain and the United States focused on studying Latin and Greek, based on the assumption that learning them would add mental discipline that helps in all aspects of life. Today, the premedical curriculum requires calculus. How often do you suppose medical doctors use calculus? About as often as they use astronomy. The calculus requirement is meant to strengthen overall intellectual ability, just by concentrating on something difficult. How well this procedure actually works is uncertain. Many people recommend that old people do crossword puzzles and Sudoku puzzles to exercise their brains. However, the research finds that when older adults work crossword puzzles, they get better at crossword puzzles, but

they don't get better at remembering where they left their keys (Salthouse, 2006).

Psychologists distinguish between near transfer and far transfer (Barnett & Ceci, 2002). Near transfer, *benefit to a new skill based on practice of a similar skill*, is a robust phenomenon, easy to demonstrate. Far transfer, *benefit from practicing something less similar*, is more difficult. Suppose you learn to solve problems like this in a physics course: A train going 25 meters per second (m/s) increases its velocity by 2 m/s each second. How fast will it be going 10 seconds from now? To solve, you multiply 2 m/s times 10 seconds (yielding an increase of 20 m/s) and add it to the original 25 m/s, for an answer of 45 m/s. Now if you face new problems about cars that increase their velocity by a certain amount per second, you should solve them easily. (That's near transfer.) But then you get this problem: Tom receives an allowance of $2 per month beginning on his sixth birthday. The allowance increases by $0.20 each month. How much will he receive on his seventh birthday? This is an example of far transfer, and most people find it difficult to solve (Bassok & Holyoak, 1989). You, of course, recognize the similarity to the train problem: You multiply $0.20/month times 12 months (yielding $2.40) and add it to the original $2, for a total of $4.40.

Far transfer does occur, but it requires extensive practice of the first skill, and even then far transfer is a small or inconsistent effect (Hertzog, 2009). Computer games that require attention, memory, and planning improve academic progress for low-performing children (Goldin et al., 2014). Practicing working memory enhances performance on other working memory tasks (near transfer) but produces no consistent benefit for unrelated cognitive tasks (Harrison et al., 2013; Heinzel et al., 2014; Jaeggi, Buschkuehl, Shah, & Jonides, 2014). Many studies have reported that bilingualism produces far-transfer benefits: On average, children who grow up speaking two or more languages show superior performance on tests of controlling attention, presumably because of their experience at shifting from one language to another

(Bialystok, Craik, Green, & Gollan, 2009). However, many unpublished studies failed to find this benefit (de Bruin, Treccani, & Della Salla, 2015). As is often the case, studies that show a significant effect are published, and studies failing to find the effect are ignored. Although bilingualism may produce benefits, those benefits have been overstated. Overall, the conclusion remains that far transfer is a weak effect.

concept check

13. What is one documented example of far transfer?

Answer

13. Playing computer games that require memory and attention provide benefits for low-performing children.

Successful and Unsuccessful Problem Solving

In this module, we have considered thinking at its best and worst—expertise and error. Experts polish their skills through extensive practice. Of course, we all have to make decisions about topics in which we are not experts. Without insisting on perfection, we can at least hold ourselves to the standard of not doing anything foolish. Perhaps if we become more aware of common errors, we can be more alert to avoid them.

Summary

- *Two types of thinking.* We often make decisions quickly and automatically, using System 1. When we recognize a problem as being more difficult, we do calculations, ponder the evidence, or in other ways engage effortful processes, using System 2. (page 263)
- *Algorithm and heuristics.* People solve problems by algorithms (ways of checking every possibility) and heuristics (ways of simplifying a problem). (page 263)
- *Maximizing and satisficing.* The maximizing strategy is to consider thoroughly every possible choice to find the best one. The satisficing strategy is to accept the first choice one finds that is good enough. People using the maximizing strategy usually make good choices but are often not fully pleased with them. The maximizing strategy is especially problematic when many choices are available. (page 263)
- *Representativeness heuristic.* If something resembles members of some category, we usually assume it too belongs to that category. However, that assumption is risky if the category is a rare one. (page 264)

- *Availability heuristic.* We generally assume that the more easily we can think of examples of some category, the more common that category is. However, this heuristic misleads us when items in rare categories get much publicity. (page 265)
- *Other errors.* People tend to be overconfident about their judgments on difficult questions. They tend to look for evidence that confirms their hypothesis instead of evidence that might reject it. They answer the same question differently when it is framed differently. They sometimes take unpleasant actions to avoid admitting that previous actions were a waste of time or money. (page 265)
- *Expertise.* Becoming an expert requires years of practice and effort, but a given amount of practice benefits some people more than others. Experts recognize and memorize familiar and meaningful patterns more rapidly than less experienced people do. (page 268)
- *Near and far transfer.* Developing skill at a task aids performance of a similar task. It seldom helps much with a dissimilar task. (page 270)

Key Terms

Answers to Other Questions in the Module

D. This illustration shows how to cut and fold an ordinary piece of paper or cardboard to match the figure with nothing left over. (page 262)

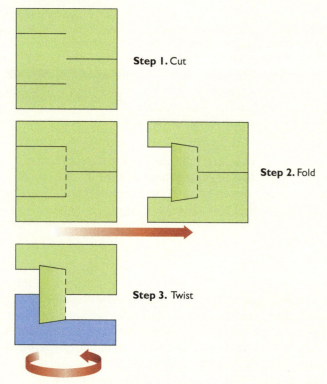

Step 1. Cut

Step 2. Fold

Step 3. Twist

E. A membrane heavy enough to keep the water in would also keep the rubber balls out. (page 262)

F. (1) The best way to attach the candle to the wall is to dump the matches from the box and thumbtack the side of the box to the wall, as shown in this picture. The tiny piece of string is irrelevant.

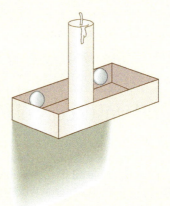

(2) The dots can be connected with four lines:

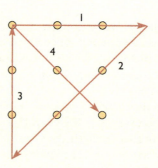

(3) One answer is three students: one psychology major, one chemistry major, and one history major. The other possibility is two students who are majoring in something else—music, for example. (If there are two music majors, all but two of them are indeed majoring in psychology etc.) (page 267)

Review Questions

1. In contrast to System 1 (or Type 1 thinking), what is true of System 2?
   (a) It is quick and almost effortless.
   (b) It evolved earlier in the animal kingdom.
   (c) It is best suited to considering and evaluating complex evidence.
   (d) It generally leads to incorrect answers.

2. What is a heuristic?
   (a) An explicit procedure for calculating an answer
   (b) A procedure that carefully tests every hypothesis before choosing an answer
   (c) A strategy for simplifying a problem

3. In decision making, what is the disadvantage of being a maximizer?
   (a) Maximizers tend to make decisions too quickly.
   (b) Maximizers tend to make worse overall decisions.
   (c) Maximizers tend to be less satisfied with their decisions.
   (d) Maximizers tend to be too influenced by what other people have chosen.

4. People who believe that violent or bizarre behavior is more common on nights of a full moon remember the few occasions that fit this expectation and decide that the results support their belief. This is an example of which heuristic?
   (a) The representativeness heuristic
   (b) The availability heuristic

5. Steve says he has a coworker who is persecuting him. You conclude that Steve is paranoid, ignoring the possibility that Steve really does have an enemy. This is a possible example of which heuristic?
   (a) The representativeness heuristic
   (b) The availability heuristic

6. Someone tells me that if I say "abracadabra" every morning, I will stay healthy. I say it daily and, sure enough, I stay healthy. I conclude that this magic word ensures health. What error of thinking have I made?
   (a) Overconfidence
   (b) Functional fixedness
   (c) Confirmation bias
   (d) The framing effect

7. People will buy meat that claims "90 percent fat free," but not one that says "contains 10 percent fat." This observation is an example of which of the following?
   (a) Overconfidence
   (b) Framing effect
   (c) Sunk cost effect
   (d) Inappropriate use of the availability heuristic

8. Why do most musicians have better-than-average hearing? And what's the evidence?
   (a) Prolonged practice improves hearing. Longitudinal studies find progressively better hearing year by year in people playing music.
   (b) Prolonged practice improves hearing. Twins with more music practice have better hearing than their twins with little or no practice.
   (c) People with better hearing are more likely than average to practice music. Longitudinal studies find no change from year to year in people practicing music.
   (d) People with better hearing are more likely than average to practice music. Twins with more music practice do not have better hearing than their twins with little or no practice.

9. As people develop expertise in a skill such as chess, what improves?
   (a) Their ability to recognize common patterns
   (b) The ratio of excitatory to inhibitory transmission in their brain
   (c) The accuracy of their vision, hearing, and other senses
   (d) Their overall memory and intelligence

10. Many people recommend that old people do crossword puzzles or similar activities to improve everyday memory. If that advice worked (and generally it doesn't), it would be an example of what?
    (a) Near transfer
    (b) Far transfer
    (c) The representativeness heuristic
    (d) The availability heuristic

Answers: 1c, 2c, 3c, 4b, 5a, 6c, 7b, 8d, 9a, 10b.

After studying this module, you should be able to:

- Discuss attempts to teach language to nonhumans.
- Describe and evaluate possible explanations for how humans are specialized to learn language.
- Distinguish between types of language impairment after brain damage.
- Describe how children develop language.
- Explain the role of eye movements in reading.

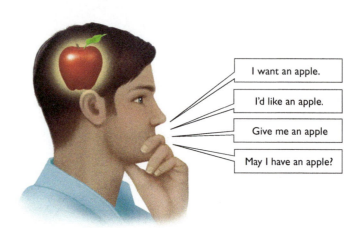

▲ **Figure 8.20** According to transformational grammar, we transform a given deep structure into any of several sentences with different surface structures.

Every species of animal has ways of communicating, but only human language has the property of productivity, *the ability to combine words into new sentences that express an unlimited variety of ideas* (Deacon, 1997). People constantly invent new sentences that no one has ever said before.

You might ask, "How do you know that no one has ever said that sentence before?" Well, of course, no one can be certain that a particular sentence is new, but we can be confident that many sentences are new (without specifying which ones) because of the vast number of possible ways to rearrange words. Imagine this exercise (but don't really try it unless you have nothing else to do with your life): Pick a sentence of more than 10 words from any book you choose. How long would you need to keep reading, in that book or any other, until you found the exact same sentence again?

In short, we do not memorize all the sentences we use. Instead, we learn rules for making and understanding sentences. The famous linguist Noam Chomsky (1980) described those rules as a transformational grammar, *a system for converting a deep structure into a surface structure.* The deep structure is the underlying logic or meaning of a sentence. The surface structure is the sequence of words as they are actually spoken or written (see ▲ Figure 8.20). According to this theory, whenever we speak, we transform the deep structure of the language into a surface structure.

Two surface structures can resemble each other without representing the same deep structure, or they can represent the same deep structure without resembling each other. For example, "John is easy to please" has the same deep structure as "Pleasing John is easy" and "It is easy to please John." These sentences represent the same idea. In contrast, consider

the sentence "Never threaten someone with a chain saw." The surface structure of that sentence maps into two deep structures, as shown in ▼ Figure 8.21.

Nonhuman Precursors to Language

Researcher Terrence Deacon once presented a talk about language to his 8-year-old's elementary school class. One child asked whether other animals have their own languages. Deacon explained that other species communicate but without the productivity of human language. The child persisted, asking whether other

Deep Structure No. 1:
You are holding a chain saw. Don't threaten to use it to attack someone!

Deep Structure No. 2:
Some deranged person is holding a chain saw. Don't threaten him!

▲ **Figure 8.21** The sentence "Never threaten someone with a chain saw" has one surface structure but two deep structures, corresponding to different meanings.

animals had at least a simple language with a few words and short sentences. No, he replied, they don't.

Then another child asked, "Why not?" (Deacon, 1997, p. 12). Deacon paused. Why not, indeed? If language is so useful to humans, why haven't other species evolved at least a little of it? And what makes humans so good at learning language?

One way to examine humans' language specialization is to ask how far another species could progress toward language. Beginning in the 1920s, several psychologists reared chimpanzees in their homes and tried to teach them to talk. The chimpanzees learned many human habits but understood only a few words and their few attempts to speak were extremely inarticulate.

Much of the problem is that chimpanzees make their sounds while inhaling, whereas humans speak while exhaling. (Give it a try. Can you say your name while inhaling?) However, chimpanzees do make hand gestures in nature. R. Allen Gardner and Beatrice Gardner (1969) taught a chimpanzee named Washoe to use the sign language of the American deaf (Ameslan). Washoe eventually learned the symbols for about 100 words, and other chimps learned to communicate with other visual symbols (see ▼ Figure 8.22).

How much do these gestures resemble language? Washoe and other chimpanzees trained in this way used their symbols almost exclusively to make requests, not to describe, and rarely in original combinations (Pate & Rumbaugh, 1983; Terrace, Petitto, Sanders, & Bever, 1979; Thompson & Church, 1980). By contrast, a human child with a vocabulary of 100 words or so links them into short sentences and frequently uses words to describe. However, Washoe did show some understanding. She usually answered "Who" questions with names, "What" questions with objects, and "Where" questions with places, even when she specified the wrong name, object, or place (Van Cantfort, Gardner, & Gardner, 1989).

More impressive results have been reported for another species, the bonobo chimpanzee, *Pan paniscus*. Bonobos' social behavior resembles that of humans in several regards: Males and females

a

b

c

d

▲ **Figure 8.22** Psychologists have tried to teach chimpanzees to communicate with gestures or symbols. (**a**) A chimp arranges plastic chips to request food. (**b**) Another chimp in her human home. (**c**) Kanzi, a bonobo, presses symbols to indicate words. (**d**) A chimp signing *toothbrush*.

▲ **Figure 8.23** Kanzi, a bonobo, points to answers on a board in response to questions he hears through earphones. Experimenter Rose Sevcik does not hear the questions, so she cannot signal the correct answer.

form strong attachments, females are sexually responsive outside their fertile period, males contribute to infant care, and adults often share food. Like humans, they stand comfortably on their hind legs, and they often copulate face-to-face. Several bonobos have learned to press keys on a board to make short sentences, as in Figure 8.22c and ▲ Figure 8.23. Unlike Washoe and other common chimpanzees, bonobos sometimes use symbols to describe events, without requesting anything. One with a cut on his hand explained that his mother had bitten him. However, unlike children, bonobos almost never use expressions of possession, such as "mine!" (Lyn, Greenfield, Savage-Rumbaugh, Gillespie-Lynch, & Hopkins, 2011).

The most proficient bonobos seem to comprehend symbols about as well as a 2- to $2^1/_2$-year-old child understands language (Savage-Rumbaugh et al., 1993). They also show considerable understanding of spoken English, following such odd commands as "bite your ball" and "take the vacuum cleaner outside" (Savage-Rumbaugh, 1990; Savage-Rumbaugh, Sevcik, Brakke, & Rumbaugh, 1992). They passed a test of responding to commands issued over earphones, to make sure the experimenter sitting nearby wasn't using "Clever Hans"-type signals, as discussed in Chapter 2 (see Figure 8.23).

Why have bonobos been more successful with language than common chimpanzees? Apparently, bonobos have a greater predisposition for this type of learning. Also, they learned by observation and imitation, which promote better understanding than the formal training methods that previous studies used (Savage-Rumbaugh et al., 1992). Finally, the bonobos began their language experience early in life.

concept check

14. Based on the studies with bonobos, can you offer advice about how to teach language to children with impaired language learning?

Answer

14. Start language learning when a child is young. Rely on imitation as much as possible instead of providing direct reinforcements for correct responses.

Human Specializations for Learning Language

Humans are clearly more adapted for language than any other species, including bonobos. Why do we learn language so easily?

Language and General Intelligence

Did we evolve language as an accidental by-product of evolving big brains? Several observations argue strongly against this idea. Dolphins and whales have even larger brains but do not develop a flexible communication system resembling human language. Some people with brain damage have less total brain mass than a chimpanzee but continue to speak and understand language.

Also, some children, up to 7 percent by some estimates, have normal intelligence in other ways but noticeable limitations in language. For example, they don't understand the difference between "Who was the girl pushing?" and "Who was pushing the girl?" (Leonard, 2007). People with a particular gene have even greater language impairments despite otherwise normal intelligence (Fisher, Vargha-Khadem, Watkins, Monaco, & Pembrey, 1998; Lai, Fisher, Hurst, Vargha-Khadem, & Monaco, 2001). They do not fully master even simple rules, such as how to form plurals of nouns.

At the opposite extreme, consider Williams syndrome, *a genetic condition characterized by mental retardation in most regards but surprisingly good use of language relative to their other abilities* (Meyer-Lindenberg, Mervis, & Berman, 2006). One child, when asked to name as many animals as he could, started with "ibex, whale, bull, yak, zebra, puppy, kitten, tiger, koala, dragon . . ." Another child could sing more than 1,000 songs in 22 languages (Bellugi & St. George, 2000). However, these children prefer 50 pennies to 5 dollars and, when asked to estimate the length of a bus, give answers such as "3 inches or 100 inches, maybe" (Bellugi, Lichtenberger, Jones, Lai, & St. George, 2000). They often show problems in attention and planning (Greer, Riby, Hamiliton, & Riby, 2013). Evidently, language ability is not the same as overall intelligence.

Language Learning as a Specialized Capacity

Susan Carey (1978) calculated that children between the ages of 1½ and 6 learn an average of nine new words per day. But how do they infer the meanings of all those words? A parent points at a frog and says "frog." How does the child guess that the word means "frog" rather than "small thing," "green thing," or "this particular frog"? Indeed, why does the child assume the sound means anything at all?

Noam Chomsky has argued that children must begin with preconceptions. Chomsky and his followers suggest that people are born with a language acquisition device, *a built-in mechanism for acquiring language* (Pinker, 1994). One line of evidence for this theory is that deaf children who are not taught a sign language invent one of their own and try to teach it to their parents or to other deaf children (Goldin-Meadow, McNeill, & Singleton, 1996; Goldin-Meadow & Mylander, 1998). Further evidence is that children learn to use complex grammatical structures, such as "Is the boy who is unhappy watching Mickey Mouse?"

Wernicke's area:
Brain damage leading to
Wernicke's aphasia usually
includes this area.

Broca's area:
Brain damage
leading to Broca's
aphasia usually
includes this area.

▲ **Figure 8.24** Brain damage that produces major deficits in language usually includes the left-hemisphere areas shown here. However, the deficits are severe only if the damage includes these areas but extends beyond them.

and muscle control. If you hear a highly emotional story, activity increases in brain areas important for emotion (Chow et al., 2013). That is, understanding language means relating it to everything else your brain does. Although Broca's area, Wernicke's area, and the surrounding areas are important, they can do nothing without connections to all of the brain.

concept check

15. **Brain-damaged patient A speaks fluently but is hard to understand, and she has trouble understanding other people's speech. Patient B understands most speech, but he speaks slowly and inarticulately, and he leaves out nearly all prepositions, conjunctions, and word endings. Which kind of aphasia does each patient have?**

Answer

15. Patient A has Wernicke's aphasia. Patient B has Broca's aphasia.

Language and the Human Brain

What aspect of the human brain enables us to learn language so easily? Studies of people with brain damage have long pointed to two brain areas as particularly important for language. People with damage in the frontal cortex, including *Broca's area* (see ▲ Figure 8.24), develop Broca's aphasia, *a condition characterized by difficulties in language production.* Serious language impairment occurs only if the damage extends beyond Broca's area, and even into the interior of the brain, but what matters here is the nature of the impairment, not the exact location of the damage. The person speaks slowly and inarticulately and is no better with writing or typing. Someone with Broca's aphasia is especially impaired with using and understanding grammatical devices such as prepositions, conjunctions, and word endings. For example, one person who was asked about a dental appointment slowly mumbled, "Yes . . . Monday . . . Dad and Dick . . . Wednesday nine o'clock . . . 10 o'clock . . . doctors . . . and . . . teeth" (Geschwind, 1979, p. 186).

People with damage in the temporal cortex, including *Wernicke's area* (see Figure 8.24), develop Wernicke's aphasia, *a condition marked by impaired recall of nouns and impaired language comprehension, despite fluent and grammatical speech.* Difficulty with nouns and impaired comprehension fit together: If you cannot remember what something is called, you will have trouble processing a sentence based on that word. Because these people omit or misuse most nouns, their speech is hard to understand. For example, one patient responded to a question about his health, "I felt worse because I can no longer keep in mind from the mind of the minds to keep me from mind and up to the ear which can be to find among ourselves" (Brown, 1977, p. 29).

However, language depends on far more than just Broca's area and Wernicke's area. If you hear a story about sights and sounds, activity increases in the brain areas responsible for vision and hearing. If you hear a story with much movement, activity increases in the areas responsible for body sensations

even though they don't hear that kind of expression very often. To pick up that kind of grammar so quickly, children must have a predisposition of some sort. Still, the exact nature of that predisposition is uncertain.

Language Development

Brain specializations facilitate language learning, but we still have to learn. Children's language learning is amazing. Nearly every child learns language, even if the parents know nothing about how to teach it.

Language in Early Childhood

■ Table 8.2 lists the average ages at which children reach various stages of language ability (Lenneberg, 1969; Moskowitz, 1978). Remember, these are averages, and children vary considerably. Progression through these stages depends largely on maturation (Lenneberg, 1967, 1969). Parents who expose their children to as much language as possible increase the children's vocabulary, but they hardly affect the rate of progression through language stages. Hearing children of deaf parents are exposed to much less spoken language, but they too progress almost on schedule.

Deaf infants babble as much as hearing infants do for the first 6 months and then start to decline. At first, hearing infants babble only haphazard sounds, but soon they start repeating the sounds they have been hearing. By age 1 year, an infant babbles mostly sounds that resemble the language the family speaks (Locke, 1994).

One of an infant's first sounds is *muh,* and that sound or something similar has been adopted by many of the world's languages to mean "mother." Infants also make the sounds *duh, puh,* and *buh.* In many languages, the word for father is similar to *dada* or *papa. Baba* is the word for father in Chinese and for grandmother in several other languages. In effect, infants tell their parents what words to use for important concepts.

By age 1½, most toddlers have a vocabulary of about 50 words, but they seldom link words together. A toddler says "Daddy" and "bye-bye" but not "Bye-bye, Daddy." In context, parents can usually discern considerable meaning in these single-word utterances. *Mama* might mean, "That's a picture of Mama," "Take me to Mama," "Mama went away and left me here," or "Mama, I'm hungry." Toddlers also communicate extensively by gestures (Behne, Carpenter, & Tomasello, 2014; Kraljevic, Cepanec, & Simlesa, 2014). So do adults, of course. (Try to explain the concept of *spiral* without moving your hands!) Toddlers also sometimes combine a word with a gesture, such as pointing at something while saying "mine" or pointing at a hat and saying "mama" to indicate mama's hat (Iverson & Goldin-Meadow, 2005). The word and gesture constitute a primitive kind of sentence. Children who convey much information by gesture alone or word plus gesture at age 1½ are likely to develop better-than-average vocabulary and complex sentence structure by age 3½ (Rowe & Goldin-Meadow, 2009).

By age 2, children start producing telegraphic phrases of two or more words, such as "more page" (read some more), "allgone sticky" (my hands are now clean), and "allgone outside" (someone has closed the door). Note the originality of such phrases. It is unlikely that the parents ever said "allgone sticky"!

By age 2½ to 3 years, most children generate sentences but with some idiosyncrasies. Many young children have their own rules for negative sentences. A common one is to add *no* or *not* to the beginning or end of a sentence, such as, "No I want to go to bed!" One little girl formed her negatives just by saying something louder and at a higher pitch. If she shrieked, "I want to share my toys!" she meant, "I do *not* want to share my toys." She had learned this rule by noting that people screamed when they told her not to do something. My son Sam made negatives for a while by adding the word *either* to the end of a sentence: "I want to eat lima beans either." He had heard people say, "I don't want to do that either."

When young children speak, they apply grammatical rules, although of course they cannot state those rules. For example, they apply the rules of English to produce such sentences as "the womans goed and doed something," or "the mans getted their foots wet." We say that children *overregularize* or *overgeneralize* the rules. My son David invented the word *shis* to mean "belonging to a female." (He apparently generalized the rule "He–his, she–shis.") Clearly, children are not just repeating what they have heard.

People have an optimal period for learning language in early childhood (Werker & Tees, 2005).

Table 8.2 Stages of Language Development

Age	Typical Language Abilities (Much Individual Variation)
3 months	Random vocalizations.
6 months	More distinct babbling.
1 year	Babbling that resembles the typical sounds of the family's language; probably one or more words including "mama"; language comprehension much better than production.
1 1/2 years	Can say some words (mean about 50), mostly nouns; few or no phrases.
2 years	Speaks in two-word phrases.
2 1/2 years	Longer phrases and short sentences with some errors and unusual constructions. Can understand much more.
3 years	Vocabulary near 1,000 words; longer sentences with fewer errors.
4 years	Close to adult speech competence.

Much of the evidence for this conclusion comes from people who learn a second language. Adults can memorize the vocabulary of a second language, but children are far better at mastering the pronunciation and somewhat better at acquiring the grammar (Huang, 2014). People who start a second language after early childhood only rarely approach the level of a native speaker. Even those who start after the first couple years of life are at a disadvantage (Abrahamsson & Hyltenstam, 2009). However, researchers find no sharp age cutoff when language suddenly becomes more difficult. The ease of learning a second language declines steadily from early childhood through the 60s and 70s (Vanhove, 2013).

16. Why do psychologists believe that even very young children learn rules of grammar?

Answer

16. Children show that they learn rules of grammar when they overgeneralize those rules, creating such words as *womans* and *goed.*

Children Exposed to No Language or Two Languages

Would children who were exposed to no language make up a new one? In rare cases, an infant who was accidentally separated from other people grew up in a forest without human contact until discovered years later. Such children not only fail to show a language of their own but also fail to learn much language after they are given the chance (Pinker, 1994). However, their development is so abnormal and their early life so unknown that we should hesitate to draw conclusions.

Better evidence comes from studies of children who are deaf. Children who cannot hear well enough to learn speech and who are not taught sign language invent their own sign language (Senghas, Kita, & Özyürek, 2004). Observations in Nicaragua found that sign language evolved over the decades. Deaf people learned sign language and taught it to the next generation, who, having learned it from early childhood, elaborated on it, made it more expressive, taught the enhanced sign language to the next generation, and so on (Senghas & Coppola, 2001).

If a deaf child starts to invent a sign language and no one responds to it, because the child meets no other deaf children and the adults fail to learn, the child gradually abandons it. If a deaf child does learn sign language, it can be a bridge to later learning a spoken language. On average, the children who are best at sign language are also best at reading English or other written languages (Andrew, Hoshooley, & Joanisse, 2014). A deaf child who is given no opportunity to learn sign language until age 12 or so struggles to develop signing skills and never catches up with those who started earlier (Harley & Wang, 1997; Mayberry, Lock, & Kazmi, 2002). This observation is our best evidence for the importance of early development in language learning: A child who doesn't learn any language while young is permanently impaired at learning one.

Many children grow up in a bilingual environment, *learning two languages*. You might guess that a bilingual person represents the languages in different brain areas. However, the research shows that both languages activate the same areas (Perani & Abutalebi, 2005). Those who are bilingual from early infancy devote more brain areas to language, including parts of both left and right hemispheres, and they develop wider connections in the brain, but the same brain areas participate in both languages (Hull & Vaid, 2007; Luk, Bialystock, Craik, & Grady, 2011; Mechelli et al., 2004; Perani & Abutalebi, 2005). If the brain represents two languages in the same places, how do bilingual people keep their languages separate? They don't, at least not completely (Thierry & Wu, 2007). They often get confused when they switch between languages (Levy, McVeigh, Marful, & Anderson, 2007; Linck, Kroll, & Sunderman, 2009).

Bilingualism has two disadvantages: Children take longer to master two languages than one, and their vocabulary lags behind that of someone who speaks only one language. Bilingual people often take longer than average to think of a word (Bialystok, Craik, & Luk, 2008). The primary advantage of bilingualism is obvious: People who know another language can communicate with more people (see ▼ Figure 8.25). A second advantage, as mentioned earlier, is that bilingual people learn to control their attention more effectively (Engel de Abreu et al., 2012; Gold, Kim, Johnson, Kryscio, & Smith, 2013). Researchers still debate the size of that effect, however.

▲ **Figure 8.25** Children who grow up in a bilingual or multilingual environment gain in their ability to communicate with more people, and possibly gain in their ability to control their attention.

concept check

17. What are the advantages and disadvantages of bilingualism?

Answer

17. Advantages: The individual can speak with more people, and perhaps improves the ability to control attention. Disadvantages: The individual takes longer to learn two languages than one, and probably will not master either language as well as someone who is learning only one language.

Understanding Language

The English language has many words with ambiguous meanings. For instance, *peck* can mean one-fourth of a bushel or to strike with a beak. *Rose* can mean a flower or the past tense of the verb *to rise*. *Desert* can mean a dry stretch of land or (with a different accent) to abandon someone. In context, however, listeners usually understand the meaning.

We become even more aware of context when we compare languages. Mandarin Chinese draws no distinctions for noun number or verb tense, and it lacks articles such as *a* and *the*. Thus, the sentence for "A man is buying an apple" is also the sentence for "The men bought apples," "A man will buy apples," and so forth. Despite this ambiguity, listeners ordinarily understand the meaning in context. If the context is insufficient, a speaker adds a word such as *tomorrow* or *yesterday*. The Malay language has one word for "you and I" and a different word for "someone else and I." English translates both words as "we." The Malaysians wonder how listeners understand this ambiguous word, just as English speakers wonder how the Chinese get by without indications of number or tense.

Understanding a Word

Context not only determines how we interpret a word, but also primes us to hear an ambiguous sound one way or another. For example, a computer generated a sound halfway between a normal *s* sound and a normal *sh* sound. When this intermediate sound replaced the *s* sound at the end of the word *embarrass*, people heard it as an *s* sound. When the same sound replaced *sh* at the end of *abolish*, people heard the same sound as *sh* (Samuel, 2001).

We also use lip-reading more than we realize to understand what we hear. If lip movements do not match the sound, we strike a compromise between what we see and what we hear (McGurk & MacDonald, 1976). In one study, students listened to a tape recording of a sentence with a sound missing (Warren, 1970). The sentence was, "The state governors met with their respective legislatures convening in the capital city." However, the sound of the first *s* in the word *legislatures*, along with part of the adjacent *i* and *l*, had been replaced by a cough or a tone. The students were asked to listen to the recording and try to identify the location of the cough or tone. None of the 20 students identified the location correctly, and half thought the cough or tone interrupted one of the other words on the tape. Even those who were told that the *s* sound was missing insisted that they clearly heard the sound *s*. The brain uses the context to fill in the missing sound.

Just as we hear the word *legislatures* as a whole, not as a string of separate letters, we interpret a sequence of words as a whole, not one at a time. Suppose you hear a tape-recorded word that is carefully engineered to sound halfway between *dent* and *tent*. The way you perceive it depends on the context:

1. When the *ent in the fender was well camouflaged, we sold the car.
2. When the *ent in the forest was well camouflaged, we began our hike.

Most people who hear sentence 1 report the word *dent*. Most who hear sentence 2 report *tent*. Now consider two more sentences:

3. When the *ent was noticed in the fender, we sold the car.
4. When the *ent was noticed in the forest, we stopped to rest.

For sentences 3 and 4, the context comes too late to help. People are as likely to report hearing *dent* in one sentence as in the other (Connine, Blasko, & Hall, 1991). Consider what this means: In the first two sentences, after *ent, the person heard only two intervening syllables before hearing fender or forest. In the second pair, five syllables intervened. Evidently, when you hear an ambiguous sound, you hold it briefly in an "undecided" state for the context to clarify it. Beyond a certain point, it is too late.

Although a long-delayed context cannot help you hear an ambiguous word correctly, it does help you understand its meaning. Consider the following sentence (Lashley, 1951):

> Rapid righting with his uninjured hand saved from loss the contents of the capsized canoe.

If you hear this sentence spoken aloud so that spelling provides no clues, you are likely at first to interpret the second word as *writing*, until you reach the final two words of the sentence. Suddenly, *capsized canoe* tells you that *righting* meant "pushing with a paddle." Only the immediate context can influence what you hear, but a delayed context can change the word's meaning.

Understanding Sentences

Making sense of language requires knowledge about the world. For example, consider the following sentences (from Just & Carpenter, 1987):

▲ **Figure 8.26** In England, a *football coach* is a bus full of soccer fans. In the United States, it's the person who directs a team of American football players.

That store sells horseshoes.
That store sells alligator shoes.

You interpret *horseshoes* to mean "shoes for horses to wear," but you interpret *alligator shoes* as "shoes made from alligator hide." Your understanding of the sentences depends on your knowledge of the world, not just the syntax of the sentences.

Here is another example:

I'm going to buy a pet hamster at the store, if it's open.
I'm going to buy a pet hamster at the store, if it's healthy.

Nothing about the sentence structure told you that *it* refers to the store in the first sentence and a hamster in the second sentence. You understood because you know that stores but not hamsters can be open, whereas hamsters but not stores can be healthy.

In short, understanding a sentence depends on your knowledge of the world and all the assumptions that you share with the speaker or writer of the sentence. Sometimes, you even have to remember where you are because the meaning of a word differs from one place to another (see ▲ Figure 8.26).

Now consider this sentence: *While Anna dressed the baby played in the crib.* Quickly: Whom did Anna dress? And who played in the crib? The addition of a comma would simplify the sentence, but even without it, English grammar prohibits "baby" from being both the object of *dressed* and the subject of *played*. If the baby played in the crib (as you no doubt answered), Anna must have dressed herself. Nevertheless, many people think Anna dressed the baby (Ferreira, Bailey, & Ferraro, 2002). When speaking or writing, it is important to try to imagine ways in which people might misunderstand you.

Limits to Our Language Understanding

Some grammatical sentences are almost incomprehensible. One example is a doubly embedded sentence—a sentence within a sentence within a sentence. A singly embedded sentence is understandable, though difficult:

The dog the cat saw chased a squirrel.
The squirrel the dog chased climbed the tree.

▲ **Figure 8.27** Most students preferred Kool-Aid made with sugar labeled "sugar" instead of sugar labeled "not cyanide," even though they had placed the labels themselves. People don't always trust the word *not*. (Based on results of Rozin, Markwith, & Ross, 1990)

In the first sentence, "the cat saw the dog" is embedded within "the dog chased a squirrel." In the second, "the dog chased the squirrel" is embedded within "the squirrel climbed the tree." So far, so good, but now consider a doubly embedded sentence:

The squirrel the dog the cat saw chased climbed the tree.

Doubly embedded sentences overburden our memory. In fact, if your memory is already burdened with other matters, you may have trouble understanding a singly embedded sentence (Gordon, Hendrick, & Levine, 2002).

Double negatives are also difficult to understand. "I would not deny that . . ." means that I agree. "It is not false that . . ." means that something is true. People often misunderstand such sentences. Have you ever seen a multiple-choice test item that asks "Which of the following is not true . . ." and then one of the choices has a *not* in it? With such items, confusion is almost certain.

Triple negatives are still worse. Consider the following sentence, which includes *four* negatives (emphasis added): "If you do *not* unanimously find from your consideration of all the evidence that there are *no* mitigating factors sufficient to *preclude* the imposition of a death sentence, then you should sign the verdict requiring the court to impose a sentence *other than* death." In Illinois some years ago, judges used to read those instructions to a jury to explain how to decide between a death penalty and life in prison. It means that if even one juror sees some reason to reject the death penalty, the jury should recommend prison instead. Do you think many jurors understood?

With a single negative, people often don't fully accept the meaning of the word *not*. Suppose a packaged food says, "Contains no rat pieces!" Does that notice encourage you to buy the product? Hardly! I was once on an airplane that turned around shortly after departure because one of its two engines failed. The attendant told the passengers what was happening, but until she said, "Please don't panic," we didn't realize there might be a reason to panic. If you ask someone for a favor and the person responds, "No problem," how do you react? The expression "no problem" implies there was almost a problem, or maybe there is a bit of a problem.

In one clever experiment, students watched an experimenter pour sugar into two jars. The students were then told to label one jar "sucrose, table sugar" and the other "not sodium cyanide, not poison." Then the experimenter made two cups of Kool-Aid, one from each jar of sugar, and asked the students to choose one to drink (see ▲ Figure 8.27). Of the 44 who expressed a preference, 35 wanted Kool-Aid made from the jar marked "sucrose," not from the one that denied having poison (Rozin, Markwith, & Ross, 1990).

Reading

Students of language distinguish between phonemes and morphemes. A **phoneme** is *a unit of sound*, such as *f* or *sh*. Machines that talk to you, such as a GPS, take a written word, break it into phonemes, and pronounce the phonemes. For some words with irregular spellings, the machine's pronunciation may be wrong or hard to understand. A **morpheme** is *a unit of meaning*. For example, the noun *thrills* has two morphemes (*thrill* and *s*). The final *s* is a unit of meaning because it indicates that the noun is plural (see ▼ Figure 8.28). *Harp* has one morpheme, and *harping* has two, but *harpoon* has just one, as it is not derived from *harp*. Morphemes help us break an

Phonemes
(units of sound):

SHAMELESSNESS

Morphemes
(units of meaning):

▲ **Figure 8.28** The word *shamelessness* has nine phonemes (units of sound) and three morphemes (units of meaning).

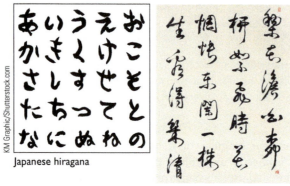

Japanese hiragana

Chinese characters

Illustration of Japanese hiragana writing and Chinese writing.

unfamiliar word into meaningful parts. For example, we can see *reinvigoration* as *re-in-vigor-ation*, meaning the process of increasing vigor again.

Readers of English and other European languages are accustomed to the idea that a letter or combination of letters represents a phoneme. However, in the Japanese *hiragana* style of writing, each character represents a syllable. In Chinese, each character represents a morpheme and ordinarily a whole word.

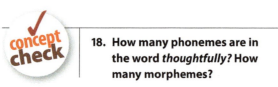

concept check

18. **How many phonemes are in the word *thoughtfully*? How many morphemes?**

Answer

18. It has seven phonemes: th-ough-t-f-u-ll-y. It has three morphemes: thought-ful-ly.

Word Recognition

Expertise develops from many years of practice, enabling someone to recognize complex patterns at a glance. Because you have been reading for hours a day, almost every day since childhood, you have developed expertise at reading. You may not think of yourself as an expert, because we usually reserve that term for someone who is far more skilled than others. Nevertheless, you recognize words instantaneously, like an expert who recognizes chess patterns at a glance.

Consider the following experiment: The investigator flashes a letter on a screen for less than a quarter-second, shows an interfering pattern, and asks, "Was it *C* or *J*?" Then the experimenter flashes an entire word on the screen under the same conditions and asks, "Was the first letter of the word *C* or *J*?" (see ▼ Figure 8.29). Which question is easier? Most people *identify the letter more accurately when it is part of a word than when it is presented by itself* (Reicher, 1969; Wheeler, 1970). This is known as the word-superiority effect.

In further research, James Johnston and James McClelland (1974) briefly flashed words on the screen and asked students to identify one letter at a marked position in each word (see ▼ Figure 8.30). On some trials, the experimenters told the students to try to see the whole word. On other trials, they showed the students exactly where the critical letter would appear on the screen and told them to focus on that spot and ignore the rest of the screen. Most students identified the critical letter more successfully when they looked at the whole word than when they focused on just the letter itself. This benefit occurs only with a real word, like COIN, not with a nonsense combination, like CXQF (Rumelhart & McClelland, 1982).

You may have experienced the word-superiority effect yourself. To pass time on long car trips, people sometimes try to find every letter of the alphabet on the billboards. It is easier to spot a letter by reading words than by checking letter by letter.

What accounts for the word-superiority effect? According to one model (McClelland, 1988; Rumelhart, McClelland, & the PDP Research Group, 1986), our perceptions and memories are represented by connections among "units" corresponding to sets of neurons. Each unit connects to other

▲ **Figure 8.29** Either a word or a single letter flashed on a screen and then an interfering pattern. The observers were asked, "Which was presented: *C* or *J*?" More of them identified the letter correctly when it was part of a word.

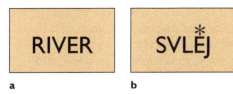

a   b

▲ **Figure 8.30** Students identified an indicated letter better when they focused on an entire word (**a**) than on a single letter in a designated spot (**b**).

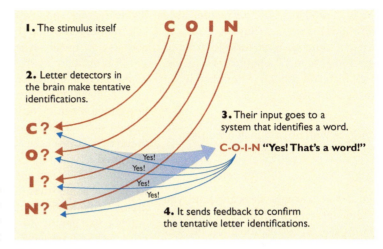

I. The stimulus itself

2. Letter detectors in the brain make tentative identifications.

3. Their input goes to a system that identifies a word.

C-O-I-N **"Yes! That's a word!"**

Yes!
Yes!
Yes!
Yes!

C ?
O ?
I ?
N ?

4. It sends feedback to confirm the tentative letter identifications.

▲ **Figure 8.31** According to one model, a visual stimulus activates certain letter units, some more strongly than others. Those letter units then activate a word unit, which in turn strengthens the letter units that compose it. For this reason, we recognize a whole word more easily than a single letter.

units (see ▶ Figure 8.31). Any activated unit excites some of its neighbors and inhibits others. Suppose units corresponding to the letters *C, O, I,* and *N* are moderately active. They excite a higher-order unit corresponding to the word *COIN*. Although none of the four letter units sends a strong message by itself, the collective impact is strong (McClelland & Rumelhart, 1981). The perception *COIN* then feeds excitation back to the individual letter-identifying units and confirms their tentative identifications.

This model helps explain our perception of ▼ Figure 8.32. You see the first and third words as *BIRD* and *PROOF*, not *BIPD* and *RROOF*. You see the second and fourth words as *DRIVE* and *FRIDAY*, not *DRIVF* and *EIRDAY*. Why? After all, the R in BIRD looks the same as the P in PROOF, and the E in DRIVE looks the same as the F in FRIDAY. When you tentatively perceive a word, the feedback strengthens the perception of the units that would make the word, and not those that would make a meaningless string of letters. Word recognition can become more complex. Consider the following sentence:

> The boy cuold not slove the porblem so he aksed for help.

Most readers "recognize" the words *could, solve, problem, and asked,* although of course they read faster if all words are spelled correctly (Rayner, White, Johnson, & Liversedge, 2006; White, Johnson, Liversedge, & Rayner, 2008). When we read, we process the context so that even out-of-place letters activate identification of the correct words. (This tendency can pose a probelm for prooofreaders, who sometimes fail to notice a misspellling!)

Reading and Eye Movements

Reading requires eye movements, of course. When psychologists monitored eye movements, they discovered that a reader's eyes move in a jerky fashion. You move your eyes steadily to follow a moving object, but when scanning a stationary object, such as a page of print, you alternate between fixations, *when your eyes are stationary,* and saccades (sa-KAHDS), *quick eye movements from one fixation point to another.* You read during fixations, not during saccades. For an average adult reader, most fixations last about 200 to 250 milliseconds. Fixations are briefer on familiar words like *legal* than on harder words like *luau* or words with more than one meaning like *lead* (Rodd, Gaskell, & Marslen-Wilson, 2002). Because

19. What evidence indicates that we do *not* read a word one letter at a time?

Answer

19. Ambiguous letters, such as those in Figure 8.32, appear to be one letter in one context and another letter in a different context. Also, a reader sometimes "recognizes" a misspelled word even when certain letters are out of order.

▲ **Figure 8.32** The combination of possible letters enables us to identify a word. Word recognition in turn helps to confirm the letter identifications.

saccades last only 25 to 50 ms, a normal reading pace is about four fixations per second (Rayner, 1998).

How much can someone read during a fixation? On average, the limit is about 11 characters at a time. To demonstrate, focus on the letter *i* marked by an arrow (↓) in these sentences:

↓

1. This is a sentence with no misspelled words.

↓

2. Xboc tx zjg rxunce with no mijvgab zucn.

If you permit your eyes to wander back and forth, you notice the gibberish in sentence 2. But as long as you dutifully keep your eyes on the fixation point, the sentence looks all right. You read the letter on which you fixated plus about three or four characters (including spaces) to the left and about seven to the right. The rest is too blurry to make it out. Therefore, you see — *ce with no m*—or possibly—*nce with no mi*—.

This limit of about 11 letters depends partly on the lighting. In faint light, your span decreases to as little as 1 or 2 letters, and your reading ability suffers accordingly (Legge, Ahn, Klitz, & Luebker, 1997). Within a large range, the limit does not depend on the size of the print (Miellet, O'Donnell, & Sereno, 2009). In the following display, again focus on the letter *i* in each sentence and check how many letters you can read to its left and right:

↓

This is a sentence with no misspelled words.

↓

This is a sentence with no misspelled words.

↓

is a sentence with no misspelled

If your reading span were limited by how many letters can fit into the fovea of your retina, you would read fewer letters as the print gets larger. In fact, you do at least as well, maybe even better, with larger print (up to a point).

The results vary from one language to another. In Japanese and Chinese, where each character conveys more information than English letters do, readers see fewer letters per fixation (Rayner, 1998). That is, the limit depends on how much meaning one can attend to at once. In Hebrew and Farsi, which are written right to left, readers read more letters to the left of fixation and fewer to the right (Brysbaert, Vitu, & Schroyens, 1996; Faust, Kravetz, & Babkoff, 1993; Malamed & Zaidel, 1993).

Reading is a strategic process of pausing longer on difficult or ambiguous words and sometimes looking back to previous words. In fact, of all eye movements while reading, about 10 to 15 percent are backward movements. One app you can get for your computer claims to increase reading speed by eliminating those backward movements. A device monitors your eye movements, so that whenever you move your eyes forward, every word you have already read goes blank. You therefore cannot go back. That procedure may indeed increase your reading speed, but sometimes you *need* to look back. Consider this sentence:

While the woman ate the spaghetti on the table grew cold.

When you first read that sentence, you thought the woman ate the spaghetti. The rest of the sentence told you that you misunderstood, so you had to look back and reread. Moving your eyes backward in a sentence is often important for understanding (Schotter, Tran, & Rayner, 2014).

 concept check

20. If a word is longer than 11 letters, will a reader need more than one fixation to read it?

Answer

20. Sometimes, but not always. Suppose your eyes fixate on the fourth letter of *memoriza-tion*. You should be able to see the three letters to its left and the seven to its right—that is, all except the final letter. Because there is only one English word that starts *memorizatio-*, you already know the word.

Language and Humanity

At the start of this module, we considered the question, "If language is so useful to humans, why haven't other species evolved at least a little of it?" None of the research answers this question, but we can speculate.

Many adaptations are much more useful on a large scale than on a small scale. For example, stinkiness is extremely useful to skunks. Being slightly stinky wouldn't help much. If you're going to rely on stink for your survival, you need a lot of it. Porcupines survive because of their long quills. Having a few short quills would be only slightly helpful. Similarly, a little bit of language development is probably an unstable condition, evolutionarily speaking. Once a species such as humans had evolved a little language, those individuals with still better language abilities would have a huge selective advantage over the others.

Summary

- *Language productivity.* Human languages enable us to create new words and phrases to express new ideas. (page 274)
- *Language training in nonhumans.* Bonobos, and to a smaller extent other species, have learned certain aspects of language.

Human evolution evidently elaborated on potentials found in our apelike ancestors but developed that potential further. (page 274)

- *Language and intelligence.* It is possible to have intelligence without language or language without other aspects of intelligence. Therefore, many psychologists regard language as a specialized capacity, not just a by-product of overall intelligence. (page 276)
- *Predisposition to learn language.* Noam Chomsky and others have argued that the ease with which children acquire language indicates that they are born with a predisposition that facilitates language learning. (page 276)
- *Brain organization and aphasia.* Brain damage, especially in the left hemisphere, impairs people's ability to understand or use language. Many brain areas contribute to language in varied ways. (page 277)
- *Stages of language development.* Children advance through several stages of language development, reflecting maturation of brain structures. From the start, children's language is creative, using the rules of language to make new word combinations and sentences. (page 277)
- *Children exposed to no language or two.* If deaf children are not exposed to language, they invent a sign language of their own. However, a deaf child who learns neither spoken language nor sign language in childhood is impaired on learning any language later. Children in a bilingual environment sometimes have trouble keeping the two languages separate but possibly gain increased ability to control attention. (page 278)
- *Understanding language.* We understand ambiguous words and sentences in context by applying the knowledge we have about the world in general. (page 279)
- *Limits to our language understanding.* Many sentences are difficult to understand, especially those with embedded clauses or with one or more negatives. (page 280)
- *Reading.* When we read, we alternate between fixation periods and saccadic eye movements. An average adult reads about 11 letters per fixation. (page 281)

Key Terms

bilingual (page 279)

Broca's aphasia (page 277)

fixation (page 283)

language acquisition device (page 276)

morpheme (page 281)

phoneme (page 281)

productivity (page 274)

saccade (page 283)

transformational grammar (page 274)

Wernicke's aphasia (page 277)

Williams syndrome (page 276)

word-superiority effect (page 282)

Review Questions

1. When bonobos learned to use symbols to communicate, what training method was used?
   - (a) Positive reinforcement
   - (b) Negative reinforcement
   - (c) Classical conditioning
   - (d) Observation and imitation

2. Someone with Broca's aphasia shows impairments most strongly with regard to which aspect of language?
   - (a) Use of nouns and memory of what the nouns mean
   - (b) Use of prepositions, word endings, and other grammatical devices
   - (c) Comprehension of speech
   - (d) Reading

3. At what age do people begin to use rules of grammar?
   - (a) Very early, even at ages 2 or 3
   - (b) When they start school
   - (c) After a few years of school
   - (d) As teenagers

4. What is the most convincing evidence that early exposure to language is necessary for language development?
   - (a) Early language exposure alters development of certain brain areas.

   - (b) It is easier to learn the correct pronunciation of a foreign language if one starts when young.
   - (c) Deaf children who do not learn any language when young are seriously impaired when they try to learn one later.

5. Suppose one sound in a word is engineered to sound halfway between *d* and *t*, or halfway between *s* and *sh*. What do you hear?
   - (a) You hear both sounds.
   - (b) You hear whichever sound is more common in your language.
   - (c) You hear the sound that makes more sense in context, unless the context is delayed.
   - (d) You hear the sound that makes more sense in context, even if the context is delayed.

6. What is meant by the "word-superiority effect"?
   - (a) Children learn to read faster by the use of phonics than by the whole-word method.
   - (b) Children learn to read faster by the whole-word method than by the use of phonics.
   - (c) People who describe an event in words remember it better than those who don't.
   - (d) You more easily recognize a letter when it is part of a word than when it is alone.

7. When we read a word, do we read it one letter at a time? And what's the evidence?
   (a) Yes, we read one letter at a time. Brain areas corresponding to the various letters become active in order, one at a time.
   (b) Yes, we read one letter at a time. The evidence is that people tell us how they read.
   (c) No, we do not. An ambiguous letter can appear to be one letter in one context and a different letter in some other context.
   (d) No, we do not. The evidence is that people tell us they read a word all at once.

8. Reading alternates between fixations and saccades. On average, a person reading an alphabetic language can read about __ characters during a fixation and about __ during a saccade.
   (a) 11 ... 11
   (b) 11 ... 0
   (c) 0 ... 11
   (d) 8 ... 3

Answers: 1d, 2b, 3a, 4c, 5c, 6d, 7c, 8b.

9 Intelligence

Alan Turing, a famous mathematician and pioneer in computer science, bicycled to and from work each day. Occasionally, the chain fell off his bicycle, and he had to replace it. Turing kept records and noticed that the chain fell off at regular intervals, after exactly a certain number of turns of the front wheel. He calculated that this number was the product of the number of spokes in the front wheel times the number of links in the chain times the number of cogs in the pedal. He deduced that the chain came loose whenever a particular link in the chain came in contact with a particular bent spoke on the wheel. He identified that spoke, repaired it, and had no more trouble with his bicycle (Stewart, 1987).

Turing's solution to his problem is impressive, but hold your applause. Your local bicycle mechanic could have solved the problem without using mathematics at all. So, you might ask, what's the point? Was Turing unintelligent? Of course not. The point is that intelligence includes both the ability to solve unfamiliar problems, as Turing showed, and practiced skills, such as those of a bicycle mechanic.

The goal of the last three chapters was to understand learning, memory, and cognition. The emphasis was on theoretical concerns first and practical applications second. Here, the emphasis shifts. Although the study of intelligence certainly raises important theoretical issues, the study of intelligence traditionally has been guided by the practical concern of measuring individual differences and predicting outcomes in school.

To repair a bicycle, you could use general problem-solving skills or specific expertise about bicycles. Either approach shows a kind of intelligence.

Bernd Opitz/Getty Images

module 9.1

Intelligence and Intelligence Tests

After studying this module, you should be able to:

- Describe *g*, the evidence for it, and the explanations for it.
- Distinguish between fluid and crystallized intelligence.
- Describe three common IQ tests.
- Describe and evaluate the evidence for hereditary and environmental influences on intellectual development.

Is there intelligent life in outer space? For decades, people have pointed huge arrays of dishes toward the stars, hoping to detect signals from alien civilizations. If we did intercept signals, would we make any sense of them? The effort assumes that intelligent life in outer space would resemble us enough to make communication possible. It is a remarkable assumption, considering that our communication with dolphins here on Earth is limited to such superficialities as "take the ball to the hoop."

Defining Intelligence

What is intelligence? Let's analyze that question before we try to answer it. If we ask what is gravity or what is magnetism, there can be only one correct answer (even if we're not sure what it is). But if we ask what is beauty, that's different. Beauty is in the eye of the beholder, and if you think something is beautiful, no one can say you are wrong. Is intelligence a "real" thing like gravity, with only one correct definition, or is it a subjective evaluation, like beauty? Or is it perhaps something in between?

Defining intelligence is not easy. Here are some attempts (Kanazawa, 2004; Sternberg, 1997; Wolman, 1989):

- The mental abilities that enable one to adapt to, shape, or select one's environment
- The ability to deal with novel situations
- The ability to judge, comprehend, and reason
- The ability to understand and deal with people, objects, and symbols
- The ability to act purposefully, think rationally, and deal effectively with the environment

None of these definitions is fully satisfactory. Note the use of ill-defined terms such as *judge, comprehend, understand,* and *think rationally.*

It would be nice if we could say that psychologists first analyzed learning, memory, and cognition and then built upon that knowledge to understand intelligence. In fact, psychological researchers began with tests of intellectual abilities, defined as the ability to do well in school. Then they conducted research to find out what the tests measure. It may strike you as odd to try to measure something before being sure what it is. However, to learn what something is, one needs research, and any good research starts with measurement.

Spearman's Psychometric Approach and the *g* Factor

One of the earliest research programs in psychology was Charles Spearman's (1904) psychometric approach to intelligence, based on *the measurement of individual differences in performance.* Spearman measured how well many people performed tasks such as following directions, judging musical pitch, matching colors, and doing arithmetic. He found that performance on any of his tasks correlated positively with performance on any of the others. Spearman therefore inferred that all the tasks have something in common. To perform well on any test of mental ability, Spearman argued, people need a *"general" ability,* which he called *g*. The symbol *g* is always italicized and lowercase, like the mathematical terms *e* (the base of natural logarithms) and *i* (the square root of –1).

To account for the fact that performances on various tasks do not correlate perfectly, Spearman suggested that each task also requires a *"specific" ability,* *s* (see ▼ Figure 9.1). Thus, intelligence consists of a general ability plus an unknown number of specific abilities, such as mechanical, musical, arithmetical,

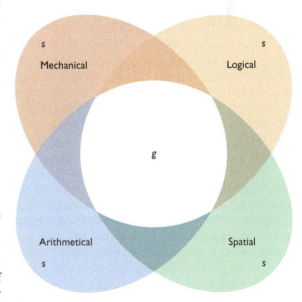

▲ **Figure 9.1** According to Spearman (1904), all intelligent abilities have an area of overlap, which he called *g* (for "general"). Each ability also depends on an *s* (for "specific") factor.

logical, and spatial abilities. Spearman called his theory a "monarchic" theory of intelligence because it included a dominant ability, or monarch (*g*), that ruled over the lesser abilities.

Later researchers confirmed that scores on virtually all kinds of cognitive tests correlate positively with one another within almost any population (Johnson, Bouchard, Krueger, McGue, & Gottesman, 2004; Johnson, te Nijenhuis, & Bouchard, 2008). You have probably noticed this trend yourself: A student who does well in one course generally does well in others also. Only under unusual conditions do most of the individuals with high scores on one kind of test get scores below average on another. For example, in one study, rural Kenyan children who did well on an academic test did poorly on a test of knowledge about traditional herbal medicines, and those who did well on the test of herbal medicines did poorly on the academic test (Sternberg et al., 2001). Presumably, the two groups of children had been exposed to different experiences.

Possible Explanations for *g*

Why do people who perform well on one type of test generally perform well on others also? The simplest interpretation is that all the tasks measure a single underlying ability. Consider an analogy with the tasks shown in ▶ **Figure 9.2**: Most people who excel at running a 100-meter race also do well at the high jump and the long jump. They have to, because all three events depend on the same leg muscles.

Similarly, perhaps people perform well on a variety of intellectual tests because all the tests depend on one underlying skill. If so, what might that skill be? One possibility is working memory (e.g., Martínez & Colom, 2009). For almost any intellectual task, holding information in memory is important, as is the ability to shift attention. However, training tasks that enhance working memory do not increase other aspects of intelligence (Harrison et al., 2013). Another possibility is speed of processing information (Coyle, Pillow, Snyder, & Kochunov, 2011). For people as for computers, processing information quickly makes it possible to complete more complicated tasks.

An alternative explanation for *g* is that several types of intelligence correlate because they grow in the same ways (Petrill, Luo, Thompson, & Detterman, 1996). By analogy, consider the lengths of three body parts—the left leg, the right arm, and the left index finger: As a rule, most people with a long left leg also have a long right arm and a long left index finger, because the factors that increase the growth of one also help the others grow— factors such as genes, health, and nutrition. Similarly, all forms of intelligence depend on genes, health, nutrition, and education. Most people who have good support for developing one intellectual skill also have good support for developing others.

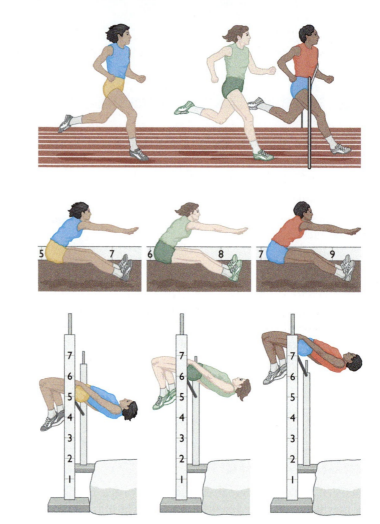

▲ **Figure 9.2** Measurements of sprinting, high jumping, and long jumping correlate with one another because they all depend on the same leg muscles. Similarly, the *g* factor that emerges in IQ testing could reflect a single ability.

Which of these examples applies to intelligence? Do the various intellectual skills correlate with one another because they all measure a single underlying ability (as do running and jumping, which require good leg muscles) or because they all grow together (as do your arms, legs, and fingers)? To some extent, both hypotheses are probably correct. Most intellectual tasks require attention, working memory, and speed. Also, independent brain functions correlate with one another because factors that promote good development of one area promote good development of all.

1. **You read about two explanations for *g*. What would each of them predict about whether something could impair intelligence in one way and spare it in another?**

Answer

1. If all intelligent abilities depend on a single underlying factor, then anything that impaired that factor (some type of brain damage, for example) would impair all the intelligent abilities. For analogy, an injury that impairs running would also impair jumping. However, if intelligent abilities correlate because they usually grow together, we can imagine something that impairs one ability much more than others—as in the case of Williams syndrome (discussed in Chapter 8). For analogy, amputating a finger does not harm the legs.

Hierarchical Models of Intelligence

Although Spearman and later researchers have regarded *g* as the key to intelligence, it does not account for everything. Spearman suggested the existence of specific (*s*) factors, but the task fell on other psychologists to try to describe these *s* factors.

Raymond Cattell (1987) drew a distinction between fluid intelligence and crystallized intelligence. The analogy is to water: Fluid water fits into any shape of container, but an ice crystal has a fixed shape. Fluid intelligence is *the power of reasoning and using information*. It includes the ability to perceive relationships, solve unfamiliar problems, and gain new knowledge. Crystallized intelligence consists of *acquired skills and knowledge and the ability to apply that knowledge in specific situations*. Fluid intelligence enables you to learn new skills in a new job, whereas crystallized intelligence includes the job skills you have already acquired. The ability to learn new words is an example of fluid intelligence, and the words already learned are part of your crystallized intelligence. Expertise, as discussed in Chapter 8, is crystallized intelligence.

Fluid intelligence reaches its peak before age 20, remains nearly steady for decades, and declines on average in old age, more in some people than others (Horn, 1968). However, crystallized intelligence, including such skills as vocabulary, remains steady or increases over age (Cattell, 1987; Salthouse, 2013). On average, younger people are more successful at solving new, unfamiliar problems, but older people do well on problems in their area of specialization. The distinction between fluid and crystallized intelligence is sharper in theory than in practice. Any task taps both crystallized and fluid intelligence to some extent.

Other researchers have described intelligence in terms of a hierarchy of several components. One analysis described those components as language, perceptual processing, and spatial relationships (Johnson & Bouchard, 2005). Another analysis described them as language, short-term memory, and reasoning (Hampshire, Highfield, Parkin, & Owen, 2012).

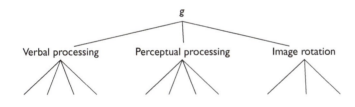

2. **Was Alan Turing's solution to the slipping bicycle chain, from the introduction to this chapter, an example of fluid or crystallized intelligence? Was the solution provided by a bicycle mechanic fluid or crystallized intelligence?**

Answer 2. Turing's solution reflected fluid intelligence, a generalized ability that could apply to any topic. The solution provided by a bicycle mechanic reflected crystallized intelligence, an ability developed in a particular area of experience.

Gardner's Theory of Multiple Intelligences

Certain critics propose to dispense with, or at least de-emphasize, the concept of *g*. According to Howard Gardner (1985, 1999), if we could test intellectual abilities in pure form, we might find multiple intelligences—*unrelated forms of intelligence*, consisting of language, musical abilities, logical and mathematical reasoning, spatial reasoning, ability to recognize and classify objects, body movement skills, self-control and self-understanding, and sensitivity to other people's social signals. Gardner argues that people can be outstanding in one type of intelligence but not others. For example, an athlete can excel at body movement skills but lack musical abilities. Someone who seems intelligent in one way may be mediocre or worse in another because different skills require not only different kinds of practice but also, perhaps, different brain specializations.

Gardner makes the important point that each person has different skills. However, the question is whether those skills represent different types of intelligence. Moreover, Gardner suggests that these types are different not just in the sense of Spearman's *s* factor—a specialization tacked onto a more general ability. Gardner argues that the different abilities are independent and unrelated. To defend Gardner's position, someone would need to demonstrate that several intellectual skills are not strongly correlated with one another. However, each of Gardner's proposed types of intelligence correlates positively with the others, except for body movement skills and possibly music (Visser, Ashton, & Vernon, 2006). Therefore, it would seem that language, logic, spatial reasoning, and all the others are different manifestations of *g*. Gardner believes that these abilities

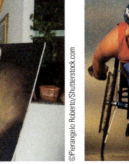

According to Howard Gardner, we have many intelligences, including mathematical ability, artistic skill, muscle skills, and musical abilities.

would stop correlating so strongly if we could measure them in pure form, without the influence of language, for example. Perhaps so, but no one knows how to measure any intellectual ability in pure form. Gardner's theory is an appealing idea without solid evidence to support it.

Parallel to the claim of multiple intelligences, many educators have embraced the concept that people vary in their learning styles. According to this view, some people are visual learners, others are verbal learners, and others learn in other ways, and teaching should be adjusted to each student's style of learning. If so, in a classroom using a highly visual style of instruction, one group of students would learn best, and in a classroom with a highly verbal style of instruction, a different group of students would learn best. In fact, almost no evidence supports this prediction, and much evidence opposes it (Pashler, McDaniel, Rohrer, & Bjork, 2008)—with the obvious exception that blind children don't learn from visual presentations and deaf children don't learn from spoken presentations. The idea of learning styles became popular without any research basis.

---

concept check ✓

3. **What evidence would we need to determine whether music, mathematics, social sensitivity, and so forth are really different kinds of intelligence or just different aspects of a single type of intelligence?**

Answer

3. We would need to determine whether ability at each kind of intelligence correlates highly with the others. If they correlate highly, they are simply different aspects of g. If they do not, and if the differences reflect more than just different amounts of practice at different skills, then they are separate kinds of intelligence.

IQ Tests

We have been discussing intelligence and IQ tests in general, and the idea of IQ tests is no doubt familiar to you, as such tests are commonplace in education. However, the time has come to consider examples in more detail.

Let's start with this analogy: You have just been put in charge of choosing the members of your country's next Olympic team. However, the Olympic rules have been changed: Each country will send only 30 men and 30 women, and each athlete must compete in every event. The Olympic committee will not describe those events until all the athletes have been chosen. Clearly, you cannot hold the usual kind of tryouts, but neither will you choose people at random. How will you proceed?

Your best bet would be to devise a test of "general athletic ability." You might measure the abilities of applicants to run, jump, change direction, maintain balance, throw and catch, kick, lift weights, respond rapidly to signals, and perform other athletic feats. You would choose the applicants with the best scores.

No doubt, your test would be imperfect. But if you want your team to do well, you need some way to measure athletic ability. Later, other people begin to use your test also. Does its wide acceptance mean that athletic ability is a single quantity? Of course not. You found it useful to act as if it were a single quantity, but you know that most great basketball players are not great swimmers or gymnasts.

Intelligence tests resemble this imaginary test of athletic ability. If you were in charge of choosing which applicants a college should admit, you would want to select those who will be the best students. Because students will study subjects that they have not studied before, it makes sense to measure a range of academic skills, not knowledge of a single topic. That is, you want a test of aptitude (*ability to learn, or fluid intelligence*) in addition to achievement (*what someone has already learned, or crystallized intelligence*). Aptitude and achievement are hard to separate. Aptitude leads to achievement, and past achievement increases future ability to learn. Still, we make an effort to separate the two.

The original goal of intelligence tests was to identify the *least* capable children, who could not learn from ordinary schooling. Before long, tests were also used to identify the best students, who would profit from accelerated classes. Similar tests are used for selecting among applicants to colleges and professional schools. Course grades are useful, too, but grading standards vary from one school to another and from one teacher to another. Objective tests help compare students from different schools and classes. They also help identify people with good abilities who for any reason failed to impress their teachers.

Intelligence quotient (IQ) tests try to *predict someone's performance in school and similar settings.* The term *quotient* originated when IQ was determined by dividing mental age by chronological age and then multiplying by 100. Mental age is *the average age of children who perform as well as this child.* Chronological age is time since birth. For example, an 8-year-old who performs like an average 10-year-old has a mental age of 10, a chronological age of 8, and an IQ of $10 \div 8 \times 100 = 125$. That method is now obsolete, but the term remains.

Two French psychologists, Alfred Binet and Theophile Simon (1905), devised the first IQ tests. The French Ministry of Public Instruction wanted a fair way to identify children who had such serious intellectual deficiencies that they needed to be placed in special classes. The school system wanted an impartial test instead of leaving the decision to someone's opinion. Binet and Simon's test measured the skills that children need for success in school, such as counting, remembering, following instructions, and understanding language.

Their test and others like it make reasonably accurate predictions. But suppose a test correctly predicts that one student will perform better than another in school. Can we then say that the first student did better *because of* a higher IQ score? No, an IQ is a measurement, not an explanation. A child doesn't do poorly because of a low IQ score any more than a basketball player misses a shot because of a low shooting average.

The Stanford-Binet Test

The test that Binet and Simon designed was later modified for English speakers by Stanford psychologists and published as the Stanford-Binet IQ test. The test's items are designated by age (see ■ Table 9.1). An item designated as "age 8," for example, will be answered correctly by 60 to 90 percent of 8-year-olds. (A higher percentage of older children answer it correctly and a lower percentage of younger children.) A child who answers correctly most of the age 8 items, but not the age 9 items, has a mental age of 8.

TABLE 9.1 Examples of the Types of Items on the Stanford-Binet Test

Age	Sample Test Item
2	Test administrator points at pictures of everyday objects and asks, "What is this?" "Here are some pegs of different sizes and shapes. See whether you can put each one into the correct hole."
4	"Why do people live in houses?" "Birds fly in the air; fish swim in the ___."
6	"Here is a picture of a horse. Do you see what part of the horse is missing?" "Here are some candies. Can you count how many there are?"
8	"What should you do if you find a lost puppy?" "Stephanie can't write today because she twisted her ankle. What is wrong with that?"
10	"Why should people be quiet in a library?" "Repeat after me: 4 8 3 7 1 4."
12	"What does regret mean?" "Here is a picture. Can you tell me what is wrong with it?"
14	"What is the similarity between high and low?" "Watch me fold this paper and cut it. Now, when I unfold it, how many holes will there be?"
Adult	"Make up a sentence using the words celebrate, reverse, and appointment." "What do people mean when they say, 'People who live in glass houses should not throw stones'"?

Source: Modified from Nietzel and Bernstein, 1987.

School psychologists are carefully trained on how to administer the test items and score the answers. A psychologist testing an 8-year-old might start with the items designated for 7-year-olds. Unless the child misses many of the 7-year-old items, the psychologist gives credit for all the 6-year-old items without testing them. If the child answers most of the 7-year-old items correctly, the psychologist proceeds to the items for 8-year-olds, 9-year-olds, and so forth, until the child begins to miss most items. At that point, the psychologist ends the test. This method is known as **adaptive testing** because *the range of items used is adapted to the performance of the individual.* Individuals proceed at their own pace, usually finishing in 45 to 90 minutes.

Stanford-Binet IQ scores are computed from tables set up to ensure that a given IQ score means the same at different ages. The mean IQ at each age is 100. A 6-year-old with an IQ score of, say, 116 has performed better on the test than 84 percent of other 6-year-olds. Similarly, an adult with an IQ score of 116 has performed better than 84 percent of other adults. The Stanford-Binet provides subscores reflecting visual reasoning, short-term memory, and other specialized skills. It also provides an overall IQ score, a verbal IQ score, and a nonverbal IQ score based on items answered by handling items instead of by speech. Someone not fluent in English might get a much higher nonverbal than verbal score.

The Wechsler Tests

IQ tests originally devised by David Wechsler, and later modified by others, known as the **Wechsler Adult Intelligence Scale–Fourth Edition (WAIS–IV)** and the **Wechsler Intelligence Scale for Children–Fifth Edition (WISC–V)**, produce the same average, 100, and almost the same distribution of scores as the Stanford-Binet. The WISC is for children up to age 16, and the WAIS is for everyone older. As with the Stanford-Binet, the Wechsler tests are administered to one person at a time (see ◄ Figure 9.3). The Stanford-Binet and Wechsler tests are the most widely used IQ tests.

A Wechsler test provides an overall IQ, a Verbal IQ, a Performance IQ (based on tasks that do not require a verbal response), and subtest scores representing working memory, verbal comprehension, processing speed, and others. Examples of working memory items are "Listen to these numbers and then repeat them: 3 6 2 5" and "Listen to these numbers and repeat them in reverse order: 4 7 6." An example of a processing speed item is "Put a slash (/) through all the circles on this page and an X through all the squares, as quickly as possible."

△ ○ □ ▱ ○ △ ▱ □ ○

▲ **Figure 9.3** Most IQ tests are administered individually. Here, a psychologist (left) records the responses by a participant (right).

Each part of the WISC-V or the WAIS–IV starts with simple questions and progresses to more difficult ones. The subscores call attention to someone's strengths and weaknesses. For example, a child who learned English as a second language might do best on items that call for nonverbal answers. Educators use Wechsler tests to identify possible learning disabilities.

Culture-Reduced Testing

If you learned English as a second language, or if you are hearing impaired, your score on the Stanford-Binet or Wechsler IQ test might seriously underestimate your abilities. "Why not translate the tests into other languages, including sign language?" you might ask. Psychologists do, but a translated item may be easier or harder than the original. For example, one part of the Stanford-Binet presents words and asks for other words that rhyme with them. Generating rhymes is easier in some languages than in others. Other items may refer to information that is familiar in one culture and unfamiliar in another. Each of these tests has been revised repeatedly to minimize items that clearly favor one culture over another, but some degree of cultural specificity remains.

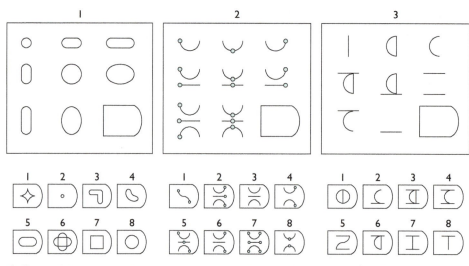

▲ **Figure 9.4** Items similar to those on Raven's Progressive Matrices test. Select the item that completes the pattern both going across and going down. (You can check your answers against answer A on page 298.)

Psychologists have tried to devise a culture-fair or culture-reduced test. Although no task is free of cultural influences, some tests are fairer than others. *The most widely used culture-reduced test* is the Progressive Matrices test devised by John C. Raven. These matrices, which *progress* gradually from easy to difficult items, attempt to measure abstract reasoning (fluid intelligence) without any use of language or reference to factual information. To answer questions on the Progressive Matrices, someone must generate hypotheses, test them, and infer rules. ▲ Figure 9.4 presents three matrices similar to those on this test. The first is relatively easy, the second is harder, and the third is harder still.

How culture-fair is the Progressive Matrices test? It requires less information than the Wechsler or Stanford-Binet tests, and requires no use of language, but it does assume familiarity with pencil-and-paper, multiple-choice tests. No test can be totally free from cultural influences, but this comes closer than most. A disadvantage is that this test provides only a single score instead of identifying someone's strengths and weaknesses.

concept check

4. **What is one advantage of the Wechsler IQ tests over Raven's Progressive Matrices? What is an advantage of the Progressive Matrices?**

Answer

4. The Wechsler tests provide separate scores for different tasks and therefore identify someone's strengths and weaknesses. Raven's Progressive Matrices are fairer for someone who is not a native speaker of English.

Individual Differences in IQ Scores

Why do some people score higher than others on IQ tests? The British scholar Francis Galton (1869/1978)[1] was the first to argue for the importance of heredity. His evidence was that politicians, judges, and other eminent and distinguished people generally had distinguished relatives. You can quickly see why this evidence does not justify a conclusion about genetics. Let's consider the better evidence we have today.

Most first-generation immigrants do not score highly on English-language intelligence tests. As a rule, their children and grandchildren get higher scores.

Robert Brenner/PhotoEdit

[1]A slash like this indicates original publication date and the date of a revised printing, such as one in translation. It does not represent Galton's birth and death dates, which were 1822–1911.

Table 9.2 Mean Correlations for the IQs of Children with Various Degrees of Genetic and Environmental Similarity

Degree of Genetic or Environmental Similarity	Correlation of IQ Scores
Parent and child	0.41
Sibling	0.47
Parent & biological child who is adopted by another family	0.23
Biological siblings who are adopted in separate families	0.23
Adoptive parent & adopted child	0.19
Unrelated children adopted in the same family	0.31
Monozygotic twins adopted in separate families	0.78
Monozygotic twins reared together	0.85
Dizygotic twins reared together	0.6

(Adapted from Plomin, DeFries, McClearn, & McGuffin, 2001)

Family Resemblances

■ **Table 9.2**, based on an extensive literature review (Plomin, DeFries, McClearn, & McGuffin, 2001), shows the correlations of IQ scores for people with various degrees of genetic relationship. These data are based mostly on European or American families.

The scores of monozygotic ("identical") twins correlate with each other about 0.85, significantly higher than dizygotic twins or non-twin siblings (Bishop et al., 2003; McGue & Bouchard, 1998). Monozygotic twins also closely resemble each other in brain volume (Posthuma et al., 2002) and in specific skills such as working memory, attention, reading, and mathematics (Koten et al., 2009; Kovas, Haworth, Dale, & Plomin, 2007; Luciano et al., 2001). The greater similarity between monozygotic than dizygotic twins implies a genetic basis. In Table 9.2, note the high correlation between monozygotic twins reared apart. That is, they strongly resemble each other on IQ tests even if they are adopted by separate sets of parents (Bouchard & McGue, 1981; Farber, 1981).

Monozygotic twins continue to resemble each other throughout life, even beyond age 80 (Petrill et al., 1998). In fact, monozygotic twins become more and more similar to each other in IQ as they grow older, indicating that the influence of genes is greater in older than in younger individuals (Davis, Haworth, & Plomin, 2009; Lyons et al., 2009). Why might that be? One reason is that older individuals have more control of their environment. Those who start with an intellectual advantage gravitate toward activities that sustain and increase that advantage. This is an example of the multiplier effect from Chapter 3: Slightly better-than-average performance early in life, perhaps genetically based, leads to encouragement and support that leads to still better performance (Dickens & Flynn, 2001).

One limitation in all this research is that most twin studies rely on data from middle-class families. Studies of impoverished families find much less evidence for a genetic influence. That is, monozygotic twins in more prosperous families resemble each other strongly, but those in impoverished families resemble each other only a little more than dizygotic twins do (Bates, Lewis, & Weiss, 2013; Nisbett et al., 2012). The probable meaning is this: For children living in a terrible environment, the chance for intellectual development is limited, regardless of their genes. For those in a satisfactory environment, genetic differences have more impact. Those with favorable genetic predispositions take advantage of their opportunities. Similarly, the influence of genetics is weak if the quality of teaching is poor. None of the children do well when the teaching is poor, regardless of genetics. With better teaching, some children advance faster than others (Taylor, Roehrig, Hensler, Connor, & Schatschneider, 2010).

Twins and Single Births

Notice in Table 9.2 that dizygotic twins resemble each other more closely than single-birth siblings do. This finding suggests an influence from being born at the same time and therefore sharing more of the environment. In support of this conclusion, researchers have found a higher correlation between the IQs of brothers born within a couple of years of each other than those born further apart (Sundet, Eriksen, & Tambs, 2008).

Adopted Children

In Table 9.2, note the correlation between unrelated children adopted into the same family, indicating an influence from shared environment (Plomin et al., 2001; Segal, 2000). However, this correlation is lower than the correlation between biological brothers or sisters. The IQs of young adopted children correlate moderately with those of their adoptive parents. As the children grow older, their IQ scores gradually correlate more with those of their biological parents and less with those of their adoptive parents (Loehlin, Horn, & Willerman, 1989; Plomin, Fulker, Corley, & DeFries, 1997; see ▼ Figure 9.5). Another interesting study examined "virtual twins"—unrelated children of the same age growing up in the same family. For example, parents might adopt two children of the same age, or have a child of their own and adopt another of the same age. In these cases, the virtual twins' IQs are moderately correlated in early childhood, and less as they grow older (Segal, McGuire, & Stohs, 2012).

The studies of adopted children imply a genetic influence from the biological parents, but another interpretation is possible. Some low-IQ parents who put their children up for adoption are impoverished and probably do not provide good prenatal care. The mother may have poor nutrition, may smoke and drink, or may in other ways put her infant at risk for reasons other than genetics. Poor prenatal care correlates with decreased IQ for the offspring throughout life (Breslau, Dickens, Flynn, Peterson, & Lucia, 2006). In short, adopted children can resemble their biological parents for nongenetic as well as genetic reasons.

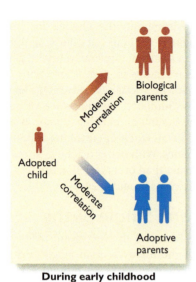 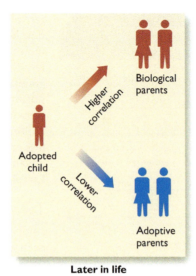

During early childhood   **Later in life**

▲ **Figure 9.5** As adopted children grow older, their IQs begin to correlate more strongly with those of their biological parents.

Gene Identification

The Human Genome Project and related research now make it possible to identify particular genes that promote intelligence. The strategy is to locate genes that are more common among those with higher IQ scores than those with lower scores, or the reverse. Similar research has been done with laboratory animals, comparing fast learners to slow learners. Dozens of genetic variations have been reported to correlate with measures of intelligence, but no common variant has a large effect (Chablis et al., 2012; Davies et al., 2015; Deary et al., 2012; Plomin et al., 2013; Rietveld et al., 2014). In short, intelligence depends on many genes making small contributions, and depends on epigenetic influences as well.

Environmental Influences and Interventions

The heritability of variations in IQ scores does not mean that genes dictate people's intellectual accomplishments. Certainly, if we gave every child either an extremely good or extremely bad environment, we could raise or lower everyone's IQ scores.

When we think about environmental influences on intelligence, we might think first about how often parents read to their children, take them to museums, and so forth. Those factors can certainly be important, but many other environmental influences deserve attention. In particular, much research

emphasizes the role of physical health early in life. Researchers have compared mean IQ scores across countries and across states within the United States. We need to be cautious here, as scores are not always comparable among countries speaking different languages. Still, the finding is that mean IQ is consistently lowest in the countries and states where children have the highest exposure to infectious diseases, such as tetanus, malaria, tuberculosis, hepatitis, cholera, and measles (Eppig, Fincher, & Thornhill, 2010, 2011). Fighting disease takes much of the body's energy, and building a brain does also. IQ scores correlate more strongly with infectious disease than with family wealth or quality of education. These results come from correlations, and as always we should beware of assuming cause and effect. ▼ Figure 9.6 shows the results across countries.

To what extent can we help low-performing children? A variety of programs have provided special interventions for children from extremely deprived homes to foster their intellectual development. Randomized controlled studies demonstrate long-term benefits from educational programs as well as from dietary supplements, especially with polyunsaturated fatty acids (Protzko, Aronson, & Blair, 2013). Although no brief educational program helps much, intensive programs occupying many hours per week for several years do produce significant, lasting benefits (Barnett, 2011; Reynolds, Temple, Ou, Arteaga, & White, 2011).

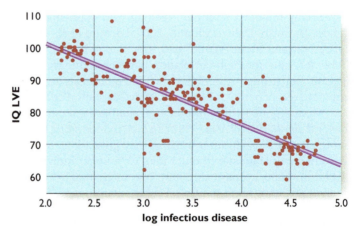

▲ **Figure 9.6** Each dot represents the results for one country. Along the x-axis is the degree of exposure to infectious disease. Along the y-axis is the mean IQ score. The correlation was –0.82. (Figure 1 part (a) from "Parasite prevalence and the worldwide distribution of cognitive ability," by C. Eppig, C. L. Fincher, & R. Thornhill, 2010. *Proceedings of the Royal Society B, 277,* pp. 3801–3808. Copyright © 2010 by the Royal Society. Reprinted with permission.)

An interesting intervention is music lessons. In one study, 6-year-olds who were randomly assigned to receive music lessons showed a gain of 1 to 2 IQ points, on the average, compared to other children (Schellenberg, 2004). Additional research indicates that children with music training show IQ advantages beyond what we can explain in terms of parental income and education (Schellenberg, 2006; Schellenberg & Mankarious, 2012).

Interventions work best if they start early. Some orphanages provide a particularly deprived environment, including poor nutrition and minimal intellectual stimulation. Most children who remain in the orphanages perform poorly on tests and in school. Those who leave the orphanages and enter adoptive families show clear improvement, with the greatest improvement evident among children adopted before age 6 months (Beckett et al., 2006; Nelson et al., 2007; van IJzendoorn, Juffer, & Poelhuis, 2005).

concept check

5. **What types of evidence support a genetic contribution to individual differences in IQ scores?**

6. **What evidence suggests an influence of infectious diseases on intellectual development?**

Answers

5. One type of evidence is that monozygotic twins resemble each other in IQ more than dizygotic twins do. A second type of evidence is that IQs of adopted children correlate significantly with those of their biological parents. 6. The mean IQ score is lowest in those countries and states where children have the highest exposure to infectious diseases.

---

in closing | module 9.1

Measuring Something We Don't Fully Understand

The standard IQ tests were devised by trial and error long before most of the discoveries about memory and cognition that we discussed in the last two chapters. We still do not understand intelligence very well. Can we measure intelligence without understanding it? Possibly so. Physicists measured gravity and magnetism long before they understood them theoretically. Maybe psychologists can do the same with intelligence.

Or maybe not. Measuring a poorly understood phenomenon is risky. Many psychologists who are dissatisfied with the current tests are striving toward better ones. Producing an improved IQ test is not as easy as it may sound.

In the meantime, the current tests have both strengths and weaknesses. An IQ test, like any other tool, can be used in constructive or destructive ways. The next module explores ways of evaluating IQ tests.

Summary

- *Defining intelligence.* Intelligence is difficult to define. Psychological researchers try to measure it, hoping to learn something from the measurements. (page 289)
- g *factor.* People's scores on almost any test of intelligent abilities correlate positively with scores on other tests. The overlap among tests is referred to as *g,* meaning the general factor in intelligence. (page 289)
- *Possible explanations for* g. Many psychologists believe the *g* factor corresponds to an ability that underlies all kinds of intelligence, such as mental speed or working memory. Another possibility is that different abilities correlate with one another because the same growth factors that promote any one of them also support the others. (page 290)
- *Fluid and crystallized intelligence.* Psychologists distinguish between fluid intelligence (reasoning ability) and crystallized intelligence (acquired and practiced skills). (page 291)
- *Intelligence as a hierarchy.* The *g* factor can be subdivided into more specific categories, such as verbal, perceptual, and image rotation; or language, short-term memory, and reasoning. (page 291)

- *One or many types of intelligence?* Howard Gardner argued that people have many independent types of intelligence, including social attentiveness, musical abilities, and motor skills. However, so far, no one has demonstrated that different types of intelligence are independent of one another. (page 291)
- *IQ tests.* The Stanford-Binet, Wechsler, and other IQ tests were devised to predict the level of performance in school. Culture-reduced tests such as Raven's Progressive Matrices are more appropriate for people not fluent in English. (page 292)
- *Hereditary influences.* Studies of twins and adopted children suggest hereditary influences on individual differences in IQ performance, although no one gene has a major effect. (page 294)
- *Environmental influences.* Intellectual development depends on many aspects of the environment, including physical health in early childhood. Extensive interventions can help children's intellectual development, if started early in life and continued for years. (page 296)

Key Terms

Answers to Other Question in the Module (page 294)

A. 1. (8); 2. (2); 3. (4) For item 3, going either across or down, add any parts that are different and subtract any parts that are the same.

Review Questions

1. What evidence did Spearman have for the existence of *g*?
   (a) Scores of monozygotic twins correlate highly with each other.
   (b) Scores on any test of intelligent performance correlate positively with scores on other tests.
   (c) Children who are identified as intellectually gifted tend to become highly productive adults.
   (d) On the average, intelligence scores are equal for males and females.

2. On average, how does intelligence change from young adulthood to old adulthood?
   (a) Both fluid and crystallized intelligence decline.
   (b) Fluid intelligence declines, but crystallized intelligence remains constant or increases.
   (c) Fluid intelligence remains constant or increases, but crystallized intelligence declines.
   (d) Both fluid and crystallized intelligence remain constant or increase.

3. Many educators maintain that different children have different learning styles, such as visual learner or auditory learner. What does the evidence say about this proposal?
   (a) Most children are visual learners and only a few are auditory learners.
   (b) Most children are auditory learners and only a few are visual learners.
   (c) About 50% are visual learners and 50% are auditory learners.

   (d) The research does not support the idea of different styles of learning.

4. What evidence would demonstrate the existence of an intellectual ability separate from *g*?
   (a) People with this ability do well on all measures of intelligent behavior.
   (b) People with this ability do not do well in school.
   (c) The ability predicts some type of intelligent behavior but has a low correlation with the tests that measure *g*.

5. What was the original purpose of Binet's first IQ test?
   (a) to select the brightest students for advanced training
   (b) to compare the performance of ethnic groups
   (c) to determine the relationship between intelligence and brain size
   (d) to identify slow learners who needed special education

6. Under what circumstances do environmental interventions most strongly promote intellectual development?
   (a) if they start in early childhood
   (b) if they take place during school hours
   (c) if they start during adolescence
   (d) if large numbers of children are taught together at the same time

Answers: 1b, 2b, 3d, 4c, 5d, 6a.

module 9.2

Evaluation of Intelligence Tests

After studying this module, you should be able to:

- Define standardization of a test.
- Explain the Flynn effect and the evidence for it.
- Describe the evidence that researchers use to measure reliability and validity.
- Define test bias and describe the evidence that researchers use to measure it.
- Discuss stereotype threat.

> Whatever exists at all exists in some amount.
> —E. L. Thorndike (1918, p. 16)

> Anything that exists in amount can be measured.
> —W. A. McCall (1939, p. 15)

> Anything which exists can be measured incorrectly.
> —D. Detterman (1979, p. 167)

All three of these quotes apply to intelligence: If intelligence exists, it must exist in some amount. It must be measurable, but it can be measured incorrectly. Exactly how accurate, useful, and fair are the IQ tests? Because much is at stake here, the conclusions are often controversial.

The Standardization of IQ Tests

In the first module, we considered examples of IQ tests. To evaluate them or any other test, we need to rely on objective evidence. The evaluation begins with standardization, *the process of evaluating the questions, establishing rules for administering a test, and interpreting the scores.* One step in this process is to find the norms, *descriptions of how frequently various scores occur.* Psychologists try to standardize a test on a large sample of people who are as representative as possible of the population.

You may sometimes hear someone use the term *standardized test* in a way that makes it sound threatening. The opposite of a standardized test is an unstandardized test, like nearly all the ones that professors give in class. Some of the questions might be confusing, and the test might be easier or harder than the professor intended. Standardizing a test improves it.

The Distribution of IQ Scores

Binet, Wechsler, and the others who devised IQ tests chose items and arranged the scoring method to establish a mean score of 100. The standard deviation is 15 for the Wechsler test, and 16 for the Stanford-Binet. As discussed in Chapter 2, the standard deviation measures variance among individuals. The standard deviation is small if most scores are close to the mean and large if scores vary widely. The scores for a large population approximate a *normal distribution*, or bell-shaped curve, as shown in ▶ Figure 9.7.

In a normal distribution, 68 percent of all people fall within one standard deviation above or below the mean, and about 95 percent are within two standard deviations. Someone with a score of 115 on the Wechsler test exceeds the scores of people within one standard deviation from the mean plus all of those

more than one standard deviation below the mean—a total of 84 percent, as shown in Figure 9.7. We say that such a person is "in the 84th percentile." Someone with an IQ score of 130 is in the 98th percentile, with a score higher than those of 98 percent of others.

In fact, however, the actual distribution of IQ scores isn't as symmetrical as the theoretical normal distribution. The mode (most common score) is about 105 instead of 100. More people score above 100 than below 100, but a slight bulge in the 60- to 85-range lowers the mean score to 100, as shown in ▼ Figure 9.8 (Johnson, Carothers, & Deary, 2008).

The bulge at the lower end represents people with disabilities, described as mentally challenged. For example, people with Down syndrome *have a variety of physical and medical impairments as a result of having an extra copy of chromosome #21. They have impairments in speech development, motor skills, memory, and cognition. However, although most qualify as intellectually impaired, they vary considerably, and some score closer to the mean of IQ* (Mégarbané et al., 2013).

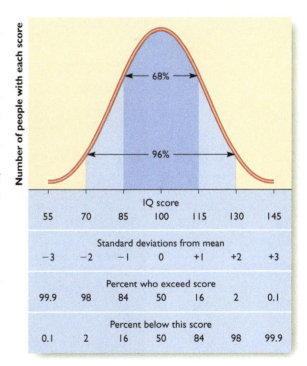

▲ **Figure 9.7** The curve shown here represents the intended distribution of scores on the Wechsler IQ test, with a standard deviation of 15 (15 points above and below the mean, which is 100).

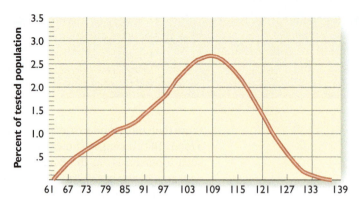

▲ **Figure 9.8** The actual distribution of scores is not quite symmetrical. The mode (most common score) is a bit higher than the mean, and more scores lie far below the mean than equally far above it. (Source: "Sex differences in variability in general intelligence," by W. Johnson, A. Carothers, & I. J. Deary, 2008. *Perspectives on Psychological Science, 3,* pp. 518–531.)

The term *mentally challenged* or *mentally disabled* refers to people more than two standard deviations below average, corresponding to an IQ score of 68 or 70, depending on the test. This cutoff is arbitrary, and a psychologist considers other observations of the person's level of functioning before making a diagnosis. In the United States, the Individuals with Disabilities Education Act requires public schools to provide "free and appropriate" education for all children regardless of their limitations. Children with mild physical or intellectual disabilities are mainstreamed as much as possible—that is, placed in the same classes as other children but with special consideration. On the plus side, children in mainstream classes develop better language abilities than those in classes limited to children with disabilities (Laws, Byrne, & Buckley, 2000). However, although children with disabilities generally report friendly relationships with their classmates, they seldom form truly close friendships (Webster & Carter, 2013).

An IQ score of 130 or more is the "gifted" range. As with a diagnosis of disabled, a label of gifted requires a judgment based on other behaviors, not just a test score. Gifted children learn rapidly without much help, seek to master knowledge, ask deep questions, and develop new ideas (Winner, 2000). Given adequate opportunities, most go on to earn advanced degrees and to make major accomplishments in science, the arts, business, or government (Kell, Lubinski, & Benbow, 2013).

Since the first IQ tests, psychologists have found that girls tend to do better than boys on certain kinds of language tasks, such as verbal fluency, whereas boys tend to do better than girls on visuospatial rotations. On the WAIS, men generally have higher scores on certain subtests, whereas women have higher scores on others (Irwing, 2012). On attention tasks, males more often focus on one item at a time whereas females spread their attention more broadly (Johnson & Bouchard, 2007). None of these differences are huge. However, by loading IQ tests with one type of item or another, test authors could have produced results favoring one gender or the other.

A person with Down syndrome.

Instead, they balanced various types of items to ensure that the mean scores of both females and males would be the same. On Raven's Progressive Matrices, even though it has only one type of item, researchers find no significant difference between males and females (Savage-McGlynn, 2012). In short, overall intelligence is equal for men and women.

7. What is meant by a "standardized" test?

The Flynn Effect

In 1920, the question "What is Mars?" was considered difficult, because most people knew little about the planets. Today, that question is easy. Researchers periodically restandardize tests to keep the overall difficulty about the same.

Eventually a pattern was clear: Every time the test authors restandardized an IQ test, they made it more difficult to keep the mean score from rising above 100. That is, *decade by decade, generation by generation, people's raw scores on IQ tests have gradually increased, and to keep up with this trend, test makers have had to make the tests harder.* This tendency is known as the Flynn effect, after James Flynn, who called attention to it and made people take it seriously (Flynn, 1984, 1999), although many other writers had noticed the trend since as early as 1936 (Lynn, 2013). The results vary across countries, tests, and periods of time, but a typical figure is about three IQ points per 10 years (Trahan, Stuebing, Fletcher, & Hiscock, 2014). If you took the same IQ test that your parents took at your age, then your score probably would be higher than theirs. If you took an IQ test from your grandparents' era, your score would be still higher.

One consequence of the Flynn effect is that if you take an IQ test and later take a restandardized form, your score will probably drop! You did not deteriorate, but you are being compared to a higher standard. For most people, a few points' change makes little difference, but for people at the low end of the distribution, the loss of a few points might qualify them for special services (Kanaya, Scullin, & Ceci, 2003). In states that use the death penalty, courts have forbidden the death penalty for people who are mentally disabled. In borderline cases, eligibility for the death penalty depends on whether someone took an IQ test before or after it was revised.

The Flynn effect—increase in IQ scores over generations—has occurred over many decades, and in nearly every group for whom we have data, including people in rural Kenya (Daley, Whaley, Sigman, Espinosa, & Neumann, 2003) and deaf children in Saudi Arabia (Bakhiet, Barakat, & Lynn, 2014). Within the United States, the effect has occurred in all ethnic groups, with larger gains by Black and Hispanic people than by non-Hispanic Whites (Rindermann & Thompson, 2013). Reports vary as to whether the Flynn effect applies mostly to fluid intelligence or crystallized intelligence (Williams, 2013).

What accounts for the Flynn effect? Here are some hypotheses, with their pros and cons (Trahan et al., 2014; Williams, 2013):

- Improved education and test-taking skills. Education is important, but it cannot account for much of the Flynn effect. The IQ improvement is just as large in 6-year-old children, who have just started school, as in older children. Also, it has occurred in rural Kenyan children, who have little schooling (Daley et al., 2003). Furthermore, strong gains are apparent for scores on

Raven's Progressive Matrices, which measures skills not taught in school.

- An increased tendency for people to marry outside their own neighborhood (Mingroni, 2004). Plant breeders have long noticed *hybrid vigor*, the improvement from crossing two genetic strains of a plant. For people, too, children have an advantage if their parents' genes are not too similar. However, the Flynn effect occurs in countries where people still stay mostly in their home village. Also, one study showed that later-born brothers within a family have an advantage over those born earlier (Sundet, Eriksen, Borren, & Tambs, 2010). That trend suggests a change in society, not anything related to their parents' genes.

- Decreases in mental retardation. Advances in medicine have decreased several types of mental retardation. However, over the decades we see an increase in the highest test scores, not just a decrease in low scores (Wai & Putallaz, 2011).

- Increased cognitive stimulation. People have been exposed to more and more stimulation over the years, beginning with radio, and then movies, television, video games, and the Internet. These experiences stimulate skills related to performance on Raven's Progressive Matrices and similar tests (Neisser, 1997). Even in rural Kenya, some homes now have television (Daley et al., 2003).

- Improved health and nutrition (Sigman & Whaley, 1998). People have been getting taller over the years also, presumably because of advances in health, improved nutrition, and decreased smoking and drinking by pregnant women. Infants today on average hold their head up earlier than in past generations. They also sit up, stand, walk, say their first word, and so forth at a younger age (Lynn, 2009). Age of holding the head up has nothing to do with education or exposure to technology, but it has much to do with early health and nutrition.

- This one sounds so odd that not many investigators have considered it: Over the years, children have had more and more exposure to artificial lights. Poultry farmers have long known that they could accelerate chickens' growth by increasing artificial lighting. Might the same be true for human growth, including brain growth?

Although performance on IQ tests has steadily increased, have people really become that much more intelligent? Do we really believe that the average person of your grandparents' generation was, by today's standards, mentally retarded (or intellectually challenged, or whatever other term you prefer)? Flynn (1998) argued that we have seen an increase in IQ scores, but not intelligence, over time. If so, we have to wonder exactly what IQ scores mean. At a minimum, it is clear that the IQ scores of people born at different times do not mean the same thing.

Evaluation of Tests

Have you ever complained about a test in school that seemed unfair? *Seeming* unfair doesn't necessarily make it unfair—and seeming fair doesn't make it fair. When psychologists want to evaluate the accuracy or fairness of a test, they examine specific kinds of evidence related to its reliability and validity.

Reliability

The **reliability** of a test is defined as *the repeatability of its scores*. If a test is reliable, it produces nearly the same results every time. To determine the reliability of a test, psychologists calculate a correlation coefficient. Recall from Chapter 2 that a correlation coefficient measures how accurately we can use one measurement to predict another. Psychologists may test the same people twice with the same test or with equivalent versions of the test and compare the two sets of scores. Or they may compare the scores on the first and second halves of the test, or the scores on the test's odd-numbered and even-numbered items. If all items measure approximately the same thing, one set of scores should correlate highly with the other. ▲ Figure 9.9 illustrates **test–retest reliability**, *the correlation between scores on a first test and a retest.* Correlation coefficients theoretically range from +1 to −1. In the real world, however, a reliability coefficient is always either zero or positive. A negative reliability would mean that most people who score high the first time they take a test do worse than average the second time. That pattern never happens.

If a test's reliability is perfect (+1), the person with the highest score on the first test also scores highest on the retest, the person who scores second highest on the first test scores second highest on the retest, and so forth. If the reliability is 0, scores vary randomly from one test to another. If people took a test in a language that none of them understood, so that they were just guessing on every item, we would expect a reliability of zero. The WISC, Stanford-Binet, Progressive Matrices, and other commonly used intelligence tests all have reliabilities above 0.9.

IQ scores are reasonably stable over time for most individuals. Scores for children under age 7 correlate

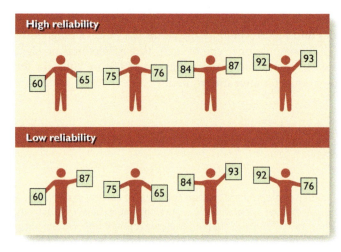

▲ **Figure 9.9** On a test with high reliability, people get similar scores each time they take the test. On a test with low reliability, scores fluctuate randomly.

only moderately well with later scores (Schneider, Niklas, & Schmiedeler, 2014), but most studies find correlations near 0.9 for adults taking the same test at times 10 to 20 years apart (Larsen, Hartmann, & Nyborg, 2008). A long-term study found that IQ scores at age 11 correlated 0.66 with scores at age 80 and 0.54 with scores at age 90 (Deary, Whiteman, Starr, Whalley, & Fox, 2004). ▼ Figure 9.10 shows the results.

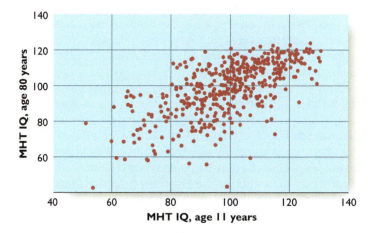

▲ **Figure 9.10** In this scatter plot, each point represents one person. The *x*-axis shows the IQ score at age 11, and the *y*-axis shows the IQ score at age 80. (MHT = the Moray House Test, a type of IQ test.) (Source: "The impact of childhood intelligence on later life: Following up the Scottish mental surveys of 1932 and 1947," by I. J. Deary, M. C. Whiteman, J. M. Starr, L. J. Whalley, & H. C. Fox, 2004. *Journal of Personality and Social Psychology, 86,* pp. 130–147.)

Validity

A test's *validity* is defined as *the degree to which evidence and theory support the interpretations of test scores for the intended purposes* (Joint Committee on Standards, 1999). In simpler terms, validity indicates how well the test measures what it claims to measure. To determine the validity of a test, researchers examine five types of evidence:

Content. The content of a test should match its purposes. A test given to job applicants should include only tasks that are important for the job. An end-of-grade test for fifth grade should correspond to the fifth-grade curriculum.

Response processes. If a test claims to measure a certain skill, then the test-takers should need to use that skill instead of using shortcuts. For example, tests of reading comprehension include something to read, followed by questions. If people can guess the answers without reading the passage, then the test isn't measuring reading comprehension (Katz, Lautenschlager, Blackburn, & Harris, 1990).

Internal structure. If a test claims to measure a single skill, such as working memory, then all the items should correlate with one another. That is, people who answer one item correctly should be more likely than average to answer the other items correctly. (Internal structure is the same idea as reliability.)

Relation to other variables. Most importantly, if a test is valid, the scores predict important kinds of performance. Scores on an interest inventory should predict which jobs or activities someone would enjoy. Results of a personality test should predict which people might develop anxiety problems or depression. Scores on an IQ test should predict grades in school. In fact, they do correlate positively with grades and achievement tests in all academic subjects (Deary, Strand, Smith, & Fernandes, 2007).

IQ tests were designed to predict school performance. Later results showed that they predicted other outcomes as well, to the surprise of almost everyone, including the authors of the tests. On average, people with higher IQ scores get better jobs than most other people and earn higher salaries (Strenze, 2007). They have fewer automobile accidents than others do (O'Toole, 1990) and are less likely to suffer post-traumatic stress disorder (Vasterling et al., 2002). They do better than others at reading maps, understanding order forms, reading bus schedules, understanding nutrition labels on foods, and taking their medicines correctly (Gottfredson, 2002a; Murray, Johnson, Wolf, & Deary, 2011). They are more likely than average to forego a smaller pleasure now in favor of a larger one later (Shamosh et al., 2008). They are more likely than average to hold attitudes that are antiracist and favorable to women's causes (Deary, Batty, & Gale, 2008). They tend to be healthier than average, to live longer (Shalev et al., 2013), and to show more creativity and leadership (Kuncel & Hezlett, 2010). Although some of these correlations are small, they indicate that IQ scores relate to real-world outcomes outside the classroom.

As you might expect, high scores predict success in scientific fields. Even among those with a master's or PhD degree, those with higher scores usually have more patents and scientific publications (Park, Lubinski, & Benbow, 2008). IQ scores also predict success on a wide variety of other jobs, especially if combined with other information (Schmidt & Hunter, 1998). According to Linda Gottfredson (2002b, pp. 25, 27), "The general mental ability factor—g—is the best single predictor of job performance . . . [It] enhances performance in all domains of work." According to Frank Schmidt and John Hunter (1981, p. 1128), "Professionally developed cognitive ability tests are valid predictors of performance on the job . . . for all jobs . . . in all settings." That is probably an overstatement. (It could hardly be an understatement!) For example,

IQ scores are probably not useful predictors of success for singers or professional athletes. Still, for many jobs, using some type of cognitive test score to select employees increases the chances that those who are hired will learn their jobs quickly and succeed at them.

Do IQ tests measure everything that we care about? Of course they don't, not even in academics. One study found that eighth graders' performance in school correlated highly with questionnaire measurements of their self-discipline (Duckworth & Seligman, 2005). College grades correlate highly with measures of effort (Credé & Kuncel, 2008) and curiosity (von Stumm, Hell, & Chamorro-Premuzic, 2011). People also vary in initiative, creativity, and other variables that are important but hard to measure.

Consequences of testing. Tests produce benefits, but also some unintended consequences. For example, in the U.S. public school system, students' scores on end-of-grade tests determine whether they advance to the next grade. The scores also influence the teachers' salaries for the next year and the amount of government support that a school receives. As a result, the best qualified teachers don't want to work at schools with low-performing students (Tuerk, 2005). Many students and teachers concentrate heavily on preparing for the tests at the expense of other educational goals. Do the tests accomplish enough good to outweigh these costs? Although opinions are strong, good research on these issues is rare (Braden & Niebling, 2005).

Special Problems in Measuring Validity

Measuring the validity of a test can be difficult. Scores on the SAT or ACT correlate only modestly

In some countries, test scores determine a student's future almost irrevocably. Students who perform well are almost assured future success, and those who perform poorly have limited opportunities.

with college grades. One reason is that college students take different courses. A student with a B average in hard courses may have done better work than a student with all A's in easy courses. If we examine data for only students taking the same courses, the test scores predict success reasonably well (Berry & Sackett, 2009).

Here is another issue: Consider data for the Graduate Record Examination (GRE), a test taken by graduate school applicants. According to one large study, grades for first-year graduate students in physics correlated 0.13 with their GRE quantitative scores and 0.19 with their verbal scores. That is, for students in physics, verbal scores predicted success better than quantitative scores did. For first-year students in English, the pattern was reversed. Their grades correlated 0.29 with their quantitative scores and 0.23 with their verbal scores (Educational Testing Service, 1994). These scores seem surprising, because physics is such a quantitative field and English is such a verbal field.

The explanation is simple: Almost all graduate students in physics have nearly the same (very high) score on the quantitative test, and almost all English graduate students have nearly the same (very high) score on the verbal test. If almost all the students in a department have nearly the same score, their scores cannot predict who will do better than others. A test predicts performance only when scores vary over a substantial range.

11. Can a test have high reliability and low validity? Can a test have low reliability and high validity?

12. If physics graduate departments tried admitting some students with low quantitative scores on the GRE and English departments tried admitting some students with low verbal scores, what would happen to the predictive validity of the tests?

Answers

11. Yes, a test can have high reliability and low validity. A measure of intelligence determined by dividing head length by head width has high reliability (repeatability) but presumably no validity. A test with low reliability cannot have high validity, however. Low reliability means that the scores fluctuate randomly. If the test scores cannot even predict a later score on the same test, then they can hardly predict anything else.

12. The predictive validity of the tests would increase. The predictive validity is low when most students have nearly the same score. It is higher when students' scores are highly variable.

Interpreting Fluctuations in Scores

Suppose on the first test in some course you get 94 percent correct. On the second test, which was equally difficult, your score is only 88 percent. Does that score indicate that you studied harder for the first test? Not necessarily. When tests are not perfectly reliable, your scores fluctuate. The lower the reliability, the greater the fluctuation.

When people lose sight of this fact, they sometimes draw unwarranted conclusions. In one study, Harold Skeels (1966) tested infants in an orphanage and identified those with the lowest IQ scores. He transferred those infants to an institution that provided more attention. Several years later, most of them showed major increases in their IQ scores. Should we conclude, as many psychologists did, that the extra attention improved the children's IQ performances? Not necessarily (Longstreth, 1981). IQ tests for infants have low reliability. The scores fluctuate widely, even from one day to the next. If someone selects infants with low scores and retests them later, their mean IQ score is almost certain to improve, simply because the scores had nowhere to go but up.

Similarly, suppose we examine people who had a perfect score on the first test in some class. What scores should we expect on the second test? On average, their scores will go down. It is not because they got overconfident and failed to study. It is because the tests are not perfectly reliable, and a certain amount of fluctuation is inevitable.

A similar trend occurs in many fields. An athlete who performs extremely well or extremely poorly one day will probably be closer to average the next time. (Someone else, who was close to average the first time, might do extremely well or poorly the next time.) If the value of a stock investment shoots way up or way down one day, the best guess is that it won't repeat its performance the next day. All of these changes merely reflect the low reliability of a single measurement.

Are IQ Tests Biased?

In addition to being reliable and valid, a test should also be unbiased—that is, equally fair and accurate for all groups. A biased test *overstates or understates the true performance of one or more groups.* If one group scores better than another, that difference by itself does not necessarily indicate bias. To take an extreme example, students who study hard in a course get better grades than those who don't study. Does that result mean the test is biased against students who don't study? No. (If you do think it is biased, then your idea of an unbiased test is one on which everyone gets the same score.) If groups really do differ in some kind of performance, the test should report that fact accurately. Measuring differences is the whole point of a test. Driver's license examinations include vision tests. Are they therefore biased against people who are blind? Again, no. The results accurately predict that blind people would be poor drivers. However, if someone were selecting applicants to be a school guidance counselor, then a vision test *would* be biased against the blind, because it would understate their ability to do the job. The point is that bias means unfairness for a particular purpose. Researchers need to determine the bias, or lack of it, for any potential use of any test.

The question of bias is an empirical question—that is, one to be decided by the evidence. In what way, if any, are IQ tests or other tests biased? Women who enter college or graduate school after age 25 generally receive better grades than their SAT scores predict (Swinton, 1987). Therefore, the tests are biased against them, even though in fact most of them have good scores. The tests are biased in the sense that a given SAT score means something different for a woman over 25 than for a 20-year-old. Why do older women get better grades than their test scores predict? Here are three hypotheses: (1) Because they have been away from school for a while, their test-taking skills are rusty.

Women who return to school after age 25 usually get better grades than their SAT scores predict. The tests are "biased" against them in the sense of underpredicting their performance.

(2) Anyone who returns to school at that point must have strong motivation. (3) A few extra years of experiences give them some advantages.

To determine whether a test is biased against groups, psychologists conduct several kinds of research. They try to identify bias both in individual test items and in the test as a whole.

Evaluating Possible Bias in Single Test Items

Suppose on a test with 100 items, one item is the 10th easiest for group A but only the 42nd easiest for group B. This pattern suggests that the item taps information or skills that are more available to group A than group B. If so, the item is biased (Schmitt & Dorans, 1990). ▶ **Figure 9.11**, an item that once appeared on the SAT, diagrams an American football field and asks for the ratio of the distance between the goal lines to the distance between the sidelines. For men, this was one of the easiest items on the test. Many women missed it, including some of the brightest women who missed almost no other questions.

The reason was that some women had so little interest in football that they did not know which

were the goal lines and which were the sidelines. The publishers of the SAT saw that this item was biased and removed it from the test.

Evaluating Possible Bias in a Test as a Whole

By definition, a biased test systematically misestimates the performance by members of some group. For example, if an IQ test is biased against Black students, then Black students who score, say, 100 will do *better* in school than White students with the same score.

Researchers have repeatedly looked for evidence of test bias. However, the evidence indicates that on average the Black students with a given IQ score or other standardized test score do about the same in school as do White students with the same score (Davis et al., 2013; McCornack, 1983; Pesta & Poznanski, 2008; Sackett, Borneman, & Connelly, 2008). The test scores do seem to be a bit less accurate in their predictions for Black students. That is, the scores underestimate performance for some and overestimate for others (Berry, Cullen, & Meyer, 2014). Why that is true is unknown.

The unpleasant fact is that White students usually receive better grades in school than Black students. The difference in IQ scores approximately matches the difference in performance. Presumably whatever is impairing performance in school is also impairing performance on the tests. The test scores make no implication about what impairs performance.

The gap between Black and White students in the United States has decreased. The gap, which

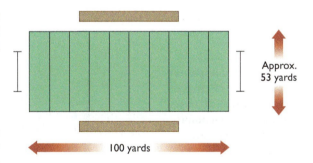

The diagram above represents a football field. What is the ratio of the distance between the goal lines to the distance between the sidelines?

a. 1.89
b. 1.53
c. 0.53
d. 5.3
e. 53

▲ **Figure 9.11** This item was eliminated from the SAT when researchers determined that it was biased against women. Some women who did very well on the rest of the test did not know which were the goal lines and which were the sidelines.

used to be about 16 points, has decreased to about 10 points. Simultaneously, Black students also increased their grades in school (Grissmer, Williamson, Kirby, & Berends, 1998). The fact that grades and test scores improved together supports the idea that the tests predict performance validly. Most of the gain in test scores occurred between 1970 and 1990, with less change since then (Dickens & Flynn, 2006; Magnuson & Duncan, 2006; Murray, 2007; Rindermann & Thompson, 2013). The improvement of Black students' IQ scores and grades presumably relates to improved health, education, and occupational opportunities for many Black families. The reason for the decreased progress since 1990 is not clear.

If IQ and SAT scores predict school performance about as well for Blacks as for Whites, then the tests are not biased, according to the definition of test bias. However, another possibility remains: Many Black students may be performing at a lower level than they could, in both school and the tests.

If so, why? Poverty (which leads to poor prenatal health and nutrition, as well as high levels of stress) is one hypothesis (Evans & Schamberg, 2009), but probably not the whole explanation. If we compare Blacks and Whites of the same socioeconomic status, a difference in scores remains, although it is smaller than usual (Magnuson & Duncan, 2006). Another possibility is impairment by low expectations and aspirations. If you think you don't have a chance anyway, maybe you don't try. On average, Black men score lower than Black women, and are less likely than Black women to attend college. That fact strongly suggests that many Black men are not giving a full effort academically (McKinnon & Bennett, 2005). We explore this possibility in the next section.

13. A company hiring salespeople proposes to test applicants on their ability to speak Spanish. Is this policy biased against people who don't speak Spanish?

Answer

13. It depends. A test is biased if it underpredicts or overpredicts performance for a group of people. If the salespeople will be working in a neighborhood with many Spanish-speaking customers, this test will accurately predict success on the job, and it would therefore be unbiased. However, if the sales staff works in a neighborhood with no need to use Spanish, the test is biased.

what's the evidence?

Stereotype Threat

Possible test bias depends not only on the test itself but also on how the test is administered and the

expectations of those being tested. Imagine you are about to take some test when someone says that "people like you"—left-handers, redheads, people who live in small towns, whatever it might be—usually don't do well on this kind of test. How will that statement affect you? You might become discouraged. Even if you don't believe the statement, it's a distraction. You worry that if you perform poorly, you confirm this hurtful expectation.

Claude Steele termed this idea **stereotype threat**—*people's perceived risk of performing poorly and thereby supporting an unfavorable stereotype about their group.* In particular, Black students who take an IQ test may fear that a poor score would support prejudices about Blacks. They may become distracted or discouraged. Let's examine Steele's study and its results.

Hypothesis If Black students believe they are taking the kind of test on which Black students in general do not perform well, then they worry that their own performance may reflect poorly on their group. They may also lose confidence. As a result, they fail to perform up to their abilities. If they are freed from this kind of concern, their performance may improve.

Method Participants were 20 Black and 20 White undergraduate students at Stanford University, a prestigious, highly selective institution. They were given a set of 27 difficult verbal questions from the Graduate Record Exam, a test intended for college seniors applying to graduate schools. Before the test, two groups (randomly assigned) received different instructions. Those in the "nondiagnostic" group were told that the researchers were studying how people solve difficult verbal problems. In contrast, participants in the "diagnostic" group were told that the research was an attempt to find each participant's strengths and weaknesses in solving verbal problems. This latter instruction was an attempt to increase students' nervousness about being evaluated.

Results Instead of simply presenting the number of correct answers for each group, the researchers adjusted the scores based on participants' SAT scores. The results in ▼ Figure 9.12 show the number of correct answers for each group *relative to the scores predicted by their verbal SAT scores.* The mean for these Black

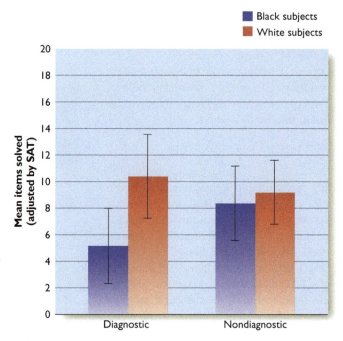

▲ **Figure 9.12** Black students who believed the test would identify their strengths and weaknesses failed to live up to their abilities. (From "Stereotype threat and the intellectual test performance of African Americans," by Claude M. Steele & Joshua Aronson, 1995. *Journal of Personality and Social Psychology, 69*, pp. 797–811.) Copyright © 1995 American Psychological Association. Reprinted with permission.

students on the verbal part of the SAT was 603, and the mean for these White students was 655. So, if the Black and White students both did as well as their SAT scores predicted, the graph would show equal performances on the test, even if the White students answered a slightly higher percentage correctly.

The results for the "nondiagnostic" group do in fact show this pattern. However, for students who were given the "diagnostic" instructions, Black students had lower scores than their SAT scores predicted. They answered fewer questions overall, and answered fewer correctly, than Black students given the "nondiagnostic" instructions. The type of instructions did not significantly affect the White students.

When interviewed afterward, the Black students who received the "diagnostic" instructions said that they felt strongly aware of the stereotype about Black students taking ability tests. They also said they felt self-doubts about possibly conforming to this stereotype (Steele & Aronson, 1995). Another study by the same researchers found that simply asking participants to indicate their race prior to the test impaired Black students' scores (Steele & Aronson, 1995).

Interpretation The results confirmed that many Black students are sensitive to a suggestion that they are taking a test on which Black students do not excel. Presumably, the worry distracts from their ability to concentrate on the questions.

Further Research on Stereotype Threat

Many further studies have been conducted on stereotype threat, and most replicate the general finding (Nguyen & Ryan, 2008; Steele, 2010). Stereotype threat also applies to other groups, such as the Turkish minority in Germany (Walton & Spencer, 2009). Informing old people (truthfully) that they have a gene that increases the risk of Alzheimer's disease decreases their self-confidence and impairs their performance on memory tests (Lineweaver, Bondi, Galasko, & Salmon, 2014).

Another stereotype is that women don't do well at math. Overall, the research indicates that thinking about the stereotype impairs women's math performance, although the effect is small and many studies fail to show it (Ganley et al., 2013; Krendl, Richeson, Kelley, & Heatherton, 2008; Picho, Rodriguez, & Finnie, 2013). Women who don't believe the stereotype or don't believe it applies to them personally show no impairment (Dar-Nimrod & Heine, 2006; Kiefer & Sekaquaptewa, 2007; Lesko & Corpus, 2006).

Asian women confront contradictory stereotypes concerning their math abilities. One stereotype is that women don't do well, but another is that Asians tend to excel on math. In several studies, researchers primed attention to being female by first giving a questionnaire about being female, or primed attention to being Asian by giving a questionnaire about family and ethnic background. In some of these studies, focusing attention on being Asian enhanced math performance whereas focusing attention on being female impaired performance, at least among those who were aware of the stereotypes (Gibson, Losee, & Vitiello, 2014; Shih, Pittinsky, & Ambady, 1999). However, the effect is a small one, and some studies fail to find it (Moon & Roeder, 2014).

Given the goal of helping all people live up to their abilities, how can we combat stereotype threat? One approach is simply to tell people about stereotype threat! In one study, researchers described math problems as diagnostic of abilities that differ between men and women. But then they told some of the women (randomly assigned) about stereotype threat and urged them not to let the stereotype bother them. Those women performed as well as men did on average (Johns, Schmader, & Martens, 2005). In several other studies, researchers asked students who lacked confidence about their test performance to write about their most important values, their most valuable characteristics, or how it would feel to be highly successful. The result was enhanced test performance (Lang & Lang, 2010; Martens, Johns, Greenberg, & Schimel, 2006; Miyake et al., 2010). Writing about worries helped also, perhaps by getting them out in the open and then dismissing them (Ramirez & Beilock, 2011). The idea is that worrying about your performance leads to "choking under pressure," just as it does for athletes (Beilock, Jellison, Rydell, McConnell, & Carr, 2006).

Benefits of writing interventions can last surprisingly long. One group of Black seventh-grade students completed a series of self-affirming writing assignments about their family, friendships, interests, and values. The result was improved grades in school for at least the next two years (Cohen, Garcia, Purdie-Vaughns, Apfel, & Brzustoski, 2009).

In most studies, the effect of stereotype threat on Black students is the equivalent of about three IQ points. However, what we don't know is the cumulative effect over years. Students who are told they aren't likely to do well in school or on tests may be discouraged from the start. Early discouragement could compound into greater discouragement later. How large might the overall effect be?

14. **How does stereotype threat affect the validity of a test?**

Answer

14. Because stereotype threat leads some people to perform at a lower level than they would otherwise, it decreases the validity of the test.

Consequences of Testing

Regardless of what we say about intelligence theoretically, testing continues for practical reasons. Just as a coach tries to choose the best players for an athletic team, colleges and employers try to choose the applicants who will learn the fastest. If people are going to make those judgments—as no doubt they will—we want them to use the best available methods and evaluate the results accurately.

Testing has consequences for the individuals who take the tests and the institutions that evaluate the scores, but it can also have another kind of consequence: If we begin to better understand the factors that influence intelligence, we may be able to do something about these factors. As a society, we would like to intervene early to help children develop as well as possible, but to make those interventions work, we need research. How important are prenatal health and early childhood nutrition? Which kinds of environmental stimulation are most effective? Are different kinds of stimulation better for different kinds of children? To answer these questions, we need good measurements—measurements that can come only from testing of some kind.

Summary

- *Standardization.* To determine the meaning of a test's scores, the authors of a test determine the mean and the distribution of scores for a random or representative sample of the population. IQ tests are revised periodically. (page 299)
- *Distribution of IQ scores.* IQ tests have a mean of 100 and a standard deviation of about 15 or 16, depending on the test. However, the mode (most frequent score) is higher than 100, and a bulge of lower scores exists. (page 299)
- *The Flynn effect.* To keep the mean score at 100, authors of IQ tests have had to revise the tests periodically, always making them more difficult. That is, raw performance has been increasing steadily. The reasons for this trend are unknown. (page 301)
- *Reliability and validity.* Tests are evaluated in terms of reliability and validity. Reliability is a measure of the repeatability of a test's scores. Validity is a determination of how well a test measures what it claims to measure. (page 302)

- *Measuring validity.* To evaluate a test's validity for a given purpose, researchers examine its content, the response processes people use while taking the test, the internal structure of the test, the scores' relationship to other variables, and the consequences of using the test. (page 303)
- *Test bias.* Bias means inaccuracy of measurement. Psychologists try to remove from a test any item that tends to be easy for one group of people to answer but difficult for another group. They also try to evaluate whether the test as a whole makes equally accurate predictions for all groups. (page 304)
- *Test anxiety and stereotype threat.* Many Black students perform worse on tests after any reminder of the stereotype of Black students scoring poorly on such tests. Awareness of stereotypes also impairs performance of other groups. However, some simple procedures can weaken this threat. (page 306)

Key Terms

bias (page 304)

Down syndrome (page 299)

Flynn effect (page 301)

norms (page 299)

reliability (page 302)

standardization (page 299)

stereotype threat (page 306)

test–retest reliability (page 302)

validity (page 303)

Review Questions

1. Theoretically, the distribution of IQ scores should have a mean of 100 and an equal number of people above and below the mean. How does the actual distribution of scores differ from this prediction?
   (a) The actual mean is 105.
   (b) The actual mean is 95.
   (c) The mode (most common score) is 105.
   (d) The mode (most common score) is 95.

2. On average, how do males and females compare in IQ?
   (a) On average, males have a higher IQ.
   (b) On average, females have a higher IQ.
   (c) On average, males and females are equal on all subtests and on overall IQ.
   (d) On average, males and females differ on certain subscores, but are equal on overall IQ.

3. Why have psychologists needed to restandardize IQ tests repeatedly over the years?
   (a) To prevent the mean from increasing above 100
   (b) To prevent the mean from decreasing below 100
   (c) To match the changes in school curricula
   (d) To measure newly evolved abilities

4. A hundred people take a test. We find that the person with the highest score on the odd-numbered items also has the highest score on the even-numbered items. Someone else has the second highest score on both sets of items, and so forth down to the 100th person. Which of the following can we conclude about this test?
   (a) It has high reliability and validity.
   (b) It has low reliability and validity.
   (c) It has high reliability and unknown validity.
   (d) It has unknown reliability but high validity.

5. At which kind of college, if any, would you expect SAT scores to have the highest validity for predicting grades?
   (a) A highly competitive college that admits only students with high SAT scores
   (b) A moderately competitive college
   (c) A college that admits everyone, ranging from those with high SAT scores to those with very low scores
   (d) No difference among colleges

6. Suppose on some new IQ test tall people generally get higher scores than short people. Which of the following would be the strongest evidence that the test is biased against short people?
   (a) The fact that short people get lower scores is in itself strong evidence that the test is biased.
   (b) It would be strong evidence if short people believed the questions were unfair to them.
   (c) It would be strong evidence if it were revealed that most of the test's authors were tall.
   (d) It would be strong evidence if someone demonstrated that short people get better grades in school than the test scores predict.

7. Which of the following is another way to state the idea of stereotype threat?
   (a) On most tests, younger people do better on reasoning and older people do better on factual knowledge.
   (b) If you expect to do poorly on a test, you probably will.
   (c) On average, test scores are higher for some groups than for others.
   (d) People tend to stay away from others whom they consider dangerous.

Answers: 1c, 2d, 3a, 4c, 5c, 6d, 7b.

10 Consciousness

©Wavebreakmedia/Shutterstock.com

What is consciousness? As William James (1892/1961) said, "Its meaning we know so long as no one asks us to define it" (p. 19). Of all the questions that humans ask, two are the most profound and the most difficult. One is why there is a universe at all. As the philosopher Gottfried Leibniz (1714) put it, "Why is there something rather than nothing?" A second profound question is why, in a universe of matter and energy, does consciousness exist? Why is electrochemical activity in your brain sometimes conscious?

Many questions about consciousness are unanswerable, at least by present methods. But that doesn't stop us from dealing with some simpler but related questions. What aspects of brain activity are necessary for consciousness? How does your conscious experience change when you are sleeping, dreaming, or under hypnosis? These questions, too, are fascinating.

We examine ourselves to try to understand consciousness.

© Forster Forest/Shutterstock.com

Conscious and Unconscious Processes

After studying this module, you should be able to:

- Explain why early psychologists abandoned the study of consciousness and why new developments now make such a study possible.

- List methods of presenting a stimulus while preventing conscious perception of it.

- Describe how a consciously perceived stimulus activates brain areas differently from the same stimulus when not consciously perceived.

- Cite evidence that the brain processes some information unconsciously.

- Discuss cases in which people in a vegetative state showed evidence of consciousness.

- Describe and evaluate evidence that brain activity responsible for a movement begins before the conscious decision to make that movement.

In the fall of 2013, the editors of *Science* invited young scientists to answer the question, "What recent discovery in your field will still be remembered 200 years from now?" They published some of the best replies in a later issue ("NextGen Speaks," 2014) and posted others online. Responses included suggestions for physics, astronomy, chemistry, biochemistry, and other fields, but no one offered a suggestion for psychology. So, what recent discovery in psychology, if any, will anyone remember 200 years from now?

Here is my guess: I predict that 200 years from now, people will remember that around the year 2000, give or take 20 years, psychologists began to study consciousness as an empirical topic.

Psychology began in the late 1800s as the scientific study of the conscious mind. However, researchers soon abandoned that effort. (Someone quipped that psychology had "lost its mind.") The behaviorists argued convincingly that consciousness is an internal, private experience that researchers cannot observe or measure. At the time they were certainly right, as they had no method to measure brain activity or anything else that might correlate with a private experience. Therefore, psychologists redefined their field as the study of behavior. Many behaviorists went well beyond saying that consciousness could not be studied, saying that it was not important. Consider these quotes:

> The essence of behaviorism is the belief that the study of man will reveal nothing except what is adequately describable in the concepts of mechanics and chemistry. (Lashley, 1923a, p. 244)

> The behaviorist may go his way . . . with the conviction that the inclusion of "mind" will add nothing to scientific psychology. (Lashley, 1923b, p. 352)

> The epoch of the I is drawing to a close. . . . Consciousness contains almost no information. (Norretranders, 1991/1998, pp. ix–xi)

Several scientists and philosophers have gone even further, suggesting that consciousness doesn't even exist, defending the paradoxical claim that your mind is a figment of your imagination!

> Just as it turned out that there was no such thing as impetus, there may be no such thing as awareness. (P. S. Churchland, 1986, p. 309)

> [T]here is no subjective feeling inside. . . . Instead, there is a description of having a feeling and a computed certainty that the description is accurate. (Graziano, 2013, pp. 20–21)

Other psychologists and philosophers have made the point that consciousness does not help us explain behavior (e.g., Wegner, 2002). They are right, at least as of today, with one exception: the behavior of talking about consciousness! Presumably we wouldn't talk about it if it didn't exist. Except for that perhaps trivial exception, we don't need the concept of consciousness for any explanation of behavior. But that misses the point: Consciousness is not something that psychologists invented to try to explain behavior. It is the thing we are trying to explain. In a universe composed of matter and energy, why is there such a thing as consciousness?

Measuring Consciousness

Although the behaviorists were right at their time that research on consciousness was impossible, times have changed. Four advances have facilitated meaningful research.

An Operational Definition of Consciousness

A dictionary might define **consciousness** as *the subjective experience of perceiving oneself and one's surroundings*. However, that definition relies on the phrase "subjective experience," which is no better defined than consciousness itself. Researchers use this operational definition: *If a cooperative person reports being conscious (aware) of one stimulus and not of another, then he or she was conscious of the first and not the second*. That definition may seem obvious, even silly, but it is useful for research purposes. An important point is that it applies only for people who speak. Because an infant cannot report being conscious of anything, the definition doesn't apply, and we cannot infer either consciousness or the lack of it. Similarly, nonhuman animals do not talk, nor do people with certain types of brain damage, but we need not assume they are unconscious.

Limited, Answerable Questions

Important questions abound: Why does consciousness exist at all? Does it have elements, analogous to the elements of chemistry? What is it good for? And so on. For the time being, we postpone the questions that are hardest to answer and focus on limited, answerable questions such as, "How does the brain activity when someone is conscious of a stimulus differ from the activity when someone is not conscious of the same or a similar stimulus?" Among the stimuli striking your receptors at any moment, you are conscious of only a few. Right now, do you smell or taste anything? What do you feel in your left leg? The back of your neck? As you turn your attention to one sensation after another, you become aware of much that had been present but unconscious until then (Lambie & Marcel, 2002).

Modern Methods to Measure Brain Activity

As discussed in Chapter 3, researchers today have several methods to record brain activity without invading the brain. The simplest are EEG and MEG, which use detectors on the scalp to measure rapid changes in the brain's electrical or magnetic activity. They identify only the approximate location of the activity, but for many purposes approximate location is good enough, and these methods detect the timing of the activity to millisecond accuracy. The fMRI method identifies the location of activity more precisely, but with less precision about timing. A researcher could use EEG, MEG, or fMRI, depending on the research question.

Ways of Controlling Consciousness of a Stimulus

The final advance comes from new methods of presenting a stimulus so that people are conscious of it sometimes and not at other times. One method is **masking**: *a word or other stimulus appears on the screen for a fraction of a second, preceded and/or followed by an interfering stimulus.* If *the interfering stimulus follows it* but doesn't precede it also, we call the procedure **backward masking**. Participants in one study watched words flash on a screen for just 29 milliseconds (ms) each. On some trials, a blank screen preceded and followed the word:

GROVE

Under those conditions, people usually identified the word, even though it flashed so briefly. On other trials, a masking pattern preceded and followed the word. Under these conditions, people almost never identified the word, and almost always insisted that they saw no word at all:

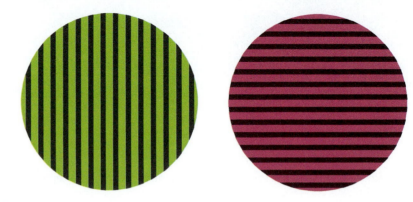

▲ **Figure 10.1** To produce binocular rivalry, look through tubes and alter the focus of your eyes until the two circles seem to merge. You will alternate between seeing red lines and seeing green lines.

 SALTY

Let's consider a second method. Suppose you see a yellow dot surrounded by blue dots on a computer screen. Then the blue dots start moving rapidly in haphazard directions. They will grab your attention so strongly that the yellow dot actually disappears from your sight for seconds at a time (Bonneh, Cooperman, & Sagi, 2001). Another possibility is for the *other dots to flash on and off, rapidly.* While they are flashing, you lose sight of the yellow dot (Kreiman, Fried, & Koch, 2002; Yuval-Greenberg & Heeger, 2013). This procedure is called **flash suppression**.

Here is a third method. Ordinarily, your two retinas see almost the same thing. Examine ▲ **Figure 10.1** to see what happens when the images conflict.

Find or make tubes like those in a roll of paper towels, so your left eye can look at Figure 10.1 through one roll and your right eye can look through the other. For a quick shortcut, you could cup your two hands to form viewing tubes, or touch your nose to the page so that your two eyes are right in front of the two images. Adjust your focus until the two circles appear to overlap. First, you will be conscious of what one eye sees—such as red and black lines. Within seconds, that perception fades and you start seeing green and black lines. Because you cannot see both images at the same time in the same place, your brain alternates between the two perceptions (Blake & Logothetis, 2002). The *alternation between seeing the pattern in the left retina and the pattern in the right retina* is known as **binocular rivalry**. (If you see well from one eye and poorly from the other eye, you might see one image almost exclusively.)

Brain Activity, Conscious or Unconscious

In each of the procedures just described, an observer is conscious of a stimulus under one condition and not under the other, but the initial processing is the same. The retina responds to the visual stimulus equally in both cases, and sends equivalent messages to the visual cortex. For about the first 200 ms, the response in the visual cortex is about the same for stimuli destined for consciousness or unconsciousness. For about the next second after that, the responses diverge. On trials when the observer does not become conscious of the stimulus, the response to it remains weak and mostly localized to the primary visual cortex. On trials when conscious processing results, the activation spreads quickly from the visual cortex to many brain areas, as shown in ▼ **Figure 10.2**, and then rebounds back from the prefrontal cortex to the primary visual cortex, magnifying and prolonging the

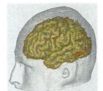

Visible words   Masked words

▲ **Figure 10.2** When people were conscious of a briefly flashed word, it activated the areas colored in the brain on the left. When masking prevented consciousness, the word activated only the areas colored on the right. (From "Cerebral mechanisms of word masking and unconscious repetition priming," by S. Dehaene, et al. *Nature Neuroscience, 4,* pp. 752–758. Copyright © 2001 Nature Publishing Group. Reprinted with permission.)

response there (Dehaene et al., 2001; Li, Hill, & He, 2014). That echo amplifies the conscious perception. People with an impaired prefrontal cortex are less likely than average to notice weak stimuli (Del Cul, Dehaene, Reyes, Bravo, & Slachevsky, 2009; Rounis, Maniscalco, Rothwell, Passingham, & Lau, 2010).

Researchers found a convenient way to label the brain response to a particular stimulus. Instead of binocular rivalry between red and green stripes, they exposed one eye to an unchanging face and the other eye to a circle that pulsated between large and small, seven times per second. Then they looked for patterns of brain activity that pulsated seven times per second. When a viewer reported seeing the flashing stimulus, researchers saw a seven per second rhythm of activity throughout a large portion of the brain (Cosmelli et al., 2004; Lee, Blake, & Heeger, 2005). When the viewer reported seeing the face, the rhythmic activity subsided, and a steadier pattern spread over the brain. In short, when you become conscious of a stimulus, it produces more brain activity and more spread of the activity across brain areas. It also produces more inhibition of other, competing brain activity (Li et al., 2014; Moher, Lakshmanan, Egeth, & Ewen, 2014). We begin to understand why it is hard to be conscious of several things at the same time: When you are conscious of something, it occupies much of your brain.

Unconscious Processing of a Suppressed Stimulus

During binocular rivalry, while you are conscious of one stimulus, what happens to the brain representation of the other one? Is it lost altogether? No, although the information doesn't spread enough to become conscious, it does spread enough for the brain to process it to a certain degree. If flash suppression or similar techniques block your awareness of a stimulus, you might still react to it emotionally—for example, if it is a picture of a spider, or a face with an emotional expression (Anderson, Siegel, White, & Barrett, 2012; Lapate, Rokers, Li, & Davidson, 2014). Suppose your eyes view different scenes on a computer screen. While you are conscious of one eye, the experimenter gradually changes the scene in the other eye to show a face. A face with an emotional expression captures your attention faster than a neutral face does (Alpers & Gerdes, 2007). If a word emerges on one side, it captures your attention faster if it is in a language you read than one you don't (Jiang, Costello, & He, 2007). That is, your brain notices that something is meaningful or important even before you become conscious of it. Unconscious processes can do a good bit more than we once imagined they could (Hassin, 2013).

Consciousness as an All-or-None Phenomenon

Does consciousness come in degrees? That is, are you ever "partly" conscious of a stimulus? Suppose we flash blurry stimuli on the screen for a split second each. On some trials people say they were conscious of the stimulus and they accurately name or describe it. On other trials they say they did not see the stimulus, although they might be able to guess with accuracy slightly better than chance (Li et al., 2014). People almost never say they were "partly conscious" of the stimulus (Sergent & Dehaene, 2004).

Studies using brain scans point to the same conclusion. On trials where someone reports consciousness of a stimulus, its excitation spreads widely in the brain. On other trials, the excitation spreads weakly and briefly. Intermediate cases do not occur. Evidently a stimulus either reaches a threshold necessary for spread, or it does not. Even with infants, the response to a stimulus is either strong and widespread, or weak and brief (Kouider et al., 2013). Consciousness of a stimulus appears to be an all-or-none phenomenon.

1. **How did researchers arrange for a stimulus to be conscious on some trials and not others?**

2. **What do people perceive during binocular rivalry?**

Answers

2. Most people perceive one stimulus and then the other, alternating.

1. Researchers presented a word for a small fraction of a second. When they simply presented the word, most people identified it. In other cases, researchers put interfering patterns before and after the word. In those cases, people were not conscious of it.

Consciousness as a Construction

When we see or hear something, we assume that we see or hear it *as it happens*. However, various studies cast doubt on that assumption. Suppose a word flashes on a screen for 29 ms followed by a masking stimulus, so that you are not conscious of the word. Then the experimenter repeats the procedure but extends the duration to 50 ms. With this longer presentation, you do see the word. More important, you don't have 29 ms of unconscious perception and 21 ms of conscious perception. Rather, the final part of that 50-ms presentation enabled you to become conscious of the first part retroactively. In some way, your brain constructed an experience of a 50-ms stimulus, even though it had to wait until the later part of the stimulus to perceive the first part.

Here is a related phenomenon. Suppose you see a display of two vertical lines:

|
|

After a delay of one- or two-tenths of a second, you see a display of circles like this:

○
○

When you report the appearance of the lines, you describe something like this:

|
|

That is, the lines appear to be displaced partly in the same direction that the circles were displaced

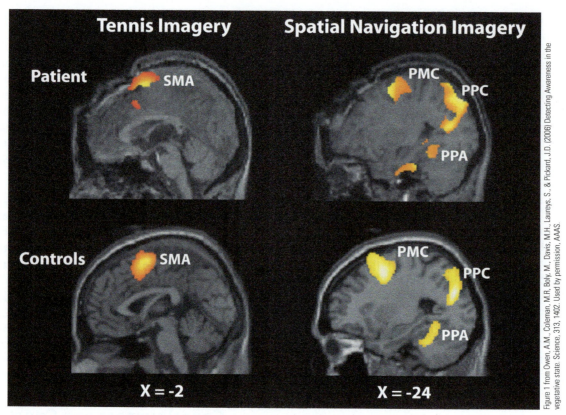

Tennis Imagery   **Spatial Navigation Imagery**

Patient   SMA   PMC   PPC   PPA

Controls   SMA   PMC   PPC   PPA

X = -2   X = -24

Figure 1 from Owen, A.M., Coleman, M.R, Boly, M., Davis, M.H., Laureys, S., & Pickard, J.D. (2006) Detecting Awareness in the vegetative state. Science, 313, 1402. Used by permission, AAAS.

▲ **Figure 10.3** The brain areas marked in red and yellow showed increased activity after instructions to imagine playing tennis or imagine walking through the house. Note the similarities between a patient in a persistent vegetative state and uninjured people. SMA = supplementary motor cortex, an area important for planning complex movements. PMC, PPC, and PPA = three areas responsible for spatial imagery and memory. (From Owen et al., 2006)

(Ono & Watanabe, 2011). The later stimulus changed your perception of the earlier stimulus. Evidently, consciousness does not occur at exactly the same time as the events. You construct a conscious perception of events that already happened.

concept check

3. **What evidence suggests that we construct a conscious perception of a stimulus afterward instead of simultaneously with it?**

Answer

3. A brief masked stimulus is not perceived consciously, but a slightly longer one is perceived as lasting the entire duration. Also, the perception of a first stimulus can be altered by a stimulus that follows it.

Can We Use Brain Measurements to Infer Consciousness?

Physicians distinguish various gradations of brain activity that relate to arousal, responsiveness, and presumed consciousness. In brain death, *the brain shows no activity and no response to any stimulus.* Most people consider it ethical to remove life support for someone who remains steadily in this condition. In a coma (KOH-muh), *caused by traumatic brain damage, the brain shows a steady but low level of activity and no response to any stimulus*, including potentially painful stimuli. In nearly all cases, someone in a coma either dies or begins to recover within a few weeks.

Someone starting to emerge from a coma enters a vegetative state, *marked by limited responsiveness, such as increased heart rate in response to pain.* Responsiveness varies between a sleeping state and a waking state, but even in the waking state, brain activity is well below normal, and the person shows no purposeful behaviors. The next step up is a minimally conscious state, in which people have brief periods of purposeful actions and speech comprehension. A vegetative or minimally conscious state can last for months or years.

Because people in a vegetative state do nothing, it is easy to assume that they are unconscious. However, new research methods challenge that assumption in certain cases. Researchers used fMRI to record the brain activity of a young woman who was in a persistent vegetative state following a traffic accident. When they instructed her to imagine playing tennis, activity increased in the same motor areas of the cortex, as if she were getting ready to hit a tennis ball. An instruction to imagine walking through her house activated the brain areas responsible for spatial navigation. When uninjured people received the same instructions, they showed activity in the same areas that this young woman did (Owen et al., 2006). ▲ Figure 10.3 shows the results.

A follow-up study of 53 other patients in a vegetative state found results similar to this in 4 of them. One of those was then asked questions such as "Do you have a brother?" and instructed to imagine playing tennis if the answer was yes, and imagine walking through his house if the answer was no. His brain responses indicated the correct answers to the first five questions. His brain showed no response at all to the sixth question, suggesting that he had fallen asleep (Monti et al., 2010).

Several other patients demonstrated apparent consciousness in other ways. For example, one viewed a face superimposed on a picture of a house. When told to pay attention to the face, activity increased in a brain area important for perceiving faces. When told to attend to the house, activity increased in a different brain area. The researchers found that about 18 percent of patients in a vegetative state after traumatic brain injury showed apparent indications of understanding spoken instructions (Fernández-Espejo & Owen, 2013).

These results suggest that at least a few patients in a vegetative state are conscious. It is an encouraging result, but also a somewhat scary one. How many times have people said something about a patient, in the patient's presence, assuming that he or she didn't hear?

Consciousness and Action

You consciously decide that three seconds from now you will pick up a pencil. Sure enough, three seconds later you pick up that pencil. You therefore conclude that your conscious decision controlled the action. But are you right about that? Did your conscious decision actually control the behavior, or did it just predict something that an unconscious process caused? And how would you know?

At least some of the time, we fool ourselves about how much control we have. Psychologist Daniel Wegner (2002) described a time when he was manipulating a joystick at a video game display, making a monkey jump over barrels . . . or at least so it seemed. Then the notice "Start game" appeared, and he realized that he hadn't been controlling anything after all. Let's consider a famous experiment that poses a serious challenge to the idea of conscious control. Interest in this experiment followed an unusual trajectory. In the first 20 years after it was published, other researchers cited it an average of just over 6 times per year. And then interest started increasing, more and more rapidly. Since 2010, it has been cited over 50 times per year, by philosophers as well as psychologists.

what's the evidence?

Consciousness and Action

Benjamin Libet and his associates measured the time when people made a conscious decision to act, the time when brain activity preparing for the movement started, and the time of the act itself. What would you guess was the order of the three events in time?

Hypothesis The researchers considered three hypotheses, any one of which would be interesting: (1) Someone becomes aware of a decision to act before relevant brain activity begins, (2) awareness starts at the same time as the brain activity, and (3) the brain activity responsible for a movement starts before a conscious decision.

Method People were instructed to make a simple movement, to flex the wrist. Although they had no choice of movement, they had complete freedom for the timing. The instruction was to flex the wrist whenever they decided to, but spontaneously, with no planning. While waiting for that spontaneous urge to occur, they were to watch a special clock like the one in ▲ Figure 10.4, on which a spot of light moved around the edge every 2.56 seconds. When they suddenly decided to flex the wrist, they were to note the position of the light at that moment, so they could report it later. In this way, the study measured, as well as anyone knows how, the time of the

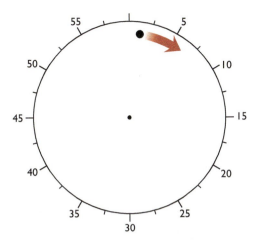

▲ **Figure 10.4** A spot of light rotated around the clock once every 2.56 seconds. Participants made a spontaneous decision to flex the wrist and noted the location of the light at the time of the decision. They remembered that time and reported it later. (From Libet, Gleason, Wright, & Pearl, 1983)

conscious decision. Meanwhile, researchers used electrodes on the scalp to detect increased activity in the motor cortex, the brain area responsible for initiating muscle movements. *The increased motor cortex activity prior to the start of the movement* is known as the readiness potential. Researchers also measured when the wrist muscles began to flex. On certain trials, the participants were told to report when they felt the wrist flex instead of the time they felt the intention to move it.

Results ▼ Figure 10.5 shows the means for a large sample. On average, people reported forming an intention of movement 200 to 300 ms before the movement (Libet, Gleason, Wright, & Pearl, 1983). (They noted the time on the clock then and reported it later.) For example, someone might report forming an intention when the light was at location 25 on the clock, 200 ms before the movement began at location 30. (Remember, the light zooms around the circle in 2.56 seconds.) In contrast, the readiness potential in the brain began 300 to 800 ms before the reported intention. Several other laboratories replicated this finding with varying procedures, confirming that the readiness potential comes before the conscious intention (Haggard & Eimer, 1999; Lau, Rogers, Haggard, & Passingham, 2004; Pockett & Miller, 2007; Trevena & Miller, 2002).

Can people report these times accurately? Recall that on certain trials the participants reported the time of the wrist motion. On these trials, people usually reported the movement within 100 ms of the actual time (Lau et al., 2004; Libet et al., 1983). From this finding, the researchers concluded that people report the time of an experience with moderate accuracy.

Interpretation These results imply that your brain starts producing a voluntary movement before you are

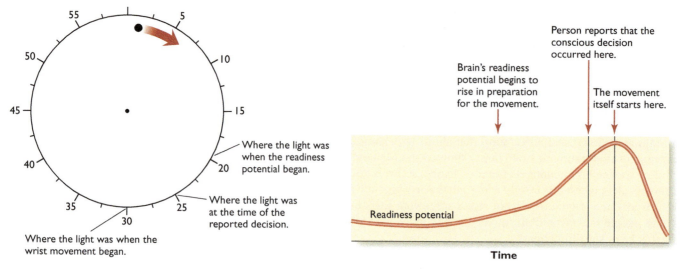

▲ **Figure 10.5** On average, the brain's readiness potential began 300 ms or more prior to the reported decision, which occurred 200 to 300 ms before the movement.

conscious of a decision to move. If so, your consciousness does not cause your action.

concept check

4. In the experiment described in the "What's the Evidence?" section, what did participants report, and when did they report it?

5. What was the order of these events: conscious decision to move, brain activity relevant to movement, and the movement itself?

Answers

4. Participants watched a special fast clock and noted the time when they made a spontaneous decision to flex the wrist. They reported it a few seconds later.
5. Measurable brain activity came first, then the perception of the conscious decision, and then the movement.

An Additional Study

Imagine yourself in this follow-up study: You watch a screen that displays a different letter of the alphabet every half-second. You choose not only when to act but which of two acts to do. At some point you spontaneously decide whether to press a button on the left or one on the right. As soon as you decide, you press the button, and you remember what letter is on the screen when you decided which button to press. Researchers record your brain activity. The result: You usually report a letter you saw within a second of making the response. The letters changed only twice per second, so the researchers could not determine the time of decision with greater accuracy. However, it wasn't necessary, because areas in the frontal and parietal cortex showed activity related to the left or right hand 7 to 10 seconds before your response (Soon, Brass, Heinze, & Haynes, 2008). That is, someone

monitoring your cortex could predict your choice a few seconds before you were aware of your decision.

How Well Can We Measure the Time of a Conscious Decision?

Although the results are clear, serious questions remain about the interpretation. People can fairly accurately report the time of a light, sound, or muscle movement, but reporting the time of a voluntary decision may be more difficult and less accurate. Perhaps people notice when they make a movement and merely guess that the decision came shortly before it. Researchers found that if they sounded a beep shortly after someone's movement, the person guessed the time of the movement later than it really was, and also guessed the time of the decision later than people usually do (Banks & Isham, 2009). That result supports the idea that reported decision times are little more than guesses.

A closely related objection is this: A spontaneous, voluntary decision is never a sudden event at a discrete time. Let's digress for a moment to discuss two types of movement. It will seem that we are way off topic, but the relevance will be clear later.

The movements we make in response to a stimulus differ from the movements we make spontaneously. Those we make in response to a stimulus are often quick, whereas spontaneous movements are almost always slower and more gradual. Imagine yourself driving along when suddenly a deer darts into the road. You swerve immediately to avoid it. In contrast, if you decide you need to get into the left lane to make a turn, you move slowly. Suppose your professor says, "When I count to three, please raise your hand." You will raise it swiftly at the count of three, in contrast to the way you slowly raise your hand in class when you want to ask a question. The gradual, spontaneous movements depend on a set of brain areas called the basal ganglia, which contribute much less when you act in response to a stimulus (Jueptner & Weiller, 1998; Turner & Anderson, 2005). People with Parkinson's disease suffer from decreased excitation into the basal ganglia. Their spontaneous, self-initiated movements are weak and slow, but they generally do better when responding to signals or instructions (Teitelbaum, Pellis, & Pellis, 1991).

Distinguishing between stimulus-elicited and self-initiated movements has an interesting consequence. Many of the old western movies featured a gunfight between a good guy and a bad guy. Always the bad guy drew his gun first, but the good guy drew faster and won the fight. Plausible? Yes. The first one to draw his gun makes a spontaneous, self-initiated movement and the second one reacts to a stimulus (the sight of the other guy going for his gun). The second one therefore draws his gun faster. It might even be an advantage to draw second (Welchman, Stanley, Schomers, Miall, & Bülthoff, 2010). Remember that, the next time you get into a gunfight.

Now, let's go back to Libet's experiment. When someone made a voluntary decision to flex the wrist, what type of movement was it? It was a spontaneous, self-initiated movement, the type that develops slowly and gradually. Asking for the time when the decision occurred assumes, falsely, that the decision occurred suddenly. Similarly, if you asked a romantic couple when they fell in love, they might tell you the time when they were sure of it, but the process had started developing long before. Perhaps what happens in Libet's study is that someone's conscious decision develops gradually, and the brain activity also develops gradually.

concept check

6. **Libet's experiment indicated that the brain activity responsible for a movement began earlier than the conscious decision to make the movement. What is the main reason to be uncertain of this conclusion?**

Answer

6. We have reasons to doubt that people can accurately state the time that a conscious decision began. Spontaneous movements and the decisions behind them develop gradually, not suddenly.

What Is the Purpose of Consciousness?

Given that the role of consciousness in decisions remains unclear at best, why do we have consciousness at all? Some theorists have argued that consciousness is an *epiphenomenon*—an accidental by-product with no purpose, like the noise a machine makes. But if consciousness does serve a purpose, what might that purpose be?

One hypothesis is that conscious thought is a way of rehearsing possibilities for future actions (Baumeister & Masicampo, 2010; Baumeister, Masicampo, & Vohs, 2011). After you do something, you might ponder, "That didn't go well.

What could I have done differently? Then what would have happened? Ah, I see. The next time I'm in a situation like this, here is what I'll do. . . ." In that way your conscious thinking modifies your behavior on some future occasion.

That sort of process occurs only when we think about something consciously. Still, the question remains, must it depend on consciousness? Could someone build a robot (presumably unconscious) that calculated possible outcomes of its future actions? If so, why do humans need to be conscious? And what, if anything, is the function of simple awareness, such as the experience you have when you see a flower or hear a melody—the kind of consciousness we probably share with many other animal species?

Many theorists seem to see the role of consciousness as an either–or question: Either consciousness is useless, or it evolved to serve a special purpose. However, the identity position on the mind–brain relationship suggests another possibility: If a certain type of brain activity *is* mental activity, then they are inseparable. You cannot have consciousness without brain activity, but you also cannot have certain kinds of brain activity without consciousness. Brains didn't evolve consciousness to solve a special task any more than brains evolved mass to solve a special task. Rather, they couldn't operate without it.

Still, that idea doesn't answer the fundamental question of *why* brain activity is mental activity. To repeat: In a universe of matter and energy, why is there such a thing as consciousness?

The questions will keep both scientists and philosophers busy for much time to come. But at least we now see consciousness as a legitimate topic for research.

in closing | module 10.1

Research on Consciousness

What outcomes can result from research on consciousness? If we better understand the types of brain activity associated with consciousness, we will be in a better position to infer consciousness, or lack of it, in people with brain damage and in infants, fetuses, and nonhuman animals. We may also be in a position to improve our speculations on the age-old philosophical question of the relationship between mind and brain.

Summary

- Psychologists long ago abandoned the study of consciousness, but today research is possible because of an operational definition, limited research questions, methods of measuring brain activity, and methods of presenting a stimulus while avoiding conscious perception. (page 313)

- Masking, flash suppression, and binocular rivalry are among the methods to present a stimulus while preventing conscious perception of it. (page 314)
- When someone is conscious of a stimulus, the stimulus activates neurons more strongly, their activity reverberates

through other brain areas, that activity rebounds to magnify the original response, and the process inhibits responses to competing stimuli. (page 314)

- The brain processes stimuli even without consciousness, enough to evaluate their importance. Unconscious processes are an important part of cognition. (page 315)
- Consciousness of a stimulus appears to be an all-or-none process. Either the brain activity spreads strongly through the brain, or it does not. (page 315)
- Conscious experience of a stimulus is a construction that can occur slightly after the stimulus itself, rather than simultaneously with it. (page 315)

- Brain scans provide suggestions of consciousness in certain patients who seem unresponsive to their environment. (page 316)
- When people report the time of a conscious decision to make a movement, brain scans indicate that the brain activity responsible for the movement began before the reported time of the conscious decision. (page 317)
- Research promotes skepticism that people can report their decision times accurately. Voluntary decisions are gradual, not sudden. (page 318)
- A possible function of conscious thought is to prepare for future action when a similar situation arises. (page 319)

Key Terms

backward masking (page 314)

binocular rivalry (page 314)

brain death (page 316)

coma (page 316)

consciousness (page 313)

flash suppression (page 314)

minimally conscious state (page 316)

masking (page 314)

readiness potential (page 317)

vegetative state (page 316)

Review Questions

1. With masking, flash suppression, or binocular rivalry, a viewer is conscious of a stimulus under one condition but not another. How does the brain representation differ as a result?
   (a) When a viewer is conscious of a stimulus, the brain activity is stronger and more widespread.
   (b) When a viewer is conscious of a stimulus, each action potential is larger and faster.
   (c) When a viewer is conscious of a stimulus, the brain activity occurs mostly in the left hemisphere.
   (d) When a viewer is conscious of a stimulus, the brain activity occurs mostly in the right hemisphere.

2. When you are conscious of one eye's stimulus during binocular rivalry, what happens to the representation of the stimulus in the other eye?
   (a) That stimulus is quickly inhibited and produces no effect.
   (b) The brain processes that stimulus enough to determine whether or not it is important.
   (c) That stimulus appears later in one of the person's dreams.
   (d) The stimulus in the other eye causes perception of a sound or a tingling touch sensation.

3. A brief masked stimulus is not perceived consciously, but a slightly longer one is perceived as lasting the entire duration. That finding supports which of these conclusions?
   (a) Much of what we do depends on unconscious processes.
   (b) We sometimes construct a conscious perception after the stimulus, not simultaneously with it.
   (c) Conscious and unconscious processes depend on different brain areas.
   (d) Consciousness depends on something outside the brain.

4. What did one woman in a vegetative state do that suggested she might be conscious?
   (a) She repeated a few words that she heard other people say.
   (b) She responded to instructions with increased activity in appropriate brain areas.
   (c) She pointed her hand toward people's voices.
   (d) She pointed her hand toward the television set.

5. In Libet's experiment, in which people reported the time of a decision to flex the wrist, why were the results relevant to philosophical questions?
   (a) The results implied that heredity and environment are equally important for controlling behavior.
   (b) The results implied that the mind is separate from the body.
   (c) The results implied that conscious decisions do not control behavior.
   (d) The results implied that human behavior depends on the same influences as the rest of the animal kingdom.

6. How do self-initiated movements differ from stimulus-elicited movements?
   (a) Stimulus-elicited movements activate more muscles, and larger muscles.
   (b) Self-initiated movements are generally briefer.
   (c) Stimulus-elicited movements depend on activity in the basal ganglia.
   (d) Self-initiated movements are generally slow and gradual.

Answers: 1a, 2b, 3b, 4b, 5c, 6d.

module 10.2

Sleep and Dreams

After studying this module, you should be able to:

- Describe how circadian rhythms affect alertness and other functions.
- Distinguish between morning and evening people.
- Discuss the consequences of jet lag and shift work.
- Explain how brain mechanisms control the circadian rhythm.
- List known functions of sleep.
- Describe the stages of sleep and characterize REM sleep.
- Discuss insomnia and other sleep problems.
- Evaluate several theories of dreaming.

Consciousness and alertness cycle daily between wakefulness and sleep. During sleep, we become less aware of our surroundings. Dreams take us to a fantasy world where impossible events seem possible. Why do we have these periods of altered consciousness?

Circadian Rhythms

Animal life follows cycles. Consider hibernation. Ground squirrels hibernate in winter, when they would have trouble finding food. The females awaken in spring as soon as food is available. The males also need to eat, but they have

The rising and setting of the sun do not produce our daily rhythm of wakefulness and sleepiness, but they synchronize the rhythm. We adjust our internally generated cycles so that we feel alert during the day and sleepy at night.

a reason to awaken earlier: The females are ready to mate as soon as they come out of their winter burrows, and each female mates only once a year. A male who awakens after the females pays for his extra rest by missing his only mating opportunity of the *entire year*. To avoid that risk, males awaken a week before the females do. They spend that week waiting—with no females, nothing to eat, and little to do except fight with one another (French, 1988).

The point is that animals have evolved internal timing mechanisms to prepare them for predictable needs. Male ground squirrels awaken not in response to their current situation but in preparation for what will happen a few days later. Similarly, birds start migrating south in the fall long before their northern homes become inhospitable.

Humans have mechanisms that prepare us for activity during the day and sleep at night. Like other animals, we generate a circadian rhythm, a *rhythm of activity and inactivity lasting about a day*. (The term *circadian* comes from the Latin roots *circa* and *dies*, meaning "about a day.") The rising and setting of the sun provide cues to reset our rhythm, but we generate the rhythm ourselves. In an environment with no cues for time, such as near-polar regions in summer or winter, most people generate a waking–sleeping rhythm a little longer than 24 hours, which gradually drifts out of phase with the clock (Palinkas, 2003).

Your circadian rhythm controls more than sleeping and waking. Over the course of a day, you vary in your hunger, thirst, urine production, blood pressure, and alertness. Your body temperature varies from 37.2°C (98.9°F) in late afternoon to 36.7°C (98.1°F) in the middle of the night (Morris, Lack, and Dawson, 1990). Most young people's mood varies over the day, reaching a peak of happiness in late afternoon (Murray et al., 2009).

Certain people have genes that alter their circadian rhythms (Jones, Huang, Ptáček, & Fu, 2013). Those with genes causing a 23-hour cycle instead of the usual 24-hour cycle get sleepy early in the evening and wake up early. They act as if they were moving at least one time zone west every day, and trying to readjust. Unlike most people, they look forward to weekends so that they can go to bed early! Other people have genes causing a longer-than-24-hour cycle, or genes decreasing the total need for sleep.

Sleepiness and alertness depend on the circadian rhythm, and not just on how long one has gone without sleep. If you have ever gone all night without sleep—as most college students do on occasion—you probably felt very sleepy between 2 and 6 A.M. But in the morning, you began feeling less sleepy, not more. You became more alert because of your circadian rhythm, even though your sleep deprivation continued.

In one study, volunteers went without sleep for three nights. Their body temperature and performance on reasoning tasks declined during the first night and then increased the next morning. During the second and third nights, their temperature and reasoning decreased more than on the first night, but they rebounded somewhat in the day (see ▶ Figure 10.6). Thus, sleep deprivation produces a pattern of progressive deterioration superimposed on the normal circadian cycle of rising and falling body temperature and alertness (Babkoff, Caspy, Mikulincer, & Sing, 1991).

7. **If you were on a submarine deep in the ocean with only artificial light that was the same at all times, what would happen to your rhythm of wakefulness and sleepiness?**

Answer

7. You would continue to produce a 24-hour circadian rhythm. The sun resets the rhythm, but you generate it within your own body.

Morning People and Evening People

People vary in their circadian rhythms. "Morning people" awaken easily, become alert quickly, and do their best work early. "Evening people" take longer to warm up in the morning (literally as well as figuratively) and do their best work in the afternoon or evening (Horne, Brass, & Pettitt, 1980). You can probably classify yourself as a morning person, evening person, or intermediate.

Morning people have advantages in several ways, especially if school or work starts early in the morning. On average, morning-type students maintain attention better in the morning, do better on tests in the morning, and get better grades, even when compared to evening-type students with the same cognitive ability and motivation (Haraszti, Ella, Gyöngyösi, Roenneberg, & Káldi, 2014; Lara, Madrid, & Correa, 2014; Preckel et al., 2013). However, male evening types have this advantage: They tend to be more extraverted, have a more active social life, and are likely to have more sex partners (Randler et al., 2012). Benjamin Franklin said, "Early to bed and early to rise makes a man healthy, wealthy, and wise." Maybe so, but someone else quipped, "Early

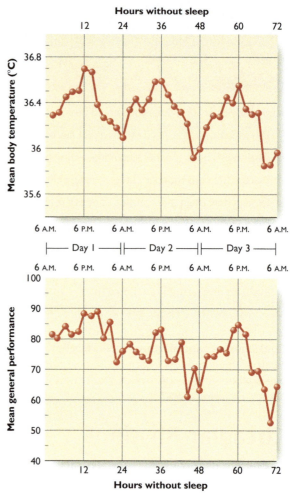

▲ **Figure 10.6** Cumulative effects of three nights without sleep: Body temperature and reasoning decrease each night and increase the next morning. They also deteriorate from one day to the next. (From Babkoff, Caspy, Mikulincer, & Sing, 1991)

to bed and early to rise and the girls will go out with other guys!"

Most young adults are either evening people or intermediate, whereas most people over age 65 are morning people. If you ask people at what time they like to go to bed when they have no obligations, their mean answer shifts later and later during the teenage years, reaches 1 to 2 A.M. at age 20, and then starts reversing, slowly and steadily over decades (Roenneberg et al., 2004). If the shift toward earlier bedtimes after age 20 were a reaction to job requirements, we might expect a sudden change, and we should predict the trend to reverse at retirement. The fact that the trend continues gradually over a lifetime suggests a biological basis. Furthermore, the same pattern occurs in other species. Older rats wake up promptly, whereas younger rats awaken more slowly and improve their performance later (Winocur & Hasher, 1999, 2004).

Age differences in circadian rhythms affect behavior in many ways. Researchers in one study

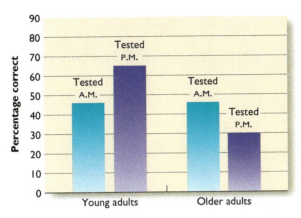

▲ **Figure 10.7** Early in the morning, older people perform as well as younger people on memory tasks. Later in the day, young people improve and older people deteriorate.

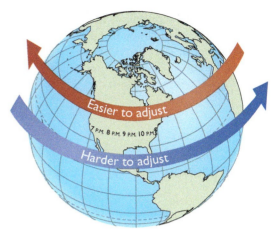

▲ **Figure 10.8** Most people suffer more serious jet lag when traveling east than when traveling west.

compared the memories of young adults (18 to 22 years old) and older adults (66 to 78 years old). Early in the morning, the older adults did about as well as the younger ones. Later in the day, the younger adults remained steady or improved, whereas the older adults deteriorated (May, Hasher, & Stoltzfus, 1993). ▲ Figure 10.7 shows the results.

8. If you are an evening person, what could you do to improve your grades?

Answer

8. Try to schedule your important classes in the afternoon instead of the morning.

Shifting Sleep Schedules

Ordinarily, the light of early morning resets the body's clock each day to keep it in synchrony with the outside world. If you travel across time zones, your internal rhythm is temporarily out of phase with your new environment. For example, if you travel from California to France, it is 7 A.M. (time to wake up) when your body says it is 10 P.M. (getting close to bedtime). You experience jet lag, *a period of discomfort and inefficiency while your internal clock is out of phase with your new surroundings.* Most people find it easier to adjust when flying west, where they go to bed later, than when flying east, where they go to bed earlier (see ▶ Figure 10.8). If you fly west, your circadian rhythm shifts a bit later each day until it catches up; if you fly east, your rhythm shifts a bit earlier each day. If you fly beyond a certain number of time zones one way or the other, it is as if your rhythm isn't sure whether to move forward or backward, and you may take a long time to readjust (Leloup & Goldbeter, 2013).

People voluntarily control their sleeping and waking times based on when they have to go to school or work, but the sun continues to rule the internal clock. Researchers asked people in Germany the times they prefer to go to bed and wake up. On business days, people throughout Germany awaken at the same time because they are all in the same time zone. However, on weekends and holidays, people in eastern Germany prefer to go to bed and wake up about half an hour earlier than those in western Germany, corresponding to the fact that the sun rises half an hour earlier in eastern Germany (Roenneberg, Kumar, & Merrow, 2007).

People in most parts of the United States have to shift their clock ahead an hour on a Sunday in March because of daylight saving time. On Monday, they awaken when the room clock tells them to, even though their internal clock thinks it is an hour earlier. Waking up while the sky is still dark doesn't effectively reset the internal clock. For at least the next week, many people have difficulty sleeping, feel fatigued, and report a decrease in overall well-being. Several reports also suggest increases in health problems and traffic accidents during the week after the switch (Harrison, 2013; Kountouris & Remoundou, 2014).

Some businesses run three work shifts, such as midnight to 8 A.M., 8 A.M. to 4 P.M., and 4 P.M. to midnight. Because few people want to work regularly on the midnight to 8 A.M. shift, many companies rotate their workers among the three shifts. Employers can ease the burden on their workers in two ways: First, when they transfer workers from one shift to another, they should transfer them to a *later* shift (Czeisler, Moore-Ede, & Coleman, 1982; see also ▼ Figure 10.9). That is, someone working from 8 A.M. to 4 P.M. shifts to the 4 P.M. to midnight time (like traveling west) instead of midnight to 8 A.M. (like traveling east). Second, employers can help workers on the night shift by providing bright lights that resemble sunlight. In one study, young

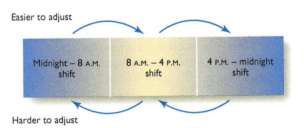

▲ **Figure 10.9** The graveyard shift is aptly named: Serious industrial accidents usually occur at night, when workers are least alert. As in jet lag, the direction of change is critical. Moving forward—clockwise—is easier than going backward.

▶ Figure 10.10 The suprachiasmatic nucleus, a small area at the base of the brain, produces the circadian rhythm. Information from the optic nerves resets the timing but doesn't produce it.

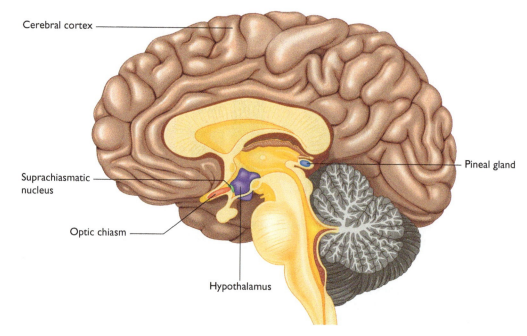

Cerebral cortex

Pineal gland

Suprachiasmatic nucleus

Optic chiasm

Hypothalamus

people exposed to very bright lights at night adjusted their circadian rhythms to the new schedule within six days. A group who worked under dimmer lights failed to alter their circadian rhythms (Czeisler et al., 1990).

9. **Suppose you are the president of a U.S. company, negotiating a business deal with someone from the opposite side of the world. Should you prefer a meeting place in Europe or on an island in the Pacific Ocean?**

Answer

9. You should prefer to meet on a Pacific island so that you will travel west.

Brain Mechanisms of Circadian Rhythms

An animal continues following a circadian rhythm of wakefulness and sleep even in an unchanging environment with a constant temperature and constant light or darkness, even if it is blind or deaf, and even after almost any intervention that increases or decreases its activity level (Richter, 1967, 1975). The circadian rhythm of sleep and wakefulness is generated within the brain by a tiny structure known as the *suprachiasmatic nucleus (SCN)*. If it is damaged, the body's activity cycles become erratic (Rusak, 1977). If cells from the SCN are kept alive outside the body, they generate a 24-hour rhythm on their own (Earnest, Liang, Ratcliff, & Cassone, 1999; Inouye &

Kawamura, 1979). Cells in other areas also produce daily rhythms, but the suprachiasmatic nucleus is the body's main clock (see ▲ Figure 10.10).

Although the SCN generates a circadian rhythm, light resets the internal clock, causing you to wake up more or less in synchrony with the sunlight. A special set of ganglion cells in the nose side of the retina (looking toward the periphery) respond to the average amount of bright light over a period of time, and send their output to the SCN, unlike other retinal cells that respond to instantaneous changes in light and darkness and send their output to the visual cortex (Berson et el., 2002). These special ganglion cells respond mainly to short-wavelength light, which computers and televisions emit in abundance. A consequence is that people who watch television or use computers late in the evening often have trouble sleeping (Czeisler, 2013; Fossum, Nordnes, Storemark, Bjorvatn, & Pallesen, 2014).

The suprachiasmatic nucleus exerts its control partly by regulating the pineal gland's secretions of the hormone *melatonin*, which is important for both circadian rhythms and many species' annual rhythms of reproduction, hibernation, and so forth (Butler et al., 2010). Ordinarily, the human pineal gland starts releasing melatonin two or three hours before bedtime. Taking a melatonin pill in the evening has little effect because you are already producing melatonin. However, if you have just flown a few time zones east and want to get to bed before you feel sleepy, then a melatonin pill can help (Deacon & Arendt, 1996).

10. **Suppose someone with intact retinas becomes blind because of damage to the visual cortex. Will that person nevertheless synchronize the circadian rhythm to the time of sunlight? Explain.**

Answer

10. Yes, someone with blindness because of cortical damage nevertheless tends to waken during times of sunlight. The average amount of bright light activates certain ganglion cells that send their output not to the visual cortex, but to the suprachiasmatic nucleus, which controls the circadian rhythm.

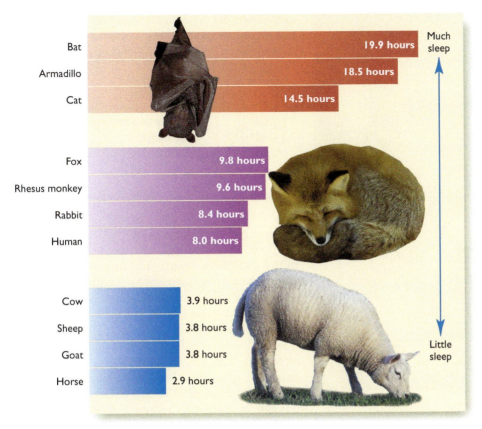

Bat	19.9 hours — Much sleep
Armadillo	18.5 hours
Cat	14.5 hours
Fox	9.8 hours
Rhesus monkey	9.6 hours
Rabbit	8.4 hours
Human	8.0 hours
Cow	3.9 hours
Sheep	3.8 hours
Goat	3.8 hours
Horse	2.9 hours — Little sleep

▲ **Figure 10.11** Predatory mammals sleep more than prey animals. Predators are seldom attacked during their sleep, but prey species need to arouse quickly from sleep to avoid being attacked. (Based on data from Zepelin & Rechtschaffen, 1974; Image credits: EcoPrint/Shutterstock.com, Ilya D. Gridnev/Shutterstock.com, Photodisc/Getty Images)

Why We Sleep

We would not have evolved a mechanism that forces us to spend one-third of our lives sleeping unless sleep did us some good. But what good does it do? Scientists have identified several benefits.

The simplest is that sleep saves energy. When NASA sent a robot to explore Mars, they programmed it to shut down at nights, when exploration would waste energy. Presumably, our ancient ancestors evolved sleep for the same reason. Sleeping mammals and birds lower their body temperatures, and all sleeping animals decrease muscle activity, saving energy. When food is scarce, people sleep longer and at a lower body temperature (Berger & Phillips, 1995).

Various animal species differ in their sleep per day in ways that make sense based on their way of life (Campbell & Tobler, 1984; Siegel, 2005). Predatory animals, including cats and bats, sleep most of the day. They get the nutrition they need from brief, energy-rich meals, and they face little danger of attack during their sleep. In contrast, horses need to spend many hours grazing, and their survival depends on running away from attackers, even at night (see ▲ Figure 10.11). They sleep little and rouse easily. Woody Allen once wrote, "The lion and the calf shall lie down together, but the calf won't get much sleep."

Animals show other sleep specializations. One species of migratory birds, bar-tailed godwits, fly for a week between their summer home in Alaska and their winter home in New Zealand. Because they are flying over the ocean with nowhere to rest, they have to fly nonstop without sleep. Many other migratory birds forage for food during the day and do their migratory flying at night, when it is cooler. That schedule leaves no time for sleep. Somehow the birds

temporarily turn off their need for sleep (Rattenborg et al., 2004). Even if those birds are kept in cages during the migratory season, they hardly sleep at all (Fuchs, Haney, Jechura, Moore, & Bingman, 2006). They show no sign of sleep deprivation, even though forcing them to stay awake at other times of the year would produce the usual impairments of learning and performance.

Whales and dolphins face a different problem: Throughout the night, they have to swim to the surface to breathe. Their solution is to sleep in half of the brain at a time so that one half or the other is always alert (Lyamin et al., 2002; Rattenborg, Amlaner, & Lima, 2000). Seals sleep this way too when they are at sea, but they shift to sleeping on both sides when they are on land (Lyamin, Kosenko, Lapierre, Mukhametov, & Siegel, 2008). During the first month after a baby whale or dolphin is born, it doesn't sleep at all, and neither does its mother (Lyamin, Pryaslova, Lance, & Siegel, 2005). Evidently, like migratory birds, they have found the secret for temporarily suppressing the need for sleep.

Some people need less sleep than others (Meddis, Pearson, & Langford, 1973), and some tolerate sleep deprivation better than others. In 1965, a San Diego high school student, Randy Gardner (see ▼ Figure 10.12), stayed awake for 11 days as a high school science project without apparent harm (Dement, 1972). On the last night, he played about 100 arcade games against sleep researcher William Dement and won every game. Just before the end of the ordeal, he held a press conference and handled himself well. He then slept for 14 hours and 40 minutes and awoke refreshed.

If a torturer prevented you from sleeping for the next 11 days, would you do as well as Randy Gardner? Probably not, for two reasons: First, Gardner knew he could quit. A sense of control makes any experience less stressful. Second, we heard about Gardner only because he tolerated sleep deprivation so well. We have no idea how many other people tried to deprive themselves of sleep but gave up.

Still, people suffer when they don't get enough sleep. Sleep-deprived people become more vulnerable to illness, especially depression and other mental illnesses (Roberts & Duong, 2014; Wulff, Gatti, Wettstein, & Foster, 2010). They suffer lapses of attention (Åkerstedt, 2007; Gvilia, Xu, McGinty, & Szymusiak, 2006) and lapses of ethical behavior (Barnes, Schaubroeck, Huth, & Ghumman, 2011). After sleep deprivation, an "awake" person has a mixture of neurons that are active and other neurons that are as inactive as if the person were asleep

▲ **Figure 10.12** Even near the end of Randy Gardner's 264 consecutive sleepless hours, he remained alert and coordinated. Observers dutifully recorded his every move.

(Vyazovskiy et al., 2011). As a result, a sleep-deprived driver is as dangerous as a drunk driver (Falleti, Maruff, Collie, Darby, & McStephen, 2003).

Sleep also strengthens learning and memory to varying degrees, depending on the type of learning (Doyon et al., 2009). When you learn something, your memory improves if you go to sleep within the next three hours (even a nap), and it deteriorates after a sleepless night (Hu, Stylos-Allan, & Walker, 2006; Korman et al., 2007; Rasch & Born, 2008; Yoo, Hu, Gujar, Jolesz, & Walker, 2007). A good night's sleep also improves learning the next day (Van der Werf et al., 2009). So beware of those all-night study sessions.

When people learn a difficult new motor task, such as a video game skill, the brain areas active during the learning become reactivated during sleep that night, replaying the same patterns they had during the day, only faster (and sometimes backward). The amount of activity in those areas during sleep predicts the amount of improvement the next day (Euston, Tatsuno, & McNaughton, 2007; Huber, Ghilardi, Massimini, & Tononi, 2004; Maquet et al., 2000; Peigneux et al., 2004). Wakefulness and sleep play complementary roles in learning. Animal researchers have demonstrated that learning

strengthens the appropriate synapses during wakefulness and weakens other synapses during sleep (Vyazovskiy, Cirelli, Pfister-Genskow, Faraguna, & Tononi, 2008).

11. **Name two important functions of sleep.**

Answer

11. Sleep conserves energy, and memories strengthen during sleep.

Stages of Sleep

In the mid-1950s, French and American researchers independently discovered a stage of sleep called *paradoxical sleep*, or rapid eye movement (REM) sleep (Dement & Kleitman, 1957a, 1957b; Jouvet, Michel, & Courjon, 1959). *During this stage of sleep, the sleeper's eyes move rapidly back and forth under the closed lids.* (The other stages of sleep are known as non-REM, or NREM, sleep.) A paradox is an apparent contradiction. REM sleep is paradoxical because it is light in some ways and deep in others. It is light because the brain is active and the body's heart rate, breathing rate, and temperature fluctuate substantially (Parmeggiani, 1982). It is deep because the large muscles of the body that control posture and locomotion are deeply relaxed. Indeed, the nerves to those muscles are virtually paralyzed at this time. REM also has features that are hard to classify as deep or light, such as penis erections and vaginal lubrication.

William Dement's early research indicated that people who were awakened during REM sleep usually reported dreaming, but people who were awakened during other periods seldom reported dreaming. Later research weakened that link, however. Adults who are awakened during REM sleep report dreams about 85 to 90 percent of the time, whereas those awakened during NREM (non-REM) sleep report dreams on 50 to 60 percent of occasions (Foulkes, 1999). REM dreams are on average longer, more complicated, and more visual, with more action by the dreamer, but not always (McNamara, McLaren, Smith, Brown, & Stickgold, 2005). Furthermore, people with certain types of brain damage have REM sleep but no dreams, and others have dreams but no REM sleep (Solms, 1997). Thus, REM is not synonymous with dreaming (Domhoff, 1999).

Nevertheless, because vivid dreams are most common during REM sleep and because the postural muscles are paralyzed during REM sleep,

▲ **Figure 10.13** Electrodes monitor the activity in a sleeper's brain, and an EEG then records and displays brain-wave patterns.

people typically do not act out their dreams. A small number of people, with a condition called *REM behavior disorder*, fail to inhibit their muscular activity during REM, and as a result, they sometimes walk around flailing their arms.

Sleep Cycles during the Night

The brain is more active than you might guess during sleep. Neurons' metabolic rate, spontaneous activity, and responsiveness to stimuli decrease less than 20 percent (Hobson, 2005). The main characteristic of sleep is an increase of inhibitory messages, preventing brain messages from reverberating widely (Massimini et al., 2005). Activity in one brain area becomes less likely to excite other areas (Esser, Hill, & Tononi, 2009). As noted in the first module of this chapter, a spread of messages through the brain is central to conscious experience, so blocking that spread decreases consciousness.

Sleep researchers distinguish among sleep stages by recording brain waves with electrodes attached to the scalp (see ▲ Figure 10.13). An **electroencephalograph (EEG)** *measures and amplifies tiny electrical changes on the scalp that reflect patterns of brain activity.* Sleep researchers *combine an EEG measure with a simultaneous measure of eye movements to produce a* **polysomnograph** (literally, "many-sleep measure"), as shown in Figure 10.14. A sleeper first enters stage 1, when the eyes are nearly motionless and the EEG shows many short, choppy waves (see ▼ Figure 10.14b) that indicate a fair amount of brain activity. Because brain cells fire out of synchrony, their activities nearly cancel each other out, like the sound of many people talking at the same time.

As sleep continues, a person progresses into stages 2, 3, and 4, as shown in ▼ Figure 10.14c through 10.14e. These stages differ in the number of long, slow waves. Stage 2 has the fewest and stage 4 has the most. These waves indicate synchrony among neurons, related to *decreased* brain activity. The waves grow larger because the little brain activity that does occur drives many neurons in synchrony. Stage 2 is also marked by **sleep spindles**, *waves of activity at about 12 to 14 per second* that result from an exchange of information between the cerebral cortex and the underlying thalamus. Sleep spindles are important for storing memory, and the improvement of memory that often occurs after sleep depends on the amount of sleep spindles (Barakat et al., 2013; Eschenko, Mölle, Born, & Sara, 2006). Preschool children's naps, which generally include much stage 2 sleep, are important for the children's memory storage (Kurdziel, Duclos, & Spencer, 2013).

A sleeper progresses through stages 2, 3, and 4 then gradually back through stages 3 and 2, and then to REM sleep. In Figure 10.14f, the EEG in REM sleep resembles that of stage 1, but the eyes move steadily. At the end of REM sleep, the sleeper cycles again through stages 2, 3, 4 and then back to 3, 2, and REM. In a healthy young adult, each cycle lasts 90 to 100 minutes on average. As shown in ▼ Figure 10.15, over the course of the night, stages 3 and 4 become shorter while REM and stage 2 increase in duration. (You may sometimes hear someone say that to get any benefit from sleep, you have to sleep through a full 90-minute cycle. They are making that up. No evidence supports that statement.)

concept check

12. **During which sleep stage is the brain least active? During which stage are the muscles least active?**

Answer

12. The brain is least active during stage 4 sleep. The muscles are least active during REM sleep.

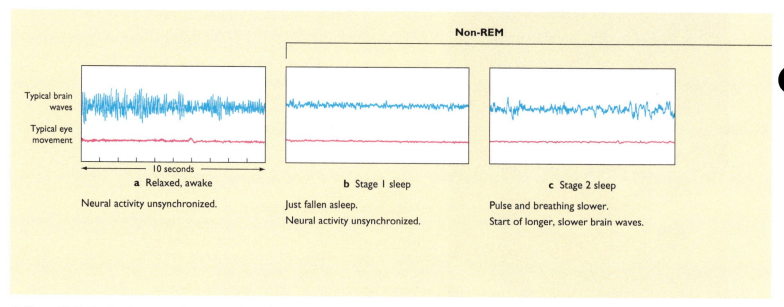

▲ **Figure 10.14** During sleep, people progress through stages of varying brain activity. The blue line indicates brain waves, as shown by an EEG. The red line shows eye movements. REM sleep resembles stage 1 sleep, except for the addition of rapid eye movements. (Courtesy of T. E. Le Vere)

▲ **Figure 10.15** This sleeper had five cycles of REM and non-REM sleep and awakened (A) briefly three times during the night. Stage 4 occupies more time earlier in the night than later. REM and stage 2 become more prevalent as the night progresses. (From Dement, 1972)

Abnormalities of Sleep

Comedian Steven Wright says that someone asked him, "Did you sleep well last night?" He replied, "No, I made a few mistakes."

We laugh because sleep isn't the kind of activity on which people make mistakes. Sometimes, however, we fail to sleep, feel poorly rested, or have bad dreams. These experiences are not "mistakes," but our sleep is not what we wanted it to be.

Insomnia

Insomnia means "lack of sleep." More specifically, insomnia is *not enough sleep for the person to feel rested the next day*. Six hours sleep could be insomnia for one person but adequate for another. Insomnia results from causes including noise, worries, indigestion, uncomfortable temperatures, use of alcohol or caffeine, and medical or psychological disorders (Ohayon, 1997). If you have persistent insomnia, consult a physician, but for occasional or minor insomnia, you can try a few things yourself:

- Keep a regular time schedule for going to bed and waking up each day.

- Spend some time in the sunlight to set your circadian rhythm.
- Minimize exposure to television and computers in the hours before bedtime.
- Avoid caffeine, nicotine, and other stimulants, especially in the evening.
- Don't rely on alcohol or tranquilizers to fall asleep. After repeated use, you may be unable to sleep without them.
- Keep your bedroom cool and quiet.
- Exercise daily but not shortly before bedtime.

Sleep Apnea

Apnea (AP-nee-uh) means "no breathing." Many people have occasional brief periods without breathing while asleep. People with sleep apnea, however, *fail to breathe for a minute or more and then wake up gasping for breath.* They may lie in bed for 8 to 10 hours but sleep less than half that time. Sleep apnea is most common in overweight middle-aged men whose breathing passages become narrower than usual. While awake, they compensate by breathing frequently and vigorously, but they cannot keep up this pattern while they are asleep (Mezzanotte, Tangel, & White, 1992).

Treatment includes recommendations to lose weight and to avoid alcohol and tranquilizers before bedtime. Surgeons can remove tissue to widen the airways. Some people with sleep apnea use a device that pumps air into a mask covering the nose and mouth during sleep, forcing the person to breathe.

Narcolepsy

Infants alternate between brief waking periods and brief sleeping periods (Blumberg, Gall, & Todd, 2014). As they grow older, they consolidate into one long

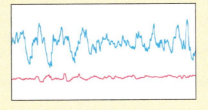

Non-REM

Typical brain waves
Typical eye movement

d Stage 3 sleep

Pulse, breathing, and brain activity slower yet.

Neural activity more synchronized.

Stages 3 and 4 dominate first half of night.

e Stage 4 sleep

Pulse, breathing, and brain activity slowest.

Brain waves highly synchronized, indicating low overall neuron activity.

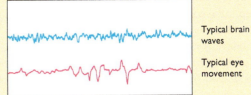

f REM (paradoxical) sleep

Eyes move back and forth.

Dreams more frequent, vivid, complex.

Brain waves desynchronized.

Postural muscles most relaxed.

Duration gets longer toward morning.

3 A.M.　　4 A.M.　　5 A.M.　　6 A.M.　　7 A.M.

2　3　2　REM　1　2　3　2 A　REM　A　A　2　REM

waking period during the day (possibly interrupted by a nap) and one long sleeping period at night. A neurotransmitter called *orexin* is important for maintaining long periods of wakefulness. People with narcolepsy lose the brain cells that produce orexin, and therefore return to a pattern resembling infants (Thanickal et al., 2000). They experience *sudden attacks of sleepiness during the day*. They also experience sudden attacks of muscle weakness or paralysis and occasional dreamlike experiences while awake. These symptoms represent intrusions of REM sleep into the waking period (Guilleminault, Heinzer, Mignot, & Black, 1998).

A combination of stimulant and antidepressant drugs maintains wakefulness during the day and blocks the attacks of muscle weakness. Future research may develop medications based on orexin, but none are available currently.

Some Other Sleep Experiences

Sleep talking is a common experience that ranges from a grunted word to a clear paragraph. Many people talk in their sleep more often than they realize because they do not remember sleep talking and usually no one else hears them. Sleep talking is most common during stage 2 sleep, but it occurs in all stages (Moorcroft, 2003). Sleep talkers

Insomnia is identified by how sleepy the person is the following day.

Helen King/Corbis

sometimes pause between utterances, as if they were carrying on a conversation. In fact, it is possible to engage some sleep talkers in a dialogue. Sleep talking is not related to mental or emotional disorders, and sleep talkers rarely say anything embarrassing. So if you talk in your sleep, don't worry about it.

Have you ever had the experience of waking up and finding yourself unable to move? If so, don't be alarmed. When you awaken, various brain areas don't necessarily all awaken at once (Krueger et al., 2008; Silva & Duffy, 2008). Occasionally, most of your cortex awakens but one part of your medulla continues sending inhibitory messages to the spinal cord, just as it does during REM sleep. You then find yourself alert, with your eyes open, but temporarily unable to move your arms or legs.

Sleepwalking tends to run (walk?) in families, mostly in children and mainly during stage 4 sleep (Dement, 1972). Some adults sleepwalk also, mostly during the first half of the night's sleep, and not while dreaming. They have clumsy, apparently purposeless movements with only limited responsiveness to their surroundings. Contrary to what you may have heard, wakening a sleepwalker is not dangerous, although it is not particularly helpful either (Moorcroft, 2003). A better idea is to guide the person gently back to bed. In addition to walking during sleep, some people have been known to eat, rearrange furniture, drive cars, and engage in sex (either by masturbation or with a partner) during sleep (Mangan, 2004). You might wonder, is the person really asleep? The answer is "sort of." As mentioned, the entire brain doesn't necessarily wake up or go to sleep all at once. Sleep can be localized to one brain area more than another. Sleepwalking occurs when the motor cortex and a few other areas are active while most of the brain remains asleep (Terzaghi et al., 2012; Zadra, Desautels, Petit, & Montplaisir, 2013).

Lucid dreaming is another example in which part of the brain is awake and another part asleep. Someone having a lucid dream is aware that it is a dream. Lucid dreaming occurs during periods of increased activity at 40 Hz (cycles per second) in the frontal and temporal cortex, with less arousal in the rest of the brain (Voss et al., 2014).

Do you ever lie in bed, trying to fall asleep, when suddenly a leg kicks? An occasional leg jerk while trying to fall asleep is common and no cause for concern. However, some people have *prolonged "creepy-crawly" sensations in their legs, accompanied by repetitive leg movements strong enough to awaken the person, especially during the first half of the night* (Moorcroft, 1993). This condition, known as periodic limb movement disorder, interrupts sleep in many people, mostly over age 50. The causes are unknown, and the best advice is to avoid factors that make the condition worse, such as caffeine, stress,

or fatigue. Tranquilizers sometimes suppress these leg movements (Schenck & Mahowald, 1996).

Nightmares are intensely unpleasant dreams. A night terror, however, *causes someone to awaken screaming and sweating with a racing heart rate, sometimes flailing with the arms and pounding the walls.* Night terrors occur during stage 3 or stage 4 sleep, not REM, and their dream content, if any, is usually simple, such as a single image. Comforting or reassuring people during a night terror is futile, and the terror simply has to run its course. Many children have night terrors, as do nearly 3 percent of adults (Mahowald & Schenck, 2005). Treatments include psychotherapy, antidepressant and antianxiety drugs, and advice to minimize stress.

concept check

13. **What experience reflects the fact that part of the brain can be awake while another is asleep?**

Answer

13. Any of the following: waking up but finding oneself unable to move, sleepwalking, or lucid dreaming.

Dreams

Even a saint is not responsible for what happens in his dreams.
—St. Thomas Aquinas

In ancient times, people believed that dreams foretold the future. Occasionally, of course, they do, either by coincidence or because the dreamer had a reason to expect some outcome. Today, scientists do not believe dreams tell us about the future, although many other people do. If you dream about a plane crash tonight, will you hesitate to take a plane trip tomorrow? If you dream your friend treats you badly or your lover is unfaithful, will you become suspicious in real life? If so, you have plenty of company (Morewedge & Norton, 2009).

If dreams do not tell us the future, what do they tell us? Can we explain or interpret dreams? Let's consider dream content.

Descriptive Studies of Dreaming

To determine dream content, some studies ask people to keep dream diaries. Another approach is to awaken people in the laboratory and ask for immediate dream reports (Domhoff, 2003). ■ Table 10.1 lists common dream themes of college students in five countries. Note the similarities across samples.

Dreams do differ among cultures in several regards (Domhoff & Schneider, 2008). For example, people in hunter-gatherer societies have many dreams about animals, and people in dangerous societies have dreams about being victims of violent aggression. People in the United States often dream of people they don't know, whereas people in India, Iran, and Japan more often dream only of the people they know (Mazandarani, Aguilar-Vafaie, & Domhoff, 2013). Still, the cross-cultural similarities in dream content are striking.

Common usage implies that dreams are happy. In the Disney movie, Cinderella sings, "A dream is a wish your heart makes." Martin Luther King Jr.'s famous "I Have a Dream" speech described a wonderful future. Calling your boyfriend or girlfriend "dreamy" would be a compliment. Sigmund Freud claimed that all dreams are based on wish fulfillment. However, Table 10.1 shows that much or most of dream content is unpleasant, such as falling, being chased, or being unable to do something. When college students recorded their dreams and their daytime experiences, 73 percent of their dreams included something threatening, as opposed to only 15 percent of their daytime activity reports (Valli, Strandholm, Sillanmäki, & Revonsuo, 2008). Curiously, 11- to 13-year-olds have

Table 10.1 Percentages of College Students Who Reported Certain Dream Topics

Dream Topic	U.S. 1958	Japan 1958	Canada 2003	Germany 2004	China 2008
Falling	83%	74%	74%	74%	87%
Being attacked or pursued	77%	91%	82%	89%	92%
Repeatedly trying to do something	71%	87%	54%	30%	74%
Schoolwork	71%	86%	67%	89%	94%
Sex	66%	68%	76%	87%	70%
Arriving too late	64%	49%	60%	68%	80%
Eating delicious food	62%	68%	31%	42%	69%
Frozen with fright	58%	87%	41%	56%	71%
Loved one dying	57%	42%	54%	68%	75%

Based on Griffith, Miyagi, & Tago (1958); Nielsen et al. (2003); Schredl, Ciric, Götz, & Wittman, 2004; Yu, 2008.

the happiest dreams on average (Foulkes, 1999). From then on, dreams get worse and worse. Sorry about that.

Although some dreams are bizarre, most are similar to what we think about in everyday life (Domhoff, 1996; Hall & Van de Castle, 1966). For example, preteens seldom dream about the opposite sex, but teenagers do (Strauch & Lederbogen, 1999). Blind people frequently dream about difficulties in locomotion or transportation (Hurovitz, Dunn, Domhoff, & Fiss, 1999). In one study, young adults indicated from a list of topics which ones were concerns to them and which ones were matters of indifference. Then they reported their dreams over three nights. They frequently dreamed of the concerns and rarely of the indifferent topics (Nikles, Brecht, Klinger, & Bursell, 1998). However, we do not dream about everything we do in daily life. People seldom dream about reading, writing, using a computer, or watching television (Schredl, 2000). They do dream about sexual and other fantasies that they don't act on in real life. For the best research on dream content, visit this website: www2.ucsc .edu/dreams.

Many questions about dreaming are difficult to answer. For example, "How accurately do we remember our dreams?" Well, how would we find out? With real events, we compare people's memories to what actually happened, but we have no way to compare dream reports to the original dreams. Or consider this apparently simple question: "Do we dream in color?" People ask because they do not remember. But how could an investigator answer the question except by asking people to remember? The best evidence we have is that, when people are awakened and asked immediately, they report color at least half of the time (Herman, Roffwarg, & Tauber, 1968; Padgham, 1975). This result does not mean that other dreams are in black and white. Perhaps the colors in those dreams are not memorable.

Do blind people have visual dreams? It depends. People who become blind because of damage to the visual cortex lose visual dreaming as well as visual imagery. People who experience eye damage after about age 5 to 7 continue to have visual dreams, although their frequency of visual dreams declines over time. People who were born blind or who became blind in early childhood have no visual imagery in their dreams. Instead, they dream of sounds, touch, smells, and tastes (Hurovitz et al., 1999).

14. How is the content of dreams similar to waking thoughts, and how is it different?

Answer

14. We mostly dream about the same topics we think about, but dreams usually feature less happy emotions.

Freud's Theory of Dreams

The Austrian physician Sigmund Freud, founder of psychoanalysis, maintained that dreams reveal the dreamer's unconscious thoughts and motivations. To understand a dream, he said, one must probe for hidden meanings. Each dream has a **manifest content**—*the content that appears on the surface*—and a **latent content**—*the hidden ideas that the dream experience represents symbolically.*

For example, Freud (1900/1955) once dreamed that one of his friends was his uncle. He worked out these associations: Both this friend and another friend had been recommended for an appointment as professor at the university. Both had been turned down, probably because they were Jews. Freud himself had been recently recommended for the same appointment, and he feared that he too would be rejected because he was Jewish. Freud's only uncle had once been convicted of illegal business dealings. Freud's father had said, however, that the uncle was not bad but just a simpleton.

How did the two friends relate to the uncle? One of the friends was in Freud's judgment a bit simpleminded. The other had once been accused of sexual misconduct. By linking these two friends to his uncle, Freud interpreted the dream as meaning, "Maybe they didn't get the university appointment because one was a simpleton (like my uncle) and the other was regarded as a criminal (like my uncle). If so, my being Jewish might not stop me from getting the appointment."

In some cases, Freud relied on individual associations, as in the dream just described, but he also assumed that certain elements have predictable meanings for most people. For example, he claimed that the number three in a dream represents a man's penis and testes. Anything long, such as a stick, represents a penis. So does anything that could penetrate the body, anything from which water flows, anything that can be lengthened, almost any tool, and anything that can fly or float—because rising is like an erection (Freud, 1935). He admitted that if you dream about a knife or an airplane, you really might be dreaming about a knife or airplane instead of a penis, but he was confident that a skilled psychoanalyst could tell the difference (even if the dreamer could not).

One of Freud's most famous dream analyses concerned a man who reported remembering a dream from when he was 4 years old (!) in which he saw six or seven white dogs with large tails sitting motionlessly in a tree outside his window. (The actual dream was of spitz dogs, although Freud wrote about them as wolves.) After a laborious line of reasoning, Freud concluded that the child had dreamed about his parents in their bedclothes—presumably white, like the dogs in the dream. The dogs' lack of motion represented its opposite—frantic sexual activity. The big tails also represented their opposite—the boy's fear of having his penis cut off. In short, said Freud, the boy had dreamed about watching his parents have sex, doggy style. Decades later, researchers located the man who had told Freud this dream. He reported that (1) he regarded Freud's interpretation of his dream as far-fetched, and (2) Freud's treatment did him no apparent good, as he spent many later years in continued treatment (Esterson, 1993).

Can anyone listen to dreams and determine hidden aspects of the dreamer's personality? Many therapists offer dream interpretations that their clients find meaningful. However, there is no way to check which interpretations are accurate and which ones are not. Freud's approach to dream analysis has been on the decline (Domhoff, 2003).

15. Are Freud's ideas on dreaming falsifiable in the sense described in Chapter 2?

Answer

15. No. A falsifiable theory makes specific predictions so that we could imagine evidence that would contradict it. Freud's dream theories make no clear predictions.

Modern Theories of Dreaming

According to the **activation-synthesis theory of dreams**, dreams occur because the cortex takes the haphazard activity that occurs during REM sleep plus whatever stimuli strike the sense organs and does

its best to make sense of this activity (Hobson & McCarley, 1977). Some aspects of dreams do appear to relate to spontaneous brain activity and various stimuli. For example, when people dream of using a toilet or trying to find a toilet, they often awaken and discover that they really do need to use a toilet. Do you ever dream that you are trying to walk or run, but you cannot move? One explanation is that the major postural muscles are really paralyzed during REM sleep. Your brain sends messages telling your muscles to move but receives sensory feedback indicating they have not moved.

However, dreams that relate to current sensations are the exception, not the rule (Foulkes & Domhoff, 2014; Nir & Tononi, 2010). Also, the activation-synthesis theory makes no clear, testable predictions. For example, the muscles are always paralyzed during REM sleep. Why don't we always dream that we cannot move? Perhaps a more serious problem for this theory is that dream experiences, although strange, do not appear to be random or haphazard.

An alternative view, known as the neurocognitive theory, is that dreaming is simply a kind of thinking, similar to daydreaming or mind wandering, that occurs under these conditions (Fox, Nijeboer, Solomonova, Domhoff, & Christoff, 2013; Solms, 2000):

- reduced sensory stimulation, especially in the brain's primary sensory areas
- reduced activity in the prefrontal cortex, important for planning and working memory
- loss of voluntary control of thinking
- enough activity in other brain areas, including those responsible for face recognition and certain aspects of motivation and emotion

In contrast to the activation-synthesis theory, which regards dreaming as a bottom-up process beginning with sensations or random activation, the neurocognitive theory regards dreaming as a top-down process, controlled by the same mechanisms as any other thought. William Domhoff (2011) compares dreaming to activity of the brain's "default network," the system active during mind wandering and daydreaming. The default network drifts from thought to thought without plan or control, much as a dream does. A sleeper's brain receives only a limited amount of sensory information. Because the primary visual and auditory areas of the brain are doing little during sleep, the rest of the brain constructs images without interference, usually focusing on something the dreamer has seen, heard, or thought about in the last several days. Occasionally a dream deals with something that was a worry long ago. For example, an older person might dream about forgetting a high school locker combination. Because of low activity in the prefrontal cortex, an area important for planning and working memory, the dream story jumps from one event to another without much continuity and without much sense of intention.

Dreams do reveal something about the dreamer's interests and personality. That is, you dream about issues that interest or worry you. However, that kind of interpretation is different from finding hidden symbolic meanings, as Freud attempted to do.

16. How does dreaming differ from other thinking?

Answer

16. Dreaming resembles other thinking, but it occurs during a time of decreased sensory input and loss of voluntary control of thinking.

The Mysteries of Sleep and Dreams

Sleep and dreams are not a state of unconsciousness but a state of reduced or altered consciousness. For example, a parent will awaken at the sound of a child softly crying. A healthy brain is never completely off duty, never completely relaxed.

Although our understanding of sleep and dreams continues to grow, major questions remain. Even such basic issues as the function of REM sleep remain in doubt. People have long found their dreams a source of wonder, and researchers continue to find much of interest and mystery.

Summary

- *Circadian rhythms.* Even in an unchanging environment, people become sleepy in cycles of approximately 24 hours. (page 321)
- *Morning and evening people.* Some people arouse quickly and reach their peak alertness early. Others increase alertness more slowly and reach their peak in late afternoon or early evening. Evening people are at a disadvantage if they need to start work or school early in the morning. (page 322)
- *Brain mechanisms of circadian rhythms.* An area of the brain generates an approximately 24-hour rhythm. Sunlight does not generate this rhythm, but it does reset it. (page 324)
- *The need for sleep.* Sleep serves several functions, including conservation of energy and an opportunity to strengthen memories. Sleep-deprived people have difficulty maintaining attention. (page 325)
- *Sleep stages.* During sleep, people cycle through sleep stages 1 through 4 and back through stages 3 and 2 to 1 again. The cycle beginning and ending with stage 1 lasts about 90 to 100 minutes. (page 326)
- *REM sleep.* A special stage known as REM sleep replaces the stage 1 periods after the first one. REM sleep is characterized by rapid eye movements, a high level of brain activity, and relaxed muscles. Dreams are common in this stage but not limited to it. (page 326)
- *Insomnia.* Insomnia—subjectively unsatisfactory sleep—results from many influences. Sleep abnormalities include sleep apnea and narcolepsy. (page 328)
- *Dream content.* More dreams are threatening than pleasant. Freud proposed that dreams are the product of unconscious motivations. Modern theorists describe dreaming as a kind of thinking that occurs under conditions of low sensory input and no voluntary control of thinking. (page 330)

Key Terms

activation-synthesis theory of dreams (page 332)
circadian rhythm (page 321)
electroencephalograph (EEG) (page 327)
insomnia (page 328)
jet lag (page 323)

latent content (page 331)
manifest content (page 331)
narcolepsy (page 329)
night terror (page 330)
periodic limb movement disorder (page 330)

polysomnograph (page 327)
rapid eye movement (REM) sleep (page 326)
sleep apnea (page 328)
sleep spindles (page 327)

Review Questions

1. If someone remains awake nonstop for three days, what happens to the person's alertness?
   (a) It decreases steadily throughout the three days.
   (b) It decreases for about one day and then remains constant.
   (c) It remains constant for at least one day, and then starts to decline.
   (d) It rises and falls on a 24-hour schedule, superimposed on a downward slope.

2. On average, how does the alertness of an older person change over the course of a day?
   (a) Alertness is highest in the morning and then decreases.
   (b) Alertness increases until about noon and then decreases.
   (c) Alertness increases throughout the day and reaches its peak in the evening.

3. What role does sunlight play, if any, in the circadian rhythm?
   (a) It determines the length of the rhythm (that is, 24 hours).
   (b) It rests the rhythm, like resetting the time on your watch.
   (c) It plays no role in the circadian rhythm.

4. Which animal species spend the greatest amount of time sleeping?
   (a) Infant whales and dolphins
   (b) Horses and related species
   (c) Predatory animals
   (d) Migratory birds

5. What do the long waves of brain activity during stage 4 sleep indicate?
   (a) Increased brain activity
   (b) Synchrony among neurons
   (c) Increased amplitude and velocity of action potentials
   (d) Muscle activity

6. Which of the following is characteristic of people with narcolepsy?
   (a) Periods of a minute or more during sleep when they fail to breathe
   (b) Repetitive leg movements during sleep that are strong enough to waken the person
   (c) A sleep pattern resembling that of an old person
   (d) Sudden intrusions of REM sleep into the waking period

7. In which of these ways is dreaming usually different from waking thought?
   (a) We dream about different topics than we think about.
   (b) Dreams are highly repetitive.
   (c) Most dreams are in black and white.
   (d) Dreams usually feature less pleasant emotions.

8. What did Freud mean by the "latent content" of a dream?
   (a) The part of the dream that repeats a person's previous dreams
   (b) The content that appears on the surface
   (c) The nonvisual aspects of the dream, such as sounds
   (d) A hidden meaning that the dream symbolizes

9. The neurocognitive theory of dreams compares dreams to what?
   (a) Mind wandering and daydreaming
   (b) Hypnosis
   (c) Recovery of repressed thoughts and memories
   (d) Meditation

Answers: 1d, 2a, 3b, 4c, 5b, 6d, 7d, 8d, 9a.

Hypnosis

After studying this module, you should be able to:

- Describe methods of inducing hypnosis.

- List uses of hypnosis that the evidence supports, and those that it does not support.

- Describe the evidence indicating that hypnosis does not improve memory.

- Discuss the issue of whether we should regard hypnosis as an altered state of consciousness.

Truth is nothing but a path traced between errors.[1]
—Franz Anton Mesmer

If a hypnotist told you that you were 4 years old and you started acting like a 4-year-old, we would say that you are a good hypnotic subject. If the hypnotist said your cousin was sitting in the empty chair in front of you and you agreed that you see her, then again, we would remark on the depth of your hypnotism.

But what if you had *not* been hypnotized and you suddenly started acting like a 4-year-old or insisted that you saw someone in an empty chair? Then psychologists would suspect that you were suffering from a serious psychological disorder. Hypnosis induces a temporary state that is sometimes bizarre. No wonder we find it so fascinating.

Hypnosis is *a condition of focused attention and increased suggestibility that occurs in the context of a special hypnotist–subject relationship.* The term *hypnosis* comes from Hypnos, the Greek god of sleep, although the similarity between hypnosis and sleep is superficial. People in both states lose initiative, and hypnotized people, like dreamers, accept contradictory information without protest. Hypnotized people, however, walk around and respond to objects in the real world. Their brain activity, unlike that during sleep, is characterized by increased activity in the prefrontal cortex, important for attention (Oakley & Halligan, 2013).

Hypnosis originated with the work of Franz Anton Mesmer (1734–1815), an Austrian physician. Mesmer sometimes treated illnesses by passing a magnet back and forth across a patient's body to redirect the flow of blood, nerve activity, and undefined "fluids." Some patients reported dramatic benefits. Later, Mesmer discovered that he could dispense with the magnet and use only his hand. From this observation, most people would conclude that the phenomenon related to the power of suggestion. Mesmer, however, drew the quirky conclusion that he did not need a magnet because *he himself* was a magnet. With that claim, he gave us the term *animal magnetism.*

After his death, others studied "animal magnetism" or "Mesmerism," eventually calling it "hypnotism." By that time, many physicians and scientists had already associated hypnosis with charlatans and hocus-pocus. Still today, some stage performers use hypnosis for entertainment. We should carefully distinguish the exaggerated claims from the legitimate use of hypnosis by licensed therapists.

Ways of Inducing Hypnosis

Mesmer thought hypnosis was a power emanating from his body. If so, only special people could hypnotize others. Today, we find that successful hypnotists need practice but no unusual powers.

The first step toward being hypnotized is agreeing to give it a try. Contrary to what you may have heard, no one can hypnotize an uncooperative person. A hypnotist tells you to sit down and relax, and you do so because you would like to experience hypnosis. The whole point of hypnosis is following the hypnotist's suggestions, and when you sit down and relax, you are already following a suggestion.

A hypnotist might then monotonously repeat something like, "You are putting everything else out of your mind except what you hear from me. You are starting to fall asleep. Your eyelids are getting heavy. Your eyelids are getting very heavy. They are starting to close. You are falling into a deep, deep sleep." A bit later (Udolf, 1981), the hypnotist might suggest something specific, such as, "After you go under

© Mary Evans Picture Library

Although Mesmer is often depicted as being able to control people irresistibly, hypnosis depends on the person's willingness.

[1]Does this seem profound? Or is it nonsense? Many statements sound profound until we try to figure out exactly what they mean.

A hypnotist induces hypnosis by repeating suggestions, relying on the hypnotized person's cooperation and willingness to accept suggestions.

hypnosis, your arm will begin to rise automatically." (Some people, eager for the hypnosis to succeed, shoot their arm up immediately and have to be told, "No, not yet. Just relax. That will happen later.") The hypnotist encourages you to relax and suggests that your arm is starting to feel lighter, as if it were tied to a helium balloon.

The hypnotist might suggest that your arm is beginning to feel strange and is beginning to twitch. The timing of this suggestion is important because when you stand or sit in one position long enough, your limbs really do tingle and twitch. If the hypnotist's suggestion comes at just the right moment, you think, "Wow, that's right. My arm does feel strange. This is starting to work!" Believing that you are being hypnotized is a big step toward actually being hypnotized.

The Uses and Limitations of Hypnosis

Hypnosis resembles ordinary suggestibility. If someone asked you to imagine a bright, sunny day, you almost certainly would, without being hypnotized. If you were asked to please stand and put your hands on your head, you probably would, again without being hypnotized. Then someone asks you to stand, flap your arms, and cluck like a chicken. You might or might not. People vary considerably in how far they will follow suggestions, either with or without hypnosis (Barnier, Cox, & McConkey, 2014). Hypnosis enhances suggestibility a little, but only a little (Kirsch & Braffman, 2001). If you are easily hypnotizable, you probably also respond strongly to books and movies, reacting almost as if the events were really happening.

What Hypnosis Can Do

One well-established effect of hypnosis is to inhibit pain. Some people undergo medical or dental

surgery with only hypnosis and no anesthesia. The benefits of hypnosis are most easily demonstrated for acute (sudden) pains, but hypnosis helps with chronic pains, too (Patterson, 2004). Hypnosis is particularly helpful for people who react unfavorably to anesthetic drugs and those who have developed a tolerance to painkilling opiates. Unfortunately, although hypnosis can relieve pain cheaply and without side effects, few physicians and hospitals use it (Yeh, Schnur, & Montgomery, 2014).

Recall from Chapter 4 that pain has both sensory and emotional components. Hypnosis alters mostly the emotional components, although it also somewhat decreases the response of brain areas responsive to the sensation (Jensen & Patterson, 2014; ▼ Figure 10.16). The mechanism of pain relief is not understood, but it does not depend entirely on either relaxation or distraction.

Another use of hypnosis is the posthypnotic suggestion, *a suggestion to do or experience something after coming out of hypnosis.* Suppose you receive a suggestion under hypnosis that whenever you see the number 1, it will look red, and when you see the number 2, it will look yellow. After you emerge from hypnosis, the researcher shows you black numbers on various backgrounds and asks you to press a key as soon as you see a number. You will have no

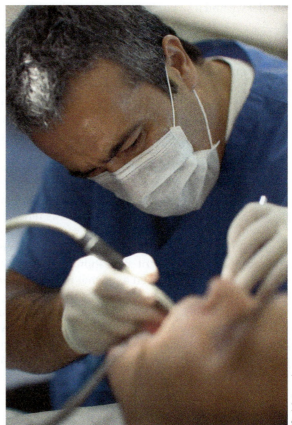

Some dentists use hypnosis to relieve pain, even for tooth extractions and root canal surgery.

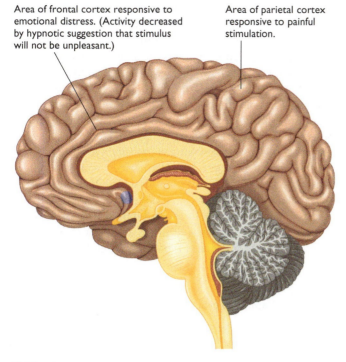

Area of frontal cortex responsive to emotional distress. (Activity decreased by hypnotic suggestion that stimulus will not be unpleasant.)

Area of parietal cortex responsive to painful stimulation.

▲ **Figure 10.16** A hypnotic suggestion to experience less pain decreases activity in the frontal cortex areas associated with emotional distress but has less effect on the sensory areas in the parietal cortex.

trouble seeing 1 or 2, but you will usually fail to see 1 or 2 (Cohen Kadosh, Henik, Catena, Walsh, & Fuentes, 2009). Until the hypnotist cancels the suggestion or it wears off, you will be like the people with synesthesia, as discussed in Chapter 4.

In one study, adults known to be easily hypnotized were randomly assigned to two groups. One group was handed a stack of 120 addressed stamped postcards and asked (without being hypnotized) to mail one back each day until they exhausted the stack. Another group was given a posthypnotic suggestion to mail one card per day. The nonhypnotized group actually mailed back more cards, but they reported that they had to remind themselves each day to mail a card. Those given the posthypnotic suggestion said they never made a deliberate effort. The idea of mailing a card just "popped into mind," providing a sudden compulsion to mail one (Barnier & McConkey, 1998).

Many therapists have given cigarette smokers a posthypnotic suggestion that they will not want to smoke. Only a few studies have compared the results to a placebo treatment. Overall, hypnosis appears to be an effective treatment, but because of the small number of studies and their varying results, the amount of benefit is uncertain (Tahiri, Mottillo, Joseph, Pilote, & Eisenberg, 2012).

What Hypnosis Does Not Do

Many of the spectacular claims about the power of hypnosis become less impressive on closer scrutiny. For instance, as in ▶ Figure 10.17, people under hypnosis can balance their head and neck on one chair and their feet on another chair and even allow someone to stand on their body! Amazing? Not really. It's easier than it looks, with or without hypnosis. Give it a try. (But don't invite someone to stand on you. Someone who does not balance correctly could injure you.)

Many people have attempted to use hypnosis to enhance memory. For example, a distressed person tells a psychotherapist, "I don't know

try it yourself

why I have such troubles. Maybe I had a bad experience when I was younger. I just can't remember." Or a witness to a crime says, "I saw the culprit for a second or two, but now I can't give you a good description." Therapists and police officers have sometimes turned to hypnosis in the hope of uncovering lost memories. As recently as the 1990s, almost one-fourth of psychotherapists believed that all memories stated under hypnosis must be true, and almost half believed that hypnosis could recover memories going back to the time of birth. Today, only about 10 percent hold either of those beliefs (Patihis, Ho, Tingen, Lilienfeld, & Loftus, 2014).

Under hypnosis, people do report additional details, mostly with great confidence. However, most of the additional details turn out to be factually wrong. Hypnotized people have an "illusion of memory," but all the evidence says that hypnosis fails to improve the accuracy of memory, and probably harms it (Mazzoni, Laurence, & Heap, 2014). Let's consider a typical study.

AP Images/Bookstaver

▲ **Figure 10.17** The U.S. Supreme Court ruled in 1987 that criminal defendants may testify about details they recalled under hypnosis. Its decision sparked this protest by the magician known as The Amazing Kreskin, who borrowed a stunt commonly used to demonstrate the power of hypnosis—standing on a person suspended between two chairs.

Hypnosis and Memory

The design of this study and several like it is simple: The experimenter presents material, tests people's memory of it, hypnotizes them, and tests their memory again (Dywan & Bowers, 1983).

Hypothesis People will remember some of the material without hypnosis and more of it after hypnosis.

Method Fifty-four people looked at 60 drawings of simple objects (e.g., pencil, hammer, or bicycle), one every 3.5 seconds. Then they were given a sheet with 60 blank spaces and asked to recall as many of the items as possible. They viewed the drawings a second and third time, and after each session, they had another chance to recall items. Each day for the next week, they again wrote a list of all the items they could remember without seeing the slides again. Finally, a week after the original slide sessions, they returned to the laboratory. Half of them, chosen at random, were hypnotized and the others were just told to relax. All were asked to recall as many of the drawings as possible.

Results ▼ Figure 10.18 shows the means for the two groups. The hypnotized people reported some items that they had not recalled before and more than the nonhypnotized group did. However, the hypnotized group also reported more incorrect items than the nonhypnotized group did.

Interpretation These results show no evidence that hypnosis improves memory. Rather, it decreases people's usual hesitance about reporting uncertain or doubtful memories. It may also cause people to confuse imagination with reality.

This study is an example of the signal-detection issue discussed in Chapter 4: A reported new memory is a

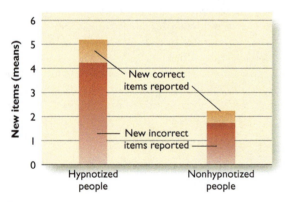

▲ **Figure 10.18** Hypnosis increased people's recall of items they had not recalled before. However, most of the new "memories" they confidently reported were incorrect. (From "The Use of Hypnosis to Aid Recall," J. Dwyan and K. Bowers, 1983. *Science, 222,* pp. 184–185. Copyright © 1983 American Association for the Advancement of Science. Reprinted with permission.)

"hit," but the number of hits, by itself, is useless information unless we also know the number of "false alarms"—reported memories that are incorrect.

In response to these results and similar ones, the American Medical Association (1986) recommended that courts of law should refuse to admit any testimony that was elicited under hypnosis, although hypnosis might be used as an investigative tool if all else fails. For example, if a hypnotized witness reports a license plate number and the police track down the car and find blood on it, the blood is certainly admissible evidence, even if the hypnotized report is not. Success stories of that type rarely if ever occur.

You may encounter the astonishing claim that hypnosis enables people to recall memories from a previous life. Hypnotized young people who claim to be recollecting a previous life most often describe the life of someone similar to themselves, married to someone remarkably similar to the current boyfriend or girlfriend. They often tell good stories, but if they are asked facts about their previous life such as whether their country is at war or what kind of money it uses, their guesses are seldom correct (Spanos, 1987–1988).

concept check

17. Name two practical applications of hypnosis.

Answer

17. Hypnosis can relieve pain, and posthypnotic suggestions help some people break unwanted habits, such as smoking.

Hypnosis and Risky Acts

Most hypnotists agree, "You don't have to worry. People will not do anything under hypnosis that they would ordinarily refuse to do." That reassurance is important for persuading you to agree to hypnosis. But is it true? How would anyone know? Do you suppose hypnotists ask clients to perform immoral acts, meet with refusals, and then report the results of these unethical experiments? Not likely. Furthermore, on the rare occasions when investigators did ask hypnotized people to perform dangerous acts, the results were hard to interpret. Here is an example.

Hypothesis Hypnotized people will sometimes perform acts that people would refuse to do otherwise.

Method Eighteen college students were randomly assigned to three groups. The investigator hypnotized those in one group, instructed the second group to pretend they were hypnotized, and simply asked the third group to participate in the study, without mentioning hypnosis. Each student was then asked to perform three acts: First, pick up a venomous snake from a box. Anyone who got too close was restrained at the last moment. Second, reach into a vat of fuming nitric acid to retrieve a coin (which was already starting to dissolve). Here, there was no last-second restraint. People who followed the instructions were told to wash their hands in warm soapy water immediately afterward. (Today's ethical procedures would prevent this study.) Third, throw the nitric acid into the face of the hypnotist's assistant. While the participant was washing hands, the researcher had replaced the nitric acid with water, but the participant had no way of knowing that.

Results Five of the six hypnotized students followed all three directions (Orne & Evans, 1965). Moreover, so did all six of those who were pretending to be hypnotized! So did two of the six who were just told to take these actions as part of an experiment with no mention of hypnosis. (Nonhypnotized subjects did, however, hesitate longer than the hypnotized subjects.)

Why would people do such extraordinary things? They explained that they trusted the experimenter: "If he tells me to do something, it can't really be dangerous."

Will hypnotized people do anything that they would otherwise refuse to do? The problem is that nonhypnotized people will sometimes perform some strange and dangerous acts either because an experimenter asked them to or on their own.

Interpretation We do not have adequate evidence to decide whether people under hypnosis will do anything that they would refuse to do otherwise because it is difficult to find anything that people will refuse to do!

Notice the importance of control groups: We cannot simply assume what people would do without hypnosis. We need to test them.

Is Hypnosis an Altered State of Consciousness?

If a hypnotist tells you, "Your hand is rising; you can do nothing to stop it," your hand might indeed rise. If you were later asked why, you might reply that you lost control of your own behavior. Still, you were not a puppet. Was the act voluntary or not? To put the question differently, is hypnosis really different from normal wakefulness?

At one extreme, some psychologists regard hypnosis as a special state of consciousness characterized by increased suggestibility. At the other extreme, some psychologists emphasize the similarities between hypnosis and normal wakeful consciousness. Most psychologists regard hypnosis as a special state in some ways but not others (Kirsch & Lynn, 1998). One way to determine whether hypnosis is a special state of consciousness is to find out whether nonhypnotized people can do everything that hypnotized people do. How convincingly could you act like a hypnotized person?

How Well Can Someone Pretend to Be Hypnotized?

In several experiments, certain college students were hypnotized and others pretended they were hypnotized. An experienced hypnotist then examined them and tried to determine which ones were really hypnotized.

Fooling the hypnotist was easier than expected. The pretenders tolerated sharp pain without flinching. They pretended to recall old memories. When they were told to sit down, they did so immediately (as hypnotized people do) without first checking to make sure they had a chair behind them (Orne, 1959, 1979). When told to experience anger, they exhibited physiological changes such as increased heart rate and sweating, just as hypnotized people do (Damaser, Shor, & Orne, 1963). Even experienced hypnotists could not identify the pretenders.

A few differences between the hypnotized people and pretenders emerged, because the pretenders did not always know how a hypnotized subject would act (Orne, 1979). For instance, when the hypnotist suggested, "You see Professor Schmaltz sitting in that chair," some of the hypnotized subjects asked with puzzlement, "How is it that I see the professor there, but I also see the chair?" Pretenders never reported seeing this double reality. At that point in the experiment, Professor Schmaltz walked into the room. "Who is that?" asked the hypnotist. The pretenders would either say they saw no one, or they would identify Schmaltz as someone else. The hypnotized subjects would say, "That's Professor Schmaltz." Some then said that they were confused about seeing the same person in two places. For some of them, the hallucinated professor faded at that moment. Others continued to accept the double image.

One study reported a way to distinguish hypnotized people from pretenders more than 90 percent of the time. But it might not be the way you would expect. Simply ask people how deeply hypnotized they thought they were, how relaxed they were, and whether they were aware of their surroundings while hypnotized. People who rate themselves as "extremely" hypnotized, "extremely" relaxed, and "totally unaware" of their surroundings are almost always pretenders. Those who were really hypnotized rate themselves as only mildly influenced (Martin & Lynn, 1996).

So, what is our conclusion? Apparently, people pretending to be hypnotized can mimic almost any effect of hypnosis that they know about. However, hypnosis is ordinarily not just role-playing. The effects that role-players learn to imitate happen spontaneously for the hypnotized people.

18. **Can hypnosis cause people to do anything they would be unwilling to do otherwise?**

Answer

18. The evidence is unclear. In certain experiments, hypnotized people have done some strange things, but so have nonhypnotized people.

Other States of Consciousness

Meditation, *a systematic procedure for inducing a calm, relaxed state through the use of special techniques*, follows traditions that have been practiced in much of the world for thousands of years, especially in India. One variety of meditation seeks "mindfulness" or thoughtless awareness, in which the person is aware of the sensations of the moment but otherwise passive. While seeking this state, the person might concentrate on a single image, or repeat a sound or a short religious statement (e.g., "om" or "God is good"). Meditators may observe their own thoughts, attempt to modify them, or distance themselves from certain thoughts. Goals of meditation vary from the development of wisdom to general well-being (Walsh & Shapiro, 2006).

Many studies document that meditation increases relaxation, decreases pain, decreases anxiety, and improves health in several ways (Hölzel et al., 2011; Wachholtz & Pargament, 2008; Yunesian, Aslani, Vash, & Yazdi, 2008). It is particularly useful for increasing people's ability to control their attention and resist distraction (MacLean et al., 2010; Mrazek, Franklin, Phillips, Baird, & Schooler, 2013).

The **déjà vu experience**, a *feeling that an event is uncannily familiar*, is fairly common in young adults and less so as people grow older (Brown, 2003). Because it takes several forms, a single explanation may not suffice. Occasionally, someone is somewhere for the first time and sees it as familiar, as if he or she had been there before. Perhaps the person really had seen something similar, possibly in a movie or photo.

More commonly, people report déjà vu in a familiar setting. You might be sitting in your room, walking down a familiar road, or having an everyday conversation, when you suddenly feel, "This has happened before!" In a sense, of course it has happened before, but your sense is not that it's just similar to a past experience. Instead, it seems *this particular* event happened before. As people talk, you feel, "I knew they were going to say that!" You could not really predict the words, but after you hear them,

Meditation excludes the worries and concerns of the day and thereby induces a calm, relaxed state.

you feel that you had been *about to* predict them. Apparently, something is triggering the brain to signal "familiar."

One man with epilepsy originating in his temporal cortex had a special feeling, an *aura*, before each of his seizures. Each aura included a strong sense of déjà vu that lasted long enough for him to move around and shift his attention from one item to another. During the aura, *whatever* he looked at seemed strangely familiar (O'Connor & Moulin, 2008). In a case like this, we can discard the hypothesis that what he saw was actually familiar. Another man with epilepsy experienced déjà vu constantly during his waking day. Everyone he met, anywhere he visited, and anything reported on a news program seemed familiar. Even when he was admitted to a hospital, he insisted that he had been treated there before. Anti-epileptic medication halted his déjà vu experiences. Brain scans suggested that his déjà vu experiences correlated with abnormal activity in parts of the temporal lobe that are important for memory (Takeda, et al., 2011).

19. What evidence shows that déjà vu does not always indicate that an experience was actually familiar?

Answer

19. A person with temporal lobe epilepsy reported an intense déjà vu experience immediately before his seizures, regardless of where he was or what he was seeing at the time.

What Hypnosis Is and Isn't

Researchers agree on a few general points: Hypnosis is not faking or pretending to be hypnotized, and it does not give people mental or physical powers that they otherwise lack. Hypnosis enables people to relax, concentrate, and follow suggestions better than they usually do. Meditation also improves concentration, often in a more lasting way.

Summary

- *Nature of hypnosis.* Hypnosis is a condition of increased concentration and suggestibility that occurs in the context of a special hypnotist–subject relationship. Psychologists distinguish the genuine phenomenon, which deserves serious study, from exaggerated claims. (page 335)
- *Hypnosis induction.* To induce hypnosis, a hypnotist asks a person to concentrate and then makes repetitive suggestions. The first steps toward being hypnotized are the willingness to be hypnotized and the belief that one is becoming hypnotized. (page 335)
- *Uses.* Hypnosis can alleviate pain, and through posthypnotic suggestion, it sometimes helps people combat bad habits. (page 336)
- *Nonuses.* Hypnosis does not give people special strength or unusual powers. It does not improve memory accuracy. When asked to report their memories under hypnosis, people report a mixture of correct and incorrect information with much confidence. (page 337)
- *Uncertain limits.* Although many hypnotists insist that hypnotized people will not do anything that they would refuse to do when not hypnotized, little evidence is available to support this claim. (page 338)
- *Hypnosis as an altered state.* Hypnosis is not greatly different from normal wakefulness, but it is also not just something that people pretend. (page 339)
- *Meditation.* Meditation increases relaxation, decreases anxiety, and enhances attention. (page 340)
- *Déjà vu.* People sometimes feel that the current experience is uncannily familiar. In some cases (probably not all) it relates to abnormal activity in brain areas responsible for memory. (page 340)

Key Terms

déjà vu experience (page 340)

hypnosis (page 335)

meditation (page 340)

posthypnotic suggestion (page 336)

Review Questions

1. In what way, if at all, can hypnosis relieve pain?
   - (a) It weakens the response of the pain receptors themselves.
   - (b) It decreases the brain's response to pain, especially to the emotional aspect.
   - (c) It causes people to say they have less pain, even though they really feel it just as much.
   - (d) It has no effect on pain.

2. What are the effects of hypnosis on memory?
   - (a) It enables people to improve their memory.
   - (b) It enables people to remember previous lives.
   - (c) It leads people to confidently report more details, most of which are wrong.

3. Why is it hard to test whether hypnosis can get people to do something they would refuse to do otherwise?
   - (a) Ethics boards refuse to let experimenters test this hypothesis.
   - (b) Anyone who conducted such a study would be banned from the profession.
   - (c) Nonhypnotized people are willing to do some strange and dangerous acts.

4. During a state of meditation, what does a person practice?
   - (a) Concentration on an image or sensation while remaining passive
   - (b) Shifting attention among several activities
   - (c) Maintaining a polite conversation
   - (d) Self-criticism

Answers: 1b, 2c, 3c, 4a.

11 Motivated Behaviors

©Spaceport9/Shutterstock.com

During the summer of 1996, the proprietors of London's Kew Gardens announced that an unusual plant, native to Sumatra and rarely cultivated elsewhere, was about to bloom for the first time since 1963. If you had been in London then, would you have made a point of visiting Kew Gardens to witness this rare event? No? What if I told you that it was a truly beautiful flower? With a lovely, sweet smell? Still no?

Then what if I told you the truth—that the flower is called the *stinking lily* or *corpse plant* because it smells like a huge, week-old carcass of rotting meat or fish. One whiff of it can make a person retch. Now would you want to visit it? If so, you would have to wait in line. When Kew Gardens announced that the stinking lily was about to bloom, an enormous crowd gathered, forming a line that stretched to the length of a soccer field (MacQuitty, 1996). When another stinking lily bloomed in Davis, California, more than 3,000 visitors came in the five days it was in bloom (Cimino, 2007).

The visitors' behavior is not unusual. People seek new and interesting experiences just out of curiosity. Even motivations with obvious biological value, such as hunger and sex, sometimes produce puzzling behaviors. Researchers have nevertheless made progress in understanding many aspects of motivation. We begin this chapter with an overview of motivation as it applies to ambition and work. Then we explore two representative and important motivations—hunger and sex.

This flower is seldom cultivated, for good reasons. Would you stand in line to visit it?

AP Images/Rich Pedroncelli

module 11.1

Work Motivation

After studying this module, you should be able to:

- Evaluate the drive, homeostasis, and incentive theories of motivation.
- Discuss the values of setting goals and deadlines.
- Describe ways to overcome temptations, including the temptation to procrastinate.
- Distinguish between the scientific management and human relations approaches to job design.
- List factors that correlate with job satisfaction.
- Distinguish between transformational leaders and transactional leaders.

One of the remarkable characteristics of human behavior is our joy of competing. People compete with one another in just about anything. One woman let her fingernails grow to 19 feet 9 inches (6 meters) to get her name in the *Guinness Book of World Records*. People compete in the mud pit belly flop contest, the wife-carrying contest, and underwater hockey. Did you know about the International Rock, Paper, Scissors Tournament? For the Krispy Kreme Challenge, contestants run 2.5 miles, eat 12 Krispy Kreme donuts, and then run back. (Anyone who vomits is disqualified.)

Tapping into people's competitive nature can be useful. A father was trying to get his son to walk from a shopping mall to the car, while the son stubbornly refused. The father tried promises, pleadings, and threats, to no avail. Then the father's friend said, "Hey, kid, I'll race you to the car!" The son took off, won the race, and everyone was happy.

Striving for excellence in school or on the job is similar. People constantly strive to beat someone else's performance or to top their own previous best.

Would you compete in the mud pit belly flop contest?

Views of Motivation

Like many other important terms in psychology, motivation is difficult to define. Let's consider several possibilities: "Motivation is what activates and directs behavior." This description sounds good, but it also fits other phenomena. For instance, light activates and directs plant growth, but we wouldn't say that light motivates plants.

"Motivation is what makes our behavior more vigorous and energetic." Alas, some motivated behavior is not vigorous at all. For example, you might be motivated to spend the next few hours sleeping.

How about this: Based on the concept of reinforcement from Chapter 6, we could define motivation as *the process that determines the reinforcement value of an outcome*. In everyday language, motivation is what makes you seek something more at one time than another. For example, you want food at some times and not others. Motivated behavior is goal-directed. If you are motivated by hunger, you try one approach after another until you find food. If you are cold, you put on heavier clothing, find a nice fireplace, or do whatever else you can to get warmer.

This definition works as a description, but it offers no theory. Let's briefly consider some influential theories with their strengths and weaknesses.

Drive Theories

One view regards motivation as a drive, *a state of unrest or irritation that energizes one behavior after another until one of them removes the irritation* (Hull, 1943). For example, if you get a splinter in your finger, the discomfort motivates you to try various actions until you remove the splinter.

According to the *drive-reduction theory* that was popular among psychologists of the 1940s and 1950s, humans and other animals eat to reduce their hunger, drink to reduce their thirst, and have sexual activity to reduce their sex drive. By this view, if you satisfy all your needs, you become inactive. The theory seems to imply that your ultimate goal is to have nothing to do. In fact, most people dislike having nothing to do! In one study, young adults were asked to sit by themselves for 6 to 15 minutes awake but otherwise doing nothing, unless they chose to flip a switch to give themselves a painful electrical shock. Even though all these people had previously said they would pay money to avoid such shocks,

Table 11.1 Three Views of Motivation

View	Basic Position	Major Weaknesses
Drive Theories According to drive theories, motivation is an irritation that continues until we find a way to reduce it.	Motivations are based on needs or irritations that we try to reduce; they do not specify particular actions.	Implies that we always try to reduce stimulation, never to increase it. Also overlooks importance of external stimuli.
Homeostasis (plus anticipation) Homeostasis is the process of maintaining a variable such as body temperature within a set range.	Motivations tend to maintain body states near some optimum intermediate level. They may react to current needs and anticipate future needs.	Overlooks importance of external stimuli.
Incentive Theories Incentives are external stimuli that attract us even if we have no biological need for them.	Motivations are responses to attractive stimuli.	Incomplete theory unless combined with drive or homeostasis.

12 of the 18 men and 6 of the 24 women gave themselves at least one shock, just to break the monotony (Wilson et al., 2014). Just try explaining that one in terms of drive-reduction theory.

Homeostasis

An advance on the idea of drive reduction is the concept of homeostasis, *the maintenance of an optimum level of biological conditions within an organism* (Cannon, 1929). The idea of homeostasis recognizes that we seek a state of equilibrium, which is not zero stimulation. For example, people make an effort to maintain a fairly constant body temperature, a steady body weight, a certain amount of water in the body, a moderate amount of sensory experience, and so on.

Our behavior also anticipates future needs. For example, you might eat a large breakfast even though you are not hungry, just because you know you will be too busy to stop for lunch. Many animals put on extra fat and fur to protect against winter's cold weather and then lose weight and shed the extra fur in spring. If you become frightened, you start to sweat in anticipation of the extra body heat you will generate while trying to escape a danger. A revised concept of homeostasis is allostasis, defined as *maintaining levels of biological conditions that vary according to an individual's needs and circumstances*. Allostasis acts to prevent difficulties instead of just correcting them after they occur (Sterling, 2012).

Incentive Theories

The drive-reduction and homeostasis concepts overlook the power of new stimuli to arouse behaviors. For example, if someone offers your favorite dessert, might you eat it even though you are not hungry? Motivation includes more than the internal forces that push us toward certain behaviors. It also includes incentives—*stimuli that pull us toward an action*. Most motivated behaviors are controlled by a combination of drives and incentives. You eat because you are hungry (a drive) and because you see appealing food (an incentive). You jump into a swimming pool on a hot day to cool your body (a drive) and because you will enjoy splashing around in the water (an incentive).

Parallel to the distinction between drives and incentives is a distinction between extrinsic motivation and intrinsic motivation. An extrinsic motivation *is based on the rewards the act might bring or the punishments it might avoid*. A drive for hunger, water, or a comfortable temperature is an extrinsic motivation. An intrinsic motivation *is based on the pleasure that the act itself provides*. For example, working a crossword puzzle or playing a video game is based on intrinsic motivation. Many if not most acts are a combination of both. For example, you might jog or exercise because you enjoy it, and also to lose weight or strengthen your muscles. You might read a textbook not only to fulfill an assignment, but also (I hope) because you find it interesting.

Table 11.1 summarizes three views of motivation.

1. **The introduction to this chapter described people who stood in line to visit a foul-smelling flower. Would that action make sense in terms of drive-reduction, incentive, or homeostasis views of motivation?**

Answer

1. The action is a response to an incentive, the opportunity for an unusual experience. It would be harder to explain in terms of drive-reduction or homeostasis.

Conflicting Motivations

You almost always have more than one motivation. Sometimes they are in harmony. Imagine yourself outside on a hot day. You would like to cool off, you are thirsty and a bit hungry, and you would like to be with your friends. Someone suggests going somewhere for a snack and a cool glass of lemonade.

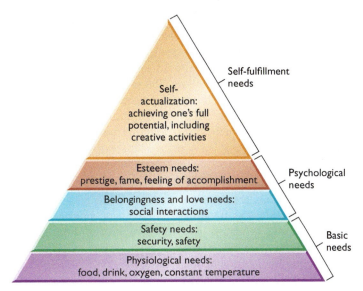

▲ **Figure 11.1** According to Maslow's hierarchy of needs, you satisfy your lower needs before moving on to your higher needs. (Based on Maslow, 1970)

You agree, satisfying all four motives—temperature regulation, thirst, hunger, and socialization. At another time, you might have motivations in conflict. You might be sleepy when your friends want to watch a late-night movie. How do we resolve such conflicts?

Abraham Maslow (1970) proposed that we resolve conflicts by a **hierarchy of needs**, *an organization from the most insistent needs to the ones that receive attention only when all others are under control*, as shown in ▲ **Figure 11.1**. If you need to breathe, fighting for oxygen takes priority over anything else. If you are hungry, thirsty, or too hot or too cold, you pursue those needs until you satisfy them. After you satisfy your basic physiological needs, you move on to your safety needs, such as security from attack and avoidance of pain. Next come your social needs, followed by your need for self-esteem. At the apex of the hierarchy is the need for **self-actualization**, *the need for creative activities to fulfill your potential.* Maslow further proposed that people who satisfy more of their higher needs tend to be mentally healthier than others.

As a generalization, Maslow's hierarchy makes the valid point that certain motivations take priority over others. However, the theory fails if we take it literally. Sometimes, escaping pain or avoiding danger is more urgent than seeking food. Might you walk through bitter cold, passing up opportunities to eat or drink, to be with someone you love? It depends: How cold is it, how hungry and

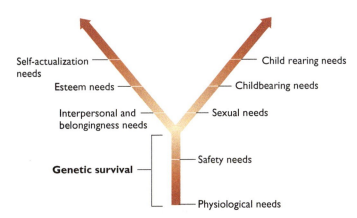

▲ **Figure 11.2** According to a revised model, people who satisfy their physiological and safety needs can branch off to emphasize one set of goals or another.

thirsty are you, and how much do you love that person? Might you risk your life to advance a cause you believe in? Some people do. Although the lower-level needs *usually* take priority over the higher needs, exceptions are common.

Further criticisms are that Maslow's theory omits parenting and overemphasizes the vague idea of self-actualization (Kenrick, Griskevicius, Neuberg, & Schaller, 2010). Also, it is culture specific. For many people in China, self-esteem and personal accomplishments are less important than the sense of belonging to one's group and one's family. ▼ **Figure 11.2** presents an alternative hierarchy of needs (Yang, 2003). According to this model, everyone has to satisfy the survival needs at the bottom. Having satisfied them, a person can branch off in either of two directions or a combination of both. The arm at the right pertains to reproduction, an essential goal for all human cultures, although not for every person within a given culture. The arm at the left pertains to expressing one's own needs. Relating to other people and belonging to a family or group are important to everyone, especially people in collectivist cultures. Self-esteem and self-actualization needs are important for people in some cultures but not others.

concept check

2. What are some criticisms of Maslow's hierarchy?

Answer

2. A lower level of need does not always take priority over one at a higher level. Maslow's hierarchy ignores parenting and overemphasizes self-actualization. Also, goals vary among cultures.

Goals and Deadlines

One of the most powerful ways to motivate anyone, including yourself, is to set a goal. Which of these goals would be best?

- I will work for an A in every course.
- I will work for at least a C average.
- I will do my best.

The research says that "do your best" is the same as no goal at all. Although it sounds good, you are never behind schedule on achieving it, so it doesn't motivate extra work. The most effective goals are specific, difficult, and realistic (Locke & Latham, 2002). A goal should be specific, because a vague goal does not tell you what to do. If a company sets a goal to "substantially increase sales," the goal is worthless, because it does not say how much or how soon. In contrast, "increase sales by 10 percent within two years" is specific enough to be effective. Workers at government agencies often have unclear or conflicting goals that change a bit after each election. Government workers without a clear goal tend to report low job satisfaction (Jung, 2014). A goal should also be difficult, or it inspires no work. A student's goal of "at least a C average" would be worthless, unless the student's previous performance was below that.

A goal must also be realistic. Especially for group work, if a goal seems beyond reach, many members of the group simply give up (Curseu, Janssen, & Meeus, 2014). If the goal for a company or a branch within the company appears extremely difficult, supervisors feel anxiety and often become rude or abusive toward their employees (Mawritz, Folger, & Latham, 2014). Workers who are trying to achieve extremely difficult goals make risky, sometimes dangerous decisions and are sometimes tempted to dishonest dealing (Schiebener, Wegmann, Pawlikowski, & Brand, 2014).

For any goal to be effective, certain conditions are necessary (Locke & Latham, 2002). One is to take the goal seriously, preferably by committing to it publicly. If you want to get better grades next semester, tell your friends about it. Also you should receive frequent feedback about your progress. If you are aiming for all A's but you get a B on a test in one course, you know you have to study harder in that course. If your goal is to increase profits by 10 percent and you learn that they are currently up 9 percent, you know you need to work a little harder. Finally, you have to believe that the reward will be worth the effort. Do you care enough about your grades to make sacrifices in your social life? Do you trust your boss to pay the bonus as promised? Some employees do, but others consider their bosses lying, cheating scoundrels (Craig & Gustafson, 1998).

▲ **Figure 11.3** The Sydney Opera House is a classic example of underestimating the time and cost to complete a project.

One other point about goals: Inappropriate goals have unfavorable consequences. Setting a goal of straight A's leads some students to take only easy courses or to drop out of interesting courses in which they are not sure they can get an A. In 1995 the Australian government set a goal for college faculty to increase their total number of publications. The result was that many professors published many short articles in seldom-read journals, increasing their quantity but decreasing the quality (Butler, 2002). If a company's goal is to get more new customers, the employees concentrate on potential new customers while largely ignoring the old customers.

Realistic Goals

Given that the best goals are high but realistic, what goal is realistic? Most Americans rate themselves as healthier than average, smarter, more creative, and better than average at almost everything. As part of their optimism, they underestimate the time they need for holiday shopping, writing a term paper, remodeling their kitchen, and almost anything they do. Companies underestimate how long they will need to bring a product to market, reorganize their sales staff, or finish a building (Dunning, Heath, & Suls, 2004). Governments underestimate the time and cost of major projects. The Sydney Opera House in Australia was expected to be completed by 1963 at a cost of $7 million. It was finally completed in 1973 at a cost of $102 million (see ▼ Figure 11.3).

Senior students at one college were asked to estimate "realistically" how soon they would complete their senior honors thesis—a major research paper. They were also asked how late they might finish if everything went wrong. On average, they finished their papers 1 week *later* than what they said was the worst-case scenario (Buehler, Griffin, & Ross, 1994). The message is to allow yourself more time than you think you need—and get started sooner than you think is necessary. Major tasks almost always take more work than expected.

The Value of Deadlines

If you had no deadlines to meet, how hard would you work? When you have a deadline, do you sometimes wait until shortly before the deadline to start working in earnest? For example, are you reading this chapter now because you have to take a test on it tomorrow? Would anyone ever finish anything if they didn't have to meet a deadline?

Procrastination (putting off work until tomorrow) is a problem for many students and workers. Here is an experiment that beautifully illustrates the phenomenon.

what's the evidence?

The Value of Deadlines

A professor set firm deadlines for one class and let another class choose their own deadlines to see whether those with evenly spaced deadlines would outperform those who had the opportunity to procrastinate (Ariely & Wertenbroch, 2002).

Hypothesis Students who are required, or who require themselves, to spread out their work will do better than those with an opportunity to wait until the end of the semester.

Method A professor taught two sections of the same course. Students were not randomly assigned to sections, but the students in the two sections had about equal academic records. The professor told one class that they had to write three papers, the first due after one-third of the semester, the second after two-thirds, and the third at the end of the semester. The other class was told that they could choose their own deadlines. They might make their three papers due after each third of the semester, all three at the end of the semester, or whatever else they chose. However, they had to decide

Fairfax Media/Getty Images

by the second day of class, and whatever deadlines they chose would be enforced. That is, a paper that missed a deadline would be penalized, even though the student could have chosen a later deadline. At the end of the course, the professor graded all the papers blind to when they had been submitted.

Results If you were in the class that could choose the deadlines, what would you do? Twelve of the fifty-one students set all three deadlines on the final day of the semester. Presumably, they reasoned that they would try to finish their papers earlier, but they would have the opportunity for extra time if they needed it. Other students, however, saw that if they set their deadlines at the end, they would expose themselves to a temptation that would be hard to resist, so they imposed earlier deadlines. Some spaced the deadlines evenly at one-third, two-thirds, and the end of the semester, and others compromised, setting deadlines for the first two papers somewhat later but not at the end of the semester.

On average, the students in the section with assigned deadlines got better grades than those who were allowed to choose their own deadlines. Of those permitted to choose their own deadlines, those who set their deadlines at approximately one-third, two-thirds, and the end of the semester did about the same as those with assigned deadlines and much better than those who set all their deadlines at the end.

Interpretation If the professor had studied only one class and let them choose their own deadlines, we could draw no conclusion from the finding that those who spread out their deadlines did the best. It could mean that early deadlines help, but it could also mean that better students set earlier deadlines. However, the early-deadline students merely matched the assigned-deadline students, whereas the late-deadline students did worse. Therefore, the conclusion follows that setting deadlines does help. If you are required to do part of your work at a time, you manage your time to accomplish it. If your deadlines are all at the end, you face a powerful temptation to delay until the end.

3. What conclusion would have followed if the early-deadline students did better than the late-deadline students did but that the class on the average did as well as the assigned-deadline students?

Answer

3. If students in the two sections had equal performance overall, we could not conclude that deadlines help. Instead, the conclusion would be that brighter students tend to set earlier deadlines.

Overcoming Procrastination

You have some work to do. It isn't due immediately, but you need to start making progress now, or you will regret it later. Procrastination is putting something off until later, based on the Latin word *cras*, meaning "tomorrow." Given the importance of working steadily toward a goal, how can we overcome the temptation to procrastinate? Part of the answer is confidence. It is hard to get started if you are not sure you can do the task well. A little encouragement or praise often helps (Fritzsche, Young, & Hickson, 2003). But if you are trying to encourage someone else, don't overdo it. Adults sometimes tell children that their latest work is wonderful and amazing. Unrealistically high praise often has a negative effect, either because the children don't believe it, or because they think they cannot continue to achieve such high standards (Brummelman, Thomaes, Orobio de Castro, Overbeek, & Bushman, 2014).

You decrease procrastination if you make a detailed plan of when, where, and how you will do something (McCrea, Liberman, Trope, & Sherman, 2008). Suppose your goal is to exercise more. Decide what kind of exercise you will do, when, and where. If you want to eat a healthier diet, decide to eat a salad

instead of a hamburger for lunch tomorrow, or vow to buy fruits and vegetables when you go to the store. If you set specific plans, then the relevant situation will evoke the behavior (Milne, Orbell, & Sheeran, 2002; Verplanken & Faes, 1999).

Here is another strategy to combat procrastination: Identify some activity that you have been procrastinating, such as cleaning your room or calling your grandparents. *Please choose an activity.* Now, estimate how likely you are to complete that activity within the next week. *Please make that estimate.* If you have followed instructions, you have just increased your probability of actually engaging in that behavior! *Simply estimating your probability of doing some desirable activity increases your probability of that action* (Levav & Fitzsimons, 2006). Psychologists call this phenomenon the **mere measurement effect.** (Of course, if you estimated your probability at zero, then this little trick isn't going to work.)

Another strategy for overcoming procrastination is to make a decision about something else first, even something unimportant. For example, if you go to a zoo, which will you visit first, elephants or hippopotamuses? Where would you prefer to go on vacation, Hawaii, the Caribbean, or France? Just after people have made quick, no-cost decisions like these, they become more likely than usual to take action of other kinds, such as buying a new computer (Xu & Wyer, 2008). They get into the mind-set of deciding and acting instead of delaying and doing nothing. (You can use this idea if you are trying to sell something. Suppose someone seems undecided about buying some product. Ask, "If you did buy one, what color would you prefer?" Making one decision primes a person to make another.)

4. How could you increase your probability of getting a good start on writing a term paper?

Answers

4. First, find some way to boost your confidence. Then make specific plans, such as, "I will spend Monday night at the library looking for materials." You could also estimate your probability of completing the first part of the paper.

Temptation

The conflict between doing some work and procrastinating it until later (so you can do something fun right now) is a typical example of temptation, or what psychologists sometimes call a "*want* versus *should* conflict." They also refer to **delay of gratification**— *declining a pleasant activity now in order to get greater pleasure later.* Temptation occurs in many other settings too. You might be tempted to cheat on a test, tell a lie on your tax form, drive above the speed limit, or engage in risky sex. Every temptation is a battle between an impulse to do something enjoyable at the moment, and an effort to resist it in favor of a later benefit (Lopez, Hofmann, Wagner, Kelley, & Heatherton, 2014). Although many types of temptation don't pertain to work, it is convenient to discuss them all here.

A procedure for measuring resistance to temptation in children goes as follows: An experimenter seats a preschool child alone in a room and explains, "Here is a marshmallow. You can have it now, or you can wait until I come back. If you wait, I'll give you a second marshmallow." So the choice is between one now and two later. Some children eagerly eat the first one, and others dutifully wait, often using strategies such as not looking at the marshmallow. (If you do an Internet search for "marshmallow experiment," you can find some entertaining videos.) Long-term follow-up studies found significant advantages for the children who waited. They show self-control and conscientious behavior at home and in school (Duckworth, Tsukayama, & Kirby, 2013). As adolescents, they were less distractible, better able to handle frustration, and better able to resist temptations. Also, they had higher than average SAT scores (Shoda, Mischel, & Peake, 1990). As middle-aged people, they were less likely to be overweight (Schlam, Wilson, Shoda, Miscle, & Ayduk, 2013).

As people advance from childhood to adulthood, they gradually improve their ability to resist temptation and delay gratification (Steinberg et al., 2009). Still, people of any age face a temptation to do something they will enjoy right now despite the disadvantage they will suffer later. Most people overestimate their ability to resist temptation, and therefore expose themselves to tempting situations (Nordgren, van Harreveld, & van der Pligt, 2009). It is better to avoid tempting situations than to try to resist temptations.

Imagine the following: You and another student show up for a research study. The researchers explain that two studies are available. One study sounds appealing. The other is difficult and painful. You are invited to flip a coin, examine it by yourself in private, and then announce who gets to be in the pleasant study. In this situation, nearly 90 percent of students claim they won the toss and get to be in the pleasant experiment. Obviously, many are lying. However, suppose you were asked whether you want to flip the coin and announce the results or let the experimenter do it. Now most people say, "Let the experimenter do it" (Batson & Thompson, 2001). They avoid putting themselves in a situation in which they know they will be tempted to cheat.

One way to overcome temptation is to commit to an action well in advance. For example, would

you prefer $500 now or $750 a year from now? You might choose the immediate $500, even though you know the delayed $750 makes logical sense. But what if you make the decision in advance? Your choice becomes $500 a year from now or $750 two years from now. Under these conditions, you will probably switch to the delayed $750, even though a year from now you might wish you had made the other choice.

If you want to resist temptations, does it help to practice resisting temptations? The answer is, as usual, "it depends." Resisting a temptation helps you resist the same temptation later. For example, if you are trying to quit smoking, and you resist the temptation to smoke right now, you improve your ability to resist the next smoking temptation (O'Connell, Schwartz, & Shiffman, 2008). However, people who have resisted one temptation often feel entitled to treat themselves in some other way. Rightly or wrongly, they think they have "used up their willpower," and they don't try as hard to resist the next temptation. Another explanation is that self-control requires attention, and people find it difficult to continue maintaining strong attention (Sripada, Kessler, & Jonides, 2014). For whatever reason, whenever you use self-control to resist a temptation in one situation, you become less likely to resist temptation in a second situation soon after it (Hofmann, Vohs, & Baumeister, 2012; Inzlicht & Schmeichel, 2012).

Your ability to resist temptation also depends on what you see other people doing. Imagine yourself in this study: An experimenter gives you a set of 20 math problems to try in the next 5 minutes. You are told to solve as many as you can, and then shred your answer sheet and report how many you solved, receiving a payment of 50 cents per answer. You see that you could easily exaggerate your number correct and increase your payment. Although an average person solves only about 7 items in the 5 minutes, most people cheat a little and report, on average, solving about 12. But now suppose that after just one minute, someone stands up, shreds his paper, announces that he got them all correct, and takes the full payment of $10. Obviously, he must be cheating, and he got away with it. How do you react? Ordinarily, his act would increase your own cheating. However, suppose he is wearing a sweatshirt from a nearby college that you consider a major rival. In that case, his cheating *decreases* your probability of cheating (Gino, Ayal, & Ariely, 2009). You say to yourself, "Hah. *Those* people act like that. We're better!"

Here's another intervention that decreases cheating: You're in an experiment similar to the one just described, but right before it you do a preliminary task of listing as many of the Ten Commandments as you can remember. Under those conditions, cheating is reduced to almost zero, even for nonreligious students! The simple reminder of ethical norms reduces the temptation to cheat (Mazar, Amir, & Ariely, 2008). One caution: These studies used U.S. and Canadian students. The results may be different in other cultures.

concept check

5. **What advice would you give someone who wants to resist a temptation?**

Answer

5. The best advice is to avoid the situation in which you might feel temptation! Second, don't expose yourself to one temptation just after successfully resisting a different type of temptation. If it is possible to make a commitment far in advance, do so. Think of people who yield to the temptation as different from yourself. Also, remind yourself of ethical norms.

Job Design and Job Satisfaction

Let's turn to some research specifically dealing with work. People work harder, more effectively, and with more satisfaction at some jobs than at others. Why?

▲ **Figure 11.4** Adherents of the scientific-management approach tried to determine the best, safest, most efficient ways to perform even simple tasks. For example, the drawing on the left shows the right way to lift a brick, and the drawing on the right shows the wrong way, according to Gilbreth (1911).

Two Approaches to Job Design

Imagine that you are starting or reorganizing a company, and you must decide how to divide the workload. Should you make the jobs challenging and interesting? Or should you make them simple and foolproof?

According to the scientific-management approach to job design, also known as *Theory X, you should experiment to find the best way to do the job, select appropriate workers, and train them well to do it the right way* (Derksen, 2014). The employer should do research to find the most efficient way to do each task, to increase speed, decrease effort, and avoid injuries (see ▲ Figure 11.4). According to this approach, you don't expect workers to take much initiative or to show creativity.

According to an alternative view, the human-relations approach to job design, also known as *Theory Y, employees like variety in their job, a sense of accomplishment, and a sense of responsibility.* Therefore, employers should enrich the jobs, giving each employee responsibility for meaningful tasks. For example, a financial services corporation that followed the scientific-management approach would have each employee keep just one kind of records for many clients, developing expertise at a narrow task. The same company, reorganized according to the human-relations approach, might put each employee in charge of fewer clients, keeping track of all the information about those clients. Employees with enriched jobs generally report greater satisfaction (Campion & McClelland, 1991). From the employer's standpoint, the enriched jobs have many advantages but two disadvantages: It takes longer to train the workers than it would with simpler jobs, and the workers performing enriched jobs expect to be paid more!

Which approach is better? It depends. Consider an analogy to education: Professor X tells students exactly what to read and precisely what to do to get a good grade. (This course is analogous to the scientific-management approach.) Professor Y outlines the general issues, lists some suggested readings, lets the students control class discussion, and invites students to create their own ideas for projects. (This course is analogous to the human-relations approach, though perhaps more extreme.) Which class would you like better?

If you are highly interested in the topic and have ideas of your own, you love Professor Y's course and consider Professor X's course tedious. But if you are taking the course just to satisfy a requirement, you appreciate the precise structure of Professor X's class. The same is true of jobs. Some workers, especially the younger and brighter ones, thrive on the challenge of an enriched job, but others prefer a simple, stable set of tasks (Arnold & House, 1980; Campion & Thayer, 1985; Hackman & Lawler, 1971).

6. "I want my employees to enjoy their work and to feel pride in their achievements." Does that statement reflect a belief in the human-relations approach or the scientific-management approach?

Answer

6. It reflects the human-relations approach.

Job Satisfaction

Your choice of career profoundly affects the quality of your life. For most of your adult life, you will spend about half of your waking hours on the job. You want to spend that time on a job you like. How much you like your job correlates strongly with your interest in the job (Nye, Su, Rounds, & Drasgow, 2012), and moderately well with your skill at performing the job (Judge, Thoresen, Bono, & Patton, 2001). The causation probably goes in several directions: High job satisfaction improves performance, good performance improves job satisfaction, and highly conscientious people tend to be satisfied with life and successful on their job (Judge et al., 2001; Tett & Burnett, 2003). However, the correlation is not high. You can probably imagine several explanations. For example, some of the people who do a job well are not highly satisfied, because they want a better job.

Obviously, job satisfaction depends largely on the job itself, including the interest level, the pay, coworkers, and management. It also depends on the worker's personality. Some people are just easier to please than others. Comparisons of identical and fraternal twins indicate that job satisfaction is highly heritable (Arvey, McCall, Bouchard, Taubman, & Cavanaugh, 1994). If your close relatives say they are happy with their jobs, you probably are also, even though you have a different job. You don't inherit your job, but you inherit your disposition. Some people find much to like about their jobs, and others find much to complain about (Ilies & Judge, 2003; Judge & Larsen, 2001; Thoresen, Kaplan, Barsky, Warren, & de Chermont, 2003).

On average, older workers express higher job satisfaction than younger workers do (Pond & Geyer, 1991). One possible explanation is that older workers have better, higher-paying jobs. Another is that today's young people are harder to satisfy than their elders ever were (Beck & Wilson, 2000). Another possibility is that many young workers start in the wrong job and find a more suitable one later. Yet another is that many young people are still considering the possibility of changing jobs. By middle age, most people reconcile themselves to whatever jobs they have.

Pay and Job Satisfaction

An employer who wants to keep workers satisfied gives careful attention to the pay scale. Obviously, workers want to be paid well, but they also need to perceive the pay scale as fair. In one classic experiment, some workers were led to believe that they had been hired in spite of less than average qualifications for the job. They worked harder than average, apparently to convince the employer that they deserved the job, but perhaps also to convince themselves that they earned their pay (J. S. Adams, 1963).

Employees who perceive their bosses as operating unfairly often start looking for another job. They also stop doing the "good citizen" behaviors that help the company, such as keeping the building tidy, helping other workers, and attending meetings after working hours (Simons & Roberson, 2003). At the opposite extreme, some workers develop an emotional commitment that leads them to work loyally and energetically, well beyond what they are paid to do (Meyer, Becker, & Vandenberghe, 2004; Seo, Barrett, & Bartunek, 2004).

Money is certainly part of anyone's work motivation. However, although pay is effective at increasing workers' quantity of output, it is much less effective for increasing quality. Quality depends much more on intrinsic motivation—enjoyment of the job itself and a feeling of accomplishment (Cerasoli, Nicklin, & Ford, 2014). For many people, work is an enjoyable, important part of who they are.

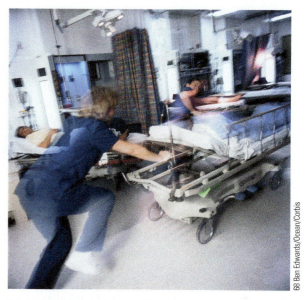

Job burnout is a serious problem for nurses and others who are expected to act positive while doing often unpleasant and challenging tasks.

7. What are some factors that contribute to high job satisfaction?

Answer

7. Factors associated with high job satisfaction include high ability to perform the job, a happy personality, a perception that the pay scale is fair, and old age.

Job Burnout

Almost any job produces some stress, but sometimes work stress gets so bad that it leaves people physically and emotionally exhausted. The term *burnout* should not be overused. If you have been working hard, but you recover after a pleasant vacation, you did not have burnout. Job burnout refers to a *long-lasting sense of mental and physical exhaustion and discouragement*. People with this condition feel detached from their job and their coworkers, and they lack any sense of accomplishment (Melamed et al., 2006). They become less effective on the job, and their health deteriorates. The long persistence of burnout has at least two possible explanations. One is that exhaustion and discouragement are a personality trait; that is, when people become depressed for any reason, they blame their jobs. The other explanation is that burnout is like

a severely shattered leg: After sustaining that kind of injury, you never completely recover ... and it doesn't take much to reinjure that leg.

Burnout is especially common among people in the helping professions, such as nurses, teachers, and therapists, who are expected to be supportive and encouraging at all times. Consider the contrast: If you work an office job, you might come in one day and tell your coworkers, "I can still do my job, but I'm going to be in a bad mood today." You cannot do that in the helping professions. Imagine you are a nurse who just cleaned up vomit for the patient in room 1, blood for the patient in room 2, and bowel movements in room 3. The patient in room 4, whom you especially liked, just died. Next you have to go into room 5 and act cheerful and supportive. Your training was in medicine, not acting, and this process of suppressing one emotion and substituting another requires enormous effort (Cheung & Tang, 2007).

Not everyone with a difficult job experiences burnout. People prone to depression are also prone to job burnout. People with a happy home life, enjoyable leisure activities, and high physical activity are unlikely to develop job burnout (Armon, 2014; Blom, Sverke, Vodin, Lindfors, & Svedberg, 2014; Sonnentag, Arbeus, Mahn, & Fritz, 2014).

8. What jobs are especially vulnerable to job burnout?

Answer

8. Job burnout is especially common in the helping professions, such as nursing or therapy.

Leadership

Your motivation to work also depends on how you perceive your organization's leadership. Some employers inspire deep loyalties and intense efforts, whereas others barely get their workers to do the minimum. (The same is true of college professors, athletic coaches, and political leaders.)

What does good leadership require? Early psychological research found no consistent personality difference between effective and ineffective leaders. Effective leaders were not consistently more gregarious, outspoken, or anything else. You know there has to be something wrong here. If good and poor leaders really do not differ, we could choose company executives, college presidents, or state governors at random. Later researchers concluded that no single personality factor is decisive because what matters is a combination of many qualities. A good leader has the right combination of personality, intelligence, expertise, motives, values, and people-handling skills (Zaccaro, 2007).

Furthermore, what constitutes good leadership depends on the situation. Just as no one is creative in all situations—a creative poet probably won't propose creative solutions to an automobile repair problem—the leadership style that succeeds in one situation may not be right for another (Vroom & Jago, 2007). A good leader of a committee meeting gives everyone a chance to express an opinion before putting an issue to a vote. Someone leading a field trip for a class of 6-year-olds makes the decisions and tells the children what to do. A dictatorial approach would almost always fail in a committee meeting, and asking the 6-year-olds to debate and vote is not ordinarily the best approach.

Industrial-organizational psychologists distinguish between transformational and transactional leadership styles. A *transformational leader articulates a vision of the future, intellectually stimulates subordinates, and motivates them to use their imagination to advance the organization.* In most cases, the idea of a visionary leader is more myth than reality. An organization functions well if leadership is shared throughout the organization, with various people taking the lead as the situation changes (Eberly, Johnson, Hernandez, & Avolio, 2013; Wang, Waldman, & Zhang, 2014). Especially in a military setting, leaders are most effective if they share the same lifestyle and risks as their subordinates (Matthews, 2014). When all goes well and the organization is thriving, people tend to perceive their leader as visionary, inspiring, and transformational.

A *transactional leader tries to make the organization more efficient at doing what it is already doing by providing rewards (mainly pay) for effective work.* Transactional leaders are often effective in organizations where activities stay the same from year to year (Lowe, Kroeck, & Sivasubramaniam, 1996). Someone can be either a transformational leader, a transactional leader, both, or neither.

---

in closing module 11.1

Work and Ambition

Unfortunately, many workers do the same job every day, with little motivation to work harder. However, the most productive people see their work as a competition. They want to make a better product, sell more of their product, write a better novel, or do whatever else they are doing better than anyone else, or at least better than their own previous performance. The best students have a similar ambition in their course work. This module has highlighted a few hints on how to facilitate the process, such as by combating the temptation to procrastinate.

Summary

- *Characteristics of motivated behaviors.* Motivated behaviors vary from time to time, from situation to situation, and from person to person. They persist until the individual reaches the goal. (page 345)
- *Motivation as drive reduction.* Some aspects of motivation can be described as drive reduction, but people strive for new experiences that do not reduce any apparent drive. (page 345)
- *Homeostasis and allostasis.* Many motivated behaviors tend to maintain body conditions and stimulation at a near-constant, or homeostatic, level. In addition, behaviors anticipate future needs. (page 346)
- *Motivation as incentive.* Motivations are partly under the control of incentives—external stimuli that pull us toward certain actions. Both drives and incentives control most motivated behaviors. (page 346)

- *Extrinsic and intrinsic motivations.* Motivations include the possible rewards and the joy of the task itself. (page 346)
- *Motivation conflict.* People seldom do anything for just one reason. In general, biological needs take priority over other motivations, but not always. (page 346)
- *Goal setting.* Setting a goal motivates strong effort if the goal is high but realistic. Other important factors include making a serious commitment to the goal, receiving feedback on progress, and believing that the goal will bring a fair reward. (page 347)
- *Making goals realistic.* People tend to underestimate how much time and effort they will need to achieve their goals. It is best to plan for more time and resources than seem necessary and to start as quickly as possible. (page 348)

- *Deadlines.* Deadlines motivate people to work harder. Setting deadlines for parts of an assignment can spread out the task. (page 348)
- *Overcoming procrastination.* People get started toward their goals if they set specific plans about what they will do, when, and where. Estimating your probability of doing something increases your chance of doing it. Making any kind of decision helps end procrastination. (page 349)
- *Delayed gratification.* People vary in whether they choose a larger reward later over a smaller one now. Children who can delay gratification show long-term advantages when they reach adolescence. It is often easier to choose the delayed reward if you make the choice far in advance. (page 349)
- *Overcoming temptations.* It is better to avoid tempting situations than to try to combat temptation. Resisting a temptation helps people to later resist the same type of temptation, but it often weakens their ability to resist other types. Seeing another person yield to temptation increases the risk of also yielding, unless one sees the other person as an outsider, different from oneself. A reminder about ethical norms decreases cheating in some situations. (page 350)
- *Job design.* The scientific-management approach emphasizes efforts to find the best, most efficient, safest way to do a job. According to the human-management approach, jobs should be made interesting enough to give workers a sense of achievement. (page 351)
- *Job satisfaction.* Job satisfaction is strongly correlated with an individual's interest in the job, and moderately correlated with good performance on the job. People with a happy disposition are more likely than others to be satisfied with their jobs, as are older workers in general. Job satisfaction also requires a perception that the pay scale is fair. (page 351)
- *Job burnout.* Some people have a long-lasting discouragement that alienates them from their job and their coworkers. (page 352)
- *Leadership.* The demands of leadership depend on the situation. Organizations generally work best if many people can take a leadership role, depending on the situation. When an organization thrives, its leader is perceived as visionary. Leaders perceived as using rewards to get employees to do their work efficiently are effective in situations when the business is stable. (page 353)

Key Terms

allostasis (page 346)

delay of gratification (page 349)

drive (page 345)

extrinsic motivation (page 346)

hierarchy of needs (page 347)

homeostasis (page 346)

human-relations approach (page 351)

incentive (page 346)

intrinsic motivation (page 346)

job burnout (page 352)

mere measurement effect (page 349)

motivation (page 345)

scientific-management approach (page 351)

self-actualization (page 347)

transactional leader (page 353)

transformational leader (page 353)

Review Questions

1. How does the concept of allostasis differ from homeostasis?
   (a) Allostasis pertains to how we maintain constancy within the body.
   (b) Allostasis pertains to how we make changes for new circumstances.
   (c) Allostasis emphasizes the importance of incentives.

2. Which of the following is NOT good advice about making a New Year's resolution?
   (a) Make your resolution realistic.
   (b) Make it general, such as "I will do my best."
   (c) Tell other people about your resolution.
   (d) Keep track of how successful you are in keeping your resolution.

3. If you are supervising employees who say they can finish a challenging job in six weeks, what kind of bonus should you promise them?
   (a) A bonus they can earn only by finishing within six weeks
   (b) A bonus they can earn by finishing within six weeks but also a not-quite-so-good bonus for finishing within eight weeks
   (c) A bonus they can earn regardless of when they finish

4. What is the usual consequence of resisting a temptation?
   (a) Regret at having resisted it
   (b) Increased probability of resisting the next temptation
   (c) Decreased probability of resisting the next temptation
   (d) A desire to brag about resisting temptation

5. Which of the following would increase your probability of contributing money to a charity?
   (a) Several weeks in advance, someone asks you to estimate your probability of contributing to the charity.
   (b) The person asking you for a contribution starts by telling you that you are a good person.
   (c) The person asking you for a contribution says your contribution is needed, because other people have not been contributing.

6. Which of these bits of advice is best for someone who is trying to resist a temptation?
   (a) Practice resisting various types of temptation.
   (b) Be confident of your ability to resist the temptation.
   (c) Watch what happens to other people who yield to temptation.
   (d) Remind yourself of ethical norms.

7. What are the main ways in which motivation affects job performance?
   (a) Extrinsic motivation increases both quality and quantity of performance.
   (b) Intrinsic motivation increases both quality and quantity of performance.
   (c) Extrinsic motivation mainly increases quantity, and intrinsic motivation mainly increases quality.
   (d) Extrinsic motivation mainly increases quality, and intrinsic motivation mainly increases quantity.

8. What is a transformational leader?
   (a) Someone who is seen as visionary and stimulating
   (b) Someone who makes an organization more efficient by proper rewards
   (c) Someone who is still learning how to be a leader
   (d) Someone who has recently changed his or her style of leadership

Answers: 1b, 2b, 3b, 4c, 5a, 6d, 7c, 8a.

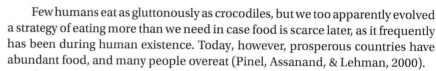

After studying this module, you should be able to:

- Name and briefly describe some short-term and long-term physiological influences on eating.
- Describe the role of the hypothalamus in food regulation.
- List examples of social influences on the amount eaten.
- Discuss possible causes of obesity.
- Define anorexia nervosa and bulimia nervosa and explain possible causes of each.

Small birds eat only what they need at the moment—mostly seeds and insects—storing almost no fat at all. Remaining as light as possible is important for flying away from predators. At the opposite extreme, predators ranging from lions to crocodiles to sharks have huge meals available when they catch something big, and nothing to eat on many other days. They eat as much as they can when they can, and then live off the stored fat during times without food. Their digestive systems are adapted to accept huge meals (Armstrong & Schindler, 2011).

Few humans eat as gluttonously as crocodiles, but we too apparently evolved a strategy of eating more than we need in case food is scarce later, as it frequently has been during human existence. Today, however, prosperous countries have abundant food, and many people overeat (Pinel, Assanand, & Lehman, 2000).

Our eating also depends on social motives. Imagine you visit your boyfriend's or girlfriend's family, and you want to make a good impression. "Dinner's ready!" You go to the dining room and find a huge meal, which your hosts clearly expect you to enjoy. Do you explain that you are not hungry because you made a pig of yourself at lunch? Probably not.

The Physiology of Hunger and Satiety

Hunger serves to keep fuel available for the body. How does your brain know how much fuel you need? The problem is more complex than keeping enough fuel in your car. You store fuel in your stomach, intestines, fat cells, liver cells, and bloodstream. Furthermore, each meal has different nutrients. It would be as if you were never sure how much fuel was already in your car's tank, or exactly what you were filling it with. The complexity of hunger requires multiple mechanisms to control intake.

Short-Term Regulation of Hunger

Ordinarily, the main factor for ending a meal is distension of the stomach and intestines. You feel full when your digestive system is full. The stomach signals its distension by nerves to the brain, and the intestines signal distension by releasing a hormone (Deutsch & Ahn, 1986; Gibbs, Young, & Smith, 1973). With familiar foods, you also calibrate approximately how much nutrition each bite contains (Deutsch & Gonzalez, 1980).

When the stomach is empty, it stimulates hunger by releasing the hormone *ghrelin* (GRELL-in). People who produce larger than average amounts of ghrelin are likely to overeat and become overweight (Karra et al., 2013). The other main factor inducing hunger is a drop in how much glucose enters the cells (see ▼ Figure 11.5). Glucose, *the most abundant sugar in the blood, is an important energy source for the body and by far the main energy source for the brain.* The body makes glucose from almost any food. If you eat too much, your body converts the excess into fats and other stored fuels. If you eat too little, you convert the stored fuels back into blood glucose. The flow of glucose from the blood into cells depends on insulin, a hormone released by the pancreas.

The hormone insulin *increases the flow of glucose and several other nutrients*

Mealtime is more than an opportunity to satisfy hunger: It is an occasion to share a pleasant experience with family or friends, to discuss the events of the day, and even to pass on cultural traditions from one generation to the next.

©Monkey Business Images/Shutterstock.com

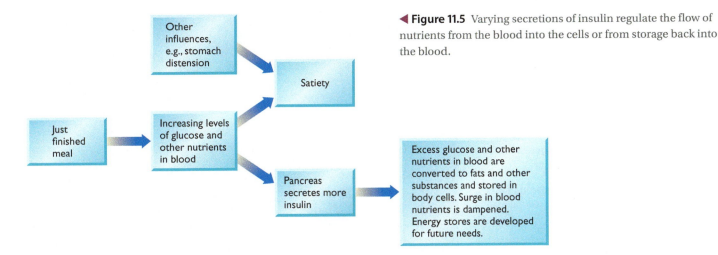

◀ **Figure 11.5** Varying secretions of insulin regulate the flow of nutrients from the blood into the cells or from storage back into the blood.

into body cells. At the beginning of a meal, before the nutrients begin to enter the blood, the brain sends messages to the pancreas to secrete insulin. Insulin promotes the movement of glucose and other nutrients out of the blood and into the cells that need fuel and into cells that store nutrients for future use.

As the meal continues, the digested food enters the blood, and almost as fast as it enters, insulin moves excess nutrients out of the blood and into the liver or fat cells. Hours after a meal, when blood glucose levels start to drop, the pancreas secretes another hormone, *glucagon,* that stimulates the liver to release stored glucose back into the blood.

As insulin levels rise and fall, hunger decreases and increases, as shown in ▶ Figure 11.6. Insulin affects hunger partly by controlling the flow of glucose and also stimulating neurons of the hypothalamus that signal satiety (Brüning et al., 2000).

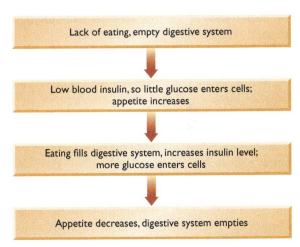

▲ **Figure 11.6** A feedback system between eating and insulin levels maintains homeostatic control of nutrition.

9. **Insulin levels fluctuate over the course of a day. Would they be higher in the middle of the day, when people tend to be hungry, or late at night, when most are less hungry?**

Answer

9. Insulin levels are higher in the middle of the day (LeMagnen, 1981). As a result, much of your meal is stored, and you become hungry again. At night, when insulin levels are lower, you draw from your supplies to make more glucose.

Long-Term Hunger Regulation

Stomach distension and the other mechanisms for ending a meal are far from perfect. For your next meal, you may eat a bit more or less than you need. If you misjudged consistently in the same direction, either you would become obese, or you would waste away.

You have long-term mechanisms to correct short-term errors. After overeating, you feel less hungry until you get back to your normal weight. If you eat too little, you feel hungrier than usual until you get back to normal. Most people's weight fluctuates from day to day but remains stable from month to month.

Your mean weight is called a set point—*a level that the body works to maintain* (see ▶ Figure 11.7). It's similar to the temperature at which you set the thermostat in your house. Maintaining constant body weight depends on *the hormone* leptin, *which the body's fat cells release in amounts proportional to their mass.* When the body gains fat, the extra leptin alters activity in neurons of the hypothalamus, causing meals to satisfy hunger

faster. Leptin is your fat cells' way to say, "The body has enough fat already, so eat less." Leptin also triggers the start of puberty: When the body reaches a certain weight, the increased leptin levels combine with other forces to induce the hormonal changes of puberty (Chehab, Mounzih, Lu, & Lim, 1997). If you lose weight, your fat cells produce less leptin, and your hunger increases.

Those few people who lack the genes to produce leptin become obese (Farooqi et al., 2001). Their brains get no signals from their fat supplies, so they feel as if they are starving. They also fail to enter puberty (Clément et al., 1998). Leptin injections greatly

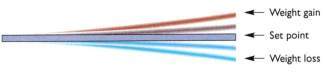

▲ **Figure 11.7** For most people, weight fluctuates around a set point, just as a diving board bounces up and down from a central position.

reduce obesity for these few people (Williamson et al., 2005). However, most obese people produce plenty of leptin but become less sensitive to it (Tups, 2009).

10. Over the past few decades, the average age of starting puberty has become younger. What is one explanation, based on this chapter?

Answer

10. People have been gaining weight and therefore producing more leptin. Leptin facilitates the onset of puberty.

Brain Mechanisms

Your appetite at any moment depends on the taste and appearance of the food, the contents of your stomach and intestines, the availability of glucose to the cells, and your body's fat supplies. It also depends on your health, body temperature, time of day, and social influences. Several parts of the hypothalamus integrate all this information and thereby determine your hunger level (see ▼ Figure 11.8).

Within the hypothalamus, an area called the arcuate nucleus has one set of neurons that receive hunger signals (e.g., "the food looks good" and "my stomach is empty") and other neurons that receive satiety signals (e.g., "my insulin level is high" and "my leptin level is high"). The output from the arcuate nucleus directs other parts of the hypothalamus to enhance or weaken salivation responses, swallowing, digestion, and the pleasure of eating (Mendieta-Zéron, López, & Diéguez, 2008). Damage in the hypothalamus impairs regulation of eating. ▲ Figure 11.9 shows an example of a rat with damage to one part of the hypothalamus, the ventromedial nucleus.

Reeves & Plum, "Hyperphagia, rage, and dementia accompanying a ventromedial hypothalamic neoplasm," Archives of Neurology 1969, Vol.20,no. 616-624.

▲ **Figure 11.9** A rat with a damaged ventromedial hypothalamus (left) has a constantly high insulin level that causes it to store most of its meal as fat. Because the nutrients do not circulate in the blood, the rat quickly becomes hungry again. This rat's excess fat prevents it from grooming its fur.

11. After damage to the ventromedial hypothalamus, an animal's weight eventually reaches a higher than usual level and then fluctuates around that amount. What has happened to the set point?

Answer

11. The set point increased.

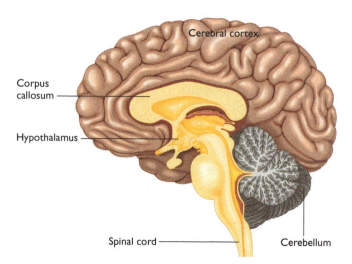

▲ **Figure 11.8** The hypothalamus, a small area on the underside of the brain, helps regulate eating, drinking, sexual behavior, and other motivated activities.

Labels: Cerebral cortex, Corpus callosum, Hypothalamus, Spinal cord, Cerebellum

iStockphoto.com/Lauri Patterson

One reason for the increased obesity in the United States over recent decades is the increase in restaurant portion sizes. Instead of a simple cheeseburger, you can now get a colossal sandwich with several meat patties and many add-ons.

Social and Cultural Influences on Eating

Insulin, leptin, and other physiological mechanisms are important, but social factors also have a major effect on what we eat, when we eat, and how much. If you eat while watching television, you tend to eat more than if you were paying full attention to your meal (van der Wal & van Dillen, 2013). When you dine with friends, on average you linger two or three times as long as you would if eating alone (Bell & Pliner, 2003), and you eat almost twice as much (de Castro, 2000). You eat a few more bites after you thought you were done, and then a few more, probably without realizing the other people's influence. Someone wants dessert, so you have one, too (Vartanian, Herman, & Wansink, 2008). Exceptions occur, of course, if you are dining with someone who might scold you for overeating (Herman, Roth, & Polivy, 2003).

Our expectations also influence our eating. Even the name of the food can influence appetite. What we now call Chilean sea bass used to be called Patagonian toothfish. Changing the name greatly increased sales. Another fish, orange roughy, used to be called "slimehead." Would you go to a restaurant and order a yummy plate of slimehead?

As an experiment, one restaurant gave every customer a free glass of wine. Half of them (chosen at random) were told it was from California (a state famous for fine wine), and the others were told it was from North Dakota (where the climate is unsuitable for growing grapes). Those who thought it was from California gave high ratings to the wine, the food, and the chef. Those who thought it was from North Dakota didn't like the wine or anything else, and mostly didn't think they would return to that restaurant (Wansink, Payne, & North, 2007).

Another influence is portion size. Over the years, portion sizes have been steadily increasing, especially in the United States (Rozin, Kabnick, Pete, Fischler, & Shields, 2003). If someone serves you a large meal, do you feel obligated to eat most of it? If you dine at an all-you-can-eat buffet (sometimes called an "all-night buffet"), do you try to get your money's worth? Researchers gave 50 percent off coupons to half the people, chosen at random, as they entered an all-you-can-eat pizza buffet. The restaurant staff recorded how much each person ate. On average, those paying full price ate a little more than four pizza slices each, and those paying half price ate slightly less than three slices each. Apparently, people ate less if they thought they had already had their money's worth (Just & Wansink, 2011).

People at a convention of nutrition experts (who you might think would know better) were asked to serve themselves ice cream. Those who were given a large bowl gave themselves almost one-third more ice cream than those given a smaller bowl (Wansink, van Ittersum, & Painter, 2006). In another fascinating study, customers at a movie theater were given a free box of popcorn, either a large box (120 g) or a huge one (240 g). Afterward, researchers weighed the remainder to determine how much people ate. People ate significantly more if they were given a huge box, even if the popcorn was very stale—14 days old! (Wansink & Kim, 2005).

However, it is unfair to put all the blame on restaurants with their large, high-calorie meals for making us fat. The people who eat large amounts of high-calorie foods in restaurants also generally eat large amounts of fats and sugars when they eat at home (Poti, Duffy, & Popkin, 2014).

Overeating has spread in other cultures, too, as they became, as some people put it, "Coca-Colonized" by Western cultures (Friedman, 2000). Consider the Native American Pima of Arizona (see ▼ Figure 11.10). Most Pima adults are obese, probably because of several genes (Norman et al., 1998), and most also have high blood pressure and type 2 diabetes. However, their ancestors—with the same genes—were not overweight. They ate the fruits and vegetables that grow in the Sonoran Desert, which are available only briefly during the year. To survive, they had to eat as much as they could whenever they could and conserve their energy as much as possible. Beginning in the 1940s, they switched to the same diet as other Americans, rich in calories and available year-round. The Pima still eat vigorously and conserve their energy by being relatively inactive, and the result is weight gain. This is a superb example of the combined influence of genetics and environment. The Pima weight problem depends on both their genes and the change in diet.

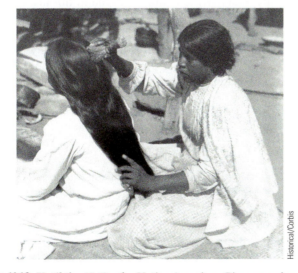 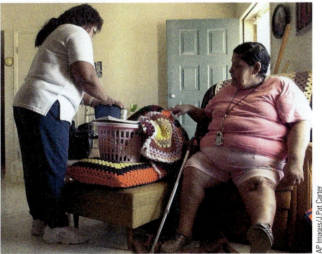

▲ **Figure 11.10** Until the 1940s, the Native American Pima remained thin eating their traditional diet of desert plants. Today, they eat the typical U.S. diet while remaining relatively inactive, and the result is high prevalence of obesity.

Eating Too Much or Too Little

Obesity has become widespread but not universal. Why do some people become obese, whereas others do not? At the other extreme, why do some people eat too little? Abnormal eating reflects a combination of physiological and social influences.

Obesity

Obesity is *the excessive accumulation of body fat.* Physicians calculate a *body mass index,* defined as weight in kilograms divided by height in meters squared (kg ÷ m²). A ratio over 25 is considered overweight, over 30 is obese, and over 40 is extremely obese (National Institutes of Health, 2000). About 30 percent of U.S. adults are obese, and another 35 percent are overweight (Marx, 2003). People become overweight because they take in more calories than they use. But *why* do they do that? A reason just mentioned was that we often have large portions of tasty food. Still, even with that food available, some people gain weight and others don't. What accounts for the difference?

The Limited Role of Emotional Disturbances

Many people, though not all, react to emotional distress by overeating. Conversely, when people

Many people with obesity feel distressed and suffer from low self-esteem because of how other people treat them.

feel good, they tend to eat less (Sproesser, Schupp, & Renner, 2014). Data from people who kept an eating diary showed that shortly after an important football or soccer game, fans of the losing team ate more than usual whereas fans of the winning team ate less (Cornil & Chandon, 2013).

Eating binges in response to stress are particularly common among people who have been dieting to lose weight (Greeno & Wing, 1994). Evidently, dieters actively inhibit their desire to eat until a stressful experience breaks their inhibitions and releases a pent-up desire to eat. If distress provokes eating binges, could it lead to obesity? A review of 15 studies found that being depressed increased one's probability of becoming obese, and being obese increased one's probability of becoming depressed (Luppino et al., 2010). However, both effects were small. In one study, 19 percent of the people with a history of serious depression became obese compared to 15 percent of other people (McIntyre, Konarski, Wilkins, Soczynska, & Kennedy, 2006).

Genetics and Energy Output

Many twin studies have shown a strong genetic influence on obesity, but the causes vary. Only about one percent of obesity cases can be traced to a single gene. Many genes—dozens at least—make small contributions to the probability of obesity. Epigenetic changes—that is, changes in the expression of genes—may be more important contributors than any common gene (Waalen, 2014). In any case, how do any of the genes affect behavior?

Many overweight people eat more than they admit, maybe even more than they admit to themselves. In one admirably simple study, researchers collected supermarket receipts and found that overweight families bought more food per person than average, especially high-fat food (Ransley et al., 2003).

In addition to consuming more energy, most overweight people have low energy output, including a low metabolic rate. Investigators compared the infants of 12 overweight mothers and 6 normal-weight mothers over their first year of life. The babies weighed about the same at birth, but 6 babies of the overweight mothers were inactive compared to the other babies and became overweight within their first year. During their first 3 months, they expended about 20 percent less energy per day than the average for other babies (Roberts, Savage, Coward, Chew, & Lucas, 1988).

Low energy expenditure is a good predictor of weight gain in adults as well. Researchers found that mildly obese people are less active than other people and spend more time sitting, even after they lose weight (J. A. Levine et al., 2005). Evidently, inactivity is a long-term habit, not just a reaction to being heavy.

Increased exercise is an important part of any weight-loss program, but one problem is that most people overestimate how many calories they burn in an exercise session. A further problem is that people who expect exercise to solve their weight problem continue to overeat (McFerran & Mukhopadhyay, 2013).

concept check

12. What evidence indicates important nongenetic influences on eating and weight gain?

Answer

12. People eat more when in social groups than when eating alone. People's expectations about foods, based on such things as the name of the food, influence intake. People eat more when portion sizes are larger.

Losing Weight

People trying to lose weight have a conflict between the motive to enjoy eating now and the motive to feel good about losing weight later. For people who struggle to lose weight, diets and most other interventions produce only small or temporary benefits. Nevertheless, advertisements for various diet programs report that many people lost a significant amount of weight. Let's assume they are telling the truth. If you hear that X number of people lost weight on some diet, how useful is that information? It's almost useless, unless you also know how long they kept it off and how many other people tried the diet without losing weight. A review of the literature found that about as many people gain weight on a diet as lose (Mann et al., 2007). More successful treatments require a change of lifestyle, including increased exercise as well as decreased eating. That combination does help, although still only 20 to 40 percent of participants keep weight off for two years or more (Powell, Calvin, & Calvin, 2007).

One of the main problems is that most people claiming to be on a diet don't stick to the diet closely, if at all. After years of big meals and low activity, it is difficult to shift to a sparse diet and heavy activity. When people gain weight, they become even more likely to give in to new temptations to overeat (Sutin et al., 2013). People are more likely to comply with recommendations for small changes: Consistently increase daily activity, drink water instead of soda drinks, eat healthier snacks, store tempting treats out of sight, and always leave at least a few bites on the plate (Poelman, de Vet, Velema, Seidell, & Steenhuis, 2014).

Weight-loss pills are only mildly effective, they produce unwanted side effects, and there is one further disadvantage: People taking these pills no longer feel much obligation to control their appetite on their own. In one study, people trying to lose weight all took a placebo, but researchers told half of them (chosen randomly) that it was a weight-loss pill. A little later, all of them had a chance to sample some candies for a "taste preference" test. Those who thought they had taken a weight-loss pill ate, on average, 29 percent more candies (Chang & Chiou, 2014).

Although the statistics about weight loss sound discouraging, you probably know people who did manage to lose weight and then kept it off. We hear about more dieting failures than successes for a simple reason: People who lose weight and keep it off don't keep seeking help (Schachter, 1982). The people who fail to lose weight show up at one weight-loss clinic after another. Therefore, the patients with difficulties seem disproportionately common.

Anorexia Nervosa

The Duchess of Windsor once said, "You can't be too rich or too thin." She may have been right about too rich, but she was wrong about too thin. Some people are so strongly motivated to be thin that they threaten their health.

Anorexia nervosa is *a condition in which someone intensely fears gaining weight and refuses to eat a normal amount. Anorexia* means "loss of appetite," but the problem is not really lack of hunger. Most people with anorexia enjoy the taste of food and even enjoy preparing it, but they express fear of eating and gaining weight. The term *nervosa*, meaning "for reasons of the nerves," distinguishes this condition from digestive disorders.

In the United States, anorexia nervosa occurs in a little less than 1 percent of women at some point in life and in about 0.3 percent of men (Hudson, Hiripi, Pope, & Kessler, 2007). It usually begins in the teenage years, and almost never after the mid-20s. Unlike other starving people, most people with anorexia run long distances, compete at sports, or are extremely active in other ways. They usually deny or understate their problem. Even when they become dangerously thin, they often describe themselves as "looking fat" and "needing to lose weight."

Anorexia nervosa stands out from other psychiatric problems in several ways. Anyone with depression, schizophrenia, alcohol or drug abuse, or an anxiety disorder has at least a 50-50 chance to have one or more of the others also, and the genes that predispose to one disorder predispose to others also (Caspi et al., 2014; Cross-Disorder Group of the Psychiatric Genomics Consortium, 2013). Most people with anorexia have a perfectionistic, obsessive-compulsive personality, but otherwise have no more likelihood of anxiety disorders than the rest of the population. The rates of alcohol or drug abuse are very low at the onset of anorexia, although they increase to normal levels later in life. Many people with anorexia do develop depression, and many therapists have therefore assumed that depression is the cause of anorexia. However, few people had depression or any other psychiatric disorder before becoming anorexic (Bühren et al., 2014; Zerwas et al., 2013), and the treatments appropriate for depression are not very effective for anorexia (Berkman, Lohr, & Bulik, 2007).

Another hypothesis is that weight loss is the primary problem, and that the emotional problems come later, as a result and not a cause. Most cases of anorexia begin with strict dieting, sometimes by ballet dancers, athletes, or others strongly motivated to lose weight. It is remarkably easy to get rats to produce several symptoms resembling anorexia, just by weight loss coupled with an opportunity for exercise: Restrict a rat to just one hour a day of eating, and provide a running wheel. Ordinarily, rats are inactive for an hour or two after eating, and then run in a wheel until their next meal. That pattern works fine if they can eat again in a few hours, but if they have to wait 23 hours, they lose weight. After losing much weight, they stop eating even when food is available, and unless rescued, they die of starvation. Why do they run so vigorously? Most laboratories are kept at about 21°C (70°F), comfortable for human experimenters, but cool for a rat, especially a few hours after its last meal. Digesting food generates heat, but within a couple hours after eating, a rat starts feeling cold, and it exercises to get warm. It has been known since the work of Curt Richter (1922) and confirmed more recently that rats in a warmer room run much less, and they maintain normal weight even if limited to one hour of eating per day (Cerrato, Carrera, Vazquez, Echevarria, & Gutiérrez, 2012; Gutiérrez, 2013).

Extending this idea to humans, the hypothesis is that someone diets to lose weight, then exercises extensively to maintain body temperature,

Place more food on the plate.

Place the plate on the scale and food on the plate.

Courtesy of Per Södersten

▲ **Figure 11.11** For treatment, someone with anorexia stays in a warm room, with restrictions on excessive activity. At mealtimes, a device connected to the plate monitors the rate of eating and compares it to the average rate. The patient tries to stay close to that rate.

loses further weight, and so forth. As with rats, people with anorexia are most active on the coldest days (Carrera et al., 2012). From this hypothesis, a treatment arose: Someone with anorexia stays in a warm room or wears a jacket to keep warm, and is required to limit physical activity. Medications (which are not very effective anyway) cease. At mealtimes, people with anorexia often fear that if they eat anything at all, they will overeat and become fat. To reduce this fear and maintain a sense of control, they eat with a scale under the plate, connected to a computer that reports the rate of eating compared to average (see ▲ Figure 11.11). Then eating is like a video game, as the person tries to eat at the recommended pace, neither too little nor too much. Six clinics using this approach with 571 patients, nearly all female, reported that 75 percent were fully recovered within 13 months of treatment, a much better success rate than with any other form of treatment (Bergh et al., 2013).

concept check

13. **What are the arguments against regarding anorexia as a result of emotional problems?**

Answer

13. Most people with anorexia had no psychiatric problems before developing anorexia. Standard forms of psychotherapy and drug therapies are not very effective with anorexia. Also, a treatment based on increasing body warmth and avoiding excessive exercise has been reported to be highly effective.

Bulimia Nervosa

Another eating disorder is bulimia nervosa (literally, "ox hunger for nervous reasons"), in which people—again, mostly women—alternate *between self-deprivation and periods of excessive eating, while feeling a loss of control*. To compensate after overeating, they may force themselves to vomit or use laxatives or enemas, or they may go through long periods of dieting and exercising. That is, they "binge and purge." In extreme eating binges, people have been known to consume up to 20,000 calories at a time (Schlesier-Stropp, 1984). A meal of a cheeseburger, fries, and a milkshake constitutes about 1,000 calories, so imagine eating that meal 20 times at one sitting. Most binges feature sweets and fats (Latner, 2003), so a better illustration of 20,000 calories would be 7 liters of chocolate fudge topping.

In the United States, about 1 percent of adult women and about 0.1 percent of adult men have bulimia nervosa (Hoek & van Hoeken, 2003). The incidence increased steadily for several decades, although it has leveled out since about 1990 (Crowther, Armey, Luce, Dalton, & Leahey, 2008). Most people recover fully or partly from bulimia, but many have lingering problems of depression (Berkman et al., 2007).

Culture is a major contributor. Bulimia was rare until the mid-1900s, and it has not been recorded in any cultures without a strong Western influence (Keel & Klump, 2003). Of course, eating binges are impossible without huge amounts of tasty food.

One hypothesis is that people with bulimia starve themselves for a while, fight their persistent feelings of hunger, and then go on an eating binge (Polivy & Herman, 1985). That idea may be on the right track, but it is incomplete. Of the people who starve themselves for days or weeks, some do develop eating binges, but others do not (Stice, 2002). The results may depend on what someone eats after a period of deprivation. Whereas most people end a fast by eating meat, fish, or eggs, people with bulimia start with desserts or snack foods (Latner, 2003).

In some ways, bulimia resembles drug addiction. The defining features of addiction are significant distress or harm, and repeated failures to quit despite a desire to do so. By that definition, people with bulimia nervosa can be described as food addicted (Meule, van Rezori, & Blechert, 2014). For some people, foods rich in fats and sugars have properties similar to addicting drugs (Hoebel, Rada, Mark, & Pothos, 1999). When someone consumes high quantities of these rich foods, especially right after a period of abstention, the result is a "high" similar to what addictive drugs provide.

To test this idea, researchers put laboratory rats on a regimen of no food for 12 hours, including the first 4 hours of their waking day, followed by a meal of sweet syrup. With each repetition of this schedule, the rats ate more and more of the syrup. Furthermore, if they were then deprived of this accustomed meal, they shook their heads and chattered their teeth much like rats going through morphine withdrawal (Colantuoni et al., 2001, 2002). The results suggest that a pattern of deprivation followed by overeating provides strong reinforcement that overwhelms other motivations.

14. **Under what circumstances would an eating binge produce an experience similar to taking an addictive drug?**

Answer

14. Eating a meal high in sugars and fats right after a deprivation period produces an experience comparable to those produced by addictive drugs.

---

in closing | module 11.2

The Complexities of Hunger

The research in this module underscores the idea that our motivations reflect a complex mixture of physiological, social, and cognitive forces. People eat for many reasons—physiological, cognitive, and social—and they abstain from food for many reasons also. To understand why people become overweight or anorexic, we have to address many types of influence. The general point is this: All our motivations interact and combine. We seldom do anything for just one reason.

Summary

- *Short-term regulation of hunger.* Meals end by several mechanisms, principally distension of the stomach and intestines. Hunger resumes when the cells begin to receive less glucose and other nutrients. The hormone insulin regulates the flow of nutrients from the blood to storage. (page 356)
- *Long-term regulation of hunger.* When someone gains weight, the fat cells increase release of leptin, which decreases hunger. When someone loses weight, fat cells decrease leptin release and hunger increases. (page 357)
- *Cognitive and social influences on eating.* People eat more in groups than when eating alone. They eat more, drink more, and enjoy their meal more when they have high expectations for the meal, based on such things as the name of the food or the supposed location of the winery. They eat more when they are offered larger portions. (page 359)
- *Obesity.* Some people are predisposed to obesity for genetic reasons. Obese people tend to be inactive and remain so even after losing weight. (page 360)

- *Weight-loss techniques.* Most people fail to lose weight for the long term by dieting, often because they fail to follow the diet. A combination of diet and exercise works better, although the success rate is still disappointing. (page 361)
- *Anorexia nervosa.* People suffering from anorexia nervosa deprive themselves of food, sometimes to a dangerous point. Most show extreme physical activity, which can be interpreted as a mechanism of temperature regulation. A therapy based on keeping the person warm, restricting exercise, and monitoring food intake has shown promise. (page 361)
- *Bulimia nervosa.* People suffering from bulimia nervosa alternate between periods of strict dieting and brief but spectacular eating binges. Bulimia has been compared to drug addiction. (page 362)

Key Terms

anorexia nervosa (page 361)

bulimia nervosa (page 362)

glucose (page 356)

insulin (page 356)

leptin (page 357)

obesity (page 360)

set point (page 357)

Review Questions

1. The main fuel of the body, especially the brain, is _____. The hormone that increases its flow into the cells is _____.
   (a) glucose . . . insulin
   (b) glucose . . . glucagon

   (c) protein . . . insulin
   (d) protein . . . glucagon

2. Which hormones strongly influence appetite?
   (a) Estradiol, testosterone, and epinephrine (adrenalin)
   (b) Insulin, epinephrine (adrenalin), and leptin
   (c) Estradiol, testosterone, and ghrelin
   (d) Insulin, ghrelin, and leptin

3. Which of these brain areas is considered most important for regulating hunger and satiety?
   (a) Hypothalamus
   (b) Corpus callosum
   (c) Locus coeruleus
   (d) Fusiform gyrus

4. Which of the following generally increases how much food people eat?
   (a) People eat more when they are alone.
   (b) People eat more when the weather is hot.
   (c) People eat more when offered a larger portion size.
   (d) People eat more if they have been inactive.

5. What led to significant weight gain among the Pimas?
   (a) A genetic change
   (b) Increased life stress
   (c) Decreased exercise
   (d) A change in diet

6. When a rat runs in a running wheel before a meal, what is the main motivation?
   (a) To increase salivation
   (b) To increase body strength
   (c) To keep warm
   (d) To increase appetite

7. Research on rats suggests that bulimia nervosa resembles what other condition?
   (a) Sleep apnea
   (b) Drug addiction
   (c) Bipolar disorder
   (d) Phobia

Answers: 1a, 2d, 3a, 4c, 5d, 6c, 7b.

module 11.3

Sexual Motivation

After studying this module, you should be able to:

- Describe the results of the Kinsey survey and other sex behavior surveys.

- State how AIDS can and cannot be transmitted between people.

- List the four stages of sexual arousal.

- Explain the roles of testosterone and estradiol in prenatal sexual development.

- Discuss the factors that cause an intersex appearance, and the policies for dealing with such cases.

- List differences between men and women with regard to sexual orientation.

- Evaluate evidence about possible influences on sexual orientation.

Alfred C. Kinsey was an outstanding interviewer who put people at ease so they could speak freely but he was also alert to probable lies.

Sexual motivation, like hunger, depends on both a physiological drive and incentives. Also like hunger, the sex drive increases during times of deprivation, at least up to a point, and people can inhibit the drive when they need to. However, the sex drive differs from hunger in important ways. We do not need to be around food to feel hungry, but many people need a partner to feel sexual arousal. We eat in public, but we have sexual activities in private.

Ultimately, hunger and sex serve important biological functions that we ordinarily don't even think about during the acts themselves. We evolved mechanisms that make us enjoy eating because eating keeps us alive. Similarly, we evolved mechanisms that make sex feel good because it leads to reproduction.

What Do People Do and How Often?

Researchers have many reasons for studying the frequency of various sexual behaviors. For example, if we want to predict the spread of AIDS, we need to know how many people are having unsafe sex and with how many partners. In addition to the scientific and medical reasons for studying sex, let's admit it: We're curious, aren't we?

The Kinsey Survey

The first important survey of human sexual behavior was conducted by Alfred C. Kinsey, an insect biologist who agreed to teach the biological portion of Indiana University's course on marriage. When he found that the library included little information about human sexuality, he conducted a survey. What started as a small-scale project for teaching purposes grew into a survey of 18,000 people.

Although Kinsey's sample was large, he obtained most of his interviews from members of cooperative organizations, ranging from fraternities to nunneries, mostly in the U.S. Midwest. Later researchers, trying harder to get representative samples of the population, obtained significantly different results.

Nevertheless, Kinsey did document the variability of human sexual behavior (Kinsey, Pomeroy, & Martin, 1948; Kinsey, Pomeroy, Martin, & Gebhard, 1953). He found some people who had rarely or never experienced orgasm. He also found a middle-aged man who reported an average of 4 or 5 orgasms per day (with a wide variety of male, female,

and animal partners) and several women who sometimes had 50 or more orgasms within 20 minutes.

Kinsey found that most people were unaware of how much sexual behavior varies. When he asked people whether they believed that "excessive masturbation" causes physical and mental illness, most said "yes." (In fact, it does not.) He then asked what

Sexual customs vary sharply from one society to another. At a Hmong festival, unmarried women toss tennis balls to potential suitors.

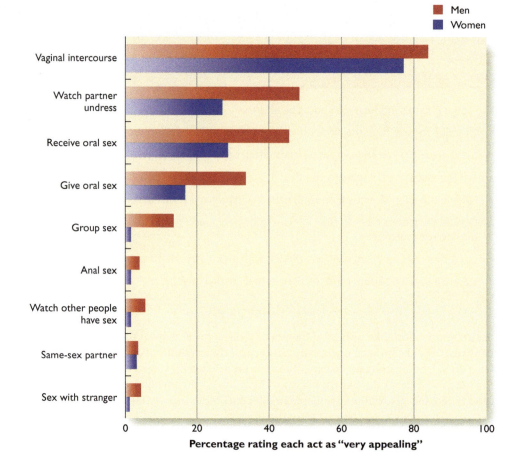

▶ **Figure 11.12** The percentage of U.S. adults who rate various sexual activities as "very appealing" as opposed to "somewhat appealing," "not appealing," or "not at all appealing." (Based on data of Laumann, Gagnon, Michael, & Michaels, 1994)

constitutes "excessive." For each person, excessive meant a little more than what he or she did. One young man who masturbated once a month said he thought three times a month would cause mental illness. A man who masturbated three times daily said he thought five times a day would be excessive. (In reaction, Kinsey defined *nymphomaniac* as "someone who wants sex more than you do.")

Later Surveys

Kinsey did not try to interview a random sample of the population because he assumed that most people would refuse to cooperate. He may have been right in the 1940s, but in later years, researchers identified random samples and got most people to cooperate (Fay, Turner, Klassen, & Gagnon, 1989; Laumann, Gagnon, Michael, & Michaels, 1994).

(Some advice if anyone ever asks you to participate in a sex survey: Legitimate researchers present their credentials to show their affiliation with a research institute. They also take precautions to guarantee the confidentiality of responses. Do not trust "researchers" who fail to show their credentials. Be wary of sex surveys by telephone. It is hard to distinguish a legitimate survey from an obscene phone call in disguise.)

A survey of a random sample of almost 3,500 U.S. adults (Laumann et al., 1994) explored what

people enjoy. ▲ Figure 11.12 shows the percentage of men and women who describe various sexual activities as "very appealing." The most popular sexual activity is vaginal intercourse, followed by watching one's partner undress and then by oral sex. Note an ambiguity: When 13 percent of men say they find group sex "very appealing," do they mean they have frequently enjoyed it or that they have fantasies about it?

Note that more men than women report enjoying every activity listed. A broader survey of 27,500 people found that in each of 29 countries, a higher percentage of men than women reported pleasure and satisfaction with their sex life (Laumann et al., 2006). However, that result may be misleading in several ways. Women who are in a committed, loving relationship report enjoying sex as much as men do (Conley, Moors, Matsick, Ziegler, & Valentine, 2011). Also, many men brag about their sexual activity, and some women understate their sexual interest (Alexander & Fisher, 2003).

▼ Figure 11.13 presents the results from a survey of nearly six thousand people in the United States. As the figure shows, frequency of sexual activity peaks in young adulthood and then declines, but even beyond age 70, nearly half of men and nearly a quarter of women remain sexually active (Herbenick et al., 2010). Another survey, including more than a thousand people, found that old people were, on average, as satisfied with their sex life as were young or middle-aged people. At all ages, the best predictor of sexual satisfaction was being in love with one's partner (Neto & Pinto, 2013).

Comparisons by Culture and Cohort

Sexual customs vary considerably among cultures and subcultures. A survey of four U.S. colleges found that the percentage of undergraduates who have had sexual intercourse ranged from 54 percent at one college to 90 percent at

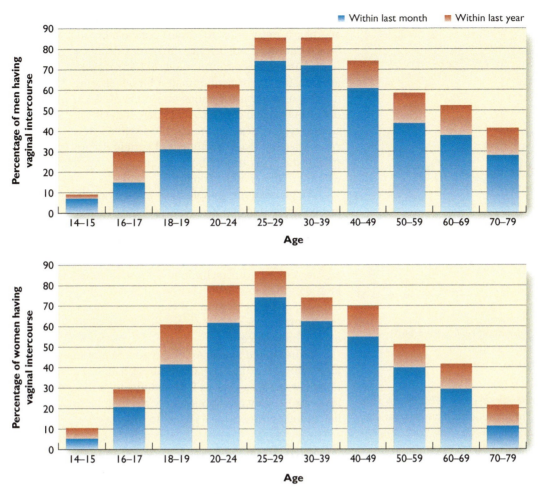

Figure 11.13 This graph shows the percentage of people who have had vaginal intercourse within the last month (blue) and within the last year (red). (From Herbenick et al., 2010)

another (Davidson, Moore, Earle, & Davis, 2008). At universities in Turkey, the percentage ranged from 32 percent of the men and 9 percent of the women at one college to 84 percent of the men and 33 percent of the women at another college (Askum & Ataca, 2007). Women in many countries in Asia and Africa have no sex before marriage, or no sex before becoming engaged. In all of these countries, more men than women have sex before marriage, some of them with prostitutes. In the United States and many countries in western Europe, men and women have sex, on average, 10 or more years before marriage (Parish, Laumann, & Mojola, 2007).

Customs also vary by historical era. For most of human history, premarital sex was uncommon and scandalous in much of the world. Since the early to mid-1900s, standards have changed in many countries. Previously, people reached puberty at about age 15 or 16 and typically got married before age 20. In the United States today, because of improved health and nutrition, the mean age of puberty is about 10 to 12, and for economic reasons, most people postpone marriage until 25 to 30. Reliable contraception prevents unwanted pregnancy. Also, movies and television bombard us with suggestions that other people are having casual sex with multiple partners. Under the circumstances, abstinence until marriage has become the exception, not the rule. Although most people still regard teenage sex as deviant, others are beginning to acknowledge that teenage sex with a romantic partner is not always harmful, and sometimes a positive experience. Nevertheless, "hooking up" without a strong personal attachment correlates

Cultures differ in their standards for public display of the human body.

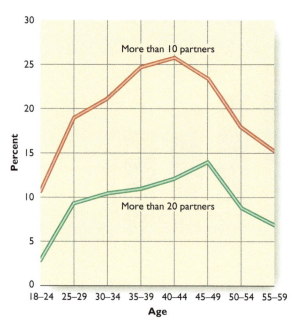

▲ Figure 11.14 The percentage of U.S. men and women reporting more than 10 or 20 sex partners in their lives. (Based on data of Laumann et al., 1994)

with depression, and adolescents who begin their sexual activity early in life tend to have less satisfactory attachments later in life (Harden, 2012, 2014).

A survey in the United States in the 1990s found the results shown in ▲ Figure 11.14 (Laumann et al., 1994). On the average, people in their 40s reported more lifetime sex partners than did people in their 50s. Obviously, your total cannot decrease as you get older. The 40-year-olds were different people from the 50-year-olds, and they had been young during an era of greater sexual freedom. This is a cohort effect, like the ones described in Chapter 5. Surveys in Finland, Brazil, and India have also found trends toward greater sexual freedom in more recent generations (Kontula & Haavio-Mannila, 2009; Paiva, Aranha, & Bastos, 2008; Sandhya, 2009).

15. Why did Kinsey's results differ from those of later surveys?

Answer

15. Kinsey interviewed a nonrandom, nonrepresentative sample of people.

Sexual Behavior in the Era of AIDS

During the 1980s, a new factor entered into people's sexual motivations: the fear of **acquired immune deficiency syndrome (AIDS)**, *a sexually transmitted disease that attacks the body's immune system.* For HIV (human immunodeficiency virus)—the virus

that causes AIDS—to spread from one person to another, it must enter the other person's blood. (The virus does not survive long outside body fluids.) The three common routes of transmission are transfusions of contaminated blood, sharing needles used for intravenous injections of illegal drugs, and sexual contact. Anal intercourse is the riskiest type of sexual contact, but vaginal intercourse is risky also. Touching and kissing do not spread the virus unless both people have open wounds that exchange blood.

For generations, people have known how to avoid contracting syphilis, gonorrhea, and other sexually transmitted diseases: Avoid sex with someone who might be infected, or use a condom. If people had consistently followed this advice, we could have eliminated those diseases long ago. The same advice is now offered to combat AIDS, and the amount of compliance varies. Information campaigns have produced clear benefits in many places.

In the United States, AIDS spread first among male homosexuals and later among heterosexuals. In parts of Africa, it affects up to one-fourth of the population between ages 15 and 50. One difficulty is that people remain symptom-free for years, so they can spread the virus long before they know they have it and before their partners have reason to suspect it.

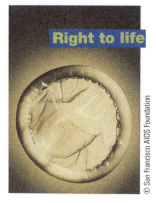

Right to life

To prevent AIDS, use condoms during sex and don't share injection needles. Advertisements such as this have prompted many people to change their behavior.

Sexual Arousal

Sexual motivation depends on both physiological and cognitive influences—that is, not just the "plumbing" of the body but also the presence of a suitable partner, a willingness to be aroused, and a lack of anxiety. William Masters and Virginia Johnson (1966) pioneered the study of human sexual response by actually observing hundreds of people masturbating or having sexual intercourse in a laboratory. They monitored people's physiological responses to sex, including heart rate, breathing, muscle tension, blood engorgement of the genitals and breasts, and nipple erection.

Their research was considered shocking, but it revolutionized our understanding in many ways. Sigmund Freud had argued (based on no data) that vaginal orgasms were superior to clitoral orgasms, which he regarded as immature. Masters and Johnson found that clitoral stimulation was almost always essential to a woman's response. Although Kinsey had reported women with multiple orgasms, most psychiatrists and physicians writing about sex (men, as you might guess) ignored or doubted those reports. Masters and Johnson found that many women can have prolonged orgasms or repeated orgasms within a short time, unlike men. Furthermore, many psychiatrists had written that women had sex mainly to have babies or to please their partners. Masters and Johnson demonstrated that women can enjoy sex as much as men do, and possibly more. Clearly, this was research with important consequences.

Masters and Johnson identified four physiological stages in sexual arousal (see ▼ Figure 11.15). During the first stage, *excitement,* a man's penis becomes erect and a woman's vagina becomes lubricated. Breathing is rapid and deep. Heart rate and blood pressure increase. Many people experience a flush of the skin, resembling a rash. Women's nipples become erect, and the breasts swell slightly for women who have not nursed a baby. Nervousness interferes with sexual excitement, as do coffee and other stimulant drugs.

Excitement remains high during the second stage, the *plateau,* which lasts for varying lengths of time depending on a person's age and the intensity of the

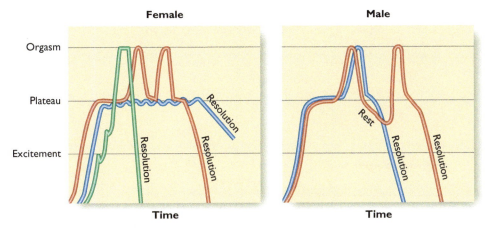

Female   **Male**

Orgasm

Plateau

Excitement

Resolution

Rest

Time   Time

▲ **Figure 11.15** Sexual arousal usually proceeds through four stages—excitement, plateau, orgasm, and resolution. Each color represents the response of a different individual. Note the variation. (After Masters & Johnson, 1966)

stimulation. Excitement builds until the third stage, a sudden release of tension known as *climax* or *orgasm,* which the entire body feels. The fourth and final stage is *resolution,* a state of relaxation. At orgasm, the pituitary gland releases the hormone *oxytocin,* which induces relaxation, decreased anxiety, and increased sense of attachment to one's partner.

As Figure 11.15 shows, the pattern of excitation varies from one person to another. During a given episode, a woman may experience no orgasm, one, or many. Most men have only one orgasm, although they can achieve orgasm again following a rest (or refractory) period that generally lasts at least an hour. Among both men and women, the intensity of an orgasm ranges from something like a sigh to an extremely intense experience.

Among men, levels of the hormone testosterone relate only weakly to frequency of sexual activity, but one interesting pattern has been reported: Single men have higher testosterone levels than men in a committed relationship, such as marriage, except for men who are in a committed relationship but still seeking additional sex partners (McIntyre, Gangestad, et al., 2006). How shall we interpret these results? One possibility is that when a man becomes completely faithful to a partner, his testosterone level drops. However, a longitudinal study supported a different interpretation: Men whose testosterone levels start lower are more likely to enter into a committed, monogamous relationship, whereas those with higher levels continue seeking multiple partners (van Anders & Watson, 2006). Women with relatively high testosterone levels also tend to seek multiple partners (van Anders, Hamilton, & Watson, 2007).

16. **Is testosterone related more to sexual activity or to seeking new partners? What evidence supports this conclusion?**

Answer

16. Testosterone relates more to seeking partners. Men with higher testosterone levels are less likely to commit themselves to a monogamous relationship.

Sexual Development and Identity

In the earliest stages of development, a human fetus has a unisex appearance (see ▼ **Figure 11.16**). One structure will eventually develop into either a penis or a clitoris. Another structure will become either a scrotum or labia. The direction of development depends on hormonal influences during prenatal

development (McFadden, 2008). Beginning in the seventh or eighth week after conception, *male fetuses secrete higher levels of the hormone* testosterone than do females (although both sexes produce some), and over the next couple of months, the testosterone causes the tiny fetal structures to grow into a penis and a scrotum. In female fetuses, with lower levels of testosterone, the structures develop into clitoris and labia instead. Levels of the *hormone* estradiol *increase more in females* than in males at this time. (*Estrogen* is a category of related chemicals, not a single chemical itself. Estradiol is an abundant type of estrogen.) Estradiol and related hormones are important for internal female development but have little effect on development of the external anatomy—penis versus clitoris and scrotum versus labia.

Remember: In humans and other mammals, high testosterone levels produce a male external anatomy, and low testosterone levels produce a female anatomy. Within normal limits, the amount of circulating estradiol does not determine male or female external appearance. Estradiol is important, however, for normal development of the internal female organs.

The sex hormones also influence brain development, producing differences between men and women in several brain areas. The mechanisms of hormonal effects differ among brain areas. In one part of the hypothalamus, hormones regulate a chemical called prostaglandin, which in turn influences the shape of neurons' dendrites (Lenz, Nugent, Haliyur, & McCarthy, 2013). In another part of the hypothalamus, hormones act by a chemical called PI3 kinase, and in still another area they act via histones (McCarthy & Arnold, 2011). Why is this important? Hormones are not the only influence on prostaglandins, PI3 kinase, or histones. Because the mechanism of sexual differentiation varies from one area to another, it is possible, in fact common, for someone's brain to be more strongly masculinized or feminized in one area than another. And that fits with what we know about behavior. You could be highly masculine or feminine in one aspect of your behavior, and not so much in another.

About 1 child in 2,000 is born with genitals that are hard to classify as male or female, and 1 or 2 in 100 have a slightly ambiguous external anatomy (Blackless et al., 2000). Ambiguity occurs most frequently if a genetic female's adrenal glands produce more than the usual amount of testosterone during a sensitive period before birth (Money & Ehrhardt, 1972). Less frequently, a genetic male develops an intermediate appearance because of an alteration

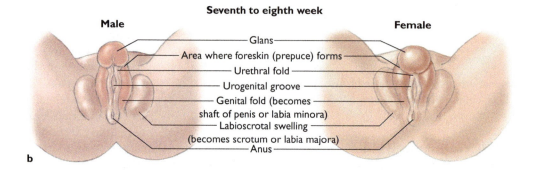

Undifferentiated before sixth week

Genital tubercle
Urethral fold
Urethral groove
Genital fold
Anal pit

a

Seventh to eighth week

Male   Female

Glans
Area where foreskin (prepuce) forms
Urethral fold
Urogenital groove
Genital fold (becomes
shaft of penis or labia minora)
Labioscrotal swelling
(becomes scrotum or labia majora)
Anus

b

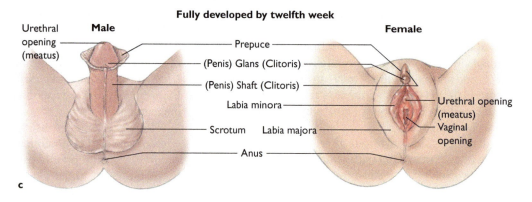

Fully developed by twelfth week

Urethral   Male   Female
opening
(meatus)   Prepuce
                  (Penis) Glans (Clitoris)
                  (Penis) Shaft (Clitoris)
                  Labia minora   Urethral opening
                                                  (meatus)
            Scrotum   Labia majora   Vaginal
                                                  opening
                  Anus

c

▲ **Figure 11.16** Male and female genitals look the same for the first six or seven weeks after conception (**a**). Differences emerge over the next couple of months (**b**) and are clear at birth (**c**).

in the gene that controls testosterone receptors (Misrahi et al., 1997). *People with an anatomy that appears intermediate between male and female* are known as intersexes. The Intersex Society of North America (**www.isna.org**) is devoted to increasing understanding and acceptance of people with ambiguous genitals.

How should parents and others treat intersexed people? For decades, the standard medical recommendation was, when in doubt, call the child female and perform surgery to make her anatomy look female. This surgery includes creating or lengthening a vagina and reducing the ambiguous penis/clitoris to the size of an average clitoris. Many cases require repeated surgery to obtain a satisfactory appearance.

This recommendation was based on the assumption that any child who looks like a girl and is treated like a girl will develop a female gender identity. Gender identity is *the sex that someone regards him- or herself as being.* No one ever had much evidence

for assuming that rearing was entirely responsible for gender identity, and later experience indicated otherwise. Follow-up studies on girls who were partly masculinized at birth but reared as females found that they are more likely than other girls to prefer boy-typical activities and interests during childhood and adolescence (Berenbaum, 1999; Berenbaum, Duck, & Bryk, 2000). The point is that we cannot count on rearing patterns to control psychological development.

Furthermore, the genital surgery—reducing or removing the penis/clitoris to make an intersex look more female—decreases sexual pleasure and the capacity for orgasm (Minto, Liao, Woodhouse, Ransley, & Creighton, 2003). An artificial vagina may be satisfactory to a male partner, but it provides no sensation or pleasure to the woman, and it requires frequent attention to prevent scar tissue. Many intersexes report that they never had a love relationship of any type (Jürgensen et al., 2013), and most of those who did, report very little sexual pleasure (van der Zwan et al., 2013). Finally, intersexed individuals object that, in many cases, physicians lied to them about the surgery and the reasons for it. Today, more and more physicians recommend that parents raise the child as the gender the genitals most resemble and perform no surgery until and unless the individual requests it. The result is that many are reared as males, instead of calling all such children female (Kolesinska et al., 2014). Many intersexed individuals prefer to remain as they are, without surgery (Dreger, 1998).

Caster Semenya, a South African runner, has won several medals in the Olympics and in World Championships. She was subjected to a test to prove that she is a woman, and was judged eligible.

Those who prefer partners of their own sex have a homosexual (gay or lesbian) orientation.

Homosexual or bisexual behavior has also been observed in hundreds of animal species. Biologists previously assumed that homosexuality occurred only in captive animals, only in hormonally abnormal animals, or only when partners of the other sex were unavailable, but the evidence has refuted these assumptions (Bagemihl, 1999). If "natural" means that something occurs in nature, then homosexuality is natural.

How many people have a homosexual orientation? You may have heard claims of "10 percent." That number is derived from Kinsey's report that about 13 percent of the men and 7 percent of the women he interviewed in the 1940s and 1950s stated a predominantly homosexual orientation. However, Kinsey did not have a random or representative sample, and later surveys have reported lower numbers.

In a random sample of 3,500 U.S. adults, 2.8 percent of men and 1.4 percent of women described themselves as having a homosexual (gay or lesbian) orientation (Laumann et al., 1994). As ▼ Figure 11.17 demonstrates, the results depend on the phrasing of the question. Many people who do not consider themselves gay or lesbian have had at least one adult homosexual experience, and more (especially males) had one in early adolescence (Laumann et al., 1994). Still more say they have felt some sexual attraction to a member of their own sex (Dickson, Paul, & Herbison, 2003).

Several other large surveys reported that 1 to 6 percent of U.S. men have a gay or bisexual orientation (Billy, Tanfer, Grady, & Klepinger, 1993; Cameron, Proctor, Coburn, & Forde, 1985; Fay et al., 1989).

 concept check

17. If a human fetus is exposed to very low levels of both testosterone and estradiol throughout prenatal development, how does the sexual anatomy appear?

18. If a human fetus is exposed to high levels of both testosterone and estradiol throughout prenatal development, how does the sexual anatomy appear?

Answers

17. A fetus exposed to very low levels of both testosterone and estradiol throughout prenatal development develops a female appearance.
18. A fetus exposed to high levels of both testosterone and estradiol develops a male appearance. High levels of testosterone lead to male anatomy; low levels lead to female anatomy. The level of estradiol is not decisive for external anatomy.

Sexual Orientation

Sexual orientation is *someone's tendency to respond sexually to male or female partners or both or neither.* People vary in their sexual orientations, just as they do in their food preferences and other motivations.

Attitudes toward homosexual relationships have varied among cultures and among historical eras.

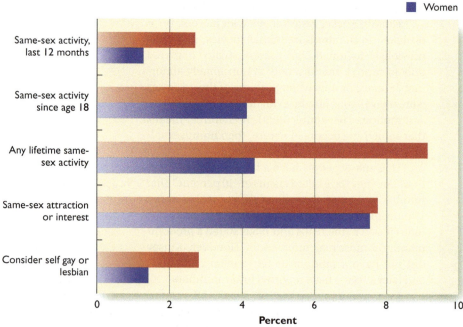

▲ **Figure 11.17** The percentages of U.S. adults who reported sexual activity or interest in sexual activity with people of their own sex. (Based on data of Laumann et al., 1994)

switching between homosexual and heterosexual attraction. However, a longitudinal study found that female bisexuality is usually stable over many years, and more women switch *to* bisexuality than *from* it (Diamond, 2008). The prevalence of male bisexuality depends on how we define it. If bisexuality consists merely in having had sex with at least one man and at least one woman, then it is fairly common. But if it consists of having sexual fantasies and sexual excitement toward both men and women, then it is considerably less common (Rieger, Chivers, & Bailey, 2005; Rieger et al., 2013).

Studying women's sexuality raised some interesting problems for researchers. Studying men is easy, because penis erection is synonymous with sexual arousal. To find out whether a man is sexually excited by males or females, attach a device to his penis and measure erections while he views photos or films of naked men or women. If you want to know whether someone might be prone to sadistic sex, show pictures of sadistic sex and measure a possible erection (Seto, Lalumière, Harris, & Chivers, 2012). So, researchers tested women by measuring vaginal secretions in response to pornographic films. Most women showed about equal responses to depictions of naked men

Surveys in other countries have reported similar or slightly lower percentages, as shown in ▼ Figure 11.18 (Izazola-Licea, Gortmaker, Tolbert, De Gruttola, & Mann, 2000; Sandfort, de Graaf, Bijl, & Schnabel, 2001; Spira & Bajos, 1993; Wellings, Field, Johnson, & Wadsworth, 1994).

Differences between Men and Women

Sexual orientation differs on the average between men and women in several regards. Most men become aware of being homosexual or heterosexual by early adolescence, and later changes are rare. Most (not all) homosexual men have a history of childhood "gender-nonconforming" (i.e., feminine-type) behaviors (Rieger, Linsenmeier, Gygax, & Bailey, 2008), which observers confirmed by watching the family's home videos. In contrast, a fair number of women develop a homosexual (lesbian) orientation in young adulthood without any previous indications (Diamond, 2007). Girls' early gender-nonconforming (i.e., masculine-type) behaviors are relatively poor predictors of sexual orientation in adulthood (Udry & Chantala, 2006).

Also, women are more likely than men to experience some sexual attraction to both men and women. Psychologists used to think that bisexuality (*attraction to both sexes*) was just a temporary transition by someone

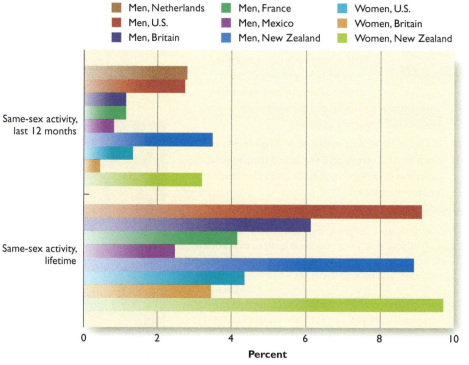

▲ **Figure 11.18** Comparisons of the results of surveys conducted in six countries, in which people were asked about homosexual experiences. (Based on data of Dickson, Paul, & Herbison, 2003; Izazola-Licea, Gortmaker, Tolbert, De Gruttola, & Mann, 2000; Laumann, Gagnon, Michael, & Michaels, 1994; Sandfort, de Graaf, Bijl, & Schnabel, 2001; Spira & Bajos, 1993; Wellings, Field, Johnson, & Wadsworth, 1994)

or women, regardless of whether they described themselves as heterosexual or lesbian, and despite protestations in some cases that they didn't enjoy any of the pictures (Chivers, Rieger, Latty, & Bailey, 2004; Peterson, Janssen, & Laan, 2010). At first, researchers were inclined to trust the physiological responses, suggesting that nearly all women are at least potentially bisexual. But then later research found that women also produced vaginal secretions in response to descriptions of violent rape (Suschinsky & Lalumière, 2011). Evidently vaginal secretions are not synonymous with sexual arousal for women, the way penis erections are for men. The researchers speculated that vaginal secretions may be a defensive reaction to prepare the woman for sexual contact, regardless of whether or not it is voluntary.

19. What are some of the ways in which men's sexuality differs from women's?

Answer

19. Nearly all men identify their sexual orientation early and cannot imagine switching. Some women discover their sexual orientation later, and a fair number have a consistent bisexual response. Measuring penis erections can accurately indicate a man's sexual interest, but vaginal secretions are not a dependable way to measure a woman's sexual interest.

Possible Influences on Sexual Orientation

Why are some people heterosexual and others homosexual? The available research suggests that genetic factors contribute to sexual orientation for both men and women. ▼ Figure 11.19 shows the results of studies concerning homosexuality in twins and other relatives of adult gays and lesbians (Bailey & Pillard, 1991; Bailey, Pillard, Neale, & Agyei, 1993). Note that homosexuality is more prevalent in their monozygotic (identical) twins than in their dizygotic (fraternal) twins. Another study with a smaller sample showed the same trends

(Kendler, Thornton, Gilman, & Kessler, 2000). However, a Swedish study that asked about "any homosexual activity" rather than sexual orientation found a smaller, less impressive genetic influence (Långström, Rahman, Carlström, & Lichtenstein, 2010). The conclusion from these studies and others is that genes do influence sexual orientation, but the magnitude of the influence is uncertain.

A study published in 1993 reported a link between homosexuality and a gene on the X chromosome, indicating inheritance from the mother's side of the family (Hamer, Hu, Magnuson, Hu, & Pattatucci, 1993). Several later studies failed to replicate this finding, but a large, more recent study again linked homosexuality to that gene, although the effect was small (Sanders et al., 2015).

The data on genetics raise an evolutionary question: How could a gene that increases homosexuality be widespread? Any gene that decreases the probability of reproducing becomes rare. One hypothesis is that homosexual people who have no children of their own might help their brothers and sisters rear children, thus passing on some of their genes. Most gay men are not especially helpful to their relatives in the United States, but they are more helpful than average in Samoa (Bobrow & Bailey, 2001; Vasey & VanderLaan, 2010). Another idea is that relatives of gay men may have larger than average families (Camperio-Ciani, Corna, & Capiluppi, 2004; Schwartz et al., 2010). However, a common estimate is that the

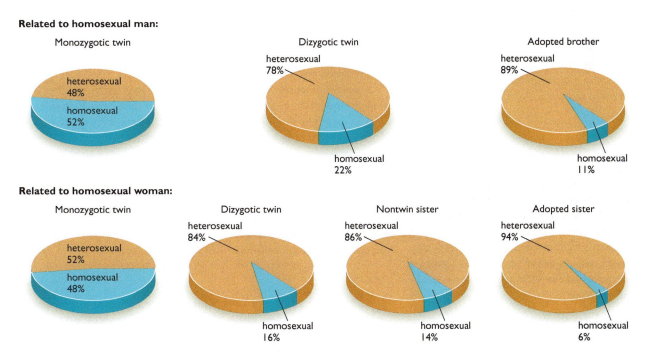

▲ **Figure 11.19** The probability of a homosexual orientation is higher among monozygotic twins of adult homosexuals than among their dizygotic twins. The probability is higher among dizygotic twins than among adopted brothers or sisters who grew up together. These data suggest a genetic role in sexual orientation. (Based on results of Bailey & Pillard, 1991; Bailey, Pillard, Neale, & Agyei, 1993)

average homosexual man has one-fifth as many children as the average heterosexual man, and it would be surprising if the brothers and sisters have enough extra children to offset this decrease. Another possibility is that sexual orientation depends on epigenetics—the activation or inactivation of a gene rather than a genetic mutation (Rice, Friberg, & Gavrilets, 2012).

Another factor in sexual orientation is biological but not genetic: The probability of a homosexual orientation is slightly elevated among men who have an older brother. Having an older sister doesn't make a difference, nor does having an older adopted brother. It also doesn't make any difference whether the older brother lived in the same house with the younger brother or somewhere else. What matters is whether the mother had previously given birth to another son (Bogaert, 2006). One hypothesis to explain this tendency is that the first son sometimes causes the mother's immune system to build up antibodies that alter development of later sons (Bogaert, 2003).

Regardless of whether the original basis is genetics, prenatal environment, or something else, the question arises of how the body differs. Adult hormone levels are *not* decisive. Most adult homosexual people have normal levels of testosterone and estradiol. Altering someone's hormone levels alters the strength of the sex drive but not sexual orientation (Tuiten et al., 2000). By analogy, changing your insulin or glucose levels affects your hunger but has little effect on what you consider good food.

However, it is possible that prenatal sex hormones influence later sexual orientation (McFadden, 2008). Presumably, if they do, they have some effect on the brain. One widely quoted and often misunderstood study reported a small but measurable difference between the brains of homosexual and heterosexual men. Let's examine the evidence.

© S. LeVay, 1991, "A Difference in Hypothalamic Structure Between Heterosexual & Homosexual Men," Science 253, 2034-1037

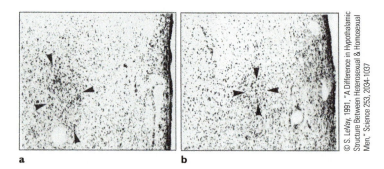

▲ **Figure 11.20** One section of the anterior hypothalamus (marked by arrows) is larger on average in the brains of heterosexual men (**a**) than in the brains of homosexual men (**b**) or heterosexual women (LeVay, 1991). Review Figure 11.8 for the location of the hypothalamus.

women. No brains of homosexual women were available. LeVay measured the sizes of four clusters of neurons in the anterior hypothalamus, including two clusters for which sex differences are common and two that are the same between the sexes.

Results Three of the four neuron clusters did not consistently vary in size among the groups LeVay studied. However, area INAH3 was on the average about twice as large in heterosexual men as it was in homosexual men and about the same size in homosexual men as in heterosexual women. ▲ Figure 11.20 shows results for two representative individuals. The size of this area was about the same in heterosexual men who died of AIDS as in heterosexual men who died of other causes, so AIDS probably did not control the size of this area.

Interpretation These results suggest that the size of the INAH3 area may relate to heterosexual versus homosexual orientation, on average. Note, however, the variation within each group. The anatomy does not correlate perfectly with behavior.

Like most studies, this one has its limitations: We do not know whether the people that LeVay studied were typical of others. One later study found that the INAH3 of homosexual men was intermediate in size between that of heterosexual men and heterosexual women (Byne et al., 2001). That study extended our knowledge by finding that the INAH3 varied among people because of differences in the size of neurons, not the number of neurons.

A major limitation is that LeVay's study does not tell us whether brain anatomy influenced people's sexual orientation or whether their sexual activities altered brain anatomy. Extensive experience modifies brain anatomy, even in adults.

So where does the research leave us? The evidence points to both genetics and prenatal environment, which probably alter certain aspects of brain anatomy in small ways. However, we need to know far more about how these biological factors interact with experience. At this point, we don't even know what kinds of experience are most relevant.

Uncertainty and tentative conclusions are not unusual in psychology. If you decide to become a psychologist, you will need to get used to the words *maybe* and *probably*. Most psychologists avoid the word *prove*. Results merely increase or decrease their confidence in a conclusion.

what's the evidence?

Sexual Orientation and Brain Anatomy

Animal studies demonstrated that one section of the anterior hypothalamus is generally larger in males than in females. This brain area is necessary for the display of male-typical sexual activity in many mammalian species, and its size depends on prenatal hormones. Might part of the anterior hypothalamus differ between homosexual and heterosexual men?

Hypothesis INAH3, a cluster of neurons in the anterior hypothalamus, will be larger on average in the brains of heterosexual than homosexual men or heterosexual women.

Method Simon LeVay (1991) examined the brains of 41 adults who died at ages 26 to 59. AIDS was the cause of death for all 19 of the homosexual men in the study, 6 of the 16 heterosexual men, and 1 of the 6 heterosexual

concept check

20. Most studies find that gay men have approximately the same levels of testosterone in their blood as heterosexual men of the same age. Do such results conflict with the suggestion that prenatal hormonal conditions can predispose certain men to homosexuality?

Answer

20. Not necessarily. The suggestion is that prenatal hormones can alter early brain development. In adulthood, hormone levels are normal, but certain aspects of brain development have already been determined.

The Biology and Sociology of Sex

Studies of sexual motivation remind us that important motives have multiple determinants, both biological and social. We engage in sexual activity because it feels good, and we have evolved mechanisms that make it feel good because sex leads to reproduction. We also engage in sexual activity because it cements a relationship with another person. Sex is one of the most powerful ways of drawing people together or tearing a relationship apart.

Society regulates sexual behavior strictly. The rules vary from one culture to another, but every culture has definite expectations about what people will do, when, and with whom. In short, we cannot make much sense of complex human behaviors without considering a range of biological and social influences.

Summary

- *Variability in human sexual behavior.* Alfred Kinsey, who conducted the first extensive survey of human sexual behavior, found that sexual activity varies more widely than most people realize. (page 365)
- *More recent surveys.* Both men and women cite vaginal intercourse as their most preferred sexual activity. Most people remain sexually active throughout life if they remain healthy and have a loving partner. (page 366)
- *Sexual arousal.* Sexual arousal proceeds through four stages: excitement, plateau, orgasm, and resolution. (page 368)
- *Development of genitals.* In the early stages of development, the human fetus possesses anatomical structures that may develop into either male genitals (if testosterone levels are high enough) or female genitals (if testosterone levels are lower). (page 369)
- *Prevalence of homosexuality.* According to surveys in several countries, 1 to 6 percent of adult men and somewhat fewer

women regard themselves as primarily or exclusively homosexual. Sexual orientation varies in degree from exclusively homosexual to exclusively heterosexual with intermediate gradations. (page 371)
- *Differences between men and women.* Bisexual orientation is more common in women than men. Measurements of penis erection accurately gauge a man's sexual interest, but vaginal secretions do not measure a woman's sexual interest. (page 372)
- *Origins of sexual orientation.* Genetic influences and prenatal environment affect sexual orientation. On the average, heterosexual and homosexual men differ in the size of a structure in the hypothalamus that contributes to certain aspects of sexual behavior. Less is known about the role of experience in the development of sexual orientation. (page 373)

Key Terms

acquired immune deficiency syndrome (AIDS) (page 368)

bisexuality (page 372)

estradiol (page 369)

gender identity (page 370)

intersexes (page 370)

sexual orientation (page 371)

testosterone (page 369)

Review Questions

1. In one survey, 40-year-olds recalled more lifetime sex partners than did 50-year-olds. What is the most likely explanation?
    (a) A difference between cohorts
    (b) Memory decay in old age
    (c) Decreased sex drive as people grow older
    (d) Different definitions of the term *sex partner*

2. Women differ most strongly from men, on average, in which of these aspects of sexual experience?
    (a) Men go through four stages of sexual arousal, whereas women go through three.

    (b) Women go through four stages of sexual arousal, whereas men go through three.
    (c) Women are more likely to experience more than one orgasm in a short time.
    (d) Men are more likely to experience more than one orgasm in a short time.

3. Which of the following results in a child with an "intersex" appearance of the genitals?
    (a) Exposure of a female fetus to higher than average levels of testosterone

(b) Exposure of a male fetus to higher than average levels of estradiol

(c) Absence of the Y chromosome

(d) Stressful experiences to the mother during pregnancy

4. Although Alfred Kinsey reported that 13 percent of men and 7 percent of women had a predominantly homosexual orientation; later surveys reported much lower numbers. Why?

(a) The prevalence of homosexuality has decreased over the last several decades.

(b) Kinsey lied about his results.

(c) Kinsey did not interview a representative sample of the population.

(d) The definition of homosexuality has changed over time.

5. In which of these ways do male homosexuals differ, on average, from male heterosexuals?

(a) Concentration of testosterone in the blood and brain

(b) Concentration of estradiol in the blood and brain

(c) Anatomy of one part of the hypothalamus

(d) Number of older sisters

Answers: 1a, 2c, 3a, 4c, 5c.

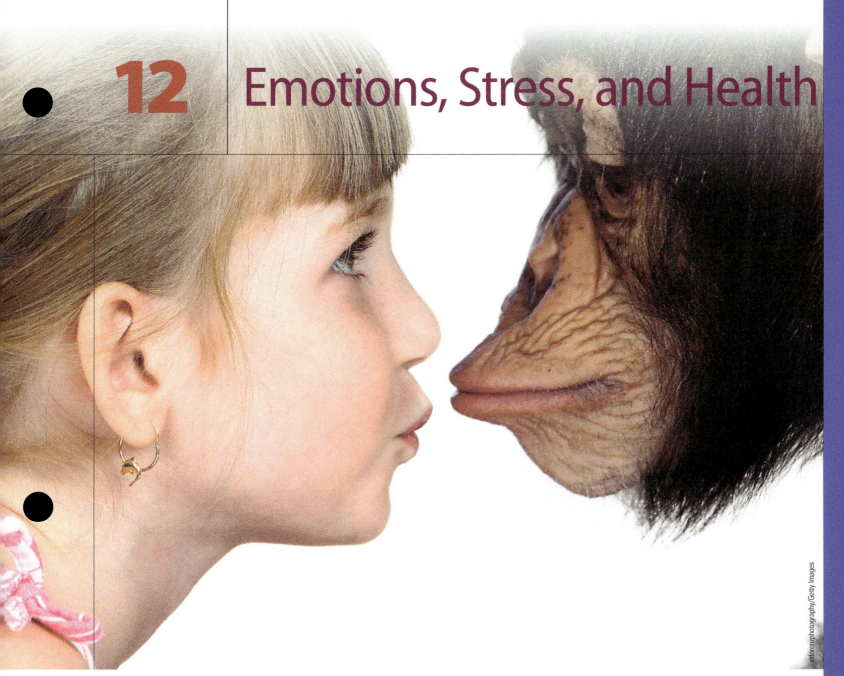

12 Emotions, Stress, and Health

milorenzphotography/Getty Images

Would you make more intelligent decisions if you could suppress your emotions, like the fictional character Spock? After brain damage that impairs emotion, people make worse than average decisions.

Suppose your romantic partner asks, "How much do you love me?" You reply, "Oh, compared to other loving couples, probably about average." "What?" your partner screams. "Average! Did you say *average*?" You are in deep trouble, even though your answer was probably true. (It is for most people. That's what "average" means!)

If that was the wrong answer, what would be better? "Forty-two cubic meters per second"? No, we don't measure love in physical units. So instead, you say, "I love you more than you can possibly imagine. More than any other person has ever loved." That was a good answer, and your partner is happy, even though the answer is almost certainly false. You get away with that answer because there is no way to check whether it is true.

When we are talking about emotions, measurement is a serious problem. Psychologists make reasonably good measurements of sensation, perception, learning, memory, and cognition. As we now move to emotion, social behavior, and personality, the measurement problems become greater, and consequently, the progress has been slower. In this chapter, we consider what psychologists have learned so far about emotions despite the difficulties.

module 12.1

The Nature of Emotion

After studying this module, you should be able to:

- Describe methods of measuring emotions, including the strengths and weaknesses of each method.
- Evaluate the James-Lange theory of emotions, and the evidence relating to it.
- Evaluate the Schachter and Singer theory, and the evidence relating to it.
- Discuss whether it makes sense to distinguish a few "basic" emotions.
- Describe an alternative to the idea of basic emotions.
- Discuss the role of emotions in moral reasoning.
- Define emotional intelligence and describe evidence relating to it.

Imagine trying to list all the emotions you feel during a day. You might include frightened, angry, sad, joyful, disgusted, worried, bored, ashamed, frustrated, contemptuous, embarrassed, surprised, proud, and confused. But which of those states are really emotions? And how many are *different* emotions instead of overlapping or synonymous conditions?

Defining the term *emotion* is difficult. Psychologists usually define it in terms of a combination of cognitions, physiology, feelings, and actions (Keltner & Shiota, 2003; Plutchik, 1982). For example, you might have the *cognition* "he was unfair to me," *physiological* changes that include increased heart rate, a *feeling* you call anger, and *behaviors* such as a clenched fist. However, that definition implies that the four components always occur together. Do they? Don't you sometimes feel fear, anger, or other emotions without knowing why?

Furthermore, it is uncertain that emotion is a natural category at all. Lisa Feldman Barrett (2012) has argued that emotions are a category that we find useful, but only in the same way that we find "weeds" to be a useful category. Nature does not distinguish between emotions and motivations any more than it does between flowers and weeds.

Measuring Emotions

Research progress depends on good measurement. Psychologists measure emotions by self-reports, behavioral observations, and physiological measures. Each method has its strengths and weaknesses.

Self-Reports

Psychologists most often measure emotions by asking people how happy they are, how nervous, and so forth. Self-reports are quick and easy, but their accuracy is limited. If you rated your happiness 4 yesterday and 7 today, it seems clear that you have become happier. But if your friend rates her happiness 6 today, are you happier today than she is? Maybe, maybe not. People rate their happiness or other emotions by comparison to how they usually feel, not in comparison to how others feel.

Linda Bartoshuk (2014) has suggested a method that offers some promise. Instead of asking for a numerical rating of an emotion, offer tones varying in loudness and ask which loudness corresponds to your current level of happiness (or sadness, anger, or whatever). For people who hear equally well, the result may be a more accurate gauge of emotions.

Behavioral Observations

We infer emotion from people's behavior and its context. If we see someone shriek and run away, we infer fear. When you were an infant, your parents must have inferred your emotions before you could report them verbally. They had to in order to teach you the words for emotions! At some point, you screamed and someone said you were "afraid." At another time, you smiled and someone said you were "happy."

We especially watch facial expressions. People sometimes control their expressions voluntarily. However, *very brief, sudden emotional expressions*, called microexpressions, are harder to control. For example, someone who is pretending to be calm or happy may show occasional brief signs of anger, fear, or sadness (Ekman, 2001). With practice (or a videotape that can be played slowly), psychologists infer emotions that people would like to hide. However, microexpressions are too infrequent to be a major source of information.

Physiological Measures

Originally, the term *emotion* referred to turbulent motion. Centuries ago, people described thunder as an "emotion of the atmosphere." Eventually, people

Ordinarily, an emotional state elicits a tendency toward vigorous action, even if we suppress that tendency. Here, a soldier disarms a mine.

▶ Figure 12.1 The autonomic nervous system consists of the sympathetic and parasympathetic nervous systems, which sometimes act in opposing ways and sometimes cooperate. The sympathetic nervous system readies the body for emergency action. The parasympathetic nervous system supports digestive and other nonemergency functions.

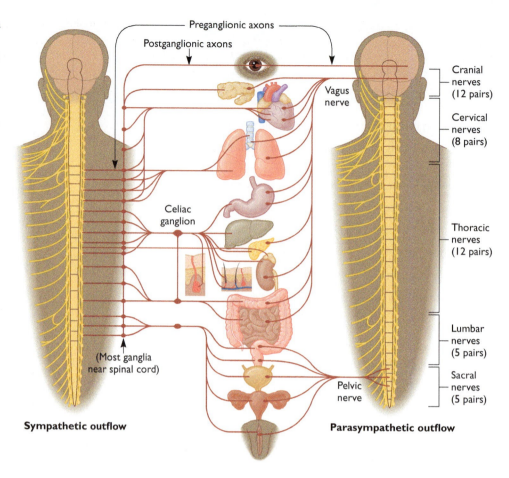

Preganglionic axons

Postganglionic axons

Vagus nerve

Celiac ganglion

(Most ganglia near spinal cord)

Pelvic nerve

Cranial nerves (12 pairs)

Cervical nerves (8 pairs)

Thoracic nerves (12 pairs)

Lumbar nerves (5 pairs)

Sacral nerves (5 pairs)

Sympathetic outflow

Parasympathetic outflow

limited the term to body motions and their associated feelings, but the idea still includes turbulent arousal.

Any stimulus that arouses emotion alters the activity of the autonomic nervous system, *the section of the nervous system that controls the organs* such as the heart and intestines. The word *autonomic* means "independent" (autonomous). Biologists once believed that the autonomic nervous system was independent of the brain and spinal cord. We now know that the brain and spinal cord regulate the autonomic nervous system, but the term *autonomic* remains.

The autonomic nervous system consists of the sympathetic and the parasympathetic nervous systems (see ▲ Figure 12.1). *Chains of neuron clusters just to the left and right of the spinal cord* comprise the sympathetic nervous system, *which arouses the body for vigorous action.* It is often called the "fight-or-flight" system because it increases your heart rate, breathing rate, sweating, and flow of epinephrine (EP-i-NEF-rin; also known as adrenaline), thereby preparing you for vigorous activity. Different situations activate different parts of the sympathetic nervous system to facilitate different kinds of activity.

The sympathetic nervous system prepares the body for a vigorous burst of activity.

The parasympathetic nervous system consists of *neurons whose axons extend from the medulla* (see Figure 12.1) *and the lower part of the spinal cord to neuron clusters near the organs. The parasympathetic nervous system decreases the heart rate and promotes digestion and other nonemergency functions.* Both the sympathetic and parasympathetic systems send axons to the heart, the digestive system, and most other organs. A few organs, such as the adrenal gland, receive only sympathetic input.

Both systems are constantly active, although one system can temporarily dominate. If you spot danger at a distance (in either time or space), you pay attention to it with mainly parasympathetic activity. If the danger is close enough to require action, you shift to vigorous sympathetic activity (Löw, Lang, Smith, & Bradley, 2008). Many situations activate parts of both systems (Berntson, Cacioppo, & Quigley, 1993). Some emergency situations increase your heart rate and sweating (sympathetic responses) and also promote bowel and bladder evacuation (parasympathetic responses). Have you ever been so frightened that you thought you might lose your bladder control?

To measure emotion, researchers measure sympathetic nervous system arousal as indicated by heart rate, breathing rate, or momentary changes in the electrical conductivity across the skin. However, remember that the sympathetic nervous system is the fight-*or*-flight system, so its responses could indicate anger, fear, or any other intense emotion. Physiological measurements do not tell us *which* emotion someone is feeling.

1. **Why should we not insist on verbal reports to infer or measure emotions?**

Answer

1. It would be impossible to teach a child (or anyone else) the words for emotions unless we had already inferred the emotions from the individual's behavior.

Emotion, Arousal, and Action

How do emotional cognitions, feelings, behavior, and arousal relate to one another? William James, the founder of American psychology, proposed one of psychology's first theories.

The James-Lange Theory of Emotions

According to common sense, you feel sad and therefore you cry. You become afraid and therefore you tremble. You feel angry and therefore your face turns red. In 1884 William James and Carl Lange independently proposed the opposite. According to the James-Lange theory, *your interpretation of a stimulus evokes autonomic changes and sometimes muscle actions. Your perception of those changes is the feeling aspect of your emotion.* In James's original article, he said simply that the situation (e.g., the sight of a bear) gives rise to an action (e.g., running away), and your perception of the action is the emotion. That is, you don't run away because you are afraid; you feel afraid because you perceive yourself running away. In response to his critics, he clarified his view (James, 1894): Obviously, the sight of a bear doesn't automatically cause you to run away. You first appraise the situation. If it is a caged bear or a circus bear, you do not run. If it appears dangerous, you do run. (Of course, you cannot really outrun a bear, but you get the point.) Your appraisal of the situation is the cognitive aspect of the emotion. Your perception of your reaction is what you *feel* as the emotion. That perception includes your muscle reactions (running away), but also your autonomic reactions (heart rate, breathing, and so forth), and your facial expression. That is,

Situation →	Appraisal →	Actions →	Perception of the actions
	= cognitive aspect of the emotion	= physiological and behavioral aspects	= feeling aspect of the emotion

As we shall see, our evaluation of this theory depends on what we mean by "the feeling aspect." The main types of evidence are that decreases in body reaction decrease emotional feelings, and increases in body reaction increase emotional feelings.

Decreased Body Reaction

According to the James-Lange theory, people with weak physiological responses still identify emotional situations cognitively, but they should have little emotional feeling. People with paralyzed muscles because of spinal cord injuries report normal or nearly normal emotions (Cobos, Sánchez, García, Vera, & Vila, 2002; Deady, North, Allan, Smith, & O'Carroll, 2010). However, they continue to feel changes in autonomic responses, such as heart rate, as well as changes in facial expression. So, contrary to the James-Lange theory, running away is not necessary for feeling fear, but other types of sensation may be.

What about people with weakened autonomic responses? In people with pure autonomic failure, *the autonomic nervous system stops regulating the organs.* That is, nothing in the nervous system influences heart rate, breathing rate, and so forth. One effect is that someone who stands up quickly faints because none of the usual reflexes kick in to prevent gravity from drawing blood from the head. With regard to emotions, affected people still recognize that some situations call for anger, fear, or sadness, but they report that their emotions feel less intense than before (Critchley, Mathias, & Dolan, 2001). The cognitive aspect of emotion remains, but the feeling is weak, as the James-Lange theory predicts.

Related evidence comes from a study of people with BOTOX (botulinum toxin) injections that temporarily paralyzed all their facial muscles. Because they were unable to smile or frown, they reported weaker than usual emotional feelings while watching short videos (Davis, Senghas, Brandt, & Ochsner, 2010).

Increased Body Reaction

Suppose researchers mold your posture and breathing pattern into the pattern typical of an emotion. Will you then feel that emotion? Have someone read these instructions to you, or read them to someone else and check what happens:

> Lower your eyebrows toward your cheeks. Sigh. Close your mouth and push your lower lip slightly upward. Sigh again. Sit back in your chair and draw your feet under the chair. Be sure you feel no tension in your legs or feet. Sigh again. Fold your hands in your lap, cupping one in the other. Drop your head, letting your rib cage fall, letting most of your body go limp, except for a little tension in the back of your neck and across your shoulder blades. Sigh again.

Most people who follow these directions report starting to feel sad (Flack, Laird, & Cavallaro, 1999;

Philippot, Chapelle, & Blairy, 2002). Instructions to hold the posture and breathing pattern characteristic of happiness, anger, or fear induce those emotions, too, although the instructions for fear sometimes induce anger and those for anger sometimes induce fear. Fear and anger are physiologically similar.

With studies like this, one worry is that the participants might guess what the experimenter is trying to demonstrate. (Recall the idea of "demand characteristics" from Chapter 2.) To conceal the purpose of the study, researchers told participants they were studying how people with paralyzed arms learn to write. They told participants to hold a pen either with their teeth or with their protruded lips, as in ▼ Figure 12.2, and then to make check marks to rate the funniness of cartoons.

a

b

▲ **Figure 12.2** Facial expression can influence mood. When people hold a pen with their teeth (a), they rate cartoons as funnier than when they hold it with their lips (b).

When they held the pen with their teeth, their faces were forced into a slight smile, and they rated the cartoons as very funny. When they held the pen with their lips, they could not smile, and they rated the cartoons as less funny (Strack, Martin, & Stepper, 1988). Try holding a pen one way and then the other while reading newspaper cartoons. Do you notice a difference? However, although a smile slightly facilitates happiness or amusement, it is not necessary for them. Children with a facial paralysis that prevents smiling can still experience joy and humor (Miller, 2007b).

try it your self

More than a century after its proposal, the James-Lange theory remains controversial (Moors, 2009). Part of the resistance to the theory depends on misunderstandings, as Laird and Lacasse (2014) have argued. Disagreement also hinges on what we mean by "emotional feeling." William James meant feeling as a sensation, and in fact it is hard to imagine where an emotional sensation could come from, other than from reactions of the body. Those who disagree with his theory seem to mean feeling in the sense of the whole experience of the emotion, including more cognitive aspects.

concept check

2. **What happens to emotions in people with conditions that weaken their autonomic responses? How do these results relate to the James-Lange theory?**

Answer 2. People with pure autonomic failure have no systematic autonomic changes, and their emotions feel weak. That result supports the predictions of the James-Lange theory.

Schachter and Singer's Theory of Emotions

The research says that once you get your body into a hunched-over posture with tension only in your neck and you are constantly sighing, you tend to feel sad. But how did you get into that posture in the first place? Ordinarily, your appraisal of the situation entered into the process.

Furthermore, how do you know whether you are angry or frightened? Anger and fear are so similar physiologically that your autonomic changes cannot tell you which one you are experiencing (Lang, 1994).

Because of such considerations, Stanley Schachter and Jerome Singer (1962) proposed a theory of how we identify one emotion from another. According to Schachter and Singer's theory of emotions (see ▼ Figure 12.3), *the intensity of the physiological state—that is, the degree of sympathetic nervous system arousal—determines the intensity of the emotion, but a cognitive appraisal of the situation identifies the type of emotion.* A given type of arousal might produce an experience of fear, anger, joy, or none of these depending on the situation. Schachter and Singer saw their theory as an alternative to the James-Lange theory, but it really addresses a different question.

The ideal test of Schachter and Singer's theory would be to wire you to someone else so that whenever the other person's heart rate, breathing rate, and so forth changed, yours would, too, at the same time and to the same degree. Then, when the other person felt an emotion, researchers would ask whether you feel it, too. That procedure is impossible with current technology, so Schachter and Singer (1962) tried a simpler procedure.

what's the evidence?

The Cognitive Aspect of Emotion

Hypothesis A drug that increases arousal will enhance whatever emotion a situation arouses, but the type of emotion will depend on the situation.

Method The experimenters put college students into different situations but gave some of them injections of epinephrine to induce (they hoped) the same physiological

Cognitive appraisal of the situation: This calls for fear.

Perception of autonomic responses: My heart is beating fast and I'm breathing hard. My fear must be intense.

▲ **Figure 12.3** According to Schachter and Singer's theory, physiological arousal determines the intensity of an emotion, but a cognitive appraisal determines which emotion one feels.

condition regardless of the situation. (Epinephrine mimics the effects of the sympathetic nervous system.) They tried to influence some participants to attribute their increased arousal to the situation and others to attribute it to the injection.

Specifically, the experimenters told certain participants that the injections would produce no important side effects. These participants would presumably notice their arousal and attribute it to the situation, feeling intense emotions. Others were told to expect side effects such as increased heart rate and butterflies in the stomach. When they felt the changes, they would presumably attribute them to the injections and not to emotional experiences. Additional participants were given one set of instructions or the other but injected with a placebo instead of epinephrine.

Participants were then placed in different situations to elicit euphoria or anger. Each student in the euphoria situation waited in a room with a playful young man who flipped paper wads into a trash can, sailed paper airplanes, built a tower with manila folders, shot paper wads at the tower with a rubber band, played with a hula hoop, and tried to get the other student to join his play. Each participant in the anger situation was asked to answer a questionnaire full of such insulting items as these:

Which member of your immediate family does not bathe or wash regularly?

With how many men (other than your father) has your mother had extramarital relationships?

4 or fewer   5–9   10 or more

Results Many students in the euphoria situation joined the playful partner (see ▼ Figure 12.4). One jumped up and down on the desk, and another opened a window and threw paper wads at passersby. The anger situation was less effective than expected, although a few students muttered angry comments or refused to complete the questionnaire.

Recall that some of the participants had been informed beforehand that the injections would produce certain autonomic effects. No matter which situation they were in, they showed only slight emotional responses. When they felt themselves sweating and their hands trembling, they said to themselves, "Aha! I'm getting the side effects, just as they said I would."

Interpretation Unfortunately, this experiment has problems that limit the conclusions. Recall that some participants were injected with a placebo instead of epinephrine. These participants showed about as much euphoria in the euphoria situation and as much anger in the anger situation as did the participants injected with epinephrine. Therefore, the epinephrine injections apparently had nothing to do with the results. If so, we are

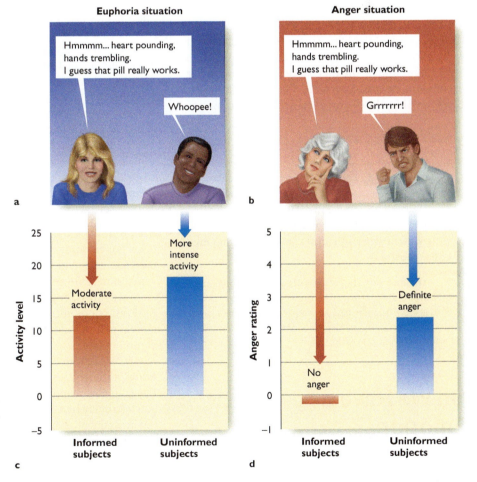

▲ **Figure 12.4** (a and b) In Schachter and Singer's experiment, people who were uninformed about the effects of epinephrine reported strong emotions appropriate to the situation. (c and d) According to Schachter and Singer, autonomic arousal controls the strength of an emotion, but cognitive factors tell us which emotion we are experiencing.

left with this unexciting summary of the results: People in a situation designed to induce euphoria act happy, and those in an anger situation act angry (Plutchik & Ax, 1967). However, if they attribute their arousal to an injection, their response is more restrained.

Despite the problems in Schachter and Singer's experiment, the idea behind it is reasonable, and other research since then has supported it in many, though not all, cases (Reisenzein, 1983). That idea, to reiterate, is that feeling more highly aroused increases the intensity of your emotion, but you evaluate the situation to determine which emotion you feel. Consider this example: A young woman interviewed young men, either on a wide, sturdy bridge, or on the wobbly Capilano Canyon suspension bridge (see ▶ Figure 12.5). After the interview, she gave each man a card with her phone number in case he wanted to ask further questions about the study. Of those interviewed on the suspension bridge, 39 percent called her, as opposed to 9 percent from the sturdy, low bridge (Dutton & Aron, 1974). The interpretation was that men on the suspension bridge experienced high arousal from the situation itself, but attributed it to the woman. ("Wow, what an exciting woman! My heart is racing!") There is, however, a problem with this study. Might the woman herself have been more excited on the suspension bridge than on the low bridge? Maybe the men were responding to her excitement, not just their own. You can begin to perceive the difficulty of doing research on emotion.

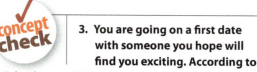

3. You are going on a first date with someone you hope will find you exciting. According to to Schachter and Singer's theory, should you plan a date walking through an art gallery or riding on roller coasters?

Answer

3. According to Schachter and Singer's theory, you should plan a date riding on roller coasters. If your date gets emotionally excited, he or she may attribute the arousal to you. (However, if you are dating someone who gets nauseated on roller coasters, you should change your strategy!)

Do We Have a Few "Basic" Emotions?

How many emotions do humans experience? Do we have a few "basic" emotions that combine to form other experiences, like the elements of chemistry? This controversy has a long history. Charles Darwin (1872/1965), noting that a few facial expressions of emotion occur throughout the world, favored the

Chris Cheadle/All Canada Photos/Getty Images

▲ **Figure 12.5** How much excitement might you feel while crossing the Capilano Canyon suspension bridge? If you met an attractive person on this bridge, might you think that person was exciting?

idea of a few basic emotions. Wilhelm Wundt, who started the first psychology laboratory, and William James, founder of American psychology, both argued against the idea of distinct categories, favoring instead the idea that one emotion grades into another.

Some psychologists have proposed a short list of emotions, such as happiness, sadness, anger, fear, disgust, and surprise. Others add more candidates, such as contempt, shame, guilt, interest, hope, pride, relief, frustration, love, awe, boredom, jealousy, regret, or embarrassment (Keltner & Buswell, 1997). Japanese people include *amae,* translated as "the pleasant feeling of depending on someone else" or "the feeling of comfort in another person's acceptance" (Doi, 1981; Niiya, Ellsworth, & Yamaguchi, 2006). Japanese are also more likely than Americans to list loneliness as an emotion (Kobayashi, Schallert, & Ogren 2003). Hindus include heroism, amusement, peace, and wonder (Hejmadi, Davidson, & Rozin, 2000).

How can we decide what is a basic emotion (if there is such a thing)? Psychologists have proposed the following criteria:

- Basic emotions should emerge early in life without requiring much experience. For example, nostalgia and pride emerge slowly and seem less basic than fear, anger, or joy. The problem with this criterion is that all emotional expressions emerge gradually. Infants' expressions at first do not distinguish among distress, anger, and fear (Messinger, 2002).

- Basic emotions should be similar across cultures. Because most emotions appear to be similar throughout human cultures, this criterion does not eliminate much.

- Each basic emotion should have a distinct physiology. If we take this criterion seriously, we should probably abandon the idea of basic emotions. Physiological reactions such as heart rate and breathing rate do not distinguish strongly between one emotion and another, although they do indicate the intensity of an emotion. Brain measurements also fail to identify which emotion someone feels. ▼ Figure 12.6 summarizes the results of many studies using PET and fMRI brain scans (see Chapter 3) to measure brain activity when different emotions were aroused in various ways (Phan, Wager, Taylor, & Liberzon, 2002). As you can see, the areas aroused by any emotion largely overlap those aroused by other emotions. A thorough review of the literature concluded that no brain area is devoted exclusively to emotion, as opposed to cognition, motivation or other processes, and that no brain area

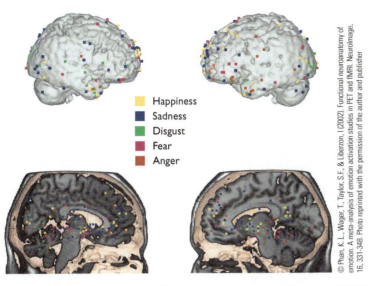

- Happiness
- Sadness
- Disgust
- Fear
- Anger

© Phan, K. L. Wager, T., Taylor, S.F., & Liberzon. I (2002). Functional neuroanatomy of emotion: A meta-analysis of emotion activation studies in PET and fMRI. NeuroImage. 16, 331-348. Photo reprinted with the permission of the author and publisher

▲ **Figure 12.6** Researchers aroused emotions in various ways and then used PET or fMRI scans to identify which brain areas became aroused. No brain area appears specific to one type of emotion. (Source: Phan, Wager, Taylor, & Liberzon, 2002)

contributes to only one type of emotion (Lindquist, Wager, Kober, Bliss-Moreau, & Barrett, 2012). A brain area might contribute mainly to pleasantness versus unpleasantness, approach versus avoidance, or strong feeling versus weak feeling, but not specifically to anger, sadness, or any other named emotion (Wilson-Mendenhall, Barrett, & Barsalou, 2013).

- Finally, each basic emotion might have its own facial expression. Most of the research has focused on this last criterion.

Producing Facial Expressions

Does each emotion have its own special expression? And why do we have facial expressions of emotions anyway?

Emotional expressions are not altogether arbitrary, as shown in ▼ Figure 12.7. When you are frightened, you open your eyes wide, increasing your ability to

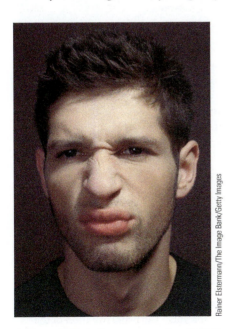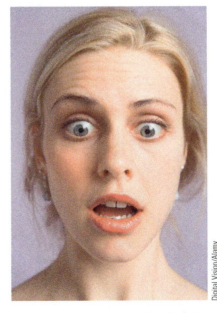

▲ **Figure 12.7** A disgust expression (left) decreases your exposure to something foul. A fear expression (right) increases your readiness to see dangers and take necessary actions.

see dangers, and you inhale deeply, preparing for possible action. If you see something disgusting, you partly close your eyes and turn your nose away from the offending object, decreasing your exposure to it (Susskind et al., 2008). Opening the eyes wide (as in fear) improves your ability to locate a potentially dangerous object. Narrowing the eyes (as in disgust) enhances your ability to identify what the object is (Lee, Mirza, Flanagan, & Anderson, 2014).

In addition, emotional expressions are specialized for communication in a social context. For example, Olympic medal winners generally smile if they are waiting for the awards ceremony with others but not if they are waiting alone (Fernández-Dols & Ruiz-Belda, 1997). Even 10-month-old infants smile more when their mothers are watching than when they are not (S. S. Jones, Collins, & Hong, 1991). Robert Provine (2000) spent many hours in shopping malls and elsewhere recording and observing laughter. He found that people laughed almost entirely when they were with friends and that the speakers laughed more than the listeners. People laughed mostly while saying something that wasn't even funny, such as, "Can I join you?" or "It was nice meeting you too." Laughter expresses friendliness.

Intentional emotional expressions seldom exactly match the spontaneous expressions. For example, the smile of a truly happy person includes movements of the mouth muscles and the muscles surrounding the eyes (see ▼ Figure 12.8a). Voluntary smiles (see ▼ Figure 12.8b) generally do not include the muscles around the eyes (Ekman & Davidson, 1993). *The full expression including the muscles around the eyes* is called the Duchenne smile, named after Duchenne de Boulogne, the first person to describe it.

Because the Duchenne smile is hard to produce voluntarily, it is a good indicator of someone's true feelings. Researchers have found that women with a Duchenne smile in their college yearbooks are more likely than other women to have happy, long-lasting marriages and to report feeling happy and competent long after their college years (Harker & Keltner, 2001). Major league baseball players with a Duchenne smile on their photos lived longer than those with less smile or no smile (Abel & Kruger, 2010).

Do we learn to make appropriate facial expressions, or are they part of our biological heritage? Irenäus Eibl-Eibesfeldt (1973, 1974) photographed people in various world cultures, documenting smiling, frowning, laughing, and crying, even in children who were born deaf and blind (see ▼ Figure 12.9). He also found that people throughout the world express a friendly greeting by briefly raising their eyebrows (see ▼ Figure 12.10). That expression has the same meaning in all cultures and the same duration— one-third of a second.

a   b

▲ **Figure 12.8** A spontaneous, happy smile (a) uses both the mouth muscles and the muscles surrounding the eyes. This expression is sometimes called the *Duchenne smile*. A voluntary smile (b) ordinarily includes only the mouth muscles. Most people cannot voluntarily activate the eye muscles associated with the Duchenne smile.

Understanding Facial Expressions

The similarity of facial expressions across cultures implies that they are unlearned, but do they always have the same meanings? Researchers asked people in different cultures to interpret six facial expressions like those in ▼ Figure 12.11. Look at each face and try to name its expression. (Please try now.)

try it your self

After researchers translated the labels into other languages, people in other cultures also identified them, though somewhat less accurately (Ekman, 1992; Ekman & Friesen, 1984; Russell, 1994). A study of the Himba people, a largely isolated group in Namibia, found that they could easily recognize expressions of happiness and fear, but they were less accurate with other expressions (Gendron, Roberson,

van der Vyver, & Barrett, 2014). At a minimum, facial expressions have regional "accents" in different cultures. Just as you understand the speech from your own region better than that from elsewhere, you recognize facial expressions more accurately among people from your own culture (Elfenbein, Beaupré, Lévesque, & Hess, 2007). Japanese and American people examined photos of Japanese faces expressing anger and disgust. Of Japanese people, 82 percent recognized the anger expression and 66 percent recognized the disgust expression. Of Americans, only 34 percent recognized anger and 18 percent recognized disgust (Dailey et al., 2010).

The ability of people throughout the world to classify these facial expressions is not strong evidence for the idea of six "basic" emotions (Barrett, Mesquita, & Gendron, 2011). First, researchers typically list six emotion names and ask which face goes with which label. If people are simply shown a face and asked to identify the expression, they are often uncertain whether an expression is sad, angry, frightened, disgusted, or something else (Pochedly, Widen, & Russell, 2012; Widen & Naab, 2012).

Second, we identify someone's emotion by context, posture, touch, tone of voice, and gestures, and not just by facial expression (Edwards, 1998; Hertenstein, Keltner, App, Bulleit, & Jaskolka, 2006). Some people, mostly women, can sense someone's fear from the smell (de Groot, Semin, & Smeets, 2014; Leppänen & Hietanen, 2003; Zhou & Chen, 2009). Consider ▼ Figure 12.12. Out of context, most people would call the expression sadness. The posture on the left confirms that judgment. However, given the posture on the right, most people call the expression fear (Aviezer et al., 2008).

Another issue: The faces in Figure 12.11 are all posed looking at the viewer. From the standpoint of experimental design, putting all

▲ **Figure 12.10** Throughout the world, people raise their eyebrows as a friendly greeting, indicating "I am glad to see you." The usual duration of the expression is one-third of a second, in all known cultures.

▲ **Figure 12.9** Even children born deaf and blind show the typical facial expressions of emotion, including laughter.

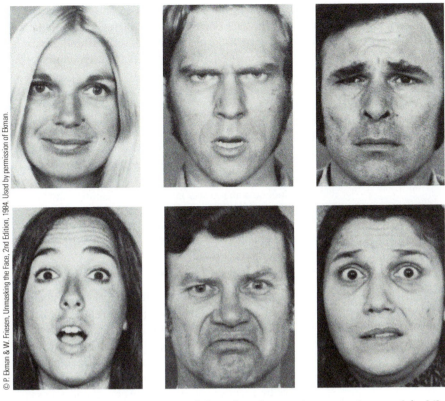

▲ **Figure 12.11** Paul Ekman has used these faces in experiments testing people's ability to recognize emotional expressions. Can you identify them? Check answer A on page 392. (From Ekman & Friesen, 1984)

the faces in the same position seems right. However, sad people almost always look down and make eye contact with you only briefly, if at all. Frightened people look at what frightens them. They make eye contact with you only if they are afraid of *you*. Examine the photos in ▲ Figure 12.13. Which expression is easier to identify? Most

a

From Angry, disgusted, or afraid? by Aviezer, H., Hassin, R. R., Ryan, J., Grady, C., Susskind, J., Anderson, A., et al. (2008). Psychological Science, 19, 724-732. Reprinted by Permission of SAGE Publications.

b

▲ **Figure 12.12** The same facial expression can look like sadness or fear depending on someone's posture. (Source: Aviezer et al., 2008)

Fear

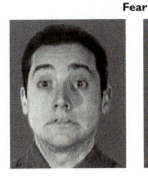 

a Direct gaze   **b** Averted gaze

© Reginald B. Adams, Jr

▲ **Figure 12.13** Most people identify fearful expressions more easily when the person is looking away.

observers identify sad or frightened expressions faster when they see someone looking away (Adams & Kleck, 2003). In contrast, happy and angry expressions are easier to identify if the person is looking directly forward (Adams & Kleck, 2005).

Sad people not only look down, but also they cry. If you see someone with a sad face and tears, you immediately identify the expression as sadness, as in ▼ Figure 12.14. Take away the tears, and you are often less certain what the expression means. You may

try it yourself

▲ **Figure 12.14** If you cover the tear with your finger, this face looks less sad. If you color the whites of the eyes slightly reddish, the face looks sadder.

describe it as awe, puzzlement, or concern (Provine, Krosnowski, & Brocato, 2009). If someone's eyes are red, they add to the impression of sadness (Provine, Cabrera, Brocato, & Krosnowski, 2011). Robert Provine and colleagues have suggested that humans evolved white scleras (the whites of our eyes) to enhance emotional communication. Other primates have dark scleras. When someone's eyes turn red, you may not be sure whether the person is sad, angry, or frightened, but certainly the person doesn't look happy (Provine, Nave-Blodgett, & Cabrera, 2013).

4. **Researchers often show a photograph and ask observers to identify the emotion. In what way might this procedure underestimate the ability to recognize emotions?**

Answer

4. We ordinarily have many other cues, including gestures, posture, tone of voice, and context. Also, it is easier to recognize expressions of sadness and fear when someone looks down or to the side.

Do Facial Expressions Indicate Basic Emotions?

The question is whether we have a few basic emotions. The research shows that people throughout the world recognize facial expressions of joy, sadness, fear, anger, disgust, and surprise, at least moderately well. However, the photos in Figure 12.11 were carefully posed to be the best possible examples so that people could recognize them accurately. In everyday life, most expressions show a mixture of emotions. If we take photographs of spontaneous everyday expressions, observers often disagree with one another, they see more than one emotion in each face, and what they see doesn't always agree with what the person in the photograph was actually experiencing (Kayval & Russell, 2013).

Furthermore, the ability of people to recognize expressions of six emotions could not tell us whether people have precisely six basic emotions. People can, with a little less accuracy, also identify an expression of contempt, which is a little different from disgust. People also readily identify expressions of pride from facial expression and posture (Tracy & Robins, 2004; Tracy, Robins, & Lagattuta, 2005). From videotapes, though not from still photographs, most people can identify expressions of peace and heroism, which Hindu people generally list as emotions (Hejmadi, Davidson, & Rozin, 2000). So if the ability to identify an expression is evidence for a basic emotion, our list should grow.

Also, we readily identify the facial expressions of sleepiness and confusion, although we probably would

not classify either of them as an emotion (Keltner & Shiota, 2003; Rozin & Cohen, 2003). So the fact that we recognize facial expressions of surprise and disgust is not strong evidence to regard them as emotions.

5. **Why is the ability to recognize the expressions of six emotions not convincing evidence that these are basic emotions?**

Answer

5. Most everyday expressions do not fit neatly into those six categories. We can also identify additional states, such as contempt and pride. Also, we can identify facial expressions of other conditions that may or may not be emotions.

An Alternative to Basic Emotions

Many psychologists doubt that it makes sense to talk about basic emotions at all (Barrett, 2006). If fear, anger, or anything else is a basic emotion, we should expect that when people show its expression, they should also show the gestures, postures, vocal intonation, and everything else that goes along with it. However, people frequently show part of one emotional expression, part of another, and a posture or gesture that doesn't fit either one (Scherer & Ellgring, 2007).

Instead of basic emotions, we might regard emotion as a series of dimensions. According to the "circumplex" model, emotions range on a continuum from pleasure to misery and along another continuum from arousal to sleepiness (Russell, 1980). ▼ Figure 12.15 shows this idea. Note that this model deals with the feeling aspect of emotion, not the cognitive aspects. For example, both anger and fear would fit near "distress" on this graph, even though we associate anger and fear with different

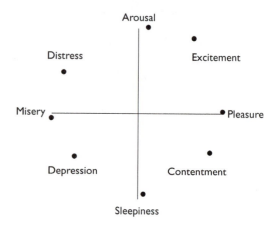

▲ **Figure 12.15** According to the circumplex model of emotion, emotional feelings occur along a continuum of arousal and another continuum of pleasure. (Figure 1 from "A circumplex model of affect," by J. A. Russell, 1980. *Journal of Personality and Social Psychology, 39,* pp. 1161–1178.)

cognitions. Other psychologists have proposed different descriptions but maintain the idea that emotions range along continuous dimensions (Watson, Wiese, Vaidya, & Tellegen, 1999; Yik, Russell, & Steiger, 2011).

6. **Why do many psychologists doubt the concept of basic emotions?**

Answer

6. People frequently show parts of several emotions instead of all the aspects of one emotion. That is, the various aspects supposedly associated with one emotion do not correlate well with one another.

Usefulness of Emotions

Presumably, emotions must be useful for something, or we would not have evolved the capacity to feel them. One function is that emotions focus our attention on important information. Your eyes and your attention turn at once toward images that evoke strong emotions, even if you are trying to pay attention to something else (Schupp et al., 2007; Yoon, Hong, Joormann, & Kang, 2009). People who are prone to anxiety are especially likely to pay attention to anything related to fear (Doty, Japee, Ingvar, & Ungerleider, 2013).

Emotions or moods also adjust our priorities. If you are running away from a mad attacker with a chainsaw, you don't stop to smell the roses. When you are in a happy mood, you expand your focus. According to Barbara Fredrickson's (2001) broaden-and-build hypothesis of positive emotions, *a happy mood increases your readiness to explore new ideas and opportunities.* You think creatively, notice the details in the background that you ordinarily overlook, and increase your pursuit of new experiences that will help maintain your happy mood (Fredrickson & Losada, 2005). That tendency relates to the fact that happiness is usually a low-intensity emotion. Very intense emotions of any type tend to narrow one's focus of attention (Gable & Harmon-Jones, 2010).

Although major depression impairs reasoning, a mildly sad mood aids reasoning under some conditions. As discussed in Chapter 11, most people overestimate their own abilities and underestimate how long a task will take. People in a happy mood are especially prone to that error. Sad people tend to be less optimistic, and therefore more realistic. However, severely depressed people are unrealistic in the other direction, by rating themselves too low and regarding easy tasks as difficult (Moore & Fresco, 2012).

Sad people generally examine the evidence more cautiously than average before making a decision. In one study, students listened to a weaker and a stronger argument concerning possible increases in student fees at their university. Students in a sad mood were more persuaded by the stronger argument, whereas students in a happy mood found both arguments about equally persuasive (Bless, Bohner, Schwarz, & Strack, 1990).

Emotions and Moral Reasoning

People often advise us not to let our emotions get in the way of our decisions. Emotions sometimes impair decisions, but they often provide a guide when we have to make a quick decision about right and wrong (Beer, Knight, & D'Esposito, 2006). Let's begin with two moral dilemmas on which well-meaning people disagree:

The Trolley Dilemma. A trolley car with defective brakes is coasting downhill toward five people lying on the tracks. You could throw a switch to divert the trolley onto a different track, where one person is lying. If you flip the switch, the trolley will kill one instead of five. Should you do it?

The Footbridge Dilemma. Another trolley with defective brakes is coasting downhill and about to kill five people. This time you are standing on a footbridge over the track. You see a way to save those five people: A fat person is beside you, leaning over. If you push him off the bridge, he will land on the track and block the trolley. (You are, let's assume, too thin to block it yourself.) Again your action would kill one to save five. Should you do it? (See ▼ Figure 12.16.)

▲ **Figure 12.16** (a) Should you flip a switch so the trolley goes down a track with one person instead of five? (b) Should you push a fat person off a bridge to save five people?

Most people say "yes" to flipping the switch in the first dilemma, although they might find it difficult. We hesitate to do something that harms someone, even when failing to act harms a greater number (DeScioli, Christner, & Kurzban, 2011; Miller, Hannikainen, & Cushman, 2014). Fewer people say they would push someone off the bridge in the second dilemma (Greene, Sommerville, Nystrom, Darley, & Cohen, 2001). Logically, the answers might be the same because the act kills one person to save five, although the situations are not quite comparable. What if you pushed someone to his death and the trolley killed the others anyway? Or what if they jumped out of the way, so that killing him was unnecessary? However, even if you were fully confident that pushing someone off a bridge would save five others, it would still be emotionally repulsive.

After people make moral decisions in cases like these, they often have trouble stating a reason for their decisions. They make a quick, emotional decision and then look for an explanation afterward (Haidt, 2001). The emotional guidance usually works. As a rule, pushing someone off a bridge is a horrendously bad idea. Your emotional reaction is a quick guide to making a decision that is almost always right.

Decisions by People with Impaired Emotions

Antonio Damasio (1994) described patients who suffered impoverished or inappropriate emotions following brain damage. One was the famous patient Phineas Gage, who in 1848 survived an accident in which an iron bar shot through his head (see ▼ Figure 12.17). More than a century and a half later, researchers examined his skull (which is still on display in a Boston museum) and reconstructed the route that the bar must have taken through his brain (Ratiu & Talos, 2004). The accident damaged

part of his prefrontal cortex. During the first months after this accident, Gage often showed little emotion, and he made poor, impulsive decisions. However, the reports at the time provided little detail. Over the years, people retold this story and elaborated on it. If you have read about this case before, you may have read some exaggerations (Kotowicz, 2007).

A patient known to us as "Elliot" provides a more recent example (Damasio, 1994). Elliot suffered damage to his prefrontal cortex during surgery to remove a brain tumor. After the operation, he showed almost no emotional expression, no impatience, no frustration, no joy from music or art, and almost no anger. He described his brain surgery and the resulting deterioration of his life with calm detachment, as if describing events that happened to a stranger. Besides his impaired emotions, he had trouble making or following reasonable plans. He could discuss the probable outcome of each possible choice but still had trouble deciding. As a result, he could not keep a job, invest his money intelligently, or maintain normal friendships.

As a rule, people with damage to one part of the prefrontal cortex (the ventromedial prefrontal cortex, to be precise) have trouble making decisions, and seem particularly impaired in what we consider moral judgment. Most people think it is okay to flip a switch to make a trolley car kill one person instead of five, but presumably you wouldn't think so if the one person who would die is your mother or your daughter. People with this type of brain damage generally say it would be okay. And they tend to make decisions like that with little hesitation (Ciaramelli, Muccioli, Làdavas, & diPellegrino, 2007; Thomas, Croft, & Tranel, 2011). The rest of us would consider the action "logical" but emotionally much too painful. If the brain damage occurs in childhood or early adolescence, the effects are even greater; for example, people say it would be okay to kill a boss you disliked, if you were sure you could get away with it (Taber-Thomas et al., 2014). That result suggests a failure to learn the rules of right and wrong that most people take for granted in a civilized society. The amygdala is the brain area primarily responsible for processing emotional information (such as feeling sad or guilty). Ordinarily, the amygdala feeds that information into the ventromedial prefrontal cortex, which weighs it when making a decision. When the connection from amygdala to cortex is broken, the result is decisions that ignore potential feelings of sadness or guilt (Shenhav & Greene, 2014). People with frontal lobe damage don't easily imagine the emotional outcomes. As Damasio (1999, p. 55) said, "Emotions are inseparable from the idea of good and evil." If you cannot imagine feeling good or bad, proud or guilty, you make bad decisions.

7. In what way does prefrontal cortex damage interfere with decision making?

Answer

7. People with damage to the prefrontal cortex cannot imagine feeling good or bad after various outcomes; therefore, they do not consider the emotional pain that a decision might cause.

Emotional Intelligence

Is reasoning about emotional issues different from reasoning about anything else? The observations on patient Elliot imply a difference, as he answers questions normally when they have nothing to do with emotional consequences. Casual observations in everyday life also suggest that reasoning about emotional topics might be special. Some people know the right thing to say to make someone else feel better. They notice subtle signals in people's facial expressions that

▲ **Figure 12.17** Phineas Gage, holding the bar that shot through part of his prefrontal cortex. The damage impaired Gage's judgment and decision-making ability.

From the collection of Jack and Beverly Wilgus

indicate who needs reassurance or a pat on the back. They know when a smile is sincere or fake. They foresee whether their romantic attachments are going well or about to break up. And other people, smart in their own way, seem clueless in emotional situations. Psychologists therefore speak of **emotional intelligence**, *the ability to perceive, imagine, and understand emotions and to use that information in making decisions* (Mayer & Salovey, 1995, 1997).

The idea of emotional intelligence quickly became popular, but the evidence behind the idea is still not strong. If the concept is going to be useful, emotional intelligence should have enough in common with other kinds of intelligence to deserve being called intelligence. However, it should not overlap too heavily with academic intelligence, or we would have no reason to talk about it separately. Most importantly, it should predict some outcome that we cannot already predict using other measures.

First, we need a way to measure emotional intelligence. Several psychologists have devised pencil-and-paper tests. Here are two example questions, reworded slightly (Mayer, Caruso, & Salovey, 2000):

1. A man has been so busy at work that he spends little time with his wife and daughter. He feels guilty for spending so little time with them, and they feel hurt. Recently, a relative who lost her job moved in with them. A few weeks later, they told her she had to leave because they needed their privacy.
On a scale from 1 to 5, where 5 is highest, rate how much this man feels:

Depressed   _____

Frustrated   _____

Guilty   _____

Energetic   _____

Happy   _____

2. A driver hit a dog that ran into the street. The driver and the dog's owner hurried to check on the dog.
On a scale from 1 to 5, where 5 means "extremely likely" and 1 means "extremely unlikely," how would the people probably feel?

The owner would feel angry at the driver.   _____

The owner would feel embarrassed at not training the dog better.   _____

The driver would feel guilty for not driving more carefully.   _____

The driver would feel relieved that it was a dog and not a child.   _____

To each of these questions, you might answer, "It depends!" You need more information about the people and the situation. Indeed, one of the key aspects of emotional intelligence is knowing what additional information to request. Still, you could do your best to answer the questions as stated. The problem then is, gulp, what are the correct answers? In fact, *are* there any correct answers, or do the answers depend on culture and circumstances?

Would you trust some experts to decide the correct answers? Maybe, but only if we can agree on who are the experts. Another method is "consensus": Researchers ask many people each question. Suppose on item 2, on the part about the driver feeling guilty, 70 percent say "5" (it is extremely likely that the driver will feel guilty). That becomes the best answer. However, an answer of "4" isn't utterly wrong. Suppose 20 percent of people answer "4," 5 percent answer "3," 4 percent answer "2," and 1 percent answer "1." Instead of counting anything right or wrong, the test adds 0.70 point for everyone who answered 5, 0.20 for everyone who answered 4, and so on. In other words, you always get part credit on any question, and you get more credit depending on how many other people agreed with you. The problem is, on a very difficult question, only the wisest people might know what is really the best answer. If the correct answer is uncommon, it will be considered wrong.

In short, an emotional intelligence question as currently constituted does not do a good job of identifying an emotional "genius." However, it does identify people who fail to answer easy questions. That by itself is worth something. People with certain kinds of brain damage or psychiatric disorders do poorly even on easy questions about emotional situations (Adolphs, Baron-Cohen, & Tranel, 2002; Blair et al., 2004; Edwards, Jackson, & Pattison, 2002; Townshend & Duka, 2003). So the test identifies "emotional stupidity," even if it doesn't identify exceptional emotional intelligence.

The key criteria for any test are reliability and validity, as discussed in Chapter 9. The authors of the current tests of emotional intelligence claim that the tests have high reliability (Mayer, Salovey, Caruso, & Sitarenios, 2001), but other researchers find problems with many of the test items and report much lower reliability (Føllesdal & Hagtvet, 2009). With regard to validity, high emotional intelligence scores are associated with high quality of friendships (Lopes et al., 2004), ability to detect the emotional content of someone's voice (Trimmer & Cuddy, 2008), and good interpersonal communication (Libbrecht, Lievens, Carette, & Côté, 2014).

However, emotional intelligence is a useful concept only if it predicts such outcomes better than we already could with other tests. Emotional intelligence scores correlate significantly with overall intelligence (Kong, 2014) and with conscientiousness and other personality factors. We can predict people's friendships, happiness, and life satisfaction moderately well from tests of academic intelligence and personality factors. What do emotional intelligence scores add to those predictions? Several studies have concluded "not much" (Amelang & Steinmayr, 2006; Gannon & Ranzijn, 2005; Karim & Weisz, 2010). So either emotional intelligence is not a useful concept, or we need to improve our measurements of it. Pencil-and-paper tests work well enough for academic intelligence, but they may not be ideal for measuring emotional responsiveness.

8. What is the main objection to "consensus" scoring?

Answer

8. A test based on consensus scoring cannot easily identify the truly outstanding individuals because it doesn't give proper credit on difficult items.

Research on Emotions

Research on emotions is fascinating but difficult. Of the various components of emotion, the cognitive and feeling aspects are the hardest to measure. Behavioral and physiological measures are more objective, but they have their own problems. The best solution is to approach any question in multiple ways. Any study has limitations, but if several different kinds of research point to the same conclusion, we gain confidence in the overall idea. That principle is, indeed, important throughout psychology: Seldom is any study fully decisive, so we strive for independent lines of research that converge on the same conclusion.

Summary

- *Measuring emotions.* Emotions are inferred, not observed directly. Researchers rely on self-reports, observations of behavior, and measurements of physiological changes. (page 379)
- *Emotions and autonomic arousal.* Many emotional states are associated with increased arousal of the sympathetic nervous system, which readies the body for emergency action. (page 380)
- *James-Lange theory.* According to the James-Lange theory of emotions, the feeling aspect of an emotion is the perception of a change in the body's physiological state. (page 381)
- *Evidence supporting the James-Lange theory.* People who lose control of their autonomic responses generally report weakened emotional feelings. Molding someone's posture and breathing pattern into the pattern typical for some emotion facilitates that emotion. (page 381)
- *Schachter and Singer's theory.* According to Schachter and Singer's theory, autonomic arousal determines the intensity of an emotion but does not determine which emotion occurs. We identify an emotion on the basis of how we perceive the situation. (page 382)
- *Do we have basic emotions?* Certain psychologists propose that we have a few basic emotions. The main evidence is that people throughout the world can recognize certain emotional expressions. However, we seldom recognize an emotion from facial expression alone; we also consider posture, context, tone of voice, and other information. Using such information, we can identify a wider range of emotional states than just a few. The fact that we recognize expressions of disgust and surprise is not decisive for calling them emotions, because we also recognize expressions of sleepiness and confusion, which most people do not regard as emotions. (page 384)
- *Alternative views.* Instead of speaking of a list of basic emotions, an alternative is to consider emotions as varying along continuous dimensions. (page 388)
- *Usefulness of emotions.* Emotions call our attention to important information and adjust our priorities to our situation in life. (page 389)
- *Emotions and moral decisions.* When we face a moral decision, we often react emotionally. Those quick emotional feelings may be an evolved mechanism to steer our behavior toward what is usually the right choice. (page 389)
- *Effects of brain damage.* People with brain damage that impairs their emotions have trouble making good decisions, especially in situations related to moral treatment of others. (page 390)
- *Emotional intelligence.* People need skills to judge other people's emotions and the probable emotional outcomes of their own actions. The ability to handle such issues may constitute "emotional intelligence." However, it is not clear that current measurements of emotional intelligence predict much that we could not already predict based on academic intelligence and certain aspects of personality. (page 390)

Key Terms

autonomic nervous system (page 380)

broaden-and-build hypothesis (page 389)

Duchenne smile (page 385)

emotional intelligence (page 391)

James-Lange theory (page 381)

microexpressions (page 379)

parasympathetic nervous system (page 381)

pure autonomic failure (page 381)

Schachter and Singer's theory of emotions (page 382)

sympathetic nervous system (page 380)

Answers to Other Questions in the Module

A. The faces express (a) happiness, (b) anger, (c) sadness, (d) surprise, (e) disgust, and (f) fear.

Review Questions

1. For which of these purposes are physiological measurements more helpful?
   (a) Determining whether someone is angry or frightened
   (b) Measuring the strength of someone's anger or fear
2. According to the James-Lange theory, which of the following is true?
   (a) You run away because you feel fear.
   (b) If you see a bear, you automatically run away from it.
   (c) Your feeling of fear is your perception of what your body is doing.
   (d) Feeling fear and running away are the same thing.
3. What happens when people adopt postures and breathing patterns characteristic of a particular emotion? How do these results relate to the James-Lange theory?
   (a) They show an enhanced tendency to feel that emotion. This result is consistent with the James-Lange theory.
   (b) They show an enhanced tendency to feel that emotion. This result is inconsistent with the James-Lange theory.
   (c) They show an enhanced tendency to feel the opposite emotion. This result is consistent with the James-Lange theory.
   (d) They show an enhanced tendency to feel the opposite emotion. This result is inconsistent with the James-Lange theory.
4. According to Schachter and Singer's theory, the intensity of an emotion depends on your ___ and your identification of which emotion you feel depends on your _____.
   (a) hypothalamus . . . amygdala
   (b) amygdala . . . hypothalamus
   (c) physiological arousal . . . appraisal of the situation
   (d) appraisal of the situation . . . physiological arousal
5. To what extent do facial expressions of emotion differ among human cultures?
   (a) The emotion expressed by a face can be recognized equally easily by people throughout the world.
   (b) People anywhere can recognize facial expressions with greater than chance accuracy, but they are more accurate with faces from their own culture.
   (c) Facial expressions differ so much that people cannot recognize expressions from another culture.

6. Why is the ability to recognize the facial expressions of emotions not good evidence for the idea of basic emotions?
   (a) People are not always accurate at recognizing these expressions.
   (b) Perhaps there are more than six basic emotions.
   (c) Each of these emotional expressions can occur in various degrees of intensity.
   (d) We also recognize facial expressions of other states that we don't regard as emotions.
7. What is one apparent advantage of feeling sad?
   (a) Sad people become more active and more ambitious.
   (b) In general, sad people are more optimistic about their future.
   (c) Sadness improves the probability of maintaining good health.
   (d) In some ways sad people are more realistic.
8. A moral dilemma such as the trolley dilemma or the footbridge dilemma pits two considerations against each other. What are they?
   (a) The desire to help yourself versus the desire to help other people
   (b) The desire to avoid pain to yourself versus the desire to avoid pain to others
   (c) The desire to help more people versus the guilt you would feel from hurting one person
   (d) The desire to save money versus the desire to enjoy an expensive treat at once
9. Tests of emotional intelligence ask questions about how someone would feel in various situations. Which of the following is a significant difficulty with such tests?
   (a) The tests take too long to administer.
   (b) It is hard to be sure what is the correct answer.
   (c) The questions are so easy that almost everyone gets the same score.
   (d) Scores on these tests correlate negatively with academic intelligence.

Answers: 1b, 2c, 3a, 4c, 5b, 6d, 7d, 8c, 9b.

After studying this module, you should be able to:

- Describe how researchers measure anxiety objectively.

- Describe how amygdala damage alters fear and anxiety.

- Evaluate the effectiveness of polygraphs ("lie detector tests").

- Distinguish among anger, disgust, and contempt.

- Discuss the role of wealth in happiness.

- List factors that influence happiness and ways to enhance happiness.

- Discuss how life satisfaction changes in old age.

The first module posed difficult theoretical questions, but we do not have to wait until we answer them. Even if we discard the concept of basic emotions, it remains convenient to talk about certain emotions, just as it is convenient to talk about Asia and Europe separately even though they constitute a single landmass. We proceed to issues of practical importance to almost everyone, especially clinical psychologists, such as controlling fear and increasing happiness. The emphasis here is on fear and happiness, because Chapter 13 discusses anger and aggressive behavior in more detail, and Chapter 15 includes sadness and depression.

Fear and Anxiety

Fear is a response to an immediate danger, whereas *anxiety* is a vague sense that "something bad might happen." The "right" level of anxiety depends on the situation. We readjust our anxiety based on our experiences.

Measuring Anxiety

When psychologists study happiness, sadness, or most other emotions, they rely largely on self-reports, because they have no reliable behavioral measure. Anxiety is different. For anxiety, researchers can use an operational definition based on behavior: **Anxiety** is *an increase in the startle reflex.* The startle reflex is the quick, automatic response that follows a sudden loud noise. Within a fifth of a second after the noise, you tense your muscles, especially your neck muscles, close your eyes, and mobilize your sympathetic nervous system to prepare for escape if necessary. The startle reflex itself is automatic, but experiences and context modify it.

Imagine yourself sitting with friends in a familiar place on a nice, sunny day when you hear a sudden loud noise. You startle, but just a bit. Now imagine yourself walking alone at night through a graveyard when you notice someone following you . . . and then you hear the same loud noise. Your startle response will be greater. The increase in the startle reflex is an objective measurement of anxiety. As you would expect, the startle reflex is enhanced for people who are prone to frequent anxieties (McMillan, Asmundson, Zvolensky, & Carleton, 2012). Happiness and anger decrease the startle reflex (Amodio & Harmon-Jones, 2011).

Learned associations also alter the startle reflex in laboratory animals. Suppose a rat frequently sees a "danger" stimulus—generally a light or a sound—before receiving a shock. Now that danger stimulus enhances the startle reflex to a loud noise. The increase in the startle reflex, reflecting anxiety, depends on activity of the amygdala (uh-MIG-duh-luh), shown in ▼ Figure 12.18 (Antoniadis, Winslow, Davis, & Amaral, 2007; Wilensky, Schafe, Kristensen, & LeDoux, 2006).

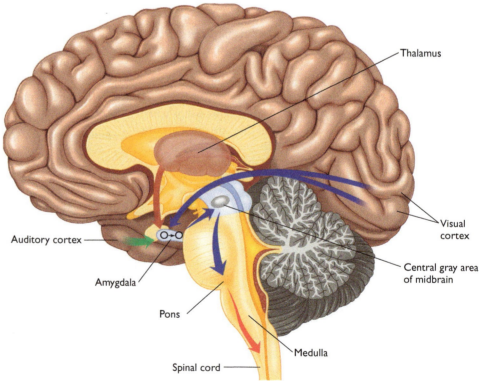

▲ **Figure 12.18** Structures in the pons and medulla control the startle response. The amygdala sends information that modifies activity in the pons and medulla. This drawing shows a human brain, although much of the research has used rats.

The figure shows a human brain, but much of the research has been conducted with laboratory animals.

Back to humans: People vary in the responsiveness of their amygdala, and therefore in their tendency toward anxiety. That tendency remains fairly consistent for an individual over time, based partly on genetics (Miu, Vulturar, Chis, Ungureanu, & Gross, 2013), and partly on epigenetics—that is, chemical changes that alter the expression of certain genes (Nikolova et al., 2014). It also depends on top-down connections from the frontal cortex that suppress the amygdala. People suffering from depression or severe anxiety have decreased activity in the frontal cortex, and therefore increased activity in the amygdala (Britton et al., 2013; Holmes et al., 2012).

People who have a highly responsive amygdala, for whatever reason, are more likely than others to report many emotionally unpleasant experiences (Barrett, Bliss-Moreau, Duncan, Rauch, & Wright, 2007). Soldiers with strong amygdala responses at the start of their service are more likely than others to report severe combat stress (Admon et al., 2009). Although soldiers experiencing a head wound leading to brain damage have a high probability of post-traumatic stress disorder (PTSD), those whose damage includes the amygdala apparently never experience PTSD (Koenigs et al., 2008). All these studies indicate that amygdala activity contributes to intense fear responses, although that is certainly not the only function of the amygdala.

People with amygdala damage no longer respond quickly the way other people do to complex emotional signals. For example, they are impaired at recognizing emotions from facial expressions (Anderson & Phelps, 2000) or tone of voice (Scott et al., 1997). Most people remember emotionally disturbing pictures better than emotionally neutral ones, but people with amygdala damage remember both kinds of photos about equally (LaBar & Phelps, 1998). A woman with damage to her amygdala in both brain hemispheres describes herself as fearless. When she watches horror movies, she experiences excitement but no fear. At an exotic pet store, people had to restrain her from trying to touch the venomous snakes and spiders. In everyday life, she enters dangerous situations without the caution other people would show. As a result, she has been robbed and assaulted several times. When she describes these events, she recalls feeling angry, but not frightened (Feinstein, Adolphs, Damasio, & Tranel, 2011). However, she did experience fear under one circumstance: When she breathed 35 percent carbon dioxide, which leaves a person gasping for breath, she reacted with panic and called it a terrible experience. Nevertheless, she agreed to do the same experiment again the next week! Furthermore, during that week she did not worry about going through the ordeal again (Feinstein et al., 2013). Evidently her amygdala is not necessary for the experience of fear, but just for processing information about possible danger.

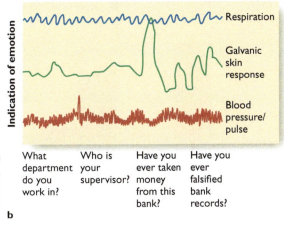

isfa/Getty Images

a   b

▲ **Figure 12.19** A polygraph operator (a) asks a series of nonthreatening questions to establish baseline readings of the subject's autonomic responses (b) and then asks questions relevant to an investigation.

Anxiety, Arousal, and Lie Detection

Let's consider an attempt to use physiological measurement of anxiety for a practical purpose, lie detection. It is, in fact, difficult to tell when someone is lying. Many people think they can detect lies by noticing fidgeting hands, or watching whether someone looks them in the eye or looks away. Those techniques are, in fact, worthless and if we ignored them, we would probably do a little better on detecting lies (ten Brinke, Stimson, & Carney, 2014). Still, the search is on for a reliable method of lie detection.

The best known attempt is the **polygraph**, or "lie detector test," which records sympathetic nervous system arousal, as measured by blood pressure, heart rate, breathing rate, and electrical conduction of the skin (see ▲ **Figure 12.19**). (Slight sweating increases electrical conduction of the skin.) The assumption is that when people lie, they feel nervous and therefore increase their sympathetic nervous system arousal.

(A bit of trivia: William Marston, the inventor of the polygraph, was also the originator of the *Wonder Woman* cartoons. Wonder Woman used a "lasso of truth" to force people to stop lying.)

The polygraph sometimes accomplishes its goal simply because an accused person hooked up to a polygraph confesses, "Oh, what's the use. You're going to figure it out now anyway, so I may as well tell you. . . ." But if people do not confess, how effectively does a polygraph detect lying?

In one study, investigators selected 50 criminal cases where two suspects took a polygraph test and one suspect later confessed to the crime (Kleinmuntz & Szucko, 1984). Thus, they had data from 100 suspects, of whom 50 were later shown to be guilty and 50 shown to be innocent. Six professional polygraph administrators examined the

concept check

9. **How could we measure anxiety levels of nonhuman animals, preverbal children, or others who cannot answer in words?**

Answer

9. Measure the strength of the startle reflex.

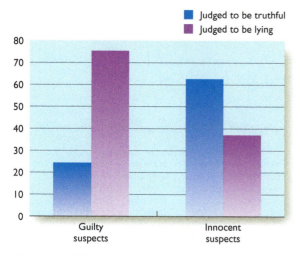

▲ **Figure 12.20** Polygraph examiners correctly identified 76 percent of guilty suspects as lying. However, they also identified 37 percent of innocent suspects as lying. (Based on data of Kleinmuntz & Szucko, 1984)

polygraph results and judged which suspects appeared to be lying. ▲ Figure 12.20 shows the results. The polygraph administrators identified 76 percent of the guilty suspects as liars but also classified 37 percent of the innocent suspects as liars.

The few other well-designed studies that have been done produced equally unimpressive results. Although many police officers still believe in polygraph testing, most researchers regard the accuracy as too uncertain for important decisions (Fiedler, Schmid, & Stahl, 2002). Polygraph results are only rarely admissible as evidence in U.S. courts. The U.S. Congress passed a law in 1988 prohibiting private employers from giving polygraph tests to employees or job applicants, except under special circumstances, and a commission of the U.S. National Academy of Sciences in 2002 concluded that polygraphs should not be used for national security clearances.

Alternative Methods of Detecting Lies

The **guilty-knowledge test**, *a modified version of the polygraph test*, produces more accurate results by *asking questions that should be threatening only to someone who knows the facts of a crime* (Lykken, 1979). Instead of asking, "Did you rob the gas station?" the interrogator asks, "Was the gas station robbed at 8 p.m.? At 10:30? At midnight? Did the robber carry a gun? A knife? A club? Was the getaway car green? Red? Blue?" Someone who shows arousal only in response to the correct details is presumed to have "guilty knowledge" that only the guilty person or someone who had talked to the guilty person would possess. The guilty-knowledge test, when properly administered, rarely classifies an innocent person as guilty (Iacono & Patrick, 1999).

Another approach for detecting lies is to ask better questions. For example, if you ask, "What were you doing at the time of the crime?" someone can repeat a rehearsed lie. However, if you ask the person to describe the event backward, liars often falter, because it is easier to remember the truth than to remember a made-up story. Also, if you ask someone detailed, unexpected questions, or ask someone to draw a picture of where they were, innocent people generally do better than those who are lying (Vrij, Granhag, & Porter, 2010). Researchers also report that when people lie, they tend to provide few details, perhaps to avoid saying something that could be shown to be wrong (DePaolo et al., 2003). These techniques help, but the point remains that we have no way to identify lying with high confidence.

---

concept check

10. **What is the main objection to polygraph tests?**
11. **How does a guilty-knowledge test differ from the usual polygraph test?**

Answers

10. A polygraph too often identifies an innocent person as lying. 11. An ordinary polygraph test asks whether you did or did not do something, and an innocent person might be nervous, even when telling the truth. A guilty-knowledge test asks questions that should cause only someone with detailed knowledge about the crime to become nervous.

Anger and Related Emotions

Anger is associated with a desire to harm people or drive them away, usually in response to a belief that someone has harmed you. Participants in one study kept an "anger diary" for a week (Averill, 1983). A typical entry was, "My roommate locked me out of the room when I went to the shower." They also described how they reacted, such as, "I talked to my roommate about it," or "I did nothing about it."

Surveys across a variety of cultures find that people experience anger frequently but seldom even consider resorting to violence (Ramirez, Santisteban, Fujihara, & Van Goozen, 2002). Chapter 13 has more to say about aggressive behavior.

Anger, disgust, and contempt are reactions to different types of offense. Anger occurs when someone interferes with your rights or expectations. Disgust is literally *dis* (bad) + *gust* (taste). In the English language, we often use the term loosely, but narrowly speaking, **disgust** refers to *a reaction to something that would make you feel contaminated if it got into your mouth* (Rozin, Lowery, et al., 1999*)*. Most people find the idea of eating feces or insects highly disgusting. We also react with disgust to moral offenses, such as when one person cheats another (Chapman, Kim, Susskind, & Anderson, 2009; Danovitch & Bloom, 2009). After experiencing disgust from a bad or offensive taste, people are more likely than usual to feel disgusted or "grossed out" by moral offenses, so evidently the two types of disgust are closely related (Erskine, Kacinik, & Prinz, 2014; Herz, 2014). **Contempt** is *a reaction to a violation of community standards,* such as when someone fails to do a fair share of the work or claims credit for something another person did (Rozin, Lowery, et al., 1999).

Happiness, Joy, and Positive Psychology

"What makes people happy?" is a more complicated question than it sounds. If we ask, "What *would* make you happy?" people often ask for more money, a better job, or other tangibles. If we ask, "What *does* make you happy?" people are more likely to cite family, friends, nature, a sense of accomplishment, music, or religious faith.

Positive psychology *studies the features that enrich life, such as happiness, hope, creativity, courage, spirituality, and responsibility* (Seligman & Csikszentmihalyi, 2000). It includes not only momentary happiness, but also subjective well-being, *a self-evaluation of one's life as pleasant, interesting, satisfying, and meaningful* (Diener, 2000).

Influence of Wealth

Are rich people happier than poor people? On average, yes, although the influence is smaller than you might guess. Not all rich people are happy, but most poor people are unhappy, especially if their friends and relatives are doing better (Fliessbach et al., 2007; Frank, 2012; Lucas & Schimmack, 2009). Health also enters into the equation. It is possible to be poor and happy, or sick and happy, but it is hard to be happy if you are both poor and sick (Smith, Langa, Kabeto, & Ubel, 2005).

As you might guess, people who have just won a lottery call themselves very happy. As you might not guess, people who won a lottery a few months ago no longer rate themselves happier than average (Diener, Suh, Lucas, & Smith, 1999; Myers, 2000). One explanation is that lottery winners get used to their new level of happiness, so a given rating doesn't mean what it used to. Also, when rich people get used to the fine things that money can buy, they get less joy from some of the ordinary pleasures of life, such as talking with friends, eating breakfast, or taking a walk in the park (Quoidbach, Dunn, Petrides, & Mikolajczak, 2010). Besides that, people are never satisfied. According to a newspaper survey, Americans earning $25,000 a year thought $50,000 a year would make them happy, but those earning $50,000 a year said they would need $100,000 a year, and those earning $100,000 a year wanted $200,000 (Csikszentmihalyi, 1999).

For many people, wealth is less important than status. When people feel prestigious and powerful, they can "be themselves" without trying to do what others want them to do (Anderson, Kraus, Galinsky, & Keltner, 2012; Kifer, Heller, Perunovic, & Galinsky, 2013).

Differences among Nations

Cross-cultural research on happiness is difficult, because it relies entirely on self-reports. Does "above-average happiness" mean the same thing to Venezuelans as it does to Bulgarians? Probably not, but for what it's worth, here are the results: In general, people in richer countries rate themselves happier than those in poorer countries, as shown in ▶ Figure 12.21 (Oishi & Schimmack, 2010). However, residents of poorer countries tend to report a higher sense of meaning and purpose in life, perhaps because poorer countries tend to be more religious (Oishi & Diener, 2014).

As a rule, when the average wealth in a country increases, average satisfaction with life also increases. However, the United States has been an exception to that rule. From 1972 until 2012, the wealth of the average person approximately doubled, while reports of well-being slightly decreased. One explanation is the increasingly uneven distribution of wealth. It used to be that the chief executive officer of a large company earned about 20 times as much as the average worker. By 2012, the chief executive earned more than 350 times as much, a ratio far higher than what almost anyone, liberal or conservative, considers fair (Kiatpongsan & Norton, 2014). So, when the statistics say that the mean wealth in the United States increased, most of the increase is due to increased wealth by the richest. Most people saw little change in their wealth, and if they compared themselves to the richest, it seemed they were doing worse than before (Sacks, Stevenson, & Wolfers, 2012).

In addition to wealth, the mean level of happiness of a country correlates positively with individual freedoms, social equality, education, good opportunities for women, and a government with little corruption (Basabe et al., 2002; Oishi & Schimmack, 2010). Happiness also correlates with tolerance for minority groups (Inglehart, Foa, Peterson, & Welzel, 2008). It is likely that a tolerant attitude leads to happiness, but it is also true that feeling happy makes people more tolerant (Ashton-James, Maddux, Galinsky, & Chartrand, 2009).

12. **Why did a doubling of the mean wealth of Americans over 30 years fail to increase mean happiness?**

Answer

12. Most of the increased wealth went to rich people. Most people's wealth did not increase much.

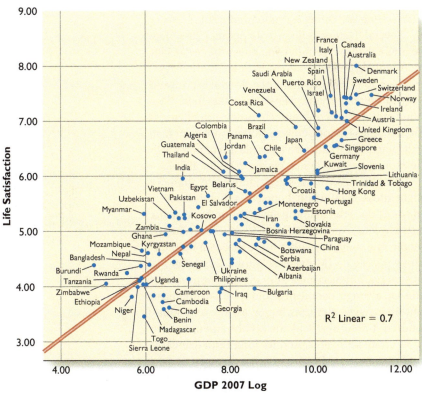

▲ **Figure 12.21** For each country, gross domestic product (GDP), a measure of wealth, is represented on the *x*-axis and an index of life satisfaction is on the *y*-axis. (From Oishi & Schimmack, 2010)

More Influences on Happiness

One of the strongest influences on happiness is people's temperament or personality. In one study, most pairs of identical twins reported almost the same level of happiness, even if they differed in their wealth, education, and job prestige (Lykken & Tellegen, 1996). Another study found that most people's reports of life satisfaction fluctuate around a stable, moderately high level (Cummins, Li, Wooden, & Stokes, 2014). This is not to say that your level of happiness cannot change, but just that it tends to stay about the same over time for most people.

How would you guess parenthood affects happiness? The answer depends on how we measure happiness. One way is to ask people to record what they are doing at various moments (in response to an unpredictable beeper) and how much they enjoy their activity. By that method, parenthood appears to be a negative influence. Being a parent, especially with a young child, entails changing diapers, caring for pain or illness, and many other chores that are unpleasant at the time. Young or unmarried parents are especially likely to find parenthood difficult. Nevertheless, if we ask people to describe their life satisfaction in general, most parents describe their children as a source of joy, because the occasional moments when a child gives a parent a hug and a smile outweigh a long series of tedious tasks. Parents are more likely than others to think frequently about the meaningfulness of life (Nelson, Kushlev, English, Dunn, & Lyubomirsky, 2013).

Several factors influence happiness less than we might expect. Wouldn't you guess that especially good-looking people would be happier than average? If you are good looking, many people smile at you and want to be your friend. However, researchers have found only a small correlation between attractiveness and happiness among college students—except that, on average, highly attractive people are happier with their romantic life (Diener, Wolsic, & Fujita, 1995).

Weather also makes less difference than we might guess. People rate themselves slightly happier on sunny days than cloudy days (Denissen, Butalid, Penke, & van Aken, 2008), but on a given day, happy people rate today's weather more pleasant than unhappy people do (Messner & Wänke, 2011). That is, most of happiness comes from inside, not from outside. On average, people in a cold state like Michigan rate themselves about as happy as those in sunny southern California (Schkade & Kahneman, 1998).

Certain life events produce long-term decreases in life satisfaction. People who get divorced show a gradual decrease in happiness in the years leading up to the divorce. They recover slowly and incompletely over the next few years (Diener & Seligman, 2004; Lucas, 2005). People who lose a spouse through death also have decreased happiness

leading up to the event (because of the spouse's failing health) and on average they recover slowly and incompletely. ▼ Figure 12.22 shows the mean results. Naturally, the results vary from one person to another. Losing a job is a similar blow to life satisfaction, and many people do not fully recover (Lucas, Clark, Georgellis, & Diener, 2004).

Many aspects of life correlate with happiness or subjective well-being. In the following list, remember that correlations do not demonstrate causation, so alternative explanations are possible.

- Married people tend to be happier than unmarried people (DeNeve, 1999; Myers, 2000), especially if it is a happy marriage (Carr, Freedman, Cornman, & Schwarz, 2014). (Well, duh!) College students with close friendships and romantic attachments are usually happier than those without such attachments (Diener & Seligman, 2002). Marriages and close social contacts are helpful in many ways (Cacioppo, Hawkley, & Berntson, 2003). Also, happy people are more likely than sad people to get married or develop friendships (Lyubomirsky, King, & Diener, 2005). (Would you want to marry or become close friends with someone who was frequently sad?)
- Happy people are more likely than average to have a sense of purpose in life, and a goal in life other than making money (Csikszentmihalyi, 1999; Diener et al., 1999; Hill & Turiano, 2014). One reason the money goal does not lead to happiness is that most people who strive to be rich do not succeed! (Nickerson, Schwarz, Diener, & Kahneman, 2003).
- Health and happiness go together, to no one's surprise (DeNeve, 1999; Myers, 2000). Health improves happiness, and a happy disposition improves habits that lead to health.
- People who have many conversations that exchange important information tend to be happier than those who engage only in small talk (Mehl, Vazire, Holleran, & Clark, 2010).
- Religious people tend to be happier than nonreligious people (Myers, 2000). That trend is stronger in countries with high attendance at religious services,

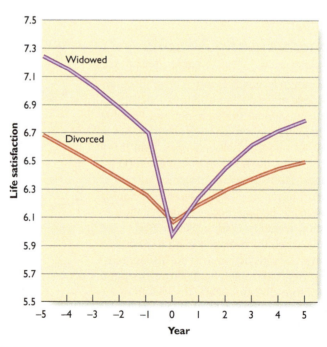

▲ **Figure 12.22** For each person, 0 marks the year of loss of a spouse through divorce or death. On the average, life satisfaction declines until the loss and gradually but incompletely recovers afterward. (From "Beyond money: Toward an economy of well-being" by E. Diener and M. E. P. Seligman, 2004. *Psychological Science in the Public Interest, 5,* 1–31. Copyright © 2004 Blackwell Publishing. Reprinted by permission.)

such as Turkey and Poland, than in countries with low attendance, such as Sweden (Gebauer, Sedikides, & Neberich, 2012). Religion's ability to enhance happiness apparently depends on building social networks, as it does not correlate significantly with private devotion (Lim & Putnam, 2010).

- People who have happy friends tend also to be happy. A massive longitudinal study suggests a cause-and-effect relationship: If your friends or other people with whom you have frequent contact become happier, then within a few months, you will probably become happier also, and a few months later, your other friends will start becoming happier (Fowler & Christakis, 2008). Evidently, happiness is contagious!

Ways to Improve Happiness

If you want to improve your happiness, your best strategy is to change your activities. A nature walk improves mood far more than most people guess (Nisbet & Zelenski, 2011). People who live near a park or other natural area tend to be happier than those who don't (White, Alcock, Wheeler, & Depledge, 2013). For students, joining a club or starting better study habits yields long-term improvements in mood and satisfaction (Sheldon & Lyubomirsky, 2006).

Some advice that will help in the long run, though not necessarily today: Keep a diary where you record the events of the day, especially the pleasant ones. Later you will get pleasure—more than you expect—from looking back and reliving these events (Zhang, Kim, Brooks, Gino, & Norton, 2014). You can also enjoy anticipating future experiences. You won't get great pleasure when you look forward to getting an object, like a new television set or a car, but looking forward to a vacation or other experience often makes people happy (Kumar, Killingsworth, & Gilovich, 2014).

Still more advice: Take out time once a week to list a few things about which you feel grateful. People who write about feeling grateful improve their life satisfaction (Emmons & McCullough, 2003; Lyubomirsky, Dickerhoof, Boehm, & Sheldon, 2011). Also, perform an occasional act of kindness for someone you hardly know (Sheldon & Lyubomirsky, 2004). In one study, experimenters asked people to rate their happiness in the morning and then gave them money, instructing them to spend it by evening. Some (chosen randomly) were told to spend it on themselves. Others were told to buy a gift for someone else. When they were questioned that evening, those who gave presents were happier, on the average, than those who spent the money on themselves (Dunn, Aknin, & Norton, 2008). Other studies confirmed that both adults and toddlers feel happier and act happier after an act of kindness to someone else (Aknin, Hamlin, & Dunn, 2012; Mongrain, Chin, & Shapira, 2011). In the words of a Chinese proverb, if you want happiness for an hour, take a nap. If you want happiness for a day, go fishing. If you want happiness for a year, inherit a fortune. If you want happiness for a lifetime, help somebody.

Age

Other things being equal, would you expect old people to be happier than young people, less happy, or about the same? ▲ Figure 12.23 shows the trend over age, according to a survey of more than 340,000 people in the United States (Stone, Schwartz, Broderick, & Deaton, 2010). Overall well-being declines from early adulthood until about age 50, on average, and then begins a steady increase as long as people remain healthy.

What explains the reported happiness of older people? One explanation is decreased stress (Stone et al., 2010). Beyond a certain age, people can stop worrying about becoming a success, paying the bills, rearing a family, and so forth. They already know how successful they are or aren't, and there is little need to continue worrying about it. Also, older people deliberately regulate their mood. They attend to happy events and turn away from unpleasant ones, especially if they are already in an unhappy mood (Isaacowitz, Toner, Goren, & Wilson, 2008). That trend varies somewhat

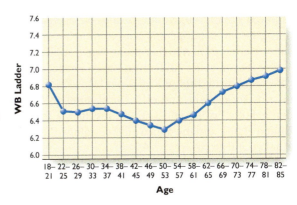

▲ **Figure 12.23** People's reported well-being reaches a low point at about age 50 and then increases, on average, as long as people remain healthy. These results represent a survey of more than 340,000 people in 2008. Source: From "A snapshot of the age distribution of psychological well-being in the United States," by A. A. Stone, Schwartz, J. E., Broderick, J. E., & Deaton, A., 2010. *Proceedings of the National Academy of Sciences, U.S.A., 107,* pp. 9985–9990.

across cultures, as older Americans are more likely to distance themselves from unpleasant information than Japanese people are (Grossman, Karasawa, Kan, & Kitayama, 2014).

The age trend also depends on when someone was born. Over 20 to 30 years, researchers repeatedly asked one set of people to rate their overall enjoyment of life. As ▼ Figure 12.24 shows, people

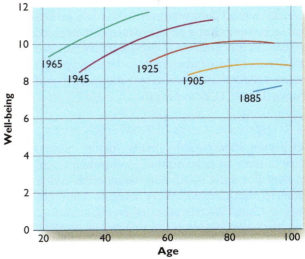

▲ **Figure 12.24** On average, people born in a given year (such as 1965 or 1945) reported greater well-being as they grew older. In addition, those born in more recent decades reported greater well-being than those born earlier. (From "The effect of birth cohort on well-being: The legacy of economic hard times," by A. R. Sutin, A. Terracciano, Y. Milaneschi, Y. An, L. Ferrucci, & A. B. Zonderman, 2013. *Psychological Science, 24,* pp. 379–385.)

reported greater enjoyment of life, on average, as they grew older, but people born in more recent decades started from a higher point than people born earlier (Sutin, et al., 2013). Those born in earlier decades had lived through the Great Depression, one or two World Wars, and other hard times that evidently left a lasting effect. These results are for the United States, and the data would certainly differ for other countries.

13. List some factors that correlate with happiness.

Answer

13. Happiness correlates positively (though not in all cases strongly) with wealth, health, living in a country that tolerates minority groups and gives high status to women, having close personal relationships, having goals in life, having substantive conversations, having happy friends, expressing gratitude, and helping others. It also increases in old age, and is greater for people born in recent decades (at least in the United States).

Sadness

If you ask people what makes them happy, you get many answers, but if you ask what makes them sad, most answers fit a pattern: People feel sad from a sense of loss. It could be death of a loved one, breakup of a romantic relationship, injury or illness, or a financial setback, but whatever it is, it is a serious loss. Sadness motivates people to restore their mood in whatever way possible. If given a choice between a small reward now and a larger one later, sad people are more likely than others to take the small reward at once (Lerner, Li, & Weber, 2013).

Crying

Sad people often react by crying. Just as cultures differ in their attitudes toward loud public laughter, they also differ in attitudes about adult crying. Adults in the United States cry far more often than those in China. Women reported crying more than men in each of 30 cultures in one survey (Becht & Vingerhoets, 2002).

Why do we cry? (Other animals don't.) Many people say that crying relieves tension and makes them feel better, but the actual effectiveness is uncertain. Certainly people relax when they *stop* crying, but the relief from stopping doesn't necessarily mean that crying was beneficial (Gross, Fredrickson, & Levenson, 1994). In one experiment, one group was encouraged to cry and another was instructed to hold back their tears while watching a sad film. Contrary to the idea that crying relieves tension, the two groups had equal tension at the end, and those who cried reported more depression (Kraemer & Hastrup, 1988). An alternative view is that the main purpose of crying is to communicate a need for sympathy and social support (Provine, Krosnowski, & Brocato, 2009).

14. What evidence conflicts with the idea that crying relieves tension?

Answer

14. People who cried during a sad movie had no less tension than people who restrained their crying, and they reported feeling more depressed.

Other Emotions

Happiness may not be the only type of "positive" emotion. For some purposes it helps to distinguish among enthusiasm, amusement, pride, awe, and several types of love. For example, people feeling happy or amused tend to become noncritical in their thinking, and they often accept weak arguments. In contrast, people experiencing a sense of awe tend to examine the evidence more carefully (Griskevicius, Shiota, & Neufeld, 2010).

Many psychologists consider surprise an emotion. It occurs when events do not match expectations. When people are surprised, they become more sensitive to dangers and turn their attention toward anything that suggests a threat (Schützwohl & Borgstedt, 2005). They also tend to remember previous events that were surprising (Parzuchowski & Szymkow-Sudziarska, 2008).

Embarrassment, shame, guilt, and pride are the self-conscious emotions. They occur when you think about how other people regard you or might regard you if they knew what you had done. The distinctions among embarrassment, shame, and guilt are not sharp, and different cultures draw the distinctions in different ways. For example, the Japanese use a word translated as *shame* far more often than the word translated into English as *embarrassment* (Imahori & Cupach, 1994). For English speakers, most causes of embarrassment fall into three categories (Sabini, Siepmann, Stein, & Meyerowitz, 2000):

- *mistakes,* such as thinking someone was flirting with you when in fact they were flirting with the person behind you
- *being the center of attention,* such as having people sing "Happy Birthday" to you
- *sticky situations,* such as having to ask someone for a major favor

Sometimes, people also feel embarrassed out of sympathy for someone else who is in an embarrassing situation (Shearn, Spellman, Straley, Meirick, & Stryker, 1999). Imagining how the other person feels causes you embarrassment, too.

Emotions and the Richness of Life

We try to feel happy as much as possible and try to avoid feeling sad, angry, or frightened, right? Well, usually but not always. People voluntarily go to movies that they know will make them sad or frightened. They ride roller coasters that advertise how scary they are. Some people seem to enjoy being angry.

Alcoholics and drug abusers experience wild swings of emotion, and many who quit say that although life is better since they quit, they sometimes miss the emotional swings. All of our emotions, within limits, provide richness to our experiences.

Summary

- *Fear and anxiety.* Anxiety can be measured objectively by variations in the startle reflex after a loud noise. (page 394)
- *Anxiety and the amygdala.* Variations in fear and anxiety relate to activity of the amygdala. People with damage to the amygdala are capable of feeling fear, but they are impaired in processing most types of information that might lead to fear. (page 394)
- *Polygraph.* The polygraph measures the activity of the sympathetic nervous system. The polygraph is sometimes used as a "lie detector." However, because the responses of honest people overlap those of liars, the polygraph makes many mistakes. (page 395)
- *Anger.* Anger arises when we perceive that someone has done something intentionally that blocks our intended actions. (page 396)
- *Positive psychology.* Positive psychology is the study of features that enrich life. (page 397)

- *Happiness and joy.* Happiness level is usually fairly stable over time. However, it decreases for years, sometimes permanently, after the death of a close loved one, divorce, loss of a job, or a disability. (page 398)
- *Increasing happiness.* Happiness increases from changes in activities, such as listing things to feel grateful about and helping other people. (page 399)
- *Happiness and age.* On average, people report increased happiness and life satisfaction as they grow older. In the United States, people born in recent decades tend to report more happiness than people born in previous decades. (page 399)
- *Sadness.* Sadness is a reaction to a loss. Crying is a way of communicating sadness or distress to others. (page 400)
- *Other emotions.* It is often helpful to distinguish several types of positive emotion such as pride, awe, and amusement. Embarrassment, shame, guilt, and pride depend on how we believe others will react to our actions. (page 400)

Key Terms

anxiety (page 394)

contempt (page 396)

disgust (page 396)

embarrassment (page 400)

guilty-knowledge test (page 396)

polygraph (page 395)

positive psychology (page 397)

subjective well-being (page 397)

Review Questions

1. Which of the following best describes the woman in the text with damage to her amygdala in both brain hemispheres?
   - (a) Unable to experience fear
   - (b) Fails to process information about possible danger
   - (c) Prone to outbursts of unprovoked anger and aggression
   - (d) Very slow to shift between happiness and sadness

2. What does a polygraph measure?
   - (a) Overall activity of the cerebral cortex
   - (b) Differences in activity between the left and right hemispheres of the cerebral cortex
   - (c) Arousal of the sympathetic nervous system
   - (d) Arousal of the parasympathetic nervous system

3. How much annual salary would it take to make the average American happy?
   - (a) $50,000
   - (b) $100,000
   - (c) $200,000
   - (d) About twice as much as the current salary, whatever that is

4. On average, people born in more recent decades are _____ than those born in earlier decades, and life satisfaction _____ as people grow older.
   - (a) happier . . . increases
   - (b) happier . . . decreases
   - (c) less happy . . . increases
   - (d) less happy . . . decreases

5. Embarrassment, shame, guilt, and pride are grouped as what category of emotions?
   - (a) Positive
   - (b) Negative
   - (c) Self-conscious
   - (d) Reactive

Answers: 1b, 2c, 3d, 4a, 5c.

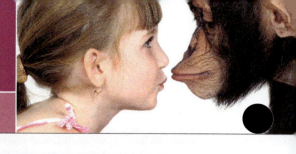

Stress, Health, and Coping

After studying this module, you should be able to:

- Describe and evaluate Selye's concept of stress.

- Discuss the difficulties of measuring stress.

- Give examples of how stress can affect health by altering behavior.

- Describe the role of cortisol and the immune system in stress effects on health.

- Explain the evidence suggesting that some people are more predisposed than others to post-traumatic stress disorder.

- List examples of ways to cope with stress.

Our emotions affect physiological processes and thereby influence health.

John Olson/Getty Images

Imagine you meet a man suffering from multiple sclerosis. Would you say, "It's his own fault. He's being punished for his sins"? Many people in previous times believed just that. We congratulate ourselves today on having learned not to blame the victim.

Or have we? We think that cigarette smokers are largely at fault if they develop lung cancer. We note that AIDS is most common among people with a history of intravenous drug use or unsafe sex. If women drink alcohol during pregnancy, we hold them partly to blame if their infants have deformities or mental retardation. As we learn more and more about the causes of various illnesses, we expect people to accept more responsibility for their own health. Nevertheless, it is easy to overstate the effect of behavior on health. Even if you are careful about your diet, exercise regularly, and avoid known risks, you could become ill anyway.

Health psychology *addresses how people's behavior influences health,* including such issues as why people smoke, why they sometimes ignore their physician's advice, and how they can reduce pain. In this module, we focus on stress, the effects of stress on health, and means of coping with stress. Stress is not itself an example of emotion, but it provokes strong emotions.

Stress

Have you ever gone without sleep several nights in a row trying to meet a deadline? Or waited in a dangerous area for someone who was supposed to pick you up? Or had a close friend suddenly not want to see you anymore? Or tried to explain why you no longer want to date someone? These experiences and countless others cause stress.

Selye's Concept of Stress

Hans Selye, an Austrian-born physician who worked at McGill University in Montreal, noticed that a wide variety of illnesses produce the same symptoms— fever, inactivity, sleepiness, loss of appetite, and release of the hormone cortisol, *which enhances metabolism and increases the supply of sugar and other fuels to the cells.* While doing laboratory research with rats, he noted that the same symptoms followed many stressful experiences, including heat, cold, confinement, the sight of a cat, or an injection of anything. He inferred that the body reacts with fever, inactivity, and so forth to any threat, and that these symptoms were the body's way of defending itself. According to Selye (1979), stress is *the nonspecific response of the body to any demand made upon it.* All demands on the body evoke responses that prepare for fighting some kind of threat.

Selye's concept of stress included any experience that changes a person's life. Getting married and being promoted are presumably pleasant experiences, but they also require changes in your life, so in Selye's sense, they produce stress. However, Selye's definition does not include the effects of anything unchanging— such as poverty, racism, or a lifelong disability. An alternative definition of stress is *"an event or events that are interpreted as threatening to an individual and which elicit physiological and behavioral responses"* (McEwen, 2000, p. 173). Because this definition highlights what an individual interprets as threatening, it recognizes that some event might be stressful to you and not someone else or to you at one time and not at another. For example, seeing a snake in your backyard could terrify one person but not another. A critical word from your boss might disturb you, but not as much if you know why your boss is in a bad mood.

Selye described the general adaptation syndrome, *the body's response to stressful events of any type.* It begins with the *alarm* stage, marked by activity of the sympathetic nervous system to prepare the body for vigorous activity. However, the sympathetic nervous system is not capable of sustained, long-term arousal. After a while, the body enters the *resistance* stage, when the adrenal glands

The stressfulness of an event depends on how we interpret it. Most people would be delighted to finish second in an Olympic event, but someone who hoped to finish first may consider it a defeat.

release cortisol and other hormones that maintain prolonged alertness. The body also saves energy by decreasing unnecessary activity. After intense, prolonged stress the body enters *exhaustion*, marked by fatigue, inactivity, and decreased ability to resist illness. For example, after an earthquake produced the Fukushima nuclear plant disaster in Japan, many families had to seek temporary shelter far from home. In the short run, they felt energized, but when they couldn't resume their normal lives, they became depressed (Brumfiel, 2013).

Measuring Stress

To do research on stress, we need to measure it. One approach is to give people a checklist of stressful experiences. For example, the Social Readjustment Rating Scale lists 43 life-change events (Holmes & Rahe, 1967). The authors of this test asked people to rate how stressful each event would be, and on that basis, they assigned each event a certain number of points, such as 100 for death of a spouse and 11 for a traffic ticket. On this questionnaire, you check the events you experienced recently, and a psychologist totals your points to measure your stress.

Checklists of this sort have serious problems. One is the assumption that many small stressors add up to the same as one large stressor. For example, graduating from college, receiving unexpected money, moving to a new address, and starting a new job are all considered stressors. According to the checklist, this combination rates almost twice as many points as you would get from a divorce. Another problem is the ambiguity of many items. You get 44 points for "change in health of a family member." You would certainly check that item if you discover that your 5-year-old son or daughter has diabetes. Should you also check it if your aunt, whom you seldom see, recovers nicely from a bout of influenza? Apparently, you get to decide what counts and what doesn't.

Moreover, a given event has different meanings depending on how people interpret the event and what they can do about it (Lazarus, 1977). Becoming pregnant is not the same for a 27-year-old married woman as for an unmarried 16-year-old. Losing a job is shattering for a 50-year-old, mildly disappointing to a 17-year-old, and trivial for an actor who works in many plays each year and never expects any of them to last long. How would you feel about winning a silver medal in the Olympics? Most of us would feel great, but many silver medal winners are disappointed that they didn't win the gold (Medver, Madey, & Gilovich, 1995). What matters is not the event itself but what it means to you.

Yet another problem with Selye's approach is that it considers all types of stressors to be equivalent, except in amount. Later research has found that personal rejection is especially troubling, such as comes from a romantic breakup, being fired from a job, or any other occasion when a person feels excluded and rejected. That type of stress is particularly likely to lead to health problems (Murphy, Slavich, Chen, & Miller, 2015).

The effects of stress depend not only on the unpleasant events ("hassles") that we have to deal with but also the pleasant events ("uplifts") that brighten our day (Kanner, Coyne, Schaefer, & Lazarus, 1981). ■ Table 12.1 presents one example of this approach. Given that the stressfulness of an event depends on our interpretation of the event, the best way to measure someone's stress is through a careful, well-structured interview that evaluates all the pluses and minuses in someone's life (Brown, 1989).

Table 12.1 Ten Common Hassles and Uplifts	
Hassles	**Uplifts**
1. Concerns about weight	1. Relating well with your spouse or lover
2. Health of a family member	2. Relating well with friends
3. Rising prices of common goods	3. Completing task
4. Home maintenance	4. Feeling healthy
5. Too many things to do	5. Getting enough sleep
6. Misplacing or losing things	6. Eating out
7. Yard work or outside home maintenance	7. Meeting your responsibilities
8. Property, investment, or taxes	8. Visiting, phoning, or writing someone
9. Crime	9. Spending time with family
10. Physical appearance	10. Home (inside) pleasing to you

Source: Kanner, Coyne, Schaefer, & Lazarus, 1981

How Stress Affects Health

People who have recently endured severe stress, such as divorce or the death of a husband or wife, have an increased risk of medical problems, ranging from life-threatening illnesses to tooth decay (Hugoson, Ljungquist, & Breivik, 2002; Lillberg et al., 2003; Manor & Eisenbach, 2003; Sbarra, Law, & Portley, 2011). How does stress lead to health problems?

Indirect Effects

Stress can influence health by altering people's behavior. For example, people who have just lost a husband or wife lose their appetite (Shahar, Schultz, Shahar, & Wing, 2001). They don't sleep well, they forget to take their medications, and some engage in risky behaviors, such as excessive drinking or overeating.

Stress also impairs health in roundabout ways. Back in the 1940s, a midwife who delivered three female babies on a Friday the 13th announced that all three were hexed and would die before their 23rd birthday. The first two did die young. As the third woman approached her 23rd birthday, she checked into a hospital and informed the staff of her fears. The staff noted that she dealt with her anxiety by extreme hyperventilation (deep breathing). Shortly before her birthday, she hyperventilated to death.

How did this happen? Ordinarily, when people do not breathe voluntarily, the carbon dioxide in their blood triggers reflexive breathing. By extreme hyperventilation, this woman exhaled so much carbon dioxide that she did not have enough left to trigger reflexive breathing. When she stopped breathing voluntarily, she stopped breathing altogether (Clinicopathologic Conference, 1967). This is a clear example of an indirect effect of emotions on health: The fact that she believed the hex caused its fulfillment.

Direct Effects

Stress also affects health more directly. Suppose you have a miserable job, you live in a war zone, or you live with someone who is often abusive. If you face a constant threat, you activate your adrenal glands to release more cortisol, which enhances metabolism and enables cells to combat stress. A moderate, brief increase in cortisol improves attention and memory (Krugers, Hoogenraad, & Groc, 2010). Stress also activates parts of your immune system, preparing it to fight anything from infections to tumors (Benschop et al., 1995; Connor & Leonard, 1998). Presumably, the reason is that throughout our evolutionary history, stressful situations often led to injury, so the immune system must be ready to fight infections. That effect made more sense when injuries were people's main source of stress. Today, the immune system reacts to the stress of such things as feeling socially rejected (Moor, Crone, & van der Molen, 2010) or giving a public lecture (Dickerson, Gable, Irwin, Aziz, & Kemeny, 2009). Your immune system fights infections by producing a fever, because most bacteria do not reproduce well at elevated temperatures (Kluger, 1991). It also conserves energy by increasing sleepiness and decreasing overall activity levels. Note the result: Intense, prolonged stress *by itself*, acting through the immune system, can lead to fever, fatigue, and sleepiness (Maier & Watkins, 1998). You may feel ill and look ill, even if you are not.

Still more prolonged stress leads to exhaustion. You feel withdrawn, your performance declines, and you complain about low quality of life (Evans, Bullinger, & Hygge, 1998). Prolonged high release of cortisol damages the hippocampus, a key brain area for memory (de Quervain, Roozendaal, Nitsch, McGaugh, & Hock, 2000; Kleen, Sitomer, Killeen, & Conrad, 2006; Kuhlmann, Piel, & Wolf, 2005). Eventually, the immune system weakens, and you become more vulnerable to illness (Cohen et al., 1998).

Heart Disease

An upholsterer repairing the chairs in a physician's waiting room once noticed that the fronts of the seats wore out before the backs. To figure out why, the physician began watching patients in the waiting room. He noticed that his heart patients habitually sat on the front edges of their seats, waiting impatiently to be called in for their appointments. This observation led to a hypothesis linking heart disease to an impatient, success-driven personality, now known as Type A personality (Friedman & Rosenman, 1974).

People with Type A personality are *highly competitive, insisting on always winning. They are impatient and often hostile.* By contrast, people with a Type B personality are *more easygoing, less hurried, and less hostile.* Heart disease correlates with Type A behavior, especially with hostility, but only weakly (Eaker, Sullivan, Kelly-Hayes, D'Agostino, & Benjamin, 2004). Heart disease also correlates with chronic anxiety (Thurston, Rewak, & Kubzansky, 2013). The best way to conduct the research is to measure personality now and heart problems later. (We want to know how personality affects heart problems, not how heart problems affect personality.) A study of that kind found a correlation of only 0.08 between hostility and heart disease (Rutledge & Hogan, 2002).

The strongest known psychological influence on heart disease is social support. People with strong friendships and family ties usually take better care of themselves and keep their heart rate and blood pressure under control (Uchino, Cacioppo, & Kiecolt-Glaser, 1996). People who learn techniques for managing stress lower their blood pressure and decrease their risk of heart disease (Linden, Lenz, & Con, 2001).

a

b

People in some cultures (**a**) live at a frantic pace. In other cultures (**b**), no one cares what time it is. Heart disease is more common in cultures with a hectic pace.

Variations in the prevalence of heart disease across cultures may depend on behavior (Levine, 1990). In some cultures, people walk fast, talk fast, wear watches, and tend to everything in a hurry. In other, more relaxed cultures, people are seldom in a rush. Almost nothing happens on schedule, but no one seems to care. As you might guess, heart disease is more common in countries with a hurried pace.

Post-Traumatic Stress Disorder

A profound result of severe stress is post-traumatic stress disorder (PTSD), *marked by prolonged anxiety and depression.* This condition has been recognized in postwar periods throughout history under such terms as "battle fatigue" and "shell shock." It also occurs in rape or assault victims, torture victims, survivors of life-threatening accidents, and witnesses to a murder. People with PTSD suffer from frequent nightmares, outbursts of anger, unhappiness, and guilt. A brief reminder of the tragic experience might trigger a flashback that borders on panic. Mild problems seem unduly stressful, even years after the event (Solomon, Mikulincer, & Flum, 1988).

However, most people who endure a traumatic event do not develop PTSD. In fact, the probability of developing PTSD correlates poorly with the stressfulness of the event, and more strongly with previous emotional difficulties (Berntsen et al., 2012; Rubin & Feeling, 2013). Many psychologists have assumed that talking to a therapist soon after a traumatic experience might be helpful. However, most studies find that such interventions have little benefit (McNally, Bryant, &

Ehlers, 2003), and often make people feel even worse (Bootzin & Bailey, 2005; Lilienfeld, 2007).

Perhaps some people are simply more vulnerable than others. Most PTSD victims have a smaller than average hippocampus, and their brains differ from the average in several other ways (Stein, Hanna, Koverola, Torchia, & McClarty, 1997; Yehuda, 1997). Given that stress releases cortisol and that high levels of cortisol damage the hippocampus, it would seem likely that high stress caused the smaller hippocampus. However, one study compared monozygotic twins in which one twin developed PTSD after wartime experiences and the other was not in battle and did not develop PTSD. The results: *Both* twins had a smaller than average hippocampus (Gilbertson et al., 2002). These results imply that the hippocampus was already small before the trauma, perhaps for genetic reasons, and having a small hippocampus increases the risk of PTSD.

concept check ✓

17. **What conclusion would follow if researchers had found that the twin without PTSD had a normal size hippocampus?**

Answer

17. If the twin without PTSD had a normal hippocampus, the conclusion would be that severe stress had damaged the hippocampus of the twin with PTSD.

Coping with Stress

How you react to an event depends not only on the event itself but also on how you interpret it. How did it compare to what you had expected? Do you think it was a one-time event or the start of a trend? Your reaction also depends on your personality. Some people keep their spirits high in the face of tragedy, whereas others are devastated by minor setbacks. Coping with stress is the process of developing ways to get through difficult times.

People cope with stress in many ways, grouped into three categories. One is problem-focused coping, *doing something to improve the situation.* Reappraisal is *reinterpreting a situation to make it seem less threatening.* Emotion-focused coping is *regulating one's emotional reaction.* Suppose you are nervous about an upcoming test. Studying harder is a problem-focused method of coping. Deciding that your grade is not very important is a reappraisal. Deep breathing exercises are an emotion-focused method. Each of these coping strategies works well under certain circumstances, and the most healthful strategy is to be flexible in picking the strategy best suited to the problem at hand (Bonanno & Burton, 2013).

The distinction among coping styles is not a firm one, however (Skinner, Edge, Altman, & Sherwood, 2003). For example, one way of coping is to seek help and support from friends. Their support helps calm emotions (emotion-focused) but also may help deal with the problem itself (problem-focused).

Problem-Focused Coping

In many cases, the best way to handle stress is to do something about the problem. In one experiment, college students in one group spent half an hour a day for three to five days writing about a deeply upsetting experience, while participants in the control group wrote about unemotional topics. All the writings were confidential, so no one received any feedback or advice. Follow-up studies found that during the succeeding months, those who had written about their upsetting experiences showed better health, better grades, and less alcohol use than those in the control group, mainly because writing about the problem helped students plan what to do the next time they faced a similar problem (Pennebaker, 1997; Pennebaker & Graybeal, 2001). Writing about a stressful experience doesn't always help, however. Researchers asked people who had recently gone through a divorce or separation to write for 20 minutes a day over three days about their deepest emotions concerning the loss of their marriage. Most of these people fared worse than those in the control group, who spent the same time writing about unemotional topics (Sbarra, Boals, Mason, Larson, & Mehl, 2013). Why emotional writing backfired in this case is not entirely clear, but the authors suggested that dwelling on a difficult experience while it is still happening is painful. The students in the previous studies were gaining perspective on experiences that had happened some time ago.

Gaining a sense of control over a situation makes it less stressful. Suppose a snowstorm has trapped you in a small cabin. You have food and fuel, but you have no idea how long you will be stuck. The snow melts five days later, enabling you to leave. Contrast that with a case where you decide to isolate yourself in a cabin for five days so you can finish a painting. In both cases, you spend five days in a cabin, but when you do it voluntarily, you know what to expect, you feel in control, and you have less stress. Hospital patients who are told exactly what to expect show less anxiety and recover more quickly than average (Van Der Zee, Huet, Cazemier, & Evers, 2002). Even people with a terminal disease feel better if they have some sense of control (Gerstorf et al., 2014).

Thinking that you have control is calming, even if you really don't. In one study, people received painfully hot stimuli to their arms while playing a video game. Participants in one group knew they had no control over the pain. Those in the other group were told (incorrectly) that they could decrease the painful

stimuli if they made the correct joystick response quickly enough. In fact, the painful stimuli varied randomly, but whenever it decreased, these people assumed they were responding "quickly enough." Those who *thought* they were in control reported less pain, and brain scans confirmed that the pain-sensitive areas of the brain responded less strongly (Salomons, Johnstone, Backonja, & Davidson, 2004).

One way to reduce stress is to get a small-scale preview of an upcoming experience. This is inoculation by *exposing yourself to small amounts of stressful events*. Armies have soldiers practice combat skills under realistic conditions. A police trainee might pretend to intervene while two people enact a violent quarrel. If you are nervous about going to your landlord with a complaint, you might practice what you plan to say while your friend plays the part of the landlord. Inoculation has helped young people suffering from "dating anxiety." Some people are so nervous about saying or doing the wrong thing that they avoid dating opportunities. By role-playing, they practice dating behaviors with assigned partners and reduce their apprehension (Jaremko, 1983).

concept check

18. Which would disrupt your studying more, your own radio or your roommate's radio? Why?

Answer

18. Your roommate's radio would be more disruptive. You can turn your own radio on or off, switch stations, or reduce the volume. You have no such control over your roommate's radio.

Coping by Reappraisal

Suppose you are in a situation that offers no control. You underwent medical tests, and you are nervously waiting for the results. While waiting, what can you do? You might reappraise the situation: "Even if the news is bad, I can handle it. It's an opportunity for me to rise to the occasion, to show how strong I can be." People who recover well from tragedies and defeats say that they try to see the positive side of any event (Tugade & Fredrickson, 2004). Most people say they want to maintain a moderately optimistic outlook even when it is not completely accurate (Armor, Massey, & Sackett, 2008).

Asmaa Waguih/Reuters/Corbis

Practicing self-defense serves as an inoculation against fear. The thought of being attacked is less frightening if you know how to handle a situation.

People who devote a short time each day to relaxation report diminished stress. Exercise works off excess energy, allowing greater relaxation.

watching an unpleasant film, even if the loved one wasn't present (Schneiderman, Zilberstein-Kra, Leckman, & Feldman, 2011). Close contact with a loved one helps even more. Researchers recorded women's reactions while they waited to receive an electric shock. At various times, each woman held her husband's hand, an unfamiliar man's hand, or no hand. As shown in ▼ Figure 12.25, on average, a woman reported less unpleasantness and lower arousal while holding her husband's hand. Holding the hand of an unfamiliar man helped less. Women who reported a highly satisfactory marriage received more benefit from holding their husband's hand than did women reporting a less satisfactory marriage (Coan, Schaefer, & Davidson, 2006).

Here is an example of reappraisal: Students were asked to restrain their emotions while examining pictures with some disturbing images, such as injured people and crying children. Those who restrained their emotions most successfully relied on reinterpreting the pictures. For example, they might regard a picture of an injured person as "someone about to receive good medical care" (Jackson, Malmstadt, Larson, & Davidson, 2000). In another study, young adults in Israel who practiced reappraisal to control their anger became more inclined to approach the Israel-Palestinian conflict with conciliation, and less likely to advocate violence (Halperin, Porat, Tamir, & Gross, 2013).

Suppose you have to give a public speech tomorrow, or meet with your boss, and you feel such high arousal that your hands are shaking and your voice is trembling. You can try to calm yourself down, but a more effective strategy is to reappraise your arousal: It's not nervousness. It's excitement! Embracing the arousal as a good thing generally leads to a more successful performance (Brooks, 2014).

Emotion-Focused Coping

Emotion-focused strategies do not solve an underlying problem, but they help you manage your reaction to it. If you feel an unpleasant emotion—fear, anger, sadness, or disgust—would it help to simply suppress your emotion and act as if you are doing okay? It might, although suppressing your emotional expressions might reduce the energy you'll have available for something else (Segerstrom & Nes, 2007). Most Europeans and North Americans find it difficult and unpleasant to suppress their emotions. However, people in Asian cultures routinely practice emotional suppression and find it much less burdensome (Butler, Lee, & Gross, 2007). In addition to actively suppressing emotions, other ways of handling them include social support, relaxation, exercise, and distraction.

Social Support

When you feel bad, do you turn to others for support? This tendency varies across cultures. An American might discuss personal problems with a friend without necessarily expecting the friend to help. In Asian cultures, anyone who knows about your problem feels obligated to help. Many Asians avoid telling people about their difficulties for fear of burdening them with an obligation (Kim, Sherman, & Taylor, 2008).

Social support is helpful in many situations. A study found that people who had recently fallen in love reacted less strongly than usual to the stress of

Relaxation

Relaxation is an excellent way to reduce unnecessary anxiety. Here are some suggestions (Benson, 1985):

• Find a quiet place, or at least a spot where the noise is not too disturbing.
• Adopt a comfortable position, relaxing your muscles. If you are not sure how to do so, start with the opposite: *Tense* all your muscles so you notice how they feel. Then relax them one by

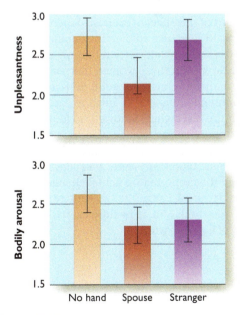

▲ **Figure 12.25** On the average, a woman exposed to the threat of an upcoming shock reported less distress while holding her husband's hand. (From Coan, Schaefer, & Davidson, 2006).

one, starting from your toes and working toward your head.

- Reduce sources of stimulation, including your own thoughts. Focus your eyes on a simple, unexciting object. Or repeat something—a word, a phrase, a prayer, perhaps the Hindu syllable *om*—whatever feels comfortable to you.
- Don't worry about anything, not even about relaxing. If worrisome thoughts pop into your head, dismiss them with "oh, well."

People who practice this or other forms of meditation report that they feel less stress. Many improve their overall health (Benson, 1977, 1985). Teachers who went through an eight-week meditation program showed benefits in handling threatening situations and in showing compassion to other people (Kemeny et al., 2012).

Exercise

Exercise also reduces stress. It may seem contradictory to say that both relaxation and exercise reduce stress, but exercise helps people relax. If you are tense about something that you have to do tomorrow, your best approach may be to put your energy to use: Exercise and relax afterward.

People in good physical condition react less strongly than average to stressful events (Crews & Landers, 1987). An event that would elevate heart rate enormously in other people elevates it only moderately in someone who has been exercising regularly. The exercise should be consistent, almost daily, but it does not need to be vigorous. In fact, strenuous activity often worsens someone's mood (Salmon, 2001).

Part of the effect of exercise depends on expectations. Researchers studied the female room attendants at seven hotels. They randomly chose certain hotels to inform these women (correctly) that their daily activities constitute good exercise that meets recommendations for a healthy, active lifestyle. When the researchers followed up four weeks later, they found that the women who were told that they were getting good exercise had in fact lost weight, and their blood pressure had decreased, even though they reported no actual change in their activities (Crum & Langer, 2007). Activity is more helpful if you think of it as healthy exercise than if you think of it as dull work.

Distraction

Another emotion-focused strategy is to distract yourself. Hospitalized patients handle their pain better if they distract themselves with a nice view, pleasant music, or other activities (Fauerbach, Lawrence, Haythornthwaite, & Richter, 2002). The Lamaze method teaches pregnant women to suppress the pain of childbirth by concentrating on breathing. Many people distract themselves from stressful or sad events by going shopping and buying themselves presents (Cryder, Lerner, Gross, & Dahl, 2008; Hama, 2001). If you find yourself brooding about some disappointment, you might feel better after reminding yourself of pleasant or successful experiences in your past (DeWall et al., 2011).

The effectiveness of distraction depends partly on people's expectations. In one study, college students were asked to hold their fingers in ice water until the sensation became too painful to endure (Melzack, Weisz, & Sprague, 1963). Some of them listened to music of their own choice and were told that listening to music would reduce the pain. Others also listened to music but were given no suggestion that it would ease the pain. Still others heard nothing but were told that a special "ultrasonic sound" was being transmitted that would lessen the pain. The group that heard music and expected it to reduce the pain tolerated the pain better than either of the other two groups did. Evidently, neither the music nor the suggestion of reduced pain is as effective as both are together.

19. Some people control anxiety with tranquilizers. In which of the three categories of coping strategy do these drugs belong?

Answer

19. Using tranquilizers is an example of emotion-focused coping.

Resilience

All of us can learn to handle stress better by using some of the techniques just described. In addition, some people seem to handle it better naturally (Haas, Omura, Constable, & Canli, 2007). We say they have **resilience**, *an ability to handle difficult situations with a minimum of distress*. A longitudinal study of police officers found that those who showed mostly positive emotions at the start were more likely than the others to handle their later stressful experiences well (Galatzer-Levy et al., 2013). A study of resilience among people of low socioeconomic status attributed part of their success to having good role models who taught them to persist through difficult situations by finding meaning in life and maintaining an optimistic viewpoint (Chen & Miller, 2012).

The best way to study resilience is to examine a large, diverse group of people before, during, and after stressful experiences to see what factors before the events predict good outcomes during and after. The U.S. Army began such a study ("The Army Study To Assess Risk and Resilience in Servicemembers") in 2010. It expects to complete the study and publish results in 2015.

Health Is Mental as Well as Medical

We have considered the ways people try to deal with stressful situations. How well do these strategies work? They work well for many people but at a cost. The cost is that coping with serious stressors requires energy. Many people who have had to cope with long-lasting stressors break their diets, resume smoking and drinking habits that they had abandoned long ago, and find it difficult to concentrate on challenging cognitive tasks (Muraven & Baumeister, 2000).

Still, in spite of the costs, an amazing number of people say that the experience of battling a chronic illness, tending to a loved one with a severe illness, or dealing with other painful experiences has brought them personal strength and an enhanced feeling of meaning in life (Folkman & Moskowitz, 2000). They found positive moments even in the midst of fear and loss. Not everyone rises to the occasion, but many do.

Summary

- *Selye's concept of stress.* According to Hans Selye, stress is "the nonspecific response of the body to any demand made upon it." Any event, pleasant or unpleasant, that brings about change in a person's life produces some measure of stress. However, this definition omits lifelong problems, such as coping with racism. By an alternative definition, stress is an event that someone interprets as threatening. (page 402)

- *Difficulties of measuring stress.* Stress checklists are problematic because many items are ambiguous. They treat all types of stress as interchangeable, although later research indicates that the stress from feeling rejected is especially hurtful. Furthermore, the stressfulness of an event depends on the person's interpretation of the event and ability to cope with it. (page 403)

- *Indirect effects on health.* Stress affects health indirectly because people exposed to stressful events often change their eating, sleeping, and drinking habits. (page 404)

- *Direct effects on health.* Stress causes increased secretion of the hormone cortisol. Brief, moderate elevations of cortisol enhance memory and immune system responses. However, prolonged cortisol damages health by impairing the hippocampus and by exhausting the immune system. (page 404)

- *Heart disease.* Research has found only a small link between emotional responses and the onset of heart disease. (page 404)

- *Post-traumatic stress disorder (PTSD).* After traumatic experiences, some people (not all) have long-lasting changes in their emotional reactions. Apparently some people are more predisposed to PTSD than others are. (page 405)

- *Coping styles.* Most strategies for dealing with stress fall into three major categories: trying to fix the problem, reappraisal, and trying to control emotions. (page 405)

- *Prediction and control.* Events are generally less stressful when people think they can predict or control them. (page 406)

- *Reappraisal.* Interpreting a situation in a new, less threatening way reduces tension. (page 406)

- *Emotion-focused coping.* Relaxation, exercise, and distraction reduce excess anxiety. (page 407)

Key Terms

cortisol (page 402)

emotion-focused coping (page 405)

general adaptation syndrome
(page 402)

health psychology (page 402)

inoculation (page 406)

post-traumatic stress disorder (PTSD)
(page 405)

problem-focused coping (page 405)

reappraisal (page 405)

resilience (page 408)

stress (page 402)

Type A personality (page 404)

Type B personality (page 404)

Review Questions

1. According to Selye's definition of stress, which one of the following would be considered stressful?
   (a) Constant quarreling with your family
   (b) Getting married
   (c) Lifelong poverty
   (d) Being a member of a minority group
2. Why does intense, prolonged stress sometimes lead to fever, fatigue, and sleepiness?
   (a) Intense stress activates the immune system.
   (b) Intense stress decreases metabolic rate.
   (c) Intense stress activates the sympathetic nervous system.
   (d) Intense stress prevents people from eating a proper diet.
3. Why is it likely that the Social Readjustment Rating Scale understates the stress levels of Type A people?
   (a) People with a Type A personality tend to lie on questionnaires.
   (b) The Social Readjustment Rating Scale measures life changes but not constant stress such as work.
   (c) People with a Type A personality feel stress only at certain times.

(d) People with a Type A personality are prone to divorce and many other life-change events.

4. Which of the following is associated with the probability of developing PTSD?
   (a) PTSD depends on the severity of the traumatic event.
   (b) People with a smaller than average hippocampus are more likely to develop PTSD.
   (c) People who talk with a therapist as soon as possible after the event can avoid PTSD.
   (d) Monozygotic twins are more likely to develop PTSD.

5. Suppose you are nervous about giving a speech before a group of 200 strangers. How could you inoculate yourself to reduce the stress?
   (a) Take some deep-breathing exercises to relax.
   (b) Practice giving your talk to a smaller group.

(c) Locate the exits of the room to increase your sense of control.
   (d) Take some pills to decrease your anxiety.

6. Suppose you have anxieties because of living in a dangerous neighborhood. Which of the following is an example of problem-based coping?
   (a) Taking tranquilizers to control anxiety.
   (b) Playing soothing music to relax yourself.
   (c) Moving to a different neighborhood.
   (d) Convincing yourself that the neighborhood isn't as dangerous as it seems.

Answers: 1b, 2a, 3b, 4b, 5b, 6c.

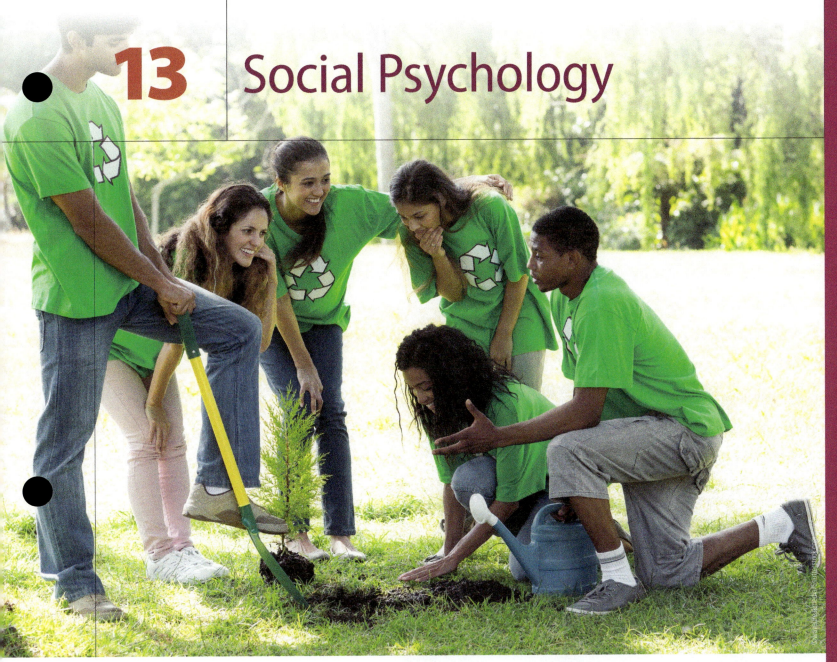

13 Social Psychology

In the *Communist Manifesto*, Karl Marx and Friedrich Engels wrote, "Mankind are more disposed to suffer, while evils are sufferable, than to right themselves by abolishing the forms to which they are accustomed. But when a long train of abuses and usurpations, pursuing invariably the same object, evinces a design to reduce them under absolute despotism, it is their right, it is their duty, to throw off such government." Fidel Castro wrote, "A little rebellion, now and then, is a good thing." Do you agree with those statements? Why or why not? Can you think of anything that would change your mind?

What if I told you that the first statement is not from the *Communist Manifesto*, but from the United States' Declaration of Independence? And what if I told you that the second quotation is from Thomas Jefferson, not Castro?

Would you agree more with these statements if they came from democratic revolutionaries instead of communist revolutionaries?

Well, those quotes did in fact come from the Declaration of Independence and Thomas Jefferson, so you can now start trying to negotiate one of the fundamental questions in social psychology: What influences your opinions?

Social psychology includes the study of attitudes, persuasion, self-understanding, and almost all everyday behaviors of relatively normal people in their relationships with others. **Social psychologists** *study social behavior and how people influence one another.*

Jim West/Alamy

Influence depends not only on what someone says but also on what the listeners think of the speaker.

After studying this module, you should be able to:

- Evaluate Kohlberg's approach to moral reasoning.
- Describe the prisoner's dilemma task.
- Explain how logical considerations can lead to cooperation.
- Describe bystander apathy and social loafing.
- List factors that correlate with aggressive behavior.

Young people, especially in the United States, look forward to becoming adults and being independent. But how independent are any of us, really? Do you make your own clothing? Will you build your own home? How much of your food do you grow or hunt? Do you perform your own medical care? Will you build your own car and pave your own roads? Of all the acts you need for survival, do you do *any* of them by yourself, other than breathe? (Even for that, you count on the government to prevent excessive air pollution.) Humans are extremely *inter*dependent. Our survival depends on cooperation.

Furthermore, most of us at least occasionally give to charity, volunteer time for worthy projects, offer directions to a stranger who appears lost, and in other ways help people who will never pay us back. Why?

Morality: Logical or Emotional?

Psychologists once regarded morality as a set of arbitrary rules, like learning to stop at a red light and go at a green light. Lawrence Kohlberg (1969; Kohlberg & Hersh, 1977) proposed instead that moral reasoning is a process that matures through a series of stages, similar to Piaget's stages of cognitive development. For example, children younger than about 6 years old say that accidentally breaking a valuable object is worse than intentionally breaking a less valuable object. Older children and adults care about intentions and not just results. The change is a natural unfolding, according to Kohlberg, not a matter of memorizing rules. As the reasoning ability matures, one moves toward making decisions based on justice and avoiding harm to others.

According to Kohlberg, to evaluate people's moral reasoning, we should ask about the reasons for their decisions, not just about the decisions themselves. In George Bernard Shaw's (1911) play *The Doctor's Dilemma*, two men are dying. The only doctor in town has enough medicine to save one of them but not both. One man is an artistic genius but dishonest, rude, and disagreeable. The other will make no great accomplishments, but he is honest and decent. The doctor, forced to choose between them, saves the honest but untalented man. Did he make the right choice? According to Kohlberg, this is the wrong question. The right question is *why* he made that choice. In the play, the doctor chose this man because he hoped to marry the wife of the artistic genius after letting him die. (What do you think about the quality of the doctor's moral reasoning?)

Kohlberg focused psychologists' attention on the reasoning processes behind moral decisions, but people usually don't deliberate about right and wrong before they act. More often, they make a quick decision and then look for reasons afterward. In the terminology of cognitive psychology (Chapter 8), we use System 1 for the initial decision, and we call upon System 2 mostly to generate logical-sounding explanations for what System 1 already decided. Consider the following: Mark and his sister Julie are college students. One summer, they traveled together and one night they stayed at a cabin in the woods. They decided it would be fun to have sex together, so they did. Julie was taking birth control pills, but Mark used a condom anyway just to be sure. Both enjoyed the experience, and neither felt hurt in any way. They decided not to do it again but to keep it as their little secret. They feel closer than ever as brother and sister. Was their action okay?

Almost everyone reacts immediately, "No! No! No!" Why? Mark and Julie used two reliable methods of birth control, and both said they enjoyed the experience and did not feel hurt. If their act was wrong, why was it wrong? When you (presumably) said that they were wrong, did you carefully reason it out? You probably decided at once, intuitively and emotionally, and then looked for a justification (Haidt, 2001, 2007).

In addition to the fact that most moral decisions are more emotional rather than logical, Kohlberg's analysis falls short in another way. According to Kohlberg, morality means seeking justice and avoiding harm to others. That description works for most Americans and Europeans, especially political liberals. However, most people in the rest of the world also consider loyalty to their group, respect for authority, and spiritual purity. For example, they would insist that incest between Mark and Julie was an impure act that defiles them spiritually, regardless of how much they say they enjoyed it (Haidt, 2012). If we care about moral thinking by all people, and not just certain types of people, we need to consider more than Kohlberg did.

1. What are some limitations of Kohlberg's approach?

Answer 1. Ordinarily, people make quick moral decisions intuitively and emotionally, rather than reasoning them out logically. Also, Kohlberg assumed that all moral decisions are based on seeking justice and avoiding harm to others. Most of the world's people also consider such matters as group loyalty, respect for authority, and spiritual purity.

Altruistic Behavior

Why do we sometimes engage in prosocial or altruistic behavior—*helping others without a benefit to ourselves?* Altruism is uncommon in other animal species. Let's qualify that: In almost every species, animals devote great energies and risk their lives to help their babies or other relatives. But they seldom do much to help unrelated individuals.

Consider this example: Each chimpanzee could pull either a rope that brought food to itself, or a rope that brought food to both itself and another chimp it sees in a nearby cage. The chimp in control seemed indifferent to the other chimp, even when the other chimp made begging gestures. Usually, the chimp pulled whichever rope was on the right regardless of whether or not it fed the other chimp (Silk et al., 2005). Similar results were reported for bonobos, gorillas, orangutans, and two monkey species (Amici, Visalberghi, & Call, 2014), although primates do show cooperative behavior in other situations (Burkart et al., 2014). In contrast, children as young as 2½ years old generally prefer a choice that brings a treat to themselves and someone else, as opposed to just themselves (Sebastián-Enesco, Hernández-Lloreda, & Colmenares, 2013), and that tendency increases as children grow older (House et al., 2013). Given a choice between two treats to themselves or one to self and one to another, 6- to 8-year-old children generally choose two for themselves, but older children and adults in some societies shift toward the sharing option (House et al., 2013). Evidently a certain amount of prosocial behavior comes naturally, and cultural influences can increase it.

Why do people do so much to help one another? You may reply that we help others because it feels good. Yes, but why does it feel good? Did we evolve genes that make altruistic behavior feel good? If so, why? No one has found such a gene, and if someone did, a theoretical question would remain about how natural selection could favor such a gene. You may reply that an altruistic gene helps the species. Yes, but if a gene helps those who *don't* have the gene as much as or more than those who do, the gene won't spread in the population. If we consider the issue in nongenetic terms, the same problem arises: If you learn a habit of helping others, including people who are not altruistic themselves, they profit and you do not. Why would you learn to act that way? Researchers have used game situations to explore these issues.

The Prisoner's Dilemma

To investigate cooperation and competition, many researchers have used the **prisoner's dilemma,** *a situation where people choose between a cooperative act*

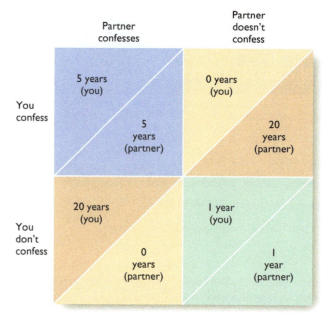

▲ **Figure 13.1** In the prisoner's dilemma, each person has an incentive to confess. But if both people confess, they suffer worse than if both had refused to confess.

and a competitive act that benefits themselves but hurts others. Imagine that you and a partner are arrested and charged with armed robbery. The police take you into separate rooms and urge each of you to confess. If neither of you confesses, the police do not have enough evidence to convict you of robbery, but they can convict you of a lesser offense with a sentence of a year in prison. If either confesses and testifies against the other, the confessor goes free and the other gets 20 years in prison. If both confess, you each get 5 years in prison. Each of you knows that the other person has the same options. ▲ Figure 13.1 illustrates the choices.

If your partner does not confess, you can confess and go free. (Let's assume you care only about yourself and not about your partner.) If your partner confesses, you still gain by confessing because you will get only 5 years in prison instead of 20. So you confess. Your partner, reasoning the same way, also confesses, so you both get 5 years in prison. If you had both kept quiet, you would have served only 1 year in prison. The situation trapped both people into uncooperative behavior.

If you and your partner could discuss your strategy, you would agree not to confess. Then, when the police took you to separate rooms, you would each hope that the other keeps the bargain. But can you be sure? Maybe your partner will double-cross you and confess. If so, you should confess, too. And if your partner does keep the bargain, what should you do? Again, it's to your advantage to confess! We're back where we started.

The two of you are most likely to cooperate if you stay in constant communication (Nemeth, 1972). If you overhear each other, you know that, if one confesses, the other will retaliate. This kind of situation occurs in real life among nations as well as individuals. During the arms race between the United States and the Soviet Union, both sides wanted a treaty to stop building nuclear weapons. However, if one country kept the agreement while the other made additional weapons, the cheater could build a military advantage. The only way to keep an agreement was to allow each side to inspect the other. Eventually, spy satellites made it possible to monitor the agreement.

The prisoner's dilemma can also be stated in terms of gains. Suppose you and another person have a choice between two moves, which we call *cooperate* and *compete.* Depending on your choices, here are the payoffs:

Here are the payoffs:

	Other person cooperates	Other person competes
You cooperate	Both win $1	Other person gains $2; you lose $2
You compete	You gain $2; other person loses $2	Both lose $1

Suppose you play this game only once with someone you will never meet. Both of you will reveal your answers by telephone to a third person. Which move do you choose? If the other person cooperates, your winning choice is *compete* because you will get $2 instead of $1. If the other person competes, again you gain by competing because you will lose just $1 instead of $2. Logically, you should compete, as should the other person, and you both lose $1. (Try to avoid getting into situations like this!) You can explore the prisoner's dilemma at this website, where you compete against a computer opponent: **http://serendip .brynmawr.edu/bb/pd.html**.

In real life, people do cooperate most of the time. What is the difference between real-life situations and the prisoner's dilemma? The main difference is that we deal with people repeatedly, not just once. If you play the prisoner's dilemma many times with the same partner, the two of you will probably learn to cooperate, especially if real rewards are at stake. Furthermore, in real life you want a reputation for cooperating, or people will stop doing business with you (Feinberg, Willer, & Schultz, 2014). Thus, here is one explanation for altruistical behavior: *People want a reputation for being fair and helpful* (McNamara, Barta, Fromhage, & Houston, 2008).

A second reason for cooperation is that *people who do cooperate punish those who don't.* In some cases, people will pay for the opportunity to punish an uncooperative person (Gächter, Renner, & Sefton, 2008). However, punishment is effective only if most people can combine efforts to punish the few who don't cooperate. If too many people become uncooperative, it is difficult or ineffective to try punishing them all (Dreber, Rand, Fudenberg, & Nowak, 2008; Herrmann, Thöni, & Gächter, 2008). Punishing uncooperative people works well in countries where most people trust one another. In countries with low trust, people react to punishment with anger rather than guilt (Balliet & Van Lange, 2013).

concept check

2. **You have read two explanations for humans' altruistic behavior. Why do both of them require individual recognition?**

Answer

2. One explanation for altruistic behavior is that cooperating builds a reputation, and a reputation requires individuals to recognize one another. The other explanation is that people who cooperate will punish those who do not. Again, to retaliate, they need to recognize who has failed to cooperate.

Accepting or Denying Responsibility toward Others

Other people can encourage us to do something we would not have done on our own. They can also inhibit us from doing something that we would have done on our own. We look around to see what others are doing—or *not* doing—and we say, "Okay, I'll do that, too." Why do people sometimes work together and sometimes ignore the needs of others?

Bystander Helpfulness and Apathy

Suppose while you are waiting at a bus stop, you see me trip and fall down, not far away. I am not screaming in agony, but I don't get up either, so you are not sure whether I need help. Would you come over and offer to help? Before you answer, try to imagine the situation in two ways: First, you and I are the only people in sight. Second, many other people are nearby, none of them rushing to my aid. Does the presence of those other people make any difference to you? (It doesn't to me. I am in the same pain regardless of how many people ignore me.)

A real-life event illustrates the issue. Late one night in March 1964, Kitty Genovese was stabbed to death near her apartment in Queens, New York. A newspaper article at the time reported that 38 of her neighbors heard her screaming for more than half an hour, but none of them called the police, each of them either declining to get involved or assuming that someone else had already called the police. Later investigations of the crime indicated that this report was greatly exaggerated (Manning, Levine, & Collins, 2007). About six people saw someone attack Genovese, and at least one or two did call the police, who did nothing. She went into the building on her own, and her attacker returned to attack again half an hour later, out of sight of witnesses, while she was too weak to scream.

Although the original newspaper article was full of errors, it prompted interest in why people often fail to help someone in distress. Are we less likely to act when we know that someone else could act? Bibb Latané and John Darley (1969) proposed that being in a crowd decreases our probability of action because of **diffusion of responsibility**: *We feel less responsibility to act when other people are equally able to act.*

In an experiment designed to test this hypothesis, a young woman ushered one or two students into a room and asked them to wait for the start of a market research study (Latané & Darley, 1968, 1969). She went into the next room, closing the door behind her. Then she played a tape recording that sounded as though she climbed onto a chair, fell off, and moaned, "Oh . . . my foot . . . I can't move it. Oh . . . my ankle . . ." Of the participants who were waiting alone, 70 percent went next door and offered to help. Of the participants who were waiting with someone else, only 13 percent offered to help.

In another study, investigators entered 400 Internet chat groups of different sizes and in each one asked, "Can anyone tell me how to look at someone's profile?" (That is, how can I check the autobiographical sketch that each chat room user posts?) The researchers found that the more people in a chat room at the time, the longer the wait before anyone answered the question. In large groups, the researchers sometimes had to post the same question repeatedly (Markey, 2000).

Diffusion of responsibility is one explanation. Each person thinks, "It's not my responsibility to help any more than someone else's." A second possible explanation is that the presence of other people who are doing nothing provides information (or misinformation). The situation is ambiguous: "Do I need to act or not?" Other people's inaction implies that the situation requires no action. In fact, the others, who are just as uncertain as you are, draw the same conclusion from *your* inaction. Social psychologists use the term pluralistic ignorance to describe *a situation in which people say nothing, and each person falsely assumes that others have a better-informed opinion.* Other people's inactivity implies that doing nothing is acceptable (a norm) and that the situation is not an emergency (information).

Social Loafing

When you take a test, you work alone, and your success depends on your own effort. However, if you work for a company that gives workers a share of the profits, your rewards depend on other workers' productivity as well as your own. Do you work as hard as you can when the rewards depend on the group's productivity?

In many cases, you do not. In one experiment, students were told to scream, clap, and make as much noise as possible, like cheerleaders at a sports event. Students either screamed and clapped alone, or acted in groups, or acted alone but *thought* other people were screaming and clapping, too. (They wore headphones so they could not hear anyone else.) Most of the students who screamed and clapped alone made more noise than those who were or thought they were part of a group (Latané, Williams, & Harkins, 1979). Social psychologists call this phenomenon social loafing—*the tendency to "loaf" (or work less hard) when sharing work with other people.*

Social loafing has been demonstrated in many situations. Suppose you are asked to "name all the uses you can think of for a brick" (e.g., crack nuts, anchor a boat, use as a doorstop) and write each one on a card. You probably fill out many cards by yourself but fewer if you are tossing cards into a pile along with other people's suggestions (Harkins & Jackson, 1985). You don't bother submitting ideas that you assume other people have already suggested.

At this point, you may be thinking, "Wait a minute. When I'm playing basketball or soccer, I try as hard as I can. I don't think I loaf." You are right; social loafing is rare in team sports because observers, including teammates, watch your performance. People work hard in groups if they expect other people to notice their effort or if they think they can

People watch other people's responses to decide how they should respond. When a group of sidewalk Santas—who had gathered in Manhattan to promote a back-rub business—came to the aid of an injured cyclist, a few Santas made the first move and the others followed.

AP Images/Marty Lederhandler

contribute something that other group members cannot (Shepperd, 1993; Williams & Karau, 1991).

concept check

3. **In a typical family, one or two members have jobs, but their wages benefit all. Why do those wage earners *not* engage in social loafing?**

Answer

3. The main reason is that the wage earners see they can make a special contribution that the others (children, injured, or retired) cannot. Also, others can easily observe their contributions.

Violent and Aggressive Behavior

During World War II, nearly all the industrialized nations were at war, the Nazis were exterminating the Jews, and the United States was preparing a nuclear bomb that it later dropped on Japan. Meanwhile, Mohandas K. Gandhi was in jail for leading a nonviolent protest march against British rule in India. The charge against Gandhi was, ironically, "disturbing the peace." Someone asked Gandhi what he thought of Western civilization. He replied that "it might be a good idea."

Cruelty and violence have always been part of human experience, just as kindness and altruism have been. But that is not to say that the balance between kindness and cruelty always remains the same. As Steven Pinker (2011) has argued, since World War II, the worldwide rate of death by war and murder has declined to its lowest level ever. Education is probably a major contributor to the decline, as are travel and communication. (It's hard to hate people after you have visited their country or played Internet games with them.) Violence is still a problem, but we can do much about it.

Causes of Anger and Aggression

According to the frustration-aggression hypothesis, *the main cause of anger and aggression is frustration—an obstacle that stands in the way of doing something or obtaining something* (Dollard, Miller, Doob, Mowrer, & Sears, 1939). However, frustration makes you angry only when you believe the other person acted intentionally. You might feel angry if someone ran down the hall and bumped into you, but probably not if someone slipped on a wet spot and bumped into you.

Leonard Berkowitz (1983, 1989) proposed a more comprehensive theory: Any unpleasant event—frustration, pain, heat, foul odors, bad news, whatever—excites both the impulse to fight and the impulse to flee. That is, it excites the sympathetic nervous system and its fight-or-flight response. Your choice to fight or flee depends on the circumstances. If someone who just annoyed you looks weak, you express your anger. If that person looks intimidating, you suppress your anger. And if the one who bumped into you is the loan and scholarship officer at your college, you smile and apologize for getting in the way.

Individual Differences in Aggression

Why are some people aggressive more often than others? One hypothesis has been that low self-esteem leads to violence. According to this idea, people who think little of themselves try to build themselves up by tearing someone else down. Some studies find a small relationship between aggressive behaviors and low self-esteem, but others find virtually no relationship between the two (Baumeister, Campbell, Krueger, & Vohs, 2003; Donnellan, Trzesniewski, Robins, Moffitt, & Caspi, 2005). No evidence indicates that low self-esteem *causes* aggressiveness. More likely, whatever life events led to low self-esteem also led to aggressiveness. Another possibility is that people who are accustomed to feeling powerful become aggressive when they find their self-confidence threatened, or when their self-esteem wavers (Fast & Chen, 2009; Zeigler-Hill, Enjaian, Holden, & Southard, 2014).

Are mentally ill patients prone to violence? Swedish researchers examined the whole country's medical and criminal records and found that people with severe mental illnesses, who constituted about 1.4 percent of the population, committed about 5 percent of the violent crimes (Fazel & Grann, 2006). However, as illustrated in ▼ Figure 13.2, the increased danger is

associated only with those mental patients who are also alcohol or substance abusers (Elbogen & Johnson, 2009). Mentally ill people without drug or alcohol abuse are no more dangerous than anyone else (Hodgins, Mednick, Brennan, Schulsinger, & Engberg, 1996).

If low self-esteem and mental illness do not predict violence, what does? Research on twins and adopted children indicates a genetic predisposition, but no single gene or small set of genes accounts for much. An influential study pointed to an interaction between genes and environment: One form of the MAO_A gene (which regulates levels of the transmitter serotonin in the brain) correlates with increased violent behavior, but only in people with a history of maltreatment during childhood (Caspi et al., 2002). Since then, most attempts to replicate this finding have been successful, though not all (e.g., McDermott, Dawes, Prom-Wormley, Eaves, & Hatemi, 2013). It is apparently a real, but small effect.

Several other factors are associated with a tendency toward violent behavior (Bushman & Anderson, 2009; Davidson, Putnam, & Larson, 2000; Glenn & Raine, 2014; Hay et al., 2011; D. O. Lewis et al., 1985; Lynam, 1996; Osofsky, 1995). Bear in mind that all of this research is correlational, and not necessarily related to a cause-and-effect relationship:

- Growing up in a violent neighborhood
- Having parents with a history of antisocial behavior
- Having a mother who smoked cigarettes or drank alcohol during pregnancy
- Poor nutrition or exposure to lead or other toxic chemicals early in life
- A history of head injury
- Not feeling guilty after hurting someone
- Weaker than normal sympathetic nervous system responses (which correlates with not feeling bad after hurting someone)
- High levels of testosterone coupled with low levels of cortisol
- A history of suicide attempts

Many people have worried that playing violent video games may increase aggressive behavior or decrease cooperative behavior. However, the best-designed studies show little or no effect (Ferguson, 2013). Pathological game playing—playing video games to the exclusion of other activities—may be linked to antisocial behavior, but in that case the likely explanation is that antisocial people enjoy violent games, rather than that the games made people antisocial.

Culture is also a powerful influence. A fascinating study documented the influence of culture on aggressive behavior even in nonhuman primates. Researchers observed one troop of baboons for

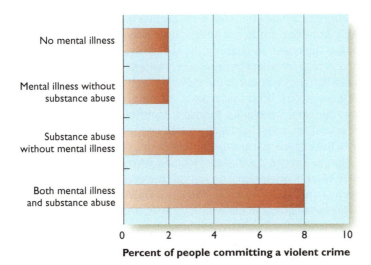

▲ **Figure 13.2** People with mental illness who are also substance abusers have an 8 percent chance of committing a violent crime within two to three years. Those who are not substance abusers are no more dangerous than the rest of the population. (Based on data from "The intricate link between violence and mental disorder," by E. B. Elbogen & S. C. Johnson, 2009. *Archives of General Psychiatry, 66,* pp. 152–161.)

Percent of people committing a violent crime (x-axis: 0, 2, 4, 6, 8, 10)

Categories (top to bottom): No mental illness; Mental illness without substance abuse; Substance abuse without mental illness; Both mental illness and substance abuse

25 years. At one point, the most aggressive males in the troop took food away from a neighboring troop. The food happened to be contaminated, and those males died. The troop then consisted of females, juveniles, and the less aggressive males. All got along well, stress levels decreased, and health improved. Over the years, new males occasionally entered the troop and adopted this troop's customs. Years later, none of the original males remained there, but the troop continued its nonaggressive tradition (Sapolsky & Share, 2004).

4. Could we decrease violent crime through better treatment of mental illness?

Answer

4. Probably not, although treating drug abuse might be effective. Aggressive behavior is often a problem among mental patients who abuse alcohol or other drugs, but mental patients without substance abuse are no more dangerous than anyone else.

Cognitive Influences on Violence

Most people think of themselves as good. Most of the time you treat other people fairly, right? You know it is wrong to hurt or cheat anyone. But at times, you might. If you serve in the police or military, certain situations might require you to shoot someone. In business, you might yield to a temptation to raise profits by doing something unfair to your competitors or risky to your customers. If so, you want to justify your actions, to make them seem acceptable.

People often justify their acts by thinking of themselves as better than the people they are hurting. In war, soldiers give their enemies a derogatory name and think of them as less than human (Lewandowsky, Stritzke, Freund, Oberauer, & Krueger, 2013). The same occurs for violence against racial minorities or other groups. Psychologists describe this process as *deindividuation* (perceiving others as anonymous, without any real personality) and *dehumanization* (perceiving others as less than human). The result is greater acceptance of violence and injustice. Certain brain areas are known to respond strongly when you interact socially with someone, or even when you see someone with whom you would like to interact socially. These brain areas hardly respond at all when you see homeless people, drug addicts, or others for whom you have a low regard (Harris & Fiske, 2006). In effect, you don't

Does playing games like this make you more prone to violence?

see them as human. (That study is one example of *social neuroscience*—the use of brain measurements to shed light on social behavior.)

People also justify their violent behavior by decreasing their own sense of identity. A soldier on duty is no longer acting as an individual making his or her own decisions. A Ku Klux Klansman wearing a hood suppresses a sense of personal identity. A criminal wearing a mask not only decreases the probability of witness identification, but also creates a distance between the "real self" and the perpetrator of the act. Even wearing sunglasses has been found to decrease people's sense of personal responsibility and to increase their probability of dishonest acts (Zhong, Bohns, & Gino, 2010).

Sexual Aggression

Rape is *sexual activity without the consent of the partner*. In one survey, about 10 percent of adult women reported that they had been forcibly raped, and another 10 percent said they had sex while incapacitated by alcohol or other drugs (Testa, Livingston, Vanzile-Tamsen, & Frone, 2003). However, the statistics vary considerably from one study to another, depending on even slight changes in the wording of the question (Hamby, 2014). Surveys that ask about "unwanted" sex report very high numbers because many people interpret "unwanted" to include times when they weren't in the mood but agreed to sex to please a partner (Hamby & Koss, 2003). With that type of wording, even most men answer yes (Struckman-Johnson, Struckman-Johnson, & Anderson, 2003).

Of all sexual assaults that legally qualify as rape, only about half the victims think of the experience as rape, and far fewer report it to the police (Fisher, Daigle, Cullen, & Turner, 2003). Most women who have involuntary sex with a boyfriend or other acquaintance do not call the event rape, especially if alcohol was involved (Kahn, Jackson, Kully, Badger, & Halvorsen, 2003). In some cases, the man does not realize that the woman considered his behavior abusive.

Rapists are not all alike. Many are hostile, distrustful men with a history of other acts of violence and criminality (Hanson, 2000). Sexually aggressive men tend to be high users of pornography (Vega & Malamuth, 2007), and rapists are much more likely than other men to enjoy violent pornography (Donnerstein & Malamuth, 1997). Another element in rape is extreme self-centeredness, or lack of concern for others (Dean & Malamuth, 1997).

Is Cooperative Behavior Logical?

Either we have evolved a tendency to help others, or we learn to. The research on the prisoner's dilemma and similar games attempts to demonstrate that cooperation and mutual aid are logical under certain conditions. You cooperate to develop a good reputation so that others will cooperate with you and not penalize you.

Do you find this explanation completely satisfactory? Sometimes, you make an anonymous contribution to a worthy cause with no expectation of personal gain, not even an improvement of your reputation. You simply wanted to help

that cause. You occasionally help someone you'll never see again while no one else is watching. Perhaps these acts require no special explanation. You have developed habits of helping for all the reasons that investigators have identified. Once you developed those habits, you generalize them to other circumstances, even when they do you no good. Yes, perhaps. Or maybe researchers are still overlooking something. Conclusions in psychology are almost never final. You are invited to think about these issues yourself and develop your own hypotheses.

Summary

- *Kohlberg's view of moral reasoning.* Lawrence Kohlberg argued that we should evaluate moral reasoning on the basis of the reasons people give for a decision rather than the decision itself. (page 413)
- *Limits to Kohlberg's views.* Kohlberg concentrated on logical reasoning. In fact, people usually act first, based on an emotional urge, and look for a justification later. Also, many people, especially in non-Western cultures, base their moral decisions on factors Kohlberg ignored, including loyalty, authority, and purity. (page 413)
- *The prisoner's dilemma.* In the prisoner's dilemma, two people can choose to cooperate or compete. The *compete* move seems best from the individual's point of view, but it is harmful to the group. (page 414)
- *Reasons for cooperation.* Studies of the prisoner's dilemma demonstrate two rational reasons for cooperation: A cooperative person enhances his or her reputation and therefore gains

cooperation from others. Also, people who cooperate punish those who do not. (page 415)
- *Bystander apathy.* People are less likely to help someone if other people are in an equally good position to help. (page 415)
- *Social loafing.* Most people work less hard when they are part of a group than when they work alone, except when they think they can make a unique contribution or if they think others are evaluating their contribution. (page 416)
- *Aggressive behavior.* Frustration or discomfort of any kind increases the probability of anger and aggression, especially if one perceives that others have caused their frustration intentionally. (page 416)
- *Cognitive factors in aggression.* People sometimes justify cruel or uncooperative behavior by lowering their opinion of the victims. People also decrease their own sense of personal responsibility. (page 418)

Key Terms

altruistic behavior (page 414)

diffusion of responsibility (page 415)

frustration-aggression hypothesis
  (page 417)

pluralistic ignorance (page 416)

prisoner's dilemma (page 414)

rape (page 418)

social loafing (page 416)

social psychologists (page 412)

Review Questions

1. How did Lawrence Kohlberg evaluate moral reasoning?
   (a) He evaluated the decisions people made on moral dilemmas.
   (b) He evaluated the reasons people gave for their decisions on moral dilemmas.
   (c) He evaluated people's actual behavior.
   (d) He evaluated other people's opinion of each person.

2. Theoretically, how can we explain why you sometimes act altruistically toward people you have never met?
   (a) You expect reciprocity ("tit for tat").
   (b) You hope to develop a reputation for being helpful.
   (c) You work to advance genes that you have in common with those people.

3. In which of the following situations would people be most likely to engage in social loafing?
   (a) Cleaning up the environment
   (b) Doing household chores
   (c) Participating on a team sport
   (d) Washing your own car

4. For which kind of person, if any, do genetic differences most strongly influence the probability of aggressive behavior?
   (a) The influence is strongest on people who grew up in supportive, middle-class families.
   (b) The influence is strongest on people who suffered maltreatment during childhood.

(c) Genes produce equally strong influences on aggressive behavior for all kinds of people.
(d) No evidence suggests a genetic influence on aggressive behavior.

5. How do deindividuation and dehumanization increase aggressive behavior?
   (a) They increase the perpetrator's sense of righteousness.
   (b) They enable the perpetrator to think of the victim as less worthy of kind treatment.
   (c) They decrease the perpetrator's self-esteem.
   (d) They enable the perpetrator to forget the event.

Answers: 1b 2b, 3a, 4b, 5b.

module 13.2

Social Perception and Cognition

After studying this module, you should be able to:

- Define the primacy effect in social psychology and give an example.
- Describe how the implicit association test measures prejudices.
- Discuss methods of overcoming prejudice.
- Distinguish among three main influences on attributions.
- Describe the actor-observer effect and the fundamental attribution error.
- Discuss cultural differences in attributions.

People generally measure their success by comparing themselves to others. You cheer yourself up by noting that you are doing better than some other people you know. You motivate yourself to try harder by comparing yourself to someone more successful (Suls, Martin, & Wheeler, 2002).

To make these comparisons, we need accurate information about other people. We also need that information to predict how others will act and whom we can trust. Social perception and cognition are *the processes for learning about others and making inferences from that information.* Social perception and cognition influence our observations, memory, and thinking.

First Impressions

Other things being equal, *the first information we learn about someone influences us more than later information does* (Jones & Goethals, 1972). This tendency is known as the primacy effect. (We also encountered the same term in Chapter 7 on memory, where it refers to the tendency to remember well the first items on a list.) For example, if you hear both favorable and unfavorable reports about a restaurant, the reports you hear first influence you the most (Russo, Carlson, & Meloy, 2006).

We form first impressions quickly and more accurately than we might guess. In one study, college students viewed three 2-second videos of several professors lecturing, without sound, and rated how good they thought these professors were. Their mean rating correlated 0.6 with the end-of-semester ratings by the students in those classes (Ambady & Rosenthal, 1993). People watching 6-second videos of music ensembles or orchestras, again without sound, performed at better than chance levels at identifying the more successful group (Tsay, 2014). People watching 10-second videos of couples could in most cases guess how much romantic interest they felt (Place, Todd, Penke, & Asendorpf, 2009). People viewing faces for just 39 milliseconds fairly accurately guessed how aggressive those people were (Carré, McCormick, & Mondloch, 2009). However, first impressions are not always accurate. Researchers asked observers to estimate the trustworthiness of people in photos. Generally, they gave high ratings to someone who was smiling, but if they later saw the same person not smiling, they gave a lower rating (Todorov & Porter, 2014). Clearly, smiling or stopping a smile does not change someone's overall trustworthiness.

First impressions can become self-fulfilling prophecies, *expectations that increase the probability of the predicted event.* Suppose a psychologist hands you a cell phone and asks you to talk with someone, while showing you a photo

Jupiter Images/Photolibrary/Getty Images

What's your first impression of this man—rich or poor? Businessman, professional athlete, or manual laborer? (Yeah, you got it right.)

supposedly of that person. Unknown to the person you are talking to, the psychologist might hand you a photo of a very attractive person or a much less attractive photo. Not surprisingly, you act friendlier to someone you regard as attractive. Besides that, if you think you are talking to someone attractive, that person reacts by becoming more cheerful and talkative. In short, your first impression changes how you act and influences the other person to live up to (or down to) your expectations (M. Snyder, Tanke, & Berscheid, 1977).

concept check

5. Why do some professors avoid looking at students' names when they grade essay exams?

Answer

5. They want to avoid being biased by their first impressions of the students.

Stereotypes and Prejudices

A **stereotype** is *a belief or expectation about a group of people.* A **prejudice** is *an unfavorable attitude toward a group of people.* It is usually associated with **discrimination**, which is *unequal treatment of different groups,* such as minority groups, the physically disabled, people who are obese, or gays and lesbians.

Throughout life, we look for patterns and we learn generalizations that help us predict later events. For example, we note similarities within a group of people, enabling us to learn what to expect of them (Martin et al., 2014). However, we also sometimes perceive a pattern too quickly and form a false stereotype. Sometimes people form an opinion about some group after observing just a single member of that group (Ranganath & Nosek, 2008).

Stereotypes are not always wrong. Who do you think gets into more fistfights on average—men or women? If you answered "men," you are supporting a stereotype, but you are correct. Similarly, who do you think is more likely to notice the subtle social connotations in conversation—a liberal arts major or an engineering major? If you said "liberal arts major," you are endorsing a stereotype, but the research supports you (Ottati & Lee, 1995). Whenever we say that culture influences

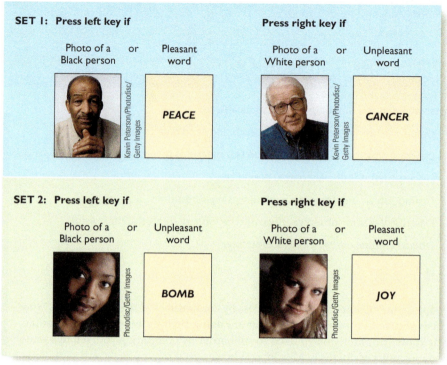

▲ **Figure 13.3** Procedures for an implicit association test to measure prejudices.

behavior, we imply that members of those cultures behave differently on average, and therefore that a stereotype about them is partly correct. However, remember that phrase "on average." Even for a mostly correct stereotype, we need to recognize exceptions to the rule.

Implicit Measures of Prejudice

Decades ago, Americans admitted their prejudices openly. Today, almost all people believe in fair treatment for everyone, or so they say. But are people as unprejudiced as they claim to be? Researchers have sought methods of measuring subtle prejudices that people do not want to admit, even to themselves.

One method is the **implicit association test (IAT)**, which *measures reactions to combinations of categories.* Imagine this example: You rest your left and right forefingers on a computer keyboard. When you see a word on the computer screen, you should press with your left finger if it is an unpleasant word, such as *death,* and press with your right finger if it is a pleasant word, such as *joy.* After a while, the instructions change. Now you should press the left key if you see the name of an insect and the right key if you see the name of a flower. Next you combine two categories: Press the left key for unpleasant words or insects and the right key for pleasant words or flowers. Then the pairings switch: Press the left key for unpleasant words or flowers and the right key for pleasant words or insects. The procedure continues, alternating between the two instructions.

Most people respond faster to the combination "pleasant or flowers" than to "pleasant or insects." The conclusion is that most people like flowers more than insects. This procedure may seem more trouble than it is worth, as people readily agree that they like flowers more than insects. However, the research established the validity of the method, which researchers then used to measure other preferences (Greenwald, Nosek, & Banaji, 2003).

Imagine yourself in this experiment: You view a computer screen that sometimes shows a photo and sometimes a word. If it is a photo of a black person or a pleasant word, press the left key. If it is a photo of a white person or an unpleasant word, press the right key. After you respond that way for a while, the rule switches to the opposite pairing. ▲ **Figure 13.3** illustrates the procedures and

The stereotype of old people as inactive has many exceptions.

▶ **Figure 13.4** summarizes the results for a group of white people. Most of them responded faster to the combinations *black/unpleasant* and *white/pleasant,* even though they claimed to have no racial prejudice (Phelps et al., 2000). With enough practice, people learn to respond just as fast to each combination, so the test is most useful for the first few trials (Hu, Rosenfeld, & Bodenhausen, 2012). In similar studies black participants show nearly equal responses to blacks and whites on average—that is, little or no prejudice (Stewart, von Hippel, & Radvansky, 2009).

The results of the implicit association test correlate only weakly with people's expressed attitudes (Greenwald, Poehlman, Uhlmann, & Banaji, 2009). However, contrary to what some theorists have assumed, it is wrong to say that the prejudices are unconscious. When people are asked about their prejudices but urged to answer *honestly,* their answers correlate more strongly with their IAT results (Phillips & Olson, 2014). Also, if people are asked to predict their results on the IAT, they do so fairly accurately (Hahn, Judd, Hirsh, & Blair, 2014). In short, most people do know their prejudices, even if they hesitate to admit them.

Researchers have also used the IAT to gauge attitudes toward men and women (Nosek & Banaji, 2001; Rudman & Goodwin, 2004), toward obese people (Agerström & Rooth, 2011), toward politicians, and others. Project Implicit on Harvard University's website provides a few implicit association tests that you can try yourself.

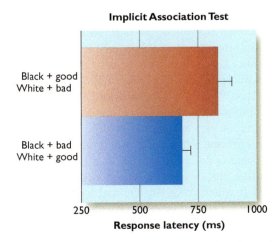

▲ **Figure 13.4** On average, white people who claimed to have no racial prejudice responded slower if they had to make one response for "black face or pleasant word" and a different response for "white face or unpleasant word" than if the pairings were reversed—black and unpleasant, white and pleasant. (From "Performance on indirect measures of race evaluation predicts amygdala activation" by E. A. Phelps, K. J. O'Connor, W. A. Cunningham, E. S. Funayama, J. C. Gatenby, J. C. Gore & M. R. Banaji, 2000. *Journal of Cognitive Neuroscience, 12,* pp. 729–738.

6. **What is the advantage of the implicit association test over asking people about their racial prejudices?**

Answer

6. The implicit association test may reveal prejudices that people don't want to admit, even to themselves.

Overcoming Prejudice

After people form a prejudice, what can overcome it? Increasing contact between groups often helps, but not always. A study of white and black college students who were assigned to be roommates found that they spent little time together at first, but over the course of a semester, they formed more favorable attitudes (Shook & Fazio, 2008). Another study found that minority students at a mostly white college came to like the college more after developing a friendship with one or more white students (Mendoza-Denton & Page-Gould, 2008). Voluntarily

People who work together for a common goal can overcome prejudices that initially divide them.

taking part in a Mexican cultural activity reduces prejudice against Mexicans (Brannon & Walton, 2013). However, white Americans who worry that they may become outnumbered tend to become more prejudiced, not less (Craig & Richeson, 2014).

A particularly effective technique is to get groups to work toward a common goal (Dovidio & Gaertner, 1999). Long ago, psychologists demonstrated the power of this technique using two arbitrarily chosen groups (Sherif, 1966). At a summer camp at Robbers Cave, Oklahoma, 11- and 12-year-old boys were divided into two groups in separate cabins. The groups competed for prizes in sports, treasure hunts, and other activities. With each competition, the antagonism between the two groups grew more intense. The boys made threatening posters, shouted insults, and engaged in food fights. (The ethics here were questionable, as the "counselors" deliberately encouraged the hostility, and never asked for informed consent to participate in an experiment.)

Then the counselors tried to reverse the hostility. First, they asked the two groups to work together to find and repair a leak in the water pipe that supplied the camp. Then they had the two groups pool their treasuries to rent a movie that both groups wanted to see. Later, they had the boys pull together to get a truck out of a rut. Gradually, hostility turned into friendship. The point is that competition breeds hostility, and cooperation leads to friendship.

The media also play a role in strengthening or weakening prejudices. In 1994, Rwanda (in south-central Africa) had a vicious civil war in which the majority Hutus, urged on by their government and Rwanda's primary radio station, killed three-fourths of the Tutsi minority. (Televisions and newspapers were rare in Rwanda, and radio was the primary means of communication and entertainment.) Later, the Hutus and surviving Tutsis lived in an uneasy truce. A radio soap opera, provided on an experimental basis to some villages and not others, described a fictional place in which one group attacked another group, but leaders spoke out against violence, and people from the two groups formed friendships. The people in villages that heard this soap opera showed increased sympathy, trust, and cooperation, breaking down the barriers between Hutus and Tutsis (Paluck, 2009).

Decreasing Prejudice by Increasing Acceptance

Most people today publicly endorse the goal of treating all people fairly, without prejudice. However, the way of expressing this goal has major effects on the result. Consider the expression "we treat all people the same." Although that goal sounds good, it seems to imply, "We expect all people to act the same." What if you are *not* the same as everyone else? You might differ from the others in racial or ethnic background, sexual orientation, or other regards. You might be older or younger than most, or the only man or only woman in the organization. Under a policy of treating everyone the same, people are supposed to ignore the fact that you are different. When people try not to notice skin color, sexual orientation, or anything else, or try to avoid seeming prejudiced, they find the effort unpleasant and tiring. The result is often an *increase* in prejudice (Legault, Gutsell, & Inzlicht, 2011; Trawalter & Richeson, 2006; Wegner, 2009). In some cases, this "we're all the same" approach has been carried so far that certain schools tried to teach about Martin Luther King, Jr., without mentioning that he was

black, or that he was fighting against racial prejudice (Apfelbaum, Paulker, Sommers, & Ambady, 2010).

An alternative is multiculturalism—*accepting, recognizing, and enjoying the differences among people and groups and the unique contributions that each person can offer.* Research shows advantages of the multiculturalism approach. When a company or other organization endorses a multiculturalist position, members of both majority and minority groups feel more comfortable (Meeussen, Otten, & Phalet, 2014; Plaut, Thomas, & Goren, 2009).

concept check

7. What would be an improvement on the advice "try to avoid seeming prejudiced"?

Answer

7. It is better to try to have a positive experience and to enjoy cultural differences.

Attribution

Yesterday, you won the state lottery, and today, classmates who previously ignored you want to be your friends. You draw inferences about their reasons. Attribution is *the set of thought processes we use to assign causes to our own behavior and that of others.*

Internal versus External Causes

Fritz Heider, the founder of attribution theory, emphasized the distinction between internal and external causes of behavior (Heider, 1958). Internal attributions are *explanations based on someone's attitudes, personality traits, abilities, or other characteristics.* External attributions are *explanations based on the situation, including events that would influence almost anyone.* An example of an internal attribution is saying that your brother walked to work this morning "because he likes the exercise." An external attribution would be that he walked "because his car wouldn't start." Internal attributions are also known as *dispositional* (i.e., relating to the person's disposition). External attributions are also known as *situational* (i.e., relating to the situation).

You make internal attributions when someone's act surprises you. For example, you draw no conclusions about someone who would like to visit Hawaii. (After all, who wouldn't?) However, if someone wants to visit northern Norway in winter, you look for something special about that person. When a man gets angry in public, most people assume he had a reason. When a woman gets equally angry in public, her behavior is more surprising, and people attribute it to her personality (Brescoll & Uhlmann, 2008).

This tendency sometimes leads to misunderstandings between members of different cultures. Each person views the other's behavior as "something I would

In the United States, a funeral usually calls for reserved behavior. Many other places expect loud wailing.

not have done" and therefore a reason to make an attribution about personality. For example, some cultures expect people to cry loudly at funerals, whereas others expect more restraint. People who are unfamiliar with other cultures may attribute a behavior to personality, when in fact it is a dictate of culture.

Harold Kelley (1967) proposed that three types of information influence us to make an internal or external attribution:

- **Consensus information** *(how the person's behavior compares with other people's behavior).* If someone behaves the same way you believe other people would in the same situation, you make an external attribution, recognizing that the situation led to the behavior. When a behavior seems unusual, you look for an internal attribution. (You can be wrong if you misunderstand the situation.)
- **Consistency information** *(how the person's behavior varies from one time to the next).* If someone almost always seems friendly, you make an internal attribution ("friendly person"). If someone's friendliness varies, you make an external attribution, such as an event that elicited a good or bad mood.
- **Distinctiveness** *(how the person's behavior varies from one situation to another).* If your friend is pleasant to all but one individual, you assume that person has done something to irritate your friend (an external attribution).

8. Juanita returns from watching *The Return of the Son of Sequel Strikes Back Again Part 2* and says it was excellent. Most other people disliked the movie. Will you make an internal or external attribution for Juanita's opinion? Why? (distinctiveness, consensus, or consistency?)

Answer

8. You probably will make an internal attribution because of consensus. When one person's behavior differs from others, we make an internal attribution.

The Actor-Observer Effect

If you see someone complaining loudly to a sales clerk, how do you react? You say, "Such an aggressive loudmouth!" When you complain equally loudly, how do you explain it? You say, "I had been treated unfairly!" *People are more likely to make internal attributions for other people's behavior and more likely to make external attributions for their own* (Jones & Nisbett, 1972). This tendency is called the **actor-observer effect**. You are an "actor" when you try to explain the causes of your own behavior and an "observer" when you try to explain someone else's behavior.

We can account for this tendency in terms of the three influences just mentioned. First, *consensus:* When you see someone angry with a sales clerk, would you be equally angry in that situation? You don't know, because you don't know the situation. But usually you are polite to salespeople, so maybe there is something unusual about that other person. Second, *consistency:* Is that other person angry all the time? Could be, so far as you know. But you know you get angry only on rare occasions. Third, *distinctiveness:* Is that other person aggressive in many situations? Could be, so far as you know. Are you aggressive in many situations? You know that you aren't.

Another explanation for the actor-observer effect is perceptual. We see other people as objects in our visual field, and we tend to think that whatever we are watching is the cause of the action. If you watch a videotape of your own behavior, you make more references to your personality than you ordinarily do (Storms, 1973), although still not as much as other people do (Hofmann, Gschwendner, & Schmitt, 2009).

An application of this idea: Suppose you watch a videotape of two people who participate equally in a conversation. You are randomly given a version of the videotape with the camera focused on one person or the other. You tend to perceive that the person you are watching dominates the conversation. Similarly, if you watch a videotape of an interrogation between a detective and a suspect, you judge the suspect's confession to be more voluntary if the camera focuses on the suspect and more coerced if the camera focuses on the detective (Lassiter, Geers, Munhall, Ploutz-Snyder, & Breitenbecher, 2002).

The Fundamental Attribution Error

A common error is *to make internal attributions for people's behavior even when we see evidence for an external influence on behavior.* This tendency is known as the **fundamental attribution error** (Ross, 1977). It is also known as the *correspondence bias,* meaning a tendency to assume a strong similarity between someone's current actions and his or her dispositions.

Imagine yourself in a classic study demonstrating this phenomenon. You are told that U.S. college students were randomly assigned to write essays praising or condemning Fidel Castro, then the communist leader of Cuba. You read an essay that praises Castro. What's your guess about the actual attitude of the student who wrote this essay?

very anti-Castro   neutral   very pro-Castro

Most U.S. students in one study guessed that the student was at least mildly pro-Castro, even though they were informed, as you were, that the author had been required to praise Castro (Jones & Harris, 1967). In a later study, experimenters explained that one student in a creative writing class had been assigned to write a pro-Castro essay and an anti-Castro essay at different times. When the participants read the two essays, most thought that the writer had changed attitudes between the two essays (Allison, Mackie, Muller, & Worth, 1993). That is, even when people are told of a powerful external reason for someone's behavior, they seem to believe the person probably had internal reasons as well.

The fundamental attribution error emerges in many settings. When we see crime, we tend to think "bad person," although sometimes the truth is closer to "bad situation." When we see poverty and failure, we think "lack of effort," even though "lack of opportunity" might be more accurate. We think our political opponents adopted their wrongheaded opinions because they are biased liberals (or conservatives), whereas we formed our own opinions entirely because of the evidence!

9. **If instead of watching someone, you close your eyes and imagine yourself in that person's position, will you be more likely to explain the behavior with internal or external attributions? Why?**

10. **How would the fundamental attribution error affect people's attitudes toward actors and actresses who portrayed likable and contemptible characters?**

Answers

9. You will be more likely to give an external attribution because you will become more like an actor and less like an observer.

10. Because of the fundamental attribution error, people tend to think that performers who portray likable characters are themselves likable, and those who play contemptible people probably resemble those characters.

Cultural Differences in Attribution and Related Matters

The fundamental attribution error varies by culture. People in Western cultures tend to make more internal (personality) attributions, whereas people in China and other Asian countries tend to make more external (situational) attributions. How would you explain the behavior of the fish designated with an arrow in this drawing? Most Americans say it is leading the others, whereas many Chinese say the other fish are chasing it (Hong, Morris, Chiu, & Benet-Martinez, 2000). That is, the cultures differ in whether they think the fish controls its own behavior or obeys the influence of the others.

try
it your
self

In many other ways, most Asian people tend to focus more on the situation and less on personality than do most people in Western cultures (Nisbett, Peng, Choi, & Norenzayan, 2001). As a result, Asians expect more change and less consistency in people's behavior from one situation to another. They are less guided by first impressions (the primacy effect mentioned earlier) than Americans are (Noguchi, Kamada, & Shrira, 2014). They are also more likely to accept contradictions and look for compromises instead of viewing one position as correct and another as incorrect. Here are a few examples:

- When given a description of a conflict, such as one between mother and daughter, Chinese students are more likely than Americans to see merit in both arguments (Peng & Nisbett, 1999).
- Far more Chinese than English-language proverbs include apparent self-contradictions, such as "beware of your friends, not your enemies" and "too humble is half proud" (Peng & Nisbett, 1999).
- Chinese people are more likely than Americans to predict that current trends—whatever they might be—will reverse themselves. If life seems to have been getting better lately, most Americans predict that things will continue getting better, whereas Chinese expect them to get worse (Ji, Nisbett, & Su, 2001).

The reported differences are interesting. Still, an important question remains: To the extent that Asian people respond differently from Western-culture people, is that difference due to ancient traditions or current conditions? Perhaps Asians notice the influence of their environment more just because their environment looks different from that of Western countries. Most Asian cities are more cluttered than American and European cities (see ▼ Figure 13.5). Researchers found that Japanese students tended to notice the background of photographs more than Americans, who focused heavily on objects in the foreground. However, after Americans viewed a series of pictures of Japanese cities, they too began paying more attention to the backgrounds (Miyamoto, Nisbett, & Masuda, 2006).

Using Attributions to Manage Perceptions of Ourselves

Even if you generally attribute your own behavior largely to external causes, you vary your attributions to try to present yourself in a favorable light. For example, you might credit your good grades to your intelligence and hard work (an internal attribution) but blame your worst grades on unfair tests (an external attribution). *Attributions that we adopt to maximize credit for success and minimize blame for failure* are called **self-serving biases**. Most Americans rate themselves above average on almost everything. Self-serving biases are, however, less prominent among Asians. One reason is that Asian culture defines self-worth in terms of fitting into the group rather than outcompeting one's peers (Balcetis, Dunning, & Miller, 2008; Heine & Hamamura, 2007).

People also protect their images with **self-handicapping strategies**, in which they *intentionally put themselves at a disadvantage to provide an excuse for failure.* Suppose you fear you will do poorly on a test. You stay out late at a party the night before. Now you can blame your low score on your lack of sleep without admitting that you might have done poorly anyway.

In one study, one group of students worked on solvable problems while others worked on a mixture of solvable and unsolvable problems. (The students did not know that some of the problems were impossible.) The experimenters told all students that they had done well. The students who had been given solvable problems (and solved them) felt good. Those who had worked on unsolvable problems were unsure in what way they had "done well." They had no confidence that they could continue to do well.

Next the experimenters told the participants that the purpose of the experiment was to investigate the effects of drugs on problem solving. Before starting on the next set of problems, each student could choose between taking a drug

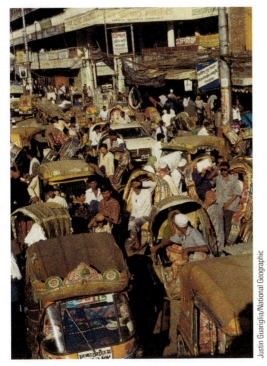

▲ **Figure 13.5** On average, Asian cities are more crowded and cluttered than U.S. and European cities.

that supposedly impaired problem-solving abilities and another drug that supposedly improved them. The participants who had worked on unsolvable problems were more likely than the others to choose the drug that supposedly impaired performance. Because they were not sure they could continue their supposedly "good" performance, they provided themselves with an excuse (Berglas & Jones, 1978).

in closing | module 13.2

How Social Perceptions Affect Behavior

We are seldom fully aware of the reasons for our own behavior, much less someone else's, but we make our best guesses. If someone you know passes by without saying "hello," you might attribute that person's behavior to absentmindedness, indifference, or hostility. You might attribute someone's friendly response to your own personal charm, the other person's extraverted personality, or that person's devious and manipulative personality. The attributions you make are sure to influence your own social behaviors.

Summary

- *First impressions.* Other things being equal, we pay more attention to the first information we learn about someone than to later information. First impressions form rapidly, and some are more accurate than we might guess. (page 421)
- *Stereotypes and prejudices.* Stereotypes are generalized beliefs about groups of people. A prejudice is an unfavorable stereotype. (page 422)
- *Measuring unconscious prejudice.* The implicit association test finds evidence of subtle prejudice, even among many people who deny having such prejudices. However, most people are aware of their prejudices, even if they don't like to admit them. (page 422)
- *Overcoming prejudice.* Working together for a common goal weakens prejudices between groups. (page 423)
- *Enjoying diversity.* A goal of treating everyone the same sometimes backfires by implying that everyone should act the same. A goal of accepting and enjoying the differences among people is generally a better goal. (page 424)
- *Attribution.* Attribution is the set of thought processes by which we assign internal or external causes to behavior.

According to Harold Kelley, we are likely to attribute behavior to an internal cause if it is consistent over time, different from most other people's behavior, and directed toward a variety of other people or objects. (page 424)

- *Actor-observer effect.* We are more likely to attribute internal causes to other people's behavior than to our own. (page 425)
- *Fundamental attribution error.* People frequently attribute people's behavior to internal causes, even when they see evidence of external influences. (page 425)

- *Cultural differences.* People in Asian cultures are less likely than those in Western cultures to attribute behavior to consistent personality traits and more likely to attribute it to the situation. (page 426)
- *Self-serving bias and self-handicapping.* People often try to protect their self-esteem by attributing their successes to skill and their failures to outside influences. They sometimes place themselves at a disadvantage to provide an excuse for failure. (page 426)

Key Terms

actor-observer effect (page 425)

attribution (page 424)

consensus information (page 425)

consistency information (page 425)

discrimination (page 422)

distinctiveness (page 425)

external attribution (page 424)

fundamental attribution error (page 425)

Implicit Association Test (IAT) (page 422)

internal attribution (page 424)

multiculturalism (page 424)

prejudice (page 422)

primacy effect (page 421)

self-fulfilling prophecy (page 421)

self-handicapping strategies (page 426)

self-serving biases (page 426)

social perception and cognition (page 421)

stereotypes (page 422)

Review Questions

1. What have social psychologists learned about first impressions of people?
   - (a) They are no more accurate than chance.
   - (b) They can be accurate, but only if the initial information combines sight and sound.
   - (c) They can influence your behavior and that of the other person also.

2. What does an implicit association test (IAT) measure?
   - (a) Reaction times
   - (b) Percent correct
   - (c) Relative activity of several brain areas
   - (d) Number of words generated in a given time

3. What is meant by "multiculturalism"?
   - (a) Trying to avoid seeming prejudiced
   - (b) Treating everyone the same
   - (c) Recognizing and enjoying the differences among people

4. Which of the following is an example of an internal attribution?
   - (a) She contributed money to charity because she is generous.
   - (b) She contributed money to charity to impress her boss, who was watching.
   - (c) She contributed money to charity because she owed a favor to the person collecting for the charity.

   - (d) She contributed money to charity because she saw other people doing the same thing.

5. On average, how do attributions differ between people in Asian countries and people in the United States?
   - (a) Asians tend to form their attributions more quickly and hold them more firmly.
   - (b) Asians form attributions about themselves and not about others.
   - (c) Asians tend to make more internal (personality) attributions.
   - (d) Asians tend to make more external (situational) attributions.

6. The self-handicapping strategy leads to which of the following?
   - (a) People take a risky gamble to try to make a big success.
   - (b) People try some task repeatedly until they get it right.
   - (c) People choose an easier task instead of one with a bigger potential reward.
   - (d) People do something to harm their own performance.

Answers: 1c, 2a, 3c, 4a, 5d, 6d.

After studying this module, you should be able to:

- Explain how psychologists measure attitudes.

- Define cognitive dissonance and describe an experiment that demonstrates it.

- Distinguish between the peripheral and central routes to persuasion.

- List some important techniques of persuasion.

- Discuss the effectiveness or ineffectiveness of fear messages.

- Describe why coercive persuasion leads to unreliable information.

You may have heard people say, "If you want to change people's behavior, you have to change their attitudes first." That sounds reasonable, but let's test it out with these questions: (1) What is your attitude about paying higher taxes? (2) If the government raises taxes, will you pay them?

Most people say their attitude is opposed to higher taxes. However, if the government did raise the taxes, almost everyone would pay them. In this case, it was easier to change behavior than to change attitudes. Also, as we shall see, changing behavior often leads to a change in attitudes. Let's explore the effects attitudes have on behavior, and the influences that change people's attitudes.

Attitudes and Behavior

An **attitude** is *a like or dislike that influences behavior* (Allport, 1935; Petty & Cacioppo, 1981). Your attitudes include an evaluative or emotional component (how you feel about something), a cognitive component (what you know or believe), and a behavioral component (what you are likely to do). Psychologists in Western cultures have typically interpreted attitudes in terms of personal likes and dislikes. In Asian cultures people's attitudes vary according to the situation

and align more closely with the goals of their family or their society (Riemer, Shavitt, Koo, & Markus, 2014).

Attitude Measurement

Psychologists commonly measure attitudes through attitude scales. On a Likert scale (named after psychologist Rensis Likert), you would check a point along a line from 1, meaning "strongly disagree," to 7, meaning "strongly agree," for each statement, as illustrated in ▼ Figure 13.6.

People's reported attitudes do not always match their behaviors. Many people say one thing and do another with regard to alcohol, safe sex, conserving natural resources, or studying hard for tests. Your attitudes are most likely to match your behavior if you have personal experience with the topic (Glasman & Albarracín, 2006). For example, if you have had experience dealing with mental patients, then you know how you react to them, and you state your attitude accordingly. Someone without experience states only a hypothetical attitude, which is less certain.

11. Suppose someone expresses a positive attitude on a Likert scale but you suspect the person really has a negative attitude. Which method from an earlier module of this chapter might confirm your suspicion?

Answer: 11. The implicit association test measures attitudes that don't match what people say.

Cognitive Dissonance and Attitude Change

Much research asks whether people's attitudes change their behavior. The theory of cognitive dissonance reverses the direction: It holds that a change in people's behavior alters their attitudes (Festinger, 1957). **Cognitive dissonance** is *a state of unpleasant tension that people experience when they hold contradictory attitudes or when their behavior contradicts their stated attitudes, especially if the inconsistency distresses them.*

Suppose you pride yourself on honesty but find yourself saying something you do not believe. You feel tension that

Indicate your level of agreement with the items below, using the following scale:

	Strongly disagree		Neutral			Strongly agree
1. Labor unions are necessary to protect the rights of workers.	1 2	3	4	5	6	7
2. Labor union leaders have too much power.	1 2	3	4	5	6	7
3. If I worked for a company with a union, I would join the union.	1 2	3	4	5	6	7
4. I would never cross a picket line of striking workers.	1 2	3	4	5	6	7
5. Striking workers hurt their company and unfairly raise prices for the consumer.	1 2	3	4	5	6	7
6. Labor unions should not be permitted to engage in political activity.	1 2	3	4	5	6	7
7. America is a better place for today's workers because of the efforts by labor unions in the past.	1 2	3	4	5	6	7

Note: Items 2, 5, and 6 are scored the opposite of 1, 3, 4, and 7.

▲ **Figure 13.6** This Likert scale assesses attitudes toward labor unions.

you can reduce in three ways: You can change what you are saying to match your attitudes, change your attitude to match what you are saying, or find an explanation that justifies your behavior under the circumstances (Wicklund & Brehm, 1976). Most research focuses on how cognitive dissonance changes people's attitudes.

Imagine yourself as a participant in this classic experiment on cognitive dissonance (Festinger & Carlsmith, 1959). The experimenters say they are studying motor behavior. They show you a board full of pegs. Your task is to take each peg out of the board, rotate it one-fourth of a turn, and return it to the board. When you finish all the pegs, you start over, rotating all the pegs again as quickly and accurately as possible for an hour. As you proceed, an experimenter silently takes notes. You find the task immensely tedious. In fact, the researchers chose this task because it was so boring.

At the end of the hour, the experimenter thanks you for participating and "explains" (falsely) that the study's purpose is to determine whether people's performance depends on their attitudes toward the task. You were in the neutral-attitude group, but those in the positive-attitude group are told before they start that they will enjoy the experience.

In fact, the experimenter continues, right now the research assistant is supposed to give that instruction to the next participant, who is waiting in the next room. The experimenter excuses himself to find the research assistant and returns distraught. The assistant is nowhere to be found, he says. He turns to you and asks, "Would you be willing to tell the next participant that you thought this was an interesting, enjoyable experiment? If so, I will pay you." Assume that you consent. After you have told someone that you enjoyed the study, what would you really think of it, assuming the experimenter paid you $1? What if he paid you $20? (This study occurred in the 1950s. In today's money, that $20 would be worth more than $150.)

After you finished describing how much fun the experiment was, you leave and walk down the hall. A representative of the psychology department greets you and explains that the department wants to learn about all the experiments and their educational value. (The answers to these questions are the real point of the experiment.) Two questions are how much you enjoyed the experiment and whether you would be willing to participate in a similar experiment later.

The students who received $20 said the experiment was boring and they wanted nothing to do with another such experiment. However, contrary to what you might guess, those who received

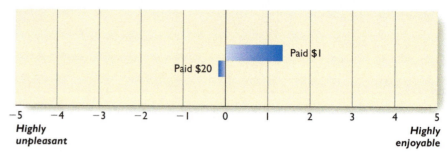

▲ **Figure 13.7** Participants were paid either $1 or $20 for telling another subject that they enjoyed an experiment (which was actually boring). Later, they were asked for their real opinions. Participants who were paid the smaller amount said that they enjoyed the study. (Based on data from Festinger & Carlsmith, 1959)

$1 said they enjoyed the experiment and would be willing to participate again (see ▲ Figure 13.7).

Why did those who received less pay say that they enjoyed participating? According to the theory of cognitive dissonance, if you accept $20 to tell a lie, you experience little conflict. You are lying, but you are doing it for $20. However, if you tell a lie for $1, do you want to think you can be bribed so cheaply? You feel cognitive dissonance—unpleasant tension from the conflict between your true attitude and what you had said about the experiment. You reduce your tension by changing your attitude, deciding that the experiment really was interesting after all. ("I learned so much about myself, like . . . uh . . . how good I am at rotating pegs.")

The idea of cognitive dissonance attracted much attention and inspired a great deal of research (Aronson, 1997). Here are two examples:

- An experimenter left a child in a room with toys but forbade the child to play with one particular toy. If the experimenter threatened the child with severe punishment for playing with the toy, the child avoided it but still regarded it as desirable. However, if the experimenter merely said that he or she would be disappointed if the child played with that toy, the child avoided the toy and said (even weeks later) that it was not a good toy (Aronson & Carlsmith, 1963).

- An experimenter asked college students to write an essay defending a position that the experimenter knew, from previous information, contradicted the students' beliefs. For example, college students who favored freer access to alcohol might be asked to write essays on why the college should increase restrictions on alcohol. Those who were told they must write the essays did not change their views significantly, but those who were asked to "please" voluntarily write the essay generally came to agree with what they wrote (Croyle & Cooper, 1983).

The general principle is that, if you entice people to do something by a minimum reward or a tiny threat so that they are acting almost voluntarily, they change their attitudes to support what they are doing. People try to seem consistent. You might be able to use this principle to your advantage: At the start of a job interview, ask why the employer chose to interview you. That question prompts the interviewer to cite something positive about you. Once you get someone to compliment you, that person seeks evidence to support the compliment.

Back to this question: If you want to change people's behavior, do you have to change their attitudes first? The results of cognitive dissonance experiments say quite the opposite: If you change people's behavior first, their attitudes will change, too.

12. Suppose your parents pay you to get a good grade in a boring course. According to cognitive dissonance theory, are you more likely to develop a positive attitude toward your studies if your parents pay you $10 or $100?

Answer

12. You will come to like your studies more if you are paid only $10. If you are paid $10, you won't be able to tell yourself that you are studying harder only for the money. Instead, you will tell yourself that you must be really interested. The theory of intrinsic and extrinsic motivation (Chapter 11) leads to the same prediction: If you study hard without any strong external reason, you perceive that you have internal reasons for studying.

Mechanisms of Attitude Change and Persuasion

The way we form or change an attitude depends on many factors, especially the importance of the topic. First let's consider your attitude toward unimportant items. You go to the supermarket to buy drinks, potato chips, and pasta sauce. You probably didn't form your attitudes toward various brands by carefully evaluating the ingredients. You might like the colorful packaging, or you saw an entertaining commercial on television, or you saw one of your friends using one of these products. When a decision seems unimportant, or when you have so many more serious concerns that you cannot devote much effort to a decision, you form or change an attitude by the **peripheral route to persuasion** that is based mostly on emotions: *If for any reason you associate something with feeling happy, you form a favorable attitude toward it* (Petty & Briñol, 2015).

In contrast, consider your approach to a highly important decision. If you are buying a new home, you carefully examine the quality of the house, the price, the neighborhood, and a great deal more. The **central route to persuasion** *requires investing enough time and effort to evaluate the evidence and reason logically about a decision.* Your emotions can still enter into the decision, but only if they are relevant. You might be in a better mood when you see one house than another just because of nicer weather or some other irrelevant factor, but you don't let that kind of emotion influence your decision. However, if the appearance of one house makes you feel cheerful, that feeling is relevant and worth considering. Similarly, you might decide to marry someone because that person makes you feel good, but not because that person is wearing an attractive outfit that makes you feel happy at the moment.

Note the similarity to a distinction from Chapter 8: The peripheral route, like System 1, gives a quick, effortless response. The central route, like System 2, devotes enough energy to consider a response carefully.

13. Suppose a well-dressed, attractive, articulate speaker presents a long list of rather weak arguments for why a college should require all seniors to take a comprehensive examination. Will this speech be more effective if the speaker is talking about your college or some other college? Why?

Answer

13. It will be more effective if it concerns some other college. When a decision is unimportant to you, you follow the peripheral route to persuasion, which attends to your emotions at the moment instead of careful examination of the evidence.

Special Techniques of Persuasion

Many people will try to persuade you to buy something, contribute to a cause, or do something else that may or may not be in your best interests. Robert Cialdini (1993) has described many techniques in the category of peripheral routes to persuasion. Let's consider a few. The goal here is not to teach you how to persuade others but to help you recognize and resist certain kinds of manipulation.

Liking and Similarity

People are more successful at persuading you if you like them or see them as similar to yourself. Suppose someone you don't know calls you and immediately asks, "How are you today?" You reply, "Okay." The reply: "Oh, I'm so glad to hear that!" Is this caller, who doesn't even know you, really delighted that you are "okay"? Or is this an attempt to seem friendly so that you will buy something? Salespeople, politicians, and others also try to emphasize the ways in which they are similar to you. For example, "I grew up in a small town, much like this one."

Here is a surprising use of this principle: If you see a lightbulb with a face on it and a message "I'm burning hot; turn me off when you leave," you are more likely to comply than if it has no face and the message "Our bulbs are burning hot; turn them off when you leave!" Simply putting a face on the bulb makes it more like *you* and therefore more worthy of your support! Similarly, a trash can with a face and the words "Please feed me food waste only" gets more compliance than a faceless can with the words "Please put in food waste only" (Ahn, Kim, & Aggarwal, 2013).

People are more likely to "help" even inanimate objects if they perceive them as similar to themselves.

Social Norms

We'll consider conformity in more detail later in this chapter, but you already know the idea: People tend to do what others are doing. A powerful influence technique is to show that many other people are doing what you want them to do. A bartender or singer with a tip jar ordinarily puts a few dollars in at the start to imply that other people have already left tips. A politician publishes photographs showing crowds of enthusiastic supporters. However, if you know that most people do not do something—for example, most people do not undergo a cancer-screening test—you become less likely to do it yourself (Sieverding, Decker, & Zimmermann, 2010).

Many hotels try to influence guests to agree to use towels more than once instead of expecting daily replacements. A typical message in the room points out that reusing towels saves energy, reduces the use of detergents that pollute the water supply, and helps protect the environment. More people agree to reuse their towels if the message adds that other guests have agreed to reuse their towels. It works even better to say that most other guests using *this room* have agreed (N. J. Goldstein, Cialdini, & Griskevicius, 2008). You conform to people similar to yourself.

Reciprocation

Civilization is based on the concept of reciprocation: If you do me a favor, then I owe you one. However, it is possible to abuse this principle. A company might hand out free samples, confident that many people who accept the samples will feel obligated to buy something in return. Someone might give you something (which maybe you didn't want), and then tell you what favor you should do in return.

Here's another version of reciprocation: An alumni organization once called me asking for a contribution. Their representative said that many other alumni were pledging $1,000, and he hoped he could count on me for the same. No, I explained, I wasn't prepared to make that kind of contribution. Oh, he responded, with a tone that implied, "too bad you don't have a *good* job like the other alumni." He then said that if I couldn't afford $1,000, how about $500? The suggestion was that we should compromise! He was giving in $500 from his original proposal, so I should give in $500 from my end.

Contrast Effects

An offer can seem good or bad, depending on how it compares to something else. A restaurant menu might list one entrée at such a high price that almost no one orders it. However, sales increase for the second most expensive item, which now seems not too expensive by contrast. A realtor might start by showing you several overpriced houses in bad condition, before showing a nicer house at a more reasonable price. If you had seen that house first, you might not have been impressed, but by contrast it seems like a good deal. Almost anything can seem good by contrast to something worse.

Foot in the Door

Sometimes, someone *starts with a modest request, which you accept, and follows with a larger request.* This procedure is called the foot-in-the-door technique. When Jonathan Freedman and Scott Fraser (1966) asked suburban residents in Palo Alto, California, to put a small "Drive Safely" sign in their windows, most agreed to do so. A couple of weeks later, other researchers asked the same residents to let them set up a large "Drive Safely" billboard in their front yards for 10 days. They also made the request to residents who had not been approached by the first researchers. Of those who had already agreed to display the small sign, 76 percent agreed to the billboard. Only 17 percent of the others agreed. Those who agreed to the first request felt they were already committed to the cause, and to be consistent, they agreed to further participation. Another study found that people who agreed to fill out a 20-minute survey became more willing a month later to take a 40-minute survey on the same topic. However, although this tendency was strong for Americans, it was weak for Chinese students. An interpretation was that Chinese culture puts less emphasis on individual consistency from one time to another (Petrova, Cialdini, & Sills, 2006).

Bait and Switch

Someone using the bait-and-switch technique *first offers an extremely favorable deal, gets the other person to commit to the deal, and then makes additional demands.* Alternatively, the person might offer a product at a low price to get customers to the store but then claim to be out of the product and try to sell something else. For example, a car dealer offers you an exceptionally good price on a new car and a generous price for the trade-in of your old car. The deal seems too good to resist. After you have committed yourself to buying, the dealer checks with the boss and returns, saying, "I'm so sorry. I forgot that this car has some special features that raise the value. If we sold it for the price I quoted, we'd lose money." So you agree to a higher price. Then the company's used car specialist looks at your old car and "corrects" the trade-in value to a lower amount. Still, you have committed yourself. You leave with a deal that you would not have accepted at the start.

That's Not All!

In the that's-not-all technique, *someone makes an offer and then improves the offer before you have a chance to reply.* The television announcer says, "Here's your chance to buy this amazing combination paper shredder and coffee-maker for only $39.95. But wait, there's more! We'll throw in a can of dog deodorant! Also this handy windshield wiper cleaner and a solar-powered flashlight and a subscription to *Modern Lobotomist!* If you call now, you get this amazing offer, which usually costs $39.95, for only $19.95! Call now!" People who hear the first offer and then the "improved" offer are more likely to comply than are people who hear the "improved" offer from the start (Burger, 1986).

You may notice a similarity among the foot-in-the-door, bait-and-switch, and that's-not-all techniques: The persuader starts with one proposal and then switches to another. The first proposal changes the listeners' state of mind, making them more open for the second proposal.

14. Identify each of the following as an example of reciprocation, the contrast effect, foot-in-the-door technique, the bait-and-switch technique, or the that's-not-all technique.

a. A credit card company offers you a card with a low introductory rate. After a few months, the interest rate on your balance doubles.

b. A store marks its prices "25 percent off," scratches that out and marks them "50 percent off!"

c. A friend asks you to help carry some supplies over to the elementary school for an afternoon tutoring program. When you get there, the principal says that one of the tutors is late and asks whether you could take her place until she arrives. You agree and spend the rest of the afternoon tutoring. The principal then talks you into coming back every week as a tutor.

Answers

14. a. bait-and-switch technique; b. either the contrast effect or the that's-not-all technique; c. foot-in-the-door technique.

Fear Messages

Some attempts at persuasion use threats, such as, "If you don't send money to support our cause, our political opponents will gain power and do terrible things." One organization appealed for contributions with a message on the envelope, "Every day an estimated 800 dolphins, porpoises, and whales will die . . . unless you act now!" (What, *me*? My contribution was supposed to save 800 marine mammals per day? How much did they think I was going to contribute?) How effective are fear messages as persuasion?

Fear messages are sometimes effective, but not always. Some countries require cigarette packages to include photos of damaged lungs or blackened teeth, and these frightening displays appear to be effective (Nan, Zhao, Yang, & Iles, 2015). However, if a message is too frightening, many people simply don't want to listen to it, or if they do listen to it, they don't believe it (Petty & Briñol, 2015). An extreme message may suggest that the problem is hopeless (Cialdini, 2003). For example, messages about global warming don't motivate many people to conserve energy, because they doubt that their behavior will make a difference (Feinberg & Willer, 2011).

Delayed Influence

Some messages have little influence at first but more later. Let's consider two examples.

The Sleeper Effect

Suppose you hear an idea from someone with poor qualifications. Because of what you think of the speaker, you reject the idea. Weeks later, you forget where you heard the idea (*source amnesia*) and remember only the idea itself. At that point, its persuasive impact may increase (Kumkale & Abarracín, 2004). If you completely forget the source, you might even claim it as your own idea! Psychologists use the term **sleeper effect** to describe *delayed persuasion by an initially rejected message*. Most studies find that the sleeper effect is very small after someone listens to a speech. That is, people who reject the speaker's message at first don't often accept it later. However, incorrect information in an entertaining television show may exert a larger sleeper effect: Viewers who disregard the information at first may begin to believe it a couple weeks later (Jensen, Bernat, Wilson, & Goonewardene, 2011).

Minority Influence

Delayed influence also occurs when a minority group proposes a worthwhile idea. It could be an ethnic, religious, political, or any other kind of minority.

The majority rejects the idea at first but reconsiders it later. If the minority continually repeats a single simple message and its members seem united, it has a good chance of eventually influencing the decision. The minority's influence often increases gradually, even if the majority hesitates to admit that the minority has swayed them (Wood, Lundgren, Ouellette, Busceme, & Blackstone, 1994). By expressing its views and demonstrating the possibility of disagreeing with the majority, the minority also prompts others to offer new ideas (Nemeth, 1986). When you disagree with what everyone else is saying, you might hesitate to speak out. When someone else objects, you feel more comfortable expressing your own idea.

One powerful example of minority influence is that of the Socialist Party of the United States, which ran candidates for elective offices from 1900 through the 1950s. No Socialist candidate was elected senator or governor, and only a few were elected to the House of Representatives (Shannon, 1955). The party's support gradually dwindled, until it stopped nominating candidates. Had they failed? No! Most of their major proposals had been enacted into law (see ■ Table 13.1). Of course, the Democrats and Republicans who voted for these changes claimed credit for the ideas.

15. At a meeting of your student government, you suggest a new method of testing and grading students. The other members immediately reject your plan. Should you give up?

Answer

15. The fact that your idea was rejected does not mean that you should give up. If you and a few allies continue to present this plan, showing apparent agreement among yourselves, the majority may eventually adopt a similar plan—probably without giving you credit for it.

Differences in Resistance to Persuasion

You may be more easily influenced at some times than at others. *Simply informing people that they are about to hear a persuasive speech activates their resistance and weakens the persuasion* (Petty & Cacioppo, 1977). This tendency is called the **forewarning effect**. Actually, the results are somewhat complex. Suppose you have a strongly unfavorable attitude toward something—increased tuition at your college, for example. Now someone tells you that a well-informed person is going to try to persuade you in favor of higher tuition. At once, before the speech even begins, your attitudes shift slightly in the direction of favoring higher

Table 13.1 Political Proposals of the U.S. Socialist Party, Early 1900s

Proposal	Eventual Fate of Proposal
Women's right to vote	Established by 19th Amendment to U.S. Constitution; ratified in 1920
Old-age pensions	Included in the Social Security Act of 1935
Unemployment insurance	Included in the Social Security Act of 1935; also guaranteed by other state and federal legislation
Health and accident insurance	Included in part in the Social Security Act of 1935 and in the Medicare Act of 1965
Increased wages, including minimum wage	First minimum-wage law passed in 1938; periodically updated since then
Reduction of working hours	Maximum 40-hour workweek (with exceptions) established by the Fair Labor Standards Act of 1938
Public ownership of electric, gas, and other utilities and of the means of transportation and communication	Utilities not owned by government but heavily regulated by federal and state government since the 1930s
Initiative, referendum, and recall (mechanisms for private citizens to push for changes in legislation and for removal of elected officials)	Adopted by most state governments

Sources: Foster, 1968; and Leuchtenburg, 1963

tuition! Exactly why is unclear, but perhaps you are telling yourself, "I guess there must be some good reason for that opinion." Then when you hear the speech itself, it does have some influence, and your attitudes shift still further, but not as much as those of someone who had not been forewarned. The warning alerts you to resist the persuasion, to criticize weak arguments, and to reject weak evidence (Wood & Quinn, 2003).

In the closely related inoculation effect, *people first hear a weak argument and then a stronger argument supporting the same conclusion.* After they have rejected the first argument, they usually reject the second one also. In one experiment, people listened to speeches *against* brushing their teeth after every meal. Some of them heard just a strong argument (e.g., "Brushing your teeth too frequently wears away tooth enamel, leading to serious disease"). Others first heard a weak argument and then the strong argument two days later. Still others first heard an argument *for* brushing teeth and then the strong argument against it. Only those who heard the weak argument against brushing resisted the influence of the strong argument. The other two groups found it highly persuasive (McGuire & Papageorgis, 1961). So if you want to convince someone, start with your strong evidence.

Coercive Persuasion

Finally, let's consider the most unfriendly kinds of persuasion. In some places, military or police interrogators have used torture (more generously known as "enhanced interrogation techniques") until suspects confessed or revealed information about subversive plots. If you were innocent, might you confess anyway, just to end the torture? Most people underestimate how painful torture can be (Nordgren, McDonnell, & Loewenstein, 2011). Any technique strong enough to get guilty people to confess gets innocent people to confess also.

Similar problems occur with what we might call "psychological torture." Suppose the police want you to confess to some crime. You agree to talk with them. After all, what do you have to lose? You're innocent, so you have nothing to hide. First the police claim your crime is horrendous and you face a stiff sentence. Then they offer sympathy and excuses, implying that if you confess, you can get a much lighter sentence. They claim that you failed a polygraph test. You stay in isolation, without food or sleep for many hours, with no promise of when, if ever, this ordeal will end. Apparently, confession is the only way you can get them to stop badgering you. Might you confess, even though you are innocent? You think, "Oh, well, eventually they will realize their mistake. They can't really convict me, because they won't have any other evidence."

Many innocent people do confess under these conditions. Unfortunately, juries consider a confession to be strong evidence, even if they know it was coerced (Kassin & Gudjonsson, 2004). Furthermore, a forced confession biases the rest of the investigation. The police look only for further evidence of your guilt, not for evidence implicating someone else, and any witness who was in doubt now testifies confidently that you were the perpetrator (Kassin, Bogart, & Kerner, 2012).

To test the effects of coercive persuasion, researchers set up this experiment: They asked pairs of students to work independently on logic problems. For half of the pairs, one of them (a confederate of the experimenter) asked for help, which the first person usually gave. Later, they were told that offering help was considered cheating. For the other pairs, the confederate did not ask for help and therefore no cheating occurred. After both completed the problems, the experimenter entered the room, accused the participant of cheating, and threatened to treat this event as harshly as any other case of academic cheating. However, the experimenter suggested they could settle the problem quickly if the student signed a confession. Under these circumstances, 87 percent of the guilty students and 43 percent of the innocent ones agreed to confess, as illustrated in ▶ Figure 13.8 (Russano, Meissner, Narchet, & Kassin, 2005). The message is that coercive techniques increase confessions by both guilty and innocent people, and therefore make the confessions unreliable evidence.

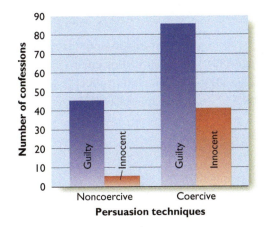

▲ **Figure 13.8** Coercive persuasion techniques increased the number of confessions by both guilty and innocent people. (Based on data of Russano, Meissner, Narchet, & Kassin, 2005)

---

in closing   module 13.3

Persuasion and Manipulation

Broadly defined, attitudes influence almost everything we do. It is important to be alert to some of the influences that might throw you off course. Advertisers, politicians, and others try to polish their techniques of persuasion, and not everyone has your best interest at heart.

Summary

- *Attitudes.* An attitude is a like or dislike that influences behavior. (page 429)

- *Cognitive dissonance.* Cognitive dissonance is a state of unpleasant tension that arises when a behavior conflicts with an attitude. People try to reduce the inconsistency, often by changing their attitudes. (page 429)

- *Persuasion.* When people consider a topic unimportant, they form attitudes based on happy or unhappy associations, often from superficial factors such as a speaker's appearance. When people care about the topic, they evaluate the evidence more carefully and consider their emotions only to the extent that they are relevant. (page 431)

- *Methods of influence.* Someone you like or consider similar to yourself is more persuasive than other people are. Being told that most people favor some idea or action makes it appealing. You may feel obligated to perform a favor for someone who did a favor for you or gave you something. An item may appear more desirable because of its contrast to something else. In the foot-in-the-door, bait-and-switch, and that's-not-all techniques, a first request makes you more likely to accept a second request. (page 431)

- *Influence of fear.* Messages that appeal to fear are sometimes effective, unless the message is too extreme or if it suggests that the problem is hopeless. (page 433)

- *Sleeper effect.* When people reject a message because of their low regard for the person who proposed it, they sometimes forget where they heard the idea and later come to accept it. (page 433)

- *Minority influence.* Although a minority may have little influence at first, it can, through persistent repetition of its message, eventually persuade the majority to adopt its position or consider other ideas. (page 433)

- *Forewarning and inoculation effects.* If people have been warned that someone will try to persuade them of something or if they have previously heard a weak version of the persuasive argument, they tend to resist the argument. (page 433)

- *Coercive persuasion.* Techniques designed to pressure a suspect into confessing decrease the reliability of the confession because, under these circumstances, many innocent people confess also. (page 434)

Key Terms

attitude (page 429)

bait-and-switch technique (page 432)

central route to persuasion (page 431)

cognitive dissonance (page 429)

foot-in-the-door technique (page 432)

forewarning effect (page 433)

inoculation effect (page 434)

peripheral route to persuasion (page 431)

sleeper effect (page 433)

that's-not-all technique (page 432)

Review Questions

1. What is meant by "cognitive dissonance"?
   (a) Harmony between attitudes and actions
   (b) Disagreement between attitudes and actions
   (c) A tendency to change your attitudes
   (d) A tendency to change your actions

2. What is the usual outcome of cognitive dissonance?
   (a) People become more consistent in their behavior.
   (b) People become more rigid in their attitudes.
   (c) People change their behavior first, and then change their attitudes.
   (d) People change their attitudes first, and then change their behavior.

3. In which of the following cases would you be most likely to follow the central route to persuasion?
   (a) A discussion about the pros and cons of a medical treatment for a condition you don't have
   (b) A discussion about proposed changes in the government of a country on the other side of the world
   (c) A discussion about the best seafood for people to eat
   (d) A discussion about the best kind of cat food (assuming you don't own a cat)

4. Suppose you want to persuade people to buy some product. Which of the following statements would probably work best?
   (a) Most of the people who have bought this product like it.
   (b) More people have bought this product this year than last year.

   (c) Ten other people that I talked to today have bought this product.
   (d) Ten of your neighbors on your own street have bought this product.

5. Someone donates a large amount to a political campaign. Later, the donor asks the elected candidate to support a project. Which of these persuasion techniques was used?
   (a) Foot-in-the-door technique
   (b) Bait-and-switch technique
   (c) That's-not-all technique
   (d) Reciprocation

6. A friend asks you to drive him to the mall. When you get there, he asks whether you could wait while he shops and then drive him home. Which of these persuasion techniques did he use?
   (a) Foot-in-the-door technique
   (b) Contrast effect
   (c) That's-not-all technique
   (d) Reciprocation

7. If you want your children to preserve the beliefs and attitudes you try to teach them, which of the following should you do?
   (a) Present only arguments in favor of those beliefs.
   (b) Expose them also to weak attacks on those beliefs.

Answers: 1b, 2c, 3c, 4d, 5d, 6a, 7b.

After studying this module, you should be able to:

- Explain theoretically why people and other animals care about physical attractiveness when choosing a mate.

- List some factors that increase the probability of forming a friendship or romantic relationship.

- Distinguish between passionate and companionate love.

William Proxmire, a former U.S. senator, used to give Golden Fleece Awards to those who, in his opinion, most flagrantly wasted the taxpayers' money. He once bestowed an award on psychologists who had received a federal grant to study how people fall in love. According to Proxmire, the research was pointless because people do not want to understand love. They prefer, he said, to let such matters remain a mystery.

This module presents the information Senator Proxmire thought you didn't want to know.

Establishing Relationships

Of all the people you meet, how do you choose those who become your friends or romantic attachments? How do they choose you?

Proximity and Familiarity

Proximity means *closeness.* (It comes from the same root as *approximate.*) Not surprisingly, we are most likely to become friends with people who live or work in proximity to us. One professor assigned students to seats randomly and followed up on them a year later. Students most often became friends with those who sat in adjacent seats (Back, Schmulkle, & Egloff, 2008). One reason proximity is important is that people who live nearby discover what they have in common. Another reason is the mere exposure effect, the principle that *the more often we come in contact with someone or something, the more we tend to like that person or object* (Saegert, Swap, & Zajonc, 1973; Zajonc, 1968).

However, familiarity does not always increase liking. Researchers contacted people who were about to go on a date arranged by an online dating service. Prior to the date, most people gave moderately high ratings on how much they expected to like the person they were about to date. After the date, more ratings went down than up (Norton, Frost, & Ariely, 2007). Becoming familiar with someone gives you a chance to find out what you have in common, but it also lets you see the other person's flaws.

Physical Attractiveness

What characteristics do you look for in a potential romantic partner? Most people have many of the same preferences regardless of whether they are male or female, homosexual or heterosexual (Holmberg & Blair, 2009). People look for intelligence, honesty, a sense of humor, and of course, physical attractiveness.

In a study long ago, psychologists arranged blind dates for 332 freshman couples for a dance before the start of classes. They asked participants to fill out questionnaires, and then ignored the questionnaires and paired students

at random. Midway through the dance, the experimenters separated the men and women and asked them to rate how much they liked their dates. The only factor that influenced the ratings was physical attractiveness (Walster, Aronson, Abrahams, & Rottman, 1966). Similarities of attitudes, personality, and intelligence counted for almost nothing. Surprising? Hardly. During the brief time they had spent together, the couples had little opportunity to learn much about each other. Intelligence, honesty, and other character values are critical for a lasting relationship but not for the first hour of a first date (Keller, Thiessen, & Young, 1996).

Later studies examined speed-dating situations, in which people briefly meet 10 to 25 other people in one evening and then report which potential partners they might like to meet for a more extended date. For both men and women, physical attractiveness was by far the main influence on their choices (Finkel & Eastwick, 2008). Although their romantic interest correlated with what they *thought* they had in common, it did not correlate with anything they *really* had in common (Tidwell, Eastwick, & Finkel, 2012). That is, speed dating is not a great way to learn much about another person.

Possible Biological Value of Attractiveness: Birds

Why do we care about physical appearance? We take its importance so much for granted that we seldom consider the question, so for a moment let's consider other species.

In many bird species, early in the mating season, females shop around and choose a brilliantly colored male that sings vigorously from the treetops. In several species, females also prefer males with especially long tails (see ▼ Figure 13.9). From an evolutionary standpoint, aren't these foolish choices? The popular males are those that risk their lives by singing loudly from the treetops, where they call the attention of predators such as hawks and eagles. They waste energy by growing bright feathers. (It takes more energy to produce bright than dull colors.) A long tail may look pretty, but it interferes with flying. Why does the female prefer a mate who wastes energy and endangers his life?

Biologists eventually decided that wasting energy and risking life were precisely the point (Zahavi & Zahavi, 1997). Only a healthy, vigorous

▲ **Figure 13.9** In some bird species, males with long tails attract more mates. Only a healthy male can afford this trait that impairs his flying ability.

male has enough energy to make bright, colorful feathers (Blount, Metcalfe, Birkhead, & Surai, 2003; Faivre, Grégoire, Préault, Cézilly, & Sorci, 2003). Only a strong male can fly despite a long tail, and only a vigorous male would risk predation by singing from an exposed perch. A colorful, singing male is showing off his health, and (perhaps) his good genes. Colorful males are also better than average at solving problems to find food (Mateos-Gonzalez, Quesada, & Senar, 2011). The female presumably does not understand why she is attracted to colorful loudmouths. She just is, because throughout her evolutionary history, most females who chose such partners produced healthier offspring than those who chose dull-colored, quiet, inactive males.

Possible Biological Value of Attractiveness: Humans

Are attractive people more likely than others to be healthy and fertile? Theoretically, they should be.

Most illnesses decrease people's attractiveness. Also, *good-looking* generally means *normal*, and normal appearance probably indicates good genes. Suppose a computer takes photographs of many people and averages their faces. The resulting composite face has about an average nose, average distance between the eyes, and so forth, and most people rate this face "highly attractive" (Langlois & Roggman, 1990; Langlois, Roggman, & Musselman, 1994; Rhodes, Sumich, & Byatt, 1999) (see ▼ Figure 13.10). It may not be the number one most attractive face, but it is among the most attractive, and it is also regarded as the most trustworthy (Sofer, Dotsch, Wigboldus, & Todorov, 2015). An attractive person has nearly average features and few irregularities—no crooked teeth, skin blemishes, or asymmetries, and no facial hair on women (Fink & Penton-Voak, 2002). Normal implies healthy. Presumably, the genes for an average face have spread in the population because of their link to success. Any face far different from the average might indicate an unfavorable mutation.

Do attractive people tend to be healthier than others? The most extensive study examined 15,000 young adults and found that those rated more attractive were healthier in almost all ways, except for having more sexually transmitted diseases (Nedelec & Beaver, 2014). So, good appearance is evidently a reasonable cue to someone's health.

Would you consider a face similar to your own to be especially attractive? Suppose we take a photograph of someone's face and let a computer morph it to look somewhat more like your face. If it was the face of someone of your own sex, you will probably regard this face as better looking than the original. If it was the face of someone of the opposite sex (and you are heterosexual), you will regard the morphed

▲ **Figure 13.10** Averaging or morphing many faces produces a generalized face that most people consider attractive. In this example, the first two faces were morphed to produce the one on the right.

face as trustworthy and likeable, but not sexually attractive (DeBruine, 2004, 2005). That is, you like to associate with someone who looks like you, but you don't want to mate someone who looks like you. Presumably the advantage is to decrease inbreeding.

16. According to evolutionary theory, attractiveness is a sign of good health. Why would it be difficult for an unhealthy individual to produce "counterfeit" attractiveness?

Answer

16. Attractive features such as bright feathers in a bird or large muscles in a man require much energy. It would be difficult for an unhealthy individual to devote enough energy to produce such features.

Similarity

The saying "opposites attract" is true for magnets. It doesn't apply to people. Most romantic partners and close friends resemble each other in age, physical attractiveness, political and religious beliefs, intelligence, education, and attitudes (Eastwick, Finkel, Mochon, & Ariely, 2007; Laumann, 1969; Lee et al., 2008; Montoya, 2008; Rushton & Bons, 2005). As a relationship matures, people's interests become more and more alike (Anderson, Keltner, & John, 2003). However, similarity of personality is not important for the success of a relationship (Montoya, Horton, & Kirchner, 2008). A relationship can work out fine if one is more extraverted and the other is more introverted. In fact, couples with highly similar personalities often find their relationship deteriorating over time (Shiota & Levenson, 2007). Another point on which similarity doesn't help is smell: Many women (unconsciously) prefer a romantic partner who does not smell too much like herself, her brothers, and other members of her family. That tendency is presumably a way to decrease the chance of mating with a close relative. Women taking birth control pills fail to show this tendency (Roberts, Gosling, Carter, & Petrie, 2008).

Members of minority groups face special difficulties. If your ethnic or religious group is greatly outnumbered where you live, your choice of potential friends or romantic partners may be limited to members of your group who do

Even when friends differ in some ways, they generally have much in common, such as interests, attitudes, and level of education.

not share your interests or members of other groups who do (Hamm, 2000).

The Equity Principle

According to exchange or equity theories, *social relationships are transactions in which partners exchange goods and services.* As in business, a relationship is most stable if both partners believe the deal is fair. It is easiest to establish a fair deal if the partners are about equally attractive and intelligent, contribute about equally to the finances and the chores, and so forth. For most couples, one partner contributes more in one way, and the other contributes more in another way.

The equity principle applies readily in the early stages of friendships or romances but less so later. You might nurse your spouse or lifelong friend through a long illness without worrying about whether you are still getting a fair deal.

Dating and Modern Technology

The Internet has added a new dimension to dating. Internet dating services introduce couples who never would have met otherwise. They bring couples together who have at least a few important aspects in common. The system is not perfect. Many people are less than honest in describing themselves. (Of course, the same is true in any dating situation.) Also, having too many choices makes it hard to consider any of them carefully, and tempts people to rely on superficial criteria (Finkel, Eastwick, Karney, Reis, & Sprecher, 2012). Despite all the information available on dating websites, most people, both men and women, react more strongly to the attractiveness of the photographs than to anything else (Sritharan, Heilpern, Wilbur, & Gawronski, 2010).

Some people also have Internet contacts with no intention of meeting face to face. They establish an online character (who may or may not look like the real person) who interacts with someone else's online character, sometimes even having on-screen sex. This type of activity apparently appeals mainly to people who do not have good real-life relationships (Scott, Mottarella & Lavooy, 2006).

Marriage and Long-Term Commitments

Most people hope to have a long-term loving relationship. Although the available research deals mainly with heterosexual marriages, the conclusions probably apply to other types of long-term commitments as well.

Is it possible to predict which marriages will succeed and which will not? To some extent, yes.

Psychologists have studied newlywed couples and compared the results to how the marriages developed later. Couples whose arguments escalate to greater and greater anger are likely to consider divorce later. Many people have been told that it is good to express their feelings fully. However, venting anger at your partner makes both of you feel bad. If your partner retaliates by screaming at you, nothing good will come of it (Fincham, 2003). Discussing a conflict calmly is important for maintaining a successful relationship (Bloch, Haase, & Levenson, 2014).

The best predictor of long-term satisfaction is much display of genuine affection between newlyweds (Graber, Laurenceau, Miga, Chango, & Coan, 2011). If your partner cheers you up when things are going badly, that's good, but often a better sign of affection is if your partner feels genuine pleasure at your successes.

In a mature, lasting relationship, a couple can count on each other for care and affection through both good times and bad times.

Apparently, other subtle cues also distinguish successful from less successful marriages. In one study, people watched 3-minute videotaped conversations between married couples and estimated how satisfied each couple was. Their estimates were then compared to reports by the couples themselves. People who reported that their own marriages were either highly satisfying or highly unsatisfying were the best at judging the quality of other couples' marriages (Ebling & Levenson, 2003).

When you hear about how many marriages end in divorce, it is easy to despair, but many marriages remain strong for a lifetime. Psychologists have maintained that a romantic relationship begins with *passionate love*, marked with *sexual desire and excitement*, and gradually develops over many years into *companionate love*, *marked by sharing, care, and protection* (Bartels & Zeki, 2000; Hatfield & Rapson, 1993; Kim & Hatfield, 2004). However, later research found that one-third or more of people who have been married for more than 30 years report that they are still "very intensely" in love (O'Leary, Acevedo, Aron, Huddy, & Mashek, 2012). Brain scans show that when they see a photo of their spouse, they get excitation in the same brain areas that show excitation in the early stages of romance (Acevedo, Aron, Fisher, & Brown, 2012). Yes, love does fade for many couples, but for some it remains strong for a lifetime.

concept check

17. **What is the best predictor of long-term success for a marriage?**

Answer

17. Consistent displays of affection and respect correlate with long-term success.

Choosing Your Partners Carefully

Life is like a roller-coaster ride in the dark: It has many ups and downs, and you never know what is going to happen next. You want to ride with someone you like and trust. Many people choose their partners poorly. In some regards, forming impressions of romantic partners is especially difficult. A person you date is trying to make a good impression, and you *hope* to like the person. As the relationship progresses, another factor kicks in: Remember from the section on persuasion that anyone you like tends to be highly persuasive. In short, it is easy to form an attachment and later regret it. Choose carefully.

Summary

- *Forming relationships.* People generally choose friends and romantic partners who live near them. In the early stage of romantic attraction, physical appearance is the key factor, but similarity of interests and goals becomes more serious later. Relationships are most likely to thrive if each person believes that he or she is getting about as good a deal as the other person is. (page 437)
- *Physical attractiveness.* Theoretically, physical attractiveness should be a cue to someone's health and therefore desirability as a mate. Someone with approximately average features is at-tractive, presumably because average features have been associated with successful breeding in the past. (page 437)
- *Marriage.* Marriage and similar relationships often break up because of problems that were present from the start, such as displays of anger. (page 439)
- *Romantic love.* Psychologists distinguish passionate love and companionate love. For many people, love fades over a life-time, but for a substantial number of people, it remains strong and passionate even after decades of marriage. (page 440)

Key Terms

companionate love (page 440)

exchange (or equity) theories (page 439)

mere exposure effect (page 437)

passionate love (page 440)

proximity (page 437)

Review Questions

1. According to evolutionary theory, which of the following is true?
   (a) The average person is highly attractive.
   (b) Someone with average features in all regards is attractive.
   (c) A person with average features is unattractive.

2. Someone your own age from another country moves next door. Neither of you speaks the other's language. Of the fol-lowing factors, which will tend to weaken the likelihood of your becoming friends?
   (a) Proximity
   (b) Familiarity
   (c) Similarity

3. What is the best advice if you have a conflict with a romantic partner?
   (a) Express your emotions fully.
   (b) Restrain your emotional display.

4. What happens to romantic love after decades of marriage?
   (a) If it remains at all, it transforms from passionate love to companionate love.
   (b) The results vary, but in many cases passionate love continues for a lifetime.

Answers: 1b, 2c, 3b, 4b.

module 13.5

Interpersonal Influence

After studying this module, you should be able to:

- Describe Asch's classic experiment demonstrating conformity.
- Discuss cultural differences in conformity.
- Evaluate Zimbardo's prison experiment.
- Describe Milgram's study on obedience.
- Give examples of group polarization and groupthink.

People influence us constantly. First, people set *norms* that define the expectations of a situation. You watch how others dress and act in any situation, and you tend to do the same. Second, they provide us with *information*. For example, if you approach a building and find crowds quickly fleeing from it and screaming, they probably know something you don't. However, people sometimes provide misinformation. In 2009, a man who had the wrong floor mat under the accelerator of his Toyota could not get his car to stop and therefore had a fatal accident. The publicity led people to believe there was something wrong with Toyotas, and suddenly a huge number of people reported problems with their Toyotas, and then with other models. Eventually people realized this was just mass hysteria, and none of the cars were defective (Fumento, 2014). Third, people influence us just by suggesting a possible action. Seeing people yawn makes you feel like yawning, too. Why? They haven't given you any new information, and you don't necessarily wish to resemble them. You copy just because seeing a yawn suggested the possibility.

Conformity

Conformity means *altering one's behavior to match other people's behavior or expectations.* In many situations, conformity is good. When you are driving, it is helpful if everyone going the same direction drives on the same side of the road. If you are having a discussion, it is helpful if everyone speaks the same language. If you go to a meeting, it is helpful if everyone arrives at about the same time.

Don't underestimate the power of conformity. Koversada, Croatia, used to be an officially nudist town. If a first-time visitor walked around the city wearing clothes, other people stopped and stared, shaking their heads with disapproval. The visitor felt

People conform to one another in their clothing and other customs.

as awkward and self-conscious as a naked person would be in a city of clothed people. Most visitors quickly undressed (Newman, 1988). If you exclaim, "I wouldn't conform," compare your own clothing right now to what others around you are wearing. Professors have sometimes noted the irony of watching a class full of students in blue jeans insisting that they do not conform to other people's style of dress (Snyder, 2003).

On many websites, users can post a comment and other users can then vote "thumbs up" or "thumbs down" to indicate their approval or disapproval. Researchers chose a few thousand new comments at random to give an initial "thumbs up." The result was a 25 percent increased percentage of "thumbs up" votes by later users, compared to average (Muchnik, Aral, & Taylor, 2013).

Do you think you conform about as much as most other people do, or more or less? *Most* U.S. students insist that they conform *less* than average. One group of students was asked, "Here is what most students at your college think about this issue . . . Now, what do you think?" Regardless of what the students were told the others thought, most students said they agreed with that position . . . while insisting that it was really their own opinion, and they weren't just going along with the crowd (Pronin, Berger, & Molouki, 2007).

Conformity to an Obviously Wrong Majority

Early research suggested that we conform our opinions when we are unsure of our own judgment (Sherif, 1935). Would we conform even we knew that everyone else was wrong? To answer that question, Solomon Asch (1951, 1956) conducted a now-famous series of experiments. He asked groups of students to look at a vertical bar, as shown in ▼ **Figure 13.11**, which he defined as the model. He showed them three other vertical bars (right half of Figure 13.11) and asked which bar was the same length as the model. As you can see, the task is simple. Asch asked the students to give their answers aloud. He repeated the procedure with 18 sets of bars.

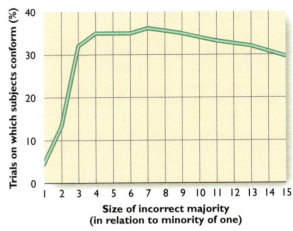

Figure 13.11 In Asch's conformity studies, a participant was asked which of three lines matched another line. Before answering, the participant heard other people answer incorrectly.

In each group, only one student was a real participant. The others were confederates who had been instructed to give incorrect answers on 12 of the 18 trials. Asch arranged for the real participant to be the next to last person in the group to announce his answer so that he would hear most of the confederates' incorrect responses before giving his own (see ▼ Figure 13.12). Would he go along with the crowd?

To Asch's surprise, 37 of the 50 participants conformed to the majority at least once, and 14 conformed on most of the trials. Asch (1955) was disturbed by these results: "That we have found the tendency to conformity in our society so strong . . . is a matter of concern. It raises questions about our ways of education and about the values that guide our conduct" (p. 34).

Why did people conform so readily? When they were interviewed after the experiment, some said they thought the rest of the group was correct or they guessed that an optical illusion was influencing the appearance of the bars. Others said they knew their conforming answers were wrong but went along with the group for fear of ridicule. The nonconformists were interesting, too. Some were nervous but felt duty bound to say how the bars looked to them. A few seemed socially withdrawn. Still others were supremely self-confident, as if to say, "I'm right and everyone else is wrong. It happens all the time." When Asch (1951, 1955) varied the number of confederates who gave incorrect answers, he found that people conformed to a group of three or four just as readily as to a larger group (see ▶ Figure 13.13). However, a participant with an ally giving correct answers conformed much less. Being a minority of one is painful, but being in a minority of two is not as bad (see ▶ Figure 13.14).

A tendency to conform can influence a person's opinion for days, but probably not forever. Young adults first rated the attractiveness of many photos of women's faces, and then saw what was reported to be the average rating by other observers. If they reexamined the photos one to three days later, they tended to shift their rating closer to what they believed other people had said. This shift evidently represents a real change of opinion, because none of the other people

Figure 13.12 Three of the participants in one of Asch's experiments on conformity. The one in the middle looking uncomfortable is the real participant. The others are the experimenter's confederates. (From Asch, 1951)

Figure 13.13 Asch found that conformity became more frequent as group size increased to about three, and then it leveled off. (Adapted from "Opinion and social pressure" by Solomon Asch, 1955 (November). *Scientific American.* Copyright © 1955 by Scientific American, Inc. All rights reserved.)

were around to imply any pressure. However, if the observers examined the photos a week later, they gave reports close to their original ratings (Huang, Kendrick, & Yu, 2014). So, although conformity's influence is strong, it is limited.

concept check

18. Are you more likely to conform to a group when you are outnumbered 5 to 1, 10 to 1, or 10 to 2?

Answer

18. You would be about equally likely to conform when outnumbered 5 to 1 or 10 to 1. Any group of 3 or more produces about the same urge to conform. However, having even one ally decreases the pressure, so you would be less likely to conform when outnumbered 10 to 2.

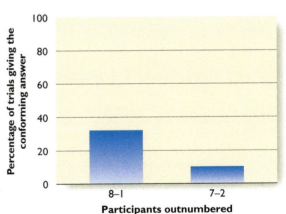

Figure 13.14 In Asch's experiments, participants who were faced with a unanimous incorrect majority conformed on 32 percent of trials. Participants who had one ally giving the correct answer were less likely to conform.

Variation in Conformity

Over the years since Asch's experiments, many similar studies have been conducted. In the United States, most studies using a design similar to Asch's show less conformity than he found in the 1950s. In most Asian countries, the percentage of conforming answers tends to be higher than in the United States, partly because people try to be polite and not embarrass the others by pointing out their error (Bond & Smith, 1996). That is, when researchers use the same procedure in different cultures, they may not be testing the same psychological processes.

Are people in certain cultures more prone to conformity as a general rule? The cultures of southern Asia, including China and Japan, are often described as "collectivist" in contrast to the "individualist" cultures of the United States, Canada, Australia, and most of Europe. According to this view, Western culture encourages originality, individualism, and uniqueness, whereas Eastern culture favors subordination of the individual to the welfare of the family or society (Takemura, 2014).

Many studies have contrasted Japanese and U.S. attitudes, mostly using college students and relying on questions like those in ■ Table 13.2. A few investigators have directly observed conformist, cooperative, and competitive behaviors in various countries.

Table 13.2	Examples of Questions to Measure Collectivist Versus Individualist Attitudes	
T	F	I take pride in accomplishing what no one else can accomplish.
T	F	It is important to me that I perform better than others on a task.
T	F	I am unique—different from others in many respects.
T	F	I like my privacy.
T	F	To understand who I am, you must see me with members of my group.
T	F	I would help, within my means, if a relative were in financial difficulty.
T	F	Before making a decision, I always consult with others.
T	F	I have respect for the authority figures with whom I interact.

Note: The first four items measure individualism; the second four measure collectivist attitudes.
Source: From Oyserman, Coon, & Kemmelmeier, 2002.

The results depend on the type of question or the type of behavior observed. Japanese culture is more collectivist than American culture in some ways, but similar to American culture in other ways (Hamamura, 2012; Oyserman, Coon, & Kemmelmeier, 2002).

Some researchers therefore suggest that the "collectivist" notion is wrong, at least for modern-day Japan (Takano & Osaka, 1999). Others point out that each country has multiple subcultures (Fiske, 2002). In many ways Tokyo is more like New York than either of those cities resembles rural areas in their own countries.

19. In what way does conformity in the United States seem to differ from conformity in Asia?

Answer

19. Americans often conform to avoid embarrassing themselves. Asians sometimes conform to the wrong opinions of others to avoid embarrassing the others.

Obedience to Authority

Ordinarily, if someone ordered you to hurt another person, you would refuse. However, certain situations exert powerful pressure.

In the early 1970s, psychologist Philip Zimbardo and his colleagues performed one of the bests known studies in social psychology. They paid college students to play the roles of guards and prisoners for two weeks during a vacation period. The researchers set up the basement of a Stanford University building as a prison and randomly assigned participants to the roles of guard or prisoner. Within six days, the researchers had to cancel the study because many of the guards were physically and emotionally bullying the prisoners (Haney, Banks, & Zimbardo, 1973). Zimbardo concluded that the situation had elicited cruel behavior. Normal, well-educated, middle-class young men, when given power over others, had quickly abused that power. The implication is that we shouldn't blame people who abuse their power, because most of us would do the same thing in that situation.

Although that conclusion may be true, the Stanford prison experiment is not solid evidence for it. Chapter 2 discussed demand characteristics, the cues that tell participants what the experimenter hopes to see. In this case, the demand characteristics were huge. After all, if they were "playing prison" for two weeks, they must have inferred that they were expected to be rude and abusive (Banuazizi & Movahedi, 1975). One of the guards recalled, decades later, "I set out with a definite plan in mind, to try to force the action, force something to happen, so that the researchers would have something to work with. After all, what could they possibly learn from guys sitting around like it was a country club?" ("The Menace Within," 2011).

Furthermore, later and fuller descriptions of the study revealed that the guards didn't have to do much inferring. During the guards' orientation session, Zimbardo had instructed them to create fear, deprive the prisoners of privacy, and give them a sense of powerlessness. A few days later, some of the guards were told that they were supposed to act tougher (Zimbardo, 2007). Under the circumstances, the guards were doing what they thought they were supposed to do.

The question remains, to what extent would normal people follow orders that might hurt someone? Let's consider in detail another of social psychology's most famous experiments.

what's the evidence?

The Milgram Experiment

If an experimenter asked you to deliver shocks to another person, starting with weak shocks and progressing to stronger ones, at what point, if any, would you refuse? Research by Stanley Milgram (1974) was inspired by reports of atrocities in the Nazi concentration camps during World War II. People who had committed the atrocities defended themselves by saying they were only obeying orders. International courts rejected that defense, and outraged people throughout the world insisted, "If I had been there, I would have refused to follow such orders" or "I would have been like the woman in the movie *Schindler's List* who risked her life to save Jewish people from the Nazi Holocaust."

Well, maybe you would have, and maybe not. It is hard to be sure what you would do in a situation you have never faced. Milgram suspected that people might yield to pressure.

Hypothesis When an authority figure gives normal people instructions to do something that might hurt another person, some of them will obey.

Method Two adult men at a time arrived at the experiment—a real participant and a confederate of the experimenter pretending to be a participant. The experimenter told them that in this study on learning, one participant would be the "teacher" and the other would be the "learner." The teacher would read lists of words through a microphone to the learner, sitting in another room. The teacher would then test the learner's memory for the words. Whenever the learner made a mistake, the teacher was to deliver an electric shock as punishment.

The experiment was rigged so that the real participant was always the teacher and the confederate was always the learner. The teacher watched as the learner was strapped into an escape-proof shock device (see ▼ Figure 13.15). The learner never received shocks, but the teacher was led to believe that he did. In fact, before the start of the study, the experimenter had the teacher feel a sample shock from the machine.

Throughout the experiment, the learner made many mistakes. The experimenter instructed the teacher to begin by punishing the learner with the 15-volt switch for his first mistake and increase by 15 volts for each successive mistake, up to the maximum of 450 volts (see ▶ Figure 13.16).

As the voltage went up, the learner in the next room cried out in pain. If the teacher asked who would take responsibility for any harm to the learner, the experimenter replied that he, the experimenter, would take responsibility but insisted, "while the shocks may be painful, they are not dangerous." When the shocks reached 150 volts, the learner begged to be let out of the experiment, complaining that his heart was bothering him. Beginning at 270 volts, he screamed in agony. At 300 volts, he shouted that he would no longer answer any questions. After 330 volts, he made no response at all. Still, the experimenter ordered the teacher to continue asking questions and delivering shocks. Remember, the learner was not really being shocked. The screams came from a recording.

Results Of 40 participants, 25 delivered shocks all the way to 450 volts. Most of those who quit did so early. Most of those who went beyond 150 volts and everyone who continued beyond 330 persisted all the way to 450. Those who delivered the maximum shock were not sadists but normal adults recruited from the community through newspaper ads. They were paid a few dollars for their services, and if they asked, they

Irena Sendler, a Polish social worker, saved the lives of more than 2,500 Jewish children from the Nazis, not giving up their whereabouts even under torture. She was later able to reunite many of the children with their families by digging up thousands of jars in which she had buried their identities and information.

were told that they could keep the money even if they quit. (Not many asked.) People from all walks of life obeyed the experimenter's orders, including blue-collar workers, white-collar workers, and professionals. Most became nervous and upset while they were supposedly delivering shocks to the screaming learner.

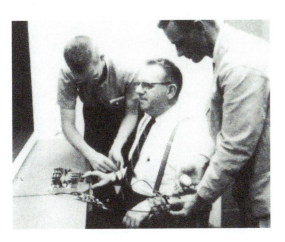

◀ **Figure 13.15** In Milgram's experiment, a rigged selection chose a confederate of the experimenter to be the "learner." Here the learner is strapped to a device that supposedly delivers shocks. (Source: https://www.youtube.com/watch?v=Jqr5-dWk6Gw)

▲ **Figure 13.16** The "teacher" in Milgram's experiment flipped switches on this box, apparently delivering stronger and stronger shocks for each successive error that the "learner" made. Although the device looked realistic, it did not actually shock the learner. (Source: https://www.youtube.com/watch?v=Jqr5-dWk6Gw)

▲ **Figure 13.17** In one variation of the procedure, the experimenter asked the teacher to hold the learner's hand on the shock plate. This close contact with the learner decreased obedience to less than half its usual level. (From Milgram's 1965 film, *Obedience*) (Source: https://www.youtube.com/watch?v=Jqr5-dWk6Gw)

Interpretation Why did so many people obey orders? One reason was that the experimenter agreed to take responsibility. (Remember the diffusion of responsibility principle.) Another reason is that the teachers identified with the experimenter and saw themselves as his assistant (Reicher, Haslam, & Smith, 2012). Also, the experimenter

started with a small request, a 15-volt shock, and gradually progressed to stronger shocks. It is easy to agree to the small request, and agreeing to that one makes it easier to agree to the next one. If you have already delivered many shocks you are unlikely to quit, because if you quit, you take responsibility for your actions. That is, if you quit after 300 volts, why didn't you quit earlier? You could no longer say, "I was just following orders."

◀ Figures 13.17 and ▼ 13.18 illustrate the results of some variations in procedure. Participants were more obedient to an experimenter who remained in the same room than to one who left. They were less obedient if they needed to force the learner's hand back onto the shock plate. If additional "teachers" divided the task—the other "teachers" being confederates of the experimenter—a participant was likely to obey if the others obeyed but unlikely if the others did not.

Still, the remarkable conclusion remains that many normal people followed orders that they thought might hurt or even kill someone. If people in this study felt compelled to obey, just imagine the pressure to obey orders from a government or military leader.

Ethical Issues Milgram's experiment told us something about ourselves that we did not want to hear. No longer could we say, "What happened in Nazi Germany could never happen here." We found that most of us do follow orders, even offensive ones. We are indebted to Milgram's study for this unpleasant but important information. However, although it is good to know about Milgram's results, you would not have enjoyed participating in his experiment. Most people found the experience upsetting and some became very distressed indeed (Perry, 2013).

A few years after Milgram's studies, the U.S. government established regulations to protect people participating in research. These regulations were a response to abusive experiments in medicine, not to Milgram's study (Benjamin & Simpson, 2009). Nevertheless, the rules apply to psychological research. In addition, psychologists have become more sensitive to the ethics of research. Today, before the start of any

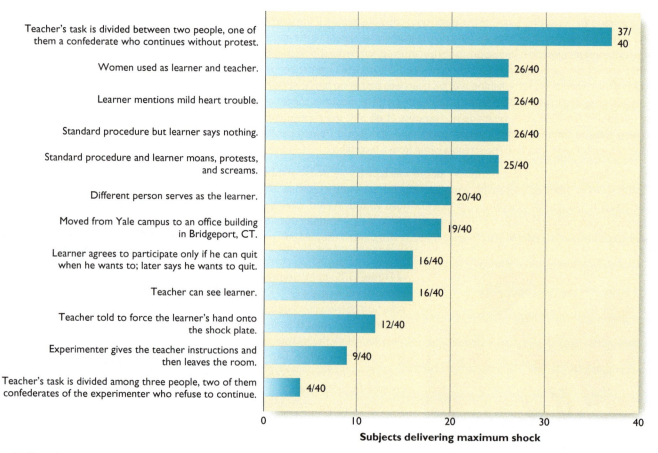

▲ **Figure 13.18** Milgram varied his procedure in many ways. Division of responsibility increased obedience. An implication of personal responsibility decreased obedience.

study—even the simplest and most innocuous—the researcher must submit a plan to an institutional committee that considers the ethics and approves or rejects the study. One of the main rules is *informed consent*. Before you participate, you must understand what is about to happen, and you must agree to it.

Could anyone replicate Milgram's research today? Psychologists long assumed that the ethical restraints would prohibit a replication (although reality television shows submit people to equal or worse experiences). However, one researcher found a way to replicate the essential aspect of the research. Milgram reported that most of the people who went beyond 150 volts continued all the way to 450. The teacher's tension and stress increased as the learner screamed and protested at the higher voltages. So Burger (2009) repeated the procedure but just until 150 volts. The result was that most people, both men and women, continued as far as 150 volts, as in Milgram's research more than 40 years earlier (Burger, 2009). The level of obedience was a bit lower than in Milgram's era, but the finding remains that most people followed orders that might hurt someone.

It is interesting to speculate about what would have happened under other conditions that Milgram didn't try. Would people quit earlier if they thought they were shocking a child? What if they were told that they would eventually trade places so that the previous learner would start delivering shocks to the teacher? How do you think the teachers would behave then? What other changes in procedure can you imagine that might influence the degree of obedience?

20. **In what way did the obedience in Milgram's experiment resemble the foot-in-the-door procedure? How did it resemble Skinner's shaping procedure?**

Answer

20. As with the foot-in-the-door procedure, Milgram started with a small request (give a small shock) and then built up. Skinner's shaping procedure also starts with an easy task and then builds to something more difficult.

Group Decision Making

An organization that needs to reach a decision often sets up a committee to consider the issues and make recommendations. A committee has more time, more information, and fewer peculiarities than any individual has. Group decisions are generally better than individual decisions, but the outcome depends on circumstances. If you and someone else are equally well informed, you probably will make a better decision together than either of you would separately. However, some groups work together better than others do. One study compared many groups that were asked to make decisions about moral judgments, visual problems, ways of dividing limited resources, and so forth. In this study, decisions were best in groups that cooperated, letting everyone participate about equally rather than letting one person dominate. Groups with a high percentage of women usually outperformed groups with mostly men, who tended to argue and compete (Wooley, Chabris, Pentland, Hashmi, & Malone, 2010). However, the results would certainly be different for groups making decisions about more technical topics. For a decision relating to nuclear engineering, for example, it would be better to have an expert on nuclear engineering than a friendly group in which everyone participates equally.

Furthermore, groups sometimes interact in unfavorable ways that stifle dissent or rush to a judgment. We'll consider how this happens.

Group Polarization

If nearly all the people who compose a group lean in the same direction on a particular issue, then a group discussion moves the group as a whole even further in that direction. This phenomenon is known as group polarization. It requires a fairly homogeneous group. If the group has several disagreeing factions, the trends are less predictable (Rodrigo & Ato, 2002).

The term *polarization* does not mean that the group breaks up into fragments favoring different positions. Rather, it means that the members of a group move *together* toward one pole (extreme position) or the other. For example, a group of people who are opposed to abortion or in favor of animal rights or opposed to gun regulations will, after discussing the issue among themselves, generally become more extreme in their views than they had been at the start (Lamm & Myers, 1978). During the discussion, if most of the members were already leaning in the same direction, they hear new arguments favoring that side of the issue and few or none for the opposition (Kuhn & Lao, 1996). For example, corporations in the United States appoint a committee of directors outside the company to set the salary for the chief executive officer. If most of them think the officer deserves a high salary, they probably vote for an even higher salary after discussing it with one another. If most favored a low salary, they choose an even lower salary after the discussion (Zhu, 2014).

21. **How would group polarization affect a jury?**

Answer

21. If most jury members lean toward a guilty or innocent verdict, they will become even more confident of their decision after a discussion. In a civil suit, if most jurors favor a strong penalty against the defendant, they will probably choose an even stronger penalty after a discussion.

Groupthink

An extreme form of group polarization, known as groupthink, occurs when *the members of a group suppress their doubts about a group's decision for fear of making a bad impression or disrupting group harmony* (Janis, 1972, 1985). The main elements leading to groupthink are overconfidence by the leadership, underestimation of the problems, and pressure to conform. Sometimes, dissenters conform on their own, and sometimes, the leadership actively urges them to conform.

A classic example of groupthink led to the Bay of Pigs fiasco of 1962. President John F. Kennedy and his advisers were considering a plan to support a small-scale invasion of Cuba at the Bay of Pigs. They assumed that a small group of Cuban exiles could overwhelm the Cuban army and trigger a spontaneous rebellion of the Cuban people against their government. Most of the advisers who doubted this assumption kept quiet. The only one who expressed doubts was told that he should loyally support the president. Within a few hours after the invasion began, all the invaders were killed or captured. The decision makers then wondered how they could have made such a stupid decision.

Another example was Japan's decision to attack the United States at Pearl Harbor in 1941. Most of the civilian leadership and the leaders of the navy doubted the wisdom of attacking, but a few leaders of the army strongly advocated the attack, and the opponents hesitated to speak out against the decision (Hotta, 2013).

Groupthink is not easy to avoid. We generally admire government or business leaders who are decisive and confident. Groupthink occurs when they become *too* decisive and confident, and when other group members hesitate to risk their status by objecting. Occasionally, some people do speak out, especially people who care deeply about an issue under discussion (Packer, 2009). To decrease groupthink, one strategy is for a leader to consult with advisers individually so they are not influenced by what they hear other advisers saying.

Fix the Situation, Not Human Nature

Certain situations bring out the worst in people, even well-educated people with good intentions. If we want to prevent people from panicking when a fire breaks out in a crowded theater, the best solution is not to remind people what to do. The solution is to build more exits. Similarly, it is difficult to teach people to behave ethically or intelligently when they are under strong pressure to conform or to obey orders. To avoid the temptation to make bad decisions, we need to choose our situations carefully.

Summary

- *Social influence.* People influence our behavior by setting norms and by offering information. We also follow others' examples just because they suggested a possible action. (page 442)
- *Conformity.* Many people conform to the majority view even when they are confident that the majority is wrong. An individual is as likely to conform to a group of three as to a larger group, but an individual with an ally is less likely to conform. (page 442)
- *Cultural differences.* Although some cultures tend to be more collectivist or conforming than others, it is an overgeneralization to regard all Asian cultures as collectivist or to assume that all members of a society are equally collectivist. (page 444)
- *Obedience.* In Milgram's obedience study, many people followed directions in which they thought they were delivering painful shocks to another person. (page 444)
- *Group polarization.* Groups of people who lean mostly in the same direction on a given issue often make more extreme decisions than most people would have made on their own. (page 447)
- *Groupthink.* Groupthink occurs when members of a cohesive group fail to express their opposition to a decision for fear of making a bad impression or harming the cohesive spirit of the group. (page 447)

Key Terms

conformity (page 442)

group polarization (page 447)

groupthink (page 447)

Review Questions

1. What did Solomon Asch's study of conformity reveal?
   (a) Americans conform to others' opinions, but people in other countries do not.
   (b) People conform on clothing, but not on opinions.
   (c) People outnumbered 10 to 1 are twice as likely to conform as those outnumbered 5 to 1.
   (d) Most people conform even when they know the majority opinion is wrong.

2. What is meant by a "collectivist" culture?
   (a) One where people subordinate their own wishes to the welfare of their society
   (b) One that encourages originality and uniqueness
   (c) One with large, densely populated cities
   (d) One where the government charges high taxes

3. Which of these criticisms seems to apply to Zimbardo's prison study?
   (a) The effect was too small to be statistically significant.
   (b) Participants were not randomly assigned to the two groups.
   (c) Later studies failed to replicate these results.

   (d) The participants were probably influenced by demand characteristics.

4. Which conclusion did Milgram draw from his obedience study?
   (a) Most people will deliver a weak shock to someone, but they refuse at higher levels.
   (b) Less-educated people will obey orders, but well-educated people refuse.
   (c) Normal people will follow orders even if it means badly hurting someone.
   (d) Stronger ethical standards need to be instituted for guiding psychological experiments.

5. What is meant by "group polarization"?
   (a) After a discussion, a group splits between those who favor one extreme opinion and those who favor the opposite extreme opinion.
   (b) After a discussion, a group that mostly favored one position at the start becomes more extreme in favoring that position.

Answers: 1d, 2a, 3d, 4c, 5b.

14 Personality

This three-dimensional jigsaw puzzle of the ocean liner *Titanic* consists of 26,000 pieces. Understanding personality is an even more complex puzzle.

Several thousand people have the task of assembling the world's largest jigsaw puzzle, with more than a trillion pieces. Cody Conclusionjumper scrutinizes 20 pieces, stares off into space, and announces, "When the puzzle is fully assembled, it will be a picture of the Sydney Opera House!" Prudence Plodder says, "Well, I don't know what the whole puzzle will look like, but I think I've found two little pieces that fit together."

Which of the two has made the greater contribution to completing the puzzle? We could argue either way. Clearly, the task requires an enormous number of small accomplishments like Prudence's. But if Cody is right, her flash of insight will be extremely valuable for assembling all the pieces. Of course, if the puzzle turns out to be a picture of a sailboat at sunset, then Cody will have misled us and wasted our time.

Some psychologists have offered grand theories about the nature of personality. Others have tried to classify personality types and understand why people act differently in specific situations. In this chapter, we explore several methods of approaching personality. In the first module, we consider some famous personality theorists, including Sigmund Freud. The second module concerns descriptions of personality. Any description is, of course, a theory, but description differs from the kinds of theories in the first module. The final module concerns personality measurements.

module 14.1

Personality Theories

After studying this module, you should be able to:

- Discuss and evaluate Sigmund Freud's theories and some of the changes he made in them.

- List Freud's stages of psychosexual pleasure.

- Define and give examples of Freud's defense mechanisms against anxiety.

- Explain what Carl Jung meant by the collective unconscious.

- Discuss how Alfred Adler advanced the idea that mental health is more than the absence of mental illness.

- Explain how the learning approach deals with apparent inconsistencies in personality.

- State the distinctive features of humanistic psychology.

> Every individual is virtually an enemy of civilization. . . . Thus civilization has to be defended against the individual. . . . For the masses are lazy and unintelligent . . . and the individuals composing them support one another in giving free rein to their indiscipline.
>
> —Sigmund Freud (1927/1961, pp. 6–8)

> It has been my experience that persons have a basically positive direction. In my deepest contacts with individuals in therapy, even those whose troubles are most disturbing, whose behavior has been most anti-social, whose feelings seem most abnormal, I find this to be true.
>
> —Carl Rogers (1961, p. 26)

What is human nature? The seventeenth-century philosopher Thomas Hobbes argued that humans are by nature selfish. Life in a state of nature, he said, is "nasty, brutish, and short." We need the government to protect ourselves from one another. The eighteenth-century political philosopher Jean-Jacques Rousseau disagreed, maintaining that people are naturally good and that governments are the problem, not the solution. Rational people acting freely, he maintained, would advance the welfare of all.

The debate between those two viewpoints survives in theories of personality (see ▼ Figure 14.1). Sigmund Freud held that people are born with impulses that must be held in check if civilization is to survive. Carl Rogers believed that

people seek good and noble goals after they have been freed from unnecessary restraints.

Which point of view is correct? Way down deep, are we good, bad, both, or neither? What is the basic nature of human personality?

The term *personality* comes from the Latin word *persona,* meaning "mask." In the plays of ancient Greece and Rome, actors wore masks to indicate their characters. Unlike a mask, however, the term *personality* implies something stable. **Personality** consists of *all the consistent ways in which the behavior of one person differs from that of others, especially in social situations.* (Differences in learning, memory, sensation, or athletic skills are generally not considered personality.)

Sigmund Freud and the Psychodynamic Approach

Sigmund Freud (1856–1939), an Austrian physician, developed the first psychodynamic theory. A **psychodynamic theory** *relates personality to the interplay of conflicting forces, including unconscious ones, within the individual.* That is, internal forces that we do not understand push us and pull us.

Freud's influence extends into sociology, literature, art, religion, and politics. And yet, here we are, about three-fourths of the way through this text on psychology, and until now, it has barely mentioned Freud. Why?

The reason is that most psychologists are highly skeptical of Freud's theories. According to

Hobbes	Rousseau
Humans are selfish	Humans are good
Government is required for protection	Government is a corrupting influence
Freud	**Rogers**
Natural impulses are detrimental to society	Natural impulses are noble and good

▲ **Figure 14.1** Sigmund Freud, like the philosopher Thomas Hobbes, stressed the more destructive aspects of human nature. Carl Rogers, like Jean-Jacques Rousseau, emphasized the more favorable aspects.

Sigmund Freud interpreted dreams, slips of the tongue, and so forth to infer unconscious thoughts and motivations.

Frederick Crews (1996, p. 63), "independent studies have begun to converge toward a verdict that was once considered a sign of extremism or even of neurosis: that there is literally nothing to be said, scientifically or therapeutically, to the advantage of the entire Freudian system or any of its constituent dogmas." Others have written, "the legend is losing its hold, fraying from all sides" (Borch-Jacobsen & Shamdasani, 2012). Not everyone agrees, of course. Still, Freud's influence within psychology today is far more limited than most people outside psychology imagine it to be.

Freud's Search for the Unconscious

Although Freud was a physician, he admitted in letters to his friends that he was never much interested in medicine. His goal was a theoretical understanding of the human mind. Early in his career, Freud worked with the psychiatrist Josef Breuer, who was treating a young woman with a fluctuating variety of physical complaints. As she talked with Breuer about her past, she described various emotionally traumatic experiences. Breuer, and later Freud, said that remembering these experiences produced catharsis, *a release of pent-up emotional tension*, thereby relieving her illness. However, later scholars who reexamined the medical records found that this woman who was so central to the history of psychoanalysis showed little or no benefit from the treatment (Ellenberger, 1972). We should not take it for granted that catharsis is a good thing. Reliving painful experiences is painful. People who are encouraged to cry during sad movies end up feeling worse, not better, than people who restrain their emotions (Kraemer & Hastrup, 1988). Expressing your anger by hitting a punching bag makes you feel greater anger, not less (Bushman, 2002).

Regardless of whether catharsis had been successful in this case, or any other, Freud began seeking a "talking cure" with other patients. He referred to *his method of explaining and dealing with personality, based on the interplay of conscious and unconscious forces*, as psychoanalysis. To this day, psychoanalysts remain loyal to some version of Freud's methods and theories, although their views have of course developed and diversified over the decades.

Central to Freud's theory was his concept of the unconscious, *a repository of memories, emotions, and thoughts, many of them illogical, that affect our behavior even though we cannot talk about them*. According to this theory, people deal with traumatic experiences and unresolved childhood conflicts by forcing certain thoughts and emotions into the unconscious mind. The goal of psychoanalysts is to bring those memories back to consciousness, producing catharsis and enabling the person to overcome irrational impulses. The psychoanalyst should listen intently to everything the patient says and help the patient explore possible meanings of each thought, memory, and action. The assumption is that simply understanding and bringing the unconscious material into consciousness is the key to psychological improvement.

So Freud said, at any rate. Later interviews with his surviving ex-patients revealed that Freud often deviated from the procedure he recommended. Sometimes he administered morphine or other drugs. In many cases he gave explicit, and often harmful, advice. In one case he urged a client who was having an affair with a married woman to divorce his wife and marry the other woman. He also told the other woman it was essential that she divorce her husband and marry this other man to save him from what Freud claimed was his "latent homosexuality." When they followed his advice, the result was the breakup of two marriages and the substitute of a new one that ended in divorce two years later. Although Freud publicly claimed that his treatment always cured his patients, his private correspondence to friends admitted that many of his cases ended badly, and few if any patients reached a full cure (Kramer, 2006).

Changes in Freud's Theory

Initially, Freud attributed neurotic behavior to recent traumatic experiences in his patients' lives. However, the recent events often seemed insufficient explanations. For a while in the early 1890s, Freud attributed patients' problems to sexual difficulties and recommended increased sexual activity as a cure (Macmillan, 1997). Then he abandoned that idea and suggested instead that the ultimate problem was sexual abuse during childhood. Freud's patients denied any such memories, but Freud put together parts of the patients' dream reports, slips of the tongue, and so forth and claimed that they pointed to early sexual abuse. He then tried to persuade his patients of these interpretations. Note the similarity to implanted memories or false memories, as discussed in Chapter 7.

A few years later, he abandoned the emphasis on childhood sexual abuse. According to Freud, he decided that his patients had "misled" him into believing they were sexually abused in early childhood (Freud, 1925). Why did Freud abandon his early theory? According to one view (Masson, 1984), Freud simply lost the courage to defend his theory. As other scholars insist, however, Freud never had any evidence for it (Esterson, 2001; Powell & Boer, 1994; Schatzman, 1992). Freud had inferred his patients' early sexual abuse despite their denials of such experiences. It was hardly fair, then, to complain that the patients had misled him into believing they had been abused.

Freud replaced the idea about early sexual abuse with theories focusing on children's sexual fantasies. Although he did not fully develop his views of girls' early sexual development, he was explicit about boys: During early childhood, every boy goes through an Oedipus complex, *when he develops a sexual interest in his mother and competitive aggression toward his father*. (Oedipus—EHD-ah-puhs— in the ancient Greek play by Sophocles unknowingly murdered his father and married his mother.) Most boys negotiate through this stage and emerge with a healthy personality, but those who fail to resolve these sexual fantasies develop long-term personality problems.

What evidence did he have for this view? Again, he had nothing that most people would consider evidence. He reconsidered the same statements his patients made to him earlier and reinterpreted them. Just as his patients denied having been sexually abused in childhood, they also denied his inferences about their childhood sexual fantasies. Freud's main reason for his interpretations was simply that he could construct a coherent story linking a patient's symptoms, dreams, and so forth to the sexual fantasies that Freud imagined they must have had (Esterson, 1993). Developmental psychologists report that they almost never see evidence of an Oedipus complex in children. Although some psychoanalysts still see merit in the idea (Luborsky & Barrett, 2006), most put little emphasis on it.

concept check

1. What was Freud's original view of the cause of personality problems, and what view did he substitute? What evidence did he have for either view?

Answer

1. Initially, Freud pointed to childhood sexual abuse. Later, he said the problem was childhood sexual fantasies, such as the Oedipus complex. His only evidence was that he thought he could infer these childhood events from his patients' dreams and symptoms.

Stages of Psychosexual Development in Freud's Theory of Personality

Right or wrong, Freud's theory is so widely known that you should understand it. One of his central points was that psychosexual interest and pleasure begin in infancy. He used the term **psychosexual pleasure** broadly to include *all strong, pleasant excitement arising from body stimulation.* He maintained that how we deal with our psychosexual development influences nearly all aspects of personality.

According to Freud (1905/1925), people have a *psychosexual energy,* which he called **libido** (lih-BEE-doh), from a Latin word meaning "desire." During infancy, libido is focused in the mouth. As the child grows older, libido flows to other body parts. Children go through five stages of psychosexual development, and each leaves its mark on the adult personality. If normal sexual development is blocked or frustrated at any stage, Freud said, part of the libido is held in **fixation** at that stage, and the person *continues to be preoccupied with the pleasure area associated with that stage.* ■ Table 14.1 summarizes these stages.

The Oral Stage

In the **oral stage**, from birth to about age 1½, *the infant derives intense pleasure from stimulation of the mouth, particularly while sucking at the mother's breast.*

According to Freud, if normal sexual development is blocked at the oral stage, the child seeks pleasure from drinking and eating and later from kissing and smoking. Like many of Freud's ideas, this one is difficult to test.

According to Freud, someone fixated at this stage continues to receive great pleasure from eating, drinking, and smoking and may also have lasting concerns with dependence and independence.

The Anal Stage

At about age 1½, children enter the **anal stage**, when *they get psychosexual pleasure from the sensations of bowel movements.* If toilet training is too strict—or too lenient—the child becomes fixated at this stage. Someone fixated at the anal stage goes through life "holding things back"—being orderly, stingy, and stubborn—or less commonly, goes to the opposite extreme, becoming messy and wasteful. (Remember the concept of "falsifiable" from Chapter 2. Can you imagine any evidence that would contradict this aspect of Freud's theory?)

The Phallic Stage

Beginning at about age 3, in the **phallic stage**, children begin to *play with their genitals* and according to Freud become sexually attracted to the opposite-sex parent. Freud claimed that every boy is afraid of having his penis cut off, whereas girls develop "penis

Table 14.1 Freud's Stages of Psychosexual Development

Stage (approximate ages)	Sexual Interests	Effects of Fixation at This Stage
Oral stage (birth to 1½ years)	Sucking, swallowing, biting	Lasting concerns with dependence and independence; pleasure from eating, drinking, and other oral activities
Anal stage (1½ to 3 years)	Expelling feces, retaining feces	Orderliness or sloppiness, stinginess or wastefulness, stubbornness
Phallic stage (3 to 5 or 6 years)	Touching penis or clitoris; Oedipus complex	Difficulty feeling closeness. Males: fear of castration Females: penis envy
Latent period (5 or 6 to puberty)	Sexual interests suppressed	—
Genital stage (puberty onward)	Sexual contact with other people	—

envy." These ideas have always been doubtful, and they have few defenders today.

The Latent Period

From about age 5 or 6 until adolescence, Freud said, most children enter a **latent period** in which they *suppress their psychosexual interest*. At this time, they play mostly with peers of their own sex. The latent period is evidently a product of European culture and does not appear in all societies.

The Genital Stage

Beginning at puberty, young people *take a strong sexual interest in other people*. This is known as the **genital stage**. According to Freud, anyone who has fixated a great deal of libido in an earlier stage has little libido left for the genital stage. But people who have successfully negotiated the earlier stages now derive primary satisfaction from sexual intercourse.

Evaluation of Freud's Stages

It is undeniable that infants get pleasure from sucking, that toddlers go through toilet training, that older children begin to notice their genitals, and that adolescents become interested in sexual contact with other people. However, the idea of fixation at various stages, central to much of Freud's thinking, is difficult to test (Grünbaum, 1986; Popper, 1986). In fact, Freud resisted any attempt to test his ideas experimentally, insisting that the only relevant data were the observations he made during psychoanalytic sessions. Many of his followers have held the same position, and the result has been alienation from the rest of psychology (Chiesa, 2010).

2. If someone has persistent problems with independence and dependence, Freud would suggest a fixation at which psychosexual stage?

Answer

2. Freud would interpret this behavior as a fixation at the oral stage.

Structure of Personality

Personality, Freud claimed, consists of three aspects: id, ego, and superego. (Actually, he used German words that mean *it*, *I*, and *over-I*. A translator used Latin equivalents instead of English words.) The **id** consists of *sexual and other biological drives* that demand immediate gratification. The **ego** is *the rational, decision-making aspect of the personality*. It resembles the concept of central executive or executive functioning, discussed in Chapter 7 (Bornstein & Becker-Matero, 2011). The **superego** contains *the memory of rules and prohibitions we learned from*

our parents and others, such as, "Nice little boys and girls don't do that." If the id produces sexual desires that the superego considers repugnant, the result is guilty feelings. Most psychologists today find it difficult to imagine the mind in terms of three warring factions, although all would agree that people sometimes have conflicting impulses.

3. What behavior would Freud expect of someone with an unusually strong superego?

Answer

3. Someone with an unusually strong superego would be unusually inhibited and dominated by feelings of guilt.

Defense Mechanisms against Anxiety

According to Freud, *the ego defends itself against anxieties by relegating unpleasant thoughts and impulses to the unconscious mind*. Among the **defense mechanisms** that the ego employs are repression, denial, rationalization, displacement, regression, projection, reaction formation, and sublimation. He saw these as normal processes that sometimes went to extremes. His daughter, Anna, developed and elaborated descriptions of these mechanisms.

Repression

The defense mechanism of **repression** is *motivated removal of something to the unconscious*—rejecting unacceptable thoughts, desires, and memories. For example, someone who has an unacceptable sexual impulse might become unaware of it. Freud maintained that people repress painful, traumatic memories. Repressed material is removed from consciousness but not forgotten. Freud once compared a repressed thought to a rowdy person expelled from a polite room who continues banging on the door, trying to get back in.

Is repression real? The evidence for it is shaky. As discussed in Chapter 7, most people remember well their most miserable experiences, unless they were very young at the time. Laboratory attempts to demonstrate repression have produced, at best, weak and ambiguous evidence (Holmes, 1990). People can and often do intentionally suppress unwanted thoughts and memories (Erdelyi, 2006). That is, they simply refuse to think about them. However, intentional suppression is not repression. According to most research, people who intentionally suppress unpleasant memories *improve* their psychological adjustment. They do not experience the distorted perceptions and pathological behaviors Freud saw as linked to repression (Rofé, 2008). The evidence suggests much reason to be skeptical of Freud's concept of repression.

Denial

The refusal to believe unpleasant information ("This can't be happening") is **denial**. Whereas repression is the motivated removal of information from consciousness, denial is an assertion that the information is incorrect, generally accompanied by a wish-fulfilling fantasy. For example, someone with an alcohol problem may insist, "I'm not an alcoholic. I can take it or leave it." Someone whose marriage is headed for divorce may insist that all is going well. People who are about to get fired may believe that they are highly successful on the job.

Rationalization

When people *attempt to show that their actions are justifiable*, they are using **rationalization**. For example, a student who wants to go to the movies says, "More studying won't do me any good anyway." Someone who takes unfair advantage of another says, "Learning to deal with disappointment will make him a better person."

Displacement

By diverting a behavior or thought away from its natural target toward a less threatening target, displacement lets people engage in the behavior with less anxiety. For example, if you are angry with your employer or your professor, you might yell at someone else.

Regression

A *return to a more immature level of functioning,* regression is an effort to avoid the anxiety of the current situation. By adopting a childish role, a person returns to an earlier, more secure, way of life. For example, after a new sibling is born, an older child may cry or pout. An adult who has just gone through a divorce or lost a job may move in with his or her parents.

Projection

Attributing one's own undesirable characteristics to other people is known as projection. If someone tells you to stop being angry, you might reply, "I'm not angry! You're the one who's angry!" Suggesting that other people have your faults might make the faults seem less threatening. For example, someone who secretly enjoys pornography might accuse other people of enjoying it. However, the research finds that people using projection do not ordinarily decrease their anxiety or their awareness of their own faults (Holmes, 1978; Sherwood, 1981).

Reaction Formation

To avoid awareness of some weakness, people sometimes use reaction formation to *present themselves as the opposite of what they really are.* In other words, they go to the opposite extreme. A man troubled by doubts about his religious faith might try to convert others to the faith. Someone with unacceptable aggressive tendencies might join a group dedicated to preventing violence.

Sublimation

The transformation of sexual or aggressive energies into culturally acceptable, even admirable, behaviors is sublimation. According to Freud, sublimation lets someone express an impulse without admitting its existence. For example, painting and sculpture may represent a sublimation of sexual impulses. Someone may sublimate aggressive impulses by becoming a surgeon. Sublimation is the one proposed defense mechanism that is associated with socially constructive behavior. However, if the true motives of a painter are sexual and the true motives of a surgeon are violent, they are well hidden indeed.

concept check

4. **Match these Freudian defense mechanisms with the situations that follow: regression, denial, projection, rationalization, reaction formation, displacement, and sublimation.**

a. A man who is angry with his neighbor goes deer hunting.
b. A smoker insists there is no convincing evidence that smoking impairs health.
c. Someone who secretly enjoys pornography campaigns to outlaw pornography.
d. A man who beats his wife writes a book arguing that people have an instinctive need for aggressive behavior.
e. Someone who has difficulty dealing with others resorts to pouting and crying.
f. A boss takes credit for an employee's idea because "If I get the credit, our department will look good and all employees will benefit."
g. Someone with an impulse to shout obscenities writes novels.

Evaluating Freud

How much credit should we give Freud? He was right that people have conflicting impulses, but that idea was hardly original with him. Yes, people have unconscious thoughts and feelings. However, that idea too had been around before Freud. Freud's elaboration on that idea was to say that the unconscious developed mostly from repressed sexual thoughts, such as boys' fear of losing the penis and girls' wish to have a penis (Borch-Jacobsen & Shamdasani, 2012; Kramer, 2006). The part that is original to Freud is the part that is most doubtful. Later psychologists discovered unconscious processes in implicit memories, subliminal perception, and so forth, but these processes are far different from the type of unconscious processes Freud emphasized.

Freud did introduce a few new ideas that have stood the test of time, such as his recognition of transference: *You might react to your therapist, or your husband or wife, or other people in a particular way because they remind you of someone else, especially your parents.* Transference was an important insight that many therapists today find helpful. Still, Freud's main lasting contribution is that he popularized psychotherapy. Others had done psychotherapy before him, but he made it seem *interesting.* Many psychotherapists today, including some who acknowledge no allegiance to Freud, try to help their clients understand where their conflicts and emotional reactions come from. They help their clients think about their developmental history and what it means. In that way, Freud deserves credit, even if most of his specific theories fail to impress.

The idea behind the psychoanalytic couch is for the client to relax and say everything that comes to mind. This was Freud's couch.

Karen Horney, a neo-Freudian, revised some of Freud's theories and paid greater attention to cultural influences. She pioneered the study of feminine psychology.

Karen Horney, a Neo-Freudian

Psychologists known as neo-Freudians kept parts of Freud's theory while modifying other aspects. One of the most influential was the German-born physician Karen Horney (HOR-nigh; 1885–1952), who kept the concept of repression but argued that penis envy in women was no more likely than womb envy in men. She also argued that women have the same drive to achievement that men do, and that women feel frustrated when forced into subordinate roles. In that way she was a forerunner to later feminist thinkers. Contrary to Freud's idea of an Oedipus complex, Horney emphasized the detrimental effects a child might feel from parental neglect or indifference.

Horney focused on what happens when someone's unrealistic view of the *ideal self* contrasts with a low evaluation of the *real self*. The constant feeling that "I should be better in so many ways" tyrannizes the person, leading to psychological distress. In pronounced cases, the result is the emotional turbulence we call neurosis. Many later psychotherapists have emphasized the same idea.

Other theorists, including Carl Jung and Alfred Adler, disagreed more sharply with Freud. Jung and Adler were at one time associates of Freud, and they shared his interest in dreams and unconscious processes. However, their interpretations of dreams and their concepts of unconscious processes differed sharply from Freud's. Each broke with Freud's theory in substantial ways and should not be classified as neo-Freudians.

Carl Jung and the Collective Unconscious

Carl G. Jung (YOONG; 1875–1961) was a Swiss physician that Freud regarded as the "heir apparent" or "crown prince" of the psychoanalytic movement, until their father–son relationship deteriorated (Alexander, 1982). Jung's theory of personality emphasized people's search for a spiritual meaning in life. In contrast to Freud, who traced much of adult personality to childhood events, Jung stressed the possibility of personality changes in adulthood. He also discussed the way people adopt a *persona,* like a role in a play. That is, people try to make a certain impression while concealing parts of their true nature.

Jung was impressed that many of his patients described dreams with no clear relation to anything in their own lives. Instead, they were similar to images that are common in the myths, religions, and artworks of cultures throughout the world. He suggested that these images arise from inborn aspects of human nature. If you dream about a beetle, Jung might relate your dream to the important role beetles have played in

Carl G. Jung rejected Freud's concept that dreams hide their meaning from the conscious mind: "To me dreams are a part of nature, which harbors no intention to deceive, but expresses something as best it can" (Jung, 1965, p. 161).

human mythology dating back to the ancient Egyptians. If you dream about a baby, he might relate the symbolism to the possibility of psychological rebirth (Lawson, 2008).

According to Jung, people have not only a conscious mind and a "personal unconscious" (equivalent to Freud's unconscious) but also a collective unconscious mind. The collective unconscious, present at birth, relates to *the cumulative experience of preceding generations.* Whereas the conscious mind and the personal unconscious vary from one person to another, the collective unconscious is similar for nearly all people. It contains archetypes, which are *vague images—* or at least the predisposition to form images—*that have always been part of the human experience.* As evidence for this view, Jung pointed out similarities in the art of cultures throughout the world (see ▼ Figure 14.2) as well as similarities in their myths and folklore.

But how did the collective experiences of our ancestors become part of our unconscious minds? Jung offered little by way of explanation, and our current understanding of biology offers no route by which an experience could get into the genes. A more realistic hypothesis is that ancient people who thought in certain ways had advantages and therefore survived long enough to become our ancestors. As a result, we evolved a tendency to think in those same ways. Along the same lines, Nicholas Wade (2009) argued that people evolved an "instinct" to be religious because through human existence, religious societies survived better than nonreligious ones did.

Another of Jung's contributions was the idea of psychological types. He believed that people's personalities fell into a few distinct categories, such as extraverted or introverted. The authors of the Myers-Briggs personality test have revived this idea, as we shall see in the third module of this chapter.

concept check ✓

5. **How does Jung's idea of the collective unconscious differ from Freud's idea of the unconscious?**

Answer

5. Jung's collective unconscious is the same for all people and is present at birth. Freud believed the unconscious developed from repressed experiences.

a

b

▲ **Figure 14.2** Carl Jung was fascinated that similar images appear in the artworks of different cultures. One recurring image is the circular mandala, a symbol of unity and wholeness. These mandalas are: **(a)** a Hindu painting from Bhutan; and **(b)** a tie-dye tapestry created in California.

Alfred Adler and Individual Psychology

Alfred Adler (1870–1937) was an Austrian physician who broke away from Freud because he believed Freud overemphasized the sex drive and neglected other influences. They parted company in 1911, with Freud insisting that women experience "penis envy" and Adler replying that women were more likely to envy men's status and power.

Adler founded a rival school of thought, which he called **individual psychology**. Adler did not mean "psychology of the individual." Rather, he meant *"indivisible psychology," a psychology of the person as a whole rather than parts* such as id, ego, and superego. Adler emphasized the importance of conscious, goal-directed behavior.

Adler's Description of Personality

Several of Adler's early patients were acrobats who had suffered childhood injuries to an arm or leg. After they worked to overcome their disabilities, they continued until they developed unusual strength and coordination. Perhaps, Adler surmised, people in general try to overcome weaknesses and transform them into strengths (Adler, 1932/1964). As infants, Adler noted, we are small, dependent, and surrounded by others who seem so superior. We try to overcome

Alfred Adler emphasized the ways in which personality depended on people's goals, especially their way of striving for a sense of superiority.

that feeling of inferiority. Occasional experiences with failure goad us to try harder. However, persistent failures and excessive criticism produce an **inferiority complex**, *an exaggerated feeling of weakness, inadequacy, and helplessness.*

According to Adler, everyone has a natural **striving for superiority**, *a desire to seek personal excellence and fulfillment.* Each person creates a master plan for achieving a sense of superiority. A typical strategy is to seek success in business, sports, or other competitive activities. People also strive for success in other ways. Someone who withdraws from life gains a sense of accomplishment or superiority from being uncommonly self-sacrificing. Someone who constantly complains about illnesses or disabilities wins a measure of control over friends and family. Another person may commit crimes to savor the attention the crimes bring. People also get a feeling of superiority by making excuses. If you marry someone who is likely to thwart your ambitions, perhaps your underlying motivation is to maintain an illusion: "I could have been a great success if my spouse hadn't prevented me." Failure to study can have a similar motivation: "I could have done well on this test, but my friends talked me into partying the night before." According to Adler, people often engage in self-defeating behavior because they are not fully aware of their goals and strategies. (Recall the concept of self-handicapping from Chapter 13.)

Adler tried to determine people's real motives. For example, he would ask someone who complained of a backache, "How would your life be different if you could get rid of your backache?" Those who eagerly said they would become more active were presumably trying to overcome their ailment. Those who said they could not imagine how their life would change, or said only that they would get less sympathy from others, were probably exaggerating their discomfort if not imagining it.

6. According to Adler, what is people's main motivation?

Answer

6. Adler said people's main motivation was striving for superiority.

Adler's View of Psychological Disorders

According to Adler, seeking success or a feeling of superiority for yourself alone is unhealthy (Adler, 1928/1964). The healthiest goal is to seek success for a larger group, such as your family, your community, your nation, or better yet, all of humanity. Adler was ahead of his time, and many psychologists since then have rediscovered this idea (Crocker & Park, 2004).

According to Adler, people's needs for one another require a social interest, *a sense of solidarity and identification with other people that leads to constructive action.* Note that social interest does not mean a desire to socialize. It means an interest in the welfare of society. People with social interest want to cooperate. In equating mental health with social interest, Adler saw mental health as a positive state, not just a lack of impairments. In Adler's view, people with excessive anxieties are not suffering from an illness. Rather, they set immature goals, follow a faulty style of life, and show little social interest. Their response to new opportunity is, "Yes, but . . ." (Adler, 1932/1964).

Adler's Legacy

Adler's influence exceeds his fame. His concept of the inferiority complex has become part of the common culture. He was the first to talk about mental health as a positive state of activity and accomplishment rather than merely the absence of impairments. Many later psychologists have endorsed this idea. Various later forms of therapy drew upon Adler's emphasis on understanding the assumptions that people make and how those assumptions influence behavior. Many psychologists also followed Adler by urging people to take responsibility for their own behavior. According to Adler, the key to a healthy personality was not just freedom from disorders but a desire for the welfare of other people.

The Learning Approach

How did you develop your personality? As discussed in Chapter 13, many social situations influence and constrain your behavior. You learn much of what we call personality in terms of what to do in one situation after another (Mischel, 1973, 1981). But situations vary, and so does your behavior. You might be honest about returning a lost wallet to its owner but lie to your professor about why your paper is late. The learning approach to personality emphasizes the ways in which we learn our social behaviors, one situation at a time. As described in the Social Learning section of Chapter 6, we learn social behaviors by vicarious reinforcement and punishment. That is, we tend to copy behaviors that were successful for other people and avoid behaviors that failed for others. We especially imitate the people whom we respect and want to resemble. For example, children watched adults choose between an apple and a banana. If all the men chose one fruit and all the women chose the other, the boys wanted what the men had and the girls wanted what the women had (Perry & Bussey, 1979).

Imitation can occur in powerful ways without our awareness. Experimenters found that when a woman ate lunch with an unfamiliar partner who appeared to be seriously overweight, the woman ate a larger and less healthful meal than when she ate with a normal-weight partner (Shimizu, Johnson, & Wansink, 2014). The experimenters' interpretation was that the presence of an overweight partner made the idea of healthful eating less salient.

Much of what we think of as personality develops at least partly by imitation. Your attitudes toward alcohol, drugs, guns, and almost anything else depend on how you saw your parents and others in your neighborhood act. If you lived in a different country, or if you lived a hundred years ago, you probably would have developed very different attitudes about women's roles, minority groups, sexual orientation, and much else.

7. Suppose someone observes your behavior over a period of time and reports that your personality seems inconsistent. How does the learning approach to personality explain that inconsistency?

Answer

7. You learn your behaviors one situation at a time. You may have learned to be friendly in one situation and not another or honest in one situation and not another.

Humanistic Psychology

Another perspective on personality, humanistic psychology, *deals with consciousness, values, and abstract beliefs, including spiritual experiences and the beliefs that people live and die for.* According to humanistic psychologists, personality depends on people's beliefs and perceptions of the world. If you *believe* that a particular experience was highly meaningful, then it *was* highly meaningful.

A psychologist can understand you only by asking you to interpret and evaluate the events of your life. (In theology, a *humanist* glorifies human potentials, generally denying or de-emphasizing a supreme being. The term *humanistic psychologist* implies nothing about someone's religious beliefs.)

Humanistic psychology emerged in the 1950s and 1960s as a protest against both behaviorism and psychoanalysis, the dominant psychological viewpoints at the time. Behaviorists and psychoanalysts often emphasize the less noble aspects of people's thoughts and actions, whereas humanistic psychologists see people as essentially good and striving to achieve their potential. Also, behaviorism and psychoanalysis, despite their differences, both assume *determinism* (the belief that every behavior has a cause) and *reductionism* (the attempt to explain behavior in terms of its component elements). Humanistic psychologists do not try to explain behavior in terms of its parts or hidden causes. They claim that people are free to make deliberate, conscious decisions. For example, people might devote themselves to a great cause, sacrifice their own well-being, or risk their lives. To a humanistic psychologist, ascribing such behavior to past reinforcements or unconscious thought processes misses the point.

Humanistic psychology has much in common with positive psychology, as discussed in Chapter 12, in that both emphasize the factors that make life meaningful and joyful. However, the two fields follow different methods (Waterman, 2013). Whereas researchers in positive psychology rely on surveys, experiments, and so forth to seek general principles, humanistic psychologists generally record narratives about individuals, using methods more like a biographer than like a scientist.

Carl Rogers and Unconditional Positive Regard

Carl Rogers, the most influential humanistic psychologist, studied theology before turning to psychology, and the influence of those early studies is apparent in his view of human nature. Rogers (1980) regarded human nature as basically good. According to Rogers, it is as natural for people to strive for excellence as it is for a plant to grow.

People evaluate themselves and their actions beginning in childhood. They develop a **self-concept**, *an image of what they really are,* and an **ideal self**, *an image of what they would like to be.* Rogers measured self-concept and ideal self by handing someone a stack of cards containing statements such as "I am honest" and "I am suspicious of others." The person would then sort the statements into piles representing *true of me* and *not true of me* or arrange them in a continuum from *most true of me* to *least true of me.* (This method is known as a *Q-sort.*) Then Rogers would provide an identical stack of cards and ask the person to sort them into two piles: *true of my ideal self* and *not true of my ideal self.* In this manner, he could compare someone's self-concept to his or her ideal self. People who perceive much discrepancy between the two generally feel distress. Humanistic psychologists try to help people overcome their distress by improving their self-concept or by revising their ideal self.

To promote human welfare, Rogers maintained that people should relate to one another with **unconditional positive regard**, a relationship that Thomas Harris (1967) described as "I'm OK—You're OK." Unconditional positive regard is *the complete, unqualified acceptance of another person*

Carl Rogers maintained that people naturally strive toward positive goals without special urging. He recommended that people relate to one another with unconditional positive regard.

as he or she is, much like the love of a parent for a child. If you feel unconditional positive regard, you might disapprove of someone's actions or intentions, but you would still accept and love the person. (This view resembles the Christian advice to "hate the sin but love the sinner.") The alternative is *conditional positive regard,* the attitude that "I shall like you only if . . . ." People who are treated with conditional positive regard feel restrained about opening themselves to new ideas or activities for fear of losing someone else's support.

Abraham Maslow and the Self-Actualized Personality

Abraham Maslow, another humanistic psychologist, complained that most psychologists concentrate on disordered personalities, assuming that personality is either normal or worse than normal. Maslow insisted, as Alfred Adler had, that personality can also be better than normal. He emphasized **self-actualization**, *the achievement of one's full potential.* The concept of self-actualization is similar to Adler's concept of striving for superiority. In fact, Adler had a clear influence on Rogers and Maslow. Adler's term "unconditional social interest" was the forerunner of unconditional positive regard.

As a first step toward describing the self-actualized personality, Maslow (1962, 1971) made a list of people who in his opinion were approaching their full potential. His list included people he knew personally as well as some from history. He sought to discover what, if anything, they had in common.

According to Maslow (1962, 1971), people with a self-actualized (or self-actualizing) personality show the following characteristics:

- An accurate perception of reality: They perceive the world as it is, not as they would like it to be. They accept uncertainty and ambiguity.

Abraham Maslow, one of the founders of humanistic psychology, introduced the concept of a "self-actualized personality," a personality associated with high productivity and enjoyment of life.

Harriet Tubman, identified by Maslow as having a self-actualized personality, was a leader of the Underground Railroad, a system for helping slaves escape from the southern states before the Civil War. Maslow defined the self-actualized personality by first identifying admirable people, such as Tubman, and then determining what they had in common.

Historical/Corbis

- Independence, creativity, and spontaneity: They make their own decisions, even if others disagree.
- Acceptance of themselves and others: They treat people with unconditional positive regard.
- A problem-centered outlook rather than a self-centered outlook: They think about how to solve problems, not how to make themselves look good. They concentrate on significant philosophical or political issues, not just on getting through the day.
- Enjoyment of life: They are open to positive experiences, including "peak experiences" when they feel truly fulfilled and content.
- A good sense of humor.

Critics have noted that, because Maslow's description is based on his own choice of examples, it may simply reflect the characteristics that he himself admired. That is, his reasoning was circular: He defined certain people as self-actualized and then inquired what they had in common to decide what "self-actualized" means (Neher, 1991). In any case, Maslow emphasized the idea of a healthy personality as something more than the absence of disorder.

8. How does humanistic psychology resemble the ideas of Alfred Adler?

Answer

8. Adler emphasized the importance of people's beliefs and the possibility of a better than normal personality. Humanistic psychology is based on Adler's approach.

In Search of Human Nature

The three most comprehensive personality theorists—Freud, Jung, and Adler—lived and worked in Austria in the early 1900s. Here we are, a century later, and most specialists in personality research neither accept those theories nor try to replace them with anything better. Recall from Chapter 1 that a good research question is interesting and answerable. Fundamental questions about human nature are extraordinarily interesting but not easily answerable. Most researchers today try to answer smaller questions about specific, measurable aspects of behavior, as the next two modules will describe. After researchers answer many of the smaller questions, perhaps they may return to the big questions of "what makes people tick?"

Summary

- *Personality.* Personality consists of the stable, consistent ways in which each person's behavior differs from that of others, especially in social situations. (page 451)
- *Psychodynamic theories.* Several historically influential theories have described personality as the outcome of unconscious internal forces. (page 451)
- *Freud.* Sigmund Freud, the founder of psychoanalysis, proposed that much of what we do and say has hidden meanings. However, most psychologists today doubt most of his interpretations of those hidden meanings. (page 451)
- *Freud's psychosexual stages.* Freud believed that many unconscious thoughts and motives are sexual in nature. He proposed that people progress through stages or periods of psychosexual development—oral, anal, phallic, latent, and genital—and that frustration at any stage fixates the libido at that stage. (page 453)
- *Defense mechanisms.* Freud and his followers argued that people defend themselves against anxiety by such mechanisms as denial, repression, projection, and reaction formation. (page 454)

- *Jung.* Carl Jung believed that all people share a collective unconscious that represents the experience of our ancestors. (page 456)
- *Adler.* Alfred Adler proposed that people's primary motivation is a striving for superiority. Each person adopts his or her own method of striving, and to understand people, we need to understand their goals and beliefs. (page 457)
- *Adler's view of a healthy personality.* According to Adler, the healthiest style of life is one that emphasizes social interest—that is, concern for the welfare of others. (page 458)
- *The learning approach.* Much of what we call personality is learned through individual experience, imitation, or vicarious reinforcement and punishment. (page 458)
- *Humanistic psychology.* Humanistic psychologists emphasize conscious, deliberate decision making. (page 458)

Key Terms

anal stage (page 453)

archetypes (page 456)

catharsis (page 452)

collective unconscious (page 456)

defense mechanism (page 454)

denial (page 454)

displacement (page 455)

ego (page 454)

fixation (page 453)

genital stage (page 454)

humanistic psychology (page 458)

id (page 454)

ideal self (page 459)

individual psychology (page 457)

inferiority complex (page 457)

latent period (page 454)

libido (page 453)

neo-Freudians (page 456)

Oedipus complex (page 452)

oral stage (page 453)

personality (page 451)

phallic stage (page 453)

projection (page 455)

psychoanalysis (page 452)

psychodynamic theory (page 451)

psychosexual pleasure (page 453)

rationalization (page 454)

reaction formation (page 455)

regression (page 455)

repression (page 454)

self-actualization (page 459)

self-concept (page 459)

social interest (page 458)

striving for superiority (page 457)

sublimation (page 455)

superego (page 454)

transference (page 455)

unconditional positive regard (page 459)

unconscious (page 452)

Review Questions

1. What did Freud mean by the term *Oedipus complex*?
   (a) A release of pent-up emotional tension
   (b) Preoccupation with the pleasure area associated with an immature stage of psychosexual development
   (c) A boy's sexual interest in his mother and hostility toward his father
   (d) The memory of rules and prohibitions that we learned from our parents and others

2. When Freud attributed adult psychological problems to childhood sexual fantasies, what evidence did he have?
   (a) His patients described sexual fantasies that they remembered from their childhood.
   (b) He conducted research on a representative sample of children.
   (c) He relied on observations that developmental psychologists had conducted on children.
   (d) He had no evidence, except for his ability to construct a story linking a patient's symptoms and dreams to early sexual fantasies that Freud inferred.

3. Freud attributed both excessive orderliness and excessive messiness to a fixation at which psychosexual stage?
   (a) Oral
   (b) Anal

   (c) Phallic
   (d) Latent

4. Suppose someone follows a variety of sexual and other impulses that most people inhibit. According to Freud, this person has:
   (a) A strong id and a weak superego
   (b) A weak superego and weak ego
   (c) A weak id and strong ego
   (d) A strong superego

5. A political candidate who is unwilling to admit a history of using drugs argues for stricter penalties against drug users. Which of Freud's defense mechanisms might be responsible for this action?
   (a) Denial
   (b) Displacement
   (c) Projection
   (d) Reaction formation

6. A man who cheats on his taxes argues that "everyone cheats on their taxes." Which of Freud's defense mechanisms might be responsible for this action?
   (a) Denial
   (b) Displacement

(c) Projection

(d) Reaction formation

7. According to Carl Jung, what is the origin of the collective unconscious?

(a) The collective unconscious develops from repressed memories of traumatic experiences or repression of unacceptable impulses.

(b) The collective unconscious develops from childhood experiences of dealing with others.

(c) The collective unconscious develops when we focus attention on one stimulus and filter out others.

(d) The collective unconscious developed from the experiences of our ancestors.

8. According to Alfred Adler, what causes anxieties and other psychological disorders?

(a) Repression of painful memories and impulses

(b) An imbalance among neurotransmitters in the brain

(c) Failure to understand the contents of the collective unconscious

(d) Seeking immature or improper goals

9. According to Carl Rogers, people feel distress when they perceive a large discrepancy between their self-concept (their real self) and their ideal self. Which other personality theorist also made this same point?

(a) Sigmund Freud

(b) Karen Horney

(c) Carl Jung

(d) Alfred Adler

Answers: 1c, 2d, 3b, 4a, 5d, 6c, 7d, 8d, 9b.

After studying this module, you should be able to:

- Distinguish the nomothetic approach from the idiographic approach, and distinguish states from traits.

- Use self-esteem as an example to illustrate the difficulty of measuring personality.

- Describe how psychologists identified the Big Five personality factors.

- List and describe the Big Five personality factors.

- Discuss the roles of heredity, age, culture, and cohort in personality development.

You will sometimes hear someone talk about the opinions or attitudes of "the average person." Are you an average person? In some ways, probably yes. You might have average height, an average amount of interest in Olympic sports, or an average attitude toward penguins. But I doubt that you or anyone you will ever meet is an average person in all regards. People's personalities differ in countless ways.

However, for research purposes, psychologists want to count all those countless ways! At least, psychologists want to identify the major dimensions along which personality varies, so that they can discover some of the causes of personality differences, and so that they can make better predictions about individuals' behavior.

Psychologists study personalities in two ways, called the nomothetic and the idiographic approaches. The word *nomothetic* (NAHM-uh-THEHT-ick) comes from the Greek *nomothetes,* meaning "legislator." The **nomothetic approach** *seeks broad, general principles of personality* based on studies of groups of people. For example, we might make the nomothetic statement that more extraverted people are more likely to introduce themselves to a stranger. Most personality research uses the nomothetic approach.

In contrast, the word *idiographic* is based on the root *idio-,* meaning "individual." (The same root appears in the word *idiosyncratic,* meaning *peculiar to an individual.*) The **idiographic approach** concentrates on *intensive studies of individuals,* looking for what makes

Like this man playing the role of a woman in Japanese kabuki theater, actors can present personalities that are very different from their private ones. All of us occasionally display temporary personalities that are different from our usual selves.

someone special (Allport, 1961). For example, a psychologist might study one person's goals, moods, and reactions. The conclusions would apply to this person and possibly no one else.

Personality Traits and States

Meteorologists distinguish between climate (the usual conditions) and weather (the current conditions). For example, the climate in Scotland is moister and cooler than the climate in Texas, but on a given day the weather could be warm in Scotland or cool in Texas. Similarly, psychologists distinguish between long-lasting personality conditions and temporary fluctuations.

A consistent tendency in behavior, such as shyness, hostility, or talkativeness, is a **trait**. In contrast, a **state** is *a temporary activation of a particular behavior.* For example, being nervous most of the time is a trait, but being afraid right now is a state. Being quiet habitually is a trait, but being quiet in the library is a state. A trait, like a climatic condition, is an average over time. However, just as climate can change, personality traits are not 100 percent permanent.

Both traits and states are descriptions of behavior, not explanations. To say that someone is nervous and quiet does not explain anything. It merely describes what we are trying to explain.

concept check

9. **Suppose someone becomes nervous as soon as he sits down in a dentist's chair. Is this experience "trait anxiety" or "state anxiety"?**

Answer

9. It is state anxiety because the situation evokes it. Trait anxiety is a tendency to become nervous in many situations.

The Search for Broad Personality Traits

According to the **trait approach to personality**, *people have consistent characteristics in their behavior.* Psychologists have described, studied, and measured many personality traits. Let's consider one example: belief in a just world. People with a strong

belief in a just world *maintain that life is fair and people usually get what they deserve* (Lerner, 1980). Here are examples of questions to measure this belief reworded from a standard questionnaire (Lipkus, 1991). Indicate your degree of agreement from 1 (complete disagreement) to 6 (complete agreement). The higher your score (scores range from 6 to 36), the greater your belief in a just world:

> People usually get the rewards and punishments they deserve.
>
> Most people who meet with misfortune did something to bring it on themselves.
>
> Most of the lucky breaks I get are earned.
>
> Promotions go to the people who work hardest.
>
> People who have no job or no money have only themselves to blame.
>
> Only rarely does an innocent person go to prison.

It is comforting to believe that life is fundamentally fair, that good deeds are rewarded and bad deeds punished. People with a strong belief in a just world usually handle stressful situations well, feeling confident that things will turn out favorably after all (Bègue & Muller, 2006; Otto, Boos, Dalbert, Schöps, & Hoyer, 2006). They are more likely than average to offer help to a person in distress or to seek revenge against whoever caused the harm, presumably to restore a sense of justice (Furnham, 2003; Kaiser, Vick, & Major, 2004). However, they are also more likely than average to "blame the victim" for an illness or other disadvantage (Ebneter, Latner, & O'Brien, 2011). (After all, if it is a just world, then people get what they deserve.) Compared to people with a low belief in a just world, people with a high belief are less likely to support preferential hiring for Blacks or women (Wilkins & Wenger, 2014). (If you believe life is already fair, you don't need to do much to improve its fairness.) The point is that a personality trait—in this case, belief in a just world—manifests itself in many ways. The way someone acts in one situation provides a clue to how that person will act in other situations.

concept check

10. **Accident victims often respond, "It could have been worse." How might this reaction relate to a belief in a just world?**

Answer

10. It seems unjust for an innocent person to sustain an injury. Minimizing the damage makes the injustice seem less.

Issues in Personality Measurement

In personality as in other areas of psychology, research progress depends on good measurement.

The problem in measuring personality is that behavior is not entirely consistent. You might be friendly toward some people and not others. You are cheerful at some times and not others. You keep some promises and not others. A researcher who watched you briefly might come to the wrong conclusions. Instead, researchers use questionnaires to ask people how they usually behave.

When people rate their own personality, can we trust them to be accurate? Most Americans rate themselves above average in almost all possible regards, whereas the British tend to be more modest, and Asians are still more modest (Baumeister, Campbell, Krueger, & Vohs, 2003; Furnham, Hosoe, & Tang, 2002). Americans who call themselves "average" are assumed to have low self-esteem, on the theory that you wouldn't *say* you were average unless you really thought you were *below* average! In many cases, your close friends would probably provide a more accurate assessment of your personality than you would yourself (Hofstee, 1994; Vazire & Carlson, 2011).

An Example of Measurement Problems: Self-Esteem

Let's consider the difficulty of measuring personality. **Self-esteem** is *the evaluation of one's own abilities, performance, and worth.* People in general, and Americans in particular, want to have high self-esteem. They do what they can to maintain it, including trying to improve their skills, or reminding themselves that they are more successful than other people in certain ways (Nussbaum & Dweck, 2008). People with high self-esteem are less likely to become depressed (Steiger, Allemand, Robins, & Fend, 2014). Psychologists have often predicted that high self-esteem should lead to increased productivity and other good outcomes. However, programs to raise people's self-esteem have had disappointing results. Praising people generally has little effect on their aggressive behavior and sometimes *decreases* school and job performance (Baumeister et al., 2003). (Perhaps people who think they are already wonderful feel little need to prove it.) Psychologists have also predicted that successful people should have high self-esteem, but many studies reported that many bright and accomplished young women report somewhat low self-esteem.

Some of the surprising or disappointing results depend on how we measure self-esteem (Blascovich & Tomaka, 1991). Here are example items from one self-esteem questionnaire:

- I feel that I have a number of good qualities.
- I can do things as well as most other people.
- At times I think I'm no good at all.
- I'm a failure.

An answer of "true" to the first two or "false" to the second two would count toward a high self-esteem score. Contrast those items to another self-esteem questionnaire, on which you answer from 1 (rarely or never) to 5 (usually or always):

- I feel that I am a beautiful person.
- I think that I make a good impression on others.
- I think that I have a good sense of humor.
- I feel that people really like me very much.

Do those items measure self-esteem or bragging? Here are true–false items from a third test of self-esteem:

- There are lots of things about myself I'd change if I could.
- I'm often sorry for the things I do.
- I'm not doing as well in school as I'd like.
- I wish I could change my physical appearance.

Do "true" answers on these items indicate low self-esteem or do they indicate high goals? Someone who says "true" is presumably striving for self-improvement. People who say "false" think they are just about perfect already.

How concerned should we be that many young women report low self-esteem? The results reflect how someone measured self-esteem. According to a careful analysis of answers to individual items, women's self-esteem is equal to men's or higher with regard to academics, emotional control, moral behavior, and many other regards. Women tend to have lower self-esteem only with regard to athletic ability (where, in fact, more men concentrate their efforts) and physical appearance, presumably because women strive for a higher standard than men do (Gentile, Grabe, Dolan-Pascoe, Twenge, & Wells, 2009).

The message, in short, is this: Personality is difficult to measure, and we should look carefully at how it was measured before we draw conclusions.

The Big Five Model of Personality

Psychologists have devised questionnaires to measure belief in a just world, self-esteem, and hundreds of other traits. Are some of these traits more important than others? Remember the principle of parsimony from Chapter 2: If we can adequately describe personality with a few traits, we should not measure more.

One way to begin is to examine our language. The English language probably has a word for every important personality trait. Although this assumption is not a necessity, it seems likely considering how much attention people pay to other people's personalities. When 168 people were asked to describe the personalities of people they knew, they generated 758 terms (Leising, Scharloth, Lohse, & Wood, 2014).

Gordon Allport and H. S. Odbert (1936) plodded through an English dictionary and found almost 18,000 words that might be used to describe personality. They deleted from this list words that were merely evaluations, such as *nasty*, and terms referring to temporary states, such as *confused*. (At least, we hope that being confused is temporary.) In the remaining list, they looked for clusters of synonyms, such as *affectionate*, *warm*, and *loving*, and kept only one of the terms. When they found opposites, such as *honest* and *dishonest*, they also kept just one term. After eliminating synonyms and antonyms, Raymond Cattell (1965) narrowed the original list to 35 traits.

Derivation of the Big Five Personality Traits

Although none of the 35 personality traits that Cattell identified are synonyms or antonyms of one another, many of them overlap. Psychologists looked for clusters of traits that correlate strongly with one another, but don't correlate with the other clusters. Using this approach, researchers found what they call the **Big Five personality traits** or **five-factor model**: *emotional stability, extraversion, agreeableness, conscientiousness, and openness to new experience* (McCrae & Costa, 1987). The case for these five traits is that (1) each correlates with many personality dimensions for which our language has a word and (2) none of these traits correlates highly with any of the other four, so they are not measuring the same thing. The Big Five dimensions are described in the following list (Costa, McCrae, & Dye, 1991):

Emotional stability is *a tendency to minimize unpleasant emotions*. The opposite term is **neuroticism**. Neuroticism correlates positively with anxiety,

hostility, self-consciousness, frequent conflicts with other people, and many physical and mental illnesses (Lahey, 2009). Therefore, emotional stability correlates with self-control, good relations with others, and mental health.

Extraversion is *a tendency to seek stimulation and to enjoy the company of other people*. The opposite of extraversion is introversion. Extraversion is associated with warmth, gregariousness, assertiveness, impulsiveness, and a need for excitement. The unpleasant side of extraversion is an increased chance of alcohol abuse and other risky behaviors (Martsh & Miller, 1997). The pleasant side is that extraverts tend to feel good and report high life satisfaction (Gale, Booth, Mottus, Kuh, & Deary, 2013). The relationship goes in both directions: Feeling happy makes people more outgoing, and outgoing behavior makes people feel happy (Lucas, Le, & Dyrenforth, 2008). Even pretending to be extraverted makes introverted people feel happier (Fleeson, Malanos, & Achille, 2002; Zelenski, Santoro, & Whelan, 2012). Many people have assumed that extraverts are the best salespeople, but the research says the best salespeople are only mildly extraverted—somewhat assertive and enthusiastic, but not overconfident or domineering (Grant, 2013).

Active, outgoing behavior   Happy feelings

Agreeableness is *a tendency to be compassionate toward others*. It implies a concern for the welfare of other people and is closely related to Adler's concept of social interest. People high in agreeableness trust other people and expect other people to trust them. They are more likely than average to have stable marriages and stable employment (Roberts et al., 2007). They are less likely than average to have prejudices (Akrami, Ekehammar, & Bergh, 2011). They recover better than average from an injury, partly because they have good social support (Boyce & Wood, 2011).

Conscientiousness is *a tendency to show self-discipline, to be dutiful, and to strive for achievement and competence*. People high in conscientiousness work hard and complete their tasks on time (Judge & Ilies, 2002). They exercise, eat a healthy diet, and in general act to advance their health and longevity (Bogg & Roberts, 2013). Agreeableness and conscientiousness both correlate with success in a wide variety of jobs (Sackett & Walmsley, 2014).

Openness to experience is *a tendency to enjoy new intellectual experiences and new ideas.* People high in this trait enjoy modern art, unusual music, and thought-provoking films and books. They enjoy meeting unusual people and exploring new ideas (McCrae, 1996).

■ Table 14.2 summarizes the five-factor model.

| 12. **Some psychologists suggest that we should divide extraversion into two traits—which they call *ambition* and *sociability*—changing the Big Five into six factors. How should psychologists determine whether to do so?** |

Answer

12. They should determine whether measures of ambition correlate strongly with measures of sociability. If so, then ambition and sociability can be considered two aspects of a single trait, extraversion. If not, then they are indeed separate personality traits.

Cross-cultural studies offer partial support to the Big Five approach. Several studies have found results consistent with the Big Five model for people in other cultures using other languages (McCrae & Costa, 1997; Yamagata et al., 2006). However, some studies do find cross-cultural differences

The Japanese artist Morimura Yasumasa re-creates famous paintings, substituting his own face for the original. People high in "openness to experience" delight in new, unusual art forms such as this.

Table 14.2 The Five-Factors Model of Personality		
Trait	**Description**	**Typical true–false question to measure it**
Emotional Stability	Resistance to unpleasant emotions	I have few major worries.
Extraversion	Seeking excitement and social contact	I make friends easily.
Agreeableness	Compassionate and trusting	I believe others have good intentions.
Conscientiousness	Self-disciplined and dutiful	I complete most tasks on time or early.
Openness	Stimulated by new ideas	I believe art is important for its own sake.

(Panayiotou, Kokkinos, & Spanoudis, 2004). A study in China identified traits corresponding to extraversion, neuroticism, conscientiousness, and loyalty to Chinese traditions (Cheung et al., 1996).

Limitations

If we want to predict who pays their bills on time, a measure of conscientiousness works well. To predict who will try a new exotic restaurant, we can rely on openness to experience. Similarly, one or another of these Big Five traits correlates well with many other aspects of behavior. But do the Big Five capture everything of importance about human behavior? Many psychologists remain unconvinced. For example, some employees steal from their company and treat coworkers abusively. Their behavior goes beyond mere lack of conscientiousness. A different kind of questionnaire, measuring integrity (honesty and virtue) provides a helpful measure (O'Neill & Hastings, 2011). Other researchers fault the Big Five approach for overlooking sense of humor, religiousness, sexiness, thriftiness, conservativeness, masculinity–femininity, and snobbishness (Paunonen & Jackson, 2000). In short, the Big Five description accounts for enough of the variability in human behavior to be useful, but for certain purposes we need to explore additional dimensions of personality.

The Origins of Personality

A description of personality differences is not an explanation. What makes some people more extraverted, emotionally stable, agreeable, conscientious, or open to experience than other people are?

Heredity and Environment

If you want evidence that heredity can influence personality, you need look no further than the nearest pet dog. For centuries, people have selectively bred dogs for their personalities, ranging from shy lapdogs to watchdogs that attack intruders.

To measure the influences of heredity on human personality, much research relies on studies of twins and adopted children. As ▼ Figure 14.3 shows, studies in five locations indicated greater similarities in extraversion between monozygotic pairs than dizygotic pairs (Loehlin, 1992). Similar research shows a hereditary component to neuroticism (Lake, Eaves, Maes, Heath, & Martin, 2000), conscientiousness (Luciano, Wainwright, Wright, & Martin, 2006), and other personality traits.

© Morimura Yasumasa

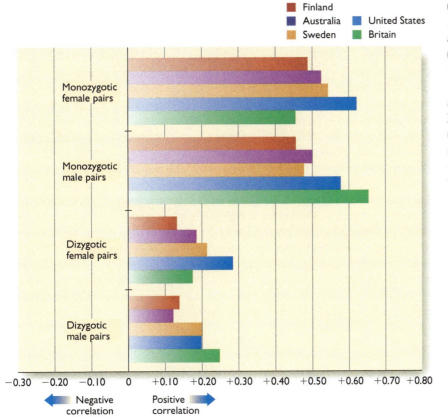

■ Finland
■ Australia   ■ United States
■ Sweden   ■ Britain

Monozygotic
female pairs

Monozygotic
male pairs

Dizygotic
female pairs

Dizygotic
male pairs

−0.30 −0.20 −0.10   0   +0.10 +0.20 +0.30 +0.40 +0.50 +0.60 +0.70 +0.80

◀ Negative   Positive ▶
  correlation   correlation

▲ **Figure 14.3** The length of each bar indicates the strength of a correlation between pairs of twins in their degree of extraversion. Correlations (similarities) were greater between monozygotic twins (who share all their genes) than between dizygotic twins (who share half their genes). (Based on data summarized by Loehlin, 1992)

(Loehlin, 1992). The results shown in Figures 14.3 and 14.4 pertain to extraversion; other studies provide a largely similar pattern for other personality traits (Heath, Neale, Kessler, Eaves, & Kendler, 1992; Loehlin, 1992; Viken, Rose, Kaprio, & Koskenvuo, 1994).

The low correlations between adopted children and adoptive parents imply that children learn rather little of their personalities by imitating their parents. (As mentioned in Chapter 5, Judith Harris made this same point.) In addition to the role of genetics, much of the variation among people's personalities relates to the unshared environment, *the aspects of environment that differ from one individual to another, even within a family.* Unshared environment includes the effects of a particular playmate, a particular teacher, an injury or illness, or any other isolated experience. Because of its idiosyncratic nature, unshared environment is difficult to investigate.

concept
check

13. **What evidence would indicate an important role of the *shared environment*—the influences that are the same for all children within a family?**

Answer

However, careful studies of the genome (all the chromosomes) have found no identifiable gene with a major effect on personality (Balestri, Calati, Serretti, & De Ronchi, 2014). At one point it appeared that a gene linked to serotonin levels in the brain might control responses to frightening stimuli. However, apparently the researchers who had failed to find such an effect failed to publish their results. If we take into account all the results, published and unpublished, that gene appears to have at most a small effect (Bastiaansen et al., 2014).

Evidently a great many genes influence personality, each in small ways, combined with environmental influences. For example, genes that increase vulnerability to neuroticism have different effects depending on the experiences someone has had (Barlow, Ellard, Sauer-Zavala, Bullis, & Carl, 2014).

Researchers have compared personalities of parents, their biological children, and their adopted children. As ▶ Figure 14.4 shows, parents' extraversion levels correlate moderately with those of their biological children but hardly at all with their adopted children. Similarly, biologically related brothers or sisters growing up together resemble each other moderately in personality, and unrelated children adopted into the same family do not

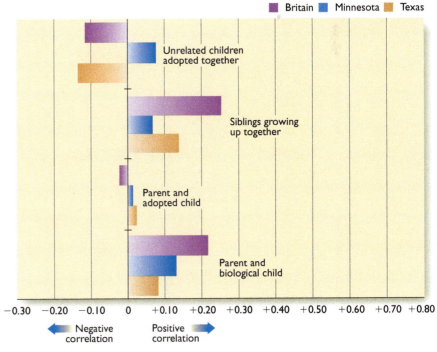

■ Britain ■ Minnesota ■ Texas

Unrelated children
adopted together

Siblings growing
up together

Parent and
adopted child

Parent and
biological child

−0.30 −0.20 −0.10   0   +0.10 +0.20 +0.30 +0.40 +0.50 +0.60 +0.70 +0.80

◀ Negative   Positive ▶
  correlation   correlation

▲ **Figure 14.4** The length and direction of each bar indicate the correlations between pairs of people in their degree of extraversion. Biological relatives (siblings or parent and child) showed low positive correlations. People related by adoption had close to zero correlations. (Based on data summarized by Loehlin, 1992)

Influences of Age, Culture, and Cohort

How much does your personality now resemble what it was in childhood? In one study, investigators followed people's behavior from age 3 to 26. Children who were fearful and easily upset at age 3 were more nervous and inhibited than others at age 26. Those who were impulsive and restless at age 3 tended to have trouble with others from then on and felt alienated from society. Those who were confident, friendly, and eager to explore their environment at 3 tended to be confident adults, eager to take charge of events (Caspi et al., 2003).

How will your personality change in the future? The older people get, the more slowly they change. In childhood, answers on a personality questionnaire correlate a modest 0.34 with a second test given 6 or 7 years later. By college age, the correlation is 0.54. It increases to 0.64 at age 30 and 0.74 at age 60

(Roberts & DelVecchio, 2000). Personality is probably even more stable than these figures suggest, because the measurements themselves are not entirely reliable (Gnambs, 2014). One reason for personality to become more fixed is that older people usually stay in the same environment, doing the same things year after year. Perhaps you can suggest additional possible explanations.

Although the differences that occur over age are not large, some trends are consistent. One trend, found in cultures throughout the world, is that middle-aged people tend to be more conscientious than teenagers (Donnellan & Lucas, 2008; McCrae et al., 2000). A simple hypothesis (not necessarily the whole explanation) is that adults are forced, whether or not they like it, to hold a job, pay the bills, repair the house, care for children, and take responsibility in other ways.

Most people reach their peak of social vitality and sensation seeking during adolescence or early adulthood and then decline gradually with further age (Roberts, Walton, & Viechtbauer, 2006). (In other words, teenagers ride roller coasters more than their grandparents do.) Older people also tend to be more emotionally stable and more agreeable (Cramer, 2003; McCrae et al., 2000). In most countries, young adults score higher on openness to new experience than older people do (Donnellan & Lucas, 2008; Roberts, Walton, & Viechtbauer, 2006). This trend is no surprise, as we see that young people enjoy new types of music, new kinds of food, new styles of clothing, and so forth. ▼ **Figure 14.5** shows

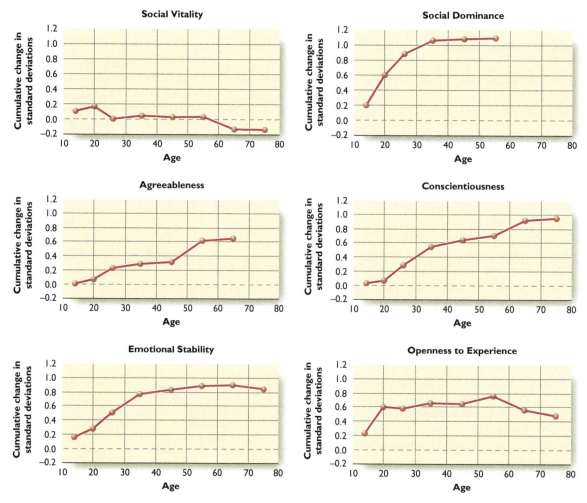

▲ **Figure 14.5** Six aspects of personality show different patterns of change over age based on the means of longitudinal research studies. The numbers along the vertical axis represent changes from the earliest age tested, measured in terms of standard deviations. (From Roberts, Walton, & Viechtbauer, 2006)

mean changes in six aspects of personality over age (Roberts, Walton, & Viechtbauer, 2006). Note that this research distinguished between two aspects of extraversion—social vitality and social dominance.

Does personality vary among cultures or countries? Research relying on self-reports encounters some difficulties. Outsiders think of Puerto Ricans as highly extraverted and Mexicans as highly sociable, but the Puerto Ricans and Mexicans don't rate themselves that way (Ramírez-Esparza, Mehl, Álvarez-Bermúdez, & Pennebaker, 2009; Terracciano et al., 2005). Countries' self-ratings on conscientiousness don't match the way outsiders would rank them, either. To some extent, the answer is just that many of our stereotypes about national character are wrong (McCrae et al., 2013). However, problems also exist in the accuracy of the measurements. When you rate your own personality, you of course rate it in comparison to people you know. If you are highly sociable, extraverted, or conscientious, but so is everyone else in your community, you rate yourself about average. Another problem relates to the way people handle rating scales. If you rated your own personality, or that of others you know, on a 0-to-10 scale, would you stay close to 5, or would you use many 0s and 10s? Most people in Japan, Hong Kong, and South Korea tend to use the middle of the scale. That is, they rate themselves and other people close to average in most regards. People in Poland, Malaysia, and several African countries tend to rate themselves and others either extremely high or extremely low (Mottus et al., 2012). The result is that self-ratings from one country are not easily comparable to those from another. The best way to compare personalities across cultures is to observe actual behavior (Heine, Buchtel, & Norenzayan, 2008).

Within the United States, personality varies, on average, among geographical areas. "Creative productivity" tends to be highest in the Northeast, Midwest, and West Coast. People in the Southeast are more likely to defend their reputation violently. People in cities tend to be more extraverted than those in rural areas. These are just a few of the differences. One reason for the differences is that the reputation of a place tends to attract like-minded people. If you read about people in Portland, Oregon, and think, "those sound like my kind of people," you might want to move there, too. Another example is that extraverts tend to seek exciting places with many opportunities to socialize, such as a large city, whereas people high in neuroticism tend to seek less threatening places (Rentfrow, Gosling, & Potter, 2008).

Finally, does personality change from one generation to the next? Remember the Flynn effect from Chapter 9: Over the years, people's performance on IQ tests has gradually increased so that each generation does better on the tests than the previous generation did. Researchers have also found generational differences in personality. For example, over the years,

beginning in the 1950s, measurements of anxiety steadily increased (Twenge, 2000). On the Children's Manifest Anxiety Scale, the mean score for all children in the 1980s was higher than the mean for mentally hospitalized children in the 1950s! Do we really have that much more anxiety than in past generations? Perhaps people's answers do not mean what they used to. However, compared to past generations, more children today have to live through their parents' divorce, and fewer live in a neighborhood with many friends and relatives. Perhaps those social changes have raised the average anxiety level.

Generations also differ in other aspects of personality. From the 1980s to 2006, American college students showed a steady increase in measures of narcissism (Twenge, Konrath, Foster, Campbell, & Bushman, 2008). Narcissism relates to self-confidence, which is generally a good thing, but it also relates to risk taking, selfishness, and troubled romantic relationships. American teenagers' desire for a high-paying job and an expensive lifestyle increased from the mid-1970s until 1990, and remained about steady since then. Meanwhile, their intention to work hard at their jobs decreased (Twenge & Kasser, 2013). The general point here is that the era in which you live exerts a major influence on personality development.

14. Why is it difficult to use self-reports to compare personality trends from one country to another?

Answer

14. When people rate themselves, they compare themselves to others within the country, and therefore, their ratings are not necessarily a good gauge of what the country as a whole does. Also, people in some countries are more likely to use the extremes of a scale, whereas those in other countries usually stay closer to the middle.

The Challenges of Classifying Personality

Personality descriptions refer to averages over time. We don't expect anyone to be equally extraverted at all times, equally conscientious, or anything else. What you do at any moment depends largely on the situation. In a sufficiently novel situation, you may be surprised by the actions of people you know well and even by your own behavior. The variation across situations makes the measurement of general tendencies difficult. Research progress always depends on good measurement, and you can see why progress in understanding personality is difficult.

Summary

- *Nomothetic and idiographic research.* Nomothetic studies examine large numbers of people briefly, whereas idiographic studies examine one or a few individuals intensively. (page 463)
- *Traits and states.* Traits are personality characteristics that persist over time; states are temporary tendencies in response to particular situations. (page 463)
- *Measurement problems.* Personality researchers rely mostly on self-reports, which are not entirely accurate. (page 464)
- *Five major traits.* Much of personality can be explained by these five traits: emotional stability, extraversion, agreeableness, conscientiousness, and openness to new experience. (page 465)
- *Determinants of personality.* Studies of twins and adopted children indicate that heredity contributes to the observed differences in personality. However, no single gene controls much of the variance. Family environment evidently contributes rather little. Some personality variation relates to unshared environment, the special experiences that vary from one person to another even within a family. (page 466)
- *Changes over age.* Compared to younger people, older people tend to be higher in conscientiousness, agreeableness, and emotional stability. They are somewhat lower in extraversion. Openness to experience decreases with age in most countries. (page 468)
- *Changes over generations.* Measurements of anxiety have gradually increased over the decades so that normal people now report anxiety levels that used to characterize people in mental hospitals. American teenagers today report more desire for wealth than teenagers of the past did, while also reporting less intention to work hard. (page 469)

Key Terms

agreeableness (page 465)

belief in a just world (page 464)

Big Five personality traits or five-factor model (page 465)

conscientiousness (page 465)

emotional stability (page 465)

extraversion (page 465)

idiographic approach (page 463)

neuroticism (page 465)

nomothetic approach (page 463)

openness to experience (page 466)

self-esteem (page 464)

state (page 463)

trait (page 463)

trait approach to personality (page 463)

unshared environment (page 467)

Review Questions

1. The trait approach to personality is an example of which of these?
   (a) The nomothetic approach
   (b) The idiographic approach

2. Someone with a strong belief in a just world would probably agree with which of the following statements?
   (a) My success or failure in life will be largely a matter of luck.
   (b) How well I succeed in life will depend on how hard I work.
   (c) If I succeed at one thing, I will probably fail at another.

3. On average, how does self-esteem compare between women and men, on average?
   (a) Women report lower self-esteem in all regards.
   (b) Women report lower self-esteem only with regard to academics.
   (c) Women report lower self-esteem only with regard to athletics and physical appearance.
   (d) Women report lower self-esteem only with regard to emotional control and moral behavior.

4. If you wanted to predict someone's happiness, which personality trait would you measure?
   (a) Openness to experience
   (b) Extraversion
   (c) Agreeableness
   (d) Conscientiousness

5. If you wanted to predict how long someone would live, which personality trait would you measure?
   (a) Openness to experience
   (b) Extraversion
   (c) Agreeableness
   (d) Conscientiousness

6. What evidence indicates that children learn little of their personality by imitating their parents?
   (a) Dizygotic twins resemble each other in personality more closely than do monozygotic twins.
   (b) Children's personality resembles that of their father more closely than that of their mother.
   (c) The personality of adopted children correlates very low with that of the adopting parents.
   (d) The personalities of today's generation differ in several ways from that of earlier generations.

7. Which of the following changes has been reported for American children and teenagers, as compared to those of previous generations?
   (a) Increased desire for wealth and an expensive lifestyle
   (b) Increased willingness to work hard
   (c) Decreased anxiety
   (d) Decreased narcissism

Answers: 1a, 2b, 3c, 4b, 5d, 6c, 7a.

module 14.3

Personality Assessment

After studying this module, you should be able to:

- Explain why people's testimonials that "this personality test described me accurately" cannot be taken as good evidence.

- Describe several objective personality tests.

- Explain how the MMPI and other tests detect when someone is lying.

- Describe the pros and cons of projective personality tests.

- Discuss the difficulty of using a personality test to diagnose an uncommon psychological disorder.

- Evaluate the usefulness of criminal profiling.

A new P. T. Barnum Psychology Clinic that just opened at your local shopping mall is offering a grand opening special on personality tests. You would like to know more about yourself, so you sign up. Here is Barnum's true–false test:

Questionnaire for Universal Assessment of Zealous Youth (QUAZY)

1.	I have never met a cannibal I didn't like.	T F
2.	Robbery is the only felony I have ever committed.	T F
3.	I eat "funny mushrooms" less frequently than I used to.	T F
4.	I don't care what people say about my nose-picking habit.	T F
5.	Sex with vegetables no longer disgusts me.	T F
6.	This time I am quitting glue sniffing for good.	T F
7.	I generally lie on questions like this one.	T F
8.	I spent much of my childhood sucking on computer cables.	T F
9.	I find it impossible to sleep if I think my bed might be clean.	T F
10.	Naked bus drivers make me nervous.	T F
11.	I spend my spare time playing strip solitaire.	T F

You turn in your answers. A few minutes later, a computer prints out your personality profile:

> You have a need for other people to like and admire you, and yet you tend to be critical of yourself. While you have some personality weaknesses, you are generally able to compensate for them. You have considerable unused capacity that you have not turned to your advantage. Disciplined and self-controlled on the outside, you tend to be worrisome and insecure on the inside. At times, you have serious doubts as to whether you have made the right decision or done the right thing. You prefer a certain amount of change and variety and become dissatisfied when hemmed in by restrictions and limitations. You also pride yourself as an independent thinker and do not accept others' statements without satisfactory proof. But you have found it unwise to be too frank in revealing yourself to others. At times you are extraverted, affable, and sociable, while at other times you are introverted, wary, and reserved. Some of your aspirations tend to be rather unrealistic. (Forer, 1949, p. 120)

Do you agree with this assessment? Did it capture your personality? Several experiments have been conducted along these lines with psychology classes (Forer, 1949; Marks & Kammann, 1980; Ulrich, Stachnik, & Stainton, 1963). Students filled out a questionnaire that looked reasonable, not with these ridiculous statements (which were included just for amusement). Several days later, each student received a sealed envelope containing a personality profile supposedly based on the students' answers to the questionnaire. The students were

People tend to accept almost any personality assessment, especially if it is stated in vague terms that people can interpret to fit themselves.

asked, "How accurately does this profile describe you?" About 90 percent rated it as good or excellent, and some expressed amazement at its accuracy. They didn't know that everyone had received exactly the same personality profile—the same one you just read.

The students accepted this personality profile partly because it vaguely describes almost everyone and partly because people accept almost *any* statement that a psychologist makes about them (Marks & Kammann, 1980). This *tendency to accept vague descriptions of our personality is known as the* Barnum effect, named after P. T. Barnum, the circus owner who specialized in fooling people out of their money.

The conclusion: Psychological testing must be done carefully. If we want to know whether a test measures personality, we cannot simply ask for people's opinions. Psychologists need to design a test carefully and then determine its reliability and validity.

Standardized Personality Tests

A **standardized test** is *one that is administered according to rules that specify how to interpret the results.* An important step for standardizing a test is to determine the distribution of scores. We need to know the mean score and the range of scores for a representative sample of the population and how these scores differ for special populations, such as people with severe depression. Given such information, we can determine whether a particular score on a personality test is within the normal range or whether it is more typical of people with a disorder.

Most of the tests published in popular magazines have not been standardized. A magazine may herald an article: "Test Yourself: How Good Is Your Marriage?" or "Test Yourself: How Well Do You Control Stress?" Unless the magazine states otherwise, you can assume that the author pulled the scoring norms out of thin air with no supporting research.

Over the years, psychologists have developed an enormous variety of tests to measure normal and abnormal personality. Let's examine a few prominent examples.

An Objective Personality Test: The Minnesota Multiphasic Personality Inventory

A widely used personality test, the **Minnesota Multiphasic Personality Inventory** (mercifully abbreviated **MMPI**), consists of *true-false questions intended to measure certain personality dimensions, especially for identifying clinical conditions.* The original MMPI, developed in the 1940s and still in use, has 550 items. *The second edition,* **MMPI–2,** published in 1990, has 567. Example items are "my mother never loved me" and "I think I would like the work of a pharmacist." (The items stated in this text are rewordings of actual items.)

The MMPI was devised *empirically*—that is, based on evidence rather than theory (Hathaway & McKinley, 1940). The authors wrote hundreds of questions that they thought might relate to personality. They put these questions to people with various psychological disorders and to a group of hospital visitors, who were assumed to be psychologically normal. The researchers selected the items that most people in any clinical group answered differently from most normal people. They assumed, for example, that if your answers resemble those of people with depression, you probably are depressed also. The MMPI includes scales for depression, paranoia, schizophrenia, and others.

Some of the items on the MMPI make sense theoretically, but others do not. For example, some items on the depression scale ask about feelings of helplessness or worthlessness, an important part of depression. But two other items on the original MMPI are "I attend religious services frequently" and "occasionally I tease animals." If you answer *false* to either of those items, you get a point on the depression scale! These items were included simply because many people with depression answered *false.* The reason is not clear, except that people feeling depressed seldom do anything they don't have to do.

Revision of the Test

The MMPI was standardized in the 1940s. As time passed, the meaning of certain items or their answers changed. For example, how would you respond to the following item?

I believe I am important.   T   F

In the 1940s, fewer than 10 percent of all people marked *true*. At the time, the word *important* meant about the same as *famous,* and people who called themselves important were thought to have an inflated view of themselves. Today, we stress that every person is important.

What about this item?

I like to play drop the handkerchief.   T   F

Drop the handkerchief, a game similar to tag, fell out of popularity in the 1950s. Most people today have never heard of the game, much less played it.

To bring the MMPI up to date, psychologists eliminated obsolete items and added new ones to deal with drug abuse, suicidal thoughts, and other issues (Butcher, Graham, Williams, & Ben-Porath, 1990). They also removed most of the items that made little sense theoretically, such as the one about teasing animals. Then they standardized the new MMPI–2 on a large representative sample of the U.S. population. The MMPI–2 has 10 clinical scales, as shown in ■ Table 14.3. The

Table 14.3 The 10 MMPI–2 Clinical Scales

Scale	Typical Item
Hypochondria (Hs)	I have chest pains several times a week. (T)
Depression (D)	I am glad that I am alive. (F)
Hysteria (Hy)	My heart frequently pounds so hard I can hear it. (T)
Psychopathic Deviation (Pd)	I get a fair deal from most people. (F)
Masculinity–Femininity (Mf)	I like to arrange flowers. (T = female)
Paranoia (Pa)	There are evil people trying to influence my mind. (T)
Psychasthenia (Obsessive–Compulsive) (Pt)	I save nearly everything I buy, even after I have no use for it. (T)
Schizophrenia (Sc)	I see, hear, and smell things that no one else knows about. (T)
Hypomania (Ma)	When things are dull I try to get some excitement started. (T)
Social Introversion (Si)	I have the time of my life at parties. (F)

items of any type are scattered throughout the test so that people won't see that "oh, this seems to be a set of items about depression." Most people get at least a few points on each scale. Higher scores indicate greater probability of psychological distress.

Detecting Deception

If you take the MMPI, could you lie to make yourself look mentally healthier than you really are? Yes. Could someone catch your lies? Probably.

The designers of the MMPI and MMPI–2 included items designed to identify lying (Woychyshyn, McElheran, & Romney, 1992). For example, consider the items "I like every person I have ever met" and "Occasionally I get angry at someone." If you answer *true* to the first question and *false* to the second, you are either a saint or a liar. On the theory that liars outnumber saints, the test counts such answers on a "lie" scale. If you get too many points on the lie scale, a psychologist distrusts your answers to the other items. Strangely enough, some people lie to try to look bad. For example, a criminal defendant might want to be classified as mentally ill. The MMPI includes items to detect that kind of faking also (Bagby, Nicholson, Bacchiochi, Ryder, & Bury, 2002).

Several other questionnaires also try to detect deception. Suppose an employer's questionnaire asks you to state how much experience you have at various skills. One of them is "determining myopic weights for periodic tables." You're not sure what that means, but you want the job. Do you claim to have extensive experience? If so, your claimed expertise will count *against* you because "determining myopic weights for periodic tables" is nonsense. The employer asked about it just to see whether you were exaggerating your qualifications on other items.

15. Suppose a person thinks "Black is my favorite color" would be a good true–false item for the depression scale of the MMPI. How would a researcher decide whether to include this item?

Answer

15. Researchers would determine whether people with depression are more likely than other people to answer *true*. If so, the item could be included.

The NEO PI-R

A more recent personality test is based on the Big Five personality model. An early version of this test measured neuroticism, extraversion, and openness to experience, abbreviated NEO. A revised test added scales for conscientiousness and agreeableness, but kept the name NEO, which is now considered just the name of the test and not an abbreviation. (It's like the company AT&T, which no longer stands for American Telephone and Telegraph. After all, how many people use telegraphs anymore?) The NEO PI-R (NEO personality inventory-revised) *includes 240 items to measure neuroticism, extraversion, openness, agreeableness, and conscientiousness*. A typical conscientiousness item resembles this:

| I keep my promises. | Very inaccurate | Moderately inaccurate | Neither | Moderately accurate | Very accurate |

Scores on this test have good reliability, about 0.9 (Gnambs, 2014). They correlate with observable behaviors, too. For example, students who score high on conscientiousness tend to spend much time studying (Chamorro-Premuzic, & Furnham, 2008). People who score high on openness are more likely than others to visit an art gallery (Church et al., 2008). The test has been translated into several other languages and seems to work reasonably well in other cultures (Ispas, Iliescu, Ilie, & Johnson, 2014; Wu, Lindsted, Tsai, & Lee, 2007). It is intended mainly to measure normal personality, as contrasted to the MMPI, which is used mainly to identify possible clinical problems.

16. For what purposes might the NEO PI-R be more suitable, and for what purposes might the MMPI be more suitable?

Answer

16. The NEO PI-R is designed to measure normal personality. The MMPI is set up to detect possible abnormalities.

The Myers-Briggs Type Indicator

The Myers-Briggs Type Indicator (MBTI) is *a test of normal personality, loosely based on Carl Jung's theories.* Jung emphasized the distinction between extraversion, which he defined as attending to the outside world, and introversion, concentrating on one's inner world. (Note the difference between his definitions and the ones more commonly used today.) He thought each person remained throughout life either extraverted or introverted. Unlike the MMPI, which gives people scores ranging continuously from zero upward on each scale, the MBTI classifies people as types. In addition to being either extraverted or introverted, each person is classed as sensing or intuitive, thinking or feeling, and judging or perceiving. For example, you might be classified as introverted-intuitive-thinking-judging. The test identifies a total of 16 personality types (McCaulley, 2000). The MBTI is more popular with businesses, which use it to describe the personalities of their employees, than with most psychologists, who are skeptical of dividing people into distinct categories. Some counselors also use the MBTI to help students choose a possible career, although other tests are more suitable for that purpose (Pulver & Kelly, 2008). You can take a simplified version of the MBTI at the website www.humanmetrics.com/cgi-win/JTypes2.asp and see how it classifies you. But remember the Barnum effect: The description may be reasonably accurate, but most people are inclined to accept almost any personality report they receive.

Someone said that there are two kinds of people—the kind who believe there are two kinds of people and the kind who don't believe it. It is tempting to divide people into personality types, but is it true that people fall into discrete groups? It would make sense to divide people into extraverted and introverted types if most people's scores were far to one end of the scale or the other. In fact, most people get scores close to the middle. Changing your answer to one question might switch you from one personality type to another, according to this test (Pittenger, 2005). Although the MBTI is a reasonable test in many regards, its insistence on putting people into distinct categories is hard to defend.

Projective Techniques

The MMPI, NEO PI-R, and Myers-Briggs Type Indicator analyze someone's personality based on self-reports. However, people don't always report honestly, and even when they intend to be honest, many people (especially people with mental disturbance) have limited insight into their own attributes (Bornstein, 2010). Therefore, many psychologists want to supplement these objective tests with other ways of assessing personality.

Sometimes when people are embarrassed to admit something about themselves, they say something like, "Let me tell you about my friend's problem and ask what my friend should do." They then describe their own problem. They are "projecting" their problem onto someone else in Freud's sense of the word—that is, attributing it to someone else.

Rather than discouraging projection, psychologists make use of it with projective techniques, which are *designed to encourage people to project their personality characteristics onto ambiguous stimuli.* Let's consider two well-known projective techniques: the Rorschach inkblots and the Thematic Apperception Test.

The Rorschach Inkblots

The Rorschach inkblots, *a projective technique based on people's interpretations of 10 ambiguous inkblots,* is the most famous, most widely used, and most controversial projective personality technique. It was created by Hermann Rorschach (ROAR-shock), a Swiss psychiatrist, who showed people inkblots and asked them to say whatever came to mind (Pichot, 1984). Other psychiatrists and psychologists gradually developed the Rorschach into the projective technique we know today.

Administering the Rorschach

The Rorschach inkblot technique consists of 10 cards similar to those in ▼ Figure 14.6, 5 of them in color. A psychologist hands you a card and

▲ **Figure 14.6** In the Rorschach inkblot technique, people examine an abstract pattern and say what it looks like.

asks, "What might this be?" The instructions are intentionally vague on the assumption that you reveal more about your personality in an ill-defined situation.

Sometimes, people's answers are revealing either immediately or in response to a psychologist's probes. Here is an example (Aronow, Reznikoff, & Moreland, 1995):

Client: Some kind of insect; it's not pretty enough to be a butterfly.

Psychologist: Any association to that?

Client: It's an ugly black butterfly, no colors.

Psychologist: What does that make you think of in your own life?

Client: You probably want me to say "myself." Well, that's probably how I thought of myself when I was younger—I never thought of myself as attractive—my sister was the attractive one. I was the ugly duckling—I did get more attractive as I got older.

Evaluation of the Rorschach

When you describe what you see in a picture, your answer undoubtedly relates in some way to your experiences, concerns, and personality. But how accurately can psychologists perceive that relationship? And if they perceive a relationship, did they really get the information from the Rorschach or from something they already knew about you?

One man described a particular inkblot as "like a bat that has been squashed on the pavement under the heel of a giant's boot" (Dawes, 1994, p. 149). Psychologist Robyn Dawes initially was impressed with how the Rorschach had revealed this client's sense of being overwhelmed and crushed by powers beyond his control. But then he realized that he had already known the man was depressed. If a client with a history of violence had made the same response, he would have focused on the aggressive nature of the giant's foot stomp. Psychologists often believe the Rorschach gave them an insight, when in fact it just confirmed an opinion they already had (Wood, Nezworski, Lilienfeld, & Garb, 2003).

James Exner (1986) developed methods to standardize the interpretations of Rorschach responses, such as counting the number of times a client mentions aggressive themes. Clinicians using this system achieve a reasonably high level of agreement in their interpretations (Viglione & Taylor, 2003). However, a high level of agreement does not necessarily mean correctness. Critics note several serious problems (Garb, Wood, Lilienfeld, & Nezworski, 2005; Lilienfeld, Wood, & Garb, 2000; Wood et al., 2003). One is that the psychologist counts the total number of pathological answers, not the percentage of replies that seem pathological. Therefore, highly talkative people are more likely to get a score that seems "disturbed." The most important objection is that the Rorschach seldom gives information that one could not obtain from biographical reports or other sources, and sometimes gives a false impression.

Critics of the Rorschach stop short of calling it completely invalid. The Rorschach does detect thought disorders (as are common in schizophrenia), has moderate validity for detecting risk of suicide, and identifies certain other personality characteristics with low to moderate accuracy (Mihura, Meyer, Dumitrascu, & Bombel, 2013). Its defenders insist that when the Rorschach is used properly, its validity is comparable to that of many other psychological tests (Society for Personality Assessment, 2005). Unfortunately, the other tests also have only low to moderate validity. Critics doubt that the Rorschach is worth the bother of administering it, and strongly insist that no one should use it to make important decisions, such as which parent should get custody of a child or which prisoners should get parole (Wood et al., 2003). Personality measurement is, frankly, difficult.

17. When a psychologist administers the Rorschach, why does he or she give only vague instructions?

Answer

17. The belief is that you reveal the most about your personality in an ill-defined, unstructured situation.

The Thematic Apperception Test

The Thematic Apperception Test (TAT) consists of pictures similar to the one shown in ▼ Figure 14.7. *The person is asked to make up a story for each picture, describing what events led up to this scene, what is happening now, and what will happen in the future.* Christiana Morgan and Henry Murray devised this test to measure people's needs (Murray, 1943). It includes 31 pictures, including some showing women, some showing men, some with both or neither, and one that is totally blank. A psychologist selects a few cards to use with a given client (Lilienfeld, Wood, & Garb, 2000).

The assumption is that when you tell a story about someone in the drawing, you probably identify with that person, and so the story is really about yourself. You might describe events and concerns that you might be reluctant to discuss openly. For example, one young man told the following story about a picture of a man clinging to a rope:

> This man is escaping. Several months ago he was beat up and shanghaied and taken aboard ship. Since then, he has been mistreated and unhappy and has been looking for a way to escape. Now the ship is anchored near a tropical island and he is climbing down a rope to the water. He will get away successfully and swim to shore. When he gets there, he will be met by a group of beautiful native women with whom he will live the rest of his life in luxury and never tell anyone what happened. Sometimes he will feel that he should go back to his old life; but he will never do it. (Kimble & Garmezy, 1968, pp. 582–583)

This young man had entered divinity school to please his parents but was unhappy there. He was wrestling with a secret desire to escape to a new life with

▲ **Figure 14.7** In the Thematic Apperception Test, people tell a story about what is going on in a picture, including what led up to this event, what is happening now, and what will happen in the future.

greater worldly pleasures. In his story, he described someone doing what he wanted to do.

Psychologists use the Thematic Apperception Test (TAT) in inconsistent ways. Many therapists interpret the results according to their clinical judgment, without any clear rules. If you took the TAT with two psychologists and said the same thing both times, they might reach different conclusions about you (Cramer, 1996).

The TAT is also used to measure people's need for achievement by counting all the times they mention achievement. It is also used to measure power and affiliation needs. These results are useful for research purposes, although not necessarily for making decisions about an individual (Lilienfeld, Wood, & Garb, 2000).

Handwriting as a Projective Technique

Based on the theory that your personality affects everything you do, some psychologists (and others) have tried analyzing people's handwriting. For example, perhaps people who dot their i's with a dash—*i*—are especially energetic, or perhaps people who draw large loops above the line—as in *allow*—are highly idealistic. Carefully collected data, however, show no dependable relationship between handwriting and personality (Tett & Palmer, 1997).

Implicit Personality Tests

Although projective tests have debatable usefulness, the motivation behind them remains: Psychologists would like to measure personality aspects that people cannot or will not discuss openly. So the search for another kind of personality test continues.

Chapter 7 distinguished between explicit and implicit memory. If you hear a list of words and try to repeat them, your recall is explicit memory. If you later use words from the list in your conversation, your use of those words constitutes implicit memory. Implicit memory can affect you without your awareness.

Analogous to that, an implicit personality test *measures some aspect of your personality without your awareness.* One example is the implicit association test. Chapter 13 described how this test could be used to measure prejudices that people do not want to admit. It can also detect other emotional reactions. For example, someone who is nervous around other people might pair social words (*party, friend, companion*) more readily with unpleasant words than with pleasant words. Someone who

©sdeva/Shutterstock.com

strongly dislikes drug users will pair drug use words with unpleasant words more strongly than most other people do. In some cases this kind of test provides useful information, such as predicting which nurses will quit a job in which they have to deal with drug users (von Hippel, Brener, & von Hippel, 2008).

Another implicit personality test is the affective priming paradigm. A participant sees first a picture (such as a butterfly or a spider) and then a word (such as *happy* or *awful*). In one version of the task, all the participant has to do is to say the word aloud. The idea is that someone afraid of spiders will be quick to say *awful* after seeing a spider, but slower to say *happy*. The delay of response might measure the strength of someone's dislike of spiders, filthiness, loneliness, or anything else.

Both the implicit association test and the affective priming paradigm can distinguish moderately well between groups who differ in their personality (Horcajo, Rubio, Aguado, Hernandez, & Marquez, 2014). However, at least at present they are not accurate enough to say anything with confidence about an individual (DeHouwer, Teige-Mocigemba, Spruyt, & Moors, 2009).

18. **What behavior do both the implicit association test and the affective priming paradigm measure?**

Answer

18. They both measure the delay of a person's response after presentation of some stimulus.

Uses and Misuses of Personality Tests

Personality tests serve several functions. Researchers use them to investigate how personality develops. Some businesses use them to help select which job applicants to hire. Clinicians use them to help identify disorders and to measure improvement during therapy.

Personality tests are useful up to a point, but we need to be aware of their limits. Suppose someone's MMPI personality profile resembles the profile typical for schizophrenia. Identifying schizophrenia or any other unusual condition is a signal-detection problem, as discussed in Chapter 4: We want to report a stimulus when it is present but not when it is absent. People without schizophrenia outnumber people with schizophrenia by about 100 to 1. Suppose a particular score on some personality test

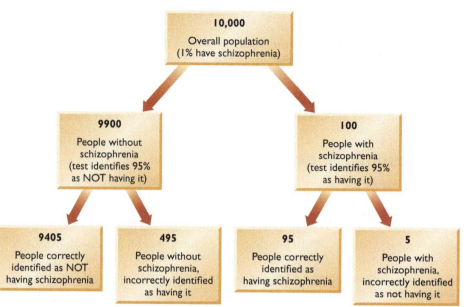

▲ **Figure 14.8** Assume that a certain profile occurs in 95 percent of people with schizophrenia and 5 percent of other people. If we relied entirely on this test, we would correctly identify 95 people with schizophrenia and misidentify 495 normal people.

is characteristic of 95 percent of people with schizophrenia, whereas 5 percent of other people also have that score. As ▲ Figure 14.8 shows, 5 percent of the total population is a larger group than 95 percent of the people with schizophrenia. Thus, if we label as "schizophrenic" everyone with a high score, we are wrong more often than right. (Recall the representativeness heuristic and the issue of base-rate information discussed in Chapter 8: Someone who seems representative of people in a rare category does not necessarily belong to that category.) Therefore, although the personality test provides a helpful clue, a psychologist looks for evidence beyond the test score before drawing a conclusion.

Personality Tests in Action: Criminal Profiling

Personality traits are moderately accurate predictors of people's behavior in certain situations. Can we go in the other direction? Can we observe a behavior and infer someone's personality? Consider crime. Criminal profiling, also known as behavioral investigative advice, attempts to infer something about the criminal from the crime itself. Although you might not have thought of it this way, criminal profiling is an application of personality testing. It assumes that people who commit similar crimes have similar personalities or backgrounds. In 1956, the New York City police asked psychiatrist James Brussel to help them find the "mad bomber" who had planted more than 30 bombs over 16 years. Brussel examined the evidence and told police the mad bomber hated the power company, Con Ed. The bomber was probably unmarried, foreign-born, probably Slavic, 50 to 60 years old, and living in Bridgeport, Connecticut. Brussel said to look for a man who dresses neatly and wears a buttoned double-breasted suit. That evidence led police directly to a suspect, George Metesky, who was wearing a buttoned double-breasted suit! Metesky confessed, and criminal profiling established itself as a powerful tool.

Well, that's the way James Brussel told the story, anyway. Sometimes people have memory distortions and hindsight bias (Chapter 7). Brussel apparently distorted his memory of what he told the police. According to police records,

Many television shows and several movies have featured a criminal profiler who examines the scene of the crime and infers the personality of the perpetrator. This idea makes for a good story, but in fact criminal profiling has much less accuracy.

Brussel didn't say the bomber was Slavic; he said German. Metesky, in fact, was Lithuanian. Brussel didn't say the bomber lived in Bridgeport, Connecticut; he said White Plains, New York, and the police spent much time fruitlessly searching for suspects in White Plains. Metesky, in fact, lived in Waterbury, Connecticut. Brussel said the bomber was 40 to 50 years old and revised his memory when Metesky turned out to be a bit older. Brussel also said the bomber had a facial scar, had a night job, and was an expert on civil or military ordnance (none of which was true). And Metesky was not wearing a buttoned double-breasted suit when the police arrested him. He was wearing pajamas. Nothing that Brussel said led the police to the mad bomber. They found Metesky because a clerk from Con Ed patiently went through years of letters the company had received until she found a threatening letter that resembled messages the mad bomber had planted (Foster, 2000).

Brussel's *reported* success in helping the police (which was really no success at all) inspired interest in criminal profiling, and today, FBI profilers consult with police on a thousand or so cases per year. How accurate are their profiles? Researchers examined 21 criminal profiles that various police departments obtained. Most statements in those profiles were useless to investigators, such as, "The offender felt no remorse" (Alison, Smith, Eastman, & Rainbow, 2003). It is possible to list many correct statements that profilers have made (Snook, Cullen, Bennell, Taylor, & Gendreau, 2008). However, the number of correct statements is meaningless unless we also know the number of incorrect statements. We also need to know whether professional profilers' surmises are more accurate than other people's guesses. Only a few studies have investigated these questions. Let's examine two of the best such studies.

what's the evidence?

Criminal Profiling

Richard Kocsis and his associates first did a study of profiling in a murder case. They provided extensive details about the murder to five professional profilers and larger numbers of police officers, psychologists, college students, and people who claimed to be psychics. Then each person tried to guess the murderer's sex, height, age,

religion, and so forth in 30 multiple-choice questions, with varying numbers of choices per item. Researchers determined the accuracy of these answers, based on facts about the actual murderer, who had in fact been caught. Random guessing would produce 8.1 correct answers for the 30 items, but no one would guess at random. Even without knowing any details about the crime, aren't you more likely to guess the murderer was a young man than an 80-year-old woman? If the crime was in the United States, you probably won't guess that the criminal was a Buddhist. And so forth. All groups did better than the random score of 8.1, but none did well. The professional profilers did the best, at 13.8 correct out of 30, and psychics did the worst, at 11.3 (Kocsis, Irwin, Hayes, & Nunn, 2000).

However, it may be hard to profile a criminal from a single crime. Kocsis (2004) therefore did a similar study concerning someone who had committed a series of 13 cases of arson (setting fires).

Hypothesis Professional profilers will guess correctly more facts about the arsonist than other people will.

Method As in Kocsis's first study, most profilers refused to participate, but three were willing. Other groups were police officers with much experience investigating arson, professional fire investigators, and sophomore chemistry majors. Each person examined all the evidence that police had assembled, including photos and descriptions of the crime scenes, statements by witnesses, shoe prints, information about how the fires were set, and so forth. The study also included a group of community college students who received *no* information about the crimes (except that they were arson), but took guesses about the arsonist anyway. Then each participant answered 33 questions about the probable arsonist. All were questions to which the researcher knew the correct answer. Examples (reworded slightly for brevity):

- The offender is: (1) male, (2) female.
- The offender is: (1) thin, (2) average, (3) solid/muscular, (4) fat.
- The offender was: (1) highly familiar with the crime locations, (2) somewhat familiar, (3) unfamiliar.
- The offender is: (1) single, (2) married, (3) living with someone, (4) divorced.
- The offender is: (1) a student, (2) unemployed, (3) employed part time, (4) a blue-collar worker, (5) a semiskilled worker, (6) a skilled or white-collar worker.
- The offender's alcohol use is: (1) none, (2) low, (3) medium, (4) in binges, (5) high.
- The offender: (1) has a previous criminal record, (2) has no previous criminal record.

Results Questions had between 2 and 9 choices each, and random guessing would produce a bit more than 10 correct answers out of 33. ▼ Figure 14.9 shows the results. The three professional profilers did the best,

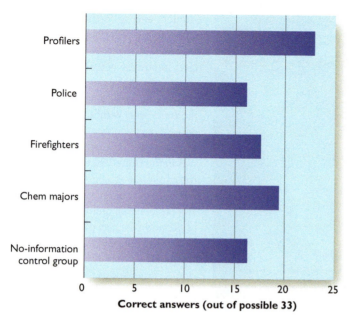

▲ **Figure 14.9** Of 33 multiple-choice questions, many of them with only 2 or 3 choices, profilers answered a mean of 23 items correctly. Random guessing would produce 10 correct. People with no information about the crime guessed more than 16 correct. (Source: Based on data from Kocsis, 2004).

but only 3 to 4 items better than the chemistry majors. (Chemistry majors were used to represent people with no relevant experience but high intelligence. Take a bow, chemistry majors.) Police and firefighters, despite their experience, did hardly better than the community college students who had no information about the crimes.

Interpretation This study has clear limitations, especially that it included only three professional profilers, just one criminal, and a set of questions that may not have been ideal. Still, the profilers did better than the

other groups, so it appears that the field is not entirely bogus. A few similar studies yielded similar results: Professional profilers do a bit better than other people, but not by much, and police investigators do no better than inexperienced people. In no case did anyone answer a very high percentage of questions correctly (Snook, Eastwood, Gendreau, Goggin, & Cullen, 2007).

A critical question remains: Did the profilers do well *enough*? On average, they answered 23 questions correctly, which is closer to the scores of people who knew nothing (16+) than to a perfect score (33). If profilers provide the police with a mixture of correct and incorrect information, is the net result to advance the investigation or lead the police astray?

19. Note the use of a control group who knew nothing about the crime. Why was this group necessary? We already knew how many answers someone would get right by random guessing.

Answer

19. No one would guess randomly. Some guesses are more likely than others regardless of the details of the crime.

Criminal profiling is not impossible. People who commit certain crimes tend to resemble each other in certain ways that research can identify (Cole & Brown, 2014; Fujita et al., 2013). However, the accuracy is analogous to predicting the weather a week or more in advance: Someone can say that one outcome is more likely than another, but the certainty is never high. Research can no doubt improve the future accuracy of criminal profiling, but police should beware of putting more confidence in a profile than it merits.

---

in closing | module 14.3

Possibilities and Limits of Personality Tests

One of most people's main topics of conversation could be described uncharitably as "gossip" or more generously as "understanding other people." Knowing about other people is important. You need to know whom to trust and whom to distrust.

Given our focus on personality, most of us tend to believe that personality is highly stable and governs a great deal of behavior. If so, someone should be able to look at a crime scene

and infer the personality of the perpetrator. Psychologists should be able to listen to people's answers to the Rorschach inkblots and discern their innermost secrets. So it might seem, but the research suggests we should be cautious. Personality is somewhat consistent, but not altogether so. Our actions depend on our situations at least as much as they depend on our personalities.

Summary

- *People's tendency to accept personality test results.* Because most people accept almost any interpretation of their personality based on a personality test, tests must be carefully scrutinized to ensure that they are measuring what they claim to measure. (page 471)

- *Standardized personality tests.* A standardized test is administered according to explicit rules, and its results are interpreted in a prescribed fashion based on the norms for the population. (page 472)

- *The MMPI.* The MMPI, a widely used personality test, consists of a series of true–false questions selected in an effort to distinguish among various personality types. The MMPI–2 is a modern version. (page 472)

- *Detection of lying.* The MMPI and other tests guard against lying by including items about common faults and rare virtues. Anyone who denies common faults or claims rare virtues is probably lying. (page 473)

- *Projective techniques.* A projective technique, such as the Rorschach inkblots or the Thematic Apperception Test, lets people describe their concerns indirectly while talking about ambiguous stimuli. The results from projective techniques have unimpressive validity for making decisions about any individual. (page 474)

- *Implicit personality tests.* The implicit association test and affective priming paradigm are attempts to measure personality traits that people do not or cannot describe about themselves. So far, such tests are useful for research but not for decisions about an individual. (page 475)

- *Uses and misuses of personality tests.* Personality tests can help assess personality, but their results should be interpreted cautiously. Because the tests are not entirely accurate, a score that seems characteristic of a psychological disorder may occur also in many people without that disorder. (page 476)

- *Criminal profiling.* Some psychologists try to aid police investigations by constructing personality profiles of the kind of person who would commit a certain crime. Research so far suggests low accuracy of personality profiles. (page 476)

Key Terms

Barnum effect (page 471)

implicit personality test (page 475)

Minnesota Multiphasic Personality Inventory (MMPI) (page 472)

MMPI–2 (page 472)

Myers-Briggs Type Indicator (MBTI) (page 473)

NEO PI-R (NEO personality inventory-revised) (page 473)

projective techniques (page 474)

Rorschach inkblots (page 474)

standardized test (page 472)

Thematic Apperception Test (TAT) (page 475)

Review Questions

1. Why does the MMPI include some items that ask about common flaws, such as, "Sometimes I think more about my own welfare than that of others"?
   (a) To measure people's tendency to lie
   (b) To identify people who are morally perfect
   (c) To measure degrees of moral imperfection

2. The NEO PI-R is based on which of the following?
   (a) Sigmund Freud's theory of personality
   (b) The five-factor model of personality
   (c) Carl Rogers's approach to personality
   (d) A combination of Carl Jung's and Alfred Adler's theories of personality

3. Which of the following is a projective technique?
   (a) A psychologist gives a child a set of puppets with instructions to act out a story about a family.
   (b) A psychologist hands you a stack of cards, each containing one word, and asks you to sort the cards into a stack that applies to you and a stack that does not.
   (c) A psychologist asks you to stare off into space and describe yourself.
   (d) A psychologist asks several of your friends to describe your personality.

4. Suppose that research using the Rorschach inkblots suggests that highly talkative people are more mentally disturbed than average. What would be a likely explanation?
   (a) The more someone says, the greater chance of saying something that's considered "disturbed."
   (b) The number of disturbed comments is multiplied by the amount of time someone takes in completing the test.
   (c) Highly talkative people really are disturbed.

5. Is a personality test more likely to be accurate in identifying common disorders or rare disorders?
   (a) Common disorders
   (b) Rare disorders

6. According to current evidence, how accurate are criminal profilers?
   (a) Their advice reliably identifies the type of person who committed a crime.
   (b) They are no more accurate than random guessing.
   (c) They are no more accurate than an inexperienced, untrained person's guesses.
   (d) Their assessments are slightly more accurate than those that an untrained person would make.

Answers: 1a, 2b, 3a, 4a, 5a, 6d.

15 Abnormal Psychology: Disorders and Treatment

Pittsburgh Steelers All-Pro linebacker James Harrison has been suspended and fined multiple times for delivering helmet-to-helmet hits to opposing players. Every time he delivers a tackle that way, he risks injury not only to the opposing player but also to himself. How does the context of sport impact how we view this behavior? How would we view it outside of the sports arena?

Over the past four months, George has injured dozens of people whom he hardly knew. Two of them needed hospital treatment. George expresses no guilt, no regrets. He says he would hit every one of them again if he got the chance. What should society do with George?

1. Send him to jail.
2. Commit him to a mental hospital.
3. Give him an award for being the best defensive player in the National Football League.

You cannot answer the question unless you know the context of George's behavior. Behavior that seems normal at a party is bizarre at a business meeting. Behavior expected of a rock star might earn a trip to the mental hospital for a college professor.

Even knowing the context of someone's behavior may not tell us whether the behavior is normal. Suppose your rich aunt Tillie starts passing out money to strangers on a street corner and plans to continue until she has exhausted her fortune. Does that sound crazy? Should you urge her to seek therapy? If so, how is she different than Warren Buffet, one of the richest men in the world, saying he will donate half of his multibillion-dollar estate to charity?

Assessing abnormal behavior is difficult. What seems abnormal for one person or in one context may be normal for someone else. Deciding what to do about abnormal behavior is often even more difficult.

After studying this module, you should be able to:

- Describe and evaluate a definition of mental illness.
- Define the biopsychosocial model of mental illness.
- Give examples of cultural influences on abnormal behavior.
- Describe *DSM-5* and give examples of the categories it lists.
- Evaluate the assumptions behind *DSM* and the categorical approach to mental illness.

Many students in medical school contract what is called "medical students' disease." Imagine reading a medical textbook that describes, say, Cryptic Ruminating Umbilicus Disorder (CRUD): "The symptoms are hardly noticeable until the condition becomes hopeless. The first symptom is a pale tongue." (You go to the mirror. You cannot remember what your tongue is supposed to look like, but it *does* look a little pale.) "Later, a hard spot forms in the neck." (You feel your neck. "Wait! I never felt *this* before! I think it's something hard!") "Just before the arms and legs fall off, the person has shortness of breath, increased heart rate, and sweating." (Already distressed, you *do* have shortness of breath, your heart *is* racing, and you *are* sweating profusely.)

Sooner or later, most medical students misunderstand the description of some disease and confuse it with their own normal condition. When my brother was in medical school, he diagnosed himself as having a rare, fatal illness, checked himself into a hospital, and wrote out his will. (He finished medical school and is still doing fine today, decades later.)

Students of psychological disorders are particularly vulnerable to medical students' disease. As you read this chapter, you may decide that you are suffering from one of the disorders you read about. Perhaps you are, but recognizing a little of yourself in the description of a disorder does not necessarily mean that you have it. Most people feel nervous occasionally, and most have mood swings and a peculiar behavior or two. A diagnosis of a psychological disorder should be reserved for people whose problems seriously interfere with their lives.

Defining Abnormal Behavior

The American Psychiatric Association (2013, p. 20) defined mental disorder as a "clinically significant disturbance in an individual's cognition, emotion regulation, or behavior that reflects a dysfunction in the psychological, biological, or developmental processes underlying mental functioning." That seems a reasonable definition, but it is not always easy in practice. Who decides whether someone has a clinically significant disturbance? Do we let people themselves decide? Do we always trust a psychiatrist or psychologist to decide? What if therapists disagree with one another? Furthermore, does the second part of that definition ("reflects a dysfunction in the psychological, biological, or developmental processes . . .") add anything? In many cases we don't know what caused someone's psychological dysfunction, but we would consider it a disorder anyway.

In previous eras, people have held many views of abnormal behavior and its causes. The idea of demon possession was popular in medieval Europe and is still common in much of the world today (van Duijl, Nijenhuis, Komproe, Gernaat, & de Jong, 2010). Although it conflicts with a scientific worldview, we understand its appeal: When someone's behavior changes drastically, we feel like saying, "That's not the person I knew."

The ancient Greeks explained behavior in terms of four fluids: An excess of blood caused a sanguine (courageous and loving) personality. An excess of phlegm caused a phlegmatic (calm) personality. Too much yellow bile made one choleric (easily angered). Too much black bile made one melancholic (sad). Although the four-fluids theory is obsolete, the terms *sanguine*, *phlegmatic*, *choleric*, and *melancholic* persist.

Traditional Chinese philosophy held that personality progresses through five states of change,

Edvard Munch (1863–1944), *Evening Melancholy* (1896). Like many of Munch's paintings, this one depicts depression and despair.

analogous to the seasons: Winter rain helps the trees (wood) grow in spring. The trees burn (fire) in summer, and the ashes return to earth in late summer. The earth can be mined for metal in autumn, and melted metal becomes a liquid, like water, completing the cycle. According to this view, personality also cycles with the seasons, and an excessive response could cause too much fear, anger, and so forth. ▶ Figure 15.1 illustrates the idea.

The Biopsychosocial Model

In Western cultures today, the predominant view is the biopsychosocial model that emphasizes *biological, psychological, and sociological aspects of abnormal behavior.* The *biological* roots of abnormal behavior include genetic factors, infectious diseases, poor nutrition, inadequate sleep, drugs, and other influences on brain functioning.

The *psychological* component includes reactions to stressful experiences. For example, people who were physically or sexually abused in childhood are more likely than others to develop psychological problems in adulthood (J. G. Johnson, Cohen, Brown, Smailes, & Bernstein, 1999). People who live in poverty are more likely to engage in risky behavior (Haushofer & Fehr, 2014).

Also, behavior must be understood in a *social* and *cultural* context. Behavior that is considered acceptable in one society might be labeled abnormal in another. For example, loud wailing at a funeral is expected in some societies, but not in others. Public drunkenness is acceptable in some cultures, but strictly forbidden in others.

▲ **Figure 15.1** In traditional Chinese philosophy, personality cycles through five stages or elements, just as the seasons do. An excessive response could lead to abnormalities.

Cultural Influences on Abnormality

We learn from our culture how to behave normally. We also learn some of the options for behaving abnormally. In part of Sudan some years ago, women had low status and very limited rights. If a woman's husband mistreated her, she had no defense. However, people believed that a woman could be possessed by a demon that caused her to lose control and scream "crazy" things that she "could not possibly believe," including insults against her own husband (!). Her husband could not scold or punish her because, after all, it was not she who was speaking, but a demon. The standard way to remove the demon was to provide the woman with the best available food, new clothing, an opportunity to spend much time with other women,

a

b

What we consider abnormal depends on the context. **(a)** People dressed as witches ski down a mountain as part of an annual festival in Belalp, Switzerland, in which dressing as witches is supposed to chase away evil spirits. **(b)** People parade through Stockholm, Sweden, on "Zombie Day." Unusual behavior is not necessarily a sign of psychological disorder.

Fans sometimes celebrate a major sports victory with a destructive rampage. In some ways, it is like running amok. People copy abnormal behavior from other people's example.

hold onto their penis constantly to prevent it from disappearing into the body (Bracha, 2006). You have probably heard the expression "to run amok." *Running amok* occurs in parts of Southeast Asia, where someone (usually a young man) runs around engaging in indiscriminate violent behavior (Berry, Poortinga, Segal, & Dasen, 1992). Such behavior is considered an understandable reaction to psychological stress.

An Australian psychiatrist found that three mental patients in a hospital had cut off one of their ears. Assuming that this behavior must be a common symptom of mental illness, he asked other psychiatrists how often they had seen the same thing. He found that ear removal occurred only at his own hospital. Apparently, after one patient cut off his ear, the other two copied (Alroe & Gunda, 1995).

freedom from work responsibilities, and almost anything else she demanded until the demon departed. You can imagine how common demon possession became (Constantinides, 1977).

More examples: *Koro*, said to be common in China, is a fear that a man's penis will retract into the body, causing death. Some men have been known to

DSM and the Categorical Approach to Psychological Disorders

If you go to a doctor's office with a complaint of headache, the doctor will ask some questions and run tests to determine the cause. Most headaches are due to tension, sleeplessness, or other simple problems, but some are due to an infection or blood clot in the brain, a tumor, or migraine. In any case, the doctor pinpoints a cause before recommending a treatment. For many years, psychiatrists and clinical psychologists expected to reach the same point: They would precisely diagnose someone's psychological problem, determine the cause, and recommend the most effective therapy. Over time, that goal has become more and more elusive.

To standardize their definitions and diagnoses, psychiatrists and psychologists developed *a reference book called* the *Diagnostic and Statistical Manual of Mental Disorders (DSM) that sets specific criteria for each psychological diagnosis.* The latest edition, *DSM-5*, was published in 2013 (American Psychiatric Association, 2013). ■ Table 15.1

In the early days of medicine, physicians provided the same treatments for all diseases (e.g., applying leeches to draw blood, as shown). Progress depended on differentiating particular disorders and developing individual treatments for each. Can we also find specific treatments for psychological disorders?

Table 15.1 Categories of Psychological Disorders According to DSM–5
Neurodevelopmental Disorders
Schizophrenia Spectrum
Bipolar and Related Disorders
Depressive Disorders
Anxiety Disorders
Obsessive-Compulsive Disorders
Trauma-Related Disorders
Dissociative Disorders
Somatic Symptom Disorders
Eating Disorders
Elimination Disorders
Sleep-Wake Disorders
Sexual Dysfunctions
Gender Dysphoria
Impulse Control Disorders
Substance Abuse and Addictions
Neurocognitive Disorders
Personality Disorders
Paraphilias
Others

Inattention

Fails to attend to details
Difficulty sustaining attention
Seems not to listen
Fails to finish tasks
Difficulty organizing an activity
Avoids tasks requiring sustained effort
Frequently loses objects
Easily distracted
Forgetful in daily tasks

Hyperactivity/Impulsivity

Often fidgets
Restless while others sit quietly
Runs about inappropriately
Excessively loud during play
Acts as if driven by a motor
Talks excessively
Blurts out answer before question is complete
Difficulty waiting his/her turn
Interrupts others

This "either–or" style of diagnosis means that people can qualify for the same diagnosis in many ways. *DSM-5* offers 227 possible combinations of symptoms for major depression, more than 23,000 for panic disorder, and more than 636,000 for post-traumatic stress disorder (PTSD) (Galatzer-Levy & Bryant, 2013)! Disorders vary in other ways, too.

DSM has helped standardize psychiatric diagnoses so that psychologists use terms like *depression, schizophrenia,* and so forth in more consistent ways than they would otherwise. However, this approach assumes that every disorder fits into one category or another, and that each troubled person can receive a single, unambiguous diagnosis. In fact, many troubled people fit several diagnoses partly and none of them perfectly (Ahn, Flanagan, Marsh, & Sanislow, 2006; Kupfer, First, & Regier, 2002). If you are suffering from depression, mania, anxiety, substance abuse, conduct disorder, obsessive-compulsive disorder, or schizophrenia, the chances are better than 50/50 that you are suffering from one or more of the others also, at least to a mild degree (Caspi et al., 2014). You might fit mainly into one diagnosis now but a different one later. Lab tests won't clarify the situation, because psychiatry has no useful lab tests. Furthermore, different disorders have many overlapping causes. The genes that increase the risk of any one disorder also increase the risk of other disorders (Cross-Disorder Group, 2013; Duncan, Pollastri, & Smoller, 2014; Schneider et al., 2014). Highly stressful experiences, such as the sudden death of a loved one, can trigger the onset of depression, anxiety, or schizophrenia (Keyes et al., 2014; Nolen-Hoeksema & Watkins, 2011). Even when therapists agree on a single diagnosis, the diagnosis doesn't reliably point the way to a treatment. Antidepressant drugs sometimes help people with disorders other than depression, and antipsychotic drugs sometimes help relieve nonpsychotic disorders (Dean, 2011).

Many psychologists who are dissatisfied with the *DSM* approach would prefer to rate each client's problems along several dimensions, instead of trying to give each person a label (Watson & Clark, 2006). For example, instead of a single diagnosis, a therapist might use ratings like this:

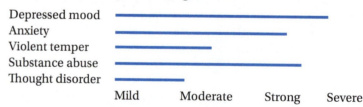

The authors of *DSM-5* moved partway in that direction, but only for personality disorders. A personality disorder is *a maladaptive, inflexible way of dealing with the environment and other people,* such as being unusually self-centered. A previous edition of *DSM* listed ten personality disorders, but clinicians found that few clients fit neatly into one label or another (Lenzenweger, Johnson, & Willett, 2004). *DSM-5* gives clinicians two options. First, they can classify someone in terms of six personality disorders, as briefly described in ■ Table 15.2. Second, if they prefer, they can dispense with labels and rate someone along several

shows the categories of disorder, in the order that *DSM-5* lists them.

For each disorder, *DSM-5* sets the criteria for making a diagnosis. For example, to qualify for a diagnosis of attention deficit/hyperactivity disorder, someone must frequently show at least six symptoms (or four if over age 17) from either of the following columns:

Table 15.2 Six Personality Disorders

Personality Disorder	Description
Antisocial personality disorder	Lack of affection for others, lack of guilt feelings
Avoidant personality disorder	Avoidance of social contact, lack of friends
Borderline personality disorder	Unstable self-image, no lasting relationships or firm decisions, repeated self-endangering behaviors
Narcissistic personality disorder	Exaggerated self-regard, disregard for others
Obsessive-compulsive personality disorder	Excessive preoccupation with details
Schizotypal personality disorder	Cognitive impairments and interpersonal deficits

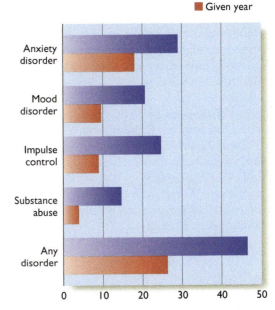

▲ **Figure 15.2** In this survey, just over one-fourth of U.S. adults suffer a psychological disorder in any given year, and nearly half do at some time in life. (Based on data of Kessler, Berglund, et al., 2005; Kessler, Chiu, et al., 2005)

dimensions, including impulsivity, suspiciousness, withdrawal, and hostility. It is fair to say that our understanding of personality disorders is in a state of flux, as is the whole concept of mental illness, but clearly the trend is toward doubting the categorical approach to mental illness.

concept check

1. **Is it possible for two people to get the same diagnosis without having many symptoms in common?**
2. **Why are many psychologists and psychiatrists skeptical of the categorical approach to mental illness?**

Answers

2. Few people exactly fit the criteria for one and only one disorder. More frequently, someone partly fits the description for two or more disorders. Also, the genetic and environmental causes of any disorder overlap those for other disorders, and the treatments designed for one disorder may be effective for others.

1. Yes. In DSM-5, many diagnoses are based on variable combinations of symptoms, such as six out of column A or six out of column B.

A further criticism is that *DSM* labels too many conditions as "mental illnesses." If you seek help to increase your enjoyment of sex, you have *sexual interest/arousal disorder* or *hypoactive sexual desire disorder*. A woman with premenstrual distress gets a diagnosis of *premenstrual dysphoric disorder*. If you get at least seven hours of sleep per night but still feel sleepy during the day, and you have trouble feeling fully awake after a sudden awakening, you have *hypersomnolence disorder*. The list goes on, with hundreds of other possibilities. Surveys have found that almost half of all people in the United States qualify for at least one *DSM* diagnosis of mental illness at some time in life (Kessler, Berglund,

Demler, Jin, & Walters, 2005; Kessler, Chiu, Demler, & Walters, 2005). Most people would prefer not to have that label, considering the stigma attached to mental illness (Corrigan, Druss, & Perlick, 2014). Once you have been labeled as mentally ill, people can interpret almost anything you do as a further manifestation of illness. You may do so yourself. Therapist Jack Huber (personal communication) says that if it were up to him, he would eliminate all the other diagnoses and just label *everyone* with "chronic human imperfection."

The most common disorders are anxiety disorders, mood disorders (e.g., depression), impulse control problems (including attention deficit disorder), and substance abuse, as shown in ▲ **Figure 15.2**. Throughout this chapter we shall discuss several of the common diagnoses listed in *DSM-5*, but remember that many troubled people don't exactly fit into any of them.

in closing module 15.1

Is Anyone Normal?

According to the studies described in this module, nearly half of all people in the United States will have a *DSM* disorder at some point in life. If those statistics are even close to accurate, one implication is obvious: Most of the people who qualify for a

psychological diagnosis are not a rare group who would stand out immediately from everyone else. At some point in your life, you may have a bout of psychological distress. If so, remember that you have plenty of company.

Summary

- *Defining mental illness.* The American Psychiatric Association defines mental disorder as a clinically significant disturbance in an individual's cognition, emotion regulation, or behavior. It is sometimes difficult to apply that definition, because of disagreements over what constitutes a significant disturbance. (page 483)
- *Views of abnormality.* In the past, people have described abnormal behavior in many ways, including spirit possession. The standard view today is that abnormal behavior results from a combination of biological, psychological, and social influences. (page 483)
- *Cultural influences.* A culture provides examples not only of how to behave normally but also of how to behave abnormally. (page 484)
- *The categorical approach.* The *Diagnostic and Statistical Manual of Mental Disorders (DSM-5)* lists possible diagnoses and the criteria for identifying each of them. (page 485)
- *Doubts about the categorical approach.* Most troubled people partly fit two or more diagnoses. Also, the genetic and environmental causes of various disorders overlap, and the treatment designed for one disorder may help with another. An alternative is to rate each person along several dimensions of distress. (page 485)

Key Terms

biopsychosocial model (page 484)

Diagnostic and Statistical Manual of Mental Disorders (DSM) (page 485)

personality disorder (page 486)

Review Questions

1. In what way does *DSM* help psychologists do research?
   (a) It tells researchers the correct way to do research.
   (b) It helps researchers find adequate samples of people with disorders.
   (c) It helps ensure that researchers identify each disorder in the same way.
   (d) It specifies the correct statistical tests to use in the research.

2. How, if at all, can therapists confirm which of two or more psychiatric diagnoses is the correct one?
   (a) An examination of the genes can determine the correct diagnosis.
   (b) Brain scans can confirm the correct diagnosis.
   (c) A blood test can confirm the correct diagnosis.
   (d) No available test can confirm one diagnosis over another.

3. Which of the following is a common criticism of *DSM*?
   (a) We don't really need to distinguish one disorder from another.
   (b) It includes only major disorders and not the common minor disorders.
   (c) It does not distinguish enough types of disorders.
   (d) It labels some nearly normal conditions as mental illnesses.

Answers: 1c, 2d, 3d.

module 15.2

Anxiety Disorders and Obsessive-Compulsive Disorder

After studying this module, you should be able to:

- Describe generalized anxiety disorder and panic disorder.
- Explain why learned avoidance responses are so resistant to extinction.
- Describe theoretically how classical conditioning could explain the onset of a phobia.
- Evaluate the limits of the classical conditioning explanation of phobia, citing observations that it does not easily explain.
- Describe obsessive-compulsive disorder.
- Explain how therapists treat phobias and obsessive-compulsive disorder.

You go to the beach, looking forward to an afternoon of swimming and surfing. Will you stay out of the water if someone tells you that a shark attacked a swimmer yesterday? What if the shark attack was a month ago? What if someone saw a small shark that did not attack anyone?

Staying out of the water because you see a shark is reasonable. Staying out because a small shark was present a few days ago is less sensible. If you refuse to look at ocean photographs because they might *remind* you of sharks, you have a serious problem. Excessive anxiety can interfere with life in many ways.

Disorders with Excessive Anxiety

Many psychological disorders are marked by anxiety and attempts to avoid anxiety. Anxiety is similar to fear, except that fear is tied to a specific situation. You might be afraid of a growling dog, but your fear subsides at a distance. Anxiety

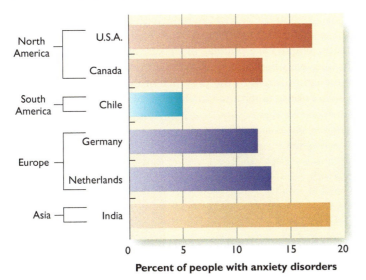

▲ **Figure 15.3** Percentage of people in six countries who have an anxiety disorder within a given year. (Based on data from "The prevalence of treated and untreated mental disorders in five countries," by R. V. Bijl, R. de Graaf, E. Hiripi, R. C. Kessler, R. Kohn, D. R. Offord, et al., 2003. *Health Affairs, 22,* pp. 122–133; and "Epidemiological study of prevalence of mental disorders in India," by M. S. Murali, 2001. *Indian Journal of Community Medicine, 26,* p. 198.)

is an apprehensive feeling you cannot easily escape. ▼ Figure 15.3 shows the prevalence of anxiety disorders in six countries (Bijl et al., 2003; Murali, 2001). Chapter 12 discussed post-traumatic stress disorder. Here we consider additional anxiety disorders.

Generalized Anxiety Disorder (GAD)

People with generalized anxiety disorder (GAD) have *frequent and exaggerated worries.* They worry that "I might get sick," "My daughter might get sick," "I might lose my job," or "I might not be able to pay my bills." Although they have no more reason for worry than anyone else, they grow so tense, irritable, and fatigued that they have trouble working, maintaining social relationships, or enjoying life (Henning, Turk, Mennin, Fresco, & Heimberg, 2007). Because anxiety is common in so many disorders, including depression, we could regard generalized anxiety as a symptom more than a disorder.

Panic Disorder (PD)

Suddenly, you feel warm all over. You breathe faster and faster, and your heart is pounding vigorously for no apparent reason. You feel dizzy and nauseated, you sweat profusely, and your hands are shaking. But within a few minutes, the episode is over and you feel normal again. No heart attack would end so quickly. What happened?

This description fits a panic attack. People with panic disorder (PD) *have frequent periods of anxiety and occasional attacks of panic—rapid breathing, increased heart rate, chest pains, sweating, faintness, and trembling.* Panic disorder occurs in 1 to 3 percent of adults at some time during their lives. It is more common in women than in men (Weissman, Warner, Wickramaratne, Moreau, & Olfson, 1997), and— like other anxiety disorders—it is more common in whites than in blacks (Gibbs et al., 2013; ▼ Figure 15.4). It is fairly common in adolescents and young adults, and its prevalence declines as people age (Swoboda, Amering, Windhaber, & Katschnig, 2003).

Several studies have shown a genetic contribution, although no single gene has a strong influence (Hettema, Neale, & Kendler, 2001; Kim, Lee, Yang, Hwang, & Yoon, 2009). People with *joint laxity* (the ability to bend fingers farther than usual, popularly called "double-jointedness") tend to experience more fears than average, and are more likely than

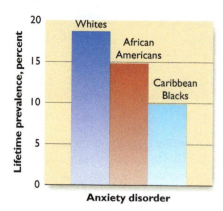

▲ **Figure 15.4** Lifetime prevalence of anxiety disorders for whites in the United States, African Americans, and Caribbean blacks who immigrated to the United States. (Based on data of Gibbs et al., 2013)

other people to develop anxiety disorders, especially panic disorder (Smith et al., 2014).

Panic disorder is linked to having strong autonomic responses, such as rapid heartbeat and **hyperventilation**, *rapid deep breathing*. Almost anything that causes hyperventilation makes the body react as if it were suffocating, thereby triggering other sympathetic nervous system responses such as sweating and increased heart rate (Coplan et al., 1998; Klein, 1993). Fluctuations in heart rate and breathing usually begin well before the panic attack itself—sometimes half an hour or more—even though the panic attack seems to occur suddenly and spontaneously (Meuret et al., 2011).

Many people with panic disorder also develop **agoraphobia** (from *agora*, the Greek word for "marketplace"), *an excessive fear of open or public places*, or **social phobia**, *a severe avoidance of other people and a fear of doing anything in public*. They develop these fears because they are afraid of being incapacitated or embarrassed by a panic attack in a public place. In a sense, they are afraid of their fear itself (McNally, 1990).

The usual treatment focuses on teaching the patient to control breathing and learning to relax (Marchand et al., 2008). Controlling stress helps also. A stressful experience doesn't trigger an immediate panic attack, but it increases the frequency of attacks over the next three months (Moitra et al., 2011). In addition, therapists help the person experience sweating and increased heart rate in a controlled setting, showing that they need not lead to a full-scale panic attack. Over a period of months, most patients can decrease or stop their panic attacks (Butler, Chapman, Forman, & Beck, 2006). However, panic disorder sometimes follows a pattern of remission and relapse—that is, disappearing for some time and then returning (Nay, Brown, & Roberson-Nay, 2013).

3. Why is agoraphobia common in people with panic disorder?

Answer

3. People with panic disorder avoid public places because they worry about embarrassing themselves by having a panic attack.

Phobia

Sometimes extreme efforts to avoid harm interfere with normal life. Let's begin with avoidance learning, which is relevant to phobias and compulsions. Suppose you learn to press a lever at least once every 10 seconds to avoid electric shocks. After you are responding consistently, the experimenter disconnects the shock generator without telling you. What will you do? You continue pressing, of course. As far as you can tell, nothing has changed, and the response still works! *Avoidance behaviors are highly resistant to extinction.*

You can see how this tendency would support superstitions. If you believe that Friday the 13th is dangerous, you are cautious on that day. If nothing goes wrong, you decide that your caution was successful. If a misfortune happens anyway, it confirms your belief that Friday the 13th is dangerous. As long as you continue an avoidance behavior, you never learn whether or not it is useful.

4. Suppose you are an experimenter, and you have trained someone to press a lever to avoid shocks. Now you disconnect the shock generator. Other than telling the person what you have done, how could you facilitate extinction of the lever pressing?

Answer

4. Temporarily prevent the person from pressing the lever. Only by ceasing to press it does the person discover that pressing is not necessary.

A **phobia** is *a fear that interferes with normal living*. It is not necessarily irrational. Many people have phobias of snakes, spiders, lightning, heights, and other items that really are dangerous. What is irrational is the degree of the fear, leading to extreme distress in the presence of the feared object. Most people with phobias are not so much afraid of the object itself but of their own reactions

Many people who watched the famous shower scene in the movie *Psycho* became afraid to take showers. Actress Janet Leigh, who portrayed the woman killed in that scene, subsequently avoided showers herself.

(Beck & Emery, 1985). They fear that they will have a heart attack or that they will embarrass themselves by trembling or fainting. Consequently, they vigorously avoid the object or any reminder of it.

Prevalence

According to a study of U.S. adults, about 11 percent of people suffer a phobia at some time in life, and 5 to 6 percent have a phobia at any given time (Magee, Eaton, Wittchen, McGonagle, & Kessler, 1996). However, phobias vary from mild to extreme, so the apparent prevalence depends on how many marginal cases we include. Common objects of phobias include public places, public speaking, heights, air travel, water travel, being observed by strangers, snakes or other dangerous animals, blood, and lightning storms (Cox, McWilliams, Clara, & Stein, 2003). Social phobia—avoidance of contact with unfamiliar people—is also common.

Acquiring Phobias

John B. Watson, one of the founders of behaviorism, was the first to argue that phobias and intense fears are learned (Watson & Rayner, 1920). To demonstrate the point, Watson set out to teach a child an intense fear. Today we would regard that plan as ethically dubious, but Watson worked before the day of institutional review boards that oversee research ethics. Watson and Rosalie Rayner studied an 11-month-old child, "Albert B.," who had previously shown no fear of animals (see ▼ Figure 15.5). They set a white rat in front of him and then struck a large steel bar behind him with a hammer. The sound made Albert whimper and cover his face. After a few repetitions, the presence of the rat made him cry and crawl away. Watson and Rayner declared that they had created a strong fear. Unfortunately, they made no attempt to extinguish it.

Almost a century later, scholars tried to discover Albert's true identity. An initial report pointed to Douglas Merritte, the young son of an unmarried woman who worked at Watson's university, Johns Hopkins. Merritte was almost exactly the same age as the child Watson and Rayner had described, so he seemed a likely candidate (Beck, Levinson, & Irons, 2009). However, a later study identified another child, also the son of an unmarried woman working

at Johns Hopkins. This child, named Albert Barger, was almost exactly the same age as Douglas Meritte, matched the weight that Watson had recorded for "Albert B.," and now seems almost certainly to have been the child Watson studied (Powell, Digdon, Harris, & Smithson, 2014).

Regardless of the identity of the child, and regardless of the questionable ethics and scientific weakness of the study, Watson and Rayner's explanation of phobias ignored important questions: First, why do many people develop phobias toward objects that have never injured them? Some people with phobias can indeed trace them to a specific frightening event (Kendler et al., 1995), but many other people cannot, and many people who do have traumatic experiences fail to develop phobias (Field, 2006). Genetic predisposition to fearfulness is part of the answer, though not the whole story (Van Houtem et al., 2013).

Furthermore, why are some phobias more common than others? And why are phobias so persistent?

5. **In classical conditioning terms, what was the conditioned stimulus (CS) in Watson and Rayner's experiment? The unconditioned stimulus (UCS)? The conditioned response (CR)? The unconditioned response (UCR)?**

Answer

5. The CS was the white rat. The UCS was the loud noise. The CR and the UCR were a combination of crying and other fear reactions.

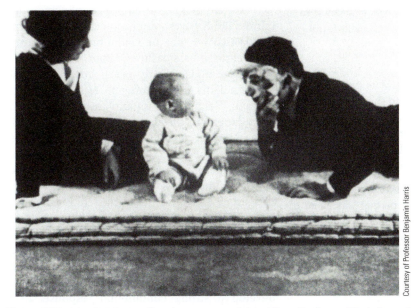

▲ **Figure 15.5** John B. Watson first demonstrated that Albert B. showed little fear of small animals. Then Watson paired a white rat with a loud, frightening noise. Albert became afraid of the white rat, as well as other small animals and odd-looking masks.

Courtesy of Professor Benjamin Harris

what's the evidence?

Learning Fear by Observation

Given that many people develop phobias without any traumatic experience, maybe they learn their phobias by watching others. Susan Mineka and her colleagues demonstrated that monkeys learn fears by observing other monkeys (Mineka, 1987; Mineka, Davidson, Cook, & Keir, 1984). This animal study sheds light on important human issues.

First Study

Hypothesis Monkeys that have seen other monkeys avoid a snake will develop a similar fear themselves.

Method Nearly all wild-born monkeys show a fear of snakes, but laboratory monkeys do not. Mineka put a laboratory-reared monkey with a wild-born monkey and let them both see a snake (see ▼ Figure 15.6). The lab monkey watched as the wild monkey shrieked and ran away. Later, Mineka tested the lab monkey's response to a snake.

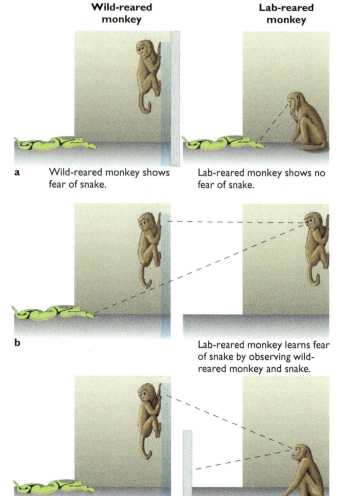

Wild-reared monkey   **Lab-reared monkey**

a   Wild-reared monkey shows fear of snake.   Lab-reared monkey shows no fear of snake.

b   Lab-reared monkey learns fear of snake by observing wild-reared monkey and snake.

c   Barrier masks snake from view of lab-reared monkey.   Lab-reared monkey does not learn fear when snake is not visible.

▲ **Figure 15.6** A lab-reared monkey learns to fear snakes from the reactions of a wild-reared monkey. But if the snake is not visible, the lab-reared monkey learns no fear.

Results When the lab monkey saw its partner shriek and run away from the snake, it too shrieked, ran away, and turned to see what it was that was frightening (see Figure 15.6b). ("Aha! Learned something today. Snakes are bad for monkeys.") It continued to fear the snake when tested by itself, even months later.

Interpretation The lab monkey may have learned a fear of snakes because it saw that its partner was afraid of snakes. But Mineka asked a further question: What was the critical experience—seeing the other monkey show fear *of snakes* or seeing the other monkey show fear *of anything*? To find out, Mineka conducted a second experiment.

Second Study

Hypothesis A monkey learns a fear from another monkey only if it sees *what* the other monkey fears.

Method A monkey reared in a lab watched a monkey reared in the wild through a window. The wild monkey saw a snake, and reacted with fear. The lab monkey saw the wild monkey's fear without seeing the snake. Later, the lab monkey was placed with a snake.

Results The lab monkey showed no fear of the snake.

Interpretation To develop a fear of snakes, the observer monkey needed to see that the other monkey was frightened of snakes, not just that it was frightened (see Figure 15.5c). Similarly, children learn fears by observing adults' fears (Dunne & Ashew, 2013).

Some Phobias Are More Common than Others

Imagine that you survey your friends. You can actually survey them, if you wish, but it's easy enough to imagine the results. You ask them:

- Are you afraid of snakes?
- Are you afraid of cars?
- Have you ever been bitten by a snake or seen someone else bitten?
- Have you ever been injured in a car accident or seen someone else injured?

You know what to expect. Far more people have been injured or seen someone injured by cars than by snakes, but far more are afraid of snakes than cars. Few people have phobias of cars, guns, tools, or electricity, even though they produce many injuries. When my son Sam was a toddler, three times that we know about he stuck his finger into an electric outlet. He even had a name for it: "Smoky got me again." But he never developed a fear of electricity or electric devices.

Why do people develop fears of some objects more readily than other objects? One explanation is that we may be evolutionarily prepared to learn certain fears easily (Öhman & Mineka, 2003; Seligman, 1971). Nearly every infant develops a fear of heights and of strangers, especially unfamiliar men. Heights and unfamiliar adult males have been dangerous throughout mammalian evolution. Less universal but still widespread are the fears of snakes, darkness, and confined spaces, which have been dangerous throughout primate (monkey and ape) evolution. Cars, guns, and electricity became dangerous only within the last few generations. Our predisposition to develop fears and phobias corresponds to how long various items have been dangerous in our evolutionary history (Bracha, 2006). In support of this idea, people who receive electric shocks paired with snake pictures quickly develop a strong conditioned response. People who receive shocks paired with pictures of houses show a much weaker response (Öhman, Eriksson, & Olofsson, 1975).

Many people are afraid of extreme heights, partly because the danger is hard to control.

a method of gradually exposing people to the object of their fear (Wolpe, 1961). Someone with a phobia of snakes, for example, is exposed to pictures of a snake in the reassuring environment of a therapist's office. The therapist might start with a cartoon drawing and gradually work up to a black-and-white photograph, a color photograph, and then a real snake (see ▼ Figure 15.7). Or the therapist might start with the snake itself (with the client's consent). The client is terrified at first, but the autonomic nervous system is not capable of sustaining a permanent panic. Gradually, the person becomes calmer and learns, "It's not that bad after all. Here I am, not far from that horrid snake, and I'm not having a heart attack." Getting the client to actively approach the feared object makes the procedure even more effective (Jones, Vilensky, Vasey, & Fazio, 2013).

Exposure therapy resembles Skinner's shaping procedure (Chapter 6). The person masters one step before going on to the next. If the distress becomes too great, the therapist then goes back several steps. Exposure is combined with social learning: The person with a phobia watches the therapist or other people display a fearless response to the object.

Most therapists do not keep handy a supply of snakes, spiders, and so forth. Increasingly, they use virtual reality (Coelho, Waters, Hine, & Wallis, 2009): The client wears a helmet that displays a virtual-reality scene, as shown in ▼ Figure 15.8. For example, a client with a phobia of heights can view going up a glass elevator or crossing a narrow bridge over a chasm. This technology provides control of the situation, including the option of quickly turning off the display. Research on this method has been limited, but so far it shows good success (McCann et al., 2014).

However, evolution is not the only explanation for why you learn a snake or spider fear more easily than a fear of houses. After all, you have often have often heard about the dangers of snake and spider bites (Tierney & Connolly, 2013). It is also easy to explain why snake phobias are more common than car or tool phobias (Mineka & Zinbarg, 2006). Okay, you have hurt yourself with tools and you have been in a car accident or seen others injured in a car accident. But how many times have you had safe experiences with tools and cars? In contrast, how often have you had safe experiences with snakes or spiders? What matters is not just the number of bad experiences but also the number of safe experiences.

Also, people most often develop phobias of objects that they cannot predict or control. If you are afraid of spiders, you must be constantly on the alert, because they could be anywhere. Lightning is also unpredictable and uncontrollable. In contrast, you don't have to worry that hammers, saws, or electric outlets will take you by surprise.

6. **Give three explanations for why more people develop phobias of snakes and spiders than of cars and guns.**

Answer

6. People may be born with a predisposition to learn fears of objects that have been dangerous throughout our evolutionary history. We more readily fear objects with which we have few safe experiences. We more readily fear objects that we cannot predict or control.

Treatment for Phobias

Phobias sometimes last for years. Remembering the discussion about avoidance learning, you see why phobias are difficult to extinguish: If you have learned to press a lever to avoid shock, you may not stop pressing long enough to find out that you no longer need to respond. Similarly, if you always avoid snakes, you don't learn that your avoidance is unnecessary or excessive.

The most successful type of therapy for phobia is exposure therapy, also known as systematic desensitization,

▲ **Figure 15.7** Here a therapist treats fear of water by exposing someone to the fear under calming conditions.

Although exposure therapy is highly effective, at least temporarily, phobias sometimes return. If you think about phobias as learned, and recall what Chapter 6 said about classical and operant conditioning, an explanation should be clear. Exposure therapy is extinction of the original learning, but extinction is merely a suppression of original learning, not an erasure of it. When time passes after an extinction procedure, spontaneous recovery is likely—that is, a return of the original learned response. In animal learning, a good way to minimize spontaneous recovery is to repeat the extinction procedure in several environments (Laborda & Miller, 2013). Similarly, exposure therapy is likely to be more effective if it is repeated in as many ways, places, and times as possible, even after the phobia appears to be gone.

▲ **Figure 15.8** Virtual reality lets a patient with a phobia of heights experience heights without leaving the therapist's office.

7. How does systematic desensitization resemble extinction of a learned shock-avoidance response?

Answer

7. To extinguish a learned shock-avoidance response, prevent the response so that the individual learns that a failure to respond is not dangerous. Similarly, in systematic desensitization, the patient is prevented from fleeing the feared stimulus. He or she learns that the danger is not as great as imagined.

Obsessive-Compulsive Disorder

People with **obsessive-compulsive disorder (OCD)** have two kinds of problems. An **obsession** is a *repetitive, unwelcome stream of thought*, such as worrying about doing something shameful. A **compulsion** is a *repetitive, almost irresistible action*. Obsessions generally lead to compulsions, as an itching sensation leads to scratching. For example, someone obsessed about dirt and disease develops compulsions of continual cleaning and washing. Someone obsessively worried about doing something shameful develops compulsive rituals that maintain rigorous self-control.

An estimated 2 to 3 percent of all people in the United States suffer from obsessive-compulsive disorder at some time in life, most of them to a mild degree, although the severe cases can be disabling (Karno, Golding, Sorenson, & Burnam, 1988). The usual age of onset is between the ages of 10 and 25. Twin studies indicate a moderate degree of genetic influence, but no single gene has been identified (Lopez-Sola et al., 2014).

Earlier editions of *DSM* listed OCD among the anxiety disorders, but *DSM-5* lists it separately. Although people with OCD do react strongly to threats,

they often report disgust more than anxiety (Pauls, Abramovitch, Rauch, & Geller, 2014). They also feel guilt over persistent impulses—perhaps an impulse to engage in a sexual act that they consider shameful, an impulse to hurt someone, or an impulse to commit suicide. In many cases these people believe that thinking something makes it more likely to happen, or that thinking about doing something contemptible is morally as bad as actually doing it (Coughtrey, Shafran, Lee, & Rachman, 2013). They decide, "I don't want to ever think that terrible thought again."

However, vigorously trying to avoid a thought makes it more intrusive. As a child, the Russian novelist Leo Tolstoy once organized a club with an unusual qualification for membership: A prospective member had to stand alone in a corner *without thinking about a white bear* (Simmons, 1949). If you think that sounds easy, try it. Ordinarily, you go months between thoughts about polar bears, but when you try *not* to think about them, you can think of little else.

Many kinds of compulsions occur. The most common compulsions are cleaning and checking. Another common one is counting one's steps, counting objects, or counting almost anything. One man with obsessive-compulsive disorder could not go to sleep at night until he had counted the corners of every object in the room to make sure that the total was evenly divisible by 16. Others have odd habits such as touching everything they see, trying to arrange objects in a completely symmetrical manner, or walking back and forth through a doorway nine times before leaving a building. Hoarding is another common compulsion.

Distrusting Memory

Many obsessive-compulsive people repeatedly check whether the doors and windows are locked and the water faucets

It's probably a long time since you last thought about polar bears. But see what happens if you are trying as hard as possible to *avoid* thinking about them.

This button says it all.

are turned off. But then they worry, "Did I *really* check them all, or did I only imagine it?" Because they distrust their memory, they check again and again.

Why do people with obsessive-compulsive disorder distrust their memory? Several studies found that repeated checking makes the memories less distinct! Suppose you check the kitchen stove to make sure it is turned off. Then you do it again and again several times. The more times you do it, the less distinctly you remember the most recent time you did so, and you might distrust your memory. Similar results have been reported for college students and for patients with obsessive-compulsive disorder (Radomsky, Dugas, Alcolado, & Lavoie, 2014; van den Hout & Kindt, 2003). A vicious cycle results: Because of repeated checking, you doubt your memory, and because you doubt your memory, you want to check again.

Therapies

Most people with obsessive-compulsive disorder eventually improve to some extent with or without treatment (Skoog & Skoog, 1999). Still, no one wants to wait years for recovery. The therapy best supported by the evidence is *exposure therapy with response prevention:* The person is simply prevented from performing the obsessive ritual (Rosa-Alcázar, Sánchea-Meca, Gómez-Conesa, & Marín-Martínez, 2008). Someone might be prevented from cleaning the house or checking the doors more than once before going to sleep. The point is to demonstrate that nothing catastrophic occurs if one leaves a little mess in the house or runs a slight risk of leaving a door unlocked.

However, although exposure therapy is the most successful procedure currently available, that is not saying much. People with OCD dislike the idea of stopping their rituals, and almost half quit the treatment without achieving any benefits. Many people respond well to a cognitive intervention to help them reinterpret their thoughts and images (Coughtrey et al., 2013). In some cases, antidepressant drugs also help.

8. **Suppose someone reports that a therapy lasting several years relieves many cases of obsessive-compulsive disorder. Should we be impressed? Why or why not?**

Answer

8. We should not be impressed. Over a long enough time, most people recover from obsessive-compulsive disorder, even without treatment.

---

in closing | module 15.2

Emotions and Avoidance

Phobias and obsessive-compulsive disorder illustrate some of the complex links between emotions and cognitions. People with phobias experience emotional attacks associated with a particular thought, image, or situation. People with obsessive-compulsive disorder experience repetitive thoughts that produce emotional distress. In both conditions, most people know that their reactions are exaggerated, but mere awareness of the problem does not correct it. Dealing with such conditions requires attention to emotions, cognitions, and the links between them.

Summary

- *Generalized anxiety disorder and panic disorder.* People with generalized anxiety disorder experience excessive anxiety much of the day, even when actual dangers are low. Panic disorder is characterized by episodes of disabling anxiety, high heart rate, and rapid breathing. (page 489)
- *Persistence of avoidance behaviors.* A learned shock-avoidance response can persist long after the possibility of shock has been removed. As with shock-avoidance responses, phobias persist because people do not discover that their avoidance behaviors are unnecessary. (page 490)
- *Phobia.* A phobia is a fear so extreme that it interferes with normal living. Phobias are learned through observation as well as through experience. (page 490)
- *Common phobias.* People are more likely to develop phobias of certain objects (e.g., snakes) than of others (e.g., cars). The most common objects of phobias have menaced humans throughout evolutionary history. They pose dangers that are difficult to predict or control, and we generally have few safe experiences with them. (page 492)
- *Exposure therapy.* A common therapy for phobia is exposure therapy, also known as systematic desensitization. The patient relaxes while being gradually exposed to the object of the phobia. (page 493)
- *Obsessive-compulsive disorder (OCD).* People with obsessive-compulsive disorder have distressing thoughts or impulses. Many also perform repetitive behaviors. (page 494)

- *Compulsive checking.* Compulsive checkers constantly double-check themselves and invent elaborate rituals. Repeatedly checking something leads to decreased confidence in the memory of having checked it. (page 495)
- *Treatments for OCD.* The most effective treatment is exposure to the source of distress while preventing the ritualized response. However, this treatment is often ineffective, partly because many patients refuse or quit the treatment. A valuable supplement is a cognitive intervention to help people reinterpret their thoughts and images. (page 495)

Key Terms

agoraphobia (page 490)

compulsion (page 494)

exposure therapy (page 493)

generalized anxiety disorder (GAD)
   (page 489)

hyperventilation (page 490)

obsession (page 494)

obsessive-compulsive disorder (OCD)
   (page 494)

panic disorder (PD) (page 489)

phobia (page 490)

social phobia (page 490)

systematic desensitization (page 493)

Review Questions

1. Panic disorder and other anxiety disorders are more common than average for which type of people?
   (a) They are more common in blacks than in whites.
   (b) They are more common in old people than in young people.
   (c) They are more common in women than in men.

2. Panic disorder and other anxiety disorders are more common than average for people with which of these physical conditions?
   (a) Joint laxity
   (b) Left-handedness
   (c) Curly hair
   (d) Near-sightedness

3. In avoidance learning, someone learns to make some response to avoid shock or other misfortune. What is unusual about this type of learning?
   (a) If the stimuli change even slightly, the response does not generalize.
   (b) After an interruption, rapid forgetting occurs.
   (c) Older individuals learn more rapidly than younger individuals.
   (d) This type of learning is highly resistant to extinction.

4. In Watson and Rayner's experiment, the conditioned stimulus was ____. The unconditioned stimulus was ____. The conditioned response was ____. (The unconditioned response was the same as the conditioned response.)
   (a) a loud noise . . . crying and other fear responses . . . a white rat
   (b) a white rat . . . crying and other fear responses . . . a loud noise

   (c) a loud noise . . . a white rat . . . crying and other fear responses
   (d) a white rat . . . a loud noise . . . crying and other fear responses

5. What did Mineka's experiments with monkeys show?
   (a) Monkeys are born with a fear of snakes.
   (b) Monkeys learn a fear of snakes only if a snake bites them.
   (c) Monkeys can learn a fear by observing another monkey's fear.
   (d) Monkeys work hard to overcome their fears.

6. The return of a phobia months or years after treatment with exposure therapy is comparable to which of these aspects of classical conditioning?
   (a) Stimulus generalization
   (b) Stimulus discrimination
   (c) Extinction
   (d) Spontaneous recovery

7. In what way do people with obsessive-compulsive disorder have an abnormal memory?
   (a) Their memory has low accuracy for the overall gist of events.
   (b) Their memory has low accuracy for details.
   (c) Their declarative memory is normal but their procedural memory is weak.
   (d) Their memory is normal but they have low confidence in their memory.

Answers: 1c, 2a, 3d, 4d, 5c, 6d, 7d.

module 15.3

Substance-Related Disorders

After studying this module, you should be able to:

- Define substance dependence or addiction.

- Explain why it is difficult to list what substances are or are not addictive.

- Discuss possible explanations for addiction.

- Describe a procedure to identify young people who may be at increased risk of alcohol abuse.

- Describe treatments for alcoholism and opiate abuse.

How would you like to volunteer for an experiment? I want to implant into your brain a little device that will automatically lift your mood. There are still a few kinks in it, but most people who have tried say that it makes them feel good at least some of the time, and some people like it a great deal.

I should tell you about the possible risks. My device will endanger your health and reduce your life expectancy. Some people believe it causes brain damage, but they haven't proved that charge, so I don't think you should worry about it. Your behavior will change a good bit, though. You may have difficulty concentrating, for example. The device affects some people more than others. If you happen to be strongly affected, you will have difficulty completing your education, getting or keeping a job, and carrying on a satisfactory personal life. But if you are lucky, you might avoid all that. Anyway, you can quit the experiment anytime you decide. You should know, though, that the longer the device remains in your brain, the harder it is to remove.

I cannot pay you for taking part in this experiment. In fact, you will have to pay me. But I'll give you a bargain rate: only $10 for the first week and then a little more each week as time passes. One other thing: Technically speaking, this experiment is illegal. We probably won't get caught, but if we do, we could both go to prison.

What do you say? Is it a deal? I presume you will say "no." I get very few volunteers. And yet, if I change the term *brain device* to *drug* and change *experiment* to *drug deal*, it is amazing how many volunteers come forward. Chapter 3 examined the effects of drugs on the brain and behavior. In this module, we focus on addiction.

Substance Dependence (Addiction)

Use and abuse of alcohol and other drugs come in all degrees, from occasional social drinking to ruinous problems. People who *are unable to* *quit a self-destructive habit* are said to have a dependence on or an addiction to it. Two major questions are what causes occasional drug use to develop into an overwhelming craving, and why some people are more vulnerable than others.

People who attend Alcoholics Anonymous for the first time often ask, "How can I tell whether I am an alcoholic?" You can consider yourself an alcoholic if you answer yes to these two questions: Does alcohol use cause serious trouble in your life? And do you sometimes decide you will quit after a certain amount, and then find yourself unable to stop at that point? The same questions apply to drug abuse and any other addiction.

Almost all addictive drugs increase the release of dopamine in a small brain area called the *nucleus accumbens,* which is apparently critical for attention and reinforcement. It is reasonable to describe addiction as something that monopolizes someone's attention (Berridge & Robinson, 1998; Koob & LeMoal, 1997; Robinson & Berridge, 2000). ▼ Figure 15.9 shows the location of the nucleus accumbens.

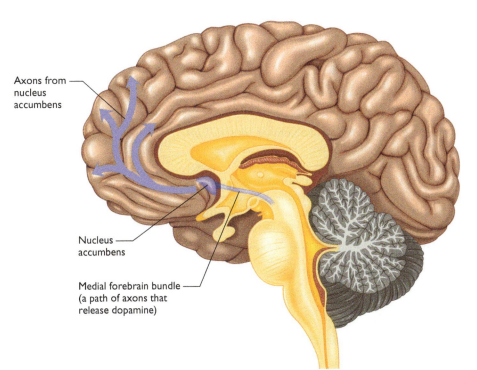

Axons from nucleus accumbens

Nucleus accumbens

Medial forebrain bundle (a path of axons that release dopamine)

▲ **Figure 15.9** The nucleus accumbens is a small brain area that is critical for the motivating effects of many experiences, including drugs, food, and sex. Most abused drugs increase the activity of the neurotransmitter dopamine in this area.

However, beware of assuming that the release of dopamine in the nucleus accumbens causes addiction. For example, compulsive gambling and video game playing have much in common with drug addictions (Gentile, 2009). After they have become addictive, they release dopamine in the nucleus accumbens (Ko et al., 2009; Koepp et al., 1998), but it would be misleading to say they became addictive *because* they release dopamine.

It is hard to put limits on what can or cannot be an addictive substance. In a hospital ward where alcoholics were being treated, one patient moved his bed into the men's room (Cummings, 1979). At first, the hospital staff ignored his curious behavior. Then, more and more patients moved their beds into the men's room. Eventually, the staff discovered what was happening. These men, deprived of alcohol, had found that by drinking about 30 liters of water per day and urinating the same amount (which was why they moved into the men's room), they could alter the acid-to-base balance of their blood enough to produce a sensation like drunkenness. (Do *not* try this yourself. Some people have died from an overdose of water.)

9. Why is it probably pointless to distinguish between substances that are and are not addictive?

Answer

9. Some people show addictions to gambling or video games, which are not substances at all. Some have managed to abuse water.

What Motivates Addictive Behavior?

The motives for initial use of alcohol or other drugs differ from those of addiction. People drink alcohol for pleasure, to relax, or to suppress social anxieties (Terlecki & Buckner, 2015). An addiction is more insistent. Terry Robinson and Kent Berridge (2000, 2001) distinguish between "liking" and "wanting." Ordinarily, you like the things you want, but not always. You might want a healthy diet but not like it, or you might like spending money but do not want to. Addicted drug users get much less pleasure ("liking") than they used to, but they continue to want the drug anyway. Why do addictive behaviors continue with such intensity?

One reason is to escape unpleasant feelings. Abstaining from a drug leads to withdrawal symptoms. Withdrawal symptoms from prolonged alcoholism include sweating, nausea, sleeplessness, and sometimes hallucinations and seizures. With opiate drugs, withdrawal symptoms include anxiety,

restlessness, vomiting, diarrhea, and sweating. Consistent cigarette smokers experience unpleasant mood when they abstain (Baker et al., 2012). Someone who *uses a drug to reduce unpleasant withdrawal symptoms* is said to have a physical dependence. However, physical dependence cannot be the whole explanation for addiction. Many users feel strong cravings long after the end of their withdrawal symptoms. A psychological dependence is a *strong desire for something without withdrawal symptoms.* For example, habitual gamblers have a psychological dependence. A psychological dependence can be extremely insistent, and the distinction between physical and psychological dependence is not always helpful.

Also, someone who takes a drug to relieve withdrawal symptoms learns its power to relieve distress, and then begins using it to relieve other kinds of displeasure. People who have quit drugs often relapse during periods of financial or social difficulties (Baker, Piper, McCarthy, Majeskie, & Fiore, 2004). Even a brief, mild stress, such as seeing unpleasant photos or remembering an unpleasant experience increases a smoker's urge to smoke (McKee et al., 2010; Vinci, Copeland, & Carrigan, 2011).

The relief-from-distress explanation works, but it seems incomplete. People often use a substance so obsessively that its effect on their lives produces more distress than it relieves. Neuroscientists have demonstrated that when an addictive behavior bombards the nucleus accumbens with massive amounts of dopamine, it stimulates synaptic changes of the same type that occur in learning. For example, after repeated cocaine use, the synapses learn to respond strongly to cocaine and reminders of cocaine, but they decrease their response to other reinforcers. The result is a craving for cocaine and decreased interest in most other activities (Lubman et al., 2009; Mameli & Lüscher, 2011). Cocaine use then becomes the only efficient way to produce the synaptic activities normally associated with pleasure (Willuhn, Burgeno, Groblewski, & Phillips, 2014). Similarly, people with nicotine addiction or other addictions report less than average enjoyment from the usual pleasures of life (Leventhal et al., 2014). Researchers have said that addiction "hijacks" the brain areas that are important for motivation and attention (Kalivas, Volkow, & Seamans, 2005; Liu, Pu, & Poo, 2005; Volkow et al., 2006).

Okay, but one problem with that statement: Saying that an addiction hijacks those brain areas makes the situation sound hopeless. Many young people who abuse alcohol or other drugs manage to quit or greatly reduce their use by age 30, even without treatment (Heyman, 2011). Even of those who don't quit early, some quit later (Genberg et al., 2011). Quitting is more likely for marijuana or amphetamine users than for heroin or cocaine users, but even for the most powerful addictions, persistent lifetime addiction is not inevitable (Calabria et al., 2010).

10. After people have quit an addiction, when are they most likely to resume the habit?

Answer

10. People are most likely to relapse into an addictive habit during times of high stress.

Alcoholism

Alcohol can be a source of pleasure in moderation, or a path to ruin in excess. Alcoholism is *the habitual overuse of alcohol.* Treating alcoholism is difficult, and the success rate is not impressive. If we could identify young people who are at high risk for alcoholism, perhaps we could initiate effective prevention. At least, psychologists would like to try.

Genetics and Family Background

Twin studies indicate a substantial genetic influence on abuse of alcohol or other drugs, in combination with environmental influences, especially the influence of neighborhood quality (Kendler, Maes, Sundquist, Ohlsson, & Sundquist, 2014; Liu, Blacker, Xu, Fitzmaurice, Lyons, & Tsuang, 2004). A genetic predisposition contributes most strongly to early-onset alcoholism. Late-onset alcoholism develops gradually over the years, affects about as many women as men, is generally less severe, and often occurs in people with no family history of alcoholism. Early-onset alcoholism develops rapidly, usually by age 25, occurs more often in men than women, is usually more severe, and shows a stronger genetic basis (Devor, Abell, Hoffman, Tabakoff, & Cloninger, 1994; McGue, 1999). Naturally, not everyone with alcoholism fits neatly into one category or the other.

Although many genes contribute in small ways, only one is known to produce effects large enough to produce results that are easily replicated. That gene affects the liver's ability to metabolize alcohol. The liver converts alcohol into a toxic substance, *acetaldehyde* (ASS-eh-TAL-de-HIDE), and then uses another enzyme to convert acetaldehyde into harmless *acetic acid*. However, people vary in the gene for that second enzyme. Those with one form of that gene are slow to convert acetaldehyde into acetic acid. If they drink much at a time, they accumulate acetaldehyde, feel ill, and experience an intense hangover. Consequently, they learn to avoid excessive alcohol (Biernacka et al., 2013). Nearly half of Southeast Asians have that form of the gene, and relatively few Asians become alcoholics or binge drinkers (Harada, Agarwal, Goedde, Tagaki, & Ishikawa, 1982; Luczak et al., 2014).

Alcoholism, of course, depends on the environment also. The prevalence of alcoholism and other kinds of substance abuse varies among cultures and subcultures. For example, alcoholism is more prevalent in Irish culture, which tolerates heavy drinking, than among Jews or Italians, who emphasize drinking in moderation (Cahalan, 1978; Vaillant & Milofsky, 1982). The incidence of alcoholism is greater than average among people who grew up in families marked by conflict, hostility, and inadequate parental supervision (Schulsinger, Knop, Goodwin, Teasdale, & Mikkelsen, 1986). Women who were sexually abused

Alcohol abuse is more common in cultures that tolerate it, such as the Irish, than in cultures that emphasize moderation.

in childhood are at increased risk for alcoholism (Kendler, Bulik, et al., 2000). Depression and alcohol abuse often go together (Creswell, Chung, Clark, & Martin, 2014).

Furthermore, individuals differ. Not all children of alcoholic parents become alcoholics themselves, and not all children who grow up in a culture that tolerates heavy drinking become alcoholics. Can we identify individuals who are highly vulnerable to alcoholism?

what's the evidence?

Predicting Alcoholism

Perhaps people's behavior might indicate who is more likely to develop alcoholism. Several studies found that many alcoholics have difficulty estimating their own degree of intoxication. This study tested whether young drinkers who underestimate their intoxication are more likely than others to become alcoholics later in life (Schuckit & Smith, 1997).

Hypothesis Men who underestimate their intoxication after moderate drinking are more likely than others to develop alcoholism later.

Method This study was limited to 18- to 25-year-old men with a close relative who was alcoholic. Presumably, many of them had a genetic predisposition toward alcoholism. After each of them drank a fixed amount of alcohol, they were asked to walk and to describe how intoxicated they felt. Experimenters measured the stagger or sway when the men walked. Ten years later, the experimenters located as many of these men as possible and interviewed them about their alcohol use.

Results Of the 81 who either did not sway much when walking or stated that they did not feel intoxicated, 51 (63 percent) became alcoholics within 10 years. Of those who clearly swayed and reported feeling intoxicated, 9 of 52 (17 percent) became alcoholics (Schuckit & Smith, 1997).

Interpretation Someone who drinks a moderate amount and starts to stagger and feel intoxicated may stop drinking at that point. Someone who shows less effect thinks, "I hold my liquor well," and continues drinking. By the time he begins to stagger, he may have drunk enough to impair his judgment. Later studies confirmed that people who don't show much effect of alcohol on their movement nevertheless show as much effect as anyone else on their cognition and self-control (Fillmore & Weafer, 2012; Miller, Hays, & Fillmore, 2012).

Although the original study examined only men, a later study found similar results for women: Women with a family history of alcoholism are more likely than average to report low intoxication and experience little body sway after drinking a moderate amount (Eng, Schuckit, & Smith, 2005).

Measuring people's body sway as they walk after drinking is a time-consuming process. Later research found it possible to achieve similar result just by asking people a few questions, such as how many drinks before you feel dizzy, how many before you stumble when walking, and how many before you slur your speech. Those who report needing more drinks to produce these effects are more likely than average to become heavy drinkers in the next few years as well as decades later (Schuckit et al., 2007; Schuckit & Smith, 2013).

concept check

11. What is one way to predict which young people will later become heavy drinkers?

Answer

11. Measure the amount of body sway after drinking, or ask people to report how many drinks they need to experience various effects. People who report experiencing little effect from a moderate amount of alcohol are more likely than average to become heavy drinkers.

Treatments

My mind is a dark place, and I should not be left alone there at night.
—Participant at Alcoholics Anonymous meeting

Of all the people who try to quit alcohol or other drugs on their own, an estimated 10 to 20 percent manage to succeed (S. Cohen et al., 1989), though many of them quit and relapse repeatedly before eventual success. However, many other people find that they cannot quit a substance abuse problem on their own. Eventually, they "hit bottom," discovering that they have damaged their health, their ability to hold a job, and their relationships with friends and family. At that point, they might seek help. Let's consider several options.

Alcoholics Anonymous

The most popular treatment for alcoholism in North America is Alcoholics Anonymous (AA), *a self-help group of people who are trying to abstain from alcohol use and help others do the same.* AA meetings take place in community halls, church basements, and other available spaces. The meeting format varies but often includes study of the book *Alcoholics Anonymous* (Anonymous, 1955) and discussions of participants' individual problems. Some meetings feature an invited speaker. The group has a strong spiritual focus, including a reliance on "a Power greater than ourselves," but no affiliation with any particular religion. Although AA imposes no requirements on its members other than making an

effort to quit alcohol, new members are strongly encouraged to attend 90 meetings during the first 90 days. The idea is to make a strong commitment. From then on, members attend as often as they like.

Millions of people have participated in the AA program. One reason for its appeal is that all its members have had similar experiences. If someone makes an excuse for drinking and says, "You just don't understand how I feel," others can retort, "Oh, yes we do!" A member who feels the urge to take a drink can phone a fellow member day or night for support. However, the other member offers support, not pampering. Fellow members help someone resist the urge to drink, but generally won't do much for someone who is already drunk. The only charge is a voluntary contribution toward the cost of renting the meeting place. AA has inspired Narcotics Anonymous (NA) and other "anonymous" self-help groups that help compulsive gamblers, compulsive eaters, and others.

Researchers find that people who regularly attend AA or NA meetings, and who have a strong commitment to the program, are more likely than other addicts to abstain from alcohol and drugs (Gossop, Stewart, & Marsden, 2008; Laffaye, McKellar, Ilgen, & Moos, 2008). However, we cannot draw a cause-and-effect conclusion. Presumably, people who attend regularly differ in many ways from those who decline to participate or who try a few times and then quit.

Antabuse

Many years ago, investigators noticed that the workers in a certain rubber manufacturing plant drank very little alcohol. The investigators linked this behavior to *disulfiram*, a chemical that was used in the manufacturing process. As mentioned, the liver converts alcohol into a toxic substance, acetaldehyde, and then converts acetaldehyde into acetic acid. Disulfiram blocks the conversion of acetaldehyde to acetic acid. When the workers exposed to disulfiram drank alcohol, they accumulated acetaldehyde, became ill, suffered hangovers, and learned to avoid alcohol.

Disulfiram, available under the trade name Antabuse, is sometimes used in treating alcoholism. *Alcoholics who take a daily Antabuse pill become sick if they have a drink.* The threat of sickness is more effective than the sickness itself (Fuller & Roth, 1979). By taking a daily Antabuse pill, a recovering alcoholic renews the decision not to drink. Anyone who takes a drink in spite of the threat becomes ill, and then either decides not to drink again . . . or decides not to take the pill again! Several other medications are also moderately effective in helping people quit alcohol. In each case, the medication is most effective for people who are strongly motivated to quit (Krishnan-Sarin, Krystal, Shi, Pittman, & O'Malley, 2007; Mason, Goodman, Chabac, & Lehert, 2006).

concept check

12. Why is it difficult to determine the effectiveness of Alcoholics Anonymous through experimental research?

Answer

12. Because Alcoholics Anonymous is a voluntary organization, people cannot be randomly assigned to participate or not participate.

Contingency Management

Another approach to treating alcoholism and other addictions is *contingency management.* Practitioners monitor alcohol use by a Breathalyzer or other drugs by urine samples. Whenever the test shows no alcohol or drugs, a therapist provides an immediate reinforcement, such as a movie pass or a voucher for a pizza.

The effectiveness of contingency management is surprising, as the rewards are small. That is, people could have abstained from alcohol and drugs and then used the money they saved to give themselves the same or greater rewards.

Evidently, there is something powerful about testing negative for drugs and then receiving an immediate reinforcement.

Opiate Dependence

Prior to 1900, opiate drugs such as morphine and heroin were considered less dangerous than alcohol (Siegel, 1987). In fact, many doctors urged patients with alcoholism to switch from alcohol to morphine. Then, around 1900, opiates became illegal in the United States, except by prescription to control pain. Opiate dependence generally has a more rapid onset than alcohol or tobacco dependence.

Treatments

Some people who are trying to quit heroin or other opiates turn to self-help groups, contingency management, and other treatments. Therapists emphasize the importance of identifying the locations and situations in which someone has the greatest cravings, and then trying to minimize exposure to those situations (Witkiewitz & Marlatt, 2004).

For those who cannot quit, researchers have sought to find a less dangerous substitute that would satisfy the craving for opiates. Heroin was originally introduced as a substitute for morphine before physicians discovered that it is even more troublesome.

The drug methadone (METH-uh-don) *is sometimes offered as a substitute for opiates.* Chemically similar to morphine and heroin, methadone can be addictive also, but it is considered a safer addiction. ■ Table 15.3 compares methadone and morphine. When methadone is taken as a pill, it enters the bloodstream gradually and departs gradually. (If morphine or heroin is taken as a pill, much

Ed Kashi/Terra/Corbis

Heroin withdrawal resembles a week-long bout of severe flu, with aching limbs, intense chills, vomiting, and diarrhea. Unfortunately, even after people have endured withdrawal, they still sometimes crave the drug.

of it is digested without reaching the brain.) Thus, methadone does not produce the "rush" associated with injected opiates, and therefore does not strongly interfere with important behaviors, such as keeping a job. Methadone satisfies the craving and blocks heroin or morphine from reaching the same receptors. However, methadone does not eliminate the addiction. People who try to reduce their use of methadone generally report that their drug craving returns. The drugs *buprenorphine* and *levo-α-acetylmethadol acetate* (LAAM) have effects similar to methadone.

Table 15.3 Comparison of Methadone and Morphine			
	Morphine	Methadone by Injection	Methadone Taken Orally
Addictive?	Yes	Yes	Weakly
Onset	Rapid	Rapid	Slow
"Rush"?	Yes	Yes	No
Relieves craving?	Yes	Yes	Yes
Rapid withdrawal symptoms?	Yes	Yes	No

concept check

13. **Many methadone clinics carefully watch patients while they are taking their pills. Why?**

Answer

13. Someone who didn't swallow the pill could dissolve it in water and inject it to get a "high" similar to that of heroin or morphine.

Substances, the Individual, and Society

Substance abuse is a big problem for everyone because of its link to crime, unemployment, drunk driving, and other threats to society. In the 1970s, the United States government declared a "war on drugs." Decades later, it seems unlikely that we shall ever declare victory in that war. Fighting addiction is more like

fighting weeds in your garden. You can never expect to eliminate all weeds forever. Your best hope is to suppress the weeds enough that they don't seriously interfere with the plants you are trying to cultivate.

Summary

- *Substance dependence.* People who find it difficult or impossible to stop using a substance are said to be dependent on or addicted to it. (page 497)
- *Addictive substances.* Addictive substances stimulate dopamine synapses in the nucleus accumbens, a brain area that is associated with attention. After people develop a compulsive habit of gambling, video game playing, or other activities, those activities also elicit dopamine release in the nucleus accumbens. (page 497)
- *Motivations behind addiction.* People with an addiction continue a habit even though they recognize that it does them more harm than good. Reasons for continued use include avoiding withdrawal symptoms and coping with distress. Also, addictive substances alter the brain's synapses to increase response to substance-related experiences and decrease response to other activities. In spite of all this, some people do manage to quit. (page 498)
- *Predisposition to alcoholism.* People who have less than average intoxication from moderate drinking are more likely than average to become heavy drinkers. (page 499)
- *Alcoholics Anonymous.* The self-help group Alcoholics Anonymous provides the most common treatment for alcoholism in North America. (page 500)
- *Antabuse.* Some alcoholics are treated with Antabuse, a prescription drug that makes them ill if they drink alcohol. (page 500)
- *Contingency management.* Rewarding people for abstaining from drugs is sometimes effective. (page 500)
- *Opiate abuse.* Some opiate users manage to quit. Others substitute methadone or buprenorphine under medical supervision. (page 501)

Key Terms

Alcoholics Anonymous (AA) (page 500)

alcoholism (page 498)

Antabuse (page 500)

dependence (or addiction) (page 497)

methadone (page 501)

physical dependence (page 498)

psychological dependence (page 498)

Review Questions

1. Nearly all addictive substances and addictive behaviors affect the brain in what way?
   (a) They cause a shift of blood flow toward mainly the right hemisphere.
   (b) They increase release of the neurotransmitter dopamine in certain brain areas.
   (c) They increase the velocity of action potentials.
   (d) They increase the rate at which nutrients cross the blood–brain barrier.

2. What happens in the brain when people repeatedly use cocaine?
   (a) Synapses in the nucleus accumbens respond less than usual to other reinforcers.
   (b) With each use of cocaine, it releases more and more dopamine in the nucleus accumbens.
   (c) Eventually the drug damages the nucleus accumbens so that it no longer responds to anything.
   (d) Cocaine begins releasing serotonin as well as dopamine in the nucleus accumbens.

3. Which of the following is true, on average, for young people who will later become heavy drinkers?
   (a) Moderate amounts fail to relieve their stress.
   (b) They show less than average body sway after drinking a moderate amount.
   (c) They sleep more than average, and sounds do not arouse them during sleep.
   (d) They tend to eat a diet with more protein than carbohydrates.

4. How does Antabuse (disulfiram) help someone quit alcohol?
   (a) It alters the taste buds.
   (b) It increases synaptic activity in the prefrontal cortex.
   (c) It blocks the breakdown of acetaldehyde.
   (d) It acts as an antidepressant.

5. What would happen if a heroin addict dissolved methadone in water and injected it, instead of swallowing it as a pill?
   (a) It would produce a "high" similar to that of heroin.
   (b) It would have no effect.
   (c) It would be fatal.
   (d) It would satisfy the craving for heroin without producing a "high."

Answers: 1b, 2a, 3b, 4c, 5a.

Mood Disorders, Schizophrenia, and Autism

After studying this module, you should be able to:

• Describe the symptoms and possible causes of major depression.

• Evaluate the advantages and disadvantages of several treatments for major depression.

• Distinguish bipolar disorder from major depression.

• List the primary symptoms of schizophrenia.

• Discuss evidence for a genetic basis of schizophrenia.

• State the neurodevelopmental hypothesis of schizophrenia, and cite evidence that supports it.

• Describe therapies for schizophrenia.

• Describe and discuss autism spectrum disorder.

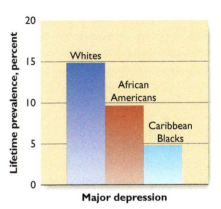

▲ **Figure 15.11** Lifetime prevalence of major depression for whites in the United States, African Americans, and Caribbean blacks who immigrated to the United States. (Based on data of Gibbs et al., 2013)

All psychological disorders range in severity, but depression, bipolar disorder, and schizophrenia are the most likely to become severe. We shall consider these conditions, along with autism, another condition that often produces long-term disability.

Depression

People sometimes call themselves depressed when they mean that they are discouraged or disappointed. A **major depression** is a *more extreme condition lasting weeks at a time, during which the person experiences little interest, pleasure, or motivation.* Sadness is characteristic of depression, but lack of happiness is even more characteristic. Many people with depression say they cannot even imagine anything that would make them happy. In one study, people had a beeper that alerted them at unpredictable times to make a note of what they were doing and how they felt about it. People with depression reported about an average number of sad experiences but few happy experiences (Peters, Nicolson, Berkhof, Delespaul, & deVries, 2003).

Nearly all people experiencing depression have sleep abnormalities (Carroll, 1980; Healy & Williams, 1988) (see ▼ Figure 15.10). They enter REM sleep

much faster than average. They wake up early and cannot get back to sleep. Two longitudinal studies found that adolescents who had trouble sleeping were more likely than average to become depressed later (Roane & Taylor, 2008; Roberts & Duong, 2014).

About 20 percent of U.S. adults are depressed at some time in life (Kessler, Berglund, Demler, Jin, & Walters, 2005). The reported prevalence varies greatly among countries, but the standards for diagnosis may not be the same everywhere. Women experience depression more than men in all cultures for which we have data (Culbertson, 1997; Cyranowski, Frank, Young, & Shear, 2000; Silberg et al., 1999).

The second module of this chapter noted that anxiety disorders are more common for whites than blacks in the United States. The same is true of depression, as shown in ▲ Figure 15.11 (Gibbs et al., 2013). That result is surprising, because stressful experiences increase the probability of depression, and on average blacks in the United States face stressful experiences more often than whites do. The explanation cannot be that blacks fail to get diagnosed, because the statistics come from extensive surveys of representative populations, not from therapists' records. Many have suggested that blacks benefit from greater social support, but data from a national survey found little difference in support received from family and friends (Mouzon, 2013, 2014). James Jackson and colleagues have suggested another possible explanation:

Normal sleep

◀ 90 minutes ▶

Depressed sleep

◀ 90 minutes ▶

▲ **Figure 15.10** During a bout of depression, people enter REM sooner than average and awaken frequently during the night.

Many poor blacks live in neighborhoods with much access to alcohol, cigarettes, and fattening foods but little availability of fresh fruits and vegetables. When faced with stress, they are likely to drink, smoke, and overeat high-fat foods—behaviors that are terrible for physical health, but sometimes effective in combating stress. In support of this hypothesis, they found that blacks with the poorest health behaviors were the least likely to react to stressful events by becoming depressed (Mezuk et al., 2010).

Although depression is a widespread problem, the good news is that few people remain permanently depressed. Typically, people have an episode of depression that lasts a few months (less commonly, years) and then they recover. However, the depression may return. Later episodes tend to be briefer but more frequent (Solomon et al., 1997). Typically, an intensely stressful event such as divorce or the death of a close loved one triggers the first episode of depression, but later episodes may occur with less provocation. It is as if the brain learns how to become depressed (Monroe & Harkness, 2005; Post, 1992). The same is true for epilepsy and migraine headaches: The more episodes one has had, the easier it is to have another one.

In a related condition, seasonal affective disorder (SAD), *people repeatedly become depressed during a particular season of the year.* It is common in Scandinavia, which has many hours of sunlight in summer and few in winter (Haggarty et al., 2002), and it is almost universal among explorers who spend long times in Antarctica (Palinkas, 2003). Although annual winter depressions receive the most publicity, annual summer depressions also occur (Faedda et al., 1993). The most effective treatment for seasonal affective disorder is exposure to a bright light for a few hours each day (Wirz-Justice, 1998). Exactly how the light produces its benefits is uncertain, but the benefits often occur rapidly, within a week.

14. How does major depression differ from sadness or discouragement?

Answer

14. Major depression is more severe than sadness and lasts months. A person with major depression finds almost no pleasure in anything.

Environmental and Genetic Influences on Depression

Depression often begins after a stressful event, especially interpersonal stress, such as the sudden death of a loved one or a feeling of rejection by a loved one (Slavich & Irwin, 2014). Still, some people become depressed more easily than others. The role of genetics is far from clear. Although studies of twins and relatives of patients with depression indicate a moderate degree of heritability (Wilde et al., 2014), extensive research on the chromosomes of thousands of people failed to identify a gene with a major effect (Major Depressive Disorder Working Group, 2013). Perhaps many uncommon genes are capable of leading to depression, or perhaps the explanation lies with epigenetics instead of chromosomal changes.

Another hypothesis is that certain genes, such as one gene that influences serotonin levels in the brain, increase the risk of depression only in people who endured major stressful experiences. After one study reported this finding (Caspi et al., 2003), many researchers attempted to replicate it, some successfully and some not (Karg, Burmeister, Shedden, & Sen, 2011). The problems with this type of research include both the difficulty of measuring depression and the difficulty of measuring stress. One study suggested that the gene in question increases the risk of depression only after interpersonal stress (death of a loved one, divorce, social rejection, etc.), and not after other types of stress (Vrshek-Schallhorn et al., 2014).

Most people with depression have relatives with depression (Kendler, Gardner, & Prescott, 1999; Lyons et al., 1998), and also relatives with other problems, such as substance abuse, antisocial personality disorder, attention deficit disorder, bulimia nervosa, migraine headaches, asthma, arthritis, and others (Fu et al., 2002; Hudson et al., 2003; Kendler et al., 1995). Many people recover from depression and then later develop anxiety disorders, substance abuse, or an eating disorder (Melvin et al., 2013). In other words, the genes or other factors that predispose to depression increase vulnerability to many disorders, not just depression.

Apparently, one thing depression has in common with so many other disorders is inflammation. Recall from Chapter 12 that highly stressful experiences activate certain aspects of the immune system, preparing the body to attack an infection. In a stressful situation, your body reacts as if it expects to be injured, and it prepares to fight the infection. The immune system increases the release of cytokines that fight infection and produce inflammation, but they also conserve energy by producing sleepiness, inactivity, and loss of appetite. Prolonged release of inflammatory cytokines can lead to depression, or to asthma, arthritis,

Smithsonian American Art Museum, Washington, DC/Art Resource, NY

Depression is most common among people who have little social support.

or other disorders (Slavich & Irwin, 2014). Many treatments that decrease inflammation also help relieve depression (Miller, Maletic, & Raison, 2009).

15. Evidently some of the same factors that lead to depression can also lead to other disorders. How might that fact complicate the search for genes linked to depression?

Answer

15. Researchers compare the genes of people with depression to those without depression. If certain genes sometimes lead to depression and sometimes lead to different problems, then the genes linked to depression will also show up frequently in the population of people without depression.

Treatments for Major Depression

The common treatments for depression are antidepressant medications and psychotherapy. Much research has addressed the effectiveness of each.

Antidepressant Medications

Three common classes of antidepressants are tricyclics, serotonin reuptake inhibitors, and monoamine oxidase inhibitors. Tricyclic drugs *interfere with the axon's ability to reabsorb the neurotransmitters dopamine, norepinephrine, and serotonin after releasing them* (see ▼ Figure 15.12b). Thus, tricyclics prolong the effect of these neurotransmitters at the synapses. Selective serotonin reuptake inhibitors (SSRIs) (e.g., fluoxetine, trade name Prozac) have a similar effect, but *block reuptake of only serotonin.* Monoamine (MAHN-oh-ah-MEEN) oxidase inhibitors (MAOIs) *block the metabolic breakdown of dopamine, norepinephrine, and serotonin* by the enzyme monoamine oxidase (MAO) (see ▼ Figure 15.12c). Thus, MAOIs also increase the effects of these neurotransmitters. People taking MAOIs must be careful with their diet, avoiding red wine, raisins, and many kinds of cheese. Psychiatrists seldom prescribe MAOIs except for patients who did not respond to the other drugs.

Based on these descriptions of antidepressants, researchers long assumed that the cause of depression was inadequate release of serotonin or other transmitters. However, antidepressant drugs alter synaptic activity within an hour

or so, whereas mood improvement begins two to three weeks later. Evidently the effect on serotonin and other transmitters is not the whole explanation of how the drugs work. It may not even be relevant. In addition to altering the neurotransmitters, prolonged use of antidepressants increases production of a chemical called BDNF (brain-derived neurotrophic factor) that over a period of weeks leads to the birth of new neurons in the hippocampus, expansion of dendrites, and improved learning (Drzyzga, Marcinowska, & Obuchowicz, 2009; Vetencourt et al, 2008). (Depression is associated with impaired learning and decreased cell growth in the hippocampus.) Those changes in the hippocampus may be the main reason for how antidepressants help, although researchers are not yet certain.

16. Tricyclics and SSRIs block reuptake of neurotransmitters. Which other drugs, discussed in Chapter 3, block reuptake also?

Answer

16. Cocaine and methylphenidate (Ritalin), discussed in Chapter 3) also block reuptake of neurotransmitters. However, the antidepressant drugs produce slower and milder effects.

Depressed Cognition and Cognitive Therapy

Suppose you fail a test. Choose your probable explanation:

- The test was difficult. Probably other students did poorly, too.

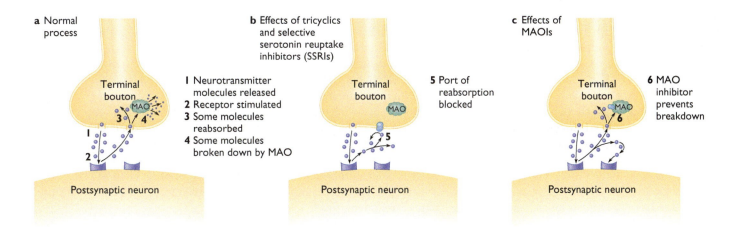

▲ **Figure 15.12** (a) Ordinarily, after the release of a neurotransmitter, some of the molecules are reabsorbed, and some are broken down by the enzyme monoamine oxidase (MAO). (b) Selective serotonin reuptake inhibitors (SSRIs) prevent reabsorption of serotonin. Tricyclic drugs prevent reabsorption of dopamine, norepinephrine, and serotonin. (c) MAO inhibitors (MAOIs) block the enzyme monoamine oxidase and thereby increase the availability of the neurotransmitter.

- Other students had a better previous background in this topic than I did.
- I didn't get a good chance to study.
- I'm just stupid. I always do badly no matter how hard I try.

The first three explanations attribute your failure to something temporary, specific, or correctable, but the fourth leaves you feeling hopeless. If you consistently make that type of attribution, you have a *pessimistic explanatory style*. People with a pessimistic style are likely to be depressed now or to become depressed in the future (Alloy et al., 1999; Haeffel et al., 2005).

Cognitive therapy focuses on changing people's thoughts and encouraging a more active life. According to Aaron Beck, a pioneer in cognitive therapy, depressed people are guided by thoughts that he calls the "negative cognitive triad of depression":

- I am deprived or defeated.
- The world is full of obstacles.
- The future is devoid of hope.

People who have these "automatic thoughts" interpret ambiguous situations to their own disadvantage (Beck, 1991). Therapists try to overcome these thoughts and get clients to reinterpret events in a more positive way. A therapist might invite the client to regard the negative thoughts as charges by a prosecuting attorney, and then act as the defense attorney to produce counterarguments.

Cognitive therapists also encourage people to become more active—to take part in more activities that might bring pleasure or a sense of accomplishment (Jacobson et al., 1996). Think about a study reported in Chapter 14: Introverts who pretended to be extraverted (i.e., more outgoing) reported feeling happier. The same applies here: Just getting people to become more active helps relieve depression.

Most people who become depressed after a highly stressful event find it helpful to talk about their reactions to that event with a therapist, and all the common types of psychotherapy appear to be approximately equal in effectiveness (Barth et al., 2013). However, continuing to talk about a stressful experience month after month does more harm than good (Curci & Rimé, 2012). Discussing a bad experience too long is rumination, which interferes with recovery. Good therapists help a patient put an experience behind them and move on with life.

Effectiveness or Ineffectiveness of Treatments

Psychotherapy and antidepressant drugs are about equally effective, but neither is highly reliable (Bortolotti, Menchetti, Bellini, Montaguti, & Berardi, 2008). If we ask what percentage of people with

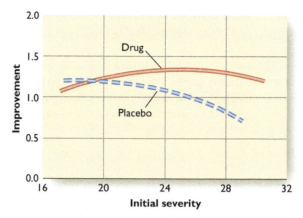

▲ **Figure 15.13** For people with mild to moderate depression, antidepressant drugs apparently produce no more apparent benefit than placebos. The drugs show a significant benefit for people with severe depression, who do not respond well to placebos. (From Kirsch et al., 2008)

depression show significant improvement, the result depends on how long the treatment lasts and how someone measures improvement, but generally about half improve. Even saying that half of the people show improvement overstates the effectiveness of the treatments. Because depression occurs in episodes, most people with no treatment at all generally improve, given enough time, and some improve within a short time. Giving a placebo increases the chance of recovery, just by the expectation of improvement. If we look at results a few months after the onset of depression, about a third of patients improve with no treatment or a placebo, and about half improve with either antidepressant drugs or psychotherapy (Hollon, Thase, & Markowitz, 2002).

▲ **Figure 15.13** summarizes the results of many studies with many antidepressant drugs. People with mild to moderate depression respond about as well to placebos as they do to the drugs. The drugs are better than placebos for people with severe depression, mainly because those people don't respond well to placebos (Kirsch et al., 2008). Other researchers reevaluated the data and confirmed that the drugs are no better than placebos for people with moderate depression (Fournier et al., 2010). Most studies used the Hamilton Rating Scale for Depression, which is not very accurate for measuring moderate levels of depression (Isaacson & Adler, 2012). Therefore it is possible that the research underestimates the benefits for patients with moderate depression. (Equally true, the results may underestimate the improvement with placebos.) Still, it is clear that antidepressant drugs are only moderately helpful for many patients, and not at all for others.

When patients fail to respond to a drug, psychiatrists sometimes increase the dosage or switch to a different drug, but no solid research supports this strategy. One study took people who failed to respond to a drug, switched them to another drug, and found that 21 percent of them improved within the next few weeks (Rush et al., 2006). Do you see a problem with this design? The problem is the lack of a control group that stayed on the first drug. We don't know whether switching drugs was the key, or whether people recovered because of more total time of treatment.

Choosing between Psychotherapy and Antidepressant Drugs

If psychotherapy helped one type of patient and antidepressants helped another type, combining the treatments should help a much larger number than either treatment alone. In fact, combining treatments improves the response for only a small percentage of people (Hollon et al., 2014; Thase, 2014). That result implies that most of the people who would respond to one type of treatment would also respond to the other.

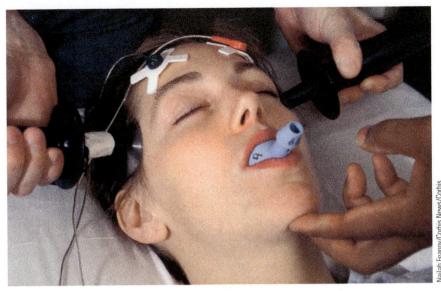

▲ **Figure 15.14** Electroconvulsive therapy is administered today only with the patient's informed consent. ECT is given in conjunction with muscle relaxants and anesthetics to minimize discomfort.

Antidepressant drugs usually show benefits a little faster. They are less expensive, and it's easier to take a pill than to spend an hour with a therapist. However, the drugs produce unpleasant side effects, such as dry mouth, difficulty urinating, or increased blood pressure. Also, many people find that after they stop taking the drugs, their depression returns within a few months. The benefits of psychotherapy usually last longer after the end of therapy (Imel, Malterer, McKay, & Wampold, 2008).

Electroconvulsive Shock Therapy

For those who don't respond to either psychotherapy or antidepressant drugs, another option is electroconvulsive therapy (ECT) (see ▲ Figure 15.14), in which *a brief electrical shock is administered across the patient's head to induce a convulsion similar to epilepsy.* ECT, widely used in the 1940s and 1950s, fell out of favor because of its history of abuse. Some patients were subjected to ECT hundreds of times without informed consent, and sometimes, ECT was used more as a punishment than a therapy.

Beginning in the 1970s, ECT made a comeback in modified form, mostly for people with severe depression who failed to respond to antidepressant drugs or patients with strong suicidal tendencies (Scovern & Kilmann, 1980). For suicidal patients, ECT has the advantage of rapid effect, often within a week. When a life is at stake, rapid relief is important. However, about half of those who respond will relapse into depression within six months unless they receive some other therapy to prevent it (Riddle & Scott, 1995).

ECT is now used only after patients have given their informed consent. The shock is less intense than previously, and the patient is given muscle relaxants to prevent injury and anesthetics to reduce discomfort. The main side effect is temporary memory impairment. How ECT works is uncertain, but it is not by causing people to forget depressing memories. ECT that is administered to just the frontal part of the brain or just the right hemisphere is as effective as whole-brain ECT but without significant memory loss (Lisanby, Maddox, Prudic, Devanand, & Sackeim, 2000; Sackeim et al., 2000).

ECT produces faster benefits than psychotherapy or antidepressant drugs, but its benefits are the least enduring. Although it has a high success rate for patients who did not respond to other treatments, only about 10 percent of hospitals in the United States offer it (Case et al., 2013).

Other Treatments

We have good reasons to expect exercise to help. Animal research has shown that steady, nonstrenuous exercise increases neuron formation in the hippocampus, known to be an important part of recovery from depression. The best study with humans showed that an increase in physical activity predicts a lower probability of later depression, and depression predicts a decrease in physical activity (Pereira, Geoffroy, & Power, 2014). That is, people who exercise feel good, and people who feel good like to exercise.

Seafood contains omega-3 fatty acids that are important for brain functioning. People who eat at least a pound (0.45 kg) of seafood per week have a decreased probability of mood disorders (Noaghiul & Hibbeln, 2003). Placebo-controlled studies have confirmed the value of omega-3 fatty acids for relieving depression (Freeman, 2009; Saris, Mischoulon, & Schweitzer, 2012).

Najlah Feanny/Corbis News/Corbis

17. Of the various treatments recommended for depression, which one(s) might be helpful for prevention, as opposed to treating a disorder that has already occurred?

Answer

17. Exercise and seafood are suitable for prevention.

Bipolar Disorder

Bipolar disorder, previously known as manic-depressive disorder, is a condition in which someone alternates between mood extremes. In many respects, mania is the *opposite of depression.* In mania, people are sometimes but not necessarily cheerful, and they are *constantly active, uninhibited, and often irritable.* They are sometimes dangerous to themselves or others. Some mental hospitals have had to disable the fire alarms, because manic patients impulsively pull the alarm every time they pass it. People with a mild degree of mania ("hypomania") are also energetic and uninhibited, but to a lesser degree. Lifetime prevalence rates vary from less than 0.5 percent in Asia to almost 1.5 percent in Europe, with the United States at about 1 percent (Johnson & Johnson, 2014).

As mentioned earlier in the chapter, many people do not fit neatly into one category. Some patients straddle the border between depression and bipolar disorder, many have bipolar disorder plus anxiety problems, and some have both the mood swings of bipolar disorder and some thought problems that are more characteristic of schizophrenia.

Treatment for bipolar disorder enables people to lead successful lives. Dr. Alice W. Flaherty is a neurologist who says having the disorder has made her more empathetic to her patients.

concept check

18. What are the similarities and differences between seasonal affective disorder and bipolar disorder?

Answer

18. Both conditions have repetitive cycles. However, people with bipolar disorder swing back and forth between depression and mania, whereas people with seasonal affective disorder alternate between depression and normal mood. Also, people with seasonal affective disorder show a regularity in timing that depends on time of year.

Effective treatments for bipolar disorder include lithium salts and anticonvulsant drugs, such as valproate (trade names Depakene, Depacote), all of which can be tolerated for long-term treatment, if the dose is carefully monitored. Psychotherapy is helpful for handling the anxiety that many patients experience (Deckersbach et al., 2014).

Schizophrenia

Many people mistakenly use the term *schizophrenia* when they mean *dissociative identity disorder*, or *multiple personality*, an uncommon condition in which people alternate personalities. The term *schizophrenia* does come from Greek roots meaning "split mind" or "shattered mind," but the idea was a split between the intellectual and emotional aspects of one personality, as if the intellect were no longer in contact with the emotions. Someone suffering from schizophrenia might express inappropriate emotion or fail to show appropriate emotion. This

separation of intellect and emotions is no longer considered a defining feature of schizophrenia, but the term remains.

To be diagnosed with schizophrenia, someone must exhibit a prolonged deterioration of daily activities such as work, social relations, and self-care, and some combination of the following: hallucinations, delusions, disorganized speech and thought, movement disorder, and loss of normal emotional responses and social behaviors. The symptoms must include at least one of the first three (delusions, hallucinations, and disorganized speech) and at least two of the five overall. As you can see, two people diagnosed with schizophrenia might have no symptoms in common.

Hallucinations, delusions, thought disorder, and movement disorder are considered positive symptoms, meaning that they are *defined by the presence of some behavior*. In contrast, negative symptoms are *defined by the absence of a behavior*. Common negative symptoms include lack of emotional expression, lack of motivation, and lack of social interactions. Curiously, most people with schizophrenia report feeling normal degrees of emotion, even when they show very little expression (Mote, Stuart, & Kring, 2014).

Hallucinations

Hallucinations are *perceptions that do not correspond to anything in the real world*, such as hearing voices that no one else hears. The voices may speak nonsense, or they may direct the person to do something. People sometimes think the voices are real, sometimes they know the voices are unreal, and sometimes they are not sure (Junginger & Frame, 1985). Spontaneous activity in the auditory cortex accompanies auditory hallucinations (Shergill, Brammer, Williams, Murray, & McGuire, 2000).

Have you ever heard a voice when you knew you were alone? I asked my class this question. At first, just a few people hesitantly raised their hands, and then more and more, until about one-fourth of the class—and I, too—admitted to hearing a voice at least once. Often, the experience occurred while someone lay in bed, just waking up. Having an occasional auditory hallucination does not mean you are losing your mind.

Delusions

A delusion is a *belief that someone holds strongly despite evidence against it*. For example, a delusion of persecution is a *belief that enemies are persecuting you*. A delusion of grandeur is a *belief that you are unusually important*, perhaps a special messenger from God. A delusion of reference is a *tendency to take all sorts of messages personally*. For example, someone may interpret a newspaper headline as a coded message of what he or she should do today.

It is hazardous to make a diagnosis of schizophrenia if the main symptom is a delusion. Suppose someone constantly sees evidence of government conspiracies in everyday events. Is that belief a delusion or merely an unusual opinion? Might it even be correct? Most people who believe they have been abducted by outer space aliens do not seem mentally ill, even though they hold implausible beliefs (Clancy, 2005). Probably most of us believe something that someone else might consider ridiculous.

Disordered Speech and Thought

Many people with schizophrenia show various problems with communication, including illogical, incoherent, distracted, or tangential speech, as if they start speaking but quickly forget what they are trying to say. Here is a quote from a person with schizophrenia (Andreasen, 1986, p. 477):

> They're destroying too many cattle and oil just to make soap. If we need soap when you can jump into a pool of water, and then when you go to buy your gasoline, my folks always thought they should get pop but the best thing to get, is motor oil, and, money.

Rick Friedman/The New York Times/Redux Pictures

Most but not all people with schizophrenia show intellectual impairments of various types, especially with attention and working memory (Hahn et al., 2012). For example, the Wisconsin Card Sorting Test asks people to sort a stack of cards by one rule (e.g., in piles by color) and then shift to a different rule (in piles by number or shape). Most people with schizophrenia have trouble shifting, as do people with frontal cortex damage.

Another characteristic of schizophrenic thought is difficulty using abstract concepts, such as interpreting proverbs literally instead of seeing the intended meaning. Here are examples (Krueger, 1978, pp. 196–197):

Proverb: People who live in glass houses shouldn't throw stones.
Interpretation: "It would break the glass."
Proverb: All that glitters is not gold.
Interpretation: "It might be brass."

concept check

19. What are typical "positive" and "negative" symptoms of schizophrenia?

Answer

19. Positive symptoms of schizophrenia include hallucinations, delusions, and thought disorder. Negative symptoms include lack of speech, lack of emotional expression, and lack of social contact.

▲ **Figure 15.15** At the memorial service for Nelson Mandela, the man who was supposedly interpreting speeches into sign language for the deaf made no sense. He was soon evaluated and admitted to a psychiatric hospital to receive treatment for schizophrenia.

Prevalence

Worldwide, about one to four people per thousand develop schizophrenia at some point in life (Brown, 2011). As with all statistics about mental illness, that figure would increase or decrease depending on how many mild cases we count. As well as researchers can reconstruct from historical records, the incidence of schizophrenia and severe mental illness in general increased from the late 1700s until about 1950. Since then, it stopped increasing and apparently started decreasing in some parts of the world (Suvisaari, Haukka, Tanskanen, & Lönnqvist, 1999; Torrey & Miller, 2001).

Schizophrenia is most frequently diagnosed in young adults in their 20s, occasionally in teenagers. It is more common in men than women, by a ratio of about 7 to 5, and on average more severe in men (Brown, 2011). Schizophrenia is more common among people who grew up in big cities than among people who grew up in rural areas or small towns (Brown, 2011). Several explanations are possible, including decreased social support, changes in diet, more exposure to toxic substances, and decreased exposure to sunlight, resulting in less absorption of vitamin D.

Decades ago, psychiatrists believed that people with schizophrenia almost invariably continued deteriorating throughout life. At the time, most such patients lived in poorly staffed, overcrowded mental hospitals, and perhaps it is no wonder that they deteriorated. Today, the prospects are more encouraging. About one-fourth of people with schizophrenia remain permanently impaired, although most of them don't get substantially worse over time. Of the others, some show good recovery after a brief episode of schizophrenia, and others alternate between periods of remission and periods of relapse (Zipursky, Reilly, & Murray, 2013).

Causes

Schizophrenia probably develops from a variety of influences. The prime candidates are genetics and prenatal environment, aggravated by stress later in life.

Genetics

The evidence for a genetic basis rests primarily on studies of twins and adopted children. Monozygotic twins have much higher overlap than dizygotic twins, indicating high heritability of schizophrenia (Cardno et al., 1999; Gottesman, 1991; Sullivan, Kendler, & Neale, 2003), and close relatives in general have an increased similarity (see ▼ Figure 15.16). Brothers and sisters of someone with schizophrenia have an increased probability of impaired memory and attention, even if they do not have other symptoms (Barch, Cohen, & Csernansky, 2014). Adopted children who have schizophrenia have more biological relatives than adoptive relatives with schizophrenia (Kety et al., 1994). However, the data on adopted children are subject to another interpretation. Many women with schizophrenia smoke and drink during pregnancy, take poor care of their health, and fail to eat a good diet. That prenatal environment can unfavorably affect a fetus's brain development.

The strongest evidence of a genetic influence would be a demonstration linking schizophrenia to a specific gene. A massive study comparing nearly 37,000 people with schizophrenia to more

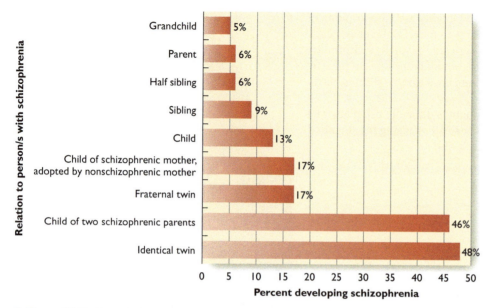

▲ **Figure 15.16** The relatives of someone with schizophrenia have an increased probability of developing schizophrenia. (Based on data from Gottesman, 1991)

than 100,000 others identified more than a hundred genes that differed in frequency between the two groups. Most of these genes influence some aspect of brain activity, but many others related to the immune system (Schizophrenia Working Group, 2014). However, none of these genes by itself has a large effect, and only four genetic differences have been repeatedly found across studies with different populations (Vieland et al., 2014).

A promising hypothesis relates schizophrenia to copy number variants (*deletions and duplications of tiny parts of a chromosome*), which have been found in about 15 percent of people with schizophrenia and fewer other people (Buizer-Voskamp et al., 2011; International Schizophrenia Consortium, 2008; Stefansson et al., 2008). Several of these errors show convincing links to schizophrenia or other cognitive deficits (Stefansson et al., 2014). Copy errors could also explain the fact that monozygotic twins are sometimes discordant for schizophrenia, because a copy error can occur in one twin and not the other (Bruder et al., 2008).

20. How could researchers explain how schizophrenia can have a strong genetic basis, even though no single gene is strongly linked with schizophrenia?

Answer

20. Brain development depends on many genes, and a disruption of any of them (including a spontaneous deletion or duplication of part of a gene) can increase the risk of schizophrenia.

The Neurodevelopmental Hypothesis

Some cases of schizophrenia probably don't result from genetic factors at all. According to the neurodevelopmental hypothesis, *schizophrenia originates with nervous system impairments that develop before birth or in early childhood, because of either genetics or early environment, especially prenatal environment* (McGrath, Féron, Burne, Mackay-Sim, & Eyles, 2003; Weinberger, 1996). Schizophrenia is known to be more common in any of these cases (Brown, 2011):

- The mother had a difficult pregnancy, labor, or delivery.
- The mother was poorly nourished during pregnancy.
- The mother had influenza, rubella, or other infection during early to mid-pregnancy.
- The mother had an extremely stressful experience early in her pregnancy.
- A mother with Rh-negative blood type has given birth to more than one baby with Rh-positive blood.
- The patient was exposed to lead or other toxins in early childhood.
- The patient was infected during childhood with the parasite *Toxoplasma gondii*, which attacks parts of the brain (Yolken, Dickerson, & Torrey, 2009). The usual route of infection with this parasite is handling cat feces (Leweke et al., 2004; Torrey & Yolken, 2005).

Furthermore, *a person born in the winter or early spring is slightly more likely to develop schizophrenia than a person born at other times* (Bradbury & Miller, 1985; Davies, Welham, Chant, Torrey, & McGrath, 2003). This season-of-birth effect occurs only in northern climates, not near the equator. No other psychological disorder has this characteristic. One possible explanation relates to the fact that influenza and other epidemics are common in the fall. If a woman catches influenza or another infection during the first or second trimester of pregnancy, her fever and the elevated activity of her immune system can impair the fetus's brain development.

Brain Abnormalities

Brain scans indicate that people with schizophrenia have, on average, decreased gray matter in several brain areas and slightly enlarged cerebral ventricles, the fluid-filled cavities of the brain (Ren et al., 2013; Wolkin et al., 1998; Wright et al., 2000). ▼ Figure 15.17 shows an example of enlarged cerebral ventricles.

Most people with schizophrenia also have smaller than average neurons (Pierri, Volk, Auh, Sampson, & Lewis, 2001; Weinberger, 1999) and fewer than average synapses, especially in the prefrontal cortex (Glantz & Lewis, 1997, 2000). One of the most impaired areas, the dorsolateral prefrontal cortex, controls aspects of working memory that are often weak in schizophrenia (Gur et al., 2000; Pearlson, Petty, Ross, & Tien, 1996; Sowell, Thompson, Holmes, Jernigan, & Toga, 1999).

However, these results must be interpreted cautiously. Many people with schizophrenia abuse alcohol or other drugs that might impair brain functioning, shrink dendrites, and so forth (Rais et al., 2008; Sullivan et al., 2000).

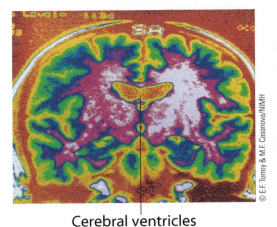

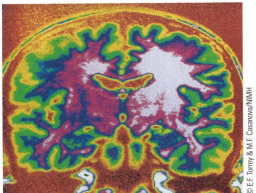

◀ **Figure 15.17** The twin on the left has schizophrenia, and the twin on the right does not. The fluid-filled ventricles are larger in the twin with schizophrenia. An enlargement of the ventricles implies a loss of brain tissue.

Cerebral ventricles

concept check

21. **Suppose someone argues that the brain abnormalities in schizophrenia indicate that brain damage causes schizophrenia. What is an alternative explanation?**

Answer

21. Perhaps schizophrenia leads to alcohol abuse, which in turn leads to brain abnormalities.

Therapies

Before the discovery of effective drugs to combat schizophrenia, many people spent years or decades in mental hospitals, growing more disoriented. The situation today is still far from ideal, but certainly better, mainly as a result of antipsychotic medications.

Medications

During the 1950s, researchers discovered the first effective antipsychotic drug—that is, *a drug that can relieve schizophrenia*. That drug was chlorpromazine (klor-PRAHM-uh-ZEEN; trade name Thorazine). Daily use of an antipsychotic drug produces variable degrees of recovery, emerging gradually in a month or more (Szymanski, Simon, & Gutterman, 1983). When affected people stop taking the drugs, the symptoms usually return (see ▼ Figure 15.18).

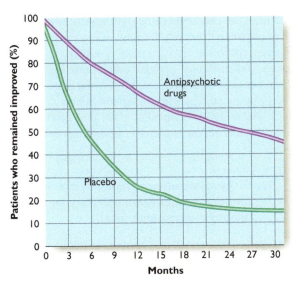

▲ **Figure 15.18** After recovery from schizophrenia, the percentage of people who remained improved for the next 2½ years was higher in the group that received continuing drug treatment than in the placebo group. (Based on Baldessarini, 1984)

Typical antipsychotic drugs block dopamine synapses in the brain (Seeman & Lee, 1975). Furthermore, large doses of amphetamines, cocaine, or other drugs that stimulate dopamine activity produce hallucinations and delusions. These observations led to the dopamine hypothesis of schizophrenia—the idea that *the underlying cause of schizophrenia is excessive release of dopamine in certain brain areas* (Hirvonen et al., 2006; Howes et al., 2009; Simpson, Kellendonk, & Kandel, 2010).

However, dopamine may not be the entire explanation. The brain's release of dopamine is regulated largely by the neurotransmitter glutamate, and several lines of evidence suggest that people with schizophrenia have deficient glutamate release in the prefrontal cortex (Lewis & Gonzalez-Burgos, 2006). Prolonged use of *phencyclidine* ("angel dust"), which inhibits glutamate receptors, produces both the positive and negative symptoms of schizophrenia (Olney & Farger, 1995).

Side Effects and Alternative Treatments

Antipsychotic drugs produce unwelcome side effects, including tardive dyskinesia (TAHRD-eev DIS-ki-NEE-zhuh), *a condition characterized by tremors and involuntary movements* (Kiriakakis, Bhatia, Quinn, & Marsden, 1998). Presumably, tardive dyskinesia relates to the fact that antipsychotic drugs block dopamine synapses, some of which control movement. Researchers have sought new drugs to combat schizophrenia without causing tardive dyskinesia.

Atypical (or *second-generation*) antipsychotic drugs, such as risperidone and clozapine, *relieve schizophrenia with less risk of tardive dyskinesia*, although some risk remains. These drugs alter activity at both dopamine and serotonin synapses. Atypical antipsychotic drugs relieve the negative symptoms of schizophrenia that most antipsychotic drugs fail to address (Davis, Chen, & Glick, 2003). However, the atypical antipsychotic drugs have side effects of their own, and it is not clear that they improve overall quality of life any better than the older drugs (P. B. Jones et al., 2006).

Many people refuse to take antipsychotic drugs, or quit them because of the side effects. A limited amount of research indicates that many of those people respond well to cognitive therapy, in some cases gaining benefits comparable to those of the antipsychotic drugs (Morrison et al., 2014). A software company has developed video games to help people with schizophrenia practice simple visual and auditory skills, on the idea that making simple skills more automatic can free the brain to concentrate on higher-order tasks. As of early 2015, the company is seeking approval from the Food and Drug Administration (FDA) in the United States. You don't need FDA approval to sell a video game, of course, but you do if you want to advertise that it has medical benefits. This would be the first time the FDA ever gave formal approval to a software program.

22. What are the advantages of atypical antipsychotic drugs?

Answer

22. Atypical antipsychotic drugs relieve the negative symptoms of schizophrenia better than the older drugs do, with less risk of tardive dyskinesia.

Autistic Spectrum Disorder

Autism is a lifelong condition characterized by impaired social contact. At one time, psychiatrists distinguished autism from a milder condition, *Asperger's syndrome*, but because the difference is just one of degree, the conditions are now combined as autism spectrum disorder. It is far more common in boys than in girls. Parents usually notice autism before age 2 and sometimes within the first weeks of life, as the infant seems not to cuddle like other infants. The main symptoms are:

- *Impaired social relationships* (little eye contact; little social contact)
- *Impaired communication* (repetitive speech; no sustained conversations)
- *Stereotyped behaviors* (repetitive movements such as flapping fingers)

However, these three aspects do not correlate highly with one another. Many people have severe symptoms in one area and only mild symptoms in another (Happé, Ronald, & Plomin, 2006). As with schizophrenia, what we call autism may represent several disorders with different causes.

In addition to the primary symptoms, most individuals with autism show other symptoms, including fluctuations of temperature regulation, insensitivity to pain, and decreased tendency to become dizzy after spinning with the lights on (Ritvo, 2006). (Curiously, they show a normal tendency to dizziness with the lights off!) Another characteristic is a tendency to focus attention narrowly on one item to the exclusion of everything else (Bryson, 2005). Many people with autism perform below average on some intellectual tasks and above average, sometimes way above average, on other tasks (Dawson, Soulières, Gernsbacher, & Mottron, 2007).

Twin studies point to a strong genetic basis. One study found 92 percent concordance for autism or related problems in monozygotic twins. That is, if one twin had autism or related problems, the probability was 92 percent that the other did also. For dizygotic twins, the concordance was only 10 percent (Bailey et al., 1995). To explain this huge discrepancy between monozygotic and dizygotic twins, one possibility is that autism depends on a combination of two or more genes. If autism requires two or three genes, dizygotic twins would have a low probability of getting the same combination. Chromosome examinations have identified dozens of genes with a small link to autism (DeRubeis et al., 2014). As with schizophrenia, many cases can be traced to a microdeletion of part of a chromosome (Iossifov et al., 2014).

Several other possible causes relate to prenatal environment. About 12 percent of mothers of autistic children, and few if any other mothers, have certain antibodies that attack the proteins of a developing brain (Braunschweig et al., 2013). Also, pregnant women are advised to take folic acid (vitamin B9), which is important for the developing nervous system. Women who get enough folic acid from pills or fresh fruits and vegetables have about half the usual probability of a child with autism (Surén et al., 2013).

Researchers have found many brain abnormalities related to autism but none that occur consistently. One of the most surprising is that about one-fifth of people with autism have large heads and brains—larger than 97 percent of everyone else (White, O'Reilly, & Frith, 2009). Evidently they have more neurons but abnormal connections among them (Ke et al., 2009). Other abnormalities include decreased number of neurons in the cerebellum and alterations of neuron structure in the cerebral cortex (Bauman & Kemper, 2005; Voineagu et al., 2011). The decrease in the cerebellum relates to the clumsiness and lack of voluntary eye movements often characteristic of autism.

Given enough patience and special education, many individuals with autism develop well enough to live reasonably normal lives. So far, no drug treatment has proved to be successful. Many desperate parents turn to untested fad treatments, which are generally a waste of effort and money (Matson, Adams, Williams, & Rieske, 2013). Autism remains a fascinating mystery.

23. Of the most common symptoms of autism, which would be considered *negative symptoms* analogous to the negative symptoms of schizophrenia?

Answer

23. Impaired social relationships and impaired communication.

Disabling Psychological Disorders

Depression, schizophrenia, and autism have at least three major points in common: First, they seriously impair people for a long time. Second, the treatment options are not yet satisfactory for any of these conditions. Third, each of them can be a result of various causes, not just one.

As you have read about these disorders, you could easily become discouraged with how little we know. An antidote to complete discouragement would be to read what the textbooks of the mid-1900s had to say. They blamed schizophrenia and autism on bad parents who failed to show their children enough love. Those days, mercifully, have passed. We don't yet have all the answers that we seek, but at least we know what the answers are *not*. That progress is worth celebrating.

Summary

- *Symptoms of depression.* People with depression find little interest or pleasure in life and have trouble sleeping. (page 503)
- *Episodes.* Depression occurs in episodes. Although the first episode is usually triggered by a stressful event, later episodes occur more easily. (page 504)
- *Antidepressant drugs.* Although antidepressants affect the synapses within an hour or so, their behavioral effects begin after two or three weeks of treatment. Perhaps they produce their benefits by enhancing cell growth in the hippocampus. (page 505)
- *Effectiveness of treatment.* About one-third of patients recover from depression spontaneously within a few months. Of patients receiving psychotherapy, antidepressant drugs, or both, a little over half recover. Antidepressants are not significantly more helpful than placebos for people with mild to moderate depression. (page 506)
- *Antidepressants or psychotherapy?* Antidepressants are convenient and less expensive than psychotherapy, but psychotherapy's effects are more likely to produce long-lasting benefits. (page 506)
- *Other treatments.* For the many people who do not respond to drugs or psychotherapy, electroconvulsive therapy (ECT) is another option. Exercise and seafood help to prevent depression. (page 507)
- *Bipolar disorder.* People with bipolar disorder alternate between periods of depression and periods of mania. (page 507)

- *Symptoms of schizophrenia.* A diagnosis of schizophrenia applies if someone has deteriorated in everyday functioning and shows other symptoms from this list: hallucinations, delusions, disorganized speech and thought, movement disorder, and loss of normal emotional responses and social behaviors. (page 508)
- *Genetic influences.* Much evidence indicates that it is possible to inherit a predisposition toward schizophrenia. A current hypothesis is that schizophrenia can result from changes in any of a large number of genes. (page 509)
- *The neurodevelopmental hypothesis.* Many researchers believe that schizophrenia originates with abnormal brain development before or around the time of birth because of either genetics or prenatal environment. Early abnormal development leaves a person vulnerable to further deterioration in adulthood. (page 510)
- *Brain abnormalities.* Many people with schizophrenia show indications of mild brain abnormalities. However, some of the damage may be due to alcohol abuse. (page 510)
- *Antipsychotic drugs.* Drugs that alleviate schizophrenia block dopamine synapses. However, all current antipsychotic drugs produce unpleasant side effects. (page 511)
- *Autism.* Autism, a condition that begins in early childhood, is characterized by impaired social contact, impaired language, and stereotyped movements. The causes apparently relate to genetics and prenatal environment. (page 512)

Key Terms

antipsychotic drugs (page 511)

atypical antipsychotic drugs (page 511)

autism spectrum disorder (page 512)

bipolar disorder (page 507)

copy number variants (page 510)

delusion (page 508)

delusion of grandeur (page 508)

delusion of persecution (page 508)

delusion of reference (page 508)

dopamine hypothesis of schizophrenia (page 511)

electroconvulsive therapy (ECT) (page 507)

hallucinations (page 508)

major depression (page 503)

mania (page 507)

monoamine oxidase inhibitors (MAOIs) (page 505)

negative symptoms (page 508)

neurodevelopmental hypothesis (page 510)

positive symptoms (page 508)

schizophrenia (page 508)

season-of-birth effect (page 510)

seasonal affective disorder (SAD) (page 504)

selective serotonin reuptake inhibitors (SSRIs) (page 505)

tardive dyskinesia (page 511)

tricyclic drugs (page 505)

Review Questions

1. Which of the following is an indication that an adolescent is more likely than average to become depressed at some later time?
   (a) The person has trouble sleeping.
   (b) The person tends to eat very spicy foods.
   (c) The person competes in sports.
   (d) The person spends much time on the phone.

2. Depression is more common among ___ than among ___, and more common among ___ than among ___.
   (a) men . . . women; whites . . . blacks
   (b) men . . . women; blacks . . . whites
   (c) women . . . men; whites . . . blacks
   (d) women . . . men; blacks . . . whites

3. What is the current status of the search for a genetic basis of depression?
   (a) Several genes have been identified with a strong link to depression.
   (b) Depression appears to have a genetic basis, but researchers have not located any gene with a significant effect.
   (c) Depression does not have a genetic basis.

4. In which of these ways does a highly stressful experience increase the risk of depression?
   (a) Prolonged stressful experiences lead to weight gain.
   (b) Prolonged stressful experiences release chemicals related to inflammation.
   (c) Prolonged stressful experiences increase heart rate and breathing rate.
   (d) Prolonged stressful experiences release chemicals related to cell division.

5. In addition to their effects on serotonin and other neurotransmitters, what other brain effect do antidepressant drugs produce?
   (a) They increase the velocity of action potentials in the cerebral cortex.
   (b) They decrease the velocity of action potentials in the cerebral cortex.
   (c) They increase production of a chemical that increases birth of new neurons in the hippocampus.
   (d) They shift blood flow from the left hemisphere of the brain to mainly the right hemisphere.

6. For depression, the treatment with the most rapid benefit is _____ and the treatment most likely to produce long-lasting benefits is _____.
   (a) antidepressant drugs . . . ECT
   (b) ECT . . . psychotherapy
   (c) psychotherapy . . . antidepressant drugs
   (d) ECT . . . antidepressant drugs

7. What dietary change is recommended for people with depression?
   (a) Avoid leafy vegetables.
   (b) Avoid red meat.
   (c) Eat more bananas.
   (d) Eat more seafood.

8. Which of the following is NOT a symptom of schizophrenia?
   (a) Alternating between one personality and another
   (b) Hallucinations and delusions
   (c) Lack of motivation
   (d) Deterioration of daily activities

9. Which of the following is the most plausible statement of the relationship between genetics and schizophrenia?
   (a) Schizophrenia depends on a single gene, which has been discovered.
   (b) Schizophrenia depends on a single gene, which has yet to be discovered.
   (c) Schizophrenia can result from a disruption of any of a large number of genes.
   (d) Schizophrenia is unrelated to genetics.

10. According to the neurodevelopmental hypothesis, what is one reason why researchers cannot find a single gene responsible for schizophrenia?
    (a) The gene is too small to be detected with current methods.
    (b) Schizophrenia depends on a combination of two genes, and both must be present.
    (c) One gene is responsible for schizophrenia in men, and a different gene in women.
    (d) Schizophrenia sometimes results from the prenatal environment instead of genetics.

11. What is the main effect that antipsychotic drugs have in common with one another?
    (a) They block activity at dopamine synapses.
    (b) They increase activity at dopamine synapses.
    (c) They increase blood flow to the brain.
    (d) They decrease blood flow to the brain.

Answers: 1a, 2c, 3b, 4b, 5c, 6b, 7d, 8a, 9c, 10d, 11a.

module 15.5

Treatment of Mental Illness

After studying this module, you should be able to:

- Distinguish among forms of psychotherapy.
- Describe how researchers evaluate the effectiveness of psychotherapy.
- Describe possible ways of providing psychotherapeutic help inexpensively to more people.
- List possible methods to prevent psychological disorders.
- Discuss the insanity defense and other societal issues related to mental illness.

Psychologists offer help for many problems. Here, psychologists comfort the relatives of people killed in an explosion.

Some nearsighted people lost in the woods were trying to find their way home. One of the few who wore glasses said, "I think I know the way. Follow me." The others burst into laughter. "That's ridiculous," said one. "How could anybody who needs glasses be our leader?"

In 1972 the Democratic Party nominated Senator Thomas Eagleton for vice president of the United States. Shortly after his nomination, he revealed that he had once received psychiatric treatment for depression. He was ridiculed mercilessly: "How could anybody who needed a psychiatrist be our leader?"

Many troubled people decline to seek help, partly because of the stigma (Corrigan, Druss, & Perlick, 2014). All of us need to consider our reactions toward the idea of therapeutic help. We also need to deal with other issues. Can society as a whole take steps to prevent psychological disorders? Under what circumstances, if any, should a criminal defendant be acquitted because of "insanity"?

Overview of Psychotherapy

Treatments for psychological disorders are of two types, medications and psychotherapy. We considered antidepressant and antipsychotic medications in the last module. We have also considered psychotherapy, but now it is time to examine it in more detail. Psychotherapy is *a treatment of psychological disorders by methods that include a personal relationship between a trained therapist and a client.*

Treatment of mental illness has changed greatly since the mid-1900s, for both scientific and economic reasons (Sanchez & Turner, 2003). If you had sought treatment in the mid-1900s, you probably would have gone to a psychiatrist, because clinical psychology was just getting started. Freud's theories were dominant, and if you went to a Freudian therapist (a psychoanalyst), you would schedule one-hour sessions, four or five days a week, for months or years. You had to pay for it yourself, because few people had health insurance, and if you did have health insurance, it didn't cover psychiatric care. (In other words, hardly anyone but the wealthy could get psychotherapy.) No research had tested the effectiveness of treatments, and so you just had to hope and trust that your treatment was appropriate. Your therapist might give you no diagnosis at all, or a vague diagnosis like "neurotic."

Today, all of that has changed. If you want treatment, you can choose among psychiatrists, clinical psychologists, social workers, and others. Therapists use many methods, not just psychoanalysis. Instead of paying for your treatment, you will probably charge it to your health maintenance organization (HMO) or other insurance program. HMOs and other insurers are unwilling to pay for more treat-

ment than necessary, or for any untested techniques. If you want to crawl naked into a hot tub with your psychotherapist to reenact the moment of birth, you are welcome to do it every day for the rest of your life, if you pay for it yourself. But if you expect insurance to pay for it, someone needs to demonstrate that this treatment is effective. Consequently, therapists have felt pressure to test their methods and adopt empirically supported treatments, *therapies demonstrated to be helpful* (APA Presidential Task Force on Evidence-Based Practice, 2006). Many therapists follow published manuals that specify exactly how to treat various disorders. Because insurers limit the number of sessions they will reimburse for a given client, therapists have worked to develop brief therapies, in which they accomplish as much as they can in a moderate number of sessions. As ▼ Figure 15.19 shows, about half of all people who enter psychotherapy show significant improvement within eight sessions (Howard, Kopta, Krause, & Orlinsky, 1986). Further research showed that for most people, lengthier treatment produces less and less benefit (Stulz, Lutz, Kopta, Minami, & Saunders, 2013). Two brief sessions per week for a few weeks might be better than one session a week for many weeks (Cuijpers, Huibers, Ebert, Koole, & Andersson, 2013).

Insurance companies might pay for a session or two if you just feel bad and need to talk to someone, but they pay for more if you have a diagnosed mental disorder. As you might guess, the consequence is that a therapist is almost certain to give you a diagnosis of some sort, no matter what your problem is. ■ Table 15.4 summarizes these changes.

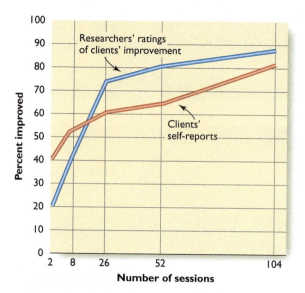

▲ Figure 15.19 The relationship of the number of psychotherapy sessions to the percentage of clients who improved. (From "The dose-effect relationship in psychotherapy," by K. I. Howard et al., 1986. *American Psychologist*, 41, pp. 159–164. By the American Psychological Association.

24. How has treatment of psychological disorders changed since the 1950s?

Answer

24. In the 1950s, psychiatrists conducted almost all psychotherapy. Today, clinical psychologists and other specialists also provide treatment. Today's therapists use a variety of empirically supported treatments, with less reliance on Freudian methods. Therapists try to achieve good results in just a few sessions, when possible, instead of proceeding for months or years. Today's therapists provide diagnoses for more disorders and define their diagnoses more carefully.

Types of Psychotherapy

Many types of psychotherapy are available, differing in their procedures and assumptions. The discussion here focuses on psychotherapy as it is practiced in the United States and Europe. Most Chinese consider it shameful to discuss personal or family matters with a stranger (Bond, 1991). Psychologists in India adapt their practice to local customs. For example, to maintain a close relationship with a client, they have to respect beliefs in astrology and other concepts that most Western psychologists dismiss (Clay, 2002).

Psychodynamic Therapies

Psychodynamic therapies *attempt to understand conflicting impulses, including some that the individual does not consciously recognize.* Both Sigmund Freud's procedure (looking for sexual motives) and Alfred Adler's procedure (looking for power and superiority motives) are psychodynamic despite the differences between them.

Psychoanalysis *tries to bring unconscious thoughts and emotions to consciousness.* It is therefore an insight-oriented therapy. Psychoanalysts offer interpretations of what the client says—that is, they try to explain the underlying meaning—and sometimes argue with a client about interpretations. They may regard a client's disagreement as resistance. For example, a client who has begun to touch on an anxiety-provoking topic may turn the conversation to something trivial or may simply "forget" to come to the next session.

One technique used in psychoanalysis is **free association**, in which *the client says everything that comes to mind*—a word, phrase, or image—without censoring anything or even speaking in complete sentences. The psychoanalyst listens for links that might tie the remarks together, on the assumption that every jump from one thought to another reveals a relationship between them. Another technique is **dream analysis**, seeking to understand symbolism in reported dreams. Even a therapist who doesn't look for deep symbolism can use dreams to understand how the client understands the world. Psychoanalysts also attend to **transference**, in which clients *transfer onto the therapist the behaviors and feelings they originally established toward their father, mother, or other important person.*

Psychoanalysts today modify Freud's approach in many ways. The goal is still to bring about a reorganization of the personality, changing a person from the inside out, by helping people understand the hidden reasons behind their actions.

Table 15.4 Changes in Psychotherapy Between the 1950s and the 21st Century		
Aspect of Therapy	**1950s**	**Early 21st Century**
Payment	By the patient or family	By health insurance
Types of therapist	Psychiatrists	Psychiatrists, clinical psychologists, others
Types of treatment	Mostly Freudian	Many types; emphasis on evidence-based treatments
Duration of treatment	Usually long, often years	A few sessions if effective; more if necessary
Diagnoses	Usually vague, such as "neurosis" or "psychosis." Often, no diagnosis.	Many diagnoses. Each carefully defined.
Treatment decisions	By the therapist and patient	By the insurer, unless the patient pays for more

▲ **Figure 15.20** A Potty Pager in a child's underwear vibrates when it becomes moist. This awakens the child, who then learns to awaken when the bladder is full.

Behavior Therapy

Behavior therapists assume that abnormal behavior is learned and can be unlearned. They identify the behavior that needs to be changed, such as a fear or bad habit, and then set about changing it through reinforcement and other principles of learning. They may try to understand the causes of a behavior as a first step toward changing it, but unlike psychoanalysts, they are more interested in changing behaviors than in understanding their hidden meanings.

Behavior therapy *begins with a clear, well-defined goal, such as eliminating test anxiety, and then attempts to achieve it through learning.* Setting a clear goal enables a therapist to judge whether the therapy is succeeding. If the client shows no improvement, the therapist changes the procedure.

One example of behavior therapy is for children who continue wetting the bed after the usual age of toilet training. The most effective procedure uses classical conditioning to train the child to wake up when the bladder is full. A small battery-powered device is attached to the child's underwear at night (see ▶ Figure 15.20). If the child urinates, the device detects the moisture and produces a vibration that awakens the child. According to one interpretation, the vibration acts as an unconditioned stimulus (UCS) that evokes the unconditioned response (UCR) of waking up. In this instance, the body itself generates the conditioned stimulus (CS): the sensation produced by a full bladder (see ▼ Figure 15.21). That sensation signals that the vibration is imminent. After a few pairings, the sensation of a full bladder is enough to wake the child.

Actually, the situation is a little more complicated. A child who awakens to go to the toilet gains rewards, as in operant conditioning (Ikeda, Koga, & Minami, 2006). Also, many children begin sleeping through the night, as hormones stop the body from producing so much urine at night (Butler et al., 2007). In any case, the alarm method is an application of behavior therapy, successful for at least two-thirds of bed-wetting children, sometimes after as few as one or two nights.

Cognitive Therapies

Suppose someone asks for your opinion and then asks someone else also. You might react, "It's good to get several opinions." Or you might feel hurt that your opinion wasn't good enough. Your emotions depend not only on the events but also on how you interpret them. Cognitive therapy *seeks to improve psychological well-being by changing people's interpretation of events* (Hofmann, Asmundson, & Beck, 2013). A cognitive therapist identifies distressing thoughts (such as "people don't like me" or "my enemies are out to get me") and encourages the client to explore the evidence behind them, much as

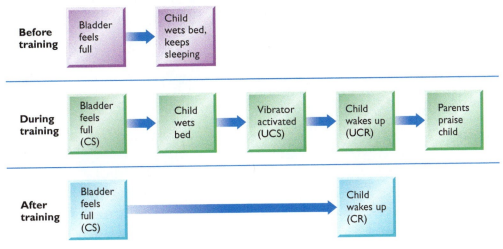

| Before training | Bladder feels full | → | Child wets bed, keeps sleeping | | | | | |

| During training | Bladder feels full (CS) | → | Child wets bed | → | Vibrator activated (UCS) | → | Child wakes up (UCR) | → | Parents praise child |

| After training | Bladder feels full (CS) | → | | | | | Child wakes up (CR) | |

◀ **Figure 15.21** At first, the sensation of a full bladder (the CS) produces no response, and the child wets the bed. The moisture causes a vibration (the UCS), and the child wakes up (the UCR). Soon the sensation of a full bladder wakens the child (CR).

An event can be upsetting or not, depending on how we interpret it.

a scientist would evaluate evidence. The therapist isn't necessarily promoting an optimistic outlook, but a realistic outlook. After all, if people really don't like you, or if you really do have enemies, you should know about it! Usually, however, the client discovers that the beliefs are unjustified. The therapist helps people identify unrealistic beliefs and abandon unrealistic goals, such as a need to excel all the time. Cognitive therapy also encourages people to find opportunities for activity, pleasure, or a sense of accomplishment.

Many therapists combine features of behavior therapy and cognitive therapy to form **cognitive-behavior therapy**, in which therapists *set explicit behavioral goals, but also try to change people's interpretation of situations.* For example, they help clients distinguish between serious problems and imagined or exaggerated problems. Then they try to change clients' behavior in handling the more serious problems.

Humanistic Therapy

As we saw in Chapter 14, humanistic psychologists believe that people can decide deliberately what kind of person to be. According to humanistic therapists, once people are freed from a feeling of rejection or failure, they can solve their own problems.

In Carl Rogers's version of humanistic therapy, **person-centered therapy**, also known as *nondirective* or *client-centered therapy, the therapist listens to the client with total acceptance and unconditional positive regard.* Most of the time, the therapist paraphrases and clarifies what the client has said, conveying the message, "I'm trying to understand the experience from your point of view." The therapist strives to be genuine, empathic, and caring, seldom if ever offering interpretation or advice. Few therapists today rely entirely on person-centered therapy,

but most therapists, regardless of other methods, follow the emphasis on listening carefully to the client and developing a caring, honest relationship between therapist and client.

concept check ✓

27. **Answer the following questions with reference to psychoanalysis, cognitive therapy, humanistic therapy, and behavior therapy.**

a. Which is least likely to offer advice and interpretations of behavior?
b. Which is least concerned with people's emotions?
c. Which focuses more on changing what people do than what they think?
d. Which two types of therapy try to change what people think?

Answers

27. a. humanistic therapy; b. behavior therapy; c. behavior therapy; d. psychoanalysis and cognitive therapy.

Family Systems Therapy

In **family systems therapy**, *the guiding assumption is that most people's problems develop in a family setting and that the best way to deal with them is to improve family relationships and communication.* A family therapist may use behavior therapy, cognitive therapy, or other techniques. What distinguishes family therapists is that they prefer to talk with two or more members of a family together. Solving most problems requires changing the family dynamics as well as any individual's behavior.

We have examined five types of psychotherapy. About half of U.S. psychotherapists profess no strong allegiance to any single method. Instead, they practice **eclectic therapy**, in which they *use a combination of methods and approaches.*

Group Therapies

The pioneers of psychotherapy saw their clients individually. Individual treatment has advantages, such as privacy. **Group therapy** is *administered to several people at once.* It first became popular for economic reasons. (Spreading the costs among several people makes it more affordable.) Soon therapists discovered other advantages to group therapy. Just meeting other people with similar

In group therapy, participants can explore how they relate to other people.

problems is reassuring. Also, group therapy lets people examine how they relate to others, practice social skills, and receive feedback (Ballinger & Yalom, 1995).

A self-help group, such as Alcoholics Anonymous, *operates much like group therapy, except without a therapist.* Each participant both gives and receives help. People who have experienced a problem can offer special insights to others with the same problem. In some places, people with mental health issues have organized self-help centers as an alternative to mental hospitals. These small, homelike environments may or may not include professional therapists. Instead of treating people as patients who need medical help, they expect people to take responsibility for their own actions. For most types of disorder, these facilities produce results equal to or better than those of mental hospitals, and the clients certainly like them better (Greenfield, Stoneking, Humphreys, Sundby, & Bond, 2008).

28. **Brief therapy is a goal or policy for many therapists. Why would it be less important in self-help groups such as Alcoholics Anonymous?**

Answer

28. One advantage of brief therapy is that it limits the expense. Expense is not an issue for self-help groups because they charge nothing other than a voluntary contribution toward rental of the facilities.

How Effective Is Psychotherapy?

Suppose you enter therapy, and six months later you and your therapist agree that you are much improved. Can we conclude that the therapy was effective? No, for several reasons (Lilienfeld, Ritschel, Lynn, Cautin, & Latzman, 2014). First, both you and your therapist want to believe the therapy worked, and so you may overestimate the degree of improvement. Second and more importantly, most psychological crises are temporary, and most people recover with or without therapy. *Improvement without therapy* is called spontaneous remission. We cannot conclude that the therapy was effective unless we see that its benefits exceed those of spontaneous recovery. People who overlook this problem sometimes endorse treatments that are ineffective or harmful.

To evaluate psychotherapy, we cannot simply compare people who did or did not choose to enter therapy. Those who sought help might differ from the others in the severity of their problems or their motivation for improvement. In the best studies, people who contact a clinic are randomly assigned to receive therapy at once or wait for therapy later. A few months later, the investigators evaluate people's improvement, often by their answers to a standardized questionnaire.

Most experiments have included only a moderate number of people. To draw a conclusion, researchers use a method called meta-analysis, *taking the results of many experiments, weighting each one in proportion to the number of participants, and determining the overall average effect.* According to a meta-analysis that pooled the results of 475 experiments, the average person in therapy showed greater improvement than 80 percent of similar people who did not receive therapy (Smith, Glass, & Miller, 1980).

One could easily complain that investigators invested much effort for little payoff. From 475 experiments, we conclude that therapy is usually better than no therapy for mild disorders. This outcome is like saying that medicine is usually better than no medicine. However, the research paved the way for more detailed studies about how therapy produces its benefits and which types of therapy are or are not effective.

a   b

Because everyone's moods and behavior fluctuate over time, an apparent improvement between (a) the start of therapy and (b) the end is hard to interpret. How much improvement is due to therapy and how much would have occurred without it?

Comparing Therapies

Next, we would like to know which kinds of therapy are most effective, or whether the answer differs for different disorders. At first the conclusion appeared stunningly simple: For a variety of disorders relating to anxiety or depression, all the mainstream types of therapy appeared nearly equal in effectiveness (Benish, Imel, & Wampold, 2008; Cuijpers, van Straten, Andersson, & van Oppen, 2008; Wampold et al., 1997). Later research qualified this statement somewhat: For several types of disorder, cognitive therapy or cognitive-behavioral therapy produces a slightly greater reduction of the target symptoms (such as anxiety), but all the common types of treatment are roughly equal for less specific goals, such as overall quality of life (Marcus, O'Connell, Norris, & Sawaqeh, 2014). (This conclusion does not apply to fad or quack treatments.)

It should be surprising that several forms of psychotherapy seem to be similar in their effectiveness, despite differences in their assumptions, methods, and goals. Evidently, they have more in common than we might have thought. One feature they share is a "therapeutic alliance"—a relationship between therapist and client characterized by acceptance, caring, respect, and attention. Second, in nearly all forms of therapy, clients talk openly and honestly about their beliefs, emotions, and personal difficulties. They examine aspects of themselves that they usually take for granted. Third, the mere fact of entering therapy improves clients' morale. Just taking action—any action—suggests that things will get better.

Finally, every form of therapy requires clients to commit themselves to change their lifestyle. Simply by coming to a therapy session, they reaffirm their commitment to feel less depressed, overcome their fears, or conquer some bad habit. Between sessions, they work to make progress that they can report at the next session. ■ Table 15.5 highlights similarities and differences among four types of therapy.

29. Name four ways in which nearly all forms of psychotherapy are similar.

Answer

29. Nearly all forms of psychotherapy include a close relationship between client and therapist, an effort to discuss personal difficulties openly, an expectation of improvement, and a commitment to make changes in one's life.

Advice for Potential Clients

At some point, you or someone close to you may be interested in seeing a psychotherapist. If so, here are some points to remember:

- Consulting a therapist does not mean that something is wrong with you. Many people simply need to talk with someone during a crisis.
- If you live in the United States, you can look up the telephone number for the Mental Health Association. Call and ask for a recommendation. You can specify how much you can pay, what kind of problem you have, and even what type of therapy you prefer. On average, people who choose their form of treatment persist with it longer and show greater benefits (Lindhiem, Bennett, Trentacosta, & McLear, 2014).
- Effective therapy depends on a good relationship between client and therapist. If you feel more comfortable talking with someone from your own culture, ethnic group, or religious background, look for such a person (La Roche & Christopher, 2008; Worthington, Kurusu, McCullough, & Sandage, 1996).
- Be skeptical of any therapist who seems overconfident. Clinical experience does not give anyone quick access to your private thoughts.

Table 15.5 Similarities and Differences among Four Types of Psychotherapy

Procedure	Psychoanalysis	Behavior Therapy	Cognitive Therapy	Person-Centered Therapy
Therapeutic alliance	√	√	√	√
Discuss problems openly	√	√	√	√
Expect improvement	√	√	√	√
Commit to make changes	√	√	√	√
Probe unconscious	√			
Specific goals		√	√	
Emphasize new learning		√		
Reinterpret situation			√	
Unconditional positive regard				√
Change thinking	√		√	

The Future of Psychotherapy and Prospects for Prevention

Sigmund Freud's procedure featured a therapist and a client for an hour at a time, four or five times a week, month after month. Today's therapists provide briefer treatments, often with a group of people at a time. Still, Alan Kazdin and his associates have argued that we will never have enough psychologists and psychiatrists to provide individual help to as many people as need help (Kazdin & Rabbitt, 2013). So, what should we do instead? Kazdin suggests therapy by telephone or the Internet, good self-help books, and informative movie and television programs. Computer programs to provide cognitive-behavioral therapy have made great advances, especially for treating anxiety (Rooksby, Elouafkaoui, Humphris, Clarkson, & Freeman, 2015). One problem with computer therapy is the threat of hacking that might invade a confidential conversation (Teachman, 2014).

A still better goal should be to prevent disorders as much as possible. Just as our society puts fluoride into drinking water to prevent tooth decay and immunizes people against contagious diseases, it can take action to prevent certain types of psychological disorders (Albee, 1986; Wandersman & Florin, 2003).

Let's distinguish prevention from intervention and maintenance. **Prevention** is avoiding a disorder from the start. **Intervention** is identifying a disorder in its early stages and relieving it, and **maintenance** is taking steps to keep a disorder from becoming more serious. Prevention takes several forms. A *universal* program targets everyone, such as an antismoking campaign, or abolition of lead-based paints and leaded gasoline. A *selective* program includes only people at risk, such as people with a family history of some disorder. An *indicated* program identifies people in the early stages of a disorder and tries to stop it. An indicated program is closer to intervention than to prevention.

Community psychologists *try to help people change their environment, both to prevent disorders and to promote a positive sense of mental well-being,* analogous to the goals set by Alfred Adler (Trickett, 2009). For example, many schools have instituted social and emotional learning programs (SEL) to teach self-management, social relationship skills, and responsible decision making. These programs reliably reduce the prevalence of conduct problems and emotional distress, but in addition they improve social skills, emotional control, and academic performance even for students who were already doing reasonably well (Durlak, Weissberg, Dymncki, Taylor, & Schellinger, 2011). Success of this type shows the potential of well-designed universal prevention programs.

Effective prevention programs need careful testing. Many interventions that sound reasonable don't work. For example, prolonged discussions of a stressful experience shortly after the event are more likely to cause than prevent posttraumatic stress disorder. "Scared straight" interventions tend to increase, not decrease, criminal behavior. Group therapy for aggressive teenagers often backfires by introducing them to potential bad influences. Several programs intended to prevent anorexia nervosa or to decrease suicide rates have in fact increased the rates (Joiner, 1999; Mann et al., 1997; Moller, 1992; Stice & Shaw, 2004; Taylor et al., 2006). The point is that we need careful research to identify effective methods of prevention and treatment (Lilienfeld, 2007; Nicholson, Foote, & Gigerick, 2009).

The best programs give participants active practice at specific behaviors, such as resisting peer pressure to risky behaviors. They build up step by step from simpler skills to more complex ones, analogous to Skinner's method of shaping. And they work with people at appropriate times in their lives. For example, AIDS prevention or pregnancy prevention should start at an age when students might begin to be sexually active, not many years earlier or many years later.

Here are examples of effective prevention programs:

- **Ban toxins.** The sale of lead-based paint has been banned because children who eat flakes of it sustain brain damage.
- **Educate pregnant women about prenatal care.** The use of alcohol or other drugs during pregnancy damages the brain of a fetus, and bacterial and viral infections during pregnancy can impair fetal brain development.
- **Outlaw smoking in public places and educate people about the risks of smoking.** Improvements in physical health improve psychological well-being, too.
- **Help people get jobs.** People who lose their jobs lose self-esteem and increase their risk of depression and substance abuse. Summer jobs for low-income teenagers decrease their probability of violent crime, not only during the summer but also long after (Heller, 2014).
- **Neighborhood improvement.** Low-income people who move from a crime-ridden neighborhood to a less distressed neighborhood experience long-term benefits in mental health (Ludwig et al., 2012).
- **Prevent bullying in school.** Children who are frequently bullied have an increased risk of anxiety, depression, and other distress throughout life (Takizawa, Maughan, & Aarseneault, 2014).

30. Why is it important to do careful research before initiating a new program to prevent a psychological disorder?

Answer

30. Some programs intended for prevention have been ineffective or counterproductive.

Social Issues Related to Mental Illness

Finally, let's consider some pubic policy issues you may face as a citizen. First, mental hospitals: Until the 1950s, huge numbers of troubled people were confined in understaffed, overcrowded state mental hospitals supported by the government. Residents included not only mental patients but also patients with Alzheimer's disease and people with mental retardation. Most of these hospitals were grim places.

In the 1950s, hospitals moved toward **deinstitutionalization**, *the removal of patients from mental hospitals,* to give them the least restrictive care possible—an idea that many people had been advocating for 100 years or more (Tuntiya, 2007). The hope

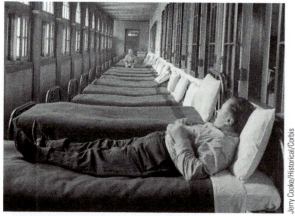

Most mental hospitals of the mid-1900s were unpleasant warehouses that provided minimal care.

was that patients would go home, free to live as normal a life as possible, while receiving outpatient care at community mental health centers, which are usually cheaper and more effective than large mental hospitals. England and Wales had 130 psychiatric hospitals in 1975 but only 12 in 2000 (Leff, 2002). The United States had almost 200,000 people in mental hospitals in 1967 and fewer than 40,000 in 2007 (Scott, Lakin, & Larson, 2008).

But what happened to people after release from the mental hospitals? Implementing good alternative care isn't easy. Policies vary from one country to another and from one part of a country to another, and the effectiveness has been undependable (Markström, 2014). Deinstitutionalization was and is a good idea in principle but only if implemented well, and too often it has not been.

The Duty to Protect

Suppose someone tells his therapist that he plans to kill a woman who refused his attentions. Months later, he really does kill her. Should her family be able to sue the therapist and collect damages?

Deinstitutionalization moved people out of mental hospitals, but many received little or no treatment after their release.

In the 1976 *Tarasoff* case, a California court ruled that *a therapist who has reason to believe that a client is dangerous to someone must warn the endangered person or take other steps to prevent harm*. That rule has become widely accepted in most of the United States and Canada, although its application is sometimes unclear (Quattrocchi & Schopp, 2005). Unfortunately, therapists don't always know who is dangerous. Issuing an unnecessary warning could increase the hostility between two people. Also, many therapists are now hesitant to take potentially violent clients, for fear of legal responsibility, and many clients decline to discuss violent impulses, for fear of involuntary commitment. The result is that many dangerous people no longer get the therapy that might help them control their violence (Bersoff, 2014; Edwards, 2014).

The Insanity Defense

Suppose someone slips into your drink a drug that causes you to hallucinate wildly. You see what looks like a hideous giant cockroach, and you kill it. Later, you discover it was not a cockroach but a person. Should you be convicted of murder? Of course not. Now suppose your own brain chemistry causes the same hallucination. You kill what you think is a giant cockroach, but it is actually a human being. Are you guilty of murder?

The tradition since Roman times has been that you are "not guilty by reason of insanity." You had no intention to do harm, and you did not know what you were doing. You should go to a mental hospital, not a prison. Most people agree with that principle in extreme cases. The problem is where to draw the line. *Insanity* is a legal term, not a psychological or medical term. According to the most famous definition of insanity, the M'Naghten rule, written in Great Britain in 1843,

> [t]o establish a defense on the ground of insanity, it must be clearly proved that, at the time of the committing of the act, the party accused was laboring under such a defect of reason, from disease of the mind, as not to know the nature and quality of the act he was doing; or if he did know it, that he did not know he was doing what was wrong. (Shapiro, 1985)

Would a diagnosis of schizophrenia or another mental illness demonstrate that someone was insane? Not by itself. What if someone committed a bizarre crime that most people couldn't imagine committing? Still no. Jeffrey Dahmer, arrested

Jeffery Dahmer, who murdered and cannibalized several men, was ruled sane. The bizarreness of the crime itself does not demonstrate legal insanity.

in 1991 for murdering and cannibalizing several men, was ruled sane and sentenced to prison. *To be regarded as insane under the M'Naghten rule, people must be so disordered that they do not understand what they are doing.* Anyone who tries to prevent the police from detecting a murder or other crime presumably did understand what he or she was doing.

An insanity verdict requires a difficult judgment about the defendant's state of mind at the time of the act. To help make that judgment, psychologists and psychiatrists are called as expert witnesses. The insanity cases that come to a jury trial are the difficult ones in which the experts disagree. In the United States, fewer than 1 percent of accused felons plead insanity, and of those, fewer than 25 percent are found not guilty (Knoll & Resnick, 2008). So, no more than 0.25 percent of all defendants are found not guilty by reason of insanity. However, those few cases get enough publicity that many people overestimate how common they are.

Another misconception is that defendants found not guilty by reason of insanity simply go free. In fact, they are almost always committed to a mental hospital, where their average stay is at least as long as the average prison term (Silver, 1995). When they are released, it is usually a "conditional release" that requires them to follow certain rules, such as continuing to take their medicine or to abstain from alcohol (Marshall, Vitaco, Read, & Harway, 2014).

31. A patient escapes from a mental hospital and commits a murder. Will this person be judged not guilty by reason of insanity?

Answer

31. Not necessarily. A defendant is insane only if the disorder prevented the person from understanding what he or she was doing.

The Science and Politics of Mental Illness

Suppose you are a storekeeper. Someone dressed as Batman stands outside your store every day shouting gibberish at anyone who comes by. Your once thriving business draws fewer and fewer customers each day. The disturbing man outside does not seem to be breaking any laws. He wants nothing to do with psychologists or psychiatrists. Should he nevertheless be forced to accept treatment for his odd behavior? If so, are we doing that for his sake or for yours as a storekeeper?

Similarly, the insanity defense and all the other issues in this module are complicated questions that require political decisions by society as a whole, not just the opinions of psychologists or psychiatrists. Regardless of what career you enter, you will be a voter and potential juror, and you will have a voice in deciding these issues. The decisions deserve serious, informed consideration.

Summary

- *Historical trends.* In the mid-1900s, people seeking psychotherapy paid for it themselves. Today, most people rely on insurance, and the insurance companies urge brief treatment with empirically supported therapies. Because they pay for more treatment if someone has a diagnosis, therapists now apply a greater variety of diagnoses, carefully described. (page 515)

- *Psychoanalysis.* Psychoanalysts try to uncover the unconscious reasons behind self-defeating behaviors. To bring the unconscious to consciousness, they rely on free association, dream analysis, and transference. (page 516)

- *Behavior therapy.* Behavior therapists set specific goals for changing a client's behavior and use learning techniques to help clients achieve those goals. (page 517)

- *Cognitive therapies.* Cognitive therapists try to get clients to replace defeatist thinking with more favorable views of themselves and the world. Many therapists combine features of behavior therapy and cognitive therapy, attempting to change people's behaviors by altering how they interpret the situation. (page 517)

- *Humanistic therapy.* Humanistic therapists, including person-centered therapists, assume that people can solve their own problems. (page 518)

- *Family systems therapy.* In many cases, an individual's problem is part of an overall disorder of family communications and expectations. Family systems therapists try to work with a whole family. (page 518)

- *Group therapies and self-help groups.* Psychotherapy is sometimes provided to people in groups, often composed of individuals with similar problems. Self-help groups provide sessions similar to group therapy but without a therapist. (page 518)

- *Effectiveness of psychotherapy.* The average person in therapy improves more than at least 80 percent of the equally troubled people not in therapy. In general, all mainstream therapies appear about equally effective, although cognitive or cognitive-behavioral therapy is somewhat better for reducing anxiety or other primary symptoms. Therapists today emphasize empirically supported therapies. (page 519)

- *Similarities among therapies.* A wide variety of therapies share certain features: All rely on a caring relationship between therapist and client. All promote self-understanding. All improve clients' morale. And all require a commitment by clients to try to make changes in their lives. (page 520)

- *Prevention.* Psychologists, especially community psychologists, seek to help people change their environment to promote mental health. (page 521)
- *Deinstitutionalization.* Few patients stay long in mental hospitals, but many patients released from mental hospitals do not receive adequate alternative care. (page 521)

- *Duty to warn.* The courts have ruled that a therapist who is convinced that a client is dangerous should warn the endangered person. (page 522)
- *The insanity defense.* Some defendants accused of a crime are acquitted for reasons of insanity, which is a legal rather than a medical or psychological concept. (page 522)

Key Terms

behavior therapy (page 517)

cognitive therapy (page 517)

cognitive-behavior therapy (page 518)

community psychologist (page 521)

deinstitutionalization (page 521)

dream analysis (page 516)

eclectic therapy (page 518)

empirically supported treatments
   (page 515)

family systems therapy (page 518)

free association (page 516)

group therapy (page 518)

intervention (page 521)

maintenance (page 521)

meta-analysis (page 519)

M'Naghten rule (page 522)

person-centered therapy (page 518)

prevention (page 521)

psychoanalysis (page 516)

psychodynamic therapies (page 516)

psychotherapy (page 515)

self-help group (page 519)

spontaneous remission (page 519)

Tarasoff case (page 522)

transference (page 516)

Review Questions

1. On average, what is the relationship between duration of psychotherapy and amount of improvement?
   (a) The rate of improvement is steady over time.
   (b) The rate of improvement starts slow, and increases in later sessions.
   (c) The rate of improvement is fastest at first, and then declines.
   (d) The rate of improvement is greater during the middle sessions than in the early ones or the later ones.

2. In psychoanalysis, for what purpose is free association used?
   (a) To help people learn to get along with other people
   (b) To gain access to unconscious thoughts
   (c) To test the client's intelligence
   (d) To enable clients to help each other when the therapist is absent

3. In which of these ways does a behavior therapist differ most sharply from a psychoanalyst?
   (a) A behavior therapist is more interested in discovering unconscious thought processes.
   (b) A behavior therapist relies more heavily on dream interpretations.
   (c) A behavior therapist sets more specific goals.
   (d) A behavior therapist practices unconditional positive regard.

4. According to a meta-analysis, how effective is psychotherapy for treating psychological disorders?
   (a) It produces benefits for almost all people in treatment.
   (b) The average person in treatment benefits more than 80 percent of people not in treatment.

   (c) It produces benefits only for a few disorders, such as phobia.
   (d) It is no more effective than a placebo.

5. In which of these ways do various forms of psychotherapy *differ* from one another?
   (a) Some types of therapy include a therapeutic alliance (close relationship between client and therapist) and others do not.
   (b) Some types of therapy imply a commitment to seek changes in one's life, and others do not.
   (c) Some types of therapy probe unconscious thoughts, and others do not.
   (d) Some types of therapy include a policy of discussing personal difficulties openly, and others do not.

6. Which type of specialist is most devoted to prevention of mental disorders?
   (a) Psychiatrists
   (b) Clinical psychologists
   (c) Community psychologists
   (d) Forensic psychologists

7. The *Tarasoff* ruling requires a therapist to warn or protect anyone whom a psychotherapy patient seriously threatens. What is one major risk that results from this policy?
   (a) A call to the threatened person might awaken him or her in the middle of the night.
   (b) Many therapists will have to be trained in certain aspects of the law.
   (c) Potentially dangerous clients may avoid psychotherapy.

Answers: 1c, 2b, 3c, 4b, 5c, 6c, 7c.

Here we are at the end of the book. As I've been writing and revising, I've imagined you sitting there reading. I've imagined a student much like I was in college, reading about psychology for the first time and often growing excited about it. I remember periodically telling a friend or relative, "Guess what I just learned about psychology! Isn't this interesting?" (I still do the same today.) I also remember occasionally thinking, "Hmm. The book says such-and-so, but I'm not convinced. I wonder whether psychologists ever considered a different explanation. . . ." I started thinking about research I might do if I became a psychologist.

I hope that you've had similar experiences yourself. I hope you've occasionally become so excited about something you read that you thought about it and told other people about it. In fact I hope you told your roommate so much about psychology that you started to become mildly annoying. I also hope you've sometimes doubted a conclusion, imagining a research project that might test it or improve on it. Psychology is still a work in progress.

Now, as I picture you reaching the end of the course, I'm not sure how you'll react. You might be thinking, "Wow, I sure have learned a lot!" Or you might be thinking, "Is that *all*?" Maybe you are reacting both ways: "Yes, I learned a lot. But it seems like there should be more. I still don't understand what conscious experience is all about, and I don't understand why I react the way I do sometimes. And this book—*wonderful as it is!*—hardly mentioned certain topics. Why do we laugh? How do we sense the passage of time? Why do people like to watch sports? Why are some people religious and others not?"

I have two good reasons for not answering all of your questions. One is that this is an introductory text and it can't go on forever. If you want to learn more, you should take other psychology courses or do additional reading. The other reason is that psychologists do not know all the answers.

Perhaps someday you'll become a researcher yourself and add to our knowledge. If not, you can try to keep up to date on current developments in psychology by reading good books and magazine articles. The magazine *Scientific American Mind* is an excellent source. One of my main goals has been to prepare you to continue learning about psychology.

Try to read critically: Is a conclusion based on good evidence? If you read about a survey, were the questions worded clearly? How reliable and valid were the measurements? Did the investigators obtain a representative or random sample? If someone draws a cause-and-effect conclusion, was the evidence based on experiments or only correlations? Even if the evidence looks solid, is the author's explanation the best one?

Above all, remember that *any* conclusion is tentative. Psychological researchers seldom use the word *prove;* their conclusions are almost always tentative. I once suggested to my editor, half seriously, that we should include in the index to this book the entry "*maybe*—see pages 1–524." We did not include such an entry, partly because I doubt anyone would have noticed the humor, and partly because our understanding of psychology isn't really that bad. Still, be leery of anyone who seems a little too certain about a great new insight in psychology. It's a long route from *maybe to definitely*.

Numbers in parentheses indicate the chapter in which a source is cited.

Abel, E. L., & Kruger, M. L. (2010). Smile intensity in photographs predicts longevity. *Psychological Science, 21,* 542–544. (12)

Abrahamsson, N., & Hyltenstam, K. (2009). Age of onset and nativelikeness in a second language: Listener perception versus linguistic scrutiny. *Language Learning, 59,* 249–306. (8)

Acevedo, B. P., Aron, A., Fisher, H. E., & Brown, L. L. (2012). Neural correlates of long-term intense romantic love. *Social Cognitive and Affective Neuroscience, 7,* 145–159. (13)

Ackerman, R. A., Kashy, D. A., Donnellan, M. B., Neppl, T., Lorenz, F. O., & Conger, R. D. (2013). The interpersonal legacy of a positive family climate in adolescence. *Psychological Science, 24,* 243–250. (5)

Ackil, J. K., Van Abbema, D. L., & Bauer, P. J. (2003). After the storm: Enduring differences in mother-child recollections of traumatic and nontraumatic events. *Journal of Experimental Child Psychology, 84,* 286–309. (7)

Adam, H., Shirako, A., & Maddux, W. W. (2010). Cultural variance in the interpersonal effects of anger in negotiations. *Psychological Science, 21,* 882–889. (5)

Adams, J. S. (1963). Wage inequities, productivity, and work quality. *Industrial Relations, 3,* 9–16. (11)

Adams, R. B., & Kleck, R. E. (2003). Perceived gaze direction and the processing of facial displays of emotion. *Psychological Science, 14,* 644–647. (12)

Adams, R. B., & Kleck, R. E. (2005). Effects of direct and averted gaze on the perception of facially communicated emotion. *Emotion, 5,* 3–11. (12)

Adler, A. (1964). Brief comments on reason, intelligence, and feeble-mindedness. In H. L. Ansbacher & R. R. Ansbacher (Eds.), *Superiority and social interest* (pp. 41–49). New York: Viking Press. (Original work published 1928) (14)

Adler, A. (1964). The structure of neurosis. In H. L. Ansbacher & R. R. Ansbacher (Eds.), *Superiority and social interest* (pp. 83–95). New York: Viking Press. (Original work published 1932) (14)

Adler, E., Hoon, M. A., Mueller, K. L., Chandrashekar, J., Ryba, N. J. P., & Zuker, C. S. (2000). A novel family of mammalian taste receptors. *Cell, 100,* 693–702. (4)

Admon, R., Lubin, G., Stern, O., Rosenberg, K., Sela, L., Ben-Ami, H., . . . Hendler, T. (2009). Human vulnerability to stress depends on amygdala's predisposition and hippocampal plasticity. *Proceedings of the National Academy of Sciences, U.S.A., 106,* 14120–14125. (12)

Adolph, K. E. (2000). Specificity of learning: Why infants fall over a veritable cliff. *Psychological Science, 11,* 290–295. (5)

Adolphs, R., Baron-Cohen, S., & Tranel, D. (2002). Impaired recognition of social emotions following amygdala damage. *Journal of Cognitive Neuroscience, 14,* 1264–1274. (12)

Adolphs, R., Damasio, H., & Tranel, D. (2002). Neural systems for recognition of emotional prosody: A 3-D lesion study. *Emotion, 2,* 23–51. (3)

Agar, W. E., Drummond, F. H., Tiegs, O. W., & Gunson, M. M. (1954). Fourth (final) report on a test of McDougall's Lamarckian experiment on the training of rats. *Journal of Experimental Biology, 31,* 307–321. (2)

Agerström, J., & Rooth, D. O. (2011). The role of automatic obesity stereotypes in real hiring decisions. *Journal of Applied Psychology, 96,* 790–805. (13)

Aglioti, S. M., Cesari, P., Romani, M., & Urgesi, C. (2008). Action anticipation and motor resonance in elite basketball players. *Nature Neuroscience, 11,* 1109–1116. (8)

Ahn, W., Flanagan, E. H., Marsh, J. K., & Sanislow, C. A. (2006). Beliefs about essences and the reality of mental disorders. *Psychological Science, 17,* 759–766. (15)

Ahn, H.-K., Kim, H. J., & Aggarwal, P. (2013). Helping fellow beings: Anthropomorphized social causes and the role of anticipatory guilt. *Psychological Science, 25,* 224–229. (13)

Ainsworth, M. D. S. (1979). Attachment as related to mother-infant interaction. In J. S. Rosenblatt, R. A. Hinde, C. Beer, & M. Busnel (Eds.), *Advances in the study of behavior* (Vol. 9, pp. 1–51). New York: Academic Press. (5)

Ainsworth, M. D. S., Blehar, M., Waters, E., & Wall, S. (1978). *Patterns of attachment.* Hillsdale, NJ: Erlbaum. (5)

Akers, K. G., Martinez-Canabal, A., Restivo, L., Yiu, A. P., De Cristofaro, A., Hsiang, H.-L., . . . Frankland, P. W. (2014). Hippocampal neurogenesis regulates forgetting during adulthood and infancy. *Science, 344,* 598–602. (7)

Åkerstedt, T. (2007). Altered sleep/wake patterns and mental performance. *Physiology and Behavior, 90,* 209–218. (10)

Aknin, L. B., Hamlin, J. K., & Dunn, E. W. (2012). Giving leads to happiness in young children. *PLoS One, 7,* e39211. (12)

Akrami, N., Ekehammar, B., & Bergh, R. (2011). Generalized prejudice: Common and specific components. *Psychological Science, 22,* 57–59. (14)

Albee, G. W. (1986). Toward a just society: Lessons from observations on the primary prevention of psychopathology. *American Psychologist, 41,* 891–898. (15)

Alcock, J. E. (2011, March/April). Back from the future: Parapsychology and the Bem affair. *Skeptical Inquirer, 35*(2), 31–39. (2)

Alexander, G. M., & Hines, M. (2002). Sex differences in response to children's toys in nonhuman primates (*Cercopithecus aethiops sabaeus*). *Evolution and Human Behavior, 23,* 467–479. (5)

Alexander, G. M., Wilcox, T., & Woods, R. (2009). Sex differences in infants' visual interest in toys. *Archives of Sexual Behavior, 38,* 427–433. (5, 14)

Alexander, I. E. (1982). The Freud-Jung relationship—the other side of Oedipus and countertransference. *American Psychologist, 37,* 1009–1018. (14)

Alexander, K. W., Quas, J. A., Goodman, G. S., Ghetti, S., Edelstein, R. S., Redlich, A. D., . . . Jones, D. P. H. (2005). Traumatic impact predicts long-term memory for documented child sexual abuse. *Psychological Science, 16,* 33–40. (7)

Alexander, M. G., & Fisher, T. D. (2003). Truth and consequences: Using the bogus pipeline to examine sex differences in self-reported sexuality. *Journal of Sex Research, 40,* 27–35. (11)

Alison, L. J., Smith, M. D., Eastman, O., & Rainbow, L. (2003). Toulmin's philosophy of argument and its relevance to offender profiling. *Psychology, Crime and Law, 9,* 173–183. (14)

Allen, H. L., Estrada, K., Lettre, G., Berndt, S. I., Weedon, M. N., Rivadeneira, F., . . . Hirschhorn, J. L. (2010). Hundreds of variants clustered in genomic loci and biological pathways affect human height. *Nature, 467,* 832–838. (3)

Allison, S. T., Mackie, D. M., Muller, M. M., & Worth, L. T. (1993). Sequential correspondence biases and perceptions of change: The Castro studies revisited. *Personality and Social Psychology Bulletin, 19,* 151–157. (13)

Alloy, L. B., Abramson, L. Y., Whitehouse, W. G., Hogan, M. E., Tashman, N. A., Steinberg, D. L., . . . Donovan, P. (1999). Depressogenic cognitive styles: Predictive validity, information processing and personality characteristics, and developmental origins. *Behaviour Research and Therapy, 37,* 503–531. (15)

Allport, G. W. (1935). Attitudes. In C. Murchison (Ed.), *A handbook of social psychology* (pp. 798–844). Worcester, MA: Clark University Press. (13)

Allport, G. W. (1961). *Pattern and growth in personality.* New York: Holt, Rinehart & Winston. (14)

Allport, G. W., & Odbert, H. S. (1936). Traitnames: A psycholexical study. *Psychological Monographs, 47*(Whole No. 211). (14)

Alpers, G. W., & Gerdes, A. B. M. (2007). Here is looking at you: Emotional faces predominate in binocular rivalry. *Emotion, 7,* 495–506. (10)

Alpert, J. L., Brown, L. S., & Courtois, C. A. (1998). Symptomatic clients and memories of childhood abuse. *Psychology, Public Policy, and Law, 4,* 941–995. (7)

Alroe, C. J., & Gunda, V. (1995). Self-amputation of the ear. *Australian and New Zealand Journal of Psychiatry, 29,* 508–512. (15)

Alter, A. L., Oppenheimer, D. M., Epley, N., & Eyre, R. N. (2007). Overcoming intuition: Metacognitive difficulty activates analytic reasoning. *Journal of Experimental Psychology: General, 136,* 569–576. (8)

Altmann, E. M., & Gray, W. D. (2002). Forgetting to remember: The functional relationship of decay and interference. *Psychological Science, 13,* 27–33. (7)

Ambady, N., & Rosenthal, R. (1993). Half a minute: Predicting teacher evaluations from thin slices of nonverbal behavior and physical attractiveness. *Journal of Personality and Social Psychology, 64,* 431–441. (13)

Amelang, M., & Steinmayr, R. (2006). Is there a validity increment for tests of emotional intelligence in explaining the variance of performance criteria? *Intelligence, 34,* 459–468. (12)

American Medical Association. (1986). Council report: Scientific status of refreshing recollection by the use of hypnosis. *International Journal of Clinical and Experimental Hypnosis, 34,* 1–12. (10)

American Psychiatric Association (2013). *Diagnostic and Statistical Manual of Mental Disorders* (fifth edition). Washington, DC: American Psychiatric Publishing. (15)

Amici, F., Visalberghi, E., & Call, J. (2014). Lack of prosociality in great apes, capuchin monkeys and spider monkeys: convergent evidence from two different food distribution tasks. *Proceedings of the Royal Society B, 281,* rspb.2014.1699. (13)

Amodio, D. M., & Harmon-Jones, E. (2011). Trait emotions and affective modulation of the startle eyeblink: On the unique relationship of trait anger. *Emotion, 11,* 47–51. (12)

Anderson, A., & Phelps, E. A. (2000). Expression without recognition: Contributions of the human amygdala to emotional communication. *Psychological Science, 11,* 106–111. (12)

Anderson, C., Kraus, M. W., Galinsky, A. D., & Keltner, D. (2012). The local-ladder effect: Social status and subjective well-being. *Psychological Science, 23,* 764–771. (12)

Anderson, C., Keltner, D., & John, O. P. (2003). Emotional convergence between people over time. *Journal of Personality and Social Psychology, 84,* 1054–1068. (13)

Anderson, D. I., Campos, J. J., Witherington, D. C., Dahl, A., Rivera, M., He, M., . . . Barbu-Roth, M. (2013). The role of locomotion in psychological development. *Frontiers in Psychology, 4,* Article 440. (5)

Anderson, E., Siegel, E., White, D., & Barrett, L. F. (2012). Out of sight but not out of mind: Unseen affective faces influence evaluations and social impressions. *Emotion, 12,* 1210–1221. (10)

Anderson, S., Parbery-Clark, A., White-Schwoch, T., & Kraus, N. (2012). Aging affects neural precision of speech encoding. *Journal of Neuroscience, 32,* 14156–14164. (4)

Anderson, S. W., Bechara, A., Damasio, H., Tranel, D., & Damasio, A. R. (1999). Impairment of social and moral behavior related to early damage in human prefrontal cortex. *Nature Neuroscience, 2,* 1032–1037. (3)

Andreano, J. M., & Cahill, L. (2006). Glucocorticoid release and memory consolidation in men and women. *Psychological Science, 17,* 466–470. (7)

Andreasen, N. C. (1986). Scale for the assessment of thought, language, and communication. *Schizophrenia Bulletin, 12,* 473–482. (15)

Andrew, D., & Craig, A. D. (2001). Spinothalamic lamina I neurons selectively sensitive to histamine: A central neural pathway for itch. *Nature Neuroscience, 4,* 72–77. (4)

Andrew, K. N., Hoshooley, J., & Joanisse, M. F. (2014). Sign language ability in young deaf signers predicts comprehension of written sentences in English. *PLoS One, 9,* e89994. (8)

Andrews, T. J., Halpern, S. D., & Purves, D. (1997). Correlated size variations in human visual cortex, lateral geniculate nucleus, and optic tract. *Journal of Neuroscience, 17,* 2859–2868. (4)

Anglin, S. M. (2014). From avoidance to approach: The effects of mortality salience and attachment on the motivation to repair troubled relationships. *Personality and Individual Differences, 66,* 86–91. (5)

Anglin, D., Spears, K. L., & Hutson, H. R. (1997). Flunitrazepam and its involvement in date or acquaintance rape. *Academy of Emergency Medicine, 4,* 323–326. (3)

Anguera, J. A., Boccanfuso, J., Rintoul, J. L., Al-Hashimi, O., Faraji, F., Janowich, J., . . . Gazzaley, A. (2013). Video game training enhances cognitive control in older adults. *Nature, 501,* 97–101. (5)

Anonymous. (1955). *Alcoholics anonymous* (2nd ed.). New York: Alcoholics Anonymous World Services. (15)

Antoniadis, E. A., Winslow, J. T., Davis, M., & Amaral, D. G. (2007). Role of the primate amygdala in fear-potentiated startle. *Journal of Neuroscience, 27,* 7386–7396. (12)

APA Presidential Task Force on Evidence-Based Practice. (2006). Evidence-based practice in psychology. *American Psychologist, 61,* 271–285. (15)

Apfelbaum, E. P., Paulker, K., Sommers, S. R., & Ambady, N. (2010). In blind pursuit of racial equality? *Psychological Science, 21,* 1587–1592. (13)

Ariely, D., & Wertenbroch, K. (2002). Procrastination, deadlines, and performance: Self-control by precommitment. *Psychological Science, 13,* 219–224. (11)

Arkes, H. R. (2013). The consequences of the hindsight bias in medical decision making. *Current Directions in Psychological Science, 22,* 356–360. (7)

Arkes, H. R., & Ayton, P. (1999). The sunk cost and Concorde effects: Are humans less rational than lower animals? *Psychological Bulletin, 125,* 591–600. (8)

Armon, G. (2014). Type D personality and job burnout: The moderating role of physical activity. *Personality and Individual Differences, 58,* 112–115. (11)

Armor, D. A., Massey, C., & Sackett, A. M. (2008). Prescribed optimism: Is it right to be wrong about the future? *Psychological Science, 19,* 329–331. (11)

Armstrong, J. B., & Schindler, D. E. (2011). Excess digestive capacity in predators reflects a life of feast and famine. *Nature, 476,* 84–87. (11)

Arnell, K. M., Killman, K. V., & Fijavz, D. (2007). Blinded by emotion: Target misses follow attention capture by arousing distractors in RSVP. *Emotion, 7,* 465–477. (7)

Arnold, H. J., & House, R. J. (1980). Methodological and substantive extensions to the job characteristics model of motivation. *Organizational Behavior and Human Performance, 25,* 161–183. (11)

Aronow, E., Reznikoff, M., & Moreland, K. L. (1995). The Rorschach: Projective technique or psychometric test? *Journal of Personality Assessment, 64,* 213–228. (14)

Aronson, E. (1997). The theory of cognitive dissonance: The evolution and vicissitudes of an idea. In C. McGarty & S. A. Haslam (Eds.), *The message of social psychology* (pp. 20–35). Cambridge, MA: Blackwell. (13)

Aronson, E., & Carlsmith, J. M. (1963). Effect of the severity of threat on the devaluation of forbidden behavior. *Journal of Abnormal and Social Psychology, 66,* 584–588. (13)

Arvey, R. D., McCall, B. P., Bouchard, T. J., Jr., Taubman, P., & Cavanaugh, M. A. (1994). Genetic influences on job satisfaction and work values. *Personality and Individual Differences, 17,* 21–33. (11)

Asch, S. E. (1951). Effects of group pressure upon the modification and distortion of judgments. In H. Guetzkow (Ed.), *Groups, leadership, and men* (pp. 177–190). Pittsburgh, PA: Carnegie Press. (13)

Asch, S. E. (1955, November). Opinions and social pressure. *Scientific American, 193*(5), 31–35. (13)

Asch, S. E. (1956). Studies of independence and conformity: I. A minority of one against a unanimous majority. *Psychological Monographs, 70*(9, Whole No. 416). (13)

Ash, R. (1986, August). An anecdote submitted by Ron Ash. *The Industrial-Organizational Psychologist, 23*(4), 8. (6)

Ashton-James, C. E., Maddux, W. W., Galinsky, A. D., & Chartrand, T. L. (2009). Who I am depends on how I feel. *Psychological Science, 20,* 340–346. (12)

Askum, D., & Ataca, B. (2007). Sexuality related attitudes and behaviors of Turkish university students. *Archives of Sexual Behavior, 36,* 741–752. (11)

Athos, E. A., Levinson, B., Kistler, A., Zemansky, J., Bostrom, A., Freimer, N., . . . Gitschier, J. (2007). Dichotomy and perceptual distortions in absolute pitch ability. *Proceedings of the National Academy of Sciences, USA, 104,* 14795–14800. (4)

Atkinson, R. C., & Shiffrin, R. M. (1968). Human memory: A proposed system and its control. In K. W. Spence & J. T. Spence (Eds.), *The psychology of learning and motivation* (Vol. 2, pp. 89–105). New York: Academic Press. (7)

Averill, J. R. (1983). Studies on anger and aggression: Implications for theories of emotion. *American Psychologist, 38,* 1145–1160. (12)

Aviezer, H., Hassin, R. R., Ryan, J., Grady, C., Susskind, J., Anderson, A., . . . Bentin, S. (2008). Angry, disgusted, or afraid? *Psychological Science, 19,* 724–732. (12)

Babkoff, H., Caspy, T., Mikulincer, M., & Sing, H. C. (1991). Monotonic and rhythmic influences: A challenge for sleep deprivation research. *Psychological Bulletin, 109,* 411–428. (10)

Back, M. D., Schmukle, S. C., & Egloff, B. (2008). Becoming friends by chance. *Psychological Science, 19,* 439–440. (13)

Baddeley, A. D. (2001). Is working memory still working? *American Psychologist, 56,* 851–864. (7)

Baddeley, A., & Hitch, G. J. (1994). Developments in the concept of working memory. *Neuropsychology, 8,* 485–493. (7)

Bagby, R. M., Nicholson, R. A., Bacchiochi, J. R., Ryder, A. G., & Bury, A. S. (2002). The predictive capacity of the MMPI-2 and PAI validity scales and indexes to detect coached and uncoached feigning. *Journal of Personality Assessment, 78,* 69–86. (14)

Bagemihl, B. (1999). *Biological exuberance.* New York: St. Martin's Press. (11)

Bahrick, H. (1984). Semantic memory content in permastore: 50 years of memory for Spanish learned in school. *Journal of Experimental Psychology: General, 113,* 1–29. (7)

Bailey, A., Le Couteur, A., Gottesman, I., Bolton, P., Simonoff, E., Yuzda, E., . . . Rutter, M. (1995). Autism as a strongly genetic disorder: Evidence from a British twin study. *Psychological Medicine, 25,* 63–78. (15)

Bailey, J. M., & Pillard, R. C. (1991). A genetic study of male sexual orientation. *Archives of General Psychiatry, 48,* 1089–1096. (11)

Bailey, J. M., Pillard, R. C., Neale, M. C., & Agyei, Y. (1993) Heritable factors influence sexual orientation in women. *Archives of General Psychiatry, 50,* 217–223. (11)

Baillargeon, R. (1986). Representing the existence and the location of hidden objects: Object permanence in 6- and 8-month-old infants. *Cognition, 23,* 21–41. (5)

Baillargeon, R. (1987). Object permanence in 3½- and 4½-month-old infants. *Developmental Psychology, 23,* 655–664. (5)

Baillargeon, R., Li, J., Ng, W., & Yuan, S. (2009). An account of infants' physical reasoning. In A. Woodward & A. Needham (Eds.), *Learning and the infant* (pp. 66–116). New York: Oxford University Press. (5)

Baird, J. C. (1982). The moon illusion: A reference theory. *Journal of Experimental Psychology: General, 111,* 304–315. (4)

Baker-Ward, L., Gordon, B. N., Ornstein, P. A., Larus, D. M., & Clubb, P. A. (1993). Young children's long-term retention of a pediatric examination. *Child Development, 64,* 1519–1533. (7)

Baker, T. B., Piper, M. E., McCarthy, D. E., Majeskie, M. R., & Fiore, M. C. (2004). Addiction motivation reformulated: An affective processing model of negative reinforcement. *Psychological Review, 111,* 33–51. (15)

Baker, T. B., Piper, M. E., Shlam, T. R., Cook, J. W., Smith, S. S., Loh, W.-Y., & Bolt, D. (2012). Are tobacco dependence and withdrawal related amongst heavy smokers? Relevance to conceptualizations of dependence. *Journal of Abnormal Psychology, 121,* 909–921. (15)

Bakhiet, S. e. F. A., Barakat, S. M. R., & Lynn, R. (2014). A Flynn effect among deaf boys in Saudi Arabia. *Intelligence, 44,* 75–77. (9)

Balcetis, E., Dunning, D., & Miller, R. L. (2008). Do collectivists know themselves better than individualists? Cross-cultural studies of the holier than thou phenomenon. *Journal of Personality and Social Psychology, 95,* 1252–1267. (13)

Baldessarini, R. J. (1984). Antipsychotic drugs. In T. B. Karasu (Ed.), *The psychiatric therapies: I. The somatic therapies* (pp. 119–170). Washington, DC: American Psychiatric Press. (15)

Balestri, M., Calati, R., Serretti, A., & De Ronchi, D. (2014). Genetic modulation of personality traits: A systematic review of the literature. *International Clinical Psychopharmacology, 29,* 1–15. (14)

Bali, V., Raisch, D. W., Moffett, M. L., & Khan, N. (2013). Determinants of nonmedical use, abuse, or dependence on prescription drugs, and use of substance abuse treatment. *Research in Social and Administrative Pharmacy, 9,* 276–287. (3)

Balliet, D., & Van Lange, P. A. M. (2013). Trust, punishment, and cooperation across 18 societies: A meta-analysis. *Perspectives on Psychological Science, 8,* 363–379. (13)

Ballinger, B., & Yalom, I. (1995). Group therapy in practice. In B. Bongar & L. E. Beutler (Eds.), *Comprehensive textbook of psychotherapy: Theory and practice* (pp. 189–204). Oxford, England: Oxford University Press. (15)

Bandura, A. (1977). *Social learning theory.* Upper Saddle River, NJ: Prentice Hall. (6)

Bandura, A. (1986). *Social foundations of thought and action.* Upper Saddle River, NJ: Prentice Hall. (6)

Bandura, A., Barbaranelli, C., Caprara, G. V., & Pastorelli, C. (2001). Self-efficacy beliefs as shapers of children's aspirations and career trajectories. *Child Development, 72,* 187–206. (6)

Bandura, A., Ross, D., & Ross, S. A. (1963). Imitation of film-mediated aggressive models. *Journal of Abnormal and Social Psychology, 66,* 3–11. (6)

Banks, W. P., & Isham, E. A. (2009). We infer rather than perceive the moment we decided to act. *Psychological Science, 20,* 17–21. (10)

Banuazizi, A., & Movahedi, S. (1975). Interpersonal dynamics in a simulated prison. *American Psychologist, 30,* 152–160. (13)

Barakat, M., Carrier, J., Debas, K., Lungu, O., Fogel, S., Vanderwalle, G., . . . Doyon, J. (2013). Sleep spindles predict neural and behavioral changes in motor sequence consolidation. *Human Brain Mapping, 34,* 2918–2928. (10)

Barlow, D. H., Ellard, K. K., Sauer-Zavala, S., Bullis, J. R., & Carl, J. R. (2014). The origins of neuroticism. *Perspectives on Psychological Science, 9,* 481–496. (14)

Barnett, K. J., Finucane, C., Asher, J. E., Bargary, G., Corvin, A. P., Newell, F. N., & Mitchell, K. J. (2008). Familial patterns and the origins of individual differences in synaesthesia. *Cognition, 106,* 871–893. (4)

Barnett, S. M., & Ceci, S. J. (2002). When and where do we apply what we learn? A taxonomy for far transfer. *Psychological Bulletin, 128,* 612–637. (8)

Barnett, W. S. (2011). Effectiveness of early educational intervention. *Science, 333,* 975–978. (9)

Barnier, A. J., Cox, R. E., & McConkey, K. M. (2014). The province of "highs": The high hypnotizable person in the science of hypnosis and in psychological science. *Psychology of Consciousness, 1,* 168–183. (10)

Barnier, A. J., & McConkey, K. M. (1998). Posthypnotic responding away from the hypnotic setting. *Psychological Science, 9,* 256–262. (10)

Baron, A., & Galizio, M. (2005). Positive and negative reinforcement: Should the distinction be preserved? *Behavior Analyst, 28,* 85–98. (6)

Barrett, L. F. (2006). Are emotions natural kinds? *Perspectives on Psychological Science, 1,* 28–58. (12)

Barrett, L. F. (2012). Emotions are real. *Emotions, 12,* 413–429. (12)

Barrett, L. F., Bliss-Moreau, E., Duncan, S. L., Rauch, S. L., & Wright, C. I. (2007). The amygdala and the experience of affect. *Social Cognitive and Affective Neuroscience, 2,* 73–83. (12)

Barrett, L. F., Mesquita, B., & Gendron, M. (2011). Context in emotion perception. *Current Directions in Psychological Science, 20,* 286–290. (12)

Barrett, L. F., Tugade, M. M., & Engle, R. W. (2004). Individual differences in working memory capacity and dual-process theories of the mind. *Psychological Bulletin, 130,* 553–573. (7)

Barron, E., Riley, L. M., Greer, J., & Smallwood, J. (2011). Absorbed in thought: The effect of mind wandering on the processing of relevant and irrelevant events. *Psychological Science, 22,* 596–601. (8)

Bartels, A., & Zeki, S. (2000). The neural basis of romantic love. *NeuroReport, 11,* 3829–3834. (13)

Barth, J., Munder, T., Gerger, H., Nüesch, E., Trelle, S., Znoj, H., . . . Cuijpers, P. (2013). Comparative efficacy of seven psychotherapeutic interventions for patients with depression: A network meta-analysis. *PLoS Medicine, 10,* e1001454. (15)

Bartlett, F. C. (1932). *Remembering.* Cambridge, England: Cambridge University Press. (7)

Bartoshuk, L. (2014). The measurement of pleasure and pain. *Perspectives on Psychological Science, 9,* 91–93. (12)

Bartoshuk, L. M. (1991). Taste, smell, and pleasure. In R. C. Bolles (Ed.), *The hedonics of taste* (pp. 5–28). Hillsdale, NJ: Erlbaum. (4)

Bartoshuk, L. M., Duffy, V. B., Lucchina, L. B., Prutkin, J., & Fast, K. (1998). PROP (6-n-propyl-thiouracil) supertasters and the saltiness of NaCl. *Annals of the New York Academy of Sciences, 855,* 793–796. (1)

Bartz, J. A., Simeon, D., Hamilton, H., Kim, S., Crystal, S., Braun, A., . . . Hollander, E. (2011). Oxytocin can hinder trust and cooperation in borderline personality disorder. *Social, Cognitive, and Affective Neuroscience, 6,* 556–563. (3)

Basabe, N., Paez, D., Valencia, J., Gonzalez, J. L., Rimé, B., & Diener, E. (2002). Cultural dimensions, socioeconomic development, climate, and emotional hedonic level. *Cognition and Emotion, 16,* 103–125. (12)

Bassok, M., & Holyoak, K. J. (1989). Interdomain transfer between isomorphic topics in algebra and physics. *Journal of Experimental Psychology: Learning, Memory, and Cognition, 15,* 153–166. (8)

Bastiaansen, J. A., Servaas, M. N., Bernard, J., Marsman, C., Ormel, J., Nolte, I. M., . . . Aleman, A. (2014). Filling the gap: Relationship between the serotonin-transporter-linked polymorphic region and amygdala activation. *Psychological Science, 25,* 2058–2066. (14)

Bates, T. C., Lewis, G. J., & Weiss, A. (2013). Childhood socioeconomic status amplifies genetic effects on adult intelligence. *Psychological Science, 24,* 2111–2116. (9)

Batson, C. D., & Thompson, E. R. (2001). Why don't people act morally? Motivational considerations. *Current Directions in Psychological Science, 10,* 54–57. (11)

Bauer, P. J., Wenner, J. A., & Kroupina, M. G. (2002). Making the past present: Later verbal accessibility of early memories. *Journal of Cognition and Development, 3,* 21–47. (7)

Baugerud, G. A., Magnussen, S., & Melinder, A. (2014). High accuracy but low consistency in children's long-term recall of a real life stressful event. *Journal of Experimental Child Psychology, 126,* 357–368. (7)

Baldauf, D., & Desimone, R. (2014). Neural mechanisms of object-based attention. *Science, 344,* 424–427. (3)

Barch, D. M., Cohen, R., & Csernansky, J. G. (2014). Altered cognitive development in the siblings of individuals with schizophrenia. *Clinical Psychological Science, 2,* 138–151. (15)

Barnes, C. M., Schaubroeck, J., Huth, M., & Ghumman, S. (2011). Lack of sleep and unethical conduct. *Organizational Behavior and Human Decision Processes, 115,* 169–180. (10)

Bauman, M. L., & Kemper, T. L. (2005). Structural brain anatomy in autism: What is the evidence? In M. L. Bauman & T. L. Kemper (Eds.), *The neurobiology of autism* (pp. 121–135). Baltimore: Johns Hopkins University Press. (15)

Baumeister, R. F. (2008). Free will in scientific psychology. *Perspectives on Psychological Science, 3,* 14–19. (1)

Baumeister, R. F., & Masicampo, E. J. (2010). Conscious thought is for facilitating social and cultural interactions: How mental simulations serve the animal-culture interface. *Psychological Review, 117,* 945–971. (10)

Baumeister, R. F., Campbell, J. D., Krueger, J. I., & Vohs, K. D. (2003). Does high self-esteem cause better performance, interpersonal success, happiness, or healthier lifestyles? *Psychological Science in the Public Interest, 4,* 1–44. (13, 14)

Baumeister, R. F., Masicampo, E. J., & Vohs, K. D. (2011). Do conscious thoughts cause behavior? *Annual Review of Psychology, 62,* 331–361. (10)

Bäuml, K.-H. T., & Samenieh, A. (2010). The two faces of memory retrieval. *Psychological Science, 21,* 793–795. (7)

Baumrind, D. (1971). Current patterns of parental authority. *Developmental Psychology Monographs, 4*(1, Pt. 2). (5)

Baxter, M. G., & Murray, E. A. (2002). The amygdala and reward. *Nature Reviews Neuroscience, 3,* 563–573. (3, 12)

Bayley, T. M., Dye, L., & Hill, A. J. (2009). Taste aversions in pregnancy. In S. Reilly & T. R. Schachtman (Eds.), *Conditioned taste aversion* (pp. 497–512). New York: Oxford University Press. (6)

Beaman, L., Duflo, E., Pande, R., & Topalova, P. (2012). Female leadership raises aspiratons and educational attainment for girls: A policy experiment in India. *Science, 335,* 582–586. (6)

Beauchamp, G. K., Cowart, B. J., Mennella, J. A., & Marsh, R. R. (1994). Infant salt taste: Developmental, methodological, and contextual factors. *Developmental Psychobiology, 27,* 353–365. (1)

Becht, M. C., & Vingerhoets, A. J. J. M. (2002). Crying and mood change: A cross-cultural study. *Cognition and Emotion, 16,* 87–101. (12)

Beck, A. T. (1991). Cognitive therapy: A 30-year retrospective. *American Psychologist, 46,* 368–375. (15)

Beck, A. T., & Emery, G. (1985). *Anxiety disorders and phobias.* New York: Basic Books. (15)

Beck, H. P., Levinson, S., & Irons, G. (2009). Finding Little Albert: A journey to John B. Watson's infant laboratory. *American Psychologist, 64,* 605–614. (15)

Beck, K., & Wilson, C. (2000). Development of affective organizational commitment: A cross-sequential examination of change with tenure. *Journal of Vocational Behavior, 56,* 114–136. (11)

Beckett, C., Maughan, B., Rutter, M., Castle, J., Colvert, E., Groothues, C., . . . Sonuga-Barke, E. J. S. (2006). Do the effects of early severe deprivation on cognition persist into early adolescence? Findings from the English and Romanian adoptees study. *Child Development, 77,* 696–711. (9)

Beer, J. S., Knight, R. T., & D'Esposito, M. (2006). Controlling the integration of emotion and cognition. *Psychological Science, 17,* 448–453. (12)

Bègue, L., & Muller, D. (2006). Belief in a just world as moderator of hostile attributional bias. *British Journal of Social Psychology, 45,* 117–126. (14)

Behne, T., Carpenter, M., & Tomasello, M. (2014). Young children create iconic gestures to inform others. *Developmental Psychology, 50,* 2049–2060. (8)

Behrens, M., Foerster, S., Staehler, F., Raguse, J.-D., & Meyerhof, W. (2007). Gustatory expression pattern of the human TAS2R bitter receptor gene family reveals a heterogenous population of bitter responsive taste receptor cells. *Journal of Neuroscience, 27,* 12630–12640. (4)

Beilock, S. L., Jelllison, W. A., Rydell, R. J., McConnell, A. R., & Carr, T. H. (2006). On the causal mechanisms of stereotype threat: Can skills that don't rely heavily on working memory still be threatened? *Personality and Social Psychology Bulletin, 32,* 1059–1071. (9)

Bell, R., & Pliner, P. L. (2003). Time to eat: The relationship between the number of people eating and meal duration in three lunch settings. *Appetite, 41,* 215–218. (11)

Bellugi, U., & St. George, M. (2000). Preface. *Journal of Cognitive Neuroscience, 12*(Suppl.), 1–6. (8)

Bellugi, U., Lichtenberger, L., Jones, W., Lai, Z., & St. George, M. (2000). I. The neurocognitive profile of Williams syndrome: A complex pattern of strengths and weaknesses. *Journal of Cognitive Neuroscience, 12*(Suppl.), 7–29. (8)

Belsky, J. (1996). Parent, infant, and social-contextual antecedents of father-son attachment security. *Developmental Psychology, 32,* 905–913. (5)

Bem, D. J. (2011). Feeling the future: Experimental evidence for anomalous retroactive influences on cognition and affect. *Journal of Personality and Social Psychology, 100,* 407–425. (2)

Bem, D. J., & Honorton, C. (1994). Does psi exist? Replicable evidence for an anomalous process of information transfer. *Psychological Bulletin, 115,* 4–18. (2)

Benish, S. G., Imel, Z. E., & Wampold, B. E. (2008). The relative efficacy of bona fide psychotherapies for treating post-traumatic stress disorder: A meta-analysis of direct comparisons. *Clinical Psychology Review, 28,* 746–758. (15)

Benjamin, L. T., Jr., & Simpson, J. A. (2009). The power of the situation. *American Psychologist, 64,* 12–19. (13)

Benschop, R. J., Godaert, G. L. R., Geenen, R., Brosschot, J. F., DeSmet, M. B. M., Olff, M., . . . Ballieux, R. E. (1995). Relationships between cardiovascular and immunologic changes in an experimental stress model. *Psychological Medicine, 25,* 323–327. (12)

Benson, H. (1977). Systemic hypertension and the relaxation response. *New England Journal of Medicine, 296,* 1152–1156. (12)

Benson, H. (1985). Stress, health, and the relaxation response. In W. D. Gentry, H. Benson, & C. J. de Wolff (Eds.), *Behavioral medicine: Work, stress and health* (pp. 15–32). Dordrecht, The Netherlands: Martinus Nijhoff. (12)

Benton, T. R., Ross, D. F., Bradshaw, E., Thomas, W. N., & Bradshaw, G. S. (2006). Eyewitness memory is still not common sense: Comparing jurors, judges and law enforcement to eyewitness experts. *Applied Cognitive Psychology, 20,* 115–129. (7)

Berenbaum, S. A. (1999). Effects of early androgens on sex-typed activities and interests in adolescents with congenital adrenal hyperplasia. *Hormones and Behavior, 35,* 102–110. (11)

Berenbaum, S. A., Duck, S. C., & Bryk, K. (2000). Behavioral effects of prenatal versus postnatal androgen excess in children with 21-hydroxylase-deficient congenital adrenal hyperplasia. *Journal of Clinical Endocrinology and Metabolism, 85,* 727–733. (5, 11)

Berger, R. J., & Phillips, N. H. (1995). Energy conservation and sleep. *Behavioural Brain Research, 69,* 65–73. (10)

Bergh, C., Callmar, M., Danemar, S., Hölcke, M., Isberg, S., Leon, M., . . . Södersten, P. (2013). Effective treatment of eating disorders: Results at multiple sites. *Behavioral Neuroscience, 127,* 878–889. (11)

Berglas, S., & Jones, E. E. (1978). Drug choice as a self-handicapping strategy in response to noncontingent success. *Journal of Personality and Social Psychology, 36,* 405–417. (13)

Berkman, N. D., Lohr, K. N., & Bulik, C. M. (2007). Outcomes of eating disorders: A systematic review of the literature. *International Journal of Eating Disorders, 40,* 293–309. (11)

Berkowitz, L. (1983). Aversively stimulated aggression: Some parallels and differences in research with animals and humans. *American Psychologist, 38,* 1135–1144. (13)

Berkowitz, L. (1989). Frustration-aggression hypothesis: Examination and reformulation. *Psychological Bulletin, 106,* 59–73. (13)

Bernardi, F., & Radl, J. (2014). The long-term consequences of parental divorce for children's educational attainment. *Demographic Research, 30,* Article 61. (5)

Bernstein, D. M., & Loftus, E. F. (2009). The consequences of false memories for food preferences and choices. *Perspectives on Psychological Science, 4,* 135–139. (7)

Bernstein, D. M., Atance, C., Loftus, G. R., & Meltzoff, A. (2004). We saw it all along. *Psychological Science, 15,* 264–267. (7)

Bernstein, I. L. (1991). Aversion conditioning in response to cancer and cancer treatment. *Clinical Psychology Review, 11,* 185–191. (6)

Berntsen, D., & Rubin, D. C. (2002). Emotionally charged autobiographical memories across the lifespan: The recall of happy, sad, traumatic and involuntary memories. *Psychology and Aging, 17,* 636–652. (7)

Berntsen, D., Johannessen, K. B., Thomsen, Y. D., Bertelsen, M., Hoyle, R. H., & Rubin, D. C. (2012). Peace and war: Trajectories of posttraumatic stress disorder symptoms before, during, and after military deployment in Afghanistan. *Psychological Science, 23,* 1557–1565. (12)

Berntson, G. G., Cacioppo, J. T., & Quigley, K. S. (1993). Cardiac psychophysiology and autonomic space in humans: Empirical perspectives and conceptual implications. *Psychological Bulletin, 114,* 296–322. (12)

Berridge, K. C., & Robinson, T. E. (1998). What is the role of dopamine in reward: Hedonic impact, reward learning, or incentive salience? *Brain Research Reviews, 28,* 309–369. (15)

Berry, C. M., & Sackett, P. R. (2009). Individual differences in course choice result in underestimation of the validity of college admission systems. *Psychological Science, 20,* 822–830. (9)

Berry, C. M., Cullen, M. J., & Meyer, J. M. (2014). Racial/ethnic subgroup differences in cognitive ability test range restriction: Implications for differential validity. *Journal of Applied Psychology, 99,* 21–37. (9)

Berry, J. W., Poortinga, Y. H., Segal, H., & Dasen, P. R. (1992). *Cross-cultural psychology.* Cambridge, England: Cambridge University Press. (15)

Bersoff, D. N. (2014). Protecting victims of violent patients while protecting confidentiality. *American Psychologist, 69,* 461–467. (15)

Berson, D. M., Dunn, F. A., & Takao, M. (2002). Phototransduction by retinal ganglion cells that set the circadian clock. *Science, 295,* 1070–1073. (10)

Bertenthal, B. I., Longo, M. R., & Kosobud, A. (2006). Imitative response tendencies following observation of intransitive actions. *Journal of Experimental Psychology: Human Perception and Performance, 32,* 210–225. (6)

Beuming, T., Kniazeff, J., Bergmann, M. L., Shi, L., Gracia, L., Raniszewska, K., . . . Loland, C. J. (2008). The binding sites for cocaine and dopamine in the dopamine transporter overlap. *Nature Neuroscience, 11,* 780-789. (3)

Bialystok, E., Craik, F. I. M., Green, D. W., & Gollan, T. H. (2009). Bilingual minds. *Psychological Science in the Public Interest, 10,* 89-129. (8)

Bialystok, E., Craik, F., & Luk, G. (2008). Cognitive control and lexical access in younger and older bilinguals. *Journal of Experimental Psychology: Learning, Memory, and Cognition, 34,* 859-873. (8)

Biederman, I., Yue, X., & Davidoff, J. (2009). Representation of shape in individuals from a culture with minimal exposure to regular, simple artifacts. *Psychological Science, 20,* 1437-1442. (4)

Biernacka, J. M., Geske, J. R., Schneekloth, T. D., Frye, M. A., Cunningham, J. M., Choi, D.-S., . . . Karpyak, V. M. (2013). Replication of genome wide association studies of alcohol dependence: Support for association with variation in *ADH1C*. *PLoS One*, e58798. (15)

Bijl, R. V., de Graaf, R., Hiripi, E., Kessler, R. C., Kohn, R., Offord, D. R., . . . Wittchen, H. U. (2003). The prevalence of treated and untreated mental disorders in five countries. *Health Affairs, 22,* 122-133. (15)

Billy, J. O. G., Tanfer, K., Grady, W. R., & Klepinger, D. H. (1993, March/April). The sexual behavior of men in the United States. *Family Planning Perspectives, 25,* 52-60. (11)

Binet, A., & Simon, T. (1905). Méthodes nouvelles pour le diagnostic du niveau intellectuel des anormaux [New methods for the measurement of the intellectual level of the abnormal]. *L'Année Psychologique, 11,* 191-244. (9)

Birak, K. S., Higgs, S., & Terry, P. (2011). Conditioned tolerance to the effects of alcohol on inhibitory control in humans. *Alcohol and Alcoholism, 46,* 686-693. (6)

Bishop, E. G., Cherny, S. S., Corley, R., Plomin, R., DeFries, J. C., & Hewitt, J. K. (2003). Development genetic analysis of general cognitive ability from 1 to 12 years in a sample of adoptees, biological siblings, and twins. *Intelligence, 31,* 31-49. (9)

Bjerkedal, T., Kristensen, P., Skjeret, G. A., & Brevik, J. I. (2007). Intelligence test scores and birth order among young Norwegian men (conscripts) analyzed within and between families. *Intelligence, 35,* 503-514. (5)

Bjorklund, D. F., & Shackelford, T. K. (1999). Differences in parental investment contribute to important differences between men and women. *Current Directions in Psychological Science, 8,* 86-92. (3)

Blackless, M., Charuvastra, A., Derryck, A., Fausto-Sterling, A., Lauzanne, K., & Lee, E. (2000). How sexually dimorphic are we? Review and synthesis. *American Journal of Human Biology, 12,* 151-166. (11)

Blair, R. J. R., Mitchell, D. G. V., Peschardt, K. S., Colledge, E., Leonard, R. A., Shine, J. H., . . . Perrett, D. I. (2004). Reduced sensitivity to others' fearful expressions in psychopathic individuals. *Personality and Individual Differences, 37,* 1111-1122. (12)

Blake, R., & Logothetis, N. K. (2002). Visual competition. *Nature Reviews Neuroscience, 3,* 13-23. (10)

Blakemore, C., & Sutton, P. (1969). Size adaptation: A new aftereffect. *Science, 166,* 245-247. (4)

Blascovich, J., & Tomaka, J. (1991). Measures of self-esteem. In J. P. Robinson, R. R. Shaver, & L. S. Wrightsman (Eds.), *Measures of personality and social psychological attitudes* (Vol. 1, pp. 115-160). San Diego, CA: Academic Press. (14)

Bless, H., Bohner, G., Schwarz, N., & Strack, F. (1990). Mood and persuasion: A cognitive response analysis. *Personality and Social Psychology Bulletin, 16,* 331-345. (12)

Bloch, L., Haase, C. M., & Levenson, R. W. (2014). Emotion regulation predicts marital satisfaction: More than a wives' tale. *Emotion, 14,* 130-144. (13)

Blom, V., Sverke, M., Bodin, L., Lindfors, P., & Svedberg, P. (2014). Work-home interference and burnout: A study based on Swedish twins. *Journal of Occupational and Environmental Medicine, 56,* 361-366. (11)

Blount, J. D., Metcalfe, N. B., Birkhead, T. R., & Surai, P. F. (2003). Carotenoid modulation of immune function and sexual attractiveness in zebra finches. *Science, 300,* 125-127. (13)

Blum, D. (1994). *The monkey wars.* New York: Oxford University Press. (2)

Blum, G. S., & Barbour, J. S. (1979). Selective inattention to anxiety-linked stimuli. *Journal of Experimental Psychology: General, 108,* 182-224. (4)

Blumberg, M. S., Gall, A. J., & Todd, W. D. (2014). The development of sleep-wake rhythms and the search for elemental circuits in the infant brain. *Behavioral Neuroscience, 128,* 250-263. (10)

Bobrow, D., & Bailey, J. M. (2001). Is male homosexuality maintained via kin selection? *Evolution and Human Behavior, 22,* 361-368. (11)

Bogaert, A. F. (2003). The interaction of fraternal birth order and body size in male sexual orientation. *Behavioral Neuroscience, 117,* 381-384. (11)

Bogaert, A. F. (2006). Biological versus nonbiological older brothers and men's sexual orientation. *Proceedings of the National Academy of Sciences, USA, 103,* 10771-10774. (11)

Bogg, T., & Roberts, B. W. (2013). The case for conscientiousness: Evidence and implications for a personality trait marker of health and longevity. *Annals of Behavioral Medicine, 45,* 278-288. (14)

Bohn, A., & Berntsen, D. (2011). The reminiscence bump reconsidered: Children's prospective life stories show a bump in young adulthood. *Psychological Science, 22,* 197-202. (7)

Bonanno, G. A., & Burton, C. L. (2013). Regulatory flexibility: An individual differences perspective on coping and emotion regulation. *Perspectives on Psychological Science, 8,* 591-612. (12)

Bonanno, G. A., & Mancini, A. D. (2008). The human capacity to thrive in the face of potential trauma. *Pediatrics, 121,* 369-375. (5)

Bond, M. H. (1991). *Beyond the Chinese face.* New York: Oxford University Press. (15)

Bond, R., & Smith, P. B. (1996). Culture and conformity: A meta-analysis of studies using Asch's (1952, 1956) line judgment task. *Psychological Bulletin, 119,* 111-137. (13)

Bonneh, Y. S., Cooperman, A., & Sagi, D. (2001). Motion-induced blindness in normal observers. *Nature, 411,* 798-801. (10)

Bonnie, R. J. (1997). Research with cognitively impaired subjects: Unfinished business in the regulation of human research. *Archives of General Psychiatry, 54,* 105-111. (2)

Boot, W. R., Simons, D. J., Stothart, C., & Stutts, C. (2013). The pervasive problem with placebos in psychology: Why active control groups are not sufficient to rule out placebo effects. *Perspectives on Psychological Science, 8,* 445-454. (2)

Bootzin, R. R., & Bailey, E. T. (2005). Understanding placebo, nocebo, and iatrogenic treatment effects. *Journal of Clinical Psychology, 61,* 871-880. (12)

Borch-Jacobsen, M., & Shamdasani, S. (2012). *The Freud files: An inquiry into the history of psychoanalysis.* New York: Cambridge University Press. (1, 14)

Borden, V. M. H., & Rajecki, D. W. (2000). First-year employment outcomes of psychology baccalaureates: Relatedness, preparedness, and prospects. *Teaching of Psychology, 27,* 164-168. (1)

Boring, E. G. (1930). A new ambiguous figure. *American Journal of Psychology, 42,* 444-445. (4)

Bornstein, R. F. (2010). Psychoanalytic theory as a unifying framework for 21st century personality assessment. *Psychoanalytic Psychology, 27,* 133-152. (14)

Bornstein, R. F., & Becker-Matero, N. (2011). Reconnecting psychoanalysis to mainsgtream psychology: Metaphor as glue. *Psychoanalytic Inquiry, 31,* 172-184. (14)

Boroditsky, L., & Gaby, A. (2010). Remembrances of times east: Absolute spatial representations of time in an Australian aboriginal community. *Psychological Science, 21,* 1635-1639. (2)

Borota, D., Murray, E., Keceli, G., Chang, A., Watabe, J. M., Ly, M., . . . Yassa, M. A. (2014). Post-study caffeine administration enhances memory consolidation in humans. *Nature Neuroscience, 17,* 201-203. (7)

Borsutzky, S., Fujiwara, E., Brand, M., & Markowitsch, H. J. (2008). Confabulations in alcoholic Korsakoff patients. *Neuropsychologia, 46,* 3133-3143. (7)

Bortolotti, B., Menchetti, M., Bellini, F., Montaguti, M. B., & Berardi, D. (2008). Psychological interventions for major depression in primary care: A meta-analytic review of randomized controlled trials. *General Hospital Psychiatry, 30,* 293-302. (15)

Bos, H. M. W., van Balen, F., & van den Boom, D. C. (2007). Child adjustment and parenting in planned lesbian-parent families. *American Journal of Orthopsychiatry, 77,* 38-48. (5)

Bos, H., & Gartrell, N. (2010). Adolescents of the USA National Longitudinal Lesbian Family Study: Can family characteristics counteract the negative effects of stigmatization. *Family Process, 49,* 559-572. (5)

Bosker, W. M., Karschner, E. L., Dayong, L., Goodwin, R. S., Hirvonen, J., Innis, R. B., . . . Ramackers, J. G. (2013). Psychomotor function in chronic daily cannabis smokers during sustained abstinence. *PLoS One, 8,* e53127. (3)

Bouchard, T. J., Jr., & McGue, M. (1981). Familial studies of intelligence: A review. *Science, 212,* 1055-1059. (9)

Bouchard, T. J., Jr., & McGue, M. (2003). Genetic and environmental influences on human psychological differences. *Journal of Neurobiology, 54,* 4-45. (5, 14)

Bouchard, T. J., Lykken, D. T., McGue, M., Segal, N. L., & Tellegen, A. (1990). Sources of psychological differences: The Minnesota study of twins reared apart. *Science, 250,* 223-228. (5)

Bowlby, J. (1973). *Attachment and loss: Vol. II. Separation.* New York: Basic Books. (5)

Bowmaker, J. K. (1998). Visual pigments and molecular genetics of color blindness. *News in Physiological Sciences, 13,* 63-69. (4)

Bowmaker, J. K., & Dartnall, H. J. A. (1980). Visual pigments of rods and cones in a human retina. *Journal of Physiology* (London), *298,* 501-511. (4)

Boyce, C. J., & Wood, A. M. (2011). Personality prior to disability determines adaptation: Agreeable individuals recover lost life satisfaction faster and more completely. *Psychological Science, 22,* 1397-1402. (14)

Boyke, J., Driemeyer, J., Gaser, C., Büchel, C., & May, A. (2008). Training-induced brain structure changes in the elderly. *Journal of Neuroscience, 28,* 7031-7035. (3)

Bracha, H. S. (2006). Human brain evolution and the "neuroevolutionary time-depth principle": Implications for the reclassification of fear-circuitry-related traits in *DSM-V* and for studying resilience to warzone-related posttraumatic stress disorder. *Progress in Neuro-Psychopharmacology and Biological Psychiatry, 30,* 827-853. (15)

Bradbury, T. N., & Miller, G. A. (1985). Season of birth in schizophrenia: A review of evidence, methodology, and etiology. *Psychological Bulletin, 98,* 569-594. (15)

Braden, J. P., & Niebling, B. C. (2005). Using the joint test standards to evaluate the validity evidence for intelligence tests. In D. P. Flanagan & P. L. Harrison (Eds.), *Contemporary intellectual assessment* (pp. 615-630). New York: Guilford Press. (9)

Brang, D., Edwards, L., Ramachandran, V. S., & Coulson, S. (2008). Is the sky 2? Contextual priming in grapheme-color synesthesia. *Psychological Science, 19,* 421-428. (4)

Brannon, T. N., & Walton, G. M. (2013). Enacting cultural interests: How intergroup contact reduces prejudice by sparking interest in an out-group's culture. *Psychological Science, 24,* 1947-1957. (13)

Braungart-Rieker, J. M., Zentall, S., Lickenbrock, D. M., Ekas, N. V., Oshio, T., & Planalp, E. (2014). Attachment in the making: Mother and father sensitivity and infants' responses during the Still-Face Paradigm. *Journal of Experimental Child Psychology, 125,* 63-84. (5)

Braunschweig, D., Krakowiak, P., Duncanson, P., Boyce, R., Hansen, R. L., Ashwood, P., . . . Van de Water, J. (2013). Autism-specific maternal autoantibodies recognize critical proteins in developing brain. *Translational Psychiatry, 3,* e277. (15)

Brédart, S., Delchambre, M., & Laureys, S. (2006). One's own face is hard to ignore. *Quarterly Journal of Experimental Psychology, 59,* 46-52. (8)

Bregman, A. S. (1981). Asking the "what for" question in auditory perception. In M. Kubovy & J. R. Pomerantz (Eds.), *Perceptual organization* (pp. 99-118). Hillsdale, NJ: Erlbaum. (4)

Bremmer, F., Kubischik, M., Hoffmann, K.-P., & Krekelberg, B. (2009). Neural dynamics of saccadic suppression. *Journal of Neuroscience, 29,* 12374-12383. (3)

Brescoll, V. L., & Uhlmann, E. L. (2008). Can an angry woman get ahead? *Psychological Science, 19,* 268-275. (13)

Breslau, N., Dickens, W. T., Flynn, J. R., Peterson, E. L., & Lucia, V. C. (2006). Low birthweight and social disadvantage: Tracking their relationship with children's IQ during the period of school attendance. *Intelligence, 34,* 351-362. (9)

Brewer, M. B., & Chen, Y.-R. (2007). Where (who) are collectives in collectivism? Toward conceptual clarification of individualism and collectivism. *Psychological Review, 114,* 131-151. (5)

Brewer, N., Weber, N., Wootton, D., & Lindsay, D. S. (2012). Identifying the bad guy in a lineup using confidence judgments under deadline pressure. *Psychological Science, 23,* 1208-1214. (7)

Britton, J. C., Grillon, C., Lissek, S., Norcross, M. A., Szuhany, K.L., Chen, G., . . . Pine, D. S. (2013). Response to learned threat: An fMRI study in adolescent and adult anxiety. *American Journal of Psychiatry, 170,* 1195-1204. (12)

Brooks, A. W. (2014). Get excited: Reappraising pre-performance anxiety as excitement. *Journal of Experimental Psychology: General, 143,* 1144-1158. (12)

Brower, K. J., & Anglin, M. D. (1987). Adolescent cocaine use: Epidemiology, risk factors, and prevention. *Journal of Drug Education, 17,* 163-180. (3)

Brown, A. S. (2003). A review of the déjà vu experience. *Psychological Bulletin, 129,* 394-413. (10)

Brown, A. S. (2011). The environment and susceptibility to schizophrenia. *Progress in Neurobiology, 93,* 23-58. (15)

Brown, G. W. (1989). Life events and measurement. In G. W. Brown & T. O. Harris (Eds.), *Life events and illness* (pp. 3-45). New York: Guilford Press. (12)

Brown, J. (1977). *Mind, brain, and consciousness.* New York: Academic Press. (8)

Brown, R., & McNeill, D. (1966). The "tip of the tongue." *Journal of Verbal Learning and Verbal Behavior, 5,* 325-337. (7)

Bruck, M., Cavanagh, P., & Ceci, S. J. (1991). Fortysomething: Recognizing faces at one's 25th reunion. *Memory and Cognition, 19,* 221-228. (4)

Bruder, C. E. G., Piotrowski, A., Gijsbers, A. A. C. J., Andersson, R., Erickson, S., Diaz de Staal, T., . . . Dumanski, J. P. (2008). Phenotypically concordant and discordant monozygotic twins display different DNA copy-number-variant profiles. *American Journal of Human Genetics, 82,* 763-771. (15)

Brumfiel, G. (2013). Fallout of fear. *Nature, 493,* 291-293. (12)

Brummelman, E., Thomaes, S., Orobio de Castro, B., Overbeek, G., & Bushman, B. J. (2014). "That's not just beautiful—that's incredibly beautiful!": The adverse impact of inflated praise on children with low self-esteem. *Psychological Science, 25,* 728-735. (11)

Brüning, J. C., Gautham, D., Burks, D. J., Gillette, J., Schubert, M., Orban, P. C., . . . Kahn, C. R. (2000). Role of brain insulin receptor in control of body weight and reproduction. *Science, 289,* 2122-2125. (11)

Bryant, F. B., & Guilbault, R. L. (2002). "I knew it all along" eventually: The development of hindsight bias in the Clinton impeachment verdict. *Basic and Applied Social Psychology, 24,* 27-41. (7)

Brysbaert, M., Vitu, F., & Schroyens, W. (1996). The right visual field advantage and the optimal viewing position effect: On the relation between foveal and parafoveal word recognition. *Neuropsychology, 10,* 385-395. (8)

Bryson, S. E. (2005). The autistic mind. In M. L. Bauman & T. L. Kemper (Eds.), *The neurobiology of autism* (pp. 34-44). Baltimore: Johns Hopkins University Press. (15)

Buck, L., & Axel, R. (1991). A novel multigene family may encode odorant receptors: A molecular basis for odor recognition. *Cell, 65,* 175-187. (4)

Buehler, R., Griffin, D., & Ross, M. (1994). Exploring the "planning fallacy": Why people underestimate their task completion times. *Journal of Personality and Social Psychology, 67,* 366-381. (11)

Bühren, K., Schwarte, R., Fluck, F., Timmesfeld, N., Krei, M., Egberts, K., . . . Herpertz-Dahlmann, B. (2014). Comorbid psychiatric disorders in female adolescents with first-onset anorexia nervosa. *European Eating Disorders Review, 22,* 39-44. (11)

Bui, D. C., Myerson, J., & Hale, S. (2013). Note-taking with computers: Exploring alternative strategies for improved recall. *Journal of Educational Psychology, 105,* 299-309. (7)

Buizer-Voskamp, J. E., Muntjewerff, J. W., Strengman, E., Sabatti, C., Stefansson, H., Vorstman, J. A. S, & Ophoff, R. A. (2011). Genome-wide analysis shows increased frequency of copy number variations deletions in Dutch schizophrenia patients. *Biological Psychiatry, 70,* 655-662. (15)

Burger, J. M. (1986). Increasing compliance by improving the deal: The that's-not-all technique. *Journal of Personality and Social Psychology, 51,* 277-283. (13)

Burger, J. M. (2009). Replicating Milgram: Would people still obey today? *American Psychologist, 64,* 1-11. (13)

Burke, K. A., Franz, T. M., Miller, D. N., & Schoenbaum, G. (2008). The role of the orbitofrontal cortex in the pursuit of happiness and more specific rewards. *Nature, 454,* 340-344. (6)

Burkart, J. M., Allon, O., Fichtel, C., Finkenwirth, C., Heschl, A., Huber, J., . . . van Schaik, P. (2014). The evolutionary origin of human hyper-cooperation. *Nature Communications, 5,* Article 4747. (13)

Burr, D. C., Morrone, M. C., & Ross, J. (1994). Selective suppression of the magnocellular visual pathway during saccadic eye movements. *Nature, 371,* 511-513. (8)

Bushdid, C., Magnasco, M. O., Vosshall, L. B., & Keller, A. (2014). Humans can discriminate more than 1 trillion olfactory stimuli. *Science, 343,* 1370-1372. (4)

Bushman, B. J. (2002). Does venting anger feed or extinguish the flame? Catharsis, rumination, distraction, anger, and aggressive responding. *Personality and Social Psychology Bulletin, 28,* 724-731. (14)

Bushman, B. J., & Anderson, C. A. (2009). Comfortably numb: Desensitizing effects of violent media on helping others. *Psychological Science, 20,* 273-277. (13)

Buss, D. M. (2000). Desires in human mating. *Annals of the New York Academy of Sciences, 907,* 39-49. (3)

Butcher, J. N., Graham, J. R., Williams, C. L., & Ben-Porath, Y. S. (1990). *Development and use of the MMPI-2 content scales.* Minneapolis: University of Minnesota Press. (14)

Butler, A. C., Chapman, J. E., Forman, E. M., & Beck, A. T. (2006). The empirical status of cognitive-behavioral therapy: A review of meta-analyses. *Clinical Psychology Review, 26,* 17-31. (15)

Butler, E. A., Lee, T. L., & Gross, J. J. (2007). Emotion regulation and culture: Are the social consequences of emotion suppression culture-specific? *Emotion, 7,* 30-48. (12)

Butler, L. (2002). A list of published papers is no measure of value. *Nature, 419,* 877. (11)

Butler, M. R., Turner, K. W., Park, J. H., Schoomer, E. E., Zucker, I., & Gorman, M. R. (2010). Seasonal regulation of reproduction: Altered role of melatonin under naturalistic conditions in hamsters. *Proceedings of the Royal Society B, 277,* 2867-2874. (10)

Butler, R. J., Holland, P., Gasson, S., Norfolk, S., Houghton, L., & Penney, M. (2007). Exploring potential mechanisms in alarm treatment for primary nocturnal enuresis. *Scandinavian Journal of Urology and Nephrology, 41,* 407–413. (15)

Byers-Heinlein, K., & Fennell, C. T. (2014). Perceptual narrowing in the context of increased variation: Insights from bilingual infants. *Developmental Psychobiology, 56,* 274–291. (5)

Byne, W., Tobet, S., Mattiace, L. A., Lasco, M. S., Kemether, E., Edgar, M. A., . . . Jones, L. B. (2001). The interstitial nuclei of the human anterior hypothalamus: An investigation of variation with sex, sexual orientation, and HIV status. *Hormones and Behavior, 40,* 86–92. (11)

Cacioppo, J. T., Hawkley, L. C., & Berntson, G. G. (2003). The anatomy of loneliness. *Current Directions in Psychological Science, 12,* 71–74. (12)

Cahalan, D. (1978). Subcultural differences in drinking behavior in U.S. national surveys and selected European studies. In P. E. Nathan, G. A. Marlatt, & T. Løberg (Eds.), *Alcoholism: New directions in behavioral research and treatment* (pp. 235–253). New York: Plenum Press. (15)

Cahill, L. (2006). Why sex matters for neuroscience. *Nature Reviews Neuroscience, 7,* 477–484. (3, 5)

Calabria, B., Degenhardt, L., Briegleb, C., Vos, T., Hall, W., . . . McLaren, J. (2010). Systematic review of prospective studies investigating "remission" from amphetamine, cannabis, cocaine or opioid dependence. *Addictive Behaviors, 35,* 741–749. (15)

Calipari, E. S., & Ferris, M. J. (2013). Amphetamine mechanisms and actions at the dopamine terminal revisited. *Journal of Neuroscience, 33,* 8923–8925. (3)

Calvo-Merino, B., Grèzes, J., Glaser, D. E., Passingham, R. E., & Haggard, P. (2006). Seeing or doing? Influence of visual and motor familiarity on action observation. *Current Biology, 16,* 1905–1910. (3)

Cameron, P., Proctor, K., Coburn, W., & Forde, N. (1985). Sexual orientation and sexually transmitted disease. *Nebraska Medical Journal, 70,* 292–299. (11)

Campbell, S. S., & Tobler, I. (1984). Animal sleep: A review of sleep duration across phylogeny. *Neuroscience and Biobehavioral Reviews, 8,* 269–300. (10)

Camperio-Ciani, A., Corna, F., & Capiluppi, C. (2004). Evidence for maternally inherited factors favouring male homosexuality and promoting female fecundity. *Proceedings of the Royal Society of London, B, 271,* 2217–2221. (11)

Campion, M. A., & McClelland, C. L. (1991). Interdisciplinary examination of the costs and benefits of enlarged jobs: A job design quasi-experiment. *Journal of Applied Psychology, 76,* 186–198. (11)

Campion, M. A., & Thayer, P. W. (1985). Development and field evaluation of an interdisciplinary measure of job design. *Journal of Applied Psychology, 70,* 29–43. (11)

Campion, M. A., & Thayer, P. W. (1989). How do you design a job? *Personnel Journal, 68,* 43–46. (1)

Campitelli, G., & Gobet, F. (2011). Deliberate practice: Necessary but not sufficient. *Current Directions in Psychological Science, 20,* 280–285. (8)

Cannon, W. B. (1929). Organization for physiological homeostasis. *Physiological Reviews, 9,* 399–431. (11)

Capela, J. P., Carmo, H., Remiao, F., Bastos, M. L., Meisel, A., & Carvalho, F. (2009). Molecular and cellular mechanisms of ecstasy-induced neurotoxicity: An overview. *Molecular Neurobiology, 39,* 210–271. (3)

Cardno, A. G., Marshall, E. J., Coid, B., Macdonald, A. M., Ribchester, T. R., Davies, N. J., . . . Murray, R. M. (1999). Heritability estimates for psychotic disorders. *Archives of General Psychiatry, 56,* 162–168. (15)

Carey, S. (1978). The child as word learner. In M. Halle, J. Bresnan, & G. A. Miller (Eds.), *Linguistic theory and psychological reality* (pp. 264–293). Cambridge, MA: MIT Press. (8)

Carlson, E. A., Hostinar, C. E., Mlinar, S. B., & Gunnar, M. R. (2014). The emergence of attachment following early social deprivation. *Development and Psychopathology, 26,* 479–489. (5)

Carlsson, K., Petrovic, P., Skare, S., Petersson, K. M., & Ingvar, M. (2000). Tickling expectations: Neural processing in anticipation of a sensory stimulus. *Journal of Cognitive Neuroscience, 12,* 691–703. (4)

Carney, R. N., & Levin, J. R. (1998). Coming to terms with the keyword method in introductory psychology: A "neuromnemonic" example. *Teaching of Psychology, 25,* 132–134. (7)

Carr, D., Freedman, V. A., Cornman, J. C., & Schwarz, N. (2014). Happy marriage, happy life? Marital quality and subjective well-being in later life. *Journal of Marriage and Family, 76,* 930–948. (12)

Carré, J. M., McCormick, C. M., & Mondloch, C. J. (2009). Facial structure is a reliable cue of aggressive behavior. *Psychological Science, 20,* 1194–1198. (13)

Carreiras, M., Seghier, M. L., Baquero, S., Estévez, A., Lozano, A., Devlin, J. T., . . . Price, C. J. (2009). An anatomical signature for literacy. *Nature, 461,* 983–986. (3)

Carrera, O., Adan, R. A. H., Gutiérrez, E., Danner, U. N., Hoek, H. W., van Elburg, A. A., & Kas, M. J. H. (2012). Hyperactivity in anorexia nervosa: Warming up not just burning-off calories. *PLoS One, 7,* e41851. (11)

Carroll, B. J. (1980). Implications of biological research for the diagnosis of depression. In J. Mendlewicz (Ed.), *New advances in the diagnosis and treatment of depressive illness* (pp. 85–107). Amsterdam: Excerpta Medica. (15)

Carstensen, L. L., Mikels, J. A., & Mather, M. (2006). Aging and the intersection of cognition, motivation, and emotion. In J. E. Birren & K. W. Schaie (Eds.), *Handbook of the psychology of aging* (6th ed., pp. 343–362). Burlington, MA: Elsevier. (5)

Case, B. G., Bertollo, D. N., Laska, E. M., Price, L. H., Siegel, C. E., Olfson, M., & Marcus, S. C. (2013). Declining use of electroconvulsive shock in United States general hospitals. *Biological Psychiatry, 73,* 119–126. (15)

Caspi, A., Houts, R. M., Belsky, D. W., Goldman-Mellor, S. J., Harrington, H. L., Israel, S., . . . Moffitt, T. E. (2014). The *p* factor: One general psychopathology factor in the structure of psychiatric disorders? *Clinical Psychological Science, 2,* 119–137. (11, 15)

Caspi, A., McClay, J., Moffitt, T. E., Mill, J., Martin, J., Craig, I. W., . . . Poulton, R. (2002). Role of genotype in the cycle of violence in maltreated children. *Science, 297,* 851–854. (13)

Caspi, A., Sugden, K., Moffit, T. E., Taylor, A., Craig, I. W., Harrington, H. L., . . . Poulton, R. (2003). Influence of life stress on depression: Moderation by a polymorphism in the 5-HTT gene. *Science, 301,* 386–389. (14, 15)

Cassia, V. M., Turati, C., & Simion, F. (2004). Can a nonspecific bias toward top-heavy patterns explain newborns' face preference? *Psychological Science, 15,* 379–383. (5)

Catmur, C., Walsh, V., & Heyes, C. (2007). Sensorimotor learning configures the human mirror system. *Current Biology, 17,* 1527–1531. (3)

Cattell, R. B. (1965). *The scientific analysis of personality.* Chicago: Aldine. (14)

Cattell, R. B. (1987). *Intelligence: Its structure, growth and action.* Amsterdam: North-Holland. (9)

Center for Psychology Workforce Analysis and Research. (2007). Doctorate Employment Survey. Washington, DC: American Psychological Association. (1)

Cepeda, N. J., Pashler, H., Vul, E., Wixted, J. T., & Rohrer, D. (2006). Distributed practice in verbal recall tasks: A review and quantitative synthesis. *Psychological Bulletin, 132,* 354–380. (7)

Cepeda, N. J., Vul, E., Rohrer, D., Wixted, J. T., & Pashler, H. (2008). Spacing effects in learning. *Psychological Science, 19,* 1095–1102. (7)

Cerasoli, C. P., Nicklin, J. M., & Ford, M. T. (2014). Intrinsic motivation and extrinsic incentives jointly predict performance: A 40-year meta-analysis. *Psychological Bulletin, 140,* 980–1008. (11)

Cerrato, M., Carrera, O., Vazquez, R., Echevarria, E., & Gutiérrez, E. (2012). Heat makes a difference in activity-based anorexia: A translational approach to treatment development in anorexia nervosa. *International Journal of Eating Disorders, 45,* 26–35. (11)

Cesarini, D., Dawes, C. T., Fowler, J. H., Johanesson, M., Lichtenstein, P., & Wallace, B. (2008). Heritability of cooperative behavior in the trust game. *Proceedings of the National Academy of Sciences, USA, 105,* 3721–3726. (5)

Cesario, J. (2014). Priming, replication, and the hardest science. *Perspectives on Psychological Science, 9,* 40–48. (2)

Chablis, C. F., Hebert, B. M., Benjamin, D. J., Beauchamp, J., Cesarini, D., van der Loos, M., . . . Laibson, D. (2012). Most reported genetic associations with general intelligence are probably false positives. *Psychological Science, 23,* 1314–1323. (9)

Chabris, C. F., & Glickman, M. E. (2006). Sex differences in intellectual performance: Analysis of a large cohort of competitive chess players. *Psychological Science, 17,* 1040–1046. (5)

Chamorro-Premuzic, T., & Furnham, A. (2008). Personality, intelligence and approaches to learning as predictors of academic performance. *Personality and Individual Differences, 44,* 1596–1603. (14)

Chang, Y. Y.-C., & Chiou, W.-B. (2014). Taking weight-loss supplements may elicit liberation from dietary control. A laboratory experiment. *Appetite, 72,* 8–12. (11)

Changeux, J.-P. (2010). Nicotine addiction and nicotinic receptors: Lessons from genetically modified mice. *Nature Reviews Neuroscience, 11,* 389–401. (3)

Chapman, H. A., Kim, D. A., Susskind, J. M., & Anderson, A. K. (2009). In bad taste: Evidence for the oral origins of moral disgust. *Science, 323,* 1222–1226. (12)

Chaudhari, N., Landin, A. M., & Roper, S. D. (2000). A metabotropic glutamate receptor variant functions as a taste receptor. *Nature Neuroscience, 3,* 113–119. (4)

Cheetham, E. (1973). *The prophecies of Nostradamus.* New York: Putnam's. (2)

Chehab, F. F., Mounzih, K., Lu, R., & Lim, M. E. (1997). Early onset of reproductive function in normal female mice treated with leptin. *Science, 275,* 88–90. (11)

Chen, D., & Haviland-Jones, J. (2000). Human olfactory communication of emotion. *Perceptual and Motor Skills, 91,* 771–781. (5)

Chen, E., & Miller, G. E. (2012). "Shift-and-persist" strategies: Why low socioeconomic status isn't always bad for health. *Perspectives on Psychological Science, 7,* 135–158. (12)

Chen, Z., Williams, K. D., Fitness, J., & Newton, N. C. (2008). When hurt will not heal. *Psychological Science, 19,* 789–795. (4)

Cheung, B. Y., Chudek, M., & Heine, S. J. (2011). Evidence for a sensitive period for acculturation: Younger immigrants report acculturating at a faster rate. *Psychological Science, 22,* 147–152. (5)

Cheung, F. M., Leung, K., Fang, R. M., Song, W. Z., Zhang, J. X., & Zhang, J. P. (1996). Development of the Chinese Personality Assessment Inventory (CPAI). *Journal of Cross-Cultural Psychology, 27,* 181–199. (14)

Cheung, F. Y.-L., & Tang, C. S.-K. (2007). The influence of emotional dissonance and resources at work on job burnout among Chinese human service employees. *International Journal of Stress Management, 14,* 72–87. (11)

Chiesa, M. (2010). Research and psychoanalysis: Still time to bridge the great divide? *Psychoanalytic Psychology, 27,* 99–114. (14)

Chivers, M. L., Rieger, G., Latty, E., & Bailey, J. M. (2004). A sex difference in the specificity of sexual arousal. *Psychological Science, 15,* 736–744. (11)

Chomsky, N. (1980). *Rules and representations.* New York: Columbia University Press. (8)

Chow, H. M., Mar, R. A., Xu, Y., Liu, S., Wagage, S., & Braun, A. R. (2013). Embodied comprehension of stories: Interactions between language regions and modality-specific neural systems. *Journal of Cognitive Neuroscience, 26,* 279–295. (8)

Church, A. T., Katigbak, M. S., Reyes, J. A. S., Salanga, M. G. C., Miramontes, L. A., & Adams, N. B. (2008). Prediction and cross-situational consistency of daily behavior across cultures: Testing trait and cultural psychology perspectives. *Journal of Research in Personality, 42,* 1199–1215. (14)

Churchland, P. S. (1986). *Neurophilosophy.* Cambridge, MA: MIT Press. (10)

Cialdini, R. B. (1993). *Influence: The psychology of persuasion* (Rev. ed.). New York: Morrow. (6, 13)

Cialdini, R. B. (2003). Crafting normative messages to protect the environment. *Current Directions in Psychological Science, 12,* 105–109. (13)

Ciaramelli, E., Muccioli, M., Làdavas, E., & DiPellegrino, G. (2007). Selective deficit in personal moral judgment following damage to ventromedial prefrontal cortex. *Social Cognitive and Affective Neuroscience, 2,* 84–92. (12)

Cimino, K. (2007, June 20). After it blooms, it will smell as bad as a blooming corpse. *News and Observer* (Raleigh, NC), p. 4B. (11)

Cislo, A. M. (2008). Ethnic identity and self-esteem: Contrasting Cuban and Nicaraguan young adults. *Hispanic Journal of Behavioral Sciences, 30,* 230–250. (5)

Clancy, S. A. (2005). *Abducted: How people come to believe they were kidnapped by aliens.* Cambridge, MA: Harvard University Press. (15)

Clark, S. E. (2012). Costs and benefits of eyewitness identification reform: Psychological science and public policy. *Perspectives on Psychological Science, 7,* 238–259. (7)

Clay, R. A. (2002, May). An indigenized psychology. *Monitor on Psychology, 33*(5), 58–59. (15)

Clearfield, M. W., & Nelson, N. M. (2006). Sex differences in mothers' speech and play behavior with 6-, 9-, and 14-month-old infants. *Sex Roles, 54,* 127–137. (5)

Clément, K., Vaisse, C., Lahlou, N., Cabrol, S., Pelloux, V., Cassuto, D., . . . Guy-Grand, B. (1998). A mutation in the human leptin receptor gene causes obesity and pituitary dysfunction. *Nature, 392,* 398–401. (11)

Clinicopathologic Conference. (1967). *Johns Hopkins Medical Journal, 120,* 186–199. (12)

Coan, J. A., Schaefer, H. S., & Davidson, R. J. (2006). Lending a hand: Social regulation of the neural response to threat. *Psychological Science, 17,* 1032–1039. (12)

Coatsworth, J. D., Maldonado-Molina, M., Pantin, H., & Szapocznik, J. (2005). A person-centered and ecological investigation of acculturation strategies in Hispanic immigrant youth. *Journal of Community Psychology, 33,* 157–174. (5)

Cobos, P., Sánchez, M., García, C., Vera, M. N., & Vila, J. (2002). Revisiting the James versus Cannon debate on emotion: Startle and autonomic modulation in patients with spinal cord injuries. *Biological Psychology, 61,* 251–269. (12)

Coelho, C. M., Waters, A. M., Hine, T. J., & Wallis, G. (2009). The use of virtual reality in acrophobia research and treatment. *Journal of Anxiety Disorders, 23,* 563–574. (15)

Cohen Kadosh, R., Henik, A., Catena, A., Walsh, V., & Fuentes, L. J. (2009). Induced cross-modal synaesthetic experience without abnormal neuronal connections. *Psychological Science, 20,* 258–265. (10)

Cohen, G. L., Garcia, J., Purdie-Vaughns, V., Apfel, N., & Brzustoski, P. (2009). Recursive processes in self-affirmation: Intervening to close the minority achievement gap. *Science, 324,* 400–403. (9)

Cohen, J. D., Noll, D. C., & Schneider, W. (1993). Functional magnetic resonance imaging: Overview and methods for psychological research. *Behavior Research Methods, Instruments, and Computers, 25,* 101–113. (3)

Cohen, M. A., Alvarez, G. A., & Nakayama, K. (2011). Natural-scene perception requires attention. *Psychological Science, 22,* 1165–1172. (8)

Cohen, M. A., Konkle, T., Rhee, J. Y., Nakayama, K., & Alvarez, G. A. (2014). Processing multiple visual objects is limited by overlap in neural channels. *Proceedings of the National Academy of Sciences (U.S.A.), 111,* 8955–8960. (8)

Cohen, M. R., & Maunsell, J. H. R. (2011). When attention wanders: How uncontrolled fluctuations in attention affect performance. *Journal of Neuroscience, 31,* 15802–15806. (8)

Cohen, N. J., & Squire, L. R. (1980). Preserved learning and retention of pattern-analyzing skill in amnesia: Dissociation of knowing how and knowing that. *Science, 210,* 207–211. (7)

Cohen, S., Frank, E., Doyle, W. J., Skoner, D. P., Rabin, B. S., & Swaltney, J. M., Jr. (1998). Types of stressors that increase susceptibility to the common cold in healthy adults. *Health Psychology, 17,* 214–223. (12)

Cohen, S., Lichtenstein, E., Prochaska, J. O., Rossi, J. S., Gritz, E. R., Carr, C. R., . . . Ossip-Klein, D. (1989). Debunking myths about self-quitting: Evidence from 10 prospective studies of persons who attempt to quit smoking by themselves. *American Psychologist, 44,* 1355–1365. (15)

Colantuoni, C., Rada, P., McCarthy, J., Patten, C., Avena, N. M., Chadcayne, A., . . . Hoebel, B. G. (2002). Evidence that intermittent, excessive sugar intake causes endogenous opioid dependence. *Obesity Research, 10,* 478–488. (11)

Colantuoni, C., Schwenker, J., McCarthy, J., Rada, P., Ladenheim, B., Cadet, J. L., . . . Hoebel, B. G. (2001). Excessive sugar intake alters binding to dopamine and mu-opioid receptors in the brain. *NeuroReport, 12,* 3549–3552. (11)

Colcombe, S., & Kramer, A. F. (2003). Fitness effects on the cognitive function of older adults: A meta-analytic study. *Psychological Science, 14,* 125–130. (5)

Cole, T., & Brown, J. (2014). Behavioural investigative advice: Assistance to investigative decision-making in difficult-to-detect murder. *Journal of Investigative Psychology and Offender Profiling, 11,* 191–200. (14)

Colizoli, O., Muirre, J. M. J., & Rouw, R. (2013). A taste for words and sounds: A case of lexical-gustatory and sound-gustatory synesthesia. *Frontiers in Psychology, 4,* Article 775. (4)

Collins, A. M., & Loftus, E. F. (1975). A spreading-activation theory of semantic processing. *Psychological Review, 82,* 407–428. (8)

Collins, A. M., & Quillian, M. R. (1969). Retrieval time from semantic memory. *Journal of Verbal Learning and Verbal Behavior, 8,* 240–247. (8)

Collins, A. M., & Quillian, M. R. (1970). Does category size affect categorization time? *Journal of Verbal Learning and Verbal Behavior, 9,* 432–438. (8)

Collins, W. A., Maccoby, E. E., Steinberg, L., Hetherington, E. M., & Bornstein, M. H. (2000). Contemporary research on parenting: The case for nature and nurture. *American Psychologist, 55,* 218–232. (5)

Coman, A., Manier, D., & Hirst, W. (2009). Forgetting the unforgettable through conversation. *Psychological Science, 20,* 627–633. (7)

Conley, T. D., Moors, A. C., Matsick, J. L., Ziegler, A., & Valentine, B. A. (2011). Women, men, and the bedroom: Methodological and conceptual insights that narrow, reframe, and eliminate gender differences in sexuality. *Current Directions in Psychological Science, 20,* 296–300. (11)

Connine, C. M., Blasko, D. G., & Hall, M. (1991). Effects of subsequent sentence context in auditory word recognition: Temporal and linguistic constraints. *Journal of Memory and Language, 30,* 234–250. (8)

Connor, T. J., & Leonard, B. E. (1998). Depression, stress and immunological activation: The role of cytokines in depressive disorders. *Life Sciences, 62,* 583–606. (12)

Constantinides, P. (1977). Ill at ease and sick at heart: Symbolic behavior in a Sudanese healing cult. In I. Wilson (Ed.), *Symbols and sentiments* (pp. 61–84). New York: Academic Press. (15)

Cooper, J., & Cooper, G. (2002). Subliminal motivation: A story revisited. *Journal of Applied Social Psychology, 32,* 2213–2227. (4)

Coplan, J. D., Goetz, R., Klein, D. F., Papp, L. A., Fyer, A. J., Leibowitz, M. R., . . . Gorman, J. M. (1998). Plasma cortisol concentrations preceding lactate-induced panic. *Archives of General Psychiatry, 55,* 130–136. (15)

Corkin, S. (1984). Lasting consequences of bilateral medial temporal lobectomy: Clinical course and experimental findings in H. M. *Seminars in Neurology, 4,* 249–259. (7)

Corkin, S. (2002). What's new with the amnesic patient H. M.? *Nature Reviews Neuroscience, 3,* 153–159. (7)

Cornil, Y., & Chandon, P. (2013). From fan to fat? Vicarious losing increases unhealthy eating, but self-affirmation is an effective remedy. *Psychological Science, 24,* 1936–1946. (11)

Corrigan, P. W., Druss, B. G., & Perlick, D. A. (2014). The impact of mental illness stigma on seeking and participating in mental health care. *Psychological Science in the Public Interest, 15,* 37–70. (15)

Cosmelli, D., David, O., Lachaux, J.-P., Martinerie, J., Garnero, L., Renault, B., . . . Varela, F. (2004). Waves of consciousness: Ongoing cortical patterns during binocular rivalry. *NeuroImage, 23,* 128–140. (10)

Costa, P. T., Jr., McCrae, R. R., & Dye, D. A. (1991). Facet scales for agreeableness and conscientiousness: A revision of the NEO personality inventory. *Personality and Individual Differences, 12,* 887–898. (14)

Coughlan, E. K., Williams, A. M., McRobert, A. P., & Ford, P. R. (2014). How experts practice: A novel test of deliberate practice theory. *Journal of Experimental Psychology: Learning Memory and Cognition, 40,* 449–458. (8)

Coughtrey, A. E., Shafran, R., Lee, M., & Rachman, S. (2013). The treatment of mental contamination: A case series. *Cognitive and Behavioral Practice, 20,* 221–231. (15)

Courage, M. L., & Howe, M. L. (2002). From infant to child: The dynamics of cognitive change in the second year of life. *Psychological Bulletin, 128,* 250–277. (5)

Cowan, N. (2010). The magical mystery four: How is working memory capacity limited, and why? *Current Directions in Psychological Science, 19,* 51–57. (7)

Cox, B. J., McWilliams, L. A., Clara, I. P., & Stein, M. B. (2003). The structure of feared situations in a nationally representative sample. *Journal of Anxiety Disorders, 17,* 89–101. (15)

Cox, J. J., Reimann, F., Nicholas, A. K., Thornton, G., Roberts, E., Springell, K., . . . Woods, C. G. (2006). An *SCN9A* channelopathy causes congenital inability to experience pain. *Nature, 444,* 894–898. (4)

Coyle, T. R., Pillow, D. R., Snyder, A. C., & Kochunov, P. (2011). Processing speed mediates the development of general intelligence (*g*) in adolescence. *Psychological Science, 22,* 1265–1269. (9)

Craig, A. D., Bushnell, M. C., Zhang, E. T., & Blomqvist, A. (1994). A thalamic nucleus specific for pain and temperature sensation. *Nature, 372,* 770–773. (4)

Craig, S. B., & Gustafson, S. B. (1998). Perceived leader integrity scale: An instrument for assessing employee perceptions of leader integrity. *Leadership Quarterly, 9,* 127–145. (11)

Craik, F. I. M., & Lockhart, R. S. (1972). Levels of processing: A framework for memory research. *Journal of Verbal Learning and Verbal Behavior, 11,* 671–684. (7)

Craig, M. A., & Richeson, J. A. (2014). More diverse yet less tolerant? How the increasingly diverse racial landscape affects White Americans' racial attitudes. *Personality and Social Psychology Bulletin, 40,* 750–761. (13)

Cramer, P. (1996). *Storytelling, narrative, and the Thematic Apperception Test.* New York: Guilford Press. (14)

Cramer, P. (2003). Personality change in later adulthood is predicted by defense mechanism use in early adulthood. *Journal of Research in Personality, 37,* 76–104. (14)

Credé, M., & Kuncel, N. R. (2008). Study habits, skills, and attitudes. *Perspectives on Psychological Science, 3,* 425–453. (9)

Creswell, K. G., Chung, T., Clark, D. B., & Martin, C. S. (2014). Solitary alcohol use in teens is associated with drinking in response to negative affect and predicts alcohol problems in young adulthood. *Clinical Psychological Science, 2,* 602–610. (15)

Crews, D. J., & Landers, D. M. (1987). A meta-analytic review of aerobic fitness and reactivity to psychosocial stressors. *Medicine and Science in Sports and Exercise, 19,* S114–S120. (12)

Crews, F. (1996). The verdict on Freud. *Psychological Science, 7,* 63–68. (14)

Critcher, C. R., & Rosenzweig, E. L. (2014). The performance heuristic: A misguided reliance on past success when predicting prospects for improvement. *Journal of Experimental Psychology: General, 143,* 480–485. (8)

Critchley, H. D., Mathias, C. J., & Dolan, R. J. (2001). Neuroanatomical basis for first- and second-order representations of bodily states. *Nature Neuroscience, 4,* 207–212. (12)

Crocker, J., & Park, L. E. (2004). The costly pursuit of self-esteem. *Psychological Bulletin, 130,* 392–414. (14)

Cross-Disorder Group of the Psychiatric Genomics Consortium. (2013). Genetic relationship between five psychiatric disorders estimated from genome-wide SNPs. *Nature Genetics, 45,* 984–994. (11, 15)

Crowley, K., Callanen, M. A., Tenenbaum, H. R., & Allen, E. (2001). Parents explain more often to boys than to girls during shared scientific thinking. *Psychological Science, 12,* 258–261. (5)

Crowther, J. H., Armey, M., Luce, K. H., Dalton, G. R., & Leahey, T. (2008). The point prevalence of bulimic disorders from 1990 to 2004. *International Journal of Eating Disorders, 41,* 491–497. (11)

Croyle, R. T., & Cooper, J. (1983). Dissonance arousal: Physiological evidence. *Journal of Personality and Social Psychology, 45,* 782–791. (13)

Crum, A. J., & Langer, E. J. (2007). Mind-set matters. *Psychological Science, 18,* 165–171. (12)

Cryder, C. E., Lerner, J. S., Gross, J. J., & Dahl, R. E. (2008). Misery is not miserly: Sad and self-focused individuals spend more. *Psychological Science, 19,* 525–530. (12)

Csikszentmihalyi, M. (1999). If we are so rich, why aren't we happy? *American Psychologist, 54,* 821–827. (12)

Cubillo, A., Halari, R., Smith, A., Taylor, E., & Rubia, K. (2012). A review of fronto-striatal and fronto-cortical brain abnormalities in children and adults with Attention Deficit Hyperactivity Disorder (ADHD) and new evidence for dysfunction in adults with ADHD during motivation and attention. *Cortex, 48,* 194–215. (8)

Cuijpers, P., Huibers, M., Ebert, D. D., Koole, S. L., & Andersson, G. (2013). How much psychotherapy is needed to treat depression? A metaregression analysis. *Journal of Affective Disorders, 149,* 1–13. (15)

Cuijpers, P., van Straten, A., Andersson, G., & van Oppen, P. (2008). Psychotherapy for depression in adults: A meta-analysis of comparative outcome studies. *Journal of Consulting and Clinical Psychology, 76,* 909–922. (15)

Culbertson, F. M. (1997). Depression and gender. *American Psychologist, 52,* 25–31. (15)

Cumming, G. (2014). The new statistics: Why and how. *Psychological Science, 25,* 7–29. (2)

Cumming, G. (2008). Replication and *p* intervals. *Perspectives on Psychological Science, 3,* 286–300. (2)

Cummings, N. A. (1979). Turning bread into stones: Our modern antimiracle. *American Psychologist, 34,* 1119–1129. (15)

Cummins, R. A., Li, N., Wooden, M., & Stokes, M. (2014). A demonstration of set-points for subjective wellbeing. *Journal of Happiness Studies, 15,* 183–206. (12)

Curci, A., & Rimé, B. (2012). The temporal evolution of social sharing of emotions and its consequences on emotional recovery: A longitudinal study. *Emotion, 12,* 1404–1414. (15)

Curseu, P. L., Janssen, S. E. A., & Meeus, M. T. H. (2014). Shining lights and bad apples: The effect of goal setting on group performance. *Management Learning, 45,* 332–348. (11)

Cyranowski, J. M., Frank, E., Young, E., & Shear, K. (2000). Adolescent onset of the gender difference in lifetime rates of major depression. *Archives of General Psychiatry, 57,* 21–27. (15)

Czeisler, C. (2013). Casting light on sleep deficiency. *Nature, 497,* S13. (10)

Czeisler, C. A., Johnson, M. P., Duffy, J. F., Brown, E. N., Ronda, J. M., & Kronauer, R. E. (1990). Exposure to bright light and darkness to treat physiologic maladaptation to night work. *New England Journal of Medicine, 322,* 1353–1359. (10)

Czeisler, C. A., Moore-Ede, M. C., & Coleman, R. M. (1982). Rotating shift work schedules that disrupt sleep are improved by applying circadian principles. *Science, 217,* 460–463. (10)

Dahl, A., Campos, J. J., Anderson, D. I., Uchiyama, I., Witherington, D. C., Ueno, M., . . . Barbu-Roth, M. (2013). The epigenesis of wariness of heights. *Psychological Science, 24,* 1361–1367. (5)

Dailey, M. N., Joyce, C., Lyons, M. J., Kamachi, M., Ishi, H., . . . Cottrell, G. W. (2010). Evidence and a computational explanation of cultural differences in facial expression recognition. *Emotion, 10,* 874–893. (12)

Daley, D., van der Oord, S., Ferrin, M., Danckaerts, M., Cortese, S., & Sonuga-Barke, E. J. S. (2014). Behavioral interventions in attention-deficit/hyperactivity disorder: A meta-analysis of randomized controlled trials across multiple outcome domains. *Journal of the American Academy of Child & Adolescent Psychiatry, 53,* 835–847. (8)

Daley, T. C., Whaley, S. E., Sigman, M. D., Espinosa, M. P., & Neumann, C. (2003). IQ on the rise: The Flynn effect in rural Kenyan children. *Psychological Science, 14,* 215–219. (9)

Dallenbach, K. M. (1951). A puzzle picture with a new principle of concealment. *American Journal of Psychology, 64,* 431–433. (4)

Damaser, E. C., Shor, R. E., & Orne, M. E. (1963). Physiological effects during hypnotically requested emotions. *Psychosomatic Medicine, 25,* 334–343. (10)

Damasio, A. (1999). *The feeling of what happens.* New York: Harcourt Brace. (3, 12)

Damasio, A. R. (1994). *Descartes' error: Emotion, reason, and the human brain.* New York: G. P. Putnam's Sons. (12)

Danovitch, J., & Bloom, P. (2009). Children's extension of disgust to physical and moral events. *Emotion, 9,* 107–112. (12)

Dar-Nimrod, I., & Heine, S. J. (2006). Exposure to scientific theories affects women's math performance. *Science, 314,* 435. (9)

Darst, C. R., & Cummings, M. E. (2006). Predator learning favours mimicry of a less-toxic model in poison frogs. *Nature, 440,* 208–211. (6)

Darwin, C. (1859). *On the origin of species by means of natural selection.* New York: D. Appleton. (1)

Darwin, C. (1871). *The descent of man.* New York: D. Appleton. (1)

Darwin, C. (1965). *The expression of emotions in man and animals.* Chicago: University of Chicago Press. (Original work published 1872) (12)

da Silva, D. D., Silva, E., Carvalho, F., & Carmo, H. (2014). Mixtures of 3,4-methylenedioxymethamphetamine (ecstasy) and its major human metabolites act additively to induce significant toxicity to liver cells when combined at low, non-cytotoxic concentrations. *Journal of Applied Toxicology, 34,* 618–627. (3)

Davenport, J. L., & Potter, M. C. (2004). Scene consistency in object and background perception. *Psychological Science, 15,* 559–564. (8)

Davidson, J. K., Sr., Moore, N. B., Earle, J. R., & Davis, R. (2008). Sexual attitudes and behavior at four universities: Do region, race, and/or religion matter? *Adolescence, 43,* 189–220. (11)

Davidson, R. J., Putnam, K. M., & Larson, C. L. (2000). Dysfunction in the neural circuitry of emotion regulation—A possible prelude to violence. *Science, 289,* 591–594. (13)

Davies, G., Armstrong, N., Bis, J. C., Bressler, J., Chouraki, V., Giddaluru, S., . . . Deary, I. J. (2015). Genetic contributions to variation in general cognitive function: A meta-analysis of genome-wide association studies in the CHARGE consortium (N = 53 949). *Molecular Psychiatry, 20,* 183–192. (9)

Davies, G., Welham, J., Chant, D., Torrey, E. F., & McGrath, J. (2003). A systematic review and meta-analysis of Northern Hemisphere season of birth studies in schizophrenia. *Schizophrenia Bulletin, 29,* 587–593. (15)

Davis, D., Dorsey, J. K., Franks, R. D., Sackett, P. R, Searcy, C. A., & Zhao, X. (2013). Do racial and ethnic group differences in performance on the MCAT exam reflect test bias? *Academic Medicine, 88,* 593–602. (9)

Davis, J. L., Senghas, A., Brandt, F., & Ochsner, K. N. (2010). The effects of BOTOX injections on emotional experience. *Emotion, 10,* 433–440. (12)

Davis, J. M., Chen, N., & Glick, I. D. (2003). A meta-analysis of the efficacy of second-generation antipsychotics. *Archives of General Psychiatry, 60,* 553–564. (15)

Davis, O. S. P., Haworth, C. M. A., & Plomin, R. (2009). Dramatic increase in heritability of cognitive development from early to middle childhood. *Psychological Science, 20,* 1301–1308. (9)

Dawes, R. M. (1994). *House of cards: Psychology and psychotherapy.* New York: Free Press. (14)

Dawson, M., Soulières, I., Gernsbacher, M. A., & Mottron, L. (2007). The level and nature of autistic intelligence. *Psychological Science, 18,* 657–662. (15)

Day, R. H. (1972). Visual spatial illusions: A general explanation. *Science, 175,* 1335–1340. (4)

de Castro, J. M. (2000). Eating behavior: Lessons from the real world of humans. *Nutrition, 16,* 800–813. (1, 11)

de Groot, A. D. (1966). Perception and memory versus thought: Some old ideas and recent findings. In B. Kleinmuntz (Ed.), *Problem solving* (pp. 19–50). New York: Wiley. (8).

de Groot, J. H. B., Semin, G. R., & Smeets, M. A. M. (2014). Chemical communication of fear: A case of male-female asymmetry. *Journal of Experimental Psychology: General, 143,* 1515–1525. (12)

De Houwer, J., Teige-Mocigemba, S., Spruyt, A., & Moors, A. (2009). Implicit measures: A normative analysis and review. *Psychological Bulletin, 135,* 347–368. (14)

de Quervain, D. J.-F., Roozendaal, B., Nitsch, R. M., McGaugh, J. L., & Hock, C. (2000). Acute cortisone administration impairs retrieval of long-term declarative memory in humans. *Nature Neuroscience, 3,* 313–314. (12)

de Waal, F. B. M. (2002). Evolutionary psychology: The wheat and the chaff. *Current Directions in Psychological Science, 11,* 187–191. (1, 3)

De Wall, C. N., MacDonald, G., Webster, G. D., Masten, C. L., Baumeister, R. F., Powell, C., . . . Eisenberger, N. I. (2010). Acetaminophen reduces social pain: Behavioral and neural evidence. *Psychological Science, 21,* 931–937. (4)

Deacon, S., & Arendt, J. (1996). Adapting to phase shifts: II. Effects of melatonin and conflicting light treatment. *Physiology and Behavior, 59,* 675–682. (10)

Deacon, T. W. (1997). *The symbolic species.* New York: W. W. Norton. (8)

Deady, D.K., North, N. T., Allan, D., Smith, M. J. L., & O'Carroll, R. E. (2010). Examining the effect of spinal cord injury on emotional awareness, expressivity and memory for emotional material. *Psychology, Health and Medicine, 15,* 406–419. (12)

Dean, C. E. (2011). Psychopharmacology: A house divided. *Progress in Neuro-Psychopharmacology & Biological Psychiatry, 35,* 1–10. (15)

Dean, K. E., & Malamuth, N. M. (1997). Characteristics of men who aggress sexually and of men who imagine aggressing: Risk and moderating variables. *Journal of Personality and Social Psychology, 72,* 449–455. (13)

Deary, I. J., Batty, G. D., & Gale, C. R. (2008). Bright children become enlightened adults. *Psychological Science, 19,* 1–6. (9)

Deary, I. J., Strand, S., Smith, P., & Fernandes, C. (2007). Intelligence and educational achievement. *Intelligence, 35,* 13–21. (9)

Deary, I. J., Whiteman, M. C., Starr, J. M., Whalley, L. J., & Fox, H. C. (2004). The impact of childhood intelligence on later life: Following up the Scottish mental surveys of 1932 and 1947. *Journal of Personality and Social Psychology, 86,* 130–147. (9)

Deary, I. J., Yang, J., Davies, G., Harris, S. E., Tenesa, A., . . . Visscher, P. M. (2012). Genetic contributions to stability and change in intelligence from childhood to old age. *Nature, 482,* 212–215. (9)

de Bruin, A., Treccani, B., & Della Salla, S. (2015). Cognitive advantage in bilingualism: An example of publication bias? *Psychological Science, 26,* 99–107. (8)

DeBruine, L. M. (2004). Facial resemblance increases the attractiveness of same-sex faces more than other-sex faces. *Proceedings of the Royal Society of London, B, 271,* 2085–2090. (13)

DeBruine, L. M. (2005). Trustworthy but not lust-worthy: Context-specific effects of facial resemblance. *Proceedings of the Royal Society of London, B, 272,* 919–922. (13)

DeCasper, A. J., & Fifer, W. P. (1980). Of human bonding: Newborns prefer their mothers' voices. *Science, 208,* 1174–1177. (5)

Deckersbach, T., Peters, A. T., Sylvia, L., Urdahl, A., Magalhaes, P. V. S., Otto, M. W., . . . Nierenberg, A. (2014). Do comorbid anxiety disorders moderate the effects of psychotherapy for bipolar disorder? Results from STEP-BD. *American Journal of Psychiatry, 171,* 178–186. (15)

De Jager, P. L., Srivastava, G., Lunnon, K., Burgess, J., Schalkwyk, L. C., Yu, L., ... Bennett, D. A. (2014). Alzheimer's disease: Early alterations in brain DNA methylation at *ANK1, BIN1, RHBDF2,* and other loci. *Nature Neuroscience, 17,* 1156–1163. (7)

Deese, J. (1959). On the prediction of occurrence of particular verbal intrusions in immediate recall. *Journal of Experimental Psychology, 58,* 17–22. (7)

Dehaene, S., Naccache, L., Cohen, L., LeBihan, D., Mangin, J.-F., Poline, J. B., . . . Riviere, D. (2001). Cerebral mechanisms of word masking and unconscious repetition priming. *Nature Neuroscience, 4,* 752–758. (10)

Dehaene, S., Pegado, F., Braga, L. W., Ventura, P., Nunez Filho, G., Jobert, A., . . . Cohen, L. (2010). How learning to read changes the cortical networks for vision and language. *Science, 330,* 1359–1364. (3)

De Houwer, J., Teige-Mocigemba, S., Spruyt, A., & Moors, A. (2009). Implicit measures: A normative analysis and review. *Psychological Bulletin, 135,* 347–368. (14)

Del Cul, A., Dehaene, S., Reyes, P., Bravo, E., & Slachevsky, A. (2009). Causal role of prefrontal cortex in the threshold for access to consciousness. *Brain, 132,* 2531–2540. (10)

DeLoache, J. S. (1989). The development of representation in young children. *Advances in Child Development and Behavior, 22,* 1–39. (5)

DeLoache, J. S., Miller, K. F., & Rosengren, K. S. (1997). The credible shrinking room: Very young children's performance with symbolic and nonsymbolic relations. *Psychological Science, 8,* 308–313. (5)

Dement, W. C. (1972). *Some must watch while some must sleep.* Stanford, CA: Stanford Alumni Association. (10)

Dement, W., & Kleitman, N. (1957a). Cyclic variations in EEG during sleep and their relation to eye movements, body motility, and dreaming. *Electroencephalography and Clinical Neurophysiology, 9,* 673–690. (10)

Dement, W., & Kleitman, N. (1957b). The relation of eye movements during sleep to dream activity: An objective method for the study of dreaming. *Journal of Experimental Psychology, 53,* 339–346. (10)

DeNeve, K. M. (1999). Happy as an extraverted clam? The role of personality for subjective well-being. *Current Directions in Psychological Science, 8,* 141–144. (12)

Denissen, J. J. A., Butalid, L., Penke, L., & van Aken, M. A. G. (2008). The effects of weather on daily mood. A multilevel approach. *Emotion, 8,* 662–667. (12)

Dennett, D. C. (2003). *Freedom evolves.* New York: Viking Press. (1)

DePaolo, B. M., Lindsay, J. J., Malone, B. E., Muhlenbruck, L., Charlton, K., & Cooper, H. (2003). Cues to deception. *Psychological Bulletin, 129,* 74–118. (12)

Derksen, M. (2014). Turning men into machines? Scientific management, industrial psychology, and the "human factor." *Journal of the History of the Behavioral Sciences, 50,* 148–165. (11)

DeScioli, P., Christner, J., & Kurzban, R. (2011). The omission strategy. *Psychological Science, 22,* 442–446. (12)

Detterman, D. K. (1979). Detterman's laws of individual differences research. In R. J. Sternberg & D. K. Detterman (Eds.), *Human intelligence* (pp. 165–175). Norwood, NJ: Ablex. (9)

Deutsch, D., Henthorn, T., Marvin, E., & Xu, H. S. (2006). Absolute pitch among American and Chinese conservatory students: Prevalence differences, and evidence for a speech-related critical period. *Journal of the Acoustical Society of America, 119,* 719–722. (4)

Deutsch, J. A., & Ahn, S. J. (1986). The splanchnic nerve and food intake regulation. *Behavioral and Neural Biology, 45,* 43–47. (11)

Deutsch, J. A., & Gonzalez, M. F. (1980). Gastric nutrient content signals satiety. *Behavioral and Neural Biology, 30,* 113–116. (11)

Devane, W. A., Hanuš, L., Breuer, A., Pertwee, R. G., Stevenson, L. A., Griffin, G., . . . Mechoulam, R. (1992). Isolation and structure of a brain constituent that binds to the cannabinoid receptor. *Science, 258,* 1946–1949. (3)

Devor, E. J., Abell, C. W., Hoffman, P. L., Tabakoff, B., & Cloninger, C. R. (1994). Platelet MAO activity in Type I and Type II alcoholism. *Annals of the New York Academy of Sciences, 708,* 119–128. (15)

DeWall, C. N., MacDonald, G., Webster, G. D., Masten, C. L., Baumeister, R. F., Powell, C., . . . Eisenberger, N. I. (2010). Acetaminophen reduces social pain: Behavioral and neural evidence. *Psychological Science, 21,* 931–937. (4)

DeWall, C. N., Twenge, J. M., Koole, S. L., Baumeister, R. F., Marquez, A., & Reid, R. W. (2011). Automatic emotion regulation after social exclusion: Turning to positivity. *Emotion, 11,* 623–636. (12)

Dewar, M., Alber, J., Butler, C., Cowan, N., & Della Salla, S. (2012). Brief wakeful resting boosts new memories over the long term. *Psychological Science, 23,* 955–960. (7)

Dewsbury, D. A. (1998). Celebrating E. L. Thorndike a century after *Animal Intelligence. American Psychologist, 53,* 1121–1124. (6)

Dewsbury, D. A. (2000). Introduction: Snapshots of psychology circa 1900. *American Psychologist, 55,* 255–259. (1)

Di Pino, G., Guglielmelli, E., & Rossini, P. M. (2009). Neuroplasticity in amputees: Main implications on bidirectional interfacing of cybernetic hand prostheses. *Progress in Neurobiology, 88,* 114–126. (4)

Diamond, L. M. (2007). A dynamical systems approach to the development and expression of female same-sex sexuality. *Perspectives in Psychological Science, 2,* 142–161. (11)

Diamond, L. M. (2008). Female bisexuality from adolescence to adulthood: Results from a 10-year longitudinal study. *Developmental Psychology, 44,* 5–14. (11)

Diaz, M., Parra, A., & Gallardo, C. (2011). Serins respond to anthropogenic noise by increasing vocal activity. *Behavioral Ecology, 22,* 332–336. (6)

Dickens, W. T., & Flynn, J. R. (2001). Heritability estimates versus large environmental effects: The IQ paradox resolved. *Psychological Review, 108,* 346–369. (3, 9)

Dickens, W. T., & Flynn, J. R. (2006). Black Americans reduce the racial IQ gap. *Psychological Science, 17,* 913–920. (9)

Dickerson, S. S., Gable, S. L., Irwin, M. R., Aziz, N., & Kemeny, M. E. (2009). Social-evaluative threat and proinflammatory cytokine regulation. *Psychological Science, 20,* 1237–1244. (12)

Dickson, N., Paul, C., & Herbison, P. (2003). Same-sex attraction in a birth cohort: Prevalence and persistence in early adulthood. *Social Science and Medicine, 56,* 1607–1615. (11)

Diener, E. (2000). Subjective well-being. *American Psychologist, 55,* 34–43. (12)

Diener, E., & Seligman, M. E. P. (2002). Very happy people. *Psychological Science, 13,* 81–84. (12)

Diener, E., & Seligman, M. E. P. (2004). Beyond money: Toward an economy of well-being. *Psychological Science in the Public Interest, 5,* 1–31. (12)

Diener, E., Suh, E. M., Lucas, R. E., & Smith, H. L. (1999). Subjective well-being: Three decades of progress. *Psychological Bulletin, 125,* 276–302. (12)

Diener, E., Wolsic, B., & Fujita, F. (1995). Physical attractiveness and subjective well-being. *Journal of Personality and Social Psychology, 69,* 120–129. (12)

Dijksterhuis, A., & Bargh, J. A. (2001). The perception-behavior expressway: Automatic effects of social perception on social behavior. *Advances in Experimental Social Psychology, 33,* 1–40. (6)

DiLalla, D. L., Carey, G., Gottesman, I. I., & Bouchard, T. J., Jr. (1996). Heritability of MMPI personality indicators of psychopathology in twins reared apart. *Journal of Abnormal Psychology, 105,* 491–499. (5)

DiMarzo, V., Goparaju, S. K., Wang, L., Liu, J., Bátkai, S., Járai, Z., . . . Kunos, G. (2001). Leptin-regulated endocannabinoids are involved in maintaining food intake. *Nature, 410,* 822–825. (3)

Dimberg, U., Thunberg, M., & Elmehed, K. (2000). Unconscious facial reactions to emotional facial expressions. *Psychological Science, 11,* 86–89. (4)

Dinstein, I., Hasson, U., Rubin, N., & Heeger, D. J. (2007). Brain areas selective for both observed and executed movements. *Journal of Neurophysiology, 98,* 1415–1427. (3)

Dobrzecka, C., Szwejkowska, G., & Konorski, J. (1966). Qualitative versus directional cues in two forms of differentiation. *Science, 153,* 87–89. (6)

Doi, T. (1981). *The anatomy of dependence.* Tokyo: Kodansha International. (12)

Dollard, J., Miller, N. E., Doob, L. W., Mowrer, O. H., & Sears, R. R. (1939). *Frustration and aggression.* New Haven, CT: Yale University Press. (13)

Domhoff, G. W. (1996). *Finding meaning in dreams: A quantitative approach.* New York: Plenum Press. (10)

Domhoff, G. W. (1999). Drawing theoretical implications from descriptive empirical findings on dream content. *Dreaming, 9,* 201–210. (10)

Domhoff, G. W. (2003). *The scientific study of dreams.* Washington, DC: American Psychological Association. (2, 10)

Domhoff, G. W. (2011). The neural substrate for dreaming: Is it a subsystem of the default network? *Consciousness and Cognition, 20,* 1163–1174. (10)

Domhoff, G. W., & Schneider, A. (2008). Similarities and differences in dream content at the cross-cultural, gender, and individual levels. *Consciousness and Cognition, 17,* 1257–1265. (10)

Dompnier, B., Darnon, C., & Butera, F. (2009). Faking the desire to learn. *Psychological Science, 20,* 939–943. (2)

Donnellan, M. B., & Lucas, R. E. (2008). Age differences in the big five across the life span: Evidence from two national samples. *Psychology and Aging, 23,* 558–566. (14)

Donnellan, M. B., Trzesniewski, K. H., Robins, R. W., Moffitt, T. E., & Caspi, A. (2005). Low self-esteem is related to aggression, antisocial behavior, and delinquency. *Psychological Science, 16,* 328–335. (13)

Donnerstein, E., & Malamuth, N. (1997). Pornography: Its consequences on the observer. In L. B. Schlesinger & E. Revitch (Eds.), *Sexual dynamics of antisocial behavior* (2nd ed., pp. 30–49). Springfield, IL: Charles C Thomas. (13)

Doty, R. L., & Kamath, V. (2014). The influences of age on olfaction: A review. *Frontiers in Psychology, 5,* Article 20. (4)

Doty, T. J., Japee, S., Ingvar, M., & Ungerleider, L. G. (2013). Fearful face detection sensitivity in healthy adults correlates with anxiety-related traits. *Emotion, 13,* 183–188. (12)

Dovidio, J. F., & Gaertner, S. L. (1999). Reducing prejudice: Combating intergroup biases. *Current Directions in Psychological Science, 8,* 101–105. (13)

Doyon, J., Korman, M., Morin, A., Dostie, V., Tahar, A. H., Benali, H., . . . Carrier, J. (2009). Contribution of night and day sleep vs. simple passage of time to the consolidation of motor sequence and visuomotor adaptation learning. *Experimental Brain Research, 195,* 15–26. (10)

Dreber, A., Rand, D. G., Fudenberg, D., & Nowak, M. A. (2008). Winners don't punish. *Nature, 452,* 348–351. (13)

Dreger, A. D. (1998). *Hermaphrodites and the medical invention of sex.* Cambridge, MA: Harvard University Press. (11)

Drew, T., Võ, M. L.-H., & Wolfe, J. M. (2013). The invisible gorilla strikes again: Sustained inattentional blindness in expert observers. *Psychological Science, 24,* 1848–1853. (4)

Drewnowski, A., Henderson, S. A., Shore, A. B., & Barratt-Fornell, A. (1998). Sensory responses to 6-n-propylthiouracil (PROP) or sucrose solutions and food preferences in young women. *Annals of the New York Academy of Sciences, 855,* 797–801. (1)

Drews, F. A., Pasupathi, M., & Strayer, D. L. (2008). Passenger and cell phone conversations in simulated driving. *Journal of Experimental Psychology: Applied, 14,* 392–400. (8)

Drzyzga, L. R., Marcinowska, A., & Obuchowicz, E. (2009). Antiapoptotic and neurotrophic effects of antidepressants: A review of clinical and experimental studies. *Brain Research Bulletin, 79,* 248–257. (15)

Dubois, F. (2007). Mate choice copying in monogamous species: Should females use public information to choose extrapair males? *Animal Behaviour, 74,* 1785–1793. (6)

DeRubeis, S., He, X., Goldberg, A. P., Poultney, C. S., Samocha, K., Cicek, A. E., . . . Buxbaum, J. D. (2014). Synaptic, transcriptional and chromatin genes disrupted in autism. *Nature, 515,* 209–215. (15)

Duckworth, A. L., & Seligman, M. E. P. (2005). Self-discipline outdoes IQ in predicting academic performance of adolescents. *Psychological Science, 16,* 939–944. (9)

Duckworth, A. L., Tsukayama, E., & Kirby, T. A. (2013). Is it really self-control? Examining the predictive power of the delay of gratification task. *Personality and Social Psychology Bulletin, 39,* 843–855. (11)

Duncan, L. E., Pollastri, A. R., & Smoller, J. W. (2014). Mind the gap. *American Psychologist, 69,* 249–268. (15)

Dunlosky, J., Rawson, K. A., Marsh, E. J., Nathan, M. J., & Willingham, D. T. (2013). Improving students' learning with effective learning techniques: Promising directions from cognitive and educational psychology. *Psychological Science in the Public Interest, 14,* 1–58. (7)

Dunn, E. W., Aknin, L. B., & Norton, M. I. (2008). Spending money on others promotes happiness. *Science, 319,* 1687–1688. (12)

Dunne, G., & Ashew, C. (2013). Vicarious learning and unlearning of fear in childhood via mother and stranger models. *Emotion, 13,* 974–980. (15)

Dunning, D., Heath, C., & Suls, J. M. (2004). Flawed self-assessment: Implications for health, education, and the workplace. *Psychological Science in the Public Interest, 5,* 69–106. (11)

Durbin, C. E., Hayden, E. P., Klein, D. N., & Olino, T. M. (2007). Stability of laboratory-assessed temperamental emotionality traits from ages 3 to 7. *Emotion, 7,* 388–399. (5)

Durgin, F. H. (2000). The reverse Stroop effect. *Psychonomic Bulletin and Review, 7,* 121–125. (8)

Durlak, J. A., Weissberg, R. P., Dymnicki, A. B., Taylor, R. D., & Schellinger, K. B. (2011). The impact of enhancing students' social and emotional learning: A meta-analysis of school-based universal interventions. *Child Development, 82,* 405–432. (15)

Dutton, D. G., & Aron, A. P. (1974). Some evidence for heightened sexual attraction under conditions of high anxiety. *Journal of Personality and Social Psychology, 30,* 510–517. (12)

Dywan, J., & Bowers, K. (1983). The use of hypnosis to enhance recall. *Science, 22,* 184–185. (10)

Eagly, A. H., & Crowley, M. (1986). Gender and helping behavior: A meta-analytic review of the social psychological literature. *Psychological Bulletin, 100,* 283–308. (5)

Eagly, A. H., & Wood, W. (1999). The origins of sex differences in human behavior. *American Psychologist, 54,* 408–423. (3)

Eaker, E. D., Sullivan, L. M., Kelly-Hayes, M., D'Agostino, R. B., Sr., & Benjamin, E. J. (2004). Anger and hostility predict the development of atrial fibrillation in men in the Framingham Offspring Study. *Circulation, 109,* 1267–1271. (12)

Earnest, D. J., Liang, F.-Q., Ratcliff, M., & Cassone, V. M. (1999). Immortal time: Circadian clock properties of rat suprachiasmatic cell lines. *Science, 283,* 693–695. (10)

Eastwick, P. W., Finkel, E. J., Mochon, D., & Ariely, D. (2007). Selective versus unselective romantic desire. *Psychological Science, 18,* 317–319. (13)

Eaton, A. A., & Rose, S. (2011). Has dating become more egalitarian? A 35 year review using *Sex Roles. Sex Roles, 64,* 843–862. (5)

Eaves, L. J., Martin, N. G., & Heath, A. C. (1990). Religious affiliation in twins and their parents: Testing a model of cultural inheritance. *Behavior Genetics, 20,* 1–22. (3)

Ebbinghaus, H. (1913). *Memory.* New York: Teachers College Press. (Original work published 1885) (7)

Eberly, M. B., Johnson, M. D., Hernandez, M., & Arolio, B. J. (2013). An integrative process model of leadership. *American Psychologist, 68,* 427–433. (11)

Ebling, R., & Levenson, R. W. (2003). Who are the marital experts? *Journal of Marriage and the Family, 65,* 130–142. (13)

Ebneter, D. S., Latner, J. D., & O'Brien, K. S. (2011). Just world beliefs, causal beliefs, and acquaintance: Associations with stigma toward eating disorders and obesity. *Personality and Individual Differences, 51,* 618–622. (14)

Educational Testing Service. (1994). *GRE 1994–95 guide.* Princeton, NJ: Author. (9)

Edwards, G. (2014). Doing their duty: An empirical analysis of the unintended effect of *Tarasoff v. Regents* on homicidal activity. *Journal of Law and Economics, 57,* 321–348. (15)

Edwards, J., Jackson, H. J., & Pattison, P. E. (2002). Emotion recognition via facial expression and affective prosody in schizophrenia: A methodological review. *Clinical Psychology Review, 22,* 789–832. (12)

Edwards, K. (1998). The face of time: Temporal cues in facial expressions of emotion. *Psychological Science, 9,* 270–276. (12)

Eibl-Eibesfeldt, I. (1973). *Der vorprogrammierte Mensch* [The preprogrammed human]. Vienna: Verlag Fritz Molden. (12)

Eibl-Eibesfeldt, I. (1974). *Love and hate.* New York: Schocken Books. (12)

Eichenbaum, H. (2002). *The cognitive neuroscience of memory.* New York: Oxford University Press. (7)

Eimas, P. D., Siqueland, E. R., Jusczyk, P., & Vigorito, J. (1971). Speech perception in infants. *Science, 171,* 303–306. (5)

Eisenberger, N. I., Lieberman, M. D., & Williams, K. D. (2003). Does rejection hurt? An fMRI study of social exclusion. *Science, 302,* 290–292. (4)

Ekman, P. (1992). Facial expressions of emotion: New findings, new questions. *Psychological Science, 3,* 34–38. (12)

Ekman, P. (2001). *Telling lies* (3rd ed.). New York: W. W. Norton. (12)

Ekman, P., & Davidson, R. J. (1993). Voluntary smiling changes regional brain activity. *Psychological Science, 4,* 342–345. (12)

Ekman, P., & Friesen, W. V. (1984). *Unmasking the face* (2nd ed.). Palo Alto, CA: Consulting Psychologists Press. (12)

El-Sheikh, M., Buckhalt, J. A., Mize, J., & Acebo, C. (2006). Marital conflict and disruption of children's sleep. *Child Development, 77,* 31–43. (5)

Elbert, T., Pantev, C., Wienbruch, C., Rockstroh, B., & Taub, E. (1995). Increased cortical representation of the fingers of the left hand in string players. *Science, 270,* 305–307. (3)

Elbogen, E. B. & Johnson, S. C. (2009). The intricate link between violence and mental disorder. *Archives of General Psychiatry, 66,* 152–161. (13, 15)

Elder, T. E. (2010). The importance of relative standards in ADHD diagnoses: Evidence based on exact birth dates. *Journal of Health Economics, 29,* 641–656. (8)

Elfenbein, H. A., Beaupré, M., Lévesque, M., & Hess, U. (2007). Toward a dialect theory: Cultural differences in the expression and recognition of posed facial expressions. *Emotion, 7,* 131–146. (12)

Elicker, J., Englund, M., & Sroufe, L. A. (1992). Predicting peer competence and peer relationships in childhood from early parent-child relationships. In R. D. Parke & G. W. Ladd (Eds.), *Family-peer relationships* (pp. 77–106). Hillsdale, NJ: Erlbaum. (5)

Elkind, D. (1984). *All grown up and no place to go.* Reading, MA: Addison-Wesley. (5)

Ellenberger, H. F. (1972). The story of "Anna O": A critical review with new data. *Journal of the History of the Behavioral Sciences, 8,* 267–279. (14)

Elliott, C. (1997). Caring about risks: Are severely depressed patients competent to consent to research? *Archives of General Psychiatry, 54,* 113–116. (2)

Else-Quest, N. M., Hyde, J. S., Goldsmith, H. H., & Van Hulle, C. A. (2006). Gender differences in temperament: A meta-analysis. *Psychological Bulletin, 132,* 33–72. (5)

Emberson, L. L., Lupyan, G., Goldstein, M. H., & Spivey, M. I. (2010). Overheard cell-phone conversations: When less speech is more distracting. *Psychological Science, 21,* 1383–1388. (8)

Emery, C. E., Jr. (1997, November/December). UFO survey yields conflicting conclusions. *Skeptical Inquirer, 21,* 9. (2)

Emmons, R. A., & McCullough, M. E. (2003). Counting blessings versus burdens: An experimental investigation of gratitude and subjective well-being in daily life. *Journal of Personality and Social Psychology, 84,* 377–389. (12)

Endress, A. D., & Potter, M. C. (2014). Large capacity temporary visual memory. *Journal of Experimental Psychology: General, 143,* 548–565. (7)

Eng, M. Y., Schuckit, M. A., & Smith, T. L. (2005). The level of response to alcohol in daughters of alcoholics and controls. *Drug and Alcohol Dependence, 79,* 83–93. (15)

Engel de Abreu, P. M. J., Cruz-Santos, A., Tourinho, C. J., Martin, R., & Bialystok, E. (2012). Bilingualism enriches the poor: Enhanced cognitive control in low-income minority children. *Psychological Science, 23,* 1364–1371. (8)

Enns, J. T., & Rensink, R. A. (1990). Sensitivity to three-dimensional orientation in visual search. *Psychological Science, 1,* 323–326. (8)

Eppig, C., Fincher, C. L., & Thornhill, R. (2010). Parasite prevalence and the worldwide distribution of cognitive ability. *Proceedings of the Royal Society B, 277,* 3801–3808. (9)

Eppig, C., Fincher, C. L., & Thornhill, R. (2011). Parasite prevalence and the distribution of intelligence among the states of the USA. *Intelligence, 39,* 155–160. (9)

Erdelyi, M. H. (2006). The unified theory of repression. *Behavioral and Brain Sciences, 29,* 499–551. (14)

Erdelyi, M. H. (2010). The ups and downs of memory. *American Psychologist, 65,* 623–633. (7)

Erel, O., & Burman, B. (1995). Interrelatedness of marital relations and parent-child relations: A meta-analytic review. *Psychological Bulletin, 118,* 108–132. (5)

Erev, I., Wallsten, T. S., & Budescu, D. V. (1994). Simultaneous over- and underconfidence: The role of error in judgment processes. *Psychological Review, 101,* 519–527. (8)

Ericsson, K. A., & Charness, N. (1994). Expert performance: Its structure and acquisition. *American Psychologist, 49,* 725–747. (8)

Ericsson, K. A., Chase, W. G., & Faloon, S. (1980). Acquisition of a memory skill. *Science, 208*, 1181–1182. (7)

Ericsson, K. A., Krampe, R. T., & Tesch-Römer, C. (1993). The role of deliberate practice in the acquisition of expert performance. *Psychological Review, 100*, 363–406. (8)

Erikson, E. H. (1963). *Childhood and society* (2nd ed.). New York: W. W. Norton. (5)

Ernhart, C. B., Sokol, R. J., Martier, S., Moron, P., Nadler, D., Ager, J. W., . . . Wolf, A. (1987). Alcohol teratogenicity in the human: A detailed assessment of specificity, critical period, and threshold. *American Journal of Obstetrics and Gynecology, 156*, 33–39. (5)

Ernst, A., Alkass, K., Bernard, S., Salehpour, M., Perl, S., Tisdale, J., & Frisén, J. (2014). Neurogenesis in the striatum of the adult human brain. *Cell, 156*, 1072–1083. (3)

Ernst, C., & Angst, J. (1983). *Birth order: Its influence on personality.* New York: Springer-Verlag. (5)

Erskine, K. J., Kacinik, N. A., & Prinz, J. J. (2011). A bad taste in the mouth: Gustatory disgust influences moral judgment. *Psychological Science, 22*, 295–299. (12)

Eschenko, O., Mölle, M., Born, J., & Sara, S. J. (2006). Elevated sleep spindle density after learning or after retrieval in rats. *Journal of Neurophysiology, 26*, 12914–12920. (10)

Eskritt, M., & Ma, S. (2014). Intentional forgetting: Note-taking as a naturalistic example. *Memory & Cognition, 42*, 237–246. (7)

Esser, S. K., Hill, S., & Tononi, G. (2009). Breakdown of effective connectivity during slow wave sleep; Investigating the mechanism underlying a cortical gate using large-scale modeling. *Journal of Neurophysiology, 102*, 2096–2111. (10)

Esterson, A. (1993). *Seductive mirage.* Chicago: Open Court. (10, 14)

Esterson, A. (2001). The mythologizing of psychoanalytic history: Deception and self-deception in Freud's accounts of the seduction theory episode. *History of Psychology, 12*, 329–352. (14)

Etcoff, N. L., Ekman, P., Magee, J. J., & Frank, M. G. (2000). Lie detection and language comprehension. *Nature, 405*, 139. (3)

Euston, D. R., Tatsuno, M., & McNaughton, B. L. (2007). Fast-forward playback of recent memory sequences in prefrontal cortex during sleep. *Science, 318*, 1147–1150. (10)

Evans, G. W., Bullinger, M., & Hygge, S. (1998). Chronic noise exposure and physiological response: A prospective study of children living under environmental stress. *Psychological Science, 9*, 75–77. (12)

Evans, G. W., & Schamberg, M. A. (2009). Childhood poverty, chronic stress, and adult working memory. *Proceedings of the National Academy of Sciences, USA, 106*, 6545–6549. (9)

Evans, J. S. B. T., & Stanovich, K. E. (2013). Dual-process theories of higher cognition: Advancing the debate. *Perspectives on Psychological Science, 8*, 223–241. (8)

Evans, S. W., Owens, J. S., & Bunford, N. (2014). Evidence-based psychosocial treatments for children and adolescents with attention-deficit/hyperactivity disorder. *Journal of Clinical Child & Adolescent Psychology, 43*, 527–551. (8)

Exner, J. E., Jr. (1986). *The Rorschach: A comprehensive system* (2nd ed.). New York: Wiley. (14)

Fabiano, G. A., Pelham, W. E., Jr., Gnag, E. M., Burrows-MacLean, L., Coles, E. K., Chaco, A., . . . Robb, J. A. (2007). The single and combined effects of multiple intensities of behavior modification and methylphenidate for children with attention deficit hyperactivity disorder in a classroom setting. *School Psychology Review, 36*, 195–216. (6)

Faedda, G. L., Tondo, L., Teicher, M. H., Baldessarini, R. J., Gelbard, H. A., & Floris, G. F. (1993). Seasonal mood disorders: Patterns of seasonal recurrence in mania and depression. *Archives of General Psychiatry, 50*, 17–23. (15)

Faivre, R., Grégoire, A., Préault, M., Cézilly, F., & Sorci, G. (2003). Immune activation rapidly mirrored in a secondary sexual trait. *Science, 300*, 103. (13)

Falleti, M. G., Maruff, P., Collie, A., Darby, D. G., & McStephen, M. (2003). Qualitative similarities in cognitive impairment associated with 24 h of sustained wakefulness and a blood alcohol concentration of 0.05%. *Journal of Sleep Research, 12*, 265–274. (10)

Fan, P. (1995). Cannabinoid agonists inhibit the activation of 5-HT3 receptors in rat nodose ganglion neurons. *Journal of Neurophysiology, 73*, 907–910. (3)

Fantz, R. L. (1963). Pattern vision in newborn infants. *Science, 140*, 296–297. (5)

Farber, S. L. (1981). *Identical twins reared apart: A reanalysis.* New York: Basic Books. (9)

Farmer-Dougan, V. (1998). A disequilibrium analysis of incidental teaching. *Behavior Modification, 22*, 78–95. (6)

Farooqi, I. S., Keogh, J. M., Kamath, S., Jones, S., Gibson, W. T., Trussell, R., . . . O'Rahilly, S. (2001). Partial leptin deficiency and human adiposity. *Nature, 414*, 34–35. (11)

Farris, C., Treat, T. A., Viken, R. J., & McFall, R. M. (2008). Perceptual mechanisms that characterize gender differences in decoding women's sexual intent. *Psychological Science, 19*, 348–354. (5)

Fast, N. J., & Chen, S. (2009). When the boss feels inadequate. *Psychological Science, 20*, 1406–1413. (13)

Fauerbach, J. A., Lawrence, J. W., Haythornthwaite, J. A., & Richter, L. (2002). Coping with the stress of a painful medical procedure. *Behaviour Research and Therapy, 40*, 1003–1015. (12)

Faust, M., Kravetz, S., & Babkoff, H. (1993). Hemispheric specialization or reading habits: Evidence from lexical decision research with Hebrew words and sentences. *Brain and Language, 44*, 254–263. (8)

Fay, R. E., Turner, C. F., Klassen, A. D., & Gagnon, J. H. (1989). Prevalence and patterns of same-gender sexual contact among men. *Science, 243*, 338–348. (11)

Fazel, S., & Grann, M. (2006). The population impact of severe mental illness on violent crime. *American Journal of Psychiatry, 163*, 1397–1403. (13)

Fazio, L. K., Barber, S. J., Rajaram, S., Ornstein, P. A., & Marsh, E. J. (2013). Creating illusions of knowledge: Learning errors that contradict prior knowledge. *Journal of Experimental Psychology: General, 142*, 1–5. (7)

Feeney, D. M. (1987). Human rights and animal welfare. *American Psychologist, 42*, 593–599. (2)

Feinberg, M., & Willer, R. (2011). Apocalypse soon? Dire messages reduce belief in global warming by contradicting just-world beliefs. *Psychological Science, 22*, 34–38. (13)

Feinberg, M., Willer, R., & Schultz, M. (2014). Gossip and ostracism promote cooperation in groups. *Psychological Science, 25*, 656–664. (13)

Feinstein, J. S., Adolphs, R., Damasio, A., & Tranel, D. (2011). The human amygdala and the induction and experience of fear. *Current Biology, 21*, 34–38. (12)

Feinstein, J. S., Buzza, C., Hurlemann, R., Follmer, R. L., Dahdaleh, N. S., Coryell, W. H., . . . Wemmie, J. A. (2013). Fear and panic in humans with bilateral amygdala damage. *Nature Neuroscience, 16*, 270–272. (12)

Fendrich, R., Wessinger, C. M., & Gazzaniga, M. S. (1992). Residual vision in a scotoma: Implications for blindsight. *Science, 258*, 1489–1491. (3)

Feng, J., Fouse, S., & Fen, G. (2007). Epigenetic regulation of neural gene expression and neuronal function. *Pediatric Research, 61(5), Part 2*, 58R–63R. (3)

Feng, J., Spence, I., & Pratt, J. (2007). Playing an action video game reduces gender differences in spatial cognition. *Psychological Science, 18*, 850–855. (5)

Ferguson, C. J. (2013). Violent video games and the Supreme Court. *American Psychologist, 68*, 57–74. (1)

Ferguson, C. J. (in press). Do angry birds make for angry children? A meta-analysis of video game influences on children's and adolescents' aggression, mental health, prosocial behavior and academic performance. *Perspectives on Psychological Science.* (13)

Fernald, D. (1984). *The Hans legacy: A story of science.* Hillsdale, NJ: Erlbaum. (2)

Fernandez, E., & Turk, D. C. (1992). Sensory and affective components of pain: Separation and synthesis. *Psychological Bulletin, 112*, 205–217. (4)

Fernández-Dols, J. M., & Ruiz-Belda, M. A. (1997). Spontaneous facial behavior during intense emotional episodes: Artistic truth and optical truth. In J. A. Russell & J. M. Fernández-Dols (Eds.), *The psychology of facial expression* (pp. 255–274). Cambridge, England: Cambridge University Press. (12)

Fernández-Espejo, D., & Owen, A. M. (2013). Detecting awareness after severe brain injury. *Nature Reviews Neuroscience, 14*, 801–809. (10)

Ferreira, F., Bailey, K. G. D., & Ferraro, V. (2002). Good-enough representations in language comprehension. *Current Directions in Psychological Science, 11*, 11–15. (8)

Festinger, L. (1957). *A theory of cognitive dissonance.* Stanford, CA: Stanford University Press. (13)

Festinger, L., & Carlsmith, J. M. (1959). Cognitive consequences of forced compliance. *Journal of Abnormal and Social Psychology, 58*, 203–210. (13)

Fiedler, K., Schmid, J., & Stahl, T. (2002). What is the current truth about polygraph lie detection? *Basic and Applied Social Psychology, 24*, 313–324. (12)

Field, A. P. (2006). Is conditioning a useful framework for understanding the development and treatment of phobias? *Clinical Psychology Review, 26*, 857–875. (15)

Fillmore, M. T., & Weafer, J. (2012). Acute tolerance to alcohol in at-risk binge drinkers. *Psychology of Addictive Behaviors, 26*, 693–702. (15)

Fincham, F. D. (2003). Marital conflict: Correlates, structure, and context. *Current Directions in Psychological Science, 12*, 23–27. (13)

Fink, B., & Penton-Voak, I. (2002). Evolutionary psychology of facial attractiveness. *Current*

Directions in Psychological Science, 11, 154–158. (13)

Finkel, E. J., & Eastwick, P. W. (2008). Speed-dating. *Current Directions in Psychological Science, 17,* 193–197. (13)

Finkel, E. J., Eastwick, P. W., Karney, B. R., Reis, H. T., & Sprecher, S. (2012). Online dating: A critical analysis from the perspective of psychological science. *Psychological Science in the Public Interest, 13,* 3–66. (13)

Fisher, B. S., Daigle, L. E., Cullen, F. T., & Turner, M. G. (2003). Acknowledging sexual victimization as rape: Results from a national-level survey. *Justice Quarterly, 20,* 535–574. (13)

Fisher, R. P., Geiselman, R. E., & Amador, M. (1989). Field test of the cognitive interview: Enhancing the recollection of actual victims and witnesses of crime. *Journal of Applied Psychology, 74,* 722–727. (7)

Fisher, S. E., Vargha-Khadem, F., Watkins, K. E., Monaco, A. P., & Pembrey, M. E. (1998). Localisation of a gene implicated in a severe speech and language disorder. *Nature Genetics, 18,* 168–170. (8)

Fiske, A. P. (2002). Using individualism and collectivism to compare cultures—A critique of the validity and measurement of the constructs: Comment on Oyserman et al. (2002). *Psychological Bulletin, 128,* 78–88. (13)

Flack, W. F., Jr., Laird, J. D., & Cavallaro, L. A. (1999). Separate and combined effects of facial expressions and bodily postures on emotional feelings. *European Journal of Social Psychology, 29,* 203–217. (12)

Flatz, G. (1987). Genetics of lactose digestion in humans. *Advances in Human Genetics, 16,* 1–77. (3)

Flavell, J. (1986). The development of children's knowledge about the appearance–reality distinction. *American Psychologist, 41,* 418–425. (5)

Fleeson, W., Malanos, A. B., & Achille, N. M. (2002). An intraindividual process approach to the relationship between extraversion and positive affect: Is acting extraverted as "good" as being extraverted? *Journal of Personality and Social Psychology, 83,* 1409–1422. (14)

Fletcher, R., & Voke, J. (1985). *Defective colour vision.* Bristol, England: Hilger. (4)

Fliessbach, K., Weber, B., Trautner, P., Dohmen, T., Sunde, U., Elger, C. E., . . . Falk, A. (2007). Social comparison affects reward-related brain activity in the human ventral striatum. *Science, 318,* 1305–1308. (12)

Flor, H., Elbert, T., Knecht, S., Wienbruch, C., Pantev, C., Birbaumer, N., . . . Taub, E. (1995). Phantom-limb pain as a perceptual correlate of cortical reorganization following arm amputation. *Nature, 375,* 482–484. (4)

Flynn, J. R. (1984). The mean IQ of Americans: Massive gains 1932 to 1978. *Psychological Bulletin, 95,* 29–51. (9)

Flynn, J. R. (1998). IQ gains over time: Toward finding the causes. In U. Neisser (Ed.), *The rising curve* (pp. 25–66). Washington, DC: American Psychological Association. (9)

Flynn, J. R. (1999). Searching for justice: The discovery of IQ gains over time. *American Psychologist, 54,* 5–20. (9)

Fodor, J. (1998). When is a dog a DOG? *Nature, 396,* 325–327. (8)

Folkman, S., & Moskowitz, J. T. (2000). Positive affect and the other side of coping. *American Psychologist, 55,* 647–654. (12)

Føllesdal, H., & Hagtvet, K. A. (2009). Emotional intelligence: The MSCEIT from the perspective of generalizability theory. *Intelligence, 37,* 94–105. (12)

Forer, B. R. (1949). The fallacy of personal validation: A classroom demonstration of gullibility. *Journal of Abnormal and Social Psychology, 44,* 118–123. (14)

Fossum, I. N., Nordnes, L. T., Storemark, S. S., Bjorvatn, B., & Pallesen, S. (2014). The association between use of electronic media in bed before going to sleep and insomnia symptoms, daytime sleepiness, morningness, and chronotype. *Behavioral Sleep Medicine, 12,* 343–357. (10)

Foster, D. (2000). *Author unknown.* New York: Henry Holt. (14)

Foster, W. Z. (1968). *History of the Communist Party of the United States.* New York: Greenwood Press. (13)

Foulkes, D. (1999). *Children's dreaming and the development of consciousness.* Cambridge, MA: Harvard University Press. (10)

Foulkes, D., & Domhoff, G. W. (2014). Bottom-up or top-down in dream neuroscience? A top-down critique of two bottom-up studies. *Consciousness and Cognition, 27,* 168–171. (10)

Fournier, J. C., DeRubeis, R. J., Hollon, S. D., Dimidjian, S., Amsterdam, J., . . . Fawcett, J. (2010). Antidepressant drug effects and depression severity. *Journal of the American Medical Association, 303,* 47–53. (15)

Fowler, J. H., Baker, L. A., & Dawes, C. T. (2008). Genetic variation in political participation. *American Political Science Review, 102,* 233–248. (5)

Fowler, J. H., & Christakis, N. A. (2008). Dynamic spread of happiness in a large social network: Longitudinal analysis over 20 years in the Framingham Heart Study. *British Medical Journal, 337,* a2338. (12)

Fox, K. C. R., Nijeboer, S., Solomonova, E., Domhoff, G. W., & Christoff, K. (2013). Dreaming as mind wandering: Evidence from functional neuroimaging and first-person content reports. *Frontiers in Human Neuroscience, 7,* Article 412. (10)

Franconeri, S. L., Alvarez, G. A., & Enns, J. T. (2007). How many locations can be selected at once? *Journal of Experimental Psychology: Human Perception and Performance, 33,* 1003–1012. (8)

Frank, M. J., & Claus, E. D. (2006). Anatomy of a decision: Striato-orbitofrontal interactions in reinforcement learning, decision making, and reversal. *Psychological Review, 113,* 300–326. (3)

Frank, R. H. (2012). The Easterlin paradox revisited. *Emotion, 12,* 1188–1191. (12)

Franke, B., Faraone, S. V., Asherson, P., Buitelaaar, J., Bau, C. H. D., Ramos-Quiroga, J. A., . . . Reif, A. (2012). The genetics of attention deficit/hyperactivity disorder in adults, a review. *Molecular Psychiatry, 17,* 960–987. (8)

Fredrickson, B. L. (2001). The role of positive emotion in psychology: The broaden-and-build theory of positive emotions. *American Psychologist, 56,* 218–226. (12)

Fredrickson, B. L., & Losada, M. F. (2005). Positive affect and the complex dynamics of human flourishing. *American Psychologist, 60,* 678–686. (12)

Freedman, J. L., & Fraser, S. C. (1966). Compliance without pressure: The foot in the door technique. *Journal of Personality and Social Psychology, 4,* 195–202. (13)

Freeman, M. P. (2009). Omega-3 fatty acids in major depressive disorder. *Journal of Clinical Psychiatry, 70,* 7–11. (15)

French, A. R. (1988). The patterns of mammalian hibernation. *American Scientist, 76,* 568–575. (10)

Frensch, P. A., & Rünger, D. (2003). Implicit learning. *Current Directions in Psychological Science, 12,* 13–18. (7)

Freud, S. (1935). *A general introduction to psycho-analysis.* New York: Liveright. (Original work published 1915) (1)

Freud, S. (1925). An autobiographical study. In J. Strachey, A. Freud, A. Strachey, & A. Tyson (Eds.), *The standard edition of the complete psychological works of Sigmund Freud* (Vol. 20, pp. 7–70). London: Hogarth Press and the Institute of Psycho-Analysis. (14)

Freud, S. (1925). *Three contributions to the theory of sex* (A. A. Brill, Trans.). New York: Nervous and Mental Disease Publishing. (Original work published 1905) (14)

Freud, S. (1955). *The interpretation of dreams* (J. Strachey, Trans.). New York: Basic Books. (Original work published 1900) (10)

Freud, S. (1961). *The future of an illusion* (J. Strachey, Trans.). New York: W. W. Norton. (Original work published 1927) (14)

Frey, S. H., Bogdanov, S. Smith, J. C., Watrous, S., & Breidenbach, W. C. (2008). Chronically deafferented sensory cortex recovers a grossly typical organization after allogenic hand transplantation. *Current Biology, 18,* 1530–1534. (3)

Fried, C. B. (2008). In-class laptop use and its effects on student learning. *Computers & Education, 50,* 906–914. (7)

Friedman, J. M. (2000). Obesity in the new millennium. *Nature, 404,* 632–634. (11)

Friedman, M., & Rosenman, R. H. (1974). *Type-A behavior and your heart.* New York: Knopf. (12)

Friedman, W. J., Reese, E., & Dai, X. (2011). Children's memory for the times of events from the past years. *Applied Cognitive Psychology, 25,* 156–165. (7)

Fritz, C. O., Morris, P. E., Bjork, R. A., Gelman, R., & Wickens, T. D. (2000). When further learning fails: Stability and change following repeated presentation of text. *British Journal of Psychology, 91,* 493–511. (7)

Fritzsche, B. A., Young, B. R., & Hickson, K. C. (2003). Individual differences in academic procrastination tendency and writing success. *Personality and Individual Differences, 35,* 1549–1557. (11)

Fu, Q., Heath, A. C., Bucholz, K. K., Nelson, E., Goldberg, J., Lyons, M. J., . . . Eisen, S. A. (2002). Shared genetic risk of major depression, alcohol dependence, and marijuana dependence. *Archives of General Psychiatry, 59,* 1125–1132. (15)

Fuchs, T., Haney, A., Jechura, T. J., Moore, F. R., & Bingman, V. P. (2006). Daytime naps in night-migrating birds: Behavioural adaptation to seasonal sleep deprivation in the Swainson's thrush, *Catharus ustulatus. Animal Behaviour, 72,* 951–958. (10)

Fujita, G., Watanabe, K., Yokota, K., Kuraishi, H., Suzuki, M., Wachi, T., & Otsuka, Y. (2013). Multivariate models for behavioral offender profiling of Japanese homicide. *Criminal Justice and Behavior, 40,* 214–227. (14)

Fuligni, A. J. (1998). The adjustment of children from immigrant families. *Current Directions in Psychological Science, 7,* 99–103. (5)

Fuller, R. A., Warren, P. H., & Gaston, K. J. (2007). Daytime noise predicts nocturnal singing in urban robins. *Biology Letters, 3,* 368–370. (6)

Fuller, R. K., & Roth, H. P. (1979). Disulfiram for the treatment of alcoholism: An evaluation in 128 men. *Annals of Internal Medicine, 90,* 901–904. (15)

Fumento, M. (2014, September/October). Runaway hysteria. *Skeptical Inquirer, 42*(5), 42–49. (13)

Furman, L. M. (2008). Attention-deficit hyperactivity disorder (ADHD): Does new research support old concepts? *Journal of Child Neurology, 23,* 775–784. (8)

Furnham, A. (2003). Belief in a just world: Research progress over the last decade. *Personality and Individual Differences, 34,* 795–817. (14)

Furnham, A., Hosoe, T., & Tang, T. L.-P. (2002). Male hubris and female humility? A crosscultural study of ratings of self, parental, and sibling multiple intelligence in America, Britain, and Japan. *Intelligence, 30,* 101–115. (14)

Furukawa, T. (1997). Cultural distance and its relationship to psychological adjustment of international exchange students. *Psychiatry and Clinical Neurosciences, 51,* 87–91. (1)

Gable, P., & Harmon-Jones, E. (2010). The blues broaden, but the nasty narrows: Attentional consequences of negative affects low and high in motivational intensity. *Psychological Science, 21,* 211–215. (12)

Gabrieli, J. D. E., Cohen, N. J., & Corkin, S. (1988). The impaired learning of semantic knowledge following bilateral medial temporal-lobe resection. *Brain and Cognition, 7,* 157–177. (7)

Gächter, S., Renner, E., & Sefton, M. (2008). The long-run benefits of punishment. *Science, 322,* 1510. (13)

Gage, F. H. (2000). Mammalian neural stem cells. *Science, 287,* 1433–1438. (3)

Galatzer-Levy, I. R., Brown, A. D., Henn-Haase, C., Metzler, T. J., Neylan, T. C., & Marmar, C. R. (2013). Positive and negative emotion prospectively predict trajectories of resilience and distress among high-exposure police officers. *Emotion, 13,* 545–553. (12)

Galatzer-Levy, I. R., & Bryant, R. A. (2013). 636,120 ways to have posttraumatic stress disorder. *Perspectives on Psychological Science, 8,* 651–662. (15)

Gale, C. R., Booth, T., Mottus, R., Kuh, D., & Deary, I. J. (2013). Neuroticism and extraversion in youth predict mental well-being and life satisfaction 40 years later. *Journal of Research in Personality, 47,* 687–697. (14)

Galef, B. G., Jr. (1998). Edward Thorndike: Revolutionary psychologist, ambiguous biologist. *American Psychologist, 53,* 1128–1134. (6)

Gallavotti, A., Zhao, Q., Kyozuka, J., Meeley, R. B., Ritter, M. K., Doebley, J. F., . . . Schmidt, R. J. (2005). The role of *barren stalk1* in the architecture of maize. *Nature, 432,* 630–635. (3)

Gallistel, C. R., & Gibbon, J. (2000). Time, rate, and conditioning. *Psychological Review, 107,* 289–344. (6)

Galton, F. (1869/1978). *Hereditary genius.* New York: St. Martin's Press. (Original work published 1869) (1, 9)

Gangestad, S. W. (2000). Human sexual selection, good genes, and special design. *Annals of the New York Academy of Sciences, 907,* 50–61. (3)

Gangestad, S. W., & Simpson, J. A. (2000). The evolution of human mating: Trade-offs and strategic pluralism. *Behavioral and Brain Sciences, 23,* 573–644. (3)

Ganley, C. M., Mingle, L. A., Ryan, A. M., Ryan, K., Vasilyeva, M., & Perry, M. (2013). An examination of stereotype threat effects on girls' mathematics performance. *Developmental Psychology, 40,* 1886–1897. (9)

Gannon, N., & Ranzijn, R. (2005). Does emotional intelligence predict unique variance in life satisfaction beyond IQ and personality? *Personality and Individual Differences, 38,* 1353–1364. (12)

Gantman, A. P., & Van Bavel, J. J. (2014). The moral pop-out effect: Enhanced perceptual awareness of morally relevant stimuli. *Cognition, 132,* 22–29. (8)

Gapin, J. I., Labban, J. D., & Etnier, J. L. (2011). The effects of physical activity on attention deficit disorder symptoms: The evidence. *Preventive Medicine, 52,* S70–S74. (8)

Gapp, K., Jawaid, A., Sarkies, P., Bohacek, J., Pelczar, P., Prados, J., . . . Mansuy, I. M. (2014). Implication of sperm RNAs in transgenerational inheritance of the effects of early trauma in mice. *Nature Neuroscience, 17,* 667–669. (3)

Garb, H. N., Wood, J. N., Lilienfeld, S. O., & Nezworski, M. T. (2005). Roots of the Rorschach controversy. *Clinical Psychology Review, 25,* 97–118. (14)

Garcia, J., Ervin, F. R., & Koelling, R. A. (1966). Learning with prolonged delay of reinforcement. *Psychonomic Science, 5,* 121–122. (6)

Garcia, J., & Koelling, R. A. (1966). Relation of cue to consequence in avoidance learning. *Psychonomic Science, 4,* 123–124. (6)

Gardner, H. (1985). *Frames of mind.* New York: Basic Books. (9)

Gardner, H. (1999). *Intelligence reframed.* New York: Basic Books. (9)

Gardner, M. (1978). Mathematical games. *Scientific American, 239*(5), 22–32. (8)

Gardner, M. (1994). Notes of a fringe watcher: The tragedies of false memories. *Skeptical Inquirer, 18,* 464–470. (7)

Gardner, R. A., & Gardner, B. T. (1969). Teaching sign language to a chimpanzee. *Science, 165,* 664–672. (8)

Gartrell, N. K., Bos, H. M. W., & Goldberg, N. G. (2011). Adolescents of the US national longitudinal Lesbian family study: Sexual orientation, sexual behavior, and sexual risk exposure. *Archives of Sexual Behavior, 40,* 1199–1209. (5)

Gautam, L., Sharratt, S. D., & Cole, M. D. (2014). Drug facilitated sexual assault: Detection and stability of benzodiazepines in spiked drinks using gas chromatography-mass spectrometry. *PLoS One, 9,* e89031. (3)

Gazzaniga, M. S. (2000). Cerebral specialization and interhemispheric communication: Does the corpus callosum enable the human condition? *Brain, 123,* 1293–1326. (3)

Geary, D. C. (2000). Evolution and proximate expression of human paternal investment. *Psychological Bulletin, 126,* 55–77. (3)

Gebauer, J. E., Sedikides, C., & Neberich, W. (2012). Religiosity, social self-esteem, and psychological adjustment: On the cross-cultural specificity of the psychological benefits of religiosity. *Psychological Science, 23,* 158–160. (12)

Gelman, R. (1982). Accessing one-to-one correspondence: Still another paper about conservation. *British Journal of Psychology, 73,* 209–220. (5)

Genberg, B. L., Gange, S. J., Go, V. F., Celentano, D. D., Kirk, G. D., & Mehta, S. H. (2011). Trajectories of injection drug use over 20 years (1988–2008) in Baltimore, Maryland. *American Journal of Epidemiology, 173,* 829–836. (15)

Gendron, M., Roberson, D., van der Vyver, J. M., & Barrett, L. M. (2014). Perceptions of emotion from facial expressions are not culturally universal: Evidence from a remote culture. *Emotion, 14,* 251–262. (12)

Genoux, D., Haditsch, U., Knobloch, M., Michalon, A., Storm, D., & Mansuy, I. M. (2002). Protein phosphatase 1 is a molecular constraint on learning and memory. *Nature, 418,* 970–975. (7)

Gentile, B., Grabe, S., Dolan-Pascoe, B., Twenge, J. M., & Wells, B. E. (2009). Gender differences in domain-specific self-esteem: A meta-analysis. *Review of General Psychology, 13,* 34–45. (14)

Gentile, D. (2009). Pathological video-game use among youth ages 8 to 18: A national study. *Psychological Science, 20,* 594–602. (15)

Geraerts, E., Schooler, J. W., Merckelbach, H., Jelicic, M., Hauer, B. J. A., & Ambadar, Z. (2007). The reality of recovered memories. *Psychological Science, 18,* 564–568. (7)

German, T. P., & Barrett, H. C. (2005). Functional fixedness in a technologically sparse culture. *Psychological Science, 16,* 1–5. (8)

Gerstorf, D., Heckhausen, J., Ram, N., Infurna, F. J., Schupp, J., & Wagner, G. G. (2014). Perceived personal control buffers terminal decline in well-being. *Psychology and Aging, 29,* 612–625. (12)

Geschwind, N. (1979). Specializations of the human brain. In *Scientific American* (Ed.), *The brain: A Scientific American book.* San Francisco: W. H. Freeman. (8)

Gibbs, J., Young, R. C., & Smith, G. P. (1973). Cholecystokinin decreases food intake in rats. *Journal of Comparative and Physiological Psychology, 84,* 488–495. (11)

Gibbs, T. A., Okuda, M., Oquendo, M. A., Lawson, W. B., Wang, S., Thomas, Y. F., & Blanco, C. (2013). Mental health of African Americans and Caribbean Blacks in the United States: Results from the national epidemiological survey on alcohol and related conditions. *American Journal of Public Health, 103,* 330–338. (15)

Gibson, C. E., Losee, J., & Vitiello, C. (2014). A replication attempt of stereotype susceptibility (Shih, Pittinsky, & Ambady, 1999). *Social Psychology, 45,* 194–198. (9)

Gibson, J. J. (1968). What gives rise to the perception of movement? *Psychological Review, 75,* 335–346. (4)

Giebel, H. D. (1958). Visuelles Lernvermögen bei Einhufern [Visual learning capacity in hoofed animals]. *Zoologische Jahrbücher Abteilung für Allgemeine Zoologie, 67,* 487–520. (1)

Gigerenzer, G. (2008). Why heuristics work. *Perspectives on Psychological Science, 3,* 20–29. (8)

Gilbert, D. T., & Wilson, T. D. (2009). Why the brain talks to itself: Sources of error in emotional prediction. *Philosophical Transactions of the Royal Society, B, 364,* 1335–1341. (8)

Gilbertson, M. W., Shenton, M. E., Ciszewski, A., Kasai, K., Lasko, N. B., Orr, S. P., . . . Pitman, R. K. (2002). Smaller hippocampal volume predicts pathological vulnerability to psychological trauma. *Nature Neuroscience, 5,* 1242–1247. (12)

Gilbreth, F. B. (1911). *Motion study.* London: Constable. (11)

Gino, F., Ayal, S., & Ariely, D. (2009). Contagion and differentiation in unethical behavior. *Psychological Science, 20,* 393–398. (11)

Glantz, L. A., & Lewis, D. A. (1997). Reduction of synaptophysin immunoreactivity in the prefrontal cortex of subjects with schizophrenia. *Archives of General Psychiatry, 54*, 660–669. (15)

Glantz, L. A., & Lewis, D. A. (2000). Decreased dendritic spine density on prefrontal cortical pyramidal neurons in schizophrenia. *Archives of General Psychiatry, 57*, 65–73. (15)

Glasman, L. R., & Albarracín, D. (2006). Forming attitudes that predict future behavior: A meta-analysis of the attitude–behavior relation. *Psychological Bulletin, 132*, 778–822. (13)

Glass, M. (2001). The role of cannabinoids in neurodegenerative diseases. *Progress in Neuro-Psychopharmacology and Biological Psychiatry, 25*, 743–765. (3)

Gleich, S., Nemergut, M., & Flick, R. (2013). Anesthetic-related neurotoxicity in young children: An update. *Current Opinion in Anesthesiology, 26*, 340–347. (5)

Glenn, A. L., & Raine, A. (2014). Neurocriminology: Implications for the punishment, prediction and prevention of criminal behaviour. *Nature Reviews Neuroscience, 15*, 54–63. (13)

Gnambs, T. (2014). A meta-analysis of dependability coefficients (test-retest reliabilities) for measures of the Big Five. *Journal of Research in Personality, 52*, 20–28. (14)

Gobet, F., & Campitelli, G. (2007). The role of domain-specific practice, handedness, and starting age in chess. *Developmental Psychology, 43*, 159–172. (8)

Goetz, T. (2011, July). The feedback loop. *Wired, 19(7)*, 125–133, 162–164. (6)

Gold, B. T., Kim, C., Johnson, N. F., Kryscio, R. J., & Smith, C. D. (2013). Lifelong bilingualism maintains neural efficiency for cognitive control in aging. *Journal of Neuroscience, 33*, 387–396. (8)

Goldin, A. P., Hermida, M. J., Shalom, D. E., Costa, M. E., Lopez-Rosenfeld, M., Segretin, M. S., ... Sigman, M. (2014). Far transfer to language and math of a short software-based gaming intervention. *Proceedings of the National Academy of Sciences (U.S.A.), 111*, 357–379. (8)

Goldin-Meadow, S., McNeill, D., & Singleton, J. (1996). Silence is liberating: Removing the handcuffs on grammatical expression in the manual modality. *Psychological Review, 103*, 34–55. (8)

Goldin-Meadow, S., & Mylander, C. (1998). Spontaneous sign systems created by deaf children in two cultures. *Nature, 391*, 279–281. (8)

Goldstein, A. (1980). Thrills in response to music and other stimuli. *Physiological Psychology, 8*, 126–129. (3, 4)

Goldstein, E. B. (1989). *Sensation and perception* (3rd ed.). Belmont, CA: Wadsworth. (4)

Goldstein, E. B. (2007). *Sensation and perception* (7th ed.). Belmont, CA: Wadsworth. (4)

Goldstein, N. J., Cialdini, R. B., & Griskevicius, V. (2008). A room with a viewpoint: Using social norms to motivate environmental conservation in hotels. *Journal of Consumer Research, 35*, 472–482. (13)

Golkar, A., Selbing, I., Flygare, O, Öhman, A., & Olsson, A. (2013). Other people as means to a safe end: Vicarious extinction blocks the return of learned fear. *Psychological Science, 24*, 2182–2190. (6)

Golombok, S., Perry, B., Burston, A., Murray, C., Mooney-Somers, J., Stevens, M., ... Golding, J. (2003). Children with lesbian parents: A community study. *Developmental Psychology, 39*, 20–33. (5)

Golubock, J. L., & Janata, P. (2013). Keeping timbre in mind: Working memory for complex sounds that can't be verbalized. *Journal of Experimental Psychology: Human Perception and Performance, 39*, 399–412. (7)

Golumbic, E. Z., Cogan, G. B., Schroeder, C. E., & Poepel, D. (2013). Visual input enhances selective speech envelope tracking in auditory cortex at a "cocktail party." *Journal of Neuroscience, 33*, 1417–1426. (4)

Gómez-Pinilla, F. (2008). Brain foods: The effects of nutrients on brain function. *Nature Reviews Neuroscience, 9*, 568–578. (2)

Gonzalez Andino, S. L., de Peralta Menendez, R. G., Khateb, A., Landis, T., & Pegna, A. J. (2009). Electrophysiological correlates of affective blindsight. *NeuroImage, 44*, 581–589. (3)

Goodall, J. (1971). *In the shadow of man.* Boston: Houghton Mifflin. (2)

Goodman, G. S., Ghetti, S., Quas, J. A., Edelstein, R. S., Alexander, K. W., Redlich, A. D., ... Jones, D. P. H. (2003). A prospective study of memory for child sexual abuse: New findings relevant to the repressed-memory controversy. *Psychological Science, 14*, 113–118. (7)

Gordon, P. C., Hendrick, R., & Levine, W. H. (2002). Memory-load interference in syntactic processing. *Psychological Science, 13*, 425–430. (8)

Gossop, M., Stewart, D., & Marsden, J. (2008). Attendance at Narcotics Anonymous and Alcoholics Anonymous meetings, frequency of attendance and substance use outcomes after residential treatment for drug dependence: A 5-year follow-up study. *Addiction, 103*, 119–125. (15)

Gottesman, I. I. (1991). *Schizophrenia genesis.* New York: W. H. Freeman. (15)

Gottfredson, L. S. (2002a). *g*: Highly general and highly practical. In R. J. Sternberg & E. L. Grigorenko (Eds.), *The general intelligence factor: How general is it?* (pp. 331–380). Mahwah, NJ: Erlbaum. (9)

Gottfredson, L. S. (2002b). Where and why g matters: Not a mystery. *Human Performance, 15*, 25–46. (9)

Graber, E. C., Laurenceau, J.-P., Miga, E., Chango, J., & Coan, J. (2011). Conflict and love: Predicting newlywed marital outcomes from two interaction contexts. *Journal of Family Psychology, 25*, 541–550. (13)

Graf, P., & Mandler, G. (1984). Activation makes words more accessible, but not necessarily more retrievable. *Journal of Verbal Learning and Verbal Behavior, 23*, 553–568. (7)

Granier-Deferre, C., Bassereau, S., Ribeiro, A., Jacquet, A.-Y., & DeCasper, A. J. (2011). A melodic contour repeatedly experienced by human near-term fetuses elicits a profound cardiac reaction one month after birth. *PLoS One, 6*, e17304. (5)

Grant, A. M. (2013). Rethinking the extraverted sales ideal: The ambivert advantage. *Psychological Science, 24*, 1024–1030. (14)

Graziadei, P. P. C., & deHan, R. S. (1973). Neuronal regeneration in the frog olfactory system. *Journal of Cell Biology, 59*, 525–530. (3)

Graziano, M. S. A. (2013). *Consciousness and the social brain.* New York: Oxford University Press. (10)

Green, D. M., & Swets, J. A. (1966). *Signal detection theory and psychophysics.* New York: Wiley. (4)

Greenberg, J., Martens, A., Jonas, E., Eisenstadt, D., Pyszczynski, T., & Solomon, S. (2003). Psychological defense in anticipation of anxiety. *Psychological Science, 14*, 516–519. (5)

Greene, J. D., Sommerville, R. B., Nystrom, L. E., Darley, J. M., & Cohen, J. D. (2001). An fMRI investigation of emotional engagement in moral judgment. *Science, 293*, 2105–2108. (12)

Greenfield, T. K., Stoneking, B. C., Humphreys, K., Sundby, E., & Bond, J. (2008). A randomized trial of a mental health consumer-managed alternative to civil commitment for acute psychiatric crisis. *American Journal of Community Psychology, 42*, 135–144. (15)

Greenhoot, A. F., Ornstein, P. A., Gordon, B. N., & Baker-Ward, L. (1999). Acting out the details of a pediatric check-up: The impact of interview condition and behavioral style on children's memory reports. *Child Development, 70*, 363–380. (7)

Greeno, C. G., & Wing, R. R. (1994). Stress-induced eating. *Psychological Bulletin, 115*, 444–464. (11)

Greenwald, A. G., & Draine, S. C. (1997). Do subliminal stimuli enter the brain unnoticed? Tests with a new method. In J. D. Cohen & J. W. Schooler (Eds.), *Scientific approaches to consciousness* (pp. 83–108). Mahwah, NJ: Erlbaum. (4)

Greenwald, A. G. (2012). There is nothing so theoretical as a good method. *Perspectives on Psychological Science, 7*, 99–108. (2)

Greenwald, A. G., Nosek, B. A., & Banaji, M. R. (2003). Understanding and using the Implicit Association Test: I. An improved scoring algorithm. *Journal of Personality and Social Psychology, 85*, 197–216. (13)

Greenwald, A. G., Poehlman, A. T., Uhlmann, E. L., & Banaji, M. R. (2009). Understanding and using the Implicit Association Test: III. Meta-analysis of predictive validity. *Journal of Personality and Social Psychology, 97*, 17–41. (13)

Greenwald, A. G., Spangenberg, E. R., Pratkanis, A. R., & Eskanazi, J. (1991). Double-blind tests of subliminal self-help audiotapes. *Psychological Science, 2*, 119–122. (4)

Greer, J., Riby, D. M., Hamilton, C., & Riby, L. M. (2013). Attentional lapse and inhibition control in adults with Williams syndrome. *Research in Developmental Disabilities, 34*, 4170–4177. (8)

Gregerson, P. K., Kowalsky, E., Lee, A., Baron-Cohen, S., Fisher, S. E., Asher, J. E., ... Li, W. T. (2013). Absolute pitch exhibits phenotypic and genetic overlap with synesthesia. *Human Molecular Genetics, 22*, 2097–2104. (4)

Griffith, R. M., Miyagi, O., & Tago, A. (1958). The universality of typical dreams: Japanese vs. Americans. *American Anthropologist, 60*, 1173–1179. (10)

Griskevicius, V., Shiota, M. N., & Neufeld, S. L. (2010). Influence of different positive emotions on persuasion processing: A functional evolutionary approach. *Emotion, 10*, 190–206. (12)

Grissmer, D. W., Williamson, S., Kirby, S. N., & Berends, M. (1998). Exploring the rapid rise in the Black achievement scores in the United States (1970–1990). In U. Neisser (Ed.), *The rising curve* (pp. 251–285). Washington, DC: American Psychological Association. (9)

Gross, J. J., Fredrickson, B. L., & Levenson, R. W. (1994). The psychophysiology of crying. *Psychophysiology, 31*, 460–468. (12)

Grossman, E. D., & Blake, R. (2001). Brain activity evoked by inverted and imagined biological motion. *Vision Research, 41*, 1475–1482. (4)

Grossman, I., Karasawa, M., Kan, C., & Kitayama, S. (2014). A cultural perspective on emotional experiences across the life span. *Emotion, 14,* 679–692. (12)

Gruber, R., Wiebe, S., Montecalvo, L., Brunetti, B., Amsel, R., & Carrier, J. (2011). Impact of sleep restriction on neurobehavioral functioning of children with attention deficit hyperactivity disorder. *Sleep, 34,* 315–323. (8)

Grueter, M., Grueter, T., Bell, V., Horst, J., Laskowski, W., Sperling, K., . . . Kennerknecht, I. (2007). Hereditary prosopagnosia: The first case series. *Cortex, 43,* 734–749. (3)

Grünbaum, A. (1986). Précis of *The foundations of psychoanalysis:* A philosophical critique. *Behavioral and Brain Sciences, 9,* 217–284. (14)

Guilleminault, C., Heinzer, R., Mignot, E., & Black, J. (1998). Investigations into the neurologic basis of narcolepsy. *Neurology, 50*(Suppl. 1), S8–S15. (10)

Guiso, L., Monte, F., Sapienza, P., & Zingales, L. (2008). Culture, gender, and math. *Science, 320,* 1164–1165. (5)

Gunaydin, L. A., Grosenick, L., Finkelstein, J. C., Kauvar, I. V., Fenno, L. E., Adhikari, A., . . . Deisseroth, K. (2014). Natural neural projection dynamics underlying social behavior. *Cell, 157,* 1535–1551. (3)

Gur, R. E., Cowell, P. E., Latshaw, A., Turetsky, B. I., Grossman, R. I., Arnold, S. E., . . . Gur, R. C. (2000). Reduced dorsal and orbital prefrontal gray matter volumes in schizophrenia. *Archives of General Psychiatry, 57,* 761–768. (15)

Gustavson, C. R., Kelly, D. J., Sweeney, M., & Garcia, J. (1976). Prey-lithium aversions: I. Coyotes and wolves. *Behavioral Biology, 17,* 61–72. (6)

Gutiérrez, E. (2013). A rat in the labyrinth of anorexia nervosa: Contributions of the activity-based rodent model to the understanding of anorexia nervosa. *International Journal of Eating Disorders, 46,* 289–301. (11)

Gvilia, I., Xu, F., McGinty, D., & Szymusiak, R. (2006). Homeostatic regulation of sleep: A role for preoptic area neurons. *Journal of Neuroscience, 26,* 9426–9433. (10)

Haarmeier, T., Thier, P., Repnow, M., & Petersen, D. (1997). False perception of motion in a patient who cannot compensate for eye movements. *Nature, 389,* 849–852. (4)

Haas, B. W., Omura, K., Constable, R. T., & Canli, T. (2007). Is automatic emotion regulation associated with agreeableness? *Psychological Science, 18,* 130–132. (12)

Habermas, T., & Bluck, S. (2000). Getting a life: The emergence of the life story in adolescence. *Psychological Bulletin, 126,* 748–769. (5)

Hackman, J. R., & Lawler, E. E., III (1971). Employee reactions to job characteristics. *Journal of Applied Psychology, 55,* 259–286. (11)

Hadar, L., & Sood, S. (2014). When knowledge is demotivating: Subjective knowledge and choice overload. *Psychological Science, 25,* 1739–1747. (8)

Haeffel, G. J., Abramson, L. Y., Metalsky, G. I., Dykman, B. M., Donovan, P., . . . Halberstadt, L. (2005). Negative cognitive styles, dysfunctional attitudes, and the remitted depression paradigm: A search for the elusive cognitive vulnerability to depression factor among remitted depressives. *Emotion, 5,* 343–348. (15)

Haggard, P., & Eimer, M. (1999). On the relation between brain potentials and the awareness of voluntary movements. *Experimental Brain Research, 126,* 128–133. (10)

Haggarty, J. M., Cernovsky, Z., Husni, M., Minor, K., Kermean, P., & Merskey, H. (2002).

Seasonal affective disorder in an arctic community. *Acta Psychiatrica Scandinavica, 105,* 378–384. (15)

Hahn, A., Judd, C. M., Hirsh, H. K., & Blair, I. V. (2014). Awareness of implicit attitudes. *Journal of Experimental Psychology-General, 143,* 1369–1392. (13)

Hahn, B., Robinson, B. M., Kaiser, S. T., Matveeva, T. M., Harvey, A. N., Luck, S. J., & Gold, J. M. (2012). Kraepelin and Bleuler had it right: People with schizophrenia have deficits sustaining attention over time. *Journal of Abnormal Psychology, 121,* 641–648. (15)

Haidt, J. (2001). The emotional dog and its rational tail: A social intuitionist approach to moral judgment. *Psychological Review, 108,* 814–834. (13)

Haidt, J. (2007). The new synthesis in moral psychology. *Science, 316,* 998–1002. (13)

Haidt, J. (2012). *The righteous mind.* New York: Pantheon. (13)

Haist, F., Gore, J. B., & Mao, H. (2001). Consolidation of human memory over decades revealed by functional magnetic resonance imaging. *Nature Neuroscience, 4,* 1139–1145. (7)

Halamish, V., & Bjork, R. A. (2011). When does testing enhance retention? A distribution-based interpretation of retrieval as a memory modifier. *Journal of Experimental Psychology: Learning, Memory, and Cognition, 37,* 801–812. (7)

Hall, C. S., & Van de Castle, R. L. (1966). *The content analysis of dreams.* New York: Appleton-Century-Crofts. (10)

Hall, J. A., & Matsumoto, D. (2004). Gender differences in judgments of multiple emotions from facial expressions. *Emotion, 4,* 201–206. (12)

Halperin, E., Porat, R., Tamir, M., & Gross, J. J. (2013). Can emotion regulation change political attitudes in intractable conflicts? From the laboratory to the field. *Psychological Science, 24,* 106–111. (12)

Halpern, D. F., Benbow, C. P., Geary, D. C., Gur, R. C., Hyde, J. S., & Gernsbacher, M. A. (2007). The science of sex differences in science and mathematics. *Psychological Science in the Public Interest, 8,* 1–51. (5)

Halpern, S. D., Andrews, T. J., & Purves, D. (1999). Interindividual variation in human visual performance. *Journal of Cognitive Neuroscience, 11,* 521–534. (4)

Hama, Y. (2001). Shopping as a coping behavior for stress. *Japanese Psychological Research, 43,* 218–224. (12)

Hamamura, T. (2012). Are cultures becoming individualistic? A cross-temporal comparison of individualism-collectivism in the United States and Japan. *Personality and Social Psychology, 16,* 3–24. (13)

Hamann, S. B., & Squire, L. R. (1997). Intact perceptual memory in the absence of conscious memory. *Behavioral Neuroscience, 111,* 850–854. (7)

Hamby, S. (2014). Intimate partner and sexual violence research: Scientific progress, scientific challenges, and gender. *Trauma, Violence, and Abuse, 15,* 149–158. (13)

Hamby, S. L., & Koss, M. P., (2003). Shades of gray: A qualitative study of terms used in the measurement of sexual victimization. *Psychology of Women Quarterly, 27,* 243–255. (13)

Hamer, D. H., Hu, S., Magnuson, V. L., Hu, N., & Pattatucci, A. M. L. (1993). A linkage between DNA markers on the X chromosome and male sexual orientation. *Science, 261,* 321–327. (11)

Hamm, J. V. (2000). Do birds of a feather flock together? The variable bases for African American, Asian American, and European American adolescents' selection of similar friends. *Developmental Psychology, 36,* 209–219. (13)

Hampshire, A., Highfield, R. R., Parkin, B. L., & Owen, A. M. (2012). Fractionating human intelligence. *Neuron, 76,* 1225–1237. (9)

Han, C. J., & Robinson, J. K. (2001). Cannabinoid modulation of time estimation in the rat. *Behavioral Neuroscience, 115,* 243–246. (3)

Haney, C., Banks, C., & Zimbardo, P. (1973). Interpersonal dynamics in a simulated prison. *International Journal of Criminology and Penology, 1,* 69–97. (13)

Hanson, K. L., & Luciana, M. (2010). Neurocognitive impairments in MDMA and other drug users: MDMA alone may not be a cognitive risk factor. *Journal of Clinical and Experimental Neuropsychology, 32,* 337–349. (3)

Hanson, R. K. (2000). Will they do it again? Predicting sex-offense recidivism. *Current Directions in Psychological Science, 9,* 106–109. (13)

Happé, F., Ronald, A., & Plomin, R. (2006). Time to give up on a single explanation for autism. *Nature Neuroscience, 9,* 1218–1220. (15)

Harada, S., Agarwal, D. P. Goedde, H. W., Tagaki, S., & Ishikawa, B. (1982). Possible protective role against alcoholism for aldehyde dehydrogenase isozyme deficiency in Japan. *Lancet, ii,* 827. (15)

Haraszti, R. A., Ella, K., Gyöngyösi, N., Roenneberg, T., & Káldi, K. (2014). Social jetlag negatively correlates with academic performance in undergraduates. *Chronobiology International, 31,* 603–612. (10)

Harden, K. P. (2012). True love waits? A sibling-comparison study of age at first sexual intercourse and romantic relationships in young adulthood. *Psychological Science, 23,* 1324–1336. (11)

Harden, K. P. (2014). A sex-positive framework for research on adolescent sexuality. *Perspectives on Psychological Science, 9,* 455–469. (11)

Hariri, A. R., Mattay, V. S., Tessitore, A., Kolachana, B., Fera, F., Goldman, D., . . . Weinberger, D. R. (2002). Serotonin transporter genetic variation and the response of the human amygdala. *Science, 297,* 400–403. (3)

Harker, L. A., & Keltner, D. (2001). Expressions of positive emotion in women's college yearbook pictures and their relationship to personality and life outcomes across adulthood. *Journal of Personality and Social Psychology, 80,* 112–124. (12)

Harkins, S. G., & Jackson, J. M. (1985). The role of evaluation in eliminating social loafing. *Journal of Personality and Social Psychology, 11,* 457–465. (13)

Harley, B., & Wang, W. (1997). The critical period hypothesis: Where are we now? In A. M. B. deGroot & J. F. Knoll (Eds.), *Tutorials in bilingualism* (pp. 19–51). Mahwah, NJ: Erlbaum. (8)

Harris, J. R. (1995). Where is the child's environment? A group socialization theory of development. *Psychological Review, 102,* 458–489. (5)

Harris, J. R. (1998). *The nurture assumption.* New York: Free Press. (5)

Harris, J. R. (2000). Context-specific learning, personality, and birth order. *Current Directions in Psychological Science, 9,* 174–177. (5)

Harris, L. T., & Fiske, S. T. (2006). Dehumanizing the lowest of the low: Neuroimaging responses to extreme out-groups. *Psychological Science, 17,* 847–853. (13)

Harris, R. J., Schoen, L. M., & Hensley, D. L. (1992). A cross-cultural study of story memory. *Journal of Cross-Cultural Psychology, 23,* 133–147. (7)

Harris, T. (1967). *I'm OK—You're OK.* New York: Avon. (14)

Harrison, T. L., Shipstead, Z., Hicks, K. L., Hambrick, D. Z., Redick, T. S., & Engle, R. W. (2013). Working memory training may increase working memory capacity but not fluid intelligence. *Psychological Science, 24,* 2409–2419. (8)

Harrison, Y. (2013). The impact of daylight saving time on sleep and related behaviours. *Sleep Medicine Reviews, 17,* 285–292. (10)

Hasel, L. E., & Kassin, S. M. (2009). On the presumption of evidentiary independence. *Psychological Science, 20,* 122–126. (7)

Hassabis, D., Kumaran, D., Vann, S. D., & Maguire, E. A. (2007). Patients with hippocampal amnesia cannot imagine new experiences. *Proceedings of the National Academy of Sciences, 104,* 1726–1731. (7)

Hassett, J. M., Siebert, E. R., & Wallen, K. (2008). Sex differences in rhesus monkey toy preferences parallel those of children. *Hormones and Behavior, 54,* 359–364. (5)

Hassin, R. R. (2013). Yes it can: On the functional abilities of the human unconscious. *Perspectives on Psychological Science, 8,* 195–207. (10)

Hastie, R., Schkade, D. A., & Payne, J. W. (1999). Juror judgments in civil cases: Hindsight effects on judgments of liability for punitive damages. *Law and Human Behavior, 23,* 597–614. (7)

Hatfield, E., & Rapson, R. L. (1993). *Love, sex, and intimacy.* New York: HarperCollins. (13)

Hathaway, S. R., & McKinley, J. C. (1940). A multiphasic personality schedule (Minnesota): I. Construction of the schedule. *Journal of Psychology, 10,* 249–254. (14)

Haueisen, J., & Knösche, T. R. (2001). Involuntary motor activity in pianists evoked by music perception. *Journal of Cognitive Neuroscience, 13,* 786–792. (6)

Haushofer, J., & Fehr, E. (2014). On the psychology of poverty. *Science, 344,* 862–867. (15)

Havlicek, J., & Roberts, S. C. (2009). MHC-correlated mate choice in humans: A review. *Psychoneuroendocrinology, 34,* 497–512. (4)

Hay, D. F., Mundy, L., Roberts, S., Carta, R., Waters, C. S., . . . van Goozen, S. (2011). Known risk factors for violence predict 12-month-old infants' aggressiveness with peers. *Psychological Science, 22,* 1205–1211. (13)

Hayes, J. E., Bartoshuk, L. M., Kidd, J. R., & Duffy, V. B. (2008). Supertasting and PROP bitterness depends on more than the *TAS2R38* gene. *Chemical Senses, 33,* 255–265. (4)

Haynes, J.-D., Katsuyuki, S., Rees, G., Gilbert, S., Frith, C., & Passingham, R. E. (2007). Reading hidden intentions in the human brain. *Current Biology, 17,* 323–328. (3)

Healy, D., & Williams, J. M. G. (1988). Dysrhythmia, dysphoria, and depression: The interaction of learned helplessness and circadian dysrhythmia in the pathogenesis of depression. *Psychological Bulletin, 103,* 163–178. (15)

Heath, A. C., Neale, M. C., Kessler, R. C., Eaves, L. J., & Kendler, K. S. (1992). Evidence for genetic influences on personality from self-reports and informant ratings. *Journal of Personality and Social Psychology, 63,* 85–96. (5, 14)

Heider, F. (1958). *The psychology of interpersonal relations.* New York: Wiley. (13)

Heine, S. J., Buchtel, E. E., & Norenzayan, A. (2008). What do cross-national comparisons of personality traits tell us? *Psychological Science, 19,* 309–313. (14)

Heine, S. J., & Hamamura, T. (2007). In search of East Asian self-enhancement. *Personality and Social Psychology Review, 11,* 4–27. (13)

Heinzel, S., Schulte, S., Onken, J., Duong, Q.-L., Riemer, T. G., Heinz, A., . . . Rapp, M. A. (2014). Working memory training improvements and gains in non-trained cognitive tasks in young and older adults. *Aging, Neuropsychology, and Cognition, 21,* 146–173. (8)

Heisz, J. J., Pottruff, M. M., & Shore, D. I. (2013). Females scan more than males: A potential mechanism for sex differences in recognition. *Psychological Science, 24,* 1157–1163. (5)

Heit, E. (1993). Modeling the effects of expectations on recognition memory. *Psychological Science, 4,* 244–251. (7)

Hejmadi, A., Davidson, R. J., & Rozin, P. (2000). Exploring Hindu Indian emotion expressions. *Psychological Science, 11,* 183–187. (12)

Heller, S. B. (2014). Summer jobs reduce violence among disadvantaged youth. *Science, 346,* 1219–1223. (15)

Hemond, C., Brown, R. M., & Robertson, E. M. (2010). A distraction can impair or enhance motor performance. *Journal of Neuroscience, 30,* 650–654. (8)

Henderson, J. M. (2007). Regarding scenes. *Current Directions in Psychological Science, 16,* 219–222. (8)

Henderson, J. M., & Hollingworth, A. (2003). Global transsaccadic change blindness during scene perception. *Psychological Science, 14,* 493–497. (8)

Hendrie, H. C. (2001). Exploration of environmental and genetic risk factors for Alzheimer's disease: The value of cross-cultural studies. *Current Directions in Psychological Science, 10,* 98–101. (7)

Henkel, L. A. (2011). Photograph-induced memory errors: When photographs make people claim they have done things they have not. *Applied Cognitive Psychology, 25,* 78–86. (7)

Henning, E. R., Turk, C. L., Mennin, D. S., Fresco, D. M., & Heimberg, R. G. (2007). Impairment and quality of life in individuals with generalized anxiety disorder. *Depression and Anxiety, 24,* 342–349. (15)

Henrich, J., Heine, S. J., & Norenzayan, A. (2010). Most people are not WEIRD. *Nature, 466,* 29. (2)

Herbenick, D., Reece, M., Schick, V., Sanders, S. A., Dodge, B., & Fortenberry, J. D. (2010). Sexual behavior in the United States: Results from a national probability sample of men and women ages 14–94. *Journal of Sexual Medicine, 7* (suppl 5), 255–265. (11)

Hergenhahn, B. R. (1992). *An introduction to the history of psychology* (2nd ed.). Belmont, CA: Wadsworth. (1)

Herkenham, M., Lynn, A. B., de Costa, B. R., & Richfield, E. K. (1991). Neuronal localization of cannabinoid receptors in the basal ganglia of the rat. *Brain Research, 547,* 267–274. (3)

Herkenham, M., Lynn, A. B., Little, M. D., Johnson, M. R., Melvin, L. S., deCosta, B. R., . . . Rice, K. C. (1990). Cannabinoid receptor localization in brain. *Proceedings of the National Academy of Sciences, USA, 87,* 1932–1936. (3)

Herman, C. P., Roth, D. A., & Polivy, J. (2003). Effects of the presence of others on food intake: A normative interpretation. *Psychological Bulletin, 129,* 873–886. (11)

Herman, J., Roffwarg, H., & Tauber, E. S. (1968). Color and other perceptual qualities of REM and NREM sleep. *Psychophysiology, 5,* 223. (10)

Herrmann, B., Thöni, C., & Gächter, S. (2008). Antisocial punishment across societies. *Science, 319,* 1362–1367. (13)

Hertenstein, M. J. (2002). Touch: Its communicative functions in infancy. *Human Development, 45,* 70–94. (5)

Hertenstein, M. J., Keltner, D., App, B., Bulleit, B. A., & Jaskolka, A. R. (2006). Touch communicates distinct emotions. *Emotion, 6,* 528–533. (12)

Hertzog, C., Kramer, A. F., Wilson, R. S., & Lindenberger, U. (2009). Enrichment effects on adult cognitive development. *Psychological Science in the Public Interest, 9,* 1–65. (8)

Herz, R. (2007). *The scent of desire.* New York: HarperCollins. (4)

Herz, R. S. (2014). Verbal priming and taste sensitivity make moral transgressions gross. *Behavioral Neuroscience, 128,* 20–28. (12)

Herz, R. S., & von Clef, J. (2001). The influence of verbal labeling on the perception of odors: Evidence for olfactory illusions? *Perception, 30,* 381–391. (4)

Hespos, S. J., Ferry, A. L., & Rips, L. J. (2009). Five-month-old infants have different expectations for solids and liquids. *Psychological Science, 20,* 603–611. (5)

Hess, T. M. (2014). Selective engagement of cognitive resources: Motivational influences on older adults' cognitive functioning. *Perspectives on Psychological Science, 9,* 388–407. (5)

Hetherington, E. M. (1989). Coping with family transitions. Winners, losers, and survivors. *Child Development, 60,* 1–14. (5)

Hetherington, E. M., Stanley-Hagan, M., & Anderson, E. R. (1989). Marital transitions: A child's perspective. *American Psychologist, 44,* 303–312. (5)

Hettema, J. M., Neale, M. C., & Kendler, K. S. (2001). A review and meta-analysis of the genetic epidemiology of anxiety disorders. *American Journal of Psychiatry, 158,* 1568–1578. (15)

Heyman, G. M. (2011). Received wisdom regarding the roles of craving and dopamine in addiction: A response to Lewis's critique of *Addiction: A disorder of choice. Perspectives on Psychological Science, 6,* 156–160. (15)

Hildreth, K., Sweeney, B., & Rovee-Collier, C. (2003). Differential memory-preserving effects of reminders at 6 months. *Journal of Experimental Child Psychology, 84,* 41–62. (5)

Hill, P. L., & Turiano, N. A. (2014). Purpose in life as a predictor of mortality across adulthood. *Psychological Science, 25,* 1482–1486. (12)

Hines, T. (2014). Neuromythology of Einstein's brain. *Brain and Cognition, 88,* 21–25. (2)

Hinze, S. R., Slaten, D. G., Horton, W. S., Jenkins, R., & Rapp, D. N. (2014). Pilgrims sailing the Titanic: Plausibility effects on memory for misinformation. *Memory & Cognition, 42,* 305–324. (7)

Hirvonen, J., van Erp, T. G. M., Huttunen, J., Aalto, S., Någren, K., Huttunen, M., . . . Hietala, J. (2006). Brain dopamine D$_1$ receptors in twins discordant for schizophrenia. *American Journal of Psychiatry, 163,* 1747–1753. (15)

Hobson, J. A. (2005). Sleep is of the brain, by the brain and for the brain. *Nature, 437,* 1254-1256. (10)

Hobson, J. A., & McCarley, R. W. (1977). The brain as a dream state generator: An activation-synthesis hypothesis of the dream process. *American Journal of Psychiatry, 134,* 1335-1348. (10)

Hodgins, S., Mednick, S. A., Brennan, P. A., Schulsinger, F., & Engberg, M. (1996). Mental disorder and crime. *Archives of General Psychiatry, 53,* 489-496. (13)

Hoebel, B. G., Rada, P. V., Mark, G. P., & Pothos, E. (1999). Neural systems for reinforcement and inhibition of behavior: Relevance to eating, addiction, and depression. In D. Kahneman, E. Diener, & N. Schwartz (Eds.), *Well-being: Foundations of hedonic psychology* (pp. 560-574). New York: Russell Sage Foundation. (11, 15)

Hoek, H. W., & van Hoeken, D. (2003). Review of the prevalence and incidence of eating disorders. *International Journal of Eating Disorders, 34,* 383-396. (11)

Hofmann, S. G., Asmundson, G. J. G., & Beck, A. T. (2013). The science of cognitive therapy. *Behavior Therapy, 44,* 199-212. (15)

Hofmann, W., Gschwendner, T., & Schmitt, M. (2009). The road to the unconscious self not taken: Discrepancies between self- and observer-inferences about implicit dispositions from nonverbal behavioural cues. *European Journal of Personality, 23,* 343-366. (13)

Hofmann, W., Vohs, K. D., & Baumeister, R. F. (2012). What people desire, feel conflicted about, and try to resist in everyday life. *Psychological Science, 23,* 582-588. (11)

Hofstee, W. K. B. (1994). Who should own the definition of personality? *European Journal of Personality, 8,* 149-162. (14)

Holcombe, A. O., & Cavanagh, P. (2001). Early binding of feature pairs for visual perception. *Nature Neuroscience, 4,* 127-128. (3)

Holden, G. W., & Miller, P. C. (1999). Enduring and different: A meta-analysis of the similarity in parents' child rearing. *Psychological Bulletin, 125,* 223-254. (5)

Hollon, S. D., DeRubeis, R. J., Fawcett, J., Amsterdam, J. D., Shelton, R. C., Zajecka, J., . . . Gallop, R. (2014). Effect of cognitive therapy with antidepressant medications vs antidepressants alone on the rate of recovery in major depressive disorder. *JAMA Psychiatry, 71,* 1157-1164. (15)

Hollon, S. D., Thase, M.. E., & Markowitz, J. C. (2002). Treatment and prevention of depression. *Psychological Science in the Public Interest, 3,* 39-77. (15)

Holmberg, D., & Blair, K. L. (2009). Sexual desire, communication, satisfaction, and preferences of men and women in same-sex versus mixed-sex relationships. *Journal of Sex Research, 46,* 57-66. (13)

Holmes, A. J., Lee, P. H., Hollinshead, M. O., Bakst, L., Roffman, J. L., Smoller, J. W., & Buckner R. L. (2012). Individual differences in amygdala-medial prefrontal anatomy link negative affect, impaired social functioning, and polygenic depression risk. *Journal of Neuroscience, 32,* 18087-18100. (12)

Holmes, D. S. (1978). Projection as a defense mechanism. *Psychological Bulletin, 85,* 677-688. (14)

Holmes, D. S. (1990). The evidence for repression: An examination of sixty years of research. In J. L. Singer (Ed.), *Repression and dissociation* (pp. 85-102). New York: Wiley. (7, 14)

Holmes, T., & Rahe, R. (1967). The social readjustment rating scale. *Journal of Psychosomatic Research, 11,* 213-218. (12)

Hölzel, B. K., Lazar, S. W., Gard, T., Shuman-Olivier, Z., Vago, D. R., & Ott, U. (2011). How does mindfulness meditation work? Proposing mechanisms of action from a conceptual and neural perspective. *Perspectives in Psychological Science, 6,* 537-559. (10)

Hong, Y., Morris, M. W., Chiu, C., & Benet-Martinez, V. (2000). Multicultural minds: A dynamic constructivist approach to culture and cognition. *American Psychologist, 55,* 709-720. (13)

Hoover, D. W., & Milich, R. (1994). Effects of sugar ingestion expectancies on mother-child interactions. *Journal of Abnormal Child Psychology, 22,* 501-515. (2)

Horcajo, J., Rubio, V. J., Aguado, D., Hernandez, J. M., & Marquez, M. O. (2014). Using the Implicit Association Test to assess risk propensity self-concept: Analysis of its predictive validity on a risk-taking behaviour in a natural setting. *European Journal of Personality, 28,* 459-471. (14)

Horn, J. L. (1968). Organization of abilities and the development of intelligence. *Psychological Review, 75,* 242-259. (9)

Horne, J. A., Brass, C. G., & Pettitt, A. N. (1980). Circadian performance differences between morning and evening "types." *Ergonomics, 23,* 29-36. (10)

Hotta, E. (2013). *Japan 1941: Countdown to infamy.* New York: Knopf. (13)

Houben, K., Wiers, R. W., & Jansen, A. (2011). Getting a grip on drinking behavior: Training working memory to reduce alcohol abuse. *Psychological Science, 22,* 968-975. (7)

House, B. R., Silk, J. B., Henrich, J., Barrett, H. C., Scelza, B. A., Boyette, A. H., . . . Laurence, S. (2013). Ontogeny of prosocial behavior across diverse societies. *Proceedings of the National Academy of Sciences (U.S.A.), 110,* 14586-14591. (13)

Howard, K. I., Kopta, S. M., Krause, M. S., & Orlinsky, D. E. (1986). The dose-effect relationship in psychotherapy. *American Psychologist, 41,* 159-164. (15)

Howard, R. W. (1999). Preliminary real-world evidence that average human intelligence really is rising. *Intelligence, 27,* 235-250. (9)

Howe, M. L., & Courage, M. L. (1993). On resolving the enigma of infantile amnesia. *Psychological Bulletin, 113,* 305-326. (7)

Howes, O. D., Montgomery, A. J., Asselin, M.-C., Murray, R. M., Valli, I., Tabraham, P., . . . Grasby, P. M. (2009). Elevated striatal dopamine function linked to prodromal signs of schizophrenia. *Archives of General Psychiatry, 66,* 13-20. (15)

Hrdy, S. B. (2000). The optimal number of fathers. *Annals of the New York Academy of Sciences, 907,* 75-96. (3)

Hróbjartsson, A., & Gøtzsche, P. C. (2001). Is the placebo powerless? *New England Journal of Medicine, 344,* 1594-1602. (4)

Hu, P., Stylos-Allan, M., & Walker, M. P. (2006). Sleep facilitates consolidation of emotional declarative memory. *Psychological Science, 17,* 891-898. (10)

Hu, X., Rosenfeld, J. P., & Bodenhausen, G. V. (2012). Combating automatic autobiographical associations: The effect of instruction and training in strategically concealing information in the autobiographical Implicit Association Test. *Behavioral Neuroscience, 23,* 1079-1085. (13)

Huang, B. H. (2014). The effects of age on second language grammar and speech production. *Journal of Psycholinguistic Research, 43,* 397-420. (8)

Huang, Y., Kendrick, K., & Yu, R. (2014). Conformity to the opinions of other people lasts for no more than 3 days. *Psychological Science, 25,* 1388-1393. (13)

Hubbs-Tait, L., Nation, J. R., Krebs, N. F., & Bellinger, D. C. (2005). Neurotoxicants, micronutrients, and social environments: Individual and combined effects on children's development. *Psychological Science in the Public Interest, 6,* 57-121. (5)

Hubel, D. H., & Wiesel, T. N. (1968). Receptive fields and functional architecture of monkey striate cortex. *Journal of Physiology* (London), *195,* 215-243. (4)

Huber, R., Ghilardi, M. F., Massimini, M., & Tononi, G. (2004). Local sleep and learning. *Nature, 430,* 78-81. (10)

Hudson, J. I., Hiripi, E., Pope, H. G., Jr., & Kessler, R. C. (2007). The prevalence and correlates of eating disorders in the National Comorbidity Survey Replication. *Biological Psychiatry, 61,* 348-358. (11)

Hudson, J. I., Mangweth, B., Pope, H. G., Jr., De Col, C., Hausmann, A., Gutweniger, S., . . . Tsuang, M. T. (2003). Family study of affective spectrum disorder. *Archives of General Psychiatry, 60,* 170-177. (15)

Hudson, W. (1960). Pictorial depth perception in subcultural groups in Africa. *Journal of Social Psychology, 52,* 183-208. (4)

Huff, D. (1954). *How to lie with statistics.* New York: W. W. Norton. (2)

Hughes, J., Smith, T. W., Kosterlitz, H. W., Fothergill, L. A., Morgan, B. A., & Morris, H. R. (1975). Identification of two related pentapeptides from the brain with potent opiate antagonist activity. *Nature, 258,* 577-579. (3)

Hugoson, A., Ljungquist, B., & Breivik, T. (2002). The relationship of some negative events and psychological factors to periodontal disease in an adult Swedish population 50 to 80 years of age. *Journal of Clinical Periodontology, 29,* 247-253. (12)

Hull, C. L. (1932). The goal gradient hypothesis and maze learning. *Psychological Review, 39,* 25-43. (1)

Hull, C. L. (1943). *Principles of behavior: An introduction to behavior theory.* New York: D. Appleton. (11)

Hull, R., & Vaid, J. (2007). Bilingual language lateralization: A meta-analytic tale of two hemispheres. *Neuropsychologia, 45,* 1987-2008. (8)

Humphreys, K. L., Eng, T., & Lee, S. S. (2013). Stimulant medication and substance use outcome: A meta-analysis. *JAMA Psychiatry, 70,* 740-749. (3)

Hunter, J. E. (1997). Needed: A ban on the significance test. *Psychological Science, 8,* 3-7. (2)

Hur, Y.-M., Bouchard, T. J., Jr., & Eckert, E. (1998). Genetic and environmental influences on self-reported diet: A reared-apart twin study. *Physiology and Behavior, 64,* 629-636. (5)

Hur, Y.-M., Bouchard, T. J., Jr., & Lykken, D. T. (1998). Genetic and environmental influence on morningness–eveningness. *Personality and Individual Differences, 25,* 917-925. (5)

Hurovitz, C. S., Dunn, S., Domhoff, G. W., & Fiss, H. (1999). The dreams of blind men and women: A replication and extension of previous findings. *Dreaming, 9*, 183–193. (10)

Huttner, H. B., Bergmann, O., Salehpour, M., Rácz, A., Tatarishvili, J., Lindgren, E., ... Frisén, J. (2014). The age and genomic integrity of neurons after cortical stroke in humans. *Nature Neuroscience, 17*, 801–803. (3)

Hyde, J. (2005). The gender similarities hypothesis. *American Psychologist, 60*, 581–592. (5)

Hyde, J. S., Lindberg, S. M., Linn, M. C., Ellis, A. B., & Williams, C. C. (2008). Gender similarities characterize math performance. *Science, 321*, 494–495. (5)

Hyde, K. L., Lerch, J., Norton, A., Forgeard, M., Winner, E., Evans, A. C., ... Schlaug, G. (2009). Musical training shapes structural brain development. *Journal of Neuroscience, 29*, 3019–3025. (3)

Hyde, K. L., & Peretz, I. (2004). Brains that are out of tune but in time. *Psychological Science, 15*, 356–360. (4)

Hyland, M. E., Alkhalaf, A. M., & Whalley, B. (2013). Beating and insulting children as a risk for adult cancer, cardiac disease and asthma. *Journal of Behavioral Medicine, 36*, 632–640. (6)

Iacono, W. G., & Patrick, C. J. (1999). Polygraph ("lie detector") testing: The state of the art. In A. K. Hess & I. B. Weiner (Eds.), *The handbook of forensic psychology* (pp. 440–473). New York: Wiley. (12)

Iggo, A., & Andres, K. H. (1982). Morphology of cutaneous receptors. *Annual Review of Neuroscience, 5*, 1–31. (4)

Ikeda, K., Koga, A., & Minami, S. (2006). Evaluation of a cure process during alarm treatment for nocturnal enuresis. *Journal of Clinical Psychology, 62*, 1245–1257. (15)

Ikonomidou, C., Bittigau, P., Ishimaru, M. J., Wozniak, D. F., Koch, C., Genz, K., ... Olney, J. W. (2000). Ethanol-induced apoptotic neurodegeneration and fetal alcohol syndrome. *Science, 287*, 1056–1060. (5)

Ilies, R., & Judge, T. A. (2003). On the heritability of job satisfaction: The mediating role of personality. *Journal of Applied Psychology, 88*, 750–759. (11)

Ilieva, I., Boland, J., & Farah, M. J. (2013). Objective and subjective cognitive enhancing effects of mixed amphetamine salts in healthy people. *Neuropharmacology, 64*, 496–505. (8)

Imahori, T. T., & Cupach, W. R. (1994). A cross-cultural comparison of the interpretation and management of face: U.S. American and Japanese responses to embarrassing predicaments. *International Journal of Intercultural Relations, 18*, 193–219. (12)

Imel, Z. E., Malterer, M. B., McKay, K. M., & Wampold, B. E. (2008). A meta-analysis of psychotherapy and medication in unipolar depression and dysthymia. *Journal of Affective Disorders, 110*, 197–206. (15)

Imhoff, M. C., & Baker-Ward, L. (1999). Preschoolers' suggestibility: Effects of developmentally appropriate language and interviewer supportiveness. *Journal of Applied Developmental Psychology, 20*, 407–429. (7)

Inglehart, R., Foa, R., Peterson, C., & Welzel, C. (2008). Development, freedom, and rising happiness. *Perspectives on Psychological Science, 3*, 264–285. (12)

Inouye, S. T., & Kawamura, H. (1979). Persistence of circadian rhythmicity in a mammalian hypothalamic "island" containing the suprachiasmatic nucleus. *Proceedings of the National Academy of Sciences, USA, 76*, 5962–5966. (10)

International Schizophrenia Consortium. (2008). Rare chromosomal deletions and duplications increase risk of schizophrenia. *Nature, 455*, 237–241. (15)

Inzlicht, M., & Schmeichel, B. J. (2012). What is ego depletion? Toward a mechanistic revision of the resource model of self-control. *Perspectives in Psychological Science, 7*, 450–463. (11)

Iossifov, I., O'Roak, B. J., Sanders, S. J., Ronemus, M., Krumm, N., Levy, D., ... Wigler, M. (2014). The contribution of *de novo* coding mutations to autism spectrum disorder. *Nature, 515*, 216–221. (15)

Irwing, P. (2012). Sex differences in *g*: An analysis of the US standardization sample of the WAIS-III. *Personality and Individual Differences, 53*, 126–131. (9)

Isaacowitz, D. M., Toner, K., Goren, D., & Wilson, H. R. (2008). Looking while unhappy. *Psychological Science, 19*, 848–853. (12)

Ispas, D., Iliescu, D., Ilie, A., & Johnson, R. E. (2014). Exploring the cross-cultural generalizability of the five-factor model of personality: The Romanian NEO PI-R. *Journal of Cross-Cultural Psychology, 45*, 1074–1088. (14)

Isaacson, G., & Adler, M. (2012). Randomized clinical trials underestimate the efficacy of antidepressants in less severe depression. *Acta Psychiatrica Scandinavica, 125*, 453–459. (15)

Iverson, J. M., & Goldin-Meadow, S. (2005). Gesture paves the way for language development. *Psychological Science, 16*, 367–371. (8)

Ivry, R. B., & Diener, H. C. (1991). Impaired velocity perception in patients with lesions of the cerebellum. *Journal of Cognitive Neuroscience, 3*, 355–366. (3)

Iyengar, S. S., & Lepper, M. R. (2000). When choice is demotivating. *Journal of Personality and Social Psychology, 79*, 995–1006. (8)

Iyengar, S. S., Wells, R. E., & Schwartz, B. (2006). Doing better but feeling worse. *Psychological Science, 17*, 143–150. (8)

Izazola-Licea, J. A., Gortmaker, S. L., Tolbert, K., De Gruttola, V., & Mann, J. (2000). Prevalence of same-gender sexual behavior and HIV in a probability household survey of Mexican men. *Journal of Sex Research, 37*, 37–43. (11)

Jackson, D. C., Malmstadt, J. R., Larson, C. L., & Davidson, R. J. (2000). Suppression and enhancement of emotional responses to unpleasant pictures. *Psychophysiology, 37*, 515–522. (12)

Jacobs, B. L. (1987). How hallucinogenic drugs work. *American Scientist, 75*, 386–392. (3)

Jacobs, J., Weidemann, C. T., Miller, J. F., Solway, A., Burke, J. F., Wei, X.-X., ... Kahana, M. J. (2013). Direct recordings of grid-like neuronal activity in human spatial navigation. *Nature Neuroscience, 16*, 1188–1190. (7)

Jacobs, J. R., & Bovasso, G. B. (2009). Re-examining the long-term effects of experiencing parental death in childhood on adult psychopathology. *Journal of Nervous and Mental Disease, 197*, 24–27. (5)

Jacobs, K. M., Mark, G. P., & Scott, T. R. (1988). Taste responses in the nucleus tractus solitarius of sodium-deprived rats. *Journal of Physiology, 406*, 393–410. (1)

Jacobson, N. S., Dobson, K. S., Truax, P. A., Addis, M. E., Koerner, K., Gollan, J. K., ... Prince, S. E. (1996). A component analysis of cognitive-behavior therapy for depression. *Journal of Consulting and Clinical Psychology, 64*, 295–304. (15)

Jaeggi, S. M., Buschkuehl, M., Shah, P., & Jonides, J. (2014). The role of individual differences in cognitive training and transfer. *Memory & Cognition, 42*, 464–480. (8)

Jaffee, S. R., Hanscombe, K. B., Haworth, C. M. A., Davis, O. S. P., & Plomin, R. (2012). Chaotic homes and children's disruptive behavior: A longitudinal cross-lagged twin study. *Psychological Science, 23*, 643–650. (5)

James, W. (1890). *The principles of psychology.* New York: Henry Holt. (1)

James, W. (1894). The physical basis of emotion. *Psychological Review, 1*, 516–529. (12)

James, W. (1961). *Psychology: The briefer course.* New York: Harper. (Original work published 1892) (10)

Janis, I. L. (1972). *Victims of groupthink.* Boston: Houghton Mifflin. (13)

Janis, I. L. (1985). Sources of error in strategic decision making. In J. M. Pennings & associates (Eds.), *Organizational strategy and change* (pp. 157–197). San Francisco: Jossey-Bass. (13)

Jaremko, M. E. (1983). Stress inoculation training for social anxiety, with emphasis on dating anxiety. In D. Meichenbaum & M. E. Jaremko (Eds.), *Stress reduction and prevention* (pp. 419–450). New York: Plenum Press. (12)

Jensen, J. D., Bernat, J. K., Wilson, K. M., & Goonewardene, J. (2011). The delay hypothesis: The manifestation of media effects over time. *Human Communication Research, 37*, 509–528. (13)

Jensen, M. P., & Patterson, D. R. (2014). Hypnotic approaches for chronic pain management. *American Psychologist, 69*, 167–177. (10)

Jensen, M. P., & Turk, D. C. (2014). Contributions of psychology to the understanding and treatment of people with chronic pain. *American Psychologist, 69*, 105–118. (6)

Ji, L-J., Nisbett, R. E., & Su, Y. (2001). Culture, change, and prediction. *Psychological Science, 12*, 450–456. (13)

Jiang, Y., Costello, P., & He, S. (2007). Processing of invisible stimuli. *Psychological Science, 18*, 349–355. (10)

Johansson, P., Hall, L., Sikström, S., & Olsson, A. (2005). Failure to detect mismatches between intention and outcome in a simple decision task. *Science, 310*, 116–119. (8)

Johansson, R., & Johansson, M. (2014). Look here, eye movements play a functional role in memory retrieval. *Psychological Science, 25*, 236–242. (7)

Johns, M., Schmader, T., & Martens, A. (2005). Knowing is half the battle. *Psychological Science, 16*, 175–179. (9)

Johnson, D. D. P., & Fowler, J. H. (2011). The evolution of overconfidence. *Nature, 477*, 317–320. (8)

Johnson, J. G., Cohen, P., Brown, J., Smailes, E. M., & Bernstein, D. P. (1999). Childhood maltreatment increases risk for personality disorders during early adulthood. *Archives of General Psychiatry, 56*, 600–606. (15)

Johnson, K. R., & Johnson, S. L. (2014). Cross-national prevalence and cultural correlates of bipolar I disorder. *Social Psychiatry and Psychiatric Epidemiology, 49*, 1111–1117. (15)

Johnson, M. K., Hashtroudi, S., & Lindsay, D. S. (1993). Source monitoring. *Psychological Bulletin, 144*, 3–28. (7)

Johnson, W., & Bouchard, T. J., Jr. (2005). The structure of human intelligence: It is verbal, perceptual, and image rotation (VPR), not fluid and crystallized. *Intelligence, 33,* 393–416. (9)

Johnson, W., & Bouchard, T. J., Jr. (2007). Sex differences in mental abilities: g masks the dimensions on which they lie. *Intelligence, 35,* 23–39. (9)

Johnson, W., Bouchard, T. J., Jr., Krueger, R. F., McGue, M., & Gottesman, I. I. (2004). Just one *g:* Consistent results from three test batteries. *Intelligence, 32,* 95–107. (9)

Johnson, W., Carothers, A., & Deary, I. J. (2008). Sex differences in variability in general intelligence. *Perspectives on Psychological Science, 3,* 518–531. (9)

Johnson, W., te Nijenhuis, J., & Bouchard, T. J., Jr. (2008). Still just 1 *g:* Consistent results from five test batteries. *Intelligence, 36,* 81–95. (9)

Johnsrude, I. S., Mackey, A., Hakyemez, H., Alexander, E., Trang, H. P., & Carlyon, R. P. (2013). Swinging at a cocktail party: Voice familiarity aids speech perception in the presence of a competing voice. *Psychological Science, 24,* 1995–2004. (4)

Johnston, J. C., & McClelland, J. L. (1974). Perception of letters in words: Seek not and ye shall find. *Science, 184,* 1192–1194. (8)

Johnston, J. J. (1975). Sticking with first responses on multiple-choice exams: For better or for worse? *Teaching of Psychology, 2,* 178–179. (8)

Johnstone, H. (1994, August 8). Prince of memory says victory was on the cards. *The Times* (London), p. 2. (7)

Joiner, T. E., Jr. (1999). The clustering and contagion of suicide. *Current Directions in Psychological Science, 8,* 89–92. (15)

Joint Committee on Standards for Educational and Psychological Testing of the American Educational Research Association, the American Psychological Association, and the National Council on Measurement in Education. (1999). *Standards for educational and psychological testing.* Washington, DC: American Educational Research Association. (9)

Jones, C. M., Braithwaite, V. A., & Healy, S. D. (2003). The evolution of sex differences in spatial ability. *Behavioral Neuroscience, 117,* 403–411. (5)

Jones, C. R., Huang, A. L., Ptácek, L. J., & Fu, Y.-H. (2013). Genetic basis of human circadian rhythm disorders. *Experimental Neurology, 243,* 28–33. (10)

Jones, C. R., Vilensky, M. R., Vasey, M. W., & Fazio, R. H. (2013). Approach behavior can mitigate predominantly univalent negative attitudes: Evidence regarding insects and spiders. *Emotion, 13,* 989–996. (15)

Jones, E. E., & Goethals, G. R. (1972). Order effects in impression formation: Attribution context and the nature of the entity. In E. Jones, D. Kanouse, H. Kelley, R. Nisbett, S. Valins, & B. Wiener (Eds.), *Attribution: Perceiving the causes of behavior* (pp. 27–46). Morristown, NJ: General Learning Press. (13)

Jones, E. E., & Harris, V. A. (1967). The attribution of attitudes. *Journal of Experimental Social Psychology, 13,* 1–24. (13)

Jones, E. E., & Nisbett, R. E. (1972). The actor and the observer: Divergent perception of the causes of behavior. In E. Jones, D. Kanouse, H. Kelley, R. Nisbett, S. Valins, & B. Wiener (Eds.), *Attribution: Perceiving the causes of behavior* (pp. 79–94). Morristown, NJ: General Learning Press. (13)

Jones, P. B., Barnes, T. R. E., Davies, L., Dunn, G., Lloyd, H., Hayhurst, K. P., . . . Lewis, S. W. (2006). Randomized controlled trial of the effect on quality of life of second- vs. first-generation antipsychotic drugs in schizophrenia. *Archives of General Psychiatry, 63,* 1079–1087. (15)

Jones, S. S., Collins, K., & Hong, H. W. (1991). An audience effect on smile production in 10-month-old infants. *Psychological Science, 2,* 45–49. (12)

Joseph, R. (2000). Fetal brain behavior and cognitive development. *Developmental Review, 20,* 81–98. (5)

Jouvet, M., Michel, F., & Courjon, J. (1959). Sur un stade d'activité électrique cérébrale rapide au cours du sommeil physiologique [On a state of rapid electrical cerebral activity during physiological sleep]. *Comptes Rendus des Séances de la Société de Biologie, 153,* 1024–1028. (10)

Judge, T. A., & Ilies, R. (2002). Relationship of personality to performance motivation: A meta-analytic review. *Journal of Applied Psychology, 87,* 797–807. (14)

Judge, T. A., & Larsen, R. J. (2001). Dispositional affect and job satisfaction: A review and theoretical extension. *Organizational Behavior and Human Decision Processes, 86,* 67–98. (11)

Judge, T. A., Thoresen, C. J., Bono, J. E., & Patton, G. K. (2001). The job satisfaction–job performance relationship: A qualitative and quantitative review. *Psychological Bulletin, 127,* 376–407. (11)

Jueptner, M., & Weiller, C. (1998). A review of differences between basal ganglia and cerebellar control of movements as revealed by functional imaging studies. *Brain, 121,* 1437–1449. (10)

Juhasz, B. J. (2005). Age-of-acquisition effects in word and picture identification. *Psychological Bulletin, 131,* 684–712. (7)

Jung, C. G. (1965). *Memories, dreams, reflections* (A. Jaffe, Ed.). New York: Random House. (14)

Jung, C. S. (2014). Organizational goal ambiguity and job satisfaction in the public sector. *Journal of Public Administration Research and Theory, 24,* 955–981. (11)

Junginger, J., & Frame, C. L. (1985). Self-report of the frequency and phenomenology of verbal hallucinations. *Journal of Nervous and Mental Disease, 173,* 149–155. (15)

Jürgensen, J., Kleinemeier, E., Lux, A., Steensma, T. D., Cohen-Kettenis, P. H., Hiort, O., . . . DSD Network Working Group. (2013). Psychosexual development in adolescents and adults with disorders of sexual development—Results from the German Clinical Evaluation Study. *Journal of Sexual Medicine, 10,* 2703–2714. (11)

Juslin, P., Winman, A., & Olsson, H. (2000). Naive empiricism and dogmatism in confidence research: A critical examination of the hard-easy effect. *Psychological Review, 107,* 384–396. (8)

Just, D. R., & Wansink, B. (2011). The flat-rate pricing paradox: Conflicting effects of "all-you-can-eat" buffet pricing. *Review of Economics and Statistics, 93,* 193–200. (11)

Just, M. A., & Carpenter, P. A. (1987). *The psychology of reading and language comprehension.* Boston: Allyn & Bacon. (8)

Kagan, J., Reznick, J. S., & Snidman, N. (1988). Biological bases of childhood shyness. *Science, 240,* 167–171. (5)

Kagan, J., & Snidman, N. (1991). Infant predictors of inhibited and uninhibited profiles. *Psychological Science, 2,* 40–44. (5)

Kahn, A. S., Jackson, J., Kully, C., Badger, K., & Halvorsen, J. (2003). Calling it rape: Differences in experiences of women who do or do not label their sexual assault as rape. *Psychology of Women Quarterly, 27,* 233–242. (13)

Kahneman, D. (2011). *Thinking, fast and slow.* New York: Farrar, Straus and Giraux. (8)

Kahneman, D., & Klein, G. (2009). Conditions for intuitive expertise: A failure to disagree. *American Psychologist, 64,* 515–526. (8)

Kahneman, D., & Tversky, A. (1973). On the psychology of prediction. *Psychological Review, 80,* 237–251. (8)

Kaiser, C. R., Vick, S. B., & Major, B. (2004). A prospective investigation of the relationship between just-world beliefs and the desire for revenge after September 11, 2001. *Psychological Science, 15,* 503–506. (14)

Kalivas, P. W., Volkow, N., & Seamans, J. (2005). Unmanageable motivation in addiction: A pathology in prefrontal-accumbens glutamate transmission. *Neuron, 45,* 647–650. (15)

Kamin, L. J. (1969). Predictability, surprise, attention, and conditioning. In B. A. Campbell & R. M. Church (Eds.), *Punishment and aversive behavior* (pp. 279–296). New York: Appleton-Century-Crofts. (6)

Kanaya, T., Scullin, M. H., & Ceci, S. J. (2003). The Flynn effect and U.S. policies. *American Psychologist, 58,* 778–790. (9)

Kanazawa, S. (2004). General intelligence as a domain-specific adaptation. *Psychological Review, 111,* 512–523. (9)

Kanazawa, S. (2012). Intelligence, birth order, and family size. *Personality and Social Psychology Bulletin, 38,* 1157–1164. (5)

Kane, M. J., Brown, L. H., McVay, J. C., Silvia, P. J., Myin-Germeys, I., & Kwapil, T. R. (2007). For whom the mind wanders, and when. *Psychological Science, 18,* 614–621. (7)

Kanizsa, G. (1979). *Organization in vision.* New York: Praeger. (4)

Kanner, A. D., Coyne, J. C., Schaefer, C., & Lazarus, R. S. (1981). Comparison of two modes of stress measurement: Daily hassles and uplifts versus major life events. *Journal of Behavioral Medicine, 4,* 1–39. (12)

Kanwisher, N., & Yovel, G. (2006). The fusiform face area: A cortical region specialized for the perception of faces. *Philosophical Transactions of the Royal Society, B, 361,* 2109–2128. (3)

Karg, K., Burmeister, M., Shedden, K., & Sen, S. (2011). The serotonin transporter promoter variant (5-HTTLPR), stress, and depression meta-analysis revisited. *Archives of General Psychiatry, 68,* 444–454. (15)

Karim, J., & Weisz, R. (2010). Cross-cultural research on the reliability and validity of the Mayer-Salovey-Caaruso Emotional Intelligence Test (MSCEIT). *Cross-Cultural Research, 44,* 374–404. (12)

Karno, M., Golding, J. M., Sorenson, S. B., & Burnam, A. (1988). The epidemiology of obsessive-compulsive disorder in five U.S. communities. *Archives of General Psychiatry, 45,* 1094–1099. (15)

Karpicke, J. D., & Blunt, J. R. (2011). Retrieval practice produces more learning than elaborative studying with concept mapping. *Science, 331,* 772–775. (7)

Karpicke, J. D., & Roediger, H. L. III (2008). The critical importance of retrieval for learning. *Science, 319,* 966–968. (7)

Karra, E., O'Daly, O. G., Choudhury, A. I., Yousseif, A., Millership, S., Neary, M. T., . . . Batterham, R. L. (2013). A link between FTO, ghrelin, and impaired brain food-cue responsivity. *Journal of Clinical Investigation, 123,* 3539–3551. (11)

Kasser, T., & Sheldon, K. M. (2000). Of wealth and death. Materialism, mortality salience, and consumption behavior. *Psychological Science, 11,* 348–351. (5)

Kassin, S. M., Bogart, D., & Kerner, J. (2012). Confessions that corrupt: Evidence from the DNA exoneration case files. *Psychological Science, 23,* 41–45. (13)

Kassin, S. M., & Gudjonsson, G. H. (2004). The psychology of confessions: A review of the literature and issues. *Psychological Science in the Public Interest, 5,* 33–67. (13)

Katz, S., Lautenschlager, G. J., Blackburn, A. B., & Harris, F. H. (1990). Answering reading comprehension items without passages on the SAT. *Psychological Science, 1,* 122–127. (9)

Kaufman, L., & Rock, I. (1989). The moon illusion thirty years later. In M. Hershenson (Ed.), *The moon illusion* (pp. 193–234). Hillsdale, NJ: Erlbaum. (4)

Kavanagh, L. C., Suhler, C. L., Churchland, P. S., & Winkielman, P. (2011). When it's an error to mirror: The surprising reputational costs of mimicry. *Psychological Science, 22,* 1274–1276. (6)

Kay, K. N., Naselaris, T., Prenger, R. J., & Gallant, J. L. (2008). Identifying natural images from human brain activity. *Nature, 452,* 352–355. (3)

Kayval, M. H., & Russell, J. A. (2013). Americans and Palestinians judge spontaneous facial expressions of emotion. *Emotion, 13,* 891–904. (12)

Kazdin, A. E., & Rabbitt, S. M. (2013). Novel models for delivering mental health services and reducing the burdens of mental illness. *Clinical Psychological Science, 1,* 170–191. (15)

Ke, X., Tang, T., Hong, S., Hang, Y., Zou, B., Zi, H., . . . Liu, Y. (2009). White matter impairments in autism: Evidence from voxel-based morphometry and diffusion tensor imaging. *Brain Research, 1265,* 171–177. (15)

Kee, N., Teixeira, C. M., Wang, A. H., & Frankland, P. W. (2007). Preferential incorporation of adult-generated granule cells into spatial memory networks in the dentate gyrus. *Nature Neuroscience, 10,* 355–362. (3, 7)

Keel, P. K., & Klump, K. L. (2003). Are eating disorders culture-bound syndromes? Implications for conceptualizing their etiology. *Psychological Bulletin, 129,* 747–769. (11)

Keele, S. W., & Ivry, R. B. (1990). Does the cerebellum provide a common computation for diverse tasks? *Annals of the New York Academy of Sciences, 608,* 179–207. (3)

Kell, H. J., Lubinski, D., & Benbow, C. P. (2013). Who rises to the top? Early indicators. *Psychological Science, 24,* 648–659. (9)

Keller, M. C., Fredrickson, B. L., Ybarra, O., Cote, S., Johnson, K., Mikels, J., . . . Wager, T. (2005). A warm heart and a clear head. *Psychological Science, 16,* 724–731. (2)

Keller, M. C., Thiessen, D., & Young, R. K. (1996). Mate assortment in dating and married couples. *Personality and Individual Differences, 21,* 217–221. (13)

Kelley, H. H. (1967). Attribution theory in social psychology. In D. Levine (Ed.), *Nebraska Symposium on Motivation* (Vol. 15, pp. 192–238). Lincoln: University of Nebraska Press. (13)

Keltner, D., & Buswell, B. N. (1997). Embarrassment: Its distinct form and appeasement functions. *Psychological Bulletin, 122,* 250–270. (12)

Keltner, D., & Shiota, M. N. (2003). New displays and new emotions: A commentary on Rozin and Cohen (2003). *Emotion, 3,* 86–91. (12)

Kemeny, M. E., Foltz, C., Cavanagh, J. F., Cullen, M., Giese-Davis, J., Jennings, P., . . . Ekman, P. (2012). Contemplative/emotion training reduces negative emotional behavior and promotes prosocial responses. *Emotion, 12,* 338–350. (12)

Kendler, K. S., Bulik, C. M., Silberg, J., Hettema, J. M., Myers, J., & Prescott, C. A. (2000). Childhood sexual abuse and adult psychiatric and substance abuse disorders in women. *Archives of General Psychiatry, 57,* 953–959. (15)

Kendler, K. S., Gardner, C. O., & Prescott, C. A. (1999). Clinical characteristics of major depression that predict risk of depression in relatives. *Archives of General Psychiatry, 56,* 322–327. (15)

Kendler, K. S., Maes, H. H., Sundquist, K., Ohlsson, H., & Sundquist, J. (2014). Genetic and family and community environmental effects on drug abuse in adolescence: A Swedish national twin and sibling study. *American Journal of Psychiatry, 171,* 209–217. (15)

Kendler, K. S., Thornton, L. M., Gilman, S. E., & Kessler, R. C. (2000). Sexual orientation in a U.S. sample of twin and nontwin sibling pairs. *American Journal of Psychiatry, 157,* 1843–1846. (11)

Kendler, K. S., Walters, E. E., Neale, M. C., Kessler, R. C., Heath, A. C., & Eaves, L. J. (1995). The structure of the genetic and environmental risk factors for six major psychiatric disorders in women. *Archives of General Psychiatry, 52,* 374–383. (15)

Kenrick, D. T., Griskevicius, V., Neuberg, S. L., & Schaller, M. (2010). Renovating the pyramid of needs: Contemporary extensions built upon ancient foundation. *Perspectives on Psychological Science, 5,* 292–314. (11)

Kerr, R., & Booth, B. (1978). Specific and varied practice of motor skill. *Perceptual and Motor Skills, 46,* 395–401. (7)

Kessler, R. C., Berglund, P., Demler, O., Jin, R., & Walters, E. E. (2005). Lifetime prevalence and age-of-onset distributions of *DSM-IV* disorders in the National Comorbidity Survey Replication. *Archives of General Psychiatry, 62,* 593–602. (15)

Kessler, R. C., Chiu, W. T., Demler, O., & Walters, E. E. (2005). Prevalence, severity, and comorbidity of 12-month *DSM-IV* disorders in the National Comorbidity Survey Replication. *Archives of General Psychiatry, 62,* 617–627. (15, 16)

Kety, S. S., Wendler, P. H., Jacobsen, B., Ingraham, L. J., Jansson, L., Faber, B., . . . Kinney, D. K. (1994). Mental illness in the biological and adoptive relatives of schizophrenic adoptees. *Archives of General Psychiatry, 51,* 442–455. (15)

Keyes, K. M., Pratt, C., Galea, S., McLaughlin, K. A., Koenen, K. C., & Shear, M. K. (2014). The burden of loss: Unexpected death of a loved one and psychiatric disorders across the life course in a national study. *American Journal of Psychiatry, 171,* 864–871. (15)

Keysar, B., & Henly, A. S. (2002). Speakers' overestimation of their effectiveness. *Psychological Science, 13,* 207–212. (5)

Keysar, B., Barr, D. J., & Horton, W. S. (1998). The egocentric basis of language use: Insights from a processing approach. *Current Directions in Psychological Science, 7,* 46–50. (5)

Kiatpongsan, S., & Norton, M. I. (2014). How much (more) should CEOs make? A universal desire for more equal pay. *Perspectives on Psychological Science, 9,* 587–593. (12)

Kifer, Y., Heller, D., Perunovic, W. Q. E., & Galinsky, A. D. (2013). The good life of the powerful: The experience of power and authenticity enhances subjective well-being. *Psychological Science, 24,* 280–288. (12)

Kiefer, A. K., & Sekaquaptewa, D. (2007). Implicit stereotypes, gender identification, and math-related outcomes. *Psychological Science, 18,* 13–18. (9)

Kiff, C. J., Lengua, L. J., & Zalewski, M. (2011). Nature and nurturing: Parenting in the context of child temperament. *Clinical Child and Family Psychology Review, 14,* 251–301. (5)

Kim, H. S., Sherman, D. K., & Taylor, S. E. (2008). Culture and social support. *American Psychologist, 63,* 518–526. (12)

Kim, J., & Hatfield, E. (2004). Love types and subjective well-being: A cross-cultural study. *Social Behavior and Personality, 32,* 173–182. (13)

Kim, J. W., & King, B. G. (2014). Seeing stars: Matthew effects and status bias in major league baseball umpiring. *Management Science, 2619–2644.* (2)

Kim, S. (1989). *Inversions.* San Francisco: W. H. Freeman. (4)

Kim, Y.-K., Lee, H.-J., Yang, J.-C., Hwang, J.-A., & Yoon, H.-K. (2009). A tryptophan hydroxylase 2 gene polymorphism is associated with panic disorder. *Behavior Genetics, 39,* 170–175. (15)

Kimble, G. A. (1961). *Hilgard and Marquis' conditioning and learning* (2nd ed.). New York: Appleton-Century-Crofts. (6)

Kimble, G. A. (1967). Attitudinal factors in eyelid conditioning. In G. A. Kimble (Ed.), *Foundations of Conditioning and Learning* (pp. 642–659). New York: Appleton-Century-Crofts (1)

Kimble, G. A. (1993). A modest proposal for a minor revolution in the language of psychology. *Psychological Science, 4,* 253–255. (6)

Kimble, G. A., & Garmezy, N. (1968). *Principles of general psychology* (3rd ed.). New York: Ronald Press. (14)

Kinsey, A. C., Pomeroy, W. B., & Martin, C. E. (1948). *Sexual behavior in the human male.* Philadelphia: Saunders. (11)

Kinsey, A. C., Pomeroy, W. B., Martin, C. E., & Gebhard, P. H. (1953). *Sexual behavior in the human female.* Philadelphia: Saunders. (11)

Kiriakakis, V., Bhatia, K. P., Quinn, N. P., & Marsden, C. D. (1998). The natural history of tardive dyskinesia: A long-term follow-up of 107 cases. *Brain, 121,* 2053–2066. (15)

Kirsch, I., Deacon, B. J., Huedo-Medina, T. B., Scoboria, A., Moore, T. J., & Johnson, B. T. (2008). Initial severity and antidepressant benefits: A meta-analysis of data submitted to the Food and Drug Administration. *PLoS Medicine, 5*(2), e45. (15)

Kirsch, I., & Lynn, S. J. (1998). Dissociation theories of hypnosis. *Psychological Bulletin, 123,* 100–115. (10)

Kirsch, J., & Braffman, W. (2001). Imaginative suggestibility and hypnotizability. *Current Directions in Psychological Science, 10,* 57–61. (10)

Kitayama, S., Park, J., Boylan, J. M., Miyamoto, Y., Levine, C. S., Markus, H. R., . . . Ryff, C. D. (2015). Expression of anger and ill health in two cultures: An examination of inflammation and cardiovascular risk. *Psychological Science, 26,* 211-220. (5)

Klahr, A. M., & Burt, S. A. (2014). Elucidating the etiology of individual differences in parenting: A meta-analysis of behavioral genetic research. *Psychological Bulletin, 140,* 544-586. (5)

Kleen, J. K., Sitomer, M. T., Killeen, P. R., & Conrad, C. D. (2006). Chronic stress impairs spatial memory and motivation for reward without disrupting motor ability and motivation to explore. *Behavioral Neuroscience, 120,* 842-851. (12)

Klein, R. A., Ratliff, K. A., Vianello, M., Adams, R. B. Jr., Bahnik, S., Bernstein, M. J., . . . Nosek, B. A. (2014). Investigating variability in replicability: A "many labs" replication project. *Social Psychology, 45,* 142-152. (2)

Klein, D. F. (1993). False suffocation alarms, spontaneous panics, and related conditions. *Archives of General Psychiatry, 50,* 306-317. (15)

Kleinmuntz, B., & Szucko, J. J. (1984). A field study of the fallibility of polygraphic lie detection. *Nature, 308,* 449-450. (12)

Kluger, M. J. (1991). Fever: Role of pyrogens and cryogens. *Physiological Reviews, 71,* 93-127. (12)

Knoll, J. L., IV, & Resnick, P. J. (2008). Insanity defense evaluations: Toward a model for evidence-based practice. *Brief Treatment and Crisis Intervention, 8,* 92-110. (15)

Ko, C.-H., Liu, G.-C., Hsiao, S., Yen, J.-Y., Yan, M.-J., . . . Chen, C.-S. (2009). Brain activities associated with gaming urge of online gaming addiction. *Journal of Psychiatric Research, 43,* 739-747. (15)

Kobayashi, F. (2011). Japanese high school students' television viewing and fast food consumption. *Nutrition & Food Science, 41,* 242-248. (2)

Kobayashi, F., Schallert, D. L., & Ogren, H. A. (2003). Japanese and American folk vocabularies for emotion. *Journal of Social Psychology, 143,* 451-478. (12)

Kochanska, G., Aksan, N., & Joy, M. E. (2007). Children's fearfulness as a moderator of parenting in early socialization: Two longitudinal studies. *Developmental Psychology, 43,* 222-237. (5)

Kocsis, R. N. (2004). Psychological profiling of serial arson offenses: An assessment of skills and accuracy. *Criminal Justice and Behavior, 31,* 341-361. (14)

Kocsis, R. N., Irwin, H. J., Hayes, A. F., & Nunn, R. (2000). Expertise in psychological profiling: A comparative assessment. *Journal of Interpersonal Violence, 15,* 311-331. (14)

Koenigs, M., Huey, E. D., Raymont, V., Cheon, B., Solomon, J., . . . & Grafman, J. (2008). Focal brain damage protects against post-traumatic stress disorder in combat veterans. *Nature Neuroscience, 11,* 232-237. (12)

Koepp, M. J., Gunn, R. N., Lawrence, A. D., Cunningham, V. J., Dagher, A., Jones, T., . . . Grasby, P. M. (1998). Evidence for striatal dopamine release during a video game. *Nature, 393,* 266-268. (3, 15)

Kohlberg, L. (1969). Stage and sequence: The cognitive-developmental approach to socialization. In D. A. Goslin (Ed.), *Handbook of socialization theory and research* (pp. 347-480). Chicago: Rand McNally. (13)

Kohlberg, L., & Hersh, R. H. (1977). Moral development: A review of the theory. *Theory into Practice, 16,* 53-59. (13)

Kolesinska, Z., Ahmed, S. F., Niedziela, M., Bryce, J., Molinska-Glura, M., Rodie, M., . . . Weintrob, N. (2014). Changes over time in sex assignment for disorders of sex development. *Pediatrics, 134,* e710-715. (11)

Kong, D. T. (2014). Mayer-Salovey-Caruso Emotional Intelligence Test (MSCEIT/MEIS) and overall, verbal, and nonverbal intelligence: Meta-analytic evidence and critical contingencies. *Personality and Individual Differences, 66* 171-175. (12)

Konkle, T., Brady, T. F., Alvarez, G. A., & Oliva, A. (2010). Scene memory is more detailed than you think: The role of categories in visual long-term memory. *Psychological Science, 21,* 1551-1556. (8)

Kontula, O., & Haavio-Mannila, E. (2009). The impact of aging on human sexual activity and sexual desire. *Journal of Sex Research, 46,* 46-56. (11)

Koob, G. F., & LeMoal, M. (1997). Drug abuse: Hedonic homeostatic dysregulation. *Science, 278,* 52-58. (15)

Koppenaal, R. J. (1963). Time changes in the strengths of A-B, A-C lists: Spontaneous recovery? *Journal of Verbal Learning and Verbal Behavior, 2,* 310-319. (7)

Koriat, A., Bjork, R. A., Sheffer, L., & Bar, S. K. (2004). Predicting one's own forgetting: The role of experience-based and theory-based processes. *Journal of Experimental Psychology: General, 133,* 643-656. (7)

Korman, M., Doyon, J., Doljansky, J., Carrier, J., Dagan, Y., & Karni, A. (2007). Daytime sleep condenses the time course of motor memory consolidation. *Nature Neuroscience, 10,* 1206-1213. (10)

Kornell, N., & Bjork, R. A. (2008). Learning concepts and categories. *Psychological Science, 19,* 585-592. (7)

Kornell, N., Castel, A. D., Eich, T. S., & Bjork, R. A. (2010). Spacing as the friend of both memory and induction in young and older adults. *Psychology and Aging, 25,* 498-503. (7)

Kornell, N., Hays, M. J., & Bjork, R. A. (2009). Unsuccessful retrieval attempts enhance subsequent learning. *Journal of Experimental Psychology: Learning, Memory, and Cognition, 35,* 989-998. (7)

Koten, J. W. Jr., Wood, G., Hagoort, P., Goebel, R., Propping, P., Willmes, K., . . . Boomsma, D. I. (2009). Genetic contribution to variation in cognitive function: An fMRI study in twins. *Science, 323,* 1737-1740. (9)

Kotowicz, Z. (2007). The strange case of Phineas Gage. *History of the Human Sciences, 20,* 115-131. (12)

Kouider, S., Stahlhut, C., Gelskov, S. V., Barbosa, L. S., Dutat, M., de Gardelle, V., . . . Dehaene-Lambertz, G. (2013). A neural marker of perceptual consciousness in infants. *Science, 340,* 376-380. (10)

Kountouris, Y., & Remoundou, K. (2014). About time: Daylight Savings Time transition and individual well-being. *Economics Letters, 122,* 100-103. (10)

Kovas, Y., Haworth, C. M. A., Dale, P. S., & Plomin, R. (2007). The genetic and environmental origins of learning abilities and disabilities in the early preschool years. *Monographs of the Society for Research in Child Development, 72,* 1-144. (9)

Koyano, W. (1991). Japanese attitudes toward the elderly: A review of research findings. *Journal of Cross-Cultural Gerontology, 4,* 335-345. (5)

Kozel, N. J., & Adams, E. H. (1986). Epidemiology of drug abuse: An overview. *Science, 234,* 970-974. (3)

Kraemer, D. L., & Hastrup, J. L. (1988). Crying in adults: Self-control and autonomic correlates. *Journal of Social and Clinical Psychology, 6,* 53-68. (12, 14)

Krähenbühl, S., & Blades, M. (2006). The effect of question repetition within interviews on young children's eyewitness recall. *Journal of Experimental Child Psychology, 94,* 57-67. (7)

Kraljevic, J. K., Cepanec, M., & Simlesa, S. (2014). Gestural development and its relation to a child's early vocabulary. *Infant Behavior & Development, 37,* 192-202. (8)

Kramer, P. D. (2006). *Freud: Inventor of the modern mind.* New York: Harper Collins. (14)

Kraushaar, J. M., & Novak, D. C. (2010). Examining the affects of student multitasking with laptops during the lecture. *Journal of Information Systems Education, 21,* 241-251. (7)

Kreiman, G., Fried, I., & Koch, C. (2002). Single-neuron correlates of subjective vision in the human medial temporal lobe. *Proceedings of the National Academy of Sciences (U.S.A.), 99,* 8378-8383. (10)

Kreiner, D. S., Altis, N. A., & Voss, C. W. (2003). A test of the effect of reverse speech on priming. *Journal of Psychology, 137,* 224-232. (4)

Kreitzer, A. C., & Regehr, W. G. (2001). Retrograde inhibition of presynaptic calcium influx by endogenous cannabinoids at excitatory synapses onto Purkinje cells. *Neuron, 29,* 717-727. (3)

Krendl, A. C., Richeson, J. A., Kelley, W. M., & Heatherton, T. F. (2008). The negative consequences of threat. *Psychological Science, 19,* 168-175. (9)

Kreskin. (1991). *Secrets of The Amazing Kreskin.* Buffalo, NY: Prometheus. (2)

Kretsch, K. S., & Adolph, K. E. (2013). Cliff or step? Posture-specific learning at the edge of a drop-off. *Child Development, 84,* 226-240. (5)

Kripke, D. F., Garfinkel, L., Wingard, D. L., Klauber, M. R., & Marler, M. R. (2002). Mortality associated with sleep duration and insomnia. *Archives of General Psychiatry, 59,* 131-136. (2)

Krishnan-Sarin, S., Krystal, J. H., Shi, J., Pittman, B., & O'Malley, S. S. (2007). Family history of alcoholism influences naloxone-induced reduction in alcohol drinking. *Biological Psychiatry, 62,* 694-697. (15)

Kross, E., Berman, M. G., Mischel, W., Smith, E. E., & Wager, T. D. (2011). Social rejection shares somatosensory representations with physical pain. *Proceedings of the National Academy of Sciences, 108,* 6270-6275. (4)

Krueger, C., & Garvan, C. (2014). Emergence and retention of learning in early fetal development. *Infant Behavior and Development, 37,* 162-173. (5)

Krueger, D. W. (1978). The differential diagnosis of proverb interpretation. In W. E. Fann, I. Karacan, A. D. Pokorny, & R. L. Williams (Eds.), *Phenomenology and treatment of schizophrenia* (pp. 193-201). New York: Spectrum. (15)

Krueger, J. M., Rector, D. M., Roy, S., Van Dongen, H. P. A., Belenky, G., & Panksepp, J. (2008). Sleep as a fundamental property of neuronal assemblies. *Nature Reviews Neuroscience, 9,* 910-919. (10)

Krueger, R. F., Markon, K. E., & Bouchard, T. J., Jr. (2003). The extended genotype: The heritability of personality accounts for the heritability of recalled family environments in twins reared apart. *Journal of Personality, 71,* 809–833. (5)

Kruger, J., Wirtz, D., & Miller, D. T. (2005). Counterfactual thinking and the first instinct fallacy. *Journal of Personality and Social Psychology, 88,* 725–735. (8)

Krugers, H. J., Hoogenraad, C. C., & Groc. L. (2010). Stress hormones and AMPA receptor trafficking in synaptic plasticity and memory. *Nature Reviews Neuroscience, 11,* 675–681. (12)

Krupa, D. J., Thompson, J. K., & Thompson, R. F. (1993). Localization of a memory trace in the mammalian brain. *Science, 260,* 989–991. (3)

Kübler-Ross, E. (1975). *Death: The final stage of growth.* Englewood Cliffs, NJ: Prentice Hall. (5)

Kuhl, P. K., Williams, K. A., Lacerda, F., Stevens, K. N., & Lindblom, B. (1992). Linguistic experience alters phonetic perception in infants by 6 months of age. *Science, 255,* 606–608. (5)

Kuhlmann, S., Piel, M., & Wolf, O. T. (2005). Impaired memory retrieval after psychosocial stress in healthy young men. *Journal of Neuroscience, 25,* 2977–2982. (12)

Kuhn, D., & Lao, J. (1996). Effects of evidence on attitudes: Is polarization the norm? *Psychological Science, 7,* 115–120. (13)

Kumar, A., Killingsworth, M. A., & Gilovich, T. (2014). Waiting for merlot: Anticipatory consumption of experiential and material purchases. *Psychological Science, 25,* 1924–1931. (12)

Kumkale, G. T., & Abarracín, D. (2004). The sleeper effect in persuasion: A meta-analytic review. *Psychological Bulletin, 130,* 143–172. (13)

Kunar, M. A., Carter, R., Cohen, M., & Horowitz, T. S. (2008). Telephone conversation impairs sustained visual attention via a central bottleneck. *Psychonomic Bulletin and Review, 15,* 1135–1140. (8)

Kunar, M. A., Rich, A. N., & Wolfe, J. M. (2010). Spatial and temporal separation fails to counteract the effects of low prevalence in visual search. *Visual Cognition, 18,* 881–897. (4)

Kuncel, N. R., & Hezlett, S. A. (2010). Fact and fiction in cognitive ability testing for admissions and hiring decisions. *Current Directions in Psychological Science, 19,* 339–345. (9)

Kupfer, D. J., First, M. B., & Regier, D. A. (2002). *A research agenda for DSM-V.* Washington, DC: American Psychiatric Association. (15)

Küpper-Tetzel, C. E. (2014). Understanding the distributed practice effect: Strong effects on weak theoretical grounds. *Zeitschrift für Psychologie, 222,* 71–81. (7)

Kurdziel, L., Duclos, K., & Spencer, R. M. C. (2013). Sleep spindles in midday naps enhance learning in preschool children. *Proceedings of the National Academy of Sciences (U.S.A.), 110,* 17267–17272. (10)

Kurihara, K., & Kashiwayanagi, M. (1998). Introductory remarks on umami taste. *Annals of the New York Academy of Sciences, 855,* 393–397. (4)

Kuroshima, H., Kuwahata, H., & Fujita, K. (2008). Learning from others' mistakes in capuchin monkeys (*Cebus apella*). *Animal Cognition, 11,* 611–623. (6)

Kvavilashvili, L., Mirani, J., Schlagman, S., Foley, K., & Kornbrot, D. E. (2009). Consistency of flashbulb memories of September 11 over long delays: Implications for consolidation and wrong time slice hypotheses. *Journal of Memory and Language, 61,* 556–572. (7)

La Roche, M., & Christopher, M. S. (2008). Culture and empirically supported treatments: On the road to a collision? *Culture and Psychology, 14,* 333–356. (15)

LaBar, K. S., & Phelps, E. A. (1998). Arousal-mediated memory consolidation: Role of the medial temporal lobe in humans. *Psychological Science, 9,* 490–493. (12)

Laborda, M. A., & Miller, R. R. (2013). Preventing return of fear in an animal model of anxiety: Additive effects of massive extinction and extinction in multiple contexts. *Behavior Therapy, 44,* 249–261. (15)

Labroo, A. A., Lambotte, S., & Zhang, Y. (2009). The "name-ease" effect and its dual impact on importance judgments. *Psychological Science, 20,* 1516–1522. (8)

Lackner, J. R. (1993). Orientation and movement in unusual force environments. *Psychological Science, 4,* 134–142. (4)

Laeng, B., Svartdal, F., & Oelmann, H. (2004). Does color synesthesia pose a paradox for early-selection theories of attention? *Psychological Science, 15,* 277–281. (4)

Laffaye, C., McKellar, J. D., Ilgen, M. A., & Moos, R. H. (2008). Predictors of 4-year outcome of community residential treatment for patients with substance use disorders. *Addiction, 103,* 671–680. (15)

Lahey, B. B. (2009). Public health significance of neuroticism. *American Psychologist, 64,* 241–256. (14)

Lai, C. S. L., Fisher, S. E., Hurst, J. A., Vargha-Khadem, F., & Monaco, A. P. (2001). A forkhead-domain gene is mutated in a severe speech and language disorder. *Nature, 413,* 519–523. (8)

Laird, J. D., & Lacasse, K. (2014). Bodily influences on emotional feelings: Accumulating evidence and extensions of William James's theory of emotions. *Emotion Review, 6,* 27–34. (12)

Lake, R. I. E., Eaves, L. J., Maes, H. H. M., Heath, A. C., & Martin, N. G. (2000). Further evidence against the environmental transmission of individual differences in neuroticism from a collaborative study of 45,850 twins and relatives on two continents. *Behavior Genetics, 30,* 223–233. (3, 5, 14)

Lakens, D., & Evers, E. R. K. (2014). Sailing from the seas of chaos into the corridor of stability: Practical recommendations to increase the informational value of studies. *Perspectives on Psychological Science, 9,* 278–292. (2)

Lamb, M. E., Orbach, Y., Hershkowitz, I., Horowitz, D., & Abbott, C. B. (2007). Does the type of prompt affect the accuracy of information provided by alleged victims of abuse in forensic interviews? *Applied Cognitive Psychology, 21,* 1117–1130. (7)

Lambie, J. A., & Marcel, A. J. (2002). Consciousness and the varieties of emotion experience: A theoretical framework. *Psychological Review, 109,* 219–259. (10)

Lamm, H., & Myers, D. G. (1978). Group-induced polarization of attitudes and behavior. *Advances in Experimental Social Psychology, 11,* 145–195. (13)

Land, E. H., Hubel, D. H., Livingstone, M. S., Perry, S. H., & Burns, M. M. (1983). Colour-generating interactions across the corpus callosum. *Nature, 303,* 616–618. (4)

Land, E. H., & McCann, J. J. (1971). Lightness and retinex theory. *Journal of the Optical Society of America, 61,* 1–11. (4)

Lansdown, T. C., & Stephens, A. N. (2013). Couples, contentious conversations, mobile telephone use and driving. *Accident Analysis and Prevention, 50,* 416–422. (8)

Lang, J. W. B., & Lang, J. (2010). Priming competence diminishes the link between cognitive test anxiety and test performance: Implications for the interpretation of test scores. *Psychological Science, 21,* 811–819. (9)

Lang, P. J. (1994). The varieties of emotional experience: A meditation on James-Lange theory. *Psychological Review, 101,* 211–221. (12)

Langberg, J. M., & Becker, S. P. (2012). Does long-term medication use improve the academic outcomes of youth with attention-deficit/hyperactivity disorder? *Clinical Child and Family Psychology Review, 15,* 215–233. (8)

Langer, E. J. (1975). The illusion of control. *Journal of Personality and Social Psychology, 32,* 311–328. (5)

Langlois, J. H., & Roggman, L. A. (1990). Attractive faces are only average. *Psychological Science, 1,* 115–121. (13)

Langlois, J. H., Roggman, L. A., & Musselman, L. (1994). What is average and what is not average about average faces? *Psychological Science, 5,* 214–220. (13)

Långström, N., Rahman, Q., Carlström, E., & Lichtenstein, P. (2010). Genetic and environmental effects on same-sex sexual behavior: A population study of twins in Sweden. *Archives of Sexual Behavior, 39,* 75–80. (11)

Langworthy, R. A., & Jennings, J. W. (1972). Oddball, abstract olfactory learning in laboratory rats. *Psychological Record, 22,* 487–490. (1)

Lapate, R. C., Rokers, B., Li, T., & Davidson, R. J. (2014). Nonconscious emotional activation colors first impressions: A regulatory role for conscious awareness. *Psychological Science, 25,* 349–357. (10)

Lara, T., Madrid, J. A., & Correa, Á. (2014). The vigilance decrement in executive function is attenuated when individual chronotypes perform at their optimal time of day. *PLoS One, 9,* e88820. (10)

Larkina, M., Güler, O. E., Kleinknecht, E., & Bauer, P. J. (2008). Maternal provision of structure in a deliberate memory task in relation to their preschool children's recall. *Journal of Experimental Child Psychology, 100,* 235–251. (5)

Larsen, L., Hartmann, P., & Nyborg, H. (2008). The stability of general intelligence from early adulthood to middle age. *Intelligence, 36,* 29–34. (9)

Larson, R. W. (2001). How U.S. children and adolescents spend time: What it does (and doesn't) tell us about their development. *Current Directions in Psychological Science, 10,* 160–164. (5)

Larzelere, R. E., Cox, R. B. Jr., & Smith, G. L. (2010). Do nonphysical punishments reduce antisocial behavior more than spanking? A comparison using the strongest previous causal evidence against spanking. *BMC Pediatrics, 10,* article 10. (6)

Larzelere, R. E., & Kuhn, B. R. (2005). Comparing child outcomes of physical punishment and alternative disciplinary tactics: A meta-analysis. *Clinical Child and Family Psychology Review, 8,* 1–37. (6)

Lashley, K. (1923a). The behavioristic interpretation of consciousness. *Psychological Bulletin, 30,* 237–272, 329–353. (10)

Lashley, K. S. (1923b). The behavioristic interpretation of consciousness II. *Psychological Review, 30,* 329–353. (10)

Lashley, K. S. (1951). The problem of serial order in behavior. In L. A. Jeffress (Ed.), *Cerebral mechanisms in behavior* (pp. 112–146). New York: Wiley. (8)

Lassiter, G. D., Geers, A. L., Munhall, P. J., Ploutz-Snyder, R. J., & Breitenbecher, D. L. (2002). Illusory causation: Why it occurs. *Psychological Science, 13*, 299–305. (13)

Latané, B., & Darley, J. M. (1968). Group inhibition of bystander intervention in emergencies. *Journal of Personality and Social Psychology, 10*, 215–221. (13)

Latané, B., & Darley, J. M. (1969). Bystander "apathy." *American Scientist, 57*, 244–268. (13)

Latané, B., Williams, K., & Harkins, S. (1979). Many hands make light the work: The causes and consequences of social loafing. *Journal of Personality and Social Psychology, 37*, 822–832. (13)

Latner, J. D. (2003). Macronutrient effects on satiety and binge eating in bulimia nervosa and binge eating disorder. *Appetite, 40*, 309–311. (11)

Lau, H. C., Rogers, R. D., Haggard, P., & Passingham, R. E. (2004). Attention to intention. *Science, 303*, 1208–1210. (10)

Laumann, E. O. (1969). Friends of urban men: An assessment of accuracy in reporting their socio-economic attributes, mutual choice, and attitude development. *Sociometry, 32*, 54–69. (13)

Laumann, E. O., Gagnon, J. H., Michael, R. T., & Michaels, S. (1994). *The social organization of sexuality: Sexual practices in the United States.* Chicago: University of Chicago Press. (11)

Laumann, E. O., Paik, A., Glassser, D. B., Kang, J.-H., Wang, T., Levinson, G., . . . Gingell, C. (2006). A cross-national study of subjective sexual well-being among older women and men: Findings from the global study of sexual attitudes and behaviors. *Archives of Sexual Behavior, 35*, 145–161. (11)

Laursen, B., Coy, K. C., & Collins, W. A. (1998). Reconsidering changes in parent-child conflict across adolescence: A meta-analysis. *Child Development, 69*, 817–832. (5)

Laws, G., Byrne, A., & Buckley, S. (2000). Language and memory development in children with Down syndrome at mainstream schools and special schools: A comparison. *Educational Psychology, 20*, 447–457. (9)

Lawson, T. T. (2008). *Carl Jung, Darwin of the mind.* London: Karnac. (14)

Lazarus, R. S. (1977). Cognitive and coping processes in emotion. In A. Monat & R. S. Lazarus (Eds.), *Stress and coping* (pp. 145–158). New York: Columbia University Press. (12)

Leach, J. K., & Patall, E. A. (2013). Maximizing and counterfactual thinking in academic major decision making. *Journal of Career Assessment, 21*, 414–429. (8)

Lee, A., Clancy, S., & Fleming, A. S. (1999). Mother rats bar-press for pups: Effects of lesions of the MPOA and limbic sites on maternal behavior and operant responding for pup-reinforcement. *Behavioural Brain Research, 100*, 15–31. (6)

Lee, D. H., Mirza, R., Flanagan, J. G., & Anderson, A. K. (2014). Optical origins of opposing facial expression actions. *Psychological Science, 25*, 745–752. (12)

Lee, K., Talwar, V., McCarthy, A., Ross, I., Evans, A., & Arruda, C. (2014). Can classic moral stories promote honesty in children? *Psychological Science, 25*, 1630–1636. (6)

Lee, L., Loewenstein, G., Ariely, D., Hong, J., & Young, J. (2008). If I'm not hot, are you hot or not? *Psychological Science, 19*, 669–677. (13)

Lee, R. A., Su, J., & Yoshida, E. (2005). Coping with intergenerational family conflict among Asian American college students. *Journal of Counseling Psychology, 52*, 389–399. (5)

Lee, S.-H., Blake, R., & Heeger, D. J. (2005). Traveling waves of activity in primary visual cortex during binocular rivalry. *Nature Neuroscience, 8*, 22–23. (10)

Leff, J. (2002). The psychiatric revolution: Care in the community. *Nature Reviews Neuroscience, 3*, 821–824. (15)

Legault, L., Gutsell, J. N., & Inzlicht, M. (2011). Ironic effects of antiprejudice messages: How motivational interventions can reduce (but also increase) prejudice. *Psychological Science, 22*, 1472–1477. (13)

Legge, G. E., Ahn, S. J., Klitz, T. S., & Luebker, A. (1997). Psychophysics of reading: XVI. The visual span in normal and low vision. *Vision Research, 37*, 1999–2010. (8)

Leibniz, G. (1714). *The Principles of Nature and Grace, Based on Reason.* Retrieved Dec. 1, 2011 from www.earlymoderntexts.com/pdfs /leibniz1714a.pdf (10)

Leising, D., Scharloth, J., Lohse, O., & Wood, D. (2014). What types of terms do people use when describing an individual's personality? *Psychological Science, 25*, 1787–1794. (14)

Lekeu, F., Wojtasik, V., Van der Linden, M., & Salmon, E. (2002). Training early Alzheimer patients to use a mobile phone. *Acta Neurologica Belgica, 102*, 114–121. (7)

Leloup, J.-C., & Goldbeter, A. (2013). Critical phase shifts slow down circadian clock recovery: Implications for jet lag. *Journal of Theoretical Biology, 333*, 47–57. (10)

LeMagnen, J. (1981). The metabolic basis of dual periodicity of feeding in rats. *Behavioral and Brain Sciences, 4*, 561–607. (11)

Lenneberg, E. H. (1967). *Biological foundations of language.* New York: Wiley. (8)

Lenneberg, E. H. (1969). On explaining language. *Science, 164*, 635–643. (8)

Lenton, A. P., Fasolo, B., & Todd, P. M. (2008). "Shopping" for a mate: Expected versus experienced preferences in online mate choice. *IEEE Transactions on Professional Communication, 51*, 169–182. (8)

Lenz, K. M., Nugent, B. M., Haliyur, r., & McCarthy, M. M. (2013). Microglia are essential to masculinization of brain and behavior. *Journal of Neuroscience, 33*, 2761–2772. (11)

Lenzenweger, M. F., Johnson, M. D., & Willett, J. B. (2004). Individual growth curve analysis illuminates stability and change in personality disorder features. *Archives of General Psychiatry, 61*, 1015–1024. (15)

Leonard, L. B. (2007). Processing limitations and the grammatical profile of children with specific language impairment. In R. V. Kail (Ed.), *Advances in child development and behavior* (Vol. 35, pp. 139–171). Oxford, England: Elsevier. (8)

Leppänen, J. M., & Hietanen, J. K. (2003). Affect and face perception: Odors modulate the recognition advantage of happy faces. *Emotion, 3*, 315–326. (12)

Lerner, J. S., Li, Y., & Weber, E. U. (2013). The financial costs of sadness. *Psychological Science, 24*, 72–79. (12)

Lerner, M. J. (1980). *The belief in a just world: A fundamental delusion.* New York: Plenum Press. (14)

Lesko, A. C., & Corpus, J. H. (2006). Discounting the difficult: How high math-identified women respond to stereotype threat. *Sex Roles, 54*, 113–125. (9)

Leuchtenburg, W. E. (1963). *Franklin D. Roosevelt and the New Deal 1932*-1940. New York: Harper & Row. (13)

Levav, J., & Fitzsimons, G. J. (2006). When questions change behavior. *Psychological Science, 17*, 207–213. (11)

LeVay, S. (1991). A difference in hypothalamic structure between heterosexual and homosexual men. *Science, 253*, 1034–1037. (11)

Leventhal, A. M., Trujillo, M., Ameringer, K. J., Tidey, J. W., Sussman, S., & Kahler, C. W. (2014). Anhedonia and the relative reward value of drug and nondrug reinforcers in cigarette smokers. *Journal of Abnormal Psychology, 123*, 375–386. (15)

Levine, J. A., Lanningham-Foster, L. M., McCrady, S. K., Krizan, A. C., Olson, L. R., Kane, P. H., . . . Clark, M. M. (2005). Interindividual variation in posture allocation: Possible role in human obesity. *Science, 307*, 584–586. (11)

Levine, R. V. (1990). The pace of life. *American Scientist, 78*, 450–459. (12)

Levine, S. C., Vasilyeva, M., Lourenco, S. F., Newcombe, N. S., & Huttenlocher, J. (2005). Socioeconomic status modifies the sex difference in spatial skill. *Psychological Science, 16*, 841–845. (5)

Levinson, D. J. (1986). A conception of adult development. *American Psychologist, 41*, 3–13. (5)

Levy, B. J., McVeigh, N. D., Marful, A., & Anderson, M. C. (2007). Inhibiting your native language. *Psychological Science, 18*, 29–34. (8)

Lewandowsky, S., Stritzke, W. G. K., Freund, A. M., Oberauer, K., & Krueger, J. I. (2013). *American Psychologist, 68*, 487–501. (13)

Leweke, F. M., Gerth, C. W., Koethe, D., Klosterkötter, J., Ruslanova, I., Krivogorsky, B., . . . Yolken, R. H. (2004). Antibodies to infectious agents in individuals with recent onset schizophrenia. *European Archives of Psychiatry and Clinical Neuroscience, 254*, 4–8. (15)

Lewis, D. A., & Gonzalez-Burgos, G. (2006). Pathophysiologically based treatment interventions in schizophrenia. *Nature Medicine, 12*, 1016–1022. (15)

Lewis, D. O., Moy, E., Jackson, L. D., Aaronson, R., Restifo, N., Serra, S., . . . Simos, A. (1985). Biopsychosocial characteristics of children who later murder: A prospective study. *American Journal of Psychiatry, 142*, 1161–1167. (13)

Lewis, M., Sullivan, M. W., Stanger, C., & Weiss, M. (1991). Self development and self-conscious emotions. In S. Chess & M. E. Hertzig (Eds.), *Annual progress in child psychiatry and child development 1990* (pp. 34–51). New York: Brunner/Mazel. (5)

Li, Q., Hill, Z., & He, B. J. (2014). Spatiotemporal dissociation of brain activity underlying subjective awareness, objective performance, and confidence. *Journal of Neuroscience, 34*, 4382–4395. (10)

Li, W., Howard, J. D., Parrish, T. B., & Gottfried, J. A. (2008). Aversive learning enhances perceptual and cortical discrimination of indiscriminable odor cues. *Science, 319*, 1842–1845. (6)

Li, Z., Chang, S.-h., Zhang, L.-y., Gao, L., & Wang, J. (2014). Molecular genetic studies of ADHD and its candidate genes: A review. *Psychiatry Research, 219*, 10–24. (8)

Libbrecht, N., Lievens, F., Carette, B., & Côté, S. (2014). Emotional intelligence predicts success in medical school. *Emotions, 14,* 64–73. (12)

Libet, B., Gleason, C. A., Wright, E. W., & Pearl, D. K. (1983). Time of conscious intention to act in relation to onset of cerebral activities (readiness potential): The unconscious initiation of a freely voluntary act. *Brain, 106,* 623–642. (10)

Lim, C., & Putnam, R. D. (2010). Religion, social networks, and life satisfaction. *American Sociological Review, 75,* 914–933. (12)

Lindquist, K. A., Wager, T. D., Kober, H., Bliss-Moreau, E., & Barrett, L. F. (2012). The brain basis of emotion: A meta-analytic review. *Behavioral and Brain Sciences, 35,* 121–202. (12)

Lineweaver, T. T., Bondi, M. W., Galasko, D., & Salmon, E. P. (2014). Effect of knowledge of APOE genotype on subjective and objective memory performance in healthy older adults. *American Journal of Psychiatry, 171,* 201–208. (9)

Lilienfeld, S. O. (2007). Psychological treatments that cause harm. *Perspectives on Psychological Science, 2,* 53–70. (12, 15)

Lilienfeld, S. O., Ritschel, L. A., Lynn, S. J., Cautin, R. L., & Latzman, R. D. (2014). Why ineffective psychotherapies appear to work: A taxonomy of causes of spurious therapeutic effectiveness. *Perspectives on Psychological Science, 9,* 355–387. (15)

Lilienfeld, S. O., Wood, J. M., & Garb, H. N. (2000). The scientific status of projective tests. *Psychological Science in the Public Interest, 1,* 27–66. (14)

Lillberg, K., Verkasalo, P. K., Kaprio, J., Teppo, L., Helenius, H., & Koskenvuo, M. (2003). Stressful life events and risk of breast cancer in 10,808 women: A cohort study. *American Journal of Epidemiology, 157,* 415–423. (12)

Lin, J. Y., Franconeri, S., & Enns, J. T. (2008). Objects on a collision path with the observer demand attention. *Psychological Science, 19,* 686–692. (8)

Linck, J. A., Kroll, J. F., & Sunderman, G. (2009). Losing access to the native language while immersed in a second language. *Psychological Science, 20,* 1507–1515. (8)

Linck, J. A., Osthus, P., Koeth, J. T., & Bunting, M. F. (2013). Working memory and second language comprehension and production: A meta-analysis. *Psychonomic Bulletin & Review, 21,* 861–883. (7)

Linden, W., Lenz, J. W., & Con, A. H. (2001). Individualized stress management for primary hypertension: A randomized trial. *Archives of Internal Medicine, 161,* 1071–1080. (12)

Lindhiem, O., Bennett, C. B., Trentacosta, C. J., & McLear, C. (2014). Client preferences affect treatment satisfaction, completion, and clinical outcome: A meta-analysis. *Clinical Psychology Review, 34,* 506–517. (15)

Lindsay, D. S., Hagen, L., Read, J. D., Wade, K. A., & Garry, M. (2004). True photographs and false memories. *Psychological Science, 15,* 149–154. (7)

Lindsay, D. S., & Read, J. D. (1994). Psychotherapy and memories of childhood sexual abuse: A cognitive perspective. *Applied Cognitive Psychology, 8,* 281–338. (7)

Lipkus, I. (1991). The construction and preliminary validation of a global Belief in a Just World scale and the exploratory analysis of the multidimensional Belief in a Just World scale. *Personality and Individual Differences, 12,* 1171–1178. (14)

Lipszyc, J., & Schachar, R. (2010). Inhibitory control and psychopathology: A meta-analysis of studies using the stop signal task. *Journal of the International Neuropsychological Society, 16,* 1064–1076. (8)

Lisanby, S. H., Maddox, J. H., Prudic, J., Devanand, D. P., & Sackeim, H. A. (2000). The effects of electroconvulsive therapy on memory of autobiographical and public events. *Archives of General Psychiatry, 57,* 581–590. (15)

Liu, F., Wollstein, A., Hysi, P. G., Ankra-Badu, G. A., Spector, T. D., Park, D, . . . Kayser, M. (2010). Digital quantification of human eye color highlights genetic association of three new loci. *PLoS Genetics, 6,* e1000934. (3)

Liu, I.-C., Blacker, D. L., Xu, R., Fitzmaurice, G., Lyons, M. J., & Tsuang, M. T. (2004). Genetic and environmental contributions to the development of alcohol dependence in male twins. *Archives of General Psychiatry, 61,* 897–903. (15)

Liu, Q., Pu, L., & Poo, M. (2005). Repeated cocaine exposure *in vivo* facilitates LTP induction in midbrain dopamine neurons. *Nature, 437,* 1027–1031. (15)

Locke, E. A., & Latham, G. P. (2002). Building a practically useful theory of goal setting and task motivation. *American Psychologist, 57,* 705–717. (11)

Locke, J. L. (1994). Phases in the child's development of language. *American Scientist, 82,* 436–445. (8)

Loeb, J. (1973). *Forced movements, tropisms, and animal conduct.* New York: Dover. (Original work published 1918) (6)

Loeber, S., Croissant, B., Heinz, A., Mann, K., & Flor, H. (2006). Cue exposure in the treatment of alcohol dependence: Effects on drinking outcome, craving and self-efficacy. *British Journal of Clinical Psychology, 45,* 515–529. (6)

Loehlin, J. C. (1992). *Genes and environment in personality development.* Newbury Park, CA: Sage. (5, 14)

Loehlin, J. C., Horn, J. M., & Willerman, L. (1989). Modeling IQ change: Evidence from the Texas adoption project. *Child Development, 60,* 993–1004. (9)

Loewi, O. (1960). An autobiographic sketch. *Perspectives in Biology, 4,* 3–25. (3)

Loftus, E. (2003). Our changeable memories: Legal and practical implications. *Nature Reviews Neuroscience, 4,* 231–234. (7)

Loftus, E. F. (1975). Leading questions and the eyewitness report. *Cognitive Psychology, 7,* 560–572. (7)

Loftus, E. F. (1993). The reality of repressed memories. *American Psychologist, 48,* 518–537. (7)

Loftus, E. F., Feldman, J., & Dashiell, R. (1995). The reality of illusory memories. In D. L. Schacter (Ed.), *Memory distortion* (pp. 47–68). Cambridge, MA: Harvard University Press. (7)

Loftus, G. R. (1996). Psychology will be a much better science when we change the way we analyze data. *Current Directions in Psychological Science, 5,* 161–171. (2)

Lomniczi, A., Loche, A., Castellano, J. M., Ronnekleiv, O. K., Bosch, M., Kaidar, G., . . . Ojeda, S. R. (2013). Epigenetic control of female puberty. *Nature Neuroscience, 16,* 281–289. (3)

Long, G. M., & Toppine, T. C. (2004). Enduring interest in perceptual ambiguity: Alternating views of reversible figures. *Psychological Bulletin, 130,* 748–768. (4)

Longstreth, L. E. (1981). Revisiting Skeels' final study: A critique. *Developmental Psychology, 17,* 620–625. (9)

Lopes, P. N., Brackett, M. A., Nezlak, J. B., Schütz, A., Sellin, I., & Salovey, P. (2004). Emotional intelligence and social interaction. *Personality and Social Psychology Bulletin, 30,* 1018–1034. (12)

Lopez, R. B., Hofmann, W., Wagner, D. D., Kelley, W. M., & Heatherton, T. F. (2014). Neural predictors of giving in to temptation in daily life. *Psychological Science, 25,* 1337–1344. (11)

Lopez-Sola, C., Fontenelle, L. F., Alonso, P., Cuadras, D., Foley, D. L., Pantelis, C., . . . Harrison, B. J. (2014). Prevalence and heritability of obsessive-compulsive spectrum and anxiety disorder symptoms: A survey of the Australian twin registry. *American Journal of Medical Genetics Part B, 165,* 314–325. (15)

Lotto, R. B., & Purves, D. (2002). The empirical basis of color perception. *Consciousness and Cognition, 11,* 609–629. (4)

Lotze, M., Grodd, W., Birbaumer, N., Erb, M., Huse, E., & Flor, H. (1999). Does use of a myoelectric prosthesis prevent cortical reorganization and phantom limb pain? *Nature Neuroscience, 2,* 501–502. (4)

Loui, P., Alsop, D., & Schlaug, G. (2009). Tone deafness: A new disconnection syndrome? *Journal of Neuroscience, 29,* 10215–10220. (4)

Löw, A., Lang, P. J., Smith, J. C., & Bradley, M. M. (2008). Both predator and prey. *Psychological Science, 19,* 865–873. (12)

Low, K. S. D., Yoon, M. J., Roberts, B. W., & Rounds, J. (2005). The stability of vocational interests from early adolescence to middle adulthood: A quantitative review of longitudinal studies. *Psychological Bulletin, 131,* 713–737. (5)

Lowe, K. B., Kroeck, K. G., & Sivasubramaniam, N. (1996). Effectiveness correlates of transformational and transactional leadership: A meta-analytic review of the MLQ literature. *Leadership Quarterly, 7,* 385–425. (11)

Lubman, D. I., Yücel, M., Kettle, J. W. L., Scaffidi, A., Mackenzie, T., Simmons, J. G., . . . Allen, N. B. (2009). Responsiveness to drug cues and natural rewards in opiate addiction. *Archives of General Psychiatry, 66,* 205–212. (15)

Luborsky, L., & Barrett, M. S. (2006). The history and empirical status of key psychoanalytic concepts. *Annual Review of Clinical Psychology, 2,* 1–19. (14)

Lucas, R. E. (2005). Time does not heal all wounds. *Psychological Science, 16,* 945–950. (12)

Lucas, R. E., Clark, A. E., Georgellis, Y., & Diener, E. (2004). Unemployment alters the set point for life satisfaction. *Psychological Science, 15,* 8–13. (12)

Lucas, R. E., Le, K., & Dyrenforth, P. S. (2008). Explaining the extraversion/positive affect relation: Sociability cannot account for extraverts' greater happiness. *Journal of Personality, 76,* 385–414. (14)

Lucas, R. E., & Schimmack, U. (2009). Income and well-being: How big is the gap between the rich and the poor? *Journal of Research in Personality, 43,* 75–78. (12)

Luciano, M., Wainwright, M. A., Wright, M. J., & Martin, N. G. (2006). The heritability of conscientiousness facets and their relationship to IQ and academic achievement. *Personality and Individual Differences, 40,* 1189–1199. (14)

Luciano, M., Wright, M. J., Smith, G. A., Geffen, G. M., Geffen, L. B., & Martin, N. G. (2001). Genetic covariance among measures of information processing speed, working memory, and IQ. *Behavior Genetics, 31,* 581–592. (9)

Luczak, S. E., Yarnell, L. M., Prescott, C. A., Myers, M. G., Liang, T., & Wall, T. L. (2014). Effects of *ALDH2*2* on alcohol problem trajectories of Asian American college students. *Journal of Abnormal Psychology, 123*, 130–140. (15)

Ludwig, J., Duncan, G. J., Gennetian, L. A., Katz, L. F., Kessler, R. C., Kling, J. R., & Sabonmatsu, L. (2012). Neighborhood effects on the long-term well-being of low-income adults. *Science, 337*, 1505–1510. (15)

Luk, G., Bialystok, E., Craik, F. I. M., & Grady, C. L. (2011). Lifelong bilingualism maintains white matter integrity in older adults. *Journal of Neuroscience, 31,* 16808–16813. (8)

Luna, B., Padmanabhan, A., & O'Hearn, K. (2010). What has fMRI told us about the development of cognitive control through adolescence? *Brain and Cognition, 72,* 101–113. (5)

Lunnon, K., Smith, R., Hannon, E., De Jager, P. L., Srivastava, G., Tolta, M., . . . Mill, J. (2014). Methylomic profiling implicates cortical deregulation of *ANK1* in Alzheimer's disease. *Nature Neuroscience, 17*, 1164–1170. (7)

Luppino, F. S., de Wit, L. M., Bouvy, P. F., Stijnen, T., Cuijpers, P., . . . Zitman, F. G. (2010). Overweight, obesity, and depression. *Archives of General Psychiatry, 67*, 220–229. (11)

Lyamin, O. I., Mukhametov, L. M., Siegel, J. M., Nazarenko, E. A., Polyakova, I. G., & Shpak, O. V. (2002). Unihemispheric slow wave sleep and the state of the eyes in a white whale. *Behavioural Brain Research, 129*, 125–129. (10)

Lyamin, O. I., Kosenko, P. O., Lapierre, J. L., Mukhametov, L. M., & Siegel, J. M. (2008). Fur seals display a strong drive for bilateral slow-wave sleep while on land. *Journal of Neuroscience, 28*, 12614–12621. (10)

Lyamin, O., Pryaslova, J., Lance, V., & Siegel, J. (2005). Continuous activity in cetaceans after birth. *Nature, 435*, 1177. (10)

Lykken, D., & Tellegen, A. (1996). Happiness is a stochastic phenomenon. *Psychological Science, 7,* 186–189. (12)

Lykken, D. T. (1979). The detection of deception. *Psychological Bulletin, 86,* 47–53. (12)

Lykken, D. T., Bouchard, T. J., Jr., McGue, M., & Tellegen, A. (1993). Heritability of interests: A twin study. *Journal of Applied Psychology, 78,* 649–661. (3)

Lykken, D. T., McGue, M., Tellegen, A., & Bouchard, T. J. (1992). Emergenesis: Genetic traits that may not run in families. *American Psychologist, 47,* 1565–1577. (3)

Lyn, H., Greenfield, P. M., Savage-Rumbaugh, S., Gillespie-Lynch, K., & Hopkins, W. D. (2011). Nonhuman primates do declare! A comparison of declarative symbol and gesture use in two children, two bonobos, and a chimpanzee. *Language & Communication, 31,* 63–74. (8)

Lynam, D. R. (1996). Early identification of chronic offenders: Who is the fledgling psychopath? *Psychological Bulletin, 120,* 209–234. (13)

Lynn, R. (2009). What has caused the Flynn effect? Secular increases in the developmental quotients of infants. *Intelligence, 37,* 16–24. (9)

Lynn, R. (2013). Who discovered the Flynn effect? A review of early studies of the secular increase of intelligence. *Intelligence, 41,* 765–769. (9)

Lyons, M. J., Eisen, S. A., Goldberg, J., True, W., Lin, N., Meyer, J. M., . . . Tsuang, M. T. (1998). A registry-based twin study of depression in men. *Archives of General Psychiatry, 55,* 468–472. (15)

Lyons, M. J., York, T. P., Franz, C. E., Grant, M. D., Eaves, L. J., Jacobson, K. C., . . . Kremen, W. S. (2009). Genes determine stability and the environment determines change in cognitive ability during 35 years of adulthood. *Psychological Science, 20,* 1146–1152. (9)

Lyubomirsky, S., Dickerhoof, R., Boehm, J. K., & Sheldon, K. M. (2011). Becoming happier takes both a will and a proper way: An experimental longitudinal intervention to boost well-being. *Emotion, 11,* 391–402. (12)

Lyubomirsky, S., King, L., & Diener, E. (2005). The benefits of frequent positive affect: Does happiness lead to success? *Psychological Bulletin, 131,* 803–855. (12)

Ma, W. J., Husain, M., & Bays, P. M. (2014). Changing concepts of working memory. *Nature Neuroscience, 17,* 347–356. (7)

Ma-Kellams, C., & Blascovich, J. (2011). Culturally divergent responses to mortality salience. *Psychological Science, 22,* 1019–1024. (5)

MacCallum, F., & Golombok, S. (2004). Children raised in fatherless families from infancy: A follow-up of children of lesbian and single heterosexual mothers at early adolescence. *Journal of Child Psychology and Psychiatry, 45,* 1407–1419. (5)

Macknik, S. L., King, M., Randi, J., Robbins, A., Teller, Thompson, J., & Martinez-Conde, S. (2008). Attention and awareness in stage magic: Turning tricks into research. *Nature Reviews Neuroscience, 9,* 871–879. (8)

MacLean, K. A., Ferrer, E., Aichele, S. R., Bridwell, D. A., Zanesco, A.P., Jacobs, T.L., . . . Saron, C.D. (2010). Intensive meditation training improves perceptual discrimination and sustained attention. *Psychological Science, 21,* 829–839. (10)

Macmillan, M. (1997). *Freud evaluated.* Cambridge, MA: MIT Press. (14)

Macnamara, B. N., Hambrick, D. Z., & Oswald, F. L. (2014). Deliberate practice and performance in music, games, sports, education, and professions: A meta-analysis. *Psychological Science, 25,* 1608–1618. (8)

MacQuitty, J. (1996, August 1). Lily the stink loses its 33-year reputation by a nose. *The Times* (London), pp. 1–2. (11)

Madson, L. (2005). Demonstrating the importance of question wording on surveys. *Teaching of Psychology, 32,* 40–43. (2)

Magee, W. J., Eaton, W. W., Wittchen, H.-U., McGonagle, K. A., & Kessler, R. C. (1996). Agoraphobia, simple phobia, and social phobia in the National Comorbidity Survey. *Archives of General Psychiatry, 53,* 159–168. (15)

Magnuson, K. A., & Duncan, G. J. (2006). The role of socioeconomic resources in the Black–White test score gap among young children. *Developmental Review, 26,* 365–399. (9)

Maguire, E. A., & Frith, C. D. (2003). Lateral asymmetry in the hippocampal response to the remoteness of autobiographical memories. *Journal of Neuroscience, 23,* 5302–5307. (7)

Mahowald, M. W., & Schenck, C. H. (2005). Insights from studying human sleep disorders. *Nature, 437,* 1279–1285. (10)

Maier, S. F., & Watkins, L. R. (1998). Cytokines for psychologists: Implications of bidirectional immune-to-brain communication for understanding behavior, mood, and cognition. *Psychological Review, 105,* 83–107. (12)

Mainland, J. D., Keller, A., Li, Y. R., Zhou, T., Trimmer, C., Snyder, L. L., . . . Matsunami, H. (2014). The missense of smell: Functional variability in the human odorant receptor repertoire. *Nature Neuroscience, 17,* 114–120. (4)

Major Depressive Disorder Working Group of the Psychiatric GWAS Consortium. (2013). A mega-analysis of genome-wide association studies for major depressive disorder. *Molecular Psychiatry, 18,* 497–511. (15)

Maki, R. H. (1990). Memory for script actions: Effects of relevance and detail expectancy. *Memory and Cognition, 18,* 5–14. (7)

Malamed, F., & Zaidel, E. (1993). Language and task effects on lateralized word recognition. *Brain and Language, 45,* 70–85. (8)

Maldonado, R., Saiardi, A., Valverde, O., Samad, T. A., Roques, B. P., & Borrelli, E. (1997). Absence of opiate rewarding effects in mice lacking dopamine D2 receptors. *Nature, 388,* 586–589. (3)

Malmquist, C. P. (1986). Children who witness parental murder: Posttraumatic aspects. *Journal of the American Academy of Child Psychiatry, 25,* 320–325. (7)

Mallpress, D. E. W., Fawcett, T. W., McNamara, J. M., & Houston, A. I. (2012). Comparing pleasure and pain: The fundamental mathematical equivalence of reward gain and shock reduction under variable interval schedules. *Journal of the Experimental Analysis of Behavior, 98,* 355–367. (6)

Mameli, M., & Lüscher, C. (2011). Synaptic plasticity and addiction: Learning mechanisms gone awry. *Neuropharmacology, 61,* 1052–1059. (15)

Mandler, G. (2013). The limit of mental structures. *Journal of General Psychology, 140,* 243–250. (7)

Mangan, M. A. (2004). A phenomenology of problematic sexual behavior. *Archives of Sexual Behavior, 33,* 287–293. (10)

Mann, T., Nolen-Hoeksema, S., Huang, K., Burgard, D., Wright, A., & Hanson, K. (1997). Are two interventions worse than none? Joint primary and secondary prevention of eating disorders in college females. *Health Psychology, 16,* 215–225. (15)

Mann, T., Tomiyama, A. J., Westling, E., Lew, A.-M., Samuels, B., & Chatman, J. (2007). Medicare's search for effective obesity treatments. *American Psychologist, 62,* 220–233. (11)

Manning, R., Levine, M., & Collins, A. (2007). The Kitty Genovese murder and the social psychology of helping. *American Psychologist, 62,* 555–562. (13)

Manor, O., & Eisenbach, Z. (2003). Mortality after spousal loss: Are there socio-demographic differences? *Social Science and Medicine, 56,* 405–413. (12)

Maquet, P., Laureys, S., Peigneux, P., Fuchs, S., Petiau, C., Phillips, C., . . . Cleeremans, A. (2000). Experience-dependent changes in cerebral activation during human REM sleep. *Nature Neuroscience, 3,* 831–836. (10)

Marchand, A., Coutu, M.-F., Dupuis, G., Fleet, R., Borgeat, F., Todorov, C., . . . Mainguy, N. (2008). Treatment of panic disorder with agoraphobia: Randomized placebo-controlled trial of four psychosocial treatments combined with imipramine or placebo. *Cognitive Behaviour Therapy, 37,* 146–159. (15)

Marcia, J. E. (1980). Identity in adolescence. In J. Adelson (Ed.), *Handbook of adolescent psychology* (pp. 159–187). New York: Wiley. (5)

Marcus, D. K., O'Connell, D., Norris, A. L., & Sawaqdeh, A. (2014). Is the dodo bird endangered in the 21st century? A meta-analysis of treatment comparison studies. *Clinical Psychology Reviews, 34,* 519–530. (15)

Marian, V., & Neisser, U. (2000). Language-dependent recall of autobiographical memories. *Journal of Experimental Psychology: General, 129,* 361–368. (7)

Markey, P. M. (2000). Bystander intervention in computer-mediated intervention. *Computers in Human Behavior, 16,* 183–188. (13)

Marks, D., & Kammann, R. (1980). *The psychology of the psychic.* Buffalo, NY: Prometheus. (2, 14)

Markström, U. (2014). Staying the course? Challenges in implementing evidence-based programs in community mental health services. *International Journal of Environmental Research and Public Health, 11,* 10752–10769. (15)

Marler, P. (1997). Three models of song learning: Evidence from behavior. *Journal of Neurobiology, 33,* 501–516. (6)

Marler, P., & Peters, S. (1981). Sparrows learn adult song and more from memory. *Science, 213,* 780–782. (6)

Marler, P., & Peters, S. (1982). Long-term storage of learned birdsongs prior to production. *Animal Behaviour, 30,* 479–482. (6)

Marriott, F. H. C. (1976). Abnormal colour vision. In H. Davson (Ed.), *The eye* (2nd ed., pp. 533–547). New York: Academic Press. (4)

Marsh, E. J., Meade, M. L., & Roediger, H. L., III. (2003). Learning facts from fiction. *Journal of Memory and Language, 49,* 519–536. (7)

Marshall, D. J., Vitacco, M. J., Read, J. B., & Harway, M. (2014). Predicting voluntary and involuntary readmissions to forensic hospitals by insanity acquittees in Maryland. *Behavioral Sciences and the Law, 32,* 627–640. (15)

Martens, A., Johns, M., Greenberg, J., & Schimel, J. (2006). Combating stereotype threat: The effect of self-affirmation on women's intellectual performance. *Journal of Experimental Social Psychology, 42,* 236–243. (9)

Martin, D., Hutchison, J., Slessor, G., Urquhart, J., Cunningham, S. J., & Smith, K. (2014). The spontaneous formation of stereotypes via cumulative cultural evolution. *Psychological Science, 25,* 1777–1786. (13)

Martin, D. J., & Lynn, S. J. (1996). The hypnotic simulation index: Successful discrimination of real versus simulating participants. *International Journal of Clinical and Experimental Hypnosis, 44,* 338–353. (10)

Martindale, C. (2001). Oscillations and analogies: Thomas Young, MD, FRS, genius. *American Psychologist, 56,* 342–345. (4)

Martínez, K., & Colom, R. (2009). Working memory capacity and processing efficiency predict fluid but not crystallized and spatial intelligence: Evidence supporting the neural noise hypothesis. *Personality and Individual Differences, 46,* 281–286. (9)

Martsh, C. T., & Miller, W. R. (1997). Extraversion predicts heavy drinking in college students. *Personality and Individual Differences, 23,* 153–155. (14)

Marx, J. (2003). Cellular warriors at the battle of the bulge. *Science, 299,* 846–849. (11)

Mawritz, M. B., Folger, R., & Latham, G. P. (2014). Supervisors' extremely difficult goals and abusive supervision: The mediating effects of hindrance stress, anger, and anxiety. *Journal of Organizational Behavior, 35,* 358–372. (11)

Maslow, A. H. (1962). *Toward a psychology of being.* Princeton, NJ: Van Nostrand. (14)

Maslow, A. H. (1970). *Motivation and personality* (2nd ed.). New York: Harper & Row. (11)

Maslow, A. H. (1971). *The farther reaches of human nature.* New York: Viking Press. (14)

Mason, B. J., Goodman, A. M., Chabac, S., & Lehert, P. (2006). Effect of oral acamprosate on abstinence in patients with alcohol dependence in a double-blind, placebo-controlled trial: The role of patient motivation. *Journal of Psychiatric Research, 40,* 383–393. (15)

Mason, D. A., & Frick, P. J. (1994). The heritability of antisocial behavior: A meta-analysis of twin and adoption studies. *Journal of Psychopathology and Behavioral Assessment, 16,* 301–323. (5)

Mason, M. F., Norton, M. I., Van Horn, J. D., Wegner, D. M., Grafton, S. T., & Macrae, C. N. (2007). Wandering minds: The default network and stimulus-independent thought. *Science, 315,* 393–395. (3)

Massimini, M., Ferrarelli, F., Huber, R., Esser, S. K., Singh, H., & Tononi, G. (2005). Breakdown of cortical effective connectivity during sleep. *Science, 309,* 2228–2232. (10)

Masson, J. M. (1984). *The assault on truth.* New York: Farrar, Straus and Giroux. (14)

Masters, W. H., & Johnson, V. E. (1966). *Human sexual response.* Boston: Little, Brown. (11)

Mateos-Gonzalez, F., Quesada, J., & Senar, J. C. (2011). Sexy birds are superior at solving a foraging problem. *Biology Letters, 7,* 668–669. (13)

Matheny, A. P., Jr. (1989). Children's behavioral inhibition over age and across situations: Genetic similarity for a trait to change. *Journal of Personality, 57,* 215–235. (5)

Matson, J. L., Adams, H. L., Williams, L. W., & Rieske, R. D. (2013). Why are there so many unsubstantiated treatments in autism? *Research in Autism Spectrum Disorders, 7,* 466–474. (15)

Matsunami, H., Montmayeur, J.-P., & Buck, L. B. (2000). A family of candidate taste receptors in human and mouse. *Nature, 404,* 601–604. (4)

Matthews, M. D. (2014). *Head strong: How psychology is revolutionizing war.* Oxford, UK: Oxford University Press. (1, 11)

Mattson, M. P., & Magnus, T. (2006). Ageing and neuronal variability. *Nature Reviews Neuroscience, 7,* 278–294. (5)

Mattson, S. N., Crocker, N., & Nguyen, T. T. (2011). Fetal alcoholism spectrum disorders: Neuropsychological and behavioral features. *Neuropsychology Review, 21,* 8–101. (5)

May, C. P., Hasher, L., & Stoltzfus, E. R. (1993). Optimal time of day and the magnitude of age differences in memory. *Psychological Science, 4,* 326–330. (10)

May, P. A., Blankenship, J., Marais, A.-S., Gossage, J. P., Kalberg, W. O., Joubert, B., . . . Seedat, S. (2013). Maternal alcohol consumption producing fetal alcohol spectrum disorders (FASD): Quantity, frequency, and timing of drinking. *Drug and Alcohol Dependence, 133,* 502–512. (5)

Mayberry, R. I., Lock, E., & Kazmi, H. (2002). Linguistic ability and early language exposure. *Nature, 417,* 38. (8)

Mayer, J. D., Caruso, D. R., & Salovey, P. (2000). Emotional intelligence meets traditional standards for an intelligence. *Intelligence, 27,* 267–298. (12)

Mayer, J. D., & Salovey, P. (1995). Emotional intelligence and the construction and regulation of feelings. *Applied and Preventive Psychology, 4,* 197–208. (12)

Mayer, J. D., & Salovey, P. (1997). What is emotional intelligence? In P. Salovey & D. J. Sluyter (Eds.). *Emotional development and emotional intelligence* (pp. 3–34). New York: Basic Books. (12)

Mayer, J. D., Salovey, P., Caruso, D. R., & Sitarenios, G. (2001). Emotional intelligence as a standard intelligence. *Emotion, 1,* 232–242. (12)

Mazandarani, A. A., Aguilar-Vafaie, M. E., & Domhoff, G. W. (2013). Content analysis of Iranian college students' dreams: Comparison with American data. *Dreaming, 23,* 163–174. (10)

Mazar, N., Amir, O., & Ariely, D. (2008). The dishonesty of honest people: A theory of self-concept maintenance. *Journal of Marketing Research, 45,* 633–644. (11)

Mazzoni, G., Laurence, J.-R., & Heap, M. (2014). Hypnosis and memory: Two hundred years of adventure and still going! *Psychology of Consciousness, 1,* 153–167. (10)

Mazzoni, G., & Memon, A. (2003). Imagination can create false autobiographical memories. *Psychological Science, 14,* 186–188. (7)

McCall, W. A. (1939). *Measurement.* New York: Macmillan. (9)

McCann, R. A., Armstrong, C. M., Skopp, N. A., Edwards-Stewart, A., Smolenski, D. J., June, J. D., . . . Reger, G. M. (2014). Virtual reality exposure therapy for the treatment of anxiety disorders: An evaluation of research quality. *Journal of Anxiety Disorders, 28,* 625–631. (15)

McCarthy, M. M., & Arnold, A. P. (2011). Reframing sexual differentiation of the brain. *Nature Neuroscience, 14,* 677–683. (11)

McCaulley, M. H. (2000). Myers-Briggs Type Indicator: A bridge between counseling and consulting. *Consulting Psychology Journal: Practice and Research, 52,* 117–132. (14)

McClelland, J. L. (1988). Connectionist models and psychological evidence. *Journal of Memory and Language, 27,* 107–123. (8)

McClelland, J. L., & Rumelhart, D. E. (1981). An interactive activation model of context effects in letter perception: Part 1. An account of basic findings. *Psychological Review, 88,* 375–407. (8)

McCornack, R. L. (1983). Bias in the validity of predicted college grades in four ethnic minority groups. *Educational and Psychological Measurement, 43,* 517–522. (9)

McCourt, K., Bouchard, T. J., Jr., Lykken, D. T., Tellegen, A., & Keyes, M. (1999). Authoritarianism revisited: Genetic and environmental influences examined in twins reared apart and together. *Personality and Individual Differences, 27,* 985–1014. (5)

McCrae, R. R. (1996). Social consequences of experiential openness. *Psychological Bulletin, 120,* 323–337. (14)

McCrae, R. R., Chan, W., Jussim, L., De Fruyt, F., Löckenhoff, C. E., De Bolle, M., . . . Terracciano, A. (2013). The inaccuracy of national character stereotypes. *Journal of Research in Personality, 47,* 831–842. (14)

McCrae, R. R., & Costa, P. T., Jr. (1987). Validation of the five-factor model of personality across instruments and observers. *Journal of Personality and Social Psychology, 52,* 81–90. (14)

McCrae, R. R., & Costa, P. T., Jr. (1997). Personality trait structure as a human universal. *American Psychologist, 52,* 509–516. (14)

McCrae, R. R., Costa, P. T., Jr., Ostendorf, F., Angleitner, A., Hrebíckova, M., Avia, M. D., . . . Smith, P. B. (2000). Nature over nurture: Temperament, personality, and life span development. *Journal of Personality and Social Psychology, 78,* 173–186. (14)

McCrea, S. M., Liberman, N., Trope, Y., & Sherman, S. J. (2008). Construal level and procrastination. *Psychological Science, 19,* 1308–1314. (11)

McCrink, K., & Wynn, K. (2004). Large-number addition and subtraction by 9-month-old infants. *Psychological Science, 15,* 776–781. (5)

McDaniel, M. A., Fadler, C. L., & Pashler, H. (2013). Effects of spaced versus massed training in function learning. *Journal of Experimental Psychology: Learning, Memory and Cognition, 39,* 1417–1432. (7)

McDaniel, M. A., Howard, D. C., & Einstein, G. O. (2009). The read-recite-review study strategy. *Psychological Science, 20,* 516–522. (7)

McDermott, R., Dawes, C., Prom-Wormley, E., Eaves, L., & Hatemi, P. K. (2013). MAOA and aggression: A gene-environment interaction in two populations. *Journal of Conflict Resolution, 57,* 1043–1064. (13)

McDougall, W. (1938). Fourth report on a Lamarckian experiment. *British Journal of Psychology, 28,* 321–345, 365–395. (2)

McElheny, V. (2004). Three Nobelists ask: Are we ready for the next frontier? *Cerebrum, 5,* 69–81. (1)

McEwen, B. S. (2000). The neurobiology of stress: From serendipity to clinical relevance. *Brain Research, 886,* 172–189. (12)

McFadden, D. (2008). What do sex, twins, spotted hyenas, ADHD, and sexual orientation have in common? *Perspectives on Psychological Science, 3,* 309–323. (11)

McFerran, B., & Mukhopadhyay, A. (2013). Lay theories of obesity predict actual mass. *Psychological Science, 24,* 1428–1436. (11)

McGovern, P. E., Glusker, D. L., Exner, L. J., & Voigt, M. M. (1996). Neolithic resinated wine. *Nature, 381,* 480–481. (3)

McGrath, J. J., Féron, F. P., Burne, T. H. J., Mackay-Sim, A., & Eyles, D. W. (2003). The neurodevelopmental hypothesis of schizophrenia: A review of recent developments. *Annals of Medicine, 35,* 86–93. (15)

McGue, M. (1999). The behavioral genetics of alcoholism. *Current Directions in Psychological Science, 8,* 109–115. (15)

McGue, M., & Bouchard, T. J., Jr. (1998). Genetic and environmental influences on human behavioral differences. *Annual Review of Neuroscience, 21,* 1–24. (9)

McGuire, S., & Clifford, J. (2000). Genetic and environmental contributions to loneliness in children. *Psychological Science, 11,* 487–491. (3)

McGuire, W. J., & Papageorgis, D. (1961). The relative efficacy of various types of prior belief-defense in producing immunity against persuasion. *Journal of Abnormal and Social Psychology, 62,* 327–337. (13)

McGurk, H., & MacDonald, J. (1976). Hearing lips and seeing voices. *Nature, 264,* 746–748. (8)

McIntyre, M., Gangestad, S. W., Gray, P. B., Chapman, J. F., Burnham, T. C., O'Rourke, M. T., . . . Thornhill, R. (2006). Romantic involvement often reduces men's testosterone levels—But not always: The moderating effect of extrapair sexual interest. *Journal of Personality and Social Psychology, 91,* 642–651. (11)

McIntyre, R. S., Konarski, J. Z., Wilkins, K., Soczynska, J. K., & Kennedy, S. H. (2006). Obesity in bipolar disorder and major depressive disorder: Results from a national community health survey on mental health and well-being. *Canadian Journal of Psychiatry, 51,* 274–280. (11)

McKee, S. A., Sinha, R., Weinberger, A. H., Sofuoglu, M., Harrison, E. L. R., . . . Wanzer, J. (2010). Stress decreases the ability to resist smoking and potentiates smoking intensity and reward. *Journal of Psychopharmacology, 25,* 490–502. (15)

McKelvey, M. W., & McKenry, P. C. (2000). The psychosocial well-being of Black and White mothers following marital dissolution. *Psychology of Women Quarterly, 24,* 4–14. (5)

McKinnon, J. D., & Bennett, C. E. (2005). *We the people: Blacks in the United States.* Washington, DC: U.S. Census Bureau. (9)

McMillan, K. A., Asmundson, G. J. G., Zvolensky, M. J., & Carleton, R. N. (2012). Startle response and anxiety sensitivity: subcortical indices of physiologic arousal and fear responding. *Emotion, 12,* 1264–1272. (12)

McMurtry, P. L., & Mershon, D. H. (1985). Auditory distance judgments in noise, with and without hearing protection. *Proceedings of the Human Factors Society* (Baltimore), pp. 811–813. (4)

McNally, R. J. (1990). Psychological approaches to panic disorder: A review. *Psychological Bulletin, 108,* 403–419. (15)

McNally, R. J., Bryant, R. A., & Ehlers, A. (2003). Does early psychological intervention promote recovery from posttraumatic stress? *Psychological Science in the Public Interest, 4,* 45–77. (12)

McNally, R. J., & Geraerts, E. (2009). A new solution to the recovered memory debate. *Perspectives on Psychological Science, 4,* 126–134. (7)

McNamara, J. M., Barta, Z., Fromhage, L., & Houston, A. I. (2008). The coevolution of choosiness and cooperation. *Nature, 451,* 189–192. (13)

McNamara, P., McLaren, D., Smith, D., Brown, A., & Stickgold, R. (2005). A "Jekyll and Hyde" within: Aggressive versus friendly interactions in REM and non-REM dreams. *Psychological Science, 16,* 130–136. (10)

Mechelli, A., Crinion, J. T., Noppeney, U., O'Doherty, J., Ashburner, J., Frackowiak, R. S., . . . Price, C. J. (2004). Structural plasticity in the bilingual brain. *Nature, 431,* 757. (8)

Meddis, R., Pearson, A. J. D., & Langford, G. (1973). An extreme case of healthy insomnia. *EEG and Clinical Neurophysiology, 35,* 213–214. (10)

Medver, V. H., Madey, S. F., & Gilovich, T. (1995). When less is more: Counterfactual thinking and satisfaction among Olympic athletes. *Journal of Personality and Social Psychology, 69,* 603–610. (12)

Meeussen, L., Otten, S., & Phalet, K. (2014). Managing diversity: How leaders' multiculturalism and colorblindness affect work group functioning. *Group Processes & Intergroup Relations, 17,* 629–644. (13)

Mégarbané, A., Noguier, F., Stora, S., Manchon, L., Mircher, C., Bruno, R., . . . Piquemal, D. (2013). The intellectual disability of trisomy 21: Differences in gene expression in a case series of patients with lower and higher IQ. *European Journal of Human Genetics, 21,* 1253–1259. (9)

Mehl, M. R., Vazire, S., Holleran, S. E., & Clark, C. S. (2010). Eavesdropping on happiness: Well-being is related to having less small talk and more substantive conversations. *Psychological Science, 21,* 539–541. (12)

Meinz, E. J., & Hambrick, D. Z. (2010). Deliberate practice is necessary but not sufficient to explain individual differences in piano sight-reading skill: The role of working memory capacity. *Psychological Science, 21,* 914–919. (8)

Melamed, S., Shirom, A., Toker, S., Berliner, S., & Shapira, I. (2006). Burnout and risk of cardiovascular disease: Evidence, possible causal paths, and promising research directions. *Psychological Bulletin, 132,* 327–353. (11)

Melchers, K. G., Ungor, M., & Lachnit, H. (2005). The experimental task influences cue competition in human causal learning. *Journal of Experimental Psychology: Animal Behavior Processes, 31,* 477–483. (6)

Mellers, B., Ungar, L., Baron, J., Ramos, J., Gurcay, B., Fincher, K., . . . Tetlock, P. E. (2014). Psychological strategies for winning a geopolitical forecasting tournament. *Psychological Sciece, 25,* 1106–1115. (8)

Meltzoff, A. N., & Moore, M. K. (1977). Imitation of facial and manual gestures by human neonates. *Science, 198,* 75–78. (3)

Melvin, G. A., Dudley, A. L., Gordon, M. S., Ford, S., Taffe, J., & Tonge, B. J. (2013). What happens to depressed adolescents? A follow-up study into early adulthood. *Journal of Affective Disorders, 151,* 298–305. (15)

Melzack, R., & Wall, P. D. (1965). Pain mechanisms: A new theory. *Science, 150,* 971–979. (4)

Melzack, R., Weisz, A. Z., & Sprague, L. T. (1963). Stratagems for controlling pain: Contributions of auditory stimulation and suggestion. *Experimental Neurology, 8,* 239–247. (12)

"The Menace Within." (2011, July/August). *Stanford Alumni Magazine.* Downloaded December 19, 2014 from alumni.stanford.edu (13)

Mendieta-Zéron, H., López, M., & Diéguez, C. (2008). Gastrointestinal peptides controlling body weight homeostasis. *General and Comparative Endocrinology, 155,* 481–495. (11)

Mendoza-Denton, R., & Page-Gould, E. (2008). Can cross-group friendships influence minority students' well-being at historically White universities? *Psychological Science, 19,* 933–939. (13)

Merckelbach, H, Dekkers, T., Wessel, I., & Roefs, A. (2003). Dissociative symptoms and amnesia in Dutch concentration camp survivors. *Comprehensive Psychiatry, 44,* 65–69. (7)

Mershon, D. H., & King, L. E. (1975). Intensity and reverberation as factors in the auditory perception of egocentric distance. *Perception and Psychophysics, 18,* 409–415. (4)

Messinger, D. S. (2002). Positive and negative: Infant facial expressions and emotions. *Current Directions in Psychological Science, 11,* 1–6. (12)

Messner, C., & Wänke, M. (2011). Good weather for Schwarz and Clore. *Emotion, 11,* 436–437. (12)

Meule, A., van Rezori, V., & Blechert, J. (2014). Food addiction and bulimia nervosa. *European Eating Disorders, 22,* 331–337. (11)

Meuret, A. E., Rosenfield, D., Wilhelm, F. H., Zhou, E., Conrad, A., . . . Roth, W. T. (2011). Do unexpected panic attacks occur spontaneously? *Biological Psychiatry, 70,* 985–991. (15)

Meyer-Lindenberg, A., Mervis, C. B., & Berman, K. F. (2006). Neural mechanisms in Williams syndrome: A unique window to genetic influences on cognition and behaviour. *Nature Reviews Neuroscience, 7,* 380–393. (8)

Meyer, J. P., Becker, T. E., & Vandenberghe, C. (2004). Employee commitment and motivation: A conceptual analysis and integrative model. *Journal of Applied Psychology, 89,* 991–1007. (11)

Mezuk, B., Rafferty, J. A., Kershaw, K. N., Hudson, D., Abdou, C. M., Lee, H., . . . Jackson, J. S.

(2010). Reconsidering the role of social disadvantage in physical and mental health: Stressful life events, health behaviors, race, and depression. *American Journal of Epidemiology, 172,* 1238–1249. (15)

Mezzanotte, W. S., Tangel, D. J., & White, D. P. (1992). Waking genioglossal electromyogram in sleep apnea patients versus normal controls (a neuromuscular compensatory mechanism). *Journal of Clinical Investigation, 89,* 1571–1579. (10)

Miellet, S., O'Donnell, P. J., & Sereno, S. C. (2009). Parafoveal magnification. *Psychological Science, 20,* 721–728. (8)

Mihura, J. L., Meyer, G. J., Dumitrascu, N., & Bombel, G. (2013). The validity of individual Rorschach variables: Systematic reviews and meta-analyses of the comprehensive system. *Psychological Bulletin, 139,* 548–605. (14)

Mikkelson, A. C., & Pauley, P. M. (2013). Maximizing relationship possibilities: Relational maximization in romantic relationships. *Journal of Social Psychology, 153,* 467–485. (8)

Milar, K. S. (2000). The first generation of women psychologists and the psychology of women. *American Psychologist, 55,* 616–619. (1)

Milgram, S. (1974). *Obedience to authority.* New York: Harper & Row. (13)

Milich, R., Wolraich, M., & Lindgren, S. (1986). Sugar and hyperactivity: A critical review of empirical findings. *Clinical Psychology Review, 6,* 493–513. (2)

Miller, A. H., Maletic, V., & Raison, C. L. (2009). Inflammation and its discontents: The role of cytokines in the pathophysiology of major depression. *Biological Psychiatry, 65,* 732–741. (15)

Miller, C. T., Dibble, E., & Hauser, M. D. (2001). Amodal completion of acoustic signals by a nonhuman primate. *Nature Neuroscience, 4,* 783–784. (4)

Miller, G. (2007a). Animal extremists get personal. *Science, 318,* 1856–1858. (2)

Miller, G. (2007b). The mystery of the missing smile. *Nature, 316,* 826–827. (12)

Miller, G. A. (1956). The magical number seven, plus or minus two: Some limits on our capacity for processing information. *Psychological Review, 63,* 81–97. (7)

Miller, J. F., Neufang, M., Solway, A., Brandt, A., Trippel, M., Mader, I., . . . Schulze-Bonhage, A. (2013). Neural activity in human hippocampal formation reveals the spatial context of retrieved memories. *Science, 342,* 1111–1114. (7)

Miller, L. C., & Fishkin, S. A. (1997). On the dynamics of human bonding and reproductive success: Seeking windows on the adapted-for human-environmental interface. In J. A. Simpson & D. T. Kenrick (Eds.), *Evolutionary social psychology* (pp. 197–235). Mahwah, NJ: Erlbaum. (2)

Miller, M. A., Hays, L. R., & Fillmore, M. T. (2012). Lack of tolerance to the disinhibiting effects of alcohol in heavy drinkers. *Psychopharmacology, 224,* 511–518. (15)

Miller, R. M., Hannikainen, & Cushman, F. A. (2014). Bad actions or bad outcomes? Differentiating affective contributions to the moral condemnation of harm. *Emotion, 14,* 573–587. (12)

Miller, S. L., & Maner, J. K. (2010). Scent of a woman: Men's testosterone responses to olfactory ovulation cues. *Psychological Science, 21,* 276–283. (4)

Milne, S. E., Orbell, S., & Sheeran, P. (2002). Combining motivational and volitional interventions to promote exercise participation: Protection motivation theory and implementation intentions. *British Journal of Health Psychology, 7,* 163–184. (11)

Milner, B. (1959). The memory defect in bilateral hippocampal lesions. *Psychiatric Research Reports, 11,* 43–52. (7)

Milton, J., & Wiseman, R. (1999). Does psi exist? Lack of replication of an anomalous process of information. *Psychological Bulletin, 125,* 387–391. (2)

Minde, K., Minde, R., & Vogel, W. (2006). Culturally sensitive assessment of attachment in children aged 18–40 months in a South African township. *Infant Mental Health Journal, 27,* 544–558. (5)

Mineka, S. (1987). A primate model of phobic fears. In H. Eysenck & I. Martin (Eds.), *Theoretical foundations of behavior therapy* (pp. 81–111). New York: Plenum Press. (15)

Mineka, S., Davidson, M., Cook, M., & Keir, R. (1984). Observational conditioning of snake fear in rhesus monkeys. *Journal of Abnormal Psychology, 93,* 355–372. (15)

Mineka, S., & Zinbarg, R. (2006). A contemporary learning theory perspective on the etiology of anxiety disorders. *American Psychologist, 61,* 10–26. (15)

Mingroni, M. A. (2004). The secular rise in IQ: Giving heterosis a closer look. *Intelligence, 32,* 65–83. (9)

Minto, C. L., Liao, L.-M., Woodhouse, C. R. J., Ransley, P. G., & Creighton, S. M. (2003). The effect of clitoral surgery on sexual outcome in individuals who have intersex conditions with ambiguous genitalia: A cross-sectional study. *Lancet, 361,* 1252–1257. (11)

Mischel, W. (1973). Toward a cognitive social learning reconceptualization of personality. *Psychological Review, 80,* 252–283. (14)

Mischel, W. (1981). Current issues and challenges in personality. In L. T. Benjamin, Jr. (Ed.), *The G. Stanley Hall Lecture Series* (Vol. 1, pp. 81–99). Washington, DC: American Psychological Association. (14)

Misrahi, M., Meduri, G., Pissard, S., Bouvattier, C., Beau, I., Loosfelt, H., . . . Bougneres, P. (1997). Comparison of immunocytochemical and molecular features with the phenotype in a case of incomplete male pseudohermaphroditism associated with a mutation of the luteinizing hormone receptor. *Journal of Clinical Endocrinology and Metabolism, 82,* 2159–2165. (11)

Mitroff, S. R., & Biggs, A. T. (2014). The ultra-rare-item effect: Visual search for exceedingly rare items is highly susceptible to error. *Psychological Science, 25,* 284–289. (4)

Miu, A. C., Vulturar, R., Chis, A., Ungureanu, L., & Gross, J. J. (2013). Reappraisal as a mediator in the link between 5-HTTLPR and social anxiety symptoms. *Emotion, 13,* 1012–1022. (12)

Miyake, A., Kost-Smith, L. E., Finkelstein, N. D., Pollock, S. J., Cohen, G. L., & Ito, T. A. (2010). Reducing the gender achievement gap in college science: A classroom study of values affirmation. *Science, 330,* 1234–1237. (9)

Miyamoto, Y., Nisbett, R. E., & Masuda, T. (2006). Culture and the physical environment. *Psychological Science, 17,* 113–119. (13)

Mobbs, D., Yu, R., Meyer, M., Passamonti, L., Seymour, B., Calder, A. J., . . . Dalgleish, T. (2009). A key role for similarity in vicarious reward. *Science, 324,* 900. (6)

Moher, J., Lakshmanan, B. M., Egeth, H. E., & Ewen, J. B. (2014). Inhibition drives early feature-based attention. *Psychological Science, 25,* 315–324. (10)

Moitra, E., Dyck, I., Beard, C., Bjornsson, A. S., Sibrava, N. J., . . . Keller, M. B. (2011). Impact of stressful life events on the course of panic disorder in adults. *Journal of Affective Disorders, 134,* 373–376. (15)

Mojtabai, R., & Olfson, M. (2008). National trends in psychotherapy by office-based psychiatrists. *Archives of General Psychiatry, 65,* 962–970. (1)

Molina, B. S. G., Hinshaw, S. P., Swanson, J. M., Arnold, L. E., Vitiello, B., Jensen, P. S., . . . the MTA Cooperative Group. (2009). The MTA at 8 years: Prospective follow-up of children treated for combined-type ADHD in a multisite study. *Journal of the American Academy of Child and Psychiatry, 48,* 484–500. (8)

Moller, H. J. (1992). Attempted suicide: Efficacy of different aftercare strategies. *International Clinical Psychopharmacology, 6*(Suppl. 6), 58–59. (15)

Mondloch, C. J., Leis, A., & Maurer, D. (2006). Recognizing the face of Johnny, Suzy, and me: Insensitivity to the spacing among features at 4 years of age. *Child Development, 77,* 234–243. (5)

Money, J., & Ehrhardt, A. A. (1972). *Man & woman, boy & girl.* Baltimore: Johns Hopkins University Press. (11)

Mongrain, M., Chin, J. M., & Shapira, L. B. (2011). Practicing compassion increases happiness and self-esteem. *Journal of Happiness Studies, 12,* 963–981. (12)

Monroe, S. M., & Harkness, K. L. (2005). Life stress, the "kindling" hypothesis, and the recurrence of depression: Considerations from a life stress perspective. *Psychological Review, 112,* 417–445. (15)

Montgomery, G., & Kirsch, I. (1996). Mechanisms of placebo pain reduction: An empirical investigation. *Psychological Science, 7,* 174–176. (4)

Montgomery, K. J., Seeherman, K. R., & Haxby, J. V. (2009). The well-tempered social brain. *Psychological Science, 20,* 1211–1213. (3)

Monti, M. M., Vanhaudenhuyse, A., Coleman, M. R., Boly, M., Pickard, J. D., Tshibanda, L., . . . Laureys, S. (2010). Willful modulation of brain activity in disorders of consciousness. *New England Journal of Medicine, 362,* 579–589. (10)

Montoya, R. M. (2008). I'm hot, so I'd say you're not: The influence of objective physical attractiveness on mate selection. *Personality and Social Psychology Bulletin, 34,* 1315–1331. (13)

Montoya, R. M., Horton, R. S., & Kirchner, J. (2008). Is actual similarity necessary for attraction? A meta-analysis of actual and perceived similarity. *Journal of Social and Personal Relationships, 25,* 889–922. (13)

Moon, A., & Roeder, S. S. (2014). A secondary replication attempt of stereotype susceptibility (Shih, Pittinsky, & Ambady, 1999). *Social Psychology, 45,* 199–201. (9)

Moor, B. G., Crone, E. A., & van der Molen, M. W. (2010). The heartbreak of social rejection: heart rate deceleration in response to unexpected peer rejection. *Psychological Science, 21,* 1326–1333. (12)

Moorcroft, W. (1993). *Sleep, dreaming, and sleep disorders: An introduction* (2nd ed.). Lanham, MD: University Press of America. (10)

Moorcroft, W. H. (2003). *Understanding sleep and dreaming.* New York: Kluwer. (10)

Moore, B. C. J. (1989). *An introduction to the psychology of hearing* (3rd ed.). London: Academic Press. (4)

Moore, D. S., & Johnson, S. P. (2008). Mental rotation in human infants. *Psychological Science, 19,* 1063–1066. (5)

Moore, M. T., & Fresco, D. M. (2012). Depressive realism: A meta-analytic review. *Clinical Psychology Review, 32,* 496–509. (12)

Moors, A. (2009). Theories of emotion causation: A review. *Cognition & Emotion, 23,* 625–662. (12)

Morewedge, C. K., & Norton, M. I. (2009). When dreaming is believing: The (motivated) interpretation of dreams. *Journal of Personality and Social Psychology, 96,* 249–264. (10)

Morris, G., Baker-Ward, L., & Bauer, P. J. (2010). What remains of that day: The survival of children's autobiographical memories across time. *Applied Cognitive Psychology, 24,* 527–544. (7)

Morris, M., Lack. L., & Dawson, D. (1990). Sleep-onset insomniacs have delayed temperature rhythms. *Sleep, 13,* 1–14. (10)

Morris, S. Z., & Gibson, C. L. (2011). Corporal punishments influence on children's aggressive and delinquent behavior. *Criminal Justice and Behavior, 38,* 818–839. (6)

Morrison, A. P., Turkington, D., Pyle, M., Spencer, H., Brabban, A., Dunn, G., . . . Hutton, P. (2014). Cognitive therapy for people with schizophrenia spectrum disorders not taking antipsychotic drugs: A single-blind randomized design. *Lancet, 383,* 1395–1403. (15)

Mosing, M. A., Madison, G., Pederson, N. L., Kuja-Halkola, R., & Ullén, F. (2014). Practice does not make perfect: No causal effect of music practice on music ability. *Psychological Science, 25,* 1795–1803. (8)

Moscovitch, M. (1985). Memory from infancy to old age: Implications for theories of normal and pathological memory. *Annals of the New York Academy of Sciences, 444,* 78–96. (7)

Moscovitch, M. (1989). Confabulation and the frontal systems: Strategic versus associative retrieval in neuropsychological theories of memory. In H. L. Roediger, III, & F. I. M. Craik (Eds.), *Varieties of memory and consciousness: Essays in honour of Endel Tulving* (pp. 133–160). Hillsdale, NJ: Erlbaum. (7)

Moscovitch, M. (1992). Memory and working-with-memory: A component process model based on modules and central systems. *Journal of Cognitive Neuroscience, 4,* 257–267. (7)

Moskowitz, B. A. (1978). The acquisition of language. *Scientific American, 239*(5), 92–108. (8)

Moss, E., Cyr, C., Bureau, J.-F., Tarabulsy, G. M., & Dubois-Comtois, K. (2005). Stability of attachment during the preschool period. *Developmental Psychology, 41,* 773–783. (5)

Mote, J., Stuart, B. K., & Kring, A. M. (2014). Diminished emotion expressivity but not experience in men and women with schizophrenia. *Journal of Abnormal Psychology, 123,* 796–801. (15)

Mottus, R., Allik, J., Realo, A., Rossier, J., Zecca, G., Ah-Kion, J., . . . Johnson, W. (2012). The effect of response style on self-reported conscientiousness across 20 countries. *Personality and Social Psychology Bulletin, 38,* 1423–1436. (14)

Mouzon, D. M., (2013). Can family relationships explain the race paradox in mental health? *Journal of Marriage and the Family, 75,* 470–485. (15)

Mouzon, D. M. (2014). Relationships of choice: Can friendships or fictive kinships explain the race paradox in mental health? *Social Science Research, 44,* 32–44. (15)

Mrazek, M. D., Franklin, M. S., Phillips, D. T., Baird, B., & Schooler, J. W. (2013). Mindfulness training improves working memory capacity and GRE performance while reducing mind wandering. *Psychological Science, 24,* 776–781. (10)

Muchnik, L., Aral, S., & Taylor, S. J. (2013). Social influence bias: A randomized experiment. *Science, 341,* 647–651. (13)

Müller, M. M., Malinowski, P., Gruber, T., & Hillyard, S. A. (2003). Sustained division of the attentional spotlight. *Nature, 424,* 309–312. (8)

Murali, M. S. (2001). Epidemiological study of prevalence of mental disorders in India. *Indian Journal of Community Medicine, 26,* 198. (15)

Muraven, M., & Baumeister, R. F. (2000). Self-regulation and depletion of limited resources: Does self-control resemble a muscle? *Psychological Bulletin, 126,* 247–259. (12)

Murphy, G. L., & Medin, D. L. (1985). The role of theories in conceptual coherence. *Psychological Review, 92,* 289–316. (8)

Murphy, M. L. M., Slavich, G. M., Chen, E., & Miller, G. E. (2015). Targeted rejection predicts decreased anti-inflammatory gene expression and increased symptom severity in youth with asthma. *Psychological Science, 26,* 111–121. (11)

Murray, C., (2007). The magnitude and components of change in the black-white IQ difference from 1920 to 1991: A birth cohort analysis of the Woodcock-Johnson standardizations. *Intelligence, 35,* 305–318. (9)

Murray, C., Johnson, W., Wolf, M. S., & Deary, I. J. (2011). The association between cognitive ability across the lifespan and health literacy in old age: The Lothian birth cohort 1936. *Intelligence, 39,* 178–187. (9)

Murray, G., Nicholas, C. L., Kleiman, J., Dwyer, R., Carrington, M. J., Allen, N. B., . . . Trinder, J. (2009). Nature's clocks and human mood: The circadian system modulates reward motivation. *Emotion, 9,* 705–716. (10)

Murray, H. A. (1943). *Thematic Apperception Test manual.* Cambridge, MA: Harvard University Press. (14)

Murrie, D. C., Boccaccini, M. T., Guarnera, L. A., & Rufino, K. A. (2013). Are forensic experts biased by the side that retained them? *Psychological Science, 24,* 1889–1897. (2)

Myers, D. G. (2000). The funds, friends, and faith of happy people. *American Psychologist, 55,* 56–67. (12)

Nadig, A. S., & Sedivy, J. C. (2002). Evidence of perspective-taking constraints in children's on-line reference resolution. *Psychological Science, 13,* 329–336. (5)

Nagy, E. (2011). Sharing the moment: The duration of embraces in humans. *Journal of Ethology, 29,* 389–393. (5)

Nahum, L., Bouzerda-Wahlen, A., Guggisberg, A., Ptak, R., & Schnider, A. (2012). Forms of confabulation: Dissociations and associations. *Neuropsychologia, 50,* 2224–2234. (7)

Nairne, J. S., Pandeirada, J. N. S., Gregory, K. J., & Van Arsdall, J. E. (2009). Adaptive memory. *Psychological Science, 20,* 740–746. (7)

Nairne, J. S., Pandeirada, J. N. S., & Thompson, S. R. (2008). Adaptive memory: The comparative value of survival processing. *Psychological Science, 19,* 176–180. (7)

Nairne, J. S., Thompson, S. R., & Pandeirada, J. N. S. (2007). Adaptive memory: Survival processing enhances retention. *Journal of Experimental Psychology: Learning, Memory, and Cognition, 33,* 263–273. (7)

Nairne, J. S., VanArsdall, J. E., Pandeirada, J. N. S., Cogdill, M., & Le Breton, J. M. (2013). Adaptive memory: The mnemonic value of animacy. *Psychological Science, 24,* 2099–2105. (7)

Nan, X., Zhao, X., Yang, B., & Iles, I. (2015). Effectiveness of cigarette warning labels: Examining the impact of graphics, message framing, and temporal framing. *Health Communication, 30,* 81–89. (13)

Napier, J. L., & Jost, J. T. (2008). Why are conservatives happier than liberals? *Psychological Science, 19,* 565–572. (2)

National Institutes of Health. (2000). *The practical guide: Identification, evaluation, and treatment of overweight and obesity in adults* (NIH Publication No. 00–4084). Washington, DC: Author. (11)

Nay, W., Brown, R., & Roberson-Nay, R. (2013). Longitudinal course of panic disorder with and without agoraphobia using the national epidemiologic survey on alcohol and related conditions (NESARC). *Psychiatry Research, 208,* 54–61. (15)

Nebes, R. D. (1974). Hemispheric specialization in commissurotomized man. *Psychological Bulletin, 81,* 1–14. (3)

Nedelec, J. L., & Beaver, K. M. (2014). Physical attractiveness as a phenotypic marker of health: An assessment using a nationally representative sample of American adults. *Evolution and Human Behavior, 35,* 456–463. (13)

Neher, A. (1991). Maslow's theory of motivation: A critique. *Journal of Humanistic Psychology, 31,* 89–112. (14)

Neisser, U. (1997). Rising scores on intelligence tests. *American Scientist, 85,* 440–447. (9)

Nelson, C. A. III, Zeanah, C. H., Fox, N. A., Marshall, P. J., Smyke, A. T., & Guthrie, D. (2007). Cognitive recovery in socially deprived young children: The Bucharest Early Intervention Project. *Science, 318,* 1937–1940 (9)

Nelson, K., & Fivush, R. (2004). The emergence of autobiographical memory: A social cultural developmental theory. *Psychological Review, 111,* 486–511. (7)

Nelson, S. K., Kushlev, K., English, T., Dunn, E. W., & Lyubomirsky, S. (2013). In defense of parenthood: Children are associated with more joy than misery. *Psychological Science, 24,* 3–10. (12)

Nemeth, C. (1972). A critical analysis of research utilizing the prisoner's dilemma paradigm for the study of bargaining. In L. Berkowitz (Ed.), *Advances in experimental social psychology* (Vol. 6, pp. 203–234). New York: Academic Press. (13)

Nemeth, C. J. (1986). Differential contributions of majority and minority influence. *Psychological Review, 93,* 23–32. (13)

Neto, F., & Pinto, M. D. (2013). The satisfaction with life across the adult life span. *Social Indicators Research, 114,* 767–784. (11)

Newcombe, N. S., Sluzenski, J., & Huttenlocher, J. (2005). Preexisting knowledge versus on-line learning. *Psychological Science, 16,* 222–227. (5)

Newman, B. (1988, September 9). Dressing for dinner remains an issue in the naked city. *The Wall Street Journal,* p. 1. (13)

Newman, E. J., Sanson, M., Miller, E. K., Quigley-McBride, A., Foster, J. L., Bernstein, D. M., &

Garry, M. (2014). People with easier to pronounce names promote truthiness of claims. *PLoS One, 9*, Article 88671. (8)

"NextGen Speaks." (2014). *Science, 343*, 24–26. (10)

Ng, S.-F., Lin, R. C. Y., Laybutt, R., Barres, R., Ownes, J. A., & Morris, M. J. (2010). Chronic high-fat diet in fathers programs beta-cell dysfunction in female rat offspring. *Nature, 467*, 963–966. (3)

Nguyen, H.-H. D., & Ryan, A. M. (2008). Does stereotype threat affect test performance of minorities and women? A meta-analysis of experimental evidence. *Journal of Applied Psychology, 93*, 1314–1334. (9)

Nicholson, H., Foote, C., & Gigerick, S. (2009). Deleterious effects of psychotherapy and counseling in the schools. *Psychology in the Schools, 46*, 232–237. (15)

Nickerson, C., Schwarz, N., Diener, E., & Kahneman, D. (2003). Zeroing in on the dark side of the American Dream: A closer look at the negative consequences of the goal for financial success. *Psychological Science, 14*, 531–536. (12)

Nickerson, R. S., & Adams, M. J. (1979). Long-term memory for a common object. *Cognitive Psychology, 11*, 287–307. (7)

Nielsen, T. A., Zadra, A. L., Simard, V., Saucier, S., Stenstrom, P., Smith, C., . . . Kuiken, D. (2003). The typical dreams of Canadian university students. *Dreaming, 13*, 211–235. (10)

Niiya, Y., Ellsworth, P. C., & Yamaguchi, S. (2006). Amae in Japan and the United States: An exploration of a "culturally unique" emotion. *Emotion, 6*, 279–295. (12)

Niki, K., & Luo, J. (2002). An fMRI study on the time-limited role of the medial temporal lobe in long-term topographical autobiographic memory. *Journal of Cognitive Neuroscience, 14*, 500–507. (7)

Nikles, C. D., II, Brecht, D. L., Klinger, E., & Bursell, A. L. (1998). The effects of current-concern and nonconcern-related waking suggestions on nocturnal dream content. *Journal of Personality and Social Psychology, 75*, 242–255. (10)

Nikolova, Y. S., Koenen, K. C., Galea, S., Wang, C.-M., Seney, M. L., Sibille, E., . . . Hariri, A. R. (2014). Beyond genotype: Serotonin transporter epigenetic modification predicts human brain function. *Nature Neuroscience, 17*, 1153–1155. (12)

Nir, Y., & Tononi, G. (2010). Dreaming and the brain: From phenomenology to neurophysiology. *Trends in Cognitive Sciences, 14*, 88–100. (10)

Nisbet, E. K., & Zelenski, J. M. (2011). Underestimating nearby nature: Affective forecasting errors obscure the happy path to sustainability. *Psychological Science, 22*, 1101–1106. (12)

Nisbett, R. E., Aronson, J., Blair, C., Dickens, W., Flynn, J., Halpern, D. F., & Turkheimer, E. (2012). Intelligence. *American Psychologist, 67*, 130–159. (9)

Nisbett, R. E., Peng, K., Choi, I., & Norenzayan, A. (2001). Culture and systems of thought: Holistic versus analytic cognition. *Psychological Review, 108*, 291–310. (13)

Noaghiul, S., & Hibbeln, J. R. (2003). Cross-national comparisons of seafood consumption and rates of bipolar disorders. *American Journal of Psychiatry, 160*, 2222–2227. (15)

Noguchi, K., Kamada, A., & Shrira, I. (2014). Cultural differences in the primacy effect for person perception. *International Journal of Psychology, 49*, 208–210. (13)

Noice, H., & Noice, T. (2006). What studies of actors and acting can tell us about memory and cognitive functioning. *Current Directions in Psychological Science, 15*, 14–18. (7)

Nolen-Hoeksema, S., & Watkins, E. R. (2011). A heuristic for developing transdiagnostic models of psychopathology: Explaining multifinality and divergent trajectories. *Perspectives on Psychological Science, 6*, 589–609. (15)

Norcross, J. C., Kohout, J. L., & Wicherski, M. (2005). Graduate study in psychology: 1971 to 2004. *American Psychologist, 60*, 959–975. (1)

Nordenström, A., Servin, A., Bohlin, G., Larsson, A., & Wedell, A. (2002). Sex-typed toy play behavior correlates with the degree of prenatal androgen exposure assessed by CYP21 genotype in girls with congenital adrenal hyperplasia. *Journal of Clinical Endocrinology and Metabolism, 87*, 5119–5124. (5, 11)

Nordgren, L. F., McDonnell, M.-H. M., & Loewenstein, G. (2011). What constitutes torture? Psychological impediments to an objective evaluation of enhanced interrogation tactics. *Psychological Science, 22*, 689–694. (13)

Nordgren, L. F., van Harreveld, F., & van der Pligt, J. (2009). The restraint bias. *Psychological Science, 20*, 1523–1528. (11)

Norman, R. A., Tataranni, P. A., Pratley, R., Thompson, D. B., Hanson, R. L., Prochazka, M., . . . Ravussin, E. (1998). Autosomal genomic scan for loci linked to obesity and energy metabolism in Pima Indians. *American Journal of Human Genetics, 62*, 659–668. (11)

Norretranders, T. (1998). *The User Illusion.* New York: Penguin books. (Original work published 1991) (10).

Norton, M. I., Frost, J. H., & Ariely, D. (2007). Less is more: The lure of ambiguity, or why familiarity breeds contempt. *Journal of Personality and Social Psychology, 92*, 97–105. (13)

Nosek, B. A., & Banaji, M. R. (2001). The go/no-go association task. *Social Cognition, 19*, 625–664. (13)

Nussbaum, A. D., & Dweck, C. S. (2008). Defensiveness versus remediation: Self-theories and modes of self-esteem maintenance. *Personality and Social Psychology Bulletin, 34*, 599–612. (14)

Nuzzo, R. (2014). Statistical errors. *Nature, 506*, 150–152. (2)

Nye, C. D., Su, R., Rounds, J., & Drasgow, F. (2012). Vocational interests and performance: A quantitative summary of over 60 years of research. *Perspectives on Psychological Science, 7*, 384–403. (11)

Oakley, D. A., & Halligan, P. W. (2013). Hypnotic suggestion: Opportunities for cognitive neuroscience. *Nature Reviews Neuroscience, 14*, 565–576. (10)

O'Connell, K. A., Schwartz, J. E., & Shiffman, S. (2008). Do resisted temptations during smoking cessation deplete or augment self-control resources? *Psychology of Addictive Behaviors, 22*, 486–495. (11)

O'Connor, A. R., & Moulin, C. J. A. (2008). The persistence of erroneous familiarity in an epileptic male: Challenging perceptual theories of déjà vu activation. *Brain and Cognition, 68*, 144–147. (10)

O'Kane, G., Kensinger, E. A., & Corkin, S. (2004). Evidence for semantic learning in profound amnesia: An investigation with patient H. M. *Hippocampus, 14*, 417–425. (7)

O'Neill, T. A., & Hastings, S. E. (2011). Explaining workplace deviance behavior with more than just the "Big Five." *Personality and Individual Differences, 50*, 268–273. (14)

O'Toole, B. I. (1990). Intelligence and behaviour and motor vehicle accident mortality. *Accident Analysis and Prevention, 22*, 211–221. (9)

Oei, N. Y. L., Both, S., van Heemst, D., & van der Grond, J. (2014). Acute stress-induced cortisol elevations mediate reward system activity during subconscious precessing of sexual stimuli. *Psychoneuroendocrinology, 39*, 111–120. (4)

Ohayon, M. M. (1997). Prevalence of *DSM–IV* diagnostic criteria of insomnia: Distinguishing insomnia related to mental disorders from sleep disorders. *Journal of Psychiatric Research, 31*, 333–346. (10)

Öhman, A., Eriksson, A., & Olofsson, C. (1975). One-trial learning and superior resistance to extinction of autonomic responses conditioned to potentially phobic objects. *Journal of Comparative and Physiological Psychology, 88*, 619–627. (15)

Öhman, A., & Mineka, S. (2003). The malicious serpent: Snakes as a prototypical stimulus for an evolved module of fear. *Current Directions in Psychological Science, 12*, 5–9. (15)

Oishi, S. (2010). The psychology of residential mobility: Implications for the self, social relationships, and well-being. *Perspectives on Psychological Science, 5*, 5–21. (5)

Oishi, S., & Diener, E. (2014). Residents of poor nations have a greater sense of meaning in life than residents of wealthy nations. *Psychological Science, 25*, 422–430. (12)

Oishi, S., & Schimmack, U. (2010). Culture and well-being: A new inquiry into the psychological wealth of nations. *Perspectives on Psychological Science, 5*, 463–471. (12)

Okasha, M., McCarron, P., McEwen, J., & Smith, G. D. (2001). Age at menarche: Secular trends and association with adult anthropometric measures. *Annals of Human Biology, 28*, 68–78. (5)

Olausson, H., Lamarre, Y., Backlund, H., Morin, C., Wallin, B. G., Starck, G., . . . Bushnell, M. C. (2002). Unmyelinated tactile afferents signal touch and project to insular cortex. *Nature Neuroscience, 5*, 900–904. (3)

O'Leary, K. D., Acevedo, B. P., Aron, A., Huddy, L., & Mashek, D. (2012). Is long-term love more than a rare phenomenon? If so, what are its correlates? *Social Psychological and Personality Science, 3*, 241–249. (13)

Oliet, S. H. R., Baimoukhametova, D. V., Piet, R., & Bains, J. S. (2007). Retrograde regulation of GABA transmission by the tonic release of oxytocin and endocannabinoids governs postsynaptic firing. *Journal of Neuroscience, 27*, 1325–1333. (3)

Olff, M., Frijling, J. L., Kubzansky, L. D., Bradley, B., Ellenbogen, M. A., Cardoso, C., . . . van Zuiden, M. (2013). The role of oxytocin in social bonding, stress regulation and mental health: An update on the moderating effects of context and individual differences. *Psychoneuroendocrinology, 38*, 1883–1894. (3)

Olney, J. W., & Farger, N. B. (1995). Glutamate receptor dysfunction and schizophrenia. *Archives of General Psychiatry, 52*, 998–1007. (15)

Olsson, M. J., Lundström, J. N., Kimball, B. A., Gordon, A. R., Karshikoff, B., Hosseini,

N., . . . Lekander, M. (2014). The scent of disease: Human body odor contains an early chemosensory cue of sickness. *Psychological Science, 25,* 817–823. (4)

O'Mahony, M. (1978). Smell illusions and suggestion: Reports of smells contingent on tones played on television and radio. *Chemical Senses, 3,* 183–189. (2)

Ono, F., & Watanabe, K. (2011). Attention can retrospectively distort visual space. *Psychological Science, 22,* 472–477. (10)

Oriña, M. M., Collins, W. A., Simpson, J. A., Salvatore, J. E., Haydon, K. C., & Kim, J. S. (2011). Developmental and dyadic perspectives on commitment in adult romantic relationships. *Psychological Science, 22,* 908–915. (5)

Orne, M. T. (1959). The nature of hypnosis: Artifact and essence. *Journal of Abnormal and Social Psychology, 58,* 277–299. (10)

Orne, M. T. (1969). Demand characteristics and the concept of quasi-controls. In R. Rosenthal & R. L. Rosnow (Eds.), *Artifact in behavioral research* (pp. 143–179). New York: Academic Press. (2)

Orne, M. T. (1979). On the simulating subject as a quasi-control group in hypnosis research: What, why, and how. In E. Fromm & R. E. Shor (Eds.), *Hypnosis: Developments in research and new perspectives* (2nd ed., pp. 519–565). New York: Aldine. (10)

Orne, M. T., & Evans, F. J. (1965). Social control in the psychological experiment: Antisocial behavior and hypnosis. *Journal of Personality and Social Psychology, 1,* 189–200. (10)

Osofsky, J. D. (1995). The effects of exposure to violence on young children. *American Psychologist, 50,* 782–788. (13)

Ottati, V., & Lee, Y. T. (1995). Accuracy: A neglected component of stereotype research. In Y. T. Lee, L. J. Jussim, & C. R. McCauley (Eds.), *Stereotype accuracy* (pp. 29–59). Washington, DC: American Psychological Association. (13)

Otto, K., Boos, A., Dalbert, C., Schöps, D., & Hoyer, J. (2006). Posttraumatic symptoms, depression, and anxiety of flood victims: The impact of the belief in a just world. *Personality and Individual Differences, 40,* 1075–1084. (14)

Otto, R. K., & Heilbrun, K. (2002). The practice of forensic psychology. *American Psychologist, 57,* 5–18. (1)

Owen, A. M., Coleman, M. R., Boly, M., Davis, M. H., Laureys, S., & Pickard, J. D. (2006). Detecting awareness in the vegetative state. *Science, 313,* 1402. (10)

Oxley, D. R., Smith, K. B., Alford, J. R., Hibbing, M. V., Miller, J. L., Scalora, M., . . . Hibbing, J. R. (2008). Political attitudes vary with physiological traits. *Science, 321,* 1667–1670. (3)

Oyserman, D., Coon, H. M., & Kemmelmeier, M. (2002). Rethinking individualism and collectivism: Evaluation of theoretical assumptions and meta-analyses. *Psychological Bulletin, 128,* 3–72. (13)

Packer, D. J. (2009). Avoiding groupthink: Whereas weakly identified members remain silent, strongly identified members dissent about collective problems. *Psychological Science, 20,* 546–548. (13)

Padgham, C. A. (1975). Colours experienced in dreams. *British Journal of Psychology, 66,* 25–28. (10)

Paiva, V., Aranha, F., & Bastos, F. I. (2008). Opinions and attitudes regarding sexuality:

Brazilian national research, 2005. *Revista de Saúde Pública, 42*(Suppl. 1). (11)

Paivandy, S., Bullock, E. E., Reardon, R. C., & Kelly, F. D. (2008). The effects of decision-making style and cognitive thought patterns on negative career thoughts. *Journal of Career Assessment, 16,* 474–488. (8)

Palinkas, L. A. (2003). The psychology of isolated and confined environments. *American Psychologist, 58,* 353–363. (10, 15)

Palop, J. J., Chin, J., & Mucke, L. (2006). A network dysfunction perspective on neurodegenerative diseases. *Nature, 443,* 768–773. (7)

Paluck, E. L. (2009). Reducing intergroup prejudice and conflict using the media: A field experiment in Rwanda. *Journal of Personality and Social Psychology, 96,* 574–587. (13)

Panayiotou, G., Kokkinos, C. M., & Spanoudis, G. (2004). Searching for the "big five" in a Greek context: The NEO-FFI under the microscope. *Personality and Individual Differences, 36,* 1841–1854. (14)

Panikashvili, D., Simeonidou, C., Ben-Shabat, S., Hanuš, L. Breuer, A., Mechoulam, E., . . . Shohami, E. (2001). An endogenous cannabinoid (2-AG) is neuroprotective after brain injury. *Nature, 413,* 527–531. (3)

Papageorgiou, K. A., Smith, T. J., Wu, R., Johnson, M. H., Kirkham, N. Z., & Ronald, A. (2014). Individual differences in infant fixation duration relate to attention and behavioral control in childhood. *Psychological Science, 25,* 1371–1379. (5)

Parish, W. L., Laumann, E. O., & Mojola, S. A. (2007). Sexual behavior in China: Trends and comparisons. *Population and Development Review, 33,* 729–756. (11)

Park, D. C., Lodi-Smith, J., Drew, L., Haber, S., Hebrank, A., Bischof, G. N., & Aamodt, W. (2014). The impact of sustained engagement on cognitive function in older adults: The Synapse Project. *Psychological Science, 25,* 103–112. (5)

Park, J., Kitayama, S., Markus, H. R., Coe, C. L., Miyamoto, Y., Karasawa, M., . . . Ryff, C. D. (2013). Social status and anger expression: The cultural moderation hypothesis. *Emotion, 13,* 1122–1131. (2)

Park, J.-Y., & Jang, S. C. (2013). Confused by too many choices? Choice overload in tourism. *Tourism Management, 35,* 1–12. (8)

Park, G., Lubinski, D., & Benbow, C. P. (2008). Ability differences among people who have commensurate degrees matter for scientific creativity. *Psychological Science, 19,* 957–961. (9)

Parke, R. D., Berkowitz, L., Leyens, J. P., West, S. G., & Sebastian, R. J. (1977). Some effects of violent and nonviolent movies on the behavior of juvenile delinquents. In L. Berkowitz (Ed.), *Advances in experimental social psychology* (Vol. 10, pp. 135–172). New York: Academic Press. (2)

Parker, E. S., Cahill, L., & McGaugh, J. L. (2006). A case of unusual autobiographical remembering. *Neurocase, 12,* 35–49. (7)

Parker, J., Wales, G., Chalhoub, N., & Harper, V. (2013). The long-term outcomes of interventions for the management of attention-deficit hyperactivity disorder in children and adolescents: A systematic review of randomized controlled trials. *Psychology Research & Behavior Management, 6,* 87–99. (8)

Parmeggiani, P. L. (1982). Regulation of physiological functions during sleep in mammals. *Experientia, 38,* 1405–1408. (10)

Parrott, A. C. (1999). Does cigarette smoking cause stress? *American Psychologist, 54,* 817–820. (3)

Parzuchowski, M., & Szymkow-Sudziarska, A. (2008). Well, slap my thigh: Expression surprise facilitates memory of surprising material. *Emotion, 8,* 430–434. (12)

Pashler, H., & Harris, C. R. (2012). Is the replicability crisis overblown? Three arguments examined. *Perspectives on Psychological Science, 7,* 531–536. (2)

Pashler, H., McDaniel, M., Rohrer, D., & Bjork, R. (2008). Learning styles: Concepts and evidence. *Psychological Science in the Public Interest, 9,* 105–119. (9)

Pasterski, V. L., Geffner, M. E., Brain, C., Hindmarsh, P., Brook, C., & Hines, M. (2005). Prenatal hormones and postnatal socialization by parents as determinants of male-typical toy play in girls with congenital adrenal hyperplasia. *Child Development, 76,* 264–278. (5)

Pate, J. L., & Rumbaugh, D. M. (1983). The language-like behavior of Lana chimpanzee: Is it merely discrimination and paired-associate learning? *Animal Learning and Behavior, 11,* 134–138. (8)

Patihis, L., Ho, L. Y., Tingen, I. W., Lilienfeld, S. O., & Loftus, E. F. (2014). Are the "memory wars" over? A scientist-practitioner gap in beliefs about repressed memory. *Psychological Science, 25,* 519–530. (7)

Patterson, D. R. (2004). Treating pain with hypnosis. *Current Directions in Psychological Science, 13,* 252–255. (10)

Patterson, T., & Hayne, H. (2011). Does drawing facilitate older children's reports of emotionally laden events? *Applied Cognitive Psychology, 25,* 119–126. (7)

Pauls, D. L., Abramovitch, A., Rauch, S. L., & Geller, D. A. (2014). Obsessive-compulsive disorder: An integrative genetic and neurobiological perspective. *Nature Reviews Neuroscience, 15,* 410–424. (15)

Paunonen, S. V., & Jackson, D. N. (2000). What is beyond the big five? Plenty! *Journal of Personality, 68,* 821–835. (14)

Paus, T., Marrett, S., Worsley, K. J., & Evans, A. C. (1995). Extraretinal modulation of cerebral blood flow in the human visual cortex: Implications for saccadic suppression. *Journal of Neurophysiology, 74,* 2179–2183. (8)

Pavlov, I. P. (1960). *Conditioned reflexes.* New York: Dover. (Original work published 1927) (6)

Pearce, J. M. (1994). Similarity and discrimination: A selective review and a connectionist model. *Psychological Review, 101,* 587–607. (6)

Pearl, P. L., Weiss, R. E., & Stein, M. A. (2001). Medical mimics. *Annals of the New York Academy of Sciences, 931,* 97–112. (8)

Pearlson, G. D., Petty, R. G., Ross, C. A., & Tien, A. Y. (1996). Schizophrenia—a disease of heteromodal association cortex. *Neuropsychopharmacology, 14,* 1–17. (15)

Peelle, J. E., Troiani, V., Grossman, M., & Wingfield, A. (2011). Hearing loss in older adults affects neural systems supporting speech comprehension. *Journal of Neuroscience, 31,* 12638–12643. (4)

Peigneux, P., Laureys, S., Fuchs, S., Collette, F., Perrin, F., Reggers, J., . . . Maquet, P. (2004). Are spatial memories strengthened in the human hippocampus during slow wave sleep? *Neuron, 44,* 535–545. (10)

Pembrey, M. E., Bygren, L. O., Kaati, G., Edvinsson, S., Northstone, K., Sjöström, M., . . . The ALSPAC Study Team. Sex-specific, male-line transgenerational responses in humans. *European Journal of Human Genetics, 14,* 159-166. (3)

Penfield, W., & Rasmussen, T. (1950). *The cerebral cortex of man.* New York: Macmillan. (3)

Peng, K., & Nisbett, R. E. (1999). Culture dialectics, and reasoning about contradiction. *American Psychologist, 54,* 741-754. (13)

Pennebaker, J. W. (1997). Writing about emotional experiences as a therapeutic process. *Psychological Science, 8,* 162-166. (12)

Pennebaker, J. W., & Graybeal, A. (2001). Patterns of natural language use: Disclosure, personality, and social integration. *Current Directions in Psychological Science, 10,* 90-93. (12)

Perani, D., & Abutalebi, J. (2005). The neural basis of first and second language processing. *Current Opinion in Neurobiology, 15,* 202-206. (8)

Pereira, S. M., Geoffroy, M.-C., & Power, C. (2014). Depressive symptoms and physical activity during 3 decades in adult life. *JAMA Psychiatry, 71,* 1373-1380. (15)

Peretz, I., Cummings, S., & Dube, M. P. (2007). The genetics of congenital amusia (tone deafness): A family-aggregation study. *American Journal of Human Genetics, 81,* 582-588. (4)

Perez, E. A. (1995). Review of the preclinical pharmacology and comparative efficacy of 5-hydroxytryptamine-3 receptor antagonists for chemotherapy-induced emesis. *Journal of Clinical Oncology, 13,* 1036-1043. (3)

Perry, D. G., & Bussey, K. (1979). The social learning theory of sex differences: Imitation is alive and well. *Journal of Personality and Social Psychology, 37,* 1699-1712. (14)

Perry, G. (2013). *Behind the shock machine: The untold story of the notorious Milgram psychology experiments.* New York: New Press. (13)

Pert, C. B., & Snyder, S. H. (1973). The opiate receptor: Demonstration in nervous tissue. *Science, 179,* 1011-1014. (3, 4)

Pesta, B. J., & Poznanski, P. J. (2008). Black–White differences on IQ and grades: The mediating role of elementary cognitive tasks. *Intelligence, 36,* 323-329. (9)

Peters, F., Nicolson, N. A., Berkhof, J., Delespaul, P., & deVries, M. (2003). Effects of daily events on mood states in major depressive disorder. *Journal of Abnormal Psychology, 112,* 203-211. (15)

Petersen, S., Schroijen, M., Mölders, C., Zenker, S., & Van den Bergh, O. (2014). Categorical introception: Perceptual organization of sensations from inside. *Psychological Science, 25,* 1059-1066. (8)

Peterson, C. (2011). Children's memory reports over time: Getting both better and worse. *Journal of Experimental Child Psychology, 109,* 275-293. (7)

Peterson, C., Warren, K. L., & Short, M. M. (2011). Infantile amnesia across the years: A 2-year follow-up of children's earliest memories. *Child Development, 82,* 1092-1105. (7)

Peterson, L. R., & Peterson, M. J. (1959). Short-term retention of individual verbal items. *Journal of Experimental Psychology, 58,* 193-198. (7)

Peterson, Z. D., Janssen, E., & Laan, E. (2010). Women's sexual responses to heterosexual and lesbian erotica: The role of stimulus intensity, affective reaction, and sexual history. *Archives of Sexual Behavior, 39,* 880-897. (11)

Petrill, S. A., Luo, D., Thompson, L. A., & Detterman, D. K. (1996). The independent prediction of general intelligence by elementary cognitive tasks: Genetic and environmental influences. *Behavior Genetics, 26,* 135-147. (9)

Petrill, S. A., Plomin, R., Berg, S., Johansson, B., Pedersen, N. L., Ahern, F., . . . McClearn, G. E. (1998). The genetic and environmental relationship between general and specific cognitive abilities in twins age 80 and older. *Psychological Science, 9,* 183-189. (9)

Petrova, P. K., Cialdini, R. B., & Sills, S. J. (2006). Consistency-based compliance across cultures. *Journal of Experimental Psychology, 43,* 104-111. (13)

Petty, R. E., & Briñol, P. (2015). Emotion and persuasion: Cognitive and meta-cognitive processes impact attitudes. *Cognition & Emotion, 29,* 1-26. (13)

Petty, R. E., & Cacioppo, J. T. (1977). Effects of forewarning of persuasive intent and involvement on cognitive responses and persuasion. *Personality and Social Psychology Bulletin, 5,* 173-176. (13)

Petty, R. E., & Cacioppo, J. T. (1981). *Attitudes and persuasion: Classic and contemporary approaches.* Dubuque, IA: William C. Brown. (13)

Pezze, M. A., Bast, T., & Feldon, J. (2003). Significance of dopamine transmission in the rat medial prefrontal cortex for conditioned fear. *Cerebral Cortex, 13,* 371-380. (6)

Pfungst, O. (1911). *Clever Hans.* New York: Holt. (2)

Phan, K. L., Wager, T., Taylor, S. F., & Liberzon, I. (2002). Functional neuroanatomy of emotion: A meta-analysis of emotion activation studies in PET and fMRI. *NeuroImage, 16,* 331-348. (12)

Phelps, E. A., O'Connor, K. J., Cunningham, W. A., Funayama, E. S., Gatenby, J. C., Gore, J. C., . . . Banaji, M. R. (2000). Performance on indirect measures of race evaluation predicts amygdala activation. *Journal of Cognitive Neuroscience, 12,* 729-738. (13)

Phelps, M. E., & Mazziotta, J. C. (1985). Positron emission tomography: Human brain function and biochemistry. *Science, 228,* 799-809. (1, 3)

Philippot, P., Chapelle, G., & Blairy, S. (2002). Respiratory feedback in the generation of emotions. *Cognition and Emotion, 16,* 605-627. (12)

Phillips, J. E., & Olson, M. A. (2014). When implicitly and explicitly measured racial attitudes align: The roles of social desirability and thoughtful responding. *Basic and Applied Social Psychology, 36,* 125-132. (13)

Phillips, T. M., & Pittman, J. F. (2007). Adolescent psychological well-being by identity style. *Journal of Adolescence, 30,* 1021-1034. (5)

Phinney, J. S. (1990). Ethnic identity in adolescents and adults: Review of research. *Psychological Bulletin, 108,* 499-514. (5)

Piaget, J. (1954). *The construction of reality in the child* (M. Cook, Trans.). New York: Basic Books. (Original work published 1937) (5)

Picho, K., Rodriguez, A., & Finnie, L. (2013). Exploring the moderating role of context on the mathematics performance of females under stereotype threat: A meta-analysis. *Journal of Social Psychology, 153,* 299-333. (9)

Pichot, P. (1984). Centenary of the birth of Hermann Rorschach. *Journal of Personality Assessment, 48,* 591-596. (14)

Pierri, J. N., Volk, C. L. E., Auh, S., Sampson, A., & Lewis, D. A. (2001). Decreased somal size of deep layer 3 pyramidal neurons in the prefrontal cortex of subjects with schizophrenia. *Archives of General Psychiatry, 58,* 466-473. (15)

Pike, J. J., & Jennings, N. A. (2005). The effects of commercials on children's perceptions of gender appropriate toy use. *Sex Roles, 52,* 83-91. (5)

Pinel, J. P. J., Assanand, S., & Lehman, D. R. (2000). Hunger, eating, and ill health. *American Psychologist, 55,* 1105-1116. (11)

Pinker, S. (1994). *The language instinct.* New York: Morrow. (8)

Pinker, S. (2011). Taming the devil within us. *Nature, 478,* 309-311. (13)

Pittenger, D. J. (2005). Cautionary comments regarding the Myers-Briggs Type Indicator. *Consulting Psychology Journal: Practice and Research, 57,* 210-221. (14)

Place, S. S., Todd, P. M., Penke, L., & Asendorpf, J. B. (2009). The ability to judge the romantic interest of others. *Psychological Science, 20,* 22-26. (13)

Plaut, D. C., & Booth, J. R. (2000). Individual and developmental differences in semantic priming: Empirical and computational support for a single-mechanism account of lexical priming. *Psychological Review, 107,* 786-823. (8)

Plaut, V. C., Thomas, K. M., & Goren, M. J. (2009). Is multiculturalism or color blindness better for minorities? *Psychological Science, 20,* 444-446. (13)

Plomin, R., Corley, R., DeFries, J. C., & Fulker, D. W. (1990). Individual differences in television viewing in early childhood: Nature as well as nurture. *Psychological Science, 1,* 371-377. (5)

Plomin, R., DeFries, J. C., McClearn, G. E., & McGuffin, P. (Eds.). (2001). *Behavioral genetics* (4th ed.) New York: Worth. (9)

Plomin, R., Fulker, D. W., Corley, R., & DeFries, J. C. (1997). Nature, nurture, and cognitive development from 1 to 16 years: A parent-offspring adoption study. *Psychological Science, 8,* 442-447. (9)

Plomin, R., Haworth, C. M. A., Meaburn, E. L., Price, T. S., Wellcome Trust Case Control Consortium 2, & Davis, O. S. P. (2013). Common DNA markers can account for more than half of the genetic influence on cognitive abilities. *Psychological Science, 24,* 562-568. (9)

Plous, S. (1993). *The psychology of judgment and decision making.* Philadelphia: Temple University Press. (8)

Plous, S. (1996). Attitudes toward the use of animals in psychological research and education. *American Psychologist, 51,* 1167-1180. (2)

Plutchik, R. (1982). A psychoevolutionary theory of emotions. *Social Science Information, 21,* 529-553. (12)

Plutchik, R., & Ax, A. F. (1967). A critique of "determinants of emotional state" by Schachter and Singer (1962). *Psychophysiology, 4,* 79-82. (12)

Pochedly, J. T., Widen, S. C., & Russell, J. A. (2012). What emotion does the "facial expression of disgust" express? *Emotion, 12,* 1315-1319. (12)

Pockett, S., & Miller, A. (2007). The rotating spot method of timing subjective events. *Consciousness and Cognition, 16,* 241-254. (10)

Poelman, M. P., de Vet, E., Velema, E., Seidell, J. C., & Steenhuis, I. H. M. (2014). Behavioural strategies to control the amount of food selected and consumed. *Appetite, 72,* 156-165. (11)

Polivy, J., & Herman, C. P. (1985). Dieting and binging: A causal analysis. *American Psychologist, 40,* 193-201. (11)

Polk, T. A., Drake, R. M., Jonides, J. J., Smith, M. R., & Smith, E. E. (2008). Attention enhances the neural processing of relevant features and suppresses the processing of irrelevant features in humans: A functional magnetic resonance imaging study of the Stroop task. *Journal of Neuroscience, 28,* 13786–13792. (8)

Pond, S. B., III, & Geyer, P. D. (1991). Differences in the relation between job satisfaction and perceived work alternatives among older and younger blue-collar workers. *Journal of Vocational Behavior, 39,* 251–262. (11)

Poole, D. A., & White, L. T. (1993). Two years later: Effect of question repetition and retention interval on the eyewitness testimony of children and adults. *Developmental Psychology, 29,* 844–853. (7)

Pope, H. G., Jr., Gruber, A. J., Hudson, J. I., Huestis, M. A., & Yurgelun-Todd, D. (2001). Neuropsychological performance in long-term cannabis users. *Archives of General Psychiatry, 58,* 909–915. (3)

Popper, K. (1986). Predicting overt behavior versus predicting hidden states. *Behavioral and Brain Sciences, 9,* 254–255. (14)

Porter, J., Craven, B., Khan, R. M., Chang, S.-J., Kang, I., Judkewicz, B., . . . Sobel, N. (2007). Mechanisms of scent-tracking in humans. *Nature Neuroscience, 10,* 27–29. (4)

Porter, S., Birt, A. R., Yuille, J. C., & Lehman, D. R. (2000). Negotiating false memories: Interviewer and rememberer characteristics relate to memory distortion. *Psychological Science, 11,* 507–510. (7)

Post, R. M. (1992). Transduction of psychosocial stress into the neurobiology of recurrent affective disorder. *American Journal of Psychiatry, 149,* 999–1010. (15)

Posthuma, D., De Geus, E. J. C., Baaré, W. F. C., Pol, H. E. H., Kahn, R. S., & Boomsma, D. I. (2002). The association between brain volume and intelligence is of genetic origin. *Nature Neuroscience, 5,* 83–84. (9)

Poti, J. M., Duffy, K. J., & Popkin, B. M. (2014). The association between fast food consumption with poor dietary outcomes and obesity among children: Is it the fast food or the remainder of the diet? *American Journal of Clinical Nutrition, 99,* 162–171. (11)

Poulin, M. J., Holman, E. A., & Buffone, A. (2012). The neurogenetics of nice: Oxytocin and vasopressin receptor genes and prosocial behavior. *Psychological Science, 23,* 446–452. (3)

Powell, L. H., Calvin, J. E., III, & Calvin, J. E., Jr. (2007). Effective obesity treatments. *American Psychologist, 62,* 234–246. (11)

Powell, R. A., & Boer, D. P. (1994). Did Freud mislead patients to confabulate memories of abuse? *Psychological Reports, 74,* 1283–1298. (14)

Powell, R. A., Digdon, N., Harris, B., & Smithson, C. (2014). Correcting the record on Watson, Rayner, and Little Albert. *American Psychologist, 69,* 600–611. (15)

Pratkanis, A. R. (1992, Spring). The cargo-cult science of subliminal perception. *Skeptical Inquirer, 16,* 260–272. (4)

Pratt, J., Radulescu, P. V., Guo, R. M., & Abrams, R. A. (2010). It's alive! Animate motion captures visual attention. *Psychological Science, 21,* 1724–1730. (8)

Preckel, F., Lipnevich, A. A., Boehme, K., Brandner, L., Georgi, K., Könen, T., . . . Roberts, R. D. (2013). Morningness-eveningness and educational outcomes: The lark has an advantage over the owl at high school. *British Journal of Educational Psychology, 83,* 114–134. (10)

Principe, G. F., Kanaya, T., Ceci, S. J., & Singh, M. (2006). Believing is seeing. *Psychological Science, 17,* 243–248. (7)

Prochnow, D., Kossack, H., Brunheim, S., Muller, K., Wittsack, H. J., Markowitsch, H.-J., & Seitz, R. J. (2013). Processing of subliminal facial expressions of emotion: A behavioral and fMRI study. *Social Neuroscience, 8,* 448–461. (4)

Pronin, E., Berger, J., & Molouki, S. (2007). Alone in a crowd of sheep: Asymmetric perceptions of conformity and their roots in an introspection error. *Journal of Personality and Social Psychology, 92,* 585–595. (13)

Pronin, E., & Kugler, M. B. (2010). People believe they have more free will than others. *Proceedings of the National Academy of Sciences, 107,* 22469–22474. (1)

Protzko, J., Aronson, J., & Blair, C. (2013). How to make a young child smarter: Evidence from the Database of Raising Intelligence. *Perspectives on Psychological Science, 8,* 25–40. (9)

Provine, R. (2000). *Laughter.* New York: Viking Press. (2, 12)

Provine, R. R. (2012). *Quirks: Yawning, laughing, crying, hiccupping, and beyond.* Boston: Harvard University Press. (5)

Provine, R. R., Cabrera, M. O., Brocato, N. W., & Krosnowski, K. A. (2011). When the whites of the eyes are red: A uniquely human cue. *Ethology, 117,* 1–5. (12)

Provine, R. R., Krosnowski, K. A., & Brocato, N. W. (2009). Tearing: Breakthrough in human emotional signaling. *Evolutionary Psychology, 7,* 52–56. (12)

Provine, R. R., Nave-Blodgett, J., & Cabrera, M. O. (2013). The emotional eye: Red sclera as a uniquely human cue of emotion. *Ethology, 119,* 1–6. (12)

Public Agenda. (2001). *Medical research: Red flags.* Retrieved February 8, 2007, from www .publicagenda.org/charts/support-stem-cell -research-can-vary-dramatically-depending -question-wording-0. (2)

Pulver, C. A., & Kelly, K. R. (2008). Incremental validity of the Myers-Briggs Type Indicator in predicting academic major selection of undecided university students. *Journal of Career Assessment, 16,* 441–455. (14)

Purves, D., & Lotto, R. B. (2003). *Why we see what we do: An empirical theory of vision.* Sunderland, MA: Sinauer Associates. (4)

Purves, D., Williams, S. M., Nundy, S., & Lotto, R. B. (2004). Perceiving the intensity of light. *Psychological Review, 111,* 142–158. (4)

Pyc, M. A., & Rawson, K. A. (2010). Why testing improves memory: Mediator effectiveness hypothesis. *Science, 330,* 335. (7)

Pyszczynski, T., Greenberg, J., & Solomon, S. (2000). Proximal and distal defense: A new perspective on unconscious motivation. *Current Directions in Psychological Science, 9,* 156–160. (5)

Quadrel, M. J., Fischhoff, B., & Davis, W. (1993). Adolescent (in)vulnerability. *American Psychologist, 48,* 102–116. (5)

Quas, J. A., Malloy, L. C., Melinder, A., Goodman, G. S., D'Mello, M., & Schaaf, J. (2007). Developmental differences in the effects of repeated interviews and interview bias on young children's event memory and false reports. *Developmental Psychology, 43,* 823–837. (7)

Quattrocchi, M. R., & Schopp, R. F. (2005). Tarasaurus rex: A standard of care that could not adapt. *Psychology, Public Policy, and Law, 11,* 109–137. (15)

Quinn, P. C., & Liben, L. S. (2008). A sex difference in mental rotation in young infants. *Psychological Science, 19,* 1067–1070. (5)

Quoidbach, J., Dunn, E. W., Petrides, K. V., & Mikolajczak, M. (2010). Money giveth, money taketh away: The dual effect of wealth on happiness. *Psychological Science, 21,* 759–763. (12)

Radoeva, P. D., Prasad, S., Brainard, D. H., & Aguirre, G. K. (2008). Neural activity within area VI reflects unconscious visual performance in a case of blindsight. *Journal of Cognitive Neuroscience, 20,* 1927–1939. (3)

Radomsky, A. S., Dugas, M. J., Alcolado, G. M., & Lavoie, S. L. (2014). When more is less: Doubt, repetition, memory, metamemory, and compulsive checking in OCD. *Behaviour Research and Therapy, 59,* 30–39. (15)

Rahman, Q., Andersson, D., & Govier, E. (2005). A specific sexual orientation-related difference in navigation strategy. *Behavioral Neuroscience, 119,* 311–316. (5)

Rais, M., Cahn, W., Van Haren, N., Schnack, H., Caspers, E., . . . Kahn, R. (2008). Excessive brain volume loss over time in cannabis-using first-episode schizophrenia patients. *American Journal of Psychiatry, 165,* 490–496. (15)

Raison, C. L., Klein, H. M., & Steckler, M. (1999). The moon and madness reconsidered. *Journal of Affective Disorders, 53,* 99–106. (2)

Rajecki, D. W., & Borden, V. M. H. (2011). Psychology degrees: Employment, wage, and career trajectory consequences. *Perspectives on Psychological Science, 6,* 321–335. (1)

Ramachandran, V. S. (2003, May). Hearing colors, tasting shapes. *Scientific American, 288*(5), 52–59. (4)

Ramachandran, V. S., & Blakeslee, S. (1998). *Phantoms in the brain.* New York: Morrow. (4)

Ramachandran, V. S., & Hirstein, W. (1998). The perception of phantom limbs: The D. O. Hebb lecture. *Brain, 121,* 1603–1630. (4)

Ramadan, A. S. E., Wenanu, O., Cock, A. D. E., Maes, V., Lheureux, P., & Mols, P. (2013). Chemical submission to commit robbery: A series of involuntary intoxications with flunitrazepam in Asian travellers in Brussels. *Journal of Forensic and Legal Medicine, 20,* 918–921. (3)

Ramírez-Esparza, N., Mehl, M. R., Álvarez-Bermúdez, J., & Pennebaker, J. W. (2009). Are Mexicans more or less sociable than Americans? Insights from a naturalistic observation study. *Journal of Research in Personality, 43,* 1–7. (14)

Ramirez, G., & Beilock, S. L. (2011). Writing about testing worries boosts exam performance in the classroom. *Science, 331,* 211–213. (9)

Ramirez, J. M., Santisteban, C., Fujihara, T., & Van Goozen, S. (2002). Differences between experience of anger and readiness to angry action: A study of Japanese and Spanish students. *Aggressive Behavior, 28,* 429–438. (12)

Randler, C., Ebenhöh, N., Fischer, A., Höchel, S., Schroff, C., Stoll, J. C., . . . Piffer, D. (2012). Eveningness is related to men's mating success. *Personality and Individual Differences, 53,* 263–267. (10)

Ranganath, K. A., & Nosek, B. A. (2008). Implicit attitude generalization occurs immediately; explicit attitude generalization takes time. *Psychological Science, 19,* 249–254. (13)

Ransley, J. K., Donnelly, J. K., Botham, H., Khara, T. N., Greenwood, D. C., & Cade, J. E. (2003). Use of supermarket receipts to estimate energy and fat content of food purchased by lean and overweight families. *Appetite, 41,* 141-148. (11)

Rasch, B., & Born, J. (2008). Reactivation and consolidation of memory during sleep. *Current Directions in Psychological Science, 17,* 188-192. (10)

Ratiu, P., & Talos, I.-F. (2004). The tale of Phineas Gage, digitally remastered. *New England Journal of Medicine, 351,* e21. (12)

Rattenborg, N. C., Mandt, B. H., Obermeyer, W. H., Winsauer, P. J., Huber, R., Wikelski, M., & Benca, R. M. (2004). Migratory sleeplessness in the white-crowned sparrow (*Zonotrichia leucophrys gambelii*). *PLoS Biology, 2,* 924-936. (10)

Raven, J. (2000). The Raven's Progressive Matrices: Change and stability over culture and time. *Cognitive Psychology, 41, 1-48.* (9)

Rayner, K. (1998). Eye movements in reading and information processing: 20 years of research. *Psychological Bulletin, 124,* 372-422. (8)

Rayner, K., White, S. J., Johnson, R. L., & Liversedge, S. P. (2006). Raeding wrods with jumbled lettres. *Psychological Science, 17,* 192-193. (8)

Raz, A., Kirsch, I., Pollard, J., & Nitkin-Kaner, Y. (2006). Suggestion reduces the Stroop effect. *Psychological Science, 17,* 91-95. (8)

Rebok, G. W., Ball, K., Guey, L. T., Jones, R. N., Kim, H.-Y., King, J. W., . . . Willis, S. L. (2014). Ten-year effects of the Advanced Cognitive Training for Independent and Vital Elderly cognitive training trial on cognition and everyday functioning in older adults. *Journal of the American Geriatric Society, 62,* 16-24. (5)

Redding, R. E. (2001). Sociopolitical diversity in psychology. *American Psychologist, 56,* 205-215. (5)

Reed, A. E., Mikels, J. A., & Simon, K. I. (2008). Older adults prefer less choice than younger adults. *Psychology and Aging, 23,* 671-675. (8)

Reed, J. M., & Squire, L. R. (1999). Impaired transverse patterning in human amnesia is a special case of impaired memory for two-choice discrimination tasks. *Behavioral Neuroscience, 113,* 3-9. (7)

Reicher, G. M. (1969). Perceptual recognition as a function of meaningfulness of stimulus material. *Journal of Experimental Psychology, 81,* 275-280. (8)

Reicher, S. D., Haslam, S. A., & Smith, J. R. (2012). Working toward the experimenter: Reconceptualizing obedience within the Milgram paradigm as identification-based followership. *Perspectives on Psychological Science, 7,* 315-324. (13)

Reinius, B., Saetre, P., Leonard, J. A., Blekhman, R., Merino-Martinez, R., Gilad, Y., . . . Jazin, E. (2008). An evolutionarily conserved sexual signature in the primate brain. *PLoS Genetics, 4,* e1000100. (5)

Reisenzein, R. (1983). The Schachter theory of emotions: Two decades later. *Psychological Bulletin, 94,* 239-264. (12)

Ren, W., Lui, S., Deng, W., Li, F., Li, M., Huang, X., . . . Gong, Q. (2013). Anatomical and functional brain abnormalities in drug-naïve first-episode schizophrenia. *American Journal of Psychiatry, 170,* 1308-1316. (15)

Rensink, R. A., O'Regan, J. K., & Clark, J. J. (1997). To see or not to see: The need for attention to perceive changes in scenes. *Psychological Science, 8,* 368-373. (8)

Rentfrow, P. J., Gosling, S. D., & Potter, J. (2008). A theory of the emergence, persistence, and expression of geographic variation in psychological characteristics. *Perspectives on Psychological Science, 3,* 339-369. (14)

Repovš, G., & Baddeley, A. (2006). The multi-component model of working memory: Explorations in experimental cognitive psychology. *Neuroscience, 139,* 5-21. (7)

Rescorla, R. A. (1968). Probability of shock in the presence and absence of CS in fear conditioning. *Journal of Comparative and Physiological Psychology, 66,* 1-5. (6)

Rescorla, R. A. (1988). Pavlovian conditioning: It's not what you think it is. *American Psychologist, 43,* 151-160. (6)

Restle, F. (1970). Moon illusion explained on the basis of relative size. *Science, 167,* 1092-1096. (4)

Revusky, S. (2009). Chemical aversion treatment of alcoholism. In S. Reilly & T. R. Schachtman (Eds.), *Conditioned taste aversion* (pp. 445-472). New York: Oxford University Press. (6)

Reyna, V. F., Chick, C. F., Corbin, J. C., & Hsia, A. N. (2014). Developmental reversals in risky decision making: Intelligence agents show larger decision biases than college students. *Psychological Science, 25,* 76-84. (8)

Reynolds, A. J., Temple, J. A., Ou, S.-R., Arteaga, I. A., & White, B. A. B. (2011). School-based early childhood education and age-28 well-being: Effects by timing, dosage, and subgroups. *Science, 333,* 360-364. (9)

Rhodes, G., Sumich, A., & Byatt, G. (1999). Are average facial configurations attractive only because of their symmetry? *Psychological Science, 10,* 52-58. (13)

Rhodes, R. A., Murthy, N. V., Dresner, M. A., Selvaraj, S., Stavrakakis, N., Babar, S., . . . Grasby, P. M. (2007). Human 5-HT transporter availability predicts amygdala reactivity *in vivo. Journal of Neuroscience, 27,* 9233-9237. (3)

Riccio, D. C. (1994). Memory: When less is more. *American Psychologist, 49,* 917-926. (7)

Rice, W. R., Friberg, U., & Gavrilets, S. (2012). Homosexuality as a consequence of epigenetically canalized sexual development. *Quarterly Review of Biology, 87,* 343-368. (11)

Richter, C. P. (1922). A behavioristic study of the activity of the rat. *Comparative Psychology Monographs, 1,* 1-55. (11)

Richter, C. P. (1967). Psychopathology of periodic behavior in animals and man. In J. Zubin & H. F. Hunt (Eds.), *Comparative Psychopathology* (pp. 205-227). New York: Grune & Stratton. (10)

Richter, C. P. (1975). Deep hypothermia and its effect on the 24-hour clock of rats and hamsters. *Johns Hopkins Medical Journal, 136,* 1-10. (10)

Riddle, W. J. R., & Scott, A. I. F. (1995). Relapse after successful electroconvulsive therapy: The use and impact of continuation antidepressant drug treatment. *Human Psychopharmacology, 10,* 201-205. (15)

Rieger, G., Chivers, M. L., & Bailey, J. M. (2005). Sexual arousal patterns of bisexual men. *Psychological Science, 16,* 579-584. (11)

Rieger, G., Linsenmeier, J. A. W., Gygax, L., & Bailey, J. M. (2008). Sexual orientation and childhood gender nonconformity: Evidence from home videos. *Developmental Psychology, 44,* 46-58. (11)

Rieger, G., Rosenthal, A. M., Cash, B. M., Linsenmeier, J. A. W., Bailery, J. M., & Savin-Williams, R. C. (2013). Male bisexual arousal: A matter of curiosity? *Biological Psychology, 94,* 479-489. (11)

Riemer, H., Shavitt, S., Koo, M., & Markus, H. R. (2014). Preferences don't have to be personal: Expanding attitude theorizing with a cross-cultural perspective. *Psychological Review, 121,* 619-648. (13)

Rietveld, C. A., Conley, D., Eriksson, N., Esko, T., Medland, S. E., Vinkhuyzen, A. A. E., . . . the Social Science Genetics Association Consortium. (2014). Replicability and robustness of genome-wide-association studies for behavioral traits. *Psychological Science, 25,* 1975-1986. (9)

Rindermann, H., & Thompson, J. (2013). Ability rise in NAEP and narrowing ethnic gaps? *Intelligence, 41,* 821-831. (9)

Ritchie, S. J., Wiseman, R., & French, C. C. (2012). Failing the future: Three unsuccessful attempts to replicate Bem's 'retroactive facilitation of recall' experiment. *PLoS One, 7,* e33423. (2)

Ritvo, E. R. (2006). *Understanding the nature of autism and Asperger's syndrome.* London: Jessica Kingsley. (15)

Roane, B. M., & Taylor, D. J. (2008). Adolescent insomnia as a risk factor for early adult depression and substance abuse. *Sleep, 31,* 1351-1356. (15)

Roberts, B. W., & DelVecchio, W. F. (2000). The rank-order consistency of personality traits from childhood to old age: A quantitative review of longitudinal studies. *Psychological Bulletin, 126,* 3-25. (14)

Roberts, B. W., Kuncel, N. R., Shiner, R., Caspi, A., & Goldberg, L. R. (2007). The power of personality. *Perspectives on Psychological Science, 2,* 313-345. (14)

Roberts, B. W., Walton, K. E., & Viechtbauer, W. (2006). Patterns of mean-level change in personality traits across the life course: A meta-analysis of longitudinal studies. *Psychological Bulletin, 132,* 1-25. (14)

Roberts, R. E., & Duong, H. T. (2014). The prospective association between sleep deprivation and depression among adolescents. *Sleep, 37,* 239-244. (10, 15)

Roberts, S. B., Savage, J., Coward, W. A., Chew, B., & Lucas, A. (1988). Energy expenditure and intake in infants born to lean and overweight mothers. *New England Journal of Medicine, 318,* 461-466. (11)

Roberts, S. C., Gosling, L. M., Carter, V., & Petrie, M. (2008). MHC-correlated odour preferences in humans and the use of oral contraceptives. *Proceedings of the Royal Society, B, 275,* 2715-2722. (4, 13)

Robertson, I. H. (2005, Winter). The deceptive world of subjective awareness. *Cerebrum, 7*(1), 74-83. (3)

Robertson, L. C. (2003). Binding, spatial attention and perceptual awareness. *Nature Reviews Neuroscience, 4,* 93-102. (3)

Robinson, T. E., & Berridge, K. C. (2000). The psychology and neurobiology of addiction: An incentive-sensitization view. *Addiction, 95*(Suppl. 2), S91-S117. (15)

Robinson, T. E., & Berridge, K. C. (2001). Incentive-sensitization and addiction. *Addiction, 96,* 103-114. (15)

Rock, I., & Kaufman, L. (1962). The moon illusion, II. *Science, 136,* 1023-1031. (4)

Rodd, J., Gaskell, G., & Marslen-Wilson, W. (2002). Making sense of semantic ambiguity: Semantic competition in lexical access. *Journal of Memory and Language, 46,* 245-266. (8)

Rodgers, J. L. (2001). What causes birth order-intelligence patterns? *American Psychologist, 56,* 505-510. (5)

Rodgers, J. L., Cleveland, H. H., van den Oord, E., & Rowe, D. C. (2000). Resolving the debate over birth order, family size, and intelligence. *American Psychologist, 55,* 599-612. (5)

Rodin, J. (1986). Aging and health: Effects of the sense of control. *Science, 233,* 1271-1276. (5)

Rodrigo, M. F., & Ato, M. (2002). Testing the group polarization hypothesis by using logit models. *European Journal of Social Psychology, 32,* 3-18. (13)

Roediger, H. L., III, & Karpicke, J. D. (2006). Test-enhanced learning. *Psychological Science, 17,* 249-255. (7)

Roediger, H. L., III, & McDermott, K. B. (1995). Creating false memories: Remembering words not presented in lists. *Journal of Experimental Psychology: Learning, Memory, and Cognition, 21,* 803-814. (7)

Roenneberg, T., Kuehnle, T., Pramstaller, P. P., Ricken, J., Havel, M., Guth, A., . . . Merrow, M. (2004). A marker for the end of adolescence. *Current Biology, 14,* R1038-R1039. (10)

Roenneberg, T., Kumar, C. J., & Merrow, M. (2007). The human circadian clock entrains to sun time. *Current Biology, 17,* R44-R45. (10)

Roese, N. J., & Vohs, K. D. (2012). Hindsight bias. *Perspectives on Psychological Science, 7,* 411-426. (7)

Rofé, Y. (2008). Does repression exist? Memory, pathogenic, unconscious and clinical evidence. *Review of General Psychology, 12,* 63-85. (14)

Rogers, C. R. (1961). *On becoming a person.* Boston: Houghton Mifflin. (14)

Rogers, C. R. (1980). *A way of being.* Boston: Houghton Mifflin. (14)

Rogler, L. H. (2002). Historical generations and psychology. *American Psychologist, 57,* 1013-1023. (5)

Rogoff, B., Morelli, G. A., & Chavajay, P. (2010). Children's integration in communities and segregation from people of different ages. *Perspectives on Psychological Science, 5,* 431-440. (5)

Rohrer, D., & Pashler, H. (2007). Increasing retention without increasing study time. *Current Directions in Psychological Science, 16,* 183-186. (7)

Rohrer, R., & Taylor, K. (2007). The shuffling of mathematics problems improves learning. *Instructional Science, 35,* 481-498. (7)

Roisman, G. I., Collins, W. A., Sroufe, L. A., & Egeland, B. (2005). Predictors of young adults' representations of and behavior in their current romantic relationship: Prospective tests of the prototype hypothesis. *Attachment and Human Development, 7,* 105-121. (5)

Rolls, E. T., & McCabe, C. (2007). Enhanced affective brain representations of chocolate in cravers vs. non-cravers. *European Journal of Neuroscience, 26,* 1067-1076. (3)

Ronen, T., & Rosenbaum, M. (2001). Helping children to help themselves: A case study of enuresis and nail biting. *Research on Social Work Practice, 11,* 338-356. (6)

Rönkä, A., Oravala, S., & Pulkkinen, L. (2003). Turning points in adults' lives: The effects of gender and the amount of choice. *Journal of Adult Development, 10,* 203-215. (5)

Rooksby, M., Elouafkaoui, P., Humphris, G., Clarkson, J., & Freeman, R. (2015). Internet-assisted delivery of cognitive behavioural therapy (CBT) for childhood anxiety: Systematic review and meta-analysis. *Journal of Anxiety Disorders, 29,* 83-92. (15)

Rosa-Alcázar, A. I., Sánchez-Meca, J., Gómez-Conesa, A., & Marín-Martínez, F. (2008). Psychological treatment of obsessive-compulsive disorder: A meta-analysis. *Clinical Psychology Review, 28,* 1310-1325. (15)

Rosch, E. (1978). Principles of categorization. In E. Rosch & B. B. Lloyd (Eds.), *Cognition and categorization* (pp. 27-48). Hillsdale, NJ: Erlbaum. (8)

Rosch, E., & Mervis, C. B. (1975). Family resemblances: Studies in the internal structure of categories. *Cognitive Psychology, 7,* 573-605. (8)

Rose, J. E., Brugge, J. F., Anderson, D. J., & Hind, J. E. (1967). Phase-locked response to low-frequency tones in single auditory nerve fibers of the squirrel monkey. *Journal of Neurophysiology, 30,* 769-793. (4)

Rose, N. S., Myerson, J., Roediger, H. L. III, & Hale, S. (2010). Similarities and differences between working memory and long-term memory: Evidence from the levels-of-processing span task. *Journal of Experimental Psychology: Learning, Memory, and Cognition, 36,* 471-483. (7)

Rose, S. A., Feldman, J. F., & Jankowitz, J. J. (2011). Modeling a cascade of effects: The role of speed and executive functioning in preterm/full-term differences in academic achievement. *Developmental Science, 14,* 1161-1175. (7)

Rosenbaum, R. S., Köhler, S., Schacter, D. L., Moscovitch, M., Westmacott, R., Black, S. E., . . . Tulving, E. (2005). The case of K. C.: Contributions of a memory-impaired person to memory theory. *Neuropsychologia, 43,* 989-1021. (7)

Ross, L. (1977). The intuitive psychologist and his shortcomings: Distortions in the attribution process. In L. Berkowitz (Ed.), *Advances in experimental social psychology* (Vol. 10, pp. 173-220). New York: Academic Press. (13)

Rothbaum, F., Weisz, J., Pott, M., Miyake, K., & Morelli, G. (2000). Attachment and culture: Security in the United States and Japan. *American Psychologist, 55,* 1093-1104. (5)

Rotton, J., & Kelly, I. W. (1985). Much ado about the full moon: A meta-analysis of lunar-lunacy research. *Psychological Bulletin, 97,* 286-306. (2)

Rouder, J. N., & Morey, R. D. (2011). A Bayes factor meta-analysis of Bem's ESP claim. *Psychonomic Bulletin & Review, 18,* 682-689. (2)

Rounis, E., Maniscalco, B., Rothwell, J. C., Passingham, R., & Lau, H. (2010). Theta-burst transcranial magnetic stimulation to the prefrontal cortex impairs metacognitive visual awareness. *Cognitive Neuroscience, 1,* 165-175. (10)

Routh, D. K. (2000). Clinical psychology training: A history of ideas and practices prior to 1946. *American Psychologist, 55,* 236-241. (1)

Rovee-Collier, C. (1997). Dissociations in infant memory: Rethinking the development of explicit and implicit memory. *Psychological Review, 104,* 467-498. (5)

Rovee-Collier, C. (1999). The development of infant memory. *Current Directions in Psychological Science, 8,* 80-85. (5)

Rowe, J. W., & Kahn, R. L. (1987). Human aging: Usual and successful. *Science, 237,* 143-149. (5)

Rowe, M. L., & Goldin-Meadow, S. (2009). Early gesture selectively predicts later language learning. *Developmental Science, 12,* 182-187. (8)

Rozin, P. (1996). Sociocultural influences on human food selection. In E. D. Capaldi (Ed.), *Why we eat what we eat* (pp. 233-263). Washington, DC: American Psychological Association. (1)

Rozin, P., & Cohen, A. B. (2003). High frequency of facial expressions corresponding to confusion, concentration, and worry in an analysis of naturally occurring facial expressions of Americans. *Emotion, 3,* 68-75. (12)

Rozin, P., Fallon, A., & Augustoni-Ziskind, M. L. (1986). The child's conception of food: The development of categories of acceptable and rejected substances. *Journal of Nutrition Education, 18,* 75-81. (1)

Rozin, P., & Fallon, A. E. (1987). A perspective on disgust. *Psychological Review, 94,* 23-41. (1)

Rozin, P., Kabnick, K., Pete, E., Fischler, C., & Shields, C. (2003). The ecology of eating: Smaller portion sizes in France than in the United States help explain the French paradox. *Psychological Science, 14,* 450-454. (11)

Rozin, P., & Kalat, J. W. (1971). Specific hungers and poison avoidance as adaptive specializations of learning. *Psychological Review, 78,* 459-486. (1, 6)

Rozin, P., Lowery, L., Imada, S., & Haidt, J. (1999). The CAD triad hypothesis: A mapping between three moral emotions (contempt, anger, disgust) and three moral codes (community, autonomy, divinity). *Journal of Personality and Social Psychology, 76,* 574-586. (12)

Rozin, P., Markwith, M., & Ross, B. (1990). The sympathetic magical law of similarity, nominal realism and neglect of negatives in response to negative labels. *Psychological Science, 1,* 383-384. (8)

Rozin, P., Markwith, M., & Stoess, C. (1997). Moralization and becoming a vegetarian: The transformation of preferences into values and the recruitment of disgust. *Psychological Science, 8,* 67-73. (1)

Rozin, P., Millman, L., & Nemeroff, C. (1986). Operation of the laws of sympathetic magic in disgust and other domains. *Journal of Personality and Social Psychology, 50,* 703-712. (1)

Rozin, P., & Pelchat, M. L. (1988). Memories of mammaries: Adaptations to weaning from milk. *Progress in Psychobiology and Physiological Psychology, 13,* 1-29. (3)

Rubin, D. C., & Feeling, N. (2013). Measuring the severity of negative and traumatic events. *Clinical Psychological Science, 1,* 375-389. (12)

Rubio-Fernández, P., & Geurts, B. (2013). How to pass the false-belief task before your fourth birthday. *Psychological Science, 24,* 27-33. (5)

Ruch, J. (1984). *Psychology: The personal science.* Belmont, CA: Wadsworth. (3)

Rudman, L. A., & Goodwin, S. A. (2004). Gender differences in automatic in-group bias: Why do women like women more than men like men? *Journal of Personality and Social Psychology, 87,* 494-509. (13)

Rumelhart, D. E., & McClelland, J. L. (1982). An interactive activation model of context effects in letter perception: Part 2. The contextual enhancement effect and some tests and extensions of the model. *Psychological Review, 89,* 60-94. (8)

Rumelhart, D. E., McClelland, J. L., & the PDP Research Group. (1986). *Parallel distributed processing.* Cambridge, MA: MIT Press. (8)

Rusak, B. (1977). The role of the suprachiasmatic nuclei in the generation of circadian rhythms in the golden hamster, *Mesocricetus auratus. Journal of Comparative Physiology A, 118,* 145–164. (10)

Rush, A. J., Trivedi, M. H., Wisniewski, S. R., Stewart, J. W., Nierenberg, A. A., . . . Fava, M. (2006). Bupropion-SR, sertraline, or venlafaxine-XR after failure of SSRIs for depression. *New England Journal of Medicine, 354,* 1231–1242. (15)

Rushton, J. P., & Bons, T. A. (2005). Mate choice and friendship in twins. *Psychological Science, 16,* 555–559. (13)

Russano, M. B., Meissner, C. A., Narchet, F. M., & Kassin, S. M. (2005). Investigating true and false confessions within a novel experimental paradigm. *Psychological Science, 16,* 481–486. (13)

Russell, J. A. (1980). A circumplex model of affect. *Journal of Personality and Social Psychology, 39,* 1161–1178. (12)

Russell, J. A. (1994). Is there universal recognition of emotion from facial expression? A review of the cross-cultural studies. *Psychological Bulletin, 115,* 102–141. (12)

Russo, J. E., Carlson, K. A., & Meloy, M. G. (2006). Choosing an inferior alternative. *Psychological Science, 17,* 899–904. (13)

Rutledge, T., & Hogan, B. E. (2002). A quantitative review of prospective evidence linking psychological factors with hypertension development. *Psychosomatic Medicine, 64,* 758–766. (12)

Ryan, J. D., Althoff, R. R., Whitlow, S., & Cohen, N. J. (2000). Amnesia is a deficit in relational memory. *Psychological Science, 11,* 454–461. (7)

Sabini, J., Siepmann, M., Stein, J., & Meyerowitz, M. (2000). Who is embarrassed by what? *Cognition and Emotion, 14,* 213–240. (12)

Sacchi, D. L. M., Agnoli, F., & Loftus, E. F. (2007). Changing history: Doctored photographs affect memory for past public events. *Applied Cognitive Psychology, 21,* 1005–1022. (7)

Sackeim, H. A., Prudic, J., Devanand, D. P., Nobler, M. S., Lisanby, S. H., Peyser, S., . . . Clark, J. (2000). A prospective, randomized, double-blind comparison of bilateral and right unilateral electroconvulsive therapy at different stimulus intensities. *Archives of General Psychiatry, 57,* 425–434. (15)

Sackett, P. R., Borneman, M. J., & Connelly, B. S. (2008). High-stakes testing in higher education and employment. *American Psychologist, 63,* 215–227. (9)

Sackett, P. R., & Walmsley, P. T. (2014). Which personality attributes are most important in the workplace? *Perspectives on Psychological Science, 9,* 538–551. (14)

Sacks, D. W., Stevenson, B., & Wolfers, J. (2012). The new stylized facts about income and subjective well-being. *Emotion, 12,* 1181–1187. (12)

Sacks, O. (2010, August 30). Face-blind. *The New Yorker, 86 (31),* 36–43. (3)

Sadri-Vakili, G., Kumaresan, V., Schmidt, H. D., Famous, K. R., Chawla, P., Vassoler, F. M., . . . Cha, J. H. J. (2010). Cocaine-induced chromatin remodeling increases brain-derived neurotrophic factor transcription in the rat medial prefrontal cortex, which alters the reinforcing efficacy of cocaine. *Journal of Neuroscience, 30,* 11735–11744. (3)

Saegert, S., Swap, W., & Zajonc, R. B. (1973). Exposure, context, and interpersonal attraction. *Journal of Personality and Social Psychology, 25,* 234–242. (13)

Sales, B. D., & Folkman, S. (2000). *Ethics in research with human participants.* Washington, DC: American Psychological Association. (2)

Salimpoor, V. N., van den Bosch, I., Kovacevic, N., McIntosh, A. R., Dagher, A., & Zatorre, R. J. (2013). Interactions between the nucleus accumbens and auditory cortices predict music reward value. *Science, 340,* 216–219. (3)

Salmon, P. (2001). Effects of physical exercise on anxiety, depression, and sensitivity to stress: A unifying theory. *Clinical Psychology Review, 21,* 33–61. (12)

Salomons, T. V., Johnstone, T., Backonja, M.-M., & Davidson, R. J. (2004). Perceived controllability modulates the neural response to pain. *Journal of Neuroscience, 24,* 7199–7203. (12)

Salthouse, T. A. (2006). Mental exercise and mental aging. *Perspectives on Psychological Science, 1,* 68–87. (8)

Salthouse, T. A. (2013). Within-cohort age-related differences in cognitive functioning. *Psychological Science, 24,* 123–130. (9)

Salvatore, J. E., Kuo, S. I.-C., Steele, R. D., Simpson, J. A., & Collins, W. A. (2011). Recovering from conflict in romantic relationships: A developmental perspective. *Psychological Science, 22,* 376–383. (5)

Sam, D. L., & Berry, J. W. (2010). Acculturation: When individuals and groups of different cultural backgrounds meet. *Perspectives on Psychological Science, 5,* 472–481. (5)

Samuel, A. G. (2001). Knowing a word affects the fundamental perception of the sounds within it. *Psychological Science, 12,* 348–351. (8)

Sanchez, L. M., & Turner, S. M. (2003). Practicing psychology in the era of managed care. *American Psychologist, 58,* 116–129. (15)

Sanders, A. R., Martin, E. R., Beecham, G. W., Guo, S., Dawood, K., Rieger, G., . . . Bailey, J. M. (2015). Genome-wide scan demonstrates significant linkage for male sexual orientation. *Psychological Medicine, 45(7),* 1379–1388. (11)

Sanders, R. E., Gonzalez, D. J., Murphy, M. D., Pesta, B. J., & Bucur, B. (2002). Training content variability and the effectiveness of learning: An adult age assessment. *Aging, Neuropsychology, and Cognition, 9,* 157–174. (7)

Sandfort, T. G. M., de Graaf, R., Bijl, R. V., & Schnabel, P. (2001). Same-sex sexual behavior and psychiatric disorders. *Archives of General Psychiatry, 58,* 85–91. (11)

Sandhya, S. (2009). The social context of marital happiness in urban Indian couples: Interplay of intimacy and conflict. *Journal of Marital and Family Conflict, 35,* 74–96. (11)

Sapolsky, R. M., & Share, L. J. (2004). A pacific culture among wild baboons: Its emergence and transmission. *PLoS Biology, 2,* 534–541. (13)

Sapp, F., Lee, K., & Muir, D. (2000). Three-year-olds' difficulty with the appearance–reality distinction: Is it real or is it apparent? *Developmental Psychology, 36,* 547–560. (5)

Saris, S., Mischoulon, D., & Schweitzer, I. (2012). Omega-3 for bipolar disorder: Meta-analyses of use in mania and bipolar depression. *Journal of Clinical Psychiatry, 73,* 81–86. (15)

Saucier, D. M., Green, S. M., Leason, J., MacFadden, A., Bell, S., & Elias, L. J. (2002). Are sex differences in navigation caused by sexually dimorphic strategies or by differences in the ability to use the strategies? *Behavioral Neuroscience, 116,* 403–410. (5)

Savage-McGlynn, E. (2012). Sex differences in intelligence in younger and older participants of the Raven's Standard Progressive Matrices Plus. *Personality and Individual Differences, 53,* 137–141. (9)

Savage-Rumbaugh, E. S. (1990). Language acquisition in a nonhuman species: Implications for the innateness debate. *Developmental Psychology, 23,* 599–620. (8)

Savage-Rumbaugh, E. S., Murphy, J., Sevcik, R. A., Brakke, K. E., Williams, S. L., & Rumbaugh, D. M. (1993). Language comprehension in ape and child. *Monographs of the Society for Research in Child Development, 58*(Serial no. 233). (8)

Savage-Rumbaugh, E. S., Sevcik, R. A., Brakke, K. E., & Rumbaugh, D. M. (1992). Symbols: Their communicative use, communication, and combination by bonobos *(Pan paniscus).* In L. P. Lipsitt & C. Rovee-Collier (Eds.), *Advances in infancy research* (Vol. 7, pp. 221–278). Norwood, NJ: Ablex. (8)

Savic, I., Berglund, H., & Lindström, P. (2005). Brain response to putative pheromones in homosexual men. *Proceedings of the National Academy of Sciences (U.S.A.), 102,* 7356–7361. (4)

Sbarra, D. A., Boals, A., Mason, A. E., Larson, G. M., & Mehl, M. R. (2013). Expressive writing can impede emotional recovery following marital separation. *Clinical Psychological Science, 1,* 120–134. (12)

Sbarra, D. A., Law, R. W., & Portley, R. M. (2011). Divorce and death: A meta-analysis and research agenda for clinical, social, and health psychology. *Perspectives on Psychological Science, 6,* 454–474. (12)

Scalera, G., & Bavieri, M. (2009). Role of conditioned taste aversion on the side effects of chemotherapy in cancer patients. In S. Reilly & T. R. Schachtman (Eds.), *Conditioned taste aversion* (pp. 513–541). New York: Oxford University Press. (6)

Scarborough, E., & Furomoto, L. (1987). *Untold lives: The first generation of American women psychologists.* New York: Columbia University Press. (1)

Schachter, S. (1982). Recidivism and self-cure of smoking and obesity. *American Psychologist, 37,* 436–444. (11)

Schachter, S., & Singer, J. (1962). Cognitive, social, and physiological determinants of emotional state. *Psychological Review, 69,* 379–399. (12)

Schacter, D. L. (1987). Implicit memory: History and current status. *Journal of Experimental Psychology: Learning, Memory, and Cognition, 13,* 501–518. (7)

Schacter, D. L., Verfaellie, M., Anes, M. D., & Racine, C. (1998). When true recognition suppresses false recognition: Evidence from amnesic patients. *Journal of Cognitive Neuroscience, 10,* 668–679. (7)

Schatzman, M. (1992, March 21). Freud: Who seduced whom? *New Scientist,* pp. 34–37. (14)

Scheele, D., Striepens, N., Güntürkün, O., Deutschländer, S., Maier, W., Kendrick, K. M., & Hurlemann, R. (2012). Oxytocin modulates social distance between males and females. *Journal of Neuroscience, 32,* 16074–16079. (3)

Scheele, D., Wille, A., Kendrick, K. M., Stoffel-Wagner, B., Becker, B., Güntürkün, O., . . . Hurlemann, R. (2013). Oxytocin enhances brain reward system responses in men viewing the face of their female partner. *Proceedings of the National Academy of Sciences (U.S.A.), 110,* 20308–20313. (3)

Schellenberg, E. G. (2004). Music lessons enhance IQ. *Psychological Science, 15,* 511–514. (9)

Schellenberg, E. G. (2006). Long-term positive associations between music lessons and IQ. *Journal of Educational Psychology, 98,* 457–468. (9)

Schellenberg, E. G., & Mankarious, M. (2012). Music training and emotion comprehension in childhood. *Emotion, 12,* 887–891. (9)

Schellenberg, E. G., & Trehub, S. E. (2003). Good pitch memory is widespread. *Psychological Science, 14,* 262–266. (4)

Schenck, C. H., & Mahowald, M. W. (1996). Long-term, nightly benzodiazepine treatment of injurious parasomnias and other disorders of disrupted nocturnal sleep in 170 adults. *American Journal of Medicine, 100,* 333–337. (10)

Schenk, T. (2006). An allocentric rather than perceptual deficit in patient D. F. *Nature Neuroscience, 9,* 1369–1370. (3)

Scherer, K. R., & Ellgring, H. (2007). Multimodal expression of emotion: Affect programs or componential appraisal patterns? *Emotion, 7,* 158–171. (12)

Schiebener, J., Wegmann, E., Pawlikowski, M., & Brand, M. (2014). Effects of goals on decisions under risk conditions: Goals can help to make better choices, but relatively high goals increase risk-taking. *Journal of Cognitive Psychology, 26,* 473–485. (11)

Schiffman, S. S., & Erickson, R. P. (1971). A psychophysical model for gustatory quality. *Physiology and Behavior, 7,* 617–633. (4)

Schizophrenia Working Group of the Psychiatric Genomics Consortium. (2014). Biological insights from 108 schizophrenia-associated genetic loci. *Nature, 511,* 421–427. (15)

Schkade, D. A., & Kahneman, D. (1998). Does living in California make people happy? *Psychological Science, 9,* 340–346. (12)

Schlam, T. R., Wilson, N. L., Shoda, Y., Mischel, W., & Ayduk, O. (2013). Preschoolers' delay of gratification predicts their body mass 30 years later. *Journal of Pediatrics, 162,* 90–93. (11)

Schlesier-Stropp, B. (1984). Bulimia: A review of the literature. *Psychological Review, 95,* 247–257. (11)

Schmid, M. C., Mrowka, S. W., Turchi, J., Saunders, R. C., Wilke, M., Peters, A. J., . . . Leopold, D. A. (2010). Blindsight depends on the lateral geniculate nucleus. *Nature, 466,* 373–377. (3)

Schmidt-Duffy, M. (2011). Modeling automatic threat detection: Development of a face-in-the-crowd task. *Emotion, 11,* 153–168. (8)

Schmidt, F. L., & Hunter, J. E. (1981). Employment testing: Old theories and new research findings. *American Psychologist, 36,* 1128–1137. (9)

Schmidt, F. L., & Hunter, J. E. (1998). The validity and utility of selection methods in personnel psychology: Practical and theoretical implications of 85 years of research findings. *Psychological Bulletin, 124,* 262–274. (9)

Schmitt, A. P., & Dorans, N. J. (1990). Differential item functioning for minority examinees on the SAT. *Journal of Educational Measurement, 27,* 67–81. (9)

Schmitt, D. P., & 118 members of the International Sexuality Description Project. (2003). Universal sex differences in the desire for sexual variety: Tests from 52 nations, 6 continents, and 13 islands. *Journal of Personality and Social Psychology, 85,* 85–104. (3)

Schmolck, H., Buffalo, E. A., & Squire, L. R. (2000). Memory distortions develop over time. *Psychological Science, 11,* 39–45. (7)

Schneider, M., Debbané, M., Bassett, A. S., Chow, E. W. C., Fung, W. L. A., van den Bree, M. B. M., . . . Eliez, S. (2014). Psychiatric disorders from childhood to adulthood in 22q11.2 deletion syndrome: Results from the International Consortium on Brain and Behavior in 22q11.2 deletion syndrome. *American Journal of Psychiatry, 171,* 627–639. (15)

Schneider, P., Scherg, M., Dosch, G., Specht, H. J., Gutschalk, A., & Rupp, A. (2002). Morphology of Heschl's gyrus reflects enhanced activation in the auditory cortex of musicians. *Nature Neuroscience, 5,* 688–694. (3)

Schneider, W., Niklas, F., & Schmiedeler, S. (2014). Intellectual development from early childhood to early adulthood: The impact of early IQ differences on stability and change over time. *Learning and Individual Differences, 32,* 156–162. (9)

Schneiderman, I., Zilberstein-Kra, Y., Leckman, J. F., & Feldman, R. (2011). Love alters autonomic reactivity to emotions. *Emotion, 11,* 1314–1321. (12)

Schnider, A. (2003). Spontaneous confabulation and the adaptation of thought to ongoing reality. *Nature Reviews Neuroscience, 4,* 662–671. (7)

Schomacher, M., Müller, H. D., Sommer, C., Schwab, S., & Schäbitz, W.-R. (2008). Endocannabinoids mediate neuroprotection after transient focal cerebral ischemia. *Brain Research, 1240,* 213–220. (3)

Schooler, C. (1972). Birth order effects: Not here, not now! *Psychological Bulletin, 78,* 161–175. (5)

Schotter, E. R., Tran, R., & Rayner, K. (2014). Don't believe what you read (only once): Comprehension is supported by regressions during reading. *Psychological Science, 25,* 1218–1226. (8)

Schredl, M. (2000). Continuity between waking life and dreaming: Are all waking activities reflected equally often in dreams? *Perceptual and Motor Skills, 90,* 844–846. (10)

Schredl, M., Ciric, P., Götz, S., & Wittman, L. (2004). Typical dreams: Stability and gender differnces. *Journal of Psychology, 138,* 485–494. (10)

Schuckit, M. A., & Smith, T. L. (1997). Assessing the risk for alcoholism among sons of alcoholics. *Journal of Studies on Alcohol, 58,* 141–145. (15)

Schuckit, M. A., & Smith, T. L. (2013). Stability of scores and correlations with drinking behaviors over 15 years for the self-report of the effects of alcohol questionnaire. *Drug and Alcohol Dependence, 128,* 194–199. (15)

Schuckit, M. A., Smith, T. L., Danko, G. P., Pierson, J., Hesselbrock, V., . . . Chan, G. (2007). The ability of the self-rating of the effects of alcohol (SRE) scale to predict alcohol-related outcomes five years later. *Journal of Studies of Alcohol, 68,* 371–378. (15)

Schulsinger, F., Knop, J., Goodwin, D. W., Teasdale, T. W., & Mikkelsen, U. (1986). A prospective study of young men at high risk for alcoholism. *Archives of General Psychiatry, 43,* 755–760. (15)

Schumann, K., & Ross, M. (2010). Why women apologize more than men: Gender differences in thresholds for perceiving offensive behavior. *Psychological Science, 21,* 1649–1655. (5)

Schumm, W. R. (2008). Re-evaluation of the "no differences" hypothesis concerning gay and lesbian parenting as assessed in eight early (1979–1986) and four later (1997–1998) dissertations. *Psychological Reports, 103,* 275–304. (5)

Schupp, H. T., Stockburger, J., Codispoti, M., Junghöfer, M., Weike, A. I., & Hamm, A. O. (2007). Selective visual attention to emotion. *Journal of Neuroscience, 27,* 1082–1089. (12)

Schützwohl, A., & Borgstedt, K. (2005). The processing of affectively valenced stimuli: The role of surprise. *Cognition and Emotion, 19,* 583–600. (12)

Schwartz, B. (2004). *The paradox of choice.* New York: HarperCollins. (8)

Schwartz, B., Ward, A., Monterosso, J., Lyubomirsky, S., White, K., & Lehman, D. R. (2002). Maximizing versus satisficing: Happiness is a matter of choice. *Journal of Personality and Social Psychology, 83,* 1178–1197. (8)

Schwartz, C. E., Wright, C. I., Shin, L. M., Kagan, J., & Rauch, S. L. (2003). Inhibited and uninhibited infants "grown up": Adult amygdalar response to novelty. *Science, 300,* 1952–1953. (5)

Schwartz, G., Kim, R. M., Kolundzija, A. B., Rieger, G., & Sanders, A. R. (2010). Biodemographic and physical correlates of sexual orientation in men. *Archives of Sexual Behavior, 39,* 93–109. (11)

Scott, L. S., & Monesson, A. (2009). The origin of biases in face perception. *Psychological Science, 20,* 676–680. (5)

Scott, N., Lakin, K. C., & Larson, S. A. (2008). The 40th anniversary of deinstitutionalization in the United States: Decreasing state institutional populations, 1967–2007. *Intellectual and Developmental Disabilities, 46,* 402–405. (15)

Scott, S. K., Young, A. W., Calder, A. J., Hellawell, D. J., Aggleton, J. P., & Johnson, M. (1997). Impaired auditory recognition of fear and anger following bilateral amygdala lesions. *Nature, 385,* 254–257. (12)

Scott, T. R., & Verhagen, J. V. (2000). Taste as a factor in the management of nutrition. *Nutrition, 16,* 874–885. (1)

Scott, V. M., Mottarella, K. E., & Lavooy, M. J. (2006). Does virtual intimacy exist? A brief exploration into reported levels of intimacy in online relationships. *CyberPsychology and Behavior, 9,* 759–761. (13)

Scovern, A. W., & Kilmann, P. R. (1980). Status of electroconvulsive therapy: Review of the outcome literature. *Psychological Bulletin, 87,* 260–303. (15)

Seamon, J. G., Lee, I. A., Toner, S. K., Wheeler, R. H., Goodkind, M. S., & Birch, A. D. (2002). Thinking of critical words during study is unnecessary for false memory in the Deese, Roediger, and McDermott procedure. *Psychological Science, 13,* 526–531. (7)

Sebastián-Enesco, C., Hernández-Lloreda, M. V., & Colmenares, F. (2013). Two and a half-year-old children are prosocial even when their partners are not. *Journal of Experimental Child Psychology, 116,* 186–198. (13)

Seeman, P., & Lee, T. (1975). Antipsychotic drugs: Direct correlation between clinical potency and presynaptic action on dopamine neurons. *Science, 188,* 1217–1219. (15)

Segal, N. L. (2000). Virtual twins: New findings on within-family environmental influences on intelligence. *Journal of Educational Psychology, 92,* 442–448. (9)

Segal, N. L., McGuire, S. A., & Stohs, J. H. (2012). What virtual twins reveal about general intelligence and other behaviors. *Personality and Individual Differences, 53,* 405–410. (9)

Segerstrom, S. C., & Nes, L. S. (2007). Heart rate variability reflects self-regulatory strength, effort, and fatigue. *Psychological Science, 18,* 275-281. (12)

Sekuler, A. B., & Bennett, P. J. (2001). Generalized common fate: Grouping by common luminance changes. *Psychological Science, 12,* 437-444. (4)

Seligman, M. E. P. (1970). On the generality of the laws of learning. *Psychological Review, 77,* 406-418. (6)

Seligman, M. E. P. (1971). Phobias and preparedness. *Behavior Therapy, 2,* 307-320. (15)

Seligman, M. E. P., & Csikszentmihalyi, M. (2000). Positive psychology. *American Psychologist, 55,* 5-14. (12)

Seligman, M. E. P., Railton, P., Baumeister, R. F., & Sripada, C. (2013). Navigating into the future or driven by the past. *Perspectives on Psychological Science, 8,* 119-141. (6)

Selye, H. (1979). Stress, cancer, and the mind. In J. Taché, H. Selye, & S. B. Day (Eds.), *Cancer, stress, and death* (pp. 11-27). New York: Plenum Press. (12)

Semmler, C., Brewer, N., & Wells, G. L. (2004). Effects of postidentification feedback on eyewitness identification and nonidentification confidence. *Journal of Applied Psychology, 89,* 334-346. (7)

Senghas, A., & Coppola, M. (2001). Children creating language: How Nicaraguan sign language acquired a spatial grammar. *Psychological Science, 12,* 323-328. (8)

Senghas, A., Kita, S., & Özyürek, A. (2004). Children creating core properties of language: Evidence from an emerging sign language in Nicaragua. *Science, 305,* 1779-1782. (8)

Senju, A., Southgate, V., Snape, C., Leonard, M., & Csibra, G. (2011). Do 18-month-olds really attribute mental states to others? A critical test. *Psychological Science, 22,* 878-880. (5)

Seo, M.-G., Barrett, L. F., & Bartunek, J. M. (2004). The role of affective experience in work motivation. *Academy of Management Review, 29,* 423-439. (11)

Sergent, C., & Dehaene, S. (2004). Is consciousness a gradual phenomenon? *Psychological Science, 15,* 720-728. (10)

Seto, M. C., Lalumière, M. L., Harris, G. T., & Chivers, M. L. (2012). The sexual responses of sexual sadists. *Journal of Abnormal Psychology, 121,* 739-753. (11)

Shafir, E. (1983). Choosing versus rejecting: Why some options are both better and worse than others. *Memory & Cognition, 21,* 546-556. (2)

Shafir, E. B., Smith, E. E., & Osherson, D. N. (1990). Typicality and reasoning fallacies. *Memory and Cognition, 18,* 229-239. (8)

Shafto, M., & MacKay, D. G. (2000). The Moses, mega-Moses, and Armstrong illusions: Integrating language comprehension and semantic memory. *Psychological Science, 11,* 372-378. (8)

Shah, A. M., & Wolford, G. (2007). Buying behavior as a function of parametric variation of number of choices. *Psychological Science, 18,* 369-370. (8)

Shahar, D. R., Schultz, R., Shahar, A., & Wing, R. R. (2001). The effect of widowhood on weight change, dietary intake, and eating behavior in the elderly population. *Journal of Aging and Health, 13,* 186-199. (12)

Shalev, I., Moffitt, T. E., Wong, T. Y., Meier, M. H., Houts, R. M., Ding, J., . . . Poulton, R. (2013). Retinal vessel caliber and lifelong neuropsychological functioning: Retinal imaging as an investigative tool for cognitive

epidemiology. *Psychological Science, 24,* 1198-1207. (9)

Shamosh, N. A., DeYoung, C. G., Green, A. E., Reis, D. L., Johnson, M. R., Conway, A. R. A., . . . Gray, J. R. (2008). Individual differences in delay discounting. *Psychological Science, 19,* 904-911. (9)

Shannon, D. A. (1955). *The Socialist Party of America.* New York: Macmillan. (13)

Shapiro, D. L. (1985). Insanity and the assessment of criminal responsibility. In C. P. Ewing (Ed.), *Psychology, psychiatry, and the law: A clinical and forensic handbook* (pp. 67-94). Sarasota, FL: Professional Resource Exchange. (15)

Shapiro, K. L., Caldwell, J., & Sorensen, R. E. (1997). Personal names and the attentional blink: A visual "cocktail party" effect. *Journal of Experimental Psychology: Human Perception and Performance, 23,* 504-514. (8)

Shaw, G. B. (1911). *The doctor's dilemma.* New York: Brentano's. (13)

Shearn, D., Spellman, L., Straley, B., Meirick, J., & Stryker, K. (1999). Empathic blushing in friends and strangers. *Motivation and Emotion, 23,* 307-316. (12)

Sheldon, K., & Lyubomirsky, S. (2004). Achieving sustainable new happiness: Prospects, practices, and prescriptions. In P. A. Linley & S. Joseph (Eds.), *Positive psychology in practice* (pp. 127-145). Hoboken, NJ: Wiley. (12)

Sheldon, K. M., & Lyubomirsky, S. (2006). Achieving sustainable gains in happiness: Change your actions, not your circumstances. *Journal of Happiness Studies, 7,* 55-86. (12)

Shenhav, A., & Buckner, R. L. (2014). Neural correlates of dueling affective reactions to win-win choices. *Proceedings of the National Academy of Sciences (U.S.A.), 111,* 10978-10983. (8)

Shenhav, A., & Greene, J. D. (2014). Integrative moral judgment: Dissociating the roles of the amygdala and ventromedial prefrontal cortex. *Journal of Neuroscience, 34,* 4741-4749. (12)

Shepard, R. N. (1990). *Mind sights.* New York: W. H. Freeman. (4)

Shepard, R. N., & Metzler, J. N. (1971). Mental rotation of three-dimensional objects. *Science, 171,* 701-703. (8)

Shepperd, J. A. (1993). Productivity loss in performance groups: A motivation analysis. *Psychological Bulletin, 113,* 67-81. (13)

Shergill, S. S., Brammer, M. J., Williams, S. C. R., Murray, R. M., & McGuire, P. K. (2000). Mapping auditory hallucinations in schizophrenia using functional magnetic resonance imaging. *Archives of General Psychiatry, 57,* 1033-1038. (15)

Sherif, M. (1935). A study of some social factors in perception. *Archives of Psychology, 27,* 1-60. (13)

Sherif, M. (1966). *In common predicament.* Boston: Houghton Mifflin. (13)

Sherwood, G. G. (1981). Self-serving biases in person perception: A reexamination of projection as a mechanism of defense. *Psychological Bulletin, 90,* 445-459. (14)

Shih, M., Pittinsky, T. L., & Ambady, N. (1999). Stereotype susceptibility: Identity salience and shifts in quantitative performance. *Psychological Science, 10,* 80-83. (9)

Shih, M., & Sanchez, D. T. (2005). Perspectives and research on the positive and negative implications of having multiple racial identities. *Psychological Bulletin, 131,* 569-591. (5)

Shimaya, A. (1997). Perception of complex line drawings. *Journal of Experimental Psychology:*

Human Perception and Performance, 23, 25-50. (4)

Shimizu, M., Johnson, K., & Wansink, B. (2014). In good company: The effect of an eating companion's appearance on food intake. *Appetite, 83,* 263-268. (14)

Shinskey, J. L., & Munakata, Y. (2005). Familiarity breeds searching. *Psychological Science, 16,* 595-600. (5)

Shiota, M. N., & Levenson, R. W. (2007). Birds of a feather don't always fly farthest: Similarity in Big Five personality predicts more negative marital satisfaction trajectories in long-term marriages. *Psychology of Aging, 22,* 666-675. (13)

Shipstead, Z., & Engle, R. W. (2013). Interference within the focus of attention: Working memory tasks reflect more than temporary maintenance. *Journal of Experimental Psychology: Learning, Memory, and Cognition, 39,* 277-289. (7)

Shoda, Y., Mischel, W., & Peake, P. K. (1990). Predicting adolescent cognitive and self-regulatory competencies from preschool conditions. *Developmental Psychology, 26,* 978-986. (11)

Shogren, E. (1993, June 2). Survey finds 4 in 5 suffer sex harassment at school. *Los Angeles Times,* p. A10. (2)

Shohamy, D., Myers, C. E., Kalanithi, J., & Gluck, M. A. (2008). Basal ganglia and dopamine contributions to probabilistic category learning. *Neuroscience and Biobehavioral Reviews, 32,* 219-236. (7)

Shook, N. J., & Fazio, R. H. (2008). Interracial roommate relationships. *Psychological Science, 19,* 717-723. (13)

Shrager, Y., Levy, D. A., Hopkins, R. O., & Squire, L. R. (2008). Working memory and the organization of brain systems. *Journal of Neuroscience, 28,* 4818-4822. (7)

Shulman, E. P. (2014). Deciding in the dark: Differences in intuitive risk judgment. *Developmental Psychology, 50,* 167-177. (5)

Sibley, M. H., Kuriyan, A. B., Evans, S. W., Waxmonsky, J. G., & Smith, B. H. (2014). Pharmacological and psychosocial treatments for adolescents with ADHD: An updated systematic review of the literature. *Clinical Psychology Review, 34,* 218-232. (8)

Siegel, J. M. (2005). Clues to the functions of mammalian sleep. *Nature, 437,* 1264-1271. (10)

Siegel, S. (1977). Morphine tolerance as an associative process. *Journal of Experimental Psychology: Animal Behavior Processes, 3,* 1-13. (6)

Siegel, S. (1983). Classical conditioning, drug tolerance, and drug dependence. *Research Advances in Alcohol and Drug Problems, 7,* 207-246. (6)

Siegel, S. (1987). Alcohol and opiate dependence: Reevaluation of the Victorian perspective. *Research Advances in Alcohol and Drug Problems, 9,* 279-314. (15)

Siegel, S., & Ramos, B. M. C. (2002). Applying laboratory research: Drug anticipation and the treatment of drug addiction. *Experimental and Clinical Psychopharmacology, 10,* 162-183. (6)

Sieverding, M., Decker, S., & Zimmermann, F. (2010). Information about low participation in cancer screening demotivates other people. *Psychological Science, 21,* 941-943. (13)

Sigman, M., & Whaley, S. E. (1998). The role of nutrition in the development of intelligence. In U. Neisser (Ed.), *The rising curve* (pp. 155-182). Washington, DC: American Psychological Association. (9)

Silberg, J., Pickles, A., Rutter, M., Hewitt, J., Simonoff, E., Maes, H., . . . Eaves, L. (1999). The influence of genetic factors and life stress on depression among adolescent girls. *Archives of General Psychiatry, 56,* 225–232. (15)

Silk, J. B., Brosnan, S. F., Vonk, J., Henrich, J., Povinelli, D. J., Richardson, A. S., . . . Schapiro, S. J. (2005). Chimpanzees are indifferent to the welfare of unrelated group members. *Nature, 437,* 1357–1359. (13)

Silva, E. J., & Duffy, J. F. (2008). Sleep inertia varies with circadian phase and sleep stage in older adults. *Behavioral Neuroscience, 122,* 929–935. (10)

Silver, E. (1995). Punishment or treatment? Comparing the lengths of confinement of successful and unsuccessful insanity defendants. *Law and Human Behavior, 19,* 375–388. (15)

Simmons, E. J. (1949). *Leo Tolstoy.* London: Lehmann. (15)

Simner, J., & Bain, A. E. (2013). A longitudinal study of grapheme-color synesthesia in childhood: 6/7 years to 10/11 years. *Frontiers in Human Neuroscience, 7,* Article 603. (4)

Simner, J., & Ward, J. (2006). The taste of words on the tip of the tongue. *Nature, 444,* 438. (4)

Simon, B., Reichert, F., & Grabow, O. (2013). When dual identity becomes a liability: Identity and political radicalism among migrants. *Psychological Science, 24,* 251–257. (5)

Simon, N. W., Mendez, I. A., & Setlow, B. (2007). Cocaine exposure causes long-term increases in impulsive choice. *Behavioral Neuroscience, 121,* 543–549. (3)

Simons, D. J. (2014). The value of direct replication. *Perspectives on Psychological Science, 9,* 76–80. (2)

Simons, D. J., & Levin, D. T. (2003). What makes change blindness interesting? *The Psychology of Learning and Motivation, 42,* 295–322. (8)

Simons, T., & Roberson, Q. (2003). Why managers should care about fairness: The effects of aggregate justice perceptions on organizational outcomes. *Journal of Applied Psychology, 88,* 432–443. (11)

Simpson, E. H., Kellendonk, C., & Kandel, E. (2010). A possible role for the striatum in the pathogenesis of the cognitive symptoms of schizophrenia. *Neuron, 65,* 585–596. (15)

Singer, T., Seymour, B., O'Doherty, J., Kaube, H., Dolan, R. J., & Frith, C. D. (2004). Empathy for pain involves the affective but not sensory components of pain. *Science, 303,* 1157–1162. (4)

Singh, M., Hoffman, D. D., & Albert, M. K. (1999). Contour completion and relative depth: Petter's rule and support ratio. *Psychological Science, 10,* 423–428. (4)

Sirin, S. R., & Fine, M. (2007). Hyphenated selves: Muslim American youth negotiating identities on the fault lines of global conflict. *Applied Developmental Science, 11,* 151–163. (5)

Skeels, H. M. (1966). Adult status of children with contrasting early life experiences. *Monographs of the Society for Research in Child Development, 31,* 1–65. (9)

Skinner, B. F. (1938). *The behavior of organisms.* New York: D. Appleton-Century. (6)

Skinner, B. F. (1990). Can psychology be a science of mind? *American Psychologist, 45,* 1206–1210. (6)

Skinner, E. A., Edge, K., Altman, J., & Sherwood, H. (2003). Searching for the structure of coping: A review and critique of category systems for classifying ways of coping. *Psychological Bulletin, 129,* 216–269. (12)

Skoog, G., & Skoog, I. (1999). A 40-year follow-up of patients with obsessive-compulsive disorder. *Archives of General Psychiatry, 56,* 121–127. (15)

Slabbekoorn, H., & den Boer-Visser, A. (2006). Cities change the songs of birds. *Current Biology, 16,* 2326–2331. (6)

Slavich, G. M., & Cole, S. W. (2013). The emerging field of human social genomics. *Clinical Psychological Science, 1,* 331–348. (3)

Slavich, G. M., & Irwin, M. R. (2014). From stress to inflammation and major depressive disorder: A social signal transduction theory of depression. *Psychological Bulletin, 140,* 774–815. (15)

Slutske, W. S., Moffitt, T. E., Poulton, R., & Caspi, A. (2012). Undercontrolled temperament at age 3 predicts disordered gambling at age 32: A longitudinal study of a complete birth cohort. *Psychological Science, 23,* 510–516. (5)

Smith, D. E., Raswyck, G. E., & Davidson, L. D. (2014). From Hofmann to the Haight Ashbury and into the future: The past and potential of lysergic acid diethylamide. *Journal of Psychoactive Drugs, 46,* 3–10. (3)

Smith, D. M., Langa, K. M., Kabeto, M. U., & Ubel, P. A. (2005). Health, wealth, and happiness. *Psychological Science, 16,* 663–666. (12)

Smith, J. M., Bell, P. A., & Fusco, M. E. (1986). The influence of color and demand characteristics on muscle strength and affective ratings of the environment. *Journal of General Psychology, 113,* 289–297. (2)

Smith, L. T. (1975). The interanimal transfer phenomenon: A review. *Psychological Bulletin, 81,* 1078–1095. (2)

Smith, M. L. (1988). Recall of spatial location by the amnesic patient H. M. *Brain and Cognition, 7,* 178–183. (7)

Smith, M. L., Glass, G. V., & Miller, T. I. (1980). *The benefits of psychotherapy.* Baltimore: Johns Hopkins University Press. (15)

Smith, T. O., Easton, V., Bacon, H., Jerman, E., Armon, K., Poland, F., & Macgregor, A. J. (2014). The relationship between benign joint hypermobility syndrome and psychological distress: A systematic review and meta-analysis. *Rheumatology, 53,* 114–122. (15)

Snook, B., Cullen, R. M., Bennell, C., Taylor, P. J., & Gendreau, P. (2008). The criminal profiling illusion: What's behind the smoke and mirrors? *Criminal Justice and Behavior, 35,* 1257–1276. (14)

Snook, B., Eastwood, J., Gendreau, P., Goggin, C., & Cullen, R. M. (2007). Taking stock of criminal profiling: A narrative review and meta-analysis. *Criminal Justice and Behavior, 34,* 437–453. (14)

Snyder, C. R. (2003). "Me conform? No way": Classroom demonstrations for sensitizing students to their conformity. *Teaching of Psychology, 30,* 59–61. (13)

Snyder, M., Tanke, E. D., & Berscheid, E. (1977). Social perception and interpersonal behavior: On the self-fulfilling nature of social stereotypes. *Journal of Personality and Social Psychology, 35,* 656–666. (13)

Society for Personality Assessment. (2005). The status of the Rorschach in clinical and forensic practice: An official statement by the Board of Trustees of the Society for Personality Assessment. *Journal of Personality Assessment, 85,* 219–237. (14)

Sofer, C., Dotsch, R., Wigboldus, D. H. J., & Todorov, A. (2015). What is typical is good: The influence of face typicality on perceived trustworthiness. *Psychological Science, 26,* 39–47. (13)

Solanto, M. V., Abikoff, H., Sonuga-Barke, E., Schachar, R., Logan, G. D., Wigal, T., . . . Turkel, E. (2001). The ecological validity of delay aversion and response inhibition as measures of impulsivity in AD/HD: A supplement to the NIMH multimodal treatment study of AD/HD. *Journal of Abnormal Child Psychology, 29,* 215–228. (8)

Solms, M. (1997). *The neuropsychology of dreams.* Mahwah, NJ: Erlbaum. (10)

Solms, M. (2000). Dreaming and REM sleep are controlled by different brain mechanisms. *Behavioral and Brain Sciences, 23,* 843–850. (10)

Solomon, D. A., Keller, M. B., Leon, A. C., Mueller, T. I., Shea, T., Warshaw, M.,. . . Endicott, J. (1997). Recovery from major depression. *Archives of General Psychiatry, 54,* 1001–1006. (15)

Solomon, Z., Mikulincer, M., & Flum, H. (1988). Negative life events, coping responses, and combat-related psychopathology: A prospective study. *Journal of Abnormal Psychology, 97,* 302–307. (12)

Solter, A. (2008). A 2-year-old child's memory of hospitalization during early infancy. *Infant and Child Development, 17,* 593–605. (7)

Song, H., & Schwarz, N. (2008). If it's hard to read, it's hard to do. *Psychological Science, 19,* 986–988. (8)

Song, H., & Schwarz, N. (2009). If it's difficult to pronounce, it must be risky. *Psychological Science, 20,* 135–138. (8)

Song, H., Stevens, C. F., & Gage, F. H. (2002). Neural stem cells from adult hippocampus develop essential properties of functional CNS neurons. *Nature Neuroscience, 5,* 438–445. (3)

Song, J.-H., & Bédard, P. (2015). Paradoxical benefits of dual-task contexts for visuomotor memory. *Psychological Science, 26,* 148–158. (7)

Sonnentag, S., Arbeus, H., Mahn, C., & Fritz, C. (2014). Exhaustion and lack of psychological detachment from work during off-job time: Moderator effects of time pressure and leisure experiences. *Journal of Occupational Health Psychology, 19,* 206–216. (11)

Sonuga-Barke, E. J. S. (2004). Causal models of attention-deficit/hyperactivity disorder: From common simple deficits to multiple developmental pathways. *Biological Psychology, 57,* 1231–1238. (8)

Soon, C. S., Brass, M., Heinze, H.-J., & Haynes, J.-D. (2008). Unconscious determinants of free decisions in the human brain. *Nature Neuroscience, 11,* 543–545. (10)

Sorge, R. E., Martin, L. J., Isbester, K. A., Sotocinal, S. G., Rosen, S., Tuttle, A. H., . . . Mogil, J. S. (2014). Olfactory exposure to males, including men, causes stress and related analgesia in rodents. *Nature Methods, 11,* 629–632. (2)

Sowell, E. R., Thompson, P. M., Holmes, C. J., Jernigan, T. L., & Toga, A. W. (1999). *In vivo* evidence for post-adolescent brain maturation in frontal and striatal regions. *Nature Neuroscience, 2,* 859–861. (1)

Spachtholz, P., Kuhbandner, C., & Pekrun, R. (2014). Negative affect improves the quality of memories: Trading capacity for precision in sensory and working memory. *Journal of Experimental Psychology: General, 143,* 1450–1456. (7)

Spanos, N. P. (1987–1988). Past-life hypnotic regression: A critical view. *Skeptical Inquirer, 12,* 174–180. (10)

Sparrow, B., Liu, J., & Wegner, D. M. (2011). Google effects on memory: Cognitive consequences of having information at our fingertips. *Science, 333,* 776-778. (7)

Spear, L. P. (2000). Neurobehavioral changes in adolescence. *Current Directions in Psychological Science, 9,* 111-114. (5)

Spearman, C. (1904). "General intelligence," objectively determined and measured. *American Journal of Psychology, 15,* 201-293. (9)

Spelke, E. S. (2005). Sex differences in intrinsic aptitude for mathematics and science? *American Psychologist, 60,* 950-958. (5)

Spellman, B. (2005, March). Could reality shows become reality experiments? *APS Observer, 18*(3), 34-35. (2)

Sperry, R. W. (1967). Split-brain approach to learning problems. In G. C. Quarton, T. Melnechuk, & F. O. Schmitt (Eds.), *The neurosciences: A study program* (pp. 714-722). New York: Rockefeller University Press. (3)

Spira, A., & Bajos, N. (1993). *Les comportements sexuels en France* [Sexual behaviors in France]. Paris: La documentation Française. (11)

Sproesser, G., Schupp, H. T., & Renner, B. (2014). The bright side of stress-induced eating. *Psychological Science, 25,* 58-65. (11)

Squire, L. R., Haist, F., & Shimamura, A. P. (1989). The neurology of memory: Quantitative assessment of retrograde amnesia in two groups of amnesic patients. *Journal of Neuroscience, 9,* 828-839. (7)

Sripada, C., Kessler, D., & Jonides, J. (2014). Methylphenidate blocks effort-induced depletion of regulatory control in healthy volunteers. *Psychological Science, 25,* 1227-1234. (11)

Sritharan, R., Heilpern, K., Wilbur, C. J., & Gawronski, B. (2010). I think I like you: Spontaneous and deliberate evaluations of potential romantic partners in an online dating context. *European Journal of Social Psychology, 40,* 1062-1077. (13)

Staddon, J. (1993). *Behaviorism*. London: Duckworth. (6)

Staddon, J. E. R. (1999). Theoretical behaviorism. In W. O'Donohue & R. Kitchener (Eds.), *Handbook of behaviorism* (pp. 217-241). San Diego, CA: Academic Press. (6)

Stallen, M., De Dreu, C. K. W., Shalvi, S., Smidts, A., & Sanfey, A. G. (2012). The herding hormone: Oxytocin stimulates in-group conformity. *Psychological Science, 23,* 1288-1292. (3)

Stalnaker, T. A., Roesch, M. R., Franz, T. M., Calu, D. J., Singh, T., & Schoenbaum, G. (2007). Cocaine-induced decision-making deficits are mediated by miscoding in basolateral amygdala. *Nature Neuroscience, 10,* 949-951. (3)

Stanley, D. J., & Spence, J. R. (2014). Expectations for replications: Are yours realistic? *Perspectives on Psychological Science, 9,* 305-318. (2)

Starr, C., & Taggart, R. (1992). *Biology: The unity and diversity of life* (6th ed.). Belmont, CA: Wadsworth. (3)

Ste-Marie, D. M. (1999). Expert-novice differences in gymnastic judging: An information-processing perspective. *Applied Cognitive Psychology, 13,* 269-281. (8)

Steele, C. (2010). *Whistling Vivaldi*. New York: W. W. Norton. (9)

Steele, C. M., & Aronson, J. (1995). Stereotype threat and the intellectual test performance of African Americans. *Journal of Personality and Social Psychology, 69,* 797-811. (9)

Stefansson, H., Meyer-Lindenberg, A., Steinberg, S., Magnusdottir, B., Morgen, K., Arnarsdottir, S., . . . Stefansson, K. (2014). CNVs conferring risk of autism or schizophrenia affect cognition in controls. *Nature, 505,* 361-366. (15)

Stefansson, H., Rujescu, D., Cichon, S., Pietiläinen, O. P. H., Ingason, A., Steinberg, S., . . . Stefansson, K. (2008). Large recurrent microdeletions associated with schizophrenia. *Nature, 455,* 232-236. (15)

Steffens, B. (2007). *Ibn al-Haytham: First scientist.* Greensboro, NC: Morgan Reynolds Publishing. (4)

Steiger, A. E., Allemand, M., Robins, R. W., & Fend, H. A. (2014). Low and decreasing self-esteem during adolescence predict adult depression two decades later. *Journal of Personality and Social Psychology, 106,* 325-338. (14)

Stein, M. B., Hanna, C., Koverola, C., Torchia, M., & McClarty, B. (1997). Structural brain changes in PTSD. *Annals of the New York Academy of Sciences, 821,* 76-82. (12)

Steinberg, L., Graham, S., O'Brien, L., Woolard, J., Cauffman, E., & Banich, M. (2009). Age differences in future orientation and delay discounting. *Child Development, 80,* 28-44. (11)

Steinhardt, P. (2014). Big Bang blunder bursts the multiverse bubble. *Nature, 510,* 9. (2)

Stella, N., Schweitzer, P., & Piomelli, D. (1997). A second endogenous cannabinoid that modulates long-term potentiation. *Nature, 382,* 677-678. (3)

Sterling, P. (2012). Allostasis: A model of predictive regulation. *Physiology & Behavior, 106,* 5-15. (11)

Sternberg, K. J., Baradaran, L. P., Abbott, C. B., Lamb, M. E., & Guterman, E. (2006). Type of violence, age, and gender differences in the effects of family violence on children's behavior problems: A mega-analysis. *Developmental Review, 26,* 89-112. (5)

Sternberg, R. J. (1997). The concept of intelligence and its role in lifelong learning and success. *American Psychologist, 52,* 1030-1037. (9)

Sternberg, R. J., Nokes, C., Geissler, P. W., Prince, R., Okatcha, F., Bundy, D. A., . . . Grigorenko, E. L. (2001). The relationship between academic and practical intelligence: A case study in Kenya. *Intelligence, 29,* 401-418. (9)

Stevens, S. S. (1961). To honor Fechner and repeal his law. *Science, 133,* 80-86. (1)

Stevenson, R. J. (2014). Flavor binding: Its nature and cause. *Psychological Bulletin, 140,* 487-510. (3)

Stewart, B. D., von Hippel, W., & Radvansky, G. A. (2009). Age, race, and implicit prejudice. *Psychological Science, 20,* 164-168. (13)

Stewart, I. (1987). Are mathematicians logical? *Nature, 325,* 386-387. (9)

Stice, E. (2002). Risk and maintenance factors for eating pathology: A meta-analytic review. *Psychological Bulletin, 128,* 825-848. (11)

Stice, E., & Shaw, H. (2004). Eating disorder prevention programs: A meta-analytic review. *Psychological Bulletin, 130,* 206-227. (15)

Stickgold, R., Malia, A., Maguire, D., Roddenberry, D., & O'Connor, M. (2000). Replaying the game: Hypnagogic images in normals and amnesics. *Science, 290,* 350-353. (7)

Stone, A. A., Schwartz, J. E., Broderick, J. E., & Deaton, A. (2010). A snapshot of the age distribution of psychological well-being in the United States. *Proceedings of the National Academy of Sciences, U.S.A., 107,* 9985-9990. (12)

Stone, V. E., Nisenson, L., Eliassen, J. C., & Gazzaniga, M. S. (1996). Left hemisphere representations of emotional facial expressions. *Neuropsychologia, 34,* 23-29. (3)

Storms, M. D. (1973). Videotape and the attribution process: Reversing actors' and observers' points of view. *Journal of Personality and Social Psychology, 27,* 165-175. (13)

Strack, F., Martin, L. L., & Stepper, S. (1988). Inhibiting and facilitating conditions of the human smile: A nonobtrusive test of the facial feedback hypothesis. *Journal of Personality and Social Psychology, 54,* 768-777. (12)

Strange, B. A., Kroes, M. C. W., Roiser, J. P., Yan, G. C. Y., & Dolan, R. J. (2008). Emotion-induced retrograde amnesia is determined by a 5-HTT genetic polymorphism. *Journal of Neuroscience, 28,* 7036-7039. (7)

Strange, D., Garry, M., Bernstein, D. M., & Lindsay, D. S. (2011). Photographs cause false memories for the news. *Acta Psychologica, 136,* 90-94. (7)

Strange, D., Sutherland, R., & Garry, M. (2004). A photographic memory for false autobiographical events: The role of plausibility in children's false memories. *Australian Journal of Psychology, 56*(Suppl. S), 137. (7)

Strauch, I., & Lederbogen, S. (1999). The home dreams and waking fantasies of boys and girls between ages 9 and 15: A longitudinal study. *Dreaming, 9,* 153-161. (10)

Strenze, T. (2007). Intelligence and socioeconomic success: A meta-analytic review of longitudinal research. *Intelligence, 35,* 401-426. (9)

Striemer, C. L., Chapman, C. S., & Goodale, M. A. (2009). "Real-time" obstacle avoidance in the absence of primary visual cortex. *Proceedings of the National Academy of Sciences, 106,* 15996-16001. (3)

Stroebe, W., & Strack, F. (2013). The alleged crisis and the illusion of exact replication. *Perspectives on Psychological Science, 9,* 59-71. (2)

Struckman-Johnson, C., Struckman-Johnson, D., & Anderson, P. B. (2003). Tactics of sexual coercion: When men and women won't take no for an answer. *Journal of Sex Research, 40,* 76-86. (13)

Stulz, N., Lutz, W., Kopta, S. M., Minami, T., & Saunders, S. M. (2013). Dose-effect relationship in routine outpatient psychotherapy: Does treatment duration matter? *Journal of Counseling Psychology, 60,* 593-600. (15)

Stuss, D. T., Alexander, M. P., Palumbo, C. L., Buckle, L., Sayer, L., & Pogue, J. (1994). Organizational strategies of patients with unilateral or bilateral frontal lobe injury in word list learning tasks. *Neuropsychology, 8,* 355-373. (7)

Sullivan, E. V., Deshmukh, A., Desmond, J. E., Mathalon, D. H., Rosenbloom, M. J., Lim, K. O., & Pfefferbaum, A. (2000). Contribution of alcohol abuse to cerebellar volume deficits in men with schizophrenia. *Archives of General Psychiatry, 57,* 894-902. (15)

Sullivan, P. F., Kendler, K. S., & Neale, M. C. (2003). Schizophrenia as a complex trait: Evidence from a meta-analysis of twin studies. *Archives of General Psychiatry, 60,* 1187-1192. (15)

Suls, J., Martin, R., & Wheeler, L. (2002). Social comparisons: Why, with whom, and with what effect? *Current Directions in Psychological Science, 11,* 159-163. (13)

Sun, Q., Townsend, M. K., Okereke, O. I., Rimm, E. B., Hu, F. B., Stampfer, M. J., . . . Grodstein, F. (2011). Alcohol consumption at midlife and successful ageing in women: A prospective cohort analysis in the Nurses' Health Study. *PLoS Medicine, 8,* e1001090. (2)

Sun, Y.-G., Zhao, Z.-Q., Meng, X.-L., Yin, J., Liu, X.-Y., & Chen, Z.-F. (2009). Cellular basis of itch sensation. *Science, 325,* 1531–1534. (4)

Sundet, J. M., Eriksen, W., Borren, I., & Tambs, K. (2010). The Flynn effect in sibships: Investigating the role of age differences between siblings. *Intelligence, 38,* 38–44. (9)

Sundet, J. M., Eriksen, W., & Tambs, K. (2008). Intelligence correlations between brothers decrease with increasing age difference. *Psychological Science, 19,* 843–847. (9)

Surén, P., Roth, C., Bresnahan, M., Haugen, M., Hornig, M., Hirtz, D., . . . Stoltenberg, C. (2013). Association between maternal use of folic acid supplements and risk of autism spectrum disorders in children. *Journal of the American Medical Association, 309,* 570–577. (15)

Suschinsky, K. D., & Lalumière, M. L. (2011). Prepared for anything? An investigation of female genital arousal in response to rape cues. *Psychological Science, 22,* 159–165. (11)

Susskind, J. M., Lee, D. H., Cusi, A., Feiman, R., Grabski, W., & Anderson, A. K. (2008). Expressing fear enhances sensory acquisition. *Nature Neuroscience, 11,* 843–850. (12)

Sutin, A. R., Costa, P. T., Jr., Chan, W., Milaneschi, Y., Eaton, W. W., Zonderman, A. B., . . . Terracciano, A. (2013). I know not to, but I can't help it: Weight gain and changes in impulsivity-related traits. *Psychological Science, 24,* 1323–1328. (11)

Sutin, A. R., Terracciano, A., Milaneschi, Y., An, Y., Ferrucci, L., & Zonderman, A. B. (2013). The effect of birth cohort on well-being: The legacy of economic hard times. *Psychological Science, 24,* 379–385. (11)

Suvisaari, J. M., Haukka, J. K., Tanskanen, A. J., & Lönnqvist, J. K. (1999). Decline in the incidence of schizophrenia in Finnish cohorts born from 1954 to 1965. *Archives of General Psychiatry, 56,* 733–740. (15)

Swan, S. H., Liu, F., Hines, M., Kruse, R. L., Wang, C., Redmon, J. B., . . . Weiss, B. (2010). Prenatal phthalate exposure and reduced masculine play in boys. *International Journal of Andrology, 33,* 259–269. (5)

Swinton, S. S. (1987). *The predictive validity of the restructured GRE with particular attention to older students* (GRE Board Professional Rep. No. 83–25P. ETS Research Rep. 87–22). Princeton, NJ: Educational Testing Service. (9)

Swoboda, H., Amering, M., Windhaber, J., & Katschnig, H. (2003). The long-term course of panic disorder—an 11 year follow-up. *Journal of Anxiety Disorders, 17,* 223–232. (15)

Szymanski, H. V., Simon, J. C., & Gutterman, N. (1983). Recovery from schizophrenic psychosis. *American Journal of Psychiatry, 140,* 335–338. (15)

Taber-Thomas, B. C., Asp, E. W., Koenigs, M., Sutterer, M., Anderson, S. W., & Tranel, D. (2014). Arrested development: early prefrontal lesions impair the maturation of moral judgment. *Brain, 137,* 1254–1261. (12)

Tahiri, M., Mottillo, S., Joseph, L., Pilote, L., & Eisenberg, M. J. (2012). Alternative smoking cessation aids: A meta-analysis of randomized controlled trials. *American Journal of Medicine, 125,* 576–584. (10)

Takano, Y., & Osaka, E. (1999). An unsupported common view: Comparing Japan and the U.S. on individualism/collectivism. *Asian Journal of Social Psychology, 2,* 311–341. (13)

Takeda, Y., Kurita, T., Sakurai, K., Shiga, T., Tamaki, N., & Koyama, T. (2011). Persistent déjà vu associated with hyperperfusion in the entorhinal cortex. *Epilepsy & Behavior, 21,* 196–199. (10)

Takemura, K. (2014). Being different leads to being connected: On the adaptive function of uniqueness in "open" societies. *Journal of Cross-Cultural Psychology, 45,* 1579–1593. (13)

Takizawa, R., Maughan, B., & Arseneault, L. (2014). Adult health outcomes of childhood bullying victimization: Evidence from a five-decade longitudinal British birth cohort. *American Journal of Psychiatry, 171,* 777–784. (15)

Talhelm, T., Zhang, X., Oishi, S., Shimin, C., Duan, D., Lan, X., & Kitayama, S. (2014). Large-scale psychological differences within China explained by rice versus wheat agriculture. *Science, 344,* 603–608. (5)

Tamietto, M., Castelli, L., Vighetti, S., Perozzo, P., Geminiani, G., Weiskrantz, L., . . . de Gelder, B. (2009). Unseen facial and bodily expressions trigger fast emotional reactions. *Proceedings of the National Academy of Sciences, 106,* 17661–17666. (3)

Tanaka, J. W., Curran, T., & Sheinberg, D. L. (2005). The training and transfer of real-world perceptual expertise. *Psychological Science, 16,* 145–151. (8)

Tannenbaum, D., Valasek, C. J., Knowles, E. D., & Ditto, P. H. (2013). Incentivizing wellness in the workplace: Sticks (not carrots) send stigmatizing signals. *Psychological Science, 24,* 1512–1522. (8)

Tarr, M. J., & Gauthier, I. (2000). FFA: A flexible fusiform area for subordinate-level visual processing automatized by experience. *Nature Neuroscience, 3,* 764–769. (3)

Taylor, C. B., Bryson, S., Luce, K. H., Cunning, D., Doyle, A. C., Abascal, L. B., . . . Wilfley, D. E. (2006). Prevention of eating disorders in at-risk college-age women. *Archives of General Psychiatry, 63,* 881–888. (15)

Taylor, J., Roehrig, A. D., Hensler, B. S., Connor, C. M., & Schatschneider, C. (2010). Teacher quality moderates the genetic effects on early reading. *Science, 328,* 512–514. (9)

Teachman, B. A. (2014). No appointment necessary: Treating mental illness outside the therapist's office. *Perspectives on Psychological Science, 9,* 85–87. (15)

Teitelbaum, P., Pellis, V. C., & Pellis, S. M. (1991). Can allied reflexes promote the integration of a robot's behavior? In J. A. Meyer & S. W. Wilson (Eds.), *From animals to animats: Simulation of animal behavior* (pp. 97–104). Cambridge, MA: MIT Press/Bradford Books (10)

ten Brinke, L., Stimson, D., & Carney, D. R. (2014). Some evidence for unconscious lie detection. *Psychological Science, 25,* 1098–1105. (12)

Terlecki, M. A., & Buckner, J. D. (2015). Social anxiety and heavy situational drinking: Coping and conformity motives as multiple mediators. *Addictive Behaviors, 40,* 77–83. (15)

Terr, L. (1988). What happens to early memories of trauma? A study of twenty children under age five at the time of documented traumatic events. *Journal of the American Academy of Child and Adolescent Psychiatry, 27,* 96–104. (7)

Terracciano, A., Abdel-Khalek, A. M., Ádám, N., Admaovová, L., Ahn, C.-k., Ahn, H.-n., . . . McCrae, R. R. (2005). National character does not reflect mean personality levels in 49 cultures. *Science, 310,* 96–100. (14)

Terrace, H. S., Petitto, L. A., Sanders, R. J., & Bever, T. G. (1979). Can an ape create a sentence? *Science, 206,* 891–902. (8)

Terzaghi, M., Sartori, I., Tassi, L., Rustioni, Y., Proserpio, P., Lorusso, G., . . . Nobili, L. (2012). Dissociated local arousal states underlying essential features of non-rapid eye movement arousal parasomnia: An intracerebral stereo-electroencephalographic study. *Journal of Sleep Research, 21,* 502–506. (10)

Testa, M., Livingston, J. A., Vanzile-Tamsen, C., & Frone, M. R. (2003). The role of women's substance use in vulnerability to forcible and incapacitated rape. *Journal of Studies on Alcohol, 64,* 756–764. (13)

Tetlock, P. E. (1992). Good judgment in international politics: Three psychological perspectives. *Political Psychology, 13,* 517–539. (8)

Tett, R. P., & Burnett, D. D. (2003). A personality trait-based interactionist model of job performance. *Journal of Applied Psychology, 88,* 500–517. (11)

Tett, R. P., & Palmer, C. A. (1997). The validity of handwriting elements in relation to self-report personality trait measures. *Personality and Individual Differences, 22,* 11–18. (14)

Thase, M. E. (2014). Combining cognitive therapy and pharmacotherapy for depressive disorders: A review of recent developments. *International Journal of Cognitive Therapy, 7,* 108–121. (15)

Thanickal, T. C., Moore, R. Y., Nienhuis, R., Ramanathan, L., Gulyani, S., Aldrich, M., . . . Siegel, J. M. (2000). Reduced number of hypocretin neurons in human narcolepsy. *Neuron, 27,* 469–474. (10)

"The medals and the damage done." (2004). *Nature, 430,* 604. (2)

Thieman, T. J. (1984). A classroom demonstration of encoding specificity. *Teaching of Psychology, 11,* 101–102. (7)

Thierry, G., & Wu, Y. J. (2007). Brain potentials reveal unconscious translation during foreign-language comprehension. *Proceedings of the National Academy of Sciences, USA, 104,* 12530–12535. (8)

Thomas, B. C., Croft, K. E., & Tranel, D. (2011). Harming kin to save strangers: Further evidence for abnormally utilitarian moral judgments after ventromedial prefrontal damage. *Journal of Cognitive Neuroscience, 23,* 2186–2196. (12)

Thomas, C., Avidan, G., Humphreys, K., Jung, K., Gao, F., & Behrmann, M. (2009). Reduced structural connectivity in ventral visual cortex in congenital prosopagnosia. *Nature Neuroscience, 12,* 29–31. (3)

Thompson, C. R., & Church, R. M. (1980). An explanation of the language of a chimpanzee. *Science, 208,* 313–314. (8)

Thomsen, L., Frankenhuis, W. E., Ingold-Smith, M., & Carey, S. (2011). Big and mighty: Preverbal infants mentally represent social dominance. *Science, 331,* 477–480. (5)

Thoresen, C. J., Kaplan, S. A., Barsky, A. P., Warren, C. R., & de Chermont, K. (2003). The affective underpinnings of job perceptions and attitudes: A meta-analytic review and integration. *Psychological Bulletin, 129,* 914–945. (11)

Thorndike, E. L. (1918). The nature, purposes, and general methods of measurements of educational products. In E. J. Ashbaugh, W. A. Averill, L. P. Ayres, F. W. Ballou, E. Bryner, B. R. Buckingham, et al. (Eds.), *The seventeenth yearbook of the National Society for the Study of Education. Part II: The measurement of educational products* (pp. 16–24). Bloomington, IL: Public School Publishing Company. (9)

Thorndike, E. L. (1970). *Animal intelligence.* Darien, CT: Hafner. (Original work published 1911) (6)

Thurston, R. C., Rewak, M., & Kubzansky, L. D. (2013). An anxious heart: Anxiety and the onset of cardiovascular diseases. *Progress in Cardiovascular Diseases, 55,* 524–537. (12)

Tidwell, N. D., Eastwick, P. W., & Finkel, E. J. (2012). Perceived, not actual, similarity predicts initial attraction in a live romantic context: Evidence from the speed-dating paradigm. *Personal Relationships, 20,* 199–215. (13)

Tierney, K. J., & Connolly, M. K. (2013). A review of the evidence for a biological basis for snake fears in humans. *Psychological Record, 63,* 919–928. (15)

Timberlake, W., & Farmer-Dougan, V. A. (1991). Reinforcement in applied settings: Figuring out ahead of time what will work. *Psychological Bulletin, 110,* 379–391. (6)

Tinbergen, N. (1958). *Curious Naturalists.* New York: Basic Books. (3)

Titchener, E. B. (1910). *A textbook of psychology.* New York: Macmillan. (1)

Todorov, A., & Porter, J. M. (2014). Misleading first impressions: Didfferent for different facial images of the same person. *Psychological Science, 25,* 1404–1417. (13)

Tolman, E. C. (1938). The determinants of behavior at a choice point. *Psychological Review, 45,* 1–41. (1)

Tolstoy, L. (1978). *Tolstoy's letters: Vol. I. 1828–1879.* New York: Charles Scribner's Sons. (Original works written 1828–1879) (5)

Tombaugh, C. W. (1980). *Out of the darkness, the planet Pluto.* Harrisburg, PA: Stackpole. (4)

Torrey, E. F., & Miller, J. (2001). *The invisible plague: The rise of mental illness from 1750 to the present.* New Brunswick, NJ: Rutgers University Press. (15)

Torrey, E. F., & Yolken, R. H. (2005). *Toxoplasma gondii* as a possible cause of schizophrenia. *Biological Psychiatry, 57,* 128S. (15)

Townshend, J. M., & Duka, T. (2003). Mixed emotions: Alcoholics' impairments in the recognition of specific emotional facial expressions. *Neuropsychologia, 41,* 773–782. (12)

Tracey, T. J. G., Wampold, B. E., Lichtenberg, J. W., & Goodyear, R. K. (2014). Expertise in psychotherapy: An elusive goal? *American Psychologist, 69,* 218–229. (8)

Tracy, J. L., & Robins, R. W. (2004). Show your pride: Evidence for a discrete emotion expression. *Psychological Science, 15,* 194–197. (12)

Tracy, J. L., Robins, R. W., & Lagattuta, K. H. (2005). Can children recognize pride? *Emotion, 5,* 251–257. (12)

Trahan, L. H., Stuebing, K. K., Fletcher, J. M., & Hiscock, M. (2014). The Flynn effect: A meta-analysis. *Psychological Bulletin, 140,* 1332–1360. (9)

Trawalter, S., & Richeson, J. A. (2006). Regulatory focus and executive function after interracial interactions. *Journal of Experimental Social Psychology, 42,* 406–412. (13)

Traxler, M. J., Foss, D. J., Podali, R., & Zirnstein, M. (2012). Feeling the past: The absence of experimental evidence for anomalous retroactive influences on text processing. *Memory & Cognition, 40,* 1366–1372. (2)

Treisman, A. (1999). Feature binding, attention and object perception. In G. W. Humphreys, J. Duncan, & A. Treisman (Eds.), *Attention, space and action* (pp. 91–111). Oxford, England: Oxford University Press. (3)

Treisman, A., & Souther, J. (1985). Search asymmetry: A diagnostic for preattentive processing of separable features. *Journal of Experimental Psychology: General, 114,* 285–310. (8)

Trevena, J. A., & Miller, J. (2002). Cortical movement preparation before and after a conscious decision to move. *Consciousness and Cognition, 11,* 162–190. (10)

Trickett, E. J. (2009). Community psychology: Individuals and interventions in community context. *Annual Review of Psychology, 60,* 395–419. (15)

Trimmer, C. G., & Cuddy, L. L. (2008). Emotional intelligence, not music training, predicts recognition of emotional speech prosody. *Emotion, 8,* 838–849. (12)

Trueblood, J. S., Brown, S. D., Heathcote, A., & Busemeyer, J. R. (2013). Not just for consumers: Context effects are fundamental to decision making. *Psychological Science, 24,* 901–908. (8)

Tsankova, N., Renthal, W., Kumar, A., & Nestler, E. J. (2007). Epigenetic regulation in psychiatric disorders. *Nature Reviews Neuroscience, 8,* 355–367. (3)

Tsay, C.-J. (2014). The vision heuristic: Judging music ensembles by sight alone. *Organizational Behavior and Human Decision Processes, 124,* 24–33. (13)

Tsilidis, K. K., Panagioutou, O. A., Sena, E. S., Aretouli, E., Evagelou, E., Howells, D. W., . . . Ioannidis, J. P. A. (2013). Evaluation of excess significance bias in animal studies of neurological diseases. *PLoS Biology, 11,* e1001609. (2)

Tsuji, S., & Cristia, A. (2014). Perceptual attunement in vowels: A meta-analysis. *Developmental Psychobiology, 56,* 179–191. (5)

Tuerk, P. W. (2005). Research in the high-stakes era. *Psychological Science, 16,* 419–425. (9)

Tugade, M. M., & Fredrickson, B. L. (2004). Resilient individuals use positive emotions to bounce back from negative emotional experiences. *Journal of Personality and Social Psychology, 86,* 320–333. (12)

Tuiten, A., Van Honk, J., Koppeschaar, H., Bernaards, C., Thijssen, J., & Verbaten, R. (2000). Time course of effects of testosterone administration on sexual arousal in women. *Archives of General Psychiatry, 57,* 149–153. (11)

Tulving, E. (1989). Remembering and knowing the past. *American Scientist, 77,* 361–367. (7)

Tulving, E., & Thomson, D. M. (1973). Encoding specificity and retrieval processes in episodic memory. *Psychological Review, 80,* 352–373. (7)

Tuntiya, N. (2007). Free-air treatment for mental patients: The deinstitutionalization debate of the nineteenth century. *Sociological Perspectives, 50,* 469–488. (15)

Tups, A. (2009). Physiological models of leptin resistance. *Journal of Neuroendocrinology, 21,* 961–971. (11)

Turner, R. S., & Anderson, M. E. (2005). Context-dependent modulation of movement-related discharge in the primate globus pallidus. *Journal of Neuroscience, 25,* 2965–2976. (10)

Tversky, A., & Kahneman, D. (1981). The framing of decisions and the psychology of choice. *Science, 211,* 453–458. (8)

Tversky, A., & Kahneman, D. (1983). Extensional versus intuitive reasoning: The conjunctional fallacy in probability judgment. *Psychological Review, 90,* 293–315. (8)

Twenge, J. M. (2000). The age of anxiety? Birth cohort change in anxiety and neuroticism, 1952–1993. *Journal of Personality and Social Psychology, 79,* 1007–1021. (14)

Twenge, J. M. (2006). *Generation me.* New York: Free Press. (5)

Twenge, J. M., & Campbell, W. K. (2008). Increases in positive self-views among high-school students. *Psychological Science, 19,* 1082–1086. (5)

Twenge, J. M., & Kasser, T. (2013). Generational changes in materialism and work centrality, 1976–2007: Associations with temporal changes in societal insecurity and materialistic role modeling. *Personality and Social Psychology Bulletin, 39,* 883–897. (14)

Twenge, J. M., Konrath, S., Foster, J. D., Campbell, W. K., & Bushman, B. J. (2008). Egos inflating over time: A cross-temporal meta-analysis of the narcissistic personality inventory. *Journal of Personality, 76,* 875–901. (14)

U.S. Department of Labor. (2008). *Occupational outlook handbook* (2008–2009 ed.). Retrieved November 9, 2008, from www.bls.gov. (1)

Uchino, B. N., Cacioppo, J. T., & Kiecolt-Glaser, J. K. (1996). The relationship between social support and physiological processes: A review with emphasis on underlying mechanisms and implications for health. *Psychological Bulletin, 119,* 488–531. (12)

Udolf, R. (1981). *Handbook of hypnosis for professionals.* New York: Van Nostrand Reinhold. (10)

Udry, J. R., & Chantala, K. (2006). Masculinity-femininity predicts sexual orientation in men but not in women. *Journal of Biosocial Science, 38,* 797–809. (11)

Ulrich, R. E., Stachnik, T. J., & Stainton, N. R. (1963). Student acceptance of generalized personality interpretations. *Psychological Reports, 13,* 831–834. (14)

Ulrich, R. S. (1984). View through a window may influence recovery from surgery. *Science, 224,* 420–421. (4)

Umanath, S., & Marsh, E. J. (2014). Understanding how prior knowledge influences memory in older adults. *Perspectives on Psychological Science, 9,* 408–426. (5)

Vaillant, G. E., & Milofsky, E. S. (1982). The etiology of alcoholism: A prospective viewpoint. *American Psychologist, 37,* 494–503. (15)

Valla, J. M., & Ceci, S. J. (2014). Breadth-based models of women's underrepresentation in STEM fields: An integrative commentary on Schmidt (2011) and Nye et al. (2012). *Perspectives on Psychological Science, 9,* 219–224. (5)

Valli, K., Strandholm, T., Sillanmäki, L., & Revonsuo, A. (2008). Dreams are more negative than real life: Implications for the function of dreaming. *Cognition and Emotion, 22,* 833–861. (10)

Vallines, I., & Greenlee, M. W. (2006). Saccadic suppression of retinotopically localized blood oxygen level-dependent responses in human primary visual area V1. *Journal of Neuroscience, 26,* 5965–5969. (8)

van Anders, S. M., Hamilton, L. D., & Watson, N. V. (2007). Multiple partners are associated with higher testosterone in North American men and women. *Hormones and Behavior, 51,* 454–459. (11)

van Anders, S. M., & Watson, N. V. (2006). Relationship status and testosterone in North American heterosexual and non-heterosexual men and women: Cross-sectional and longitudinal data. *Psychoneuroendocrinology, 31,* 715–723. (11)

Van Cantfort, T. E., Gardner, B. T., & Gardner, R. A. (1989). Developmental trends in replies to Wh-questions by children and chimpanzees. In R. A. Gardner, B. T. Gardner, & T. E. Van Cantfort (Eds.), *Teaching sign language to chimpanzees* (pp. 198–239). Albany: State University of New York Press. (8)

van den Hout, M., & Kindt, M. (2003). Repeated checking causes memory distrust. *Behaviour Research and Therapy, 41,* 301–316. (15)

van der Wal, R. C., & van Dillen, L. F. (2013). Leaving a flat taste in your mouth: Task load reduces taste perception. *Psychological Science, 24,* 1277–1284. (11)

Van der Werf, Y. D., Altena, E., Schoonheim, M. M., Sanz-Arigita, E. J., Vis, J. C., De Rijke, W., & Van Someren, E. J. (2009). Sleep benefits subsequent hippocampal functioning. *Nature Neuroscience, 12,* 122–123. (10)

Van Der Zee, K. I., Huet, R. C. G., Cazemier, C., & Evers, K. (2002). The influence of the premedication consult and preparatory information about anesthesia on anxiety among patients undergoing cardiac surgery. *Anxiety, Stress, and Coping, 15,* 123–133. (12)

van der Zwan, Y. G., Janssen, E. H. C. C., Callens, N., Wolffenbuttell, K. P., Cohen-Kettenis, P. T., van den Berg, M., . . . Beerendonk, C. (2013). Severity of virilization is associated with cosmetic appearance and sexual function in women with congenital adrenal hyperplasia: A cross-sectional study. *Journal of Sexual Medicine, 10,* 866–875. (11)

van Duijl, M., Nijenhuis, E., Komproe, I. H., Gernaat, H. B. P. E., & de Jong, J. T. (2010). Dissociative symptoms and reported trauma among patients with spirit possession and matched healthy controls in Uganda. *Cultural Medicine and Psychiatry, 34,* 380–400. (15)

Vanhove, J. (2013). The critical period hypothesis in second language acquisition: A statistical critique and reanalysis. *PLoS One, 8,* e69172. (8)

Van Houtem, C. M. H. H., Laine, M. L., Boomsma, D. I., Ligthart, L., van Wijk, A. J., & De Jongh, A. (2013). A review and meta-analysis of the heritability of specific phobia subtypes and corresponding fears. *Journal of Anxiety Disorders, 27,* 379–388. (15)

Van Ijzendoorn, M. H., & Bakermans-Kranenburg, M. J. (2012). A sniff of trust: Meta-analysis of the effects of intranasal oxytocin administration on face recognition, trust to in-group, and trust to out-group. *Psychoneuroendocrinology, 37,* 438–443. (3)

van IJzendoorn, M. H., Juffer, F., & Poelhuis, C. W. K. (2005). Adoption and cognitive development: A meta-analytic comparison of adopted and nonadopted children's IQ and school performance. *Psychological Bulletin, 131,* 301–316. (9)

Vandello, J. A., Bosson, J. K., Cohen, D., Burnaford, R. M., & Weaver, J. R. (2008). Precarious manhood. *Journal of Personality and Social Psychology, 95,* 1325–1339. (5)

Vartanian, L. R., Herman, C. P., & Wansink, B. (2008). Are we aware of the external factors that influence our food intake? *Health Psychology, 27,* 533–538. (11)

Vasey, P. L., & VanderLaan, D. P. (2010). An adaptive cognitive dissociation between willingness to help kin and nonkin in Samoan *Fa'afafine. Psychological Science, 21,* 292–297. (11)

Vasterling, J., Duke, L. M., Brailey, K., Constans, J. I., Allain, A. N., & Sutker, P. B. (2002). Attention, learning, and memory performances and intellectual resources in Vietnam veterans: PTSD and no disorder comparisons. *Neuropsychology, 16,* 5–14. (9)

Vazire, S., & Carlson, E. N. (2011). Others sometimes know us better than we know ourselves. *Current Directions in Psychological Science, 20,* 104–108. (14)

Vega, V., & Malamuth, N. M. (2007). Predicting sexual aggression: The role of pornography in the context of general and specific risk factors. *Aggressive Behavior, 33,* 104–117. (13)

Verplanken, B., & Faes, S. (1999). Good intentions, bad habits, and effects of forming implementation intentions on healthy eating. *European Journal of Social Psychology, 29,* 591–604. (11)

Verrey, F., & Beron, J. (1996). Activation and supply of channels and pumps by aldosterone. *News in Physiological Sciences, 11,* 126–133. (1)

Vetencourt, J. F. M., Sale, A., Viegi, A., Baroncelli, L., DePasquale, R., . . . Maffei, L. (2008). The antidepressant fluoxetine restores plasticity in the adult visual cortex. *Science, 320,* 385–388. (15)

Vieland, V. J., Walters, K. A., Lehner, T., Azaro, M., Tobin, K., Huang, Y., & Brzustowicz, L. M. (2014). Revisiting schizophrenia linkage data in the NIM repository: Reanalysis of regularized data across multiple studies. *American Journal of Psychiatry, 171,* 350–359. (15)

Viglione, D. J., & Taylor, N. (2003). Empirical support for interrater reliability of Rorschach Comprehensive System scoring. *Journal of Clinical Psychology, 59,* 111–121. (14)

Viken, R. J., Rose, R. J., Kaprio, J., & Koskenvuo, M. (1994). A developmental genetic analysis of adult personality: Extraversion and neuroticism from 18 to 59 years of age. *Journal of Personality and Social Psychology, 66,* 722–730. (5, 14)

Vinci, C., Copeland, A. L., & Carrigan, M. H. (2011). Exposure to negative affect cues and urge to smoke. *Experimental and Clinical Psychopharmacology, 20,* 47–55. (15)

Visser, B. A., Ashton, M. C., & Vernon, P. A. (2006). Beyond *g:* Putting multiple intelligences theory to the test. *Intelligence, 34,* 487–502. (9)

Vohs, K. D., & Schooler, J. W. (2008). The value of believing in free will: Encouraging a belief in determinism increases cheating. *Psychological Science, 19,* 49–54. (1)

Voineagu, I., Wang, X., Johnston, P., Lowe, J. K., Tian, Y., . . . Geschwind, D. H. (2011). Transcriptomic analysis of autistic brain reveals convergent molecular pathology. *Nature, 474,* 380–384. (15)

Vokey, J. R., & Read, J. D. (1985). Subliminal messages: Between the devil and the media. *American Psychologist, 40,* 1231–1239. (4)

Volkow, N. D., Wang, G.-J., & Fowler, J. S. (1997). Imaging studies of cocaine in the human brain and studies of the cocaine addict. *Annals of the New York Academy of Sciences, 820,* 41–55. (3)

Volkow, N. D., Wang, G.-J., Fowler, J., Gatley, S. J., Logan, J., Ding, Y.-S., . . . Pappas. N. (1998). Dopamine transporter occupancies in the human brain induced by therapeutic doses of oral methylphenidate. *American Journal of Psychiatry, 155,* 1325–1331. (3)

Volkow, N. D., Wang, G.-J., Telang, F., Fowler, J. S., Logan, J., Childress, A.-R., . . . Wong, C. (2006). Cocaine cues and dopamine in dorsal striatum: Mechanism of craving in cocaine addiction. *Journal of Neuroscience, 26,* 6583–6588. (15)

von Hippel, W., Brener, L., & von Hippel, C. (2008). Implicit prejudice toward injecting drug users predicts intentions to change jobs among drug and alcohol nurses. *Psychological Science, 19,* 7–11. (14)

von Stumm, S., Hell, B., & Chamorro-Premuzic, T. (2011). The hungry mind: Intellectual curiosity is the third pillar of academic performance. *Perspectives on Psychological Science, 6,* 574–588. (9)

Voss, U., Holzmann, R., Hobson, A., Paulus, W., Koppehele-Gossel, J., Klimke, A., & Nitsche, M. A. (2014). Induction of self-awareness in dreams through frontal low current stimulation of gamma activity. *Nature Neuroscience, 17,* 810–812. (10)

Vrij, A., Granhag, P. A., & Porter, S. (2010). Pitfalls and opportunities in nonverbal and verbal lie detection. *Psychological Science in the Public Interest, 11,* 89–121. (12)

Vroom, V. H., & Jago, A. G. (2007). The role of the situation in leadership. *American Psychologist, 62,* 17–24. (11)

Vrshek-Schallhorn, S., Mineka, S., Zinbarg, R. E., Craske, M. G., Griffith, J. W., Sutton, J., . . . Adam, E. K. (2014). Refining the candidate environment: Interpersonal stress, the serotonin transporter polymorphism, and gene-environment interactions in major depression. *Clinical Psychological Science, 2,* 235–248. (15)

Vyazovskiy, V. V., Cirelli, C., Pfister-Genskow, M., Faraguna, U., & Tononi, G. (2008). Molecular and electrophysiological evidence for net synaptic potentiation in wake and depression in sleep. *Nature Neuroscience, 11,* 200–208. (10)

Vyazovskiy, V. V., Olcese, U., Hanlon, E. C., Nir, Y., Cirelli, C., . . . Tononi, G. (2011). Local sleep in awake rats. *Nature, 472,* 443–447. (10)

Vygotsky, L. S. (1978). *Mind in society.* Cambridge, MA: Harvard University Press. (5)

Waalen, J. (2014). The genetics of human obesity. *Translational Research, 164,* 293–301. (11)

Wachholtz, A. B., & Pargament, K. I. (2008). Migraines and meditation: Does spirituality matter? *Journal of Behavioral Medicine, 31,* 351–366. (10)

Wade, K. A., Garry, M., Read, J. D., & Lindsay, D. S. (2002). A picture is worth a thousand lies: Using false photographs to create false childhood memories. *Psychonomic Bulletin and Review, 9,* 597–603. (7)

Wade, N. (2009). *The faith instinct.* New York: Penguin. (14)

Wager, T. D., & Atlas, L. Y. (2013). How is pain influenced by cognition? Neuroimaging weighs in. *Perspectives on Psychological Science, 8,* 91–97. (3)

Wager, T. D., Scott, D. J., & Zubieta, J.-K. (2007). Placebo effects on human μ-opioid activity during pain. *Proceedings of the National*

Academy of Sciences (U.S.A.), 104, 11056–11061. (4)

Wagner, A. D., Desmond, J. E., Demb, J. B., Glover, G. H., & Gabrieli, J. D. E. (1997). Semantic repetition priming for verbal and pictorial knowledge: A functional MRI study of left inferior prefrontal cortex. Journal of Cognitive Neuroscience, 9, 714–726. (3)

Wai, J., & Putallaz, M. (2011). The Flynn effect puzzle: A 30-year examination from the right tail of the ability distribution provides some missing pieces. Intelligence, 39, 443–455. (9)

Wainright, J. L., Russell, S. T., & Patterson, C. J. (2004). Psychosocial adjustment, school outcomes, and romantic relationships of adolescents with same-sex parents. Child Development, 75, 1886–1898. (5)

Wald, G. (1968). Molecular basis of visual excitation. Science, 162, 230–239. (4)

Waller, N. G., Kojetin, B. A., Bouchard, T. J., Jr., Lykken, D. T., & Tellegen, A. (1990). Genetic and environmental influences on religious interests, attitudes, and values: A study of twins reared apart and together. Psychological Science, 1, 138–142. (3)

Walsh, R., & Shapiro, S. L. (2006). The meeting of meditative disciplines and Western psychology. American Psychologist, 61, 227–239. (10)

Walster, E., Aronson, E., Abrahams, D., & Rottman, L. (1966). Importance of physical attractiveness in dating behavior. Journal of Personality and Social Psychology, 4, 508–516. (13)

Walters, E. T. (2009). Chronic pain, memory, and injury: Evolutionary clues from snail and rat nociceptors. International Journal of Comparative Psychology, 22, 127–140. (4)

Walton, G. M., & Spencer, S. J. (2009). Latent ability. Psychological Science, 20, 1132–1139. (9)

Wampold, B. E., Mondin, G. W., Moody, M., Stich, F., Benson, K., & Ahn, H. (1997). A meta-analysis of outcome studies comparing bona fide psychotherapies: Empirically, "All must have prizes." Psychological Bulletin, 122, 203–215. (15)

Wandersman, A., & Florin, P. (2003). Community interventions and effective prevention. American Psychologist, 58, 441–448. (15)

Wang, C., Jiang, Y., Ma, J., Wu, H., Wacker, D., Katritch, V., . . . Xu, H. E. (2013). Structural basis for molecular recognition at serotonin receptors. Science, 340, 610–614. (3)

Wang, D., Waldman, D. A., & Zhang, Z. (2014). A meta-analysis of shared leadership and team effectiveness. Journal of Applied Psychology, 99, 181–198. (11)

Wang, M.-T., Eccles, J. S., & Kenny, S. (2013). Not lack of ability but more choice: Individual and gender differences in choice of careers in science, technology, engineering, and mathematics. Psychological Science, 24, 770–775. (5)

Wang, X., Jiao, Y., Tang, T., Wang, H., & Lu, Z. (2013). Altered regional homogeneity patterns in adults with attention-deficit hyperactivity disorder. European Journal of Radiology, 82, 1552–1557. (8)

Wansink, B., & Kim, J. (2005). Bad popcorn in big buckets: Portion size can influence intake as much as taste. Journal of Nutrition Education and Behavior, 37, 242–245. (11)

Wansink, B., Payne, C. R., & North, J. (2007). Fine as North Dakota wine: Sensory expectations and the intake of companion foods. Physiology & Behavior, 90, 712–716. (11)

Wansink, B., & van Ittersum, K. (2003). Bottoms up! The influence of elongation on pouring and consumption volume. Journal of Consumer Research, 30, 455–463. (5)

Wansink, B., van Ittersum, K., & Painter, J. E. (2006). Ice cream illusions—Bowls, spoons, and self-served portion sizes. American Journal of Preventive Medicine, 31, 240–243. (11)

Warren, R. M. (1970). Perceptual restoration of missing speech sounds. Science, 167, 392–393. (4, 8)

Warren, R. M. (1999). Auditory perception. Cambridge, England: Cambridge University Press. (4)

Washington, E. (2006). Female socialization: How daughters affect their legislator fathers' voting on women's issues (Working Paper No. 11924). Cambridge, MA: National Bureau of Economic Research. (2)

Wason, P. C. (1960). On the failure to eliminate hypotheses in a conceptual task. Quarterly Journal of Experimental Psychology, 12, 129–140. (8)

Waterman, A. S. (2013). The humanistic psychology-positive psychology divide. American Psychologist, 68, 124–133. (14)

Waters, E., Merrick, S., Treboux, D., Crowell, J., & Albersheim, L. (2000). Attachment security in infancy and early adulthood: A twenty-year longitudinal study. Child Development, 71, 684–689. (5)

Watrous, A. J., Tandon, N., Conner, C. R., Pieters, T., & Ekstrom, A. D. (2013). Frequency-specific network connectivity increases underlie accurate spatiotemporal memory retrieval. Nature Neuroscience, 16, 349–356. (7)

Watson, D., & Clark, L. A. (2006). Clinical diagnosis at the crossroads. Clinical Psychology, 13, 210–215. (15)

Watson, D., Wiese, D., Vaidya, J., & Tellegen, A. (1999). The two general activation systems of affect: Structural findings, evolutionary considerations, and psychobiological evidence. Journal of Personality and Social Psychology, 76, 820–838. (12)

Watson, J. B. (1913). Psychology as the behaviorist views it. Psychological Review, 20, 158–177. (1)

Watson, J. B. (1919). Psychology from the standpoint of a behaviorist. Philadelphia: Lippincott. (1)

Watson, J. B. (1925). Behaviorism. New York: W. W. Norton. (1, 6)

Watson, J. B., & Rayner, R. (1920). Conditioned emotional reactions. Journal of Experimental Psychology, 3, 1–14. (1)

Watson, J. M., Balota, D. A., & Roediger, H. L., III (2003). Creating false memories with hybrid lists of semantic and phonological associates: Over-additive false memories produced by converging associative networks. Journal of Memory and Language, 49, 95–118. (7)

Webster, A. A., & Carter, M. (2013). A descriptive examination of the types of relationships formed between children with developmental disability and their closest peers in inclusive school settings. Journal of Intellectual & Developmental Disability, 38, 1–11. (9)

Wegner, D. M. (2002). The illusion of conscious will. Cambridge, MA: MIT Press. (1, 10)

Wegner, D. M. (2009). How to think, say, or do precisely the worst thing for any occasion. Science, 325, 48–50. (13)

Wei, Y., Yang, C.-R., Wei, Y.-P., Zhao, Z.-A., Hou, Y., Schatten, H., & Sun, Q.-Y. (2014). Paternally induced transgenerational inheritance of susceptibility to diabetes in mammals.

Proceedings of the National Academy of Sciences, 111, 1873–1878. (3)

Weinberger, D. R. (1996). On the plausibility of "the neurodevelopmental hypothesis" of schizophrenia. Neuropsychopharmacology, 14, 1S–11S. (15)

Weinberger, D. R. (1999). Cell biology of the hippocampal formation in schizophrenia. Biological Psychiatry, 45, 395–402. (15)

Weiskrantz, L., Warrington, E. K., Sanders, M. D., & Marshall, J. (1974). Visual capacity in the hemianopic field following a restricted occipital ablation. Brain, 97, 709–728. (3)

Weissman, M. M., Leaf, P. J., & Bruce, M. L. (1987). Single parent women: A community study. Social Psychiatry, 22, 29–36. (5)

Weissman, M. M., Warner, V., Wickramaratne, P., Moreau, D., & Olfson, M. (1997). Offspring of depressed parents. Archives of General Psychiatry, 54, 932–940. (15)

Welchman, A. E., Stanley, J., Schomers, M. R., Miall, R. C., & Bülthoff, H. H. (2010). The quick and the dead: When reaction beats intention. Proceedings of the Royal Society B, 277, 1667–1674. (10)

Wellings, K., Field, J., Johnson, A., & Wadsworth, J. (1994). Sexual behavior in Britain: The national survey of sexual attitudes and lifestyles. New York: Penguin. (11)

Wellman, H. M., Cross, D., & Watson, J. (2001). Meta-analysis of theory-of-mind development: The truth about false beliefs. Child Development, 72, 655–684. (5)

Wells, G. L., Malpass, R. S., Lindsay, R. C. L., Fisher, R. P., Turtle, J. W., & Fulero, S. M. (2000). From the lab to the police station. American Psychologist, 55, 581–598. (7)

Wells, G. L., Memon, A., & Penrod, S. D. (2006). Eyewitness evidence: Improving its probative value. Psychological Science in the Public Interest, 7, 45–75. (7)

Wells, G. L., Olson, E. A., & Charman, S. D. (2003). Distorted retrospective eyewitness reports as functions of feedback and delay. Journal of Experimental Psychology: General, 9, 42–52. (7)

Werker, J. F., & Tees, R. C. (2005). Speech perception as a window for understanding plasticity and commitment in language systems of the brain. Developmental Psychobiology, 46, 233–251. (8)

Wethington, E., Kessler, R. C., & Pixley, J. E. (2004). Turning points in adulthood. In O. G. Brim, C. D. Ryff, & R. C. Kessler (Eds.), How healthy are we? (pp. 586–613). Chicago: University of Chicago Press. (5)

Wheeler, D. D. (1970). Processes in word recognition. Cognitive Psychology, 1, 59–85. (8)

Wheeler, M. E., & Treisman, A. M. (2002). Binding in short-term visual memory. Journal of Experimental Psychology: General, 131, 48–64. (3)

White, M. P., Alcock, I., Wheeler, B. W., & Depledge, M. H. (2013). Would you be happier living in a greener urban area? A fixed-effects analysis of panel data. Psychological Science, 24, 920–928. (12)

White, S. J., Johnson, R. L., Liversedge, S. P., & Rayner, K. (2008). Eye movements when reading transposed text: The importance of word-beginning letters. Journal of Experimental Psychology: Human Perception and Performance, 34, 1261–1276. (8)

White, S., O'Reilly, H., & Frith, U. (2009). Big heads, small details and autism. Neuropsychologia, 47, 1274–1281. (15)

Wichman, A. L., Rodgers, J. L., & MacCallum, R. C. (2006). A multilevel approach to the relationship between birth order and intelligence. *Personality and Social Psychology Bulletin, 32,* 117–127. (5)

Wicklund, R. A., & Brehm, J. W. (1976). *Perspectives on cognitive dissonance.* Hillsdale, NJ: Erlbaum. (13)

Widen, S. C., & Naab, P. (2012). Can an anger face also be scared? Malleability of facial expressions. *Emotion, 12,* 919–925. (12)

Wilde, A., Chan, H.-N., Rahman, B., Meiser, B., Mitchell, P. B., Schofield, P. R., & Green, M. J. (2014). A meta-analysis of the risk of major affective disorder in relatives of individuals affected by major depressive disorder or bipolar disorder. *Journal of Affective Disorders, 158,* 37–47. (15)

Wilensky, A. E., Schafe, G. E., Kristensen, M. P., & LeDoux, J. E. (2006). Rethinking the fear circuit. *Journal of Neuroscience, 26,* 12387–12396. (12)

Wilkins, L., & Richter, C. P. (1940). A great craving for salt by a child with corticoadrenal insufficiency. *Journal of the American Medical Association, 114,* 866–868. (1)

Wilkins, V. M., & Wenger, J. B. (2014). Belief in a just world and attitudes toward affirmative action. *Policy Studies Journal, 42,* 325–343. (14)

Williams, C. L., Barnett, A. M., & Meck, W. H. (1990). Organizational effects of early gonadal secretions on sexual differentiation in spatial memory. *Behavioral Neuroscience, 104,* 84–97. (5)

Williams, K. D., & Karau, S. J. (1991). Social loafing and social compensation: The effects of expectations of co-worker performance. *Journal of Personality and Social Psychology, 61,* 570–581. (13)

Williams, L. M. (1994). Recall of childhood trauma: A prospective study of women's memories of child sexual abuse. *Journal of Consulting and Clinical Psychology, 61,* 1167–1176. (7)

Williams, R. L. (2013). Overview of the Flynn effect. *Intelligence, 41,* 753–764. (9)

Williams, R. W., & Herrup, K. (1988). The control of neuron number. *Annual Review of Neuroscience, 11,* 423–453. (3)

Williamson, D. A., Ravussin, E., Wong, M.-L., Wagner, A., DiPaoli, A., Caglayan, S., . . . Licinio, J. (2005). Microanalysis of eating behavior of three leptin deficient adults treated with leptin therapy. *Appetite, 45,* 75–80. (11)

Willuhn, I., Burgeno, L. M., Groblewski, P. A., & Phillips, P. E. M. (2014). Excessive cocaine use results from decreased phasic dopamine signaling in the striatum. *Nature Neuroscience, 17,* 704–709. (15)

Wilson, T. D., Reinhard, D. A., Westgate, E. C., Gilbert, D. T., Ellerbeck, N., Hahn, C., . . . Shaked, A. (2014). Just think: The challenges of the disengaged mind. *Science, 345,* 75–77. (11)

Wilson, J. R., & the editors of *Life.* (1964). *The mind.* New York: Time. (4)

Wilson, R. I., & Nicoll, R. A. (2002). Endocannabinoid signaling in the brain. *Science, 296,* 678–682. (3)

Wilson-Mendenhall, C. D., Barrett, L. F., & Barsalou, L. W. (2013). Neural evidence that human emotions share core affective properties. *Psychological Science, 24,* 947–956. (12)

Wimmer, H., & Perner, J. (1983). Beliefs about beliefs: Representation and constraining function of wrong beliefs in young children's understanding of deception. *Cognition, 13,* 103–128. (5)

Winer, G. A., & Cottrell, J. E. (1996). Does anything leave the eye when we see? Extramission beliefs of children and adults. *Current Directions in Psychological Science, 5,* 137–142. (4)

Winer, G. A., Cottrell, J. E., Gregg, V., Fournier, J. S., & Bica, L. A. (2002). Fundamentally misunderstanding visual perception: Adults' belief in visual emissions. *American Psychologist, 57,* 417–424. (4)

Winner, E. (1986, August). Where pelicans kiss seals. *Psychology Today,* 24–35. (5)

Winner, E. (2000). Giftedness: Current theory and research. *Current Directions in Psychological Science, 9,* 153–156. (9)

Winocur, G., & Hasher, L. (1999). Aging and time-of-day effects on cognition in rats. *Behavioral Neuroscience, 113,* 991–997. (10)

Winocur, G., & Hasher, L. (2004). Age and time-of-day effects on learning and memory in a non-matching-to-sample test. *Neurobiology of Aging, 25,* 1107–1115. (10)

Winocur, G., Moscovitch, M., & Sekeres, M. (2007). Memory consolidation or transformation: Context manipulation and hippocampal representations of memory. *Nature Neuroscience, 10,* 555–557. (7)

Wirz-Justice, A. (1998). Beginning to see the light. *Archives of General Psychiatry, 55,* 861–862. (15)

Witkiewitz, K., & Marlatt, G. A. (2004). Relapse prevention for alcohol and drug problems: That was Zen, this is Tao. *American Psychologist, 59,* 224–235. (15)

Witt, J. K., Linkenauger, S. A., & Proffitt, D. R. (2012). Get me out of this slump! Visual illusions improve sports performance. *Psychological Science, 23,* 397–399. (4)

Witthoft, N., & Winawer, J. (2013). Learning, memory, and synesthesia. *Psychological Science, 24,* 258–263. (4)

Wojcik, S. P., Hovasapian, A., Graham, J., Motyl, M., & Ditto, P. H. (2015). Conservatives report, but liberals display, greater happiness. *Science, 347,* 1243–1246. (2)

Wolfe, J. M., Horowitz, T. S., & Kenner, N. M. (2005). Rare items often missed in visual searches. *Nature, 435,* 439–440. (4)

Wolkin, A., Rusinek, H., Vaid, G., Arena, L., Lafargue, T., Sanfilipo, M., . . . Rotrosen, J. (1998). Structural magnetic resonance image averaging in schizophrenia. *American Journal of Psychiatry, 155,* 1064–1073. (15)

Wolman, B. B. (1989). *Dictionary of behavioral science* (2nd ed.). San Diego, CA: Academic Press. (9)

Wolpe, J. (1961). The systematic desensitization treatment of neuroses. *Journal of Nervous and Mental Disease, 132,* 189–203. (15)

Wolraich, M. L., Lindgren, S. D., Stumbo, P. J., Stegink, L. D., Appelbaum, M. I., & Kiritsy, M. C. (1994). Effects of diets high in sucrose or aspartame on the behavior and cognitive performance of children. *New England Journal of Medicine, 330,* 301–307. (2)

Wood, J. M., Nezworski, T., Lilienfeld, S. O., & Garb, H. N. (2003). *What's wrong with the Rorschach?* San Francisco: Jossey-Bass. (14)

Wood, S., Hanoch, Y., Barnes, A., Liu, P.-J., Cummings, J., Bhattacharya, C., & Rice, T. (2011). Numeracy and Medicare Part D: The importance of choice and literacy for numbers in optimizing decision making for Medicare's prescription drug program. *Psychology & Aging, 26,* 295–307. (8)

Wood, W., & Eagly, A. H. (2002). A cross-cultural model of the behavior of women and men: Implications for the origins of sex differences. *Psychological Bulletin, 128,* 699–727. (5)

Wood, W., Lundgren, S., Ouellette, J. A., Busceme, S., & Blackstone, T. (1994). Minority influence: A meta-analytic review of social influence processes. *Psychological Bulletin, 115,* 323–345. (13)

Wood, W., & Quinn, J. M. (2003). Forewarned and forearmed? Two meta-analytic syntheses of forewarnings of influence appeals. *Psychological Bulletin, 129,* 119–138. (13)

Wooding, S., Kim, U., Bamshad, M. J., Larsen, J., Jorde, L. B., & Drayna, D. (2004). Natural selection and molecular evolution in *PTC,* a bitter-taste receptor gene. *American Journal of Human Genetics, 74,* 637–646. (1)

Woods, J. H., & Winger, G. (1997). Abuse liability of flunitrazepam. *Journal of Clinical Psychopharmacology, 17*(Suppl. 3), S1–S57. (3)

Wooley, A. W., Chabris, C. F., Pentland, A., Hashmi, N., & Malone, T. W. (2010). Evidence for a collective intelligence factor in the performance of human groups. *Science, 330,* 686–688. (13)

Worthington, E. L., Jr., Kurusu, T. A., McCullough, M. E., & Sandage, S. J. (1996). Empirical research on religion and psychotherapeutic processes and outcomes: A 10-year review and research prospectus. *Psychological Bulletin, 119,* 448–487. (15)

Woychyshyn, C. A., McElheran, W. G., & Romney, D. M. (1992). MMPI validity measures: A comparative study of original with alternative indices. *Journal of Personality Assessment, 58,* 138–148. (14)

Wright, D. B., & Skagerberg, E. M. (2007). Postidentification feedback affects real eyewitnesses. *Psychological Science, 18,* 172–178. (7)

Wright, I. C., Rabe-Hesketh, S., Woodruff, P. W. R., David, A. S., Murray, R. M., & Bullmore, E. T. (2000). Meta-analysis of regional brain volumes in schizophrenia. *American Journal of Psychiatry, 157,* 16–25. (15)

Wright, L. (1994). *Remembering Satan.* New York: Knopf. (7)

Writing Group for the Women's Health Initiative Investigators. (2002). Risks and benefits of estrogen plus progestin in healthy postmenopausal women. *Journal of the American Medical Association, 288,* 321–333. (2)

Wu, K., Lindsted, K. D., Tsai, S.-Y., & Lee, J. W. (2007). Chinee NEO-PI-R in Taiwanese adolescents. *Personality and Individual Differences, 44,* 656–667. (14)

Wulff, K., Gatti, S., Wettstein, J. G., & Foster, R. G. (2010). Sleep and circadian rhythm disruption in psychiatric and neurodegenerative disease. *Nature Neuroscience, 11,* 589–599. (10)

Wundt, W. (1896/1902). *Outlines of psychology* (C. H. Judd, Trans.). New York: Gustav Sechert. (Original work published 1896) (1)

Wundt, W. (1862/1961). Contributions to the theory of sensory perception. In T. Shipley (Ed.), *Classics in psychology* (pp. 51–78). New York: Philosophical Library. (Original work published 1862) (1)

Wyart, C., Webster, W. W., Chen, J. H., Wilson, S. R., McClary, A., Khan, R. M., & Sobel, N. (2007). Smelling a single component of male sweat alters levels of cortisol in women. *Journal of Neuroscience, 27,* 1261–1265. (4)

Xu, A. J., & Wyer, R. S., Jr. (2008). The comparative mind set. *Psychological Science, 19,* 859–864. (11)

Yaakobi, E., Mikulincer, M., & Shaver, P. R. (2014). Parenthood as a terror management mechanism: The moderating role of attachment orientations. *Personality and Social Psychology Bulletin, 40,* 762-774. (5)

Yamagata, S., Suzuki, A., Ando, J., One, Y., Kijima, N., Yoshimura, K., . . . Jang, K. L. (2006). Is the genetic structure of human personality universal? A cross-cultural twin study from North America, Europe, and Asia. *Journal of Personality and Social Psychology, 90,* 987-998. (14)

Yang, K.-S. (2003). Beyond Maslow's culture-bound linear theory: A preliminary statement of the double-Y model of basic human needs. *Nebraska Symposium on Motivation, 49,* 175-255. (11)

Yau, J. M., Celnik, P., Hsiao, S. S., & Desmond, J. E. (2014). Feeling better: Separate pathways for targeted enhancement of spatial and temporal touch. *Psychological Science, 25,* 555-565. (3)

Yeh, V. M., Schnur, J. B., & Montgomery, G. H. (2014). Disseminating hypnosis to health care settings: Applying the RE-AIM framework. *Psychology of Consciousness, 1,* 213-228. (10)

Yehuda, R. (1997). Sensitization of the hypothalamic-pituitary-adrenal axis in posttraumatic stress disorder. *Annals of the New York Academy of Sciences, 821,* 57-75. (12)

Yeomans, M. R., Tepper, B. J., Rietzschel, J., & Prescott, J. (2007). Human hedonic responses to sweetness: Role of taste genetics and anatomy. *Physiology & Behavior, 91,* 264-273. (1)

Yik, M., Russell, J. A., & Steiger, J. H. (2011). A 12-point circumplex structure of core affect. *Emotion, 11,* 705-731. (12)

Ying, Y.-W., Han, M., & Wong, S. L. (2008). Cultural orientation in Asian American adolescents: Variation by age and ethnic density. *Youth and Society, 39,* 507-523. (5)

Yolken, R. H., Dickerson, F. B., & Torrey, E. F. (2009). Toxoplasma and schizophrenia. *Parasite Immunology, 31,* 706-715. (15)

Yoo, S.-S., Hu, P. T., Gujar, N., Jolesz, F. A., & Walker, M. P. (2007). A deficit in the ability to form new human memories without sleep. *Nature Neuroscience, 10,* 385-392. (10)

Yoon, K. L., Hong, S. W., Joormann, J., & Kang, P. (2009). Perception of facial expressions of emotion during binocular rivalry. *Emotion, 9,* 172-182. (12)

Yousem, D. M., Maldjian, J. A., Siddiqi, F., Hummel, T., Alsop, D. C., Geckle, R. J., . . . Doty, R. L. (1999). Gender effects on odor-stimulated functional magnetic resonance imaging. *Brain Reseearch, 818,* 480-487. (4)

Yu, C. K.-C. (2008). Typical dreams experienced by Chinese people. *Dreaming, 18,* 1-10. (10)

Yunesian, M., Aslani, A., Vash, J. H., & Yazdi, A. B. (2008). Effects of transcendental meditation on mental health: A before-after study. *Clinical Practice and Epidemiology in Mental Health, 4,* 25. (10)

Yuval-Greenberg, S., & Heeger, D. J. (2013). Continuous flash suppression modulates cortical activity in early visual cortex. *Journal of Neuroscience, 33,* 9635-9643. (10)

Zaccaro, S. J. (2007). Trait-based perspectives of leadership. *American Psychologist, 62,* 6-16. (11)

Zadra, A., Desautels, A., Petit, D., & Montplaisir, J. (2013). Somnambulism: Clinical aspects and pathophysiological hypotheses. *Lancet Neurology, 12,* 285-294. (10)

Zahavi, A., & Zahavi, A. (1997). *The handicap principle.* New York: Oxford University Press. (13)

Zajonc, R. B. (1968). Attitudinal effects of mere exposure. *Journal of Personality and Social Psychology, 9*(Monograph Suppl. 2, Pt. 2). (13)

Zaleskiewicz, T., Gasiorowska, A., & Kesebir, P. (2013). Saving can save from death anxiety: Mortality salience and financial decision-making. *PLoS One, 8,* e79407. (5)

Zaragoza, M. S., Payment, K. E., Ackil, J. K., Drivdahl, S. B., & Beck, M. (2001). Interviewing witnesses: Forced confabulation and confirmatory feedback increase false memories. *Psychological Science, 12,* 473-477. (7)

Zarkadi, T., Wade, K. A., & Stewart, N. (2009). Creating fair lineups for suspects with distinctive features. *Psychological Science, 20,* 1448-1453. (7)

Zehr, D. (2000). Portrayals of Wundt and Titchener in introductory psychology texts: A content analysis. *Teaching of Psychology, 27,* 122-126. (1)

Zelenski, J. M., Santoro, M. S., & Whalen, D. C. (2012). Would introverts be better off if they acted more like extraverts? Exploring emotional and cognitive consequences of counterdispositional behavior. *Emotion, 12,* 290-303. (14)

Zentner, M., & Mitura, K. (2012). Stepping out of the caveman's shadow: Nations gender gap predicts degree of sex differentiation in mate preferences. *Psychological Science, 23,* 1176-1185. (3)

Zepelin, H., & Rechtschaffen, A. (1974). Mammalian sleep, longevity, and energy metabolism. *Brain, Behavior, and Evolution, 10,* 425-470. (10)

Zerwas, S., Lund, B. C., Von Holle, A., Thornton, L. M., Berrettini, W. H., Brandt, H., . . . Bulik, C. M. (2013). Factors associated with recovery from anorexia nervosa. *Journal of Psychiatric Research, 47,* 972-979. (11)

Zhang, T., Kim, T., Brooks, A. W., Gino, F., & Norton, M. I. (2014). A "present" for the future: The unexpected value of rediscovery. *Psychological Science, 25,* 1851-1860. (12)

Zhang, W., & Luck, S. J. (2008). Discrete fixed-resolution representations in visual working memory. *Nature, 453,* 233-235. (8)

Zhang, X., & Firestein, S. (2002). The olfactory receptor gene superfamily of the mouse. *Nature Neuroscience, 5,* 124-133. (4)

Zhong, C.-B., Bohns, V. K., & Gino, F. (2010). Good lamps are the best police: Darkness increases dishonesty and self-interested behavior. *Psychological Science, 21,* 311-314. (13)

Zhou, W., & Chen, D. (2009). Fear-related chemosignals modulate recognition of fear in ambiguous facial expressions. *Psychological Science, 20,* 177-183. (12)

Zeigler-Hill, V., Enjaian, B., Holden, C. J., & Southard, A. C. (2014). Using self-esteem instability to disentangle the connection between self-esteem level and perceived aggression. *Journal of Research in Personality, 49,* 47-51. (13)

Zhu, D. H. (2014). Group polarization in board decisions about CEO compensation. *Organization Science, 25,* 552-571. (13)

Zihl, J., von Cramon, D., & Mai, N. (1983). Selective disturbance of movement vision after bilateral brain damage. *Brain, 106,* 313-340. (3)

Zimbardo, P. G. (2007). *The Lucifer effect: Understanding how good people turn evil.* New York, NY: Random House. (13)

Zipursky, R. B., Reilly, T. J., & Murray, R. M. (2013). The myth of schizophrenia as a progressive brain disease. *Schizophrenia Bulletin, 39,* 1363-1372. (15)

Zoëga, H., Valdimarsdóttir, U. A., & Hernández-Díaz, S. (2012). Age, academic performance, and stimulant prescribing for ADHD: A nationwide cohort study. *Pediatrics, 130,* 1012-1018. (8)

Zolotor, A. J., & Puzia, M. E. (2010). Bans against corporal punishment: A systematic review of the laws, changes in attitudes and behaviours. *Child Abuse Review, 19,* 229-247. (6)

Zuriff, G. E. (1995). Continuity over change within the experimental analysis of behavior. In J. T. Todd & E. K. Morris (Eds.), *Modern perspectives on B. F. Skinner and contemporary behaviorism* (pp. 171-178). Westport, CT: Greenwood Press. (6)

approach or a single way of using an item, 266-267, *266*

Functionalism emphasis on studying what the mind does, instead of the structures that compose it, 16

Functional magnetic resonance imaging (fMRI) procedure that uses magnetic detectors outside the head to compare the amounts of hemoglobin with and without oxygen in different brain areas, 80-81, *81*, 384-385, *385*

Fundamental attribution error tendency to make internal attributions for people's behavior even when we see evidence for an external influence on behavior, 425-426

Fusiform gyrus, 75

g general intellectual ability, 289-290, *289*, *290*

GABA (gamma-amino-butyric acid), *63*, 69, 148

GAD (generalized anxiety disorder), 489

Gage, Phineas, 390

Galton, Francis, 294

Gandhi, Mohandas K., 416

Ganglion cells neurons in the eye that receive input from bipolar cells, which in turn receive input from the visual receptors, 105, *105*

Ganzfeld procedure, 32, *32*

Gardner, Beatrice, 275

Gardner, Howard, 291-292

Gardner, R. Allen, 275

Gardner, Randy, 325, *326*

Gates, 59, *60*

Gate theory idea that pain messages must pass through a gate, presumably in the spinal cord, that can block the messages, 117, *118*

GDP (gross domestic product), *397*

Gender
apologies, 171
appeal of various sex acts, 366, *366*
and depression, 503
development, influences on, 171-173
differences in sexual orientation, 372-373
influence of on development, 171-173
IQ tests, 300-301
number of sexual partners, 368, *368*
reasons for differences, 173

Gender identity sex that someone regards himself or herself as being, 370

Gender role pattern of behavior that a person is expected to follow because of being male or female, 173, *174*

"General" ability, 289, *289*

General adaptation syndrome the body's response to stressful events of any type, 402-403

General intelligence and language, 276

Generalization, 199

Generalized anxiety disorder (GAD) disorder in which people have frequent and exaggerated worries, 489

Generativity vs. stagnation, *163*, 164

Genes inherited structures that control the chemical reactions that direct development, 88-89, *88*

Genetics
alcoholism, 499-500
autism spectrum disorder, 512
behavior, influence on, 93-94
depression, 504-505
environmental modification of genetic effects, 94
heritability in humans, estimation of, 91-93
intelligence quotient (IQ), 295
intelligence tests, 295-296
more complex view of, 90-91
obesity, 360
obsessive-compulsive disorder (OCD), 494
panic disorder (PD), 489
personality, 466-467
phobias, 491
principles, 88-93
schizophrenia, 509-510, *510*
sex-linked and sex-limited genes, 89-90

Genitals, *370*

Genital stage according to Freud, period when someone becomes sexually interested in other people, *453*, 454

Genital surgery, 370

Genovese, Kitty, 415

Gestalt psychology a field that emphasizes perception of overall patterns, 130-132

g factor, 289-290

GHB (gamma hydroxybutyrate), 68, *71*

Ghrelin, 356

Gifted children, 300

Glaucoma, *103*

Glia cells that support the neurons in many ways such as insulating them, synchronizing activity among neighboring neurons, and removing waste materials, 57

Glucagon, 357

Glucose most abundant sugar in the blood, an important source of energy for the body and almost the only source the brain uses, 356

Glutamate, *63*, 69, 148

Goals and deadlines, 347-350

Golden Fleece Awards, 437

Goodall, Jane, 36, *37*

Good figure in Gestalt psychology, the tendency to perceive simple, symmetrical figures, 131, 132, *132*

Graduate Record Examination (GRE), 304

Grandeur, delusion of, 508

Grasp reflex, 95, *95*

Graveyard shift, *323*

GRE (Graduate Record Examination), 304

Gross domestic product (GDP), *397*

Group decision making, 447-448

Group polarization tendency for people who lean in the same direction on a particular issue to become more extreme in that position after discussing it with one another, 447

Group therapy treatment that is administered to several people at once, 518-519, 521

Groupthink tendency for people to suppress their doubts about a group's decision for fear of making a bad impression or disrupting group harmony, 447-448

Guilty-knowledge test modified version of the polygraph test that produces more accurate results by asking questions that should be threatening only to someone who knows the facts of a crime, 396

Habituation decreased response to a repeated stimulus, 75-76, 150-151

Hair cells, *113*

Hallucination perception that does not correspond to anything in the real world, 508

Hallucinogen drug that induces sensory distortions, 67-68, *71*

Hambrick, Jim, 197

Hammer, 113, *113*

Handwriting, 475

Happiness, 396-400, *397*

Harris, Judith Rich, 177-178

Harris, Thomas, 459

Harrison, James, 482

Hartley, David, *16*

Hassles, 403, *403*

Hawks, 102

al-Haytham, Ibn, *16*, 101

Health, effect of stress on, 404-405

Health maintenance organizations (HMOs), 7, 515

Health psychologists, 21

Health psychology field that addresses how people's behavior influences health, 402

Hearing
in infancy, 150-151
overview of, 112-114
pitch perception, 114-115
similarities with vision, 130-132
sound localization, 115

Hearing aids, 113

Heart disease, 404-405

Heider, Fritz, 424

Helmholtz, Hermann von, 106-107

Hemisphere the left or right half of the forebrain, 74, *74*

Hering, Ewald, 107

Heritability estimate of the variance within a population that is due to heredity, 91-93

Heroin, 69, *71*, 501

Hertz (Hz) cycles (vibrations) per second, 112

Heuristic strategy for simplifying a problem and generating a satisfactory guess, 263

Hierarchy of needs organization from the most insistent needs to the ones that receive attention only when all others are under control, 346-347, *347*

Hindsight bias tendency to mold our recollection of the past to fit how events later turned out, 235

Hippocampus large forebrain structure in the interior of the temporal lobe, 76, 242, 243, *243*

Histamine, *63*

Histones, 90, *90*, 369

Histone tail, *90*

HIV (human immunodeficiency virus), 368

H. M., 242, 243, 245

Hobbes, Thomas, *451*

Homeostasis maintenance of an optimum level of biological conditions within an organism, 346, *346*

Homosexuality. *See* **Sexual orientation**

Hormone chemical released by glands and conveyed by the blood to alter activity in various organs, 82, *83*

Horney, Karen, 456

Huichol tribe, 67

Hull, Clark, 19

Human factors specialist (or ergonomist) someone who tries to facilitate the operation of machinery so that ordinary people can use it efficiently and safely, 8, *12*

Human Genome Project, 296

Humanistic psychology field emphasizing consciousness, values, and abstract beliefs, including spiritual experiences and the beliefs that people live and die for, 458-460

Humanistic therapy, 518

Human-relations approach (also known as Theory Y) idea that employees like variety in their job, a sense of accomplishment, and a sense of responsibility, 351

Hume, David, *16*

Hunger motivation
brain mechanisms, 358
overeating and undereating, 360-363
physiology of hunger and satiety, 356-358
social cultural influences on eating, 359

Hybrid vigor, 301

Hypermnesia gain of memory over time, 233

Hyperopia, *103*

Hypersomnolence disorder, 487

Hyperventilation rapid deep breathing, 490

Hypnosis condition of increased suggestibility that occurs in the context of a special hypnotist-subject relationship, *16* as an altered state of consciousness, 339 and the brain, 337 introduction to, 335 and memory, 338, *338* uses and limitations of, 336-339 ways of inducing, 335-336

Hypoactive sexual desire disorder, 487

Hypochondria, *472*

Hypomania, *472*

Hypothalamus structure just below the thalamus, important for hunger, thirst, temperature regulation, sex, and other motivated behavior
definition of, 81
hormones, 82
hunger regulation, 357-358, *358*
illustrations of, *73*, *76*, *83*
sexual orientation, 374, *374*

Hypothesis clear predictive statement, 27, *28*

Hysteria, *472*

Hz (Hertz), 112

IAT (implicit association test) procedure that measures reactions to combinations of categories, such as "flowers" and "pleasant," 422-423

Id according to Freud, sexual and other biological drives that demand immediate gratification, 454

Ideal self image of what one would like to be, 456, 459

Identity, and sexual development, 369-371

Identity achievement outcome of having explored various possible identities and then making one's own decisions, 166

Identity crisis concerns with decisions about the future and the quest for self-understanding, 166

Identity development, 163-164, 166

Identity diffusion condition in which someone has not yet given serious thought to making decisions and has no clear sense of identity, 166

Identity foreclosure state of reaching firm decisions without much thought, 166

Identity moratorium state of considering the issues but not yet making decisions, 166

Identity vs. role confusion, *163*

Idiographic approach personality study that concentrates on intensive studies of individuals, 463

Illusory correlation apparent relationship based on casual

damage to the cochlea, hair cells, or auditory nerves, 113

Nervous system cells, 57–58

Neurocognitive theory, 332

Neurodevelopmental hypothesis idea that schizophrenia originates with nervous system impairments that develop before birth or in early childhood because of either genetics or early environment, especially prenatal environment, 510

Neurons cells of the nervous system that receive information and transmit it to other cells by conducting electrochemical impulses, 58
action potential, 58–60, *59*, *60*, *62*, *128*
nervous system cells, 57–58
synapses, 60–63, *60*, *61*

Neuroscience, 21

Neuroticism tendency to experience unpleasant emotions frequently, 465

Neurotransmitter chemical that activates receptors on other neurons
and antidepressants, 505, *505*
and behavior, 63–64
definition of, 60
overview of, *63*

Nicotine, 70

Nightmares, 330

Night terror condition that causes someone to awaken screaming and sweating with a racing heart rate, sometimes flailing with the arms, 330

95 percent confidence intervals range within the true population mean probably lies, with 95 percent certainty, 46–47, *46*

Nitric oxide, 63

Nobel Peace Prize, *232*

Nobel Prize, *17*, 184, 264

Nomothetic approach personality study that seeks broad, general principles of personality, 463

Nonhumans, ethical concerns in research, 48

Nontraditional families, 178

Nonvisual senses
chemical senses, 119–122
cutaneous senses, 116–118, *117*
hearing, 112–115
vestibular sense, 115–116

Norepinephrine, 63, 505, *505*

Normal distribution (or normal curve) symmetrical frequency of scores clustered around the mean, 45, 299–300, *300*

Norms description of how frequently various scores occur, 299

Nostradamus, 31, *31*

Note taking, 231

Nucleus, *88*

Nucleus accumbens, 84, 497–498, *497*

Obedience to authority, 444–447

Obesity excessive accumulation of body fat, *359*, 360

Objective personality test, 472–473

Object permanence idea that objects continue to exist even when we do not see or hear them, 152–154, *153*

Object size, 135

O'Brien, Dominic, 215

Observational research designs
case history, 36, *42*
comparison of, *42*
correlational studies, 39–41, *42*
naturalistic observation, 36, *42*
surveys, 37–39, *42*

Obsession repetitive, unwelcome stream of thought, 494–495

Obsessive-compulsive disorder (OCD) condition with repetitive thoughts and actions
and anorexia nervosa, 361
distrusting memory, 494–495
prevalence, 494
therapies, 495

Obsessive-compulsive personality disorder, *487*

Occam, William of, 29

Occam's razor, 29

Occipital cortex, *128*

Occipital lobe area of the cerebral cortex located at the rear of the head, specialized for vision, 74–75, *74*

Odbert, H. S., 465

Oedipus complex according to Freud, period when a boy develops a sexual interest in his mother and competitive aggression toward his father, 452

Old age, 168–169

Olfaction sense of smell, 120–122, *121*

Olfactory bulb, *76*, *121*

Olfactory nerve, *121*

Omega-3 fatty acids, 507

Open-mindedness, 29–30

Openness to experience tendency to enjoy new intellectual experiences and new ideas, 466, *466*

Operant-conditioning chamber, 199, *200*

Operant conditioning (or instrumental conditioning) process of changing behavior by providing reinforcement or punishment after a response
additional phenomena of, 199
applications of, 202–203
categories of reinforcement and punishment, 198, *198*
vs. classical conditioning, *199*
definition of, 196
primary and secondary reinforcers, 196–197
punishment, 197–198, *198*
reinforcement, *195*, 196–198
schedules of reinforcement, 201–202, *201*

Skinner and shaping of responses, 199–202
Thorndike on, 194–196

Operation according to Piaget, a reversible mental process, 155

Operational definitions statement that specifies the operations (or procedures) used to produce or measure something; ordinarily a way to give it a numerical value, 34

Opiate dependence, 501, *501*

Opiates either natural drugs derived from the opium poppy, or synthetic drugs with a chemical structure resembling natural opiates, 68, *119*

Opponent-process theory theory that we perceive color in terms of a system of paired opposites: red *versus* green, yellow *versus* blue, and white *versus* black, 107–108

Optical illusions misinterpretation of a visual stimulus, 136–138, *136–137*

Optic chiasm, 105, *105*

Optic nerve set of ganglion cell axons that turn around and exit the eye, *102*, 105, *105*

Oral stage according to Freud, period when an infant derives intense psychosexual pleasure from stimulation of the mouth, particularly while sucking at the mother's breast, 453, *453*

Orexin, 329

Orgasm. See Sexual motivation

Orne, Martin, 43

Otolith organs, 116, *116*

Otoliths, 116, *116*

Ovary, *83*

Overconfidence, 266

Overeating, 359–363

Owls, 102, *103*

Oxytocin, 84, 369

p < **0.05** statement that the probability that randomly generated results would resemble the observed results is less than 5 percent, 46

Pacinian corpuscle, *117*

Pain, 117–118

Pancreas, *83*

Panic disorder (PD) condition marked by frequent periods of anxiety and occasional attacks of panic—rapid breathing, increased heart rate, chest pains, sweating, faintness, and trembling, 489–490

Paradoxical sleep, 326

Paranoia, *472*

Parasympathetic nervous system neurons whose axons extend from the medulla and the lower part of the spinal cord to neuron clusters near the organs; it decreases the heart rate and promotes digestion

and other nonemergency functions, 82, *82*, 380–381, *380*

Parathyroid, *83*

Parental conflict, 178–179

Parenthood and happiness, 398

Parenting styles, 177–178

Parietal cortex, *337*

Parietal lobe structure just anterior (forward) from the occipital lobe, specialized for the body senses, including touch, pain, temperature, and awareness of the location of body parts in space, *74*, 76

Parkinson's disease condition that affects about 1 percent of people over the age of 50; the main symptoms are difficulty initiating voluntary movement, slow movement, tremors, rigidity, and depressed mood, 63

Parsimony (literally, stinginess) principle that, when given a choice among explanations that seem to fit the facts, we prefer the one whose assumptions are fewer, simpler, or more consistent with other well-established theories, 29–32

Passionate love stage in a relationship when sexual desire, romance, and friendship increase in parallel, 440

Pattern recognition, 269, *269*, *270*

Patterns, perceiving and recognizing, 128–132

Pavlov, Ivan P., *17*, 184–188, 190

Pavlovian conditioning, 184. *See also* **Classical conditioning**

Pay scale, 352

PCP (phencylidine), *71*

PD (panic disorder), 489–490

Pearl Harbor attack, 448

Pearson, Lucy, 197

Peptide transmitters, 60

Perceived intensity, *17*

Perception interpretation of sensory information, 100. *See also* **Sensation**

Periodic limb movement disorder (restless leg syndrome) condition marked by unpleasant sensations in the legs and repetitive leg movements strong enough to interrupt sleep, 330

Peripheral nervous system bundles of axons that convey messages between the spinal cord and the rest of the body, 73, *73*

Peripheral route to persuasion use of superficial factors to persuade people, such as repetition of a message or prestige of the speaker, 431

Permissive parents those who are warm and loving but undemanding, 177

Perpetual motion machine, 29–30, *30*, 262

Persecution, delusion of, 508

Persistent vegetative state, 316–317, *316*

Persona, 456

"personal fable," 166–167

Personality all the consistent ways in which the behavior of one person differs from that of others, especially in social situations
assessment of, 471–478
definition of, 451
origins of, 466–469
psychodynamic theory, 451–456
structure of, 454
theories of, 451–460
traits, 463–469

Personality assessment
criminal profiling, 476–478, *478*
implicit personality tests, 475–476
introduction to, 471
Minnesota Multiphasic Personality Inventory (MMPI), 472–473
Myers-Briggs Type Indicator (MBTI), 473
NEO PI-R (NEO personality inventory-revised), 473
objective personality test, 472–473
projective techniques, 474–475
standardized tests, 472
uses and misuses of, 476, *476*

Personality disorder maladaptive, inflexible way of dealing with the environment and other people, 485–486, *487*

Personality psychologist, *12*

Personality theories
collective unconscious, 456
humanistic psychology, 458–460
individual psychology, 457–458
learning approach, 458
neo-Freudians, 456
psychodynamic theory, 451–456
self-actualization, 357, 459–460
unconditional positive regard, 459

Personality traits
Big Five model of personality, 465–466, *466*
issues in personality measurement, 464
origins of, 466–469
search for broad traits, 463–465
and states, 463

Person-centered therapy (nondirective or client-centered therapy) procedure in which a therapist listens to the client with total acceptance and unconditional positive regard, 518, *520*

Persuasion, 202–203
coercive persuasion, 434–435
mechanisms of attitude change and, 431–435
resistance to, 433–434